CONTEMPORARY CRIMINAL LAW

■ ■ ■

Mark Osler

Professor and Robert and Marion Short
Distinguished Chair in Law
University of St. Thomas Law School (MN)

AMERICAN CASEBOOK SERIES®

WEST
ACADEMIC
PUBLISHING

American Casebook Series is a trademark registered in the U.S. Patent and Trademark Office.

© 2018 LEG, Inc. d/b/a West Academic
    444 Cedar Street, Suite 700
    St. Paul, MN 55101
    1-877-888-1330

West, West Academic Publishing, and West Academic are trademarks of West Publishing Corporation, used under license.

Printed in the United States of America

ISBN: 978-1-68328-875-6

PREFACE

Teaching criminal law is important work. Some of our students will go on to work in the field, determining the fate and freedoms of defendants and protecting communities. The introductory class in criminal law is their first glance of this world—a sphere that is complicated, deeply moral, compelling, and central to the organization of a functioning society. It is important they learn about criminal law as it exists now.

In creating a new text that reflects the real world of contemporary criminal law, I decided to diverge from the predominant model in several ways.

First, I have approached criminal law the way I was trained to do as a federal prosecutor, with a focus on elements as the building block of a case. It is the elements of crime that structure the book, that are at the center of the exercises, and that guide the selection of cases. Theory is discussed in the last chapter of the book, rather than the first. It makes more sense to first examine the structure of criminal law, especially for beginning students.

Second, common law is not a significant part of this book. Common law crimes were banished from American jurisdictions decades ago; it is senseless to teach 21st-century students common-law cases that reflect an entire system that has passed from existence. Principles can be taught just as effectively from contemporary cases that do not involve the theft of cravats or the archaic deliberations of the Queen's Bench. Criminal law is about deep human tragedy; it needn't go far from today's cases to be interesting, grounded, and instructive.

Third, I have deviated from the conventional practice of jumping from one jurisdiction to another as cases proceed in a chapter. That creates a false impression of uniformity in diverse jurisdictions, fails to reflect the coherence found within most penal codes, and is just plain confusing. In this book I use federal code and case law, which is relevant everywhere in the United States.

Fourth, the exercises often involve the exercise of discretion by someone working within the system—a prosecutor, judge, defense attorney, or probation officer—rather than putting the student in the position of an academic who is critiquing the law. Focusing on the importance of discretion presents earthy challenges and better reflects the real world of criminal law.

Fifth, two individual chapters cover the important issues relating to narcotics and firearms cases, including elements (such as chemical testing for drugs and illegal modification for guns) that are not found with other crimes. Immigration also receives its own chapter. A teacher cannot responsibly ignore all of these subjects, given their importance in modern criminal law.

Finally, I will never exclude the facts from a case. It is essential that students understand the impact crime and criminal law have on individuals and communities, and that is best conveyed by revealing the facts that lead us to court.

The book is structured to first introduce the basic elements, and then to cover a variety of types of crimes before moving on to accessory liability, conspiracy, and defenses. It ends with a discussion of sentencing and a concluding chapter on theory. In each of the issue-specific chapters, the same pattern will be followed. First, the crime is defined in terms of elements. Next, cases are presented that allow students to think through those elements and their proofs. After that, an exercise is provided that allows the student to actively see how those elements work within a discrete set of facts.

Criminal law should never be boring. It is too important for that. In attempting to create a book that fits with the contemporary world of criminal law, I hope to help teachers engage their students in a way that reveals the fascinating and very human realm of criminal law as it really works.

MARK OSLER

SUMMARY OF CONTENTS

TABLE OF CONTENTS

TABLE OF CASES

The principal cases are in bold type.

CONTEMPORARY CRIMINAL LAW

CHAPTER ONE

ELEMENTS AND THE DEFINITION OF CRIMES

■ ■ ■

Criminal law looms large in our national imagination. It wells up in the headlines, the back pages, and the police car slowly driving down a dark street. Each case is a study in tragedy.

The purpose of this book is to describe the shape of criminal law in the United States in the 21st Century. Modern criminal law is distinct from earlier eras in two crucial ways. First, relatively new crimes involving narcotics and firearms—things that were barely regulated a century ago—dominate the dockets in many of our criminal courts. Second, the common law has essentially become extinct as American jurisdictions have crafted statutes which sharply define the growing number of acts subject to criminal sanctions.

In this new world of criminal law, elements are at the center of the criminal process. An element is a discrete fact that a jury must find true beyond a reasonable doubt—by trial or by plea—if a conviction is to be obtained. Statutes define crimes by setting out the elements that comprise that crime.

For example, one element of murder is that someone died. Because death is an element of murder, if death hasn't occurred, a murder has not taken place.

One way to think about the relationship between crimes and elements is to imagine a fast-food restaurant. A relatively small number of ingredients—cheese, beef, lettuce, chicken, etc.—are used to make the items on the menu in different combinations. Without an ingredient, the menu item is not properly made. In criminal law, those ingredients are elements, and the charge is a menu item. A taco requires a tortilla, beef, cheese, and lettuce. A murder requires identification of the killer, a malicious mind, an actual death, and causation of that death.

Some elements (like certain ingredients in some types of fast food) recur in nearly every crime. Identification of the responsible person, for example, will be an element in every crime we study. Others are used often, on occasion or infrequently.

Criminal law practitioners view their work in terms of elements, because it is the elements of a crime that structure their tasks. A prosecutor can prove a case only if she can present evidence establishing the truth of each element beyond a reasonable doubt, so much of her job is matching evidence to elements. For a defense attorney in trial, the goal is to show reasonable doubt as to at least one element, requiring a deep understanding of how those elements work.

In this chapter, we will discuss five types of elements:

1) Identification

2) Elements that go to actions (actus reus)

3) Elements that go to mental state (mens rea)

4) Elements that go to jurisdiction

5) Other types of elements, including scientific findings, prior criminal history, and facts relating to a victim such as age.

A. THE ELEMENT OF IDENTIFICATION

The single most common element is also the most important in many contested cases: That the defendant is the person who committed the crime. Evidence including eyewitness testimony, fingerprints, DNA, and confessions can all be used to prove identification, and defenses such as alibi are used to show reasonable doubt as to the government's proofs.

The most difficult identity cases can be those in which only circumstantial evidence is involved. Read the following case while picking out and listing the evidence going to identity.

UNITED STATES V. CHAPPELL
307 Fed. Appx. 275 (11th Cir. 2009)

PER CURIAM:

After a jury trial, Carey Gilbert Chappell appeals his conviction for bank robbery, in violation of 18 U.S.C. § 2113(a). After review, we affirm. . . .

Because Chappell challenges the sufficiency of the government's evidence that he was the bank robber, we review the evidence linking Chappell to the robbery.

On August 14, 2006, at 11:07 a.m., a SunTrust Bank on Gray Highway in Macon, Georgia was robbed. That morning, Wyvonia Gillespie, the bank's customer service representative, saw an African-American man run toward and enter the bank. The man had a white T-shirt or towel over his head and was screaming for help. The white covering was stained with a red substance that appeared to be blood.

Once inside the bank, the man staggered around and then tried to go through a locked teller door. When he was unsuccessful, the man's demeanor suddenly changed. He stated, "this is a robbery," jumped over a teller station, pointed pepper spray at the teller, Kecia Cooper, and said "[g]ive me the money." The man grabbed Cooper's teller drawer containing $7,980, jumped back over the counter and left the bank. Cooper described the robber as about 5′5″ with a small build.

As the robber fled, a bank customer, Nathaniel Dunn, was walking up to the bank. Dunn saw a man wearing dark clothing and a white towel over his face run out and go behind a nearby dumpster. When Dunn approached the dumpster, the man said he would shoot Dunn if he did not get back, and Dunn retreated. Moments later, Dunn saw the man get on a bicycle and leave the area.

Police found the teller drawer in the grass near the dumpster. Inside the dumpster was a small canister of pepper spray and a white T-shirt with orange stains, which later were determined to be ketchup. Police also found a partial shoe track on the teller counter, probably from a tennis shoe. The only identifiable print, a partial palmprint found inside the bank, did not match Chappell. Of the money taken, only five $20 bills were "bait bills," meaning their serial numbers had been recorded. Thus, of the $7,980 taken in the robbery, only $100 was in bait bills.

Photographs taken by the bank's security camera show a dark-skinned man in dark clothing with a white cloth covering his head and face. Because of this cloth covering, none of the eyewitnesses saw the robber's face clearly enough to identify him. Neither Gillespie nor Cooper was able to identify Chappell in a lineup, and Dunn was not asked to view a lineup.

Although none of the eyewitnesses could identify Chappell, the government presented a constellation of circumstantial evidence that Chappell was the bank robber. For example, on the morning of the bank robbery, between 10:00 a.m. and 12:30 p.m., Michael Preston, Jr., bumped into Chappell (whom he knew as "Gee") at a Circle-K convenience store behind the SunTrust bank. Chappell was dressed in black and wearing "a white scarf thing" around his head. Chappell asked Preston if he wanted to make some money, and Preston responded he did not.

Around 11:30 that morning, Melando Hollings, who lived near the SunTrust bank, found a man on his porch. The man was wearing a dark shirt and was "scrunched down" on the floor of the porch looking out at the street. Hollings described the man as sweaty. When Hollings asked what the man was doing on his porch, the man asked Hollings for a ride to the Fort Hill area and told Hollings he had money. Hollings refused, went into his home and got his handgun. Hollings stood in the door and asked the man to leave. The man asked Hollings to "give [him] a minute and [he'll] go." The man then left.

Approximately twenty minutes after the robbery, Detective Robert Shockley was in Hollings's neighborhood behind the bank looking for the bank robbery suspect. Shockley knocked on the door, and Hollings answered. Hollings gave Shockley a description of the man he found on his porch. Two days later, Hollings identified Chappell in a photo lineup. Hollings also identified Chappell at trial as the man on his porch.

Several people who knew Chappell testified that he: (1) never had much money; (2) did not have a job; (3) did not own a car; (4) was a small man; (5) was from the Fort Hill area of Macon; (6) rode a bicycle; and (7) always wore black clothing. When Chappell was arrested in a motel three days after the bank robbery, police found approximately $300 in new clothing, including two black shirts still in the shopping bag and a pair of sports shoes, and a blue Chevrolet Caprice. Chappell had only $18, however, and the serial numbers did not match the stolen bait bills.

Subsequent police investigation revealed that, on the afternoon of the bank robbery, Chappell purchased the Chevrolet from Hollis Hunt for $2,500 in cash. According to Hunt, Chappell approached him and asked to buy the Chevrolet. Chappell paid in twenty, fifty and hundred dollar bills and did not ask for a bill of sale. Two days later, the police interviewed Hunt about the sale. Hunt gave the police the $1,000 that was left of the money Chappell had paid him, but none of the serial numbers matched the bait bills from the robbery.

The government also called three witnesses who were housed at the Dooly County jail with Chappell, all of whom testified that Chappell confessed to the robbery. James Williams knew Chappell before they were incarcerated. Williams testified that on June 5, 2006, Chappell offered to sell Williams some jewelry he said he had stolen from a jewelry store. Williams declined, and they parted ways.

On July 4, 2006 Williams saw Chappell again. Chappell was looking for money and told Williams that Hollis Hunt owed him money for the jewelry. Williams took Chappell to Hunt to get the money. However, after Chappell left Hunt, he told Williams he still needed money and asked Williams if he would "be down with hitting a bank with him." The next day, Williams, who was out on bond for unrelated drug offenses, had his bond revoked and was placed in the Dooly County jail ("Dooly").

While at Dooly, Williams encountered Chappell, who admitted to Williams he had robbed a bank and explained that the police did not have the right money as evidence in his trial because he had switched the bank robbery money with Hunt. Chappell told Williams that the government had "nothing on him" and he was "going to trial."

Corey Sheffield was housed next to Chappell for two weeks. During that time, Chappell told Sheffield that he: (1) had committed the bank robbery, but police did not have any evidence; (2) wrapped a towel around his head to hide his face during the robbery; (3) put ketchup on the towel to pretend someone had hit him; (4) obtained the teller drawer by threatening the teller with pepper spray; (5) rode off on his bike after the robbery; (6) threw the fifty dollar bills away because they had dye on them; and (7) used some of the money to buy a car and new clothes and hid the rest.

Kenyon Gresham, who was Chappell's cellmate at Dooly, testified that Chappell said he: (1) had robbed a bank on Gray Highway; (2) was supposed to rob the bank with someone else, but the other person was "locked up" so he did the robbery by himself; (3) put a towel over his face so that the camera could not see him and jumped over the counter to grab the money; (4) had a bottle of mace with him during the robbery; (5) after the robbery, ran onto a porch, where someone gave him a brown shirt to wear, and, after police left the area, ran back to the Fort Hill area; (5) threw away some of the bills that could not be spent because they "wasn't no good"; and (6) used some money to buy a Caprice and let a girl keep the rest. . . .

To be convicted of bank robbery under § 2113(a), the government must prove beyond a reasonable doubt that the defendant, through use of intimidation or force and violence, took money that was in possession of a bank. *See* 18 U.S.C. § 2113(a). Chappell argues that the government failed to prove that he was the bank robber, stressing the absence of physical evidence linking him to the crime.[2]

The government's evidence established that: (1) in the month leading up to the robbery, Chappell tried to recruit a friend to help him rob a bank; (2) Chappell was in the vicinity of the bank on the morning of the robbery wearing, like the bank robber, a white "scarf thing" on his head and asking a friend if he wanted to make some money; (3) Chappell remained in the bank's vicinity just after the robbery and was found sweating and crouched on the stranger's porch while watching the street—i.e., hiding; (4) Chappell offered the stranger money if he would transport him out of the neighborhood; (5) Chappell was known to wear black and ride a bicycle and the bank robber wore black and fled the scene on a bicycle; and (6) Chappell did not have a job, money or a car before the bank robbery, but suddenly, on the afternoon of the robbery, had $2,500 in cash to buy a car.

In addition, the government presented three witnesses, Williams, Sheffield and Gresham, who testified that Chappell confessed to them that he robbed a bank and gave them details that were consistent with the modus operandi of the SunTrust robber. From this evidence, a reasonable jury could conclude beyond a reasonable doubt that Chappell was the SunTrust bank robber.

Further, contrary to Chappell's contention, his conviction did not rest entirely on this "jailhouse confession" testimony, and the other evidence summarized above provides compelling circumstantial proof that Chappell was the SunTrust robber. The absence of fingerprint or other physical evidence does not render the jury's verdict unreasonable given the circumstantial evidence that Chappell was the SunTrust bank robber. *See United States v. Calderon,* 127 F.3d 1314, 1324 (11th Cir.1997) (explaining that a jury verdict must stand "unless no trier of fact could have found guilt beyond a reasonable doubt" (quotation marks omitted)).

EXERCISE

Remember that the job of a defense attorney at trial is usually to convince the jury that there is reasonable doubt as to at least one element of the crime. As a defense attorney for Mr. Chappell in the case above, what would you emphasize in seeking to show a jury reasonable doubt as to identity?

Sometimes evidence of "prior bad acts" are allowed into evidence in order to show identity.[1] This is sometimes troubling, as it runs the danger of suggesting to a jury that a defendant is guilty simply because he has committed a similar crime in the past. Because of the negative impact on the defendant's case of allowing the jury to know about prior alleged misdeeds, prior bad acts are often ferociously litigated. In the case below, Judge Richard Posner of the Seventh Circuit considered such evidence in terms of mathematical probabilities.

UNITED STATES V. VANCE
764 F. 3d 667 (7th Cir. 2014)

POSNER, CIRCUIT JUDGE.

David Vance, along with Alton Marshall and Henry Bluford, were charged with having committed two bank robberies in Chicago in 2007, 18 U.S.C. § 2113(a), as well as related crimes, such as conspiring to rob the banks. 18 U.S.C. § 371. Vance also was charged with the more serious offense of killing a person during the commission of a bank robbery. 18 U.S.C. § 2113(e).

Marshall and Bluford, but not Vance, pleaded guilty. Vance was tried by a jury, and Marshall testified at the trial. The jury convicted Vance, and the judge sentenced him to terms of years on all counts except the one charging the killing; for that the judge sentenced him to life in prison. . . .

According to Marshall's testimony, the night before the first of the two bank robberies Vance suggested to him that they commit robberies that night. Marshall agreed, and that night the pair robbed a seafood restaurant, a Mexican restaurant, and a diner. They wore ski masks (the same ones used later in the bank robberies) and gloves. Vance carried a long-barreled .44 caliber revolver, the same model later used in both bank robberies. Vance told Marshall that he (Vance) would approach the counter to get the

---

[1]   Federal Rule of Evidence 404(b).

restaurant's money while Marshall "watch[ed] his back," and that was how they conducted two of the restaurant robberies. In the third, the robbery of the Mexican restaurant, both men approached the counter and ordered the employees there to open the register.

Vance argues that Marshall's testimony about the three restaurant robberies should not have been admitted; that if believed all it proved was that Vance had a propensity to commit robberies, and propensity evidence is not admissible, lest it prejudice the jurors against the defendant, causing them to convict even if the evidence of his guilt of the crime that he is being tried for is weak.

But Rule 404(b) of the Federal Rules of Evidence, the source of the prohibition against introducing evidence of a defendant's propensity to commit crimes, allows (in subsection (b)(2)) the admission of evidence of other crimes besides the one the defendant is charged with if that evidence pertains to, among other things, "identity," in this case Vance's identity as one of the masked bank robbers. Similarities between the restaurant robberies and the bank robberies supported an inference that if, as Marshall testified, Vance had been one of the restaurant robbers he probably had been one of the bank robbers as well. Remember that in two of the restaurant robberies Vance had rushed the counter where the money was kept while Marshall watched the patrons (though, in the third both had rushed the counter). There had been a "rusher" in the bank robberies as well, and if Vance had been the rusher in the restaurant robberies this made it more likely that he had also been the rusher in the bank robberies—and whoever rushed the counter in the second bank robbery was also the teller's killer. Vance brandished a .44 caliber revolver in the restaurant robberies, as he did in one of the bank robberies. And Marshall and Vance trusted each other enough as accomplices in robbery—as shown by their joint commission of the three restaurant robberies—to make it seem likely that Vance was also a participant in the bank robberies, to which Marshall had already confessed.

This body of evidence was not conclusive in identifying Vance as one of the bank robbers, but it was not so flimsy that it had to be excluded on the ground that its probative value was outweighed by its prejudicial effect. Weakest was the caliber evidence, since .44 caliber revolver ammunition is common. But there are a number of equally or more common calibers of such ammunition, such as .22, .32, .357. 38, and .45, so the fact that .44 is common does not negate an inference that Vance is likely to have been armed with the same weapon in both robberies (rather than that another of the robbers just happened to have a weapon of the identical caliber), thus increasing the likelihood that he was the killer in the bank robbery. Moreover, when several pieces of evidence point in the same direction, the probability that it's the right direction is greater than the probability that any one of the pieces is accurate. Suppose the probability that the first piece of evidence is accurate—and thus that Vance was indeed one of the bank robbers—is .50, that the probability that the second is accurate is .40, but that the probability that the third is accurate is only .10. Still, the likelihood that none of the evidence is accurate—and Vance therefore was not one of the bank robbers after all—is lower when the third piece of evidence is considered than when it is not; excluding it in our example would raise the probability of erroneous identification of Vance as one of the bank robbers from 27 to 30 percent. $((1 - .5) \times (1 - .4) \times (1 - .1) = .27; (1 - .5) \times (1 - .4) = .30.)$

It could be (though is not) argued that since Marshall was the source of the evidence of Vance's participation in the restaurant robberies and also the evidence of his participation in the bank robberies, the restaurant-robberies evidence had no probative value; if the jury thought Marshall was telling the truth about the bank robberies, that was enough to nail Vance; if they disbelieved him, his testimony about the restaurant robberies was irrelevant because Vance wasn't on trial for those robberies. But that analysis is incomplete. The restaurant evidence if believed showed that Marshall and Vance were partners in crime and thus increased the likelihood that Vance had participated in the bank robberies, "rushed the counter," and shot the teller with a .44 caliber pistol.

When other-crimes evidence is used for a proper purpose, such as to determine identity, rather than for the improper purpose of demonstrating that the defendant has a propensity to commit crimes (he committed a prior crime, so probably he committed the crime he's currently accused of), it is important both that the proof value of the evidence not be substantially outweighed by its prejudicial effect and that the jury be carefully instructed to limit its consideration to the effect of the evidence to determining identity. As this court explained in *United States v. Gomez,* No. 12–1104, p. 24 (7th Cir. Aug. 18, 2014) (en banc), regarding the first of these requirements, the relevance of the evidence for a proper purpose "must be established through a chain of reasoning that does not rely solely on the forbidden inference that the person has a certain character and acted in accordance with that character on the occasion charged in the case. If the proponent [the prosecutor] can make this initial showing, the district court must in every case assess whether the probative value of the other-act evidence is substantially outweighed by the risk of unfair prejudice and may exclude the evidence under Rule 403 if the risk is too great. The court's Rule 403 balancing should take account of the extent to which the non-propensity fact for which the evidence is offered actually is at issue in the case."

Vance's identity as one of the bank robbers is of course at issue in this case, and the evidence that he was one of them does not depend on inferring that if he had committed robberies in the past he was likely to have committed the robbery that he was charged with in the present case. . . .

[Vance] takes the extreme position that the evidence of the restaurant robberies had only "very small" or even zero probative value, mainly because Marshall testified, and Vance did not deny, that they were long-time friends and so the evidence concerning the restaurant robberies merely confirmed that acknowledged fact. Actually it did more; it pointed to Vance as the probable triggerman in the bank robbery. In all three restaurant robberies Vance was the robber who rushed the counter while Marshall watched his back (although Marshall did join him at the counter in one of the robberies). The fact that when Vance and Marshall robbed together (at least when they robbed together on the night before the first bank robbery) Vance rushed the counter makes it more likely that he also rushed the counter at the second bank, where the teller was killed; video surveillance evidence showed that whoever rushed the counter at the second bank shot the teller moments later. Furthermore, there is a difference between partnership in robberies and a personal friendship. If Vance and Marshall were partners in robbery, there is at least some likelihood that in a robbery at which Marshall is conceded to have been present (the bank robbery), one of the other robbers was indeed Vance.

Granted, the evidence of the restaurant robberies did not have a *great* deal of probative value—but for a reason that does not help Vance's defense. It had very limited *incremental* probative value because the *other* evidence of Vance's guilt (discussed next) was very strong. But by the same token the incremental prejudicial effect of the evidence regarding the restaurant robberies must also have been slight, because for an effect to be prejudicial means that it may actually have swayed the jury's decision. If conviction was a forgone conclusion, the evidence of the restaurant robberies was icing on the cake; the government didn't need it to convict Vance.

The other evidence of Vance's guilt included Marshall's eyewitness testimony about the bank robberies, DNA evidence implicating Vance, the identification of Vance as one of the robbers by a teller at the first bank robbed and also by Vance's own girlfriend, and testimony by Marshall's girlfriend that further implicated Vance. Taken all in all, this evidence, wholly apart from the evidence about the restaurant robberies, was compelling. Even without that evidence, no reasonable jury could have acquitted Vance.

The teller testified that she recognized Vance, whom she had known since childhood, as the robber who approached her and demanded money. Marshall's girlfriend testified that Vance, Marshall, and Bluford arrived at her apartment the evening before the day planned for the second robbery (although that robbery did not actually take place for another two days) and that Vance was carrying bags of guns and ammunition. She also testified that Marshall had confessed to her that he had committed the second bank robbery along with Vance and Buford and that Vance had been "the man with the gun going over the counter," and thus the killer. Vance's girlfriend testified that she recognized him in a surveillance photograph taken during the first bank robbery.

Vance's counsel tries to pick apart the government's evidence—other than that of Marshall's girlfriend, which by itself would have been sufficient to convict Vance, since Marshall's confession to her, made before he had cut a plea deal with the government in exchange for testifying against Vance, was recorded by the wire that the FBI had given her to wear. Counsel notes, however, that Marshall had lied repeatedly in his dealings with the prosecutors and claims that this proved him to have been a "pathological liar" none of whose testimony should have been believed. Counsel also argues that the DNA evidence should not have been admitted and that the female teller and Vance's girlfriend could not have identified him because the robber whom they identified as Vance was masked.

The jury was entitled to reject these arguments. Regarding Marshall's lies, *falsus in uno, falsus in omnibus* (false in one thing—or for that matter more than one thing—therefore false in everything) is not a doctrine of American law, *United States v. Edwards,* 581 F.3d 604, 612 (7th Cir.2009), and isn't even true. When Mary McCarthy famously said of Lillian Hellman "that every word she writes is a lie, including 'and' and 'the,' " Hellman sued her for defamation. (She died before judgment, and her estate dropped the suit, even though New York had abrogated the common law rule that an action for defamation does not survive the victim's death. N.Y. Estates, Powers & Trusts Law § 11–3.2(b).) The jury was entitled to believe Marshall's testimony that Vance was one of his accomplices in the bank robberies, as well as in the restaurant robberies, and also that Vance had admitted to him after the second robbery to having shot the teller who died.

EXERCISE

You are a prosecutor in the U.S. Attorney's office. An FBI agent brings you a file on a bank robbery case against Daniel Swampcutt. During the robbery, the robber wore a mask along with jeans and a white t-shirt. The only thing that links Swampcutt to the robbery is the fact that the demand note given to the teller was written on the back of Mr. Swampcutt's business card. The robber was reported by the teller as being male and about 5'10". Mr. Swampcutt (a realtor) is 6'1". The teller also said that she did not get a good look at the robber because of the mask, but the teller believed that the robber was "probably black." Mr. Swampcutt is white. Swampcutt has a prior conviction for robbery of a post office, and was charged by acquitted of another robbery involving a convenience store. He has no other criminal history.

You have three choices: you can accept the case, you can decline it, or you can ask the agent to gather more evidence. The decision is yours alone to make. Which do you choose? If you want more evidence, what will you ask the agent to look into?

B. ACTION ELEMENTS (ACTUS REUS)

Nearly all crimes require proof that the defendant performed some action: fired a shot, possessed a drug, or took money from a bank, for example. A much smaller group of crimes require the omission of an action, such as the failure to report a crime in certain situations.

Action elements (traditionally referred to as the "actus reus" of the case) are usually easy to identify on the face of a statute. Action elements are often proven by the same evidence that proves up identity, including eyewitness testimony, but it is important to keep these two elements distinct.

Action elements are often tied up in issues of causation, which combine an action (shooting a gun) with an outcome (the death of a victim who is shot). Action and outcome elements are sometimes broken out into two parts and at other times are combined and considered together. Crimes where the required action is possession (of a gun or firearm, for example) merit special attention, since the definition of "possession" can include actions other than our normal understanding of holding an object.

1. CAUSATION

The ideas of "cause-in-fact" and "proximate cause" used in torts also come into play in criminal cases. A cause-in-fact (sometimes called a "but-for" cause) is one that is necessary for the result to have occurred. For example, in a murder the defendant having fired a gun might be a cause-in-fact, if the murder could not have been accomplished without the firearm. Proximate cause is an evaluation of how close a cause is to the harm; there are limits to how far back we can go in chain of causal events. For example, the fact that a manufacturer made a gun may be a cause-in-fact for a murder, but we are unwilling as a society to say that the proximity of that action is close enough to the killing to create criminal liability.

PAROLINE v. UNITED STATES
134 S. Ct. 1710 (2014)

JUSTICE KENNEDY delivered the opinion of the Court.

This case presents the question of how to determine the amount of restitution a possessor of child pornography must pay to the victim whose childhood abuse appears in the pornographic materials possessed. The relevant statutory provisions are set forth at 18 U.S.C. § 2259. Enacted as a component of the Violence Against Women Act of 1994, § 2259 requires district courts to award restitution for certain federal criminal offenses, including child-pornography possession.

Petitioner Doyle Randall Paroline pleaded guilty to such an offense. He admitted to possessing between 150 and 300 images of child pornography, which included two that depicted the sexual exploitation of a young girl, now a young woman, who goes by the pseudonym "Amy" for this litigation. The question is what causal relationship must be established between the defendant's conduct and a victim's losses for purposes of determining the right to, and the amount of, restitution under § 2259. . . .

One person whose story illustrates the devastating harm caused by child pornography is the respondent victim in this case. When she was eight and nine years old, she was sexually abused by her uncle in order to produce child pornography. Her uncle was prosecuted, required to pay about $6,000 in restitution, and sentenced to a lengthy prison term. The victim underwent an initial course of therapy beginning in 1998 and continuing into 1999. By the end of this period, her therapist's notes reported that she was " 'back to normal' "; her involvement in dance and other age-appropriate activities, and the support of her family, justified an optimistic assessment. App. 70–71. Her functioning appeared to decline in her teenage years, however; and a major blow to her recovery came when, at the age of 17, she learned that images of her abuse were being trafficked on the Internet. *Id.,* at 71. The digital images were available nationwide and no doubt worldwide. Though the exact scale of the trade in her images is unknown, the possessors to date easily number in the thousands. The knowledge that her images were circulated far and wide renewed the victim's trauma and made it difficult for her to recover from her abuse. As she explained in a victim impact statement submitted to the District Court in this case:

> "Every day of my life I live in constant fear that someone will see my pictures and recognize me and that I will be humiliated all over again. It hurts me to know someone is looking at them—at me—when I was just a little girl being abused for the camera. I did not choose to be there, but now I am there forever in pictures that people are using to do sick things. I want it all erased. I want it all stopped. But I am powerless to stop it just like I was powerless to stop my uncle. . . . My life and my feelings are worse now because the crime has never really stopped and will never really stop. . . . It's like I am being abused over and over and over again." *Id.,* at 60–61.

The victim says in her statement that her fear and trauma make it difficult for her to trust others or to feel that she has control over what happens to her. *Id.,* at 63.

The full extent of this victim's suffering is hard to grasp. Her abuser took away her childhood, her self-conception of her innocence, and her freedom from the kind of nightmares and memories that most others will never know. These crimes were compounded by the distribution of images of her abuser's horrific acts, which meant the wrongs inflicted upon her were in effect repeated; for she knew her humiliation and hurt were and would be renewed into the future as an ever-increasing number of wrongdoers witnessed the crimes committed against her.

Petitioner Paroline is one of the individuals who possessed this victim's images. In 2009, he pleaded guilty in federal court to one count of possession of material involving the sexual exploitation of children in violation of 18 U.S.C. § 2252. 672 F.Supp.2d 781, 783 (E.D.Tex.2009). Paroline admitted to knowing possession of between 150 and 300 images of child pornography, two of which depicted the respondent victim. *Ibid.* The victim sought restitution under § 2259, asking for close to $3.4 million, consisting of nearly $3 million in lost income and about $500,000 in future treatment and counseling costs. App. 52, 104. She also sought attorney's fees and costs. 672 F.Supp.2d, at 783. The parties submitted competing expert reports. They stipulated that the victim did not know who Paroline was and that none of her claimed losses flowed from any specific knowledge about him or his offense conduct. *Id.,* at 792, and n. 11; App. 230.

After briefing and hearings, the District Court declined to award restitution. 672 F.Supp.2d, at 793. The District Court observed that "everyone involved with child pornography—from the abusers and producers to the end-users and possessors—contribute[s] to [the victim's] ongoing harm." *Id.,* at 792. But it concluded that the Government had the burden of proving the amount of the victim's losses "directly produced by Paroline that would not have occurred without his possession of her images." *Id.,* at 791. The District Court found that, under this standard, the Government had failed to meet its burden of proving what losses, if any, were proximately caused by Paroline's offense. It thus held that "an award of restitution is not appropriate in this case." *Id.,* at 793.

As a general matter, to say one event proximately caused another is a way of making two separate but related assertions. First, it means the former event caused the latter. This is known as actual cause or cause in fact. The concept of actual cause "is not a metaphysical one but an ordinary, matter-of-fact inquiry into the existence . . . of a causal relation as laypeople would view it." 4 F. Harper, F. James, & O. Gray, Torts § 20.2, p. 100 (3d ed. 2007).

Every event has many causes, however, see *ibid.,* and only some of them are proximate, as the law uses that term. So to say that one event was a proximate cause of another means that it was not just any cause, but one with a sufficient connection to the result. The idea of proximate cause, as distinct from actual cause or cause in fact, defies easy summary. It is "a flexible concept," *Bridge v. Phoenix Bond & Indemnity Co.,* 553 U.S. 639, 654, 128 S.Ct. 2131, 170 L.Ed.2d 1012 (2008), that generally "refers to the basic requirement that . . . there must be 'some direct relation between the injury asserted and the injurious conduct alleged,'" *CSX Transp., Inc. v. McBride,* 564 U.S. ___, ___, 131 S.Ct. 2630, 2645, 180 L.Ed.2d 637 (2011) (ROBERTS, C.J., dissenting) (quoting *Holmes v. Securities Investor Protection Corporation,* 503 U.S. 258, 268, 112 S.Ct. 1311, 117 L.Ed.2d 532

(1992)). The concept of proximate causation is applicable in both criminal and tort law, and the analysis is parallel in many instances. 1 W. LaFave, Substantive Criminal Law § 6.4(c), p. 471 (2d ed. 2003) (hereinafter LaFave). Proximate cause is often explicated in terms of foreseeability or the scope of the risk created by the predicate conduct. See, *e.g., ibid.*; 1 Restatement (Third) of Torts: Liability for Physical and Emotional Harm § 29, p. 493 (2005) (hereinafter Restatement). A requirement of proximate cause thus serves, *inter alia,* to preclude liability in situations where the causal link between conduct and result is so attenuated that the consequence is more aptly described as mere fortuity. *Exxon Co., U.S.A. v. Sofec, Inc.,* 517 U.S. 830, 838–839, 116 S.Ct. 1813, 135 L.Ed.2d 113 (1996).

All parties agree § 2259 imposes some causation requirement. The statute defines a victim as "the individual harmed as a result of a commission of a crime under this chapter." § 2259(c). The words "as a result of" plainly suggest causation. See *Pacific Operators Offshore, LLP v. Valladolid,* 565 U.S. ___, ___, 132 S.Ct. 680, 690–691, 181 L.Ed.2d 675 (2012); see also *Burrage v. United States,* 571 U.S. ___, ___, 134 S.Ct. 881, 886–887, 187 L.Ed.2d 715 (2014). And a straightforward reading of § 2259(c) indicates that the term "a crime" refers to the offense of conviction. Cf. *Hughey v. United States,* 495 U.S. 411, 416, 110 S.Ct. 1979, 109 L.Ed.2d 408 (1990). So if the defendant's offense conduct did not cause harm to an individual, that individual is by definition not a "victim" entitled to restitution under § 2259.

The most difficult aspect of this inquiry concerns the threshold requirement of causation in fact. To be sure, the requirement of proximate causation, as distinct from mere causation in fact, would prevent holding any possessor liable for losses caused in only a remote sense. But the victim's costs of treatment and lost income resulting from the trauma of knowing that images of her abuse are being viewed over and over are direct and foreseeable results of child-pornography crimes, including possession, assuming the prerequisite of factual causation is satisfied. The primary problem, then, is the proper standard of causation in fact. . . .

The traditional way to prove that one event was a factual cause of another is to show that the latter would not have occurred "but for" the former. This approach is a familiar part of our legal tradition, see 1 LaFave § 6.4(b), at 467–468; Prosser and Keeton § 41, at 266, and no party disputes that a showing of but-for causation would satisfy § 2259's factual-causation requirement. Sometimes that showing could be made with little difficulty. For example, but-for causation could be shown with ease in many cases involving producers of child pornography, see § 2251(a); parents who permit their children to be used for child-pornography production, see § 2251(b); individuals who sell children for such purposes, see § 2251A; or the initial distributor of the pornographic images of a child, see § 2252.

In this case, however, a showing of but-for causation cannot be made. The District Court found that the Government failed to prove specific losses caused by Paroline in a but-for sense and recognized that it would be "incredibly difficult" to do so in a case like this. 672 F.Supp.2d, at 791–793. That finding has a solid foundation in the record, and it is all but unchallenged in this Court. See Brief for Respondent Amy 63; Brief for United States 19, 25. But see Supp. Brief for United States 8–10. From the victim's perspective, Paroline was just one of thousands of anonymous possessors. To be sure, the victim's precise degree of trauma likely bears a relation to the total number of offenders; it would probably be less if only 10 rather than thousands had seen her images. But it is not possible to prove that her losses would be less (and by how much) but for one possessor's individual role in the large, loosely connected network through which her images circulate. See Sentencing Comm'n Report, at ii, xx. Even without Paroline's offense, thousands would have viewed and would in the future view the victim's images, so it cannot be shown that her trauma and attendant losses would have been any different but for Paroline's offense. That is especially so given the parties' stipulation that the victim had no knowledge of Paroline. See *supra,* at 1736–1737.

Recognizing that losses cannot be substantiated under a but-for approach where the defendant is an anonymous possessor of images in wide circulation on the Internet, the victim and the Government urge the Court to read § 2259 to require a less restrictive causation standard, at least in this and similar child-pornography cases. They are correct to note that courts have departed from the but-for standard where circumstances warrant, especially where the combined conduct of multiple wrongdoers produces a bad outcome. See *Burrage,* 571 U.S., at ___, 134 S.Ct., at 890 (acknowledging "the undoubted reality that courts have not *always* required strict but-for causality, even where criminal liability is at issue").

The victim and the Government look to the literature on criminal and tort law for alternatives to the but-for test. The Court has noted that the "most common" exception to the but-for causation requirement is applied where "multiple sufficient causes independently . . . produce a result," *ibid.*; see also 1 LaFave § 6.4(b), at 467–469; 1 Restatement § 27, at 376. This exception is an ill fit here, as all parties seem to recognize. Paroline's possession of two images of the victim was surely not sufficient to cause her entire losses from the ongoing trade in her images. Nor is there a practical way to isolate some subset of the victim's general losses that Paroline's conduct alone would have been sufficient to cause. See Brief for United States 26, n. 11.

Understandably, the victim and the Government thus concentrate on a handful of less demanding causation tests endorsed by authorities on tort law. One prominent treatise suggests that "[w]hen the conduct of two or more actors is so related to an event that their combined conduct, viewed as a whole, is a but-for cause of the event, and application of the but-for rule to them individually would absolve all of them, the conduct of each is a cause in fact of the event." Prosser and Keeton § 41, at 268. The Restatement adopts a similar exception for "[m]ultiple sufficient causal sets." 1 Restatement § 27, Comment *f*, at 380–381. This is where a wrongdoer's conduct, though alone "insufficient . . . to cause the plaintiff's harm," is, "when combined with conduct by other persons," "more than sufficient to cause the harm." *Ibid*. The Restatement offers as an example a case in which three people independently but simultaneously lean on a car, creating enough combined force to roll it off a cliff. *Ibid*. Even if each exerted too little force to move the car, and the force exerted by any two was sufficient to the move the car, each individual is a factual cause of the car's destruction. *Ibid*. The Government argues that these authorities "provide ample support for an 'aggregate' causation theory," Brief for United States 18, and that such a theory would best effectuate congressional intent in cases like this, *id.,* at 18–19. The victim says much the same. Brief for Respondent Amy 42–43. . . .

Contrary to the victim's suggestion, this is not akin to a case in which a "gang of ruffians" collectively beats a person, or in which a woman is "gang raped by five men on one night or by five men on five sequential nights." Brief for Respondent Amy 55. First, this case does not involve a set of wrongdoers acting in concert, see Prosser and Keeton § 52, at 346 (discussing full liability for a joint enterprise); for Paroline had no contact with the overwhelming majority of the offenders for whose actions the victim would hold him accountable. Second, adopting the victim's approach would make an individual possessor liable for the combined consequences of the acts of not just 2, 5, or even 100 independently acting offenders; but instead, a number that may reach into the tens of thousands. See Brief for Respondent Amy 65.

The contention that the victim's entire losses from the ongoing trade in her images were "suffered . . . as a proximate result" of Paroline's offense for purposes of § 2259 must be rejected. But that does not mean the broader principles underlying the aggregate causation theories the Government and the victim cite are irrelevant to determining the proper outcome in cases like this. The cause of the victim's general losses is the trade in her images. And Paroline is a part of that cause, for he is one of those who viewed her images. While it is not possible to identify a discrete, readily definable incremental loss he caused, it is indisputable that he was a part of the overall phenomenon that caused her general losses. Just as it undermines the purposes of tort law to turn away plaintiffs harmed by several wrongdoers, it would undermine the remedial and penological purposes of § 2259 to turn away victims in cases like this.

With respect to the statute's remedial purpose, there can be no question that it would produce anomalous results to say that no restitution is appropriate in these circumstances. It is common ground that the victim suffers continuing and grievous harm as a result of her knowledge that a large, indeterminate number of individuals have viewed and will in the future view images of the sexual abuse she endured. Brief for Petitioner 50; Brief for Respondent Wright 4; Brief for United States 23; Brief for Respondent Amy 60. Harms of this sort are a major reason why child pornography is outlawed. See *Ferber,* 458 U.S., at 759, 102 S.Ct. 3348.

The unlawful conduct of everyone who reproduces, distributes, or possesses the images of the victim's abuse—including Paroline—plays a part in sustaining and aggravating this tragedy. And there can be no doubt Congress wanted victims to receive restitution for harms like this. The law makes restitution "mandatory," § 2259(b)(4), for child-pornography offenses under Chapter 110, language that indicates Congress' clear intent that victims of child pornography be compensated by the perpetrators who contributed to their anguish. It would undermine this intent to apply the statute in a way that would render it a dead letter in child-pornography prosecutions of this type.

Denying restitution in cases like this would also be at odds with the penological purposes of § 2259's mandatory restitution scheme. In a sense, every viewing of child pornography is a repetition of the victim's abuse. One reason to make restitution mandatory for crimes like this is to impress upon offenders that their conduct produces concrete and devastating harms for real, identifiable victims. See *Kelly, supra,* at 49, n. 10, 107 S.Ct. 353 ("Restitution is an effective rehabilitative penalty because it forces the defendant to confront, in concrete terms, the harm his actions have caused"). It would be inconsistent with this purpose to apply the statute in a way that leaves offenders with the mistaken impression that child-pornography possession (at least where the images are in wide circulation) is a victimless crime.

If the statute by its terms required a showing of strict but-for causation, these purposes would be beside the point. But the text of the statute is not so limited. Although Congress limited restitution to losses that are the "proximate result" of the defendant's offense, such unelaborated causal language by no means requires but-for causation by its terms. See *Burrage,* 571 U.S., at ___, 134 S.Ct., at 888 (courts need not read phrases like "results from" to require but-for causality where there is "textual or contextual" reason to conclude otherwise). As the authorities the Government and the victim cite show, the availability of alternative causal standards where circumstances warrant is, no less than the but-for test itself as a default, part of the background legal tradition against which Congress has legislated, cf. *id.,* at ___, 134 S.Ct., at 889–890. It would be unacceptable to adopt a causal standard so strict that it would undermine congressional intent where neither the plain text of the statute nor legal tradition demands such an approach.

In this special context, where it can be shown both that a defendant possessed a victim's images and that a victim has outstanding losses caused by the continuing traffic in those images but where it is impossible to trace a particular amount of those losses to the individual defendant by recourse to a more traditional causal inquiry, a court applying § 2259 should order restitution in an amount that comports with the defendant's relative role in the causal process that underlies the victim's general losses. The amount would not be severe in a case like this, given the nature of the causal connection between the conduct of a possessor like Paroline and the entirety of the victim's general losses from the trade in her images, which are the product of the acts of thousands of offenders. It would not, however, be a token or nominal amount. The required restitution would be a reasonable and circumscribed award imposed in recognition of the indisputable role of the offender in the causal process underlying the victim's losses and suited to the relative size of that causal role. This would serve the twin goals of helping the victim achieve eventual restitution for all her child-pornography losses and impressing upon offenders the fact that child-pornography crimes, even simple possession, affect real victims.

EXERCISE

Generally, murder statutes outlaw intentionally or recklessly causing the death of another. Imagine that Patty and Laurence share an apartment. Laurence has weak legs and is scared of falling when he gets out of the tub, and asks Patty for advice. Patty tells him that there is a "handy bar" underneath a towel rack to the left of the tub, and that Laurence simply needs to move the towel rack then clutch that bar as he gets out of the tub. Laurence had never noticed that bar, and only moved into the apartment the previous week. The two were not getting along, and Patty was upset at the way that Laurence parked his car in the spot that she had always used.

Patty knows, but Laurence does not, that the "handy bar" she referred to is a pipe that has become electrified due to an exposed electrical line touching the pipe behind the wall. Predictably, Laurence grabs the bar as he gets out of the bath and then dies when he is electrocuted. Is there cause-in-fact to support a murder charge against Patty? What about proximate cause?

2. POSSESSION

Because much of criminal law involves forbidden objects such as drugs and guns, possessing those objects often serves as the action element of a criminal violation. The act of possessing something is easy to prove if there is strong evidence (such as video) showing the defendant holding the forbidden object. It is more difficult when the case lacks such evidence.

UNITED STATES V. JAMESON
478 F. 3d 1204 (10th Cir. 2007)

PAUL KELLY, JR., CIRCUIT JUDGE.

Defendant-Appellant Christopher Jameson appeals from his conviction, after a jury trial, for being a felon in possession of a firearm in violation of 18 U.S.C. § 922(g)(1). . . .

In the early morning hours of August 27, 2004, Sergeant Vaughn Allen of the Salt Lake County Sheriff's Department was on patrol in Salt Lake County, Utah. He observed a maroon colored Dodge Stratus pull out of an apartment complex and turn eastbound onto a main thoroughfare. The officer noticed that the car's taillights were not working, and he initiated a traffic stop. The car pulled into a gas station and stopped in a well-lit area.

When the officer turned his spotlight onto the car, he saw that there were four occupants. He observed a male occupant in the front passenger seat lean forward and appear to rummage through the glove compartment. He also observed a male occupant in the rear passenger-side seat drop his shoulder and lean forward, as if he were retrieving or concealing something on the floor. The officer later determined that the man in the front passenger seat was Terry Paswaters and that the man in the rear passenger-side seat was Mr. Jameson. Mr. Jameson's brother, Cody Jameson, occupied the rear driver's-side seat while Sarah Maciano, the owner of the car, was the driver.

Sergeant Allen approached the vehicle from the driver's side and pointed his flashlight into the car to look for weapons in plain view. He noticed food and other debris on the floor. Because of Mr. Paswaters' movement toward the glove box and Mr. Jameson's movement toward the floor, the officer testified that he was concerned about the occupants hiding drugs or drug paraphernalia, and also about the possibility (attendant to every stop) that the occupants might be armed. III R. at 17–18. But, despite shining his flashlight into the car to look for such items, he initially saw none. *Id.* at 22. . . .

Sergeant Allen then conducted a search of the car to inventory its contents. During the search, he discovered a World War II-era bayonet sitting on the back seat. As he reached for the bayonet, he noticed a small, unloaded .22 caliber pistol and a key chain on the floor in front of where Mr. Jameson had been sitting. Sergeant Allen testified that the pistol lay exactly where Mr. Jameson's feet would have been before he exited the car. A subsequent examination of the pistol failed to recover any fingerprints, nor were investigators able to determine who owned or used the pistol.

To establish a violation of 18 U.S.C. § 922(g)(1), the government had to prove: (1) that Mr. Jameson had previously been convicted of a felony, (2) that he thereafter knowingly possessed a firearm, and (3) that such possession was in or affected interstate commerce. *United States v. Michel,*

446 F.3d 1122, 1128 (10th Cir.2006). On appeal, Mr. Jameson challenges only the sufficiency of the evidence with respect to his knowing possession.

As we have repeatedly held, possession can be actual or constructive. *Id.* Actual possession exists when a person has direct physical control over a firearm at a given time. *See United States v. Munoz,* 150 F.3d 401, 416 (5th Cir.1998); *see also United States v. Bowen,* 437 F.3d 1009, 1017 (10th Cir.2006). Constructive possession exists when a person "knowingly holds the power and ability to exercise dominion and control over [a firearm]." *United States v. Lopez,* 372 F.3d 1207, 1211 (10th Cir.2004). When a defendant has exclusive possession of the premises on which a firearm is found, knowledge, dominion, and control can be properly inferred because of the exclusive possession alone. *United States v. Avery,* 295 F.3d 1158, 1177 (10th Cir.2002). However, when "two or more people occupy a given space . . . the government is required to meet a higher burden in proving constructive possession." *Michel,* 446 F.3d at 1128. In other words, in joint occupancy cases, knowledge, dominion, and control may not be inferred simply by the defendant's proximity to a firearm. Instead, the government must "present evidence to show some connection or nexus between the defendant and the firearm." *Id.*

To be clear, when the government seeks to convict a defendant under § 922(g)(1), and the firearm was found in an area occupied by two or more persons, it must prove either (1) actual possession, or (2) constructive possession by way of demonstrating a nexus between the defendant and the firearm. Of course, what constitutes a sufficient nexus is the next issue. In this regard, our precedent is, admittedly, cryptic.

We have held that "*knowledge* and *access* are required to prove that [a] defendant knowingly held the power to exercise dominion and control over [a] firearm." *United States v. Colonna,* 360 F.3d 1169, 1179 (10th Cir.2004). Stated another way, "where the defendant in a joint occupancy situation has knowledge of and access to the weapons, there is a sufficient nexus to infer dominion and control." *Id.* Thus, if there is sufficient evidence to infer that a defendant had knowledge of and access to a firearm, there is also sufficient evidence to infer that he had dominion and control over the firearm, and, consequently, that he constructively possessed the firearm.

Proximity alone, however, is insufficient to establish knowledge and access to (and dominion and control over) a firearm in a joint occupancy case. *See United States v. Hishaw,* 235 F.3d 565, 572 (10th Cir.2000) (citing *United States v. Reece,* 86 F.3d 994, 996 (10th Cir.1996)). But when combined with other evidence in the case linking the defendant to the firearm, proximity is material and probative evidence that may be considered in deciding whether a defendant had knowledge of and access to (and dominion and control over) the contraband. *See United States v. Ortiz-Ortiz,* 57 F.3d 892, 895 (10th Cir.1995); *United States v. Espinosa,* 771 F.2d 1382, 1397 (10th Cir.1985).

Thus, the rule is as follows: (1) proximity alone may not establish knowledge and access in a joint occupancy case, (2) neither may proximity alone support a finding of dominion and control in a joint occupancy case, (3) evidence of knowledge and access gives rise to a permissive inference of dominion and control, (4) evidence of knowledge and access may be proved by direct evidence, or inferred from circumstantial evidence, so long as the circumstantial evidence includes something other than mere proximity, (5) proximity may be considered with other evidence in the case to support an inference of knowledge and access, and dominion and control over the firearm. This is the practical effect of our requirement that there be a "nexus" between a defendant and a firearm in a constructive possession, joint-occupancy case.

In this case, the government could have proven the "knowingly possessed" element of § 922(g)(1) in one of two ways. First, it could have shown that Mr. Jameson actually possessed the pistol-that he had direct, physical control over it. Alternatively, it could have shown constructive possession-that he had knowledge of and access to, and thus dominion and control over, the pistol, so long as the constructive possession was supported by more than Mr. Jameson's mere proximity to the pistol. Upon review of the evidence, we conclude that there was sufficient evidence for a reasonable jury to find either actual or constructive possession.

Sergeant Allen testified that, as he approached the car, he saw Mr. Jameson lean forward, as though he "was trying to retrieve something from or conceal something underneath the seat in front of him." III. R. at 17. Sergeant Allen also testified that he didn't see the pistol initially because it was underneath Mr. Jameson's foot. *Id.* at 43. Sergeant Allen eventually found the pistol in the exact spot where Mr. Jameson's foot had been. *Id.* at 43–44. He testified that it was obvious where the pistol was located and that, after Mr. Jameson left the vehicle, the pistol was not concealed by anything. *Id.* at 23. Although Mr. Jameson argues that the car was not well lit when Sergeant Allen inspected it, and that the floor was cluttered with garbage such that the pistol was not clearly visible, Sergeant Allen was adamant in his testimony. We may not upset the jury's credibility determination on appeal. *See United States v. Silvers,* 84 F.3d 1317, 1328 (10th Cir.1996).

From this evidence, a reasonable juror could infer that Mr. Jameson had actual physical control of the pistol when the car was pulled over and that he was trying to hide it underneath the seat or under his foot as Sergeant Allen approached. Similarly, a reasonable juror could easily have inferred that Mr. Jameson had knowledge of and access to the pistol and consequently, dominion and control, satisfying all the elements of constructive possession. This is not a case, as Mr. Jameson suggests, where "the Government only showed that [he] was present inside a car with three others where a gun was found." Aplt. Br. at 17–18. Instead, this is a case where Mr. Jameson's proximity to the pistol was coupled with Mr. Jameson's furtive movements, *see Bowen,* 437 F.3d at 1014–16, his inferred physical contact with the pistol (his foot was on top of it), and the pistol's being in plain view and easily retrievable to a passenger in Mr. Jameson's seat, *see United States v. Gorman,* 312 F.3d 1159, 1164 (10th Cir.2002). Sergeant Allen's testimony that the parking lot was clearly lit adds credibility to his other testimony and thus strengthens the inferences a reasonable juror could draw from it. These facts allow for a reasonable inference of actual possession or constructive possession, and they certainly demonstrate a nexus between Mr. Jameson and the pistol. Accordingly, there was sufficient evidence to show that Mr. Jameson knowingly possessed the pistol.

EXERCISE

Tony is a convicted felon who is prohibited from possessing a firearm under federal law. His prior conviction was for a very minor role in a narcotics operation, and did not involve the possession or the use of firearms. After serving the entire term of his state sentence (he did not receive parole because of smuggling violations while in prison), he is released and moves back in with his wife, Lenore. When he moves his stuff in, Lenore shows him a loaded gun that she keeps in a cupboard by the front door. The cupboard is unlocked and easily accessible. "This is for home protection, only, Tony" she tells him, "so use it only if you need it for that." Tony nods.

The police later get a tip that Tony possesses a gun, search the house, and find the loaded gun in the cupboard. They determine that the gun has, in fact, traveled in interstate commerce. Lenore tells the police about the conversation recounted above, and insists that Tony never touched the gun. You are the prosecutor. Under the standards set out in the *Jameson* case above, should Tony be charged as a felon in possession of a firearm?

3.   OMISSION

While most criminal statutes address affirmative actions, a relatively few criminalize a *failure* to act. These crimes usually have as an element not only a failure to act but the presence of some duty to take action resting in the law, a relationship, or a contract. Many crimes of omission deal with failure to adhere to regulations or report certain issues or crimes.

UNITED STATES V. PARK
421 U.S. 658 (1975)

MR. CHIEF JUSTICE BURGER delivered the opinion of the Court.

Acme Markets, Inc., is a national retail food chain with approximately 36,000 employees, 874 retail outlets, 12 general warehouses, and four special warehouses. Its headquarters, including the office of the president, respondent Park, who is chief executive officer of the corporation, are located in Philadelphia, Pa. In a five-count information filed in the United States District Court for the District of Maryland, the Government charged Acme and respondent with violations of the Federal Food, Drug and Cosmetic Act. Each count of the information alleged that the defendants had received food that had been shipped in interstate commerce and that, while the food was being held for sale in Acme's Baltimore warehouse following shipment in interstate commerce, they caused it to be held in a building accessible to rodents and to be exposed to contamination by rodents. These acts were alleged to have resulted in the food's being adulterated within the meaning of 21 U.S.C. ss 342(a)(3) and (4), in violation of 21 U.S.C. s 331(k).

Acme pleaded guilty to each count of the information. Respondent pleaded not guilty. The evidence at trial demonstrated that in April 1970 the Food and Drug Administration (FDA) advised respondent by letter of insanitary conditions in Acme's Philadelphia warehouse. In 1971 the FDA found that similar conditions existed in the firm's Baltimore warehouse. An FDA consumer safety officer testified concerning evidence of rodent infestation and other insanitary conditions discovered during a 12-day inspection of the Baltimore warehouse in November and December 1971. He also related that a second inspection of the warehouse had been conducted in March 1972. On that occasion the inspectors found that there had been improvement in the sanitary conditions, but that 'there was still evidence of rodent activity in the building and in the warehouses and we found some rodent-contaminated lots of food items.' App. 23.

The Government also presented testimony by the Chief of Compliance of the FDA's Baltimore office, who informed respondent by letter of the conditions at the Baltimore warehouse after the first inspection. There was testimony by Acme's Baltimore division vice president, who had responded to the letter on behalf of Acme and respondent and who described the steps taken to remedy the insanitary conditions discovered by both inspections. The Government's final witness, Acme's vice president for legal affairs and assistant secretary, identified respondent as the president and chief executive officer of the company and read a bylaw prescribing the duties of the chief executive officer. He testified that respondent functioned by delegating 'normal operating duties,' including sanitation, but that he retained 'certain things, which are the big, broad, principles of the operation of the company,' and had 'the responsibility of seeing that they all work together.' Id., at 41.

At the close of the Government's case in chief, respondent moved for a judgment of acquittal on the ground that 'the evidence in chief has shown that Mr. Park is not personally concerned in this Food and Drug violation. The trial judge denied the motion, stating that United States v.

Dotterweich, 320 U.S. 277, 64 S.Ct. 134, 88 L.Ed. 48 (1943), was controlling.

Respondent was the only defense witness. He testified that, although all of Acme's employees were in a sense under his general direction, the company had an 'organizational structure for responsibilities for certain functions' according to which different phases of its operation were 'assigned to individuals who, in turn, have staff and departments under them.' He identified those individuals responsible for sanitation, and related that upon receipt of the January 1972 FDA letter, he had conferred with the vice president for legal affairs, who informed him that the Baltimore division vice president 'was investigating the situation immediately and would be taking corrective action and would be preparing a summary of the corrective action to reply to the letter.' Respondent stated that he did not 'believe there was anything (he) could have done more constructively than what (he) found was being done.' App. 43–47.

On cross-examination, respondent conceded that providing sanitary conditions for food offered for sale to the public was something that he was 'responsible for in the entire operation of the company,' and he stated that it was one of many phases of the company that he assigned to 'dependable subordinates.' Respondent was asked about and, over the objections of his counsel, admitted receiving, the April 1970 letter addressed to him from the FDA regarding insanitary conditions at Acme's Philadelphia warehouse.

He acknowledged that, with the exception of the division vice president, the same individuals had responsibility for sanitation in both Baltimore and Philadelphia. Finally, in response to questions concerning the Philadelphia and Baltimore incidents, respondent admitted that the Baltimore problem indicated the system for handling sanitation 'wasn't working perfectly' and that as Acme's chief executive officer he was responsible for 'any result which occurs in our company.' Id., at 48–55.

At the close of the evidence, respondent's renewed motion for a judgment of acquittal was denied. The relevant portion of the trial judge's instructions to the jury challenged by respondent is set out in the margin. Respondent's counsel objected to the instructions on the ground that they failed fairly to reflect our decision in United States v. Dotterweich, supra, and to define "responsible relationship." The trial judge overruled the objection. The jury found respondent guilty on all counts of the information, and he was subsequently sentenced to pay a fine of $50 on each count.

The Court of Appeals reversed the conviction and remanded for a new trial. That court viewed the Government as arguing 'that the conviction may be predicated solely upon a showing that . . . (respondent) was the President of the offending corporation,' and it stated that as 'a general proposition, some act of commission or omission is an essential element of every crime.' It reasoned that, although our decision in United States v. Dotterweich, supra, 320 U.S., at 281, 64 S.Ct., at 136–137, had construed the statutory provisions under which respondent was tried to dispense with the traditional element of "awareness of some wrongdoing," the Court had not construed them as dispensing with the element of 'wrongful action.' The Court of Appeals concluded that the trial judge's instructions 'might well have left the jury with the erroneous impression that Park could be found guilty in the absence of 'wrongful action' on his part,' 499 F.2d, at 841–842, and that proof of this element was required by due process.

We granted certiorari because of an apparent conflict among the Courts of Appeals with respect to the standard of liability of corporate officers under the Federal Food, Drug, and Cosmetic Act as construed in United States v. Dotterweich, supra, and because of the importance of the question to the Government's enforcement program. We reverse. . . .

The rationale of the interpretation given the Act in Dotterweich, as holding criminally accountable the persons whose failure to exercise the authority and supervisory responsibility reposed in them by the business organization resulted in the violation complained of, has been confirmed in our subsequent cases. Thus, the Court has reaffirmed the proposition that 'the public interest in the purity of its food is so great as to warrant the imposition of the highest standard of care on distributors.' Smith v. California, 361 U.S. 147, 152, 80 S.Ct. 215, 218, 4 L.Ed.2d 205 (1959). In order to make 'distributors of food the strictest censors of their merchandise,' ibid., the Act punishes 'neglect where the law requires care, or inaction where it imposes a duty.' Morissette v. United States, supra, 342 U.S., at 255, 72 S.Ct., at 246. 'The accused, if he does not will the violation, usually is in a position to prevent it with no more care than society might reasonably expect and no more exertion than it might reasonably exact from one who assumed his responsibilities.' Id., at 256, 72 S.Ct., at 246. Cf. Hughes, Criminal Omissions, 67 Yale L.J. 590 (1958). Similarly, in cases decided after Dotterweich, the Courts of Appeals have recognized that those corporate agents vested with the responsibility, and power commensurate with that responsibility, to devise whatever measures are necessary to ensure compliance with the Act bear a 'responsible relationship' to, or have a 'responsible share' in, violations.

Thus Dotterweich and the cases which have followed reveal that in providing sanctions which reach and touch the individuals who execute the corporate mission-and this is by no means necessarily confined to a single corporate agent or employee-the Act imposes not only a positive duty to seek out and remedy violations when they occur but also, and primarily, a duty to implement measures that will insure that violations will not occur. The requirements of foresight and vigilance imposed on responsible corporate agents are beyond question demanding, and perhaps onerous, but they are no more stringent than the public has a right to expect of those who voluntarily assume positions of authority in business enterprises whose services and products affect the health and well-being of the public that supports them. Cf. Wasserstrom, Strict Liability in the Criminal Law, 12 Stan.L.Rev. 731, 741–745 (1960). . . .

We are satisfied that the Act imposes the highest standard of care and permits conviction of responsible corporate officials who, in light of this standard of care, have the power to prevent or correct violations of its provisions.

EXERCISE

You are a defense attorney representing a client, Lynette, who has been charged with the offense of "maintaining a building used to traffic narcotics." Your client tells you that she owns a house that is not her residence. She rented it out for many years, but during a period that it was vacant two years ago she agreed to let her niece, Justine, live there. A few months later, Justine let her boyfriend, Laurence, move in with her. A few months ago, your client was driving past this house and decided to stop in. Upon entering, she saw that the kitchen table was covered with small bags of crack and piles of small bills. Furious at this evidence of drug dealing, she told Justine that she had to move out immediately. Your client then left for Florida, where she spends the winter. While there, she called the house where Justine and Laurence lived, and no one answered. Your client took this to mean that they had, in fact, moved out. Then, one week ago, the police searched the house, arrested Justine and Laurence for selling crack, and then indicted your client for maintaining a building used to traffic narcotics.

Lynette asks if she should fight the charges and wants to know what her chances would be at trial. What do you say?

4. INVOLUNTARY ACTS

Another issue with action elements can be the voluntariness of an act—that is, whether the person chose to do the prohibited thing. We tend not to want to punish people for things they do not control, since that does not fit any rational goal of criminal law.

Section 2.01(2) of the Model Penal Code, which serves as the basis for some state statutes in this and other areas, describes the following as "not voluntary acts":

(a) a reflex or convulsion;

(b) a bodily movement during unconsciousness or sleep;

(c) conduct during hypnosis or resulting from hypnotic suggestion;

(d) a bodily movement that otherwise is not a product of the of the effort or determination of the actor, either conscious or habitual.

The question of voluntariness often is folded into a consideration of the element of intent, a state of mind element explored in the next section.

The case below addresses both a statute and a sentencing guideline that can be triggered by a failure to act. The court discusses the sentencing guideline, because the defendant had pled guilty to a violation of the statute, leaving only the sentencing provision at issue on appeal.

UNITED STATES V. FLORES-ALEJO

531 Fed. Appx. 422 (5th Cir. 2013)

PER CURIAM:

On July 4, 2010, police in Arlington, Texas, arrested Defendant-Appellant Lorenzo Flores-Alejo for driving while intoxicated with a child passenger. Tex. Penal Code Ann. § 49.045. Flores was convicted and sentenced to three years' imprisonment. While he was awaiting transfer to state prison to serve this sentence, agents of U.S. Immigration and Customs Enforcement (ICE) discovered him in Tarrant County Jail. Immigration records showed that Flores—a Mexican national—had illegally entered the United States three times between 1993 and 2000, and had been ordered removed or granted voluntary return each time. He reentered this country (after having been ordered removed) two months before his DWI arrest.

Flores was charged in a single count under the part of 8 U.S.C. § 1326(a) that provides punishment for an alien who has been "found in" the United States after having been deported. The government also alleged that Flores was subject to an increased statutory maximum punishment because he had committed certain crimes before his previous deportation. 8 U.S.C. § 1326(b)(1), (2). Flores pled guilty without a plea agreement. In the "Factual Resume" underlying his plea, he stipulated that he had been discovered in Tarrant County Jail.

The probation officer recommended increasing Flores's criminal history score by two points under the Sentencing Guidelines because he had been found in this country "while under [a] criminal justice sentence"—namely, the sentence imposed for his DWI conviction. U.S.S.G. § 4A1.1(d) (2011). Flores objected on two grounds. First, he argued that § 4A1.1(d) does not apply when an illegal-reentry defendant is found by immigration officials while he is in state custody. This argument was foreclosed by our decision in *United States v. Santana-Castellano,* 74 F.3d 593 (5th Cir.1996). He also argued that applying § 4A1.1(d) would violate the Fifth and Eighth Amendments by increasing his punishment based on an involuntary act that bore no relation to his culpability—remaining in the United States due to his incarceration. . . .

"The clear language in 8 U.S.C. § 1326(a)(2) provides three separate occasions upon which a deported alien may commit [an illegal-reentry] offense: 1) when he illegally enters the United States; 2) when he attempts to illegally enter the United States; or 3) when he is at any time found in the United States." *Santana-Castellano,* 74 F.3d at 597; *accord United States v. Mendez-Cruz,* 329 F.3d 885, 888–89 (D.C.Cir.2003).

Flores was charged under the "found in" prong, which "prohibits deported aliens, who have illegally reentered the United States, from remaining in the country." *Santana-Castellano,* 74 F.3d at 597. In *Santana-Castellano,* we held that a person who violates the "found in" prong commits a continuing offense that begins when he enters this country:

Where a deported alien enters the United States and remains here with the knowledge that his entry is illegal, his remaining here until he is "found" is a continuing offense because it is "an unlawful act set on foot by a single impulse and operated by an unintermittent force," to use the Supreme Court's language. *See United States v. Midstate Horticultural Co.,* 306 U.S. 161, 166 [59 S.Ct. 412, 83 L.Ed. 563] (1939). That "force" is the alien's knowledge that his entry is illegal due to his prior deportation, and his apparent intent to remain in the United States.

Id. at 598 (citation altered). We further held that this continuing offense ends only when immigration officials discover the violator's unlawful presence. *Id.* A "found in" offense thus is initiated by, but separate from, the act of reentering. . . .

At the heart of Flores's appeal is his contention that the Constitution prohibits a defendant from being punished—or in his case, from being subjected to increased punishment—for an involuntary act. He relies on *Robinson v. California,* 370 U.S. 660, 660 n. 1, 667, 82 S.Ct. 1417, 8 L.Ed.2d 758 (1962), in which the Supreme Court reversed the petitioner's conviction under a statute that criminalized the status of "be[ing] addicted to the use of narcotics." Imprisonment for such an offense "inflicts a cruel and unusual punishment" because even if a violator became addicted to narcotics through prior, voluntary use, "proof of the actual use of narcotics" was not required to convict. *Id.* at 665, 667, 82 S.Ct. 1417. Because the statute imposed criminal penalties for being afflicted with "an illness which may be contracted innocently or involuntarily," it could not withstand constitutional scrutiny.2 *Id.* at 667, 82 S.Ct. 1417.

Robinson subsequently has been interpreted to mean that, under the Eighth Amendment, "criminal penalties may be inflicted only if the accused has committed some act, has engaged in some behavior, which society has an interest in preventing, or perhaps in historical common law terms, has committed some *actus reus.*" *Powell v. Texas,* 392 U.S. 514, 533, 88 S.Ct. 2145, 20 L.Ed.2d 1254 (1968) (plurality opinion) (Marshall, J.). Extending this reasoning, Flores argues that applying § 4A1.1(d) because he remained in the United States while under a criminal justice sentence was impermissible because Texas officials actively prevented him from leaving this country and thereby ending his § 1326 offense. *See United States v. Ayala,* 35 F.3d 423, 425 (9th Cir.1994) ("To avoid being 'found in' the United States, a deported alien can either not re-enter the United States or, if he has already re-entered the United States, he can leave.").

Flores misapprehends the nature of the "relevant conduct" that triggered § 4A1.1(d)'s application to his Guidelines calculation. U.S.S.G. § 4A1.1 cmt. n. 4. Although some affirmative act is typically required for a criminal conviction, a *failure* to act in violation of a legal duty also can give rise to criminal liability. *See generally* Wayne R. LaFave, *Criminal Law* § 6.2 (5th ed.2010). This concept is woefully familiar to the American taxpayer, who may be punished for willfully failing to file a return if required by law to do so. *See* 26 U.S.C. § 7203; *Cheek v. United States,* 498 U.S. 192, 201–04, 111 S.Ct. 604, 112 L.Ed.2d 617 (1991).

A § 1326 "found in" offense is no different. As we discussed in *Santana-Castellano,* 74 F.3d at 598, a "found in" violation occurs when a deported alien remains in the United States knowing that his continued presence is unlawful, and he is subsequently found by immigration officials. Stated differently, the deported alien's reentry immediately gives rise to a duty to leave this country; his apparently intentional failure to do so is unlawful. *Id.; see also Ayala,* 35 F.3d at 425. Because an alien's prior deportation generally imparts to him the knowledge that reentering and staying would violate federal law, there will be precious few instances in which a violator will be unaware of his duty to leave this country after reentry. *See Santana-Castellano,* 74 F.3d at 598; *see also Lambert v. California,* 355 U.S. 225, 229, 78 S.Ct. 240, 2 L.Ed.2d 228 (1957) (holding, with respect to an ordinance requiring convicted felons present in Los Angeles to register with the police, that due process required "actual knowledge of the duty to register or proof of the probability of such knowledge and subsequent failure to comply").

In keeping with the continuing nature of Flores's § 1326 offense, we must view as a whole the voluntary acts he committed while illegally remaining in this country (reentering this country and driving while intoxicated) and his purportedly involuntary act (failing to leave while in state custody). To be sure, Flores hardly could have satisfied his legal duty to leave this country when he was in the hands of law enforcement. *See* LaFave, *supra,* § 6.2(c) ("[O]ne cannot be criminally liable for failing to do an act that he is physically incapable of performing."). But neither could he have failed to recognize that committing a crime in this country would likely prolong his unlawful presence. In effect, Flores argues that he cannot be held responsible for § 4A1.1(d) purposes when his affirmative acts have forced him to commit an unlawful omission. This is akin to blaming gravity for one's fall after jumping off a bridge.

EXERCISE

What if the defendant in the case above had been held prisoner in a locked closet by an ex-wife rather than detained by the government? Should that change the court's analysis of involuntariness?

C. STATE OF MIND ELEMENTS (MENS REA)

State of mind elements require the government to prove what a defendant knew, intended, or planned. A few criminal acts—mostly minor, like driving without a license—require no state of mind. These are sometimes referred to as "strict liability crimes."

State of mind elements can be proven most easily where a defendant admits that they had a particular state of mind, but often the proofs of this kind of element come in through circumstantial evidence such as behavior of the defendant that would comport with a particular thought. For example, if a defendant goes to a known cocaine dealer, says he wants "one kilo, packaged," pays the dealer and receives a kilo of cocaine, jurors might reasonably conclude that he knew that he was purchasing an illegal substance, cocaine.

The two most common state of mind elements are knowledge and intent. Though they are often found together as elements of a criminal statute, they have distinct meanings and sometimes require different proofs. For example, consider a defendant charged with knowingly possessing a controlled substance with the intent to distribute it. Knowledge and intent are both usually required elements of such crimes. Specifically, the government must prove both that the defendant *knew* that what he possessed was an illegal drug and that he *intended* to distribute it to others. The fact that he told his girlfriend that he "had a lot of crack" shows knowledge of the illegal substance he had, while offering it for sale to an undercover agent shows intent to distribute.

1. KNOWLEDGE

Knowledge is one of the most ubiquitous criminal elements. Section 2.02(2)(b) of the Model Penal Code directs that "A person acts knowingly with respect to a material element of an offense when: (i) if the element involves the nature of his conduct or the attendant circumstances, he is aware that his conduct is of that nature or that such circumstances exist; and (ii) if the element involves a result of his conduct, he is aware that it is practically certain that his conduct will cause such a result."

UNITED STATES V. PENNINGTON

20 F. 3d 593 (5th Cir. 1994)

JERRY E. SMITH, CIRCUIT JUDGE:

On September 17, 1992, Pennington and Margiotta, inexperienced truckers who lived in Miami, had just completed a delivery that left them in Laredo, Texas. Pennington contacted a broker to determine whether there were any loads in the West Texas area bound for Florida. The broker informed him that a load of unglazed Mexican tile in Rio Grande City needed to be shipped to Miami.

The defendants testified that they left Laredo around noon and arrived at the warehouse office in Rio Grande City at approximately 3:00 p.m. They talked to the warehouse owner and made arrangements for the shipment. They then drove to the warehouse across town and backed their trailer up to the loading dock, where it was loaded for about thirty minutes. The trailer had been empty prior to loading, and the defendants testified that they did not observe the entire loading process, but neither did they observe anyone place anything other than the tiles in the trailer.

After the trailer was loaded, the defendants went back to the office, picked up the bill of lading, and headed toward Edinburg to spend the night. They arrived in Edinburg at around 6:30 p.m. and parked the rig in a truck stop. Because each pallet of tile weighed approximately 3200 pounds, the trailer was not locked. The defendants checked into a motel and went to sleep.

The defendants left Edinburg the next day at around 2:00 p.m. and went to a truck stop in Harlingen to weigh their truck. After determining that their drive axle was overweight, they adjusted the fifth wheel to try to redistribute the weight. The adjustment did not correct the weight problem, so they left Harlingen overweight. They also spent several hours copying the log book information into a separate log book for Pennington because of a new federal regulation.

Margiotta drove the stretch between Harlingen and Sarita, arriving at approximately 7:00 p.m. As he approached the primary inspection area at the Sarita check point, Margiotta held the bill of lading out the window. Customs agent Jerry Welsh took the bill of lading and asked the defendants standard questions about the load and their nationality. He noticed that the bill of lading was dated July 16, 1992, two months earlier. He asked Margiotta when he had loaded his truck, and Margiotta responded that he had done so the day before.

Welsh asked whether he could look in the back of the truck, and the defendants consented. When Margiotta opened the doors, Welsh observed pallets of tile but did not see anything else at that time. Welsh did not detect any odor, either. Welsh climbed into the trailer and began counting the pallets. He saw several cardboard boxes, picked one up, and noticed a perfume smell. Welsh came out of the trailer and asked Margiotta to move the trailer to the secondary inspection area. A narcotics dog indicated that drugs were present in the cardboard boxes; one of the boxes was removed from the trailer and opened. Marihuana was discovered in the boxes, and the defendants were arrested.

After the defendants were read their *Miranda* warnings, each agreed to talk to Welsh. Both defendants denied knowing that the marihuana was in the truck and disclaimed any knowledge of how it got there. Welsh asked Pennington to speculate about how 591 pounds of marihuana could get into the back of the trailer, to which Pennington responded, "I don't want to talk about it anymore.". . .

To establish possession of marihuana with intent to distribute, the government must prove beyond a reasonable doubt (1) knowing (2) possession of marihuana (3) with intent to distribute it. . . .

The knowledge element in a possession case can be inferred from control of the vehicle in some cases; when the drugs are hidden, however, control alone is not sufficient to prove knowledge. *United States v. Garza,* 990 F.2d 171, 174 (5th Cir.), *cert. denied,* 510 U.S. 926, 114 S.Ct. 332, 126 L.Ed.2d 278 (1993). Since the marihuana was not concealed in a hidden compartment, the government contends that the jury was entitled to infer knowledge of the marihuana from the ownership and control of the trailer. Defendants claim, however, that the marihuana *was* hidden in the trailer, and therefore, other evidence was required to prove knowledge.

The threshold issue is whether the marihuana was "hidden" in the trailer, requiring the government to have produced further evidence of knowledge. We conclude that the marihuana was hidden. The government merely asserts that the marihuana was "stacked in the midst" of the cargo and not "hidden in a secret compartment." But the control of the vehicle will suffice to prove knowledge only where the drugs "are clearly visible or readily accessible." *United States v. Richardson,* 848 F.2d 509, 513 (5th Cir.1988). In *Garza,* 990 F.2d at 174 nn. 10 & 12, the court determined that drugs concealed in burlap sacks stacked on and behind lime boxes in the trailer of a truck were not in "plain view" or "readily accessible." The drugs need not be concealed in "hidden compartments," *id.* at 174 n. 12; even though the sacks were visible from outside the trailer, the court held that the government was required to show more than control of the vehicle.

In *Gonzalez-Lira,* 936 F.2d at 192, the court required additional proof of knowledge even though the border agent could smell the marihuana from the rear of the trailer. Here, the marihuana was concealed in boxes that were stacked in spaces between the pallets. The boxes were not visible from outside the trailer and there was no noticeable odor of marihuana. Therefore, the government could not rely upon the control of the vehicle as proof of knowledge of the marihuana.

Additional evidence of guilt may come from nervousness, inconsistent statements, implausible stories, or possession of large amounts of cash by the defendants. *United States v. Shabazz,* 993 F.2d 431, 442 (5th Cir.1993). The government claims that the following factors add to the inference of knowledge: (1) the circuitous route taken by the defendants; (2) the length of time taken; (3) the explanation of the trip offered by defendants; and (4) their disheveled appearance, despite ten hours' sleep.

Defendants claim that they were not nervous, they took the route suggested by their broker, their stories were consistent, and their explanation was not implausible. In particular, the defendants note that the trailer was never locked and that had they known of the marihuana, they certainly would have locked it. Agent Welsh confirmed that the trailer was unlocked at the checkpoint. Furthermore, the defendants note that they did not supervise the loading of the pallets, and the government presented no evidence of fingerprints on the boxes. They did not have large sums of money, they did not attempt to flee, the bill of lading was not falsified, *see supra* note 1, the defendants did not appear nervous when the trailer was searched, their stories were consistent with each other's, and their stories did not change over time. Moreover, the fact that they drove the truck overweight, risking a likely ticket and inspection, indicates a lack of knowledge.

Nevertheless, evidence of the defendants' circuitous route and the timing of their trip supported the jury's conclusion that they had picked up a load of marihuana. The jury was free to choose among reasonable constructions of the evidence, *Bell,* 678 F.2d at 549; the focus is not on "whether the trier of fact made the *correct* guilt or innocence determination, but rather whether it made a *rational* decision to convict or acquit." *Herrera v. Collins,* 506 U.S. 390, ___, 113 S.Ct. 853, 861, 122 L.Ed.2d 203 (1993). After weighing the evidence, the jury chose to disbelieve the defendants' story and concluded that they were guilty beyond a reasonable doubt. There was sufficient evidence to support that conclusion.

EXERCISE

Go back over the *Pennington* case and make two lists: one setting out the facts that would tend to show that the defendants knew that there was marijuana in the truck, and one listing the facts that tend to show the defendants did *not* know about the marijuana. Looking at these two lists, how would you vote as a juror, knowing that the government carried the burden of proving knowledge beyond a reasonable doubt?

UNITED STATES V. SHAW
670 F. 3d 360 (1st Cir. 2012)

HOWARD, CIRCUIT JUDGE.

A jury convicted the defendant, Hazen Shaw, on one count of possessing an unregistered short-barreled shotgun in violation of the National Firearms Act. 26 U.S.C. §§ 5861(d), 5871. At trial, he moved for a judgment of acquittal, Fed.R.Crim.P. 29, contending that the Government failed to present sufficient evidence that he knew the shotgun's barrel was shorter than 18 inches, the statutory characteristic subjecting the weapon to the Act. *See* 26 U.S.C. § 5845(a). The trial court denied the motion, and Shaw now appeals his conviction. . . .

The question on appeal is one of sufficing of the evidence, so we recite the relevant factual background in the light most favorable to the verdict. *See United States v. Gonzalez-Ramirez*, 561 F.3d 22, 24 (1st Cir.2009). On a Sunday afternoon in November 2008, state law enforcement officers received a complaint about gunshots being fired in a wooded residential area in Springfield, Maine. Upon responding, State Trooper Barry Meserve was informed by a resident that the suspected vehicle had just sped away from the scene; Trooper Meserve pursued the departing taillights. The vehicle took flight down the dirt road, and a chase ensued. With considerable effort, including the aid of other officers and two road blocks, the police finally stopped the vehicle. Still not dissuaded, the driver rammed his sedan into a police vehicle parked behind him. Two officers rapidly approached the sedan on foot with weapons drawn, demanding that the driver show his hands. Maine Warden Service Sergeant Ronald Dunham heard "the action of a gun" like a "pump-action gun being operated" and saw the driver "rifling the action of [the] gun." Shaw, the automobile's driver, then put his hands out the window and was immediately apprehended. He was the only person in the car, and a 12 gauge sawed-off "Mossberg 500A" shotgun was found lying near him within ready reach. The sound heard by Dunham was later attributed to the weapon being unloaded.

Shaw was arrested for eluding a police officer and for reckless conduct. A subsequent search of the automobile revealed various items, including two knives and a hatchet, as well as a 20 gauge shotgun with a sawed-off stock in the trunk. A single expelled or spent 12 gauge shotgun round was found between the driver and passenger seats. Shaw himself was carrying, in a pack and on his hunting belt, different types of ammunition, some boxed and some loose. Additional evidence suggested that Shaw had been engaging in some type of hunting activity while seated in his car, by shooting at game from his open car window.

State Trooper Michael Johnston, an evidence technician, arrived at the scene and quickly noticed that the 12 gauge shotgun appeared to be too short for federal guidelines. He further observed that the stock of the weapon had been cut off and covered with duct tape, the gun's barrel "look[ed] like it also had been cut," and "a homemade sling" was attached "in the form of a yellow-like nylon rope." The outside of the gun barrel still bore printing indicating that the original barrel length had been 28 inches. While the weapon's overall length was about 29 inches, the barrel itself, measured internally, was sixteen-and-a-quarter inches in length. Because the length of the shortened barrel of the 12 gauge was less than 18 inches, the weapon was subject to federal registration requirements. *See* 26 U.S.C. §§ 5845(a), 5861(d). . . .

While the defendant's knowledge is at the heart of this appeal, the statute itself does not expressly contain a mens rea requirement. The United States Supreme Court addressed this statutory silence in *Staples v. United States,* 511 U.S. 600, 114 S.Ct. 1793, 128 L.Ed.2d 608 (1994). There, the defendant had been convicted of possessing an unregistered "machinegun" firearm in violation of section 5861(d). 511 U.S. at 614, 114 S.Ct. 1793. The firearm, a semiautomatic AR-15 rifle had been modified to render it capable of fully automatic firing; the modified firing feature subjected the weapon to the Act's registration requirement as a machinegun. *See id.; see also* 26 U.S.C. § 5845(a)(6), (b) (defining "machinegun" firearm). The trial court had not required the jury to find that the defendant knew that the weapon possessed the characteristic (which resulted largely by an internal modification) rendering it a machinegun under the statute. *Staples,* 511 U.S. at 603–04, 114 S.Ct. 1793. Overturning Staples' conviction, the Court held that the government "should have been required to prove beyond a reasonable doubt that [Staples] knew the weapon he possessed had the characteristics that brought it within the statutory definition of a machinegun," reasoning that Congress had not clearly dispensed with the common law mens rea requirement. *Id.* at 602, 616–20, 114 S.Ct. 1793.

The government assumes that *Staples'* scienter requirement applies in this case involving a sawed-off weapon. For purposes of our analysis, so will we.

The defendant contends that the record contains "no evidence that he knew the barrel of the shotgun was less than 18 inches." According to Shaw, the one-and-three-quarters inch difference between the barrel's actual length, measured internally, and the prescribed length cannot support the proposition that he could have determined its length just by looking at it. Thus, he argues, establishing knowledge required evidence that he was the person who actually shortened the barrel from its original length, or that he owned the gun long enough "to become sufficiently well acquainted with its characteristics to have ascertained its length with the precise degree of accuracy (a margin of error of less than 10 percent)" for him to have visually discerned that the barrel was shorter than 18 inches. He also discounts the evidence of flight as readily susceptible to explanations other than culpable knowledge of gun barrel length.

After carefully examining the record, we conclude that it contains sufficient evidence to support the jury's finding beyond a reasonable doubt that Shaw knew that the barrel of the 12 gauge sawed-off shotgun was shorter than 18 inches. His acquaintance with the particular weapon, his familiarity with firearms generally, and the external and readily observable shortened feature of the gun's sawed-off barrel permitted the jury to infer Shaw's knowledge relative to barrel length. We explain below.

First, the evidence allowed the jury to rationally infer that Shaw was well acquainted with this particular shotgun, which had a shortened stock covered with duct tape and an immediately apparent sawed-off barrel. *See United States v. Giambro,* 544 F.3d 26, 30 (1st Cir.2008) (sufficient evidence of scienter based in part on defendant's familiarity with the particular weapon). There was evidence that he was engaging in some type of hunting excursion and that he fired the 12 gauge from inside the confines of his automobile through an open window. Indeed, the gun bore a "homemade sling" of "yellow-like nylon rope," apparently for ease of use. Also, there was evidence that Shaw deftly unloaded the shotgun while seated in a constricted area, the driver's seat of his vehicle, while law enforcement officers descended upon him with guns drawn amidst an intense effort to secure his custody.

Maneuvering the shotgun inside the close confines of his car during his sport and during the highly charged circumstances of his apprehension provides ample factual foundation for the jury to rationally conclude that he was quite familiar with this particular weapon and appreciated its smaller stature—including the short barrel feature. *See Staples,* 511 U.S. at 615 n. 11, 114 S.Ct. 1793 (noting that defendant's use of the weapon can make its regulated characteristics immediately apparent); *United States v. Jones,* 222 F.3d 349, 352 (7th Cir.2000) (noting that evidence defendant observed and handled the sawed-off shotgun can be sufficient for jury to reasonably infer his knowledge of the weapon's statutory characteristic relative to length of gun or length of barrel); *cf. United States v. Michel,* 446 F.3d 1122, 1131 (10th Cir.2006) (collecting cases on same, but holding that where "government presented absolutely no evidence that [defendant] ever observed or handled the gun," the record was insufficient to establish defendant's mens rea relative to barrel length); *United States v. Nieves-Castaño,* 480 F.3d 597, 601–02 (1st Cir.2007) (finding scienter evidence insufficient where defendant had not observed the relevant external feature of the weapon, observation of weapon would not alert a layman to such relevant feature, and defendant had not used the gun to know that it operated as a machinegun).

Second, the evidence allowed the jury to rationally infer that Shaw was familiar with firearms, more so than an average layman, and thus able to meaningfully distinguish between the physical characteristics and capabilities of different guns, including the Mossberg. *See Giambro,* 544

F.3d at 30 (court's holding on sufficiency of scienter evidence was based in part on defendant's heightened knowledge and interest in firearms). For example, he was wearing a pack of ammunition suitable to different shotguns and different hunting purposes, and had more of such ammunition in a hunting-style belt holder and strewn inside his vehicle. Also, he chose to use his 12 gauge shotgun in his sporting activity that day, with its crude strap apparently for ease of use and with its shortened stock and barrel, rather than using the 20-gauge found in the trunk, which had a shortened stock but a much-longer intact barrel. Shaw's possession of two different shotguns of distinctly different barrel lengths and with varying ammunition, and his apparent hunting propensity and peculiar use of the short-barrel gun allowed the jury to conclude that he was an experienced hunter who understood the desirability of different weapons in different circumstances. This evidence allowed the jury to infer that Shaw knew about distinct characteristics of different guns generally, and particularly those of his Mossberg pump. *See Giambro,* 544 F.3d at 30. And again, Shaw's aptitude in maneuvering the 12 gauge inside his vehicle for sport and during the charged interaction with law enforcement further displayed his knowledge about and experience with shotguns.

Third, the shortened nature of the shotgun's barrel is an external characteristic, and the evidence permitted the jury to infer that the barrel length of less than 18 inches was readily observable to the defendant. *See Giambro,* 544 F.3d at 30 (scienter evidence found sufficient based in part on the visual appearance of short barrel, which revealed that the statutory characteristics were "evident from looking at the weapon"). Trooper Johnston testified that the barrel looked like a portion had been cut off, and its outside still bore printing indicating that the barrel's original length had been 28 inches, a significant stretch lengthier than the sixteen-and-a-quarter inches. *See Staples,* 511 U.S. at 615 n. 11, 114 S.Ct. 1793 (noting that defendant's knowledge of the regulated characteristic can be inferred from "any external indicators signaling the nature of the weapon"). Moreover, Johnston had immediately noticed the short stature of the 12-gauge barrel when he arrived at the scene, raising his concern about whether it measured the requisite 18 inches. *See Giambro,* 544 F.3d at 30 (noting testimony that police detective recognized the weapon to be a firearm subject to federal regulation due to its short barrels "as soon as he saw it").

Evidence relating to how the gun barrel was measured also is telling. Special Agent Kenneth Stengel of the Bureau of Alcohol, Tobacco, Firearms and Explosives testified that he followed standard procedure when measuring the barrel's length, which involved closing the bolt of the shotgun, inserting a wooden dowel, and measuring the dowel mark to the bolt face. Stengel testified that this process, which is performed on the inside of the barrel, resulted in "measur[ing] to the furthest point on the barrel" as a "way of giving the benefit of the doubt to the defendant." This testimony gives rise to a reasonable inference that the shotgun barrel when viewed externally appeared to be even shorter than the internally measured sixteen-and-a-quarter inches. Moreover, the weapon's barrel was in fact one-and-three-quarters inches shorter than the prescribed minimum. *See United States v. Green,* 435 F.3d 1265, 1273 (10th Cir.2006) (holding that evidence of knowledge about barrel length was sufficient in part because shotgun barrel was 16.5 inches; witness testified that the barrel appeared short and "anyone who looked quickly at the gun would notice it was short or that the barrel had been sawed off"); *Miller,* 255 F.3d at 1287 (evidence that shotgun barrel was fifteen-and-one-half inches permitted jury to infer that defendant knew barrel was shorter than eighteen inches); *Moore,* 97 F.3d at 564 (the jury could have reasonably inferred defendant's knowledge that rifle was shorter than 16 inches by observing the weapon, which was thirteen-and-one-sixteenth inches long).

Other evidentiary details provided the jury with indicia that, from looking at the weapon, the defendant would have known that the barrel was shorter than 18 inches. Photographs of the scene were displayed to the jury, including one depicting the interior of the front seat of the vehicle where the 12-gauge was resting pointed toward the floorboard. Another photograph displayed the shotgun on the vehicle's hood beside a tape measure showing the overall gun length. These pictures gave the jury the opportunity to see the weapon—and its barrel—in proportion to other real life objects, and even juxtaposed with a tape measure.

Moreover, the gun was admitted into evidence, allowing jurors to see the weapon for themselves. Thus, the jury had ample opportunity to reach its own determination as to whether the statutorily prescribed short barrel length was clear from simply looking at the shotgun. *See Giambro,* 544 F.3d at 30 (noting that "[t]he jury saw the weapon and therefore could reach its own determination of whether the characteristics were clear from simply looking at the [weapon]"); *United States v. Ortiz,* 966 F.2d 707, 712 (1st Cir.1992) (noting that "jurors are neither required to divorce themselves from their common sense nor to abandon the dictates of mature experience"); *see also United States v. Sanders,* 520 F.3d 699, 701 (7th Cir.2008) (noting that jury could infer that defendant knew barrel length was shorter than 18 inches from evidence that defendant handled the shotgun if its appearance would have revealed that characteristic); *Green,* 435 F.3d at 1273 (upholding conviction for possession of unregistered firearm under section 5861(d) where testimony established that sawed-off shotgun with barrel of 16.5 inches obviously appeared short and "jurors were permitted to examine the shotgun firsthand, allowing them to make their own conclusions as to whether it was apparent the gun was sawed-off").

Despite this record panoply on scienter, Shaw contends that his case fails to reach the quantum of sufficient evidence set forth in *Giambro.* Seeking to negate any inference that he is knowledgeable about guns and their distinguishing characteristics, Shaw asserts that the evidence against him cannot compare to Giambro's extensive gun collection (more than 200 weapons) and ready discernment that two had been seized—the evidentiary display of his "specialized knowledge and interest in firearms." *Giambro,* 544 F.3d at 30. That there may have been extensive evidence in *Giambro,* however, does not diminish the meaningful evidence here that Shaw was well acquainted with the particular 12 gauge shotgun at issue, and with shotguns in general.

Shaw also relies on the fact that the discrepancy between the actual barrel length and the required eighteen inches amounts to only one-and-three-quarters inches. We disagree that evidence of a special ability to calculate length based purely on visual inspection was necessary for the jury to reasonably conclude that the defendant knew that the Mossberg's barrel was shorter than 18 inches. As we observed earlier, the evidence permitted the jury to conclude that the barrel's length visually appeared to be some stretch shorter than the actual internal measurement of sixteen-and-a-quarter inches. In any event, the totality of the evidence permitted the jury to conclude for itself that the barrel appeared shorter than 18 inches.

EXERCISE

The element of knowledge can be hard to prove because it is within the defendant's head. What two types of evidence would be best to prove the element of knowledge in a case where a defendant received a box of narcotics in the mail, but was arrested before opening it and claimed that he did not know the contents?

A tricky area regarding the knowledge element is sex crimes based on age including child porn and what is often referred to as "statutory rape." Many jurisdictions have decided that a prosecutor need not prove that the defendant knew a victim was below a certain age in such cases, creating a form of "strict liability" in which the defendant can be found guilty even if he or she was ignorant or was misled regarding the victim's age.

Sometimes, a "mistake of age" defense is allowed in these circumstances even if knowledge of age is not an element the government must prove, as in the case below.

UNITED STATES V. U.S. DISTRICT COURT FOR THE CENTRAL DISTRICT OF CALIFORNIA

858 F. 2d 534 (9th Cir. 1988)

KOZINSKI, CIRCUIT JUDGE:

Defendants are charged with violating 18 U.S.C. § 2251(a) (Supp. IV 1986), which prohibits the production of materials depicting a minor engaged in sexually explicit conduct. We consider whether they may present evidence that they reasonably believed the minor in question was an adult. . . .

The basic facts are uncontested. In 1984, defendant James Marvin Souter, Jr., a so-called talent agent, hired 16-year-old Traci Lords to appear in a film to be produced by defendants Ronald Renee Kantor and Rupert Sebastian McNee. The film, *Those Young Girls,* was produced on August 2, 1984, and showed Lords engaging in sexually explicit conduct. While the depicted conduct, as described in the briefs, falls far outside the bounds of good taste, the government does not claim that the film is obscene under the standard of *Miller v. California,* 413 U.S. 15, 93 S.Ct. 2607, 37 L.Ed.2d 419 (1973). Rather, the theory of the prosecution, founded on solid Supreme Court authority, is that defendants may be punished for producing nonobscene films that depict minors engaging in sexually explicit conduct. *See New York v. Ferber,* 458 U.S. 747, 102 S.Ct. 3348, 73 L.Ed.2d 1113 (1982).

Defendants do not dispute the government's theory, nor do they suggest that Lords was in fact an adult. They protest only that they were seriously misled. According to their counsel, Lords and her agent perpetrated a massive fraud on what is euphemistically called the adult entertainment industry; purveyors of smut from coast to coast were taken in by an artful, studied and well-documented charade whereby Lords successfully passed herself off as an adult. Defendants proposed to introduce evidence of the charade at trial.

The government moved in limine to bar defendants from presenting this evidence. Because knowledge of the minor's age is not an element of the offense as defined by section 2251(a), the government argued, good-faith mistake could not be a defense. Defendants in turn moved to dismiss the indictment for failure to specify knowledge of the minor's age as an element, arguing that the statute would violate the first amendment and due process if the government were not required to prove scienter as part of its prima facie case.

The district court denied both motions. It concluded that neither the statute, nor due process, nor the first amendment requires the government to prove that defendants knew their subject was a minor. *United States v. Kantor,* 677 F.Supp. 1421, 1426–29 (C.D.Cal.1987). Nevertheless, the court noted that strict liability for criminal offenses appears to be justified only "(1) where the legislature grants the privilege to engage in the activity; (2)

where the deterrent effect of a severe penalty is necessary to prevent harm to the public interest; and (3) where basic notions of fairness are not upset by criminal conviction." *Id.* at 1433. Finding that the first condition did not apply and the other two cut in favor of permitting a reasonable mistake of age defense, the district court ruled that defendants would be allowed to present their evidence.

The government has petitioned for a writ of mandamus; defendants Kantor and McNee, whose trial has been stayed by the district court pending our disposition of the government's petition, have entered an opposition arguing that the statute should be interpreted to require the government to prove scienter as to age in its prima facie case or, at least, to permit defendants to prove reasonable mistake of fact as an affirmative defense. . . .

Defendants concede that section 2251(a) also does not, on its face, make reasonable mistake of age an affirmative defense. Nevertheless, they contend that we must construe the statute as implicitly providing for such a defense in order to save it from constitutional infirmity. Specifically, they argue that the defense is required by the free speech and press clause of the first amendment, and by the due process clause of the fifth amendment. We need consider only the first of these.

We begin by acknowledging that the statute at issue regulates speech, albeit speech that is not protected by the first amendment. *See Ferber,* 458 U.S. at 763–64, 102 S.Ct. at 3357–58. Because protected and unprotected speech are "often separated . . . only by a dim and uncertain line," *Bantam Books, Inc. v. Sullivan,* 372 U.S. 58, 66, 83 S.Ct. 631, 637, 9 L.Ed.2d 584 (1963), however, we must be careful to ensure that, in regulating unprotected speech, Congress does not also chill speech that is protected. *See Bose Corp. v. Consumers Union of the United States, Inc.,* 466 U.S. 485, 505, 508, 104 S.Ct. 1949, 1962, 1963, 80 L.Ed.2d 502 (1984) (the Court must "confine the perimeters of any unprotected category within acceptably narrow limits in an effort to ensure that protected expression will not be inhibited"). As the Supreme Court stated in *Smith v. California,* 361 U.S. 147, 152–53, 80 S.Ct. 215, 218–19, 4 L.Ed.2d 205 (1959), "[t]here is no specific constitutional inhibition against making the distributors of food the strictest censors of their merchandise, but the constitutional guarantees of the freedom of speech and of the press stand in the way of imposing a similar requirement on the bookseller."

As noted, no one claims that *Those Young Girls* is obscene; the film would therefore enjoy the protection of the first amendment were it not for its depiction of a minor. The age of the subject thus defines the boundary between speech that is constitutionally protected and speech that is not. The question we must resolve is whether Congress may subject a defendant to strict liability for misjudging the precise location of that boundary.

... a speaker may not be put at complete peril in distinguishing between protected and unprotected speech. Otherwise, he could only be certain of avoiding liability by holding his tongue, causing him "to make only statements which 'steer far wide[ ] of the unlawful zone.' " *New York Times Co. v. Sullivan,* 376 U.S. 254, 279, 84 S.Ct. 710, 725, 11 L.Ed.2d 686 (1964) (quoting *Speiser v. Randall,* 357 U.S. 513, 526, 78 S.Ct. 1332, 1342, 2 L.Ed.2d 1460 (1958)). As the Court noted only this Term, "a rule that would impose strict liability on a publisher for [unprotected speech] would have an undoubted 'chilling' effect on speech ... that does have constitutional value." *Hustler Magazine v. Falwell,* ___ U.S. ___, 108 S.Ct. 876, 880, 99 L.Ed.2d 41 (1988).

Section 2251(a) will have precisely this effect, defendants tell us, unless they are permitted to present a reasonable mistake of age defense. They point out that an actor's chronological age cannot be precisely ascertained from his appearance. Some 16- or 17-year-olds may look older and more sophisticated than their peers; 19- or 20-year-olds may look youthful and immature. The Court recognized as much in *Ferber* when it noted that "if it were necessary for literary or artistic value, a person over the statutory age who perhaps looked younger could be utilized."

458 U.S. at 763, 102 S.Ct. at 3357. Age may also be ascertained on the basis of other evidence: birth certificates, driver's licenses or other identification; statements of those acquainted with the actor; reputation in the community. But, defendants argue, none of these sources is infallible: Documents can be, and frequently are, forged; people can be mistaken or lie; reputations may be based on unfounded rumor rather than fact.

Defendants contend that they were the victims of such deceit and misapprehension, proffering a catalogue of materials with which they expect to prove their contention if allowed to address the issue at trial. First, they intend to present photographic and testimonial evidence that Lords appeared physically mature when she made the film (in which she purportedly played an adult), and that her demeanor, sophistication and apparent sexual experience belied her minority. Second, they propose to show that Lords and those responsible for her employment used California photographic identification, other official documents, release forms and statements of her agent and others to misrepresent her age. Third, defendants propose to introduce evidence that Lords was widely understood to be an adult: her prior appearances in the mass-market men's magazines *Penthouse* and *Cavalier* which, according to industry custom and perception, reliably investigate the age of their models; her prior and subsequent appearances in other X-rated films; the nationwide distribution, with apparent impunity, of materials depicting her in sexually explicit activities; and the fact that, despite Lords' popularity and renown, no one learned or suggested that she was a minor until two years after *Those Young Girls.*

This scenario points to a serious dilemma faced by those who produce and distribute adult films: There is no way of being absolutely sure that an actor or actress who is youthful in appearance is not a minor. Even after taking the most elaborate steps to determine how old the subject is, as defendants claim they did here, a producer may still face up to ten years in prison and a $100,000 fine for each count. 18 U.S.C. § 2251(d) (Supp. IV 1986) (first offense). This must be a sobering thought for individuals wishing to cast young adults in sexually explicit films and other materials. Producers will almost certainly be deterred from producing such materials depicting youthful-looking adult actors; such actors may have considerable difficulty in finding producers willing to cast them; audiences wishing to view films featuring such actors would be denied the opportunity. *Cf. United States v. Sherin,* No. 86-CR-480, slip op. at 22 (S.D.N.Y. Jan. 28, 1987) (construing "knowingly" in 18 U.S.C. § 2252 (Supp. IV 1986) to require proof of scienter because distributors, facing strict liability, "would almost certainly censor films depicting adults engaging in sexually explicit conduct").

Our reading of the relevant Supreme Court opinions, particularly *Smith v. California,* suggests that the first amendment does not permit the imposition of criminal sanctions on the basis of strict liability where doing so would seriously chill protected speech. While Congress may take steps to punish severely those who knowingly subject minors to sexual exploitation, and even those who commit such abuse recklessly or negligently, it may not impose very serious criminal sanctions on those who have diligently investigated the matter and formed a reasonable good-faith belief that they are engaged in activities protected by the first amendment. "Freedoms of expression require 'breathing space,' " *Hustler Magazine,* 108 S.Ct. at 880 (quoting *Philadelphia Newspapers, Inc. v. Hepps,* 475 U.S. 767, 772, 106 S.Ct. 1558, 1561, 89 L.Ed.2d 783 (1986)); imposition of major criminal sanctions on these defendants without allowing them to interpose a reasonable mistake of age defense would choke off protected speech. . . .

The result we reach is no doubt counterintuitive. Section 2251(a) is designed to promote "a government objective of surpassing importance," *Ferber,* 458 U.S. at 756–57, 102 S.Ct. at 3354–55; indeed, the protection of our young from sexual abuse may be among the most important functions of a civilized society. At the same time, the first amendment interest we are protecting—the right to produce salacious movies—is intrinsically unworthy of much solicitude. Nevertheless, the first amendment is as close to an absolute as we have in our jurisprudence: Speech shielded by the amendment's protective wing must remain inviolate regardless of its inherent worth. The distaste we may feel as individuals toward the content or message of protected expression cannot, of course, detain us from discharging our duty as guardians of the Constitution. . . .

EXERCISE

From the perspective of a practitioner, there can be a big difference between an element (a fact that must be proven by the prosecutor beyond a reasonable doubt) and an affirmative defense (where a defense attorney can win an acquittal by proving a fact or set of facts, usually by a preponderance of the evidence).

Imagine that you are a judge considering a case involving the use of a minor in pornography. The prosecution has submitted a report from an expert saying that a reasonable person could tell from the face of the image itself that the person depicted was a minor. The defense contests that conclusion, but does not have an expert. If the law did not provide you with direction, would you (1) rule that the defendant's knowledge of the age of the victim-actress had to be proven by the government as an element, (2) hold that the defense could raise lack of knowledge (mistake of fact) as an affirmative defense, or (3) find that there is strict liability on the issue of knowledge, and the defendant is unable to challenge the case based on ignorance of that fact?

2. INTENT

Many statutes explicitly include an express element of intent to commit a specific act, which is sometimes referred to as "specific intent," as distinct from the general intent to commit a wrongful act. For example, fraud usually requires a specific intent to deceive the victims of the fraud,[2] and drug trafficking statutes usually require that intent to distribute be proven for felony possession of narcotics charges.[3] These statutes mandate that prosecutors prove up what the defendant meant to have happen in the future.

Below, let's consider two views on the proofs showing intent in a narcotics case—first from the District Court judge, and then from the Court of Appeals.

UNITED STATES V. CAMPOS

132 F. Supp. 2d 1181 (N.D. Iowa 2001)

BENNETT, CHIEF JUDGE.

On February 5, 2001, the case against Campos proceeded to trial before a jury. At trial, the government called three law enforcement officers to testify, and introduced the following items seized from Campos's bedroom: 50.6 grams of methamphetamine; a .38 caliber Lorcin handgun; an ammunition clip full of .38 ammunition; a box of ammunition; and several forms of false identification. At the close of the government's case, Campos moved for judgment of acquittal pursuant to Federal Rule of Criminal

---

[2] I.e., 18 U.S.C. § 1037(a)(2) (relaying email "with the intent to deceive or mislead recipients. . . .")

[3] I.e., 21 U.S.C. § 841(a).

Procedure 29. The court reserved ruling on this motion. In his defense, Campos testified along with one of his roommates, namely, Jose Novoa. At the conclusion of all of the evidence, Campos renewed his motion for judgment of acquittal, and, once again, the court reserved ruling on the motion. On February 6, 2001, the jury returned a verdict of guilty as to the charge of possession of methamphetamine with intent to distribute. . . .

In order to convict Campos of possessing methamphetamine with the intent to distribute it, under 21 U.S.C. § 841(a), the government had to show beyond a reasonable doubt, that: (1) Campos was in possession of methamphetamine; (2) Campos knew that he was, or intended to be, in possession of a controlled substance; and (3) Campos intended to distribute some or all of the controlled substance to another person. Thus, the government had to prove that Campos knowingly possessed the methamphetamine with the intent to distribute. . . .

At trial, the government presented the testimony of Sioux City police officer Brad Downing. Officer Downing testified that on September 2, 2000, he, and police officer De Faris, were dispatched to the residence of 1723 Center Street in Sioux City, because of a complaint from a citizen regarding marijuana plants being grown behind the 1723 Center Street residence. After arriving at the 1723 Center Street address, officer Downing contacted all three of the occupants who resided in that residence, and obtained both verbal and written consent to search the residence for drugs. The three residents were Campos, Jose Novoa, and the Calixto family. Officer Downing testified that no illegal items were found in either bedroom belonging to the Calixto family or Jose Novoa. In searching Campos's bedroom, however, officer Downing testified that he located several items located in, and around, a shoe box on the floor, near Campos's bed. Specifically, in the shoe box, officer Downing located a plastic bag containing methamphetamine, a .38 caliber Lorcin handgun, an ammunition clip full of .38 ammunition, a box of ammunition, and numerous false identifications. The government also presented the testimony of Special Agent Michael Hill of the Drug Enforcement Administration ("DEA"). Special Agent Hill testified that, based on his education, training and experience, the quantity of the methamphetamine discovered in Campos's bedroom (50.6 grams), the presence of a firearm and ammunition in close proximity to the drugs, and the presence of false identifications are all evidence consistent with the distribution of methamphetamine.

In his defense, Campos called his roommate, Jose Novoa, who testified that although he never witnessed Campos directly ingest the methamphetamine, he witnessed Campos arrange the methamphetamine in a line formation, presumably to ingest soon thereafter. Thereafter, Campos himself testified that he was addicted to methamphetamine and that the 50.6 grams of methamphetamine that the police recovered from his bedroom was for his personal use only.

Here, the fighting issue is whether the 50.6 grams of methamphetamine found in Campos's bedroom was for his personal use only. At trial, Campos readily conceded that he was in possession of the methamphetamine, however, he argued that he did not possess the methamphetamine with the intent to distribute it. At the close of the government's case, this court characterized the weight of the evidence presented by the government against Campos for possession with intent to distribute as "razor thin." The court maintains this view of the government's evidence. Although the government introduced the 50.6 grams of methamphetamine found in Campos's bedroom, as well as a firearm (unloaded), ammunition and various false identifications, all of which were discovered in the immediate vicinity of the methamphetamine, officer Downing testified that, in addition to discovering these items, he also discovered a butane lighter near the methamphetamine, and a pen casing in the dining room of the residence. That pen casing was subsequently analyzed and determined to have methamphetamine residue on the tip of it. Campos testified that he was a user of methamphetamine and that one of the ways he ingested methamphetamine was with the pen casing that officer Downing discovered. As this court mentioned earlier, the government did endeavor to call into question Campos's credibility by honing in on the implausibility of Campos's testimony as to how he came into possession of the methamphetamine and firearm. Campos testified that he purchased from some unknown individual at a bar the methamphetamine for $200.00 and the .38 Lorcin handgun for $50.00. Campos also testified that the same individual gave him the box of ammunition for free. While the court finds this portion of Campos's testimony incredible, the court finds the portion of Campos's testimony that he was a user of methamphetamine credible. The court makes this finding based on the undisputed fact that methamphetamine residue was present on the tip of a pen casing found in Campos's residence, and officer Downing's testimony that Campos was the only one in the 1723 Center Street residence who possessed methamphetamine. This evidence corroborates Campos's testimony that he was, in fact, a user of methamphetamine. The question, therefore, becomes whether, in addition to using the methamphetamine himself, Campos also possessed the methamphetamine with the intent to distribute it?. . . .

While the court finds that the presence of a firearm and the false identifications are consistent with drug trafficking, *see United States v. Bryson,* 110 F.3d 575, 585 (8th Cir.1997) (holding that evidence of a loaded firearm next to drug related items is probative of intent to distribute) and *United States v. Walcott,* 61 F.3d 635, 638 (8th Cir.1995) (holding that the use of aliases and other conduct to hide identification is consistent with involvement in the drug trade), the court does not find them to be probative of drug trafficking in this case, because of the presence of user paraphernalia discovered in Campos's residence. In its opening statement and closing argument, the government repeatedly indicated that there was a lack of user paraphernalia to support an inference that Campos was only a user. This was not the case however. Indeed, the pen casing with methamphetamine residue was discovered in Campos's residence, and in light of the evidence that Campos was the only individual in the residence who possessed methamphetamine, the inference is strong that he was using the methamphetamine with that pen casing. Additionally, the court finds it especially significant that the government's strategy in this case to show Campos's intent to distribute methamphetamine was based not on the presence of distribution paraphernalia, but on the lack of any user paraphernalia. *Cf. Moore,* 212 F.3d at 444 (explaining that intent to distribute may be established by circumstantial evidence, including such things, as quantity, purity and presence of firearms, cash, packaging material, or other distribution paraphernalia); *Boyd,* 180 F.3d at 980 (stating that evidence showing intent to distribute narcotics includes the quantity of the drug, the purity of the drug, presence of firearms, cash, and packaging material); *Schubel,* 912 F.2d at 956 (explaining that the presence of equipment to weigh and measure the narcotics, paraphernalia used to aid in their distribution, large sums of cash, and presence of firearms are common indicia of drug trafficking and are all circumstantial evidence of intent to distribute). This court instructed the jury that the burden is always upon the prosecution to prove guilt beyond a reasonable doubt, and unless the prosecution proves beyond a reasonable doubt that Campos has committed each and every essential element of the offense charged in the indictment, you must find Campos not guilty of the offense charged. In weighing the evidence, the court is of the view that the government did not meet its burden in this case. . . .

Although the court concluded earlier regarding Campos's motion for judgment of acquittal that there was sufficient evidence presented by the government to support Campos's conviction, that result was reached only when construing the evidence in the light most favorable to the guilty verdict, giving the government all reasonable inferences that may be drawn from the evidence. Applying the less restrictive standard for review applicable to motions for new trial, however, the court concludes that the evidence weighs heavily enough against the verdict that a miscarriage of justice may have occurred in this case. Therefore, the court will set aside the verdict in this case and grant Campos's motion for new trial.

UNITED STATES V. CAMPOS
306 F. 3d 577 (8th Cir. 2002)

HANSEN, CIRCUIT JUDGE.

A jury found Erick Arias Campos guilty of possession with intent to distribute 50 grams or more of methamphetamine in violation of 21 U.S.C. § 841(a)(1), (b)(1)(B)(viii) (1994). The district court granted Campos's motion for a new trial on the basis that the jury's verdict preponderated against the evidence such that a miscarriage of justice may have occurred. We reverse.

Campos possessed 50.6 grams of methamphetamine. A large quantity of narcotics is indicative of an intent to distribute, and we have previously held that possession of approximately 50 grams of methamphetamine is consistent with an intent to distribute. *See United States v. Schubel,* 912 F.2d 952, 956 (8th Cir.1990). It was not implausible for the jury to infer that his intent to distribute was sufficiently established by the other evidence in addition to that of drug quantity. *See United States v. Alvarez,* 254 F.3d 725, 727 (8th Cir.2001) (affirming jury verdict on charge of possession with intent to distribute when defendant was found to possess only 2.4 grams of methamphetamine at time of arrest).

The government introduced additional evidence that we have previously held supports a finding of possession with intent to distribute: the presence of a firearm and attendant ammunition. "Because a gun is 'generally considered a tool of the trade for drug dealers, [it] is also evidence of intent to distribute.' " *United States v. White,* 969 F.2d 681, 684 (8th Cir.1992) (quoting *Schubel,* 912 F.2d at 956); *see also Boyd,* 180 F.3d at 980–81 (concluding that firearm located next to bag of approximately 33.72 grams of cocaine indicated intent to distribute); *United States v. Bryson,* 110 F.3d 575, 585 (8th Cir.1997) (stating that firearm found near drug-related items suggests intent to distribute); *United States v. Brett,* 872 F.2d 1365, 1370 (8th Cir.) (considering presence of firearm evidence of intent to distribute), *cert. denied,* 493 U.S. 932, 110 S.Ct. 322, 107 L.Ed.2d 312 (1989).

Campos also possessed numerous false identification cards. Campos stated that he used the false documents to conceal his illegal alien status from his employer; however, we have previously held that false identification documents and the use of aliases is consistent with involvement in the drug trade. *See Boyd,* 180 F.3d at 981; *United States v. Walcott,* 61 F.3d 635, 638 (8th Cir.1995), *cert. denied,* 516 U.S. 1132, 116 S.Ct. 953, 133 L.Ed.2d 877 (1996). This is particularly relevant here because law enforcement found the documents, the gun, and the ammunition in the same container that stored Campos's methamphetamine beside his bed. *Cf. United States v. Rogers,* 939 F.2d 591, 595 (8th Cir.) (holding that close personal connection to location that contains drug-related items is probative of intent to distribute), *cert. denied,* 502 U.S. 991, 112 S.Ct. 609, 116 L.Ed.2d 632

(1991). It was the jury's role to determine what weight to give to this relevant evidence.

Campos testified that he regularly used methamphetamine and ordinarily purchased an "8-ball" (3.5 grams) for his personal use for $70. When he was arrested, however, he possessed roughly fourteen times the amount of methamphetamine he claimed to ordinarily possess for his personal use. The government introduced law enforcement testimony that this quantity of methamphetamine was worth between $1000 and $1500 in the Sioux City market, but according to Campos's testimony, he paid a person, whose name he did not know and whom he had met for the first time at a bar the night before, a mere $200 for the drugs. The district court found this portion of Campos's testimony incredible but still found Campos's assertion that he was merely a user credible.

We understand that the district court was free to believe some, all, or none of Campos's testimony. Campos claimed to be an addicted user of methamphetamine, but the evidence presented at trial does not support his assertion. Campos's roommate testified that he had seen Campos with methamphetamine in his possession arranged in lines and ready to use, but admitted on cross-examination that he never witnessed Campos actually ingest the drug. The arresting officer stated that Campos did not exhibit any indication that he was under the influence of methamphetamine nor did Campos have any user paraphernalia on his person at the time of arrest. Law enforcement found only a butane lighter (which could be used to smoke methamphetamine) in close proximity to the methamphetamine, and a pen casing with methamphetamine residue elsewhere in the residence.

While the standard of review certainly favors the district court's decision, we cannot say in this case that the evidence "preponderate[s] heavily against the verdict, such that it would be a miscarriage of justice to let the verdict stand." *See United States v. Martinez,* 763 F.2d 1297, 1313 (11th Cir.1985). Although the government did not set forth any evidence that Campos possessed razor blades, cutting agents, packaging material, or a scale, for example, we believe that the other undisputed evidence presented strongly correlates his intent to distribute and is more than strong enough to defeat Campos's motion for a new trial. At this juncture, the question is not what evidence the government did not have; rather, the test is how strong the evidence the government did introduce was. We respectfully disagree with the district court's assessment that the government's case was "razor thin."

Even if Campos was a methamphetamine user, the jury was faced with deciding his intent in possessing 50.6 grams of methamphetamine worth between $1000 and $1500 for which he said he paid only $200, particularly given his testimony that he was working as a day laborer tearing off roofs for cash payments. The district court made much of the pen casing with methamphetamine residue found in the common dining room in reaching its conclusion "that the government did not meet its burden in this case" to prove that Campos held the methamphetamine for distribution. (D. Ct. Order at 19.) Just because one is a drug user, however, does not preclude one from also intending to distribute drugs: it is common knowledge, we believe, that drug users often turn to dealing drugs to finance their habits.

After twice reading the entire transcript of the trial and the district court's well-written posttrial order, we are satisfied that the evidence was more than legally sufficient for the jury to find that Campos intended to distribute the methamphetamine, and we conclude that it is highly unlikely that a miscarriage of justice occurred when the jury found Campos guilty as charged.

EXERCISE

As a legislator, would you favor a law which made possession of a certain amount of narcotics (i.e., over 50 grams of methamphetamine) presumptive proof of an intent to distribute?

UNITED STATES V. SCHREIBER
458 Fed. Appx. 672 (9th Cir. 2011)

Before: EBEL, BERZON, and N.R. SMITH, CIRCUIT JUDGES.

MEMORANDUM

Defendant-Appellant Bonnie Schreiber appeals her convictions for mail fraud, wire fraud, and theft, arguing that there was insufficient evidence presented at trial to support those convictions. Having jurisdiction under 28 U.S.C. § 1291, we reject that argument and affirm her convictions. Although Schreiber also argues that defense counsel provided ineffective representation during trial, we decline to address that issue on direct appeal.

We review de novo the sufficiency of the evidence to support Schreiber's convictions, determining "whether after viewing the evidence in the light most favorable to the prosecution, any rational trier of fact could have found the essential elements of the crime beyond a reasonable doubt." *United States v. Tucker,* 641 F.3d 1110, 1118–19 (9th Cir.2011) (internal quotation marks omitted).

The jury convicted Schreiber of two counts of mail fraud, in violation of 18 U.S.C. § 1341, and one count of wire fraud, in violation of 18 U.S.C. § 1343. There was sufficient evidence presented at trial from which a rational jury could have found beyond a reasonable doubt all of the elements necessary to convict Schreiber of mail and wire fraud. *See United States v. Pelisamen,* 641 F.3d 399, 409 (9th Cir.2011) (stating elements of wire fraud); *United*

States v. Van Alstyne, 584 F.3d 803, 814 (9th Cir.2009) (mail fraud); *United States v. Crandall,* 525 F.3d 907, 911 n. 3 (9th Cir.2008) (mail and wire fraud).

Schreiber argued that the government failed to prove intent to defraud based upon her representations that she remained disabled. The evidence showed, however, that Schreiber was leading an active lifestyle that included hunting, fishing, boating, camping, riding horses and snowmobiles, frequently cutting wood to heat her home, and training as a member of the local volunteer fire department. Although Schreiber reported to her doctors and therapist that she hunted, fished, horseback-rode, and "was out in the countryside," she also warned a neighbor that, if anyone came around asking if she did any work outside, to answer that he did not know. In addition, Schreiber continued to certify that she remained unable to work in order to obtain workers' compensation benefits. Viewing this evidence in the light most favorable to the government, a rational trier of fact could have found that Schreiber was no longer disabled and thus guilty of mail and wire fraud.

The jury also convicted Schreiber of theft of more than $1,000 from the United States, in violation of 18 U.S.C. § 641. The evidence presented at trial, as set forth above, was sufficient for a rational jury to find that Schreiber knowingly stole money belonging to the United States by continuing to collect workers' compensation benefits in excess of $68,000 after she regained the ability to work. *See United States v. Seaman,* 18 F.3d 649, 650 (9th Cir.1994) (stating elements of theft from the United States).

EXERCISE

In the case above, what would you argue as a defense attorney? Would you focus more on what Ms. Schreiber's could do physically, or what was in her mind?

D. JURISDICTIONAL ELEMENTS

A court cannot issue a judgment unless it has jurisdiction, and it is the government's burden to show the jurisdiction of the court. There are two types of jurisdictional elements. First, in all cases the government must show that the crime in some way occurred within the physical boundaries of a court's jurisdiction. Second, in federal cases a particular element often must be proven in order to make the case federal; for example, a bank robbery can only be a *federal* crime if the bank is insured by the federal government.[4] Jurisdictional elements are sometimes omitted or implied in

---

[4]   18 U.S.C. § 2113(a) & (f).

boilerplate element descriptions, but failure to prove up these elements can be fatal to the government's case.

UNITED STATES V. MCNEAL
865 F. 2d 1167 (10th Cir. 1989)

MCWILLIAMS, CIRCUIT JUDGE.

On September 6, 1985, two persons held up a credit union in Kansas City, Kansas, and escaped with $4,966.09. During the course of the robbery one of the robbers took a Colt Diamondback .38 caliber revolver from the security guard at the credit union. On July 11, 1986, Jockenna O'Neal was arrested on a disturbance charge and at the time of her arrest she had in her possession a Colt Diamondback .38 caliber revolver. O'Neal stated that she had purchased the revolver from Terry McNeal in April 1986. A check of the serial number revealed that the weapon recovered from O'Neal was the weapon taken in the credit union robbery. The investigating officers then showed O'Neal a series of surveillance photos taken during the course of the robbery, and she identified Terry McNeal and his brother, Bobby McNeal, as the two robbers. . . .

The two suspects who robbed the credit union wore disguises and large dark sunglasses. One wore a striped shirt and a fishing hat. The other wore an Afro wig, was dressed in a blue jogging suit and had a woman's facial make-up.

As indicated, the robbers made a successful escape from the scene of the robbery. Apparently the "break" in the case occurred some ten months later when Jockenna O'Neal was arrested and the revolver taken from her at the time of her arrest was determined, through a check of the serial number, to be the revolver taken from the guard in the robbery of the credit union. O'Neal told the police investigating the case, and later so testified at trial, that she bought the revolver from Terry McNeal in April 1986. She also identified the robbers in the surveillance photos taken during the robbery as Terry and Bobby McNeal.

It was established at trial, at least *prima facie,* that the robber, who assaulted the security guard and knocked the guard down three times during the assault, stole his gun and pistol-whipped him was the person wearing the fishing hat, and that the robber wearing the Afro wig was the person who went behind the teller's cage, fired his pistol at the security guard, and demanded money from the tellers. The government's theory of the case was that Terry McNeal was the robber in the fishing hat who assaulted the security guard, and Bobby McNeal was the robber who collected the money in the teller's cage.

The testimony of the eye witnesses to the robbery, however, was not uniform. The security guard who was assaulted, and from whom the Colt Diamondback revolver was taken, could not identify either of the defendants as being one of the robbers. A customer who was in the credit union at the time of the robbery identified Terry McNeal as being the one who assaulted the guard, but he was unable to identify Bobby McNeal as the other robber. Paulette Reyes, a teller, incorrectly identified Terry McNeal as the robber who went behind the teller's cage and collected the money. However, Pamela Hecht, an assistant manager, testified that it was Terry McNeal who assaulted the guard and identified Bobby McNeal as the robber who went behind the teller's cage and obtained the money.

Defense counsel called another customer and another teller who could not identify either of the defendants as the robbers. Terry McNeal called several witnesses in an attempt to establish his alibi. However, neither Terry nor Bobby McNeal testified. . . .

Count 1 charged a violation of 18 U.S.C. § 2113(a) and (d). Section (a) provides that whoever by force takes money belonging to a "bank" or "credit union" shall be fined not more than $5,000 or imprisoned not more than 20 years, or both. Section (d) provides that whoever violates section (a) and in so doing assaults a person by use of a dangerous weapon shall be fined not more than $10,000 or imprisoned not more than 25 years, or both. Section (f) provides that the term "bank" includes "any bank the *deposits* of which are insured by the Federal Deposit Insurance Corporation" (emphasis added). Section (h) states that the term "credit union" includes a "[s]tate-chartered credit union the *accounts* of which are insured by the Administrator of the National Credit Union Administration" (emphasis added). 18 U.S.C. § 2113 (1984).

The credit union in the instant case was a state-chartered credit union. The government alleged in each of the three counts that the "*deposits* of Mid-American Credit Union, Challenger, K.C. office were insured by the National Credit Union Administration" (emphasis added). Why the government eschewed the use of the term "accounts," and used the term "deposits," is not clear. In drawing an indictment, the safer course is to use the language of the statute. In any event, according to appellant, the use of the term "deposit" is appropriate where a bank is involved, but inappropriate where a credit union is involved and, therefore, is fatal to the indictment. In other words, appellant argues that referring to "deposits" of the credit union, instead of "accounts," which is the statutory language, renders the entire indictment subject to a motion to dismiss for failure to state an offense. Appellant further contends that this error was compounded by the court's instructions, which also referred to the credit union's "deposits," as opposed to "accounts."

Appellant has not drawn our attention to any case holding that an allegation in an indictment that a state-chartered credit union had its "deposits"-as opposed to "accounts"-insured by the National Credit Union Administration is such a departure from the statute as to render an indictment subject to a motion to dismiss for failing to charge a crime. An indictment is sufficient if it contains the elements of the offense charged and fairly informs the defendant of the charge against which he must defend, and, secondly, enables him to plead an acquittal or conviction in bar of future prosecutions for the same offense. *United States v. Darrell,* 828 F.2d 644, 647 (10th Cir.1987) (citing *United States v. Rudetsky,* 535 F.2d 556, 562 (10th Cir.), *cert. denied,* 429 U.S. 820, 97 S.Ct. 68, 50 L.Ed.2d 81 (1976)); *United States v. Salazar,* 720 F.2d 1482 (10th Cir.1983), *cert. denied,* 469 U.S. 1110, 105 S.Ct. 789, 83 L.Ed.2d 783 (1985). Although it is quite true that the statute refers to a bank's "deposits," and a credit union's "accounts," we decline to hold that referring to a credit union's "deposits," instead of "accounts," is fatal.

An essential element in each of the three counts was that the "Mid-American Credit Union, Challenger, K.C. office" had its "deposits," or accounts, regardless of how such be characterized, insured by the National Credit Union Administration. Absent federal insurance there would be no federal jurisdiction and, in such circumstance, the McNeals would have been prosecuted in the state courts of Kansas. Appellant, however, contends that the evidence in the instant case was insufficient to establish that the credit union carried federal insurance. Such is not our reading of the record.

In the present case, exhibit 26 is a certificate from the National Credit Union Administration showing that a predecessor credit union to Mid-American was federally insured. There was testimony that Mid-American did not receive a yearly updated certificate, even though insurance premiums were paid by wire transfer the first of each year for the preceding year. Mary Pope, a senior vice president of Mid-American, testified that the deposits of Mid-American were federally insured on the date of the robbery and exhibits 27 and 28 were offered and received into evidence in support of her testimony regarding federal insurance.

In aid of our analysis is *United States v. Bolt,* 776 F.2d 1463 (10th Cir.1985). In *Bolt,* we held that an FDIC certificate, a cancelled premium check, and testimony from a bank's vice president that bank deposits were federally insured constituted sufficient proof of federal insurance. *Id.* at 1471. *Bolt* is distinguished from *United States v. Platenberg,* 657 F.2d 797 (5th Cir.1981), where a seven-year-old certificate, and nothing more, was held to be insufficient to show federal insurance on the date of a robbery. All things considered, there was sufficient evidence to show that Mid-American had federal insurance.

EXERCISE

　　The case above hints at the consequences when a prosecutor forgets to line up clear proofs of an essential element. The element of federal insurance of a bank is so mundane that it almost begs to be ignored—but if it is, a defendant may be acquitted on the defendant's motion for a directed verdict.

As one might expect, prosecutors have developed methods to avert such catastrophes. One tool popular with practitioners in criminal law is sometimes referred to as "The Matrix." It is simply a chart with boxes, used to catalogue the evidence gathered that goes to each element of the crime. Along the horizontal axis (on the top) are listed the elements of the crime. Below each element are listed the discrete proofs for each element, listed separately. For example, here is a matrix for the *Campos* case set out earlier in this chapter (assuming that the defendant had confessed before trial to the things he testified about on the stand, and that jurisdiction was stipulated to by the parties):

Identity	Possession	Methamphetamine (chemistry)	Knowledge	Intent
Confessed	Confessed	Lab test	Confessed	Large amount
Seized from his room	Seized from area he controlled		Circumstances (not hidden)	Firearm nearby
				Fake ID
				Housemates did not see him use meth
				Claimed he only paid $200 for it

The matrix serves several important functions. For the prosecutor, it allows her to match up evidence with elements to evaluate the strength of her case and determine what further investigation is necessary. At trial, it is a kind of checklist for what evidence must be admitted. For a defense attorney, the matrix will direct him to the government's weakest element. In the *Campos* case, that is clearly the element of intent.

Create a matrix of your own for bank robbery under 18 U.S.C. § 2113(a) in the McNeal case above, assuming that the tellers reported to investigator the facts that happened at the bank, and that a video camera recorded the scene.

———————

Federal jurisdiction is limited to the bounds granted by the Constitution. That means that often a discrete fact must be proven to show that such jurisdiction applies. Note that this is distinct from geographic jurisdiction—both must be present. Sometimes, though, they seemingly combine as the element showing federal jurisdiction is rooted in geography.

UNITED STATES V. IVANOV
175 F. Supp. 2d 367 (D. Conn. 2001)

THOMPSON, DISTRICT JUDGE.

Defendant Aleksey Vladimirovich Ivanov ("Ivanov") has been indicted, in a superseding indictment, on charges of conspiracy, computer fraud and related activity, extortion and possession of unauthorized access devices. Ivanov has moved to dismiss the indictment on the grounds that the court lacks subject matter jurisdiction. Ivanov argues that because it is alleged that he was physically located in Russia when the offenses were committed, he can not be charged with violations of United States law. For the reasons set forth below, the defendant's motion is being denied.

Online Information Bureau, Inc. ("OIB"), the alleged victim in this case, is a Connecticut corporation based in Vernon, Connecticut. It is an "e-commerce" business which assists retail and Internet merchants by, among other things, hosting their websites and processing their credit card data and other financial transactions. In this capacity, OIB acts as a financial transaction "clearinghouse", by aggregating and assisting in the debiting or crediting of funds against each account for thousands of retail and Internet purchasers and vendors. In doing so, OIB collects and maintains customer credit card information, merchant account numbers, and related financial data from credit card companies and other financial institutions.

The government alleges that Ivanov "hacked" into OIB's computer system and obtained the key passwords to control OIB's entire network. The government contends that in late January and early February 2000, OIB received from Ivanov a series of unsolicited e-mails indicating that the defendant had obtained the "root" passwords for certain computer systems operated by OIB. A "root" password grants its user access to and control over an entire computer system, including the ability to manipulate, extract, and delete any and all data. Such passwords are generally reserved for use by the system administrator only.

The government claims that Ivanov then threatened OIB with the destruction of its computer systems (including its merchant account database) and demanded approximately $10,000 for his assistance in making those systems secure. It claims, for example, that on February 3, 2000, after his initial solicitations had been rebuffed, Ivanov sent the following e-mail to an employee of OIB:

[name redacted], now imagine please Somebody hack you network (and not notify you about this), he download Atomic software with more than 300 merchants, transfer money, and after this did 'rm-rf/' and after this you company be ruined. I don't want this, and because this i notify you about possible hack in you network, if you want you can hire me and im allways be check security in you network. What you think about this?

The government contends that Ivanov's extortionate communications originated from an e-mail account at Lightrealm.com, an Internet Service Provider based in Kirkland, Washington. It contends that while he was in Russia, Ivanov gained access to the Lightrealm computer network and that he used that system to communicate with OIB, also while he was in Russia. Thus, each e-mail sent by Ivanov was allegedly transmitted from a Lightrealm.com computer in Kirkland, Washington through the Internet to an OIB computer in Vernon, Connecticut, where the e-mail was opened by an OIB employee.

The parties agree that the defendant was physically located in Russia (or one of the other former Soviet Bloc countries) when, it is alleged, he committed the offenses set forth in the superseding indictment. . . .

As noted by the court in *United States v. Muench,* 694 F.2d 28 (2d Cir.1982), "[t]he intent to cause effects within the United States . . . makes it reasonable to apply to persons outside United States territory a statute which is not expressly extraterritorial in scope." *Id.* at 33. "It has long been a commonplace of criminal liability that a person may be charged in the place where the evil results, though he is beyond the jurisdiction when he starts the train of events of which that evil is the fruit." *United States v. Steinberg,* 62 F.2d 77, 78 (2d Cir.1932). "[T]he Government may punish a defendant in the same manner as if [he] were present in the jurisdiction when the detrimental effects occurred.". . .

Here, all of the intended and actual detrimental effects of the substantive offenses Ivanov is charged with in the indictment occurred within the United States. In Counts Two and Three, the defendant is charged with accessing OIB's computers. Those computers were located in Vernon, Connecticut. The fact that the computers were accessed by means of a complex process initiated and controlled from a remote location does not alter the fact that the accessing of the computers, i.e. part of the detrimental effect prohibited by the statute, occurred at the place where the computers were physically located, namely OIB's place of business in Vernon, Connecticut.

Count Two charges further that Ivanov obtained something of value when he accessed OIB's computers, that "something of value" being the data obtained from OIB's computers. In order for Ivanov to violate § 1030(a)(4), it was necessary that he do more than merely access OIB's computers and view the data. *See United States v. Czubinski,* 106 F.3d 1069, 1078 (1st Cir.1997) ("[M]erely viewing information cannot be deemed the same as obtaining something of value for purposes of this statute." . . . "[T]his section should apply to those who steal information through unauthorized access . . . ."). The indictment charges that Ivanov did more than merely gain unauthorized access and view the data. Ivanov allegedly obtained root access to the OIB computers located in Vernon, Connecticut. Once Ivanov had root access to the computers, he was able to control the data, e.g., credit card numbers and merchant account numbers, stored in the OIB computers; Ivanov could copy, sell, transfer, alter, or destroy that data. That data is intangible property of OIB. . . .

At the point Ivanov gained root access to OIB's computers, he had complete control over that data, and consequently, had possession of it. That data was in OIB's computers. Since Ivanov possessed that data while it was in OIB's computers in Vernon, Connecticut, the court concludes that he obtained it, for purposes of § 1030(a)(4), in Vernon, Connecticut. The fact that Ivanov is charged with obtaining OIB's valuable data by means of a complex process initiated and controlled from a remote location, and that he subsequently moved that data to a computer located in Russia, does not alter the fact that at the point when Ivanov first possessed that data, it was on OIB's computers in Vernon, Connecticut. . .

Based on the foregoing, this court concludes that the Hobbs Act encompasses not only all extortionate interference with interstate commerce by means of conduct occurring within the United States, but also all such conduct which, although it occurs outside the United States, affects commerce within the borders of the United States. Therefore, it is immaterial whether Ivanov's alleged conduct can be said to have taken place entirely outside the United States, because that conduct clearly constituted "interference with interstate commerce by extortion", *Stirone*, 361 U.S. at 215, 80 S.Ct. 270, in violation of the Hobbs Act. Consequently, the court has jurisdiction over this charge against him.

EXERCISE

Lonny McDonahue is a resident of Ireland and resided there at the time of his alleged crime. His ex-wife lives in Danbury, Connecticut.

McDonahue guesses his ex-wife's Facebook password and logs onto Facebook as her. He views her messages and posts, careful to leave nothing disturbed so as not to get caught. The Facebook data he views might be located in a server in the United States, Canada, Taiwan, or Brazil. At no point does McDonahue enter the United States. Under the statute described in the case above, does a federal prosecutor in Connecticut have jurisdiction to bring the case?

All cases have geographic jurisdictional elements, and in federal cases there are often additional facts that have to be proven (such as federal insurance of a bank) to show the jurisdiction of federal courts. But does a defendant have to *know* that these jurisdictional facts exist?

UNITED STATES V. EPSKAMP
832 F. 3d 154 (2d Cir. 2016)

STRAUB, CIRCUIT JUDGE:

Defendant-Appellant Nicolas Epskamp appeals from a judgment entered June 24, 2015 in the Southern District of New York (Richard J. Sullivan, *Judge*). The judgment followed a seven day jury trial in which Epskamp was found guilty of both counts in a two-count superseding indictment charging him with (1) conspiracy to possess with intent to distribute a controlled substance on board an aircraft registered in the United States, in violation of 21 U.S.C. §§ 812, 959(b)(2), and 960(a)(3); and (2) possessing with intent to distribute a controlled substance on board an aircraft registered in the United States, in violation of 21 U.S.C. §§ 812, 959(b)(2), and 18 U.S.C. § 2. The controlled substance alleged to be involved in each count was 5 kilograms and more of mixture and substances containing a detectable amount of cocaine, a violation of 21 U.S.C. § 960(b)(1)(B). The District Court principally sentenced Epskamp to 264 months of incarceration. . . .

The evidence produced at trial revealed that the investigation leading to Epskamp's arrest commenced in October 2011 when the United States Drug Enforcement Administration ("DEA") was informed by an American airplane charter company that a Lebanese individual was seeking to charter a flight from the Dominican Republic to Antwerp, Belgium in November 2011. The company told the DEA that two foreign nationals would be transporting a substantial quantity of narcotics on the flight in approximately 20 to 30 suitcases.

After receiving this information, the DEA—in conjunction with a specialized narcotics division of the Dominican National Police—commenced surveillance of La Romana Airport, located approximately 65 miles east of the Dominican capital, Santo Domingo. The Dominican police involved in the operation recruited two undercover pilots, Carlos Medina ("UC-1") and Danny Jesus ("UC-2") and arranged for them to be introduced to Rawson "Roy" Watson, a British citizen who was involved in the scheme. . . .

Intercepted communications over the following weeks reveal the various logistical challenges facing those who seek to smuggle large quantities of narcotics over international borders. The flight was repeatedly delayed and rescheduled throughout November. The chartered aircraft was searched by a Dominican police unit unaffiliated with the investigation. Although the search did not yield any evidence—the plane had not yet been laden with cocaine—the search convinced the participants that they would need to obtain a new aircraft, specifically an aircraft registered in the United States, which would draw less suspicion from Dominican authorities.

After these setbacks, Watson left the Dominican Republic for several weeks, telling UC-1 that he was visiting Lebanon and the Netherlands. The two remained in contact via email, with Watson proposing solutions to the challenges they had been facing at La Romana Airport, including developing a dummy flight plan indicating the charter aircraft was bound for Africa, rather than Belgium, and also bribing a Dominican military officer. *See United States v. Epskamp*, No. 1:12-cr-00120-RJS-2, ECF Docket No. 190 at 414–22.

In early December 2011, Watson returned to the Dominican Republic with Pako Podunajec, a Dutch citizen who testified as a cooperating witness for the government at trial. Podunajec—who spoke Dutch, English, German, Spanish, and Croatian—was to serve as translator between Watson and two Colombian nationals who would ultimately supply the conspirators with 1,000 kilograms of cocaine.

Around the same time, on December 4, 2011, Defendant-Appellant Epskamp, who is also a Dutch citizen, likewise traveled from the Netherlands to the Dominican Republic, where he checked into a hotel in Santo Domingo. Podunajec testified that he was instructed by Watson to visit Epskamp and provide him with $2,000 in cash that the Colombians had given to Watson. He further testified that Watson told him that Epskamp—to whom Watson referred as the "Journalist" or "Journey"— would be traveling to Belgium from the Dominican Republic with "the thousand keys of cocaine." Joint App'x at 193. When Podunajec visited Epskamp at his hotel and provided him with the $2,000, the two had a brief conversation in Dutch, during which Epskamp asked whether he would be leaving soon and whether he would be heading to Africa or Belgium. Podunajec responded that he should ask "Ali"—the Lebanese individual arranging for the shipment in conjunction with Watson—but that he believed Epskamp would be leaving soon for Belgium with "the thousand keys of cocaine." *Id.* Epskamp told Podunajec that he was participating in the scheme to pay off a drug debt. He further explained that, in order to play his role as courier, he had been instructed to "take the flight, be like a millionaire on the flight," *id.* at 194, and in return his debt would be forgiven and he would be paid an additional 50,000 euros. . . .

On December 15, 2011—at 3:45 a.m.—Watson collected Epskamp at the hotel near La Romana Airport. During this time, Watson communicated with "Ali" via BlackBerry Messenger. Ali repeatedly asked Watson about the status of the "Journalist," and further instructed that the pair put on their "uniforms." *See United States v. Epskamp*, No. 1:12-cr-00120-RJS-2, ECF Docket No. 188 at 200–205.

Watson and Epskamp proceeded to the airport, where they met with the two undercover pilots, one of whom carried an audio and video recording device.

Epskamp was, according to the testimony of UC-1, "dressed very, very elegantly, as a gentlemen, as a real executive, with a jacket, a tie, and a scarf." Joint App'x at 254. Watson was dressed to look like a member of the flight crew. *Id.* The pair proceeded through the VIP terminal of La Romana Airport and boarded a charter airplane bearing an "N" registration number on its tail, indicating registration in the United States. On board the aircraft, strewn about the cabin, were approximately 20 suitcases containing over 1,000 kilograms of cocaine that had previously been loaded by the Colombian members of the conspiracy. UC-1 testified that there were so many suitcases in the cabin that he "had to walk on top of suitcases because the aisles were blocked by them." *Id.* at 257. He further testified that he discreetly opened two or three suitcases and was able to "confirm that there were those square-shaped packages of cocaine that [are] commonly used to pack [narcotics]" within the suitcases. *Id.*

As those onboard the plane waited to depart, an airport official approached the aircraft and informed Epskamp that he had to disembark and speak with an immigration official. Epskamp returned to the terminal while Watson remained on the plane. Dominican police officers then arrested Epskamp and Watson. A subsequent search of the aircraft revealed approximately 1,000 kilograms of cocaine, divided into approximately 1,000 bricks. A number of Epskamp's personal belongings were also found on the plane.

In November 2012, Epskamp was transferred to the United States and brought to the Southern District of New York for trial. . . .

Epskamp was convicted for possessing with intent to distribute a controlled substance aboard an aircraft registered in the United States, a crime under 21 U.S.C. § 959(b)(2), and conspiring to do the same. Section 959(b) specifically states that:

> It shall be unlawful for any United States citizen on board any aircraft, or any person on board an aircraft owned by a United States citizen or registered in the United States, to—
>
>> (1) manufacture or distribute a controlled substance or listed chemical; or
>>
>> (2) possess a controlled substance or listed chemical with intent to distribute. . . .

Epskamp next argues that a non-citizen defendant can only be liable under § 959(b) if they know that the aircraft upon which they are committing unlawful acts is registered in the United States or owned by a United States citizen. He contends the government failed to adduce sufficient evidence that he possessed such knowledge and further argues that the District Court erred in instructing the jury that, in order to find him guilty, "the defendant need not know that the narcotics would be or were possessed on board an aircraft that was registered in the United States" and again that "[t]he defendant doesn't have to know that the aircraft was registered in the United States." Joint App'x at 283–84. We disagree and conclude both that the District Court's instructions appropriately reflected the law and that, accordingly, the government was not required to adduce evidence of Epskamp's knowledge concerning the aircraft's registration.

Simply stated, nothing in the statute obliges the government to prove that Epskamp knew the aircraft was registered in the United States. To be sure, § 959(b) does contain a jurisdictional component; it limits its application to "any United States citizen on board any aircraft, or any person on board an aircraft owned by a United States citizen or registered in the United States." 21 U.S.C. § 959(b). But we have "repeatedly . . . refused to find knowledge of the jurisdictional fact to be an essential element in prosecutions under" various criminal statutes requiring, for instance, that the criminal acts affect interstate or foreign commerce. *United States v. Eisenberg*, 596 F.2d 522, 526 (2d Cir. 1979) ("The element of interstate transportation is merely a jurisdictional element, for which proof of the fact of transportation is proof enough."); *see also United States v. Green*, 523 F.2d 229, 233–34 (2d Cir. 1975) ("A substantive violation of 18 U.S.C. § 659 does not require knowledge of the interstate or foreign character of the goods. It is therefore unnecessary to prove such knowledge in order to establish a conspiracy violation." (internal citations omitted)); *United States v. Herrera*, 584 F.2d 1137, 1150 (2d Cir. 1978) ("Substantive cases brought under [18 U.S.C.] § 1952 have been uniform in their holdings that it is unnecessary to prove a defendant had actual knowledge of the jurisdictional element, and that he actually agreed and intended to use interstate facilities to commit a crime.").

The obvious exception to this rule is when the statute itself *requires* knowledge of the jurisdictional element. Such is the case with *other* subsections in the current version of § 959, which proscribe, for instance, the manufacture or distribution of chemicals "knowing, or having reasonable cause to believe that the controlled substance will be unlawfully imported into the United States." 21 U.S.C. § 959(a). Epskamp disproves his own argument by citing to *United States v. Londono-Villa*, 930 F.2d 994, 999 (2d Cir. 1991), in which we reversed a conviction under § 959(a) because the government failed to "establish that the defendant knew the narcotics were to be imported into the United States." But in *Londono-Villa*, we observed that the government was only required to prove that knowledge "[i]n light of Congress's conjoining the knowledge/intent requirement with the term 'import' " within that particular subsection. *Id.* at 998. We also stated that Congress could have used "one of its other formulations that would plainly reach all actors outside of the United States who contribute to the international movement of narcotics *regardless of their knowledge or intent as to destination*." *Id.* (emphasis added). Congress used just such a formulation in § 959(b) and, accordingly, there was no need for the government to establish that Epskamp knew the aircraft was registered in the United States.

EXERCISE

Imagine that you are an associate at a large Washington D.C. law firm. You have been assigned to a group that does governmental relations. One client of the firm is the International Couriers Group, a company that employs people to carry valuable and sensitive cargo on aircraft to international destinations. Several couriers working for ICG have been convicted of smuggling drugs on US planes, and they have hired your firm to seek a change in the law at issue in the *Epskamp* case, 21 U.S.C. § 959(b).

Specifically, ICG would like to insert into 21 U.S.C. § 959(b) a provision that would require prosecutors prove that the defendant knew that they had boarded an aircraft owned by a United States citizen or registered in the United States.

You have a meeting with a Senator who may be sympathetic to this change. What is your best argument for this amendment?

E. OTHER ELEMENTS

There is a wide array of elements that are particular to certain types of cases. For example, in the sample matrix in a narcotics case in the preceding section, there are five key elements, four of which we have already studied: Identity, an action element (possession), and two state of mind elements (knowledge and intent). There is a fifth key element, too: Chemical composition of the substance at issue. Below we will take a look at a few of the most common "miscellaneous" elements.

1. CHEMICAL COMPOSITION

In narcotics cases, the government must prove that the substance at issue is chemically identical to a substance that is prohibited. That is a scientific question, and is usually proven either by expert reports and testimony or through stipulation by the parties. Where the defense calls into question the chemical composition of a narcotic, things can become quite complex. Consider, for example, a fragment of the opinion in *United States v. Amar*, 714 F. 2d 238 (3d Cir. 1983) discussing the efforts at trial on behalf of one of the defendants, Marshall Stillman:

> The court instructed the jury that it must determine, beyond a reasonable doubt, that the substance was heroin or any isomer of heroin. The court refused to give the instruction proffered by Stillman that "[o]nly the optical isomers of heroin are included." The court characterized Stillman's instruction as "argumentative,

lengthy and . . . confusing to the jury." On appeal Stillman claims that the failure to so instruct the jury was reversible error.

To understand Stillman's argument, it is necessary to distinguish between isomers generally and optical isomers, which are a type of isomer. Isomers are substances with the same chemical composition but different structural arrangement. The number of isomers a substance may theoretically have is a function of the complexity of its chemical formula. Because heroin has a complex chemical formula, $C_{21}H_{23}NO_5$, the many constituent atoms could be arranged in a large variety of different structures. While that theoretical possibility may be of experimental interest, defendants presented no evidence that it did or could have any practical significance in this case.

Under the statute, Schedule I controlled substances are defined to include the isomers of enumerated substances. The Code of Federal Regulations defines "isomer" as "the optical isomer" for all but specified substances. 21 C.F.R. § 1308.02(c). Optical isomers, so termed because they rotate a beam of polarized light, are the mirror image of each other. We do not understand the government to dispute Stillman's claim that heroin as referred to in Schedule I of the criminal statute is limited to heroin or its optical isomer. Instead, it is the government's claim that because its evidence conclusively showed that the substance was heroin within the more restrictive meaning, appellants were in no way harmed by the court's refusal to give the instructions they requested.

In cases where the drugs are not seized and the defendant does not confess or stipulate to the chemical composition of the drugs this can be a difficult element to prove, since it will rely on proof through expert testimony.

UNITED STATES V. BAGGETT
890 F. 2d. 1095 (10th Cir. 1990)

SEYMOUR, CIRCUIT JUDGE.

On November 23, 1987, Barbara Baggett made the first of a number of phone calls to Steve Daniels, a suspected drug dealer. On November 29, she made three more calls to Daniels, all recorded by the police, in which she arranged to purchase some cocaine and heroin, and to meet Daniels at a specified time and place. *See* Government Exhibits Nos. 61, 124, and 125; rec., vol. XI, at 1257–60. At the prescribed location, an Oklahoma City police officer and an agent with the Oklahoma Bureau of Narcotics and Dangerous Drugs twice observed Steve Daniels meeting with a "white female" driving a car registered to Barbara Baggett. Rec., vol. XV, at 2017.

It is during these two meetings that the exchange of heroin allegedly occurred, and it is on this day, November 29, that Baggett is charged with the possession of heroin and with making three telephone calls to facilitate the distribution of the drug. . . .

In assessing the sufficiency of the evidence for a criminal conviction, we must view all the evidence, both direct and circumstantial, in the light most favorable to the Government. Taken together with all reasonable inferences to be drawn from such evidence, we must determine whether the evidence is sufficient to establish guilt beyond a reasonable doubt. *Glasser v. United States,* 315 U.S. 60, 80, 62 S.Ct. 457, 469, 86 L.Ed. 680 (1942); *United States v. Blandin,* 784 F.2d 1048, 1050 (10th Cir.1986). In addition, "our review here does not include assessing the credibility of witnesses; that task is reserved for the jury." *United States v. Levario,* 877 F.2d 1483, 1485 (10th Cir.1989).

It is not necessary that the Government have direct evidence to support a conviction for possession.

But where, as in this case, the Government fails to seize and analyze the chemical composition of the alleged narcotic substance, there must be enough circumstantial evidence to support an inference that the defendant actually did possess the drugs in question. *See, e.g., United States v. Hill,* 589 F.2d 1344, 1348–50 (8th Cir.1979); *United States v. Iacopelli,* 483 F.2d 159, 161 (2d Cir.1973).

The circumstantial evidence that Baggett actually possessed the drugs in question is not strong. The three telephone calls of November 29 do make clear that she arranged for a purchase of a controlled substance on that day. Additionally, some four months later, on March 31, 1988, Baggett confessed to two police officers that during November of 1987 she had used "about a half a pill or balloon of heroin a day and that towards the end of the month she was up to using a whole pill or balloon of heroin per day." Rec., vol. XVI, at 2194. However, the Government must put forth some evidence to show that Baggett actually possessed heroin on the day in question. Such evidence may include "evidence of the physical appearance of the substance involved in the transaction, evidence that the substance produced the expected effects when sampled by someone familiar with the illicit drug, evidence that the substance was used in the same manner as the illicit drug, testimony that a high price was paid in cash for the substance, evidence that transactions involving the substance were carried on with secrecy or deviousness, and evidence that the substance was called by the name of the illegal narcotic by the defendant or others in [her] presence. . . ." *United States v. Dolan,* 544 F.2d 1219, 1221 (4th Cir.1976). *See also United States v. Scott,* 725 F.2d 43, 44–46 (4th Cir.1984).

Little of the relevant information listed in *Dolan* has been presented as evidence here. Both Detective Janice Stupka and Agent Lonnie Wright observed a meeting between Steve Daniels and a "white female." The first meeting took place inside Daniels' car and lasted for about three minutes; the second occurred outside the vehicles, and consisted of only "a brief contact with each other." Rec., vol. XV, at 2018.

Neither Wright nor Stupka saw any money or narcotics exchanged at either of the two meetings. Rec., vol. XI, at 1274–75; rec., vol. XV, at 2027. No witness for the Government testified to seeing a drug exchange between Daniels and Baggett, or to seeing Baggett with heroin at any time on November 29. The Government put forward no evidence other than Stupka and Wright's testimony to show that a transaction actually took place.

If the prosecution is not going to present direct evidence of drug possession, its circumstantial evidence must include some testimony linking defendant to an observed substance that a jury can infer to be a narcotic. The Government here has presented us with no case in which a conviction was upheld without evidence that the defendant possessed a substance and that the substance was a narcotic. Courts typically require much stronger evidence before holding it sufficient to meet the Government's burden of proof. *See, e.g., Scott,* 725 F.2d at 46 (finding that "[e]very fact listed in *Dolan* for establishing circumstantially the illegal character of the [substance] possessed by the defendant was present"). . . .

In sum, we conclude that the Government's evidence is insufficient to sustain the possession conviction.

EXERCISE

The case above calls into question two distinct elements. What are they? What might be two kinds of evidence the government could try to find through investigation that would address the deficiencies in those two elements?

2. CRIMINAL HISTORY

A few statutes require a prior conviction as an element to a crime. For example, 18 U.S.C. § 922(g)(1) bars the possession of a firearm by someone who has been convicted of a felony. A complication arises with this: usually evidence of prior convictions are barred at trial, as they tend to prejudice the jury against the defendant. It is difficult to fulfill the spirit of that limitation while allowing the government to prove up the element of a prior conviction.

OLD CHIEF V. UNITED STATES
519 U.S. 172 (1997)

JUSTICE SOUTER delivered the opinion of the Court.

Subject to certain limitations, 18 U.S.C. § 922(g)(1) prohibits possession of a firearm by anyone with a prior felony conviction, which the Government can prove by introducing a record of judgment or similar evidence identifying the previous offense. Fearing prejudice if the jury learns the nature of the earlier crime, defendants sometimes seek to avoid such an informative disclosure by offering to concede the fact of the prior conviction. The issue here is whether a district court abuses its discretion if it spurns such an offer and admits the full record of a prior judgment, when the name or nature of the prior offense raises the risk of a verdict tainted by improper considerations, and when the purpose of the evidence is solely to prove the element of prior conviction. We hold that it does.

In 1993, petitioner, Old Chief, was arrested after a fracas involving at least one gunshot. The ensuing federal charges included not only assault with a dangerous weapon and using a firearm in relation to a crime of violence but violation of 18 U.S.C. § 922(g)(1). . . .

The earlier crime charged in the indictment against Old Chief was assault causing serious bodily injury. Before trial, he moved for an order requiring the Government "to refrain from mentioning—by reading the Indictment, during jury selection, in opening statement, or closing argument—and to refrain from offering into evidence or soliciting any testimony from any witness regarding the prior criminal convictions of the Defendant, *except* to state that the Defendant has been convicted of a crime punishable by imprisonment exceeding one (1) year." App. 6. He said that revealing the name and nature of his prior assault conviction would unfairly tax the jury's capacity to hold the Government to its burden of proof beyond a reasonable doubt on current charges of assault, possession, and violence with a firearm, and he offered to "solve the problem here by stipulating, agreeing and requesting the Court to instruct the jury that he has been convicted of a crime punishable by imprisonment exceeding one (1) yea[r]." *Id.,* at 7. He argued that the offer to stipulate to the fact of the prior conviction rendered evidence of the name and nature of the offense inadmissible under Rule 403 of the Federal Rules of Evidence, the danger being that unfair prejudice from that evidence would substantially outweigh its probative value.

The Assistant United States Attorney refused to join in a stipulation, insisting on his right to prove his case his own way, and the District Court agreed, ruling orally that, "If he doesn't want to stipulate, he doesn't have to." *Id.,* at 15–16. At trial, over renewed objection, the Government introduced the order of judgment and commitment for Old Chief's prior conviction. This document disclosed that on December 18, 1988, he "did knowingly and unlawfully assault Rory Dean Fenner, said assault resulting in serious bodily injury," for which Old Chief was sentenced to five years' imprisonment. *Id.,* at 18–19. The jury found Old Chief guilty on all counts, and he appealed.

The Ninth Circuit addressed the point with brevity:

> "Regardless of the defendant's offer to stipulate, the government is entitled to prove a prior felony offense through introduction of probative evidence. . . .

In dealing with the specific problem raised by § 922(g)(1) and its prior-conviction element, there can be no question that evidence of the name or nature of the prior offense generally carries a risk of unfair prejudice to the defendant. That risk will vary from case to case, for the reasons already given, but will be substantial whenever the official record offered by the Government would be arresting enough to lure a juror into a sequence of bad character reasoning. Where a prior conviction was for a gun crime or one similar to other charges in a pending case the risk of unfair prejudice would be especially obvious, and Old Chief sensibly worried that the prejudicial effect of his prior assault conviction, significant enough with respect to the current gun charges alone, would take on added weight from the related assault charge against him. . . .

Given these peculiarities of the element of felony-convict status and of admissions and the like when used to prove it, there is no cognizable difference between the evidentiary significance of an admission and of the legitimately probative component of the official record the prosecution would prefer to place in evidence. For purposes of the Rule 403 weighing of the probative against the prejudicial, the functions of the competing evidence are distinguishable only by the risk inherent in the one and wholly absent from the other. In this case, as in any other in which the prior conviction is for an offense likely to support conviction on some improper ground, the only reasonable conclusion was that the risk of unfair prejudice did substantially outweigh the discounted probative value of the record of conviction, and it was an abuse of discretion to admit the record when an admission was available. What we have said shows why this will be the general rule when proof of convict status is at issue, just as the prosecutor's choice will generally survive a Rule 403 analysis when a defendant seeks to force the substitution of an admission for evidence creating a coherent narrative of his thoughts and actions in perpetrating the offense for which he is being tried.

The judgment is reversed, and the case is remanded to the Ninth Circuit for further proceedings consistent with this opinion.

EXERCISE

You are a defense attorney representing Elmer Clancy, who has been charged with being a felon in possession of a firearm. He has two prior felonies under state law. One is for illegally brewing beer for distribution (he gave the beer to neighbors as gifts). He pled guilty to this crime twenty years ago and was sentenced to pay a $950 fine. The second is for fraudulently obtaining cable television service, which he accomplished by tapping into some wires behind his house. He pled guilty and received a sentence of one year probation five years ago.

Do you want to stipulate to the fact of an unstated prior conviction under *Old Chief*?

3. STATUS OF THE VICTIM

Some statutes include an element that is rooted in a status of the victim—usually related to the victim's age, disability, or professional status. For example, 18 U.S.C. § 1114 bars the killing of any officer or employee of the United States government while that employee is engaged in official duties. Statutory rape charges similarly require that the government prove up the age of the victim (though, as already discussed, they do not always require that the government prove that the defendant *knew* the age of the victim).

In some instances, status of the victim is an element because it is essential to the interest being protected—for example, elder abuse laws will specify that the victim must be elderly, since their interests lie at the root purpose of the law. Under many federal statutes, the victim's status (as a federal employee, usually) is the hook used to establish federal jurisdiction, such as in the case below.

UNITED STATES V. KIRKLAND
12 F. 3d 199 (11th Cir. 1994)

PER CURIAM:

Michael Wayne Kirkland was convicted in the United States District Court for the Middle District of Florida for killing an "officer or employee of the Postal Service" engaged in the performance of his duties, in violation of 18 U.S.C. § 1114 (count one); assaulting a person having custody of mail matter, in violation of 18 U.S.C. § 2114 (count two); and stealing the United States mail, in violation of 18 U.S.C. § 1708 (count three). The sole issue on appeal is whether the victim, an employee of a private company which contracts with the United States Postal Service (Postal Service) to provide drivers to operate vehicles transporting mail matter, was an "officer or employee of the Postal Service" within the meaning of § 1114. We hold that he was not and vacate Kirkland's conviction on count one. . . .

The victim in this case, Donald Cook, was employed by A & S Transportation Corporation, a company that contracted with the Postal Service to furnish drivers for the collection of mail and its delivery to various post offices. Such "contract drivers" are not part of the postal career service entitled to the benefits and protections of the civil service laws, as set forth at 39 U.S.C. § 1001(b). Their wages and benefits are provided directly by the contractor and are governed by the Service Contract Act of 1965 (the "SCA"), 41 U.S.C. §§ 351–358, which sets minimum labor standards for the protection of the employees of contractors with the United States government.1 While on the job, contract drivers are required to carry an identification badge indicating the name of the operator of the vehicle, the employing contractor and the post office to which he is assigned. Appearing at the top of the badge is the caption "NON POSTAL SERVICE CONTRACTOR EMPLOYEE." (*See* Def.Exh. 1).

Section 1114 prohibits the killing or attempted killing of various federal officials, officers and employees in the performance of their official duties, including "any officer or employee of the Postal Service." 18 U.S.C. § 1114. The statute does not define "officer or employee."

Kirkland advances several arguments in support of his contention that a contract driver is not an "officer or employee of the Postal Service." He first focuses on 39 U.S.C. § 1001(a), which states that "[e]xcept as otherwise provided in this title, the Postal Service shall appoint all officers and employees of the Postal Service." 39 U.S.C. § 1001(a). He maintains that, because Cook was not appointed by the Postal Service, he cannot be considered an "officer or employee of the Postal Service.". . .

We hold that the language of § 1114 referring to "any officer or employee of the Postal Service" unambiguously applies only to those officers or employees directly employed by the Postal Service, and does not plainly encompass contract drivers. . . .

The cases cited by the government for the proposition that § 1114 should be broadly construed to safeguard the person of all those discharging federal functions are no more illuminating on the specific issue at hand than is the legislative history. In only one case cited by the government was the court required to determine whether liability under § 1114 is limited to the murder or attempted murder of persons directly employed by the United States. *See United States v. Schaffer,* 664 F.2d 824 (11th Cir.1981). In *Schaffer,* a panel of this court concluded that an employee of a privately owned security service under contract with the United States Marshal to provide security for federal prisoners undergoing treatment at a particular hospital was within the class of persons protected by § 1114. *See id.* at 825. However, section 1114 explicitly refers to the killing or attempted killing of "any United States marshal or deputy marshal *or person employed to assist such marshal or deputy marshal.*" 18 U.S.C. § 1114 (emphasis added). This expansive language is lacking with respect to "any officer or employee of the Postal Service.". . . .

In view of the foregoing, we hold that the protection afforded by § 1114 does not extend to contract drivers for the Postal Service and we vacate Kirkland's conviction on count one. . . .

REVERSED and REMANDED for entry of a judgment of acquittal as to count one.

EXERCISE

The cost of failing to identify or prove an element can be quite high for the prosecutor and the public safety interests she is protecting. Note the impact of the failure to prove the status element in the case above—an acquittal is ordered on the murder count, leaving only convictions for assault and theft. If, as a prosecutor, this case had been brought to you for consideration at the investigative stage, what might you have done with it? Would you have asked the investigators to search for specific additional evidence?

CHAPTER TWO

CRIMES CAUSING DEATH

■ ■ ■

In nearly every criminal code, the harshest penalties are assigned to those crimes in which the death of a person is caused by the defendant's actions. In some American jurisdictions (including the federal system),[1] the penalty of execution is still available for this most-serious of crimes.

That means that the definition of crimes resulting in death is particularly important, since the stakes are so high. Sadly, the definitions we use are rooted in a long and murky history and staked to mental states that are difficult to define and subject to confusion and speculation by juries. We order homicides according to what the defendant was *thinking* rather than what she was *doing*. Thus, a woman who plans to kill her abusive husband and does so will potentially face a first-degree murder charge, while a man who tortures and sexually abuses a woman—and accidentally kills her in the process—may not be eligible for that same charge, since he did not plan for or intend his victim's death.

Most American jurisdictions have at least four categories of crimes involving death: First degree murder, second-degree murder, voluntary manslaughter, and involuntary manslaughter. To that list, some jurisdictions add the additional crimes of capital murder, third-degree murder, and/or negligent homicide. Further complicating things are doctrines like felony-murder, which allow someone to be charged with a first or second degree murder for a death that occurs in the course of another felony, such as robbery, even in the absence of premeditation or intent to kill.

All of these crimes have three elements in common: identification of the killer, actual death of a victim, and causation of the death. Beyond these common elements, they are differentiated principally by state of mind elements and elements relating to the circumstances surrounding the killing. The rest of this chapter will focus on those distinctions. They matter, because the charge of conviction determines the possible sentence. In the federal system, first-degree murder can be punished with a maximum sentence of death,[2] second degree murder with life in prison,[3]

---

[1] 18 U.S.C. § 3591.

[2] 18 U.S.C. § 1111(b).

[3] Id.

voluntary manslaughter with a term of 15 years in prison,[4] and involuntary manslaughter with a term of eight years in prison.[5]

Because Second-Degree Murder has fewer elements than First-Degree Murder, we will examine it first.

A. SECOND DEGREE MURDER

Federal law defines first and second degree murder together in 18 U.S.C. § 1111(a):

Murder is the unlawful killing of a human being with malice aforethought. Every murder perpetrated by poison, lying in wait, or any other kind of willful, deliberate, malicious, and premeditated killing; or committed in the perpetration of, or attempt to perpetrate, any arson, escape, murder, kidnapping, treason, espionage, sabotage, aggravated sexual abuse or sexual abuse, child abuse, burglary, or robbery; or perpetrated as part of a pattern or practice of assault or torture against a child or children; or perpetrated from a premeditated design unlawfully and maliciously to effect the death of any human being other than him who is killed, is murder in the first degree.

Any other murder is murder in the second degree.

Setting aside for a moment the complexities of first degree murder in this statute, let's consider the elements of Second Degree Murder in the federal courts:

1) Within the special maritime and territorial jurisdiction of the United States.

2) Identification of the killer,

3) Actual death,

4) Causation of the death by the defendant,

5) Unlawfulness, and

6) Malice aforethought.

Two of these elements are particularly thorny: unlawfulness and malice aforethought. "Unlawfulness" means that the killing was not justified under the law—for example, a soldier killing an enemy combatant during war is not considered murder because it is justified, and a killing in self-defense is sometimes also justified (we will examine the doctrine of self-defense at the end of this chapter).

---

4   18 U.S.C. § 1112(b).

5   Id.

"Malice aforethought" is archaic and confusing language. On the surface, this appears to be a description of premeditation, but it is not.

The *Milton* case below addresses the definition of "malice aforethought" and involves an odd quirk in federal law: even though the defendant was acquitted in state court of second degree murder, the federal trial judge in a subsequent firearms case sentenced him as if he had been convicted of 18 U.S.C. § 1111, pursuant to a provision of the federal sentencing guidelines called "relevant conduct."

UNITED STATES V. MILTON

27 F. 3d 203 (6th Cir. 1994)

KEITH, CIRCUIT JUDGE.

On September 26, 1992, Milton and his friend Lorenzo Colbert ("Low") met at Milton's Burt Street residence in Detroit, Michigan and arranged to sell drugs to Melvin Beasley ("Beasley"). Unbeknownst to Beasley, Milton planned to sell him chalk instead of cocaine. Later that day, Milton and Low, both armed with .45 caliber semi-automatic pistols, met Beasley and Anthony Fountain ("Fountain") at a gas station and completed the deal. Beasley paid Milton $2,700 for the chalk. After the deal, Milton and Low left the gas station to return to Burt Street. After Beasley discovered the drugs were fake, he followed Milton and Low. At a stop-light, Beasley pulled alongside Milton's and Low's car. Before any conversation occurred, Fountain saw Low cock his gun and he ducked under the dashboard. From where Fountain hid, he heard four shots fired. During the shooting, Beasley was shot in the head and later died from his wounds.

[handwritten margin note: Fountain said he ducked + only heard shots]

[handwritten margin note: Low fired 4 shots, shooting Beasley in the head - he died from his wounds]

Two days later, the Detroit Police executed a search warrant at Milton's Burt Street residence where they recovered Milton's gun and arrested him. Once in custody, Milton gave a statement about the events and admitted he knew Beasley and had arranged the fake drug deal. When questioned about the shooting, Milton stated:

[handwritten margin note: Milton said he knew Beasley + set up a fake drug deal]

> A: While I was stopped at the light, Melvin [Beasley] pulled up next to us on the right side. Melvin just looked at me, like saying, man, why did you do this to me. As Melvin had pulled up, Low rolled down the window. Then the light turned green. I was starting to turn infront [sic] of traffic to run. Before I started to turn and while Melvin was looking at me the way he was, I fired one shot that broke out their rear door window of the car Melvin was in. I aimed to shoot the back window out just to scare him. Then I started the turn, that's when Low pointed his gun out the window and fired two shots that I'm sure of. As I turned and was going down French Road, I saw the car still there at the light. I just saw the front of the car. I didn't see that Melvin had been shot.

[handwritten margin note: Milton said he fired one shot at back window to scare]

[handwritten margin note: Low fired 2 shots]

Q: What type of gun did you fire into Melvins [sic] car.

A: It was a black .45 automatic.

Q: Where is that gun at now.

A: It was on Burt Rd., but I think the police got it now.

Q: What type of gun did Low have.

A: It was also a black .45.

Q: Where is the gun Low had.

A: He should have it. . . .

Q: Did Low say anything about the shooting at all.

A: Low was just saying, 'I killed him, I killed him, killed both of them.' I told Low he didn't kill them, he just shot through the window. . . .

For Guidelines purposes, 18 U.S.C. § 1111(a) defines murder as "the unlawful killing of a human being with malice aforethought." *See* U.S.S.G. § 2A1.2 (stating the Guidelines definition of second degree murder appears at 18 U.S.C. §§ 1111 and 1112). First degree murder is defined as any murder "perpetrated by poison, lying in wait, or any kind of wilful, deliberate, malicious, and premeditated killing." *See* 18 U.S.C. § 1111(a). Second degree murder is defined as any other murder. *Id.* Second degree murder, therefore, requires a finding of malice aforethought. *See United States v. Bordeaux,* 980 F.2d 534, 536 (8th Cir.1992), *United States v. Lesina,* 833 F.2d 156, 159 (9th Cir.1987) (citing *United States v. Celestine,* 510 F.2d 457, 459 (9th Cir. 1975)).

The Sixth Circuit has not heretofore defined malice aforethought. Other courts of appeals, however, have defined malice aforethought. The Eighth Circuit stated that "[m]alice may be established by evidence of conduct which is 'reckless and wanton, and a gross deviation from a reasonable standard of care, of such nature that a jury is warranted in inferring that defendant was aware of a serious risk of death or serious bodily harm.'" *See United States v. Black Elk,* 579 F.2d 49, 51 (8th Cir.1978) (citing *United States v. Cox,* 509 F.2d 390, 392 (D.C.Cir.1974)). The Ninth Circuit defined malice aforethought as including "the state of mind with which one intentionally commits a wrongful act without legal justification or excuse." *United States v. Celestine,* 510 F.2d 457, 459 (9th Cir.1975). The *Celestine* panel further noted that malice aforethought "may be inferred from circumstances which show 'a wanton and depraved spirit, a mind bent on evil mischief without regard to its consequences.'" *Id.* . . . .

Here, the district court held a man accountable for second degree murder using a foreseeability standard. We are disturbed by the district court's failure to make any findings relevant to the elements of second degree murder. The court did not find that Milton acted with malice aforethought—in fact, no reference to malice aforethought appears within the sentencing transcript. District courts should consider specifically the elements of cross-referenced conduct. . . .

Although the district court erred by failing to make specific findings as to the elements of second degree murder, we review applications of the Guidelines *de novo,* and therefore must find that Milton's actions indicate he acted with malice aforethought. Milton, unprovoked, fired at least two shots into the victim's car. Despite Milton's statement that he only meant to scare Beasley, from his actions we infer that he must have been aware of a risk of death or serious bodily injury. Milton's gross deviation from a reasonable standard of care established the requisite malice aforethought to hold him accountable for second degree murder. Based upon a *de novo* review of the record, we find Milton's actions satisfied the requisite elements and we affirm the district court's cross-reference to the second degree murder Guideline.

[handwritten margin note: Even though he only meant to scare, he was aware of the risk of serious bodily harm or death.]

[handwritten note: holding]

EXERCISE

David and Paul are shooting at cans in a vacant lot with a rifle. They are in a national park area when they do this. They have set the cans up along a fence next to a berm; they know that the bullets will go into the earthen berm harmlessly.

As dusk falls, a car pulls up and parks directly in front of where they were shooting. A man gets out of the car and David calls out to him, informing him that he is blocking their shooting range. The man shrugs and says "I gotta go get some stuff for my kids."

Enraged, David and Paul decide to continue shooting at the cans, which are just a few feet from the car. Paul misses the cans and his bullet goes through the side of the car. It kills a child inside the car and wounds another. The children could not be seen from outside of the car. David and Paul both claim that they had no idea there were children in the car.

You are the prosecutor. Will you charge Paul with murder with malice aforethought? *[handwritten: Yes, they deviated from a reasonable standard of care, but were not aware of serious risk of death or serious bodily harm.]*

In allowing second degree murder to be based either on intent to kill *or* reckless actions likely to cause serious injury or death, the federal law diverges from many state formulas, which include a second degree murder statute which requires intent to kill and a third degree murder law which encompasses reckless behavior.

UNITED STATES V. HOUSER
130 F. 3d 867 (9th Cir. 1997)

CANBY, CIRCUIT JUDGE:

The facts as shown by the prosecution's evidence were as follows. Houser and the victim, Angela Rae LaSarte, had dated off and on for about two years prior to her death. Houser was frequently violent toward LaSarte, often after bouts of heavy drinking. On the night in question, Houser had been drinking at Bobbi's Bar in Plummer, Idaho, for almost five hours. Houser left the bar briefly about 10:00 p.m. but then returned to have one last drink with his friend, Chris Biles. Houser saw LaSarte sitting in the bar with a friend, Nick Parker. An argument ensued between Houser and Parker, during which Houser attempted to strike Parker with a beer bottle.

Biles then physically removed Houser from the bar, but Houser returned shortly thereafter and became involved in a dispute with Biles. Houser became angry, went outside, and began kicking and punching Biles' truck. Biles came out to stop him. While Biles and Houser were arguing, LaSarte and Parker-as well as most of the bar's patrons-left the bar to observe the argument.

Eventually, Houser walked back to the cab of his truck and most of the patrons re-entered the bar. LaSarte, however, remained outside and watched Houser. Houser took a handgun from his truck, pumped a cartridge into the chamber of the gun, held the gun behind his back, and began walking towards the bar.

LaSarte then began walking toward Houser. They met in the middle of the street for a few seconds; neither spoke to or struggled with the other. After four or five seconds Houser brought his right arm to the left side of LaSarte's neck and shot her. Houser then knelt to the ground beside LaSarte. A spectator, Kim DeLorme, rushed to help LaSarte, and Houser pointed his gun at her. Houser then ran into the bar, but bar patrons subdued and restrained him. LaSarte died later that evening from the gunshot wound.

Houser's view of events at the bar differed in crucial ways from that of the prosecution's witnesses. Houser testified that he got his gun out of the truck so he could scare the patrons that had gathered outside. He stated that he knew the gun was loaded, but did not know that a round was in the firing chamber. He also stated that he did not know the safety was off. He testified that, when he and LaSarte met in the parking lot, she attempted to wrest the gun from him and, in doing so, caused the accidental discharge of the weapon. After she fell and he knelt beside her, he got up and ran into the bar to call 911, but was subdued before he could do so.

Houser was subsequently convicted by a jury of murder in the second degree, in violation of 18 U.S.C. § 1111, and use of a firearm during and in relation to a crime of violence, in violation of 18 U.S.C. § 924(c). This appeal followed. . . .

conviction + appeal

Houser next challenges a different instruction regarding malice. The district court instructed the jury that it could find the malice aforethought necessary to convict Houser of second-degree murder if it concluded either that Houser killed LaSarte deliberately and intentionally, or that Houser killed LaSarte recklessly with extreme disregard for human life. Houser contends that this instruction was erroneous because at common law, he asserts, "extreme disregard" referred to acts endangering the populace at large, and could not be applied to acts directed solely at the person killed. *See Colorado v. Jefferson,* 748 P.2d 1223, 1228 (Colo.1988). Houser argues that his acts were directed only at LaSarte, and consequently could not constitute "extreme disregard.". . .

jury instruction

Houser contention

It is true that some state courts have required the general malice referred to by Houser, but our circuit has not. Although we have not addressed Houser's precise argument, our cases clearly indicate that a jury can convict a defendant of second-degree murder under an "extreme disregard" theory even if the acts causing the victim's death were reckless only toward the victim herself. In *United States v. Lesina,* 833 F.2d 156, 159 (9th Cir.1987), we indicated that an instruction on "extreme disregard for human life" was proper for second-degree murder in a case where the danger appeared to be only to the victim. In other cases describing the level of malice required for second-degree murder, we have not required extreme disregard for life to encompass more than disregard for the victim's life. For example, in *United States v. Boise,* 916 F.2d 497 (9th Cir.1990), we upheld a conviction for second-degree murder where the defendant had killed a small child through "two blunt force blows to the head." The acts causing death in *Boise* were clearly directed solely at the victim; we nevertheless concluded that "the jury could rationally conclude beyond a reasonable doubt that Boise displayed 'a wanton and depraved spirit, a mind bent on evil mischief without regard to its consequences.'" *Id.* at 500.3 Similarly, in *United States v. Celestine,* 510 F.2d 457, 459 (9th Cir.1975), we upheld a second-degree murder conviction where the defendant killed a young woman by beating her with his fists and by repeatedly kicking a stick into her vagina. There, too, the acts causing death were directed solely at the deceased; again, we concluded that "[t]he act attributed to the [defendant] certainly permits, if it does not require, the conclusion that the homicide was accompanied by a callous and wanton disregard of human life." *Id.* at 459; *accord Starr v. Lockhart,* 23 F.3d 1280, 1292 (8th Cir.1994) (same); *United States v. Black Elk,* 579 F.2d 49, 50–51 (8th Cir.1978). In the face of these cases, the district court's instruction on "extreme disregard" cannot be regarded as erroneous.

Holding

---

yes – should be
aware of serious
risk of harm

EXERCISE

You are a federal prosecutor presented with a case by an FBI agent. The target of that investigation was late for work at a federal facility. When he arrived at work, he found the door to his workplace inexplicably locked. He knocked on the door several times and got no response. Frustrated, he fired his legally-carried handgun into the door. One of the bullets struck and killed a person on the other side who had come to let him in after hearing his knocks. Is there sufficient evidence to support a charge of second-degree murder under 18 U.S.C. § 1111?

B. FIRST DEGREE MURDER

Again, first degree murder is described in 18 U.S.C. § 1111(a):

(a) Murder is the unlawful killing of a human being with malice aforethought. Every murder perpetrated by poison, lying in wait, or any other kind of willful, deliberate, malicious, and premeditated killing; or committed in the perpetration of, or attempt to perpetrate, any arson, escape, murder, kidnapping, treason, espionage, sabotage, aggravated sexual abuse or sexual abuse, child abuse, burglary, or robbery; or perpetrated as part of a pattern or practice of assault or torture against a child or children; or perpetrated from a premeditated design unlawfully and maliciously to effect the death of any human being other than him who is killed, is murder in the first degree.

Any other murder is murder in the second degree.

(b) Within the special maritime and territorial jurisdiction of the United States.

First Degree Murder, then, has the same elements as Second Degree Murder with the additional requirement that at least one of four other elements must be present:

1) Committed within the maritime or territorial jurisdiction of the United States,

2) Identification of the killer,

3) Actual death,

4) Causation of the death by the defendant,

5) Unlawfulness, and

6) Malice aforethought.

7) At least one of the following must also be proven:

     A) premeditation,

Elements

B) that the death was caused in the course of committing arson, escape, murder, kidnapping, treason, espionage, sabotage, sexual abuse, burglary or robbery,

C) perpetrated as part of an assault or torture against at least one child, or

D) that the death was caused during a premeditated attempt to kill someone other than the actual victim.

Two of these last elements in the alternative (7(A) & (D) in the list above) require premeditation, while the remaining two describe a "felony-murder rule" which allows for prosecution of a first-degree murder even in the absence of premeditation if the killing takes place in the course of one of the enumerated felonies. These two groups play out very differently in terms of the proofs required of the government if they are going to receive a conviction. First, let's consider premeditation.

1. PREMEDITATION

Premeditation can be a difficult concept, particularly where little planning was involved in the murder.

UNITED STATES V. THOMAS
664 F. 3d 217 (8th Cir. 2011)

WOLLMAN, CIRCUIT JUDGE.

Shanon Thomas was convicted of first-degree murder in violation of 18 U.S.C. §§ 1111, 113, and 1153, and sentenced to life imprisonment. He appeals from his conviction, arguing that the district court1 erred in denying his motion to suppress, his motion for judgment of acquittal, and his motion for a mistrial. We affirm.

I.

On the evening of April 17, 2010, Thomas and his girlfriend, Marissa Mackey, found that Mackey's residence had been vandalized. They suspected that Dawn Starlin, Mackey's neighbor across the back alley and Thomas's former girlfriend, was the culprit. After discovering the vandalism, Thomas retrieved a gun from his sister's residence and left it behind Mackey's home. Thomas and Mackey then went out to a bar with some friends. When they returned home Thomas went outside, and Starlin, who was sitting in a chair in her backyard, began taunting him about his relationship with Mackey. Thomas retrieved the gun he had left earlier that evening, walked towards Starlin, and shot her multiple times. Starlin was found dead outside her home early in the morning on April 18, 2010.

Around four o'clock that afternoon, Thomas requested that the officers investigating Starlin's death come to his mother's home to speak with him. Upon arrival, the officers saw Thomas hugging his mother, who was crying.

Thomas waved the officers inside. When the officers entered the house Thomas acted as though he expected to leave with them, saying "let's go," and stepping towards them. Officer Grunder then asked Thomas why he did "it" and whether he had been drinking. Thomas responded only that he had not been drinking. Grunder next asked Thomas where he had gotten the gun, Thomas replied that he had obtained it earlier the night of April 17th. Grunder asked where the gun was, to which Thomas replied that it was gone and that he "didn't mean to gun her down."

Grunder testified that he thought he had enough probable cause to arrest Thomas after the last statement. Thomas was not advised of his *Miranda* rights before this conversation, which lasted only a minute or two. Thomas was placed under arrest and taken from his mother's home to the police station, where, after being advised of his *Miranda* rights, he made a full confession. The following day, at the Dakota County Jail, Thomas was again informed of his *Miranda* rights and interviewed, and he confessed again. . . .

Confessed to the murder twice

Testimony

The trial focused on Thomas's mental state at the time of the shooting. The jury was presented with the evidence of Thomas's confessions through the testimony of the FBI agents who had investigated the case. Additionally, Justina Tuttle and Waylon Wabasha testified that they had been socializing with Thomas and Mackey on the evening of April 17th. Tuttle and Wabasha both testified that Thomas had left Mackey's house and returned a few minutes later with a gun. Later in the evening, after the four of them returned from a bar and went inside Mackey's house, Thomas went outside for a few minutes. Upon returning, Thomas said that he had shot Starlin. Thomas's mother testified that when Thomas came to her house on the afternoon of April 18, 2010, he confessed to her that he had shot Starlin. Thomas's sister, Dezarae Thomas, and her boyfriend, Roger Saul, testified that Thomas had retrieved the gun from Dezarae Thomas's house around nine or ten o'clock the evening of April 17th.

The jury's verdict that Thomas's action was premeditated and thus constituted first-degree murder is amply supported by the evidence. The district court properly instructed the jury that a killing is premeditated when it results from planning or deliberation, that the time needed for premeditation varies with the circumstances, and that the killer must be conscious of his intent to kill. *United States v. Haskell,* 468 F.3d 1064, 1074 (8th Cir.2006). The jury heard evidence of Thomas and Starlin's romantic history, as well as the tension that developed when Thomas became involved with Mackey. Thomas retrieved a gun from his sister's home and left it behind Mackey's home on the evening of April 17, 2010. Hours later, after being spoken to and taunted by Starlin, who was unarmed and seated, Thomas retrieved the gun. He walked toward Starlin and fired multiple shots. The jury could reasonably have concluded that Thomas formed the requisite intent when he initially brought the gun to Mackey's house, when he picked the gun up and walked towards Starlin, or in the moment before he started firing. Because there are multiple constructions of the evidence that support the jury's verdict, the district court did not err in denying the motion for judgment of acquittal.

[handwritten note: District court did not err in denying motion for judgment of acquittal]

EXERCISE

Roberta lives with her sister, Florence. There is a lot of tension between the two over finances, as their home is very much in need of repair.

One night after dinner, Roberta finds some money that Florence has hidden from her. Angry, she confronts Florence, who says she hid it from Roberta because Roberta "would just waste it." Florence then goes to the barn to check on something there. Roberta follows her, and then burns down the barn by dropping a lit match into dry straw near the door. She had the matches with her, as usual, since she is a smoker. She later told investigators that when she realized Florence was in the barn, she "had to do it."

Assuming federal jurisdiction, does this crime meet the standard of "premeditated" murder described in the *Thomas* case?

The proofs of premeditation are often circumstantial, particularly in a case where a killer acts alone and no discussion or joint action prior to the act can be used to prove up that element.

UNITED STATES V. SHAW
701 F. 2d 367 (5th Cir. 1983)

JERRE S. WILLIAMS, CIRCUIT JUDGE.

Late Christmas night, 1980, Kenneth Brinkley was driving his automobile down a secluded two-lane highway in the sparsely populated area of Mississippi known as the Natchez Trace Parkway. With him in the car were his son, his fiancé, Linda Johnson, and her children, twelve-year-old Lachelle and nine-year-old Terrell Johnson. The three children were sleeping in the back seat. While passing the Ballard Creek rest area, Brinkley noticed a parked pickup truck, which appeared to be a dark-colored, red and white late model Ford with chrome trim on the side. Brinkley had seen no other vehicles on the road. Immediately after Brinkley passed the rest area, a rifle shot ripped through the car's back seat. The bullet struck the young Johnson boy in the legs and hit his sister in the hip.

Brinkley quickly sought help in the nearby town of Mathiston, telling the local police where the shooting had taken place and describing the pickup he had seen in the Ballard Creek rest area immediately prior to the shooting. Relying on this information, three officers proceeded to the Trace Highway about a half mile north of the rest area. After waiting approximately ten or fifteen minutes they saw a late model, two-tone pickup approaching from the south at 35 to 40 miles per hour. Shaw was apprehended in the truck after a chase in which speeds exceeded 110 miles per hour. Shaw was frisked and told his vehicle fit the description of one at the scene of the shooting. He was arrested for speeding and driving while intoxicated, handcuffed, and placed in a patrol car.

After Shaw got out of the truck, one of the officers shined a light through its open door and saw four bullets on the floor on the driver's side. Another officer then released the seat latch and folded back the driver's seat. Behind the seat, fully cocked, was a .35 caliber rifle. Shaw was read his *Miranda* rights and told of the traffic charges. He made no statement to police. Shaw was then driven to the sheriff's office in Ackerman, Mississippi. After he was again read his *Miranda* rights, he indicated that he wished to answer questions. Shaw told the sheriff that he had been "driving around" on the Natchez Trace Highway and stopped at "a pull-off place" because he was sick. He emphatically denied that he had fired his gun since deer hunting that afternoon.

Later that same night young Terrell Johnson died of his wounds. . . .

Shaw next challenges the sufficiency of the evidence to support the jury's verdict of guilty of first degree murder under 18 U.S.C. § 1111. He does not assert that the government failed to prove that he killed Terrell Johnson. The evidence clearly established that he fired the fatal shot. He does argue, however, that the government's evidence is insufficient to support the first degree murder conviction because it failed to establish that he committed the homicide with premeditation.

In determining the sufficiency of the evidence, a court of appeals must view the evidence and all reasonable inferences which may be drawn therefrom, in the light most favorable to the government. *Glasser v. United States,* 315 U.S. 60, 80, 62 S.Ct. 457, 469, 86 L.Ed. 680 (1942). We will affirm if "any rational trier of fact could have found the essential elements of the crime beyond a reasonable doubt." *Jackson v. Virginia,* 443 U.S. 307, 319, 99 S.Ct. 2781, 2789, 61 L.Ed.2d 560 (1979).

Section 1111 retains a common law distinction between second degree murder, which requires a killing with malice aforethought, and first degree murder, which in addition to malice aforethought requires a killing with premeditation and deliberation. Although it is clear that deliberation and premeditation under § 1111 involve a prior design to commit murder, no particular period of time is necessary for such deliberation and premeditation. *See United States v. Blue Thunder,* 604 F.2d 550, 553 (8th Cir.) *cert. denied,* 444 U.S. 902, 100 S.Ct. 215, 62 L.Ed.2d 139 (1979); *United States v. Brown,* 518 F.2d 821, 826 (7th Cir.), *cert. denied,* 423 U.S. 917, 96 S.Ct. 225, 46 L.Ed.2d 146 (1975). There must be some appreciable time for reflection and consideration before execution of the act, although the period of time "does not require the lapse of days or hours or even minutes." *Bostic v. United States,* 94 F.2d 636, 638 (D.C.Cir.1937), *cert. denied,* 303 U.S. 635, 58 S.Ct. 523, 82 L.Ed. 1095 (1938).

The distinction which marks the line between "deliberation" sufficient to support a conviction of first degree murder and the lesser killing with malice which supports conviction of second degree murder is less than clear. Commentators agree that the difference between the two standards is vague and obscure, *see* W. LaFave & A. Scott, *Criminal Law* § 73 (1972); Cardozo, *Law and Literature and Other Essays,* 99–100 (1931). Perhaps the best that can be said of deliberation is that it requires a "cool mind" that is capable of reflection, and of premeditation that it requires that the one with the "cool mind" did, in fact, reflect, at least for a short period of time before his act of killing. LaFave, *supra* at 563. We are aided in our analysis of this element by the specific wording of the federal statute. If the evidence supports a finding that Shaw was "lying in wait", he shall be guilty of murder in the first degree. With these standards in mind, we turn to our consideration of the evidence offered at Shaw's trial.

Brinkley, the driver of the car in which the children were riding, and Mrs. Johnson, the children's mother, both testified that they were certain that the shooting had occurred almost immediately after their car had passed the Ballard Creek rest stop. Both explained that their certainty was due to the fact that Brinkley, a long distance truck driver, had previously had an accident on the Natchez Trace Highway and that he was looking for his "special tree" a mile and a half north of the Ballard Creek rest stop in order to show Mrs. Johnson where the accident had taken place. Three police officers and one FBI agent testified that there was a "mashed down area" behind two large oak trees on the east side of the highway at the Ballard Creek rest stop. The indentation was described as three or four inches deep and approximately six feet long, including an area where it appeared the leaves had been kicked aside to accommodate a person's elbows. According to the local sheriff, the appearance of the leaves left the "impression there that appeared that someone had been lying behind these trees, concealing himself from the Natchez Trace."

Two witnesses, Ann and Lee Avery, driving together on the Natchez Trace Highway approximately an hour before the shooting occurred, testified that they had come across a "pretty late model" two-tone Ford pickup of a "light and dark" color, pulled off the side of the road. The truck's lights were off, and a man was leaning out of the driver's window, pointing a rifle down the highway in the direction the two were heading. Lee Avery testified that the truck looked silver or gray and blue or maroon. He also identified the rifle as a "lever-action" type with a curved lever as was the rifle belonging to Shaw. Avery was sure of this identification of the gun because he owned an identical rifle of a different caliber. On cross-examination Shaw

admitted being in the same area with his truck at the time described by
the Averys. A park officer testified that on the evenings of December 22
and 23, he had seen a pickup "just like" Shaw's with its lights off parked
near Ballard Creek. The truck was the same color and model as Shaw's,
but had no license plates on the rear and did not have a dog pen in the back
as did Shaw's the night he was arrested.

Although Shaw had originally denied that he had fired his gun on the night
of the 25th, his story at trial was basically that he had been drinking and
"riding around" on Christmas night and decided to go to the Natchez Trace
in order to "headlight some deer". He pulled over near the Old Trace rest
stop, saw a deer crossing the highway in front of him, and shot at it.
Believing he had hit the deer, he turned off the truck lights and left the
truck to go after the animal. At that time, he heard a car approaching from
the south. Aware that his possession of a rifle was illegal, he attempted to
conceal himself behind a pine tree on the side of the road. Simultaneously,
he slipped and fell, and as he hit the ground, the rifle discharged and the
Brinkley car passed in front of him.

None of the evidence corroborated Shaw's story. Brinkley and Mrs. Johnson
testified that the truck's grill was facing them as they approached, not
parked heading up the highway as Shaw claimed. Both were certain the
shooting had taken place at the Ballard Creek, not the Old Trace rest stop,
as claimed by Shaw. Although Shaw explained that he was on the deserted
highway after midnight with a loaded high powered rifle because he was
pursuing a shot deer, the evidence strongly suggested that no shot had been
fired prior to the one that killed the Johnson child. Despite an exhaustive
search, no spent shell was ever located, at either Ballard Creek or the Old
Trace. In addition, police discovered five live rounds in the cab of the truck,
four on the floor, and one jammed in the gun's magazine. If one adds the
shell that killed the child, the total number of bullets retrieved was seven—
the maximum capacity of the rifle. If Shaw's story about having shot the
deer were truthful, there would have been eight shells—one over the
maximum capacity of the rifle.

It is uncontroverted that Shaw was on the Natchez Trace Highway after
midnight with a fully loaded rifle, and that he fired the shot which killed
the child. There is scant explanation for the shooting, save his unsupported
story that he was attempting to pursue a wounded deer. Testimony by the
Averys and the park ranger support an inference that Shaw had been
parked on the highway, once with his lights off and his rifle aimed down
the road, on an earlier occasion. Shaw evaded apprehension when first
confronted by the police. The fact of the hollowed-out area of leaves at
Ballard Creek contradicts his version of the facts and bolsters that he was
lying in wait to take aim at a passing car. And most important, Shaw
repeatedly changed his story, and admitted that his statements to the
police and FBI on December 26 and December 27 were a lie.

The government's case was largely circumstantial. But, whether the evidence is direct or circumstantial, the scope of the review of the evidence is the same. *See United States v. Bell,* 678 F.2d 547, 549 n. 3 (5th Cir.) (en banc), *cert. granted,* 459 U.S. 1034, 103 S.Ct. 444, 74 L.Ed.2d 600 (1982). Accepting all reasonable inferences and credibility choices gathered from the evidence in the light most favorable to the government, we must decide if the jury's verdict was supportable. It is not necessary that the evidence exclude every reasonable hypothesis of innocence or be totally inconsistent with every conclusion except that of guilt. *Id.* at 549. We will reverse only if a reasonably minded jury must necessarily have entertained a reasonable doubt of the defendant's guilt. *United States v. Alonzo,* 681 F.2d 997, 1000 (5th Cir.1982); *United States v. Herman,* 576 F.2d 1139, 1144 (5th Cir.1978). We are convinced that the evidence presented in this case permitted a reasonable jury to conclude that Shaw's story was false, that he was lying in wait behind the trees at Ballard Creek, and that he formed a conscious choice to shoot at the Brinkley's passing car. The totality of the evidence supports the jury's finding of premeditation and guilt as charged.

Holding

EXERCISE

You are an Assistant United States Attorney working in the major crimes unit. An investigator from the United States Army brings you a potential case involving a shooting death on an Army base.

The victim was Dwight Smith, a drill instructor on the base. He was performing a training exercise with a group of about 20 soldiers that involved running to a bunker, taking cover, then firing live ammunition at targets that popped up about 80 yards away in a series of fake buildings. Smith directed the exercise from a small observation tower about 10 feet from the ground which was to the side of and slightly behind the firing line, away from the direction of fire.

During the exercise, a soldier located at the end of the group closest to Smith pivoted sideways and fired at the him, killing him. At the time, Smith was observing silently and had done nothing to provoke the shooting. The soldier who shot Smith was not known to have any problems with Smith and had a clean disciplinary and criminal history. The shooter refuses to make a statement regarding the incident, and talked to no one about it before or after the shooting.

Do you think there is sufficient evidence of premeditation to charge this as a first-degree murder?

To differentiate between first and second degree murder, at the very least "premeditation" must be something more than just forming intent.

What that "something extra" should be has sometimes proven difficult to define.

UNITED STATES V. BELL

819 F. 3d 310 (7th Cir. 2016)

ROVNER, CIRCUIT JUDGE.

In 2011, Bell and Dixon were cellmates in the United States Penitentiary in Terre Haute, Indiana. The cell they shared was located on the ground floor in Unit E-1 of the Terre Haute facility, a two-level unit which was triangular in shape and housed some 121 inmates. Inmate cells occupied two legs of the triangle, with correctional staff offices and activity, shower, and laundry rooms occupying the third leg. A recreational "day room" occupied the center of the unit. Six security cameras were positioned throughout the tier, and although none were positioned so as to record activity occurring within individual cells (except as might be revealed by an open cell door), the cameras did record what occurred in the common area of the tier outside of the cells. Video recorded on the evening of June 18, 2011, revealed the following sequence of events.

At approximately 6:45 p.m., Bell emerged from Cell 103, the cell that he shared with Dixon, and walked two doors down to Cell 105, which was occupied by Brian Pendelton. Bell was wearing a white t-shirt and khaki pants, and he appeared to have something in his right hand, which he kept in his pants pocket as he walked toward Pendelton's cell. When Bell arrived at Cell 105, he opened the cell door with his left hand, keeping his right hand in his pocket. He then entered the cell and closed the door behind him.

In the meantime, Dixon emerged from Cell 103, milled around the cell doorway for a moment, and eventually sat down in a chair just outside of the cell, facing a television in the day room. At one point, while Bell was inside of Cell 105, it appears from the video that Dixon turned to look in the direction of that cell.

Bell emerged from Cell 105 roughly 70 seconds after he entered. When he left the cell, he was shirtless and carrying a t-shirt in his right hand. In his left hand, it appears he was carrying a long, slender object. Bell walked, unhurried, back to his own cell. As he approached, Dixon arose from his chair and entered Cell 103 ahead of Bell.

Dixon re-emerged from Cell 103 some 25 seconds later and walked to Cell 113 near the end of the row of cells, carrying clothing in his right hand. His path took him directly by Pendelton's cell, number 105, the door to which was open.

Pendelton was struggling to lift himself off the floor and walk out of his cell as Dixon passed. He was, according to witness testimony, bleeding profusely from a stab wound to the left carotid artery on his neck. From the video recording, it appears that Dixon turned in the direction of Pendelton and the open door to Cell 105 as he walked by, but Dixon continued walking without pause toward the end of the row.

When he arrived at Cell 113, Dixon stepped inside for a period of approximately 20 seconds. The door to the cell was ajar during that period, and another inmate could be seen on the video surveillance standing near the cell's sink. Dixon left the cell again carrying clothing, walked to a trash can in the eastern portion of the day room and placed the clothing in the trash can underneath other objects already in it, and fluffed the trash on top before walking away.

At that point in time, Bell left Cell 103, clad once again in a white t-shirt and carrying a towel, and proceeded to one of the showers along the south portion of the unit.

Pendelton, meanwhile, after emerging from Cell 105 bleeding, had collapsed on the day room floor as he tried unsuccessfully to reach a correctional staff officer who was walking out of his office in response to a panic alarm Pendelton had sounded. Prison staff came to his aid but were unsuccessful in saving his life. An autopsy would later disclose that he bled to death from the stab wound to his left neck; he also had two superficial stab wounds to his back that likely were non-fatal. . . .

Bell was charged with committing first degree murder within the territorial jurisdiction of the United States. 18 U.S.C. § 1111 defines murder as "the unlawful killing of a human being with malice aforethought." The statute defines first degree murder to include, *inter alia,* "[e]very murder perpetrated by poison, lying in wait, or any other kind of willful, deliberate, malicious, and premeditated killing[.]" Murders that do not fall into that group or that are otherwise identified in the statute as felony murders, constitute second degree murders. Thus, setting aside felony murders, it is premeditation that, in the main, distinguishes first from second degree murder. *United States v. Delaney,* 717 F.3d 553, 556 (7th Cir.2013). And, of course, the government alleged here that Bell's killing of Pendelton was premeditated.

Premeditation requires planning and deliberation beyond the simple conscious intent to kill. There must be an appreciable elapse of time between the formation of a design and the fatal act, *see id.* at 556 (quoting *Fisher v. United States,* 328 U.S. 463, 467 n. 3, 66 S.Ct. 1318, 1320 n. 3, 90 L.Ed. 1382 (1946)), although no specific period of time is required. *See id.* at 557 (quoting district court's jury instruction); *United States v. Brown,* 518 F.2d 821, 826 (7th Cir.1975); *see also United States v. Begay,* 673 F.3d 1038, 1043 (9th Cir.2011) (en banc); *United States v. Mulder,* 273 F.3d 91, 117 (2d Cir.2001) (quoting *United States v. Shaw,* 701 F.2d 367, 393 (5th Cir.1983), *abrogated on other grounds by Greer v. Miller,* 483 U.S. 756, 763, 107 S.Ct. 3102, 3108, 97 L.Ed.2d 618 (1987)). But more is required than

[handwritten margin notes:] Bell charged with 1st degree murder

1st degree murder definition

Govt. said Bell's killing was premeditated

★ Appreciable elapse of time + deliberation

the simple passage of time: the defendant must, in fact, have deliberated during that time period. *See Fisher,* 328 U.S. at 467 n. 3, 66 S.Ct. at 1320 n. 3 (quoting district court's jury instruction); *United States v. Catalan-Roman,* 585 F.3d 453, 474 (1st Cir.2009) ("it is the fact of deliberation, of second thought[,] that is important") (quoting *United States v. Frappier,* 807 F.2d 257, 261 (1st Cir.1986)); *see also Shaw,* 701 F.2d at 393. Premeditation may, of course, be proved circumstantially. *See Brown,* 518 F.2d at 826.

The jury in this case was given an instruction on premeditation that was consistent with the criteria we have just described, and Bell raises no objection to the adequacy of the instruction. His contention, as we have said, is that the evidence on the element of premeditation was too thin to support the jury's finding of guilt. We will sustain the jury's verdict so long as there was sufficient evidence, viewed favorably to the government, to permit a rational jury to find the essential elements of the offense to have been proven beyond a reasonable doubt. *See Musacchio v. United States,* ___U.S. ___, 136 S.Ct. 709, 715, 193 L.Ed.2d 639 (2016) (quoting *Jackson v. Virginia,* 443 U.S. 307, 319, 99 S.Ct. 2781, 2789, 61 L.Ed.2d 560 (1979)).

Having reviewed the trial record, we are satisfied that the jury could reasonably find that Bell both had time to contemplate killing Pendelton and did, in fact, deliberate on the murder before he actually killed Pendelton. The circumstances suggest that Bell left his cell with a plan already in place to kill his fellow prisoner.

First, Bell walked out of his cell with something in his hand, and when he arrived at Pendelton's cell, he used his other hand to open the cell door. One could reasonably surmise from what occurred next, and from the sharpened rod that Dixon subsequently left in the trash can, that Bell had a weapon in his hand, and so was walking to Pendelton's cell prepared to engage in violence. *See Begay,* 673 F.3d at 1044 ("Carrying the murder weapon to the scene is strong evidence of premeditation.") (collecting cases). Second, Bell was in Pendelton's cell for only a relatively brief period, and there were no real signs of a struggle left either in the cell or on Bell's person. Although there was blood everywhere in the cell, which is not surprising given the nature of Pendelton's injuries, nothing in his cell was knocked over or obviously out of place. This suggests that Bell did not stab Pendelton in the heat of an argument, for example, but rather that he entered the cell with a plan to kill Pendelton and executed his design quickly and efficiently. *Cf. United States v. Esquer,* 459 F.2d 431, 432–33 (7th Cir.1972) (testimony that defendant prisoner left his position behind steam table in dining room serving line, walked to center of room where victim was sitting, and attacked him from behind, seizing him around the neck and stabbing him in the back, was sufficient to support finding of premeditation). Third, the actions of both Bell and Dixon appear to have been coordinated, as evidenced by the way in which Dixon left their cell shortly after Bell did, took up post in a chair outside the cell while Bell was inside of Pendelton's cell, preceded Bell back into their cell as Bell returned, left the cell again a short time later with the bundle of clothes, and ultimately disposed of the clothing and weapon in the day room trash can. Fourth, both Bell and Dixon appeared to take these actions in a calm, unhurried, and deliberate manner, which is somewhat inconsistent with the possibility that Pendelton's murder was an unexpected or unplanned crime.

calm + unhurried

We may assume that the jury could have rejected this interpretation of events, concluded that premeditation had not been proven, and acquitted Bell of first degree murder on that basis. But the only question for us is whether a rational jury could have found premeditation beyond a reasonable doubt on these facts, and for the reasons we have outlined, we believe that it could have done so. Bell's actions—seemingly calm, deliberate, and efficient—and the evident concert of action between him and Dixon, reasonably indicate that the killing of Pendelton was pre-planned and therefore premeditated. *See Brown,* 518 F.2d at 826 ("deliberation and premeditation involve a prior design to commit a murder"). And even if Bell had not already deliberated and settled on a design to kill Pendelton before he left the cell he shared with Dixon—which the facts strongly suggest he did—he had an additional moment during his walk to Cell 105 during which to contemplate the matter, and the jury reasonably could have concluded, in light of the way events transpired, that this was an "appreciable" period of time during which Bell considered and settled upon what he was about to do. In short, the evidence supports the jury's determination that this was a "pondered" rather than a "spontaneous" killing. *Delaney,* 717 F.3d at 557.

— evidence supports jury's determination

EXERCISE

Daniel is an inmate in a federal prison. He decides to eat lunch with Harvey, a fellow inmate. During lunch, they begin to discuss politics, and their views diverge. Daniel (a liberal Democrat) knew that Harvey was a very conservative man before they began their discussion. They are sitting facing one another across the table. Daniel does not appear upset, but suddenly reaches across the table and grabs Harvey's fork. He then lunges over the table at Harvey, stabbing him in the neck with the fork. Harvey almost immediately dies of his injuries. As Harvey struggles for life, Daniel tries to give him CPR. Could Daniel's actions be considered pre-meditated?

2. FELONY-MURDER

18 U.S.C. § 1111(a) allows a killing to be defined as first-degree murder if the death was caused in the course of committing arson, escape, murder, kidnapping, treason, espionage, sabotage, sexual abuse, burglary

or robbery, or as part of an assault or torture against at least one child. Does this context replace the usual requirement of proving premeditation and malice aforethought?

UNITED STATES V. GARCIA-ORTIZ
528 F.3d 74 (1st Cir. 2008)

TORRUELLA, CIRCUIT JUDGE.

José A. García-Ortiz ("García") was convicted of intentionally obstructing and delaying commerce by robbery, armed robbery, and first degree murder. . . .

Facts

At approximately 11:30 a.m. on December 9, 2000, Rafael Rivera-Aguayo ("Rivera"), a security guard for Ralph's Food Warehouse ("RFW"), escorted RFW's manager, Edgardo Figueroa-Rosa ("Figueroa"), to his car. They were going to the bank to deposit $63,000 in cash from the previous day's sales. As the two men exited the supermarket and walked toward the car, Figueroa noticed a green four-door car—later identified as a Dodge Intrepid—which he found suspicious because of the way it was parked. Figueroa opened the door of his car for Rivera to get in, and he walked around the back of the car to get in on the driver's side. Before he was fully seated, Figueroa saw two people running towards the car through his rear-view mirror. One of them grabbed Rivera and a struggle ensued. During the struggle Figueroa heard a gunshot, and he got down on the ground. After hearing gunshots, Rivera returned fire and killed one of the assailants, Reinaldo Rolón Rivera ("Rolón"). Rivera saw a person with white tennis shoes walk around the back of the car. Figueroa remained on the ground, and he saw someone running towards his car wearing a white shirt and jeans. The person ran towards Figueroa as he heard voices from the Intrepid yelling "kill him." The assailant took the bag of money from Figueroa who kept his eyes and hands on the ground and begged for mercy. Figueroa heard two more shots and then the Intrepid sped away. Rivera was wounded and in a state of shock.

No one saw their faces

Two RFW employees saw the assailants' silhouettes, but did not see their faces. They saw someone jump out of the car, take the money, and then get back in the car and speed away. The employees identified one of the assailants as wearing blue jeans and a blue t-shirt with white stripes. Another witness saw the assailants, but he could only provide vague descriptions of them. The police recovered a .357 Magnum, short-barrel revolver at the scene of the crime and took it as evidence. The Intrepid, reported stolen by its owner in November 2000, was later recovered only five minutes away from RFW. One of its side windows had a bullet hole in it, the back window was completely broken, the back seat bore a blood stain, and there were shell casings in the car. According to forensic analysis, a total of three guns were fired during the robbery. The police collected copious amounts of forensic evidence from the Intrepid.

During its investigation, the FBI came to believe that García may have been involved in the robbery. García had been photographed with the deceased assailant at a mechanic shop that had been under surveillance prior to the RFW robbery. The owner of the shop was suspected of being part of an organization involved in armed robberies.

García, along with others, was subpoenaed to the FBI office in San Juan to provide blood, hair, saliva, and fingerprint samples. He went to the FBI office, accompanied by counsel, and during a consensual body search, the FBI discovered what looked like a bullet wound. García's wound was later x-rayed, and the FBI found metallic residue consistent with such a wound. DNA evidence performed at the FBI lab confirmed that DNA in the Intrepid matched García's DNA and excluded all other suspects. . . .

blood in car matched García's DNA

On Count Three, first degree murder, the judge gave the following jury instruction:

To kill with malice aforethought ordinarily means either to kill another person deliberately and intentionally or to act with callous and wanton disregard for life. However, the government need only prove that the killing resulted from a commission of an enumerated felony, that is, interference with commerce by robbery, in order to establish to [sic] requisite of malice aforethought.

Jury instruction

Accordingly, to be guilty of first degree murder by the virtue of federally [sic] murder rule, the defendant need only have committed the underlying felony, that is, interference with commerce by robbery, and a person, such as an alleged accomplice Reinaldo Rolón Rivera was killed.

García argues that the court's instruction that he was guilty of felony murder if he engaged in "interference with commerce by robbery" instead of "robbery" alone permitted the jury to convict him of murder in the first degree by his alleged mere interference with commerce during a robbery, which he claims is not an underlying felony enumerated in 18 U.S.C. § 1111(a). García contends that under the court's instruction, the jury was required to believe that interference with commerce during a robbery was an enumerated felony when the jury might otherwise have found that it was not. . . .

— García contention

The Government argues that the "robbery" that is listed in § 1111(a) clearly refers to a violation of 18 U.S.C. § 1951, which requires that robbery affect interstate commerce. We agree. . . .

— government argument

García is also mistaken in his belief that the indictment had to charge that he personally killed his accomplice. Section 1111 does not require that the defendant himself pull the trigger. In *United States v. Shea*, 211 F.3d 658 (1st Cir.2000), we said that "under the felony murder rule adopted by section 1111[ ] . . . , the killing [during the] robbery was first-degree murder by those who perpetrated the robbery, regardless of who pulled the trigger or any individual intent." *Id*. at 674. García was convicted of

Section 1111

[handwritten in left margin: Holding]

perpetrating the robbery. This is the case because "the statute was intended to adopt the felony murder rule, and for a stated felony [—here, robbery—] the 'malice' element is satisfied by the intent to commit the unlawful felony."

EXERCISE

Donald and his friend Mick are on a cross-country driving adventure. They run out of money in the middle of the country, though, and take to sleeping in the car. They also steal gas by going to rural stations that do not require pre-payment, then driving off without paying.

Fearing that their car has been identified in these thefts, Donald and Mick meet up with an old friend in a town along the way, hoping to swap cars with him. The friend is happy to oblige, but tells Donald and Mick that the car they are getting was stolen from a parking lot in the next state. Donald and Mick agree to the deal, then they exchange keys and transfer their things to the new car.

At this point, the friend gets upset and wants to undo the deal. After a brief argument, Donald pulls a gun from his pocket, shoots the friend and he dies.

The underlying crime that Donald and Mick have committed is a violation of 18 U.S.C. § 2313, which outlaws the knowing receipt of a stolen vehicle that has crossed state lines after being stolen. Can Mick be charged with felony-murder under 18 U.S.C. § 1111(a)?

[handwritten: yes, the killing was done under the robbery]

One area of contention in some felony-murder cases is the relationship between the underlying crime and the killing.

UNITED STATES V. SABA
526 Fed. Appx. 489 (6th Cir. 2013)

COOK, CIRCUIT JUDGE.

A jury convicted Rami Ikbal Saba of kidnapping and other crimes. The victim, Donald Dietz, has not been found and at trial was presumed to be dead. During sentencing, the government urged the district court to apply the felony-murder guideline, *see* U.S.S.G. § 2A1.1, by cross-referencing the kidnapping guideline. The district court, pointing to the absence of evidence regarding how or when Dietz died, refused and sentenced Saba to 389 months' imprisonment. The government now appeals, challenging the procedural reasonableness of Saba's sentence and seeking resentencing with application of the felony-murder guideline to specify a life sentence.

The kidnapping guideline directs courts to apply the felony-murder guideline "[i]f the victim was killed under circumstances that would constitute murder under 18 U.S.C. § 1111." U.S.S.G. § 2A4.1(c)(1). And § 1111, which codifies the common law doctrine of felony murder, provides, "Every murder [committed] . . . in the perpetration of . . . kidnapping . . . is murder in the first degree." 18 U.S.C. § 1111(a). The government argues that the evidence showed by a preponderance of the evidence that Saba's kidnapping resulted in Dietz's death. *See United States v. White,* 551 F.3d 381, 383 (6th Cir.2008) (explaining that sentencing factors need be proven only by a preponderance of the evidence). The district court found, however, that the evidence failed even under the preponderance standard.

As the government recognizes, we review this factual finding for clear error and review Saba's sentence for reasonableness under the abuse-of-discretion standard of review. *Gall v. United States,* 552 U.S. 38, 46, 128 S.Ct. 586, 169 L.Ed.2d 445 (2007); *United States v. Fore,* 507 F.3d 412, 414–15 (6th Cir.2007). Procedural unreasonableness results when a district court selects a sentence based on clearly erroneous facts. *Gall,* 552 U.S. at 51, 128 S.Ct. 586. We discern clear error only when we are "left with the definite and firm conviction that a mistake has been committed." *United States v. Orlando,* 363 F.3d 596, 603 (6th Cir.2004) (internal quotation mark omitted). Whether the district court properly interpreted the applicability of the felony-murder guideline is a factor we consider in our reasonableness calculus. *See United States v. Shor,* 549 F.3d 1075, 1077 n. 1 (6th Cir.2008).

[handwritten margin note: procedural unreasonableness]

The government argues that it need not show Saba intended to kill Dietz. No quarrel there; the intent to kidnap alone satisfies the *mens rea* needed to apply the felony-murder doctrine. *See United States v. Pearson,* 159 F.3d 480, 485 (10th Cir.1998) ("In the typical case of felony murder, there is no malice in 'fact' with respect to the homicide; the malice is supplied by the 'law.' There is an intended felony and an unintended homicide. The malice which plays a part in the commission of the felony is transferred by the law to the homicide." (quoting 2 Charles E. Torcia, *Wharton's Criminal Law* § 147 (15th ed.1994))). Yet to trigger a life sentence, the government needed to show that Saba murdered Dietz "in the perpetration of" the kidnapping. 18 U.S.C. § 1111(a). In other words, the government needed to show that Saba's act in furtherance of kidnapping caused Dietz's death. *See United States v. Martinez,* 16 F.3d 202, 208 (7th Cir.1994) ("The application of felony murder principles does not require . . . a finding that the death was in furtherance of the felony, but only that the act that *caused* the death was in furtherance of the felony."). Thus, the government needed to show, by a preponderance of the evidence, at least one act on Saba's part that both furthered the kidnapping and caused Dietz's death.

[handwritten margin note: Government argument]

The government lists the following as support for applying the felony-murder guideline: (1) Dietz was presumed dead; (2) the district court itself

[handwritten note at bottom: support for applying the felony murder guideline]

noted that "there was no dispute that Dietz was dead"; (3) the district court chose to apply a two-level enhancement to Saba's sentence for his failure to release Dietz within 30 days, *see* U.S.S.G. § 2A4.1(b)(4)(A); (4) Saba purchased pepper spray and a stun gun before kidnapping Dietz; (5) Saba assumed Dietz's identity in an effort to seize Dietz's life savings; (6) Saba impersonated Dietz in an attempt to convince Dietz's brother that Dietz was leaving the country; (7) Saba contacted Dietz's power and telephone companies to terminate Dietz's accounts; (8) Saba contacted the post office to have Dietz's mail forwarded; (9) Saba had an emotional breakdown during a religious counseling session in jail; and (10) Saba told his fellow inmates that "[t]hings moved faster than what they were supposed to."

Like the district court, we note the absence of factual support tying the death to the kidnapping. First, Dietz's death alone does not establish an act by Saba that caused it. At best, the government's evidence only supports the conclusion that Dietz was kidnapped and died. And no evidence establishes that Dietz was released, so the district court could apply the kidnapping guideline that punishes a failure to release within 30 days. Saba's identity theft and impersonation might establish Saba's knowledge of Dietz's death, but not its cause. Last, Saba's conversations with jail inmates offer no confirmation that Saba killed Dietz. There being no evidence of the cause of death, the possibility that something other than Saba's act in furtherance of kidnapping caused Dietz's death requires us to affirm the district court's judgment. *Cf. United States v. Wheaton*, 517 F.3d 350, 369 (6th Cir.2008) (holding that, even when the district court incorrectly describes the evidence, "the fact that there *is* evidence in the record to support [its] finding is sufficient to preclude us from second guessing the court's determination"). Because the district court committed no clear error in evaluating the applicability of the felony-murder guideline, we cannot find Saba's sentence to be procedurally unreasonable or an abuse of discretion.

We affirm the judgment of the district court.

EXERCISE

Jacqueline and John decide that they are going to kidnap the child of a wealthy businessman and demand money in exchange for the child's release. They are not aware that the child suffers from a severe food allergy, however. They hold the victim in reasonably decent conditions within the confines of their home. For eight days they await payment, and the child appears to be reasonably healthy. However, they then feed the child a sandwich containing peanut butter, and the child dies of an allergic reaction.

Is this felony-murder under the analysis set out by Judge Cook in the *Saba* case? *yes, in the perpetration of kidnapping— feeding him to keep him alive*

Felony Murder is sometimes hidden within other statutes, as well. Generally, we see this as an additional penalty for the underlying felony when one outcome is the death of one or more people. For example, 8 U.S.C. § 1324 addresses alien smuggling. One provision of that statute, 8 U.S.C. 1324(a)(1)(B)(iv), provides that a defendant found in violation of the alien smuggling provisions "resulting in the death of any person, be punished by death or imprisoned for any term of years or for life. . . ." While intent, recklessness, or negligence don't need to be shown in such felony murder prosecutions, other issues such as proximate cause can be important.

United States v. Pineda-Doval

614 F. 3d 1019 (9th Cir. 2010)

B. Fletcher, Circuit Judge:

Early in the morning on August 7, 2008, Pineda-Doval loaded twenty men, women, and children into a Chevrolet Suburban. The car was not equipped with rear seats or safety belts. All of his passengers were illegal aliens. Eighteen of them crowded into the back of the Suburban, and two pregnant women sat in the front seat next to Pineda-Doval, the driver.

Customs and Border Patrol ("CBP") Agent Corey Lindsay was driving south on Red Cloud Mine Road, a remote dirt road in southern Arizona that is believed by Border Patrol to be popular with alien smugglers. He passed Pineda-Doval, who was driving in the opposite direction, and saw that the Suburban was crowded with passengers. Agent Lindsay radioed for assistance and turned his car around to follow Pineda-Doval. The defendant quickly realized that he was being pursued, made a U-turn, and started driving towards Mexico. Agent Lindsay did the same. Though Pineda-Doval was forced to drive slowly because of the state of the road and weight of his car, he tried to lose Agent Lindsay several times by hitting the brakes or attempting to pull into the brush. Some passengers grew frightened and yelled at the defendant to stop. He refused.

Pineda-Doval then turned left onto the paved, two-lane Martinez Lake Road. Heading east, he accelerated to about 50–55 miles per hour, occasionally reaching speeds of about 70 miles per hour. Agent Lindsay continued to trail him.

Meanwhile, Agent Clinton Russell responded to Agent Lindsay's request for assistance and drove west on Martinez Lake Road, heading in the direction of the defendant and Agent Lindsay. He carried with him a controlled tire deflation device ("CTDD"), also called a "spike strip." A CTDD is a tool used by Border Patrol to stop fleeing vehicles. It consists of a series of x-shaped plastic links that, when expanded, can cover one lane of traffic. Hollow tubes are embedded along the plastic strip. When a vehicle drives over an expanded CTDD, the hollow tubes pierce the tires, causing air to gradually escape, disabling the vehicle.

Agent Russell had never used a CTDD before. Between them, Agents Russell and Lindsay had witnessed over 100 CTDD deployments, many of them involving SUVs that were overloaded with passengers. Neither of them had ever seen a spiked vehicle roll over. Pineda-Doval had twice before been the target of a spike strip. On both occasions he had been transporting illegal aliens. The first time he managed to swerve around the CTDD, but the next time he was successfully stopped and apprehended by Border Patrol.

Neither agents had used the spike strip before

Agent Russell stopped at a point on Martinez Lake Road where the road was relatively flat and there was little traffic. He placed the collapsed CTDD on one side of the road and hid in the brush on the opposite side of the road, ready to pull the CTDD across the pavement when Pineda-Doval approached. Agent Russell radioed Agent Lindsay and advised him of the location of the spike strip. About one and a half miles from Agent Russell's location, when Pineda-Doval was traveling about 45 miles per hour, Agent Lindsay turned on his vehicle's lights and siren. When Pineda-Doval did not yield, Agent Lindsay told Agent Russell to deploy the spike strip.

Agent Russell waited until the Suburban was approximately 80 to 100 feet away and then yanked the spike strip across the road. Pineda-Doval shouted to his passengers, "Commend yourselves to God, because we are being pursued." He swerved across the westbound lane of traffic and onto the dirt shoulder, trying to drive around the CTDD, but it caught his right rear tire. He immediately swerved back onto the paved road. The weight of his unsecured passengers suddenly shifted, and the front edge of the Suburban "tripped" into the asphalt. Passengers were thrown from the Suburban as it rolled once on its side and then once more end-to-end, finally coming to rest right side up but facing the wrong direction. Five passengers died at the scene, and five more died at hospitals as a result of injuries sustained in the crash.

Charges

Pineda-Doval was charged with ten counts of transportation of illegal aliens resulting in death, 8 U.S.C. § 1324(a)(1)(A)(ii), (a)(1)(B)(iv), one count of transportation of illegal aliens placing in jeopardy the life of any person, 8 U.S.C. § 1324(a)(1)(A)(ii), (a)(1)(B)(iii), and one count of reentry after deportation, 8 U.S.C. § 1326(a). . . .

Argument

Pineda-Doval argues that his conviction must be vacated because the jury instructions did not require the jury to find that his transportation was the proximate cause of the deaths of his ten passengers. "A proximate cause is one which played a substantial part in bringing about the death, so that the death was the direct result or a reasonably probable consequence of the defendant's speed or condition or manner of driving." *United States v. Main,* 113 F.3d 1046, 1050 (9th Cir.1997).

The defendant was charged and convicted of violating 8 U.S.C. § 1324(a)(1)(A)(ii), (a)(1)(B)(iv), which has five elements: The defendant must have (1) known or been in reckless disregard of the fact that the person he was transporting was (2) an alien who was (3) in the United States illegally; (4) the defendant must have transported the alien in order to help him or her enter or remain in the United States illegally; and (5) the defendant's transportation must have resulted in the death of some person.

5 elements

With respect to the final element, the district court instructed the jury as follows:

> As used in these instructions and the form of the verdict, "resulted in death" means that the death of a person occurred in the course of the transportation of an illegal alien and was related to the transportation of an illegal alien. You must find that during the course of the transportation *the defendant exposed* individuals to one or more life-threatening conditions and the life-threatening condition(s) was *a cause* in the deaths of those named in the enumerated counts of the indictment. (Emphasis added.)

– jury instruction

Pineda-Doval argues that this definition of "resulting in death" misstated the law because the instructions should have required the Government to prove that "the defendant exposed" his passengers to life-threatening conditions *and* that his transportation was the proximate cause of the ten deaths.

Pineda-Doval argument

The district court relied on *United States v. Matus-Leva,* 311 F.3d 1214 (9th Cir.2002), for its definition of "resulting in death." This court in *Matus-Leva* considered the question of whether § 1324(a)(1)(B)(iv) has a mens rea requirement. We held that a defendant need not have intended his conduct to have "resulted in death" to be guilty under § 1324(a)(1)(B)(iv). *Id.* at 1219. Rather, the defendant need only have been aware that he was engaging in conduct that allowed others "*to be exposed* to life-threatening conditions during the smuggling process." *Id.* (emphasis added). The issue in *Matus-Leva* was mental state, not causation. To answer the question of whether § 1324(a)(1)(B)(iv) requires only but-for causation or also proximate causation, we must look elsewhere.

A "basic tenet of criminal law" is that, when a criminal statute requires that the defendant's conduct has resulted in an injury, "the government must prove that the defendant's conduct was the legal or proximate cause of the resulting injury." *United States v. Spinney,* 795 F.2d 1410, 1415 (9th Cir.1986). In *Spinney,* the defendant was convicted of conspiracy to commit simple assault and fined for being convicted of a "misdemeanor resulting in death." 18 U.S.C. § 3623(a)(4) (Supp. II 1985) (current version at 18 U.S.C. § 3571(b)(4)). Spinney and a friend intended to scare the victim, but things "got out of hand" and his co-conspirator shot and killed the victim. *Spinney,* 795 F.2d at 1413. The defendant argued that he was not guilty because his co-conspirator's actions constituted a superseding cause of the victim's death. *Id.* at 1415. This court agreed that the statute required the Government to prove proximate cause, but affirmed the defendant's conviction because the victim's death was an "entirely foreseeable" result of the conspiracy. *Id.* at 1416. Pineda-Doval argues that, just as the offense "misdemeanor resulting in death" includes a proximate cause requirement, so too should "transportation of illegal aliens resulting in death.". . . .

We presume that the Government must prove proximate cause whenever the charged offense requires a certain result. . . .

. . . there is no reason why the general rule that the Government must prove proximate cause should not apply to 8 U.S.C. § 1324(a)(1)(A)(ii) & (a)(1)(B)(iv), or why we should depart from *Spinney* and *Main*. Therefore, we hold that a defendant may be found guilty of transportation of illegal aliens resulting in death only if the Government proves beyond a reasonable doubt that the defendant's conduct was the proximate cause of the charged deaths.

Generally, "[t]o prove proximate cause, the government must establish that the harm was a foreseeable result of the conduct." *Hanousek,* 176 F.3d at 1123 (citing *Main,* 113 F.3d at 1049). Proximate cause is drawn more broadly when the intervening action was not a coincidence or unrelated to the defendant's prior conduct, but rather was a response to that conduct. "Foreseeability is required as to the former, but in the latter instance the question is whether the intervening act was abnormal—that is, whether, looking at the matter with hindsight, it seems extraordinary." 2 Wayne R. LaFave, *Substantive Criminal Law* § 14.5(d), at 453 (2d ed.2003); *see also People v. Schmies,* 44 Cal.App.4th 38, 51 Cal.Rptr.2d 185, 194 (Ct.App.1996) (holding that officers' conduct was in response to defendant's fleeing the scene, therefore officers' conduct constituted a superseding cause only if it was "unusual, abnormal, or extraordinary"). The Border Patrol agents deployed the CTDD in response to Pineda-Doval's illegal actions, therefore the question here is whether the actions of the Border Patrol were extraordinary. At trial, the Government should have been required to prove that " 'any variation between the result intended [by Pineda-Doval] and the result actually achieved [was] not so extraordinary that it would be unfair to hold the defendant responsible for the actual result.' " *Spinney,* 795 F.2d at 1415 (quoting W. LaFave & A. Scott, *Criminal Law* § 35, at 246 (1972)).

Pineda-Doval's failed attempt to swerve around the spike strip was the proximate cause of the deaths of ten individuals. It was entirely foreseeable that the Border Patrol would deploy a CTDD against the defendant's Suburban and that Pineda-Doval's dangerous driving would end in an accident. Pineda-Doval must have known that Agents Russell and Lindsay would try to stop him by using a CTDD, since he had been the target of a spike strip twice before. He also must have known that he was in danger;

when he saw the spike strip being drawn across the road, he shouted to his passengers, "Commend yourselves to God, because we are being pursued." Pineda-Doval was in a police chase, traveling at 45 miles per hour, in an overcrowded vehicle that lacked seat belts—and then deliberately and sharply swerved off the road. No reasonable jury could have found that a car accident was an extraordinary result.

EXERCISE

Landon owns a coffee shop on federal land. He has one competitor within that federal enclave, who has been very successful. Landon decides to burn down his competitor's shop, but does not want to hurt anyone. He waits until the middle of the night when the shop is closed, then pours gasoline all around the wooden exterior of the building. He then lights it on fire and begins to flee. As he runs away, he hears something in the competitor's shop and turns around. There is a man—who had been sleeping in the shop for some reason—stumbling from the building engulfed in flames. Landon runs back and tries to put out the fire on the man's clothes by waving his jacket, but fails. The man then dies. Could Landon be found guilty of first or second degree murder under 18 U.S.C. § 1111(a)? *yes, could have expected someone to be there or get hurt*

C. VOLUNTARY MANSLAUGHTER

Manslaughter is a category of crime resulting in death that is less severely punished than murder. 18 U.S.C. § 1112 sets out the elements for two distinct crimes: voluntary manslaughter and involuntary manslaughter. Either form of manslaughter is distinct from murder because it is a killing "without malice":

(a) Manslaughter is the unlawful killing of a human being without malice. It is of two kinds:

Voluntary—Upon a sudden quarrel or heat of passion.

Involuntary—In the commission of an unlawful act not amounting to a felony, or in the commission in an unlawful manner, or without due caution and circumspection, of a lawful act which might produce death.

(b) Within the special maritime and territorial jurisdiction of the United States.

The elements of a voluntary manslaughter under this statute are:

1) Committed within the maritime or territorial jurisdiction of the United States,

2) Identification of the killer,

3) Actual death,

4)   Causation of the death by the defendant (upon a sudden quarrel or heat of passion), and

5)   Unlawfulness.

Oddly, one of the things described in the statute—"upon a sudden quarrel or heat of passion"—is not usually an element in the sense that the prosecution wants to prove it up. Instead, it is a fact that the *defense* will often raise in order to reduce the charge from murder. The case below will help explain that mechanism.

UNITED STATES V. QUINTERO
21 F. 3d 885 (9th Cir. 1994)

LAY, SENIOR CIRCUIT JUDGE:

Two days after A.B.Q. was born, her parents, Lopez Quintero and his wife, Gina Quintero, gave her to her maternal aunt and uncle for adoption. Before the adoption was completed, however, the aunt and uncle were involved in a serious automobile accident, leaving the uncle hospitalized for a one-month period. During this time, A.B.Q., then two years old, was returned to her natural parents. The Quinteros had three other children.

Testimony at trial indicated that on the morning of A.B.Q.'s death, Quintero and his four-year-old son, L.M.Q., were outside with A.B.Q. Quintero maintains that as he was pumping air into a tire of his pickup truck, A.B.Q. fell from the truck bed, where she had been playing with L.M.Q., and hit her head. The government contends that Quintero chased A.B.Q. and struck multiple blows to her head and body with his hand. L.M.Q. was the sole witness.

Quintero carried A.B.Q., who was dazed but still breathing, inside and asked his wife to look after her. A short while later, Gina called out to Quintero that A.B.Q. had stopped breathing. Quintero revived her with mouth-to-mouth resuscitation and went back outside to work on the truck. A.B.Q. soon stopped breathing again and could not be revived.

Quintero refused to take his daughter to a hospital for fear that he and Gina would be accused of child neglect and that their son would be taken from them. Instead, Quintero put A.B.Q.'s body, wrapped in a blanket, into the truck, and he, along with Gina and L.M.Q., drove out to find a place to bury her. Finding the ground too hard to dig, Quintero built a fire and burned A.B.Q.'s body. To avoid identification of the remains, he removed the head with a shovel and left it at a different location several miles away.

Authorities soon began an investigation into the whereabouts of the child. Eventually, Gina confessed and received a grant of immunity from prosecution in exchange for her willingness to testify against Quintero at trial. Quintero was indicted for first degree murder. L.M.Q. was allowed to testify at trial via closed-circuit television.

At the close of the evidence, the district court granted Quintero's motion for judgment of acquittal as to the charge of first degree murder. The court then submitted the case to the jury with instructions regarding second degree murder and, at defendant's request, voluntary and involuntary manslaughter. The jury found Quintero not guilty of second degree murder and guilty of voluntary manslaughter. At sentencing, the court departed from the Sentencing Guideline range calculated for Quintero of 70 to 87 months and sentenced Quintero to 108 months in prison, based upon Quintero's treatment of A.B.Q.'s body after her death. This appeal followed. . . .

Quintero first argues that the evidence was insufficient to support a conviction for voluntary manslaughter. Quintero contends that there was no evidence of any heat of passion or provocation, and that therefore, since the jury determined that Quintero was not guilty of murder, the only crime he could be guilty of is involuntary manslaughter. We disagree.

In reviewing the sufficiency of the evidence supporting Quintero's conviction, our role is limited. We must determine only whether, after viewing the evidence in the light most favorable to the prosecution, *any* rational trier of fact could have found the essential elements of voluntary manslaughter beyond a reasonable doubt. *Dallas v. Arave,* 984 F.2d 292, 295 (9th Cir.1993); *see Jackson v. Virginia,* 443 U.S. 307, 319, 99 S.Ct. 2781, 2789, 61 L.Ed.2d 560 (1979). Voluntary manslaughter is defined as "the unlawful killing of a human being without malice. . . . [u]pon a sudden quarrel or heat of passion." 18 U.S.C. § 1112(a) (1988). Quintero contends that the government must prove "sudden quarrel or heat of passion" as an essential element of the crime before a defendant can be convicted of voluntary manslaughter and that it failed to do so.

Quintero's argument fails to recognize the government's contention that Quintero was guilty of murder, and not a lesser included offense. Voluntary manslaughter is a lesser included offense within the crimes of first and second degree murder. *United States v. Roston,* 986 F.2d 1287, 1290 (9th Cir.), *cert. denied,* 510 U.S. 874, 114 S.Ct. 206, 126 L.Ed.2d 163 (1993); *United States v. Celestine,* 510 F.2d 457, 460 (9th Cir.1975). Under Federal Rule of Criminal Procedure 31(c), a defendant may be found guilty of an offense with which he was not charged only if it is "necessarily included" within the charged offense. To be "necessarily included," the elements of the lesser offense, voluntary manslaughter, must be a subset of the elements of the greater offense, murder. *See Schmuck v. United States,* 489 U.S. 705, 716, 109 S.Ct. 1443, 1450, 103 L.Ed.2d 734 (1989); *United States v. Garcia,* 7 F.3d 885, 890 (9th Cir.1993). Manslaughter is thus distinguished from murder, which the law defines as "the unlawful killing of a human being with malice aforethought," 18 U.S.C. § 1111(a) (1988), by the *absence* of malice, one of murder's essential elements. *United States v.*

Wagner, 834 F.2d 1474, 1487 (9th Cir.1987), *cert. denied,* 510 U.S. 1134, 114 S.Ct. 1110, 127 L.Ed.2d 420 (1994).

When a defendant charged with murder introduces evidence of sudden quarrel or heat of passion, the evidence acts in the nature of a defense to the murder charge. *See id.; United States v. Alexander,* 471 F.2d 923, 943 (D.C.Cir.1973). The defendant attempts to negate the malice element by claiming, in essence, that she was not acting maliciously because some extreme provocation, beyond what a reasonable person could be expected to withstand, severely impaired her capacity for self-control in committing the killing. *See Wagner,* 834 F.2d at 1487. Once such evidence is raised, the burden is on the government to prove beyond a reasonable doubt the *absence* of sudden quarrel or heat of passion before a conviction for murder can be sustained. *United States v. Lesina,* 833 F.2d 156, 160 (9th Cir.1987); *see Mullaney v. Wilbur,* 421 U.S. 684, 704, 95 S.Ct. 1881, 1892, 44 L.Ed.2d 508 (1975).

It is *not,* however, the burden of the government to also prove the *presence* of sudden quarrel or heat of passion before a conviction for voluntary manslaughter can stand in a murder trial. *See Alexander,* 471 F.2d at 942–43. When a defendant is charged with murder, a conviction for the lesser included offense of voluntary manslaughter means that the government failed to prove all of murder's essential elements. *See Beck v. Alabama,* 447 U.S. 625, 633, 100 S.Ct. 2382, 2387, 65 L.Ed.2d 392 (1980) (stating that conviction for lesser included offense occurs "in cases in which the proof failed to establish some element of the crime charged"). To require the government to prove sudden quarrel or heat of passion in such circumstances would impermissibly add to the "subset" of elements that makes up the lesser included offense. *See Schmuck,* 489 U.S. at 716, 109 S.Ct. at 1450. It could also lead to "the ludicrous result that a jury which finds the evidence in balance on the question of provocation can convict the defendant *neither* of second degree murder *nor* of manslaughter." *Alexander,* 471 F.2d at 942. This the law does not require. *Id.* at 942–47.

To convict a defendant charged with murder of voluntary manslaughter, the government must prove that (1) the defendant intentionally inflicted an injury upon another from which the other died; and (2) the homicide was committed without justification or excuse. *Id.* at 947; *accord United States v. Holmes,* 632 F.2d 167, 170 (1st Cir.1980) (per curiam). Intent without malice, not the heat of passion, is the defining characteristic of voluntary manslaughter. *See Alexander,* 471 F.2d at 947 n. 56; *see also* 2 Charles E. Torcia, *Whorton's Criminal Law* § 153 (14th ed. 1979) (observing that voluntary manslaughter is "an intentional killing" where the heat of passion takes the place of malice). If malice is proven, the crime becomes second degree murder, *Wagner,* 834 F.2d at 1487; if intent is not proven, the crime becomes involuntary manslaughter, *Alexander,* 471 F.2d at 947 n. 56; *see United States v. Skinner,* 667 F.2d 1306, 1309–10 & n. 1.

(9th Cir.1982) (recognizing that involuntary manslaughter is a lesser included offense of murder and voluntary manslaughter, and stating that "[i]nvoluntary manslaughter is an unintentional homicide"), *cert. denied,* 463 U.S. 1229, 103 S.Ct. 3569, 77 L.Ed.2d 1410 (1983). Sudden quarrel or heat of passion are simply not essential elements of voluntary manslaughter, and therefore, they need not be proven by evidence beyond a reasonable doubt.4 *Alexander,* 471 F.2d at 943.

In order to obtain a jury instruction regarding voluntary manslaughter in a murder trial, a defendant must demonstrate to the court that sufficient evidence exists to allow a reasonable jury to conclude that the defendant was acting out of passion rather than malice. *Roston,* 986 F.2d at 1290–91. The defendant in this case succeeded in making that showing. In so doing, he did not waive his right to now challenge the sufficiency of the evidence that led to his conviction. Our role on appeal, however, is confined to determining whether a jury could reasonably find that the government presented sufficient evidence to conclude beyond a reasonable doubt that the defendant intentionally committed an unexcused killing of a human being. We believe that it could.

From the jury's verdict, it is apparent that the jury concluded that the government had established beyond a reasonable doubt that Quintero intentionally killed his daughter without excuse or justification. It is also apparent that the jury did not believe beyond a reasonable doubt that Quintero acted with malice aforethought. The evidence supports these findings. The jury heard testimony from Quintero's wife, Gina, that Quintero had a history of beating A.B.Q. and that after he carried her inside on the day she received her fatal injury, Quintero promised A.B.Q. that he would never lay a hand on her again. Gina also testified that when *[Gina's testimony]* she asked A.B.Q., "Who's mean at you?," she replied, "Daddy." Later, when Gina and Quintero fought about going to the police, Gina testified that Quintero told her that he had killed A.B.Q.—and that he then corrected himself to say it was an accident. At one point, Quintero allegedly threatened to "do the same thing" to Gina and their son L.M.Q. as he had done to A.B.Q.

The sole eyewitness to the incident by the pickup truck, L.M.Q., testified that Quintero had hit A.B.Q. with his hand, and that A.B.Q. fell to the *[L.M.Q. testimony]* ground with her nose bleeding. After she fell, L.M.Q. testified, she was dead. When specifically asked what happened to A.B.Q., L.M.Q. testified, "My dad kill her." He drew a picture, which was admitted into evidence, illustrating what he saw.

In addition, the jury heard testimony casting doubt on Quintero's version of the events. Quintero claimed that A.B.Q. was injured when she fell from the back of the truck. A forensic pathologist testified, however, that there were no well-documented cases of fatal injuries to children caused by falls from the height of a pickup truck bed. While agreeing that such injuries

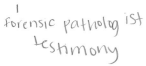

were not absolutely impossible, the expert testified that "it would be extremely rare and extremely unlikely."

This review of the evidence is by no means exhaustive. It demonstrates, however, that a rational jury could have found beyond a reasonable doubt that Quintero intentionally killed A.B.Q. At the same time, there was very little evidence of Quintero's state of mind at the time of the killing. The government argued at trial that he acted with malice, claiming that it was "just not possible" for a two-year-old child to provoke the "heat of passion" adequate to cause a reasonable person to lose control. For his part, Quintero argued that the death was accidental, but he requested the voluntary manslaughter instruction because "the Government's theory in this case is that Mr. Quintero got mad at this little girl and hit her. And if that's true, that's a sudden rage, and it could be voluntary also." Quintero did not have to prove the alleged sudden quarrel or heat of passion; once the issue was introduced and the instruction granted, the government had the burden to prove the absence of a sudden quarrel or heat of passion beyond a reasonable doubt. *Lesina*, 833 F.2d at 160. The lack of evidence as to what Quintero's state of mind actually was could allow a reasonable jury to conclude that sufficient doubt existed about the heat of passion to prevent the government from meeting its burden. The voluntary manslaughter verdict would then be appropriate. *See Alexander*, 471 F.2d at 945 n. 54. Because a rational jury could have reached the result obtained here, we affirm.

Holding

EXERCISE

Imagine that you are a federal judge considering a guilty plea agreed to by the parties. The defendant is a woman, Sharon Lee, who killed an abusive partner on a military base. The victim/abuser had twice been convicted of domestic assault, once against the Ms. Lee and once against another woman. In addition, the police had been called to the residence of the defendant and victim on two prior occasions when neighbors heard violent acts being committed.

At the time of the crime, the Ms. Lee asserts that the victim beat her with his fist and a bat. A surveillance video in the alley where this occurred confirms her account. She went to the hospital and received treatment in the form of fifteen stitches on her face. She was held overnight at the hospital for observation. In the morning, Ms. Lee left the hospital without being discharged, went to a gun store, and purchased a firearm and ammunition. The store owner informed her he was offering a handgun use and safety class that afternoon. Ms. Lee went and had lunch, then returned to the store for the class. She then returned to her residence and shot and killed the victim/abuser as he slept on the couch.

Imagine that precedent specifically bars the use of a self-defense claime where the victim is asleep. The government has agreed to a guilty plea to the charge of voluntary manslaughter. They offer this as a replacement to a murder charge, not as a lesser included offense. Do you accept that plea and the parties' claim that each element has been met?

Some jurisdictions clearly define Voluntary Manslaughter to include the element of intent: that is, they require a finding that the killer intended the death of the victim during the heat of passion.[6] New York's law requires that the prosecutor prove an intent to at least "cause serious physical injury," in combination with actions that cause death.[7]

The federal law described here does not expressly require intent, but instead infers it by the fact that the killing occurred in a context where the killer was in the heat of passion. Even the title of the crime—"Voluntary" manslaughter—seems to assume that intent is an element.

UNITED STATES V. SERAWOP
410 F.3d 656 (10th Cir. 2005)

EBEL, CIRCUIT JUDGE.

On November 2, 2002, Ernestina Moya, left her home on the Ute Indian reservation in northeastern Utah to serve a 12-day jail sentence for providing false information to a police officer. She left her nephew and three children, including three-month-old Beyonce Serawop, at home with Beyonce's father, Redd Rock Serawop. Beyonce had been sick before Moya left, and she cried almost constantly while Moya was away. Serawop had also just started a new job at a bottling company that week.

At approximately 1:30 a.m. on November 3, 2002, Serawop called for an ambulance and reported that Beyonce was having difficulty breathing. When she arrived at the hospital, Beyonce was limp, pale, and not breathing or moving on her own. A spinal tap produced blood, indicating she had suffered a head trauma. Beyonce was life-flighted to Primary Children's Hospital in Salt Lake City, where she was pronounced dead.

The medical examiner who performed the autopsy on Beyonce found rib fractures and contusions on her face and concluded her death was caused by three skull fractures along the left side of her skull, which were consistent with a blunt force trauma. According to the medical examiner, Beyonce would have been unable to cry or eat after she sustained these injuries, as they would have immediately rendered her unconscious. The medical examiner also testified that, because an infant's skull is relatively

---

[6]   E.g. Kansas Statutes 21–3403.

[7]   N.Y. Penal Law § 125.20.

malleable, it would require a considerable amount of force to compress the head to the point where the skull fractures.

Serawop gave several conflicting versions of what occurred. Initially, he told emergency room doctors that when he checked on Beyonce in the night he found she had inexplicably stopped breathing. Later, Serawop said that his 17-month-old son hit Beyonce in the head with a child's cup and that one of the children may have dropped her. In subsequent FBI interviews, Serawop said he tripped over a shoe and fell with Beyonce in his arms, causing her to hit her head on the edge of the television stand, and then revised his story to assert that he accidentally dropped his daughter and that her head struck the bathroom counter as she fell.

Conflicting versions of what occurred [margin note]

At trial, the Government asked the jury to convict Serawop of second degree murder. The Government relied on the evidence of multiple blows to Beyonce's face, head, and body; the inconsistencies in Serawop's stories; and the medical testimony about the amount of force required to cause Beyonce's death.

In defense, Serawop did not dispute that he had caused the death of Beyonce but instead argued he was guilty of only involuntary manslaughter or, in the alternative, voluntary manslaughter. Specifically, Serawop argued that Beyonce's death was caused by a single accidental fall and that there was doubt about the amount of force, as applied to her body, necessary to cause her injuries on impact—particularly given Serawop's size and the weight and relative strength of the infant's head and neck. Serawop also argued that the injuries to Beyonce's face and ribs were consistent with him attempting to perform CPR. Thus, he argued, he was guilty of involuntary manslaughter at most.

In the alternative, Serawop argued that if the jury found he used extreme force, then that force was used in a heat of passion arising out of the frustration, stress, and exhaustion caused by Beyonce's consistent crying and Moya's absence. If this was the case, he said, he should be convicted of voluntary manslaughter.

The district court instructed the jury on second degree murder and the lesser included offenses of voluntary and involuntary manslaughter. The jury convicted Serawop of voluntary manslaughter, and this appeal followed.

DISCUSSION

Serawop argument [margin note]

Serawop argues that the district court improperly instructed the jury regarding voluntary manslaughter's mental state. In particular, he contends that voluntary manslaughter requires the Government to prove an intentional or reckless killing as an element of the offense and that the district court committed prejudicial error by not instructing the jury to this effect in this case. We agree.

I. Mental State Required for Voluntary Manslaughter

As an initial matter, we must determine what mental state is required for the federal crime of voluntary manslaughter. "[D]etermining the mental state required for commission of a federal crime requires 'construction of the statute and . . . inference of the intent of Congress.' " *Staples v. United States,* 511 U.S. 600, 605, 114 S.Ct. 1793, 128 L.Ed.2d 608 (1994) (quoting *United States v. Balint,* 258 U.S. 250, 253, 42 S.Ct. 301, 66 L.Ed. 604 (1922)) (ellipsis in original). Thus, determining the mental state required under the federal voluntary manslaughter statute is a question of statutory construction we review de novo. *United States v. McVeigh,* 153 F.3d 1166, 1193 (10th Cir.1998).

A. Statutory language

Voluntary manslaughter is one offense within a hierarchy of federal homicides. Both voluntary and involuntary manslaughter are established in a single statute, which provides:

> Manslaughter is the unlawful killing of a human being without malice. It is of two kinds:
>
> Voluntary—Upon a sudden quarrel or heat of passion.
>
> Involuntary—In the commission of an unlawful act not amounting to a felony, or in the commission in an unlawful manner, or without due caution and circumspection, of a lawful act which might produce death.

18 U.S.C. § 1112(a). In contrast, the more serious murder offenses are defined as follows:

> Murder is the unlawful killing of a human being with malice aforethought. Every murder perpetrated by poison, lying in wait, or any other kind of willful, deliberate, malicious, and premeditated killing; or committed in the perpetration of, or attempt to perpetrate, any arson, escape, murder, kidnapping, treason, espionage, sabotage, aggravated sexual abuse or sexual abuse, child abuse, burglary, or robbery; or perpetrated as part of a pattern or practice of assault or torture against a child or children; or perpetrated from a premeditated design unlawfully and maliciously to effect the death of any human being other than him who is killed, is murder in the first degree.
>
> Any other murder is murder in the second degree.

18 U.S.C. § 1111(a).

Unlike many modern penal codes, these federal homicide statutes fail to articulate expressly which mental states are required for each of the various offenses. In the case of voluntary manslaughter, the statute requires only the "unlawful killing of a human being without malice . . .

[u]pon a sudden quarrel or heat of passion." 18 U.S.C. § 1112(a). Except for this express exclusion of malice, the statute is silent as to the mental state required for conviction. Moreover, the statute fails even to define the mental element it specifically excludes—malice.

Although our case law has consistently held that the "distinguishing element" among varying degrees of federal homicide is the defendant's mental state, *see, e.g., United States v. Sarracino,* 340 F.3d 1148, 1162 (10th Cir.2003), we have not yet fully articulated the precise mental state required for voluntary manslaughter. Therefore, our task is to determine, given this sparse statutory language and its placement within the hierarchy of federal homicides, what mental state Congress intended for voluntary manslaughter.

B. Interpretative rules

It is certainly true that "federal crimes are defined by statute rather than by common law." *United States v. Oakland Cannabis Buyers' Coop.,* 532 U.S. 483, 490, 121 S.Ct. 1711, 149 L.Ed.2d 722 (2001). However, the Supreme Court has repeatedly held that statutory silence as to mental state in a federal criminal statute does not necessarily mean that Congress intended to dispense with a conventional mens rea element. *Staples,* 511 U.S. at 605, 114 S.Ct. 1793. To the contrary, "some indication of congressional intent, express or implied, is required to dispense with mens rea as an element of the crime.". . .

Manslaughter developed at common law as a less culpable form of homicide for which a lesser sentence seemed justified. Initially, all homicides were unlawful and punished by death, with exception only for a narrow class of homicides committed in the enforcement of justice. *Mullaney v. Wilbur,* 421 U.S. 684, 692, 95 S.Ct. 1881, 44 L.Ed.2d 508 (1975). In response to this widespread use of capital punishment, ecclesiastic jurisdiction developed to reduce what would have been death to a one-year sentence, a branded thumb, and the forfeiture of all of one's goods. *Id.* Later, however, English rulers grew "concerned with the accretion of ecclesiastic jurisdiction at the expense of the secular" and enacted a series of statutes limiting ecclesiastic jurisdiction's benefits only to those unlawful homicides committed without malice—homicides designated as "manslaughter." *Id.* at 692–93, 95 S.Ct. 1881.

The common law defined manslaughter as the unlawful killing of another without malice, *Stevenson v. United States,* 162 U.S. 313, 320, 16 S.Ct. 839, 40 L.Ed. 980 (1896), and recognized two types, voluntary and involuntary manslaughter. *See Mullaney,* 421 U.S. at 694 n. 14, 95 S.Ct. 1881. The presence or absence of malice marked the boundary which separated the crimes of murder and manslaughter. *Id.* Today, malice still distinguishes federal murder from federal manslaughter. *Compare United States v. Lofton,* 776 F.2d 918, 920 (10th Cir.1985) (articulating malice as element of both first and second degree murder), *with* 18 U.S.C. § 1112 (defining both voluntary and involuntary manslaughter as "without malice").

1.   Defining murder mens rea

Serawop's basic argument is that § 1112 incorporates the common law understanding of voluntary manslaughter as a homicide that would constitute murder but for the fact that the killing was committed in the heat of passion. Therefore, we start with an overview of the mens rea element of murder. Second degree murder is the catch-all murder offense. *See* 18 U.S.C. § 1111 (defining second degree murder as "[a]ny other murder" not enhanced to first degree). Our case law defines second degree murder as an unlawful killing with malice. *Pearson,* 203 F.3d at 1270(interpreting 18 U.S.C. § 1111(a)).

In *Pearson,* we defined the mental element of second degree murder as requiring either (1) general intent to kill, (2) intent to do serious bodily injury, (3) depraved heart recklessness; or (4) a killing in the commission of a felony that is not among those specifically listed in the first degree murder statute. *Id.* at 1271. These mental states make up the core murder intent.

second degree murder elements

First degree murder, on the other hand, is a more serious offense that requires proof of something in addition to this basic murder intent. *See Wood,* 207 F.3d at 1228. While second degree murder requires only a general intent, meaning that the defendant "is aware that the result is practically certain to follow from his conduct, whatever his desire may be as to that result," *Welch,* 327 F.3d at 1095 n. 13; *accord Soundingsides,* 820 F.2d at 1242, first degree murder requires additional proof of a specific intent—including premeditation, deliberation, or a killing in the commission of certain enumerated felonies. *Wood,* 207 F.3d at 1228; *see also United States v. Bailey,* 444 U.S. 394, 405, 100 S.Ct. 624, 62 L.Ed.2d 575 (1980).

2nd degree

1st degree

Despite these distinct mental state requirements for these different degrees of murder, we have always said that "malice" is an element of *both* first and second degree murder. *Lofton,* 776 F.2d at 920. Although we have sometimes been less than precise in our language—suggesting in *Pearson,* for example, that second degree murder's malice element is satisfied simply by establishing one of the enumerated mental states—malice is actually a legal term of art. *See Browner,* 889 F.2d at 551.

Malice is not satisfied simply by killing with an intentional or reckless mental state; instead, malice specifically requires committing the wrongful act without justification, excuse, or mitigation. *See* 50 *Am.Jur.2d Homicide* § 37 (1999) ("[Malice] is said to include all those states and conditions of mind which accompany a homicide committed *without legal excuse or extenuation.*") (emphasis added); *Black's Law Dictionary* 976 (8th ed.2004) (defining "malice" as "intent, *without justification or excuse,* to commit a

Malice

wrongful act") (emphasis added); 40 *C.J.S. Homicide* § 33 (1991) ("Malice has been defined as consisting of the intentional doing of a wrongful act toward another *without legal justification, excuse, or mitigation.")* (emphasis added). The Supreme Court has also described malice as "lack of provocation." *Patterson v. New York,* 432 U.S. 197, 216, 97 S.Ct. 2319, 53 L.Ed.2d 281 (1977).

Thus, when we say that a murder must be committed "with malice," we mean not just that it requires a particular murderous intent but, more to the point, that it must also be "without legal justification, excuse, or mitigation." This is why, in *Lofton,* we held that to establish malice the prosecution must prove beyond a reasonable doubt the *absence* of heat of passion when it is an issue in the case. *Lofton,* 776 F.2d at 920.Heat of passion is one legal excuse pursuant to which what would otherwise constitute murder is mitigated to a less culpable offense of manslaughter— because with heat of passion, "malice" in the sense of "lack of provocation" no longer exists. *See id.*

2. Defining voluntary manslaughter mens rea

This takes us directly to the issue at hand, determining what "without malice . . . [u]pon a sudden quarrel or heat of passion" means in the context of 18 U.S.C. § 1112(a) and what mental state is intended by this language. The common law recognized "heat of passion" as one mitigating factor pursuant to which an otherwise intentional or reckless killing would constitute the less serious offense of voluntary manslaughter and be, because of that mitigating circumstance, "without malice." *See Mullaney,* 421 U.S. at 693, 95 S.Ct. 1881; *see also* 2 Wharton's CRIM. LAW § 155 (15th ed.) ("As a concession to human frailty, a killing [in the heat of passion], *which would otherwise constitute murder,* is mitigated to voluntary manslaughter.") (emphasis added); 2 Wayne R. LaFave, *Substantive Criminal Law* § 15.2, at 493 (2d ed.2003) (hereinafter *"LaFave")* ("The usual view of voluntary manslaughter thus presupposes an intent to kill (or perhaps to do serious injury or to engage in very reckless conduct), holding that *in spite of the existence of this bad intent* the circumstances may reduce the homicide to manslaughter.") (emphasis added).

As the Fifth Circuit explained:

> [t]he separate offense of voluntary manslaughter emerged [at common law] as an intentional killing that is nonetheless deemed to be without malice because it occurs in what the courts called "the heat of passion," a passion of fear or rage in which the defendant loses his normal self-control as a result of circumstances that would provoke such a passion in an ordinary person, but which did not justify the use of deadly force. Again, the federal statute simply declares the language of the common-law offense, and so when the defendant . . . actuated by a sudden passion of fear or rage arising from attendant circumstances that

would provoke such passion in an ordinary person, kills intentionally (or with one of the other mental states that constitutes malice), the killing is nevertheless deemed to be in the *absence of malice* under the federal statute. The malice that would otherwise attach is *negated* by the fact that the intentional killing occurred in the heat of passion in response to a sufficient provocation.

Browner, 889 F.2d at 552 (citations omitted).

We agree with the Fifth Circuit that this common law understanding is carried into § 1112 where "[v]oluntary manslaughter encompasses all of the elements of murder: it requires proof of the physical act of unlawfully causing the death of another, and of the mental state that *would* constitute malice, but for the fact that the killing was committed in adequately provoked heat of passion or provocation." *Id.* at 553. Thus, the only difference between second degree murder and voluntary manslaughter in the homicide hierarchy is that voluntary manslaughter is committed in the heat of passion, and the presence of this mitigating factor negates the malice that would otherwise attach given an intentional or reckless mental state. *See id.*

only difference between 2nd degree murder + voluntary manslaughter

While our court has not yet reached this issue directly, our case law directly supports this understanding. We have, without much detailed discussion, consistently noted that "heat of passion" in the voluntary manslaughter context has the effect of "negating" malice. *Lofton,* 776 F.2d at 920 ("The heat of passion defense is directly at odds with malice . . . the defense serves to negative malice.") (quotation and citation omitted); *United States v. Scafe,* 822 F.2d 928, 932 (10th Cir.1987) ("Malice is negated by heat of passion.").

Although we have used this language of negation in reference to malice, we have never suggested that heat of passion eliminates the requirement of an intentional or reckless killing implicit in the common law and in the structure of the homicide hierarchy. To the contrary, we have frequently referred to voluntary manslaughter as a general intent crime. *See, e.g., Soundingsides,* 820 F.2d at 1242; *United States v. Hatatley,* 130 F.3d 1399, 1405 (10th Cir.1997); *see also United States v. Fortier,* 180 F.3d 1217, 1228 (10th Cir.1999). Thus, malice is negated in the voluntary manslaughter context only in the sense that the killing is no longer "without excuse" as it would have to be to establish malice for second degree murder. . . .

Therefore, taking this all together, we read the statutory language of 18 U.S.C. § 1112 in accordance with our sister circuits' interpretations and with the history of the common law. Voluntary manslaughter requires proof beyond a reasonable doubt that the defendant acted, while in the heat of passion or upon a sudden quarrel, with a mental state that would otherwise constitute second degree murder—either a general intent to kill, intent to do serious bodily injury, or with depraved heart recklessness. . . .

voluntary manslaughter

We REVERSE the judgment of the district court and REMAND the case for a new trial on voluntary and involuntary manslaughter. The jury's guilty verdict on the lesser-included offense of voluntary manslaughter constituted an "implicit acquittal on the charge of second degree murder" and so he may only be retried on these lesser offenses.

EXERCISE

After coming home from work, David retreats to his basement to clean a gun he has recently purchased from a friend. While he is there, his wife Mavis comes down to talk to him. She is upset that he has spent money on a gun, when they have urgent medical bills that require their attention.

As they argue, Mavis tries to take the gun (a 9mm semi-automatic handgun) away from David, grabbing it by the barrel but never removing the obviously unloaded gun from his hands. Their screaming escalates as they back away from one another. David reaches into a bin beside him, pulls out a clip of ammunition, pushes it into the gun, and fires three times at Mavis. The first shot hit her arm, and she fell to the ground. The second shot, fired immediately after, missed her by several feet. The third shot, fired several seconds later, was fired at the ceiling but ricocheted and hit Mavis in the heart, killing her. David admits that he killed Mavis, but says he just intended to scare her. As a defense attorney, what is your best argument that he is guilty of voluntary manslaughter rather than murder? *heat of passion*

D. INVOLUNTARY MANSLAUGHTER

Let's go back to 18 U.S.C. § 1112 to develop the elements of involuntary manslaughter:

(a) Manslaughter is the unlawful killing of a human being without malice. It is of two kinds:

Voluntary—Upon a sudden quarrel or heat of passion.

Involuntary—In the commission of an unlawful act not amounting to a felony, or in the commission in an unlawful manner, or without due caution and circumspection, of a lawful act which might produce death.

(b) Within the special maritime and territorial jurisdiction of the United States.

The elements of involuntary manslaughter are:

1) Committed within the maritime or territorial jurisdiction of the United States,

2) Identification of the killer,

3) Actual death,

elements of involuntary manslaughter

4) Causation of the death,

5) Unlawfulness, and

6) At least one of the following:

    a) the killing occurred during the commission of a misdemeanor.

    b) the killing occurred during the commission of a lawful act without due caution and circumspection.

    c) the killing occurred during the commission of a lawful act in an unlawful manner.

Perhaps most commonly, involuntary homicide will be charged where the second factor of the last element is present—that is, where "the killing occurred during the commission of a lawful act without due caution and circumspection." In those cases, some level of negligence must be proven. The question of how much negligence is necessary is something addressed in case law.

UNITED STATES V. SCHMIDT
626 F. 2d 616 (8th Cir. 1980)

HANSON, SENIOR DISTRICT JUDGE.

At about midnight on June 30–July 1, 1979, one Mark Von Heeder was driving his car eastward on U. S. Highway 18 out of Mission, South Dakota, within the confines of the Rosebud Indian Reservation. He was carrying one passenger. As Von Heeder approached the Antelope Housing Community, less than a mile east of Mission, a car driven by appellant Clarence Frederick Schmidt, carrying four passengers, crossed the highway in front of him, proceeding southward out of the north turnoff to the Antelope Community. Von Heeder's car hit Schmidt's in its right rear quarter panel, turned over several times, and came to rest on its side off the southeast corner of the intersection; Schmidt's car veered into a field on the southwest side of the highway. Von Heeder died at the scene of the accident, apparently from a broken neck. There were no other fatalities.

Schmidt, an Indian, was charged by grand jury indictment with one count of involuntary manslaughter in violation of 18 U.S.C. ss 1153 and 1112. The indictment charged that he did unlawfully kill a human being while engaging in the commission in an unlawful manner and without due caution and circumspection, of a lawful act which might produce death, to-wit: in operating or driving a motor vehicle while under the influence of intoxicants, and without due caution and circumspection, and as a result did collide with an automobile, which caused the death of Mark D. Von Heeder, a human being . . . .

Trial was to a jury upon Schmidt's plea of not guilty; the jury returned a verdict of guilty. This appeal is from the judgment of conviction entered on that verdict. The only issue is whether the evidence is sufficient to sustain the conviction. Specifically, Schmidt's argument is that the evidence proves his simple negligence at most, but not the gross negligence required for conviction of involuntary manslaughter under 18 U.S.C. s 1112. It is established that conviction of this crime requires adequate proof that the defendant acted grossly negligently in that he acted with a wanton or reckless disregard for human life, knowing that his conduct was a threat to the lives of others or having knowledge of such circumstances as could reasonably have enabled him to foresee the peril to which his act might subject others. See United States v. Keith, 605 F.2d 462 (9th Cir. 1979) and cases cited therein. The district court so instructed the jury.

Issue

Schmidt's argument

As Schmidt acknowledges, the verdict of the jury must be sustained if there is substantial evidence in the record to support it, taking the view of the evidence most favorable to the government. Glasser v. United States, 315 U.S. 60, 80, 62 S.Ct. 457, 470, 86 L.Ed. 680; United States v. Cox, 580 F.2d 317, 323 (8th Cir. 1978), cert. denied, 439 U.S. 1075, 99 S.Ct. 851, 59 L.Ed.2d 43 (1979). Taking that view, and recognizing that there are conflicts in the testimony, we find substantial support in the evidence for each of the following propositions: that Schmidt was intoxicated at the time of the accident; that the brakes on the car he was driving were not in proper working order and had indeed failed to work properly earlier in the evening while Schmidt was driving the car; that immediately before the accident Schmidt "took off fast" toward the highway from a point about 100 feet north of it; that he proceeded across the highway without stopping at the stop sign posted for his lane of traffic; and that he knew or should have known Von Heeder's car was approaching because the passenger sitting with him in the front seat saw Von Heeder's headlights and warned Schmidt to stop by using the emergency brake if necessary. We hold that the jury could conclude from this evidence, taking the rest of the evidence into consideration, that Schmidt was beyond a reasonable doubt guilty of a wanton or reckless disregard for human life, and that he knew his conduct was a threat to the lives of others or had knowledge that could reasonably have enabled him to foresee the peril. This disposes of the only question raised by Schmidt on appeal. Accordingly, the judgment of conviction must be affirmed.

Holding

EXERCISE

You are called to jury duty in federal court, and are selected as the foreperson on a jury hearing a case similar in facts to *Schmidt*. Because you are a law student, you are asked by the other jurors to define what "wanton or reckless disregard for human life" means. You send a note to the judge asking for a definition, but she responds by telling the jury to "rely on your own best understanding of what those words mean."

One of the other jurors says that she is uncomfortable with this language because "it seems like you can be convicted just for making an innocent mistake." Another argues that "it's like if you sneeze while you are driving, you can get locked up for homicide."

What do you tell them?

extreme lack of care for the well-being or rights of another individual

UNITED STATES V. ERIC B.

86 F. 3d 869 (9th Cir. 1996)

MANUEL L. REAL, DISTRICT JUDGE:

On the afternoon of September 7, 1994, Eric B., then twelve-years-old, received a gun from a friend at school. Eric B. was aware that two bullets were in the weapon when he took possession of the gun.

Beginning on his bus ride home from school to Chilchinbeto, a small Navajo community in Arizona, and throughout the rest of the afternoon, Eric B. showed the gun to several of his schoolmates. After arriving in Chilchinbeto, Eric B. showed the gun to a ten-year-old named Jimmy Sharkey. Aware that the gun was loaded, Eric B. pointed the gun at Jimmy. Shortly thereafter, Eric B. and Jimmy went to a field, where Eric B. shot one bullet at some rocks. Eric B. then unscrewed the barrel, dropped the spent casing on the ground, removed the one remaining bullet and put it in his pocket.

Eric B. went on to have several encounters with other juveniles in which Eric B. would point the gun at the person and pull the trigger. Samantha Charlie, a fifteen-year-old, was one such person. After pointing the empty gun at Samantha, Eric B. pulled the remaining bullet from his pocket and put it back in the gun. Eric B. then offered the gun to Samantha and suggested she go shoot Tamara Zonnie, one of Samantha's friends.

Next, Eric B. took the now loaded gun and came across eleven-year-old Myron Redmoustache. Eric B. pointed the loaded gun at Myron and pulled the trigger. The gun did not fire.

Finally, just minutes after leaving Myron, Eric B. came across some juveniles playing in an area known as "the bridge." One of these juveniles was seven-year-old Nathan Crank. Eric B. pointed the gun at Nathan and shot him in the forehead. Eric B. then gave the gun to a boy named Tyrell and instructed him to hide the gun.

Within a few hours of the shooting, tribal police arrested Eric B. and placed him in custody. That evening tribal authorities notified the FBI of the shooting. On September 8, 1994, the FBI contacted the United States Attorney and the tribal authorities about the case. The grand jury issued a subpoena for Eric B.'s school records on September 9, 1994, and FBI agents met with tribal authorities on that same day. FBI agents stayed in Chilchinbeto until the 10th of September, during which time the FBI requested information regarding any prior juvenile adjudication Eric B. may have had.

On September 12, 1994, an FBI agent interviewed the juvenile who had given Eric B. the gun. On that same day, the agent interviewed Eric B. and received documentation from tribal authorities that Eric B. had no prior delinquency history. The FBI never undertook jurisdiction of the case, leaving the matter to the tribal court.

On September 15, 1994, the United States Attorney filed an Information charging the juvenile with committing an act of delinquency—second degree murder. Federal authorities arrested and placed Eric B. into federal custody on September 16, 1994, Eric B. making his initial appearance that same day. Trial was later set for October 14, 1994.

The district court held a disposition hearing on December 12, 1994, at which time it permitted the victim's family to be present. The district court also received several letters from the public expressing concern about the facts of the case and beseeching the court to ensure justice was done. . . .

After a one day trial, the district court found Eric B. not guilty of second degree murder under 18 U.S.C. § 1111. However, the district court did find the government had proven beyond a reasonable doubt defendant was guilty of the lesser included offense of involuntary manslaughter. *See* 18 U.S.C. § 1112.

Eric B. claims the government presented insufficient evidence to prove the requisite elements of involuntary manslaughter. Specifically, the evidence failed to support the court's finding that Eric B.'s actions demonstrated "a wanton and reckless disregard for human life."

To that end, counsel for Eric B. claims the juvenile had neither "actual knowledge that his conduct was a threat to the lives of others" nor did he have "knowledge of such circumstances as could reasonably be said to have made foreseeable to him the peril to which his acts might subject others." *United States v. Keith,* 605 F.2d 462 (9th Cir.1979) (citing *United States v. Pardee,* 368 F.2d 368 (4th Cir.1966)). Eric B. claims that due to his age and intelligence level he did not fully understand the consequences of his actions. Further, according to Eric B., the government did not present evidence that he, in fact, realized the bullet was in the gun at the time of the shooting. Plainly stated, Eric B. would have us find on this record that as a matter of law the shooting was an accident, and he did not understand the danger present in playing with the gun in this manner.

Contrary to argument that Eric B. did not foresee his acts creating peril for others, the government points to Eric B.'s conduct and testimony concerning such conduct. Eric B. knew the gun contained two bullets after he received it. He pointed the loaded gun at Jimmy Sharkey and shortly thereafter fired it at some rocks. After the gun went off, Eric B. unscrewed the cylinder, dropped the spent casing on the ground and put the remaining bullet in his pocket.

These acts alone demonstrate that the juvenile had a sufficient degree of sophistication and understanding of the gun's operation, and the corresponding cause and effect of firing a loaded weapon, to foresee the consequences of his actions and the peril created by aiming a loaded gun at another human being. Later, Eric B. again pointed the gun at another child, Samantha Charley, and she heard the trigger being pulled. Eric B. showed her the gun, put in the remaining bullet and told her to go shoot Tamara Zonnie. Eric B. repeated this exact conduct with Myron Redmoustache, but this time the gun was loaded. It did not go off.

Eric B.'s final act simply repeated the same conduct which he had engaged in throughout that day. But this time, Eric B. pointed the gun at a seven-year-old boy and shot him in the head. He intended to point the gun at the victim and he pulled the trigger just like he had several times before.

The circumstances leading up to the fatal shot and the final act itself demonstrate more than sufficient evidence to conclude that Eric B. *Holding* reasonably foresaw his acts created peril to the victim. Therefore, the district court correctly denied Eric B.'s motion for judgment of acquittal.

EXERCISE

Damien drives a postal truck. While backing into a loading dock at the main post office (on federal land), he noticed something behind him. He stopped, got out of the truck to investigate, and found that several young children were playing a game on the ground where he was about to park his vehicle. He told them to "get out of here!" and they appeared to start moving. He then got in his truck and backed up, killing one of the children. His mirrors did not show the area directly behind the truck, and Damien had disabled the back-up camera because it made him jumpy. As a prosecutor, do you feel you have enough evidence to charge Damien with Involuntary Manslaughter under 18 U.S.C. § 1112? *he should have reasonably foresaw his acts created to the victim— didn't check to see if they left - disabled backup camera*

E. SELF-DEFENSE

As reflected in the use of the word "unlawful" in the statutes on homicide, we consider some killings to be justified and lawful (as opposed to the "unlawful" killings addressed in 18 U.S.C. §§ 1111 & 1112). Killing by soldiers during wartime and inserting lethal agents during legal executions are just two examples of lawful taking of human life. Another type of justified killing is that which is done in self-defense. Self-defense is a defense to any of the charges described in this chapter, and is the justification for many shootings by both civilians and the police. Self-defense cases can involve difficult questions relating to the severity of the threat, the necessity of a lethal response, and the other options for safety that might be available.

In one famous case, the doctrine of self-defense was even allowed where the defendants shot and killed federal agents. In one of several cases involving conflicts between federal authorities and the Branch Davidian religious sect near Waco, Texas, the defendants were acquitted after asserting a self-defense claim to a charge of aiding and abetting the murder of federal agents. Some were convicted of aiding and abetting voluntary manslaughter, though, and appealed the refusal of the trial court to give an instruction of self-defense on that charge. Notably, the court required the government to prove that the killing was *not* self-defense on the murder charge. Because the burden did not shift to the defense, self-defense was not technically an affirmative defense in this case.

UNITED STATES V. BRANCH
91 F. 3d 699 (5th Cir. 1996)

PATRICK E. HIGGINBOTHAM, CIRCUIT JUDGE:

This is an appeal of six defendants convicted of federal crimes for their role in the dramatic and tragic events at Mount Carmel outside Waco, Texas during the early months of 1993. A firefight erupted when federal agents from the Bureau of Alcohol, Tobacco, and Firearms attempted to execute a search and arrest warrant on February 28, 1993. Four agents and three residents of the compound lost their lives. Each defendant now challenges his conviction and sentence.

I.

The Branch Davidians are a 65-year-old sect originally affiliated with the Seventh Day Adventist Church. Their faith urges a life of Bible study with emphasis on an imminent, apocalyptic confrontation between the Davidians and the "beast". The group's leader, Vernon Howell, instructed members to arm themselves in preparation for the final battle. Howell changed his name to David Koresh in 1990 and preached that "if you can't kill for God, you can't die for God." He told his followers that the "beast" included the U.S. Government and, specifically, the ATF.

Koresh and other Davidians stockpiled weapons and ammunition. They fortified the compound called Mount Carmel, building a two-foot high concrete barrier and an underground bunker. Koresh used "Bible studies" to instruct the residents in the use of firearms. In short, the Davidians turned Mount Carmel into a small fortress. The ATF discovered that the Davidians had amassed weapons, including fully automatic machineguns and hand grenades. On February 25, 1993, ATF agents obtained an arrest warrant for Koresh and a search warrant for the Mount Carmel compound.

The ATF decided to execute the search and arrest warrant on February 28, 1993, but, as it was to learn, the element of surprise had been lost. Around 8:00 A.M., an undercover ATF agent, Roberto Rodriguez, visited the Davidian compound and spoke with Koresh. During the conversation, Koresh took a phone call. When he returned, a visibly shaken Koresh told Rodriguez, "Robert, neither the AFT or National Guard will ever get me. They got me once, they'll never get me again." Koresh then walked over to the windows and looked toward the farmhouse used by the undercover ATF agents. He turned to Rodriguez and said, "They're coming, Robert. The time has come." Rodriguez left the compound around 9:00 A.M. and advised the ATF that Koresh had learned of the raid at least forty-five minutes earlier. The ATF decided to proceed with the arrest and search warrants.

When the ATF's decision to continue was made, approximately 115 men, women, and children, ranging in age from 6 months to 70 years, resided at Mount Carmel. The ATF plan called for ATF agents, who were transported to the compound in two cattle trailers, to quickly unload and encircle the compound, while National Guard helicopters conducted a diversionary raid on the rear of the Mount Carmel compound.

The plan quickly went awry. The helicopters did not arrive until after the ATF agents had begun unloading from the cattle trailers. As the agents unloaded, gunfire erupted from the compound. The agents returned fire. In the ensuing gunbattle, four agents and three Davidians were killed. Twenty-two ATF agents and four Davidians were wounded.

The FBI then surrounded the compound, and, for 51 days, law enforcement and the Davidians were at a stand-off. During the stand-off, approximately 30 Davidians left the compound and were taken into custody. On April 19, FBI agents attempted to end the stand-off by flooding the compound with gas, but the Davidians did not leave. Around noon, the Davidians set the compound on fire. Seventy-five of the remaining 84 occupants perished in the blaze. . . .

The Government dismissed the charges against one of the twelve Davidians, Kathryn Schroeder, pursuant to a plea bargain. After a jury trial lasting nearly two months, the jury acquitted four of the Davidians on all counts on which they were charged. . . . The jury acquitted all eleven of the defendants on Count 2 for aiding and abetting the murder of federal agents but convicted Avraam, Branch, Castillo, Fagan, and Whitecliff on the lesser-included offense of aiding and abetting the voluntary manslaughter of federal agents. . . .

The district court instructed the jury that to convict the defendants of murder under Count 2, it had to find beyond a reasonable doubt that "the Defendant under consideration did not act in self-defense or defense of another." The court explained self-defense and the defense of another, and then turned to the lesser-included offense of voluntary manslaughter.

[handwritten margin note: had to find that they were not acting in self defense]

Avraam, Branch, Castillo, and Whitecliff argue that self-defense is also a defense to voluntary manslaughter. The Davidians requested an instruction to that effect and objected at the charge conference to its omission. . . .

Holding

We hold that the district court was not obligated to give the proposed self-defense instruction and did not err in the instruction it gave. It is true, as a general proposition, that self-defense and the related defense of another are affirmative defenses to both murder and voluntary manslaughter. However, these general principles must accommodate a citizen's duty to accede to lawful government power and the special protection due federal officials discharging official duties. *See United States v. Feola,* 420 U.S. 671, 679, 95 S.Ct. 1255, 1261, 43 L.Ed.2d 541 (1975). "We do not need citizen avengers who are authorized to respond to unlawful police conduct by gunning down the offending officers." *United States v. Johnson,* 542 F.2d 230, 233 (5th Cir.1976). Other, non-violent remedies are available. *Id.*

We need not explore the law of self-defense in confrontations between citizens and law enforcement officers to answer the question asked in this case. As we will explain, a reasonable juror could not doubt that the defendants knew their targets were federal agents. Equally, the defendants responded to the agents' lawful force with a deadly barrage of gunfire. Given the extraordinary amount of automatic and large-caliber gunfire that the defendants rained upon persons they knew were federal agents, the law offers no shelter for pleas that the defendant used only force that was "responsive to excessive force." The legal claim simply has no factual leg.

That the district court allowed self-defense to the murder charges is nothing about which the defendants can complain. Whether correct or not, we need not decide. That instruction regarding murder seeds no right to a similar plea of self-defense to voluntary manslaughter. Our issue is error, not symmetry.

In sum, the evidence did not require the proposed self-defense instruction. Of course, the defendants may have feared for their life once gunfire erupted, but that fear does not warrant a self-defense instruction. There must be sufficient evidence from which a reasonable juror might infer, at a minimum, either that 1) the defendants did not know the ATF agents' identity, *see United States v. Morton,* 999 F.2d 435, 437–38 (9th Cir.1993), or that 2) the ATF agents' use of force, viewed from the perspective of a reasonable officer at the scene, was objectively unreasonable under the circumstances. *See United States v. Span,* 970 F.2d 573, 577 (9th Cir.1992), *cert. denied,* 507 U.S. 921, 113 S.Ct. 1283, 122 L.Ed.2d 676 (1993). That evidence was not adduced at trial.

The record belies the defendants' contention that they did not know the identity of the ATF agents outside the compound on February 28th. In addition to their long preparation for the arrival of law officers, Koresh and the defendants had specific knowledge well in advance that the raid of February 28th was coming. On the morning of the raid, Koresh told the ATF's undercover agent, Roberto Rodriguez, who briefly visited the Davidians that morning, that "neither the ATF or National Guard will ever get me. They got me once and they'll never get me again." Koresh repeatedly said, "They're coming, Robert. They're coming." Several Davidians overheard Koresh's remarks. Other residents also learned of the impending ATF raid. Craddock, for example, learned that David Jones had heard that seventy-five ATF agents had arrived at the airport and that there might be a raid.

Even if we assume that not every defendant had been forewarned of this specific raid, the record demonstrates beyond doubt that by the time the agents arrived at the compound, defendants knew the agents' identity as federal law enforcement officers. ATF Special Agent Roland Ballesteros, who was one of the first agents to approach the front of the compound after the raid began, testified that as he ran toward the front door of the compound, he saw David Koresh standing in the open front doorway. Ballesteros yelled loudly "Police! Lay down!" and "Search Warrant!" to Koresh several times. Koresh responded by asking "What's going on?" and Ballesteros again yelled "Search Warrant! Lay Down!" As Ballesteros approached the doorway, Koresh "made some kind of smirk" and then closed the door. Ballesteros testified that "there was no doubt in my mind that [Koresh] knew who we were and what we were there for." Other agents also testified that they heard shouts of "Police", "Search Warrant," and "Federal agents" as they exited the cattle trailers and approached the compound.

Even though a reasonable juror could doubt that the Davidians heard the repeated cries of "police" and "search warrant", a reasonable juror could not overlook the visible indicators of the agents' identity. The Davidians point out that neither the cattle trailers nor the helicopters had government markings on them. However, most of the ATF agents, including the first agents to approach the compound, wore "full raid gear." This gear included military-style helmets and black, bullet-resistant vests. Significantly, the vests had a large, gold ATF badge and the words "ATF" and "Police" inscribed in bright yellow, inch-high letters on their fronts. "ATF" and "Police" were also emblazoned on the back of the vests in large, yellow letters visible at a distance. Some agents wore "baseball" hats with a large yellow badge on the front. These markings were plainly visible in the broad daylight that morning and informed anyone who looked that these were federal law enforcement officials.

EXERCISE

The trial court in the *Branch* case instructed the jurors that they could acquit the defendants on the charge of aiding and abetting the murder of federal agents if the government failed to prove beyond a reasonable doubt that the defendants did NOT act in self-defense.

Imagine that you are a prosecutor in this case at a hearing on the jury instructions prior to trial. What arguments would you make to support the assertion that the *absence* of self-defense should not be an element the jury has to find under these facts?

———————

What if the defendant provokes the threatening behavior? This is an issue that often rises out of the murky swamp of facts surrounding a killing. The traditional rule is that a claim of self-defense can be countered if the prosecution can show that either the defendant was the aggressor or had the reasonable ability to retreat from the situation without resorting to lethal force.

If the defendant was the initial aggressor, there can be the further question of whether or not the victim responded to the aggression by escalating the situation to the degree that lethal force was justified.

UNITED STATES V. GARCIA
625 F. 2d 162 (7th Cir. 1980)

PELL, CIRCUIT JUDGE.

Appellants Eugene Pete Garcia, Joe Anthony Contreras, and David Lucero, inmates at the federal penitentiary at Marion, Illinois, were convicted by a jury of second degree murder and the illegal conveyance of a weapon within the prison, in violation of 18 U.S.C. ss 1111, and 1792, respectively. The convictions arose out of the violent killing of Michael Martinez, another inmate at Marion, who was stabbed to death in the prison by appellants on November 6, 1978.

The essential facts are not in significant dispute. Appellants introduced testimony of Marion inmates that Martinez had threatened Garcia's life prior to the fight between the two that led to Martinez's untimely death. The inmates also testified that Martinez had started the fight by attacking Garcia with a knife. Garcia, apparently, successfully repelled the attack with the aid of Contreras and Lucero. This stage of the fight occurred behind a partially closed door, thus out of the sight of the guards who were the prosecution's main witnesses. The struggle, however, soon moved into a corridor where guards testified to seeing all three appellants chasing Martinez down the hall, catching him, and stabbing him to death while ignoring the guards' orders to stop.

At trial, appellants did not contest that they were responsible for Martinez's death; rather, they relied solely on a theory of self-defense. Garcia claimed he killed Martinez while defending himself from the original attack by Martinez, and Contreras and Lucero maintained they were merely aiding Garcia's defense. On this appeal, appellants raise a variety of complaints regarding the trial which we shall consolidate and address in turn below. . . .

Appellant Garcia objects to an instruction given to the jury on the issue of provocation which he contends improperly created the impression that he might have provoked the attack by Martinez. The trial judge instructed the jury:

self defense

> A person who initially provokes the use of force against himself or another is justified in the use of force in defense only if the force used against him or another is so great that he reasonably believes that he is in danger of death or great bodily harm, and he has exhausted every reasonable means to escape the danger, other than the use of force which is likely to cause death or great bodily harm to the other person.

Jury instruction

Garcia protests that there was no evidence presented at trial suggesting he provoked the dispute with Martinez, and therefore, that the issue should not have been submitted to the jury.

Garcia contention

We believe the trial judge correctly ruled that the issue of provocation was a question of fact for the jury to consider. The Government presented eyewitness testimony that the appellants chased Martinez down a cellblock corridor before catching him, holding him, and stabbing him to death. Garcia himself testified that he obtained a knife in anticipation of a meeting with Martinez and that it was he who originally approached Martinez immediately prior to the fight. Although the defense presented inmates who testified that Martinez initiated the original fight prior to the chase, we hold that the ultimate resolution of the issue was properly a question submitted to the jury and that they were appropriately instructed.

EXERCISE

Leonard owes money to Joan. While shopping for groceries, she sees Leonard in the store. They get into a dispute about the debt, which escalates to yelling. Joan, frustrated, throws a can of corn at Leonard, who pulls out a knife and threatens to kill Joan. She responds by backing away down the aisle two yards, getting her gun out of her purse, and shooting Leonard. He dies. Assuming that the traditional rules regarding duty to retreat and initial aggression apply, and that you are the prosecutor in her case, would you charge her with some form of homicide?

Some jurisdictions bar or limit the use of this defense if the defendant had the reasonable ability to retreat to safety rather than use lethal force. In other words, it is not a justifiable killing if the shooter could have safely removed herself from the situation.[8]

In some states, the "Castle Doctrine" or a "Stand Your Ground" law has eliminated or altered this traditional rule (that a defendant cannot claim self-defense if he had a reasonable ability to retreat from the situation instead of using lethal force). The Castle Doctrine derives from common law, and allows the use of lethal force within one's home without a duty to retreat,[9] and in some jurisdictions has been extended to allow for the use of lethal force within the home to prevent a felony even if there is no threat to the inhabitants.[10] "Stand Your Ground" laws go even further: they allow for the use of lethal force outside of the home without a duty to retreat to safety.[11]

The Castle Doctrine has limits; even at home it is problematic where someone picks a fight and then uses lethal force when the victim responds.

UNITED STATES V. PETERSON
483 F. 2d 1222 (DC Cir. 1973)

Spottswood W. Robinson, III, Circuit Judge:

The events immediately preceding the homicide are not seriously in dispute. The version presented by the Government's evidence follows. Charles Keitt, the deceased, and two friends drove in Keitt's car to the alley in the rear of Peterson's house to remove the windshield wipers from the latter's wrecked car. While Keitt was doing so, Peterson came out of the house into the back yard to protest. After a verbal exchange, Peterson went back into the house, obtained a pistol, and returned to the yard. In the meantime, Keitt had reseated himself in his car, and he and his companions were about to leave.

Upon his reappearance in the yard, Peterson paused briefly to load the pistol. "If you move," he shouted to Keitt, "I will shoot." He walked to a point in the yard slightly inside a gate in the rear fence and, pistol in hand, said, "If you come in here I will kill you." Keitt alighted from his car, took a few steps toward Peterson and exclaimed, "What the hell do you think you are going to do with that?" Keitt then made an about-face, walked back to his car and got a lug wrench. With the wrench in a raised position, Keitt advanced toward Peterson, who stood with the pistol pointed toward him.

---

[8]　E.g. New York Penal Law § 35–15(2)(a).

[9]　E.g., Hawaii Statute § 703–304(5)(B)(i).

[10]　E.g. Colorado Revised Statute 18–1–704.5(2).

[11]　E.g. Florida Statutes Title XLVI, Chapter 776.102.

Peterson warned Keitt not to "take another step" and, when Keitt continued onward shot him in the face from a distance of about ten feet. Death was apparently instantaneous. Shortly thereafter, Peterson left home and was apprehended 20-odd blocks away.

This description of the fatal episode was furnished at Peterson's trial by four witnesses for the Government. Peterson did not testify or offer any evidence, but the Government introduced a statement which he had given the police after his arrest, in which he related a somewhat different version. Keitt had removed objects from his car before, and on the day of the shooting he had told Keitt not to do so. After the initial verbal altercation, Keitt went to his car for the lug wrench, so he, Peterson, went into his house for his pistol. When Keitt was about ten feet away, he pointed the pistol "away of his right shoulder;" adding that Keitt was running toward him, Peterson said he "got scared and fired the gun. He ran right into the bullet." "I did not mean to shoot him," Peterson insisted, "I just wanted to scare him."

At trial, Peterson moved for a judgment of acquittal on the ground that as a matter of law the evidence was insufficient to support a conviction. The trial judge denied the motion. After receiving instructions which in two respects are challenged here, the jury returned a verdict finding Peterson guilty of manslaughter. Judgment was entered conformably with the verdict, and this appeal followed. . . .

More than two centuries ago, Blackstone, best known of the expositors of the English common law, taught that "all homicide is malicious, and of course, amounts to murder, unless . . . *justified* by the command or permission of the law; *excused* on the account of accident or self-preservation; or *alleviated* into manslaughter, by being either the involuntary consequence of some act not strictly lawful, or (if voluntary) occasioned by some sudden and sufficiently violent provocation.

Tucked within this greatly capsulized schema of the common law of homicide is the branch of law we are called upon to administer today. No issue of justifiable homicide, within Blackstone's definition is involved. But Peterson's consistent position is that as a matter of law his conviction of manslaughter—alleviated homicide—was wrong, and that his act was one of self-preservation—excused homicide. The Government, on the other hand, has contended from the beginning that Keitt's slaying fell outside the bounds of lawful self-defense. The questions remaining for our decision inevitably track back to this basic dispute.

Self-defense, as a doctrine legally exonerating the taking of human life, is as viable now as it was in Blackstone's time, and in the case before us the doctrine is invoked in its purest form. But "[t]he law of self-defense is a law of necessity;" the right of self-defense arises only when the necessity begins, and equally ends with the necessity; and never must the necessity be greater than when the force employed defensively is deadly. The "necessity must bear all semblance of reality, and appear to admit of no other alternative, before taking life will be justifiable as excusable." Hinged on the exigencies of self-preservation, the doctrine of homicidal self-defense emerges from the body of the criminal law as a limited though important exception to legal outlawry of the arena of self-help in the settlement of potentially fatal personal conflicts.

So it is that necessity is the pervasive theme of the well defined conditions which the law imposes on the right to kill or maim in self-defense. There must have been a threat, actual or apparent, of the use of deadly force against the defender. The threat must have been unlawful and immediate. The defender must have believed that he was in imminent peril of death or serious bodily harm, and that his response was necessary to save himself therefrom. These beliefs must not only have been honestly entertained, but also objectively reasonable in light of the surrounding circumstances. It is clear that no less than a concurrence of these elements will suffice.

Here the parties' opposing contentions focus on the roles of two further considerations. One is the provoking of the confrontation by the defender. The other is the defendant's failure to utilize a safe route for retreat from the confrontation. . . .

The second aspect of the trial judge's charge as to which Peterson asserts error concerned the undisputed fact that at no time did Peterson endeavor to retreat from Keitt's approach with the lug wrench. The judge instructed the jury that if Peterson had reasonable grounds to believe and did believe that he was in imminent danger of death or serious injury, and that deadly force was necessary to repel the danger, he was required neither to retreat nor to consider whether he could safely retreat. Rather, said the judge, Peterson was entitled to stand his ground and use such force as was reasonably necessary under the circumstances to save his life and his person from pernicious bodily harm. But, the judge continued, if Peterson could have safely retreated but did not do so, that failure was a circumstance which the jury might consider, together with all others, in determining whether he went further in repelling the danger, real or apparent, than he was justified in going.

Peterson contends that this imputation of an obligation to retreat was error, even if he could safely have done so. He points out that at the time of the shooting he was standing in his own yard, and argues he was under no duty to move. We are persuaded to the conclusion that in the circumstances presented here, the trial judge did not err in giving the instruction challenged.

Within the common law of self-defense there developed the rule of "retreat to the wall," which ordinarily forbade the use of deadly force by one to whom an avenue for safe retreat was open. This doctrine was but an application of the requirement of strict necessity to excuse the taking of human life, and was designed to insure the existence of that necessity.

Even the innocent victim of a vicious assault had to elect a safe retreat if available, rather than resort to defensive force which might kill or seriously injure.

In a majority of American jurisdictions, contrarily to the common law rule, one may stand his ground and use deadly force whenever it seems reasonably necessary to save himself. While the law of the District of Columbia on this point is not entirely clear, it seems allied with the strong minority adhering to the common law. In 1856, the District of Columbia Criminal Court ruled that a participant in an affray "must endeavor to retreat, . . . that is, he is obliged to retreat, if he can safely." The court added that "[a] man may, to be sure, decline a combat when there is no existing or apparent danger, but the retreat to which the law binds him is that which is the consequence." In a much later era this court, adverting to necessity as the soul of homicidal self-defense, declared that "no necessity for killing an assailant can exist, so long as there is a safe way open to escape the conflict." Moreover, the common law rule of strict necessity pervades the District concept of pernicious self-defense, and we cannot ignore the inherent inconsistency of an absolute no-retreat rule. Until such time as the District law on the subject may become more definitive, we accept these precedents as ample indication that the doctrine of retreat persists.

That is not to say that the retreat rule is without exceptions. Even at common law it was recognized that it was not completely suited to all situations. Today it is the more so that its precept must be adjusted to modern conditions nonexistent during the early development of the common law of self-defense. One restriction on its operation comes to the fore when the circumstances apparently foreclose a withdrawal with safety. The doctrine of retreat was never intended to enhance the risk to the innocent; its proper application has never required a faultless victim to increase his assailant's safety at the expense of his own. On the contrary, he could stand his ground and use deadly force otherwise appropriate if the alternative were perilous, or if to him it reasonably appeared to be. A slight variant of the same consideration is the principle that there is no duty to retreat from an assault producing an imminent danger of death or grievous bodily harm. "Detached reflection cannot be demanded in the presence of an uplifted knife," nor is it "a condition of immunity that one in that situation should pause to consider whether a reasonable man might not think it possible to fly with safety or to disable his assailant rather than to kill him."

The trial judge's charge to the jury incorporated each of these limitations on the retreat rule. Peterson, however, invokes another—the so-called "castle" doctrine. It is well settled that one who through no fault of his own is attacked in his home is under no duty to retreat therefrom. The oft-repeated expression that "a man's home is his castle" reflected the belief in olden days that there were few if any safer sanctuaries than the home. The "castle" exception, moreover, has been extended by some courts to encompass the occupant's presence within the curtilage outside his dwelling. Peterson reminds us that when he shot to halt Keitt's advance, he was standing in his yard and so, he argues, he had no duty to endeavor to retreat.

No duty to retreat b/c of castle doctrine

Despite the practically universal acceptance of the "castle" doctrine in American jurisdictions wherein the point has been raised, its status in the District of Columbia has never been squarely decided. But whatever the fate of the doctrine in the District law of the future, it is clear that in absolute form it was inapplicable here. The right of self-defense, we have said, cannot be claimed by the aggressor in an affray so long as he retains that unmitigated role. It logically follows that any rule of no-retreat which may protect an innocent victim of the affray would, like other incidents of a forfeited right of self-defense, be unavailable to the party who provokes or stimulates the conflict. Accordingly, the law is well settled that the "castle" doctrine can be invoked only by one who is without fault in bringing the conflict on. That, we think, is the critical consideration here.

We need not repeat our previous discussion of Peterson's contribution to the altercation which culminated in Keitt's death. It suffices to point out that by no interpretation of the evidence could it be said that Peterson was blameless in the affair. And while, of course, it was for the jury to assess the degree of fault, the evidence well nigh dictated the conclusion that it was substantial.

EXERCISE

Assume that you are a defense attorney advising a client accused of manslaughter. The reasoning in the *Peterson* case is binding precedent in your district.

Your client, Milt Robinson, was throwing rocks at cars driving too fast past his house. It bothered him that people would speed down that stretch of road. It was his way of trying to control traffic. After a while he gave up and started to mow his lawn. As he did so, a car drove over the sidewalk and onto his lawn. An angry man got out of the car and pointed at a dent. As the angry man got back into his car, Mr. Robinson stepped into his house, got his rifle, and then shot the man dead as he started the car.

Mr. Robinson explains that he had to shoot the angry man because it seemed clear that the man was going to drive the car into the side of his house or drive over him if he had the chance.

Mr. Robinson wants to know if he can claim self-defense. What do you tell him? *No, he could have retreated*

There often is overlap between the issues of self-defense and the kind of provocation by the victim that leads to manslaughter. A victim's threatening behavior might be enough to reduce a charge from murder to manslaughter, but not quite enough to create a total self-defense claim. This kind of case is sometimes referred to as an "imperfect" self-defense case, and sometimes is accounted for at sentencing either informally or (as in the case below) through sentencing guidelines.

UNITED STATES V. TRUJILLO

2010 WL 5476756 (D. N.M., Dec. 1, 2010)

JAMES O. BROWNING, DISTRICT JUDGE.

Trujillo requests a downward departure and variance for a total sentence of ten years and one day, because the crime was aberrant behavior for Trujillo and because the victim, Brian Lester Sam, was the initial aggressor. Trujillo contends that this offense is his first contact with law enforcement, and that he has no prior juvenile arrests, adjudications or adult arrests or convictions. Trujillo further contends that he was not looking for trouble, and the facts of this case are unlikely to occur again, so Trujillo is unlikely to reoffend. Trujillo argues, therefore, that the shooting Sam is aberrant to Trujillo's nature and background. *[handwritten: Trujillo contention]*

Trujillo contends that Sam provoked the killing because Sam was the initial aggressor. Trujillo alleges that he and Sam were friends and relatives. According to Trujillo's account of the crime, on the night of the killing, Sam and his brother, Arlonzo, were at Trujillo's mother's residence. They were watching television and drinking. Sam was intoxicated and quarreled with Arlonzo. Trujillo and his brother, Lewis, separated Sam and Arlonzo, and Lewis and Arlonzo left Trujillo's mother's residence, leaving Trujillo alone with Sam. Sam began to quarrel with Trujillo. Trujillo attempted to walk away, and Sam followed him outside, poking at Trujillo as if Sam had a knife, and Trujillo believed Sam had a knife. During the quarrel, Sam referenced Trujillo's firearm, and Sam knew where Trujillo kept the firearm, which led Trujillo to fear that Sam might access the firearm. With Sam following, Trujillo retrieved the firearm from his bedroom and pointed it at Sam, expecting Sam to back down. Sam did not back down. Sam cursed at Trujillo and stated that Trujillo did not have the courage to shoot him. Sam then moved towards Trujillo. Fearing that Sam was moving to attack him and believing himself in danger, Trujillo took two steps back and intentionally shot Sam once in the side. . . .

The United States argues that, at best, Trujillo's version of the events the night of the crime makes the killing imperfect self-defense. The United States argues that Trujillo has already pled to manslaughter instead of second-degree murder with which the grand jury charged him, and that *[handwritten: U.S. argument]* further reducing his sentence would, in effect, credit him twice for the victim's initial aggression. *See Cannon v. Mullin,* 383 F.3d 1152, 1167 (10th Cir.2004) ("[S]ome courts and commentators refer to manslaughter as an 'imperfect' self-defense—that is, although the defendant cannot satisfy all the elements of self-defense, he is less culpable because he can satisfy some of the elements." (citing 2 Wayne R. LaFave, *Substantive Criminal Law* § 10.4(i) (2d ed.2003)). . . .

The Court believes a 7 level downward departure is warranted, because Sam provoked Trujillo. . . . The Court grants Trujillo's request for a downward departure. "Victim misconduct is an encouraged basis for departure under U.S.S.G. § 5K2.10. . . ." *Koon v. United States,* 518 U.S. 81, 83 (1996). *Accord United States v. LaVallee,* 439 F.3d 670, 708 (10th Cir.2006). U.S.S.G. § 5K2.10 provides:

If the victim's wrongful conduct contributed significantly to provoking the offense behavior, the court may reduce the sentence below the guideline range to reflect the nature and circumstances of the offense. In deciding whether a sentence reduction is warranted, and the extent of such reduction, the court should consider the following:

(1)   The size and strength of the victim, or other relevant physical characteristics, in comparison with those of the defendant.

(2)   The persistence of the victim's conduct and any efforts by the defendant to prevent confrontation.

(3)   The danger reasonably perceived by the defendant, including the victim's reputation for violence.

(4)   The danger actually presented to the defendant by the victim.

(5)   Any other relevant conduct by the victim that substantially contributed to the danger presented.

(6)   The proportionality and reasonableness of the defendant's response to the victim's provocation.

On balance, the Court concludes that these factors militate in favor of departing downward. The record does not reveal any information about the size and strength of the victim, or otherwise indicate the first factor is particularly important. The second factor—the persistence of the victim's conduct and any efforts by the defendant to prevent confrontations—is prevalent in this case and counsels in favor of a downward departure. The third factor—the danger reasonably perceived by the defendant, including the victim's reputation for violence—also supports departing downward. The Court does not have any indication of the victim's reputation for violence, but the Court believes that the defendant reasonably perceived himself to be in danger. The Court believes the fourth factor—the danger actually presented to the defendant by the victim—is fairly neutral. The Court finds there was a danger and a confrontation, but Sam does not appear to have had a knife, although it appears that Trujillo's belief that Sam had a knife was reasonable in this case. The fifth factor—any other relevant conduct of the victim that substantially contributed to the danger presented—further supports departing downward. Sam questioned Trujillo's willingness to use the firearm and moved towards him when Trujillo was pointing the firearm at Sam. The sixth and final factor—the proportionality and reasonableness of the defendant's response to the victims's provocation—cuts against departing downward because shooting Sam was an excessive response to Sam's behavior. In sum, the Court concludes that some factors are not present or neutral, one factor cuts against a downward departure, but the balance of the factors suggest that there was provocation in this case warranting a downward departure. And while victim misconduct not sufficient to warrant application in certain situations—such as cases of criminal sexual abuse—the Court believes that victim misconduct is an appropriate basis for a downward departure in a case of assault and manslaughter.

EXERCISE

Dwight is deer hunting on state land. While walking through the woods, he hears a gunshot from close by. He is alarmed to see his neighbor, Old Deaf Frank, firing at him with a rifle. Frank is elderly and hard of hearing, which Dwight well knows from their many arguments relating to a property line dispute (and also from his nickname). Clearly, Frank is out hunting deer (he is wearing an orange vest and hat) and has mistaken Dwight for a deer. Dwight decides to run for it but trips and falls, breaking his ankle. He can no longer move, but Frank is advancing on him and reloading. Dwight, fearing imminent death, shoots Frank, who dies. The whole thing occurs in a national park, granting federal jurisdiction.

You are a prosecutor in the district where this occurred. The sheriff has talked to Frank's family and they want Dwight to be prosecuted. There are no other witnesses, and Dwight tells the story related above, which is consistent with readily available facts including Dwight's broken ankle and shell casings indicating several shots fired by Frank in that area (and one by Dwight).

Your supervisor tells you that you can take the case and prosecute to the fullest extent, take the case and offer a plea with a mitigated sentence as in the case above, or just not take the case at all. Which do you choose?

offer a plea with a mitigated sentence

CHAPTER THREE

VIOLENT CRIMES (OTHER THAN HOMICIDE)

■ ■ ■

Violent crimes are generally considered those unlawful actions that either involve physical force or the threat of physical force to compel a result. Though homicide is the best-known example of a violent crime, it is not the only one. Some violent crimes are categorized as sex offenses, and will be discussed in a later chapter. Some other non-homicide violent crimes—including assault, kidnapping, and robbery—are primary topics within criminal law. Those are the focus of this chapter.

These crimes are also often viewed as more serious than other kinds of offenses, and penalties for these crimes are often (though not always) more severe than those exacted for similar crimes that lack the element of violence. For example, the sentence for a robbery is likely to be greater than the sentence for a theft of the same amount of money. In part, this is because violent crimes involve a physical injury or the potential of physical injury, which are viewed as a more significant harm than simply a financial injury.

What we term "violent crimes" do not necessarily require that an act of physical violence be completed; often, it is the *threat* of violence that fulfils the action element of a statute. For example, the action element of a bank robbery which makes it a crime of violence can be fulfilled either through the use of physical force (such as punching a teller) or through the threat of such force (i.e., a threatening demand note). How concrete a threat needs to be in order to have an action categorized as a "violent" crime is the subject of a very real and substantive debate, in both proving up an element of violence and in considering enhanced penalties that often apply when a defendant's criminal history includes priors that are considered to be violent.

We will start with a discussion of how violent crimes are defined. From that point, three discrete violent crimes will be explored: robbery, assault, and kidnapping. Terrorism will also be discussed, as it is usually based on an underlying violent crime.

A. DEFINING "VIOLENT CRIMES"

Unfortunately, there is no one accepted definition of "violent crime." It is not unusual to hear experienced prosecutors argue that a simple narcotics transaction, free of threat or physical violence, is properly considered a "crime of violence" because violence is inherent in the drug trade. Others would counter that a simple commercial transaction, even of illegal substances, cannot be considered a crime of violence on its face.

The federal Sentencing Guidelines provide for enhancements where a defendant has previously committed a "crime of violence," and defines such a crime this way:

> § 4B1.2 Definitions of Terms Used in Section 4B1.1
>
> (a)   The term "crime of violence" means any offense under federal or state law, punishable by imprisonment for a term exceeding one year, that—
>
>   (1)   has as an element the use, attempted use, or threatened use of physical force against the person of another, or
>
>   (2)   is murder, voluntary manslaughter, kidnapping, aggravated assault, a forcible sex offense, robbery, arson, extortion, or the use or unlawful possession of a firearm described in 26 U.S.C. § 5845(a) or explosive material as defined in 18 U.S.C. § 841(c).

Section (a)(1) above contains a classic and nearly indisputable definition of a violent crime. Section (a)(2), however, incorporates a series of crimes (murder, manslaughter, kidnapping, aggravated assault, forcible sex offenses, robbery) which already fit the definition under (a)(1) before veering off into less firm territory (arson, extortion, and the use or unlawful possession of a certain firearms). Firearms described in 26 U.S.C. 5845(a) include short-barreled shotguns, meaning that the mere possession of a short-barreled shotgun is a "crime of violence" under this definition.

Another (largely similar though not identical) federal definition, embedded within the federal code at 18 U.S.C. § 924(e)(2)(B), is discussed in the case below.

BEGAY v. UNITED STATES
553 U.S. 137 (2008)

JUSTICE BREYER delivered the opinion of the Court.

The Armed Career Criminal Act imposes a special mandatory 15-year prison term upon felons who unlawfully possess a firearm and who also have three or more previous convictions for committing certain drug crimes or "violent felon[ies]." 18 U.S.C. § 924(e)(1). The question in this case is whether driving under the influence of alcohol is a "violent felony" as the Act defines it. We conclude that it is not. . . .

Federal law prohibits a previously convicted felon from possessing a firearm. § 922(g)(1). A related provision provides for a prison term of up to

10 years for an ordinary offender. § 924(a)(2). The Armed Career Criminal Act imposes a more stringent 15-year mandatory minimum sentence on an offender who has three prior convictions "for a violent felony or a serious drug offense." § 924(e)(1).

The Act defines a "violent felony" as "any crime punishable by imprisonment for a term exceeding one year" that

> "(i) has as an element the use, attempted use, or threatened use of physical force against the person of another; or

> "(ii) is burglary, arson, or extortion, involves use of explosives, or otherwise involves conduct that presents a serious potential risk of physical injury to another." § 924(e)(2)(B).

We here consider whether driving under the influence of alcohol (DUI), as set forth in New Mexico's criminal statutes, falls within the scope of the second clause.

The relevant background circumstances include the following: In September 2004, New Mexico police officers received a report that Larry Begay, the petitioner here, had threatened his sister and aunt with a rifle. The police arrested him. Begay subsequently conceded he was a felon and pleaded guilty to a federal charge of unlawful possession of a firearm in violation of § 922(g)(1). Begay's presentence report said that he had been convicted a dozen times for DUI, which under New Mexico's law becomes a felony (punishable by a prison term of more than one year) the fourth (or subsequent) time an individual commits it. The sentencing judge consequently found that Begay had at least three prior convictions for a crime "punishable by imprisonment for a term exceeding one year." 377 F.Supp.2d 1141, 1143 (NM 2005). The judge also concluded that Begay's "three felony DUI convictions involve conduct that presents a serious potential risk of physical injury to another." *Id.*, at 1145. The judge consequently concluded that Begay had three or more prior convictions for a "violent felony" and should receive a sentence that reflected a mandatory minimum prison term of 15 years. *Ibid.*

Begay, claiming that DUI is not a "violent felony" within the terms of the statute, appealed. The Court of Appeals panel by a vote of 2 to 1 rejected that claim. 470 F.3d 964 (C.A.10 2006). Begay sought certiorari, and we agreed to decide the question. . . .

New Mexico's DUI statute makes it a crime (and a felony after three earlier convictions) to "drive a vehicle within [the] state" if the driver "is under the influence of intoxicating liquor" (or has an alcohol concentration of .08 or more in his blood or breath within three hours of having driven the vehicle resulting from "alcohol consumed before or while driving the vehicle"). §§ 66–8–102(A), (C).

In determining whether this crime is a violent felony, we consider the offense generically, that is to say, we examine it in terms of how the law defines the offense and not in terms of how an individual offender might have committed it on a particular occasion. . . .

We also take as a given that DUI does not fall within the scope of the Act's *clause (i)* "violent felony" definition. DUI, as New Mexico defines it, nowhere "has as an element the use, attempted use, or threatened use of physical force against the person of another." 18 U.S.C. § 924(e)(2)(B)(i).

Finally, we assume that the lower courts were right in concluding that DUI involves conduct that "presents a serious potential risk of physical injury to another." § 924(e)(2)(B)(ii). Drunk driving is an extremely dangerous crime. In the United States in 2006, alcohol-related motor vehicle crashes claimed the lives of more than 17,000 individuals and harmed untold amounts of property. Even so, we find that DUI falls outside the scope of clause (ii). It is simply too unlike the provision's listed examples for us to believe that Congress intended the provision to cover it.

In our view, the provision's listed examples—burglary, arson, extortion, or crimes involving the use of explosives—illustrate the kinds of crimes that fall within the statute's scope. Their presence indicates that the statute covers only *similar* crimes, rather than *every* crime that "presents a serious potential risk of physical injury to another." § 924(e)(2)(B)(ii). If Congress meant the latter, *i.e.,* if it meant the statute to be all encompassing, it is hard to see why it would have needed to include the examples at all. Without them, clause (ii) would cover *all* crimes that present a "serious potential risk of physical injury." *Ibid.* Additionally, if Congress meant clause (ii) to include *all* risky crimes, why would it have included clause (i)? A crime which has as an element the "use, attempted use, or threatened use of physical force" against the person (as clause (i) specifies) is likely to create "a serious potential risk of physical injury" and would seem to fall within the scope of clause (ii). . . .

In our view, DUI differs from the example crimes—burglary, arson, extortion, and crimes involving the use of explosives—in at least one pertinent, and important, respect. The listed crimes all typically involve purposeful, "violent," and "aggressive" conduct. 470 F.3d, at 980 (McConnell, J., dissenting in part); see, *e.g., Taylor, supra,* at 598, 110 S.Ct. 2143 ("burglary" is an unlawful or unprivileged entry into a building or other structure with "intent to commit a crime"); ALI Model Penal Code § 220.1(1) (1985) ("arson" is causing a fire or explosion with "the purpose of," *e.g.,* "destroying a building . . . of another" or "damaging any property . . . to collect insurance"); *id.,* § 223.4 (extortion is "purposely" obtaining property of another through threat of, *e.g.,* inflicting "bodily injury"); *Leocal, supra,* at 9, 125 S.Ct. 377 (the word " 'use' . . . most naturally suggests a higher degree of intent than negligent or merely accidental conduct" which fact helps bring it outside the scope of the statutory term "crime of violence"). That conduct is such that it makes more likely that an offender, later possessing a gun, will use that gun deliberately to harm a victim. Crimes committed in such a purposeful, violent, and aggressive manner are "potentially more dangerous when firearms are involved." 470 F.3d, at 980 (McConnell, J., dissenting in part). And such crimes are "characteristic of the armed career criminal, the eponym of the statute." *Ibid.*

By way of contrast, statutes that forbid driving under the influence, such as the statute before us, typically do not insist on purposeful, violent, and aggressive conduct; rather, they are, or are most nearly comparable to, crimes that impose strict liability, criminalizing conduct in respect to which the offender need not have had any criminal intent at all. The Government argues that "the knowing nature of the conduct that produces intoxication combined with the inherent recklessness of the ensuing conduct more than suffices" to create an element of intent. Brief for United States 35. And we agree with the Government that a drunk driver may very well drink on purpose. But this Court has said that, unlike the example crimes, the conduct for which the drunk driver is convicted (driving under the influence) need not be purposeful or deliberate. See *Leocal, supra,* at 11, 125 S.Ct. 377 (a DUI offense involves "accidental or negligent conduct"); see also 470 F.3d, at 980 (McConnell, J., dissenting in part) ("[D]runk driving is a crime of negligence or recklessness, rather than violence or aggression").

When viewed in terms of the Act's basic purposes, this distinction matters considerably. As suggested by its title, the Armed Career Criminal Act focuses upon the special danger created when a particular type of offender—a violent criminal or drug trafficker—possesses a gun. See *Taylor, supra,* at 587–588, 110 S.Ct. 2143; 470 F.3d, at 981, n. 3 (McConnell, J., dissenting in part) ("[T]he title [of the Act] was not merely decorative"). In order to determine which offenders fall into this category, the Act looks to past crimes. This is because an offender's criminal history is relevant to the question whether he is a career criminal, or, more precisely, to the kind or degree of danger the offender would pose were he to possess a gun.

In this respect—namely, a prior crime's relevance to the possibility of future danger with a gun—crimes involving intentional or purposeful conduct (as in burglary and arson) are different from DUI, a strict-liability crime. In both instances, the offender's prior crimes reveal a degree of callousness toward risk, but in the former instance they also show an increased likelihood that the offender is the kind of person who might deliberately point the gun and pull the trigger. We have no reason to believe that Congress intended a 15-year mandatory prison term where that increased likelihood does not exist.

Were we to read the statute without this distinction, its 15-year mandatory minimum sentence would apply to a host of crimes which, though dangerous, are not typically committed by those whom one normally labels "armed career criminals." See, *e.g.,* Ark.Code Ann. § 8–4–103(a)(2)(A)(ii) (2007) (reckless polluters); 33 U.S.C. § 1319(c)(1) (individuals who negligently introduce pollutants into the sewer system); 18 U.S.C. § 1365(a) (individuals who recklessly tamper with consumer products); § 1115 (seamen whose inattention to duty causes serious accidents). We have no reason to believe that Congress intended to bring within the statute's scope these kinds of crimes, far removed as they are from the deliberate kind of behavior associated with violent criminal use of firearms. The statute's use of examples (and the other considerations we have mentioned) indicate the contrary. . . .

EXERCISE

Imagine that you are a lobbyist for an anti-drunk driving group. You are tasked with the job of convincing Congress to expressly define drunk driving as a crime of violence. What are your best arguments? What counter-arguments do you anticipate?

B. ROBBERY

Though it is sometimes classified as a property crime, robbery has as an essential element the use or threat of force. Generally, the elements of robbery will consist of the following (plus a federal jurisdiction element, such as the federal insurance of a bank, in federal cases):

1) Identification of the defendant,

2) The use of force or the threat of force

3) To take the property of another from the person or presence of the victim

4) With the intent of depriving the victim of that property.

Though most robberies lack a federal nexus, there are significant exceptions. Most notably, bank robberies are often taken as federal crimes, though they are also illegal under state laws.

In some bank robbery cases, the question of whether force or the threat of force was used can raise interesting questions, particularly where a threat is not clear or specific.

UNITED STATES V. BURNLEY

533 F. 3d 901 (7th Cir. 2008)

WOOD, CIRCUIT JUDGE.

Walter Burnley was convicted after a jury trial on four counts of bank robbery, 18 U.S.C. § 2113(a), and was sentenced to a total of 262 months' imprisonment. On appeal, Burnley argues that the Government failed to prove that either he or his accomplice used force or intimidation to obtain the stolen money, and thus that three of his convictions should be overturned. We conclude that the jury was entitled to find intimidation under the circumstances of this case and affirm.

On April 25, 2006, Burnley entered a branch of Associated Bank in Beloit, Wisconsin, clad in a baseball cap pulled low over his eyes, with safety goggles placed over a pair of sunglasses. At the time, Burnley was 33 years old, 5'8" tall, and approximately 220 pounds. After waiting his turn in line, Burnley reached the lone teller and pulled out a purse. According to the teller, Burnley then leaned toward her and said, "Fill the bag and do not give me the dye pack." The frightened teller put $4,661 in the purse and, as Burnley had instructed, omitted the dye pack. Burnley then fled.

Two weeks later, on May 9, Burnley (again using his safety goggles) visited a different branch of Associated Bank in Beloit. This time when he reached the teller, he told her not to "do anything stupid" and warned that he would kill her if she gave him a dye pack or bait bills. He then pushed a black bag toward her, and she filled the bag with $1,514 in unmarked bills.

That evening Burnley met Lisa Harding, a 20-year-old crack addict, through a mutual friend. Two days later, on May 12, Burnley enlisted Harding to rob a branch of Anchor Bank in Janesville, Wisconsin. Harding, who also was charged but wound up testifying for the government, entered the bank at Burnley's direction and ordered a teller to "put all of your money in this bag but no dye pack." When the teller appeared confused, Harding, a woman of slight build, repeated the demand louder and "a little more forcefully." This teller also complied, giving her $2,069 without a dye pack. Harding then departed.

Four days after that, on May 16, Burnley and Harding arranged for another robbery, which was to be their last. The target was a branch of the First National Bank in Beloit. This time, both of them entered the bank. Burnley, whose face was concealed by a painter's mask, stood back near the door while Harding approached the teller's window and said, "I need you to do me a favor, I need you to put all the money in the bag." After the bag was full, Harding confirmed with the teller that there was no dye pack in the bag and apologized for making her "so nervous." Burnley and Harding left the bank with $2,472.

The statute under which Burnley was convicted defines "bank robbery" as using "force and violence, or intimidation" to take bank funds from an employee. See 18 U.S.C. § 2113(a). Burnley does not dispute that he did all of these things during the second robbery, but now he argues that during the other three holdups he and Harding did not use force or do or say anything that amounted to "intimidation." Instead, he points out that either he or Harding simply demanded money, got it, and left. Under no objective standard, he claims, could one say that the government demonstrated that the tellers were put in fear. Our consideration of this argument is heavily influenced by the procedural posture in which it reaches us. Burnley did not move for a judgment of acquittal on this or any other basis. See FED.R.CRIM.P. 29. Furthermore, he did not raise this argument in any other way before the district court. Our review of the jury's verdict is thus only for plain error. We will reverse only if the convictions "amounted to a manifest miscarriage of justice," *United States v. Rock,* 370 F.3d 712, 714 (7th Cir.2004) (quotation marks and citation omitted).

These were not violent robberies, and so the government did not rely on the "force" or "violence" options provided by § 2113(a). Instead, it recognized that it had to prove that Burnley and Harding used "intimidation" to take the banks' money. We have defined intimidation under § 2113(a) as "saying or doing something in such a way as would place a reasonable person in fear." *United States v. Clark,* 227 F.3d 771, 775 (7th Cir.2000) (quotation marks, brackets, and citation omitted). Intimidation "exists in situations where the defendant's 'conduct and words were calculated to create the impression that any resistance or defiance by the teller would be met with force.'" *Id.* (quoting *United States v. Jones,* 932 F.2d 624, 625 (7th Cir.1991)). The intimidation element is satisfied if an ordinary person would reasonably feel threatened under the circumstances. *United States v. Hill,* 187 F.3d 698, 702 (7th Cir.1999). How the teller who encountered the defendant felt at the time is "probative of whether a reasonable person would have been afraid under the same circumstances," *id.,* even though the ultimate standard is an objective one. The defendant does not have to make an explicit threat or even announce that he is there to rob the bank. Credibly implying that a refusal to comply with a demand for money will be met with more forceful measures is enough. See, *e.g., United States v. Kelley,* 412 F.3d 1240, 1244–45 (11th Cir.2005); *United States v. Gilmore,* 282 F.3d 398, 402–03 (6th Cir.2002); *Clark,* 227 F.3d at 775; *Hill,* 187 F.3d at 701; *United States v. McCarty,* 36 F.3d 1349, 1357 (5th Cir.1994); *United States v. Hummasti,* 986 F.2d 337, 338 (9th Cir.1993); *United States v. Smith,* 973 F.2d 603, 604–05 (8th Cir.1992); *United States v. Henson,* 945 F.2d 430, 439–40 (1st Cir.1991).

Our recent cases illustrate the point. In *Clark* the defendant entered the bank and slid a note to the teller instructing her to "remain calm and place all of your twenties, fifties, and hundred dollar bills on the counter and act normal for the next fifteen minutes." When the confused teller did not respond, the defendant clarified, "Yes, Ma'am, this is a holdup." 227 F.3d at 773. On appeal we held that the defendant's command that the teller "give him money not belonging to him" could constitute intimidation. *Id.* at 775. Similarly, in *Hill* the defendant said to the teller, "Give me all your money," adding that he did not want any of her "funny money." He then barked, "Hurry up, hurry up, bitch." 187 F.3d at 699–700. That was enough to constitute intimidation even though the defendant maintained that a reasonable person should not have been frightened because he was of medium height and build, did not carry a weapon, and spoke softly. *Id.* at 701–02.

This case is no different. Newly appointed appellate counsel criticizes the government for failing to elicit more evidence about how the tellers reacted to the demands received from Burnley and Harding, but the record is underdeveloped because her predecessor, during opening and closing arguments, conceded that robberies had been committed. Had these arguments been preserved, we would have a better record on which to decide where the objective line lies between intimidating conduct that violates § 2113(a) and statements that fall short of intimidation, because of their sheer implausibility or other reasons why the listener would not be frightened. But, assuming generously that counsel's statements conceding the robberies did not amount to waiver (which would preclude review altogether), see *United States v. Rusan,* 460 F.3d 989, 993–94 (8th Cir.2006); *United States v. Bentson,* 947 F.2d 1353, 1356 (9th Cir.1991), these points have been forfeited. The record adequately shows that in each of the three contested robberies, Burnley or Harding conveyed to the teller a demand for the bank's money and made it clear that the teller was not to put a dye pack or bait bills in with the currency. The tellers understood from the words and context that these were not polite requests that could be ignored, they felt compelled to comply, and there was some evidence that they experienced fear or nervousness. That is enough, under the plain-error standard that applies in this case, to uphold Burnley's convictions.

EXERCISE

Describe at least two possible mistakes made by the defense attorney at trial in the *Burnley* case.

Which of the robberies described in the *Burnley* case involved the least convincing proof of intimidation?

Where physical force or threat is not emphasized or cleanly shown, the violent crime of robbery may look similar to non-violent crimes including burglary and extortion. The sorting-out often takes place at sentencing rather than trial or plea. In the federal system, the sentencing guidelines sometimes contain enhancement factors for crimes such as theft where there was "the conscious or reckless risk of death or serious bodily injury" present,[1] but the case was not taken as a robbery. This deferral to sentencing of "gray-area" factors is fairly common, and other instances of this dynamic will arise as we move forward in studying other areas of criminal law.

UNITED STATES V. WILLIAMS
841 F. 3d 656 (4th Cir. 2016)

FLOYD, CIRCUIT JUDGE:

Ernest Lee Williams, Jr., was charged with attempting to enter a bank with the intent to commit a felony affecting it, and a larceny, all in violation of 18 U.S.C. § 2113(a). Williams pleaded guilty to the charge, and was then sentenced under the robbery guideline, U.S.S.G § 2B3.1. Williams appeals his sentence, arguing that the robbery guideline is inapplicable in this case because his indictment contained no mention of the robbery element of force and violence, intimidation, or extortion. We agree with Williams, and we therefore vacate his sentence and remand this matter for resentencing.

I.

On January 21, 2014, Williams approached a Southern Bank building (the "Bank") in Rocky Mount, North Carolina, while wearing gloves and covering his face in a hood. Williams entered the Bank's exterior doors into an anteroom, but before he could enter past the interior doors, a teller who believed she recognized Williams from a previous robbery locked both the interior and exterior doors. The teller then asked Williams through an intercom whether Williams had an account with the Bank, and Williams replied that he did, but that he had left his bank card in his car. The teller unlocked the exterior doors, and instructed Williams to use the drive-up window. Williams returned to his car, but then drove off.

The police were notified and given a description of Williams's vehicle. The police stopped Williams shortly thereafter, and in a show-up, Williams was identified by a Bank employee as the person who had tried to enter earlier. After being read his rights, Williams admitted to the police that—in need of money—he cased the Bank, and then wore gloves and covered part of his face. He had neither a gun nor a note with him when he tried to enter the Bank. Williams insisted that he had simply planned to tell the bank tellers to put the Bank's money in his bag.

On August 27, 2014, a federal grand jury in the Eastern District of North Carolina indicted Williams for violating 18 U.S.C. § 2113(a). In relevant part, the grand jury charged Williams with "attempt[ing] to enter a bank . . . with the intent to commit in such bank a felony affecting such bank, in

---

[1]　United States Sentencing Guideline § 2B1.1(b)(15)(A).

violation of a statute of the United States, and a larceny, all in violation of Title 18, United States Code, Section 2113(a)." J.A. 7. On January 6, 2015, Williams pleaded guilty to the charge.

Violations of § 2113(a) are potentially covered by four Sentencing Guideline sections—of relevance here are U.S.S.G. § 2B3.1 (Robbery) and § 2B2.1 (Burglary). Following the plea, the probation officer calculated Williams's imprisonment range under the Guidelines by using the robbery guideline, U.S.S.G. § 2B3.1. Specifically, the probation officer calculated Williams's imprisonment range at 37 to 46 months. This range derived from a total offense level of 19 and a criminal history category of III. Section 2B3.1 provided a base offense level of 20, which was increased by two levels because Williams's crime targeted a financial institution. See U.S.S.G § 2B3.1(b)(1). The resulting offense level of 22 was then reduced by three levels for acceptance of responsibility, resulting in a final offense level of 19.

Williams objected to the application of U.S.S.G. § 2B3.1 to his offense. Williams contended that the indictment to which he pleaded guilty described an attempted burglary, not an attempted robbery, because it did not reference force or violence. Thus, as between the two relevant guidelines that could apply to a violation of § 2113(a)—the robbery guideline and the burglary guideline—Williams insisted that he should be sentenced under the latter. Williams reasoned that if the burglary guideline was used, his total offense level would be 10, which in this case would yield an imprisonment range of only 10 to 16 months.

The probation officer, meanwhile, contended that the robbery guideline applied in this case, because it—unlike the burglary guideline—contained an enhancement accounting for the fact that Williams targeted a financial institution.

On April 8, 2015, Williams's sentencing hearing took place. After hearing both sides' arguments, the district court was convinced that the robbery guideline was appropriate in this case because it addressed the targeting of financial institutions. The district court found Williams's imprisonment range under the robbery guideline to be 37 to 46 months, and sentenced him to a term of 38 months. This appeal followed.

II.

On appeal, Williams contends that his sentence should have been calculated using the burglary guideline, rather than the robbery guideline. We review challenges to the district court's guideline selection de novo. United States v. Davis, 202 F.3d 212, 218 (4th Cir. 2000). We agree with Williams that the district court's selection of the robbery guideline was erroneous, because only the burglary guideline applies here.

A.

The Sentencing Guidelines direct a sentencing court to "[d]etermine the offense guideline section . . . applicable to the offense of conviction." U.S.S.G. § 1B1.2(a). At times, however, "the offense of conviction 'appears to fall under the express terms of more than one guideline [.]' " United States v. Boulware, 604 F.3d 832, 836 (4th Cir. 2010) (brackets omitted) (quoting United States v. Lambert, 994 F.2d 1088, 1092 (4th Cir. 1993)). In such cases, "the sentencing court must choose the guideline that is 'most applicable' by comparing the guideline texts with the charged misconduct, rather than the statute (which may outlaw a variety of conduct implicating several guidelines) or the actual conduct (which may include factors not elements of the indicted offense)." Id. (emphasis added) (internal quotation marks and brackets omitted) (quoting Lambert, 994 F.2d at 1092).

The charge that Williams pleaded guilty to plainly describes an attempted burglary, not an attempted robbery. Williams was charged with a violation of § 2113(a), which provides:

> Whoever, by force and violence, or by intimidation, takes, or attempts to take, from the person or presence of another, or obtains or attempts to obtain by extortion any property or money or any other thing of value belonging to, or in the care, custody, control, management, or possession of, any bank . . .; or

> Whoever enters or attempts to enter any bank . . ., or any building used in whole or in part as a bank . . ., with intent to commit in such bank . . ., or part thereof, so used, any felony affecting such bank . . . and in violation of any statute of the United States, or any larceny—

> Shall be fined under this title or imprisoned not more than twenty years, or both.

18 U.S.C. § 2113(a). "As its text makes clear, subsection 2113(a) can be violated in two distinct ways: (1) bank robbery, which involves taking or attempting to take from a bank by force [and violence], intimidation, or extortion; and (2) bank burglary, which simply involves entry or attempted entry into a bank with the intent to commit a crime therein." United States v. Almeida, 710 F.3d 437, 440 (1st Cir. 2013)(emphasis added).

Williams was indicted for attempting to enter a bank with an intent to commit a felony and larceny therein—i.e., a bank burglary. Moreover, his indictment failed to reference "the element of 'force and violence, or [extortion or] intimidation' which is required for conviction of bank robbery" under § 2113(a). United States v. Ketchum, 550 F.3d 363, 365 n.1 (4th Cir. 2008) (quoting United States v. Carter, 540 F.2d 753, 754 (4th Cir. 1976)). Therefore, when one compares the applicable burglary and robbery guidelines with the language of Williams's indictment, it is clear that Williams should have been sentenced under the burglary guideline.

B.

In selecting the robbery guideline over the burglary guideline, the district court stressed that only the robbery guideline contained an enhancement for the targeting of financial institutions (the "Bank Enhancement") like the one Williams targeted. The government defends this selection by citing two unpublished Fourth Circuit cases that justified the use of the robbery guideline for a § 2113(a) violation on the basis of the Bank Enhancement: United States v. Sutton, 401 Fed.Appx. 845 (4th Cir. 2010) (per curiam), and United States v. Johnson, 68 Fed.Appx. 402 (4th Cir. 2003) (per curiam). Because those cases do not justify imposing a robbery guideline-based sentence on a defendant that only pleaded guilty to an attempted burglary, the district court's selection was erroneous.

To begin, Johnson is distinguishable. Johnson held that where an indictment for violating § 2113(a) charges an attempt to obtain property from a bank via extortion, the robbery guideline is more appropriate than the extortion guideline because only the robbery guideline "permits an enhancement for attempting to obtain money from a bank." 68 Fed.Appx. at 405. In Johnson, however, the indictment charged the elements of both robbery and extortion, id. and so the Bank Enhancement merely functioned as a sensible tie-breaker between the robbery and extortion guidelines. In contrast, only the burglary guideline applies in this case, because Williams's indictment omits the robbery element of force and violence, intimidation, or extortion. As such, Johnson provides no sanction for the district court's use of the inapplicable robbery guideline.

Sutton is distinguishable for similar reasons. As in Johnson, a panel of this Court in Sutton relied on the Bank Enhancement in selecting the robbery guideline over an alternative guideline (there, the burglary guideline) to sentence a defendant convicted of violating § 2113(a). Sutton, 401 Fed.Appx. at 847–48. But as in Johnson, the panel in Sutton was satisfied that the indictment at issue actually described "robberies." Id. at 848. Because Williams's indictment cannot be read to describe even an attempted robbery, the government's reliance on Sutton here is misplaced.

C.

In this case, the precedent we find most instructive is this Court's published decision in Boulware. There, the indictment charged the defendant with making a false statement to a bankruptcy court via nondisclosure of prior bankruptcies; however, the indictment did not charge that the nondisclosure was part of a plan to defraud creditors. Boulware, 604 F.3d at 835–36. This Court reasoned that the perjury guideline should apply, rather than the fraud guideline, because the perjury guideline best fit the offense described in the indictment. Id. at 836. It so held despite the objecting party's observation that the fraud guideline contained a specific offense characteristic referencing bankruptcy proceedings, while the perjury guideline lacked any analogous provision.

Id. This Court dismissed that observation as being "of little consequence," reasoning that the fraud guideline was unfitting where "the gravamen of the charge was that [the defendant] interfered with the bankruptcy court's administration of justice, not that she defrauded any creditors." Id.

Likewise, the robbery guideline's use of the Bank Enhancement is of little consequence here, because the gravamen of Williams's charge was that he attempted to commit a burglary, not a robbery. Simply put, where an indictment omits an element of an offense, the guideline corresponding to that offense is inapplicable, even if the alternative guideline's provisions do not account for certain details that the indictment charges. . . .

III.

For the foregoing reasons, we vacate Williams's sentence, and remand this case to the district court for resentencing under the burglary guideline.

EXERCISE

Leona is desperate for money and resolves to rob a bank. She composes a demand note, which reads "Give me all the money! Put it in a bag! If you do not give me all of the money in your drawer, I will kill you with my gun and my knife, which I have with me." Leona did not have a gun or knife.

Going forward with her plan, Leona enters the bank and goes up to a teller window. The teller, however, has stepped away. Leona looks around, and sees several bound stacks of $20 bills on the counter on the other side of the teller window. She scoops them up, puts them in the bag, and leaves. No one notices. She is later caught based on the bank video (it turns out a security worker there knows Leona and was able to identify her).

You are the prosecutor in Leona's case. Will you seek an indictment for bank robbery from the Grand Jury?

A primary defense in many robbery trials centers on the element of identification, particularly where the robber took significant measures to conceal identity.

UNITED STATES V. STOKES
631 F. 3d 802 (6th Cir. 2011)

Stokes was indicted for robbing three Memphis banks with the use of a firearm. A jury ultimately found him guilty of two of the robberies, both of the same branch of Trust One Bank. In all three robberies, the perpetrator entered the bank wearing a mask or hat and carrying a pillowcase with a heavy object in the bottom. Witnesses in each robbery described the perpetrator as a dark-skinned male, between 5'11" and 6' tall, and between

200 and 250 pounds. In the last of the three robberies (of which Stokes was not convicted) the robber fired a shot inside a branch of the Regions Bank. The police did not release information about the shot to the media.

The robberies were investigated by members of the Memphis Police Department's Safe Streets Task Force. Stokes came to the investigators' attention after a police informant led officers to Stokes's co-defendant, Casanyl Valentine, who was trying to sell dye-stained cash in the Memphis area.

Because cash taken in the robberies had been given to the robber with dye packs that would later explode, investigators believed the person selling the cash would have information about the crimes. Officers arrested Valentine, who did not meet the physical description of the perpetrator in the three robberies. Valentine told the officers that he hired people to carry out bank robberies for him. Valentine gave officers details of the three robberies, describing the location and procedure of each, and mentioning that a shot had been fired in one robbery.

Valentine told police that all three robberies had been carried out by Stokes. Investigators then pulled a booking photo of Stokes and compared it to a surveillance photo from one of the robberies. The officers concluded that the photos matched. They also showed the booking photo to Valentine, who confirmed that it depicted the person he had hired to carry out the robberies. . . .

At trial, the Government called four witnesses: Sarah Britt, a Trust One teller who had been present during both of that branch's robberies; Justin Levick, an assistant vice-president of Trust One; FBI Special Agent Kay; and Teresa Thomas, a teller who was present during the robbery of Regions Bank. Britt and Kay both provided testimony relevant to the identity of the Trust One robber. In particular, Kay testified regarding Stokes's confession to the crimes.

On appeal, Stokes claims that there was insufficient evidence presented at trial to support his conviction. More specifically, Stokes contends that the evidence does not "sustain a finding that [Stokes] committed the crimes in question." This claim is unavailing because the jury could reasonably rely on the testimony of Sarah Britt and on the evidence of Stokes's own confession to conclude that Stokes was the robber. *See United States v. Lawrence,* 391 Fed.Appx. 480, 483 (6th Cir.2010).

Stokes's brief presents several arguments for why Britt's identification was not reliable. However, Britt's testimony provided the jury with several reasonable grounds for relying on her identification. Therefore, taking the evidence in the light most favorable to the prosecution, Britt's testimony could support a reasonable jury's finding that Stokes carried out the Trust One robberies. *See Jackson v. Virginia,* 443 U.S. 307, 319, 99 S.Ct. 2781, 61 L.Ed.2d 560 (1979).

Stokes identifies the following weaknesses in Britt's identification: the robber's face was covered during the first robbery and partially obscured by sunglasses in the second; Britt testified that she knew it was the same man in both robberies only from his voice, but she had not heard his voice since the robberies; Britt identified someone other than Stokes as resembling the robber in a photographic line up she was shown in the weeks following the robbery (this line up did not contain a photo of Stokes); the robbery was a very stressful and short experience for Britt, thereby decreasing the credibility of her recollection; roughly two years had elapsed since the bank robberies at the time Britt identified Stokes in the courtroom; and Stokes was the only person in the courtroom who could come close to matching the robber's physical description. However, Stokes acknowledges that Britt's testimony was not tainted by any constitutional violation, and his attorney was able to point out each of these weaknesses during cross examination.

Further, Britt's testimony provided the jury with ample grounds for relying on Britt's identification to conclude that Stokes had committed the robberies. Britt detailed the robberies at some length, and stated that she had walked the robber from drawer to drawer in the bank and followed him as he left the branch in order to read the license plate numbers of the getaway vehicles. She also testified that she was able to see the robber's face during the second robbery, and that it was clearly the same man who had previously robbed the bank based on his voice alone. Britt also stated that the two robberies were carried out in a similar fashion, further supporting her testimony that the same perpetrator committed both crimes. This testimony, taken in the light most favorable to the government, supports the conclusion that Stokes committed the robberies.

———————

EXERCISE

Should it matter that Britt, the witness-teller, made a false identification in the photographic lineup? What arguments could a defense attorney base on this fact for use in closing?

C. ASSAULT

Like many jurisdictions, the federal system has different culpability levels for assault ranging from simple assault (which can be a misdemeanor)[2] to aggravated assault that involves weapons and/or injury.[3]

Simple assault does not require physical contact, but just the threat of injury. In many jurisdictions, assault statutes cover what was traditionally

———————

[2]   18 U.S.C. § 111(a).

[3]   18 U.S.C. § 111(b).

defined as "battery." Battery (a word related to "battering") traditionally was the crime of harmfully using physical force against another person. Modern assault statutes incorporate both physical contact-based battery and causing the fear of such physical contact, and many jurisdictions no longer refer to "battery" in their criminal codes.

"Simple assault" has been defined as "either a willful attempt to inflict injury upon the person of another, or by a threat to inflict injury upon the person of another which, when coupled with an apparent present ability, causes a reasonable apprehension of immediate bodily harm."[4] The distinction between simple assault and a more serious version, traditional battery, can sometimes be more difficult than you might expect.

Based on that definition, the elements of a simple assault (in addition to jurisdictional elements) would typically be:

1) Identification of the defendant as the actor,

2) That the defendant either

    a) attempted to inflict injury on another, or

    b) Made a threat to inflict injury, and

3) That the action or threat caused a reasonable apprehension of immediate bodily harm.

This last element is unusual in that it refers to the state of mind of the *victim*, rather than the offender.

Because simple assault is a misdemeanor under federal law, and thus subject to a one-year term of imprisonment at most, the dividing line between simple assault and other forms of assault can be very important.

UNITED STATES V. VALLERY
437 F. 3d 626 (7th Cir. 2006)

KANNE, CIRCUIT JUDGE.

The government appeals from the district court's sentencing of Roosevelt Vallery as a misdemeanant following his conviction under 18 U.S.C. § 111(a). It is the government's contention that the indictment properly alleged a felony rather than a misdemeanor. Vallery's conviction is not in dispute. A fair reading of the statute requires us to conclude that the misdemeanor provision of § 111(a) applies to all conduct prohibited by the subsection. Having determined that Vallery's conviction was for a misdemeanor, we affirm his twelve-month sentence. . . .

The criminal statute involved in this case is 18 U.S.C. § 111. It provides:

    (a) In general.—Whoever—

---

[4] United States v. Joe, 831 F. 2d 218, 220 (10th Cir. 1987).

(1) forcibly assaults, resists, opposes, impedes, intimidates, or interferes with any person designated in section 1114 of this title while engaged in or on account of the performance of official duties; or

(2) forcibly assaults or intimidates any person who formerly served as a person designated in section 1114 on account of the performance of official duties during such person's term of service, shall, where the acts in violation of this section constitute only simple assault, be fined under this title or imprisoned not more than one year, or both, and in all other cases, be fined under this title or imprisoned not more than 8 years, or both.

(b) Enhanced penalty.—Whoever, in the commission of any acts described in subsection (a), uses a deadly or dangerous weapon (including a weapon intended to cause death or danger but that fails to do so by reason of a defective component) or inflicts bodily injury, shall be fined under this title or imprisoned not more than 20 years, or both.

The designation in 18 U.S.C. § 1114 includes federal corrections officers. Correctional Officer Ron Garver was employed at the Federal Correctional Institution in Greenville, Illinois. On July 24, 2003, he was instructed to escort Roosevelt Vallery, an inmate, to the lieutenant's office. Garver found Vallery in the food services area and told Vallery to come with him to the lieutenant's office. Garver escorted Vallery alone and unrestrained. Garver noticed Vallery growing increasingly nervous and evasive as they approached the lieutenant's office, so Garver directed Vallery into a restroom to strip search him for contraband.

As Vallery removed his clothes, his apprehension intensified. When Vallery got to his underwear, Vallery pushed Garver out of his way and ran into an empty toilet stall. Garver followed Vallery into the stall and repeatedly yelled for Vallery to stop. When Garver entered the stall, he saw Vallery remove an object from his underwear and throw it into the toilet. Garver attempted to prevent Vallery from flushing the item by placing his arm around Vallery's neck and shoulder and pulling back. Vallery backed Garver into the stall to break Garver's hold and then flushed the item.

During the melee, Garver used his free hand to radio for help. Other officers soon arrived, handcuffed Vallery, and placed him in a special housing unit. Garver received minor injuries during the struggle and his uniform was ripped; Vallery was unharmed. Vallery later told investigators that the contraband he flushed down the toilet was a shank.

The facts described above were presented to a federal grand jury in the Southern District of Illinois. The grand jury returned the following one-count indictment:

THE GRAND JURY CHARGES:

On or about July 24, 2003, in Bond County, Illinois, in the Southern District of Illinois,

ROOSEVELT D. VALLERY,

defendant herein, did knowingly and forcibly assault, resist, impede, and interfere with Ron Garver, a Federal Correctional Officer, while he was engaged in his official duties, to wit: conducting a visual search and restraining a federal inmate attempting to dispose of contraband, in violation of Title 18, United States Code, Sections [sic] 111(a)(1).

A jury trial ensued. Vallery objected to the government's proposed jury instruction on non-simple assault arguing that because the government did not allege physical force in the indictment, Vallery had only been charged with simple assault, a misdemeanor offense. The district court agreed and refused to give the government's proposed felony instruction.

A verdict form was submitted to the jury which contained two blanks. Under the first blank was typed "(Guilty/Not Guilty)" and under the second blank was typed "(assaulting, resisting, impeding or interfering with)". The judge explained to the jury that it should determine whether Vallery was guilty or not guilty and enter that determination in the first blank. The judge further explained that if the determination was guilty, the specific conduct that the jury found Vallery committed should be entered in the second blank. The jury returned a guilty verdict and wrote the words "resisting, impeding, interfering with" on the special verdict form.

Following Vallery's conviction, the probation officer concluded in the presentence report ("PSR") that Vallery had been convicted of a felony offense subject to a statutory maximum term of imprisonment of up to eight years. The PSR's calculation of Vallery's sentencing guideline range was 51–63 months' imprisonment. Vallery objected, arguing that he had only been convicted of a simple assault and was therefore subject to the one-year maximum sentence. Finding that Vallery was charged only with a misdemeanor, the district court imposed a sentence of twelve months' imprisonment. . . .

[W]e first address the government's argument that Vallery's indictment did allege physical contact. If so, then there is no need for us to deal with the meaning of § 111. But as it was raised for the first time at oral argument, this argument is waived. In any event, we reject the government's premise that all "restrainings" necessarily involve physical contact and conclude the indictment did not allege physical contact.

We now turn to the same statutory issue as was twice before the district court—that is, whether Vallery's indictment, which did not allege physical contact, charged him under § 111 with a felony or a misdemeanor. Section

111 is designed to protect certain federal officers and employees of the United States performing their official duties by criminalizing assaults against them. *United States v. Feola,* 420 U.S. 671, 678–84, 95 S.Ct. 1255, 43 L.Ed.2d 541 (1975). In 1994, Congress added the misdemeanor simple assault provision to § 111(a) by amendment. Violent Crime Control and Law Enforcement Act of 1994, Pub.L. No. 103–322, § 320101(a)(1), 108 Stat. 1796, 2108.

Adhering to *Jones v. United States,* 526 U.S. 227, 119 S.Ct. 1215, 143 L.Ed.2d 311 (1999), several other circuits have found post-1994 amendment § 111 to constitute three separate offenses: first, misdemeanor simple assault under § 111(a); second "all other cases" felony assault under § 111(a); and third, felony assault involving a deadly or dangerous weapon or resulting in bodily injury under § 111(b).

Because Vallery was charged with violating § 111(a) but not § 111(b), only the first two offenses, simple assault and felony "all other cases" assault, are relevant here. The government's argument is that the indictment properly alleged "all other cases" felonious assault by including in its allegations that Vallery resisted, impeded and interfered with Garver, and, therefore, that the district court was wrong to rule that it only alleged simple assault because physical contact was not alleged.

The linchpin in the government's argument is that the "physical contact rule" of felonious assault, in which physical contact is an element of the crime, applies only to the "assault prong" of § 111(a)(1) and not to the other prohibited conduct—namely, resisting, opposing, impeding, intimidating, and interfering with. Therefore, the government concludes, physical contact is not required to rise to the level of a felony for violations of § 111(a) other than "assaults," and its absence in the indictment does not preclude a felony conviction. Vallery, on the other hand, argues that the misdemeanor simple assault provision must be applied to all conduct prohibited by § 111(a)(1). Because we are presented with the issue of statutory interpretation, a question of law, we review de novo. *United States v. Jones,* 372 F.3d 910, 911–12 (7th Cir.2004). . . .

Although not mentioned by either side, we must interpret § 111 taking into account the meaning of the statute as a whole. The government's argument that simple assault applies only to the "assault prong" of § 111(a)(1) makes little sense when considering § 111(a)(2), which punishes one who "assaults or intimidates" a former federal officer. If simple assault did not apply to the remainder of § 111(a)(1), we would be left with two unavailing alternatives before us: either simple assault does not apply to § 111(a)(2) at all; or that the simple assault provision applies only to the word "assault" of §§ 111(a)(1) and (a)(2). The former does little to carry out the purpose of the statute because it would afford greater protection to those without present federal authority by making all assaults against them felonies. The latter would require us to glean an "assault prong" from two subsections and apply the simple assault clause. But without a good reason to do so, we cannot disregard the statutory structure of § 111(a) in this manner, particularly where the text clearly directs that "acts in violation of this *section* constitute only simple assault." *Contra Jones,* 526 U.S. at 239, 119 S.Ct. 1215 (interpreting statute contrary to structure to avoid "grave and doubtful constitutional questions").

Moreover, in addition to the plain language of the statute, case law supports Vallery by stating or implying that the simple assault provision applies to the entirety of § 111(a). . . . Of the remaining cases we reviewed, none referred to the "assault" of § 111(a)(1) as a term of art, as the government advocates, even when discussing the meaning of simple assault.

The government's position further erodes when we consider its practical effects. Because of the overlapping nature of many of the terms, it is difficult to imagine a situation in which one who assaults an officer does not also simultaneously resist, oppose, impede, intimidate, or interfere with that officer. If the misdemeanor provision was as narrow as the government would have us believe, then prosecutors could avoid a lesser-included offense simply by omitting "assault" from the indictment. We cannot assume that it was Congress's intent to amend a statute with no de facto application. We hold the simple assault provision of § 111(a) applies to all violations of § 111(a), not merely to "assaults."

Turning to Vallery's indictment, the language closely follows the language of § 111(a) sufficiently to allege the elements of simple assault. However, physical contact was not explicitly or, as previously discussed, implicitly alleged; therefore, we agree with the district court's conclusion that Vallery was not charged with, and could not be convicted of, "all other assaults." Because Vallery was charged only with a misdemeanor and not a felony, he was subject to a statutory maximum term of imprisonment of only one year, not eight. Neither the government nor Vallery otherwise challenges the reasonableness of Vallery's sentence of twelve months' imprisonment. *See generally United States v. Mykytiuk,* 415 F.3d 606 (7th Cir.2005).

III. CONCLUSION

For the foregoing reasons, the sentence imposed by the district court is AFFIRMED.

EXERCISE

If you were the prosecutor, how could you have drafted the indictment differently so as to avoid the problem raised on appeal?

One of the issues that often comes up with assault is enhancement for the use of a "dangerous weapon." In many jurisdictions, this will elevate the charge to "aggravated assault." Generally, an object can be considered a dangerous weapon in one of two circumstances. First, some objects—most notably, firearms—are designed expressly to be used as dangerous weapons. They are machines designed to inflict injury. Second, nearly any object can be used with the intent to kill, and in these circumstances it is the use of the object, not its design, that categorizes it as a "deadly weapon."

UNITED STATES V. GHOLSTON
932 F. 2d 904 (11th Cir. 1991)

PER CURIAM:

Defendant Ben Gholston brings this appeal from his conviction on a two-count indictment charging him with assault on a federal official and committing such an assault with a dangerous weapon under 18 U.S.C. § 111. . . .

The record shows that the assault in this case occurred when Gholston overturned a desk onto a receptionist at a local office of the Social Security Administration and then hit her in the neck with his hand. Gholston's counsel notes that the district court may have erred in not granting his motion for judgment of acquittal because a desk cannot be considered a "dangerous weapon" within the meaning of section 111. We, however, agree with defense counsel that this argument lacks any merit. "The determination whether an object constitutes a 'dangerous weapon' turns not on the object's latent capability alone, but also on the manner in which the object was used." *United States v. Guilbert,* 692 F.2d 1340, 1343 (11th Cir.1982), *cert. denied,* 460 U.S. 1016, 103 S.Ct. 1260, 75 L.Ed.2d 487 (1983). Thus, we and other courts have found that pool sticks, *see id.* at 1343–44, broken bottles, *see Thornton v. United States,* 268 F.2d 583, 584 (D.C.Cir.1959), and chairs, *see United States v. Johnson,* 324 F.2d 264, 266 (4th Cir.1963) can be considered a dangerous weapon under the appropriate circumstances. In this case, we believe that a jury could have reasonably found that a desk, overturned onto a person, is also a dangerous weapon.

———————————

EXERCISE

In the *Gholson* case, the court notes that the victim was assaulted both with the desk and the defendant's hand. In this situation, do you think a person's hand should independently be considered a deadly weapon? If so, what problems would that raise in other cases?

———————————

Where an aggravated assault is predicated on the use of a dangerous weapon, sometimes that raises tricky issues of intent—including the question of whether the necessary intent was not just to use the object, but to use it as a weapon.

UNITED STATES V. ARRINGTON
309 F. 3d 40 (D.C. Cir. 2002)

GARLAND, CIRCUIT JUDGE:

Defendant Derrek Arrington appeals from his conviction for using a dangerous weapon—to wit, an automobile—to forcibly assault, resist, oppose, impede, intimidate, or interfere with three United States Park Police officers, in violation of 18 U.S.C. § 111(a) and (b). We reject Arrington's contention that the district court plainly erred in instructing the jury, as well as his contention that the evidence presented at trial was insufficient to sustain his conviction.

On May 10, 2000, Arrington was indicted on four counts of violating federal law. Count 1 charged him with using a dangerous weapon to forcibly assault, resist, oppose, impede, intimidate, or interfere with three federal officers engaged in the performance of their duties, in violation of 18 U.S.C. § 111(a) and (b). . . .

According to the government's evidence at trial, the case began on April 13, 2000, when United States Park Police officers Jonathan Daniels, Martin Yates, and Troy Eliason stopped Arrington's car because it lacked a front license plate. As Arrington produced his license and registration, Daniels observed a small ziplock bag with a residue of white powder on the floorboard. Upon Daniels' signal, the three officers retreated to the rear of the car, where Daniels informed them of the suspected drug paraphernalia and of his intention to ask Arrington and his (unidentified) passenger to get out of the car.

The officers then returned to the front of the automobile and asked Arrington to step outside. When Arrington instead reached for the gear shift, Daniels and Eliason reached through the open driver-side door and grabbed him around the upper body, while Yates leaned in from the passenger's side to turn off the ignition. With all three officers still reaching inside the car, and two of them holding onto his body, the defendant shifted into drive and "floored it." 9/14/00 p.m. Tr. at 36. Although Yates was caught by the frame of the car door, he soon extricated himself, as did Eliason. Daniels, however, was dragged by Arrington's car for at least 50 feet, through an intersection, before he was able to free himself and fall to the ground.

All three Park Police officers then returned to their cars and pursued Arrington in what became a high speed chase. Arrington eventually lost control of his car and crashed into a curb, whereupon he fled on foot with the officers in pursuit. Daniels and an off-duty Metropolitan Police Department officer who had joined the chase finally caught up with Arrington. Yates and the off-duty officer testified that, during the ensuing struggle, Arrington shot Daniels in the face with a handgun. Yates and the other officer eventually subdued Arrington and arrested him.

Arrington testified at trial in his own defense, and the story he told of his flight from the traffic stop diverged significantly from that of the officers. Arrington testified that he decided to drive off because he felt threatened by the police. According to the defendant, he never had physical contact with any of the officers, and no officer had any part of his body in the car at the time Arrington drove off. After leading the officers on the car chase, Arrington jumped out of his car and began to run. According to Arrington, two officers caught up with him and wrestled him to the ground. During the struggle, a gun Arrington was carrying in his pocket accidentally discharged, and the bullet hit Officer Daniels.

The jury convicted Arrington on Counts 1 and 4, but deadlocked on Counts 2 and 3—the attempted murder and discharging-a-firearm counts. The latter two counts were retried twice (along with a new, additional count), each trial ending in deadlock. After the third trial, the government dismissed the outstanding counts and the district court sentenced the defendant to 240 months' imprisonment on Counts 1 and 4. Arrington's only challenge here is to his conviction, on Count 1, for violating 18 U.S.C. § 111(a) and (b). . . .

We turn next to the elements of § 111(b), and here, too, find some common ground. Again, the statutory language makes clear that, to qualify under this subsection, the defendant must: (1) use a deadly or dangerous weapon; (2) in the commission of any of the acts described in the prior subsection. In addition, although the language merely states that the defendant must "use[ ]" the weapon, the government agrees—as do we—that: (3) the defendant must use the weapon intentionally. *See* Appellee's Br. at 26. As the Supreme Court stated in *United States v. Feola,* "in order to incur criminal liability under § 111 an actor must entertain . . . the criminal intent to do the acts therein specified," 420 U.S. at 686, 95 S.Ct. at 1264– 65, and the act specified in § 111(b) is the use of a deadly weapon. Accordingly, intent to use the weapon is a necessary element, and a defendant who does so purely by accident does not come within the scope of § 111(b).

We now reach the point of the parties' dispute. The foregoing is sensible enough, Arrington says, when the weapon at issue is one that is inherently deadly, like a gun. But what if the weapon is one that is deadly only if used in a certain manner, like Arrington's car? To this query, the government responds that a distinction between the two kinds of weapons is indeed appropriate. For an object that is not inherently deadly, the government concedes that the following additional element is required: (4) the object must be capable of causing serious bodily injury or death to another person *and* the defendant must use it in that manner. Appellee's Br. at 19; *see United States v. Murphy,* 35 F.3d 143, 147 (4th Cir.1994); 1 LEONARD B. SAND ET AL., MODERN FEDERAL JURY INSTRUCTIONS (CRIMINAL) ¶ 14.01, at 14–25 (2002); 2 KEVIN F. O'MALLEY ET AL., FEDERAL JURY PRACTICE & INSTRUCTIONS (CRIMINAL) § 24.06, at 68, 71 (5th ed.2000). That is, for a car to qualify as a deadly weapon, the defendant must use it as a deadly weapon and not simply as a mode of transportation.

Arrington, however, asks us to add a fifth requirement. It is not enough, he argues, that a defendant intend to use the object; nor is it enough that he actually use the object in a deadly manner. In addition, Arrington contends, the defendant must *intentionally use the object as a weapon.*

We must state at the outset that, in light of the other elements of the (b) offense, we see little practical difference between the positions of the parties. When asked at oral argument to posit a set of circumstances in which adding Arrington's fifth element would make a difference, the government was unable to suggest one. Arrington, for his part, did propose such a scenario: he contended that without the fifth element, a jury could convict a defendant for using a car merely as a means of escape, rather than as a deadly or dangerous weapon. Although the government agrees that the use of a car merely to effectuate an escape would not qualify under the statute, it contends that its construction of § 111(a) and (b) would exclude a conviction for such use. Appellee's Br. at 20–21. We agree. The use of a car purely for flight would not satisfy the fourth element of § 111(b): that the object be used in a deadly or dangerous manner. Nor would Arrington's scenario satisfy the first element of § 111(a), applicable to the (b) offense by incorporation, because it would not involve the element of force.

In the end, however, the decisive question is not whether the element Arrington proposes would make any difference in this or other cases, but whether Congress intended it to be an element of the offense. We discern no evidence of such congressional intent. Arrington's proposed element is certainly not suggested by the language of § 111(b), which simply requires that the defendant "use" a deadly or dangerous weapon in the commission of the acts described in § 111(a). Nor is § 111(b) bereft of a *mens rea* requirement. Conviction requires both the intent to commit one of the acts specified in § 111(a), and the intent to use the object that constitutes the deadly weapon. . . .

Having determined the elements of the § 111(b) offense, we now proceed to Arrington's argument that the district court erroneously instructed the jury as to those elements in two respects. The first of these—Arrington's contention regarding § 111(b)'s dangerous weapon element—is readily dismissed. Although the court instructed that the government had to prove both that Arrington committed one of the acts specified in § 111(a) "while using a deadly or dangerous weapon," and that he "intentionally" used the weapon, 9/18/00 a.m. Tr. at 20–21, Arrington contends that the court should also have required the government to prove that he intentionally used his car as a weapon. Since, as we have just held, that kind of intent is not an element of the offense, the court's failure to so instruct the jury did not constitute error. . . .

Arrington contends that the evidence presented at his trial was insufficient to support his conviction under § 111(b). Our review of such a challenge is limited to determining "whether, after viewing the evidence in the light most favorable to the prosecution, *any* rational trier of fact could have found the essential elements of the crime beyond a reasonable doubt." *Jackson v. Virginia,* 443 U.S. 307, 319, 99 S.Ct. 2781, 2783, 61 L.Ed.2d 560 (1979) (emphasis in original).

Although Arrington does not dispute that the evidence was sufficient to satisfy the requirements of § 111(a), *see* Appellant's Br. at 11; Reply Br. at 3 n.1, he contends that it did not meet the additional requirements of § 111(b). In his view, the evidence "established no more than that [he] used his car to try to flee from the officers." Appellant's Br. at 17. There was, to be sure, evidence from which a reasonable jury could have reached that conclusion: namely, Arrington's own testimony that he had no physical contact with the officers and that no part of any of their bodies was in the car at the time he hit the gas. But we are required to view the evidence in the light most favorable to the prosecution, not the defendant, and from that perspective there is no question that a reasonable juror could have found a violation of § 111(b).

The Park Service officers testified that they reached into Arrington's car and grabbed the defendant around his upper body. At that point, Arrington reached down, put the gearshift into the drive position, and "took off"— throwing two of the officers away from the car and dragging another for at least 50 feet through an intersection. Such testimony was sufficient for a reasonable juror to find that Arrington forcibly assaulted the officers, that he did so intentionally, that he used his car in the commission of that assault, that he used his car intentionally, and that he used the car as a deadly weapon. Nothing more is required to sustain a conviction for violating § 111(b).

EXERCISE

Rutherford B. Larson walked into a bar despite the fact that he was a recovering alcoholic who had (until that night) been sober for three years. That night, as he sat on a barstool with a beer, a man jostled him as he squeezed past. Larson called out to him, but could not get his attention. Then, trying to get the man to come back, he threw a glass bowl of assorted nuts in the man's direction. It hit the man on the head.

You represent Mr. Larson as a federal defender (the bar was on an Army base), and he has been charged with assault with a deadly weapon under 18 U.S.C. § 111(b). You meet with him, and he says that he wanted the bowl to hit the wall and shatter, so the man would turn around; he did not intend to hit the man with it. "If I don't have a good chance at winning, though," he tells you, "I just want to plead guilty to the assault with a deadly weapon charge and tell the court that I'm really sorry. But. . . do you think I have any decent shot at getting acquitted of that charge?"

What do you tell him?

———————

Domestic violence and stalking statutes generally describe a particular kind of assault, as those laws usually prohibit either physically injuring someone or putting them in fear of injury. Importantly, many of these statutes allow for the action element to be fulfilled in others ways, such as through the violation of a protective order or causing emotional distress through harassment. One such statute is found at 18 U.S.C. § 2261A:

Whoever—

(1) travels in interstate or foreign commerce or is present within the special maritime and territorial jurisdiction of the United States, or enters or leaves Indian country, with the intent to kill, injure, harass, intimidate, or place under surveillance with intent to kill, injure, harass, or intimidate another person, and in the course of, or as a result of, such travel or presence engages in conduct that—

> **(A)** places that person in reasonable fear of the death of, or serious bodily injury to—
>
> > **(i)** that person;
> >
> > **(ii)** an immediate family member (as defined in section 115) of that person; or
> >
> > **(iii)** a spouse or intimate partner of that person; or
>
> **(B)** causes, attempts to cause, or would be reasonably expected to cause substantial emotional distress to a person described in clause (i), (ii), or (iii) of subparagraph (A); or

(2) with the intent to kill, injure, harass, intimidate, or place under surveillance with intent to kill, injure, harass, or intimidate another person, uses the mail, any interactive computer service or electronic communication service or electronic communication system of interstate commerce, or any other facility of interstate or foreign commerce to engage in a course of conduct that—

(A) places that person in reasonable fear of the death of or serious bodily injury to a person described in clause (i), (ii), or (iii) of paragraph (1)(A); or

(B) causes, attempts to cause, or would be reasonably expected to cause substantial emotional distress to a person described in clause (i), (ii), or (iii) of paragraph (1)(A),

shall be punished as provided in section 2261(b) of this title.

Cyberstalking is an important and emerging issue that continues to be defined by statutes and courts. Because it can consist of assault or harassment exclusively through the use of words by an unseen person, this form of crime is fundamentally different than the way assault is often envisioned as a bar fight or domestic dispute that becomes violent.

UNITED STATES V. SAYER
748 F.3d 425 (1st Cir. 2014)

LYNCH, CHIEF JUDGE.

This case challenges the constitutionality of the cyberstalking statute, 18 U.S.C. § 2261A. Shawn Sayer pled guilty to one count of cyberstalking and was sentenced to sixty months' imprisonment, the statutory maximum. Sayer appeals, on constitutional grounds, from the district court's denial of his motion to dismiss the cyberstalking charge in the indictment. He also appeals from his sentence, arguing that he was eligible for a downward departure from a Guidelines sentence and so his sentence above the Guidelines range was unreasonable. We affirm.

I.

A. *Factual Background*

The facts are not disputed on appeal.

Sayer and the victim in this case, Jane Doe, had dated in Maine starting some time in 2004 until Jane Doe ended their relationship in January 2006. After their break-up, Sayer persistently stalked and harassed Jane Doe for over four years. At first, Sayer showed up at stores and other places where he knew that Jane Doe would be. In response, Jane Doe changed her routine and gave up activities she loved for fear of seeing Sayer. She also acquired a protection order against him in state court.

Later, in the fall of 2008, Sayer started to use the internet to induce anonymous third parties to harass Jane Doe. Specifically, several unknown men came to Jane Doe's house in Maine one day in October 2008 claiming that they had met her online and were seeking "sexual entertainment." Jane Doe was "shock[ed]" and "terrified" by these "dangerous"-looking men and decided to stay with a friend because she no longer felt safe in her home. She later discovered an online ad in the "casual encounters" section of Craigslist, a classified advertisements website, that had pictures of her in lingerie that Sayer had taken while they were dating. The ad gave detailed directions to her home and described a list of sexual acts she was supposedly willing to perform. Jane Doe did not place these ads nor did she authorize Sayer to place them.

The unwanted visits from men seeking sex persisted for eight months until June 2009, when Jane Doe changed her name and moved to her aunt's house in Louisiana to escape from Sayer and this harassment. Jane Doe began a new career and felt safe for a couple of months until August 25, 2009, when an unknown man showed up at her home in Louisiana and addressed her by her new name. Jane Doe said "the hairs on [her] arms stood up," as she had not told anyone except for a neighbor and her parents that she was moving. The man said he had met her online and was seeking a sexual encounter, having seen pictures of her on an adult pornography site. When Jane Doe later searched the internet, she found videos of herself and Sayer engaged in consensual sexual acts from when they were dating on at least three pornography sites. Several of the websites included Jane Doe's name and then-current Louisiana address. One site encouraged viewers to write to Jane Doe and tell her what they thought of the videos.

Jane Doe contacted the police again in late September 2009 because someone had posted a fraudulent account in her name on Facebook, a social networking site, which included sexually explicit pictures of her. The false Facebook account was created on August 21, 2009 from 24 Marion Avenue in Biddeford, Maine, which had an unsecured wireless network; Sayer lived at 23 Marion Avenue. The police found videos of Jane Doe "engaged in sexually explicit activity" that had been posted to adult pornography sites on August 22, 25, and 29, 2009.

On November 5, 2009, the police searched Sayer's home pursuant to a warrant. They found two desktop computers that lacked hard drives and an empty laptop computer case. Sayer said that his computers had been hacked, so he had thrown out the hard drives. He also said he had thrown out his laptop after spilling water on it. The police did not believe him because they had seen "dozens of computer components scattered throughout his house."

The police seized a Nikon digital camera during this search. Although Sayer had said there were no pictures of Jane Doe on it, a forensic analysis of the camera uncovered a picture of Jane Doe in a sexual position and another photo of her engaged in a sex act.

In December 2009, Jane Doe again contacted the police to report another fake profile that had been created under her name on MySpace, another social networking site. The profile had both her old and new names, her

Louisiana address, and links to adult pornography sites hosting sex videos of Jane Doe.

The fake MySpace account was associated with multiple IP addresses from unsecured wireless networks in Saco, Maine, near where Sayer lived. A business with one of the unsecured networks had surveillance, which had captured an old green pickup truck resembling Sayer's green 1999 Ford truck parked outside for twenty minutes at about the same time that the fake MySpace account was being accessed. No one was seen getting into or out of the truck during the time that it was parked there.

Jane Doe returned to Maine the first week of November 2009 because the men that Sayer sent to her Louisiana home had scared her aunt and cousin, with whom she was staying. The cyberstalking charge in this case only encompasses Sayer's harassment of Jane Doe from "July 2009, the exact date being unknown, until about November 2009." However, Sayer continued to harass Jane Doe after she returned to Maine. As a result of new fraudulent accounts Sayer posted in Jane Doe's name soliciting sex from strangers, as many as six different men per night showed up at her home in June 2010. The police searched Sayer's home again on July 1, 2010. Forensic analysis of a laptop computer they seized showed that Sayer had created "numerous fake profiles" through Yahoo! Messenger, an online chat service, using some variation of Jane Doe's name, between June and November 2009. All of the profiles had sexually suggestive or explicit pictures of Jane Doe and in many cases directed viewers to sex videos of her on adult pornography sites. In many instances, Sayer, posing as Jane Doe, chatted with men online and encouraged them to visit Jane Doe at her home in Louisiana.

Jane Doe said Sayer did not stop sending men to her home until he was arrested by state police in July 2010 for violating a protection order she had against him. . . .

Jane Doe also testified at the sentencing hearing and recounted the progression of Sayer's stalking and harassment starting in 2006, when she ended their relationship, up until he was arrested in July 2010. She explained that what started out as "creepiness," with Sayer showing up at the places she frequented, "quickly . . . turned into something very scary." Jane Doe described the impact of Sayer's cyberstalking in particular, saying:

> From November [2008] until [Sayer] was arrested in July of 2010 man after man showed up at my house. It didn't matter the time of day; . . . I couldn't open my windows to let the fresh air in. I couldn't keep my blinds open to light. I felt scared to walk 25 feet out to my car. No longer was I afraid of just [Sayer]; I was afraid of any man who came near me because he was a potential predator. . . . It's very hard to sleep at night when there are

> predators coming to your home and banging on your windows. It's very hard to do anything. It's hard to live.
>
> [Sayer] had every intention o[f] terrorizing me and maybe even hurting me. I don't know how many times [a detective] called me up to say, . . . [Sayer] has planned a gang bang at your home tonight; you may not go home. Don't go home. It's not a safe place. . . .
>
> I can't even describe to you, really, in the words that I'm telling you how this has impacted my life. . . . I am forever changed. I will truly never be safe. . . . And so I am fearful of what happens when [Sayer] does get out of jail. . . . He knows what he did. He purposely did it. And I'm not so sure that it won't happen again. . . .

Under § 2261A(2)(A), a defendant must first have the intent "to kill, injure, harass, or place [a victim] under surveillance with intent to kill, injure, harass, or intimidate, or cause substantial emotional distress." Second, the defendant must engage in a "course of conduct" that actually "causes substantial emotional distress . . . or places [the victim] in reasonable fear of . . . death . . . or serious bodily injury. . . ." 18 U.S.C. § 2261A(2)(A). Sayer argues that because his course of conduct involved speech, or online communications, it cannot be proscribed in accord with the First Amendment. This argument is meritless.

"[I]t has never been deemed an abridgement of freedom of speech or press to make a course of conduct illegal merely because the conduct was in part initiated, evidenced, or carried out by means of language, either spoken, written, or printed." *Giboney v. Empire Storage & Ice Co.,* 336 U.S. 490, 502, 69 S.Ct. 684, 93 L.Ed. 834 (1949). For example, in Giboney the Court held that enjoining otherwise lawful picketing activities did not violate the First Amendment where the sole purpose of that picketing was to force a company to enter an unlawful agreement restraining trade in violation of a state criminal statute. *Id.* at 501–02, 69 S.Ct. 684. Speech integral to criminal conduct is now recognized as a "long-established category of unprotected speech." *Stevens,* 559 U.S. at 471, 130 S.Ct. 1577. Sayer's online communications fall in this category.

Sayer does not claim that his acts of creating false online advertisements and accounts in Jane Doe's name or impersonating Jane Doe on the internet constitute legal conduct. In fact, he has admitted that his conduct, which deceptively enticed men to Jane Doe's home, put Jane Doe in danger and at risk of physical harm. To the extent his course of conduct targeting Jane Doe involved speech at all, his speech is not protected. Here, as in *Giboney,* it served only to implement Sayer's criminal purpose. *See United States v. Rowlee,* 899 F.2d 1275, 1278 (2d Cir. 1990) (applying *Giboney* exception to a conspiracy charge because the "act of conspiracy" does not implicate protected speech); *United States v. Varani,* 435 F.2d 758, 762 (6th

Cir.1970) (explaining that, as in the crimes of perjury, bribery, extortion and threats, and conspiracy, "speech is not protected by the First Amendment when it is the very vehicle of the crime itself").

The Eighth Circuit rejected a similar First Amendment challenge to § 2261A(2)(A) in *United States v. Petrovic,* 701 F.3d 849 (8th Cir.2012). There, the defendant had created a website with links to images of his ex-wife "in the nude or engaging in sex acts" with him. *Id.* at 853. The defendant also sent sexually explicit pictures of his ex-wife to her work, her boss, and her relatives. *Id.* The court held that these "communications," which resulted in the defendant's § 2261A(2)(A) conviction, were integral to criminal conduct and unprotected under *Giboney,* as they carried out the defendant's extortionate threats to harass and humiliate his ex-wife if she terminated their sexual relationship. *Id.* at 855. As in *Petrovic,* Sayer points to no lawful purpose of the communications at issue here that would take them outside the *Giboney* exception. *Cf. United States v. Clemens,* 738 F.3d 1, 12–13 (1st Cir.2013) (rejecting as-applied challenge to criminal threat statute, 18 U.S.C. § 875(c), where jury could reasonably conclude that defendant's speech received no First Amendment protection). Nor can we surmise any on this record. Rather, his conduct lured potentially dangerous men to Jane Doe's doorstep, men whom Jane Doe was not free to ignore. As a result, § 2261A(2)(A) has been constitutionally applied to Sayer.

EXERCISE

In the Sayer case, the judge departed upward from the federal sentencing guidelines and imposed a five-year sentence of imprisonment, the statutory maximum and likely a longer sentence than if simple assault had been the basis of the charge. At sentencing, the court explained its reasoning:

> [T]here are factors here that the sentencing commission simply has not considered in the guideline analysis. And they are, for example, the use of anonymous third parties to harass the victim and the extra danger that that caused . . . [where the victim] has no idea of the limits [these third parties] might go to; the effect of posting on the Internet her identity, address, intimate details, all of which, as we know, is permanent, unlike situations where stalking occurred in a different era without the Internet; the many involvements that this defendant had with law enforcement, which did not deter him until the final arrest; and the ongoing obsession that he apparently had. . . .

Do you think this sentence was justified by the facts? Does gender matter in your consideration of this case and others like it, and would it matter if gender was reversed?

D. KIDNAPPING

The federal statute governing kidnapping, 18 U.S.C. § 1201, defines kidnapping as occurring when the defendant "unlawfully seizes, confines, inveigles, decoys, kidnaps, abducts, or carries away and holds for ransom or reward or otherwise any person, except in the case of a minor by the parent thereof, when" federal jurisdiction applies. The elements of a federal kidnapping charge where federal jurisdiction is based on interstate transportation of the defendant are:

1)   Identification of the defendant,

2)   the transportation in interstate commerce

3)   of an unconsenting person

4)   who is held for ransom, reward, or otherwise, and

5)   that these acts are done knowingly and willingly.[5]

Kidnapping includes an unusual element: the state of mind of the *victim*, rather than the defendant (in that the victim is unconsenting). We see this elsewhere in sexual assault statutes, where the consent of the victim can be a defense.

As with sexual assault, proofs going to the lack of consent of the victim can be complicated by ambiguous actions by the victim during the course of the event. In these cases, there may be different mental states of the victim (or at least the appearance of different mental states) at different points in time.

UNITED STATES V. IVY

929 F. 2d 147 (5th Cir. 1991)

W. EUGENE DAVIS, CIRCUIT JUDGE:

In September 1989, Charles Ivy drove from Memphis, Tennessee to Oxford, Mississippi to the mobile home of his estranged wife, Patricia Ivy. Neither Patricia nor her ten-year-old daughter Deanie were in the trailer when he arrived. Patricia was on a date with Alvin King. When Patricia and King returned, Charles shot King in the head as King sat at the wheel of his car. Patricia testified that Charles ordered her out of the car and into the trailer at gun point. Once they were in the trailer he pistol-whipped Patricia rendering her unconscious.

After Patricia regained consciousness, Charles ordered her to drive him to a relative's home. He threatened to shoot her in the back if she tried to escape. They then drove to the home of Charles' relative, David Carruthers. Charles left his car at Patricia's trailer. Without Patricia's knowledge, Charles hid his pistol at the Carruthers'. Charles then drove Patricia back

---

5   United States v. Osborne, 68 F. 3d 94, 100 (5th Cir. 1995).

to her trailer so he could obtain the cash she had left there. While there, Patricia picked up her stash of cocaine. The Ivys then left for Memphis. They spent the night in a motel just across the Tennessee state line.

The next morning the two went to the home of Charles' sister Ruthie Johnson, where they stayed for several days. Members of the Johnson family testified that Patricia had many opportunities to escape or seek help during this period, but did not. While at the Johnsons', Patricia and Charles went shopping, to a concert, and to a movie. Patricia testified, however, that Charles ordered her not to tell his family what had happened. She said that he monitored her closely during their stay in the Johnson home.

Charles and Patricia left the Johnsons' and traveled for two days through Arkansas, Missouri, and Illinois. The Ivys returned to the Johnson home briefly, but left again. Charles took Patricia back to the same Memphis motel where they had stayed the night of the shooting. Both went in to register, but Charles left the keys in the ignition. When Charles became distracted, Patricia ran out of the lobby and escaped in the car. She had no money so she returned to the Johnsons' to call her mother. Patricia's mother advised her to contact the police, which Patricia did immediately.

At trial, counsel questioned Patricia about why she had not attempted to escape or seek help earlier. She explained that during her four-year marriage to Charles, he repeatedly abused her physically and mentally. Patricia also testified that she was afraid Charles would kill her daughter if she tried to escape. She said Charles had told her that he knew how to construct and detonate a pipe bomb. The police found an explosive device in Charles' car along with an accurate diagram describing how to make a bomb.

Patricia admitted that she consented to sex during the four-day ordeal because she was afraid to deny Charles. She explained that she did not feel safe asking Charles' family for help because they did not like her and were unable to control Charles anyway. . . .

Ivy argues first that the district court erred in denying his motion for judgment of acquittal on the interstate kidnapping charge. In making a sufficiency of the evidence inquiry, we consider the evidence in a light most favorable to the verdict and determine whether a rational fact-finder could have found the defendant guilty beyond a reasonable doubt. *United States v. Bell,* 678 F.2d 547, 549 (5th Cir. Unit B 1982) (en banc), *aff'd,* 462 U.S. 356, 103 S.Ct. 2398, 76 L.Ed.2d 638 (1983).

Ivy argues that a rational trier of fact could not have found beyond a reasonable doubt that he kidnapped Patricia because the evidence showed that Patricia consented to being taken across the Tennessee state line. *United States v. Chancey,* 715 F.2d 543, 546 (11th Cir.1983) (if interstate transportation is by consent there is no kidnapping). Ivy argues that the following testimony established that Patricia accompanied him voluntarily:

— He and Patricia amicably met and socialized together in the weeks before the alleged abduction.

— Patricia never even attempted to escape or seek help although she had many opportunities.

— Patricia knew that he did not have the gun as they departed for Memphis.

— She consented to sexual intercourse with him.

— During the alleged abduction, Patricia shared drugs with him, went shopping, went to a concert, and went to a drive-in movie.

— Patricia acted normally during their stay at the Johnsons', not like someone being held against her will.

Ivy relies primarily on *United States v. Chancey*. In *Chancey*, the Eleventh Circuit reversed a kidnapping conviction on the ground that no rational jury could have concluded that the alleged victim was transported involuntarily. The court noted that the victim did not take advantage of numerous opportunities to escape or seek help (including a discussion with a police officer), was seen behaving playfully with the defendant, and agreed voluntarily to frequent sexual intercourse with the defendant. *Id.* at 544–45. The victim testified that she was too afraid to seek help, but the court determined that her testimony was inherently incredible. *Id.* at 547.

Ivy's violent behavior at the beginning of the alleged abduction distinguishes this case from *Chancey*. Charles shot King in the head while Patricia watched. Charles then pistol-whipped Patricia rendering her unconscious. These violent acts immediately before Patricia's abduction together with Charles' longstanding abusive behavior toward her gave Patricia good reason to believe Charles' threats to kill her and members of her family.

Ivy's argument, at bottom, rests on a complaint that the jury refused to credit his testimony and the testimony of his family members. According to Charles, the testimony summarized above conclusively established that Patricia willingly accompanied him. Patricia disputed or explained this testimony. This conflict in testimony made the issue ripe for the trier of fact. Our review of the record persuades us that the jury could have easily accepted Patricia's version of the facts and rejected the testimony of Charles and his family members.

———————

EXERCISE

Prosecutors will sometimes use a timeline to properly order events and focus on the time period they believe is most relevant (and, often, to emphasize the evidence that most favors their case).

Create a timeline of events for the Ivy case. How much of that time is really relevant to the kidnapping charge? For what element? If this was a state kidnapping charge, how much of the timeline would be relevant?

——————————

Not all kidnapping cases involve transportation of the victim. In some instances, the victim is restrained from movement, and that fulfills the action element for kidnapping, provided that the victim is held for "ransom or reward or otherwise."[6]

UNITED STATES V. ROBERT FORD
726 F. 3d 1028 (8th Cir. 2013)

SMITH, CIRCUIT JUDGE.

Robert Ford was charged with sexual abuse of an incapacitated person, in violation of 18 U.S.C. §§ 2242(2), 2246(2)(A), and 1152 ("Count 1") and kidnapping, in violation of 18 U.S.C. §§ 1201(a)(2) and 1152 ("Count 2"). A jury acquitted Ford of sexual abuse but convicted him of kidnapping. On appeal, Ford contends that his acquittal on the sexual abuse count requires an acquittal on the kidnapping count as a matter of law. . . .

On the night of June 29, 2011, Christina Weston, her cousin, Eric Sherman, her friend, Shelly Red Earth, and her former romantic interest, Ford, consumed alcohol and fell asleep at Weston's house. Sherman testified that the next morning he and Red Earth heard a "muffled commotion" coming from Weston's bedroom. When Sherman went to investigate, he encountered Ford, who had just exited Weston's bedroom and shut the door. Ford looked upset and said, "Your cousin is having a fit, an attack. You better go check on her." Sherman knocked on the door and went into Weston's room where he found her traumatized. She was seated on the floor with her legs curled up, rocking back and forth and sobbing. Sherman observed red marks on Weston's arms that had not been there the night before. When Sherman asked Weston what happened, Weston pointed to the door and said, "That f* * * * *g Bob," referring to Ford. Sherman then went to look for Ford, but he had departed. Weston was taken to the hospital. After hospital staff physically examined Weston, she told them that she had been barricaded in her room and sexually assaulted. Ford's DNA was present on swabs taken from Weston at the hospital. . . .

——————————

[6]   18 U.S.C. § 1201(a).

The instructions for Count 2 stated, in pertinent part:

> For you to find Robert Ford guilty of Count 2 of the indictment, the prosecution must prove the following four essential elements beyond a reasonable doubt:
>
> *One,* Robert Ford unlawfully seized or confined Christina Weston without her consent;
>
> *Two,* Robert Ford held Christina Weston for the purpose of preventing her from reporting a sexual attack;
>
> *Three and four,* that Christina Weston is an Indian; and that the offense took place in Indian Country, namely at Flandreau, in Indian Country, in the District of South Dakota.

During the course of its deliberations, the jury sent three questions to the court. The first question was, "Do we have to prove guilty on Count 1 to find guilty on Count 2?" After entertaining arguments from counsel, the court sent the following supplemental instruction to the jury:

> As you were instructed in Final Instruction Number Three, the jury needs to find that Robert Ford held Christina Weston for the purpose of preventing her from reporting a sexual attack. This element, along with all the other elements, must be proven beyond a reasonable doubt to find the Defendant guilty on Count Two. To find the Defendant guilty on Count Two, you do not need to find the Defendant guilty on Count One. . . .

Later, the court received a second question from the jury specifically concerning the first element of Count 2. It asked, "On Count 2, can we have a further definition of 'unlawfully seized or confined' without her consent?" After entertaining arguments from counsel on this instruction, the court submitted the following supplemental instruction to the jury:

The victim's lack of consent is a fundamental element of kidnapping. Kidnapping implies an unlawful physical or mental restraint or detention for an appreciable period of time against the person's will and with a willful intent to confine or detain the victim. . . .

The federal kidnapping statute imposes criminal liability upon "[w]hoever unlawfully seizes, confines, inveigles, decoys, kidnaps, abducts, or carries away and holds for ransom or reward or otherwise any person." 18 U.S.C. § 1201(a). Of particular relevance in the present case is the "or otherwise" element. *Id.* "We have noted that the 'or otherwise' requirement has been broadly interpreted and have held that it is met if the person kidnapped was taken for some reason that the defendant considered of sufficient benefit to him, or for " 'some purpose of his own.' " *United States v. Bordeaux,* 84 F.3d 1544, 1548 (8th Cir.1996) (quoting *United States v. Eagle Thunder,* 893 F.2d 950, 953 (8th Cir.1990) (quoting *United States v. Melton,* 883 F.2d 336, 338 (5th Cir.1989))).

Here, the district court stated:

> Ford argues that the jury could not have reasonably concluded that he held the victim for the purpose of preventing her from reporting a sexual attack because the jury found Ford not guilty of the charged sexual assault. Put differently, Ford contends that the victim could not have intended to report a sexual attack because according to the jury verdict, no sexual attack took place. Ford's reasoning is flawed because he implicitly argues that in order for one to report an alleged crime against a defendant, or at least to have the intent to do so, the defendant must be guilty of the alleged crime. Ford cites no case law to support his position[,] and the court finds that his position is not true either logically or practically. An individual can report what he or she perceives to be a crime even if no actual crime took place. To conclude otherwise would undermine the role of criminal investigations and the judicial process as a whole. Hence, the court finds that Ford's argument that a not guilty verdict for the sexual assault charge precludes a guilty verdict for the kidnapping charge lacks merit.
>
> Ford also argues that the evidence presented at trial was insufficient to prove beyond a reasonable doubt that he had the necessary intent to commit a kidnapping, namely that he held the victim for the purpose of preventing her from reporting a sexual attack. Here, after hearing all the evidence, the jury reasonably concluded that the victim intended to report a sexual attack at the time [that] Ford held her. Indeed, the victim reported the sexual attack once she had the opportunity. She immediately told a witness about the events that took place while defendant and the victim were in the victim's bedroom, the place where the alleged confinement took place. The victim then went to the Flandreau hospital that same day to have a rape kit administered, and she also reported the incident to the Flandreau police and made a statement to the FBI. The fact that defendant was later acquitted of the sexual assault crime does not negate the fact that the victim intended to report the attack at the time she was confined.

As Ford argues, much of the district court's analysis deals with Weston's intent to report a sexual attack, as opposed to evidence proving that Ford had the purpose of preventing Weston from reporting a sexual attack. But, in the present case, Weston's intent to report a sexual attack is quite relevant to establishing Ford's subjective purpose to prevent her from reporting a sexual attack. Weston testified that Ford sexually assaulted her, barricaded the door when she tried to leave the room, and prevented her from having access to her cell phone. Weston reported that Ford had sexually assaulted her as soon as she had the opportunity to do so.

Furthermore, Weston's allegation was corroborated by the testimony of Sherman and Red Earth, photographs, and DNA evidence.

In *Bordeaux,* four men left an all-night drinking party sometime after 6:30 a.m. 84 F.3d at 1546. As they were driving, they observed an injured man, Williams, walking down the road. *Id.* The men stopped and offered Williams a ride to his mother's house. *Id.* However, the driver took the car to a different location, where the occupants exited the car and battered Williams. *Id.* The men then placed Williams back into the car and drove him to another location where they continued the physical assault. *Id.* Two of the four men were convicted of kidnapping, in violation of § 1201(a)(2). *Id.* On appeal, the defendants challenged the sufficiency of the evidence, arguing that "the government did not prove that Williams was held for 'ransom or reward or otherwise,' as required by 18 U.S.C. § 1201(a)." *Id.* at 1548. We found that [i]t was reasonable for the jury to infer that the purpose of the kidnapping was to assault Williams and that he was put back in the car to enable the defendants to continue the assault at a more isolated location and thus prevent detection. Both reasons constitute a sufficient benefit to the defendants.

Id. Similar to *Bordeaux,* here "[i]t was reasonable for the jury to infer that" Ford's purpose in kidnapping Weston was to prevent Weston from reporting a sexual attack. *See id.* That "reason[ ] constitute[d] a sufficient benefit to [Ford]" under § 1201(a). *See id.*

EXERCISE

The language of 18 U.S.C. § 1201(a) is somewhat confusing in requiring that a kidnapping be for "ransom or reward or otherwise." Does the language in this element place any effective limitation on what might be considered kidnapping?

E. TERRORISM

"Terrorism" (at least under federal law) is usually describing a violent crime already criminalized, plus an element of motive. Here is how the federal statute, 18 U.S.C. § 2331, defines terrorism within the United States:

(5) the term "domestic terrorism" means activities that—

    (A) involve acts dangerous to human life that are a violation of the criminal laws of the United States or of any State;

    (B) appear to be intended—

        (i) to intimidate or coerce a civilian population;

(ii) to influence the policy of a government by intimidation or coercion; or

(iii) to affect the conduct of a government by mass destruction, assassination, or kidnapping; and

(C) occur primarily within the territorial jurisdiction of the United States.

Individual terrorism statutes, however, often lack the motive element included in section (5)(B) above. For example, here is the statute covering the bombing of public spaces, found in the Terrorism chapter of the U.S. code at 18 U.S.C. § 2332:

(a) Offenses.—

(1) In general.—Whoever unlawfully delivers, places, discharges, or detonates an explosive or other lethal device in, into, or against a place of public use, a state or government facility, a public transportation system, or an infrastructure facility—

(A) with the intent to cause death or serious bodily injury, or

(B) with the intent to cause extensive destruction of such a place, facility, or system, where such destruction results in or is likely to result in major economic loss,

shall be punished as prescribed in subsection (c).

(2) Attempts and conspiracies.—Whoever attempts or conspires to commit an offense under paragraph (1) shall be punished as prescribed in subsection (c).

(b) Jurisdiction.—There is jurisdiction over the offenses in subsection (a) if—

(1) the offense takes place in the United States and—

(A) the offense is committed against another state or a government facility of such state, including its embassy or other diplomatic or consular premises of that state;

(B) the offense is committed in an attempt to compel another state or the United States to do or abstain from doing any act;

(C) at the time the offense is committed, it is committed—

(i) on board a vessel flying the flag of another state;

(ii) on board an aircraft which is registered under the laws of another state; or

(iii) on board an aircraft which is operated by the government of another state;

(D) a perpetrator is found outside the United States;

(E) a perpetrator is a national of another state or a stateless person; or

(F) a victim is a national of another state or a stateless person;

(2) the offense takes place outside the United States and—

(A) a perpetrator is a national of the United States or is a stateless person whose habitual residence is in the United States;

(B) a victim is a national of the United States;

(C) a perpetrator is found in the United States;

(D) the offense is committed in an attempt to compel the United States to do or abstain from doing any act;

(E) the offense is committed against a state or government facility of the United States, including an embassy or other diplomatic or consular premises of the United States;

(F) the offense is committed on board a vessel flying the flag of the United States or an aircraft which is registered under the laws of the United States at the time the offense is committed; or

(G) the offense is committed on board an aircraft which is operated by the United States.

(c) **Penalties.**—Whoever violates this section shall be punished as provided under section 2332a(a) of this title.

(d) **Exemptions to jurisdiction.**—This section does not apply to—

(1) the activities of armed forces during an armed conflict, as those terms are understood under the law of war, which are governed by that law,

(2) activities undertaken by military forces of a state in the exercise of their official duties; or

(3) offenses committed within the United States, where the alleged offender and the victims are United States citizens and the alleged offender is found in the United States, or where jurisdiction is predicated solely on the nationality of

the victims or the alleged offender and the offense has no substantial effect on interstate or foreign commerce.

EXERCISE

Reading the exemptions listed in Section (d)(3), of 18 U.S.C. § 2332, could the statute apply to domestic terrorism, such as the bombing of a federal building?

A similar federal statute, 18 U.S.C. § 2332a, is titled "Use of Weapons of Mass Destruction." § 2332a is unusual in that the text of that statute does not explicitly include a state of mind element. This became an issue in one of the most significant terrorism cases in American history.

UNITED STATES V. McVEIGH
153 F. 3d 1166 (10th Cir. 1998)

EBEL, CIRCUIT JUDGE.

Defendant-appellant Timothy J. McVeigh ("McVeigh") was tried, convicted, and sentenced to death on eleven counts stemming from the bombing of the Alfred P. Murrah Federal Building ("Murrah Building") in Oklahoma City, Oklahoma, that resulted in the deaths of 168 people. . . . We affirm.

BACKGROUND

At 9:02 in the morning of April 19, 1995, a massive explosion tore apart the Murrah Building in Oklahoma City, Oklahoma, killing a total of 168 people and injuring hundreds more. On August 10, 1995, a federal grand jury returned an eleven-count indictment against McVeigh and Terry Lynn Nichols ("Nichols") charging: one count of conspiracy to use a weapon of mass destruction in violation of 18 U.S.C. § 2332a and 18 U.S.C. § 2(a) & (b); one count of use of a weapon of mass destruction in violation of 18 U.S.C. § 2332a and 18 U.S.C. § 2(a) & (b); one count of destruction by explosives in violation of 18 U.S.C. § 844(f) and 18 U.S.C. § 2(a) & (b); and eight counts of first-degree murder in violation of 18 U.S.C. §§ 1111 & 1114 and 18 U.S.C. § 2(a) & (b). . . .

At the guilt phase of trial, which encompassed twenty-three days of testimony, the government proved the following set of facts. The destruction of the Murrah Building killed 163 people in the building and five people outside. Fifteen children in the Murrah Building day care center, visible from the front of the building, and four children visiting the building were included among the victims. Eight federal law enforcement officials also lost their lives. The explosion, felt and heard six miles away, tore a gaping hole into the front of the Murrah Building and covered the streets with glass, debris, rocks, and chunks of concrete. Emergency workers who reported to the scene made heroic efforts to rescue people still trapped in the building.

The Murrah Building was destroyed by a 3,000–6,000 pound bomb comprised of an ammonium nitrate-based explosive carried inside a rented Ryder truck. In the fall of 1994, McVeigh and Nichols sought, bought, and stole all the materials needed to construct the bomb. First, on September 30, 1994, and October 18, 1994, McVeigh purchased a total of 4,000 pounds of ammonium nitrate from the McPherson branch of the Mid-Kansas Cooperative using the alias "Mike Havens." Second, in October of 1994, McVeigh and Nichols stole seven cases of Tovex explosives and a box of Primadet nonelectric blasting caps from the Martin Marietta rock quarry near Marion, Kansas. Third, on October 21, 1994, McVeigh purchased three drums of nitromethane at a race track outside of Dallas, Texas. Prior to the nitromethane purchase, McVeigh had sought bomb ingredients, including nitromethane, both in person and through the use of a prepaid telephone calling card under the name "Daryl Bridges." Using various aliases, McVeigh and Nichols rented a number of storage lockers in Kansas where they stored the bomb components. In order to fund their conspiracy, McVeigh and Nichols robbed a gun dealer in Arkansas in November of 1994.

In a letter to Michael and Lori Fortier written around September of 1994, McVeigh disclosed that he and Terry Nichols had decided to take some type of positive offensive action against the federal government in response to the government's siege of the Branch Davidians in Waco, Texas in 1993. On a subsequent visit to their home, McVeigh told the Fortiers that he planned to blow up a federal building. McVeigh later informed the Fortiers that he wanted to cause a general uprising in America and that the bombing would occur on the anniversary of the end of the Waco siege. McVeigh rationalized the inevitable loss of life by concluding that anyone who worked in the federal building was guilty by association with those responsible for Waco.

McVeigh stated that he had figured out how to make a truck into a bomb using fifty-five-gallon drums filled with ammonium nitrate combined with explosives stolen from the quarry. McVeigh demonstrated the shaped charge be intended to use for the bomb by arranging soup cans on the floor in the same triangle shape in which he was going to place fifty-five-gallon barrels filled with ammonium nitrate combined with nitromethane in the truck. McVeigh also diagramed the truck, barrels, and fusing system on a piece of paper, and stated that he intended to use a Ryder truck. McVeigh told the Fortiers that he chose the Murrah Building as the target because he believed that (1) the orders for the attack at Waco emanated from the building, (2) the building housed people involved in the Waco raid, and (3) the building's U-shape and glass front made it an easy target. On a later trip through Oklahoma City, McVeigh showed Michael Fortier the Murrah Building, asking Fortier whether he thought a twenty-foot rental truck would fit in front of the building.

Also, towards the end of 1994, McVeigh typed a number of letters discussing the justified use of violence against federal agents as retaliation for the events in Waco. McVeigh told his sister and one of his friends that he had moved from the propaganda stage to the action stage in his dispute with the federal government. McVeigh then warned his sister that "something big" was going to happen in April, and asked her to extend her April 1995 Florida vacation. He also instructed her not to write to him any more lest she incriminate herself. The manner in which the bombing was carried out closely tracked several books bought by McVeigh, which he often encouraged his friends to read, describing how to make a powerful bomb mixing ammonium nitrate with nitromethane and romanticizing self-declared patriots who blow up federal buildings. McVeigh was familiar with explosives and had detonated a pipe bomb prior to the attack on the Murrah Building.

From April 14 to 18, 1995, McVeigh stayed at the Dreamland Motel located in Junction City, Kansas. On April 14, 1995, McVeigh purchased a 1977 yellow Mercury Marquis from Junction City Firestone in Junction City, Kansas. While waiting to take possession of the car from the dealer, McVeigh made a phone call using the Bridges calling card to Elliott's Body Shop ("Elliott's") in Junction City, Kansas, seeking a twenty-foot Ryder truck for a one-way rental to Omaha. McVeigh also called Nichols.

During the search of the blast site, the FBI located the rear axle of the Ryder truck used to carry the bomb. The vehicle identification number from the axle matched that of the Ryder truck rented to McVeigh by Elliott's on April 15, 1995, and picked up by McVeigh two days prior to the blast. McVeigh rented the truck under the name "Robert King" using a phony South Dakota drivers license that Lori Fortier had helped McVeigh create.

McVeigh drove to Oklahoma City in the rented Ryder truck, which he had made into a bomb, parking the vehicle in front of the Murrah Building and running to the yellow Mercury that he and Nichols had stashed as a getaway car in a nearby alley a couple of days before the bombing. A Ford key fitting the Ryder truck was found in an alley near where McVeigh had told Michael Fortier that the getaway car would be parked. McVeigh hand-printed a sign inside the yellow Mercury, "Not Abandoned; Please do not tow; will move by April 23 (Needs Battery & Cable)." McVeigh deliberately parked the car so that a building would stand between the car and the blast, shielding McVeigh from the explosion. The bomb then exploded. Just 77 minutes after the blast, Oklahoma State Trooper Charles Hanger ("Hanger") stopped the yellow Mercury driven by McVeigh because the car had no license tags. The stop occurred between mile markers 202 and 203 on Interstate 35, just before the exit for Billings, Oklahoma, precisely 77.9

miles north of the Murrah Building. Before he was stopped by Hanger, McVeigh was headed northbound away from Oklahoma City towards Kansas. A person driving the posted speed limit would have reached the point of the stop 75 minutes after leaving the Murrah Building. If McVeigh had left the Murrah Building right after the bombing, he would have arrived at the Billings exit around 10:17 a.m., the approximate time of the stop.

Hanger arrested McVeigh upon discovering that he was carrying a concealed, loaded gun. Hanger transported McVeigh to Noble County Jail in Perry, Oklahoma, where McVeigh was booked and incarcerated for unlawfully carrying a weapon and transporting a loaded firearm. Noble County authorities took custody of McVeigh's clothing and property, including earplugs, and issued him prison garb. Two days later, on April 21, 1995, the federal government filed a Complaint against McVeigh for unlawful destruction by explosives. Oklahoma then transferred McVeigh to federal custody on the federal bombing charges. An FBI test performed later found that McVeigh's clothing and the earplugs contained explosives residue, including PETN, EGDN, and nitroglycerine—chemicals associated with the materials used in the construction of the bomb.

A subsequent inventory search of the yellow Mercury uncovered a sealed envelope containing documents arguing that the federal government had commenced open warfare on the liberty of the American people and justifying the killing of government officials in the defense of liberty. Finally, three days after the arrest, Hanger found a Paulsen's Military Supply business card on the floor of his cruiser bearing McVeigh's fingerprints. McVeigh had written on the back of the card, "TNT @ $5/stick Need more" and "Call After 01, May, See if I can get some more." . . .

D. CRIMINAL INTENT AND LESSER-INCLUDED OFFENSES

McVeigh argues that the district court improperly instructed the jury regarding the intent elements of the mass destruction crimes with which he was charged and that the district court erred in refusing to instruct the jury on lesser-included offenses for the mass destruction offenses and the first-degree murder charges. In particular, he contends that: (1) 18 U.S.C. § 2332a (1994) and 18 U.S.C. § 844(f) (1994) require the government to prove a specific intent to kill as an element of those crimes and the district court erred in failing to instruct on that element. . . .

1. Standard of Review

Whether § 2332a and § 844(f) have as an element the specific intent to kill are questions of statutory construction, and so are reviewed de novo. *See United States v. Agnew,* 931 F.2d 1397, 1407 (10th Cir.1991). Whether § 2332a and § 844(f) have any lesser-included offenses are also questions of law and will be reviewed de novo. *See United States v. Duran,* 127 F.3d 911,

914 (10th Cir.1997), *cert. denied,* 523 U.S. 1061, 118 S.Ct. 1389, 140 L.Ed.2d 648 (1998). We review for abuse of discretion whether the evidence warranted an instruction regarding second-degree murder as a lesser-included offense of first-degree murder. *See id.*

2. Analysis

a. Criminal Intent on Mass Destruction Offenses

McVeigh contends that one of the elements of the mass destruction offenses charged in Counts I, II, and III is a specific intent to kill when the charge is that deaths were caused by a bombing. He argues that the district court should have construed 18 U.S.C. § 2332a and 18 U.S.C. § 844(f) as containing two levels of criminal intent, comparable to first-degree and second-degree murder, and as a result, the government should have been required to prove a specific intent to kill as an element of the crimes charged.

i. 18 U.S.C. § 2332a

Count I charged McVeigh with conspiring to use a weapon of mass destruction against persons in the United States and against property that was owned and used by the United States and by an agency of the United States, in violation of 18 U.S.C. § 2332a. Count II charged McVeigh with using and aiding and abetting the use of a weapon of mass destruction against persons in the United States, in violation of 18 U.S.C. § 2332a and 18 U.S.C. § 2.

The version of 18 U.S.C. § 2332a(a) in effect at the time of the bombing provided:

> **Offense.**—A person who uses, or attempts or conspires to use, a weapon of mass destruction—
>
> (1)   against a national of the United States while such national is outside of the United States;
>
> (2)   against any person within the United States; or
>
> (3)   against any property that is owned, leased or used by the United States or by any department or agency of the United States, whether the property is within or outside of the United States,
>
> shall be imprisoned for any term of years or for life, and if death results, shall be punished by death or imprisoned for any term of years or for life.

From the plain language of the statute, it is clear that "intent to kill" is not a statutorily required element of § 2332a(a). In fact, no level of intent is specified.

When Congress fails to specify the degree of criminal intent required for a statutory offense, courts will either read in a level of intent or hold that the statute creates a strict liability crime. *See* 1 Wayne R. LaFave & Austin W. Scott, Jr., *Substantive Criminal Law* § 3.8(a), at 342 (1986). "[S]ilence on this point by itself does not necessarily suggest that Congress intended to dispense with a conventional mens rea element, which would require that the defendant know the facts that make his conduct illegal." *Staples v. United States,* 511 U.S. 600, 605, 114 S.Ct. 1793, 128 L.Ed.2d 608 (1994). "On the contrary, we must construe the statute in light of the background rules of the common law, in which the requirement of some *mens rea* for a crime is firmly embedded." *Id.* (citation omitted); *see also Morissette v. United States,* 342 U.S. 246, 263, 72 S.Ct. 240, 96 L.Ed. 288 (1952) ("[M]ere omission . . . of any mention of intent will not be construed as eliminating that intent from the crimes denounced.").

In light of the nature of the offense at issue and the severity of the prescribed punishments, we do not believe that § 2332a is a strict liability crime. *See Staples,* 511 U.S. at 606–07, 114 S.Ct. 1793 (interpretation of statutes silent as to *mens rea* as imposing strict liability is generally limited to "public welfare" or "regulatory" offenses); *Morissette,* 342 U.S. at 251–61, 72 S.Ct. 240 (reviewing history of the common law and the rise of regulatory offenses); LaFave & Scott, *supra,* at 342–44. Thus, we must decide the appropriate level of intent to read into the statute.

In *United States v. Bailey,* 444 U.S. 394, 406, 100 S.Ct. 624, 62 L.Ed.2d 575 (1980), the Supreme Court indicated that we should consider the mental state necessary for each separate element of a statute. We find two elements in §§ 2332a(a)(2) and (a)(3) as they existed at the time of the bombing: first, using, or attempting or conspiring to use, a weapon of mass destruction, and second, doing so against persons in the United States or against "any property that is owned, leased or used by the United States or by any department or agency of the United States . . ."

We conclude that the intent standard of "knowingly" is appropriate for each of the elements of a § 2332a violation. *See Bailey,* 444 U.S. at 408, 100 S.Ct. 624 ("[E]xcept in narrow classes of offenses, proof that the defendant acted knowingly is sufficient to support a conviction."); *see also Staples,* 511 U.S. at 619, 114 S.Ct. 1793 (adopting "knowingly" standard in face of congressional silence as to intent); *Posters 'N' Things, Ltd. v. United States,* 511 U.S. 513, 523, 114 S.Ct. 1747, 128 L.Ed.2d 539 (1994) (same); *Agnew,* 931 F.2d at 1408 (same); *United States v. Swindler,* 476 F.2d 167, 169–70 (10th Cir.1973) (same); 1 Edward J. Devitt *et al., Federal Jury Practice & Instructions* § 17.02, at 606 (4th ed. 1992) ("Most federal criminal statutes . . . require proof that a defendant act knowingly or wilfully or have knowledge with regard to one or more essential elements of the crime defined by that statute."). Thus, we conclude that § 2332a(a)(2) requires the government to prove that McVeigh (1) knowingly used, or attempted or conspired to use, a weapon of mass destruction, and (2) knowingly did so against persons in the United States. Section § 2332a(a)(3) requires the government to prove that McVeigh (1) knowingly used, or attempted or conspired to use, a weapon of mass destruction, and (2) knowingly did so against "any property that is owned, leased or used by the United States or by any department or agency of the United States."

EXERCISE

The statute at issue in the McVeigh case plainly does not contain an element requiring that the government prove a state of mind. The Circuit Court rejects out of hand that this could be a strict liability crime, asserting that "In light of the nature of the offense at issue and the severity of the prescribed punishments, we do not believe that § 2332a is a strict liability crime." Is this conclusion justified? What problems could arise if 18 U.S.C. § 2332a was construed as a strict liability crime with no requirement of a mental state?

Not all terrorism cases involve direct involvement in violent acts. Federal statutes also prohibit the material support (or funding) of terrorism, an area that steps close to free speech. Below is a civil case that addresses the criminal statute.

HOLDER V. HUMANITARIAN LAW PROJECT
561 U.S. 1 (2010)

CHIEF JUSTICE ROBERTS delivered the opinion of the Court.

Congress has prohibited the provision of "material support or resources" to certain foreign organizations that engage in terrorist activity. 18 U.S.C. § 2339B(a)(1). That prohibition is based on a finding that the specified organizations "are so tainted by their criminal conduct that any contribution to such an organization facilitates that conduct." Antiterrorism and Effective Death Penalty Act of 1996 (AEDPA), § 301(a)(7), 110 Stat. 1247, note following 18 U.S.C. § 2339B (Findings and Purpose). The plaintiffs in this litigation seek to provide support to two such organizations. Plaintiffs claim that they seek to facilitate only the lawful, nonviolent purposes of those groups, and that applying the material-support law to prevent them from doing so violates the Constitution. In particular, they claim that the statute is too vague, in violation of the Fifth Amendment, and that it infringes their rights to freedom of speech and association, in violation of the First Amendment. We conclude that the material-support statute is constitutional as applied to the particular activities plaintiffs have told us they wish to pursue. We do not, however, address the resolution of more difficult cases that may arise under the statute in the future.

I

This litigation concerns 18 U.S.C. § 2339B, which makes it a federal crime to "knowingly provid[e] material support or resources to a foreign terrorist organization." Congress has amended the definition of "material support or resources" periodically, but at present it is defined as follows:

> [T]he term 'material support or resources' means any property, tangible or intangible, or service, including currency or monetary instruments or financial securities, financial services, lodging, training, expert advice or assistance, safehouses, false documentation or identification, communications equipment, facilities, weapons, lethal substances, explosives, personnel (1 or more individuals who may be or include oneself), and transportation, except medicine or religious materials.

§ 2339A(b)(1); see also § 2339B(g)(4).

The authority to designate an entity a "foreign terrorist organization" rests with the Secretary of State. 8 U.S.C. §§ 1189(a)(1), (d)(4). She may, in consultation with the Secretary of the Treasury and the Attorney General, so designate an organization upon finding that it is foreign, engages in "terrorist activity" or "terrorism," and thereby "threatens the security of United States nationals or the national security of the United States." §§ 1189(a)(1), (d)(4). " '[N]ational security' means the national defense, foreign relations, or economic interests of the United States." § 1189(d)(2). An entity designated a foreign terrorist organization may seek review of that designation before the D.C. Circuit within 30 days of that designation. § 1189(c)(1).

In 1997, the Secretary of State designated 30 groups as foreign terrorist organizations. See 62 Fed.Reg. 52650. Two of those groups are the Kurdistan Workers' Party (also known as the Partiya Karkeran Kurdistan, or PKK) and the Liberation Tigers of Tamil Eelam (LTTE). The PKK is an organization founded in 1974 with the aim of establishing an independent Kurdish state in southeastern Turkey. . . .

Plaintiffs in this litigation are two U.S. citizens and six domestic organizations: the Humanitarian Law Project (HLP) (a human rights organization with consultative status to the United Nations); Ralph Fertig (the HLP's president, and a retired administrative law judge); Nagalingam Jeyalingam (a Tamil physician, born in Sri Lanka and a naturalized U.S. citizen); and five nonprofit groups dedicated to the interests of persons of Tamil descent. Brief for Petitioners in No. 09–89, pp. ii, 10 (hereinafter Brief for Plaintiffs); App. 48. In 1998, plaintiffs filed suit in federal court challenging the constitutionality of the material-support statute, § 2339B. Plaintiffs claimed that they wished to provide support for the humanitarian and political activities of the PKK and the LTTE in the form of monetary contributions, other tangible aid, legal training, and political advocacy, but that they could not do so for fear of prosecution under § 2339B. 9 F.Supp.2d, at 1180–1184.

Given the complicated 12-year history of this litigation, we pause to clarify the questions before us. Plaintiffs challenge § 2339B's prohibition on four types of material support—"training," "expert advice or assistance," "service," and "personnel." They raise three constitutional claims. First, plaintiffs claim that § 2339B violates the Due Process Clause of the Fifth Amendment because these four statutory terms are impermissibly vague. Second, plaintiffs claim that § 2339B violates their freedom of speech under the First Amendment. Third, plaintiffs claim that § 2339B violates their First Amendment freedom of association.

Plaintiffs do not challenge the above statutory terms in all their applications. Rather, plaintiffs claim that § 2339B is invalid to the extent it prohibits them from engaging in certain specified activities. See Brief for Plaintiffs 16–17, n. 10. With respect to the HLP and Judge Fertig, those activities are: (1) "train[ing] members of [the] PKK on how to use humanitarian and international law to peacefully resolve disputes"; (2) "engag [ing] in political advocacy on behalf of Kurds who live in Turkey"; and (3) "teach[ing] PKK members how to petition various representative bodies such as the United Nations for relief." 552 F.3d, at 921, n. 1; see 380 F.Supp.2d, at 1136. With respect to the other plaintiffs, those activities are: (1) "train[ing] members of [the] LTTE to present claims for tsunami-related aid to mediators and international bodies"; (2) "offer[ing] their legal expertise in negotiating peace agreements between the LTTE and the Sri Lankan government"; and (3) "engag[ing] in political advocacy on behalf of Tamils who live in Sri Lanka." 552 F.3d, at 921, n. 1; see 380 F.Supp.2d, at 1137. . . .

The First Amendment issue before us is more refined than either plaintiffs or the Government would have it. It is not whether the Government may prohibit pure political speech, or may prohibit material support in the form of conduct. It is instead whether the Government may prohibit what plaintiffs want to do—provide material support to the PKK and LTTE in the form of speech.

Everyone agrees that the Government's interest in combating terrorism is an urgent objective of the highest order. See Brief for Plaintiffs 51. Plaintiffs' complaint is that the ban on material support, applied to what they wish to do, is not "necessary to further that interest." *Ibid.* The objective of combating terrorism does not justify prohibiting their speech, plaintiffs argue, because their support will advance only the legitimate activities of the designated terrorist organizations, not their terrorism. *Id.,* at 51–52.

Whether foreign terrorist organizations meaningfully segregate support of their legitimate activities from support of terrorism is an empirical question. When it enacted § 2339B in 1996, Congress made specific findings regarding the serious threat posed by international terrorism. See AEDPA §§ 301(a)(1)–(7), 110 Stat. 1247, note following 18 U.S.C. § 2339B (Findings and Purpose). One of those findings explicitly rejects plaintiffs' contention that their support would not further the terrorist activities of the PKK and LTTE: "[F]oreign organizations that engage in terrorist activity are so tainted by their criminal conduct that *any contribution to such an organization* facilitates that conduct." § 301(a)(7) (emphasis added).

Plaintiffs argue that the reference to "any contribution" in this finding meant only monetary support. There is no reason to read the finding to be so limited, particularly because Congress expressly prohibited so much more than monetary support in § 2339B. Congress's use of the term "contribution" is best read to reflect a determination that any form of material support furnished "to" a foreign terrorist organization should be barred, which is precisely what the material-support statute does. Indeed, when Congress enacted § 2339B, Congress simultaneously removed an exception that had existed in § 2339A(a) (1994 ed.) for the provision of material support in the form of "humanitarian assistance to persons not directly involved in" terrorist activity. AEDPA § 323, 110 Stat. 1255; 205 F.3d, at 1136. That repeal demonstrates that Congress considered and rejected the view that ostensibly peaceful aid would have no harmful effects.

We are convinced that Congress was justified in rejecting that view. The PKK and the LTTE are deadly groups. "The PKK's insurgency has claimed more than 22,000 lives." Declaration of Kenneth R. McKune, App. 128, ¶ 5. The LTTE has engaged in extensive suicide bombings and political assassinations, including killings of the Sri Lankan President, Security Minister, and Deputy Defense Minister. *Id.,* at 130–132; Brief for Government 6–7. "On January 31, 1996, the LTTE exploded a truck bomb filled with an estimated 1,000 pounds of explosives at the Central Bank in Colombo, killing 100 people and injuring more than 1,400. This bombing was the most deadly terrorist incident in the world in 1996." McKune Affidavit, App. 131, ¶ 6.h. It is not difficult to conclude as Congress did that the "tain[t]" of such violent activities is so great that working in coordination with or at the command of the PKK and LTTE serves to legitimize and further their terrorist means. AEDPA § 301(a)(7), 110 Stat. 1247.

Material support meant to "promot[e] peaceable, lawful conduct," Brief for Plaintiffs 51, can further terrorism by foreign groups in multiple ways. "Material support" is a valuable resource by definition. Such support frees up other resources within the organization that may be put to violent ends.

It also importantly helps lend legitimacy to foreign terrorist groups—legitimacy that makes it easier for those groups to persist, to recruit members, and to raise funds—all of which facilitate more terrorist attacks. "Terrorist organizations do not maintain *organizational* 'firewalls' that would prevent or deter . . . sharing and commingling of support and benefits." McKune Affidavit, App. 135, ¶ 11.

"[I]nvestigators have revealed how terrorist groups systematically conceal their activities behind charitable, social, and political fronts." M. Levitt, Hamas: Politics, Charity, and Terrorism in the Service of Jihad 2–3 (2006). "Indeed, some designated foreign terrorist organizations use social and political components to recruit personnel to carry out terrorist operations, and to provide support to criminal terrorists and their families in aid of such operations." McKune Affidavit, App. 135, ¶ 11; Levitt, *supra,* at 2 ("Muddying the waters between its political activism, good works, and terrorist attacks, Hamas is able to use its overt political and charitable organizations as a financial and logistical support network for its terrorist operations").

Money is fungible, and "[w]hen foreign terrorist organizations that have a dual structure raise funds, they highlight the civilian and humanitarian ends to which such moneys could be put." McKune Affidavit, App. 134, ¶ 9. But "there is reason to believe that foreign terrorist organizations do not maintain legitimate *financial* firewalls between those funds raised for civil, nonviolent activities, and those ultimately used to support violent, terrorist operations." *Id.,* at 135, ¶ 12. Thus, "[f]unds raised ostensibly for charitable purposes have in the past been redirected by some terrorist groups to fund the purchase of arms and explosives." *Id.,* at 134, ¶ 10. See also Brief for Anti-Defamation League as *Amicus Curiae* 19–29 (describing fundraising activities by the PKK, LTTE, and Hamas); *Regan v. Wald,* 468 U.S. 222, 243, 104 S.Ct. 3026, 82 L.Ed.2d 171 (1984) (upholding President's decision to impose travel ban to Cuba "to curtail the flow of hard currency to Cuba—currency that could then be used in support of Cuban adventurism"). There is evidence that the PKK and the LTTE, in particular, have not "respected the line between humanitarian and violent activities." McKune Affidavit, App. 135, ¶ 13 (discussing PKK); see *id.,* at 134 (LTTE).

The dissent argues that there is "no natural stopping place" for the proposition that aiding a foreign terrorist organization's lawful activity promotes the terrorist organization as a whole. *Post,* at 2736. But Congress has settled on just such a natural stopping place: The statute reaches only material support coordinated with or under the direction of a designated foreign terrorist organization. Independent advocacy that might be viewed as promoting the group's legitimacy is not covered. See *supra,* at 2721–2723.

Providing foreign terrorist groups with material support in any form also furthers terrorism by straining the United States' relationships with its allies and undermining cooperative efforts between nations to prevent terrorist attacks. . . .

For example, the Republic of Turkey—a fellow member of NATO—is defending itself against a violent insurgency waged by the PKK. Brief for Government 6; App. 128. That nation and our other allies would react sharply to Americans furnishing material support to foreign groups like the PKK, and would hardly be mollified by the explanation that the support was meant only to further those groups' "legitimate" activities. From Turkey's perspective, there likely are no such activities. See 352 F.3d, at 389 (observing that Turkey prohibits membership in the PKK and prosecutes those who provide support to that group, regardless of whether the support is directed to lawful activities). . . .

At bottom, plaintiffs simply disagree with the considered judgment of Congress and the Executive that providing material support to a designated foreign terrorist organization—even seemingly benign support—bolsters the terrorist activities of that organization. That judgment, however, is entitled to significant weight, and we have persuasive evidence before us to sustain it. Given the sensitive interests in national security and foreign affairs at stake, the political branches have adequately substantiated their determination that, to serve the Government's interest in preventing terrorism, it was necessary to prohibit providing material support in the form of training, expert advice, personnel, and services to foreign terrorist groups, even if the supporters meant to promote only the groups' nonviolent ends. . . .

All this is not to say that any future applications of the material-support statute to speech or advocacy will survive First Amendment scrutiny. It is also not to say that any other statute relating to speech and terrorism would satisfy the First Amendment. In particular, we in no way suggest that a regulation of independent speech would pass constitutional muster, even if the Government were to show that such speech benefits foreign terrorist organizations. We also do not suggest that Congress could extend the same prohibition on material support at issue here to domestic organizations. We simply hold that, in prohibiting the particular forms of support that plaintiffs seek to provide to foreign terrorist groups, § 2339B does not violate the freedom of speech.

EXERCISE

Imagine that one of the groups involved in the *Humanitarian Law Project* case decided to go ahead and funnel money to the PKK anyways, having received assurances that the money would be used only for humanitarian purposes—and specifically, the building of a school. The money is given, the school is built, and the donor is able to verify the money given was used to build that specific school.

You are a federal prosecutor, and the FBI has brought you a potential case against this donor. Do you accept or decline the case?

CHAPTER FOUR

SEX CRIMES

■ ■ ■

Traditionally, sex crime was largely limited to forcible rape. Modern criminal codes, however, include statutes that criminalize a variety of behaviors beyond forcible rape, such as non-consensual sex.[1] In fact, the word "rape" is not found in some state codes, which utilize broader terms such as "criminal sexual conduct."[2]

As American jurisdictions have recognized the harms of sex that may not constitute forcible rape yet are non-consensual or otherwise problematic, the criminal code has become more comprehensive and complex. In addition to prohibiting certain physical sexual acts, federal law and many states also criminalize prostitution and sex trafficking and the production, transfer, and possession of images involving minors engaged in sex acts. This chapter will first address criminal sexual acts and contacts, and then discuss sex trafficking and child porn.

Federal law now bars a wide variety of sexual acts or sexual contact, including in the following circumstances:

— Sex procured by force or the threat of force (18 U.S.C. § 2241(a))

— Sex procured by coercion (18 U.S.C. § 2242),

— Non-consensual sex (18 U.S.C. § 2241(b), § 2242(2) & § 2244(b)),

— Sex with minors (18 U.S.C. § 2241(c) & § 2243).

As with other types of crime, differentiating things that sound similar—such as "coercive sex" and "non-consensual sex"—becomes very important. Some of these crimes can serve as lesser-included crimes of the others. For example, sex procured by force is necessarily non-consensual.

An element of each of these crimes is that a "sexual act" or "sexual contact" must have taken place (or, in some cases, been attempted). Modern statutes take care to define these action elements broadly so as to allow cases to proceed regardless of the gender of the offender and victim and in cases where sexual acts other than intercourse have occurred. In the federal system, 18 U.S.C. § 2246 defines those terms:

---

[1]   E.g. Minnesota Statute § 609.3451.

[2]   E.g. Michigan Penal Code § 750.520b.

(2) the term "sexual act" means—

(A) contact between the penis and the vulva or the penis and the anus, and for purposes of this subparagraph contact involving the penis occurs upon penetration, however slight;

(B) contact between the mouth and the penis, the mouth and the vulva, or the mouth and the anus;

(C) the penetration, however slight, of the anal or genital opening of another by a hand or finger or by any object, with an intent to abuse, humiliate, harass, degrade, or arouse or gratify the sexual desire of any person; or

(D) the intentional touching, not through the clothing, of the genitalia of another person who has not attained the age of 16 years with an intent to abuse, humiliate, harass, degrade, or arouse or gratify the sexual desire of any person;

(3) the term "sexual contact" means the intentional touching, either directly or through the clothing, of the genitalia, anus, groin, breast, inner thigh, or buttocks of any person with an intent to abuse, humiliate, harass, degrade, or arouse or gratify the sexual desire of any person. . . .

A. SEX PROCURED BY FORCE OR THE THREAT OF FORCE

Many of the crimes commonly categorized as "sex crimes" could also be described as violent crimes. This is most clearly true of forcible rape, which traditionally includes the element of the use of force or the threat of force. For example, the federal statute for Aggravated Sexual Abuse (18 U.S.C. § 2241) describes three ways that the crime can be committed. The first of these three constitutes a traditional forcible rape statute:

(a) By force or threat.—Whoever, in the special maritime and territorial jurisdiction of the United States or in a Federal prison, or in any prison, institution, or facility in which persons are held in custody by direction of or pursuant to a contract or agreement with the head of any Federal department or agency, knowingly causes another person to engage in a sexual act—

(1) by using force against that other person; or

(2) by threatening or placing that other person in fear that any person will be subjected to death, serious bodily injury, or kidnapping;

or attempts to do so, shall be fined under this title, imprisoned for any term of years or life, or both.

Under this part of the statute, five elements must be proven:

1) Federal jurisdiction (i.e., in a federal prison)

2) Identification

3) Knowingly

4) Caused another person to engage in a sexual act

5) By using force or putting the person in fear of death, serious bodily injury, or kidnapping.

There are really two action elements at work here. One is the action of the defendant, in using force or threat. The other is actually an action involving the victim (the "sexual act"), caused by the defendant. Note that the statute requires that the victim engage in a sexual act, not the defendant; this allows for someone who causes a victim to have sex with someone other than that defendant to be prosecuted.

One question raised by this statute is what constitutes "force" in this context:

UNITED STATES V. BUCKLEY
195 F. 3d 1034 (8th Cir. 1999)

MORRIS SHEPPARD ARNOLD, CIRCUIT JUDGE.

Following a jury trial, John Buckley was convicted of one count of aggravated sexual abuse by the use of force and two counts of sexual abuse of a minor. On appeal, he challenges only his conviction for aggravated sexual abuse, contending that the government failed to prove that he used force against the victim. We affirm the judgment of the trial court.

The pertinent statutory provision forbids "knowingly caus[ing] another person to engage in a sexual act ... by using force against that other person." *See* 18 U.S.C. § 2241(a)(1). The element of force may be established, *inter alia,* by showing that the defendant used physical force sufficient to overcome, restrain, or injure the victim. *See United States v. Allery,* 139 F.3d 609, 611 (8th Cir.1998), *cert. denied,* 524 U.S. 962, 118 S.Ct. 2389, 141 L.Ed.2d 754 (1998).

Mr. Buckley was the boyfriend of the victim's stepsister, and he and the 15-year-old victim were social friends. At trial, the victim testified that while she was resting at the home of Mr. Buckley and her stepsister, Mr. Buckley approached her on the bed. He turned her toward him, removed her clothing, got on top of her, and had intercourse with her, causing her pain and bleeding. She further testified that although she was crying and nodded "yes" when he asked her whether it hurt and whether she wanted him to stop, he paused only momentarily, and although she attempted to push him off her, she was unable to do so because of his size. We note, moreover, that the doctor who examined the victim at the hospital on the day of the incident testified that she found lacerations and abrasions consistent with the victim's version of the events. Viewing the record in the light most favorable to the verdict, as we must, we conclude that the evidence was sufficient to allow a reasonable jury to find that the element of force was proved beyond a reasonable doubt. *See United States v. Goodlow,* 105 F.3d 1203, 1206 (8th Cir.1997).

Accordingly, we affirm.

EXERCISE

Imagine the facts in *Buckley*, but with a crucial difference: The victim is larger and stronger than the offender. The sexual event occurred the same way, but ended after a few seconds of sexual penetration the victim was able to push the defendant away. In light of the statute and elements described above, should this change in facts affect the outcome?

no? Still an element of force

The evaluation of what might constitute a sufficient force or threat often is deeply engaged in context, including the power dynamic between the defendant and the victim and the setting of the event.

UNITED STATES V. DENJEN
258 F. Supp. 2d 194 (E.D.N.Y. 2003)

GERSHON, DISTRICT JUDGE.

On October 17, 2002, defendant, Randy Denjen, a lieutenant at the Metropolitan Detention Center ("MDC") in Brooklyn, New York, pleaded guilty to Counts Two and Seven of a seven count indictment, that is, to causing the victim to engage in sexual contact by threatening and placing her in fear, in violation of 18 U.S.C. § 2242(1), and to making a false statement to the FBI regarding the sexual contact, in violation of 18 U.S.C. § 1001.

With regard to the sexual offense charge, Denjen allocuted to causing the victim to engage in sexual contact by placing her in fear that, if she did not comply with his sexual advances, she would receive sanctions, such as more time in disciplinary segregation. The sexual offense carries a base level of 27 under the Sentencing Guidelines, U.S.S.G. § 2A3.1. The Second Addendum to the Pre-Sentence Report ("PSR") recommends: a two level enhancement because the victim was a person in a correctional facility, § 2A3.1(b)(3)(B); a two level enhancement for obstruction of justice under application note 8 to § 3C1.1; a base level offense of 6 for the false statement count, which is grouped with the above count, and; an adjustment for acceptance of responsibility of –3, §§ 3E1.1(a) and (b)(2).

The PSR also recommends a four level enhancement for the use of force under U.S.S.G. § 2A3.1(b)(1) which states, "If the offense was committed by the means set forth in 18 U.S.C. § 2241(a) or (b), increase by 4 levels." Section 2241(a) provides in pertinent part:

> (a) By force or threat. Whoever, ... in a Federal prison, knowingly causes another person to engage in a sexual act-
>
> (1) by using force against that other person; or
>
> (2) by threatening or placing that other person in fear that any person will be subjected to death, serious bodily injury, or kidnapping; or attempts to do so, shall be fined under this title, imprisoned for any term of years or life, or both.

Defendant has sought an evidentiary hearing as to the use of force enhancement. The government's position is that the enhancement is applicable.

On February 27, 2003, this court held an evidentiary hearing solely to address the dispute as to the applicability of the use of force enhancement. The parties agreed that the entire conduct of defendant was to be considered relevant conduct in making this determination. The government must prove the use of force by a preponderance of the evidence.

The Meaning of "Force"

"Force" is not defined in Section 2241(a) or in the Sentencing Guidelines. However, the Court of Appeals for the Second Circuit, relying on the legislative history, held that "[t]he statute requires only the use of 'force,' not of 'significantly violent action or threats.' The legislative history indicates that a specific intent of Congress was to reduce the necessity of demonstrating the use of excessive force in order to provide greater protection for the victim." *United States v. Lauck,* 905 F.2d 15, 18 (2d Cir.1990). The Court also held that "the requirement of force may be satisfied by a showing of ... the use of such physical force as is sufficient to overcome, restrain, or injure a person." *Id.* at 17.

[handwritten: satisfying the "force" requirement]

The 'force' that the statute condemns is ... force that, by being used against the other person, results in a sexual contact. The force does not have to be part of the sexual contact itself, but must be used only in order to make the contact. If ... the sexual contact resulted from a restraint upon the other person that was sufficient that the other person could not escape the sexual contact, that is sufficient ...."

Id. at 18. It is immaterial that the defendant did not use a weapon, did not threaten or harm the victim, and did not inflict pain on her. *Id.* The force required by the statute has been described as including the use of a threat of harm sufficient to coerce or compel submission by the victim. *United States v. Fire Thunder,* 908 F.2d 272, 274 (8th Cir.1990). A finding of force has also been based upon the disparity in size and coercive power between

[handwritten: Force~ use of threat or harm sufficient to coerce or compel submission by the victim]

the defendant and his victim, for example, when the defendant is an adult male and the victim is a child. *United States v. Bordeaux,* 997 F.2d 419, 421 (8th Cir.1993). And in *United States v. Lucas,* 157 F.3d 998, 1002 (5th Cir.1998), the court found force based upon the disparity in power between a jail warden and an inmate, combined with physical restraint.

The Hearing

The sole witness at the hearing was the victim. She was entirely honest and candid, equally so on cross examination as on direct. Even defense counsel acknowledged, "certainly on one point I agree wholeheartedly with [government counsel], this witness was a very credible witness." The evidence at the hearing established the following facts.

The victim, twenty-four years old at the time of the hearing, and the mother of two young children, is from London. She was arrested at John F. Kennedy airport on July 8, 2001 for importing ecstasy into the United States.

On the night of November 24, 2001, the victim was in solitary confinement, on a suicide watch, at the MDC awaiting sentencing on her plea of guilty to the importation charge. She was in a tiny cell containing a mattress on a cinder block or cement platform that was situated lengthwise along the wall. Based upon the pictures submitted into evidence and her testimony, the distance between the door to her cell and the bed was only a few feet. The victim thought that the cell was underground, like a "dungeon." The cell was isolated from the rest of the prison, and there were no guards or inmates anywhere near it, with the exception of the lieutenant's office down the corridor. Lieutenants have more authority than corrections officers, and they are responsible for discipline and punishment. Denjen was a lieutenant and occupied the office down the corridor from the victim's cell on November 24, 2001. At time of the attacks, Denjen was 6'5" tall and weighed 285 pounds, and the victim was 5'7" tall and weighed 108 pounds.

At approximately midnight, Denjen began talking to the victim, through the window in her cell door, about her sexuality. He then unlocked the victim's cell door, entered her cell and asked her, "what about me and you?" She told him that "I don't see you like that," meaning that he was not her type and that she wouldn't think of sleeping with someone like him. She told him "you're a lieutenant, I'm an inmate, it just doesn't work, it is disgusting." She also told him that she hadn't bathed for many days and that she felt dirty. Denjen said, "it doesn't matter." Denjen then tried to kiss her and push his tongue into her mouth. He unzipped his pants and took her hand and placed it on his penis while he masturbated. The victim testified that, at this point, she felt physically sick and scared. She said that she didn't want to get him angry because she was afraid that he would hurt her; in her words, "look how big he is." He told her that he wanted to touch her, that she should "think about it" and he would return. He left her in the cell and locked the door. The victim testified that, before Denjen touched her, she didn't really know what was going on and that she was not afraid to tell him "no." She testified that, "[i]t wasn't until I realized what was going on that I kept my mouth shut."

After about fifteen minutes, Denjen returned, opened the cell door and entered the cell. He asked the victim if she had "thought about it," and she said, "Lieutenant, I'm sorry, I don't find you attractive and I don't like you in that way, I am an inmate, you're a lieutenant." She testified that she just kept repeating herself, but he told her that "it doesn't matter." He kissed her and tried to push his tongue in her mouth, but she clenched her teeth. He asked her to kiss his penis, she paused, but eventually did so because, "I thought I had no choice and I was scared and I didn't know what to do." He grabbed the bottom of her jumpsuit, pulled her to him, unbuttoned two buttons and then shoved his hand down into her jumpsuit and touched her sexually. He left again, locking the door behind him.

After he left, she "was walking up and down the cell talking out loud to God asking him what to do, I don't know what to do, I don't know what to do, oh, my God, help me, oh, my God, oh, my God, what do I do. I was freaking out, I didn't know what to do. I was so scared, I didn't know what to do."

After approximately five minutes, Denjen returned with cigarettes, but then left to get a lighter. When he returned she went up to the door with the cigarette in her mouth hoping that he might not come right into the cell. However, he came into her cell, removed the cigarette from her mouth and began kissing her "all over my mouth trying to put his tongue in my mouth." He told her "that's it and he wanted more and I must take off my jumpsuit and leave one leg in so that it is quick, easy for me to put my clothes on if somebody comes." She was standing when she took off her jumpsuit, but then sat down on the mattress because she didn't want him to see her naked. He stood in front of her, held out his penis and told her to kiss it. She did so "a little bit." He then told her to "spread it." She spread her legs a little as she was sitting, but, "I wasn't going to spread my legs that way so he came between me and opened my legs." He spread her legs wide with his body and told her to lie down on the bed. She wouldn't lie back lengthwise, the way he wanted her to, so he pushed her shoulders back across the bed until her head and shoulders were pushed against the wall. She was curled up against the wall with her legs up. She did not resist being pushed down.

The victim testified that "he was in a really bad way, he was in a mess and he was shaking all over the place and trying to put his penis inside me and he just couldn't do it because he was in such a frantic mess and eventually he managed to put it in. He was on my stomach, he's got a big stomach." She couldn't breath because he was so heavy. She just turned her head and closed her eyes. She said that there was no way she could have escaped from under his body. When asked why she didn't scream out when Denjen first began his attack, the victim answered, "[s]cream out and get

didn't resist b/c
could've gotten
into trouble or
killed

strangled, no." She testified that she did not attempt to make any noise or draw attention to herself from anywhere else in the MDC at the time of this attack because "[i]t's impossible to do that." Even with the door open, there was "[n]o way whatsoever, not a single soul would have heard me and if they did they work for him anyway so." When asked why she did not physically resist when he made these sexual advances, the victim testified, "[i]t would be silly to, I mean I could get myself into trouble, he could have killed me down there, no one would have known different. I just wanted to survive and get it over with as soon as possible."

Denjen stopped the attack when he heard the keys of another corrections officer entering the unit. When the female officer reached the cell door, Denjen told her that, "I've got somebody in here" and the officer said, "oh, have you, okay." At that point Denjen left with the officer.

Defendant's Arguments

Denjen argues that he did not use force because he did not physically restrain the victim and that the victim made no effort to fight him off. Denjen argues that there must be more force than the normal physical force of contact during sex, since, in any sexual act, there will be some physical force between the parties. He also argues that the victim could have tried to escape and that there was some avenue to at least get out of the immediate area of the attack because the door was wide open during the attacks. Finally, defendant argues that the fact that the victim was previously arrested for physically assaulting a woman in England, who was bigger than she was, shows that, if she had really wanted to fight Denjen off, she would have at least attempted to do so.

Conclusion

The evidence amply supports a finding that Denjen used force when he sexually attacked the victim and that the sexual contact was a result of the force he used against her.

To begin with, she was locked in an isolated cell to which Denjen had the key, and Denjen had complete control over her. Even when the door was open, she was restrained from getting out of her cell by his presence between her and the door. Thus, there was no means of physical escape. Even if she could have maneuvered around him and gotten through the door and out into the corridor, which is highly unlikely given Denjen's size compared to the size of the doorway, she had nowhere to go, and her testimony that no one would have heard her had she screamed was uncontested. Thus, the victim was physically trapped, either by the locked door when Denjen was not there or by Denjen's enormous physical presence. Second, Denjen used physical force to make sexual contact with the victim when he kept trying to stick his tongue in her mouth, when he grabbed her jumpsuit, pulled her to him, shoved his hands into her jumpsuit and touched her sexually, and when he physically pushed her legs apart, pushed her back against the wall and pinned her down with his weight while he had intercourse with her. All of this occurred after her repeated statements that she did not want to have sex with him.

The victim testified that she told Denjen "no" until he made it clear that he was going to proceed to sexually assault her no matter what she did. As was clear from the testimony, she was in a state of dread. Her fear that any further physical resistance would have resulted only in harm to her was completely reasonable given his size and his behavior. Therefore, the fact that she did not engage in greater physical resistance than set forth here in no way mitigates against a finding of force.

The facts of this case are similar to those in *United States v. Lucas,* 157 F.3d 998 (5th Cir.1998), where a county jail warden was found to have used force against his inmate victim when he summoned her to a relatively secluded location, locked the door so she could not escape his advances and pressed her against a table in such a way that she could not leave. The court stated that "the disparity in power between a jail warden and an inmate, combined with physical restraint, is sufficient to satisfy the force requirement of § 2241." *Id.* at 1002. The court found that, even if the warden had not locked the door, the warden pressing her against the table and thereby blocking her means of egress, sufficed to constitute force. *Id.* at 1002 n. 9. The *Lucas* court was not deterred from finding the use of force by the fact that the victim did not protest when summoned by the warden nor by the fact that the victim did not try to fight off her attacker. Here also, the victim was in a completely secluded area, her egress was blocked by Denjen standing between her and the cell door as well as by his physical weight pressing her against the bed during one of the sexual attacks. Indeed, that the victim was locked in her cell in between attacks and was repeatedly forced to submit to Denjen shows an even greater degree of coercion and force than *Lucas,* where there was only one attack, and there was no finding of a disparity in size between the victim and the defendant.

In sum, the standard of force, as set forth by the Court of Appeals for the Second Circuit in *Lauck* has been met. The sexual contact resulted from a restraint upon the victim that was sufficient that she could not escape it. *Lauck,* 905 F.2d at 18. The four level enhancement under § 2A3.1(b)(1) will be applied.

––––––––––––

EXERCISE

These cases note that there is no statutory definition for what constitutes "force." Imagine that you are a staff member working for a member of Congress who would like to fix this problem. Draft a workable definition for use with 18 U.S.C. § 2241. When you do so, consider the fact that many facts will differ from case to case, including the relative size of the defendant and victim, the nature of the force used, and the context of the assault.

The *threat* of force can also fulfill the action element of 18 U.S.C. § 2241(a), provided that the threat places the victim "in fear that any person will be subjected to death, serious bodily injury, or kidnapping."

UNITED STATES V. HOLLY
488 F. 3d 1298 (10th Cir. 2007)

MURPHY, CIRCUIT JUDGE.

Melvin Holly was convicted by a jury on fourteen criminal counts, including five counts of felony deprivation of rights under color of law involving aggravated sexual abuse. In the district court's instruction to the jury on the definition of aggravated sexual abuse, the court informed the jury it need not find actual violence and could infer the requisite degree of force from a disparity in size or coercive power. It further explained the jury could alternatively find the requisite fear element if there was a fear of some bodily harm, which could also be inferred from a disparity in size or power, or control over the victim's everyday life. On appeal, Holly argues the district court erroneously instructed the jury on the definition of aggravated sexual abuse. . . .

Holly, the sheriff of Latimer County, was indicted in a fifteen-count superseding indictment that charged eight counts of misdemeanor deprivation of rights under color of law in violation of 18 U.S.C. § 242; five counts of felony deprivation of rights under color of law involving aggravated sexual abuse in violation of 18 U.S.C. § 242; one count of making a false statement in violation of 18 U.S.C. § 1001; and one count of tampering with a witness in violation of 18 U.S.C. § 1512(a)(2)(C). The indictment arose out of a series of sexual assaults perpetrated by Holly against inmates and employees of the Latimer County Jail, as well as the daughter of an employee of the jail. Following a five-day jury trial, Holly was convicted on all counts except one count of misdemeanor deprivation of rights under color of law. Holly challenges his conviction only as to the five counts of felony deprivation of rights. On each of these five counts, the jury found the deprivation of rights involved aggravated sexual abuse.

With respect to the five counts at issue in this appeal, there was testimony presented at trial that Holly had nonconsensual sex with four inmates at the Latimer County Jail and attempted to have sex with another whose resistance ultimately deterred him. Each of the five victims testified at trial. Summer Hyslop testified that Holly took her from the jail to his farm where he parked the car, told her to get into the back seat, and then proceeded to rape her. She explained she did not run away because she was scared he would shoot her. In addition, Hyslop stated that on another occasion, Holly raped her on the floor of his office at the jail. Vicki Fowler testified that Holly forced her to have sex with him in his office after allowing her to make a personal phone call. Amber Helmert related a situation in which Holly attempted to have sex with her in his office after calling her to the office using the pretext of a family emergency. Helmert testified that she yelled and physically resisted him, ultimately causing him to stop the assault. Although her resistance prevented Holly from having sex with her, Helmert testified that he penetrated her vaginal area with his finger. Rebecca Foreman testified that Holly took her from the jail to a trailer in a nearby town where he made sexual advances and proceeded to have sex with her against her will. April Partain testified that Holly had sex with her in his office against her will and that she did not fight back because she was afraid of his reaction. Partain explained she had sex with Holly on multiple occasions.

While each of the victims testified she was scared at the time of the sexual assaults, only Helmert referenced any specific threat made by Holly during the sexual encounter. Each victim did, however, testify that Holly was wearing a gun just prior to the sexual assault and placed it within reach while the incidents occurred. Helmert further elaborated that Holly looked repeatedly at his gun just prior to the sexual assault and threatened to "get to" her family, including her nine-year-old sister, if she did not cooperate. Hyslop, Foreman, and Partain all admitted, either in their trial testimony or in a prior statement, that they had sex or flirted with Holly partially for the benefits and jail privileges they received as a result. Only Helmert testified she physically resisted Holly's advances. . . .

In formulating its jury instruction on aggravated sexual abuse, the district court rejected Holly's requested jury instruction that simply quoted the aggravated sexual abuse statutory language. It instead gave the following instruction:

> The term "aggravated sexual abuse" means that a person was caused to engage in a sexual act by another's use of force against that person or by threatening or placing that person in fear that any person will be subjected to death, serious bodily injury, or kidnapping. . . .

jury instruction

> You may find that the defendant's conduct involved aggravated sexual abuse if you find that he used force during the alleged sexual assault. To establish force, the government need not demonstrate that the defendant used actual violence. The requirement of force may be satisfied by a showing of restraint sufficient to prevent the victim from escaping the sexual conduct. Force may also be implied from a disparity in coercive power or in size between the defendant and the victim or from the disparity in coercive power, combined with physical restraint.

force — actual violence or coercive power

Alternatively, you may find the defendant's conduct involved aggravated sexual abuse if you find the defendant placed the victim in fear of death, serious bodily injury, or kidnapping. The requirement of fear may be satisfied when the defendant's actions implicitly place the victim in fear of some bodily harm. Like force, fear can be inferred from the circumstances, particularly a disparity in power between the defendant and the victim. Further, a defendant's control over a victim's everyday life can generate fear.

force or threat

. . . Because aggravated sexual abuse is not defined in § 242, the statute necessarily requires reference to 18 U.S.C. § 2241, the federal aggravated sexual abuse statute. Under § 2241(a), an individual commits aggravated sexual abuse if he "knowingly causes another person to engage in a sexual act—(1) by using force against that other person; or (2) by threatening or placing that other person in fear that any person will be subjected to death, serious bodily injury, or kidnapping." Thus, although Holly's convictions on the challenged counts were pursuant to § 242, these convictions turn on whether his acts violated the substantive provisions of § 2241.

Holly argues the district court erroneously instructed the jury on the definition of aggravated sexual abuse. While he does not dispute the general definition of aggravated sexual abuse drawn directly from the statutory language of § 2241, he contends the district court erred in its subsequent explanation of the requisite elements of a violation. He argues the language of the jury instruction at issue eliminated the government's burden of proving the fear of serious bodily harm. . . .

Holly argument "fear"

Holly challenges the district court's jury instruction on the element of fear in two respects. First, he argues it was error to instruct the jury that "[t]he requirement of fear may be satisfied when the defendant's actions implicitly place the victim in fear of some bodily harm." Second, he argues it was error to allow the jury to infer fear from "a disparity in power between the defendant and the victim" or "a defendant's control over a victim's everyday life." Because the district court's use of language suggesting the victim need only be placed in fear of "some bodily harm" impermissibly reduced the degree of fear necessary to sustain a conviction, this court concludes the instruction on fear was erroneous.

As noted above, a defendant commits aggravated sexual abuse in violation of § 2241(a)(2) only "by threatening or placing [another] person in fear that any person will be subjected to death, serious bodily injury, or kidnapping." Although the victim's fear may alone support a conviction without the use of actual force, a specific and severe form of fear is required.

It is this heightened degree of fear that distinguishes *aggravated* sexual abuse from the separate crime of sexual abuse set forth in 18 U.S.C. § 2242. A violation of § 2242(1) merely requires that the defendant "causes another person to engage in a sexual act by threatening or placing that other person in fear (other than by threatening or placing that other person in fear that any other person will be subjected to death, serious bodily injury, or kidnapping)." Thus, § 2242(1) sets forth a lesser degree of fear than § 2241(a)(2). A defendant commits sexual abuse if he places the victim in fear, but commits aggravated sexual abuse only if that fear rises to the level of fear of death, serious bodily injury, or kidnapping.

The jury instruction given by the district court failed to make this critical distinction between §§ 2241(a)(2) and 2242(1). Although the court began by paraphrasing the statutory language of § 2241(a)(2), it then used language more closely resembling that of § 2242(1). By instructing the jury that the fear element is satisfied by fear of "some bodily harm," the district court eliminated the heightened degree of fear required to support a conviction for aggravated sexual abuse. . . .

Because the jury instruction did not clearly require the jury to find the heightened level of fear of death, serious bodily injury, or kidnapping necessary to convict Holly of felony deprivation of rights under color of law, involving aggravated sexual abuse, the instruction was erroneous.

instruction was erroneous

Having resolved that the jury was instructed on two independent bases for conviction, force and fear, one of which was proper and one of which was erroneous, this court must now resolve whether any of Holly's convictions on Counts II, IV, V, VI, and VII can nevertheless be affirmed. This determination requires an analysis of whether harmless error review is applicable and, if so, whether the instructional error was harmless as to any count of conviction. . . .

This court's review of Helmert's testimony at trial renders it certain that the requisite element of fear of death, serious bodily injury, or kidnapping was "uncontested and supported by overwhelming evidence, such that the jury verdict would have been the same absent the error." *Neder,* 527 U.S. at 17, 119 S.Ct. 1827. A thorough examination of the entire trial transcript further confirms this conclusion.

At trial, Helmert testified as follows:

Q. [Prosecutor] What happened at that point?

A. [Helmert] At that point, I go—my back is towards the door and I go—and he grabs me and he said—and I said, "Get away from me."

And he says that if he can't get to me, he'll get to my family, and my little sister is cute too. He goes, "Your little sister is awfully cute too." And my little sister is nine years old.

Q. Did that upset you?

A. Yes, very much.

And I go to turn around and he's looking at—his gun is sitting on the table and he's looking at his gun the whole time, you know, or he would look down at it. And he pushed me up beside the door and pushed me down on the ground and he had his hand over my mouth and he's kissing my neck and he starts to kiss my neck and I keep on moving it and I'm trying to push him off and he puts his hands—his hand down there and touched me, and then I started kicking. I got off and he said, "Get up," he said, "You are too loud," and then he said a cuss word and he said, "You are too loud, get out of my office."

This testimony provides overwhelming evidence that Holly placed Helmert in fear that either she or her nine-year-old sister would be subjected to death, serious bodily injury, or kidnapping.

———————

EXERCISE

Is it rational that the differentiation point in these laws is what type of harm is threatened? Other aspects of the situation may be more important. For example, in this situation the predominate power dynamic is likely not the words used in a threat, but the roles of sheriff and inmate.

As a legislator, what better ways might there be to distinguish more serious crimes involving sex from those that are less serious?

B. SEX PROCURED BY COERCION

18 U.S.C. § 2242(1) covers conduct where sex is procured by coercion which can include threats or fear of something less than physical harm:

Whoever, in the special maritime and territorial jurisdiction of the United States or in a Federal prison, or in any prison, institution, or facility in which persons are held in custody by direction of or pursuant to a contract or agreement with the head of any Federal department or agency, knowingly—

(1) causes another person to engage in a sexual act by threatening or placing that other person in fear (other than by threatening or placing that other person in fear that any person will be subjected to death, serious bodily injury, or kidnapping). . . .

Under this part of the statute, five elements must be proven:

1) Federal jurisdiction (i.e., in a federal prison)

2) Identification

3) Knowingly

4)   Caused another person to engage in a sexual act

5)   By threatening or placing that other person in fear.

It is the last of these elements that will often prove most challenging for the prosecutor, particularly where a defense of consent is raised—that is, where the defendant asserts that the victim consented to the sexual act rather than submitting under threat or because of fear.

UNITED STATES V. JOHNS

15 F. 3d 740 (8th Cir. 1993)

HEANEY, SENIOR CIRCUIT JUDGE.

Dale Thomas Johns was convicted of two counts of carnal knowledge of a female under age sixteen, 18 U.S.C. §§ 1153, 2032; one count of rape, 18 U.S.C. §§ 1153, 2031; and five counts of sexual abuse, 18 U.S.C. §§ 1153, 2242(1). He received concurrent sentences of 108 months imprisonment for each count. Johns raises several challenges to his convictions and sentence.

I.

Johns is a member of the Red Lake Band of Ojibwa Indians. He met S.D., an Ojibwa woman, in Minneapolis when he was a chemical dependency counselor and she was seeking help to deal with drinking and other personal problems. S.D. and her daughter C.D. moved in with Johns, and S.D. and Johns began an intimate relationship. In 1982, when C.D. was twelve, they moved to the Red Lake Indian Reservation, where Johns studied traditional Indian religion and spiritual practices and began conducting doctoring ceremonies in the family residence. Johns assumed the role of father as well as spiritual teacher in the household, and C.D. became his primary assistant when conducting ceremonies. Johns also worked for the Red Lake Social Services Department.

C.D. testified that Johns sexually abused her from 1984 until 1991, when she was age fourteen to twenty-one. C.D. recounted numerous occasions during which Johns engaged in oral, anal, and vaginal intercourse with her. As a parent, Johns controlled her movements and activities both inside and outside the home and was able to command her absence from school or work in order to engage in sex. As a spiritual teacher and medicine man who made C.D. his primary assistant, Johns ensured time alone with C.D. before and after religious ceremonies because according to tradition no one could disturb the medicine man and his assistant during these times. He taught her that events in her life, including the abuse, were ordained by the spirits and that harm would come to her or loved ones if she disrespected the spirits. Johns told C.D. she was his wife, she belonged to him, and one day she was to have his children so he could pass along his pipe and his feathers to them.

S.D. and C.D. moved off the reservation in 1991 after C.D. reported the sexual abuse to her mother. A jury convicted Johns of eight counts of sexual misconduct occurring between December 1985 and August 1991, and Johns appeals.

II.

A.

Johns first challenges the sufficiency of the evidence to support the five counts of sexual abuse, claiming there was no evidence he placed C.D. in fear. Prosecution under 18 U.S.C. § 2242(1) requires that the defendant knowingly ... cause[ ] another person to engage in a sexual act by threatening or placing that other person in fear (other than by threatening or placing that other person in fear that any person will be subjected to death, serious bodily injury, or kidnaping); . . . .

Johns challenging sufficiency of evidence

Johns argues that the "placing in fear" element was not satisfied because, by her own testimony, C.D. states that she feared rejection by the spirits rather than actual harm to herself or others, and that sort of fear is not contemplated by the statute. We disagree with Johns' characterization of C.D.'s testimony. C.D. testified that Johns yelled at her and hit and slapped her, and that she was afraid of what he would do to her. T. 425, 444–45, 461. She also testified Johns taught her that rejection by the spirits would result in harm to her or a loved one, such as illness or inability to have children, and that the way to avoid spiritual rejection was to follow his dictates. T. 406, 425–26, 430, 444–46, 462, 471.

That C.D. attributed some, though not all, of her fears of harm to the spirits rather than directly to Johns simply reflects the fact that Johns cultivated C.D.'s fear and compliance through his position as spiritual teacher and healer and his selection of her as his primary assistant in conducting religious ceremonies. He framed his behavior, and hers, in terms of roles determined by the spirits. For example, when C.D. was sixteen, Johns said he would perform a ceremony to stop his feelings for her. C.D. testified that she told him not to do it because I was so scared of, I mean, you know, he always would say that we can stop, we can stop. But then right away he would start saying that stuff would happen to me because I wasn't living my role, and I wasn't following the ways, you know, the traditional ways. I mean, God, I was scared. I didn't know what was going to happen. I mean, you don't know what the spirits are going to do. T. 445–46. His intertwining of purportedly spiritual teachings with sexual abuse of C.D. accentuated, not diminished, the fear C.D. felt.

Johns also fails to acknowledge the fear generated by his dominance of every aspect of C.D.'s life over a period of years: choosing her clothes, isolating her from friends and her biological father, controlling her activities, pulling her out of school to engage in sex, and constantly changing household rules and becoming enraged when they were not followed.

Apart from mischaracterizing C.D.'s testimony, Johns suggests that the level of fear to which she testified is insufficient under the statute. The statute and the case law indicate otherwise. By expressly excluding fear of death, serious bodily injury, or kidnaping, which are covered in a separate statute, section 2242(1) envisions a lesser degree of fear. . . . The record contains ample evidence to support the jury's conclusion that Johns caused C.D. to engage in sexual acts by placing her in fear.

EXERCISE

The Johns case is made more difficult for the defense because of the age of the defendant and the use of both physical violence and spiritual threats. If the victim were an adult and the fear generated solely through the use of spiritual threats, should the same result be reached? As a defense attorney, how might you argue that spiritual threats are not sufficient for conviction?

C. NON-CONSENSUAL SEX

Contemporary law recognizes not only that sexual acts can be illegal when they are forced or coerced, but when they occur with a lack of consent from one of the parties involved. This is an area of law that is quickly developing, as American jurisdictions pay more attention to protecting the sexual autonomy of those who might be subjected to sexual abuse not accompanied by explicit or implicit threats. There are two conditions where non-consensual sex is charged. The first is where a conscious victim simply does not consent to the sex, or changes their mind as the sexual act occurs. The second is when the victim is impaired or unconscious—circumstances that will be discussed in the next section.

1. NON-CONSENSUAL SEX WITH A CONSCIOUS VICTIM

The first situation—where a conscious, non-impaired victim does not give consent—is described in 18 U.S.C. § 2244(b), which provides:

(b) In other circumstances.—Whoever, in the special maritime and territorial jurisdiction of the United States or in a Federal prison, or in any prison, institution, or facility in which persons are held in custody by direction of or pursuant to a contract or agreement with the head of any Federal department or agency, knowingly engages in sexual contact with another person without that other person's permission shall be fined under this title, imprisoned not more than two years, or both.

elements of non-consentual sex [handwritten margin note]

Five elements must be proven:

1) Federal jurisdiction (i.e., in a federal prison)

2) Identification

3) Knowingly

4) Engaged in sexual contact with another person

5) Without the permission of the other person.

There are three critical differences between the elements of this statute and the others we have examined.

First, § 2244(b) requires sexual *contact* rather than a sexual *act*. Under 18 U.S.C. § 2246(3), sexual contact can consist of actions including the intentional touching of the inner thigh over clothing, provided that it is for the purpose of sexual gratification.

Second, the other statutes require that the prosecutor prove causation—that the defendant caused the victim to engage in a sexual act. Under this statute, it only requires that the defendant engage in the sexual contact.

Finally, § 2241(1) (covering sexual acts procured by force or threat of death, serious bodily injury, or kidnapping) and § 2242(1) (covering sexual acts procured by coercion) both have elements requiring the proof of a positive action by the defendant—force, threat, or coercion. This statute, in contrast, merely requires proof of the defendant's lack of consent.

Altogether, these elements allow prosecutors to charge "groping" incidents that may be fleeting and anonymous.

UNITED STATES V. ERRAMILLI

788 F. 3d 723 (7th Cir. 2015)

TINDER, CIRCUIT JUDGE.

Srinivasa Erramilli has been caught three times fondling unsuspecting women on airplanes. Once in 1999 and once in 2002, he took a window seat behind a young woman, and when she appeared to fall asleep, he reached forward and fondled one of her breasts. Then, in 2011, he took a middle seat between a woman and her husband (who was coincidentally blind in the eye closest to him), and when the woman appeared to fall asleep, he fondled her inner thigh. It is this latter incident that led to Erramilli's conviction for abusive sexual contact in this case. At trial, the government introduced evidence of his prior acts pursuant to Federal Rule of Evidence 413. On appeal, Erramilli argues that his prior acts should have been excluded and that, even if they were properly admitted, the jury instruction on their use was improper. We disagree; therefore, we affirm.

argues that prior acts should have been excluded [handwritten note]

I. BACKGROUND

In June 2011, Susan and Vincent Domino took a trip to Las Vegas for their thirty-fourth wedding anniversary. On June 14, their trip came to an end, and they boarded their return flight to Chicago on Southwest Airlines. Because of Southwest's open boarding policy, the Dominos were free to choose their seats. Vincent is blind in his right eye, so the Dominos generally sit on the right side of the plane, allowing him to see the flight attendants when drinks are served. This time was no exception: the Dominos sat toward the back of the plane, on the right side of the center aisle. Vincent took the aisle seat, as he thought he might need to use the restroom during the flight. Susan was tired and thought she might be getting sick; she chose the window seat so she could lay her head against the side of the plane and get some rest.

Meanwhile, Erramilli had been in Las Vegas on business and had booked the same return flight to Chicago. The flight was full, and Erramilli was the last to board, so he took the only seat available to him: the seat between the Dominos. By that time, Susan had crossed her left leg over her right and was leaning against the window. She remained in that position as the plane took off and eventually she succeeded in falling asleep. At some point after takeoff, however, she felt something brush against her leg, and she jolted awake. Not seeing anything suspicious, she assumed the contact was accidental, so she moved a little closer to the window and went back to sleep. A little later, Susan was awakened once more when she felt some pressure on her upper thigh, "like somebody was kneading it." She turned, bumped Erramilli's knee, and said, "Oh, excuse me." Erramilli said nothing in response; instead, he folded his arms on the seatback tray in front of him and put his head down. A little drowsy and still unsure of what was happening, Susan curled up again and tried to go back to sleep.

As the plane approached Chicago, Susan ordered a cup of coffee, then she leaned back in her seat and closed her eyes. She began to wonder whether someone had been touching her leg during the flight, and she opened her eyes to find that Erramilli had turned his legs toward her. Thinking that was strange, she closed her eyes again for a moment and then reopened them. At that point, Erramilli reached his left hand across his body and, while concealing it with a newspaper, slid his hand up her shorts and squeezed her inner thigh. Then, as Susan put it, she "lost control."

Susan turned and struck Erramilli, then she called him a "pig" and a "pervert." He asked what she was doing, and she responded, "You know what you were doing." Erramilli said, "I don't know what you are talking about." Then, Susan told Vincent what happened and asked for the authorities. Erramilli pleaded with them not to call the authorities, saying that his wife and two children were waiting for him and that they could "settle this in a civil matter." By this time, he was sweating profusely. He also said something to the effect of, "I thought you liked it." Eventually,

Vincent pressed the flight attendant call button, but the plane was already descending into Chicago, and the flight attendants could not immediately come to their aid. As soon as the plane arrived at the gate, Erramilli got up and tried to exit, but Vincent blocked him in. Then, a flight attendant arrived and escorted the three of them into the jetway, where they met with officers from the Chicago Police Department. Susan told her story to the police, and later, the FBI.

On November 1, 2011, a grand jury returned an indictment against Erramilli, charging him with two counts of abusive sexual contact under 18 U.S.C. § 2244, which applies to acts committed on aircraft pursuant to 49 U.S.C. § 46506(1). Under the statute, "the term 'sexual contact' means the intentional touching, either directly or through the clothing, of the genitalia, anus, groin, breast, inner thigh, or buttocks of any person with an intent to abuse, humiliate, harass, degrade, or arouse or gratify the sexual desire of any person." 18 U.S.C. § 2246(3). The first count of the indictment charged Erramilli under 18 U.S.C. § 2244(a)(2), based on the contact that occurred while Susan was asleep. However, the government voluntarily dismissed that count during trial, after concluding that there was insufficient evidence that Erramilli made contact with Susan's inner thigh (or any other area listed in the statute) while she was asleep. The second count charged Erramilli under 18 U.S.C. § 2244(b), which proscribes "knowingly engag[ing] in sexual contact with another person without that other person's permission." This charge was based on the contact that occurred after Susan awoke but without her permission.

The government filed a motion *in limine* under Federal Rule of Evidence 413, asking the district court to admit evidence of two prior sexual assaults committed by Erramilli. In response, Erramilli argued that such evidence should be excluded under Federal Rule of Evidence 403because its probative value was substantially outweighed by the danger of unfair prejudice. The district court disagreed and granted the government's motion. However, the court cautioned that "the proper focus of the trial must be the underlying conduct that supports the instant offense, rather than the prior offenses," and it directed the government to "limit its presentation to evidence that is necessary to convey the essential facts underlying the two prior offenses" and "limit emotional testimony from the prior victims."

At trial, the government presented testimony regarding Erramilli's prior acts. First, one of his prior victims testified that on August 30, 1999, when she was twenty-seven years old, she was seated next to a window on a flight from Detroit to Chicago. At some point during the flight, she placed her right arm on the armrest and leaned her head against the window, hoping to take a nap. Then, she felt a hand reach between her right arm and her body, grazing the side of her breast. At first, she thought it must have been a child playing, but then it happened again, and she grew suspicious. Then it happened a third time, only the contact with her breast was more substantial and obviously intentional. This time, she grabbed the hand and turned around to see who it was. It was Erramilli. The woman took a few minutes to process things, then she went to the back of the plane to tell the flight attendants what happened. Ultimately, Erramilli pled guilty to an Illinois battery charge.

previous battery

Next, the government presented the testimony of a former FBI agent who interviewed Erramilli following an incident that occurred on a flight from San Jose to Detroit on February 6, 2002. During the interview, Erramilli explained that although he had been upgraded to first class, he took a window seat behind an eighteen-year-old woman in coach. The woman was initially resting her head on a pillow positioned against the window, but eventually she removed the pillow. At that point, Erramilli reached forward to touch her breast. The woman clamped down on his arm with her elbow, which Erramilli took to mean that she wanted him to touch her. Erramilli admitted to the FBI agent that he was excited when he touched the woman's breast and that he had "a little bit of an erection." Ultimately, he pled guilty to abusive sexual contact in the U.S. District Court for the Eastern District of Michigan. . . .

- previous abusive sexual contact

On appeal, Erramilli argues that the district court abused its discretion in admitting the evidence of his prior sexual assaults. . .

Generally, evidence of prior crimes cannot be used to support a propensity inference, that is, "to prove a person's character in order to show that on a particular occasion the person acted in accordance with the character." Fed.R.Evid. 404(b)(1). Such evidence may only be used for other purposes, such as proving "motive, opportunity, intent, preparation, plan, knowledge, identity, absence of mistake, or lack of accident." Fed.R.Evid. 404(b)(2). However, "[i]n a criminal case in which a defendant is accused of a sexual assault, the court may admit evidence that the defendant committed any other sexual assault," and "[t]he evidence may be considered on any matter to which it is relevant." Fed.R.Evid. 413(a). Thus, "[e]vidence that tends to show that a criminal defendant has a propensity to commit crimes ordinarily is excluded from trial, but Rule 413 makes an exception where past sexual offenses are introduced in sexual assault cases." *Foley,* 740 F.3d at 1086. . . .

purpose of admitting prior crimes

Erramilli makes a feeble attempt to argue that his prior sexual assaults were not relevant, but they were relevant for at least two purposes. First, they were relevant as propensity evidence, because "the simple fact that [he] had done it before makes it more likely that he did it again." *Rogers,* 587 F.3d at 821. Erramilli complains that his prior assaults had several distinguishing characteristics and were committed long before 2011, but these arguments go to the probative value of the prior assaults, not their relevance. Rule 401 requires only that the evidence have "any tendency to make a fact more or less probable than it would be without the evidence," and the fact that Erramilli sexually assaulted women who were trying to sleep while onboard aircraft in 1999 and 2002 tends to make it more probable that he committed another such assault in 2011.

Second, Erramilli's prior sexual assaults were relevant to prove that he knowingly engaged in "sexual contact," which is required for a conviction under 18 U.S.C. § 2244(b). In order to prove that element of the offense, the government had to establish that Erramilli intentionally touched Susan Domino's inner thigh "with an intent to abuse, humiliate, harass, degrade, or arouse or gratify the sexual desire of any person." 18 U.S.C. § 2246(3). At trial, Erramilli argued that the government failed to prove the "sexual arousal" element, and he also suggested that his touching of Susan's leg was accidental. The fact that he was admittedly motivated by sexual desire when he committed the prior assaults tends to prove otherwise. Thus, those prior assaults were relevant to prove his intent in this case.

Erramilli also argues that his prior sexual assaults should have been excluded because their probative value was substantially outweighed by the danger of unfair prejudice. After determining that the evidence is admissible under Rule 413, "the district court is required to consider whether it should exclude the evidence under Rule 403." *Foley,* 740 F.3d at 1088. "Our role on appeal, however, is not to apply the Rule 403 balancing test *de novo* but to review the district court's decision for an abuse of discretion." *Id.* In this case, we cannot conclude that the district court abused its discretion because the probative value of Erramilli's prior sexual assaults was substantial and the danger of unfair prejudice was low.

At trial, Erramilli pursued two avenues of defense. First, he argued that Susan's account of what happened was incredible and that he simply never touched her inner thigh. This position made the use of Erramilli's past sexual assaults highly probative as propensity evidence because it bolstered Susan's testimony that she was sexually assaulted. *See United States v. McGuire,* 627 F.3d 622, 627 (7th Cir.2010) ("The evidence was material because the defense was that [the victim] was a liar. . . . The evidence of the other boys established the defendant's propensity for, and *modus operandi* of, molestation of young boys and by doing so bolstered [the victim's] testimony."). Second, Erramilli argued that the government failed to prove that the contact he made with Susan's leg was intended for sexual arousal or gratification. In fact, he suggested that any contact was merely accidental. The evidence of Erramilli's past sexual assaults was highly probative of his intent because it had a tendency to refute this defense.

Erramilli attempts to minimize the probative value of his prior sexual assaults by pointing out several ways in which they were different from what he did to Susan Domino, but we agree with the district court's conclusion that the differences are insignificant and that the offenses are overwhelmingly similar. True, the prior offenses were committed against younger women, and they involved Erramilli reaching forward to touch the breast of a woman seated in front of him rather than reaching across his body to touch the inner thigh of a woman seated beside him, but all three offenses were crimes of opportunity in which Erramilli furtively groped unsuspecting women who were seated near him on airplanes. The offenses need not be identical to have substantial probative value. . . .

In sum, Erramilli's prior sexual assaults were admissible under Rule 413 because they were relevant to prove his propensity to commit the charged offense, as well as the requisite intent for that offense, and the district court did not abuse its discretion in refusing to exclude the evidence under Rule 403.

— Holding

EXERCISE

Why was the prior bad act evidence so important to the government? Could they have succeeded without it? *it proves intent and Erramilli was saying he didn't do it - his word against hers- no witnesses*

As a prosecutor would you have charged the defendant in the Erramilli case under a more serious statute, requiring force, threat, or coercion? *maybe. She did have no "escape" she was in the window seat blocked by both Erramilli and her husband.*

Non-consensual sex often occurs when there is no discussion prior to the sexual contact in the affirmative or the negative. This raises the question of whether the government must prove that the defendant knew that the victim was not consenting.

UNITED STATES V. HAWKINS
603 Fed. Appx. 239 (5th Cir. 2015)

PER CURIAM:

Ruel Hawkins performed oral sex on his 18-year old niece. Because this act took place at a park within the jurisdiction of Fort Hood, he was charged with the federal crime of abusive sexual contact. *See* 18 U.S.C. § 2244(b). Appealing his conviction after a bench trial, Hawkins contends that offense requires proof that he believed the sexual contact occurred without the victim's permission, proof which he believes is absent in his case.

The testimony at trial, viewed in the light most favorable to the guilty verdict, included the following: On August 5, 2013, at around 4:00 a.m., 54-year old Hawkins sent a text message to his niece asking if she wanted to exercise that morning. Although the two had worked out at the Fort Hood gym just days earlier, Hawkins falsely informed his niece that the gym had not opened. Instead, Hawkins proposed the more isolated Belton Lake Recreational Area. She agreed to go with him, and Hawkins picked her up about an hour later.

It was still dark when they arrived. Hawkins suggested they start with abdominal exercises. He told his niece to lay on her back and move her legs up and down "like scissors." When she became sore, she allowed Hawkins to massage her stomach. He then moved his hand into her pants. She said, "Uncle Ruel, I don't think you should be doing that." Hawkins then pulled her underwear back and performed oral sex on her for about five seconds.

His niece jumped up, grabbed her phone, and quickly walked away. She felt scared and began crying. Hawkins ran after her, apologizing and asking her to come back. Fearful, she started running. She flagged down a passing truck and told the driver, "my uncle just molested me."

The driver called police, who arrested Hawkins. Later that day, Hawkins met with Agent Daniel Chadwick and gave a statement after waiving his *Miranda* rights. In that statement, Hawkins denied touching his niece in any sexual manner.

The government charged Hawkins with violating 18 U.S.C. § 2244(b), which makes it illegal in the territorial jurisdiction of the United States to "knowingly engage[ ] in sexual contact with another person without that person's permission." Hawkins elected to have a bench trial and chose to testify. On the stand, Hawkins admitted that he lied to Agent Chadwick and recounted a very different story than the one he told the day of the incident. In this version, Hawkins admitted that he touched his niece's vagina and performed oral sex on her but only because she asked him to do so. The district court returned a guilty verdict.

At trial, Hawkins never argued that the government was required to prove that he knew he lacked permission to engage in the sexual contact. However, in a post-trial motion for bond pending appeal, Hawkins claimed that the statute does require this knowledge and the government failed to prove it. The district court denied his motion, assuming without deciding that Hawkins was correct about the statute but holding that the evidence established satisfied any such *mens rea* requirement.

Hawkins's appeal thus raises two questions: Does a conviction under Section 2244(b) require proof that the defendant knew the sexual contact took place without the victim's permission? If so, did that proof exist in Hawkins's case?

No court of appeals has addressed whether the knowledge element of Section 2244(b) applies to the victim's lack of permission. As a grammatical matter, Hawkins concedes that "knowingly" modifies "engages in sexual contact" rather than the phrase "without that person's permission." But Hawkins asks us to follow the approach of *United States v. X-Citement Video, Inc.*, 513 U.S. 64, 115 S.Ct. 464, 130 L.Ed.2d 372 (1994). In that case, the Supreme Court found a *mens rea* requirement that lacked grammatical support in a child pornography statute because of the presumption that "a scienter requirement . . . appl[ies] to each of the statutory elements that criminalize otherwise innocent conduct." *Id.* at 71–72, 115 S.Ct. 464. The government responds that legislative history supports the plain language of Section 2244(b), *see United States v. Chatman,* 2008 WL 2127947, at *2 (D.Or. May 20, 2008), as do comparable state sexual assault statutes that do not require knowledge as to consent in similar circumstances.

The Second Circuit faced similar arguments in a Section 2244(b) case, but found it unnecessary to resolve the statutory question because sufficient evidence supported the conviction even assuming a *mens rea* requirement applied to the "without that person's permission" element. *See United States v. Cohen,* 2008 WL 5120669, at *2 (2d Cir. Dec.8, 2008). The same is true in Hawkins's case.

Substantial evidence exists from which the trier of fact could have found beyond a reasonable doubt that Hawkins knew he did not have his niece's permission to engage in sexual contact. And contrary to Hawkins's argument that any such holding is speculative because a finding on this issue was not made below, the district court reached this exact conclusion when it denied the motion for bond pending appeal, stating that "the trial record clearly established that the Defendant knew that he did not have permission to engage in sexual contact with victim." We agree.

For starters, his niece never gave Hawkins permission to touch her in a sexual way, strong evidence that Hawkins knew he lacked permission to do so. *See, e.g., Cohen,* 2008 WL 5120669, at *2 (finding the lack of permission probative of the defendant's knowledge that he lacked permission). Second, his niece immediately said "I don't think you should be doing that," conveying to Hawkins that he did not have permission to touch her sexually. Third, his niece jumped up and ran away shocked and crying, providing evidence that she had a nonpermissive demeanor during the encounter. Hawkins counters these points by parsing his niece's words and proof of her demeanor, arguing that she equivocated by saying "should" and pointing to physical evidence that allegedly undercuts her testimony. But the district court did not credit Hawkins's interpretation of the evidence, and given that we must view all evidence to favor the verdict, we will not either.

In many cases, establishing any one of the aforementioned facts may be enough to support a finding beyond a reasonable doubt that the defendant knew the sexual contact took place without the victim's permission, but here there is even more. The familial relationship and vast age difference between Hawkins and his niece cast serious doubt on his claim that he thought he had her permission to engage in sexual contact. *See, e.g., Cohen,* 2008 WL 5120669, at *2 (holding that the circumstances surrounding the defendant and victim's relationship were probative of knowledge). And Hawkins's deceptive plan—tricking his niece into going to an isolated area early in the morning by lying about the gym being closed—indicates that he knew his behavior would not meet with approval. That he apologized right after the incident further establishes his guilty state of mind. So does the fact that he initially denied any sexual contact took place, only to change his story at trial by admitting that it did occur but he thought it was consensual. All this evidence more than establishes Hawkins's guilt beyond a reasonable doubt even assuming the statute includes the *mens rea* requirement he advocates.

The conviction therefore is AFFIRMED.

EXERCISE

Imagine that you were the prosecutor in the *Hawkins* case, but with a few different facts. First, imagine that the defendant and the victim were the same age, not related to one another, and married. Second, imagine that the incident described happened in the married couple's home. Would that context change your decision to charge the case? If so, how do you justify that decision?

2. NON-CONSENSUAL SEX WITH AN IMPAIRED OR UNCONSCIOUS VICTIM

Two federal statutes bar non-consensual sex with a victim that is impaired or unconscious.

18 U.S.C. § 2241(b) allows a sentence up to life in prison if a defendant either "renders another person unconscious" or uses drugs or an intoxicant to "to substantially impair the ability of that other person to appraise or control conduct" before engaging in a sexual act with that person on federal land or in a federal prison.

18 U.S.C. § 2242(2) offers the same penalty (life) and requirement of a federal nexus, but simply prohibits engaging "in a sexual act with another person if that other person is (A) incapable of appraising the nature of the conduct; or (B) physically incapable of declining participation in, or communicating unwillingness to engage in, that sexual act. . . ."

UNITED STATES V. BETONE
636 F. 3d 384 (8th Cir. 2011)

MURPHY, CIRCUIT JUDGE.

A jury convicted Jeffrey Betone of two counts of sexual abuse, and the district court sentenced him to 151 months. Betone challenges his sentence and the sufficiency of the evidence supporting his convictions. We affirm.

In 2005 Betone was 19 years old and lived on the Cheyenne River Indian Reservation. He was homosexual but not "out" to his family or community. One evening in March 2005, Betone and Tate Jensen were guests at a drinking party at the home of Sherry Turning Heart. The other guests left in the early hours of the next day, but Jensen and Betone spent the night because they were both too drunk to go home. Jensen slept on the living room couch and Betone on the floor beside him. The only other people in the house were Turning Heart and her ten year old son, who were both sleeping upstairs.

At this point the men's accounts diverge. Betone testified that he and Jensen talked as they lay in the dark and that he believed Jensen was "coming on" to him. Betone began fondling Jensen's thigh and genitals. Jensen undid his own belt and pants, and Betone fellated him. After a few minutes, a light came on and footsteps could be heard. Jensen pushed Betone away. Turning Heart's son came into the room, followed by Turning Heart. Jensen testified that he passed out on Turning Heart's couch and awoke only when the light came on. He says he never consented to oral sex. At some point after Turning Heart came downstairs, Jensen assaulted Betone. Betone then fled the house.

Tribal police found Betone walking home drunk and barefoot, his mouth bloody and his nose broken. He claimed to have fallen down, but the skeptical police took him to an emergency room. Two months later Turning Heart told a tribal officer friend that she had seen Jensen and Betone doing "something [she] did not want to see," but no one investigated further until 2008. Jensen claims he was too ashamed to report the incident.

Three years later, Betone had sex with Valance Blue Arm, a 30 year old man. The two met when Betone drove up to Blue Arm on the street and offered him a ride. Even though Blue Arm was just down the street from his home, he accepted. Betone offered Blue Arm a beer and a cigarette and then drove to his own home instead of Blue Arm's.

Blue Arm has diminished mental capacity. According to Blue Arm's sister, he "is always scared" and functions "like a little boy," watching children's television programs every day. A tribal officer had noticed Blue Arm around the reservation, "always . . . talking to himself." On the day of his encounter with Betone, Blue Arm was wearing many layers of clothes and underwear as customary with him. Betone later acknowledged that Blue Arm "might have been slow."

Betone cajoled Blue Arm into entering his house. Once inside, Betone fellated Blue Arm twice and later they had anal sex. According to Betone, Blue Arm kissed him back, confirmed that he wanted to have sex, put condoms on Betone, and was sexually aroused. Blue Arm claimed to the contrary that Betone told him he "was not allowed to go anywhere" and locked the door behind him. Blue Arm says he did not resist Betone's sexual advances because he was afraid he would get in trouble if he attacked Betone before "the police were informed." Blue Arm said that he was afraid to resist or leave and that he never consented.

Later that day Blue Arm checked himself into an emergency room. Hospital employees prepared a rape kit from Blue Arm and called police. After interviewing Blue Arm, federal agents learned from tribal police of the earlier incident with Jensen. While in custody, Betone told police he had "thought [oral sex with Jensen] was consensual, but I guess it wasn't" and that Jensen had not moved during the encounter.

The government charged Betone with three counts of sexual abuse:

> (1)   knowingly engaging in a sexual act with Jensen while Jensen was "incapable of appraising the nature of the conduct" or "physically incapable of declining participation in, or communicating unwillingness to engage in, that sexual act," 18 U.S.C. § 2242(2);

> (2)   knowingly causing Blue Arm to engage in oral sex "by threatening or placing [him] in fear (other than . . . fear [of anyone's] death, serious bodily injury, or kidnapping)," *id.* § 2242(1); and

> (3)   causing Blue Arm to engage in anal sex through threats or fear, *id.*

Betone stipulated to federal Indian country jurisdiction under 18 U.S.C. § 1153.

Jensen, Blue Arm, and Betone all testified at trial. The jury convicted Betone of the first two counts and acquitted him of the third. At sentencing, the district court applied the vulnerable victim enhancement under U.S.S.G. § 3A1.1(b) to both convictions. Each enhancement increased Betone's offense level by two levels. The district court sentenced Betone to 151 months, the low end of his resulting guideline range. Betone now challenges the sufficiency of the evidence and the application of the vulnerable victim enhancement to both counts.

We review de novo challenges to the sufficiency of evidence presented at trial, viewing the evidence in the light most favorable to the verdict and drawing all reasonable inferences in its favor. *United States v. Coleman,* 584 F.3d 1121, 1125 (8th Cir.2009).

According to Jensen, Betone began fellating him while he was asleep. That testimony alone establishes the elements of § 2242(2). *See United States v. Carter,* 410 F.3d 1017, 1027 (8th Cir.2005) (elements established where defendant performed oral sex on victim who was intoxicated and drowsy); *United States v. Kirkie,* 261 F.3d 761, 768 (8th Cir.2001) (victim testimony suffices). Betone points to small differences among the accounts of Jensen, Turning Heart, and her son, such as whether Turning Heart found Jensen on the couch or in the bathroom. Jensen's testimony alone supports the conviction, however, and is internally consistent.

Only Betone testified that Jensen was awake when oral sex began. In convicting Betone on this count, the jury evidently credited Jensen over Betone. Witness credibility is quintessentially "the province of the jury." *Kirkie,* 261 F.3d at 768. Betone's conviction for sexually abusing Jensen should be affirmed.

EXERCISE

The incident between Betone and Jensen in the case above occurred in 2005 but was not investigated until 2008. In terms of proving the crucial element of incapacitation, is this a problem?

If you were the prosecutor in this case, you would have the discretion to charge both the Jensen and Blue Arm incidents or just one or the other. Which option would you choose?

The United States Code of Military Justice contains similar provisions to the primary federal code, and applies to the same kind of factual situations (which often involve heavy drinking by both the defendant and the victim).

UNITED STATES V. CARTRIGHT

2013 WL 4734520 (U.S. Air Force Court of Military Appeals, 2013)

PER CURIAM:

On 11 October 2008, Airman First Class (A1C) AL and a male friend from her duty section (A1C DL) spent the night at the appellant's off-base house following a going-away party for a co-worker. They watched football, drank, and socialized. A1C AL ended up sleeping on a futon couch next to A1C DL, without incident.

The following evening, all three went out to dinner and then visited two bars where they had several alcoholic drinks. They returned to the appellant's off-base house, where they again watched football and the appellant had a few more drinks. While watching television, A1C AL and the appellant sat on a futon and A1C DL sat on a couch near the futon. A1C AL changed into shorts offered to her by the appellant and laid down on the futon to go to sleep while the appellant was sitting on the edge of the futon watching television.

The last thing A1C AL recalled before falling asleep was the appellant spilling his drink. She then awoke and realized something was happening. She became aware the appellant had his hands inside her shorts and underwear, touching her genitals though not penetrating her. She grabbed his arm and pulled his hand out. She asked him what he was doing, to which he responded "it was okay, it was okay" and then rolled away from her to the other side of the futon. He appeared drunk to A1C AL. Although she was frightened, A1C AL believed the incident was over and subsequently went back to sleep after moving away from the appellant on the futon.

A1C AL was awakened again. This time, she was lying on her back and the appellant was somewhat on top of her. Her shorts and underwear were pulled halfway down between her hips and knees and his head was near her crotch. She sat up, pushed him off and asked what he was doing. Again, the appellant stopped, answered "it's okay, it's okay," rolled over and appeared to go back to sleep.

About 15 minutes later, A1C AL got up, went into the bathroom, and texted a male Airman she was dating at the time. He did not respond, so A1C AL evaluated a number of different options, ranging from calling various friends or coworkers, to waking up A1C DL. She ultimately decided leaving was not logistically possible, so she returned to the futon, turned on the television, and tried to stay awake. She positioned herself as far as possible from the appellant and stayed on top of the blankets.

The appellant rolled over and tried to put the blanket on top of her and slide his hands down her shorts. She quickly grabbed his arm, placed it around her stomach, and told him he could cuddle with her but she did not "want to do anything" with him. The appellant said something A1C AL could not understand and then appeared to go back to sleep. A1C AL sat up and continued to watch television until the appellant got up for the day.

After the appellant awoke and went to shower, A1C AL fell back asleep. Later, she and A1C DL got up and the appellant cooked them breakfast. The appellant was their ride so the two watched television while waiting for the appellant to drive them back to the base. A1C DL testified that the appellant did not appear impaired or hung over that morning.

After the appellant dropped them off at the base, A1C AL told A1C DL what had happened the previous night. A1C DL testified that A1C AL did not appear upset and she described the incident rather jokingly, laughingly referring to the appellant as "Mr. Clean" because he had a bald head. About a week later, A1C DL told the appellant what A1C AL was saying, and the appellant said he did not remember anything about the incident and was upset that no one had told him earlier. According to A1C DL, when he told A1C AL that the appellant had no memory of the incident, she said if he did these things while drunk and did not recall it, she was "cool with it" and didn't want to make things awkward between them. A1C DL relayed this to the appellant.

Approximately one week later, A1C AL's supervisor, who had learned about the incident from another source, asked A1C AL if what she heard—that the appellant had acted in the manner described above—was true.

A1C AL confirmed that it was and eventually provided oral and written statements to agents of the Air Force Office of Special Investigations (OSI).

When questioned by OSI agents about the events of that evening under rights advisement, the appellant said he had been drinking heavily and did not remember anything from the time he fell asleep on the futon next to A1C AL until the next morning when he awoke. He also told the agents A1C DL had informed him that A1C AL had previously made similar allegations about inappropriate sexual advances by two other male airmen in her unit, though A1C DL denied making such a statement. . . .

The appellant was charged with engaging in abusive sexual contact with A1C AL when she was "substantially incapacitated," in violation of Article 120(h), UCMJ. The offense of abusive sexual contact piggybacks the definition of aggravated sexual assault found in Article 120(c)(2), UCMJ. *United States v. Wilkins,* 71 M.J. 410, 412 (C.A.A.F. 2012).

As such, the elements of both offenses are identical except that abusive sexual contact requires "sexual contact" instead of a "sexual act." *Id.* When those two statutes are considered in conjunction with each other, abusive sexual contact is committed when a person "engages in [sexual contact] with another person of any age if that other person is substantially incapacitated or substantially incapable of—

   (A) appraising the nature of the sexual [contact];

   (B) declining participation in the sexual [contact]; or

   (C) communicating unwillingness to engage in the sexual [contact]."

At trial, the defense requested a specifically crafted instruction defining "substantially incapacitated" as:

   A degree of mental impairment due to alcohol, drugs, or other circumstances, which has left a person unable to have awareness of themselves, their mental processes and their surroundings and unable to respond in any way, to include verbally or physically, to external stimuli.

The military judge denied that request and instead used the following instruction:

   That level of mental impairment due to consumption of alcohol, drugs, or similar substance; while asleep or unconscious; or for other reasons which rendered the alleged victim unable to appraise the nature of the sexual conduct at issue, unable to physically communicate unwillingness to engage in the sexual conduct at issue, or otherwise unable to make or communicate competent decisions.

. . . The military judge properly instructed the panel on the issue of consent, namely that "consent means words or overt acts indicating a freely given agreement to the sexual conduct by a competent person." He also informed the panel members that they must find beyond a reasonable doubt that A1C AL did not consent. Absent evidence to the contrary, we presume that members understand and follow the military judge's instructions. *United States v. Quintanilla,* 56 M.J. 37, 83 (C.A.A.F. 2001). In doing so and then finding the appellant guilty, the members were convinced beyond a reasonable doubt that A1C AL did not consent, because she was not a "competent person who freely agreed" to the sexual activity since she was asleep when it occurred.

EXERCISE

Imagine that you are a juror in a case where the defendant is charged with a sexual act involving an incapacitated victim—a woman who has fallen asleep after a heavy bout of drinking. An objective observer has testified that the victim verbally agreed to intercourse before passing out. Will that evidence of a prior agreement influence your consideration of guilt or innocence?

The physically disabled, including the elderly, are often the victims of sexual abuse that is non-consensual but does not involve the use of force. The inability or limited ability of a person to either give consent or deny it due to a disability adds a troubling dimension to these cases, and raises the risk that the law will serve to deprive disabled people any access to sexuality.

UNITED STATES V. JAMES
810 F. 3d 674 (9th Cir. 2016)

TALLMAN, CIRCUIT JUDGE:

T.C. is severely disabled by cerebral palsy. Although T.C. was twenty-eight years old at the time of the sexual assault, she cannot care for herself and needs assistance from others with all of the major activities of daily living, including eating, grooming, and using the bathroom. She cannot walk without assistance. She must be lifted in and out of her wheelchair, into which she is fastened with a seatbelt in order to keep her from falling out when her limbs spasm uncontrollably. When T.C. is in the wheelchair, she can only use her feet to move around. When not in the wheelchair, she "can scoot herself kind of Army style on the floor, or she sits with her legs outward and she'll hop." She has no use of her hands and is incapable of lifting heavy objects.

It is difficult even for those who know T.C. to communicate with her or to understand her attempts at speech. T.C.'s tongue is enlarged and her voice box is thicker than normal, thus making her largely non-verbal. She communicates primarily through nodding her head yes or no in response to questions and grunting. Her full time caretaker of eight and one-half years testified that her responses are frequently inappropriate or nonsensical to the questions or situation. Her uncle testified that T.C. sometimes "gets mad" and "kind of like growls and give[s] you the mean look" if he changes a channel away from a program she prefers watching on television. T.C.'s caretaker testified she "kn[ew] about" an instance where T.C. bit a person she did not like, and that T.C. can cry and express anger. When T.C. finishes using the toilet, she will moan or grunt to indicate she is done. These examples are reflective of the extent of T.C.'s communicability.

On August 3, 2011, a family member caught James having sex with T.C. on the porch of her grandparents' home, covered with only a blanket. The incident occurred inside the boundaries of the Fort Apache Reservation within Indian Country. Because James was adopted by the victim's grandparents—who also raised T.C. following the death of her mother during childbirth—T.C. is legally James' niece. The aunt who discovered James lying on top of T.C. called for an ambulance, which rushed T.C. to the nearest clinic for a medical examination. A sexual assault nurse examiner conducted a vaginal examination and observed that T.C. had torn tissue and was bleeding from a laceration. The nurse testified that T.C. was unresponsive to her efforts at the clinic to obtain a medical or event history.

James admitted to investigators that he had sex with T.C. During interviews with an agent from the Bureau of Indian Affairs ("BIA"), James confessed to removing T.C. from her wheelchair and lifting her onto a bed, after which he took off her pants and underpants, pulled down his pants, and penetrated her vaginally with his digit and penis. James also said he had been drinking, he was "ashamed," and it was not the victim's fault. In a written statement—introduced at trial—James wrote: "I'm ashamed and confusted [sic]. I don't know what made me do what I did. . . . I will not forgive me [sic] but I do ask God for forgiveness. [T.C.] is not to bleame [sic] either. She was incent [sic] of all things." When a BIA agent questioned James about the statement, James responded: "It was intercourse, but it wasn't like sex, you know? . . . [W]ith her, she's just laying there but, I mean, you are inside her and you are moving up and down." James also informed the BIA agent that T.C. cannot talk, only "ma[ke] noises."

Because the sexual assault took place on the Fort Apache Indian Reservation, James could be indicted only by the federal government since the state of Arizona has no jurisdiction there. *See United States v. Mitchell*, 502 F.3d 931, 946 (9th Cir.2007 (noting that enacted statutes have given the federal government limited jurisdiction over certain major crimes committed on Native American land); *cf.* 18 U.S.C. § 1162 (noting Arizona is *not* one of the six enumerated states that have "jurisdiction over offenses committed by or against Indians in the areas of Indian country"). On November 1, 2011, a federal grand jury returned an indictment charging James with two counts of sexual abuse in violation of 18 U.S.C. § 2242(2)(B). For reasons unknown, the Government did not charge James in the indictment under § 2242(2)(A), nor did it offer an expert at trial to establish her cognitive impairments, relying instead on lay testimony from family members, caregivers, the nurse, and the BIA agent.

A three-day jury trial began on July 30, 2013. The investigating BIA agent testified that he was unable to ask T.C. about the event because he could not communicate with her, but he videotaped his contact with her and that was shown to the jury during the trial. The jury returned a guilty verdict on both counts of sexual abuse. Though James moved for a judgment of acquittal under Federal Rule of Criminal Procedure 29(a) both at the close of the Government's case and again at the close of trial, the district court reserved its ruling on both occasions to await the jury's verdict. The jury convicted. After post-trial briefing and oral argument, the district court granted James' Rule 29 motion and entered its Judgment of Acquittal on September 26, 2013. The Government timely appealed. We have jurisdiction under 28 U.S.C. § 1291, and we reverse. . . .

This case turns on the breadth of the "physically incapable" standard in § 2242(2)(B) for punishing a sexual act with an individual with the physical incapacity to decline participation in or communicate unwillingness to engage in the act. The statutory definitions provided in 18 U.S.C. § 2246 do not define "physically incapable," nor did Congress provide context for this term in the legislative history. While no federal court has definitively addressed the issue, we hold that "physically incapable" under § 2242(2)(B) should be defined broadly and not confused with the more narrow "physically helpless" standard employed by the district court. As so interpreted, we think the Government provided sufficient evidence to permit the question to proceed to the jury. The resulting guilty verdict meets the standard of *Jackson*. *See Jackson,* 443 U.S. at 320, 99 S.Ct. 2781.

Due to the lack of congressional direction and germane federal precedent, the district court opted to draw a parallel between the federal statute's "physically incapable" language and the "physically helpless" language employed by some states in their rape schemes—holding essentially that T.C. would need to be totally physically helpless in order for the jury to convict James under § 2242(2)(B). *See, e.g.,* Conn. Gen.Stat. § 53a–71(a)(3); N.Y. Penal Law § 130.35(2). The district court may have relied on this parallel because some states' definitions of "physically helpless" similarly discuss an inability to communicate. For example, both Oregon and New York define the term "physically helpless" as "a person [who] is unconscious or for any other reason is physically unable to communicate unwillingness to [engage in a sexual] act." Or.Rev.Stat. § 163.305; N.Y. Penal Law § 130.00(7); *see also* Tenn.Code § 39–13–501(5).

But relying on state law as the district court did is problematic. First, the Supreme Court has held that "in the absence of a plain indication of an intent to incorporate diverse state laws into a federal criminal statute, the meaning of the federal statute should not be dependent on state law." *United States v. Turley,* 352 U.S. 407, 411, 77 S.Ct. 397, 1 L.Ed.2d 430 (1957); *see also Taylor v. United States,* 495 U.S. 575, 591, 110 S.Ct. 2143, 109 L.Ed.2d 607 (1990). We find this guidance particularly applicable here. State law statutory schemes are very different from federal law because state law punishes the broad category of non-consensual rape—but federal law has no such counterpart. Noticeably absent from 18 U.S.C. § 2242 is a provision punishing non-consensual sexual intercourse. The scope of conduct punished by federal law is therefore narrower than the scope of conduct punished by state law. *See United States v. Cabrera-Gutierrez,* 756 F.3d 1125, 1134 (9th Cir.2014) ("Nonconsensual intercourse with a mentally and physically capable individual not involving a threat or the use of fear might violate Or.Rev.Stat. § 163.425, but it would not violate 18 U.S.C. § 2242.").

Second, the district court followed the line of state case law that construes the term "physically helpless" very narrowly. *See State v. Fourtin,* 307 Conn. 186, 52 A.3d 674 (2012); *People v. Huurre,* 193 A.D.2d 305, 603 N.Y.S.2d 179 (N.Y.App.Div.1993). Although both cases involved victims who suffer from cerebral palsy as T.C. does, the district court ignored the differences between the legal terms "physically incapable" and "physically helpless." In *Fourtin,* a 4–3 decision, the majority held a woman who could not walk or talk nonetheless failed to meet the physically helpless standard because she could nonverbally communicate her unwillingness to engage in the sexual act by biting, kicking, and screaming. 307 Conn. 186, 52 A.3d at 689. Rather than apply a common sense interpretation of the term, *Fourtin* explained that " 'physically helpless' has a particular statutory meaning that requires *more than* a showing that a victim is totally physically incapacitated." *Id.* (emphasis added); *see also id.* at 682 ("[N]o one would dispute that the victim is physically helpless in the ordinary sense of that term."). In *Huurre,* the state appellate court held that the victim was able to nonverbally communicate her unwillingness to do something by making guttural noises. 603 N.Y.S.2d at 306–07. Although the state had not sustained its burden in presenting evidence sufficient to demonstrate the victim was physically helpless, *Huurre* noted that the state had sustained its burden of showing an inability to consent "by reason of a mental defect." *Id.* at 310, 603 N.Y.S.2d 179.

However, the term "physically helpless" has various interpretations in other states. *See, e.g., Dabney v. State,* 326 Ark. 382, 930 S.W.2d 360 (1996) (rejected by the majority in *Fourtin*). *Dabney* found evidence sufficient to find the victim physically helpless where she was "blind, mentally impaired, partially handicapped, and unable to speak," and "could only grunt, raise her hand, and shake her head from side to side." *Id.* at 361–62. "Granted, the victim was not completely physically incapacitated, but this is not what the statute requires; it only requires physical helplessness, not total incapacity." *Id.* at 362. As another example, Iowa punishes sex with an individual who is "mentally incapacitated, physically incapacitated, or physically helpless." Iowa Code § 709.4(d). The state defines these terms separately: "Physically helpless" means a person who "is unable to communicate an unwillingness to act because the person is unconscious, asleep, or is otherwise physically limited," and "[p]hysically incapacitated" means a person who "has a bodily impairment or handicap that substantially limits the person's ability to resist or flee." *Id.* § 709.1A. These statutes demonstrate that the concept of being "physically helpless" need not be as narrow as defined by Connecticut or New York and that "physically incapable" is a separate, broader standard.

Nothing compels us to adopt Connecticut and New York's narrow formulation of "physically helpless" over the broader approach taken by other states. The federal statute itself does not use the term "physically helpless" and the district court erred in defining "physically incapable" so narrowly. "Physically helpless" and "physically incapable" are two separate standards. "Physically helpless" suggests a lack of physical ability to do anything while "physically incapable" is a term that is more susceptible to application to various factual situations that can come before a jury. A victim could have a physical incapacity to decline participation or be incapable of communicating unwillingness to engage in a sexual act and still not be physically helpless.

We find our support in differentiating the broader "physically incapable" standard from the more narrow "physically helpless" standard relied upon by the district court when we look to federal applications of § 2242(2)(B). For example, we have held in the context of sentencing that a defendant had committed an act in violation of § 2242 where the victim "repeatedly gained and lost consciousness" and "was unconscious or nearly so" when the defendant engaged in intercourse with her. *United States v. Morgan,* 164 F.3d 1235, 1237–38 (9th Cir.1999). The Eighth Circuit has similarly held that sufficient evidence supported finding the victim physically incapable where "the lingering effects of the marijuana may have hindered her ability to object straightaway to the abuse," even though the victim was conscious at the time of the sexual assault. *United States v. Carter,* 410 F.3d 1017, 1028 (8th Cir.2005); *see also United States v. Barrett,* 937 F.2d 1346, 1348 (8th Cir.1991) (upholding conviction where the victim, though not fully awake until penetration, "vaguely remember[ed] someone pulling off her jeans and underwear").

These federal cases support our conclusion by indicating that a defendant may be convicted under § 2242(2)(B) where the victim had some awareness of the situation and—while not completely physically helpless—was physically hampered due to sleep, intoxication, or drug use and thereby rendered physically incapable.

Most compellingly, "whether a victim is physically helpless at any given moment is largely a question of fact for the jury to decide." *Fourtin,* 307 Conn. 186, 52 A.3d at 695 (Norcott, Eveleigh, & Harper, JJ., dissenting) (quoting *State v. Stevens,* 311 Mont. 52, 53 P.3d 356, 361 (2002)); *see also State v. Tapia,* 751 N.W.2d 405, 407 (Iowa Ct.App.2008) (same); *State v. Rush,* 278 N.J.Super. 44, 650 A.2d 373, 374 (App.Div.1994) ("It is thus for the jury and not the judge to determine whether, as a matter of fact, a victim's condition meets the physically helpless standard."). The district court wisely deferred making a final decision until after the jury had spoken. It erred on this record by not abiding by its verdict.

After surveying the dearth of case law, we find the cases more persuasive which punish conduct under the broader "physically incapable" standard rather than the narrower "physically helpless" standard because it will allow more cases to be submitted to the good judgment of a jury. A jury could properly convict under § 2242(2)(B) for sexual acts committed against a victim who cannot verbally articulate her lack of consent—"physically incapable of communicating unwillingness"—as well as a victim who cannot physically resist the sexual act—"physically incapable of declining participation." We hold that the district court erred by, in essence, requiring the Government to prove T.C. was physically helpless in order to allow the jury's verdict to stand.

Now that we have settled the proper legal standard, applying the facts of this case is straightforward. We hold that the Government proffered sufficient evidence—when viewed in the light most favorable to it—to allow a rational juror to conclude beyond a reasonable doubt that T.C. was physically incapable of declining participation in, or communicating her unwillingness to engage in, a sexual act with James. *See Jackson,* 443 U.S. at 320, 99 S.Ct. 2781.

The Government presented evidence that witnesses—even those who knew her well—could not always understand T.C. *Cf. Fourtin,* 307 Conn. 186, 52 A.3d at 680 (reasoning that "all the . . . witnesses testified that, sometimes with the aid of a communication board and at other times, with appropriate gestures, the [victim] was able to make herself understood." (alterations in original)). Although James was T.C.'s uncle by adoption, he had never resided with her, and the evidence demonstrated they never spent any appreciable time together before James sexually assaulted her. Nothing indicates he knew her well enough to understand her or could otherwise understand her attempts at communication.

Furthermore, while T.C. had some minimal means of communicating, the evidence demonstrated that she had difficulty communicating even with her longtime caregivers, close family members, the emergency room nurse, and investigators. During the physical examination after the attack, T.C. could not communicate with the treating nurse—even through yes or no questions—nor did she seem to understand the nurse's inquiries or directives. James himself admitted that she was like a limp doll who "just lay[ ] there" during his assault. Thus, the facts presented at trial are sufficient to permit a juror to find that T.C.'s cerebral palsy was sufficiently severe that it rendered her incapable of being understood by others, and thereby incapable of communicating to James her unwillingness to participate in the sexual act.

The evidence also suffices to show that T.C. was physically incapable of declining participation in a sexual act with James. T.C. does not have use of her arms, cannot lift heavy objects, and would not be capable of pushing someone off who was lying on top of her. She is unable to feed or groom herself. She cannot walk nor get into or out of her wheelchair without assistance. James had to physically lift her from the wheelchair to the bed, and then he had to disrobe the victim before penetration. The facts presented at trial would permit a rational juror to find that T.C.'s cerebral palsy rendered her physically incapable of declining participation in this unwanted sexual act.

We emphasize that our holding does not preclude someone suffering from a physical disability from ever having consensual sexual intercourse. Someone may suffer from a physical disability and retain sufficient mental functional capacity to consent. It is one thing to impose *per se* legal violations with respect to minors and those who cannot comprehend the nature of the act under § 2242(2)(A); it is quite another to say the law is designed in this manner for individuals who suffer solely from a physical disability.

The legislative history of § 2242(2) is clear that "[l]*ack* of consent by the victim is not an element of the offense, and the prosecution need not introduce evidence of lack of consent or of victim resistance." H. Rep. No. 99–594, at 16 (emphasis added). This makes sense, as it would be very difficult to prove a sleeping or intoxicated person—who could not provide any verbal or non-verbal cues—did not consent to the sexual act. But we do not think this means that in the case of a severe physical disability the jury cannot consider the *presence* of consent when determining physical incapacity.

KOZINSKI, CIRCUIT JUDGE, dissenting:

I am puzzled and confused by Part III of the opinion. My colleagues work hard to prove that the district court read 18 U.S.C. § 2242(2)(B) too narrowly, but I'm not sure how the majority's reading is any different from that of the district court—or mine, for that matter. The whole enterprise seems misguided because the statute is clear and thus not reasonably susceptible to conflicting interpretations.

Here's what the statute says:

> Whoever . . . knowingly . . . engages in a sexual act with another person if that other person is . . . physically incapable of declining participation in, or communicating unwillingness to engage in, that sexual act . . . shall be fined under this title and imprisoned for any term of years or for life.

18 U.S.C. § 2242. What this means is perfectly clear: The government must prove that the alleged victim had a physical impairment and that this impairment made it impossible for her to say no to ("communicat[e] unwillingness to engage in") or otherwise indicate nonconsent to ("declin[e] participation in") sexual acts. There must be enough evidence for the jury to find beyond a reasonable doubt that the victim could not indicate, by word or deed, her lack of assent to a proposed sexual contact. Insofar as the majority tries to squeeze any more meaning out of these words—such as the possibility that the government could prove a violation by showing the victim could not actually fight off her assailant, *see* maj. at 679, 682–83—I must respectfully disagree. The statute is simply not susceptible to any such interpretation.

I also disagree with the methodology employed by the majority in seeking to pump up the statute beyond its ordinary meaning. The majority purports to find the statute crystal clear, maj. at 679 n. 5, but then decides it must pick between broader and narrower interpretations of the statutory language. It opts for the broader one because "it will allow more cases to be submitted to the good judgment of a jury." *Id.* at 682. This rule of acerbity, *i.e.,* the rule of lenity stood on its head, is not how the criminal law is supposed to work. People must have fair notice of what is legal and what is illegal, which is why we apply the rule of lenity when confronted with an ambiguous criminal statute. *See Liparota v. United States,* 471 U.S. 419, 427, 105 S.Ct. 2084, 85 L.Ed.2d 434 (1985). The function of the jury is to find facts and determine guilt by applying known legal standards, not to make up the law as it goes along. The majority's "let the jury decide what's illegal" approach is unwise and, most likely, unconstitutional. I emphatically disapprove of it.

The majority finds yet another reason for giving section 2242(2)(B) a capacious interpretation: According to the majority, we must read section 2242(2)(B) more broadly than analogous state laws because "state law punishes the broad category of non-consensual rape—but federal law has no such counterpart." Maj. at 679. This is a legislative choice Congress was free to make; it gives us no license to stretch other provisions of federal law beyond their natural meaning. The question "is not what Congress would have wanted but what Congress enacted." *Republic of Argentina v. Weltover, Inc.,* 504 U.S. 607, 618, 112 S.Ct. 2160, 119 L.Ed.2d 394 (1992) (internal quotation marks omitted). Our task is to construe the language as written, not to fill in what we perceive to be gaps in the statute.

In any event, all of these interpretive calisthenics are beside the point. As I said at the outset, the statute speaks for itself: A jury can convict only if it has proof that the victim could not physically express her lack of consent to the defendant's sexual advances. Because the government chose to prosecute James under subsection (2)(B) (dealing with physical incapacity) rather than subsection (2)(A) (dealing with mental incapacity), we must assume that T.C. was capable of understanding and consenting to sexual intercourse with James. The only question is whether she was able to communicate lack of consent if she chose not to participate.

It's quite clear that the district judge understood and applied this standard. I can do no better than to quote the district judge's own review of the evidence:

In her opening statement, the government's counsel said, "[The victim] communicates primarily nonverbally with gestures and sounds. *She can say yes or no.*" The government's witnesses included Special [Agent] Adrian Jim, Patricia Shands, Mark Quay, and Jodie Quay.

Special Agent Adrian Jim testified that when he first met with the victim, she was crying and "[i]t didn't seem like she wanted to talk to us." He testified that he interviewed the victim on a second visit, and the video recording of the second interview was played for the jury. *The video showed the victim nodding her head in agreement and shaking her head for disagreement. Special Agent Jim testified that during the second interview the victim responded to his questions by nodding her head for yes and shaking her head for no.*

Patricia Shands, the victim's direct caregiver, testified that part of the victim's school program involv[ed] practicing language skills, such as "sounding out our ABCs and her vowels," working on the alphabet, and using flash cards with pictures to practice the sounds of letters. Ms. Shands testified that when the victim gets out of her wheelchair, she chooses where she wants to sit. Ms. Shands also testified that the victim requires assistance to use the toilet, but "she'll moan when she's done" so that a caregiver can help her get back to her wheelchair. Ms. Shands testified that the victim can talk, but sometimes she has difficulty understanding the victim, and it is easier for the victim to show you something than to tell you. She also testified that the victim has many friends at school, and *she can express anger and dislike for someone.* Ms. Shands testified that *the victim communicates by nodding or shaking her head and making grunting sounds.* She further testified that the victim can communicate her needs and desires, such as when she needs to go to the bathroom, when she is finished using the toilet, when she wants to go play on the computer, when she wants to play games, when she wants to do something, and *when she does not want to do something.*

Mark Quay, the victim's uncle, testified that the victim understands both English and Apache and *responds to questions by nodding her head for yes and shaking her head for no.* He testified that she does not talk much, but she can talk. Mr. Quay testified that sometimes she expresses that she loves him by hugging him. He said that when he comes to her house, she always points at him and says "Mark" or "uncle." He also testified that *if you change the television channel when the victim does not want you to, she gets mad, growls, and gives you a mean look.* Mr. Quay further explained that when the victim gives you a mean look it looks like the mean look that others give.

Jodi Quay, the victim's aunt, testified that on August 3, 2011, she saw the Defendant and the victim talking and laughing together, communicating. Ms. Quay also testified that she can communicate with the victim, and *the victim nods her head for yes and shakes her head for no.*

At the time the Court reserved ruling on Defendant's Rule 29 motion, the evidence showed that the victim was physically able to communicate her unwillingness to engage in a sexual act and physically able to decline participation in a sexual act by head movements and vocalizations such as growling. As in [*State v. Fourtin,* 307 Conn. 186, 52 A.3d 674 (2012)] and [*People v. Huurre,* 193 A.D.2d 305, 603 N.Y.S.2d 179 (1993)], the government may have been able to present evidence that the victim was "incapable of appraising the nature of the conduct"—such as evidence of mental limitations, developmental delay, and lack of knowledge about sex—sufficient to support a conviction under § 2242(2)(A). But the government did not charge Defendant under § 2242(2)(A). The victim's mental limitations likely affected her ability to know what she should and should not be unwilling to do, but § 2242(2)(B) requires evidence that the victim is *physically incapable* of expressing unwillingness or declining participation. The evidence presented by the government at trial was not sufficient for a jury to reasonably find that the victim was "physically incapable of declining participation in, or communicating unwillingness to engage in, that sexual act." *United States v. James,* No. CR-11-08206-PCT-NVW, 2013 WL 5423979, at *5–*6 (D.Ariz. Sept. 26, 2013) (emphasis added) (citations omitted).

As the district court recognized, the government simply did not introduce the type of evidence that would allow "*any* rational trier of fact" to conclude that T.C.'s physical limitations rendered her incapable of declining participation or communicating unwillingness. *Jackson v. Virginia,* 443 U.S. 307, 319, 99 S.Ct. 2781, 61 L.Ed.2d 560 (1979). Significantly, the government never elicited testimony from a witness who knew T.C. that she was physically incapable of expressing her refusal or disagreement. The fact that T.C. was nonresponsive during her medical examination, *see* maj. at 682–83, is wholly irrelevant. *See State v. Fourtin,* 307 Conn. 186, 52 A.3d 674, 689–90 (concluding that a victim's failure to communicate with physicians "simply is not probative of whether the victim was unable to communicate *to the defendant* that his sexual advances were unwelcome"). The nurse's testimony that T.C. "could not say yes or no" to simple questions tells us nothing about whether T.C. was physically incapable of communicating. All the nurse *observed* was that T.C. did not respond.

It's possible that T.C. didn't comprehend the situation, either when she was with James or with the nurse. *See* maj. at 682–83. But because the government didn't charge James under section 2242(2)(A), T.C.'s mental capacity to "apprais[e] the nature of the conduct" was never at issue before the jury and is not at issue now. We therefore must presume her limitations were purely physical, and that her comprehension of the situation was no different from that of any other adult woman. The majority's periodic references to T.C.'s mental capacity betray its effort to justify James's conviction under a provision he was not charged with violating.

The majority ultimately lists a number of facts that are pretty much beside the point and thus cannot overcome the solid wall of evidence that T.C. was capable of communicating her lack of consent when she was so inclined. For example, the majority's reliance on the fact that T.C.'s caretaker and guardians can't always understand her specific needs, maj. at 676–77, 682, is not the least bit helpful. Evidence that it's hard to understand T.C.'s "wants or needs" doesn't demonstrate that she is incapable of expressing her unhappiness with a situation. Witnesses familiar with T.C. agreed that she can express disapproval with head nods, grunts, moans, growls, tears and mean looks similar to those given by able-bodied people. The majority is right that the video introduced into evidence "was powerful corroborative evidence for the jury's consideration of the testimony offered by those who knew her best," maj. at 678 n. 2: The video confirms that T.C. could express a simple concept like "no" by physically verbalizing that word. While those who knew T.C. testified that people less familiar with her might not be able to understand the exact message she is trying to convey with her growls or grunts, none of them said that she was unable to communicate a simple concept like "no" by means of head shaking, mean looks, crying or kicking. This testimony, along with the video showing T.C. saying the word "no," gives rise to only one conclusion: T.C. had multiple ways to "communicat[e] unwillingness" that a reasonable person unfamiliar with her could understand.

The majority also notes that "James had to physically lift [T.C.] from the wheelchair to the bed, and then he had to disrobe [her]." Maj. at 682. But this only proves that T.C. was unable to get out of her wheelchair or disrobe herself—which everyone agrees was the case. It has nothing to do with her ability to communicate, verbally or nonverbally. Even if T.C. had affirmatively consented, James would still have had to lift and disrobe her in order to consummate the act.

Finally, the fact that James said T.C. was "just laying there" during intercourse, *see id.,* doesn't show that she *couldn't* say "no." By characterizing the sexual act as "unwanted," *id.,* the majority engages in circular logic: If T.C. was physically capable of declining participation, she would have done so; therefore her failure to resist must mean she couldn't. This begs the question because we don't know that the sexual act was "unwanted." The fact that the government doesn't have to prove nonconsent under section 2242(2)(B) doesn't make lack of evidence of affirmative consent dispositive.

The majority claims that its holding "does not preclude someone suffering from a physical disability from ever having consensual sexual intercourse." Maj. at 683. I'm not so sure. James will go to prison, likely for many years, because he had sex with someone whose physical handicap impaired her ability to communicate, even though those who knew her testified that she could physically convey the idea of "no" when she wanted to. Today's opinion will make others more reticent about engaging in sex with people who are physically impaired. Their already difficult task of seeking out a partner for sexual gratification will become even more daunting.

Adopting a reading of the statute "that allow[s] more cases to be submitted to the good judgment of a jury" will deter all those who do not wish to submit their lives to the judgment of a jury, which I'm guessing includes most people. T.C. herself, for example, will never have sex again; who'd be foolish enough to risk it? If we're going to let juries impose lifetime sex bans on disabled individuals, it should only be by Congress speaking in far clearer terms. *Cf. City of Cleburne v. Cleburne Living Center,* 473 U.S. 432, 442–43, 105 S.Ct. 3249, 87 L.Ed.2d 313 (1985) (noting that how mentally disabled persons "[are] to be treated under the law is . . . very much a task for legislators . . . and not by the perhaps ill-informed opinions of the judiciary").

In the end, the majority faults James for not trying to prove consent as a defense. Maj. at 683. But the absence of an affirmative defense does not lower the government's burden to prove the elements of the crime. Because the government didn't (and couldn't) prove one such element beyond a reasonable doubt, I would affirm the sound judgment of the district court.

EXERCISE

Imagine that you are a criminal investigator looking into an incident on federal land. A 35-year-old woman, Tina, who suffers from Down's Syndrome and is non-verbal but able to communicate by writing, was camping with her sister, Rosa. They each had a separate tent. At night, Rosa awoke when she heard Tina having sex with a man. The sister chased the man out. As he left, he said "I was just visiting and. . . ." Rosa retrieved Tina's writing pad and pencil, which was in her tent with her, and finds that it is blank.

Tina writes to Rosa "It is ok, go away." Rosa takes Tina to the Emergency Room, where the attending nurse finds evidence of intercourse but no injury or indications of struggle.

As the investigator, you interview both Rosa and Tina. Rosa is very protective of her sister and explains that "she does whatever people tell her to do." She also is certain that Tina did not know the man prior to the incident. Tina will only write "OK" in answer to any question you pose, and seems emotionally closed-off.

You also are able to find and interview the man who had intercourse with Tina, based on camping records. He admits the sex act, explains that he was just looking for someone to talk to, and Tina seemed "nice." He says that she "wasn't all there, kind of," but also that she "seemed to want it by the way she was touching me all over."

Should you recommend the case for prosecution?

D. SEX INVOLVING MINORS

While adults can lack the capacity to consent to sex because of a temporary impairment or a permanent disability, children are generally considered to simply not have the legal ability to consent to sex. This legal rule exists for an important purpose: to protect children from sexual relationships with adults, who inherently have disproportionate power over a child. "Statutory rape" laws often, but not always, require that the defendant be significantly older than the victim.

Within the federal system, the primary statutory rape statute is found at 18 U.S.C. § 2243, and contains some fairly typical language which complicates the element of knowledge:

> **(a) Of a minor.**—Whoever, in the special maritime and territorial jurisdiction of the United States or in a Federal prison, or in any prison, institution, or facility in which persons are held in custody by direction of or pursuant to a contract or agreement with the head of any Federal department or agency, knowingly engages in a sexual act with another person who—
>
> > **(1)** has attained the age of 12 years but has not attained the age of 16 years; and
> >
> > **(2)** is at least four years younger than the person so engaging;
>
> or attempts to do so, shall be fined under this title, imprisoned not more than 15 years, or both. . . .

(c) Defenses.—

(1) In a prosecution under subsection (a) of this section, it is a defense, which the defendant must establish by a preponderance of the evidence, that the defendant reasonably believed that the other person had attained the age of 16 years.

(2) In a prosecution under this section, it is a defense, which the defendant must establish by a preponderance of the evidence, that the persons engaging in the sexual act were at that time married to each other.

(d) State of mind proof requirement.—In a prosecution under subsection (a) of this section, the Government need not prove that the defendant knew—

(1) the age of the other person engaging in the sexual act; or

(2) that the requisite age difference existed between the persons so engaging.

A separate statute, 18 U.S.C. § 2241(c), covers sex with children under twelve, with a harsher possible penalty of life in prison, and 18 U.S.C. § 2244(a)(3) incorporates the language quoted above to criminalize sexual contact (which can be less intrusive than sexual acts) with minors under 16.

The elements of 18 U.S.C. § 2243(a) are:

1)   Federal jurisdiction,

2)   Identification,

3)   Knowing engagement in a sexual act,

4)   With a person under 16, and

5)   At least a four-year age gap between the defendant and victim.

It is the knowledge element that is tricky here. As paragraph (d) makes clear, what the defendant must know is that he or she is engaging in a sex act rather than the age of the victim or the existence of a four-year age gap. This is a form of strict liability, which shifts to the defendant the responsibility of determining the age of the victim.

Unlike some criminal codes, though, this federal law does allow for an affirmative defense—one where the defendant bears the burden of production and proof—that the defendant reasonably believed the victim to be of age.

UNITED STATES V. WHITE CALF

634 F. 3d 453 (8th Cir. 2011)

RILEY, CHIEF JUDGE.

In June 2008, nineteen-year-old White Calf graduated from high school. White Calf invited classmates and friends to a party at his house on the Pine Ridge Indian Reservation in South Dakota. Everyone at the party became intoxicated, even though Pine Ridge is a "dry" reservation under Indian law.

Thirteen-year-old L.R.F. arrived late to the party. White Calf had not invited L.R.F. to the party. L.R.F.'s aunts, S.R.F. (age 18) and M.T.B. (age 16), allowed L.R.F. to tag along. S.R.F. and M.T.B. instructed L.R.F. to lie about her age at the party.

S.R.F. and White Calf were friends and high school classmates. White Calf and L.R.F. did not know one another before the night of the party, June 29–30, 2008. At some point after L.R.F. met White Calf, she lied and told him she was 15 years old. After L.R.F. and White Calf began kissing, L.R.F. told White Calf, "I am only 13." White Calf responded, "age don't matter." L.R.F. and White Calf flirted, hugged, and kissed.

S.R.F. unsuccessfully tried to break up the couple when she saw them kissing. White Calf told S.R.F. to leave the couple alone. S.R.F. later told White Calf that L.R.F. was "younger than what [L.R.F.]'s telling [White Calf]" and younger than D.B., a 15-year-old attendee of the party. White Calf thought D.B. was 14 or 15 years old.

S.R.F.'s attempts to separate L.R.F. from White Calf upset L.R.F. L.R.F. cried and later fell asleep in a bedroom. When L.R.F. woke up, White Calf was penetrating her vagina with his penis. As L.R.F. began to push White Calf away, Oglala Sioux Department of Public Safety Officer Llewellyn Preston Good Voice Flute, who was investigating a report of a loud party involving alcohol, entered the room. Officer Good Voice Flute observed White Calf and L.R.F., each naked below the waist, engaged in sexual intercourse. Specifically, Officer Good Voice Flute saw White Calf standing at the foot of the bed between L.R.F.'s legs, with his hands on L.R.F.'s hips, moving back and forth. L.R.F. was moaning, and Officer Good Voice Flute heard "[s]ex; skin slapping together." Officer Good Voice Flute ordered White Calf and L.R.F. to dress and leave the bedroom.

Officer Good Voice Flute asked White Calf and L.R.F. their ages. White Calf told Officer Good Voice Flute he was 21 and L.R.F. was 19. L.R.F. did not correct White Calf, but later lied and said she was 16. Officer Good Voice Flute was skeptical because, in his opinion, L.R.F. was small and looked like a "grade schooler." In a police cruiser, out of Officer Good Voice Flute's presence, White Calf threatened L.R.F. by telling her he would have someone beat her up if she told law enforcement the truth. White Calf instructed L.R.F. to tell law enforcement "we weren't doing nothing."

FBI Special Agent Sherry Rice interviewed White Calf. White Calf told Special Agent Rice that S.R.F. "brought her little sister," whom he did not know, to his party. White Calf estimated L.R.F. was 17 years old. White Calf initially denied having sex with L.R.F., saying his pants were still on when Officer Good Voice Flute entered the bedroom, but later recanted and admitted to having sexual intercourse with L.R.F. White Calf reported L.R.F. was flirting with him, and he did not know her name at the time. According to White Calf, L.R.F. took him to the bedroom and took her pants off. White Calf put on a condom and "was having sex when the police arrived." Toxicological tests indicated White Calf's blood alcohol content was .25. L.R.F.'s blood alcohol content was .18.

In September 2008, a grand jury returned an indictment charging White Calf with sexual abuse of a minor, in violation of 18 U.S.C. §§ 1153, 2243(a), and 2246(2)(A). The indictment alleged White Calf "did knowingly engage, and attempt to engage, in a sexual act with [L.R.F.], a child who had attained the age of 12 years, but who had not attained the age of 16 years, and who was at least four years younger than" White Calf.

In July 2009, the district court held a three-day trial on the indictment. At trial, White Calf testified on his own behalf, (1) denying he had sexual intercourse with L.R.F., because Officer Good Voice Flute interrupted him before he could do so, and (2) stating he reasonably believed L.R.F. was 17 years old when he tried to have sexual intercourse with her.

White Calf—
1. denying sex
2. reasonably believed she was 17 yrs old

The district court, employing a general verdict form, instructed the jury to find White Calf guilty if, among other things, the jury found White Calf attempted to sexually abuse or did sexually abuse L.R.F. The jury found White Calf guilty, and the district court sentenced him to 33 months imprisonment. White Calf appeals. . . .

White Calf argues the district court abused its discretion by failing to instruct the jury that (1) the jury could consider White Calf's intoxication when evaluating the affirmative defense set forth in 18 U.S.C. § 2243(c)(1), and (2) the government was required to prove White Calf knew L.R.F. was not yet 16 years old. . . .

At common law, voluntary intoxication was a not a defense to criminal activity. *See Montana v. Egelhoff,* 518 U.S. 37, 45, 116 S.Ct. 2013, 135 L.Ed.2d 361 (1996). In the 19th Century, American courts "carved out an exception to the common law's traditional across-the-board condemnation of the drunken offender, allowing a jury to consider a defendant's intoxication when assessing whether he possessed the mental state needed to commit the crime charged, where the crime was one requiring a 'specific intent.'" *Id.* at 46, 116 S.Ct. 2013. No such exception was created for general intent crimes.

voluntary intoxication is not a defense to criminal activity

Sexual abuse of a minor is a general intent crime, but attempted sexual abuse of a minor is a specific intent crime. *See United States v. Kenyon,* 481

F.3d 1054, 1069–71 (8th Cir.2007). *Cf. United States v. Robertson,* 606 F.3d 943, 954–55 (8th Cir.2010) (distinguishing attempted aggravated sexual abuse, a specific intent crime, from aggravated sexual abuse, a general intent crime). The district court instructed the jury that White Calf's voluntary intoxication was not a defense to the substantive offense of sexual abuse of a minor, but voluntary intoxication was a possible defense to the alternatively charged crime of attempted sexual abuse of a minor. The district court instructed the jury as follows:

> *[handwritten in margin: District Court Jury Instruction]*
>
> With regard to the crime of sexual abuse of a minor, it is not necessary that the government prove that the defendant intended to commit the crime of sexual abuse of a minor. The government must prove beyond a reasonable doubt that the defendant knowingly engaged in a sexual act with [L.R.F]. Therefore, the fact that the defendant may have been intoxicated is not to be considered by you in determining whether he committed the crime of sexual abuse of a minor.
>
> With regard to the crime of attempt to sexually abuse a minor, the government must prove that the defendant intended to commit the crime of sexual abuse of a minor. Being under the influence of alcohol provides a legal excuse for the commission of a crime only if the effect of the alcohol makes it impossible for the defendant to have the intent to commit the crime. Evidence that defendant acted while under the influence of alcohol may be considered by you, together with all the other evidence, in determining whether or not he did in fact have the intent to commit the crime of sexual abuse of a minor.

White Calf does not dispute that the foregoing instruction correctly states the law. White Calf objected to the instruction because it failed to "indicate [ ] that intoxication should also be considered by the jury in considering the defense." He asked for the following additional instruction:

> Another issue in this case is whether Roman White Calf reasonably believed that [L.R.F.] had attained the age of 16 years on June 30, 2008. Evidence of his intoxication may also be considered by you in determining whether he reasonably believed [L.R.F.] had attained the age of 16 years.

The district court declined to give the additional instruction.

The district court did not abuse its discretion in overruling White Calf's objection and declining to submit White Calf's proffered additional instruction to the jury. The district court correctly relied on *United States v. Weise,* 89 F.3d 502, 505 (8th Cir.1996), in which we held "the reasonableness of [a defendant's] belief is not measured through the eyes of a reasonably intoxicated person." In *Weise,* we affirmed the district court's explicit instruction to the jury "to disregard Weise's intoxication when deciding if Weise's [defense of self-defense] was founded on reasonably perceived circumstances." *Id.* (citing *United States v. Yazzie,* 660 F.2d 422, 431 (10th Cir.1981)).

EXERCISE

It appears that White Calf was asserting the affirmative defense allowed for in paragraph (c)(1) of 18 U.S.C. § 2243: "In a prosecution under subsection (a) of this section, it is a defense, which the defendant must establish by a preponderance of the evidence, that the defendant reasonably believed that the other person had attained the age of 16 years."

As a policy matter, do you think Congress should clarify the statute and state that the affirmative defense allowed for in that statute can take into account the inebriation of the defendant?

One issue with statutory rape cases is the use of the victim as a witness. Often, prosecutors wish to avoid traumatizing the victim through testimony, and due to their youth child victims sometimes give inconsistent versions of events. That means that a victim's initial statement to a third party about the abuse—sometimes referred to as an "outcry"—can be crucial evidence in this kind of case. In the case below, pay attention to the efforts of the prosecution to bring in hearsay statements that probably played a large role in the jury's understanding of the events at issue.

UNITED STATES V. JENNINGS
496 F. 3d 344 (4th Cir. 2007)

NIEMEYER, CIRCUIT JUDGE:

Ryan Jennings, age 24, was convicted for repeatedly touching a 13-year-old girl's buttocks, inner thighs, and genitalia during a "red-eye" transcontinental flight from San Diego, California, to Washington, D.C. (Dulles International Airport in Virginia), in violation of 18 U.S.C. § 2244(a)(3) (criminalizing "abusive sexual contact" with a minor).

On appeal, Jennings contends (1) that the testimony of passengers relating statements made by the 13-year-old girl to the passengers regarding Jennings' abuse was improperly admitted into evidence under an exception to the hearsay rule; (2) that the district court erred in instructing the jury that the government need not prove that Jennings knew the victim's age to prove a conviction under § 2244(a)(3); and (3) that the district court abused its discretion in giving a "deliberate ignorance" instruction to the jury.

We conclude that the hearsay testimony of two passengers about what the child said to them fell within the excited utterance exception to the hearsay rule, Federal Rule of Evidence 803(2); that § 2244(a)(3) does not require that the defendant know the victim's age; and that the district court did not abuse its discretion in giving a deliberate ignorance instruction. Accordingly, we affirm the judgment of the district court.

I

On the evening of December 18, 2005, the mother of Casey, a 13-year-old girl within days of her 14th birthday, and Ryan, an 11-year-old boy, accompanied her children through security at the San Diego International Airport to the gate of their red-eye flight to Dulles International Airport, where their father was to pick them up to spend the Christmas holiday with him. The children's mother waited with them at the departure gate for half an hour, and then departed. Ryan Jennings, age 24, who was booked on the same flight, sat across from the children in the departure gate's waiting area. After their mother left, Jennings struck up a conversation with them, asking if they were traveling alone, to which Casey responded, "Yes." Linda Columbus, a fellow passenger on the flight, overheard Jennings say to the children, "Everybody tells you not to talk to strangers, but I'm cool."

After boarding the plane, Casey sat in seat 7A, the window seat, and her brother sat in seat 6A, a window seat directly in front of her. Jennings took seat 7B, directly next to Casey, even though his assigned seat was ten rows back. Jennings told Casey he wanted to sit next to her because he "thought [she] was beautiful." Another male passenger sat in seat 7C, the aisle seat.

A few minutes into the flight, Jennings made attempts to engage Casey in conversation. Casey smelled alcohol on Jennings' breath (he had been partying prior to arriving at the airport). Casey asked Jennings how old he was, and he answered, "21," even though he was 24. Jennings, on the other hand, did not want to know how old Casey was, saying, "In my mind, you are 18. I want to make this right." Jennings then expressed his belief to Casey that it was "really wrong" that a friend of his had been charged with statutory rape, "because if two people want to be together, then they should, regardless of age." While saying this, Jennings placed his left hand on Casey's inner right thigh. Casey crossed her legs in an attempt to get it off, but Jennings left his hand there. By this time, the male passenger in seat 7C was asleep.

When the fasten-seatbelt sign was turned off, Casey got up to go to the lavatory. As Casey moved past Jennings toward the aisle, Jennings "grabbed [her] butt, and then his fingers touched [her] vagina."

After returning from the lavatory, Casey noticed that Jennings had raised the armrest separating his seat from hers. He was also drinking from a bottle of wine. Jennings complained that he was cold, and Casey offered him a blanket that she had brought along. After covering himself with the blanket, Jennings tried to cover Casey's legs with it as well. Casey resisted, saying that she was "really hot," but Jennings persisted. After he covered Casey's legs, Jennings again placed his left hand on Casey's inner thigh. When Jennings leaned in to give Casey a kiss on the cheek, he spilled wine on the blanket. Jennings cursed at his clumsiness, seized the blanket, and went to the lavatory to clean it off. While Jennings was gone, Casey tried to convince her brother to move back to seat 7B and sit by her, but Ryan said that he was sleeping and was too tired to move. Jennings returned from cleaning the blanket and tried again to cover Casey and himself with the blanket. This time, Casey grabbed the blanket and put it into her backpack.

The absence of cover did not deter Jennings, and he again put his left hand on Casey's inner thigh. Casey again crossed her legs, but this did not discourage Jennings. He hooked his hand between Casey's crossed legs, using the opportunity to reach under Casey and rub her buttocks. With his hand between Casey's legs, Jennings rubbed Casey's buttocks and inner thighs constantly for 15 minutes. Casey did not say anything because she "was scared" and "shocked." She "just thought that if [she] pretended to be sleeping, that maybe he would get bored and go away." Jennings asked Casey for her telephone number, saying, "Maybe we could hook up when we get back to San Diego."

Eventually Jennings got up to sit between Casey's brother Ryan in seat 6A and Karen Schmidt in seat 6C, in the row directly in front of Casey. Ryan was still sleeping, and Jennings began to talk to Schmidt. Casey testified that she overheard Jennings tell Schmidt that he thought Casey was beautiful, to which Schmidt asked, "Well, do you know how old she is?" Jennings replied, "No," and Schmidt told him that Casey was 13 or 14. "It doesn't matter," Jennings said. Schmidt testified that Jennings "reeked" of alcohol and that he continued to drink from his bottle of wine. Jennings repeatedly told Schmidt how "hot" he thought Casey was, and that he wanted to join the "mile high club" with her. Schmidt told Jennings, "I'm sure this isn't the first time you've done this." "No, it's not," Jennings replied, "I have always had a thing for young girls."

Jennings' conversation with Schmidt ended abruptly when Jennings again spilled wine, which landed on the feet and bag of the passenger slumbering in seat 7C. That passenger moved, leaving Casey alone to stretch out over the three seats in the row. Jennings asked Casey if she wanted him to return and sit next to her. Casey said, "No," but Jennings ignored Casey's response, moved her feet, sat down, and placed her legs on his lap. Casey told Jennings that she had overheard his conversation with Schmidt and that she knew that he knew her age. Jennings grimaced and said that it did not matter, "because in his mind, [she] was still 18." Jennings suggested that Casey take out her blanket again so nobody would see what was going to happen. Casey pretended not to hear Jennings and put on her iPod. Throughout this conversation, Jennings was rubbing Casey's lower legs.

Linda Columbus, the fellow passenger who had observed Jennings talking to the children at the departure gate, saw that Jennings was seated next to Casey and leaning in close to her. Alarmed, she contacted a flight attendant and requested that Jennings be moved to a seat away from Casey. The flight attendant ordered Jennings to sit in his assigned seat, and five minutes thereafter Casey moved to sit next to her brother.

When Casey sat down in seat 6B between her brother and Schmidt, Casey felt "shocked, angry, kind of like confused." Schmidt asked Casey what had happened, and Casey recounted in detail Jennings' words and actions. As Casey did so, she "became hysterical" and began to cry.

The plane landed approximately an hour and a half after Jennings was moved to his assigned seat. When the plane stopped at the arrival gate, Jennings, with his hood pulled over his head, rushed to the front of the plane to talk to Casey. Casey, who "was still crying," exited the aircraft as quickly as she could, pretending not to see Jennings. Jennings caught up to Casey and said, "Casey, I'm sorry the flight attendants [ ] had to move me." Casey kept on walking, grabbing her brother to speed him up. Jennings stopped following them as they left the gate terminal, at which point Casey paused and broke down into tears. Linda Columbus witnessed Jennings talk to Casey and Casey's immediate tearful reaction. Columbus approached Casey to ask if she was okay. "Tears were streaming down her face," Columbus testified. "She couldn't really speak. She was really upset." Columbus testified that when she asked what had happened, Casey exclaimed that Jennings had "touched her butt and between her legs." Columbus sent the children on to meet their father, and then she went in search of security. She found the pilots of their flight and reported what Casey had told her. The captain of the flight approached Jennings and detained him until airport security arrived.

Based on the special aircraft jurisdiction of the federal criminal laws provided by 49 U.S.C. § 46506(1), Jennings was indicted in one count for abusive sexual contact of a minor, in violation of 18 U.S.C. § 2244(a)(3). Before trial, Jennings filed a motion *in limine* that Karen Schmidt and Linda Columbus not be permitted to testify about the statements made to them by Casey concerning Jennings' conduct. The district court denied the motions, finding that the statements were admissible under Federal Rule of Evidence 803(2) (the "excited utterance" exception to the hearsay rule). Jennings renewed the objection during the trial.

At trial, the district court instructed the jury that Jennings' knowledge of Casey's age was not an element of the offense. Jennings did not object to the instruction; indeed, he explicitly agreed to it.

[handwritten margin note: motion denied]

After the jury returned a guilty verdict, Jennings filed a motion for a new trial, claiming for the first time that 18 U.S.C. § 2244(a)(3) required the government to prove, as an element of the offense, that he knew of Casey's age. The district court denied the motion, construing § 2244(a)(3) *not* to require that the defendant have knowledge of the victim's age.

On appeal, Jennings claims that the district court abused its discretion in admitting Schmidt and Columbus' testimony about what Casey had told them; in denying the motion for a new trial, arguing that § 2244(a)(3) required the government to prove beyond a reasonable doubt that he knew of Casey's age; and in giving a "deliberate ignorance" instruction to the jury.

II

Jennings contends first that the district court abused its discretion in admitting the hearsay statements of Karen Schmidt and Linda Columbus, passengers to whom Casey had related what had occurred on the flight.

The government offered the testimony of Schmidt and Columbus, claiming that it was admissible under either Federal Rule of Evidence 803(1) (permitting admission of "statement[s] describing or explaining an event or condition made while the declarant was perceiving the event or condition, or immediately thereafter") or Rule 803(2) (permitting admission of "statement[s] relating to a startling event or condition made while the declarant was under the stress of excitement caused by the event or condition"). Schmidt's testimony related to statements Casey made to her five minutes after Jennings was removed from his seat and Casey moved to seat 6B, next to Schmidt. After Casey moved, Schmidt asked her what happened. Casey, who later testified she was "shocked, angry, and confused" at the time, began to recount Jennings' misdeeds, and she quickly began to "unravel," sob, and become "hysterical." Casey told Schmidt "what happened," and "what was said and how [Jennings] touched [her]," telling her how Jennings repeatedly rubbed her inner thigh, locked his hand between her crossed legs in order to rub her buttocks, stroked her neck and hair, kissed her on her cheek and neck, and grabbed her buttocks when she passed by him on the way to the lavatory.

Linda Columbus' testimony related to statements made by Casey immediately after Jennings had spoken to her upon departing the aircraft. In the gate after exiting the aircraft, Jennings said to Casey, "Casey, I'm sorry the flight attendants had to move me." Casey stopped walking and broke down into tears, whereupon Columbus testified that, after witnessing this, she immediately approached Casey, who then blurted out that Jennings had "touched her butt and between her legs."

The district court admitted the testimony of both Schmidt and Columbus as excited utterances under Rule 803(2), although later, the court thought that the testimony might better have been admitted under Federal Rule of Evidence 803(1) (the present sense impression exception).

To qualify under the excited utterance exception, (1) the declarant must have "experienced a startling event or condition"; (2) she must have related the statement "while under the stress or excitement of that event or condition, not from reflection"; and (3) the statement or utterance must have "related[ed] to the startling event or condition." *Morgan v. Foretich,* 846 F.2d 941, 947 (4th Cir.1988); Fed.R.Evid. 803(2). The justification for admitting an excited utterance as an exception to the hearsay rule is based on the "assumption that an excited declarant will not have had time to reflect on events to fabricate." *Morgan,* 846 F.2d at 946. Additionally, errors in memory will have had less time to accumulate.

The testimony of Karen Schmidt related statements made by Casey five minutes after Jennings was moved to his assigned seat and while Casey was in a state of shock, anger, and confusion. Shortly after Casey began relating the events that had just occurred, she broke down crying and became hysterical. In view of what Casey had experienced at the hands of Jennings during the course of the flight over a lengthy period of time, we have little difficulty concluding that Casey was making statements about a startling event, as that term is used in the Rule. Jennings grabbed Casey's buttocks and touched her genitalia, repeatedly and methodically groped her upper and inner thighs, and locked his hand between her crossed legs in order to reach under her to grab her buttocks. While doing this, he spoke approvingly of statutory rape, told Casey to retrieve her blanket so that nobody would see what was going to happen, and advocated "hooking up" with Casey once they both returned to San Diego.

Just as we readily conclude that Casey was relating a startling event, we also readily conclude that Casey recounted the events to Schmidt while Casey was "under the stress of excitement caused by the event." *Morgan,* 846 F.2d at 947. In reaching this conclusion, we have considered relevant factors such as "(1) the lapse of time between the event and the declarations; (2) the age of the declarant; (3) the physical and mental state of the declarant; (4) the characteristics of the event; and (5) the subject matter of the statements." *Id.* Casey clearly made the statements while under stress caused by Jennings' abusive sexual contact. Even though Casey waited five minutes before moving to sit next to Schmidt, she remained "shocked, angry, and . . . confused" and "started talking right away," as she began to recount Jennings' misdeeds to Schmidt. She then began to "unravel," sob, and become "hysterical." Even Jennings has not suggested that the statements made by a 13-year-old in these circumstances were in any sense fabricated. While Jennings does not contend that Casey's statements were fabrications, he does argue that the time elapsed—five minutes—made them deliberative statements and not excited utterances. He asserts that Casey had made a deliberate choice not to contact a flight attendant when Jennings was away from her, maintaining that Casey's failure to report the abuse to flight attendants at her earliest opportunity precludes the government from using Casey's statements made to Schmidt. *See Morgan,* 846 F.2d at 948. Jennings' reliance upon *Morgan,* however, is completely misplaced. *Morgan* does not create a rule that requires children to report sexual abuse at the earliest opportunity in order for their statements to be considered excited utterances. To the contrary, it affirmatively rejected such a mechanical approach to the excited utterance exception. In *Morgan,* we were concerned that courts would "place undue emphasis on the spontaneity requirement in child sexual abuse cases," and so we sought to focus their attention "not only simply on the time between the abuse and the declaration," but *also* on "the child's first real opportunity to report the incident." *Id.* at 947–48. *Morgan* thus elongated the temporal view courts should take when considering whether a child was in an excited state, and it eschewed the use of the very type of bright-line rule that Jennings would have us adopt. In this case, Casey stated that she did not report the abuse to flight attendants because she was "scared." Indeed, she was not free of Jennings' influence to have a real opportunity of reporting the incidents until after she was safely with her father in the airport.

[handwritten margin note: scared + not free of Jennings' influence]

At bottom, the analysis must focus on whether the declarant's statement was trustworthy by being made in circumstances where it would not be reasonable to conclude that the declarant fabricated the statement or incorrectly remembered the events related. *Morgan,* 846 F.2d at 947–48. The lapse of time between the event and the declaration is just one of several factors to consider in the analysis. *Id.* at 947.

In this case we have little difficulty in concluding that Casey's statements to Schmidt related a startling event and were made while Casey was still under the stress of the event. Therefore, they were properly admitted under the excited utterance exception to the hearsay rule.

[handwritten margin note: Statements were properly admitted]

————————

EXERCISE

An important area of discretion accorded to prosecutors is choosing the witnesses they call. In the case above, the prosecutor could have chosen to rely on Casey's hearsay statements (the outcries to other passengers) in lieu of having Casey herself take the stand. There is a trade-off; hearsay testimony is less reliable, but it is an act of compassion to spare the child victim the trauma of the courtroom. If you were the prosecutor in this case, would you take the risk of not calling Casey to the stand?

E. PROSTITUTION AND SEX TRAFFICKING

Some consensual sex among adults is illegal in most places: that is, when sex is paid for. In some places, focus among American law enforcement has shifted from prostitutes to those who recruit, manage, and otherwise profit from them.

A long-standing federal statute on this kind of sex trafficking is the Mann Act, first enacted in 1910 and codified at 18 U.S.C. § 2421:

> Whoever knowingly transports any individual in interstate or foreign commerce, or in any Territory or Possession of the United States, with intent that such individual engage in prostitution, or in any sexual activity for which any person can be charged with a criminal offense, or attempts to do so, shall be fined under this title or imprisoned not more than 10 years, or both.

While § 2421 prohibits the actual movement of a prostitute, 18 U.S.C. § 2422 strikes more broadly:

> **(a)** Whoever knowingly persuades, induces, entices, or coerces any individual to travel in interstate or foreign commerce, or in any Territory or Possession of the United States, to engage in prostitution, or in any sexual activity for which any person can be charged with a criminal offense, or attempts to do so, shall be fined under this title or imprisoned not more than 20 years, or both.

> **(b)** Whoever, using the mail or any facility or means of interstate or foreign commerce, or within the special maritime and territorial jurisdiction of the United States knowingly persuades, induces, entices, or coerces any individual who has not attained the age of 18 years, to engage in prostitution or any sexual activity for which any person can be charged with a criminal offense, or attempts to do so, shall be fined under this title and imprisoned not less than 10 years or for life.

Taken together, these statutes give prosecutors potent tools to go after sex traffickers.

UNITED STATES v. MI SUN CHO
713 F. 3d 716 (2d Cir. 2013)

PER CURIAM:

Defendant-appellant Mi Sun Cho was convicted by a jury in the United States District Court for the Southern District of New York (Kimba M. Wood, *Judge*) of one count of conspiring to violate sex trafficking laws in violation of 18 U.S.C. §§ 2241 and 2422 and two substantive sex trafficking counts in violation of 18 U.S.C. §§ 2241 and 2. Cho raises several challenges to her conviction. First, she contends that there was insufficient evidence to establish that she transported Mei Hua Jin, a prostitute, in interstate commerce in violation of 18 U.S.C. § 2421or caused Jin to be so transported under 18 U.S.C. § 2(b). . . .

In October 2010, after losing money gambling at a casino, Mei Hua Jin telephoned Cho from Atlantic City to see whether Cho could find her employment as a prostitute. Cho was aware that Jin was calling from Atlantic City. Cho had extensive contacts in the sex-trafficking industry and worked to provide prostitutes to brothels, often determining prostitutes' placement based on their age and physical appearance. Cho and Jin had previously worked together at a Connecticut brothel and at a prostitution business that Cho operated in Manhattan. After receiving Jin's phone call, Cho arranged to have one of her contacts inform Jin that a position at a Manhattan brothel was available. This contact was a confidential informant ("CI") for law enforcement who had a lengthy relationship with Cho in the sex-trafficking industry. On October 7, 2010, the CI spoke with Jin about traveling from Atlantic City to New York so that she could be placed at the Manhattan brothel designated by Cho.

On October 8, after speaking to Cho and the CI, Jin bought a bus ticket with her own money and traveled from Atlantic City to Manhattan. She then took the subway to Flushing, where Cho and the CI awaited her arrival. The three then began driving to the Manhattan brothel, though Cho was dropped off at home before Jin and the CI reached their destination. The brothel rejected Jin because she was too old, and Jin then returned to Flushing.

On October 25, 2011, the Government filed a three-count Superseding Indictment. As relevant to this appeal, Count Two charged Cho with transporting Jin from New Jersey to New York to work at a brothel, and willfully causing her to be so transported in violation of 18 U.S.C. §§ 2241 and 2. On November 7, 2011, after a five-day trial, the jury convicted Cho of all three counts. After the verdict, Cho renewed her motion under Rule 29 of the Federal Rules of Criminal Procedure for a judgment of acquittal on Counts Two and Three. In the alternative, Cho requested a new trial on those counts pursuant to Rule 33. The district court denied Cho's motion, finding that there was ample evidence to support the jury's verdict. Applying a four-level leadership enhancement under U.S.S.G. § 3B1.1(a), the district court sentenced Cho to an aggregate term of 70 months' imprisonment, to be followed by two years of supervised release, and a $300 special assessment. . . [*sentence*]

Cho argues that the district court erred in denying her Rule 29 motion for judgment of acquittal on Count Two, because there was insufficient evidence to establish that she transported Jin in interstate commerce or caused her to be so transported. We disagree. . . .

Under 18 U.S.C. § 2421, it is a crime to "knowingly transport[ ] any individual in interstate or foreign commerce . . . with intent that such individual engage in prostitution, or in any sexual activity for which any person can be charged with a criminal offense." 18 U.S.C. § 2421. "A defendant will be deemed to have transport[ed] an individual under Section 2421 where evidence shows that the defendant personally or through an agent performed the proscribed act of transporting." *United States v. Holland,* 381 F.3d 80, 86 (2d Cir.2004) (alteration in original) (internal quotation marks omitted). As the district court properly instructed the jury, without objection from defense counsel:

[handwritten: Jury instruction]

> The prosecution does not need to prove that the defendant personally transported the individual across a state line. This element is satisfied if you find that the defendant prearranged the transportation of a person across a state line and that the defendant personally or through an agent arranged intrastate transportation as a continuation of the interstate travel.

J. App'x 97.

[handwritten: Next jury instruction — No objection to either]

Similarly, and also without objection, the district court instructed the jury that Cho could be found guilty under 18 U.S.C. § 2(b) "even if she acted through someone who was entirely innocent of the crimes charged in the indictment, even if [she] acted through a government agent." *See United States v. Ordner,* 554 F.2d 24, 29 (2d Cir.1977) ("It is . . . well recognized that the guilt or innocence of the intermediary under a § 2(b) charge is irrelevant").

Viewed in the light most favorable to the government, the evidence at trial established that Jin called Cho from Atlantic City, seeking a job as a prostitute. Cho put Jin in contact with the CI, who spoke with her about traveling to New York to engage in prostitution. Jin traveled from Atlantic City to New York, where Cho and the CI picked her up. Cho then had the CI drive Jin to Manhattan so that Jin could work in a brothel.

Cho does not dispute that one who arranges another's transportation across state lines for purposes of prostitution violates § 2421. She contends, however, that she did not "arrange" Jin's interstate travel because she did not pay for Jin's ticket or book her passage. We disagree. By agreeing, either directly or through the CI, to provide a prostitution job for Jin, and by coordinating and prearranging the date and time on which she would travel, Cho arranged for Jin to travel from New Jersey to New York to engage in prostitution. Moreover, by providing the CI to drive Jin on the last, intrastate leg of her interstate trip, Cho directly organized Jin's transportation in interstate commerce. Like the Fifth Circuit, which reached the same result on indistinguishable facts, we conclude that this was sufficient evidence from which a rational jury could find the elements of the offense satisfied. *See, e.g., United States v. Clemones,* 577 F.2d 1247, 1253 (5th Cir.1978) (holding that defendant transported prostitute under 18 U.S.C. § 2421, where defendant arranged via telephone for prostitute to cross state line, then drove prostitute to defendant's brothel upon her arrival in defendant's state). Accordingly, we decline to disturb the jury's verdict.

EXERCISE

Consider the following fictional situation.

You are the prosecutor in the *Cho* case. You did not originally intend to charge Ms. Cho, but she turned out to be an important potential witness in the case against a much more important person, the operator of the Manhattan brothel. It turns out that the primary target, the brothel-owner, is Cho's nephew. In order to get Cho to testify against her nephew, you charge her and threaten her with a potential 70-month sentence unless she cooperates with the prosecution of her nephew. She both refuses to cooperate against her nephew and goes to trial.

At sentencing, do you still ask for the threatened 70-month sentence? What negative consequences might flow from a failure to do so?

In addition to the traditional Mann Act provisions of 18 U.S.C. § 2421 and § 2422, the federal penal code now includes 18 U.S.C. § 1591, which allows for prosecution where a trafficker deals in children or uses "force, fraud, or coercion." This newer statute was first enacted in 2000.

UNITED STATES V. TODD
627 F. 3d 329 (9th Cir. 2009)

NOONAN, CIRCUIT JUDGE:

Jerome Eugene Todd appeals his conviction of three counts of sex trafficking in violation of 18 U.S.C. § 1591(a)(1) and one count of conspiracy to engage in sex trafficking in violation of 18 U.S.C. § 371. We affirm the convictions.

The statute, captioned the Trafficking Victim's Protection Act (TVPA), is a new effort to deal with a social ill whose international as well as interstate dimensions have invited federal attention and action. The TVPA was enacted in December 2000 and amended, as relevant here, in December 2003, July 2006 and December 2008. The statute focuses on those (usually men) who make money out of selling the sexual services of human beings (usually women) they control and treat as their profit-producing property.

Subtitled "Sex trafficking of children or by force, fraud, or coercion," the law strikes at two particularly vicious permutations of commercialized sex: at the exploitation of minors in the business of selling sex and at the use of criminal means to produce the product being sold. This case falls into the second slot.

FACTS

We state the facts as to Todd's treatment of four women:

Todd and Kelsey Kirschman. Just eighteen in January 2005, Kelsey was still in high school in Bellingham. Todd, age 26, was not working but had cash. They dated, going to dinner and to the movies. In May 2006, Todd suggested they get a place together. He also told her that they could get rich together if she worked as a prostitute. He would advertise her in the *Seattle Weekly*. She agreed. He ran the ad with a picture of her, offering "full service" for $200. Calls came in from men, and she responded to them. She gave up a job at Fred Meyer because Todd wanted her available for prostitution 24/7. Todd also arranged for her services to be posted on *Craigslist*. At Todd's direction, she also "walked the track," that is, she hung out in an area frequented by prostitutes and potential customers. Todd laid down rules for her to obey. As she testified, "You had to, basically, do everything he wanted." Most basically, "You had to give him all the money." Todd allotted Kelsey $35 each day to pay for condoms, food, and gas.

Todd maintained his rules psychologically by making Kelsey feel that she was "nothing." He maintained his rules physically by beating her "from head to toe," blacking one of her eyes and chipping one of her teeth. When she was 2 ½ months pregnant, he demanded that she abort the child, and she complied. She tried to hide some of her earnings as a prostitute from Todd, but he found them and confiscated them. She did not leave him because she thought that she "had nowhere else to go," was "scared," and had lived "under this man's rules" for a year and a half.

Reduced to this state of dependence, Kelsey performed a number of acts by agreement with Todd to further his traffic in the bodies of other women. She "groomed" Whitney T.—that is, coached her—as to how she should conduct herself as a prostitute working for Todd. She placed ads in *Craigslist* and *Seattle Weekly* advertising the sexual availability of Whitney and two other women who came to work for Todd as prostitutes. She rented hotel rooms for these women to use with customers, provided them with cellphones to receive calls from customers, and purchased condoms for them to supply to customers. In these actions, she collaborated with Todd.

Todd and Whitney T. Whitney T., aged twenty, met Todd at a party in October 2006. Whitney was the unmarried mother of a young child. She was unemployed and living with a girlfriend in Everett. She and Todd liked each other and began a relationship. Todd had no job but he wore nice clothes and had cash. Whitney learned eventually that his income came from Kelsey's work as a prostitute.

In January 2007, Todd told Whitney that if she too worked as a prostitute for a couple of years she could have nice cars and a nice house. In February 2007, Whitney went on her first call. She moved into an apartment with

Todd and Kelsey. Todd advertised her services on *Craigslist* and the *Seattle Weekly*. Todd imposed the rules that Whitney earn $500 in a day and that she turn the money over to him. She believed that Todd would beat her if she held any money back. She saw Todd beat Kelsey for violating one of his rules and was herself beaten by him for breaking his rule against speaking to black pimps.

Whitney T. twice left Todd and twice voluntarily returned to him. On July 3, 2007, she left him for good. She continued to work as a prostitute on her own.

Todd and Whitney E. Todd met Whitney E., aged eighteen, in June 2007. She had dropped out of high school, had left her father's home and her mother's home, was using drugs, was living with a boyfriend, and had been working for a week as a prostitute. The day after she met Todd, her boyfriend suggested that she work for Todd. The next day she began to work for him as a prostitute. He gave her a cellphone and clothes from Wal-Mart. He advertised her on *Craigslist*. He told her that he expected her to service five customers per day and earn at least $900. He put her in an apartment with a prostitute who worked for his cousin, Trent. Trent told her he would enforce Todd's rules physically. In July 2007, Todd himself assaulted her when she questioned one of his rules. She telephoned her mother for help and later the same day left the apartment with her mother and reported the assault to the police.

Todd and Jemelle L. Todd met Jemelle on her twentieth birthday in July 2007. She was living with her mother and working as a caregiver. They began to date. Todd had no job but had cash. In October 2007, she leased a house, and she and Todd moved in together.

Jemelle had previously engaged in four or five acts of prostitution. Todd now told her it would be an easy way to make money and have nice things. Todd gave her a phone to take calls from customers, and she began to respond to them after initially protesting. Todd advertised her availability in the *Seattle Weekly* and on the internet without her knowledge or consent. Todd told her that his rule was that she provide "full service," charge $200 per customer, report the transaction by telephone and turn all the money over to him. He provided her with marijuana.

Jemelle was scared seeing Todd beat Kelsey, and she was scared by his threat that she would regret it if she left him. Once she attempted to leave and he "pushed me down." The indictment covered the use of Jemelle from October 2007 to November 2007.

PROCEDURE

On November 21, 2007, Todd was indicted. On February 8, 2008, a superseding indictment was returned. Trial began May 12, 2008. After seven days, the jury found Todd guilty on all counts. Both before and after the verdict Todd moved for a judgment of acquittal.

On September 29, 2008, Todd was sentenced to five years imprisonment for conspiracy to violate the TVPA; to twenty-six years to run concurrently on each of the TVPA counts involving respectively Whitney T., Whitney E., and Jemelle; and to ten years on the count of transporting a prostitute in interstate commerce.

Todd does not appeal his conviction or sentence on the count of transportation of a prostitute. He appeals his conviction on all of the other counts.

ANALYSIS

The Statute.

Sex trafficking of children or by force, fraud, or coercion

(a) Whoever knowingly—

(1) in or affecting interstate or foreign commerce, or within the special maritime and territorial jurisdiction of the United States, recruits, entices, harbors, transports, provides, or obtains by any means a person; or

(2) benefits, financially or by receiving anything of value, from participation in a venture which has engaged in an act described in violation of paragraph (1),

knowing that force, fraud, or coercion described in subsection (c)(2) will be used to cause the person to engage in a commercial sex act, or that the person has not attained the age of 18 years and will be caused to engage in a commercial sex act, shall be punished as provided in subsection (b).

(b) The punishment for an offense under subsection(a) is—

(1) if the offense was effected by force, fraud, or coercion or if the person recruited, enticed, harbored, transported, provided, or obtained had not attained the age of 14 years at the time of such offense, by a fine under this title and imprisonment for any term of years not less than 15 or for life; or

(2) if the offense was not so effected, and the person recruited, enticed, harbored, transported, provided, or obtained had attained the age of 14 years but had not attained the age of 18 years at the time of such offense, by a fine under this title and imprisonment for not less than 10 years or for life.

(c) In this section:

(1) The term "commercial sex act" means any sex act, on account of which anything of value is given to or received by any person.

(2) The term "coercion" means—

(A) threats of serious harm to or physical restraint against any person;

(B) any scheme, plan, or pattern intended to cause a person to believe that failure to perform an act would result in serious harm to or physical restraint against any person; or

(C) the abuse or threatened abuse of law or the legal process.

(3) The term "venture" means any group of two or more individuals associated in fact, whether or not a legal entity.

18 U.S.C. § 1591.

We consider the statutory elements in turn.

Effect on interstate or foreign commerce. The TVPA was enacted after Congress took a substantial amount of evidence on the traffic in the sexual services of women based on importing women from around the world by force or fraud. *See* Victims of Trafficking and Violence Protection Act of 2000, Pub.L. No. 106–386, 114 Stat. 1464, 1466 (2000). Congress concluded that prostitution in American cities encouraged and enlarged the market for this traffic from abroad. *Id.* Sex traffic is a global matter.

In addition to its effect on foreign commerce, sex traffic in this case was conducted by advertising across state lines and so affected interstate commerce.

The TVPA is unlike the Violence Against Women Act of 1994, 42 U.S.C. § 13981, which sought to protect women by making gender-motivated crimes of violence actionable and was found to be beyond the power of Congress because its subject matter was not commerce. *United States v. Morrison,* 529 U.S. 598, 120 S.Ct. 1740, 146 L.Ed.2d 658 (2000). The TVPA deals with commerce within the power of Congress to regulate. The defendant does not question the act's constitutionality.

Todd's knowledge. Here is a crux. Could Todd have known when he soft-soaped Whitney T., Whitney E., and Jemelle L. to go to work for him that later "force, fraud, or coercion would be used" to cause each of them to engage in commercial sex? How does anyone "know" the future?

What the statute means to describe, and does describe awkwardly, is a state of mind in which the knower is familiar with a pattern of conduct. If "to know" is taken in the sense of being sure of an established fact, no one "knows" his own or anyone else's future. As William Shakespeare said of time in Sonnet 115, its "million'd accidents creep in" and nothing is completely stable, no plan is beyond alteration. When an act of Congress requires knowledge of a future action, it does not require knowledge in the sense of certainty as to a future act. What the statute requires is that the defendant know in the sense of being aware of an established modus operandi that will in the future cause a person to engage in prostitution.

The government's evidence showed that Todd had such awareness when he persuaded Whitney T. to work for him. He had an established practice of living off the earnings of Kelsey, doing so by rules controlling her work and payment of the proceeds to him. The jury could conclude that Todd knew he would follow the same pattern with Whitney T. and then with Whitney E. and Jemelle L. Just as a mother who has had one child in school and prepared his lunch knows that she will prepare the school lunch for her second child, just as a judge knows that his law clerks will use Westlaw, so Jerome Todd knew that he would use coercion to cause his sex workers to make money for him.

The findings of the jury. The jury was instructed:

> The defendant is charged with count 2 of the first superseding indictment with sex trafficking, in violation of Title 18, United States Code, Sections 1591(a)(1) and 1591(b)(1). In order for the defendant to be found guilty of that charge, the government must prove each of the following elements beyond a reasonable doubt:

> First, beginning in or about February 2007, and continuing through in or about July 2007, the defendant knowingly did recruit, entice, harbor, transport, provide, or obtain a person, that is, [Whitney T.];

> Second, the defendant did so knowing that force, fraud, or coercion would be used to cause [Whitney T]. to engage in a commercial sex act; and

> Third, the defendant's actions were in or affecting interstate commerce.

The jury answered these questions affirmatively as to Whitney T. and answered the same questions affirmatively as to Whitney E. and Jemelle L. The evidence of Todd's knowledge of his own modus operandi in securing an income from prostitution by a pattern of coercion was sufficient to support the jury's verdict.

The knowledge required of the defendant is such that if things go as he has planned, force, fraud or coercion will be employed to cause his victim to engage in a commercial sex transaction. That required knowledge brings the predictable use of force, fraud, or coercion into the definition of the defendant's crime.

The sentence. Section (b) is entitled "The punishment for an offense under subsection (a)". Section (b), therefore, does not create a new crime. It specifies the penalties for each of the crimes set out in (a). Two of these crimes depend on the age of the victim. The third crime is referenced summarily as an offense "effected by force, fraud or coercion." The summary reference does not enlarge the crime identified in (a). Section (b) is punishing the act identified in (a). A defendant who satisfies the elements of subsection (a) "*shall be* punished as provided in subsection (b)." 18 U.S.C. § 1591(a) (emphasis added). This reading comports with Congress's desire that the "sentencing provision of section 1591(b) . . . *correspond fully* with the language in the substantive offense provision in section 1591(a)." H.R.Rep. No. 108–264, pt. 1, at 20 (2003) (emphasis added).

The evidence was enough to support Todd's conviction on the counts of sex trafficking.

EXERCISE

Imagine that the defendant in the *Todd* case had done nothing more than convince the women victims to become prostitutes and then kept some of their earnings, without the beatings and threats that became part of those relationships. As a prosecutor, would you charge him under 18 U.S.C. § 1591? Do you have probable cause as to each element of the crime?

F. CHILD PORNOGRAPHY

With the advent of the internet, prior tactics used to address the use of children in pornography became obsolete. The internet allowed for an easy, cheap, and sometimes anonymous way to distribute material produced through the sexual exploitation of children. In part to address these changes, Congress created a new statute, 18 U.S.C. § 2252A:

(a) Any person who—

> **(1)** knowingly mails, or transports or ships using any means or facility of interstate or foreign commerce or in or affecting interstate or foreign commerce by any means, including by computer, any child pornography;

> **(2)** knowingly receives or distributes—

>> **(A)** any child pornography that has been mailed, or using any means or facility of interstate or foreign commerce shipped or transported in or affecting interstate or foreign commerce by any means, including by computer; or

(B) any material that contains child pornography that has been mailed, or using any means or facility of interstate or foreign commerce shipped or transported in or affecting interstate or foreign commerce by any means, including by computer;

(3) knowingly—

(A) reproduces any child pornography for distribution through the mails, or using any means or facility of interstate or foreign commerce or in or affecting interstate or foreign commerce by any means, including by computer; or

(B) advertises, promotes, presents, distributes, or solicits through the mails, or using any means or facility of interstate or foreign commerce or in or affecting interstate or foreign commerce by any means, including by computer, any material or purported material in a manner that reflects the belief, or that is intended to cause another to believe, that the material or purported material is, or contains—

(i) an obscene visual depiction of a minor engaging in sexually explicit conduct; or

(ii) a visual depiction of an actual minor engaging in sexually explicit conduct;

(4) either—

(A) in the special maritime and territorial jurisdiction of the United States, or on any land or building owned by, leased to, or otherwise used by or under the control of the United States Government, or in the Indian country (as defined in section 1151), knowingly sells or possesses with the intent to sell any child pornography; or

(B) knowingly sells or possesses with the intent to sell any child pornography that has been mailed, or shipped or transported using any means or facility of interstate or foreign commerce or in or affecting interstate or foreign commerce by any means, including by computer, or that was produced using materials that have been mailed, or shipped or transported in or affecting interstate or foreign commerce by any means, including by computer;

(5) either—

(A) in the special maritime and territorial jurisdiction of the United States, or on any land or building owned by, leased to, or otherwise used by or under the control of the United States Government, or in the Indian country (as defined in section 1151), knowingly possesses, or knowingly accesses with intent to view, any book, magazine, periodical, film, videotape, computer disk, or any other material that contains an image of child pornography; or

(B) knowingly possesses, or knowingly accesses with intent to view, any book, magazine, periodical, film, videotape, computer disk, or any other material that contains an image of child pornography that has been mailed, or shipped or transported using any means or facility of interstate or foreign commerce or in or affecting interstate or foreign commerce by any means, including by computer, or that was produced using materials that have been mailed, or shipped or transported in or affecting interstate or foreign commerce by any means, including by computer;

(6) knowingly distributes, offers, sends, or provides to a minor any visual depiction, including any photograph, film, video, picture, or computer generated image or picture, whether made or produced by electronic, mechanical, or other means, where such visual depiction is, or appears to be, of a minor engaging in sexually explicit conduct—

(A) that has been mailed, shipped, or transported using any means or facility of interstate or foreign commerce or in or affecting interstate or foreign commerce by any means, including by computer;

(B) that was produced using materials that have been mailed, shipped, or transported in or affecting interstate or foreign commerce by any means, including by computer; or

(C) which distribution, offer, sending, or provision is accomplished using the mails or any means or facility of interstate or foreign commerce,

for purposes of inducing or persuading a minor to participate in any activity that is illegal; or

(7) knowingly produces with intent to distribute, or distributes, by any means, including a computer, in or affecting interstate or foreign commerce, child pornography that is an adapted or modified depiction of an identifiable minor.

shall be punished as provided in subsection (b).

Subsection (b), in turn, provides for a number of strict sentences, including a five year mandatory sentence for any violation except under subsections (5) and (7) above. Note that each subsection has a distinct action element, ranging from simple possession to distribution of child pornography.

In a possession of child pornography case, the element of possession can create many of the same issues we see in other cases with that element, such as the possession of drugs or firearms. This becomes especially important where the contraband is discovered in a neutral location—such as a shared computer—rather than in someone's hand.

UNITED STATES V. SMITH

739 F. 3d 843 (5th Cir. 2014)

FORTUNATO P. BENAVIDES, CIRCUIT JUDGE:

The United States appeals a Rule 29 judgment of acquittal following James William Smith's conviction for knowing possession of child pornography, 18 U.S.C. § 2252A(a)(5)(B). We reverse.

The resolution of this appeal turns on a single question: did prosecutors present sufficient evidence that Smith was in knowing possession of the child pornography recovered from his shared computer? At trial, the prosecution produced uncontroverted evidence that someone intentionally downloaded videos of child pornography to Smith's computer during a period when Smith and two roommates, girlfriend Elizabeth Penix and long-time friend Joshua Jolly, were the regular and exclusive users of the computer. Employment records eliminated Penix as a suspect, and Jolly denied any knowledge of the files or associated software. Smith did not testify. Undisputed expert testimony indicated that the files were intact, that no special skill was required to download or access them, and that the files were so explicitly named that the individual downloading them must have known of their content. After deliberating for a few hours, the jury returned a guilty verdict.

Following the conviction, Smith filed a timely motion for new trial, FED.R.CRIM.P. 33, and separate motion for acquittal, FED.R.CRIM.P. 29. The district court rejected his arguments for a new trial, but entered judgment of acquittal, finding the evidence insufficient to sustain the verdict. *See generally United States v. Smith,* No. 1:ll-cr-114, slip op. (N.D.Miss. Nov. 26, 2012), ECF No. 85. After reviewing the record under the applicable standard, we find sufficient evidence for the jury to conclude beyond a reasonable doubt that Smith was in knowing possession of child pornography at the time the files were downloaded. . . .

Smith was convicted of knowing possession of child pornography in violation of 18 U.S.C. § 2252A(a)(5)(B). Accordingly, the evidence is sufficient to sustain his conviction if a rational juror could find beyond a reasonable doubt that Smith (1) knowingly (2) possessed (3) material containing an image of child pornography (4) that was transported in interstate or foreign commerce by any means. *See Moreland,* 665 F.3d at 149. Here, Smith argues that the evidence is insufficient to establish his possession of the files, and that, regardless, there is no evidence that he knew the files contained child pornography. The other elements are not in dispute.

In cases involving child pornography or other contraband, possession may be actual or constructive. *Moreland,* 665 F.3d at 149–150 (citing *United States v. Mergerson,* 4 F.3d 337, 348 (5th Cir.1993)). Actual possession "means the defendant knowingly has direct physical control over a thing at a given time." *United States v. Munoz,* 150 F.3d 401, 416 (5th Cir.1998). Where the contraband consists of computer files, the volitional downloading of those files entails control sufficient to establish actual possession. *United States v. Haymond,* 672 F.3d 948, 956 (10th Cir.2012). Actual possession, like constructive possession, may be proven by direct or circumstantial evidence. . . .

The prosecution's case is not complicated. It begins with the uncontroverted premises that someone used Frostwire software to seek out and download 26 videos of child pornography to Smith's computer, that there were only three possible suspects (Smith, Penix, and Jolly), and that Penix was not using the computer at the time the files were downloaded. The prosecution then introduced Jolly's testimony, in which he denied downloading the files and indicated that he did not know much about computers. Smith, meanwhile, did not testify. Taken in the light most favorable to the verdict, and even inferring nothing from Smith's decision not to testify, these facts appear to implicate Smith.

We must, however, consider countervailing evidence. Although Jolly testified that he is an auto mechanic and does not know much about computers, he conceded that he uses the internet often, and forensic analysis revealed that he had used Smith's computer regularly. Uncontroverted testimony from expert witnesses indicated that the Frostwire software is not difficult to use, requiring nothing more than entering search terms and selecting videos. This suggests that, even if Jolly does not know much about computers, he was likely still capable of using the Frostwire software to download the files. In addition, Jolly had no explanation whatsoever for where he had been on the dates in question. Smith, meanwhile, offered an alibi via the testimony of his girlfriend and his parents. These three witnesses testified that Smith had been at his parents' home on dates in question, rendering it impossible for him to have downloaded the files. They provided various documents in support of this alibi. The fact that Smith, without even testifying, offered an alibi—while Jolly, who did testify, offered none—certainly weakens the case against Smith.

Yet we must remain mindful that it is the sole province of the jury to assess the credibility of the testimony given at trial, and we must consider all evidence in the light most favorable to the guilty verdict rendered. *Sanchez,* 961 F.2d at 1173. With that in mind, it is not unreasonable for the jury to credit Jolly's testimony over the testimony of Penix and the Smiths. For example, the documentation provided in support of the alibi, while generally corroborating the broad storyline provided by the witnesses, does not actually indicate that Smith was at his parents' home when the files were downloaded. Moreover, the prosecution introduced evidence that Penix had entirely changed her account of one of the relevant dates, and that Mrs. Smith had originally made no mention of her son's visits when questioned by police. The jury may have been skeptical of the alibi in light of these discrepancies. But for whatever reason, it is clear from the verdict that the jurors in this case simply chose to believe Jolly instead of his girlfriend and his parents. It is well within their discretion to do so. *See Sanchez,* 961 F.2d at 1175 (upholding conviction for conspiracy where jury chose to believe the testimony of the undercover officer in spite of countervailing testimony and the fact that the testimony was the "sole inculpatory evidence" against defendant).

The district court, however, acquitted Smith on the basis that "it is just as likely that Joshua Jolly downloaded the child pornography onto the computer as Smith did." *Smith,* No. 1:ll-cr-114, at 11. As a purely theoretical statement, this may be true. But the question is not whether, in terms of metaphysical probability, it is "equally likely" that Jolly downloaded the files. The question is whether *this* evidence, *taken in the light most favorable to the verdict,* offers "nearly equal circumstantial support" for competing explanations. *United States v. Terrell,* 700 F.3d 755, 760 (5th Cir.2012). For the reasons already described, we believe that it does not. Moreover, it is well established that "[t]he evidence need not exclude every reasonable hypothesis of innocence," *id.,* and "the jury is free to choose among reasonable constructions of the evidence," *Bliss,* 491 Fed.Appx. at 492. The jury has done so here, and its verdict must not be disturbed. *United States v. Woerner,* 709 F.3d 527, 537 (5th Cir.2013).

Nonetheless, Smith urges this Court to find, as we did in *Moreland,* that there is no evidence to support "knowledge of" or "access to" the child pornography. Smith Br. at 12, ECF No. 32. The language Smith invokes is a component of constructive possession analysis. See *Mergerson,* 4 F.3d at 349. Constructive possession is "ownership, dominion or control over an illegal item itself[,] or dominion or control over the premises in which the item is found." *Id.* (citation omitted). When illegal files are recovered from shared computers, courts permit an inference of constructive possession where the files' nature and location are such that computer's owner must be aware of them. Such an inference, however, must be supported by evidence that "the defendant had knowledge of and access to" the files. *Moreland,* 665 F.3d at 150.

In the present case, there is no reason to require the knowledge and access necessary to support an inference of constructive possession, because the evidence is sufficient for a jury to find actual possession at the time of download. As a consequence, we need not address Smith's arguments regarding the complex nature of the Windows directory or file paths. Nor must we determine whether the evidence is sufficient to support an alternate finding of constructive possession under the assumption that Smith did not download the files. . . .

[handwritten margin note: No reason to require knowledge + access b/c the evidence is sufficient]

Before reversing the judgment of acquittal, we must also find sufficient evidence that Smith knowingly possessed the child pornography. 18 U.S.C. § 2252A(a)(5)(B). The knowledge requirement extends both to the age of the performers and to the pornographic nature of the material. *United States v. X-Citement Video, Inc.,* 513 U.S. 64, 78, 115 S.Ct. 464, 130 L.Ed.2d 372 (1994). Here, undisputed expert testimony indicates that someone searched for and selected these files for download. Each file name included an explicit description of the type of sexual act performed, in addition to the word "child," "pre-teen," or the age of the minor depicted. These file names were presented to the jury, who reasonably concluded that the person selecting and downloading these files must have understood the illegal nature of the content. *See Woerner,* 709 F.3d at 537 ("[T]heir content was evident from their file names, undercutting any potential argument that they were downloaded by mistake."). More significantly, 19 of the 26 files were previewed at the time of download. So it seems clear that the person downloading the files knew both the age of the performers and the sexually explicit nature of the material.

We conclude, therefore, that the prosecution presented sufficient evidence such that the jury could find, beyond a reasonable doubt, that Smith downloaded the files and knew what he was downloading. Given that the nature of the files and the interstate transport are not in dispute, the evidence is thus sufficient to sustain a conviction of knowing possession of child pornography under 18 U.S.C. § 2252A(a)(5)(B).

Smith asks that we instruct the district court to consider whether a new trial is warranted on grounds not previously raised. Smith, however, has shown no error or abuse of discretion in the district court's adjudication of his motion for a new trial, and we find none in the record. Accordingly, we deny that request. Consequently, and for the reasons stated herein, we REVERSE the judgment of acquittal and remand for sentencing.

[handwritten margin note: Reverse judgement of acquittal]

———————

EXERCISE

One role of the prosecutor is to direct the investigation. Many—perhaps even most—trials lost by the government actually fail at the investigative stage, particularly when not enough work is done to prove up key elements or properly establish the weakness in a case. If you were the prosecutor in the *Smith* case, what additional work might you have asked the investigating agents to do before charging the case?

Under 18 U.S.C. § 2252(a)(2), it is illegal to "distribute" child pornography. In the modern era of technology, though, it is sometimes challenging to define what counts as "distribution."

UNITED STATES V. GRZYBOWICZ
747 F. 3d 1296 (11th Cir. 2014)

CARNES, CHIEF JUDGE:

The facts that gave rise to this case could make any parent reluctant to let a friend look after her child, even for as little as five or ten minutes, and even in a public place.

I.

Michael Grzybowicz and Patricia Cochrum worked at the same restaurant. As friends, they planned a joint trip to an amusement park with their families to celebrate her birthday. The plan was that she would bring her boyfriend and two kids, while Grzybowicz would bring his wife and son. Grzybowicz may have known all along that his wife would not be coming because she did not like Cochrum, whom she suspected—without any basis so far as the record shows—of having an affair with her husband. In any event, after leading Cochrum to believe that his family would be with him, Grzybowicz showed up at the park by himself on February 17, 2011, claiming that his wife and son were both sick. Cochrum was there with her boyfriend and her two children, a five-year-old son and a two-year-old daughter. They entered the amusement park at 10:07 a.m.

After the group had been enjoying the amusements at the park for about four hours, Grzybowicz insisted that Cochrum ride a roller coaster with her boyfriend while he looked after her two children. She accepted what appeared to be a kind offer from her coworker and friend, entrusting her children to him in that public place for a total of five to ten minutes. At the beginning of the roller coaster ride Cochrum could see Grzybowicz and her children, but she soon lost sight of them. From the evidence at trial, the best estimate is that Cochrum and her boyfriend got on the ride a short time before 2:08 p.m., and security camera recordings show that they got off of it at 2:14 p.m. They then rejoined Grzybowicz and the two children.

The group left the park at 2:38 p.m., which was four-and-a-half hours after they had entered it.

On the car ride home from the amusement park, Cochrum's daughter complained that her genital area was hurting. Cochrum was not too alarmed because she assumed that the complaint was about a rash that the little girl had had for awhile. When they got home, Cochrum changed her daughter's diaper and noticed that its adhesive straps were not placed the same way that she had placed them earlier that day, which she would later realize was "a red flag." At the time, however, Cochrum dismissed it because her daughter occasionally played with her diaper straps. What had happened to the two-year old girl might have gone undetected but for events at the Grzybowicz house.

Two days after the trip to the amusement park, on the morning of February 19, 2011, Grzybowicz's wife, Bette Schuster, examined his cellphone. She noticed that he had received a text message from a sender she did not know. Schuster regularly checked her husband's cellphone because, as we mentioned before, she suspected him of having an affair with Cochrum. Her suspicion was ironic because Schuster herself was having an affair with a police officer named Richard Bartholomay, who had slept at the Grzybowicz home the night before.

In any event, when she checked the outbox of Grzybowicz's phone that morning, Schuster saw four photographs that had been sent from his phone to an email address she did not recognize. The photographs depicted: (1) a man's hand opening the vagina of a small child wearing a yellow dress; (2) the man's finger inserted into the child's vagina; (3) the man's hand pulling back a diaper to reveal the child's vagina; and (4) the child's diaper and exposed vagina. Schuster immediately showed the photographs on the phone to Bartholomay and then called the police department.

When Officer Frank Gay arrived at the residence in response to the call, Schuster handed him her husband's cellphone and showed him the photographs. Officer Gay then awoke Grzybowicz, who was asleep in one of the bedrooms, and asked him to go to the police station and talk to an investigator. He agreed to do so. He also consented to a search of his home, his cellphone, and his laptop computer.

Grzybowicz's computer and cellphone, both of which were manufactured outside of the United States, were sent for forensic analysis by Agent Daniel Ogden. The examination showed that the computer contained two user profiles. One of them, which was labeled "New," was password protected and had been created on February 11, 2011, less than a week before the trip to the amusement park. (Although Schuster shared the laptop with her husband, she did not know the password for his protected profile or even how a person could create a user profile.)

Agent Ogden gained access to Grzybowicz's password-protected user profile and used it to find 79 images of child pornography on the computer, including two of the four photographs of the little girl being exposed and molested that were also on Grzybowicz's cellphone. Some of those 79 child pornography images on the user profile had been deleted, some were stored in temporary internet files, and some were saved in a file folder labeled "Pictures." The images stored in that folder included depictions of infants and young girls with their vaginas exposed.

The "New" user profile's internet history also contained links to Grzybowicz's Yahoo account, which is the email address to which the four graphic photographs of the little girl's vagina that were found on Grzybowicz's cellphone had been sent. That was the same email address his wife had seen but not recognized when she inspected the cell phone the morning of February 19, 2011. In addition, the "New" user profile also contained download information, including the file name, for at least one of the images sent from his cellphone to that email address. And it had several links to a file-sharing website for child pornography.

Analysis of Grzybowicz's cellphone revealed that the four photographs of a little girl's vagina that his wife had discovered on his cell phone were created between 2:08 and 2:12 p.m. on February 17, 2011, which was during the five to ten minutes that he had been alone with Cochrum's two-year-old daughter and five-year-old son. Those four digital images had been sent from Grzybowicz's cell phone to his Yahoo account, links to which had been found in the user profile that he kept password-protected and hidden from his wife. They were sent from his cellphone to his Yahoo account that same day, around 2:45 p.m., which was seven minutes after he left the amusement park.

Cochrum later identified the dress visible in the four photographs on Grzybowicz's cell phone as the yellow and white-striped dress that her daughter was wearing when she had entrusted the little girl to Grzybowicz's care. She gave the dress to the police.

Grzybowicz was indicted on charges of sexual exploitation of a minor to produce child pornography, in violation of 18 U.S.C. § 2251(a) (Count 1); distribution of child pornography, in violation of 18 U.S.C. § 2252A(a)(2) (Count 2); and possession of child pornography, in violation of 18 U.S.C. § 2252A(a)(5)(B) (Count 3). During the four-day trial, the government called six witnesses, including Agent Ogden, Cochrum, and Grzybowicz's wife; it introduced into evidence the four photographs that Grzybowicz's wife had found on his cell phone, several of the other pornographic images that had been found on his computer, and the yellow dress worn by Cochrum's daughter during the visit to the amusement park. Based on that dress, Cochrum identified her daughter as the small child depicted in the explicit photographs that were on Grzybowicz's cellphone, two of which had been downloaded onto his computer. . . .

In its final charge, the district court instructed the jury on the essential elements of each of the charged counts, including the required nexus between the child pornography and interstate commerce and the definition of child pornography. The court told the jury that child pornography is the visual depiction of an actual minor engaged in "sexually explicit conduct," which includes "lascivious exhibition of the genitals or pubic area." The court defined "lascivious exhibition" as the "indecent exposure of the genitals or pubic area, usually to incite lust," and it instructed the jury on a number of factors that it could consider in making that determination. Specifically referring to Count 2 of the indictment, the court instructed the jury that to "distribute" child pornography "means to deliver or transfer possession of it to someone else, with or without any money involved in the transaction." Neither side objected to the court's instructions.

[handwritten margin note: court's jury instruction on child pornography]

The jury found Grzybowicz guilty on all three counts. He filed a motion for a new trial under Federal Rule of Criminal Procedure 33(a), claiming. . . that the government had failed to present any evidence that he distributed child pornography to another person or that the child pornography had been transported in interstate or foreign commerce, as required to sustain his conviction on Count 2. . . .

His conviction under Count 2 for distributing child pornography, in violation of 18 U.S.C. § 2252A(a)(2), is another matter. The difference between this count and the other two is that distribution is an element of the § 2252A(a)(2) crime, and there is no evidence that Grzybowicz sent the images of child pornography to anyone other than himself. As Grzybowicz argues, the government offered no proof that he transferred the images to, or even made them available to, another person. Although links to a child pornography file-sharing website were found on his computer, there is no evidence that the child pornography images on his computer were stored in a shared folder accessible to others or were ever uploaded to any publicly accessible website.

We have not yet defined the term "distribute" for purposes of § 2252A(a)(2), and neither has Congress. We start here with its plain and ordinary meaning. *See Smith v. United States,* 508 U.S. 223, 228, 113 S.Ct. 2050, 2054, 124 L.Ed.2d 138 (1993) ("When a word is not defined by statute, we normally construe it in accord with its ordinary or natural meaning."); *United States v. Silvestri,* 409 F.3d 1311, 1333 (11th Cir.2005) (explaining that when terms are not defined by statute, "[c]ourts must assume that Congress intended the ordinary meaning of the words it used") (quotation marks omitted). The word "distribute" ordinarily means to deliver, give out, dispense, or disperse to others. *See United States v. Probel,* 214 F.3d 1285, 1288 (11th Cir.2000) (explaining, in the context of a guidelines enhancement for distributing child pornography, that "the term 'distribution' should be given its ordinary meaning of 'to dispense' or 'to give out or deliver'"); *see also Black's Law Dictionary* 508 (8th ed.2004) (defining "distribute" as to "apportion," "deliver," or "disperse"); *Random House Webster's Unabridged Dictionary* 572 (2d ed.2001) (defining "distribute" as to "deal out," "disperse," or "pass out or deliver . . . to intended recipients"); *Webster's Third New International Dictionary* 660 (1986) (defining "distribute" as to "divide among several or many," "dispense," or "apportion esp[ecially] to members of a group"). Implicit in the cited definitions is the notion that the item being distributed is delivered to someone other than the person who does the delivering. We do not commonly speak of delivering to ourselves things that we already have. Our pattern jury instructions make the point that: "To 'distribute' something means to deliver or transfer possession of it to *someone else. . . .*" 11th Cir. Pattern Jury Instr. (Crim.) 83.4A (emphasis added). That part of the pattern instructions was given to the jury in this case, without objection from either side. . . .

The evidence presented at trial showed that Grzybowicz sent four images of child pornography from his cellphone to his personal email account and then downloaded at least two of those images onto his computer. The evidence also showed that, counting those two images, he had a total of 79 images of child pornography on his computer, which were either deleted, stored in temporary internet files, or saved in a pictures folder, and that his internet history contained links to a child pornography file-sharing website. But there is no evidence at all that Grzybowicz shared with others any of the illicit images found on his cellphone or computer or put them where they could be shared without any further action on his part. There is no evidence that he uploaded images to the file-sharing website found in his internet history, or to any website for that matter, nor is there any evidence that the images stored on his computer were accessible to other users of the file-sharing website. Speculation and conjecture is not enough. *See United States v. Mendez,* 528 F.3d 811, 814 (11th Cir.2008) ("When the government relies on circumstantial evidence, reasonable inferences, not mere speculation, must support the conviction."); *Shaffer,* 472 F.3d at 1224 (suggesting that the distribution element of § 2252A(a)(2)(B) would not be met where a defendant "save[d] the illicit images and videos in a computer folder not susceptible to file sharing"). For all that we can tell from the record, the file-sharing website that Grzybowicz frequented may not even have been linked to a peer-to-peer network, which would allow other users to directly access files saved in a shared folder on his computer. *See Kernel Records Oy v. Mosley,* 694 F.3d 1294, 1305 (11th Cir.2012) (noting that peer-to-peer networks, unlike other methods of distributing files over the internet, allow users to directly access files stored on remote computers through the use of specialized software). And there is no evidence that any of the child pornography images were saved in a shared folder.

It is not enough that Grzybowicz sent the four pictures he took with his cell phone to his own email address. By doing that, he may have taken a step in the direction of distributing those images to others but the statute does not criminalize taking steps toward distribution or getting ready to distribute, it criminalizes distribution. *See* 18 U.S.C. § 2252A(a)(2) ("Any person who . . . knowingly . . . distributes. . . .").

Because it did not present any evidence that Grzybowicz transferred child pornography to others or "freely allowed them access to his computerized stash of images," *see Shaffer,* 472 F.3d at 1223, the government failed to establish "distribution" within the meaning of § 2252A(a)(2). For that reason, we vacate his conviction on Count 2.

government failed to establish "distribution"

EXERCISE

In the case above, the defendant's transfer of the images from his phone to his email account could have helped him preserve the images or hide them from others. As the sentencing judge, would you take that action into account and give the defendant a higher sentence?

CHAPTER FIVE

PROPERTY CRIMES

■ ■ ■

Like murder, theft and its variations are part of all modern criminal codes. And just as nearly all of the variations on murder share the element of actual death, the variations on theft almost always have as an element the wrongful taking of another person's property.

In this chapter, we will discuss four crimes that are commonly charged where property has been taken in the absence of violence: Larceny, burglary, embezzlement, and fraud. We will also consider two important but less prominent property crimes: extortion and money laundering.

Larceny is the simplest. Usually it encompasses what we think of as theft: taking someone else's property without their consent. Historically, that taking needed to be intended to deprive the owner of the item permanently, but modern statutes sometimes blur or dispose of that element. The distinctive aspect of larceny is taking someone's property without permission.

Burglary is usually, but not always, a crime involving property. It typically requires proof that the defendant illegally entered a building with the intent to commit a crime. In some places, the intent can be formed after the illegal entry, however.[1] Importantly, burglary can be fulfilled by crimes other than theft, though usually it is rooted in a theft. For example, if a defendant illegally entered a building with the intent to commit a sexual assault, that will usually constitute a burglary. The distinctive element of burglary is illegal entry into a building.

Embezzlement is a special variation on theft, and normally requires that the defendant converted to his or her own use property that was entrusted to them. For example, if a bank teller steals the money from a till, it will often be considered an embezzlement since the teller was entrusted with the handling of that cash. The distinctive element of embezzlement is that the offender was trusted with the property.

Fraud involves taking someone's property through false pretenses. In a fraud, unlike a straight larceny, it is common for the victim to consent to the taking of property; the key is that they granted this consent because of misrepresentations by the defendant. The distinctive element of fraud is deception.

---

[1]   E.g., Arizona Revised Statute § 13–1506(A)(1).

The definitions of property crime have had to adjust as property has changed. In the contemporary world, things like access to computers and information have value that earlier generations could not imagine. Even our identity is a form of property subject to theft, a crime that has been made easier with the expansion of information technology. As we deal with property crime, this broader idea of what has value will inform our analysis.

A. LARCENY

Larceny is a simple theft. Generally, it will require that the following elements be proven:

1. Identification of the offender

2. The taking of a thing of value

3. Without the consent of the owner

4. With the intent to deprive the owner of the value of that thing.

Sometimes, though, criminal codes will omit the last element above in certain situations. For example, under some criminal laws it may be larceny to go joyriding in a car, even if it is the joyrider's intent to return the car to the owner in fine shape.[2]

The overwhelming majority of property crimes, especially simple larceny, end up in state court. However, some larcenies that involve the taking of money or physical property have a federal nexus, such as theft from a post office or a federally insured bank. In addition, newer federal statutes criminalize the theft of computer data and even a person's identity. All of these will be addressed.

1. THEFT OF PHYSICAL PROPERTY

Like other crimes that can be accomplished by one or two people outside the presence of others, the element of identification is often at issue in larceny cases involving the theft of property.

UNITED STATES V. LEKE
237 Fed. Appx. 54 (6th Cir. 2007)

McKINLEY, DISTRICT JUDGE.

In the early morning of December 2, 2006, nearly $40,000.00 was stolen from an ATM located at a branch of Regions Bank in Trenton, Tennessee. Five individuals worked at this branch-Defendant Adam Leke, Shawn Howard, Patsy Hickerson, Louise Prince, and Sheila Lewis. Once the bank became aware of the theft, it sent two security officers-Scott Coggins and

---

[2] E.g. Minnesota Statutes Annotated § 609.52(Subd. 2)(17)

Ronnie Gross-to investigate. Shawn Howard, Patsy Hickerson, Scott Coggins, and Ronnie Gross were the key Government witnesses at Leke's trial.

Shawn Howard testified that he and Defendant Leke worked as tellers at the branch of Regions Bank from which the money had been stolen. He stated that on December 1, 2005, he and Leke began their work duties as usual. Between 10:00 and 11:30 a.m., they went to the ATM, where they serviced the machine and replenished it by placing about $40,000.00 into the machine. Howard testified that he and Leke usually performed these duties together, but that if one was absent, the other did them alone. After they serviced the machine, Howard left for lunch. He testified that when he returned, he learned that the Defendant had been out to the ATM alone to fix a deposit printer error. The day then continued as usual. Howard testified that he left work between 3:00 and 4:00 p.m., went to his night classes around 6:00 p.m., and then returned to his home for the night around 9:00 p.m. His wife and his mother-in-law spent the night there as well. He went to work as usual the next morning. When he went out to balance the ATM, however, both doors swung open, and the cassettes containing the money in the machine were missing. When bank officials arrived to investigate, Howard told them that he believed it had to be an inside-job because "there were no marks in the outside of the ATM and the locks weren't damaged." Howard told the bank officials that he suspected the Defendant.

Howard further testified that accessing the ATM at the bank required both a key and a combination and that it only took between thirty and forty-five seconds to unlock the safe by turning the key and performing the combination. Of the five employees, only he, Sheila Lewis, and the Defendant knew the combination to the ATM, but he believed that it was written down somewhere at the bank. The key was kept in an unlocked drawer in the bank. To Howard's knowledge, the combination had never been changed since he had begun working at the bank in September 2004. Howard also testified that if the ATM's door was ever left unlocked, a keypad inside the bank would so indicate.

Finally, Howard testified that the Defendant told his coworkers at the bank that he planned to quit his job in January and return to Phoenix, where he had once lived, and that the Defendant sometimes discussed his financial problems.

At trial, Shawn Howard's wife testified that on December 1, 2005, Howard left work to go to school and then returned to their home between 8 p.m. and 9 p.m. and did not leave again until he went to work the next morning.

Patsy Hickerson, the supervisory teller at the bank, also testified at trial. She told the jury that on December 1, 2006, she was at work with Shawn Howard, Louise Prince, and the Defendant. Sheila Lewis was out that day having a tooth pulled. Hickerson testified that she filled the cassettes up with money for Howard and the Defendant to put in the ATM. She noted that she never took the money to the ATM herself because she was too short to service the machine. She then told the jury that when Howard was at lunch that day, the Defendant went out to the ATM alone to replace a printer ribbon. Hickerson then testified that the next morning, someone at the ATM security office called to alert them that something was wrong with the ATM. Shawn Howard went to see what was wrong and when he returned he said that the four cassettes containing all the money in the ATM were missing.

The next witness at trial was Scott Coggins, a security officer for Regions Bank. Coggins conducted the internal investigation for Regions Bank concerning the burglary of the ATM machine. He testified that he learned of the burglary when Shawn Howard called him and told him that customers were denied transactions because the ATM was empty and that when he checked the machine, the money cassettes were missing. When he arrived at the bank to inspect the ATM, he observed that there were "no tool marks, no pry marks, no cut marks . . . . no damage to the machine whatsoever" and concluded that it was an inside job. He then testified that he learned that only three individuals had access to the ATM combination-Patsy Hickerson, Shawn Howard, and the Defendant.

Coggins first interviewed Shawn Howard whom he concluded was honest, forthright, and "gave no appearance of deception." He then interviewed Patsy Hickerson who told him that she never performed maintenance on the ATM because she was too short. He then interviewed the Defendant and knew "within five minutes . . . there was no doubt in [his] mind that he was involved" because his statements were not "jibing" and "his mannerisms showed deception." Coggins and his partner notified law enforcement and relayed to them the results of their investigation. Based on that information, the officers detained the Defendant as a suspect in the case.

Coggins also testified that their computers revealed that the ATM was broken into at 1:43 a.m. on December 2nd. The Defendant told Coggins that he was at Andrew Ward's house from 10 p.m. that evening until 7 a.m. the next morning.

Scott Coggins' partner, Ronnie Gross, also testified at trial. Gross was also a security officer with Regions Bank and conducted the initial internal investigation into the ATM incident with Scott Coggins. Like Coggins, he testified that his investigation revealed that 1) the ATM had not been physically broken into; and 2) only three people-Shawn Howard, Patsy Hickerson, and the Defendant-knew the combination to the ATM safe. He also testified that the ATM's security alarm went off at about 1:30 a.m. on the morning of December 2nd; that a security camera had been turned so that it would be out of focus; and that the security camera showed that the money was taken from the ATM in fifty-one seconds.

During the interview of the Defendant, the Defendant gave Gross the names of two individuals he believed could have committed the theft. The Defendant told Gross the individuals probably split the money. When Gross asked the Defendant what these individuals may have done with the cassettes the money was in, he responded that most criminals discard things in "the bottoms." The Defendant then agreed to take the investigators to "the bottoms" so they could look for the cassettes. The Defendant told them there were three locations the cassettes could be. The Defendant took them to the first location-a creek-where they looked for 15 or 20 minutes. He then took them to a second location, where the investigators found three of the cassettes. They were between eight and ten miles from the bank branch where the ATM was located.

Soon after this, the investigators allowed the Defendant to speak briefly with his girlfriend. When she left, the Defendant told the investigators, "I think I've hurt myself." The Defendant then said he was finished talking with the investigators.

The Government's final witness was Andrew Ward, Leke's co-conspirator who pled guilty. At the outset, Ward admitted that he had a prior record for theft of property and burglary. He also testified that he had entered a guilty plea in this case for conspiracy and that he had an agreement with the Government in which he would get less time for his crime if he told the truth.

Ward testified that he and the Defendant were good friends and that they had grown up together. He said the Defendant came up with the plan and told him that he had left the doors unlocked on the ATM machine. He said the Defendant explained to him how to open the machine to get the money and how to avoid the security cameras. He testified that he had never worked at a bank and did not know anything about how ATM machines worked. He testified that after he removed the money from the ATM, he and the Defendant drove to "the bottoms" to dispose of the cassettes. Soon thereafter, Ward bought a new Ford Explorer for his girlfriend. He paid the $2,000.00 down payment in twenty dollar bills. When he learned from the Defendant that the police had found the cassettes, he went on a "shopping spree." By the time the FBI interviewed him, he only had $8500.00 left, which he gave to them.

From the record, it appears that the only defense witness at trial was the Defendant's former girlfriend, now wife, Tamaba Leke. She testified that she and the Defendant had a number of twenty dollar bills because they had each taken out $300.00 loans from Cash Express on December 15th. The receipts from Cash Express were entered into evidence.

At the conclusion of the trial, the jury found the Defendant guilty of conspiracy, embezzlement, and bank larceny. . . .

For bank larceny, under 18 U.S.C. § 2113(b), the two key elements which the Government must prove beyond a reasonable doubt are:

1)   the carrying away of bank property or money exceeding $1,000; and

2)   the specific intent to steal.

United States v. Marshall, 248 F.3d 525, 536 (6th Cir.2001).

The Defendant-Appellant argues that there was insufficient evidence presented at trial to support a conviction of bank larceny. Specifically, the Defendant-Appellant argues that this case is unlike *United States v. Marshall,* where the Sixth Circuit held that a conviction of bank larceny was supported by evidence that 1) the defendant had been experiencing financial difficulties; 2) had access to the money and the opportunity to steal; and 3) his wealth suddenly increased immediately after the larceny. 248 F.3d 525, 535 (6th Cir.2001). The Defendant-Appellant argues that in his case there is no physical evidence which connects him to the crime and no evidence that he experienced sudden, unexplained wealth.

However, the circumstantial evidence in this case was substantial. Testimony revealed that there were no signs of a forced entry into the ATM, suggesting an inside job; the ATM had just been filled with $40,000.00; the Defendant-Appellant told investigators he was with co-conspirator Andrew Ward on the morning of the crime; Ward had unexplained wealth after the crime; and the Defendant took investigators to the discarded ATM money cassettes. Further, the *Marshall* court specifically recognized that "circumstantial evidence alone is sufficient to sustain a conviction and such evidence need not remove every reasonable hypothesis except that of guilt." 248 F.3d 525, 536 (quoting *United States v. Vannerson,* 786 F.2d 221, 225 (6th Cir.1986)).

Accordingly, we hold there was sufficient evidence upon which a reasonable jury could have found the Defendant guilty of bank larceny.

EXERCISE

In the *Leke* case, the prosecution brought in evidence that the defendant "planned to quit his job in January and return to Phoenix, where he had once lived, and that the Defendant sometimes discussed his financial problems." What element does this evidence go towards proving? If you were the defense attorney, would you object to the introduction of that evidence as being substantially more prejudicial than probative to an element (under Federal Rule of Evidence 403)?

Also, note that the defendant in *Leke* was an employee of the victim bank. If you were the prosecutor, would you consider charging him under an embezzlement statute that covered "larceny by employees of a bank of money entrusted to them?"

---

18 U.S.C. § 1708 bars the simple theft of mail along with other offenses:

> Whoever steals, takes, or abstracts, or by fraud or deception obtains, or attempts so to obtain, from or out of any mail, post office, or station thereof, letter box, mail receptacle, or any mail route or other authorized depository for mail matter, or from a letter or mail carrier, any letter, postal card, package, bag, or mail, or abstracts or removes from any such letter, package, bag, or mail, any article or thing contained therein, or secretes, embezzles, or destroys any such letter, postal card, package, bag, or mail, or any article or thing contained therein; or

> Whoever steals, takes, or abstracts, or by fraud or deception obtains any letter, postal card, package, bag, or mail, or any article or thing contained therein which has been left for collection upon or adjacent to a collection box or other authorized depository of mail matter; or

> Whoever buys, receives, or conceals, or unlawfully has in his possession, any letter, postal card, package, bag, or mail, or any article or thing contained therein, which has been so stolen, taken, embezzled, or abstracted, as herein described, knowing the same to have been stolen, taken, embezzled, or abstracted—

> Shall be fined under this title or imprisoned not more than five years, or both.

Even though this statute does not state an intent requirement, the standard jury instructions used in the Ninth Circuit read one into that law:

8.138 MAIL THEFT

(18 U.S.C. § 1708)

The defendant is charged in [Count_____ of] the indictment with mail theft in violation of Section 1708 of Title 18 of the United States Code. In order for the defendant to be found guilty of that charge, the government must prove each of the following elements beyond a reasonable doubt:

First, there was [[a letter] [a postal card] [a package] [a bag] [mail]] [[in the mail] [in a private mail box] [at a post office] [in a letterbox] [in a mail receptacle] [in a mail route] [in an authorized depository for mail matter] [in possession of a letter or mail carrier]];

Second, the defendant stole the [letter] [postal card] [package] [bag] [mail] from the [mail] [post office] [letter box][a private mail box][mail receptacle] [mail route] [authorized depository for mail matter] [mail carrier]; and

Third, at the time the defendant stole the [letter] [postal card] [package] [bag] [mail], the defendant intended to deprive the owner, temporarily or permanently, of its use and benefit.

Comment

A jury may infer that the defendant stole an item of mail if a properly addressed and recently mailed item was never received by the addressee and was found in the defendant's possession. See United States v. Ellison, 469 F.2d 413, 415 (9th Cir.1972).

Pattern jury instructions do not have the power of precedent, even when they are authorized by the Circuit Court itself. Only a prior published opinion of that court or the Supreme Court can have that effect.

UNITED STATES V. WILLIAM

491 Fed. Appx. 821 (9th Cir. 2012)

Daniel William appeals his conviction after a jury trial for mail theft and possession of stolen mail under 18 U.S.C. § 1708, for which he was sentenced to five years of probation and three months of imprisonment. We have jurisdiction pursuant to 28 U.S.C. § 1291, and we reverse.

1.   The district court improperly instructed the jury in a manner that permitted the inference that an element of the crime, which the government was required to prove beyond a reasonable doubt, had been fulfilled. "When, as here, a defendant objects to an instruction at trial, we review the district court's formulation of the instructions for an abuse of discretion." *United States v. Warren,* 25 F.3d 890, 898 (9th Cir.1994).

The jury was instructed that to establish mail theft under 18 U.S.C. § 1708, the government was required to prove beyond a reasonable doubt that it was William's intent to "deprive the owner temporarily or permanently of [the letter's] use and benefit." The district court's instruction that the jury may infer that William "stole" the letter if it was "properly addressed and recently mailed," "never received by the addressee," and "found in [his] possession," could have been understood by the jury as relieving the government of its burden to prove that William intended to deprive the recipients, temporarily or permanently of the letter. Yet, although William "possessed" the letters, they could not have been received by the addressees—regardless of whether William had stolen them—as they had been placed in the mailbox so recently that delivery could not have occurred if Williams had not taken the mail from the mailbox. William's testimony was that he intended to return the letters to the postal box for delivery.

Thus, by permitting the jury to rely on the fact of possession while disregarding the timing of the possession, the instruction could have been understood as relieving the government of its burden to prove intent. "[W]here intent is a necessary element of the crime, it is error for the court to instruct the jury that it may, but is not required to, infer the requisite intent from an isolated fact. There can be no presumption as to intention which would permit the jury to make an assumption which all the evidence considered together does not logically establish." *United States v. Rubio-Villareal,* 967 F.2d 294, 298–99 (9th Cir.1992) (en banc) (quoting *Baker v. United States,* 310 F.2d 924, 930–31 (9th Cir.1962), cert. denied, 372 U.S. 954, 83 S.Ct. 952, 9 L.Ed.2d 978 (1963)).

The government maintains that the presumption that the defendant "stole" the mail goes only to the identity of the person who took the mail and not to the intent to deprive. But in common parlance (and in the dictionary, in which a "thief" is "one who steals," 17 Oxford English Dictionary 934 (2d ed.1989)), "stole" connotes more than just taking something (as confirmed by the statutory language, which is "steals, takes, or abstracts"). Moreover, William admitted that he had taken the mail, so the jury would have thought there was no point instructing it regarding a presumption on that question. As a result, the jury most likely understood the presumption as going both to the taking and the state of mind that accompanied the taking.

"A jury instruction need not be unconstitutional for us to find it defective." *Warren,* 25 F.3d at 898 (citations omitted). The jury instruction at issue in this appeal was "misleading," "inadequately guided the jury's deliberation," and "improperly intruded on the fact finding process." *Id.* Because the jury instruction undermined the basis for William's defense, we find that there was a reasonable probability that it affected the verdict. *Rubio-Villareal,* 967 F.2d at 296 n. 3. We thus reverse William's conviction.

EXERCISE

Intriguingly, in the *William* case, the Ninth Circuit reversed the conviction even though the District Court had precisely followed the language of the comment to the Ninth Circuit's own pattern instructions. There is yet another twist here, as revealed in a later footnote to the opinion:

> The government also submits that there is no mens rea requirement in the statute, but recognizes that it has waived this argument by requesting the model instruction. We therefore do not address this question. Nor, for the same reason, do we address the government's argument that under the statute, "taking" is sufficient, and "stealing" need not be proven.

> The statute itself allows prosecution either if the item is "taken" (which does not require intent to retain it, by the government's argument) or "stolen"

(which does require intent). If the government had made this claim—that the statute has no mens rea requirement—in the trial court, should it have prevailed? Do you think the statute should be read as having an intent requirement, even though it does not contain one on its face?

Larceny is distinct from robbery in that it does not require violence or the threat of violence. The distinction, however, goes beyond that one element. This difference becomes important when a defense attorney tries to argue that larceny is a "lesser included offense" of robbery, giving a jury an option that allows conviction with less serious sentencing consequences.

CARTER V. UNITED STATES
530 U.S. 255 (2000)

JUSTICE THOMAS delivered the opinion of the Court.

In *Schmuck v. United States,* 489 U.S. 705, 109 S.Ct. 1443, 103 L.Ed.2d 734 (1989), we held that a defendant who requests a jury instruction on a lesser offense under Rule 31(c) of the Federal Rules of Criminal Procedure must demonstrate that "the elements of the lesser offense are a subset of the elements of the charged offense." *Id.,* at 716, 109 S.Ct. 1443. This case requires us to apply this elements test to the offenses described by 18 U.S.C. §§ 2113(a) and (b) 1994 ed. and Supp. IV). The former punishes "[w]hoever, by force and violence, or by intimidation, takes . . . from the person or presence of another . . . any . . . thing of value belonging to, or in the . . . possession of, any bank. . . ." The latter, which entails less severe penalties, punishes, *inter alia,* "[w]hoever takes and carries away, with intent to steal or purloin, any . . . thing of value exceeding $1,000 belonging to, or in the . . . possession of, any bank. . . ." We hold that § 2113(b) requires an element not required by § 2113(a)—three in fact—and therefore is not a lesser included offense of § 2113(a). Petitioner is accordingly prohibited as a matter of law from obtaining a lesser included offense instruction on the offense described by § 2113(b).

I

On September 9, 1997, petitioner Floyd J. Carter donned a ski mask and entered the Collective Federal Savings Bank in Hamilton Township, New Jersey. Carter confronted a customer who was exiting the bank and pushed her back inside. She screamed, startling others in the bank. Undeterred, Carter ran into the bank and leaped over the customer service counter and through one of the teller windows. One of the tellers rushed into the manager's office. Meanwhile, Carter opened several teller drawers and emptied the money into a bag. After having removed almost $16,000 in currency, Carter jumped back over the counter and fled from the scene. Later that day, the police apprehended him.

A grand jury indicted Carter, charging him with violating § 2113(a). While not contesting the basic facts of the episode, Carter pleaded not guilty on the theory that he had not taken the bank's money "by force and violence, or by intimidation," as § 2113(a) requires. Before trial, Carter moved that the court instruct the jury on the offense described by § 2113(b) as a lesser included offense of the offense described by § 2113(a). The District Court, relying on *United States v. Mosley,* 126 F.3d 200 (C.A.3 1997), denied the motion in a preliminary ruling. At the close of the Government's case, the District Court denied Carter's motion for a judgment of acquittal and indicated that the preliminary ruling denying the lesser included offense instruction would stand. The jury, instructed on § 2113(a) alone, returned a guilty verdict, and the District Court entered judgment pursuant to that verdict.

The Court of Appeals for the Third Circuit affirmed in an unpublished opinion, relying on its earlier decision in *Mosley.* Judgment order reported at 185 F.3d 863 (1999). While the Ninth Circuit agrees with the Third that a lesser offense instruction is precluded in this context, see *United States v. Gregory,* 891 F.2d 732, 734 (C.A.9 1989), other Circuits have held to the contrary, see *United States v. Walker,* 75 F.3d 178, 180 (C.A.4 1996); *United States v. Brittain,* 41 F.3d 1409, 1410 (C.A.10 1994). We granted certiorari to resolve the conflict, 528 U.S. 1060, 120 S.Ct. 613, 145 L.Ed.2d 508 (1999), and now affirm. . . .

Turning to the instant case, the Government contends that three elements required by § 2113(b)'s first paragraph are *not* required by § 2113(a): (1) specific intent to steal; (2) asportation; and (3) valuation exceeding $1,000. The statute provides:

"§ 2113. Bank robbery and incidental crimes

"(a) Whoever, by force and violence, or by intimidation, takes, or attempts to take, from the person or presence of another, or obtains or attempts to obtain by extortion any property or money or any other thing of value belonging to, or in the care, custody, control, management, or possession of, any bank, credit union, or any savings and loan association. . .

. . .

"Shall be fined under this title or imprisoned not more than twenty years, or both.

"(b) Whoever takes and carries away, with intent to steal or purloin, any property or money or any other thing of value exceeding $1,000 belonging to, or in the care, custody, control, management, or possession of any bank, credit union, or any savings and loan association, shall be fined under this title or imprisoned not more than ten years, or both; or

"Whoever takes and carries away, with intent to steal or purloin, any property or money or any other thing of value not exceeding $1,000 belonging to, or in the care, custody, control, management, or possession of any bank, credit union, or any savings and loan association, shall be fined not more than $1,000 or imprisoned not more than one year, or both."

A "textual comparison" of the elements of these offenses suggests that the Government is correct. First, whereas subsection (b) requires that the defendant act "with intent to steal or purloin," subsection (a) contains no similar requirement. Second, whereas subsection (b) requires that the defendant "tak[e] and carr[y] away" the property, subsection (a) only requires that the defendant "tak[e]" the property. Third, whereas the first paragraph of subsection (b) requires that the property have a "value exceeding $1,000," subsection (a) contains no valuation requirement. These extra clauses in subsection (b) "cannot be regarded as mere surplusage; [they] mea[n] something." *Potter v. United States,* 155 U.S. 438, 446, 15 S.Ct. 144, 39 L.Ed. 214 (1894). . . .

We turn now to Carter's more specific arguments concerning the "extra" elements of § 2113(b). While conceding the absence of three of § 2113(b)'s requirements from the text of § 2113(a)—(1) "intent to steal or purloin"; (2) "takes *and carries away,*" *i.e.,* asportation; and (3) "value exceeding $1,000" (first paragraph)—Carter claims that the first two should be deemed implicit in § 2113(a), and that the third is not an element at all.

As to "intent to steal or purloin," it will be recalled that the text of subsection (b) requires a specific "intent to steal or purloin," whereas subsection (a) contains no explicit *mens rea* requirement of any kind. Carter nevertheless argues that such a *specific intent* requirement must be deemed implicitly present in § 2113(a) by virtue of "our cases interpreting criminal statutes to include broadly applicable scienter requirements, even where the statute by its terms does not contain them." *United States v. X-Citement Video, Inc.,* 513 U.S. 64, 70, 115 S.Ct. 464, 130 L.Ed.2d 372 (1994). Properly applied to § 2113, however, the presumption in favor of scienter demands only that we read subsection (a) as requiring proof of *general intent*—that is, that the defendant possessed knowledge with respect to the *actus reus* of the crime (here, the taking of property of another by force and violence or intimidation).

Before explaining why this is so under our cases, an example, *United States v. Lewis,* 628 F.2d 1276, 1279 (C.A.10 1980), cert. denied, 450 U.S. 924, 101 S.Ct. 1375, 67 L.Ed.2d 353 (1981), will help to make the distinction between "general" and "specific" intent less esoteric. In *Lewis,* a person entered a bank and took money from a teller at gunpoint, but deliberately failed to make a quick getaway from the bank in the hope of being arrested so that he would be returned to prison and treated for alcoholism. Though this defendant knowingly engaged in the acts of using force and taking money (satisfying "general intent"), he did not intend permanently to deprive the bank of its possession of the money (failing to satisfy "specific intent"). See generally 1 W. LaFave & A. Scott, Substantive Criminal Law § 3.5, p. 315 (1986) (distinguishing general from specific intent).

The presumption in favor of scienter requires a court to read into a statute only that *mens rea* which is necessary to separate wrongful conduct from "otherwise innocent conduct." *X-Citement Video, supra,* at 72, 115 S.Ct. 464. In *Staples v. United States,* 511 U.S. 600, 114 S.Ct. 1793, 128 L.Ed.2d 608 (1994), for example, to avoid criminalizing the innocent activity of gun ownership, we interpreted a federal firearms statute to require proof that the defendant knew that the weapon he possessed had the characteristics bringing it within the scope of the statute. *Id.,* at 611–612, 114 S.Ct. 1793. See also, *e.g., Liparota v. United States,* 471 U.S. 419, 426, 105 S.Ct. 2084, 85 L.Ed.2d 434 (1985); *Morissette,* 342 U.S., at 270–271, 72 S.Ct. 240. By contrast, some situations may call for implying a specific intent requirement into statutory text. Suppose, for example, a statute identical to § 2113(b) but without the words "intent to steal or purloin." Such a statute would run the risk of punishing seemingly innocent conduct in the case of a defendant who peaceably takes money believing it to be his. Reading the statute to require that the defendant possess general intent with respect to the *actus reus—i.e.,* that he know that he is physically taking the money—would fail to protect the innocent actor. The statute therefore would need to be read to require not only general intent, but also specific intent—*i.e.,* that the defendant take the money with "intent to steal or purloin."

In this case, as in *Staples,* a general intent requirement suffices to separate wrongful from "otherwise innocent" conduct. Section 2113(a) certainly should not be interpreted to apply to the hypothetical person who engages in forceful taking of money while sleepwalking (innocent, if aberrant activity), but this result is accomplished simply by requiring, as *Staples* did, general intent—*i.e.,* proof of knowledge with respect to the *actus reus* of the crime. And once this mental state and *actus reus* are shown, the concerns underlying the presumption in favor of scienter are fully satisfied, for a forceful taking—even by a defendant who takes under a good-faith claim of right—falls outside the realm of the "otherwise innocent." Thus, the presumption in favor of scienter does not justify reading a specific intent requirement—"intent to steal or purloin"—into § 2113(a).

Independent of his reliance upon the presumption in favor of scienter, Carter argues that the legislative history of § 2113 supports the notion that an "intent to steal" requirement should be read into § 2113(a). Carter points out that, in 1934, Congress enacted what is now § 2113(a), but with the adverb "feloniously" (which all agree is equivalent to "intent to steal") modifying the verb "takes." Act of May 18, 1934, ch. 304, § 2(a), 48 Stat. 783. In 1937, Congress added what is now § 2113(b). Act of Aug. 24, 1937, ch. 747, 50 Stat. 749. Finally, in 1948, Congress made two changes to § 2113, deleting "feloniously" from what is now § 2113(a) and dividing the "robbery" and "larceny" offenses into their own separate subsections. 62 Stat. 796.

Carter concludes that the 1948 deletion of "feloniously" was merely a stylistic change, and that Congress had no intention, in deleting that word, to drop the requirement that the defendant "feloniously" take the property—that is, with intent to steal. Such reasoning, however, misunderstands our approach to statutory interpretation. In analyzing a statute, we begin by examining the text, see, *e.g., Estate of Cowart v. Nicklos Drilling Co.,* 505 U.S. 469, 475, 112 S.Ct. 2589, 120 L.Ed.2d 379 (1992), not by "psychoanalyzing those who enacted it," *Bank One Chicago, N.A. v. Midwest Bank & Trust Co.,* 516 U.S. 264, 279, 116 S.Ct. 637, 133 L.Ed.2d 635 (1996) (SCALIA, J., concurring in part and concurring in judgment). While "feloniously" no doubt would be sufficient to convey a specific intent requirement akin to the one spelled out in subsection (b), the word simply does not appear in subsection (a).

Contrary to the dissent's suggestion, *post,* at 2176–2177, this reading is not a fanciful one. The absence of a specific intent requirement from subsection (a), for example, permits the statute to reach cases like *Lewis,* see *supra,* at 2168, where an ex-convict robs a bank because he wants to be apprehended and returned to prison. (The Government represents that indictments on this same fact pattern (which invariably plead out and hence do not result in reported decisions) are brought "as often as every year," Brief for United States 22, n. 13.) It can hardly be said, therefore, that it would have been absurd to delete "feloniously" in order to reach such defendants. And once we have made that determination, our inquiry into legislative motivation is at an end. Cf. *Bock Laundry Machine Co.,* 490 U.S., at 510–511, 109 S.Ct. 1981. . . .

Turning to the second element in dispute, it will be recalled that, whereas subsection (b) requires that the defendant "tak[e] and carr[y] away the property," subsection (a) requires only that the defendant "tak[e]" the property. Carter contends that the "takes" in subsection (a) is equivalent to "takes and carries away" in subsection (b). While Carter seems to acknowledge that the argument is at war with the text of the statute, he urges that text should not be dispositive here because nothing in the evolution of § 2113(a) suggests that Congress sought to discard the asportation requirement from that subsection.

But, again, our inquiry focuses on an analysis of the textual product of Congress' efforts, not on speculation as to the internal thought processes of its Members. Congress is certainly free to outlaw bank theft that does not involve asportation, and it hardly would have been absurd for Congress to do so, since the taking-without-asportation scenario is no imagined hypothetical. See, *e.g., State v. Boyle,* 970 S.W.2d 835, 836, 838–839

(Mo.Ct.App.1998) (construing state statutory codification of common-law robbery to apply to defendant who, after taking money by threat of force, dropped the money on the spot). Indeed, a leading treatise applauds the deletion of the asportation requirement from the elements of robbery. See 2 LaFave & Scott, Substantive Criminal Law § 8.11, at 439. No doubt the common law's decision to require asportation also has its virtues. But Congress adopted a different view in § 2113(a), and it is not for us to question that choice.

There remains the requirement in § 2113(b)'s first paragraph that the property taken have a "value exceeding $1,000"—a requirement notably absent from § 2113(a). Carter, shifting gears from his previous arguments, concedes the textual point but claims that the valuation requirement does not affect the *Schmuck* elements analysis because it is a *sentencing factor,* not an element.

We disagree. The structure of subsection (b) strongly suggests that its two paragraphs—the first of which requires that the property taken have "value exceeding $1,000," the second of which refers to property of "value not exceeding $1,000"—describe distinct offenses. Each begins with the word "[w]hoever," proceeds to describe identically (apart from the differing valuation requirements) the elements of the offense, and concludes by stating the prescribed punishment. That these provisions "stand on their own grammatical feet" strongly suggests that Congress intended the valuation requirement to be an element of each paragraph's offense, rather than a sentencing factor of some base § 2113(b) offense. *Jones v. United States,* 526 U.S. 227, 234, 119 S.Ct. 1215, 143 L.Ed.2d 311 (1999). Even aside from the statute's structure, the "steeply higher penalties"—an enhancement from a 1-year to a 10-year maximum penalty on proof of valuation exceeding $1,000—leads us to conclude that the valuation requirement is an element of the first paragraph of subsection (b). See *Castillo v. United States,* 530 U.S. 120, 127, 120 S.Ct. 2090, 147 L.Ed.2d 94; *Jones,* 526 U.S., at 233, 119 S.Ct. 1215. Finally, the constitutional questions that would be raised by interpreting the valuation requirement to be a sentencing factor persuade us to adopt the view that the valuation requirement is an element. See *id.,* at 239–252, 119 S.Ct. 1215.

We hold that § 2113(b) is not a lesser included offense of § 2113(a), and therefore that petitioner is not entitled to a jury instruction on § 2113(b). The judgment of the Third Circuit is affirmed.

It is so ordered.

JUSTICE GINSBURG, with whom JUSTICE STEVENS, JUSTICE SOUTER, and JUSTICE BREYER join, dissenting.

At common law, robbery meant larceny *plus* force, violence, or putting in fear. Because robbery was an aggravated form of larceny at common law, larceny was a lesser included offense of robbery. Congress, I conclude, did not depart from that traditional understanding when it rendered "Bank robbery and incidental crimes" federal offenses. Accordingly, I would hold that petitioner Carter is not prohibited as a matter of law from obtaining an instruction on bank larceny as a lesser included offense. The Court holds that Congress, in 18 U.S.C. § 2113, has dislodged bank robbery and bank larceny from their common-law mooring. I dissent from that determination. . . .

EXERCISE

Lesser included offenses are important in criminal law because they allow a jury to choose to convict the defendant of something even while they reject the most serious charge. Because juries often resolve disputes by making compromises, the existence of a lesser included charge can mean at once both that the prosecution is more likely to get a conviction (of some kind) and that the defense will be able to avoid the most serious charge and the sentence that would result. Presumably, that is why the defense attorney in *Carter* wanted the inclusion of that lesser included offense.

If the trial court in the *Carter* case had allowed the instruction on bank larceny and you were the defense attorney, what argument would you make that the element of "force or intimidation" included in bank robbery was not proven beyond a reasonable doubt?

Theft is a crime that sometimes works within larger markets—people steal goods to sell rather than use themselves. Sometimes, thieves sell to a "fence," who then re-sells the stolen goods, often while hiding the nefarious origins of their product. That means that prosecutors can more efficiently effect change by going after these *buyers* of stolen goods (the "fence") who create the demand for a stolen item; that way, law enforcement can dry up the market for stolen goods and potentially solve a larger problem while incarcerating fewer people. That tactic was made easier when Congress passed a statute, 18 U.S.C. § 2322, which specifically addresses "chop shops" that buy stolen cars.

UNITED STATES V. UDER
98 F. 3d 1039 (8th Cir. 1996)

McMILLIAN, CIRCUIT JUDGE.

On October 20, 1994, Uder, along with seven other individuals, was charged in an eight-count indictment. Uder was charged in two of the counts, one alleging that he and his co-defendants knowingly operated a chop shop in violation of 18 U.S.C. § 2322(a)(1), (b), and the other alleging that he and four of his co-defendants knowingly tampered with and altered the vehicle identification number on a stolen car, in violation of 18 U.S.C. § 511. By the time of trial on July 19, 1995, all of Uder's co-defendants had entered into plea or cooperation agreements with the government, and Uder was the only defendant left to stand trial.

The government called ten witnesses for its case in chief, including several of Uder's former co-defendants. According to the government witnesses, Uder worked at an auto body shop in Fair Grove, Missouri, which operated under the name Heavy Truck and Car Sales and was owned and operated by an individual named Lloyd Dale Hightower. In November of 1993, Hightower was serving time in a federal prison for possession of methamphetamine with intent to distribute and conspiracy to transport stolen cars. Nevertheless, Hightower was able to direct illegal operations and related activities at the shop through an associate, Robert Moon, and Hightower's wife, Margaret Eaves (formerly Margaret Hightower), who lived next door to the shop. Hightower would allegedly purchase a salvaged vehicle at minimal cost, have the car cut up for parts while keeping the frame, then have the body of a stolen car assembled on the frame of the salvaged car, and have the vehicle identification number plates from the salvaged car switched to the stolen car. He would then sell the rebuilt car at a substantial profit. (This practice is referred to as "body swinging" or "swinging.") The government's evidence indicated that during the winter of 1993–1994, as part of Hightower's operation, a salvaged 1993 Suburban was legitimately purchased in Louisiana. The 1993 Suburban was cut up for parts at Hightower's shop and the frame salvaged. Then, a stolen 1994 Suburban was rebuilt on the salvaged frame and was retagged to bear the vehicle identification number and other identifying parts from the 1993 model.

One of the government witnesses, Mike Willis, testified that he worked at Hightower's shop but did legitimate body work. He testified that, on January 1, 1994, he was visiting in Eaves' home. Based upon his observations and what he heard, he became suspicious of the activities that were taking place next door at the shop. The next day he left a message with FBI agent Al Stiffler to report that a "swing" of a Suburban was in progress at Hightower's shop. Willis implicated Hightower, Eaves, and Moon, and testified that a man referred to as "Robert" was apparently also involved in the "swing." The following day, Willis saw Stiffler and a state patrol officer at the shop.

Moon, who had originally been charged in the indictment, testified under a plea agreement that during 1993 and 1994 he was in the business of stealing cars for chop shops, including Hightower's. He testified that, in October or November of 1993 (before Hightower's incarceration), he saw Hightower obtain the 1993 Suburban and he saw the car chopped up and the vehicle identification number being saved. The frame and engine were taken to an auto frame shop owned by Chris Brown, in Lebanon, Missouri, to have the frame straightened. After Hightower was incarcerated, he allegedly agreed to pay Moon $2,000.00 to steal a Suburban and change the bodies before selling it. Moon further testified that he and Charles Berry Roberson (apparently the person whom Willis heard referred to as "Robert") stole the 1994 Suburban. Moon then hired Mat Lowrance and Uder (who were associated with another auto body chop shop called Auto Mart, which was owned by Kenny Smith), to do the body work on the Suburbans for $600 each.

The salvaged frame was brought to Hightower's shop from Lebanon. Over the course of January 1 and January 2, 1994, Uder and Lowrance completed the body work for the "swing," with the exception of a broken distributor that needed replacing, and transferred the vehicle identification number and other identifying plates to the newly rebuilt car. The next day, January 3, 1994, Uder and Lowrance were returning to fix the broken distributor when they were waved off as they approached Hightower's shop, apparently because the police were there. They, in turn, also waved off Moon as he approached the shop.

Consequently, Uder and Lowrance did not replace the broken distributor as planned. That evening, Lowrance, Uder, and Moon allegedly met at the Auto Mart in Lebanon, Missouri. Kenny Smith and one of his employees, Frank Rodden, were also present. Afterward, Uder allegedly removed from Hightower's shop some of the parts that had been taken out of the interior of the salvaged Suburban, and he delivered those parts to Kenny Smith, who had bought them from Eaves.

Other witnesses testifying for the government under a plea agreement or a grant of immunity were Roberson (who had allegedly helped steal the 1994 Suburban), Lowrance (who, with Uder, allegedly did the body work for the "swing"), Rodden (an employee of Kenny Smith at the Auto Mart), and Eaves (Hightower's wife). They generally corroborated the story told by Moon. The government also called as trial witnesses the owner of the stolen 1994 Suburban, law enforcement officers who were involved in the investigation (including FBI agent Stiffler), and an expert who testified about how chop shops operate.

After the government rested, Uder moved for a directed verdict or judgment of acquittal on grounds of insufficiency of the evidence. The motion was denied. Uder rested without presenting any further evidence. Uder timely objected to several of the jury instructions given by the district court, including Instruction No. 13. The case was then submitted to the jury following closing arguments. The jury found Uder guilty of knowingly operating a chop shop and not guilty of knowingly tampering with or altering a vehicle identification number. . . .

Uder also argues that the evidence was insufficient as a matter of law to support the jury's guilty verdict on the count charging him with conducting operations in a chop shop, in violation of 18 U.S.C. § 2322(a)(1). Uder contends that the government's evidence was insufficient because it failed to establish that he knew that the 1994 Suburban was stolen or otherwise unlawfully obtained. Uder maintains that this was an element of the government's burden of proof, based upon the definition of "chop shop" contained in 18 U.S.C. § 2322(b). Uder argues "there is no direct evidence that [he] knew the vehicle was stolen," and "[t]here is conflicting evidence from which inferences might be drawn which is [sic] as consistent with innocence as guilt." Brief for Appellant at 13–14.

In response, the government argues that it was only required to prove that Uder acted knowingly in conducting operations of the chop shop, not that he had specific knowledge of the facts which made the chop shop fall within the statutory definition. On this point, the government compares 18 U.S.C. § 2322 to 18 U.S.C. § 1955(a) (the federal illegal gambling business law). For example, the government contends, the mere "wrench man" is criminally responsible for a chop shop's operations even though he may not personally know the unlawful origin of a particular vehicle or the intended disposition of the vehicle. In the alternative, the government argues that, even if it were required to prove Uder's knowledge that the 1994 Suburban was stolen, there was ample evidence supporting such an inference.

Although we do not necessarily agree with the government's assertion that "[a]ny degree of participation in a chop shop, other than as customer, should be within the 'conduct' provision of § 2322(a)," Brief for Appellee at 32, we conclude that the evidence of intent was sufficient to support the jury's verdict in the present case. Because we hold that the evidence overwhelmingly supported a finding of guilty knowledge under any reasonable interpretation of the jury instruction setting forth the elements of the offense (which Uder has not challenged), we find it unnecessary at this time to define the exact scope of the intent element of 18 U.S.C. § 2322(a)(1).

EXERCISE

Here is the instruction on the elements that the court gave the trial jury in Uder:

> "*One,* the defendant, during the period alleged, conducted operations in a chop shop; and, *Two,* the defendant did so knowingly. . . . the term 'chop shop' means any building, lot, facility, or other structure or premise where one or more persons engage in receiving, concealing, destroying, disassembling, dismantling, reassembling, or storing any passenger motor vehicle or passenger motor vehicle part which has been unlawfully obtained in order to alter, counterfeit, deface, destroy, disguise, falsify, forge, obliterate, or remove the identity, including the vehicle identification number or derivative thereof, of such vehicle or vehicle part and to distribute, sell, or

dispose of such vehicle or vehicle part in interstate or foreign commerce."

The Court of Appeals ruled without determining whether or not the government should have to prove that the defendant knew that a car was stolen. If the law does require such an element of knowledge be proven, what problems might that raise for the government? Could it change the way that chop shops do business? What could they do to avoid criminal liability?

2. THEFT OF NON-PHYSICAL PROPERTY

A transition to an information economy has meant that theft of valuable property is no longer limited to physical property, and the law has adjusted to this. Modern federal criminal law protects things like trade secrets and personal identity, which can have financial value just as physical property might.

a. Theft of Trade Secrets

A number of federal criminal statutes protect property that takes the form of information rather than money or a physical object. Some are remarkably specific: 18 U.S.C. § 2319B, for example, bars making a copy of a movie by filming it while it shows in a theater. Others strike more broadly, leaving definitional problems as to what constitutes property in the form of trade secrets.

UNITED STATES V. NOSAL
844 F. 3d 1024 (9th Cir. 2016)

MCKEOWN, CIRCUIT JUDGE:

Nosal worked at the executive search firm Korn/Ferry International when he decided to launch a competitor along with a group of co-workers. Before leaving Korn/Ferry, Nosal's colleagues began downloading confidential information from a Korn/Ferry database to use at their new enterprise. Although they were authorized to access the database as current Korn/Ferry employees, their downloads on behalf of Nosal violated Korn/Ferry's confidentiality and computer use policies. In 2012, we addressed whether those employees "exceed [ed] authorized access" with intent to defraud under the CFAA. *United States v. Nosal (Nosal I)*, 676 F.3d 854 (9th Cir. 2012) (en banc). Distinguishing between access restrictions and use restrictions, we concluded that the "exceeds authorized access" prong of § 1030(a)(4) of the CFAA "does not extend to violations of [a company's] use restrictions." *Id.* at 863. We affirmed the district court's dismissal of the five CFAA counts related to Nosal's aiding and abetting misuse of data accessed by his co-workers with their own passwords.

. . . When Nosal left Korn/Ferry, the company revoked his computer access credentials, even though he remained for a time as a contractor. The company took the same precaution upon the departure of his accomplices, Becky Christian and Mark Jacobson. Nonetheless, they continued to access the database using the credentials of Nosal's former executive assistant, Jacqueline Froehlich-L'Heureaux ("FH"), who remained at Korn/Ferry at Nosal's request. . . .

Korn/Ferry's bread and butter was identifying and recommending potential candidates for corporate positions. In 2004, after being passed over for a promotion, Nosal announced his intention to leave Korn/Ferry. Negotiations ensued and Nosal agreed to stay on for an additional year as a contractor to finish a handful of open searches, subject to a blanket non-competition agreement. As he put it, Korn/Ferry was giving him "a lot of money" to "stay out of the market."

During this interim period, Nosal was very busy, secretly launching his own search firm along with other Korn/Ferry employees, including Christian, Jacobson and FH. As of December 8, 2004, Korn/Ferry revoked Nosal's access to its computers, although it permitted him to ask Korn/Ferry employees for research help on his remaining open assignments. In January 2005, Christian left Korn/Ferry and, under instructions from Nosal, set up an executive search firm—Christian & Associates—from which Nosal retained 80% of fees. Jacobson followed her a few months later. As Nosal, Christian and Jacobson began work for clients, Nosal used the name "David Nelson" to mask his identity when interviewing candidates.

The start-up company was missing Korn/Ferry's core asset: "Searcher," an internal database of information on over one million executives, including contact information, employment history, salaries, biographies and resumes, all compiled since 1995. Searcher was central to Korn/Ferry's work for clients. When launching a new search to fill an open executive position, Korn/Ferry teams started by compiling a "source list" of potential candidates. In constructing the list, the employees would run queries in Searcher to generate a list of candidates. To speed up the process, employees could look at old source lists in Searcher to see how a search for a similar position was constructed, or to identify suitable candidates. The resulting source list could include hundreds of names, but then was narrowed to a short list of candidates presented to the client. Korn/Ferry considered these source lists proprietary.

Searcher included data from a number of public and quasi-public sources like LinkedIn, corporate filings and Internet searches, and also included internal, non-public sources, such as personal connections, unsolicited resumes sent to Korn/Ferry and data inputted directly by candidates via Korn/Ferry's website. The data was coded upon entry; as a result, employees could run targeted searches for candidates by criteria such as age, industry, experience or other data points. However, once the information became part of the Searcher system, it was integrated with other data and there was no way to identify the source of the data.

Searcher was hosted on the company's internal computer network and was considered confidential and for use only in Korn/Ferry business. Korn/Ferry issued each employee a unique username and password to its computer system; no separate password was required to access Searcher. Password sharing was prohibited by a confidentiality agreement that Korn/Ferry required each new employee to sign. When a user requested a custom report in Searcher, Searcher displayed a message which stated: "This product is intended to be used by Korn/Ferry employees for work on Korn/Ferry business only."

Nosal and his compatriots downloaded information and source lists from Searcher in preparation to launch the new competitor. Before leaving Korn/Ferry, they used their own usernames and passwords, compiling proprietary Korn/Ferry data in violation of Korn/Ferry's computer use policy. Those efforts were encompassed in the CFAA accounts appealed in *Nosal I. See* 676 F.3d at 856.

After Nosal became a contractor and Christian and Jacobson left Korn/Ferry, Korn/Ferry revoked each of their credentials to access Korn/Ferry's computer system. Not to be deterred, on three occasions Christian and Jacobson borrowed access credentials from FH, who stayed on at Korn/Ferry at Nosal's request. In April 2005, Nosal instructed Christian to obtain some source lists from Searcher to expedite their work for a new client. Thinking it would be difficult to explain the request to FH, Christian asked to borrow FH's access credentials, which Christian then used to log in to Korn/Ferry's computer system and run queries in Searcher. Christian sent the results of her searches to Nosal. In July 2005, Christian again logged in as FH to generate a custom report and search for information on three individuals. Later in July, Jacobson also logged in as FH, to download information on 2,400 executives. None of these searches related to any open searches that fell under Nosal's independent contractor agreement.

In March 2005, Korn/Ferry received an email from an unidentified person advising that Nosal was conducting his own business in violation of his non-compete agreement. The company launched an investigation and, in July 2005, contacted government authorities. . . .

The jury convicted Nosal of two counts of trade secret theft under the EEA: Count 5 charged "unauthorized downloading, copying and duplicating of trade secrets" in violation of 18 U.S.C. §§ 1832(a)(2) & (a)(4); and Count 6 charged unauthorized receipt and possession of stolen trade secrets in violation of 18 U.S.C. § 1832(a)(3) & (a)(4). Both counts relate to Christian's use of FH's login credentials to obtain three source lists of CFOs from Searcher. Count 6 also included a "cut and paste" of a list of executives derived from Searcher. Christian emailed Nosal the resulting lists, which contained candidate names, company positions and phone numbers. Nosal primarily challenges the sufficiency of the evidence on the trade secret counts. . . .

Violation of the EEA requires, among other things, "intent to convert a trade secret" and "intending or knowing that the offense will[ ] injure [an] owner of that trade secret. . . ." 18 U.S.C. § 1832(a). The jury instruction for Count 5—downloading, copying and duplicating trade secrets—set out the following elements:

> 1.　At least one of the three source lists is a trade secret (requiring agreement on which one);
>
> 2.　Nosal knew that the source list was a trade secret;
>
> 3.　Nosal knowingly, and without authorization, downloaded, copied or duplicated the trade secret;
>
> 4.　Nosal intended to convert the trade secret to the economic benefit of someone other than the owner;
>
> 5.　Nosal knew or intended that the offense would injure the trade secret owner; and
>
> 6.　The trade secret was related to or included in a product in interstate commerce.

The instruction for Count 6—receiving and possessing trade secrets—replaced the third element with a requirement of knowing receipt or possession of a trade secret with the knowledge that it was "stolen or appropriated, obtained, or converted without authorization" and added the "cut and paste" list as one of the possible trade secrets.

Nosal argues that the government failed to prove: 1) secrecy and difficulty of development, because the search information was derived from public sources and because there was no evidence the source lists had not been circulated outside Korn/Ferry; 2) knowledge of trade secret status; and 3) knowledge of injury to, or an intent to injure, Korn/Ferry.

The notion of a trade secret often conjures up magic formulas, like Coca Cola's proprietary formula, technical drawings or scientific data. So it is no surprise that such technically complex cases have been brought under the EEA. *See, e.g., United States v. Chung*, 659 F.3d 815, 819 (9th Cir. 2011) (documents related to space shuttles and rockets); *United States v. Yang*, 281 F.3d 534, 540 (6th Cir. 2002) (scientific research in adhesives); *United States v. Hsu*, 155 F.3d 189, 191–92 (3d Cir. 1998) (processes, methods and formulas for manufacturing an anti-cancer drug).

But the scope of the EEA is not limited to these categories and the EEA, by its terms, includes financial and business information. The EEA defines a trade secret as all forms and types of financial, business, scientific, technical, economic, or engineering information, including . . . compilations . . . if (A) the owner thereof has taken reasonable measures to keep such information secret; and (B) the information derives independent economic value, actual or potential, from not being generally known to, and not being readily ascertainable through proper means by the public. . . .

18 U.S.C. § 1839(3).

The thrust of Nosal's argument is that the source lists are composed largely, if not entirely, of public information and therefore couldn't possibly be trade secrets. But he overlooks the principle that a trade secret may consist of a compilation of data, public sources or a combination of proprietary and public sources. It is well recognized that

> it is the secrecy of the claimed trade secret as a whole that is determinative. The fact that some or all of the components of the trade secret are well-known does not preclude protection for a secret combination, compilation, or integration of the individual elements. . . . [T]he theoretical possibility of reconstructing the secret from published materials containing scattered references to portions of the information or of extracting it from public materials unlikely to come to the attention of the appropriator will not preclude relief against the wrongful conduct. . . .

Restatement (Third) of Unfair Competition § 39 cmt. f (1995). . . .

The source lists in question are classic examples of a trade secret that derives from an amalgam of public and proprietary source data. To be sure, some of the data came from public sources and other data came from internal, confidential sources. But cumulatively, the Searcher database contained a massive confidential compilation of data, the product of years of effort and expense. Each source list was the result of a query run through a propriety algorithm that generates a custom subset of possible candidates, culled from a database of over one million executives. The source lists were not unwashed, public-domain lists of all financial executives in the United States, nor otherwise related to a search that could be readily completed using public sources. Had the query been "who is the CFO of General Motors" or "who are all of the CFOs in a particular industry," our analysis might be different. Instead, the nature of the trade secret and its value stemmed from the unique integration, compilation, cultivation, and sorting of, and the aggressive protections applied to, the Searcher database.

Nosal takes the view that the source lists are merely customer lists that cannot be protected as trade secrets. This characterization attempts to sidestep the unique nature of the source lists, which are the customized product of a massive database, not a list of well-known customers.

Regardless, courts have deemed customer lists protectable trade secrets. *See, e.g., Hollingsworth Solderless Terminal Co. v. Turley*, 622 F.2d 1324, 1332–33 (9th Cir. 1980) (setting out in detail how to analyze whether a customer list is a trade secret); *Hertz v. Luzenac Grp.*, 576 F.3d 1103, 1114 (10th Cir. 2009) (holding that a customer list may be a trade secret where "it is the end result of a long process of culling the relevant information from lengthy and diverse sources, even if the original sources are publicly available").

Our approach is not novel. This case is remarkably similar to *Conseco Finance Servicing Corp. v. North American Mortgage Co.*, 381 F.3d 811 (8th Cir. 2004). Conseco was a financial services company that issued subprime mortgages. *Id.* at 814. It generated potential customer leads through a database of information on over 40 million individuals. *Id.* at 815. A computer program compiled lists of potential customers, which were sent to branch offices as "customer lead sheets," coded from most promising (red) to decent (blue). *Id.* Several departing staff took copies of the lead sheets and went to work for a competitor. *Id.* at 816. Even though all the information in the lead sheets was public, the Eighth Circuit held that they were trade secrets: they "are a product of a specialized—and apparently quite effective—computer program that was uniquely Conseco's." *Id.* at 819.

Nosal also takes aim at the secrecy of the three source lists in question, an argument that is intertwined with his public domain/compilation claim. The jury heard more than enough evidence to support its verdict. Christian acknowledged that the only place she could obtain the source lists she needed was on Korn/Ferry's computer system. Notably, some of the downloaded information came from a source list for an engagement that was opened only twelve days prior to the April 12 downloads underlying the trade secret counts.

Although Nosal claims that Korn/Ferry's sharing of lists with clients and others undermined this claim of secrecy, witnesses who worked at Korn/Ferry did not budge in terms of procedures undertaken to keep the data secret, both in terms of technology protections built into the computer system and the limitations on distribution of the search results. For example, the Vice-President of Information Services testified that, to her knowledge, the source lists had never been released by Korn/Ferry to any third parties. As a matter of practice, Korn/Ferry did not show source lists to clients. In the occasional instance when a client was given a source list or shown one at a pitch, it was provided on an understanding of confidentiality, and disclosing the lists was contrary to company policy. It is also well established that "confidential disclosures to employees, licensees, or others will not destroy the information's status as a trade secret." Restatement (Third) of Unfair Competition § 39 cmt. f (1995).

In light of the above, it would be naive to conclude that Nosal was unaware that the information pirated by Christian included trade secrets or that the piracy would harm Korn/Ferry. As a former senior executive at Korn/Ferry, Nosal was deeply familiar with the competitive advantage Searcher provided, and was cognizant of the measures the company took to protect the source lists generated. He signed a confidentiality agreement stating that "information databases and company records are extremely valuable assets of [Korn/Ferry's] business and are accorded the legal protection applicable to a company's trade secrets." The source lists were also marked "Korn/Ferry Proprietary & Confidential." While a label or proprietary marking alone does not confer trade secret status, the notice and protective measures taken by Korn/Ferry significantly undermine Nosal's claim he was unaware the source lists were trade secret information.

EXERCISE

Examine the six elements described by the Court in the *Nosal* case. If you were the defense attorney at trial, which element would you be most aggressive in attacking in your efforts to show reasonable doubt?

b. Identity Theft

In a modern interconnected world, a person's identity can be stolen for access to money, the privileges of citizenship, and other things of value. These crimes (if prosecuted under provisions such as 18 U.S.C. § 1028A, "Aggravated identity theft") present an interesting state of mind element: The government must prove that the defendant knew that he or she was stealing an actual person's identity.

In the case below, the defendant was remarkably committed to obscuring his own true identity. In a footnote, the court noted that "To the date of this writing the Defendant, who has refused to provide his name, has not been affirmatively identified and is referred to as 'John Doe.'"

UNITED STATES v. DOE
842 F. 3d 1117 (9th Cir. 2016)

GARBIS, SENIOR DISTRICT JUDGE:

Appellant John Doe appeals from his convictions of aggravated identity theft under 18 U.S.C. § 1028A, for knowingly possessing and using the name, birth date, and social security number of another person when he applied to renew a Nevada driver's license and when he submitted a Form I-9 Employment Eligibility Verification form to his employer.

Doe contends that the Government failed to prove an element of the offense—specifically that he knew that the false identity he used belonged to a real person. He also challenges the reasonableness of his 78-month sentence.

This case presents the question, not previously addressed by this Court, of whether evidence of a defendant's repeated submission of false identifying information as part of successful applications to a government agency is sufficient to permit a reasonable jury to find that the defendant knew that the information belonged to a real person. We hold that it is and that Doe's convictions were thus based upon sufficient evidence. We also hold that the district court did not abuse its discretion with regard to Doe's sentence. . . .

The victim of Doe's identity theft, referred to herein as "V," was born in San Jose, California in 1963 and, in or about 1977, was assigned a social security number and card. No later than 1987, V's uncle sold V's birth certificate and provided his social security number to a man, not identified at trial. In 1987, someone, most likely Doe, used V's birth certificate, name, and social security number to obtain a "replacement" social security card from the Social Security Administration. For some 27 years, until Doe's arrest in 2014, V's identification was used without his authorization, most likely by Doe. In this regard, V received notices from the Social Security Administration (approximately every three years) that his name and social security number were being used in connection with multiple jobs in different places, including Nevada, with which V had no connection.

The evidence establishes that Doe's use of V's identity began no later than 2002 when Doe obtained a driver's license upon an application to the Nevada Department of Motor Vehicles ("DMV") that contained Doe's photograph but V's name and birth date. Doe renewed this license multiple times by resubmitting V's identifying information and had such a license in his possession when arrested in 2014.

On or around May 15, 2013, Doe submitted such a driver's license together with a social security card with V's number to Doe's employer with a Form I-9 Employment Eligibility Verification.

The unauthorized use of V's identity caused him problems for approximately three decades. In the 1990s, his driver's license was suspended twice—including once while he was employed as a truck driver—because of DUIs committed in a different state by another person using his social security number. Tax refund checks due to him from the IRS were sent to a person in Nevada using his social security number. His wages were garnished three times to pay child support for children that were not his. More likely than not, these problems were caused by Doe's misuse of V's identity. In any event, it is clear that in 2013 V's unemployment benefits were halted because of child support payments owed (and not made) by Doe. V contacted Doe's employer to notify it that an employee was unlawfully using his identity.

On or around June 4, 2014, Doe was arrested in connection with a fraud investigation conducted by the Nevada DMV and the Department of Homeland Security. At that time, he was found to be in possession of a Nevada driver's license bearing his photo and V's identification information.

In this case, Doe was charged with two counts of aggravated identity theft under 18 U.S.C. § 1028A, unlawful production of an identification document under 18 U.S.C. § 1028(a)(1), and false attestation in an immigration matter in violation of 18 U.S.C. § 1546(b)(3). At trial, he was convicted on all charges. The district court sentenced Doe to 78 months of incarceration. . . .

Title 18 U.S.C. § 1028A provides that a person who "knowingly transfers, possesses, or uses, without lawful authority, a means of identification of another person" in connection with an enumerated felony shall be sentenced to two years imprisonment. 18 U.S.C. § 1028A (2012).

To prove a violation of § 1028A, the Government must prove beyond a reasonable doubt that:

> 1.   The defendant knowingly transferred or used a means of identification of another person without legal authority;
>
> 2.   The defendant knew the means of identification belonged to a real person; and
>
> 3.   The defendant did so in relation to one of the crimes enumerated in 18 U.S.C. § 1028A(c). . . .

Doe does not debate the Government's proof of the first and third elements. Doe was proven to have used V's means of identification without legal authority. And the use was proven to be in relation to crimes enumerated in 18 U.S.C. § 1028A(c), i.e., the violations of 18 U.S.C. §§ 1028(a)(1) and 1546(b)(3) for which he was convicted in the instant case.

Doe acknowledges that the Government proved that V was a real person. Doe contends however, that, without *direct* proof of his knowledge (such as proof that he knew V or had any connection to the sale of V's birth certificate and identifying information), the evidence was insufficient to establish his knowledge that V was a real person. The Court does not agree.

While direct evidence of the knowledge element is often presented in § 1028A prosecutions, this Court has recognized that the element can be proven by circumstantial evidence. *See Miranda-Lopez*, 532 F.3d at 1040 (citing *United States v. Villanueva-Sotelo*, 515 F.3d 1234, 1249 (D.C. Cir. 2008) ("[P]roving the defendant knew the stolen identification belonged to another person should present no major obstacle, as such knowledge will often be demonstrated by the circumstances of the case.")). Thus, the issue here presented is whether the circumstantial evidence was sufficient to establish Doe's knowledge that the identity of V was that of a real person.

When "determining the sufficiency of circumstantial evidence, the question is not whether the evidence excludes every hypothesis except that of guilt but rather whether the trier of fact could reasonably arrive at its conclusion." *Nevils*, 598 F.3d at 1165 (quoting *United States v. Eaglin*, 571 F.2d 1069, 1076 (1977)).

The Government presented ample circumstantial evidence to establish Doe's knowledge that V was a real person. Most persuasive was proof of Doe's repeated success in obtaining renewed Nevada driver's licenses bearing Doe's photograph and V's name, date of birth, and social security number. In this regard, the Government introduced copies of applications to the DMV for Nevada driver's licenses and state identity cards in V's name. The "image history" associated with the applications dating back to 2002 showed photographs of Doe taken when he applied for reissuances of the driver's license and/or identity cards in V's name. Denise Riggleman, a DMV Compliance Enforcement Investigator, described the process involved in obtaining a new license or identity card through the Nevada DMV. Ms. Riggleman testified that new applicants must present proof of identity documents, such as a social security card or birth certificate, along with their applications to a DMV technician in person. This information is input into the DMV computer system, and the actual license is mailed to the applicant seven to ten days later.

In addition, the Government proved that Doe had submitted such a Nevada driver's license and a social security card in V's name as proof of identity in connection with an I-9 Employment Verification Form that he submitted to his employer.

In regard to the knowledge element of the § 1028A charge, the district court instructed the jury:

> Repeated and successful testing of the authenticity of a victim's identifying information by submitting it to a government agency, bank or other lender is circumstantial evidence that you may consider in deciding whether the defendant knew the identifying information belonged to a real person as opposed to a fictitious one. It is up to you to decide whether to consider any such evidence and how much weight to give it.

The jury found Doe guilty on both § 1028A charges.

This Court holds that the evidence of Doe's repeated successful use of V's identity in applications subject to scrutiny was sufficient to permit the jury to find that he knew that V was a real person. . . .

Doe, asserting that he is a Mexican national, contends that it was unreasonable for the jury to find that he knew how U.S. government agencies and their verification procedures worked. His not being a citizen, although a resident, of the United States is a fact that the jury could have considered relevant but does not render the jury's finding unreasonable. As stated in *Gomez-Castro*, 605 F.3d at 1249 (affirming the conviction of a citizen of the Dominican Republic), "[K]nowledge [of verification processes] can be inferred reasonably based on ordinary human experience for which no special proof is required; a trier of fact can rely on common sense.". . .

In sum, the Court holds that the circumstantial evidence presented, establishing Doe's repeated successful use of V's identification information, sufficed to permit the jury to find that he knew that V was a real person. Hence, he was properly convicted on two counts charging aggravated identity theft in violation of 18 U.S.C. § 1028A.

EXERCISE

Doe makes clear that aggravated identity theft under 18 U.S.C. § 1028A is only a crime if it is an actual person's identity that is being used (and the defendant knows that); creating a false identity from scratch does not create the same criminal liability, at least under these statutes. What policy motivation would justify differentiating identity theft from use of a made-up identity?

B. BURGLARY

Generally, burglary requires that the following elements be proven:

1) Identification,

2) Entry into (or presence in) a building, and

3) Intent to commit a felony within that building.

Statutes, however, vary widely in defining the elements of burglary. Variations can differ based on whether the entry itself needs to be illegal, when intent must be formed (before or after the entry), and what kind of structure must be entered.

Most burglaries (like other property crimes) are pursued in state courts. Some federal statutes do cover burglary in some instances. For example, 18 U.S.C. § 2118(b) provides:

> Whoever, without authority, enters or attempts to enter, or remains in, the business premises or property of a person registered with the Drug Enforcement Administration under section 302 of the Controlled Substances Act (21 U.S.C. 822) with the intent to steal any material or compound containing any quantity of a controlled substance shall, except as provided in subsection (c), be fined under this title or imprisoned not more than twenty years, or both, if (1) the replacement cost of the controlled substance to the registrant was not less than $500, (2) the person who engaged in such entry or attempted such entry or

who remained in such premises or property traveled in interstate or foreign commerce or used any facility in interstate or foreign commerce to facilitate such entry or attempt or to facilitate remaining in such premises or property, or (3) another person was killed or suffered significant bodily injury as a result of such entry or attempt.

Regardless of statute, though, identification of the defendant as the burglar is always an element, and it is this element that very often is challenged by the defense. The nature of burglary—furtive and tending towards the avoidance rather than the engagement of others—means that offenders often take great pains to conceal their identity.

UNITED STATES V. MARTIN
866 F. 2d 972 (8th Cir. 1989)

HENLEY, SENIOR CIRCUIT JUDGE.

According to the testimony of Fred King, a police informant, Martin and Emerson committed burglary of a drug store in New Hope, Minnesota, on May 16, 1987, and took approximately $950.00 worth of codeine, Ritalin and other controlled substances. King's testimony was corroborated by the identification testimony of an employee of the drug store who observed Martin and Emerson "casing" the store the day before the burglary. In addition, on May 20, 1987, at approximately 1:00 a.m., Chief of Police Kelly Shannon of Frazee, Minnesota stopped a car after observing the driver leave the vehicle, walk up to the front door of a drug store, and apparently investigate the lock. Martin was later identified as the driver, and Emerson as a passenger. Shannon observed that Martin was wearing a booster coat (a coat with compartments in its lining, often used in burglaries and thefts) and, after Martin consented to a search of the trunk of the vehicle, Shannon observed a four-foot railroad bar, pry pliers, drills and other tools. A buck knife and large screwdriver were also observed under the front seat. Shortly after Shannon permitted the vehicle to depart, he learned via radio that the car bore the registration sticker of another vehicle. Although he decided to stop the car, he was unable to catch it.

Thereafter, on May 22, 1987, Detective Walter Powers of the Hennepin County Sheriff's Department applied for a search warrant for Martin and his car. In his application, Powers indicated that on May 19, 1987 the manager of a truck stop reported that a man wearing a blue booster coat and driving a car with a license plate registered to Martin attempted to steal several T-shirts. In addition, Powers included Shannon's statement that he believed Martin and Emerson were "casing" a drug store in Frazee, and indicated that Martin had a criminal record, including burglary and robbery convictions. The warrant was approved by a state judge, and authorized a search for:

Burglary tools, including but not limited to, crowbars and vice grips. A booster coat described as being a dark blue parka with a red and black lining. Items to show constructive possession of the vehicle.

The warrant was executed later that day, and a number of items were seized from Martin's car including the booster coat, numerous tools, and a bag of pills and a lock pick found in the arm rest under the rear passenger side ashtray. Martin was arrested shortly thereafter. On May 28, 1987 Powers applied for a warrant to search Emerson's home, listing in the application the same information submitted in conjunction with the request to search Martin's car, and extensive information revealed by King. The warrant was executed, several items were seized, and Emerson was placed under arrest.

Martin and Emerson were indicted June 17, 1987. Adopting the recommendation of the magistrate to whom the matter had been referred for an evidentiary hearing, the district court denied both defendants' motions to suppress. The court also denied Emerson's motion for severance and various additional pretrial motions, and the matter proceeded to trial. The defendants' post-trial motions were denied, and this appeal followed. . . .

Our review of the record in light of the principles delineated above leads us to conclude that the evidence was sufficient to support Emerson's conviction as to both counts in question. Contrary to Emerson's assertion, King's testimony was not the only evidence implicating Emerson in the New Hope burglary; various personnel at the drug store also identified Emerson as one of the individuals casing the store. In addition, Officer Shannon's testimony concerning the defendants' behavior in Frazee, Shannon's observation of burglary tools, and the items seized from both defendants' vehicles provided a substantial basis for the jury's verdict. Although there is no direct evidence of the defendants' intent to distribute the stolen narcotics, it is rare that direct evidence of intent will ever exist, and consequently we have previously held that intent may be proved with circumstantial evidence. *E.g., United States v. Hudson,* 717 F.2d 1211, 1213 (8th Cir.1983). In short, Emerson has not sustained his heavy burden of establishing that the evidence is insufficient to establish his guilt. Hence, we conclude that this claim is without merit.

EXERCISE

In challenging the proofs of identification, defense attorneys often emphasize the kinds of evidence that were *not* brought before the jury by the prosecution. For example, it is common for a defense attorney to argue that the lack of fingerprint evidence at a crime scene can go towards reasonable doubt on the element of identity. If you were the defense attorney representing Emerson in the case above, what "missing" evidence would you have described in your closing argument?

Burglary is usually, but not always, a property crime. We may think of it as involving someone breaking into a building to steal things, and that very often is the fact situation burglary cases present. However, it can encompass cases where another crime is intended.

UNITED STATES V. EAGLE BEAR
507 F. 3d 688 (8th Cir. 2007)

COLLOTON, CIRCUIT JUDGE.

A jury convicted Russell Eagle Bear of burglary, assault with a dangerous weapon, and assault by striking, beating, or wounding. The jury acquitted Eagle Bear on one count of assault with a dangerous weapon. He appeals the sufficiency of the evidence on two of the counts, and challenges an evidentiary ruling of the district court. We affirm. . . .

The fourth count of the indictment accused Eagle Bear of committing burglary in the early morning hours of October 28, 2005. Eagle Bear's brother Gerald had just learned that he had been defeated in his bid for a seat on the tribal council. At a party the next morning, Gerald became offended when LeRoy Morrison, Jr., asserted that everyone disliked Gerald and that he had lost the election because he did not show respect for others. This remark upset Gerald, and when he told Eagle Bear about the dispute, the two brothers decided to visit the Morrison home. The Morrisons testified that the Eagle Bear brothers broke into the house, and that Eagle Bear assaulted LeRoy Morrison, Jr., and his brother Ashley. The jury convicted Eagle Bear of burglary in connection with this incident.

Eagle Bear also challenges the sufficiency of the evidence presented against him with respect to the burglary count. Federal law incorporates state law with respect to burglaries committed in Indian country. 18 U.S.C. § 1153. The elements of burglary under South Dakota law require proof that the perpetrator unlawfully entered or unlawfully remained in an occupied structure with intent to commit a crime. South Dakota law requires an unlawful entry, but not necessarily a forced entry, to violate the statute. S.D. Codified Laws § 22–32–1; *State v. Peck,* 82 S.D. 561, 150 N.W.2d 725, 727 (1967). Eagle Bear argues that there was insufficient evidence on the element of unlawful entry or remaining, because he was legally allowed into the Morrison house.

Four members of the Morrison household testified that the front door of their house was locked, and that Eagle Bear and his brother entered without permission. Eagle Bear counters that police found no evidence of forcible entry at the Morrison residence, that an investigating officer believed the Morrisons had left the door unlocked, and that his brother, Gerald Eagle Bear, testified that the Morrisons had allowed the pair into the house.

When presented with conflicting testimony, of course, the jury was entitled to weigh the credibility of the witnesses and determine the disputed facts. Whether or not the door to the Morrison home was locked, the jury reasonably could have credited the testimony of the Morrisons that none of them granted permission for the Eagle Bear brothers to enter the house. This evidence was thus sufficient to establish an unlawful entry by Eagle Bear.

EXERCISE

In the *Eagle Bear* case, there was no evidence of a forced entry. Instead, the court relies on evidence that the defendant did not have permission to enter the residence.

Imagine a situation in which a couple divorces and the ex-wife receives ownership of the house. The ex-husband has a key, and regularly uses it to enter the house to pick up the daughter of the couple. One night he uses the key to enter the house and sexually assaults the ex-wife. As a prosecutor, what additional information would you want as you considered whether or not to charge burglary in addition to sexual assault?

A burglary does not require completion of the underlying crime—just that the person enter (or, under some statutes, unlawfully remain within) a building with the intent to commit a crime. Under some laws, it is not necessary to show that the entry itself be illegal. For example, the federal law (18 U.S.C. § 2113(a)) covering both robbery and burglary of a bank does not require that the entry be illegal, so long as the intent to commit a crime exists at the time of the entry:

> . . . Whoever enters or attempts to enter any bank, credit union, or any savings and loan association, or any building used in whole or in part as a bank, credit union, or as a savings and loan association, with intent to commit in such bank, credit union, or in such savings and loan association, or building, or part thereof, so used, any felony affecting such bank, credit union, or such savings and loan association and in violation of any statute of the United States, or any larceny—
>
> Shall be fined under this title or imprisoned not more than twenty years, or both.

In the case below, the court has to sort out whether an offense should be classified as an attempted robbery or an attempted burglary for purposes of sentencing, when it is clear that the defendant entered the bank while it was open for business.

UNITED STATES V. WILLIAMS

841 F.3d 656 (4th Cir. 2016)

FLOYD, CIRCUIT JUDGE:

Ernest Lee Williams, Jr., was charged with attempting to enter a bank with the intent to commit a felony affecting it, and a larceny, all in violation of 18 U.S.C. § 2113(a). Williams pleaded guilty to the charge, and was then sentenced under the robbery guideline, U.S.S.G § 2B3.1. Williams appeals his sentence, arguing that the robbery guideline is inapplicable in this case because his indictment contained no mention of the robbery element of force and violence, intimidation, or extortion. We agree with Williams, and we therefore vacate his sentence and remand this matter for resentencing.

I.

On January 21, 2014, Williams approached a Southern Bank building (the "Bank") in Rocky Mount, North Carolina, while wearing gloves and covering his face in a hood. Williams entered the Bank's exterior doors into an anteroom, but before he could enter past the interior doors, a teller who believed she recognized Williams from a previous robbery locked both the interior and exterior doors. The teller then asked Williams through an intercom whether Williams had an account with the Bank, and Williams replied that he did, but that he had left his bank card in his car. The teller unlocked the exterior doors, and instructed Williams to use the drive-up window. Williams returned to his car, but then drove off.

The police were notified and given a description of Williams's vehicle. The police stopped Williams shortly thereafter, and in a show-up, Williams was identified by a Bank employee as the person who had tried to enter earlier. After being read his rights, Williams admitted to the police that—in need of money—he cased the Bank, and then wore gloves and covered part of his face. He had neither a gun nor a note with him when he tried to enter the Bank. Williams insisted that he had simply planned to tell the bank tellers to put the Bank's money in his bag.

On August 27, 2014, a federal grand jury in the Eastern District of North Carolina indicted Williams for violating 18 U.S.C. § 2113(a). In relevant part, the grand jury charged Williams with "attempt[ing] to enter a bank . . . with the intent to commit in such bank a felony affecting such bank, in violation of a statute of the United States, and a larceny, all in violation of Title 18, United States Code, Section 2113(a)." J.A. 7. On January 6, 2015, Williams pleaded guilty to the charge.

Violations of § 2113(a) are potentially covered by four Sentencing Guideline sections—of relevance here are U.S.S.G. § 2B3.1(Robbery) and § 2B2.1 (Burglary). Following the plea, the probation officer calculated Williams's imprisonment range under the Guidelines by using the robbery guideline, U.S.S.G. § 2B3.1. . . .

Williams objected to the application of U.S.S.G. § 2B3.1 to his offense. Williams contended that the indictment to which he pleaded guilty described an attempted burglary, not an attempted robbery, because it did not reference force or violence. Thus, as between the two relevant guidelines that could apply to a violation of § 2113(a)—the robbery guideline and the burglary guideline—Williams insisted that he should be sentenced under the latter. Williams reasoned that if the burglary guideline was used, his total offense level would be 10, which in this case would yield an imprisonment range of only 10 to 16 months.

The probation officer, meanwhile, contended that the robbery guideline applied in this case, because it—unlike the burglary guideline—contained an enhancement accounting for the fact that Williams targeted a financial institution.

On April 8, 2015, Williams's sentencing hearing took place. After hearing both sides' arguments, the district court was convinced that the robbery guideline was appropriate in this case because it addressed the targeting of financial institutions. The district court found Williams's imprisonment range under the robbery guideline to be 37 to 46 months, and sentenced him to a term of 38 months. This appeal followed.

II.

On appeal, Williams contends that his sentence should have been calculated using the burglary guideline, rather than the robbery guideline. We review challenges to the district court's guideline selection de novo. United States v. Davis, 202 F.3d 212, 218 (4th Cir. 2000). We agree with Williams that the district court's selection of the robbery guideline was erroneous, because only the burglary guideline applies here. . . .

The charge that Williams pleaded guilty to plainly describes an attempted burglary, not an attempted robbery. Williams was charged with a violation of § 2113(a), which provides:

> Whoever, by force and violence, or by intimidation, takes, or attempts to take, from the person or presence of another, or obtains or attempts to obtain by extortion any property or money or any other thing of value belonging to, or in the care, custody, control, management, or possession of, any bank . . .; or

> Whoever enters or attempts to enter any bank . . ., or any building used in whole or in part as a bank . . ., with intent to commit in such bank . . ., or part thereof, so used, any felony affecting such

bank . . . and in violation of any statute of the United States, or any larceny—

Shall be fined under this title or imprisoned not more than twenty years, or both.

18 U.S.C. § 2113(a). "As its text makes clear, subsection 2113(a) can be violated in two distinct ways: (1) bank robbery, which involves taking or attempting to take from a bank by force [and violence], intimidation, or extortion; and (2) bank burglary, which simply involves entry or attempted entry into a bank with the intent to commit a crime therein." United States v. Almeida, 710 F.3d 437, 440 (1st Cir. 2013) (emphasis added).

Williams was indicted for attempting to enter a bank with an intent to commit a felony and larceny therein—i.e., a bank burglary. Moreover, his indictment failed to reference "the element of 'force and violence, or [extortion or] intimidation' which is required for conviction of bank robbery" under § 2113(a). United States v. Ketchum, 550 F.3d 363, 365 n.1 (4th Cir. 2008) (quoting United States v. Carter, 540 F.2d 753, 754 (4th Cir. 1976)). Therefore, when one compares the applicable burglary and robbery guidelines with the language of Williams's indictment, it is clear that Williams should have been sentenced under the burglary guideline. . . .

For the foregoing reasons, we vacate Williams's sentence, and remand this case to the district court for resentencing under the burglary guideline.

EXERCISE

Note that in the *Williams* case, it really doesn't matter if the defendant intended to commit a larceny or a robbery once he was inside—either way, what he intended would fulfill the burglary element. Here, the court construed the crime as an "attempted" burglary. Looking at the statute as quoted in the case, could one reasonably argue that the crime was a completed burglary rather than an attempt?

C. EMBEZZLEMENT

If the distinctive element of robbery is force or intimidation and the distinctive element of burglary is the entry of a building, the similarly distinctive element of embezzlement is trust. In embezzlement cases, the government has to not only prove a wrongful taking, but that the defendant was—at least at some point—trusted with possession of the property.

UNITED STATES V. SAYKLAY

542 F. 2d 942 (1976)

GEE, CIRCUIT JUDGE:

Yvonne Sayklay appeals her jury conviction of embezzlement under 18 U.S.C. 656 (1970), claiming that the trial court erred in failing to grant her motion for acquittal based on either a failure of proof or a variance between the accusation and the proof. Reluctantly we conclude that the trial court should have granted the motion for acquittal, and we reverse and grant defendant's motion.

We do so reluctantly because the facts clearly show a violation of 18 U.S.C. s 656 (1970) in that the defendant willfully misapplied the moneys, funds and credit of the bank. She did not, however, embezzle the bank's funds, and this is the offense of which she has been convicted. The defendant was a bookkeeper at the Bank of El Paso in El Paso, Texas. As such, she had access to other bank employees' account numbers, to a check-encoding machine, and to blank counter checks. This she employed to acquire blank counter checks and encode other employees' account numbers on them. She then cashed the encoded checks through a teller. Knowing that the teller would verify only the accounts' status, not the owner of the accounts, she signed her own name to the checks. When they arrived at the bookkeeping department, the defendant destroyed them. Inevitably, one of the employee-victims of the siphoning noticed the discrepancy. Her report provoked an investigation that led to the defendant. The government filed an information (the defendant having waived indictment) charging the defendant with five counts of embezzlement in violation of 18 U.S.C. s 656 (1970). After the government's evidentiary presentation, the defense moved for a judgment of acquittal that the trial judge denied. The jury later convicted the defendant on all five counts.

Long ago the Supreme Court defined "embezzlement" as "the fraudulent appropriation of property by a person to whom such property has been entrusted, or into whose hands it has lawfully come." Moore v. United States, 160 U.S. 268, 269, 16 S.Ct. 294, 295, 40 L.Ed. 422 (1895). See United States v. Trevino, 491 F.2d 74, 75 (5th Cir. 1974); United States v. Kehoe, 365 F.Supp. 920, 923 (S.D.Tex.1973). To support its charges, then, the government had to show that the defendant converted funds in her lawful possession. The government argues that it did so by showing that as a bank employee she was entrusted with all the tools needed to acquire the funds held in the other employees' accounts. With these tools she had access to the funds by means of her plan, and thus constructively possessed the funds in a manner sufficient to meet the possession element of embezzlement.

It is not so: the defendant at no time was entrusted with or came into lawful possession of the funds. Unlike funds in possession of a bank president or a teller, the funds she stole were not entrusted to her in any capacity whatever for the use and benefit of the bank. See United States v. Northway, 120 U.S. 327, 331, 7 S.Ct. 580, 30 L.Ed. 664 (1886) (president); Navarro v. United States, 218 F.2d 360, 361 (5th Cir. 1955) (teller). Even if access to the funds were equivalent to constructive possession, the only way she could get that access would be by unlawful means. Cf. Williams v. United States, 208 F.2d 447 (5th Cir. 1953), cert. denied, 347 U.S. 928, 74 S.Ct. 531, 98 L.Ed. 1081 (1954)(serviceman guilty of theft, not embezzlement, when he requisitioned propeller with intent to steal it and propeller would not normally have come into his possession). Absent initial lawful possession of the funds she stole, the defendant cannot be found guilty of embezzlement.

"Embezzlement" is a technical term, see United States v. Wilson, 500 F.2d 715, 720 (5th Cir. 1974), imbued with a specific meaning. To uphold a conviction for embezzlement under these facts would confuse the distinction that Congress clearly drew between embezzlement and other forms of conversion. See United States v. Beard, 436 F.2d 1084, 1089–90 (5th Cir. 1971). And it remains true that penal statutes are to be strictly construed, with ambiguities resolved in favor of leniency. See United States v. Enmons, 410 U.S. 396, 411, 93 S.Ct. 1007, 35 L.Ed.2d 379 (1973); United States v. Quinn, 514 F.2d 1250, 1259 (5th Cir. 1975). The defendant's wrongful actions render her an undeserving candidate for application of the principle, but doubtless most who require its assistance have been and will be undeserving. More is at stake here than convicting a wrongdoer of something: fidelity to Congress' clear purpose and refusal to convict anyone of a crime of which he has not been and cannot be, on the facts proved guilty. The essence of embezzlement lies in breach of a fiduciary relationship deriving from the entrustment of money. In this case the defendant's position at the bank aided her in her crime, but it did not place her in lawful possession of others' funds that she converted to her own use. This is a hard case, but the bad law (if such it be) was made when Congress chose to carry forward the technical and antediluvian elements by which the Supreme Court long ago distinguished embezzlement from similar crimes.

The government's choice of offense and failure to present evidence establishing an essential element of the offense requires that the trial court's refusal to grant the defendant's motion for acquittal be

REVERSED AND RENDERED.

EXERCISE

Imagine that you are a judge with two sentencings in the same afternoon. The first is the *Sayklay* case above. The second is an identical case from another bank, the only difference being that the defendant in that case was in fact a low-paid teller who did simply took money from her till and was caught. The teller was a first offender with one arrest (for reckless driving) on her record. Assuming the same amount of loss in both cases, would you sentence them to different terms? If so, what is your basis for differentiating between these two defendants?

Embezzlement can involve tricky state of mind elements. For example, while it is common for an embezzlement statute to require proof that a defendant knew he or she was wrongful in depriving someone else of money, that does not mean that the government must prove that the defendant *knew* that the action taken was contrary to a specific statute. The difference is subtle, but can be crucial in embezzlement and other cases.

UNITED STATES V. WISEMAN
274 F. 3d 1235 (9th Cir. 2001)

CYNTHIA HOLCOMB HALL, CIRCUIT JUDGE:

These criminal prosecutions stem from certain transactions involving ERISA pension benefit plans administered by Center Art Galleries ("CAG") for its employees. Mett founded CAG, a retail art gallery, in 1973 and served as its president and sole shareholder. Wiseman served as a vice-president, responsible for staff training and art acquisition. Both defendants also served on the CAG board of directors. In 1977, CAG established two pension benefit plans for its employees. Both plans were funded solely by CAG contributions, and both were covered by ERISA. At all relevant times, Mett and Wiseman served as trustees for both plans, while CAG served as the plan administrator.

CAG fell on hard times in the early 1990s. In 1990, as a result of a federal investigation into CAG's sales practices, Mett, Wiseman, and CAG were indicted, tried and convicted of felony art fraud. The prosecution, coupled with a general downturn in the Hawaiian economy, proved devastating to CAG's financial health. Between March 1990 and November 1991, in order to meet CAG's financial obligations, Mett and Wiseman withdrew approximately $1.6 million from the pension plans and deposited the funds into CAG's general operating accounts. At no time during 1990 and 1991 did the defendants inform their employees of these transactions. CAG also did not disclose the withdrawal transactions on the 1990 Form 5500 that it filed with the IRS in connection with one of the benefit plans.

On June 27, 1996, a federal grand jury returned a 16 count indictment against the defendants in connection with the pension plan withdrawals. At trial, the defense turned on whether the defendants possessed the requisite specific intent when they arranged the withdrawals. While admitting that they withdrew funds from the pension plans, the defendants characterized the withdrawals as "loans" necessary to carry CAG through rough financial times. According to the defendants, their actions were intended to benefit their employees, who would otherwise have been laid off and faced with unemployment. The defendants further argued that the employees implicitly authorized, or would have authorized the withdrawals had they known of them. On June 25, 1997, the jury convicted the defendants on 15 counts, finding them guilty of embezzling from a pension benefit plan, in violation of 18 U.S.C. § 664. . . .

Before their retrial and before agreeing to a bench trial, Defendants proposed a jury instruction that would have required the government to "prove beyond a reasonable doubt that the defendants took money from the funds knowing that it was illegal to do so" to convict Defendants of violating 18 U.S.C. § 664. The district court correctly rejected Defendants' proposed instruction.

A person violates § 664 if he "embezzles, steals, or unlawfully and willfully abstracts or converts to his own use or to the use of another" assets belonging to an employee pension benefit plan subject to ERISA. 18 U.S.C. § 664. In Defendants' prior appeal in this case, we explained that "the essence [of a § 664 offense] is theft and in the context of . . . pension funds the offense includes a taking or appropriation that is unauthorized, if accomplished with specific criminal intent." *Mett,* 178 F.3d at 1067 (alteration in original) (quoting *United States v. Andreen,* 628 F.2d 1236, 1243 (9th Cir.1980)). "The act to be criminal must be willful, which means an act done with a fraudulent intent or a bad purpose or an evil motive." *Andreen,* 628 F.2d at 1241. While the defendant must "knowingly act [ ] wrongfully to deprive another of property," there is no requirement that the defendant also know his conduct was illegal. *United States v. Ford,* 632 F.2d 1354, 1362 (9th Cir.1980), *overruled on other grounds by United States v. DeBright,* 730 F.2d 1255, 1259 (9th Cir.1984) (en banc). . . .

Defendants also requested that the district court instruct the jury, "Since [the defendants] are accused of stealing the plan funds rather than borrowing them, the government must prove beyond a reasonable doubt that the funds at issue were not loaned to [Center Art Galleries ('CAG')]". The instruction further would have required the jurors to acquit if they had "a reasonable doubt as to whether the defendants intended to borrow the money rather than steal it." According to Defendants, because the government's theory of the case was that the transfers from the pension plan to CAG were the result of theft or embezzlement, the government needed to prove that the transfers were not actually loans. Defendants argue that the district court's failure to abide by the law as stated in their proposed instruction resulted in a constructive amendment of the indictment in violation of *Stirone v. United States,* 361 U.S. 212, 80 S.Ct.

270, 4 L.Ed.2d 252 (1960), and *United States v. Shipsey,* 190 F.3d 1081 (9th Cir.1999). We disagree.

Evidence that Defendants borrowed the plan funds may be relevant to their criminal intent. *Cf. Mett,* 178 F.3d at 1068. Intent to repay generally is not a defense to embezzlement, however. *See United States v. Ross,* 206 F.3d 896, 899 (9th Cir.2000). Nor is it a defense to conversion. *See Thordarson,* 646 F.2d at 1335 n. 22 (noting that conversion can be accomplished "without any intent to keep possession, so long as the property is misused or abused" (citing *Morissette v. United States,* 342 U.S. 246, 271–72, 72 S.Ct. 240, 96 L.Ed. 288 (1952))). The government thus did not need to disprove Defendants' intent to borrow the funds to convict them of embezzlement.

EXERCISE

In the typical embezzlement case, funds are taken for personal use. In the *Wiseman* case, they were being taken to save a business, albeit a closely-held business.

If, in fact, the sole purpose of the transfer of funds in *Wiseman* was to save the business, and you were the defense attorney, what defense might you assert?

The type of trust involved in an embezzlement case, and the harm done by the loss, can both be factors at sentencing. Even though these are usually sentencing factors rather than elements going to guilt, they can play a large role in shaping the eventual outcome in a criminal case.

UNITED STATES V. MOLNAR
590 F. 3d 912 (8th Cir. 2010)

BEAM, CIRCUIT JUDGE.

Miklos Molnar appeals his sentence following his plea of guilty to embezzlement. Though his calculated guideline range was ten to sixteen months, the district court varied upward and sentenced Molnar to sixty-months' imprisonment followed by two years of supervised release. We reverse and remand for resentencing.

I.   BACKGROUND

Since 1987, Molnar worked as a police officer in Van Buren, Arkansas. In August 2000, Molnar joined the Drug Enforcement Administration Task Force. In this capacity, Molnar had access to seized drug funds, and he was in charge of the Van Buren Police Department evidence room-one of only three people with a key to this room. Molnar testified at the sentencing hearing that at some point in 2006, he used money from the evidence room to pay personal bills. Initially, he tried to repay the money with his own funds. However, the scheme eventually "got out of control" and he began using one sum of seized money to pay back other seized funds. This process occurred over a two-year period.

A local prosecutor became suspicious when he noticed that Molnar deposited a $1,000 check for "drug buy" money into his personal account. When confronted by the Chief of Police about this, Molnar explained that he had used his personal funds for "drug buy" money and was simply reimbursing himself for the $1,000. The Chief told him not to make this practice a habit because it did not look good. The prosecutor had also complained that Molnar was slow to return $19,000 in funds that a state court ordered were to be returned to a party from whom the funds were confiscated. When the Chief inquired about this situation, Molnar indicated that he could produce the $19,000. However, when the Chief ordered him to go to the evidence room and produce the money, Molnar acknowledged that he could not and admitted to taking seized money from the evidence room for personal use. Molnar pleaded guilty to embezzlement and paid full restitution to the police department.

During sentencing, the following colloquy took place between the district court and the Van Buren Police Chief, discussing the nature of the funds in the evidence room:

> THE COURT: Are some of those funds then used to say purchase drugs or for undercover type activity?
>
> A: No. The Van Buren Police Department itself does not do that, Your Honor. It's something that would, if that money was going to be converted to that use, we would give it to Marc McCune, the prosecutor's office, and let him in turn distribute that through drug buy money or however he wanted to do that.
>
> THE COURT: But these funds would not be drug-couldn't be classified then as potential drug buy money?
>
> A: No. It had not reached that far yet.
>
> THE COURT: But that could have been the use for these funds at some point?
>
> A: It could have been; yes, sir.
>
> THE COURT: And that is done from time to time by your department? Do you use these funds or similar funds to purchase-
>
> A: The Van Buren Police Department itself does not have a so-called drug buy fund. Individual officers, narcotic officers are responsible for drug buy money that they receive from Marc

McCune, the Prosecuting Attorney. The city itself does not have [a] so-called drug buy fund account; no.

Later, when Molnar was on the witness stand, the district court similarly questioned him about the issue.

THE COURT: Could any of funds that you admittedly embezzled, $50,997, could that have been used for drug buy money in any sense?

A: It could have been converted by the prosecutor's office to that, Your Honor, once it's turned over to them.

THE COURT: But if the money is not there, you would have difficulty in turning anything over, would you not?

A: Yes, sir.

Prior to pronouncing sentence, the district court sustained Molnar's two objections to the presentence investigation report (PSIR), reiterated that he had previously notified the parties of his possible intent to impose either an upward departure or variance, and set forth the statutory penalties for the offense. The court found that Molnar's offense level was twelve but added two levels for violation of the fiduciary trust relationship. Molnar's criminal history category was one and the advisory guideline range was ten to sixteen months. After taking one last round of argument from counsel, the court noted it had reviewed the sentencing factors reflected in 18 U.S.C. § 3553(a), and announced that it would sentence Molnar to a term of sixty-months' imprisonment followed by two years of supervised release.

The court found that Molnar's crime violated the public trust in law enforcement, stating that "[l]awbreaking by a high-ranking police officer promotes disrespect for the law and must be addressed at this sentencing." The district court also stated it was concerned that "some of these funds that were used and utilized were not available to the DEA where those funds could have been used to purchase drugs from drug dealers, so I think your activities have significantly impaired multiple drug prevention work." Immediately following this statement, the court asked Molnar's counsel whether he had any objections to the court's stated intentions beyond what had already been raised, and counsel replied that he did not have any further objections.

II. DISCUSSION

Molnar argues that the district court committed a procedural sentencing error by relying on clearly erroneous factual findings with regard to Molnar's actions significantly impairing department drug prevention work, i.e., the inability of the department to use seized funds for "drug buy" money due to Molnar's actions. Because Molnar did not object to this alleged error before the district court, we review for plain error. *United States v. Miller,* 557 F.3d 910, 916 (8th Cir.2009). To establish plain error,

Molnar must prove that (1) there was error, (2) the error was plain, and (3) the error affected his substantial rights. *United States v. Olano,* 507 U.S. 725, 732, 113 S.Ct. 1770, 123 L.Ed.2d 508 (1993). An error affects a substantial right if the error was prejudicial. *Id.* at 734, 113 S.Ct. 1770. In the sentencing context, an error is prejudicial only if the defendant proves a reasonable probability that he would have received a lighter sentence but for the error. *United States v. Pirani,* 406 F.3d 543, 552 (8th Cir.2005) (en banc). However, a fourth *Olano* factor dictates that we will exercise our discretion to correct such an error only if the error "seriously affect[s] the fairness, integrity, or public reputation of judicial proceedings." *Olano,* 507 U.S. at 732, 113 S.Ct. 1770 (alteration in original) (internal quotations and citations omitted).

We find that the district court's assertion that Molnar's actions hindered drug task force agents from having adequate "drug buy" money was inaccurate and, therefore, was error. And, we find that this error was plain because there was no evidence that undercover drug task force work was actually impaired. Instead, the record showed that Molnar originally became the target of suspicion after the prosecutor noticed he had deposited a $1,000 check for "drug buy" money into his personal account, but Molnar was never accused of embezzling this particular sum of money. With regard to the $19,000 in confiscated funds, while perhaps Molnar's actions delayed the individual with rights to the $19,000 from reclaiming his seized cash in a timely manner, there was no evidence that drug task force agents confronted similar problems.

Furthermore, the error was plain under clearly established Arkansas law, which would not have allowed drug task force officers to walk into the evidence room, take cash, and use the cash to make controlled drug buys. As the Arkansas Court of Appeals noted in *State v. Hammame,* 102 Ark. App. 87, 282 S.W.3d 278, 281 (2008), the process is more complex than that. Instead, a prosecuting attorney must initiate forfeiture proceedings that do not in any way involve the seizing agency. *Id.;* Ark.Code Ann. § 5–64–505(e), (f), (h), (i). In fact, the seizing agency has no claim to the property unless and until it is ordered forfeited by the court, and even at that point, where the money is distributed is statutorily conditioned. *Hammame,* 282 S.W.3d at 281. Finally, "known owners or interest holders are entitled to seized property if it is not forfeited." *Id.* (citing Ark.Code Ann. § 5–64–505(g)(3)(C), (g)(5)(A)(iii)(b)).

Accordingly, the seized money being stored in the evidence room certainly could not have been the direct source for "drug buy" money—i.e., a DEA agent could not simply walk into the evidence room, take money, and use it for a drug buy. Furthermore, under the facts of this case, the seized money could not have been an indirect source for "drug buy" money because there is no evidence that the court ordered money forfeited, that forfeited money was designated for use as "drug buy" money, but then the money was unavailable for use. There was simply no testimony or other evidence that drug task force agents were "significantly impaired" in their abilities to perform drug prevention work due to Molnar's actions. Accordingly, the district court's reference to "drug buy" money to justify a substantial upward variance to Molnar's sentence was plain error.

The next question is whether this error affected Molnar's substantial rights, which in this context means whether Molnar can prove he would have received a lighter sentence absent the error. Having carefully reviewed the sentencing transcript, we find that Molnar can meet this burden. The district court seemed especially interested in the idea that drug task force agents were hampered in their duties due to money missing from the Van Buren Police Department evidence room. The district court questioned two witnesses about the issue at the sentencing hearing, and reiterated this concern when pronouncing Molnar's sentence. Though the district court did mention one other factor in its decision to vary upward, we find that given the extent of the variance, there is a reasonable probability that had the district court not plainly erred in considering the facts relating to "drug buy" money, it would not have varied upward to the extent—275%—that it did.

7Finally, we consider the fourth *Olano* factor and find that leaving the error uncorrected would result in a miscarriage of justice substantially affecting the fairness, integrity or public reputation of the proceedings. *Olano,* 507 U.S. at 732, 113 S.Ct. 1770. On numerous past occasions where a defendant has met his burden of proving that there is a reasonable probability he would have received a lighter sentence absent plain error, we have exercised our discretion under the fourth factor and vacated the sentence. *E.g., United States v. Nahia,* 437 F.3d 715, 717 (8th Cir.2006) (holding that we felt "compelled" to follow circuit precedent and vacate for resentencing when defendant had met the first three *Olano* factors, even without a more stringent analysis of the fourth factor). Accordingly, we follow circuit precedent and vacate Molnar's sentence and remand to the district court for resentencing.

III. CONCLUSION

For the reasons stated herein we reverse the sentence and remand to the district court for resentencing.

EXERCISE

If you were the prosecutor in the Molnar case, what arguments would you make on remand (that is, the re-sentencing of the case after this decision) in order to convince the judge to issue the same sentence again?

D. FRAUD

The distinctive element in fraud cases is deception. The definition of fraud overlaps with crimes known in some jurisdictions as "larceny by trick" and "false pretenses." Most commonly, fraud is understood to be the intentional use of wrongful deception for personal gain. That doesn't mean, of course, that it is always easy to tell when deception is being used.

UNITED STATES V. STEPHENS

421 F.3d 503 (7th Cir. 2005)

ILANA DIAMOND ROVNER, CIRCUIT JUDGE.

Wayne Stephens was employed as a manager in a technical support unit for Accenture's New York office when he repeatedly used an "add to pay" function on his time and expense reports to obtain a total of approximately $67,395 in unauthorized cash advances for personal use. That conduct resulted in his criminal conviction for wire fraud in violation of 18 U.S.C. § 1343.

In his position at Accenture, Stephens was required to use the computer program called Automatic Remote Time and Expense System (ARTES) to file a bi-weekly time and expense report (hereinafter "expense report") that was used in calculating his paycheck. Through ARTES, employees would input information regarding expenses incurred, and Accenture would use that information to bill the client and to reimburse the employee in the paycheck. Employees could request reimbursement for business-related expenses by filling in the fields labeled "expenses without receipt," "expenses with receipt," and "business meals." In addition, the form included a "add to pay/deduct from pay" line which allowed employees to add to or deduct from their paychecks. The "deduct from pay" line could be used for certain personal expenses, such as charges incurred by employees as a result of personal telephone calls or use of a concierge service that Accenture operated for its employees.

The proper use of the "add to" function was at issue in the trial. Some testimony indicated that the "add to" function was to be used only for business-related expenses such as expenses related to international assignments or employee relocations. Stephens, on the other hand, argued that there was no policy related to the use of that function, and that it could be used for personal expenses. Prior to January 2000, Accenture's written Policy 526 stated that "[c]ash advances are not provided via time reports nor through petty cash in the offices." In January 2000, however, that policy was replaced by Policy 63.044, which did not contain that sentence. Policy 526 was in place at the time Stephens was hired, but Policy 63.044 had subsumed it by the time of the criminal actions.

Therefore, during the time period of the conduct at issue here, Accenture did not have a written policy regarding the availability of cash advances through the time and expense reports. Accenture's Policy 63.044 did expressly allow the use of corporate credit cards for cash advances or for personal expenses, but further declared that Accenture had no liability for the balance on the accounts and that employees were required to directly pay the entire balance on their monthly statements.

Once an employee completed the expense report, it was sent electronically to Accenture's processing center and its payroll department, where the employee's check was automatically generated based upon that information and deposited into the employee's bank account. Approximately 5% of the expense reports were audited after they were submitted. In addition, the expense reports contained a field for the name of the employee's supervisor, and a copy of the expense report was automatically sent to that designated supervisor upon submission. The supervisor could also access a supervisee's expense report by using the "auditor's view" of the ARTES program and typing in the supervisee's identification number.

When Stephens was hired in May 1999, his supervisor was Sandra Lieb-Gieger. Lieb-Gieger required Stephens to submit his expense report to her the day before it was due. She would then review it and once approved, would personally submit it to the processing center. While Lieb-Gieger was his supervisor, Stephens often recorded business expenses, but never sought a cash advance using the "add to" function. He also consistently entered Lieb-Gieger's name in the reviewer field. Beginning in March 2000, Neil Penney became Stephens' supervisor. Penney did not preapprove expense reports prior to submission to the processing department. Instead, Penney allowed Stephens to submit the expense reports directly to the processing department, but required Stephens to e-mail a copy to him. Penney testified, however, that he did not check those expense reports and did not notice when his supervisees failed to e-mail copies to him.

In March 2000, shortly after Penney became his supervisor, Stephens submitted his expense report and e-mailed a copy to Penney. Stephens did not request a cash advance through the "add to" function on that expense report. Beginning on April 30, 2000, however, Stephens began utilizing the "add to" function to secure cash advances. His April 30 expense report requested a cash advance in the amount of $7,800. Stephens did not include Penney's name in the reviewer field of that expense report, instead designating himself as his own reviewer, and he did not e-mail a copy to Penney. He also requested reimbursement for business expenses in the amount of $78.00. The government argued at trial that Stephens used the $7,800 figure in the "add to" function because, if confronted, he could argue that it reflected his business expenses of $78.00 and was a mistake in the placement of the decimal point.

Stephens continued that use of the "add to" function for the next six expense reports. On each of six expense reports between April 30 and July 31, 2000, Stephens requested cash advances in amounts between $9,800 and $9,985, increasing his cash advance yield to $67,395. None of those reports were reviewed by Penney because Stephens did not e-mail a copy to Penney and did not include Penney's name in the reviewer field, thus bypassing the automatic sending of the report to Penney.

In his August 15, 2000, expense report, Stephens deviated from his previous pattern of keeping his requests slightly under the $10,000 mark. Instead, he requested a cash advance of $22,980. That request was noticed by Accenture's audit team, and Stephens was fired on August 23, 2000 based on unauthorized cash advances.

Stephens was subsequently convicted of wire fraud and sentenced to 21 months' imprisonment, 2 years supervised release, and $50,000 in restitution. He appeals that conviction, alleging that the evidence was insufficient to support the jury verdict. . . .

In order to convict Stephens of wire fraud under 18 U.S.C. § 1341, the jury had to find that: (1) there was a scheme to defraud; (2) wires were used in furtherance on the scheme; and (3) Stephens participated in the scheme with the intent to defraud. *Owens,* 301 F.3d at 528. Stephens contends that the jury could not rationally find either a scheme to defraud or the intent to defraud. Instead, Stephens contends that the evidence at best establishes simple theft. He argues that the government failed to demonstrate that Accenture's policy expressly prohibited Stephens from making requests for personal cash advances. Furthermore, he asserts that the government failed to establish that he made affirmative misrepresentations or misleading statements when seeking the cash advances or that he engaged in elaborate efforts to conceal his cash requests.

In determining whether conduct evinced a scheme to defraud, the Supreme Court has noted that the words "to defraud" in the mail fraud statute "refer 'to wronging one in his property rights by dishonest methods or schemes,' and 'usually signify the deprivation of something of value by trick, deceit, chicane or overreaching.' " *McNally v. United States,* 483 U.S. 350, 358, 107 S.Ct. 2875, 97 L.Ed.2d 292 (1987), quoting *Hammerschmidt v. United States,* 265 U.S. 182, 188, 44 S.Ct. 511, 68 L.Ed. 968 (1924); . . . . We have previously held that "a necessary element of a scheme to defraud is the making of a false statement or material misrepresentation, or the concealment of a material fact." *Williams v. Aztar Indiana Gaming Corp.,* 351 F.3d 294, 299 (7th Cir.2003). We have held that the concept includes both statements that the defendant knows to be false, as well as a "half truth" that the defendant knows to be misleading and which the defendant expects another to act upon to his detriment and the defendant's benefit. *Emery v. American General Finance, Inc.,* 71 F.3d 1343, 1346 (7th

Cir.1995). In *Emery,* we further noted that "[a] half truth, or what is usually the same thing a misleading omission, is actionable as fraud . . . if it is intended to induce a false belief and resulting action to the advantage of the misleader and the disadvantage of the misled." *Id.* at 1348. The mere failure to disclose information will not always constitute fraud, but an omission accompanied by acts of concealment or affirmative misrepresentations can constitute fraud.

The government presented sufficient evidence for a rational jury to find a scheme to defraud. Stephens utilized the cash advance field in his expense report although the money was not sought for any purpose related to work. A jury could find that the request for funds on that expense report carried the implied representation that it was for purposes related to work. Moreover, even if a jury were inclined to believe Stephens that he thought the "add to" line could be used to receive cash advances that he could subsequently repay using the "deduct from" line, a jury could find that Stephens' actions were inconsistent with that use of the "add to" option. The sheer frequency of his requests, along with the increasingly large amounts requested, belie any intention of repaying the funds and are inconsistent with what an employee could reasonably believe an employer would allow. Accenture allowed the use of credit cards for cash advances, but held the employee responsible for clearing the balances on a monthly basis. Given those conditions on the use of the credit card, the contention that Stephens' actions were a proper use of the "add to" function need not be credited. Accordingly, a jury could find that Stephens used that function in a[n] improper manner to obtain corporate funds for personal use.

Moreover, a jury could find that Stephens engaged in a number of actions to conceal his acquisition of the cash. Accenture maintained a system of supervisor review to ensure that only authorized expenses were allowed. When Lieb-Gieger was Stephens' supervisor, she reviewed his expense reports prior to submission, and Stephens never attempted to seek cash advances using the "add to" function. He also did not do so in his first expense report under his new supervisor, Penney. With his second expense report under Penney's supervision, Stephens did not use the "add to" function, but included his own name rather than Penney's in the reviewer field and did not forward a copy of the report to Penney via e-mail. Only when those actions went unchallenged, indicating that his expense reports were not being monitored, did Stephens proceed to use the "add to" line to acquire cash.

Even then, he structured his first request in a manner to avoid suspicion, seeking $7,800 under the "add to" function while seeking $78.00 in payment for proper business expenses. A jury could find that the amounts were calculated to provide him with a plausible explanation if the "add to" request was noticed, in that he could claim that it merely reflected the $78.00 business expenses and he misplaced the decimal point. When that request was successful, Stephens increased the amount of the requests, but kept the amount just under the $10,000 amount that could possibly trigger an audit-another indication that he was attempting to avoid detection.

Stephens nevertheless argues that he made no misrepresentations or misleading omissions, and that his actions therefore constitutes simple thefts at worst. A similar argument was made, unsuccessfully, in *United States v. Lack,* 129 F.3d 403, 406 (7th Cir.1997), a case which involved mail fraud. Lack was employed as a materials manager by Dairyland Power Cooperative ("Dairyland"), responsible for the sale of scrap or salvage items on behalf of Dairyland. *Id.* at 404. In that capacity, he devised a scheme to steal money from Dairyland. He accomplished this by opening a checking account in the name of Darrell H. Lack, d/b/a Dairyland Power Conversion, division of Midwest Computer. *Id.* at 404–05. Bank statements were mailed to Lack providing a record of all action on that account. *Id.* at 405. When Lack sold a scrap or salvage item to a buyer, he would deposit the check in that checking account rather than forwarding it to his employer. *Id.* Occasionally, he would forward a check in a smaller amount to his employer Dairyland, with the original purchaser listed as remittur. *Id.* That check would either be delivered or mailed to Dairyland. *Id.* Lack argued that his actions constituted a series of simple thefts rather than a scheme to defraud, because he merely took the funds that were meant for Dairyland, but did not do so by means of deception. *Id.* at 406. We rejected that argument.

We held that the pattern of deceit and the use of false pretenses by Lack constituted a scheme to defraud. *Id.* Essentially, Lack obtained funds meant for one purpose (implicitly at least representing to the buyers that they were paying the proper party for the purchases), converted them to his own personal use, and then engaged in conduct designed to deceive his employer so as to prevent the employer from obtaining knowledge of his improper use of the money. *Id.* That is similar to the scheme in the present case. Stephens obtained funds through the "add to" provision meant to clear an existing personal expense balance that Accenture owed employees. He then converted them to his own personal use even though he knew Accenture did not owe him any money and that his use was unrelated to his employment. In order to evade detection, he misrepresented the name of his reviewer on the form, failed to send the copy to his supervisor as required, and structured his requests and his other expense requests so as to avoid an audit. That evinces the type of pattern of deceit that properly demonstrates a scheme to defraud.

Stephens also contends that the jury lacked sufficient evidence to find an intent to defraud. The intent requirement targets "a willful act by the defendant with the specific intent to deceive or cheat, usually for the purpose of getting financial gain for one's self or causing financial loss to another." *Owens,* 301 F.3d at 528. Because direct evidence of fraudulent intent is rare, " 'specific intent to defraud may be established by circumstantial evidence and by inferences drawn from examining the scheme itself that demonstrate that the scheme was reasonably calculated to deceive persons of ordinary prudence and comprehension.' " *Id.,* quoting *Paneras,* 222 F.3d at 410.

Examination of the scheme in this case provides ample evidence that it was reasonably calculated to deceive. Stephens began his "add to" request only after changing supervisors and ascertaining that his new supervisor was not monitoring the expense reports. He structured his requests so as to avoid detection, beginning with an amount that resembled his proper business expenses so as to provide him with an explanation if it were detected. After that request was successful, he continued the requests, keeping them near, but not over, the $10,000 mark that could plausibly trigger an audit. In each case, he prevented detection by failing to correctly identify his reviewer on the form and by failing to e-mail a copy to his supervisor. Those actions were reasonably calculated to deceive his employer as to the unauthorized cash payments he was receiving. The evidence was sufficient to support the jury verdict here.

EXERCISE

It is hard not to notice that Accenture—a consulting company that advises companies on how to be more efficient and productive—had systems and oversight procedures that made it relatively easy for the defendant in *Stephens* to commit fraud. In a criminal case, is it at all relevant that the victim was ineffective at preventing fraud? If so, should this matter regardless of whether the victim is a large corporation or an elderly individual?

Good faith can sometimes serve as a defense to fraud charges. If a defendant truly believed what they were saying to be true—even if it was in fact misleading—this sometimes will be seen as something other than a fraudulent statement, and the proofs going to that element will fail. Showing that kind of good faith belief can be a challenge to the defense, of course, particularly if the fraudulent transaction lead to the enrichment of the defendant.

UNITED STATES V. DUPRE
339 F. Supp. 2d 534 (S.D.N.Y. 2004)

COTE, DISTRICT JUDGE.

The Government has moved *in limine* to exclude mental health evidence that it anticipates defendant Roberta Dupre will offer at trial. Dupre seeks to offer evidence that she was acting in good faith during the time of the fraud alleged here because of her belief that she is guided by God. For the following reasons, the motion is granted. . . .

On March 22, 2004, Roberta Dupre and Beverly Stambaugh were indicted for wire fraud, 18 U.S.C. § 1343, and conspiracy to commit wire fraud, 18 U.S.C. § 371. The indictment alleged that from October 2002 to February 2004, Dupre and Stambaugh operated a scheme to defraud potential investors by falsely inducing them to pay "advance fees" in order to secure the release and distribution of approximately $9 billion in frozen funds purportedly belonging to the family of former Filipino president Ferdinand Marcos. Dupre and Stambaugh allegedly promised investors a return of approximately $1 million for each $1,000 invested. . . .

Dupre argues that the testimony of a psychologist will assist the jury in determining whether she was acting in good faith, and therefore should be admitted. On October 1, Dupre submitted a written forensic psychological evaluation that documents her psychologist's findings and concludes that Dupre suffers from Bipolar Disorder with Psychotic Features and a personality disorder, both of which result in her sometimes "misperceiv[ing] important aspects of reality." The evaluation asserts that such misperceptions affect "her thinking about the investment project and her beliefs about the Lord's role and her own role in this project." . . .

Dupre is charged with one count of wire fraud, 18 U.S.C. § 1343, and one count of conspiracy to commit wire fraud, 18 U.S.C. § 371. The wire fraud statute assigns penalties to anyone who,

> having devised or intending to devise any scheme or artifice to defraud, or for obtaining money or property by means of false or fraudulent pretenses, representations, or promises, transmits or causes to be transmitted by means of wire . . . communication in interstate or foreign commerce, any writings . . . or sounds for the purpose of executing such scheme or artifice.

18 U.S.C. § 1343. An essential element of this crime is intent to defraud. The Government must prove that the defendant engaged or participated in a fraudulent scheme with an understanding of its fraudulent or deceptive character and with an intention to be involved in the scheme and to help it succeed with a purpose of causing actual financial harm to another. *United States v. Guadagna,* 183 F.3d 122, 129 (2d Cir.1999). Under the wire fraud statute, even false representations or statements or omissions of material facts do not amount to a fraud unless done with fraudulent intent. *Id.* However misleading or deceptive a plan may be, it is not fraudulent if it was devised or carried out in good faith. A defendant's honest belief in the truth of representations made by her is a complete defense, however inaccurate the statements may turn out to be. Nevertheless, fraudulent intent may be proven by showing that the defendant made misrepresentations with knowledge that the statements were false. *Id.* Moreover,

where some immediate loss to the victim is contemplated by a defendant, the fact that the defendant believes (rightly or wrongly) that he will 'ultimately' be able to work things out so that the victim suffers no loss is no excuse for the real and immediate loss contemplated to result from defendant's fraudulent conduct.

United States v. Rossomando, 144 F.3d 197, 201 (2d Cir.1998). Thus, intent is an essential element of the wire fraud statute. . . .

A district court may admit the testimony of an expert if her knowledge will "assist the trier of fact to understand the evidence or to determine a fact in issue." Fed.R.Evid. 702. District courts serve a "gatekeeping" function and must ensure that an expert's testimony "rests on a reliable foundation and is relevant to the task at hand." *Daubert v. Merrell Dow Pharmaceuticals, Inc.,* 509 U.S. 579, 597, 113 S.Ct. 2786, 125 L.Ed.2d 469 (1993). *See also Wills v. Amerada Hess Corp.,* 379 F.3d 32, 48 (2d Cir.2004). Like all evidence, such expert testimony must "make the existence of any fact that is of consequence to the determination of the action more probable or less probable than it would be without the evidence," Fed.R.Evid. 401, and may be excluded if its "probative value is substantially outweighed by the danger of unfair prejudice, confusion of the issues, or misleading the jury." Fed.R.Evid. 403. *See United States v. Mulder,* 273 F.3d 91, 101 (2d Cir.2001).

There are special concerns for relevance and potential jury confusion in the case of expert testimony regarding mental disease evidence offered in an attempt to negate the intent element of an offense. Testimony about mental disease should not be allowed where it is offered to support the conclusion, or will mislead the jury into concluding, that the defendant was temporarily insane, that the disease caused the defendant to commit the crime or otherwise impaired her ability to exert volitional control, or that the disease impaired the defendant's ability to reflect on the consequences of her conduct. . . .

Dupre proposes to offer the testimony of a clinical psychologist in an effort to negate the *mens rea* elements of her charged offenses. In support of this testimony, Dupre submitted a lengthy forensic psychological evaluation prepared by the psychologist based in large part on six hours of clinical interviews, as well as data from a series of psychological tests, prior statements made by Dupre in connection with this case, and a review of journals written by Dupre during the time of the charged offense conduct. The evaluation describes Dupre's life history from childhood to the present as it bears on her psychological condition, the history of Dupre's religious beliefs, a recitation of Dupre's account of the events leading to her arrest and her understanding of her current legal problems, psychological findings based on a mental status exam and behavioral observations, psychological findings based on psychological testing such as the PAI (Personality Assessment Inventory), MMPI-2 (Minnesota Multiphasic

Personality Inventory-2), and Rorschach (Exner's Comprehensive System), and a formal diagnosis.

The evaluation begins by describing Dupre's religious background and the development of her belief system. Dupre was raised in what she describes as a strict, Catholic family. The report describes that Dupre's mother was often emotionally and occasionally physically abusive towards her during her childhood. The report also describes successive stressful experiences throughout the course of her life, such as three divorces, losing various jobs, moving around the country, and enduring back surgery and a hysterectomy. In the late 1970s she heard God speaking to her as she suffered a heart attack. The evaluation indicates that when her father died on June 30, 1987, "this was the point that the Lord marked as the beginning of her 'faith walk,'" wherein she "finally surrendered herself to complete trust" in God. She describes her international finance "company," Global Exchange, which is apparently the vehicle for the fraud alleged here, as having the goal of "the creation of a foundation to spread evangelism." Dupre reports that she first heard God's voice thirty-nine years ago, and that she developed the habit of "journaling" what she heard God telling her. She reportedly hears God's voice "inside her own head," except for one occasion when she heard God's voice coming from outside herself.

The evaluation also provides details about how Dupre's religious beliefs have affected her participation in the investment scheme at the heart of this case. Dupre reports becoming involved in the scheme in the Philippines in 1994, which she "attributes directly to hearing a message from God to do so." Indeed, she reports that she was specially selected by God to participate in the scheme. The evaluation describes how Dupre worked with a woman in the Philippines on the scheme, and how she "felt that there were things she was not being told," but she explains that she could not have questioned her participation in the scheme because "her conviction was that she was 'led by the Lord.'" Dupre states that the scheme is part of a "shift taking place in the financial world" where the "wealth of the wicked" will end up in the "hands of the righteous," and expresses confidence that "when the frozen funds are released, this will be the beginning of the 'end time harvest,'" which will place some of the money into the hands of the righteous.

In describing the diagnostic results from psychological testing, the evaluation provides an overall assessment of Dupre's cognitive abilities and emotional well-being. On one hand, the evaluation describes Dupre's thought processes as "quite difficult, and at times impossible, to follow, particularly when she is discussing the investment project." Dupre's testing results are apparently "noteworthy in underscoring the defensive functions of Ms. Dupre's grandiose beliefs, such that in times of stress and distress, she is likely to cling to these ideas with increased rigidity and intensity." According to the evaluation, at such times Dupre "is likely to have difficulties separating reality from fantasy," and she may "come to hasty conclusions with only cursory attention paid to relevant information." On the other hand, the evaluation describes how Dupre is "grossly cognitively intact and of above average intelligence," as well as "clearly capable of good judgment." According to the evaluation, as a result, "at some times she is able to perceive things realistically and exhibit cognitive flexibility, while at others, she limits the information to which she attends, misperceives important aspects of reality, and exhibits rigidity in her thinking."

Pursuant to the *Diagnostic and Statistical Manual of Mental Disorders, Fourth Edition* (DSM-IV), the evaluation consequently diagnoses Dupre as having Bipolar Disorder with Psychotic Features and a personality disorder and concludes that

> Ms. Dupre's intense, pervasive religious beliefs significantly interfere with her ability to see her involvement in the 'investment project' in a realistic manner and significantly contribute to her ongoing conviction that she has been involved in a legitimate enterprise with benevolent intentions.

Nonetheless, the evaluation also stresses that Dupre's "difficulties with reality testing, while at times substantial, are not pervasive, and are currently not posing any interference at this juncture with her maintaining a basically accurate understanding of legal proceedings."

Determining whether to admit this particular type of expert testimony can be challenging due to the ethereal line prior cases have drawn between impermissible mental disease evidence addressing a defendant's inability to engage in normal reflection, and permissible mental disease evidence advancing a "legitimate" *mens rea* theory. Nonetheless, Rule 403, Fed.R.Evid., mandates that courts weigh the probative nature of evidence against factors such as its capacity to mislead or confuse the jury, and to exclude evidence where the latter factors substantially outweigh its probative qualities. On balance, the expert testimony proffered in this case demonstrates a substantial capacity to mislead the jury, while providing little additional helpful information to the jury. Much of the evaluation underscores Dupre's belief that she has been compelled to participate in the scheme by God. She claims that God instructed her to participate, and that she was being "led by the Lord" throughout her participation. Such evidence is strongly suggestive of "volitional" evidence that is foreclosed by the IDRA, as evidence of the defendant's inability to control her behavior. *See Cameron,* 907 F.2d at 1066. The presentation of such evidence to the jury creates a substantial risk that it will be used for an impermissible purpose during deliberations. Moreover, this evidence is inextricably linked to other aspects of the psychological evaluation, because it forms an important basis for the conclusions therein. Attempting to parse out objectionable components would severely undercut the basis for the testimony in the first place, and would render it unhelpful to the jury.

The evaluation also suffers from problems of generality that make it insufficiently probative to overcome the possible prejudice and confusion such testimony could cause. The analysis indicates that Dupre's condition is not all-encompassing, that she is "clearly capable of good judgment," and that her difficulties with reality testing, although at times substantial, are not pervasive. Given that she has the capacity to perceive things realistically and exhibits cognitive flexibility, the usefulness of the expert testimony in determining whether Dupre was lucid *during the course* of her participation in a complex, multi-year scheme is substantially reduced. The report's acknowledgment of the defendant's largely intact cognitive system significantly reduces any probative value the report could have on the question of whether Dupre's perception of reality was consistently clouded for such an extended period of time.

Other conclusions about the times when Dupre *does* suffer from her condition are too general to be helpful. For example, the conclusion that Dupre is vulnerable to episodes of affective disturbance and depression that "interfere with her functioning" is not helpful in determining precisely how such episodes would interfere with her functioning, and is similar to the excluded conclusion in *Schneider,* 111 F.3d at 202, that the defendant's mental condition produced "impaired judgment." Finally, the bulk of the evaluation simply restates claims made by Dupre, and consequently is unhelpful under the Rule 702 analysis of *DiDomenico.*

In sum, the report causes great concern for its capacity to mislead and confuse the jury, and to permit the defendant to put an impermissible theory of justification before the jury without meeting her burden of presenting the affirmative defense of insanity. Moreover, it does not offer useful admissible evidence that Dupre may have been continuously affected by her condition throughout the years and in connection with the many, various tasks in which she participated with the alleged fraud. It also substantially restates evidence that can easily be developed through other sources. Therefore, since its limited probative value is substantially outweighed by the danger of unfair prejudice, confusion of the issues, and its tendency to mislead the jury, the proffered expert testimony based on the psychologist's evaluation is excluded.

CONCLUSION

The Government's request to exclude the defendant's proffered expert mental health evidence is granted.

EXERCISE

The defendant in *Dupre* did not seek to be found not guilty by reason of insanity. Rather, she wanted to use mental health as a way to challenge the government's ability to prove her state of mind.

Courts often struggle with issues relating to mental health, and that will be the focus of a later chapter here. In those cases, expert testimony is crucial. Had the defense produced to the court a more thorough expert report, might they have been successful? What should the defense have sought to add to the report?

E. EXTORTION

While robbery occurs when an offender gets money or other property through threats of violence, extortion is defined as obtaining property through threats that may or may not promise the potential of violence. The federal Hobbes Act defines "extortion" broadly to include getting someone's property with their consent through "fear."[3]

If Dave shows Ronald a gun and says he will shoot him if Ronald doesn't give him his wallet, that fits the definition of robbery as already discussed. If instead Dave tells Ronald that if he doesn't give up his wallet Dave will publish embarrassing photos of Ronald, that is extortion (but not robbery). One challenge in extortion cases can be that much of the behavior that makes up the crime is legal; it is only a holistic view of the actions that show it to be "wrongful."

UNITED STATES V. COSS
677 F. 3d 278 (6th Cir. 2012)

KAREN NELSON MOORE, CIRCUIT JUDGE.

This direct criminal appeal concerns the conviction of defendants Scott Edward Sippola ("Sippola") and Allison Lenore Coss ("Coss") for extortion of a celebrity. Sippola and Coss challenge the sufficiency of the indictment forming the basis for their convictions, as well as the constitutionality of the extortion statute under which they were charged. They also appeal the district court's determination that they were not entitled to a downward adjustment for acceptance of responsibility pursuant to § 3E1.1 of the United States Sentencing Guidelines("U.S.S.G."). Because the indictment was sufficient, the extortion statute is constitutional, and their sentences were properly imposed, we AFFIRM the defendants' convictions and sentences.

---

[3]   18 U.S.C. § 1951(b)(2).

I. BACKGROUND AND PROCEDURAL HISTORY

A. Background

In April 2004, John Stamos ("Stamos"), a well-known actor, visited the Walt Disney World resort area in Orlando, Florida with a group of male friends. During the trip, Stamos met Coss, who was seventeen years old at the time, at an eighteen-and-over night club at Pleasure Island. Coss gave Stamos her phone number and, the following day, Stamos invited Coss and her girlfriend, Qynn, to join Stamos and his friends in a guided tour of the Disney parks. That evening Coss and Qynn also attended a party at Stamos's hotel room. Alcohol was served at the party, and Coss testified that illegal drugs, including cocaine and ecstasy, were used by attendees. Photographs of Stamos and Coss were taken during the party. Prior to leaving Florida, Stamos and Coss exchanged email addresses.

Stamos and Coss corresponded periodically for five or six years following their meeting in Florida. In addition, in October 2005, Coss flew to Chicago to visit Stamos while he was filming an episode of the television show "ER." Stamos characterized their relationship as "friends," R. 13 (Trial Tr. at 367:15, 368:19), and testified that their email correspondence was "sweet" and "flirty," *id.* at 368:12–22. Coss also testified that she considered Stamos a "friend," R. 114 (Trial Tr. at 812:9–10), although she maintained that they kissed while in Florida and Chicago, *id.* at 766:9–769:17, 772:2–3.

In 2008, Coss began dating Sippola. After Sippola saw photographs that Coss had of Stamos from the trip to Florida in 2004, Sippola suggested that they attempt to sell them. Subsequently, the two devised and executed a plan to obtain money from Stamos in exchange for the photographs. The scheme involved the creation of two fictitious personas through whom Coss and Sippola initiated email correspondence with Stamos: "Jessica T." and "Brian L."

On September 15, 2009, Coss and Sippola sent Stamos an email purporting to be from "Jessica Taylor" via the email address "jessi_t0909@yahoo.com." In the email, "Jessica Taylor" claimed to be a seventeen-year-old girl whom Stamos had impregnated during a sexual encounter while on vacation. On September 19, 2009, after receiving no response from Stamos, Coss and Sippola sent a second email from the "Jessica Taylor" email account that urged Stamos to respond and stated: "That night was full of drinking and drugs and I am sure you do not want any of those pictures to get out." Tr. Exh.App. at 2. Stamos sent both emails from "Jessica Taylor" to his lawyer, and his lawyer sent a cease-and-desist letter to the email account. Stamos did not receive any further emails from "Jessica Taylor."

In October 2009, Coss initiated email correspondence with Stamos, which continued through the end of November 2009. Throughout this correspondence, Coss relayed to Stamos that someone, whom she later identified as "Brian," had obtained "bad" photographs from the night of the party in April 2004. *See, e.g.,* Tr. Exh.App. at 11, 19. In subsequent emails, Coss told Stamos that there were pictures of them using drugs and "trashing the hotel room." *Id.* at 19. Coss also told Stamos that "Brian" was threatening to sell the photographs to a tabloid unless Coss purchased the photographs from him, and Coss asked for Stamos's assistance in resolving the matter.

Eventually, Coss suggested that Stamos and "Brian" communicate directly regarding Stamos's potential purchase of the photographs. Coss and Sippola, pretending to be "Brian," then initiated correspondence with Stamos regarding his purchase of the photographs from the email address "bdawgs8181 @yahoo.com." By this point in the communications, Stamos's lawyer had contacted law enforcement and the Federal Bureau of Investigation ("FBI") had launched an investigation. The FBI advised Stamos on correspondence with "Brian" from this point forward. Eventually Stamos and "Brian" reached agreement on a purchase price of $680,000 for the photographs. Arrangements were made for one of Stamos's associates to provide "Brian" with $680,000 in cash in exchange for the photographs outside of a private airport in Marquette, Michigan. Coss and Sippola were arrested near the scene of the planned exchange several hours prior to its scheduled execution.

B. Procedural History

On May 11, 2010, Coss and Sippola were indicted on one count of conspiracy to extort money by use of interstate communications in violation of 18 U.S.C. §§ 371 and 875(d) (Count One) and two counts of transmission of interstate communications of threat to injure the reputation of another with intent to extort money in violation of 18 U.S.C. §§ 875(d) and 2(a) (Counts Two and Three). On July 6, 2010, Coss and Sippola each moved to dismiss the indictment claiming that it was defective insofar as it failed to allege facts constituting a violation of 18 U.S.C. § 875(d) and that 18 U.S.C. § 875(d) was unconstitutionally vague and overbroad. The district court denied their motions because they were untimely and without merit. The case then proceeded to trial and the jury returned a verdict of guilty on all counts as to both defendants. Coss and Sippola were each sentenced to forty-eight months of imprisonment on Count One and twenty-four months of imprisonment on Counts Two and Three to be served concurrently. Coss and Sippola timely appeal their convictions and sentences.

II. ANALYSIS

A. Indictment

Coss and Sippola argue that, in order to avoid constitutional infirmities, 18 U.S.C. § 875(d) must be "read narrowly, so as to prohibit only *unlawful* threats" and not merely *wrongful* threats. Appellant Coss Br. at 20 (emphasis added); Appellant Sippola Br. at 20 (emphasis added). However, they also argue that if the statute is construed to prohibit *unlawful* threats, then the indictment failed to allege facts sufficient to constitute a violation of the statute. We consider each argument in turn. . . .

2. Sufficiency of the Indictment

The district court "read[ ] into 18 U.S.C. § 875(d) the requirement that the threat must be wrongful" and held that the indictment was "not deficient." R. 73 (Dist. Ct. Op. at 2). Both determinations are questions of law that we review de novo. *United States v. McMurray,* 653 F.3d 367, 370 (6th Cir.2011) ("We review de novo challenges to the sufficiency of an indictment."); *United States v. Batti,* 631 F.3d 371, 375 (6th Cir.2011) ("A matter requiring statutory interpretation is a question of law requiring de novo review. . . .") (internal quotation marks omitted).

a. Meaning of 18 U.S.C. § 875(d)

The "starting point" for any question of statutory interpretation "is the language of the statute itself." *Batti,* 631 F.3d at 375(internal quotation marks omitted). Title 18 U.S.C. § 875(d) provides as follows:

> Whoever, *with intent to extort* from any person, firm, association, or corporation, any money or other thing of value, transmits in interstate or foreign commerce any communication containing *any threat to injure the property or reputation* of the addressee or of another or the reputation of a deceased person or any threat to accuse the addressee or any other person of a crime, shall be fined under this title or imprisoned not more than two years, or both.

(emphasis added). The precise meaning of "extort" and "threat" in the context of 18 U.S.C. § 875(d) is an issue of first impression in the Sixth Circuit. However, in a well-reasoned, thorough opinion, the Second Circuit considered questions as to the meaning of 18 U.S.C. § 875(d) similar to those presented here. *See United States v. Jackson,* 180 F.3d 55 (2d Cir.1999), *reh'g granted,* 196 F.3d 383 (2d Cir.1999) (holding failure to instruct jury on wrongfulness element to be harmless error under *Neder v. United States,* 527 U.S. 1, 119 S.Ct. 1827, 144 L.Ed.2d 35 (1999)), *cert. denied,* 530 U.S. 1267, 120 S.Ct. 2731, 147 L.Ed.2d 993 (2000). We find the Second Circuit's analysis persuasive and agree that 18 U.S.C. § 875(d) should be interpreted to criminalize only threats that are "wrongful."

The Second Circuit concluded that a "wrongfulness" requirement was implicit in 18 U.S.C. § 875(d) by analyzing the structure and substance of 18 U.S.C. § 875 as a whole, the ordinary meaning of extortion, and 18 U.S.C. § 875(d)'s legislative history. Its reasoning on each point is persuasive. The Second Circuit noted that each of the various subsections in 18 U.S.C. § 875 criminalizes conduct "that plainly is inherently wrongful." *Id.* at 67. Subsection (a) criminalizes a "demand or request for a ransom or reward for the release of any kidnaped person," 18 U.S.C. § 875(a), while subsections (b) and (c) both criminalize a "threat to kidnap" or a "threat to injure the person of another," 18 U.S.C. § 875(b), (c). That these subsections all criminalize "conduct that plainly is inherently wrongful" suggests that Congress also meant to criminalize "inherently wrongful" conduct in subsection (d)—that is "inherently wrongful" threats to property or reputation. *Jackson,* 180 F.3d at 67.

The "intent to extort" element of § 875(d) supports the conclusion that Congress intended to criminalize only wrongful threats. While admittedly the statute does not define extortion, the term's plain meaning, as well as its definition in other statutory contexts, illuminates its significance with respect to § 875(d). As the Second Circuit noted, the definition of "extort" in *Black's Law Dictionary* is "[t]o gain by *wrongful* methods, to obtain in an unlawful manner. . . ." *Id.* at 69 (emphasis added). The Hobbs Act defines extortion as "obtaining of property from another, with his consent, induced by *wrongful* use of actual or threatened force, violence, or fear, or under color of official right." *Id.* at 67 (quoting 18 U.S.C. § 1951(b)(2)) (internal quotation marks omitted) (emphasis in original). As evidenced by the fairly extensive legislative history surveyed by the Second Circuit, there is strong evidence to suggest that Congress intended extortion to mean the same thing in 18 U.S.C. § 875 as it does in the Hobbs Act. *See id.* at 68–70 (discussing how the predecessor to the Hobbs Act, the Anti-Racketeering Act of 1934, 18 U.S.C. § 420a–420e, was enacted almost contemporaneously with the predecessor to 18 U.S.C. § 875). Thus, by including "intent to extort" as an element of § 875(d), Congress linked the statute to the broader concept of extortion, which carries with it the use of a *wrongful* threat to procure something of value.

While Coss and Sippola agree that Congress meant to criminalize something more than "threats to reputation," they argue that the something more must be not merely "wrongful" but "unlawful." Coss and Sippola argue that this strict interpretation is necessary because the term "wrongful" is so ambiguous as to render the statute constitutionally infirm. However, Coss and Sippola overlook the fact that to accept their interpretation of § 875(d) would be to unmoor the crime of extortion in a significant respect from its historically understood meaning. *See id.* at 68–69 (discussing the "generally accepted definition" of extortion). Moreover, as exemplified by the Second Circuit's analysis of what constitutes a wrongful threat, the meaning of wrongfulness is sufficiently circumscribed and readily understandable in this context.

The law of extortion has always recognized the paradox that extortion often criminalizes the contemporaneous performance of otherwise independently lawful acts. *See United States v. Valenzeno,* 123 F.3d 365, 372 n. 3 (6th Cir.1997) (Moore, J., concurring) (noting extensive literature regarding the "paradox in the law of blackmail"). Scholars have struggled to reconcile this paradox, both by adducing a principled explanation for the distinction between lawful bargaining and criminal extortion, and by justifying extortion's criminalization in law and economics terms. *See generally*

James Lindgren, *Unraveling the Paradox of Blackmail,* 84 COLUM. L.REV. 670 (1984) (discussing the theories of prominent scholars such as Arthur Goodhart, Robert Nozick, Lawrence Friedman, Richard Posner, and Richard Epstein).

Arguably, none of these scholarly efforts has been entirely successful; the precise contours of what does and does not constitute extortion remain undefined and often riddled with inconsistency and circularity in a variety of criminal contexts. *See, e.g., id.* (discussing inherent flaws in all prominent theories); *see also* Stuart P. Green, *Theft by Coercion: Extortion, Blackmail, and Hard Bargaining,* 44 WASHBURN L.J. 553, 554–55 (2005) (discussing inadequacy of theories as explanatory frameworks in the white-collar criminal context and arguing for insertion of an unlawful-threat requirement to provide clarity and coherence to the law of extortion). We recognize that the present inquiry implicates these conceptual challenges. However, we need not reconcile the entire law of extortion. We must discern only the meaning of Congress's language in 18 U.S.C. § 875(d) in the context before us.

The *Jackson* court did not have occasion to decide whether an "unlawful," as opposed to "wrongful," threat requirement should be read into 18 U.S.C. § 875(d). In *Jackson,* the government argued that the statute criminalized *all* threats to reputation, while the defendant argued that the statute criminalized only *wrongful* threats to reputation. *See* 180 F.3d at 66. The Second Circuit agreed with the defendant and, in adopting the wrongful-threat reading, described "the type of threat to reputation . . . [that] has no nexus to a claim of right" as one kind of "inherently wrongful" threat. *Id.* at 70. The Second Circuit provided examples to illustrate the dividing line between wrongful threats and permissible threats, justified by a "claim of right." *See id.* at 70–71. By dissecting the logic of these examples, we are convinced of the virtue of the Second Circuit's reasoning. Consider, first, the most classic extortion scenario where individual X demands money from individual Y in exchange for individual X's silence or agreement to destroy evidence of individual Y's marital infidelity. In this instance, the threat to reputation is wrongful because individual X has no claim of right against individual Y to the money demanded. This is clear because as soon as the marital infidelity is exposed individual X loses her ability to demand the money from individual Y. Individual X's only leverage or claim to the money demanded from individual Y is the threat of exposing the marital infidelity and, thus, individual X's threat has no nexus to a true claim of right. By way of contrast, consider the Second Circuit's example of a country club manager who threatens to publish a list of members delinquent in their dues if the members do not promptly pay the manager their outstanding account balances. *Id.* at 71. In that instance, there is a nexus between the threat and a claim of right: The duty of the members to pay the country club the outstanding dues exists independently of the threat and will continue to exist even if the club manager publishes the list as threatened. The law recognizes the club manager's threat as a lawful and valid exercise of his enforcement rights and, therefore, does not criminalize his conduct as extortion.

The questions posed by the parties require us to apply and expand upon this logic provided in *Jackson*. At first blush, it is not entirely clear that the parties' arguments are so different from each other. At least some "wrongful" threats under the Second Circuit's "claim of right" definition would also be unlawful in a criminal or civil sense—such threats could implicate defamation or fraud. Moreover, identification of a "claim of right" requires reference to preexisting legal standards and thereby utilizes these standards in distinguishing lawful from unlawful conduct. Nevertheless, the two standards implicate an important difference. To require that a threat be unlawful would be to require that the prosecution demonstrate beyond a reasonable doubt that the threat in question was independently illegal in either the criminal or civil sense. We see no reason, nor any historical or statutory basis, for reading such a requirement into 18 U.S.C. § 875(d).

The crime of extortion has never been defined strictly in terms of the lawfulness or unlawfulness of one of the actor's underlying supporting actions. Indeed, the hallmark of extortion, and its attendant complexities, is that it often criminalizes conduct that is otherwise lawful. *See* Lindgren, *supra* at 680 ("The paradox of blackmail, however, lies precisely in the fact that the crime may involve acts, or threatened acts, that would be legitimate when taken in isolation."). Thus, to adopt the position that Coss and Sippola advocate would be to depart in a significant respect from the traditional understanding of extortion. *See* Green, *supra* at 580 (recognizing that limiting extortion to unlawful threats would exclude "threats to expose embarrassing true information" which "cultural understanding traditionally associated with the offense of blackmail"). Such a significant departure is unwarranted where there is no indication that this was Congress's intention, and, as the Second Circuit's analysis illustrates, the "claim of right" wrongfulness standard is readily discernible and easily understandable.

Accordingly, we affirm the district court's holding that 18 U.S.C. § 875(d) carries with it an implicit "wrongful threat" requirement. Doing so harmonizes subsection (d) with subsections (a), (b), and (c) of 18 U.S.C. § 875, and the "intent to extort" element of subsection (d) itself. It also aligns § 875(d) with the commonly understood meaning of extortion. Utilizing this interpretation of the statute, we now consider whether the indictment alleged sufficient facts to charge Coss and Sippola under 18 U.S.C. § 875(d). . . .

Having determined that a wrongful-threat requirement is implicit in 18 U.S.C. § 875(d), we can easily conclude that the indictment was sufficient. The indictment specifically alleged that the defendants acted "with intent to extort" and that the communications they used contained "a wrongful threat to injure the reputation of the addressee." *See id.* at 1, 8–9; *cf. Heller,* 579 F.2d at 999 (holding indictment to be "fatally defective" for failing to "charge" the defendant with the "intent to extort" in a prosecution under 18 U.S.C. § 875(a)). From the facts alleged in the indictment, a jury could reasonably conclude that both of these allegations were true.

The indictment set out Coss's and Sippola's scheme involving the creation of fictitious personas "Jessica Taylor" and "Brian L." in order to induce Stamos to pay $680,000 in exchange for the photographs by threatening otherwise to sell the photographs to a tabloid magazine and damage Stamos's reputation. *See* R. 17 (Indictment ¶¶ 6–9). The threat that Coss and Sippola made—that they would sell the photographs to a tabloid unless Stamos paid them $680,000 in cash—was wrongful because Coss and Sippola had no claim of right to $680,000 in cash from Stamos. Their only leverage for obtaining this money was the threat of selling the photographs to a tabloid, as evidenced by the fact that if they had actually sold the photographs to a tabloid, they would have no longer had a basis for insisting that Stamos pay them $680,000 in cash. Thus, because Coss and Stamos were not using their threat to collect on a debt owed to them, or to exercise any other claim of right against Stamos, their threat had no nexus to a valid claim of right and was wrongful. Moreover, this wrongful threat was made with the deliberate intention of extracting the desired sum of money from Stamos. The indictment alleged an elaborate scheme that Coss and Sippola carefully executed over time to achieve their desired result. From these allegations, a jury could also conclude that both Coss and Sippola acted with the "intent to extort."

Although Coss and Sippola are correct that they may have had a lawful right to possess the photographs and a lawful right to offer Stamos the opportunity to purchase the photographs, their conduct became unlawful when their offer to Stamos was made in the form of a wrongful threat accompanied by an intent to extort.

EXERCISE

You are a federal prosecutor. A famous 40-year-old actress, Danisha Redframe, has contacted the FBI about an extortion case. She asserts that ten years ago, before she was very famous, photographs of a sexual nature were taken by a third party, a photographer named Rudy K. Savage. The photos depict her (at 30) with an 18-year-old man named Tim Theobolt. Both are depicted naked in the photographs, and the photos would embarrass Ms. Redframe if they were to be released.

The FBI has forwarded to you a case file that includes the photographs and an email from Mr. Theobolt in which he demands "$10,000 finally, or I will sell the pictures of us to a tabloid." Based on that information, you file a complaint against Mr. Theobolt, and he is arrested. You have not yet taken the case to the Grand Jury for indictment.

After Theobolt is arrested you are contacted by an attorney who represents him. He provides you with additional information, all of which turns out to be verified and credible, and asks that you dismiss the complaint and drop the case. Two facts are especially relevant. First, he includes an affidavit from Savage, the photographer, stating that is was Redframe who asked him to take the photograph, recruited Theobolt to be in the photo, and paid him for the photos (which he then provided in print form to both Redframe and Theobolt). A copy of a $350 check later in the week from Redframe to Savage is also provided. Second, Theobolt's attorney provides a series of emails between Redframe and Theobolt in which Theobolt asks to be paid for his "modeling" and notes that "you said we would work that out later." Redframe emailed back "We will work that out when I decide how to use these."

Redframe verifies those facts, but says she never intended to actually pay Theobolt since he was "a lucky nobody who got a picture with me out of it."

Do you indict the case?

Federal law, under the Hobbes Act, 18 U.S.C. § 1951(b)(2), also allows charges of extortion where a public official tries to get something of value by using his or her position "under color of official right." Many public corruption cases are brought under this clause.

UNITED STATES V. BLAGOJEVICH
794 F. 3d 729 (7th Cir. 2015)

EASTERBROOK, CIRCUIT JUDGE.

Rod Blagojevich was convicted of 18 crimes after two jury trials. The crimes include attempted extortion from campaign contributors, corrupt solicitation of funds, wire fraud, and lying to federal investigators. The first trial ended with a conviction on the false-statement count and a mistrial on the others after the jury could not agree. The second trial produced convictions on 17 additional counts. At the time of his arrest in December 2008, Blagojevich was Governor of Illinois; the state legislature impeached and removed him from office the next month. The district court sentenced Blagojevich to 168 months' imprisonment on the counts that authorize 20-year maximum terms, and lesser terms on all other counts.

The events leading to Blagojevich's arrest began when Barack Obama, then a Senator from Illinois, won the election for President in November 2008. When Obama took office in January 2009, Blagojevich would appoint his replacement, to serve until the time set by a writ of election. See *Judge v. Quinn,* 612 F.3d 537 (7th Cir.2010). Before the 2008 election, federal agents had been investigating Blagojevich and his associates. Evidence from some of those associates had led to warrants authorizing the interception of Blagojevich's phone calls. (The validity of these warrants has not been contested on this appeal.) Interceptions revealed that Blagojevich viewed the opportunity to appoint a new Senator as a bonanza.

Through intermediaries (his own and the President-elect's), Blagojevich sought a favor from Sen. Obama in exchange for appointing Valerie Jarrett, who Blagojevich perceived as the person Sen. Obama would like to have succeed him. Blagojevich asked for an appointment to the Cabinet or for the President-elect to persuade a foundation to hire him at a substantial salary after his term as Governor ended, or find someone to donate $10 million and up to a new "social-welfare" organization that he would control. The President-elect was not willing to make a deal, and Blagojevich would not appoint Jarrett without compensation, saying: "They're not willing to give me anything except appreciation. Fuck them."

Blagojevich then turned to supporters of Rep. Jesse Jackson, Jr., offering the appointment in exchange for a $1.5 million "campaign contribution." (We put "campaign contribution" in quotation marks because Blagojevich was serving his second term as Governor and had decided not to run for a third. A jury was entitled to conclude that the money was for his personal benefit rather than a campaign.) Blagojevich broke off negotiations after learning about the wiretaps, and he was arrested before he could negotiate with anyone else.

The indictment charged these negotiations as attempted extortion, in violation of 18 U.S.C. §§ 2 and 1951, plus corrupt solicitation of funds (18 U.S.C. §§ 371 and 666(a)(1)(B)) and wire fraud (18 U.S.C. §§ 1343 and 1346). The indictment also charged Blagojevich with other attempts to raise money in exchange for the performance of official acts, even though federal law forbids any payment (or agreement to pay), including a campaign contribution, in exchange for the performance of an official act. See *McCormick v. United States,* 500 U.S. 257, 111 S.Ct. 1807, 114 L.Ed.2d 307 (1991).

Blagojevich now asks us to hold that the evidence is insufficient to convict him on any count. The argument is frivolous. The evidence, much of it from Blagojevich's own mouth, is overwhelming. To the extent there are factual disputes, the jury was entitled to credit the prosecution's evidence and to find that Blagojevich acted with the knowledge required for conviction.

But a problem in the way the instructions told the jury to consider the evidence requires us to vacate the convictions on counts that concern Blagojevich's proposal to appoint Valerie Jarrett to the Senate in exchange for an appointment to the Cabinet. A jury could have found that Blagojevich asked the President-elect for a private-sector job, or for funds that he could control, but the instructions permitted the jury to convict even if it found that his only request of Sen. Obama was for a position in the Cabinet. The instructions treated all proposals alike. We conclude, however, that they are legally different: a proposal to trade one public act for another, a form of logrolling, is fundamentally unlike the swap of an official act for a private payment.

Because the instructions do not enable us to be sure that the jury found that Blagojevich offered to trade the appointment for a private salary after leaving the Governorship, these convictions cannot stand. . . .

McCormick describes the offense as a quid pro quo: a public official performs an official act (or promises to do so) in exchange for a private benefit, such as money. See also *United States v. Sun-Diamond Growers of California,* 526 U.S. 398, 404–05, 119 S.Ct. 1402, 143 L.Ed.2d 576 (1999); *United States v. McDonnell,* 2015 U.S.App. LEXIS 11889 (4th Cir. July 10, 2015). A political logroll, by contrast, is the swap of one official act for another. Representative A agrees with Representative B to vote for milk price supports, if B agrees to vote for tighter controls on air pollution. A President appoints C as an ambassador, which Senator D asked the President to do, in exchange for D's promise to vote to confirm E as a member of the National Labor Relations Board. Governance would hardly be possible without these accommodations, which allow each public official to achieve more of his principal objective while surrendering something about which he cares less, but the other politician cares more strongly.

A proposal to appoint a particular person to one office (say, the Cabinet) in exchange for someone else's promise to appoint a different person to a different office (say, the Senate), is a common exercise in logrolling. We asked the prosecutor at oral argument if, before this case, logrolling had been the basis of a criminal conviction in the history of the United States. Counsel was unaware of any earlier conviction for an exchange of political favors. Our own research did not turn one up. It would be more than a little surprising to Members of Congress if the judiciary found in the Hobbs Act, or the mail fraud statute, a rule making everyday politics criminal.

1Let's work this through statute by statute. Section 1951, the Hobbs Act, which underlies Counts 21 and 22, forbids interference with commerce by robbery or extortion. Blagojevich did not rob anyone, and extortion, a defined term, "means the obtaining of property from another, with his consent, induced by wrongful use of actual or threatened force, violence, or fear, or under color of official right" (§ 1951(b)(2)). The indictment charged Blagojevich with the "color of official right" version of extortion, but none of the evidence suggests that Blagojevich claimed to have an "official right" to a job in the Cabinet. He did have an "official right" to appoint a new Senator, but unless a position in the Cabinet is "property" from the President's perspective, then seeking it does not amount to extortion. Yet a political office belongs to the people, not to the incumbent (or to someone hankering after the position). *Cleveland v. United States,* 531 U.S. 12, 121 S.Ct. 365, 148 L.Ed.2d 221 (2000), holds that state and municipal licenses, and similar documents, are not "property" in the hands of a public agency.

That's equally true of public positions. The President-elect did not have a property interest in any Cabinet job, so an attempt to get him to appoint a particular person to the Cabinet is not an attempt to secure "property" from the President (or the citizenry at large). . . .

The prosecutor insists, however, that Blagojevich's situation is different and uncommon because he sought a post in the Cabinet for himself. It isn't clear to us that this is unusual. The current Secretary of State was appointed to that position from a seat in the Senate, and it wouldn't surprise us if this happened at least in part because he had performed a political service for the President.

Ambassadors, too, come from the House or Senate (or from state politics) as part of political deals. Some historians say that this is how Earl Warren came to be Chief Justice of the United States: he delivered the California delegation at the 1952 Republican convention to Eisenhower (rather than Senator Taft) in exchange for a commitment to appoint him to the next vacancy on the Supreme Court. See, e.g., Morton J. Horwitz, *The Warren Court and the Pursuit of Justice* 7 (1998); Arthur Paulson, *Realignment and Party Revival: Understanding American Electoral Politics at the Turn of the Twenty-First Century* 86 (2000). Whether this account is correct is debatable, see Jim Newton, *Justice for All: Earl Warren and the Nation He Made* 6–11 (2006), and Chief Justice Warren himself denied that a deal had been made (though perhaps a political debt had been incurred), *The Memoirs of Earl Warren* 250–61 (1977). If the prosecutor is right, and a swap of political favors involving a job for one of the politicians is a felony, then if the standard account is true both the President of the United States and the Chief Justice of the United States should have gone to prison. Yet although historians and political scientists have debated whether this deal was made, or whether if made was ethical (or politically unwise), no one to our knowledge has suggested that it violated the statutes involved in this case. . . .

Put to one side for a moment the fact that a position in the Cabinet carries a salary. Suppose that Blagojevich had asked, instead, that Sen. Obama commit himself to supporting a program to build new bridges and highways in Illinois as soon as he became President. Many politicians believe that public-works projects promote their re-election. If the prosecutor is right that a public job counts as a private benefit, then the benefit to a politician from improved chances of election to a paying job such as Governor—or a better prospect of a lucrative career as a lobbyist after leaving office—also would be a private benefit, and we would be back to the proposition that all logrolling is criminal. Even a politician who asks another politician for favors only because he sincerely believes that these favors assist his constituents could be condemned as a felon, because grateful constituents make their gratitude known by votes or post-office employment.

What we have said so far requires the reversal of the convictions on Counts 5, 6, 21, 22, and 23, though the prosecutor is free to try again without reliance on Blagojevich's quest for a position in the Cabinet. (The evidence that Blagojevich sought money in exchange for appointing Valerie Jarrett to the Senate is sufficient to convict, so there is no double-jeopardy obstacle to retrial. See *Burks v. United States,* 437 U.S. 1, 98 S.Ct. 2141, 57 L.Ed.2d 1 (1978).) Because many other convictions remain and the district judge imposed concurrent sentences, the prosecutor may think retrial unnecessary—but the judge may have considered the sought-after Cabinet appointment in determining the length of the sentence, so we remand for re-sentencing across the board.

EXERCISE

Imagine a case in which the Governor of Maryland calls a business owner. "If you hire my daughter," he tells the business owner. "I'll make sure that you get the state contract you want. And if you don't hire her, for at least $90,000 a year, there is no way you are getting that contract." Is this extortion or mere log-rolling as that is described in *Blagojevich*?

F. MONEY LAUNDERING

Sometimes, property crimes involve hiding, using, or moving property rather than taking it. We see this in money laundering statutes, which generally criminalize transactions that involve money that is either promoting crime, is the proceeds of crime, or both. Prosecutions for money laundering are often used as a way of addressing underlying crimes like narcotics and human trafficking.

CUELLAR V. UNITED STATES
553 U.S. 550 (1994)

JUSTICE THOMAS delivered the opinion of the Court.

This case involves the provision of the federal money laundering statute that prohibits international transportation of the proceeds of unlawful activity. Petitioner argues that his conviction cannot stand because, while the evidence demonstrates that he took steps to hide illicit funds *en route* to Mexico, it does not show that the cross-border transport of those funds was designed to create the appearance of legitimate wealth. Although we agree with the Government that the statute does not require proof that the defendant attempted to "legitimize" tainted funds, we agree with petitioner that the Government must demonstrate that the defendant did more than merely hide the money during its transport. We therefore reverse the judgment of the Fifth Circuit.

On July 14, 2004, petitioner Humberto Fidel Regalado Cuellar was stopped in southern Texas for driving erratically. Driving south toward the Mexican border, about 114 miles away, petitioner had just passed the town of Eldorado. In response to the officer's questions, petitioner, who spoke no English, handed the officer a stack of papers. Included were bus tickets showing travel from a Texas border town to San Antonio on July 13 and, in the other direction, from San Antonio to Big Spring, Texas, on July 14. A Spanish-speaking officer, Trooper Danny Nuñez, was called to the scene and began questioning petitioner. Trooper Nuñez soon became suspicious because petitioner was avoiding eye contact and seemed very nervous. Petitioner claimed to be on a 3-day business trip, but he had no luggage or extra clothing with him, and he gave conflicting accounts of his itinerary. When Trooper Nuñez asked petitioner about a bulge in his shirt pocket, petitioner produced a wad of cash that smelled of marijuana.

Petitioner consented to a search of the Volkswagen Beetle that he was driving. While the officers were searching the vehicle, Trooper Nuñez observed petitioner standing on the side of the road making the sign of the cross, which he interpreted to mean that petitioner knew he was in trouble. A drug detection dog alerted on the cash from petitioner's shirt pocket and on the rear area of the car. Further scrutiny uncovered a secret compartment under the rear floorboard, and inside the compartment the officers found approximately $81,000 in cash. The money was bundled in plastic bags and duct tape, and animal hair was spread in the rear of the vehicle. Petitioner claimed that he had previously transported goats in the vehicle, but Trooper Nuñez doubted that goats could fit in such a small space and suspected that the hair had been spread in an attempt to mask the smell of marijuana.

There were signs that the compartment had been recently created and that someone had attempted to cover up the bodywork: The Beetle's carpeting appeared newer than the rest of the interior, and the exterior of the vehicle appeared to have been purposely splashed with mud to cover up toolmarks, fresh paint, or other work. In the backseat, officers found a fast-food restaurant receipt dated the same day from a city farther north than petitioner claimed to have traveled. After a check of petitioner's last border crossing also proved inconsistent with his story, petitioner was arrested and interrogated. He continued to tell conflicting stories about his travels. At one point, before he knew that the officers had found the cash, he remarked to Trooper Nuñez that he had to have the car in Mexico by midnight or else his family would be "floating down the river." App. 50.

Petitioner was charged with attempting to transport the proceeds of unlawful activity across the border, knowing that the transportation was designed "to conceal or disguise the nature, the location, the source, the ownership, or the control" of the money. 18 U.S.C. § 1956(a)(2)(B)(i). After a 2-day trial, the jury found petitioner guilty. The District Court denied petitioner's motion for judgment of acquittal based on insufficient evidence and sentenced petitioner to 78 months in prison, followed by three years of supervised release.

On appeal, a divided panel of the Fifth Circuit reversed and rendered a judgment of acquittal. 441 F.3d 329 (2006). Judge Smith's majority opinion held that, although the evidence showed that petitioner concealed the money for the purpose of transporting it, the statute requires that the purpose of the transportation itself must be to conceal or disguise the unlawful proceeds. . . .

As noted, petitioner was convicted under § 1956(a)(2)(B)(i), which, in relevant part, makes it a crime to attempt to transport "funds from a place in the United States to . . . a place outside the United States . . . knowing that the . . . funds involved in the transportation . . . represent the proceeds of some form of unlawful activity and knowing that such transportation . . . is designed in whole or in part . . . to conceal or disguise the nature, the location, the source, the ownership, or the control of the proceeds of specified unlawful activity." Accordingly, the Government was required in this case to prove that petitioner (1) attempted to transport funds from the United States to Mexico, (2) knew that these funds "represent[ed] the proceeds of some form of unlawful activity," *e.g.,* drug trafficking, and (3) knew that "such transportation" was designed to "conceal or disguise the nature, the location, the source, the ownership, or the control" of the funds.

It is the last of these that is at issue before us, viz., whether petitioner knew that "such transportation" was designed to conceal or disguise the specified attributes of the illegally obtained funds. In this connection, it is important to keep in mind that the critical transportation was not the transportation of the funds within this country on the way to the border. Instead, the term "such transportation" means transportation "from a place in the United States to . . . a place outside the United States"—here, from the United States to Mexico. Therefore, what the Government had to prove was that petitioner knew that taking the funds to Mexico was "designed," at least in part, to conceal or disguise their "nature," "location," "source," "ownership," or "control."

Petitioner argues that the evidence is not sufficient to sustain his conviction because concealing or disguising a listed attribute of the funds during transportation cannot satisfy the "designed . . . to conceal" element. Citing cases that interpret the identical phrase in the transaction provision to exclude "mere spending," petitioner argues that the transportation provision must exclude "mere hiding." Otherwise, petitioner contends, all cross-border transport of illicit funds would fall under the statute because people regularly make minimal efforts to conceal money, such as placing it inside a wallet or other receptacle, in order to secure it during travel. The Government responds that concealment during transportation is sufficient to satisfy this element because it is circumstantial evidence that the ultimate purpose of the transportation—*i.e.,* its "design"—is to conceal or disguise a listed attribute of the funds. This standard would not criminalize all cross-border transport of illicit funds, the Government argues, because, just as in the transaction cases, the statute encompasses only *substantial* efforts at concealment. As a result, the Government agrees with the Court of Appeals that a violation of the transportation provision cannot be established solely by evidence that the defendant carried money in a wallet or concealed it in some other conventional or incidental way. See 478 F.3d, at 291 (characterizing the defendant's transportation of money in a box in *United States v. Dimeck,* 24 F.3d 1239, 1246 (C.A.10 1994), as a "minimal attempt at concealment" that is distinguishable from petitioner's "effort to hide or conceal" the funds).

We agree with petitioner that merely hiding funds during transportation is not sufficient to violate the statute, even if substantial efforts have been expended to conceal the money. . . .

Even with abundant evidence that petitioner had concealed the money in order to transport it, the Government's own expert witness—ICE Agent Richard Nuckles—testified that the purpose of the transportation was to compensate the leaders of the operation. Tr. 179 (Oct. 12, 2004), App. 64–65 ("[T]he bulk of [the money] generally goes back to Mexico, because the smuggler is the one who originated this entire process. He's going to get a large cut of the profit, and that money has to be moved back to him in Mexico"). The evidence suggested that the secretive aspects of the transportation were employed to *facilitate* the transportation, see 478 F.3d, at 289 (noting that "concealment of the funds during the U.S. leg of the trip [was] a vital part of the transportation design or plan"), but not necessarily that secrecy was the *purpose* of the transportation. Agent Nuckles testified that the secretive manner of transportation was consistent with drug smuggling, see Tr. 179–180, App. 65–66, but the Government failed to introduce any evidence that the reason drug smugglers move money to Mexico is to conceal or disguise a listed attribute of the funds. . . .

In sum, we conclude that the evidence introduced by the Government was not sufficient to permit a reasonable jury to conclude beyond a reasonable doubt that petitioner's transportation was "designed in whole or in part . . . to conceal or disguise the nature, the location, the source, the ownership, or the control of the proceeds." § 1956(a)(2)(B)(i).

The provision of the money laundering statute under which petitioner was convicted requires proof that the transportation was "designed in whole or in part . . . to conceal or disguise the nature, the location, the source, the ownership, or the control" of the funds. § 1956(a)(2)(B)(i). Although this element does not require proof that the defendant attempted to create the appearance of legitimate wealth, neither can it be satisfied solely by evidence that a defendant concealed the funds during their transport. In this case, the only evidence introduced to prove this element showed that petitioner engaged in extensive efforts to conceal the funds *en route* to Mexico, and thus his conviction cannot stand. We reverse the judgment of the Fifth Circuit.

―――――――

EXERCISE

In describing the elements of this kind of money laundering, the Supreme Court in *Cueller* lays out that the government must prove "that petitioner (1) attempted to transport funds from the United States to Mexico, (2) knew that these funds "represent[ed] the proceeds of some form of unlawful activity," *e.g.,* drug trafficking, and (3) knew that "such transportation" was designed to "conceal or disguise the nature, the location, the source, the ownership, or the control" of the funds." Given that merely concealing the money did not fulfill the third element, what additional facts might have made this a win for the government?

CHAPTER SIX

NARCOTICS

■ ■ ■

The criminalization of narcotics has profoundly affected criminal law. The sheer number of narcotics cases in the federal and state systems dictates that narcotics needs to be part of any study of criminal law as a whole.

Unlike violent and property crimes, in the broader scope of history narcotics only recently became subject to criminal law. Until the beginning of the 20th century, criminal law simply did not address the issue and narcotics were not only legal but largely unregulated (with the exception of some laws directed at opium dens). That changed in the first half of the 20th century, as tax and regulatory laws began to take aim at the problem. The Pure Food and Drug Act of 1906[1] took the relatively innocuous step of requiring disclosure of psychoactive ingredients, and the Harrison Narcotics Act of 1914[2] required those who sold cocaine and opium to register and pay a special tax. It was not until the 1950's that the major federal anti-drug laws began to take shape.

The second half of the 20th century saw a very different trajectory. A national "War on Drugs" was waged by the federal government and many states, resulting in a dramatic upswing in the number of narcotics cases, convictions, and sentences. Narcotics became not only an area of specialization for investigators, prosecutors, and defense attorneys, but the primary focus for law enforcement in many communities.

Narcotics is not only a newer area of criminal law than those discussed previously, but it is fundamentally different as well. More than nearly any other type of crime, narcotics cases often involve large networks and conspiracies. It also differs from crimes of violence, sex crimes, and property crimes in that those other types of crime are oppositional—that is, the victim does not welcome the criminal behavior. Narcotics trafficking is different because those who would be directly harmed, drug users, are seeking out the criminal transaction. One concern often expressed about narcotics trafficking is the problem of collateral violence between drug dealers and crimes committed by those who are using illegal narcotics.

Those who violate narcotics laws range from the casual marijuana user to the international trafficker importing heroin into the United States. The

---

[1]   34 Stat. 768 (1906), *amended by* 37 Stat. 416 (1912).

[2]   38 Stat. 785, 785–90, *amended by* 40 Stat. 1130 (1919) (repealed 1970).

contemporary statutes on narcotics generally distinguish between more and less culpable cases through a focus on three factors: the action taken (i.e., possession or distribution), the type of drug involved, and the amount of the drug. Narcotics crime is also unusual in that it is an area of near complete overlap between federal and state laws; nearly any type of drug case can be taken to either state or federal courts for prosecution.

For most narcotics crimes, the elements are relatively similar:

1) Identity

2) Action (possession, distribution, etc.)

3) Intent

4) knowledge (that a controlled substance is involved)

5) Chemical composition of the substance at issue.

The last of these, as a scientific factor, is relatively unusual. Because statutes (generally referred to as "schedules") define certain chemicals as illegal, this kind of scientific proof is necessary.

In this chapter, we will explore the elements of action, intent, knowledge, and chemical composition before we move on to examine a law that targets large-scale drug networks and another that is rooted in an otherwise legal action (making a phone call) when that action is related to drug trafficking.

A. ACTION ELEMENTS

Federal law criminalizes a number of actions relating to narcotics. 21 U.S.C. § 844(a) covers simple possession of narcotics. 21 U.S.C. § 841(a) outlaws the more serious crimes of manufacturing, distributing, dispensing, and possessing with the intent to manufacture, distribute, or dispense illegal drugs. Which drugs can be subject to criminal law—and their relative degree of illegality—is set out in the schedules in 21 U.S.C. § 812.

The action elements in a drug crime (possession, manufacturing, distributing, dispensing, and possessing with intent) are distinct and important to define. For example, at sentencing the difference between a case predicated on a charge of simple possession and another based on a charge of possession with intent to distribute can sometimes be measured in decades.

1. SIMPLE POSSESSION

Those who possess narcotics for their own use are generally subject to less serious charges and penalties than those who manufacture it or distribute it to others. Simple possession cases do not require proof of any action beyond the mere possession of the illegal drugs, but that can still be challenging. In the federal code, simple possession of narcotics is outlawed under 21 U.S.C. § 844(a), which provides:

> It shall be unlawful for any person knowingly or intentionally to possess a controlled substance unless such substance was obtained directly, or pursuant to a valid prescription or order, from a practitioner, while acting in the course of his professional practice, or except as otherwise authorized by this subchapter or subchapter II of this chapter. . . . Any person who violates this subsection may be sentenced to a term of imprisonment of not more than 1 year, and shall be fined a minimum of $1,000, or both, except that if he commits such offense after a prior conviction under this subchapter or subchapter II of this chapter, or a prior conviction for any drug, narcotic, or chemical offense chargeable under the law of any State, has become final, he shall be sentenced to a term of imprisonment for not less than 15 days but not more than 2 years, and shall be fined a minimum of $2,500, except, further, that if he commits such offense after two or more prior convictions under this subchapter or subchapter II of this chapter, or two or more prior convictions for any drug, narcotic, or chemical offense chargeable under the law of any State, or a combination of two or more such offenses have become final, he shall be sentenced to a term of imprisonment for not less than 90 days but not more than 3 years, and shall be fined a minimum of $5,000.

Thus, federal law makes first-time simple possession of narcotics a misdemeanor. However, for those with a prior conviction it establishes mandatory minimum sentences of 15 days (with one prior) and 90 days incarceration (with two). There is also an alternative to this misdemeanor that is available in cases involving small amounts of narcotics: 21 U.S.C. § 844A allows for a civil penalty (sometimes referred to as a "ticket offense"). That means that simple possession cases can generally be taken either as a misdemeanor or a civil offense, leaving this decision in the discretion of the prosecutor.

a. Constructive Possession

The easiest possession cases for the prosecution are those where the defendant is found holding the drug in their hand or in their pocket. When the defendant is not actively holding the narcotics when found by the police, prosecutors often rely on a theory of "constructive possession."

UNITED STATES V. DORMAN
860 F. 3d 675 (DC Cir. 2017)

ROGERS, CIRCUIT JUDGE:

The principal question in this appeal is whether the government met its burden to show beyond a reasonable doubt that Harold A. Dorman constructively possessed PCP seized from the laundry room of his mother's home. Constructive possession of unlawful controlled substances is an expansive concept that this court has held requires a showing of more than mere residence in a jointly occupied home where drugs and guns are found in generally accessible areas and are not in plain view. Because Dorman's constructive possession of a gun and ambiguous apology to his mother fail to fill the evidentiary void, we reverse in part and remand for resentencing.

I.

The seizure of the drugs and firearms from Dorman's mother's home resulted from an investigation of a robbery at a Kay Jewelers store in Maryland on October 22, 2013. Two diamond rings were taken from the fingers of a sales clerk, and the robber was captured on video getting into a white Dodge Charger. The car was identified as a rental car on loan to Dorman's father. Dorman matched the physical description of the robber, and was known by law enforcement to be facing charges in Pennsylvania for the attempted robbery of a jewelry store. Another videotape showed Dorman exiting the Dodge Charger at a 7–11 convenience store in Maryland two days after the robbery. The Dodge Charger was also spotted by FBI Special Agent Catherine Hanna several days before the robbery in an area she knew to be frequented by Dorman, with whom she had previous interactions. With a GPS tracking system, the Dodge Charger was found parked near 2317 Chester Street, S.E., Washington, D.C., which public records (including a prior arrest record) listed as Dorman's address. FBI agents subsequently observed the car parked across the street from that address.

The home at 2317 Chester Street, S.E. consisted of two floors and a basement. The basement, which was not locked off from the main floor, included a family room and closet at the base of the stairs, and a laundry room and a bedroom off a hallway; it also had an external exit at the rear. The entrance to the basement bedroom was around a corner from the laundry room. The bedroom contained men's sneakers and clothing, as well as judicial court papers in Dorman's name, and was decorated with a painting of him playing football.

Pursuant to the execution of a search warrant for 2317 Chester Street, S.E., law enforcement officers seized an array of contraband unrelated to the Kay Jewelers robbery: (1) a Glock 9-millimeter handgun loaded with a 30-round extended magazine hidden underneath a couch cushion in the living room on the first floor; (2) a one-ounce vial of PCP on the living room floor either inside or behind a vase, among other drug paraphernalia (approximately fifty glass vials in a large plastic bag, and scales and small plastic baggies in a baby formula container) elsewhere in the room; (3) an empty gun box for a Glock .40 caliber handgun on the basement stairs; (4) a loaded Ruger 9-millimeter pistol wedged between the mattress and box spring of the bed in the basement bedroom, with a digital scale, plastic baggies, and boxes of .40 caliber Smith and Wesson ammunition nearby; (5) a 15.2 ounce Tropicana juice bottle filled to the brim with PCP on the floor of the basement laundry room; and (6) a trash bag containing fifty or more empty prescription pill bottles for oxymorphone underneath a blanket in the hallway in the basement. Although the search did not produce the stolen rings, packaging and price tags for jewelry from other stores was found in the home.

Dorman was indicted on three counts: Count 1, unlawful possession with intent to distribute 100 grams or more of PCP, in violation of 21 U.S.C. § 841(a)(1) & (b)(1)(A)(iv); Count 2, unlawful possession of a firearm or ammunition by a person convicted of a felony, in violation of 18 U.S.C. § 922(g)(1); and Count 3, using, carrying, and possessing a firearm during a drug trafficking offense, in violation of 18 U.S.C. § 924(c)(1). The district court denied his motion to suppress the items seized during the search.

At trial, Dorman's mother appeared as a government witness. She testified that her son stayed in many places, but conceded to having told the grand jury that 2317 Chester Street, S.E. was his "home base." Trial Tr. 107 (July 9, 2014). She had "fixed up" the basement bedroom for him, *id.* at 122, and identified as his some of the items in the room. She also explained that when at her home, although he did not always sleep in the basement bedroom, to her knowledge no one else slept there. Multiple individuals had keys to the home, including Dorman's father and Cleavan Hill, a family friend who lived at the home; the son of Dorman's mother's boyfriend also had a key and temporarily lived at the home in 2012, but had apparently lost the key since then. Only Dorman and his mother had keys to the basement bedroom, although she admitted on cross-examination that the door "was open all the time." *Id.* at 151. Dorman, his mother, Hill, the mother's boyfriend, and possibly the boyfriend's son did laundry in the basement laundry room. Various other individuals also frequented 2317 Chester Street, S.E., including Dorman's friends regardless of whether he was there at the time. Hill testified that on several occasions he had let people in the home at Dorman's request when no one else was there.

The jury found Dorman guilty as charged, and the district court denied his motions for acquittal and a new trial. Considering Counts 1 and 2 together, the district court sentenced Dorman to concurrent terms of seventy months' imprisonment on each of these counts, and to a consecutive term of sixty months' imprisonment on Count 3, and thirty-six months' supervised release. Dorman appeals, challenging his convictions on three grounds, of which only his sufficiency challenge warrants extended discussion.

II.

"Criminal possession ... may be either actual or constructive." *United States v. Alexander*, 331 F.3d 116, 127 (D.C. Cir. 2003). Constructive possession is a potentially expansive concept, and this court has limited its reach. The government must prove beyond a reasonable doubt that "the defendant knew of, and was in a position to exercise dominion and control over, the contraband." *United States v. Littlejohn*, 489 F.3d 1335, 1338 (D.C. Cir. 2007) (quoting *United States v. Byfield*, 928 F.2d 1163, 1166 (D.C. Cir. 1991)); *see United States v. Staten*, 581 F.2d 878, 883–84 (D.C. Cir. 1978). This avoids ensnaring "incidental bystander[s]" who happen to be in the wrong place at the wrong time. *United States v. Pardo*, 636 F.2d 535, 549 (D.C. Cir. 1980). The court has addressed the sufficiency of the evidence of dominion and control in three circumstances: First, the court has held the evidence of constructive possession is sufficient when contraband is found in a home or bedroom where the defendant was the sole occupant. *See, e.g., United States v. Dykes*, 406 F.3d 717, 722 (D.C. Cir. 2005); *United States v. Morris*, 977 F.2d 617, 620 (D.C. Cir. 1992). Second, where the defendant shares a home or bedroom with other persons, the court has held the evidence of dominion and control is sufficient only where there was additional evidence linking the defendant to the contraband. *See, e.g., United States v. Boyd*, 803 F.3d 690, 693 (D.C. Cir. 2015); *United States v. Walker*, 99 F.3d 439, 441 (D.C. Cir. 1996). Third, where law enforcement encountered the defendant in close proximity to the contraband, the court has held the evidence of constructive possession was sufficient where there is "evidence of some other factor—including connection with [contraband], proof of motive, a gesture implying control, evasive conduct, or a statement indicating involvement in an enterprise." *Alexander*, 331 F.3d at 127 (quoting *United States v. Moore*, 104 F.3d 377, 381 (D.C. Cir. 1997)). Here, the government sought to establish Dorman's possession of the gun in the basement bedroom under the first line of cases and his possession of the PCP under the second.

Dorman contends that the evidence linking him to the drugs and guns was insufficient because he was not present when the items were seized and it was unreasonable to infer beyond a reasonable doubt that he constructively possessed the items discovered in areas of the home that were accessible to many individuals. He was neither the lessee nor owner of 2317 Chester Street, S.E., and there was no evidence of mail addressed to him at that address; paperwork from his arrest in Pennsylvania in the basement bedroom listed 142 Yuma Street, S.E., Washington, D.C., as his address. The evidence neither showed that all of the items in the basement bedroom belonged to him, nor how his belongings had come to rest there or how long the seized items had been there. He points to this court's precedent holding that an occasional or even frequent occupant of premises is not presumed to possess everything contained at those premises, *see United States v. Zeigler*, 994 F.2d 845, 848 (D.C. Cir. 1993), and contrasts the evidence in his case to that in *Walker*, 99 F.3d at 441, where at the time of the search and seizure the defendant was "surrounded by drug paraphernalia in the open" and drugs were "all over the floor" of a neighboring room. In Dorman's view, his case is more like *United States v. Thorne*, 997 F.2d 1504, 1510 (D.C. Cir. 1993), where there was non-exclusive use of a bedroom and no drugs or drug paraphernalia were in plain view. The government rejects the notion that any of these cases require reversal because, in its view, when considered together the evidence of Dorman's primary occupancy of the basement bedroom, the combination of drugs and guns in the home, including some readily apparent drug paraphernalia, and his mother's testimony that he phoned and told her "I'm sorry" while the search warrant was being executed made it reasonable for the jury to conclude that Dorman constructively possessed the drugs and guns.

This court must "view[ ] the evidence in the light most favorable to the prosecution," *Boyd*, 803 F.3d at 692 (quoting *Jackson v. Virginia*, 443 U.S. 307, 319, 99 S.Ct. 2781, 61 L.Ed.2d 560 (1979)), not distinguishing between direct and circumstantial evidence, and "giving full play to the right of the jury to determine credibility, weigh the evidence and draw justifiable inferences of fact," *United States v. Vega*, 826 F.3d 514, 522 (D.C. Cir. 2016) (quoting *Dykes*, 406 F.3d at 721). The government fails to meet its burden of proof, however, if the evidence leaves a jury to "base a verdict on mere speculation." *United States v. Gaskins*, 690 F.3d 569, 578 n.3 (D.C. Cir. 2012) (quoting *United States v. Teffera*, 985 F.2d 1082, 1088 (D.C. Cir. 1993)).

A.

The evidence regarding the contents of the basement bedroom and his mother's testimony established that Dorman was the sole occupant of the basement bedroom, even if he did not have exclusive control inasmuch as his mother stored some belongings there. *See Morris*, 977 F.2d at 620; *Dykes*, 406 F.3d at 722. It also established that he exercised dominion and control over the bed where the gun was found. *See United States v. Edelin*, 996 F.2d 1238, 1241 (D.C. Cir. 1993). Dorman's mother testified that, as far as she observed, Dorman alone slept in the room and photo exhibits showed his personal papers and effects next to the bed. Although Dorman was in police custody when the search warrant was executed a couple of hours later, he was home the night before, which narrowed the time when someone else could have stashed the gun in the basement bedroom without it being discovered by him. *Cf. United States v. Johnson*, 592 F.3d 164, 168–69 (D.C. Cir. 2010). We therefore affirm his conviction on Count 2, unlawful possession of ammunition or a firearm by a convicted felon, under 18 U.S.C. § 922(g)(1), based on his constructive possession of the gun found in the basement bedroom and the parties' stipulation that Dorman had a prior felony conviction. *See United States v. Bryant*, 523 F.3d 349, 354 (D.C. Cir. 2008).

B.

The evidence of Dorman's constructive possession of the PCP is more attenuated. "The natural inference is that those who live in a house know what is going on inside, particularly in the common areas." *United States v. Jenkins*, 928 F.2d 1175, 1179 (D.C. Cir. 1991). But the court has emphasized the importance of distinguishing between drugs found in plain view in a common area and those that are hidden. *See United States v. Harris*, 515 F.3d 1307, 1310 (D.C. Cir. 2008). "[A] contrary view could unfairly sweep up unwitting roommates or housemates and subject them to the harsh criminal punishments associated with drug crimes." *Id.* Constructive possession of contraband found in a shared space in the defendant's home can be shown only where it was kept in plain view, *see, e.g., Jenkins*, 928 F.2d at 1179; *Harris*, 515 F.3d at 1310; *United States v. Davis*, 562 F.2d 681, 685 (D.C. Cir. 1977), or where there is additional evidence, including the defendant's presence and conduct at the time of the search or an item in his control, linking him to the contraband, *see, e.g., Johnson*, 592 F.3d at 168–69; *Jenkins*, 928 F.2d at 1179; *see also Thorne*, 997 F.2d at 1510–11.

There is no evidence that PCP or PCP drug paraphernalia were in plain view in the common areas of Dorman's mother's home. As described by Agent Hanna, the seizing officer, neither container of PCP was in plain view. The PCP in the laundry room was on the floor, on the right side of the washing machine, and Agent Hanna described it as not "necessarily" visible from the front upon approach. Trial Tr. 9 (July 9, 2014). Similarly, Agent Hanna testified that the PCP in the living room was in a vial found either inside or behind a floral vase sitting on the floor beside the television, but not in "plain view." Trial Tr. 179 (July 8, 2014). "[A] large plastic bag containing smaller glass vials with black screw tops" was found on a chair in the living room, Trial Tr. 185 (July 8, 2014), but neither trial testimony nor the government's supplemental appendix shows that the vials were visible to a passerby. Even assuming the empty prescription pill bottles found in the basement hallway could be used to transport PCP, they were in a trash bag covered by a blanket.

Nor was Dorman physically present or behaving suspiciously during the search of his mother's home. That absence "magnifies the importance of these evidentiary holes in the government's case." *United States v. Lawrence*, 471 F.3d 135, 142 (D.C. Cir. 2006).

Nor did the evidence in Dorman's basement bedroom link him to the PCP. The government points to the plastic baggies and a digital scale found in the basement bedroom, Appellee Br. 50, but the government's expert testified that PCP is distributed in glass or plastic bottles, not plastic baggies, and is measured by bottle size rather than by weight. The government also points to the gun in Dorman's bedroom mattress, relying on cases upholding constructive possession convictions on the theory that "drugs and guns go together." *Johnson*, 592 F.3d at 169 (quoting *Jenkins*, 928 F.2d at 1179); *see United States v. McLendon*, 378 F.3d 1109, 1113 & n.4 (D.C. Cir. 2004). The link between guns and drugs is an example of a "plus factor[ ]" that, when " 'coupled with proximity,' " can support a finding of constructive possession. *United States v. Booker*, 436 F.3d 238, 242 (D.C. Cir. 2006) (quoting *Alexander*, 331 F.3d at 127). Here there was no such close physical proximity between Dorman and the PCP. *Compare In re Sealed Case*, 105 F.3d 1460, 1464 (D.C. Cir. 1997) *with Booker*, 436 F.3d at 242–43, *and Moore*, 104 F.3d at 381. The gun in the basement bedroom, then, was not a "plus factor" to Dorman's proximity to the PCP in the laundry room; it was the primary connection. Relying on the evidence of his constructive possession of the gun in his basement bedroom to support his constructive possession of PCP elsewhere would stretch the "drugs and guns" observation beyond its common usage, piling inference upon inference. *Cf. Pereira v. United States*, 347 U.S. 1, 16, 74 S.Ct. 358, 98 L.Ed. 435 (1954) (Minton, J., concurring in part and dissenting in part). In *Jenkins*, 928 F.2d at 1179, where ammunition was found in the defendant's private bedroom and drug paraphernalia and remnants were found in plain view in common areas, the court held that the evidence was "just barely" sufficient to prove constructive possession of drugs. The government cites no case and the court is aware of none holding that constructive possession of a gun in one room by itself can prove constructive possession of drugs in a separate common area. *Cf. Johnson*, 592 F.3d at 169; *United States v. Dunn*, 846 F.2d 761, 764 (D.C. Cir. 1988). The absence of case law is not surprising: Because there are many lawful reasons to have a gun, a court cannot lightly infer that a gun is being used to protect a drug stash.

The government suggests that the gun, with its handle protruding from the mattress, "was positioned for easy access should someone intrude into the bedroom, so as to protect the major stash of PCP around the corner in the laundry room." Appellee Br. 44. This theory is undermined by "the spatial separation between the defendant, the gun, and the drugs." *Booker*, 436 F.3d at 242–43. In *Booker*, the court held that "a rational juror could reasonably conclude Booker constructively possessed the gun lying next to his drugs," *id.* at 243, rather than in a different room as here. Additionally, Booker was "never more than 50–80 feet away," from the contraband. *Id.* at 242. The evidence here is more akin to that in *In re Sealed Case*, 105 F.3d at 1464–66, where the court held that the evidence failed to show the defendant, who was in a restaurant, constructively possessed a gun found under the driver's seat of a parked car from which his brother sold drugs; even assuming the defendant knew of the gun and was a joint participant in an ongoing drug trafficking enterprise, the evidence failed to show the defendant was "in a position to exercise dominion and control over the gun," *id.* at 1464. So, too, here as the PCP was found in common areas of the home beyond Dorman's presence or control.

Of course, the evidence showed that his mother's home, which she described as Dorman's "home base," contained drugs and drug paraphernalia in several rooms, and Hill's description of visitors at Dorman's request lends weight to a reasonable jury finding that unlawful drug activities were going on in the mother's home. But evidence of participation in an ongoing drug business by itself would not ordinarily support a finding of constructive possession, *see id.*, and here, despite what the jury could reasonably infer was Dorman's frequent presence in his mother's home, there was no evidence that Dorman exercised knowing dominion and control over the PCP. The stipulation informing the jury that Dorman had a prior felony conviction did not identify the offense. Agent Hanna testified there was no tangible evidence, such as fingerprints or DNA evidence, connecting Dorman to the contraband found in 2317 Chester Street, S.E. Fingerprints recovered from the prescription pill bottles found in the basement hallway matched those of Khalid Davis and Ibrahim Ahmed Adam Mohamed, and while Davis may have had a phone contact with Dorman, no evidence connected either Davis or Mohamed to the PCP or the guns. Too many other individuals had access to the home whose activities were not specifically described. Suspicion, much less speculation, is insufficient to demonstrate that the government has met its burden of proof. *See Gaskins*, 690 F.3d at 578 n.3; *United States v. Salamanca*, 990 F.2d 629, 638 (D.C. Cir. 1993).

Nor does Dorman's apology to his mother fill the evidentiary gap. "The trouble with absence of evidence is that it is consistent with *any* hypothesis." *Pardo*, 636 F.2d at 549 (quoting *United States v. Holland*, 445 F.2d 701, 703 (D.C. Cir. 1971)) (emphasis in original). Dorman had phoned his mother while the search warrant was being executed. According to her, she told him the police were "all over my house" and that she was "upset and yelling about the situation." Trial Tr. 137 (July 9, 2014). Dorman responded "Ma, I'm sorry." *Id.* at 143. The government suggests this testimony was "devastating" to Dorman because it was an admission the contraband was his. Appellee Br. 46. Although "I'm sorry" may be a capacious statement, the evidence never established what he was sorry for or even that he knew drugs had been discovered in his mother's home. The record does not indicate when during the search the phone call occurred. Dorman's mother was outside "for two hours in the hot sun" during the search, Trial Tr. 156 (July 9, 2014), leaving unclear whether she knew of the drugs when he phoned. Theoretically, Dorman could have been apologizing because he brought the PCP into her home, but it is at least as likely that he could have been apologizing because of his robbery at Kay Jewelers, for which he had just been arrested, or just to calm down his mother who was extremely upset. Dorman's statement is not in the nature of a vague expression of guilt that can only be understood as a confession to one particular criminal act, *see United States v. Brinson-Scott*, 714 F.3d 616, 624 (D.C. Cir. 2013), and leaves the jury to speculate about what he meant.

In sum, the government's attempt to demonstrate there was sufficient evidence of Dorman's constructive possession of the PCP fails under the court's precedent. True, his bedroom was around the corner from the laundry room, a gun was found in his bedroom, and the home contained some non-PCP drug paraphernalia in plain view, but multiple individuals had a key or otherwise had access to the home when Dorman was not present and no tangible evidence connected him to the PCP, which was not found in plain view. Viewed cumulatively in the light most favorable to the government, the evidence is equivocal about Dorman's relationship to the PCP and his ability to exercise dominion and control over it, and is thus insufficient to show, under Count 1, that he constructively possessed 100 grams or more of PCP with intent to distribute. *See United States v. Douglas*, 482 F.3d 591, 596–97 (D.C. Cir. 2007). This also means, notwithstanding the sufficiency of the evidence that Dorman constructively possessed a firearm under Count 2, that there was insufficient evidence of a drug trafficking offense to support his Section 924(c) conviction under Count 3. *See United States v. Kelly*, 552 F.3d 824, 832 (D.C. Cir. 2009). We therefore reverse the judgment of conviction on Counts 1 and 3.

EXERCISE

The opinion in *Dorman* recognizes that to show constructive possession "The government must prove beyond a reasonable doubt that 'the defendant knew of, and was in a position to exercise dominion and control over, the contraband.' "

Granny Annie lives in her lifelong home with her adult daughter and two grandchildren. One of the grandchildren, Tommy, smokes pot regularly. He keeps his supply of marijuana in a jar on the coffee table in the living room next to an identical jar in which Granny Annie maintains a supply of hard candy for visitors. Granny Annie knows the marijuana is there, and knows that it is marijuana. She doesn't use it, or really approve of Tommy using it, but she does not view it as a "big deal," so long as Tommy and her daughter (a recovering opioid addict) stay away from harder drugs.

Is Granny Annie in violation of 21 U.S.C. § 844(a)? How should a prosecutor approach the case against her?

Possession can be difficult to prove in those cases where the defendant did not exclusively or primarily control the space in which the narcotics were found. In the case below, the court examines the evidence going towards actual possession of narcotics that was not observed.

UNITED STATES V. CLARK

740 F. 3d 808 (2d Cir. 2014)

JON O. NEWMAN, CIRCUIT JUDGE:

This appeal of a criminal conviction presents extraordinary facts that challenge a reviewing court to take seriously its constitutional obligation to assure that evidence resulting in a conviction was sufficient to permit a jury reasonably to find guilt beyond a reasonable doubt. Jeremiah K. Clark appeals from the March 7, 2012, judgment of the District Court for the Northern District of New York (William M. Skretny, District Judge), convicting him, after a jury trial, of being a felon in possession of a firearm (Count I) and possession of a controlled substance (Count II). We have affirmed the conviction on Count I in a Summary Order filed today. In this opinion, we reverse the conviction on Count II.

Background

On Nov. 16, 2002, officers from the City of Lockport Police Department (Lockport, N.Y.) and the Niagara County Sheriff's Office (Lockport, N.Y.), responded to a 911 call reporting that a group of men, possibly armed, had just left Gonzo's Bar in Lockport in a white Jeep Cherokee after trying to "jump somebody." When the officers arrived at the bar, they saw Clark and three others sitting in the Cherokee. The facts of the ensuing confrontation, detailed in a Summary Order filed today, are not relevant to the issue decided in this opinion, except to note that the police found a firearm in the Cherokee and arrested Clark. In this opinion, we are concerned only with the facts occurring after Clark's arrest.

Niagara County Deputy Sheriff Anthony Giamberdino placed Clark, alone, in the rear compartment of his police cruiser. Clark was handcuffed with his hands behind his back. Niagara County Deputy Sheriff Gary May testified that the link between the two bracelets of the handcuffs was no longer than one or one and one-half inches. City of Lockport Police Officer Steven Abbott testified that before Clark was placed in the car, he patted down his waist, pockets, pant legs, and coat, looking for weapons. Nothing was found. The ride from the scene of the arrest to the Lockport police station lasted about one minute. After arriving at the police station, May helped Clark, still handcuffed, out of the car. Clark was then escorted into the booking area of the police station.

Once Clark was out of the police car, Giamberdino lifted the cushion of the back seat out and up, making visible the space between the back of the back-seat cushion and the bottom of the back-seat back rest. In that space he saw a quantity of a white powdery substance that later analysis determined was crack cocaine. Giamberdino also testified that he had checked this space before starting his evening shift, nothing was there at that time, and Clark was the first person to occupy the back seat of the car that evening.

Deputy Sheriff May testified that as Clark got out of the car and walked past him, he did not see any white powdery substance on his hands, pants, or jacket. Nor did he see any white powdery substance on the back seat until the seat was lifted up. No glassine envelope or other container was found in the police car or on Clark's person.

Discussion

. . .

In our view, this record does not permit an affirmance on Count 2. Several facts are not in dispute: (1) Clark was patted down for weapons before being placed in a police car; (2) no object large enough to contain a substantial quantity of crack cocaine was noticed; (3) Clark was then placed in the back of a police car with his hands handcuffed securely behind his back; (4) the ride to the police station took about one minute; (5) shortly after Clark got out of the vehicle, with his hands still handcuffed behind his back, a police officer lifted the back seat cushion sufficiently to disclose the space between the back edge of the back-seat cushion and the lower edge of the back-seat back rest; (6) in that space the officer found a quantity of crack cocaine measuring more than five inches in length and about one inch wide, and of sufficient depth such that some quantities of crumbled crack cocaine are visible above the layer of fully powdered crack cocaine (a photograph of the crack cocaine appears in the Appendix to this opinion); (7) no traces of crack cocaine were observed on Clark's clothing or on his hands; (8) no glassine envelope or similar container customarily used for holding a quantity of crack cocaine was found in the police car, nor was Clark observed to have discarded such a container after leaving the police car.

There are only three possible ways that this quantity of crack cocaine could have been secreted in the space in which it was discovered. (1) Clark might have removed the quantity from his person or clothing and wedged it into the space underneath the seam where the back-seat cushion meets the back-seat back rest; (2) someone other than Clark might have inadvertently left the crack cocaine in that space before Clark entered the police car; (3) someone other than Clark might have deliberately placed the crack cocaine in that space after Clark got out of the police car. Clark's conviction for possessing crack cocaine is valid only if a jury could reasonably find the first possibility beyond a reasonable doubt.

We cannot say it is an absolute impossibility for a person with his hands securely handcuffed behind his back to extract a substantial quantity of crack cocaine from his person or clothing and wedge it into the space where the quantity was found without leaving a trace of cocaine on his fingers or clothing, but we can say that the possibility of such an occurrence is so exceedingly remote that no jury could *reasonably* find *beyond a reasonable doubt* that it happened. The remote possibility is diminished virtually to zero by the fact that no glassine envelope or other packaging material was found in the police vehicle or on Clark's person. It taxes credulity to think that Clark carried such a quantity of crack cocaine loose in his pocket and, while handcuffed, extracted it from his pocket and secreted it where it was found, all without leaving a trace on his person or clothing.

Whether or not the extraordinary improbability of circumstances necessary for conviction on Count II in fact occurred, it is better to honor the constitutional standard of proof beyond a reasonable doubt by appropriate appellate review than to require Clark to serve three extra years, in addition to the ten years for Count I, for an offense of which he is highly likely to be innocent.

It has been said that it is better to let ten guilty persons go free than to convict one innocent person. In the past, some have favored higher ratios. However one prefers to quantify an unacceptable risk of convicting the innocent, it is difficult to imagine a case where the possibility that an innocent person has been convicted of an offense is greater than the one now before us.

Conclusion

The judgment is affirmed with respect to Count I and reversed with respect to Count II.

EXERCISE

The *Clark* case involves crack cocaine found in a police car. Is the government attempting to prove actual possession or constructive possession?

b.   Possession of Marijuana That Is Legal Under State Law

Many states have legalized the simple possession of marijuana for recreational use and others allow it for medicinal purposes. This conflicts with the language of the federal statute at 21 U.S.C. § 844(a). The conflict between the federal and state laws has spanned several administrations.

GONZALEZ V. RAICH
545 U.S. 1 (2005)

JUSTICE STEVENS delivered the opinion of the Court.

California is one of at least nine States that authorize the use of marijuana for medicinal purposes. The question presented in this case is whether the power vested in Congress by Article I, § 8, of the Constitution "[t]o make all Laws which shall be necessary and proper for carrying into Execution" its authority to "regulate Commerce with foreign Nations, and among the several States" includes the power to prohibit the local cultivation and use of marijuana in compliance with California law.

I

California has been a pioneer in the regulation of marijuana. In 1913, California was one of the first States to prohibit the sale and possession of marijuana, and at the end of the century, California became the first State to authorize limited use of the drug for medicinal purposes. In 1996, California voters passed Proposition 215, now codified as the Compassionate Use Act of 1996. The proposition was designed to ensure that "seriously ill" residents of the State have access to marijuana for medical purposes, and to encourage Federal and State Governments to take steps toward ensuring the safe and affordable distribution of the drug to patients in need. The Act creates an exemption from criminal prosecution for physicians, as well as for patients and primary caregivers who possess or cultivate marijuana for medicinal purposes with the recommendation or approval of a physician. A "primary caregiver" is a person who has consistently assumed responsibility for the housing, health, or safety of the patient.

Respondents Angel Raich and Diane Monson are California residents who suffer from a variety of serious medical conditions and have sought to avail themselves of medical marijuana pursuant to the terms of the Compassionate Use Act. They are being treated by licensed, board-certified family practitioners, who have concluded, after prescribing a host of conventional medicines to treat respondents' conditions and to alleviate their associated symptoms, that marijuana is the only drug available that provides effective treatment. Both women have been using marijuana as a medication for several years pursuant to their doctors' recommendation, and both rely heavily on cannabis to function on a daily basis. Indeed, Raich's physician believes that forgoing cannabis treatments would certainly cause Raich excruciating pain and could very well prove fatal.

Respondent Monson cultivates her own marijuana, and ingests the drug in a variety of ways including smoking and using a vaporizer. Respondent Raich, by contrast, is unable to cultivate her own, and thus relies on two caregivers, litigating as "John Does," to provide her with locally grown marijuana at no charge. These caregivers also process the cannabis into hashish or keif, and Raich herself processes some of the marijuana into oils, balms, and foods for consumption.

On August 15, 2002, county deputy sheriffs and agents from the federal Drug Enforcement Administration (DEA) came to Monson's home. After a thorough investigation, the county officials concluded that her use of marijuana was entirely lawful as a matter of California law. Nevertheless, after a 3-hour standoff, the federal agents seized and destroyed all six of her cannabis plants.

Respondents thereafter brought this action against the Attorney General of the United States and the head of the DEA seeking injunctive and declaratory relief prohibiting the enforcement of the federal Controlled Substances Act (CSA), 84 Stat. 1242, 21 U.S.C. § 801 et seq., to the extent it prevents them from possessing, obtaining, or manufacturing cannabis for their personal medical use. In their complaint and supporting affidavits, Raich and Monson described the severity of their afflictions, their repeatedly futile attempts to obtain relief with conventional medications, and the opinions of their doctors concerning their need to use marijuana. Respondents claimed that enforcing the CSA against them would violate the Commerce Clause, the Due Process Clause of the Fifth Amendment, the Ninth and Tenth Amendments of the Constitution, and the doctrine of medical necessity.

The District Court denied respondents' motion for a preliminary injunction. *Raich v. Ashcroft,* 248 F.Supp.2d 918 (N.D.Cal.2003). Although the court found that the federal enforcement interests "wane[d]" when compared to the harm that California residents would suffer if denied access to medically necessary marijuana, it concluded that respondents could not demonstrate a likelihood of success on the merits of their legal claims. *Id.,* at 931.

A divided panel of the Court of Appeals for the Ninth Circuit reversed and ordered the District Court to enter a preliminary injunction. *Raich v. Ashcroft,* 352 F.3d 1222 (2003). The court found that respondents had "demonstrated a strong likelihood of success on their claim that, as applied to them, the CSA is an unconstitutional exercise of Congress' Commerce Clause authority." *Id.,* at 1227. The Court of Appeals distinguished prior Circuit cases upholding the CSA in the face of Commerce Clause challenges by focusing on what it deemed to be the *"separate and distinct class of activities"* at issue in this case: "the intrastate, noncommercial cultivation and possession of cannabis for personal medical purposes as recommended by a patient's physician pursuant to valid California state law." *Id.,* at 1228. The court found the latter class of activities "different in kind from drug trafficking" because interposing a physician's recommendation raises different health and safety concerns, and because "this limited use is clearly distinct from the broader illicit drug market-as well as any broader commercial market for medicinal marijuana-insofar as the medicinal marijuana at issue in this case is not intended for, nor does it enter, the stream of commerce." . . .

Shortly after taking office in 1969, President Nixon declared a national "war on drugs." As the first campaign of that war, Congress set out to enact legislation that would consolidate various drug laws on the books into a comprehensive statute, provide meaningful regulation over legitimate sources of drugs to prevent diversion into illegal channels, and strengthen law enforcement tools against the traffic in illicit drugs. That effort culminated in the passage of the Comprehensive Drug Abuse Prevention and Control Act of 1970, 84 Stat. 1236.

This was not, however, Congress' first attempt to regulate the national market in drugs. Rather, as early as 1906 Congress enacted federal legislation imposing labeling regulations on medications and prohibiting the manufacture or shipment of any adulterated or misbranded drug traveling in interstate commerce. Aside from these labeling restrictions, most domestic drug regulations prior to 1970 generally came in the guise of revenue laws, with the Department of the Treasury serving as the Federal Government's primary enforcer. For example, the primary drug control law, before being repealed by the passage of the CSA, was the Harrison Narcotics Act of 1914, 38 Stat. 785 (repealed 1970). The Harrison Act sought to exert control over the possession and sale of narcotics, specifically cocaine and opiates, by requiring producers, distributors, and purchasers to register with the Federal Government, by assessing taxes against parties so registered, and by regulating the issuance of prescriptions.

Marijuana itself was not significantly regulated by the Federal Government until 1937 when accounts of marijuana's addictive qualities and physiological effects, paired with dissatisfaction with enforcement efforts at state and local levels, prompted Congress to pass the Marihuana Tax Act, 50 Stat. 551 (repealed 1970). Like the Harrison Act, the Marihuana Tax Act did not outlaw the possession or sale of marijuana outright. Rather, it imposed registration and reporting requirements for all individuals importing, producing, selling, or dealing in marijuana, and required the payment of annual taxes in addition to transfer taxes whenever the drug changed hands. Moreover, doctors wishing to prescribe marijuana for medical purposes were required to comply with rather burdensome administrative requirements. Noncompliance exposed traffickers to severe federal penalties, whereas compliance would often subject them to prosecution under state law. Thus, while the Marihuana Tax Act did not declare the drug illegal *per se,* the onerous administrative requirements, the prohibitively expensive taxes, and the risks attendant on compliance practically curtailed the marijuana trade.

Then in 1970, after declaration of the national "war on drugs," federal drug policy underwent a significant transformation. A number of noteworthy events precipitated this policy shift. First, in *Leary v. United States,* 395 U.S. 6, 89 S.Ct. 1532, 23 L.Ed.2d 57 (1969), this Court held certain provisions of the Marihuana Tax Act and other narcotics legislation unconstitutional. Second, at the end of his term, President Johnson fundamentally reorganized the federal drug control agencies. The Bureau of Narcotics, then housed in the Department of the Treasury, merged with the Bureau of Drug Abuse Control, then housed in the Department of Health, Education, and Welfare (HEW), to create the Bureau of Narcotics and Dangerous Drugs, currently housed in the Department of Justice. Finally, prompted by a perceived need to consolidate the growing number of piecemeal drug laws and to enhance federal drug enforcement powers, Congress enacted the Comprehensive Drug Abuse Prevention and Control Act.

Title II of that Act, the CSA, repealed most of the earlier antidrug laws in favor of a comprehensive regime to combat the international and interstate traffic in illicit drugs. The main objectives of the CSA were to conquer drug abuse and to control the legitimate and illegitimate traffic in controlled substances. Congress was particularly concerned with the need to prevent the diversion of drugs from legitimate to illicit channels.

To effectuate these goals, Congress devised a closed regulatory system making it unlawful to manufacture, distribute, dispense, or possess any controlled substance except in a manner authorized by the CSA. 21 U.S.C. §§ 841(a)(1), 844(a). The CSA categorizes all controlled substances into five schedules. § 812. The drugs are grouped together based on their accepted medical uses, the potential for abuse, and their psychological and physical effects on the body. §§ 811, 812. Each schedule is associated with a distinct set of controls regarding the manufacture, distribution, and use of the substances listed therein. §§ 821–830. The CSA and its implementing regulations set forth strict requirements regarding registration, labeling and packaging, production quotas, drug security, and recordkeeping. *Ibid.*; 21 CFR § 1301 *et seq.* (2004).

In enacting the CSA, Congress classified marijuana as a Schedule I drug. 21 U.S.C. § 812(c). This preliminary classification was based, in part, on the recommendation of the Assistant Secretary of HEW "that marihuana be retained within schedule I at least until the completion of certain studies now underway." Schedule I drugs are categorized as such because of their high potential for abuse, lack of any accepted medical use, and absence of any accepted safety for use in medically supervised treatment. § 812(b)(1). These three factors, in varying gradations, are also used to categorize drugs in the other four schedules. For example, Schedule II substances also have a high potential for abuse which may lead to severe psychological or physical dependence, but unlike Schedule I drugs, they have a currently accepted medical use. § 812(b)(2). By classifying marijuana as a Schedule I drug, as opposed to listing it on a lesser schedule, the manufacture, distribution, or possession of marijuana became a criminal offense, with the sole exception being use of the drug as part of a Food and Drug Administration preapproved research study. §§ 823(f), 841(a)(1), 844(a); see also *United States v. Oakland Cannabis Buyers' Cooperative,* 532 U.S. 483, 490, 121 S.Ct. 1711, 149 L.Ed.2d 722 (2001).

The CSA provides for the periodic updating of schedules and delegates authority to the Attorney General, after consultation with the Secretary of Health and Human Services, to add, remove, or transfer substances to, from, or between schedules. § 811. Despite considerable efforts to reschedule marijuana, it remains a Schedule I drug.

III

Respondents in this case do not dispute that passage of the CSA, as part of the Comprehensive Drug Abuse Prevention and Control Act, was well within Congress' commerce power. Brief for Respondents 22, 38. Nor do they contend that any provision or section of the CSA amounts to an unconstitutional exercise of congressional authority. Rather, respondents' challenge is actually quite limited; they argue that the CSA's categorical prohibition of the manufacture and possession of marijuana as applied to the intrastate manufacture and possession of marijuana for medical purposes pursuant to California law exceeds Congress' authority under the Commerce Clause.

In assessing the validity of congressional regulation, none of our Commerce Clause cases can be viewed in isolation. As charted in considerable detail in *United States v. Lopez,* our understanding of the reach of the Commerce Clause, as well as Congress' assertion of authority thereunder, has evolved over time. The Commerce Clause emerged as the Framers' response to the central problem giving rise to the Constitution itself: the absence of any federal commerce power under the Articles of Confederation. For the first century of our history, the primary use of the Clause was to preclude the kind of discriminatory state legislation that had once been permissible. Then, in response to rapid industrial development and an increasingly interdependent national economy, Congress "ushered in a new era of federal regulation under the commerce power," beginning with the enactment of the Interstate Commerce Act in 1887, 24 Stat. 379, and the Sherman Antitrust Act in 1890, 26 Stat. 209, as amended, 15 U.S.C. § 2 *et seq.*

Cases decided during that "new era," which now spans more than a century, have identified three general categories of regulation in which Congress is authorized to engage under its commerce power. First, Congress can regulate the channels of interstate commerce. *Perez v. United States,* 402 U.S. 146, 150, 91 S.Ct. 1357, 28 L.Ed.2d 686 (1971). Second, Congress has authority to regulate and protect the instrumentalities of interstate commerce, and persons or things in interstate commerce. *Ibid.* Third, Congress has the power to regulate activities that substantially affect interstate commerce. *Ibid.; NLRB v. Jones & Laughlin Steel Corp.,* 301 U.S. 1, 37, 57 S.Ct. 615, 81 L.Ed. 893 (1937). Only the third category is implicated in the case at hand.

Our case law firmly establishes Congress' power to regulate purely local activities that are part of an economic "class of activities" that have a substantial effect on interstate commerce. . . .

Our decision in *Wickard,* 317 U.S. 111, 63 S.Ct. 82, 87 L.Ed. 122, is of particular relevance. In *Wickard,* we upheld the application of regulations promulgated under the Agricultural Adjustment Act of 1938, 52 Stat. 31, which were designed to control the volume of wheat moving in interstate and foreign commerce in order to avoid surpluses and consequent abnormally low prices. The regulations established an allotment of 11.1 acres for Filburn's 1941 wheat crop, but he sowed 23 acres, intending to use the excess by consuming it on his own farm. Filburn argued that even though we had sustained Congress' power to regulate the production of goods for commerce, that power did not authorize "federal regulation [of] production not intended in any part for commerce but wholly for consumption on the farm." *Wickard,* 317 U.S., at 118, 63 S.Ct. 82. Justice Jackson's opinion for a unanimous Court rejected this submission. He wrote:

> "The effect of the statute before us is to restrict the amount which may be produced for market and the extent as well to which one may forestall resort to the market by producing to meet his own needs. That appellee's own contribution to the demand for wheat may be trivial by itself is not enough to remove him from the scope of federal regulation where, as here, his contribution, taken together with that of many others similarly situated, is far from trivial." *Id.,* at 127–128, 63 S.Ct. 82.

Wickard thus establishes that Congress can regulate purely intrastate activity that is not itself "commercial," in that it is not produced for sale, if it concludes that failure to regulate that class of activity would undercut the regulation of the interstate market in that commodity.

The similarities between this case and *Wickard* are striking. Like the farmer in *Wickard,* respondents are cultivating, for home consumption, a fungible commodity for which there is an established, albeit illegal, interstate market. Just as the Agricultural Adjustment Act was designed "to control the volume [of wheat] moving in interstate and foreign commerce in order to avoid surpluses . . ." and consequently control the market price, *id.,* at 115, 63 S.Ct. 82, a primary purpose of the CSA is to control the supply and demand of controlled substances in both lawful and unlawful drug markets. See nn. 20–21, *supra.* In *Wickard,* we had no difficulty concluding that Congress had a rational basis for believing that, when viewed in the aggregate, leaving home-consumed wheat outside the regulatory scheme would have a substantial influence on price and market conditions. Here too, Congress had a rational basis for concluding that leaving home-consumed marijuana outside federal control would similarly affect price and market conditions.

More concretely, one concern prompting inclusion of wheat grown for home consumption in the 1938 Act was that rising market prices could draw such wheat into the interstate market, resulting in lower market prices.

Wickard, 317 U.S., at 128, 63 S.Ct. 82. The parallel concern making it appropriate to include marijuana grown for home consumption in the CSA is the likelihood that the high demand in the interstate market will draw such marijuana into that market. While the diversion of homegrown wheat tended to frustrate the federal interest in stabilizing prices by regulating the volume of commercial transactions in the interstate market, the diversion of homegrown marijuana tends to frustrate the federal interest in eliminating commercial transactions in the interstate market in their entirety. In both cases, the regulation is squarely within Congress' commerce power because production of the commodity meant for home consumption, be it wheat or marijuana, has a substantial effect on supply and demand in the national market for that commodity. . . .

In assessing the scope of Congress' authority under the Commerce Clause, we stress that the task before us is a modest one. We need not determine whether respondents' activities, taken in the aggregate, substantially affect interstate commerce in fact, but only whether a "rational basis" exists for so concluding. . . . Given the enforcement difficulties that attend distinguishing between marijuana cultivated locally and marijuana grown elsewhere, 21 U.S.C. § 801(5), and concerns about diversion into illicit channels, we have no difficulty concluding that Congress had a rational basis for believing that failure to regulate the intrastate manufacture and possession of marijuana would leave a gaping hole in the CSA. Thus, as in *Wickard,* when it enacted comprehensive legislation to regulate the interstate market in a fungible commodity, Congress was acting well within its authority to "make all Laws which shall be necessary and proper" to "regulate Commerce . . . among the several States." U.S. Const., Art. I, § 8. That the regulation ensnares some purely intrastate activity is of no moment. As we have done many times before, we refuse to excise individual components of that larger scheme.

EXERCISE

The *Gonzalez* case held that federal authorities can prosecute marijuana possession. That leaves in the hands of prosecutors the discretion to decide whether or not to do so.

Imagine that you are the United States Attorney in a state where marijuana is legal under state law for recreational use. If you were given authority by the attorney general to establish policy at the local level on the use of that discretion, what would your policy guidance be regarding when marijuana possession can be taken as a federal crime under 21 U.S.C. § 844(a)?

2. DISTRIBUTION AND DISPENSING OF NARCOTICS

The primary federal narcotics statute, 21 U.S.C. § 841(a) is actually quite simple:

(a) Unlawful acts

Except as authorized by this subchapter, it shall be unlawful for any person knowingly or intentionally—

> **(1)** to manufacture, distribute, or dispense, or possess with intent to manufacture, distribute, or dispense, a controlled substance; or
>
> **(2)** to create, distribute, or dispense, or possess with intent to distribute or dispense, a counterfeit substance.

21 U.S.C. § 802(7) defines a "counterfeit substance" as knock-offs of legal pharmaceuticals: "a controlled substance which, or the container or labeling of which, without authorization, bears the trademark, trade name, or other identifying mark, imprint, number, or device, or any likeness thereof, of a manufacturer, distributor, or dispenser other than the person or persons who in fact manufactured, distributed, or dispensed such substance and which thereby falsely purports or is represented to be the product of, or to have been distributed by, such other manufacturer, distributor, or dispenser." It is the first sub-paragraph—covering "manufacture, distribute, or dispense, or possess with intent to manufacture, distribute, or dispense, a controlled substance—that much more often will be the basis of a federal narcotics case.

Distribution of narcotics is distinct from mere possession on the action element alone, and requires different proofs.

a. Distribution for No Remuneration

We often consider drug trafficking to be synonymous with drug sales, but the controlling statutes (at least in the federal system) use a variety of terms which may or may not require a traditional commercial transaction. A sale requires proof of two actions: providing the product, and payment. Distribution, on the other hand, can involve only one: the provision of the product from one person to another.

UNITED STATES v. WASHINGTON
41 F. 3d 917 (4th Cir. 1994)

RUSSELL, CIRCUIT JUDGE:

The defendant, Raymond L. Washington, was convicted of possession of cocaine with intent to distribute in violation of 21 U.S.C. § 841(a)(1). He appeals the district court's refusal to reduce his charge to simple possession of cocaine under 21 U.S.C. § 844(a). We affirm.

I.

In March 1992, during a search incident to a lawful arrest for illegally operating a motor vehicle, Washington was found in possession of 12.1 grams of cocaine base, or "crack" cocaine. The arresting officers also found a pager and a $20 bill on Washington and a 9mm pistol in the car between the driver's seat and the transmission hump. The officers did not find any drug paraphernalia that would indicate that Washington planned to sell cocaine: the car contained no packaging materials, such as vials, plastic baggies, sandwich bags, or corners of plastic bags, and no weighing apparatus, such as a scale.

At trial, Washington testified that he was a serious drug user. He said that he had used cocaine for four years and had been hospitalized three times for drug abuse. He testified that he used about 4.5 grams of cocaine per day and that the cocaine found on his person was for his own use. Washington's girlfriend testified that Washington used drugs "a lot" and "very often." She confirmed that he had been hospitalized for drug abuse.

On cross-examination, however, Washington admitted that, although he did not have a job, he paid $450 for the cocaine. He explained that he received the money to purchase the cocaine from his friends, who gave him the money because he could purchase cocaine at a good price. He testified that he planned to return to his friends with the cocaine, which they would use together. When asked whether he intended to share the cocaine with somebody else, Washington responded in the affirmative.

A grand jury indicted Washington for one count of possession with the intent to distribute in excess of five grams of cocaine base in violation of 21 U.S.C. § 841(a)(1), and one count of intentional use of a firearm in relationship to a drug trafficking crime in violation of 18 U.S.C. § 924(c)(1) and § 2. The jury returned a verdict of guilty to the possession offense and not guilty to the firearm offense. The district court sentenced Washington to 210 months imprisonment.

Washington was represented at trial and on this appeal by court-appointed counsel. Washington's counsel filed a notice of appeal on Washington's behalf but, after reviewing the entire record, determined that there was no merit to Washington's appeal. Pursuant to the guidelines set forth in *Anders v. California,* 386 U.S. 738, 87 S.Ct. 1396, 18 L.Ed.2d 493 (1967), counsel nonetheless submitted a brief and appeared at oral argument on Washington's behalf. In accordance with the requirements of *Anders,* furthermore, we have examined the entire record in this case and have found no other meritorious issues for appeal.

On October 5, 1994, one week after the Court heard arguments in this case, the Clerk of the Court notified Washington that he had the right under *Anders* to file a *pro se* supplemental brief. The Clerk allowed Washington

30 days to file a supplemental brief. Washington did not submit such a brief, and the 30-day period has expired.

II.

The record clearly demonstrates that Washington was not involved in any way in the trafficking of drugs. He did not sell drugs, and he was not a courier of drugs. He simply bought cocaine, which he planned to use himself and to share with his friends. However, Washington's intent to share the cocaine with others is sufficient for a court to find that he possessed drugs with intent to distribute.

Distribution under 21 U.S.C. § 841(a)(1) is not limited to the sale of controlled substances. *United States v. Baswell,* 792 F.2d 755, 760 n. 7 (8th Cir.1986). "Facilitation of the sale of narcotics" was prohibited before Congress enacted § 841. 21 U.S.C. § 174 (repealed 1970). Section 841, part of the Comprehensive Drug Abuse Prevention and Control Act of 1970 (the "1970 Act"), 21 U.S.C. § 801 *et seq.,* proscribes "distribution" of controlled substances, as opposed to "facilitation of sale." *See United States v. Hernandez,* 480 F.2d 1044, 1046 (9th Cir.1973). The term "distribute" means "to deliver . . . a controlled substance. . . ." 21 U.S.C. § 802(11). "Deliver" means "the actual, constructive, or attempted transfer of a controlled substance . . . whether or not there exists an agency relationship." 21 U.S.C. § 802(8). Thus, in enacting the 1970 Act, Congress intended to proscribe a range of conduct broader than the mere sale of narcotics.

Sharing drugs with another constitutes "distribution" under § 841(a)(1). *United States v. Ramirez,* 608 F.2d 1261, 1264 (9th Cir.1979) ("In the instant case, there is direct evidence that appellant engaged in the 'distribution' of cocaine; although apparently no commercial scheme is involved, his sharing the cocaine . . . constitutes 'distribution' for purposes of 21 U.S.C. § 841(a)(1)."); *United States v. Meyers,* 601 F.Supp. 1072, 1074 (D.Or.1984) ("The concept of 'distribution' includes sharing drugs with a third party, and is not limited to commercial ventures.").

Washington testified at trial that he intended to share the cocaine in his possession with his friends. This admission was enough to demonstrate that he possessed the cocaine "with intent to distribute."

The Ninth Circuit considered almost the exact same factual situation in *United States v. Wright,* 593 F.2d 105 (9th Cir.1979). In *Wright,* a friend gave the defendant $20 and asked him to purchase heroin so that the two of them could use it together; the defendant left the friend's dwelling, bought the heroin, and returned to the friend's dwelling, where they snorted the heroin together. *Id.* at 108.

The district court in *Wright* had refused to give the defendant's proposed jury instruction that would have directed the jury, if it found that the defendant acquired the heroin in a joint venture with the friend and used the heroin only with the friend, to conclude that there was no distribution of heroin. Instead, the district court instructed the jury simply that "distribute" meant "to transfer or deliver a substance either directly or by means of another person." *Id.* at 106. The defendant based his jury instruction on *United States v. Swiderski,* 548 F.2d 445 (2d Cir.1977), in which the Second Circuit held that:

> where two individuals simultaneously and jointly acquire possession of a drug for their own use, intending only to share it together, their crime is . . . simple joint possession, without any intent to distribute the drug further. Since both acquire possession from the outset and neither intends to distribute the drug to a third person, neither serves as a link in the chain of distribution.

> *Id.* at 450. Although the defendant in *Wright* purchased the heroin alone, he argued that the purchase was part of a joint venture with the friend; thus, there was no distribution of heroin to the friend because the friend was in constructive possession of the heroin at the time he made the purchase. *Wright,* 593 F.2d at 108. The Ninth Circuit, concluding that "Congress intended to prevent individuals from acquiring drugs for whatever purpose on behalf of others and then transferring the drugs to those others," rejected the defendant's joint venture theory and upheld the district court's jury instruction. *Id. See also United States v. Speer,* 30 F.3d 605, 608–09 (5th Cir.1994) (following *Wright*).

We agree with the court in *Wright* that a defendant who purchases a drug and shares it with a friend has "distributed" the drug even though the purchase was part of a joint venture to use drugs. Washington and his friends were clearly engaged in a joint venture: the friends gave Washington money to purchase cocaine, and Washington went out and purchased cocaine that all would use. The joint venture, however, does not alter the fact that Washington, from the time he purchased the cocaine until the time he was found with it, intended to distribute the cocaine to his friends. Although Washington did not intend to sell the cocaine to his friends, he intended to deliver cocaine to those friends. Under § 841(a)(1), Washington's intent to deliver cocaine to his friends constituted an "intent to distribute."

Washington's trial testimony that he intended to share the cocaine with his friends was, in itself, sufficient evidence for the jury to find him guilty of possession with intent to distribute. The government did not need to demonstrate an intent to distribute based upon the quantity of cocaine found on Washington and from the other circumstances of the case.

The judgment of the district court is affirmed.

EXERCISE

Rich is at a party at Dwight's house. Dwight is lining up some cocaine on a table, preparing to snort it. Dwight had brought the cocaine with him to the party, hoping to use it himself. Rich spots him and asks if he can have some, and after a little hesitation, Dwight says "sure, go ahead." Rich snorts a line of the cocaine.

Has Dwight committed the federal crime of distribution of illegal narcotics under 21 U.S.C. § 841(a)?

b. Distribution/Dispensing by Licensed Doctors

Many highly addictive drugs—including opioids—are available by prescription. Doctors are licensed to dispense these drugs by the Drug Enforcement Administration. However, even licensed dispensers can be convicted of illegal distribution of narcotics under 21 U.S.C. § 841(a). To do so, however, the prosecution must prove an additional element.

UNITED STATES V. TRAN TRONG CUONG M.D.
18 F.3d 1132 (4th Cir. 1994)

CHAPMAN, SENIOR CIRCUIT JUDGE:

Appellant Tran Trong Cuong, M.D. (Tran) is a physician educated in Paris, France and admitted to practice medicine in the Commonwealth of Virginia since 1973. He is registered as a practitioner with the Drug Enforcement Administration and authorized to prescribe controlled substances listed in Schedules II, III, IV and V as set forth in 21 U.S.C. § 812. He was indicted under 21 U.S.C. § 841(a)(1) for knowingly and willfully distributing and dispensing by prescription various quantities of Schedule II through V controlled substances outside the usual course of medical practice and for other than legitimate medical purposes. The indictment contained 136 counts of unlawful distribution of the drugs and a separate count for criminal forfeiture of property allegedly used in connection with these offenses, as provided by 21 U.S.C. § 853. Following a jury trial, Tran was convicted of 127 counts, and the jury returned a special verdict supporting forfeiture of certain real estate located in Alexandria, Virginia. He was acquitted of eight counts, and one count was dismissed prior to the verdict.

Tran was sentenced to 97 months in prison, ordered to pay a special assessment of $6,350, and an order of forfeiture was entered as to the real estate. Tran now appeals. . . .

Tran is accused of unlawfully prescribing controlled substances to a total of 30 patients between April 1989 and January 1992. The indictment charges that 1,711 prescriptions were written to these 30 individuals during the time alleged in the indictment and these prescriptions included drugs such as Percodan from Schedule II, Vicodin and Tylenol with codeine from Schedule III, and Valium and Zanax from Schedule IV. The testimony showed that approximately 4,000 of Tran's prescriptions were filled during 1991 at 35 pharmacies close to his office. A pharmacist testified that he had called Tran in February 1990 about one of his patients who was getting controlled substances from other doctors, and William Jennings, an inspector from the Virginia Department of Health professions testified that he had warned Tran that Tran was "being conned" into prescribing narcotics to patients who were known drug abusers.

The government presented seven former patients, who testified that Tran's physical examinations had been perfunctory, that they faked their symptoms of pain and illness in order to obtain prescriptions to feed their addictions, that Tran frequently reminded them that he could not give them medication unless they told him they were in pain, and that Tran suggested that they fill the prescriptions at different pharmacies. Some of the witnesses asked for drugs by name, and one testified that he received prescriptions in return for doing repair work at Tran's office. Several witnesses testified that they were asked to sign written release forms acknowledging the addictive potential and dangers of the drugs that were being prescribed.

The DEA obtained a search warrant for the doctor's office and obtained patient files and the office cash payment ledger. From these records it appeared that Tran charged $35 for issuing the desired prescriptions and the patient files reflected that he kept many patients on narcotics and tranquilizers for years when their complaints were for headaches, backaches and other subjective ailments.

Most of the prescriptions were not refillable and this required the patients to come back to the doctor each time they wanted a refill and obtain a new prescription and pay his $35 fee. There was testimony that he advised patients that they needed to have different complaints of pain in different parts of the body because it would look bad if they were taking these drugs for ailments that persisted too long.

Two undercover Alexandria police officers testified that they went to the doctor's office without an appointment to seek narcotic "scripts," the street name for narcotics prescriptions. Tran saw one of these undercover agents eight times over two months in early 1991, spent no more than five minutes with him on each visit and prescribed controlled substances on each visit. These officers testified that the doctor did not perform any medical examinations of them and that one advised him "I'd like to feel a little mellowed out."

One of these officers dressed very shabbily and poured Bourbon whiskey over his clothes. He testified that he told Tran he was in need of Percodan to get through the winter as a construction laborer. Tran refused to prescribe Percodan, a Schedule II drug, but did give him a prescription for Vicodin, a Schedule III drug.

The government called a medical expert, Dr. Alan MacIntosh, a Board certified family physician who had practiced for 32 years. He had reviewed 33 charts of patients listed in the indictment and prepared a written report summarizing the information on each chart. He prepared an exhibit which correlated 1800 narcotics prescriptions with specific patients. He had reviewed the grand jury testimony of some of the patients as well as the DEA undercover reports. He had also examined the waivers or releases that Tran had required some patients to sign. He gave his opinion that after a few days the continued use of narcotics for most of the complaints shown in the files would do no medical good and would possibly be harmful because such drugs would lead to addiction, and that these prescriptions were totally unreasonable and not appropriate care for a family physician. . . .

Tran argues that the evidence was insufficient to convict him of any offense, and that this insufficiency was most apparent as to the 80 counts in which the patients, who had received four prescriptions each, did not testify. As to these counts, he claims that there is no proof of his criminal intent in issuing the prescriptions, nor was there proof that his actions "exceeded the bounds of 'professional practice'" as required by *United States v. Moore,* 423 U.S. 122, 142, 96 S.Ct. 335, 345, 46 L.Ed.2d 333 (1975) (footnote omitted).

A.

First, we must consider what proof is required in the prosecution of a physician under this statute. Section 841(a) of Title 21 of the United States Code provides, in part: "(a) . . . it shall be unlawful for any person knowingly or intentionally—(1) to . . . distribute, . . . a controlled substance. . . ." In order to secure a conviction under this section the government must prove beyond a reasonable doubt that (1) defendant knowingly or intentionally distributed the controlled substance alleged in the indictment, and (2) at the time of such distribution the defendant knew that the substance distributed was a controlled substance under the law. There is no dispute that the prescriptions written by Tran were drugs that appear on Schedules II through V of the Controlled Substances Act, 21 U.S.C. § 801 et seq., and therefore are "controlled substances" and may not be lawfully distributed other than as provided by law.

Tran is a licensed physician under the laws of Virginia, and a licensed practitioner with the Drug Enforcement Administration. As such, he is authorized to write prescriptions for controlled substances in the care and treatment of his patients. The court in *Moore, supra,* held, "[T]he scheme of the statute, viewed against the background of the legislative history, reveals an intent to limit a registered physician's dispensing authority to the course of his 'professional practice.'" 423 U.S. at 140, 96 S.Ct. at 344. Therefore, a licensed physician who prescribes controlled substances outside the bounds of his professional medical practice is subject to prosecution and is no different than "a large-scale 'pusher.'" *Id.* at 143, 96 S.Ct. at 345.

B.

First, Tran contends that the court and the prosecution used a medical malpractice standard rather than a criminal standard to judge his actions. At times the court did confuse the two standards. When Dr. MacIntosh was testifying, the court advised him, "The standard is whether a reasonably prudent physician would do it." Later the court commented, "whether it is within the standard of care of a family practitioner" and "like you use in a civil case, whether in the usual course of treating a patient by the average family practitioner. . . ." These statements reflect the use of a negligence standard. A criminal prosecution requires more-that is, proof beyond a reasonable doubt that the doctor was acting outside the bounds of professional medical practice, as his authority to prescribe controlled substances was being used not for treatment of a patient, but for the purpose of assisting another in the maintenance of a drug habit or of dispensing controlled substances for other than a legitimate medical purpose, i.e. the personal profit of the physician.

The record discloses that the court's definition of the criminal standard was correct when he instructed the jury at the conclusion of the case. In explaining the essential elements of the case, he charged:

> The third element, no legitimate medical purpose. The final element the government must prove beyond a reasonable doubt is that the defendant prescribed the drug other than for legitimate medical purpose and not in the usual course of medical practice.

> In making a medical judgment concerning the right to treatment for an individual patient physicians have discretion to choose among the wide range of available options. Therefore, in determining whether defendant acted without a legitimate medical purpose, you should examine all the defendant's actions and the circumstances surrounding them.

> For example, evidence that a doctor warns his patients to fill their prescription at different drug stores, prescribes drugs without performing any physical examinations or only very superficial ones, or ask [sic] patients about the amount or type of drugs they want, may suggest that the doctor is not acting for a legitimate medical purpose than a [sic] outside the usual course of medical practice. These examples are neither conclusive nor exhaustive. They are simply meant to give you an idea of the kind of behavior from which you may conclude that a doctor was not prescribing drugs for a legitimate medical purpose and was not acting in the usual course of medical practice.

A doctor dispenses a drug in good faith in medically treating a patient, then the doctor has dispensed the drug for a legitimate medical purpose in the usual course of medical practice. That is, he has dispensed the drug lawfully. Good faith in this context means good intentions in the honest exercise of best professional judgment as to a patient's need. It means the doctor acted in accordance with what he believed to be proper medical practice.

If you find the defendant acted in good faith in dispensing the drug, then you must find him not guilty.

The instructions given the jury include a satisfactory definition of the actions of a physician which are outside the course of professional medical practice. The standard used by the court "without a legitimate medical purpose" does appear to be more strict than that required by *Moore* and therefore was to defendant's benefit.

EXERCISE

Adderall is a prescription drug intended to treat ADHD and narcolepsy. It contains amphetamine salts. Amphetamine is a drug that has long been subject to trafficking prosecutions when sold outside of the medical delivery system. It is often abused by those who seek to heighten their focus and lengthen their attention span, such as truck drivers and law students. If a doctor prescribed Adderall to a law student knowing that it is unlikely that the student actually suffers from narcolepsy (as she claims), is that doctor in violation of 21 U.S.C. § 841(a)?

c. Simple Possession of Narcotics as a Lesser Included Offense to Distribution of Narcotics

Simple possession of narcotics is often used as a lesser-included offense in cases where the crime of possession of narcotics with the intent to distribute is charged. That's because the elements of simple possession are a sub-set of intent to distribute—the greater charge is the same as the lessor except for the addition of the intent requirement.

The same is not true of distribution of narcotics, however.

UNITED STATES V. AMBRIZ
727 F. 3d 378 (5th Cir. 2013)

JENNIFER WALKER ELROD, CIRCUIT JUDGE:

Defendant-Appellant Juvenal Ambriz appeals his conviction of a single count of distribution of a controlled substance in violation of 21 U.S.C. § 841(a)(1). For the following reasons, we AFFIRM.

I.

On the evening of January 5, 2012, Drug Enforcement Administration (DEA) Agent Jason Cloutier went to Jaguars Gold Club in an undercover capacity. At about 2:00 a.m., Agent Cloutier approached a male patron in the club and indicated that he was looking for some cocaine. The patron sold Agent Cloutier two small baggies of cocaine in exchange for $40.00. Agent Cloutier noted that the patron was wearing a white hooded sweatshirt and had a thin goatee and small teardrop tattoo on his face. About an hour later, Agent Cloutier and his partner saw the patron get into the passenger seat of a white Chevy Blazer.

Agent Cloutier relayed this information to other officers, who initiated a traffic stop shortly after the Blazer left Jaguars. The officers observed a man with a thin goatee, teardrop tattoo, and white hooded sweatshirt in the passenger seat. Upon inspecting the man's driver's license, the officers identified him as Juvenal Ambriz. A consensual search of Ambriz's person yielded six baggies of similar manufacture, contents, and quantity to the baggies Agent Cloutier had purchased. The deputies seized the cocaine and released Ambriz to preserve the integrity of the undercover operation.

A grand jury indicted Ambriz with a single count of distribution of a controlled substance in violation of § 841(a)(1). The case proceeded to trial on May 16, 2012. Two of the district court's rulings are relevant here. First, the district court denied Ambriz's request for a jury instruction that simple possession of a controlled substance in violation of 21 U.S.C. § 844(a) is a lesser-included offense of distribution of a controlled substance in violation of § 841(a)(1). Second, the district court denied Ambriz's motion in limine to exclude evidence regarding the six baggies of cocaine found on Ambriz's person at the time of his arrest. Ultimately, the jury found Ambriz guilty of distribution of a controlled substance. The district court sentenced Ambriz to 18 months in prison and a three-year term of supervised release. Ambriz timely appealed.

II.

On appeal, Ambriz argues that (1) the district court erred when it denied him a lesser-included-offense instruction; and (2) the district court's admission into evidence of the baggies of cocaine violated Rule 403 of the Federal Rules of Evidence. We address each argument in turn.

A.

Ambriz must satisfy a two-pronged inquiry to demonstrate that he was entitled to a lesser-included-offense instruction. *See United States v. Cooper,* 714 F.3d 873, 879 (5th Cir.2013); *see also United States v. Browner,* 889 F.2d 549, 550–51 (5th Cir.1989) (*Browner I*) (citing *Schmuck v. United States,* 489 U.S. 705, 716, 109 S.Ct. 1443, 103 L.Ed.2d 734 (1989)). First, he must show that the elements of simple possession are a "subset" of the elements of distribution. *Cooper,* 714 F.3d at 879. Second, he must show that, based on the evidence presented at trial, a rational jury could have acquitted him of distribution and convicted him of simple possession. *Id.* We review the first prong *de novo* and the second under an abuse-of-discretion standard. *United States v. Finley,* 477 F.3d 250, 256 (5th Cir.2007).

Our analysis starts and ends with the first prong. In accordance with the Supreme Court's guidance in *Schmuck,* we employ an elements-based test to determine whether the elements of one offense are a subset of the elements of another. *See United States v. Browner,* 937 F.2d 165, 168, 172 (5th Cir.1991) (*Browner II*) (interpreting *Schmuck* to adopt a "strict statutory elements test"). Thus, we compare "the statutory elements of the offenses in question, and not . . . [the] conduct proved at trial" to determine whether one offense is a subset of the other. *United States v. Estrada-Fernandez,* 150 F.3d 491, 494 (5th Cir.1998) (quoting *Schmuck,* 489 U.S. at 716–17, 109 S.Ct. 1443). In performing this test, we construe the relevant criminal statutes in accordance with ordinary principles of statutory interpretation. *See Carter v. United States,* 530 U.S. 255, 260–61, 120 S.Ct. 2159, 147 L.Ed.2d 203 (2000). For the elements of the lesser offense to be a subset of the charged offense, it must be "impossible to commit the [charged offense] without first having committed the lesser." *Schmuck,* 489 U.S. at 719, 109 S.Ct. 1443 (citations omitted).

Here, the offenses at issue are identical except in the obvious respect: one requires possession and the other requires distribution. *Compare United States v. Krout,* 66 F.3d 1420, 1431 (5th Cir.1995) (explaining that the elements of simple possession of a controlled substance are "(1) the knowing possession (2) of a controlled substance"), *with United States v. Sotelo,* 97 F.3d 782, 789 (5th Cir.1996)(recognizing that the elements of distribution of a controlled substance are "that the defendant (1) knowingly (2) distributed (3) the controlled substance"). Thus, the central issue is whether one must *necessarily* possess a controlled substance in order to distribute it.

The answer is no. Our precedent demonstrates that "possession" and "distribution," though overlapping, are distinct concepts. "Possession" can be either actual or constructive. *See United States v. Galvan-Garcia,* 872 F.2d 638, 640 (5th Cir.1989). Constructive possession is the "ownership, dominion, or control over . . . contraband, or . . . dominion over the premises in which the contraband is found." *United States v. Hinojosa,* 349 F.3d 200, 203 (5th Cir.2003) (citations omitted). "Distribution," on the other hand, includes acts "in furtherance of transfer or sale, such as arranging or supervising the delivery." *United States v. Suarez,* 155 F.3d 521, 525 (5th Cir.1998) (citing *United States v. Lechuga,* 888 F.2d 1472, 1478 (5th Cir.1989)). We have held that distribution "is broad enough to include acts that traditionally perhaps would have been defined as mere aiding and abetting." *United States v. Oquendo,* 505 F.2d 1307, 1310 n. 1 (5th

Cir.1975). Thus, a defendant can engage in acts of distribution without actually or constructively possessing the relevant contraband.

Our holding in *United States v. Glenn* illustrates this point. There, we upheld a § 841(a) distribution conviction against a defendant who did not possess the contraband at issue:

> As discussed above, the testimony of the undercover officer, Delco, combined with the tape recording of the March 18th sale of seven rocks of crack, sufficiently supports that Terry constructively delivered the crack through Glenn by instructing him to sell to Delco. Delco also testified that she paged Terry several times on March 22, 1991, and that she spoke with Anthony Moore and Terry about purchasing another $100 worth of crack. From the last recorded telephone call between Terry and Delco, Delco interpreted Terry's statements to mean that Terry had arranged for someone to sell her the crack because he was very busy at the time. He then put someone else, Byron Rice, on the telephone to speak with her. Rice actually sold Delco the crack later that night and indicated to her that he worked for Terry. This evidence was sufficient to show the constructive delivery of crack by Terry through Rice, thus supporting Terry's distribution conviction.

No. 93–4311, 1994 WL 24871, at *2 (5th Cir. Jan. 10, 1994) (unpublished but persuasive). Similarly, this court has upheld § 841(a)distribution convictions against physicians who have prescribed, but not actually or constructively possessed, the controlled substance at issue. *See, e.g., United States v. Rosen,* 582 F.2d 1032, 1034–36 (5th Cir.1978) (upholding a distribution conviction against a physician who advised his patients to fill prescriptions at different drug stores); *cf. United States v. Harrison,* 651 F.2d 353, 354–55 (5th Cir.1981) (upholding a distribution conviction against a physician who "would make up fictitious names for prescriptions, or ask the 'patient' to supply him with names to be used" at the pharmacy).

Moreover, we recently reached the same conclusion in a different context. In *United States v. Woerner,* we evaluated whether possession of child pornography is a lesser-included offense of distribution of child pornography. 709 F.3d 527 (5th Cir.2013). As here, the central question was whether distribution necessarily required possession. We said no:

> A defendant need not possess child pornography to distribute it, [*United States v. Chiaradio,* 684 F.3d 265, 280 (1st Cir.2012)] ("One can envision circumstances in which an individual could be guilty of distribution without ever obtaining possession of (or even coming into contact with) the contraband. For example, the broker of a deal between a person who has child pornography and a person who wishes to procure it may be guilty of distribution but not guilty of possession."), and, *vice versa,* a defendant need not distribute child pornography to possess it, *United States v.*

Goluba, 672 F.3d 304, 307 (5th Cir.2012) ("[T]he forensic analysis of [the defendant]'s computers 'revealed that [he] did not distribute his collection of child pornography.' "). For that reason, we join the First and Seventh Circuits in holding that possession of child pornography is not the lesser-included offense of distribution of child pornography. . . .

Id. at 539 (internal citations omitted).

For all of these reasons, we join the Sixth, Seventh, and Tenth Circuits in concluding that simple possession of a controlled substance in violation of § 844(a) is not a lesser-included offense of distribution of a controlled substance in violation of § 841(a)(1).

EXERCISE

The fact that simple possession is not a lesser-included offense of distribution of narcotics does not mean that someone who was charged with distribution can't plead down to simple possession—in most places, that just requires that a new charge be entered before or at the change-of-plea hearing.

Under the facts described in the *Ambriz* case, what might the defense attorney emphasize in trying to convince the prosecutor to plead the case out to a charge of simple possession, a misdemeanor?

3. MANUFACTURE OF NARCOTICS

Proof of the action element in manufacture of narcotics is usually straightforward. If a defendant is caught making methamphetamine in a home lab, for example, that is clearly the act of manufacturing a narcotic. More difficult cases usually involve narcotics that are naturally occurring, including marijuana.

UNITED STATES V. WOOD
57 F. 3d 913 (10th Cir. 1995)

SEYMOUR, CHIEF JUDGE.

Thomas Nathaniel Wood and David Leslie Wood were charged with manufacturing marijuana in violation of 21 U.S.C. § 841(a)(1), (b)(2), and 18 U.S.C. § 2, possessing marijuana with intent to distribute in violation of 21 U.S.C. § 841(a)(1) and 18 U.S.C. § 2, maintaining a place for the purpose of manufacturing, distributing or using marijuana in violation of 21 U.S.C. § 856(a)(1) and 18 U.S.C. § 2, and conspiring to commit the above offenses in violation of 21 U.S.C. § 846. A fifth count charging both defendants with managing a building for the purpose of unlawfully manufacturing, distributing, or using marijuana in violation of 21 U.S.C. § 856(a)(2) was dismissed prior to trial. A jury convicted both defendants on all the remaining counts. The trial judge sentenced Thomas Wood to 97 months and David Wood to 78 months. Defendants appeal, challenging both their convictions and their sentences. We affirm.

I.

The evidence at trial, viewed most favorably to the government, *see United States v. Richard,* 969 F.2d 849, 856 (10th Cir.), *cert. denied,* 506 U.S. 887, 113 S.Ct. 248, 121 L.Ed.2d 181 (1992) and 506 U.S. 1065, 113 S.Ct. 1009, 122 L.Ed.2d 157 (1993), establishes the following facts. Eugene Norwell, a law enforcement officer with the National Forest Service, was performing aerial surveillance on June 10, 1993 for the Forest Service when he observed three patches of marijuana growing on National Forest land. The next day he did a ground check of the area he had spotted, traveling beyond the end of a Forest Service spur road about twenty yards to the first patch of seven marijuana plants. On a path further into the woods he discovered a second patch of fifty-three plants and ten yards beyond he found a third patch of twenty-eight plants. Officer Norwell testified that the plants were growing out of man-made mounds and that the vegetation around the plants had been cut away with a sharp instrument in order to expose the plants to sunlight. He further testified that the patches were located away from recreation areas in a remote place without hiking trails that received very little traffic.

Officer Norwell arranged for the installation of a remote camera system at the second patch which would begin videotaping whenever anything moved into its range. Gary Rose, another Forest Service law enforcement officer, set up the camera ten to fifteen feet away from the plants in the second patch. He returned to check the camera about fifteen times before it was removed. On June 29, when he returned to service the camera, he noticed fresh tire tracks and footprints in the area. He reviewed the videotape, which showed that two individuals had been in the patch on June 26. Officer Norwell identified one of them as defendant Thomas Wood. The other person was subsequently determined to be Thomas Wood's brother, defendant David Wood. Defendants appeared to be "working" the plants, topping them to promote a greater volume of growth. On August 3 when Officer Rose returned, he noticed footprints and found that, although the plants had previously been observed to be drying out and turning yellow due to the lack of rain, they now had better color, indicating that someone had been at the patch to water and fertilize the plants. He had also discovered a milk jug cap in the area. The videotape showed that defendants had been at the patch July 24, grooming the plants and carrying plastic jugs. On September 27 when Officer Rose went to the patch, he noticed some tire tracks on the service road and discovered that the plants at the first patch were missing, although the camera did not show any activity at the second patch. When he returned on October 12, he noticed a set of tracks leading into the area. Several of the plants at the other patches had been removed and the remaining plants had been heavily trimmed. The videotape revealed that defendants groomed the patch on October 9. On October 20, the officers removed the remaining twenty-four plants from the second and third patches and took samples of them.

Federal agents executed a search warrant on October 30 at the home of Thomas Wood's parents, where Mr. Wood had lived during the summer. The agents discovered a paper sack containing marijuana in an upstairs bedroom, a zig-zag roll of papers, marijuana seeds, a pipe containing marijuana, ziplock baggies, and a statement of earnings. In addition, an agent saw a set of scales, a roach clip, and marijuana seeds in the front seat of an automobile parked in the front yard and belonging to Thomas Wood. The agent also observed the root of a marijuana plant protruding from the back of the closed car trunk. Upon opening the trunk, the agents discovered twelve freshly pulled marijuana plants. When agents executed a search warrant at David Wood's residence, they discovered a small portable set of scales next to a box of plastic baggies, marijuana seeds, pipes, hemostats, roach clips, six one-quart baggies of processed marijuana, and seven marijuana stalks.

Thomas Wood testified that he lived with his parents in their house two months a year and lived the remainder of the year in Arkansas. He admitted visiting the marijuana patches, asserting that he and his brother had come across them while looking for landscape plants pursuant to a Forest Service permit. He denied planting, grooming, or watering the marijuana, although he did admit he had picked some leaves for personal use. He also admitted throwing down some seeds by the Kiamichi River several miles from the three patches under surveillance and stated that the plants in the car had come from the river. He said that he and his brother had agreed to go to the three patches and took turns driving there. David Wood's testimony was consistent with that of his brother. Both defendants admitted using marijuana and growing it for personal use but denied selling it or growing the plants in the three patches. . . .

Both defendants contend that the evidence was insufficient to support their convictions for manufacturing marijuana in violation of 21 U.S.C. § 841(a)(1). For purposes of section 841(a)(1), "[t]he term 'manufacture' means the production, preparation, propagation, compounding, or processing of a drug or other substance, . . . and includes any packaging or repackaging of such substance." 21 U.S.C. § 802(15). "The term 'production' includes the manufacture, planting, cultivation, growing, or harvesting of a controlled substance." *Id.* § 802(22). The evidence at trial is clearly sufficient to support defendants' convictions for manufacturing marijuana. Although they contend that they only picked some leaves, the evidence that they cultivated, grew and/or harvested marijuana is substantial. We thus affirm their convictions on this charge.

EXERCISE

Rachel is a resident of a small town, and her backyard abuts a national forest. She enjoys walking through the forest with her dog, Maisie. One day Rachel and Maisie are out for one of their walks when Rachel sees two teenagers fussing over some plants off the trail. Maisie bounds over to them and they draw guns. Rachel rushes over to defuse the situation, and realizes that the teenagers are growing marijuana in the forest.

Upset about this intrusion on her sanctuary, Rachel returns the next day with her brother and a wheelbarrow. She cuts down all of the marijuana, hauls it out, and loads it onto her brother's truck. Her brother has promised that he will sell it in a nearby city and give her half of the proceeds (which he does). Could Rachel be prosecuted for the manufacture of marijuana?

B. INTENT

Though intent is an element in all drug crimes—in that the action element must have been intended rather than accidental—it most often is at issue in possession with intent to distribute cases, especially where the defendant argues that the drug amount found was for personal use rather than distribution. In those cases where the amount of drugs at issue could conceivably be for personal use, contextual facts become very important.

UNITED STATES V. BURKLEY
513 F. 3d 1183 (10th Cir. 2008)

MCKAY, CIRCUIT JUDGE.

Following a jury trial, Defendant was convicted of possessing marijuana with intent to distribute in violation of 21 U.S.C. § 841(a)(1) (count one), carrying a firearm during and in relation to a drug trafficking crime in violation of 18 U.S.C. § 924(c)(1)(A) (count two), and being an unlawful user of marijuana in possession of firearms and ammunition in violation of 18 U.S.C. § 922(g)(3) (count three). He was sentenced to a total of 120 months' imprisonment. The district court also entered a verdict and order of forfeiture with respect to the firearms, ammunition, and currency found in Defendant's vehicle at the time of his arrest. We have jurisdiction over this appeal under 28 U.S.C. § 1291.

BACKGROUND

Defendant's convictions stem from a search of his vehicle pursuant to a traffic stop and arrest. A police officer responding to a disturbance call at the Broadway Village Apartments in Oklahoma City, Oklahoma, was driving approximately one-and-a-half car lengths behind Defendant when Defendant made a right turn from the highway onto the access road for that apartment complex without signaling his intention to turn. The officer, who was driving a marked patrol car, turned into the apartment complex after Defendant. Defendant then began using his turn signal while going around bends and curves in the winding roadway. The officer initiated a traffic stop based on Defendant's initial failure to signal and subsequent use of his turn signal where it was not necessary.

The officer approached Defendant's car and instructed him to roll down his window. When Defendant complied, the officer noticed the strong smell of marijuana emanating from inside of the car. Defendant admitted that he did not have a driver's license. The officer also observed marijuana residue on Defendant's shirt, and Defendant admitted that he had been smoking marijuana earlier that evening. The officer decided to place Defendant under arrest. Two other officers, having responded to the initial disturbance call at the apartment complex, arrived to assist the arresting officer. Defendant, who is paralyzed from the waist down, informed the officers that he would need them to retrieve his wheelchair from the back seat in order for him to exit the vehicle. Defendant also told the officers that he had a weapon in the car. When the officers opened the back door of the vehicle to retrieve the wheelchair, they observed a .50 caliber Desert Eagle handgun tucked into the folds of the wheelchair and a Carbon-15 handgun on the floorboard, both within Defendant's reach. After assisting Defendant into the wheelchair, one of the officers conducted a patdown search of Defendant and found two baggies of marijuana, a prescription bottle of medication, and over $3000 in cash inside Defendant's pants.

The officers then searched the vehicle. Under the driver's seat, the officers discovered a digital scale and two cell phones, which rang continuously during the search. The officers found a magazine and rounds for the Desert Eagle in the center console and a loaded magazine for the other handgun on the rear floorboard. On the back seat, the officers discovered a black bag containing cash, marijuana, ammunition, and bottles of prescription medication. Hidden under the back seat were five, vacuum-sealed bundles of U.S. currency. The total amount of marijuana found in the vehicle and in Defendant's possession was 157 grams; the total amount of money was $242,250.

After being arrested and advised of his rights, Defendant told officers that he owned the guns found in his car and carried them for his personal protection. He denied selling drugs, but admitted using marijuana on a regular basis for alleged medicinal purposes. He stated that the money found in the vehicle was given to him by a man he knew only as "Broadway" for the purpose of booking rap groups from St. Louis. Although he claimed to have known Broadway for seven or eight years, Defendant could not provide a last name for Broadway nor give any information regarding Broadway's current whereabouts.

Before trial, the court denied Defendant's motions for suppression of the evidence seized pursuant to the traffic stop and arrest and for severance of count one from counts two and three. The court also denied Defendant's motion for acquittal, which he initially made at the close of the government's case-in-chief. After the jury convicted Defendant on all three counts of the indictment, the district court entered a verdict and order of forfeiture of the firearms, ammunition, and currency found in the search of Defendant's vehicle and sentenced Defendant to a total of 120 months' imprisonment. Defendant now appeals. . . .

Defendant argues that there was insufficient evidence to support his convictions on counts one and two. We review a challenge to the sufficiency of the evidence de novo, "view[ing] the evidence in the light most favorable to the government in order to determine whether all of the evidence, both direct and circumstantial, together with the reasonable inferences to be drawn therefrom, 'convinces us that a rational factfinder could reasonably have found' the appellant guilty of the crime charged beyond a reasonable doubt." . . .

"To sustain a conviction of possession with intent to distribute under 21 U.S.C. § 841(a)(1), the government must prove that a defendant: (1) possessed a controlled substance, (2) knew he possessed a controlled substance, and (3) intended to distribute the controlled substance." *United States v. Jenkins,* 175 F.3d 1208, 1215–16 (10th Cir.1999) (internal quotation marks omitted). Defendant does not contest his knowing possession of marijuana. Rather, he argues that he only possessed marijuana for personal use and that the amount of marijuana found in his vehicle and on his person was insufficient to sustain a conviction for possession with intent to distribute.

As an initial matter, we note that the jury heard expert testimony that the amount of marijuana in this case was more consistent with possession for distribution than possession for personal use. Moreover, Defendant's drug possession was not the only evidence supporting a finding of intent to distribute. In addition to the marijuana, Defendant was in possession of two handguns and a large amount of ammunition, a digital scale, and $242,250 in currency. *See United States v. Sanders,* 341 F.3d 809, 816 (8th Cir.2003) ("Even a small amount of contraband may combine with circumstantial evidence to support a finding of intent to distribute."); *Martinez,* 938 F.2d at 1083 (holding that firearms, scales, and large sums of cash are probative of participation in drug distribution because they are "tools of the trade"). Most of the money was bundled in vacuum-sealed bags, and an expert witness testified that drug dealers often bundle money in this way to make it easier to conceal and transport and to avoid detection by drug-sniffing dogs. *See United States v. $242,484.00,* 389 F.3d 1149, 1162 (11th Cir.2004) ("Wrapping cash in cellophane-type material is a technique known to be used by drug dealers to prevent discovery by drug-sniffing dogs."); *see also United States v. $252,300.00 in U.S. Currency,* 484 F.3d 1271, 1275 (10th Cir.2007) (stating the fact that a large amount of currency "was bundled in stacks held by rubber bands and wrapped in cellophane . . . must be given significant probative value"). The jury heard evidence from an Internal Revenue Service employee that Defendant had no apparent legitimate source of income, further supporting an inference that the money was derived from drug transactions. Defendant also possessed more than one cell phone, which an expert witness testified is a common practice in the drug trade. *Cf. United States v. Cox,* 934 F.2d 1114, 1121 (10th Cir.1991) (indicating that possession of pager is evidence of intent to distribute). Defendant asserts that there is an innocent explanation for all of this evidence. However, viewing the evidence in the light most favorable to the government, we conclude that a rational juror could find beyond a reasonable doubt that Defendant knowingly possessed marijuana with the intent to distribute.

EXERCISE

One of the factors the Court in *Burkley* relied on in finding intent to distribute was that the defendant was unemployed.

Imagine that you are a federal prosecutor who is presented with a potential case by a police officer who works on a state/federal drug task force. You have discretion to take relatively small drug cases, but can also decline them. The defendant was found with two grams of cocaine and $420 in small bills (mostly $10s). He is unemployed, and made no statement. Do you take the case?

C. KNOWLEDGE

Because of the logistics of storing and transporting narcotics, which require some measure of secrecy, defendants sometimes challenge the element of knowledge. The government bears the burden of proving that the defendant knew that that substance they were possessing or distributing or manufacturing was a controlled substance.

UNITED STATES V. LOUIS
861 F. 3d 1330 (11th Cir. 2017)

WILSON, CIRCUIT JUDGE:

The burden is on the government to prove all elements of a crime beyond a reasonable doubt. *See In re Winship,* 397 U.S. 358, 364, 90 S.Ct. 1068, 1072, 25 L.Ed.2d 368 (1970). When a man's liberty is at stake, we must be vigilant with this burden. The government failed to offer evidence from which a reasonable jury could find that Terry Pierre Louis had knowledge that the boxes placed in the backseat of his car contained a controlled substance. Without proof of this essential element, the government has failed to meet its burden. Therefore, we must reverse.

I.

In September 2015, Customs and Border Protection received a tip that the *Ana Cecilia*, a coastal freighter used to export goods from the United States to Haiti, was returning from Haiti to Miami carrying narcotics. When the boat arrived Customs agents boarded the vessel and searched for narcotics for four days. None were found. At one point during the search, Louis, an employee of Ernso Borgella, the owner of the *Ana Cecilia*, brought the confined crewmembers food. Following the unsuccessful search, Customs set up surveillance of the *Ana Cecilia*.

During the surveillance, an agent observed the deck watchman go inside the ship and come out carrying two large cardboard boxes. Agents later watched as a forklift picked up two boxes and drove them off the *Ana Cecilia*. Borgella was following the forklift and speaking to its driver, who placed the two boxes on the dock where an unidentified man covered them with a tarp. Later on, Borgella directed a white Nissan to park near the boxes and then reached inside the passenger rear seat and opened the door. Two unidentified men then loaded the boxes into the back seat of a white Nissan. Louis then began to slowly drive the Nissan to the front of the shipyard, while Borgella walked alongside it. Once outside the front gate of the shipyard, the Nissan was stopped by unmarked law enforcement vehicles with lights and sirens. Louis then exited the car and began to run. One of the agents pursued Louis, but lost sight of him in the shipyard. The agents found Borgella and detained him. The agents searched the Nissan and found two sealed boxes in the back seat containing 111 bricks of cocaine.

Louis was charged with (1) conspiracy to possess with intent to distribute cocaine, in violation of 21 U.S.C. §§ 841(b)(1)(A) and 846, and (2)possession with intent to distribute cocaine, in violation of 21 U.S.C. § 841(a)(1) and (b)(1)(A). During the two-day trial, the government put forth evidence including surveillance photos and videos showing that Louis was near the *Ana Cecilia*, that he drove a car containing boxes of cocaine, and that he ran when confronted by law enforcement. Following the government's case-in-chief, the defense moved for an acquittal, the motion was denied, and the defense rested. A jury found Louis guilty on both counts. Louis moved for an acquittal again after the jury verdict but his motion was denied. Despite Louis's motions at sentencing for a role reduction and safety-valve relief, he was sentenced to 151 months' imprisonment. . . .

To sustain a conviction of the substantive offense of possession under § 841, the government must prove knowing possession of a controlled substance with intent to distribute it. *See United States v. Figueroa*, 720 F.2d 1239, 1244 (11th Cir. 1983). The government must therefore prove that the defendant knew "the substance [wa]s a controlled substance." *See, e.g., United States v. Sanders*, 668 F.3d 1298, 1309 (11th Cir. 2012) (per curiam) (internal quotation marks omitted); *United States v. Gomez*, 905 F.2d 1513, 1514 (11th Cir. 1990).

Recently in *McFadden v. United States*, the Supreme Court reemphasized this knowledge requirement. 576 U.S ___, ___, 135 S.Ct. 2298, 2302, 192 L.Ed.2d 260 (2015). Justice Thomas, writing for a near unanimous court, wrote that § 841 "requires the [g]overnment to establish that the defendant knew he was dealing with 'a controlled substance.'" *See id.* The Court rejected the government's proposed broader definition that the knowledge requirement would be met if the "defendant knew he was dealing with an illegal or regulated substance under *some* law." *See id.* at 2306 (internal quotation marks omitted) (emphasis added).

Following the clear guidance set forth in *McFadden*, to prove that Louis "knowingly or intentionally . . . possess[ed] with intent to . . . distribute . . . a controlled substance" under § 841 the government would have to prove that Louis knew the boxes contained a controlled substance, and not just contraband illegal under *some* law.

III.

After a careful review of the record and the parties' briefs, we conclude that no reasonable jury could find from the little evidence presented during the two-day trial that Louis is guilty of violating § 846 and § 841 beyond a reasonable doubt. Viewing the evidence in the light most favorable to the government, we can infer that Louis's presence and flight are evidence that he knew he was involved in something criminal. We cannot find, however, that the government proved beyond a reasonable doubt that Louis knew the boxes placed in his car contained a controlled substance. And because the evidence does not prove that Louis knew that the boxes contained a controlled substance, the evidence does not prove that he knew he was involved in a conspiracy to possess a controlled substance.

During a short trial, the government presented evidence that Louis was seen around the shipyard (where he worked) and was seen near Borgella (his employer). The government relied heavily on evidence that Louis fled when suddenly surrounded by law enforcement. The government's case was built upon inferences from Louis's presence and flight. However, the government presented no evidence that Louis knew that there was a controlled substance (as opposed to any other contraband) within the sealed boxes placed by others in his backseat. No one testified as to Louis's knowledge and Louis himself did not testify.

We recognize that "[e]vidence of flight is admissible to demonstrate . . . guilt," *United States v. Blakey*, 960 F.2d 996, 1000 (11th Cir. 1992), and Louis's flight might be persuasive evidence that he knew the boxes contained contraband illegal under some law. But the evidence is not enough to prove that Louis knew the boxes contained a controlled substance. *See McFadden,* 135 S.Ct. at 2302; *Sanders,* 668 F.3d at 1309.

In addition to Louis's flight, the government relies on Louis's presence and interactions around the shipyard. But the government puts forth no evidence of any conversations where Louis was informed of a plan regarding a controlled substance. There is no evidence, circumstantial or otherwise, strong enough to prove beyond a reasonable doubt that Louis knew that there was a controlled substance in the boxes. The government's evidence of presence and flight was simply not enough to support a finding of knowledge beyond a reasonable doubt.

Neither are we persuaded by an entrustment theory, which attempts to imply knowledge when there is evidence of a high quantity of drugs because "a 'prudent smuggler' is not likely to entrust such valuable cargo to an innocent person without that person's knowledge." *See United States v. Quilca-Carpio,* 118 F.3d 719, 722 (11th Cir. 1997) (per curiam). We do not find *Quilca-Carpio* sufficiently analogous here, as Louis's presence with the boxes was only brief. In *Quilca-Carpio,* the defendant checked an unusually heavy roller-bag as his own luggage on an international flight from Lima, Peru to the United States. *See id.* at 721–22. However, Louis was in the Nissan only briefly as he slowly drove with Borgella walking alongside the car. Indeed, Louis was never left completely alone with the boxes, like the defendant in *Quilca-Carpio.* This hardly supports a conclusion that Louis was sufficiently entrusted with the cocaine to establish his knowledge, and it is surely not enough to prove his knowledge beyond a reasonable doubt.

IV.

The government is charged with proving "beyond a reasonable doubt . . . *every fact* necessary to constitute the crime with which [the defendant] is charged." *See Winship,* 397 U.S. at 364, 90 S.Ct. at 1073 (emphasis added). We must hold the government accountable to this burden. While the circumstances presented by the government here might show that it is more likely than not that Louis knew that the boxes contained some sort of contraband, the permissible inferences do not support a holding that the government proved that Louis *knew* this was a conspiracy involving a controlled substance or that he knew he was in possession of a controlled substance. Without this requisite showing of knowledge, the government has failed to prove every fact necessary to meet its burden.

———————

EXERCISE

Robert works at an auto repair shop. His boss, Laurence, asks him to take a box and deliver it to "a guy who will be waiting in his car in the McDonald's parking lot at 11th Street." Robert asks what is in the box and Laurence responds "don't ask, but if you make the delivery there is $500 in it for you.

And maybe some cocaine." Robert is stopped by the police on his way to the McDonald's. The box contained three kilos of cocaine. Laurence, upon being interviewed, reveals what Robert told him.

If you are the prosecutor presented with this case, do you think there is sufficient evidence to go forward against Robert for possession with intent to distribute cocaine?

While the prosecution must show that the defendant knew that they possessed/distributed/manufactured a controlled substance, it isn't always required that the government prove that the defendant knew *which* controlled substance was at issue.

UNITED STATES v. RAMOS
814 F. 3d 910 (8th Cir. 2016)

GRUENDER, CIRCUIT JUDGE.

Mary Ann Ramos and her son, Earl James Ramos, were convicted on several drug-distribution counts. Mary Ramos argues that the district court erred by denying her motion for judgment of acquittal. Both defendants contend that the court improperly calculated their advisory sentencing guidelines range. We affirm.

I.

Mary Ramos managed an iWireless store in Cedar Rapids, Iowa. On May 28, 2013, two Drug Enforcement Administration ("DEA") agents posed as customers and entered her store. When the agents asked Mary if she sold "potpourri," Mary nodded and retrieved packets labeled "Mr. Happy" and "Mr. Nice Guy." The agents selected cotton-candy-flavored "Mr. Nice Guy." While walking to the register, Mary asked if the agents needed rolling papers. They declined and then paid $26.75 for the 10.2 gram packet. Although the "Mr. Nice Guy" packet bore a label indicating that its contents were "100% Cannabinoid Free/DEA Compliant," later testing at a DEA laboratory revealed that the packet contained organic plant material sprayed with the Schedule I controlled substance XLR-11, a synthetic cannabinoid.

Several weeks later, a confidential informant working with the Tri-County Drug Enforcement Task Force called Mary and asked to meet at 9:50 p.m. When Mary asked what the caller was "trying to get," the informant requested "Mr. Nice Guy" and "whatever jar you got." Mary said that she had "Blue" but did not have "Mr. Nice Guy." Mary instead offered the caller "Mr. Happy" and "Insane," which were available in quantities of twelve and ten grams, respectively. The informant asked for "Mr. Happy," and he stated that he wished to spend "around 80 or 90" on "the bath salt" and the "Mr. Happy." Mary drove to meet the informant at a gas station in a nearby town and sold the informant one packet of "Mr. Happy" and one jar of "Blue" for a total of $75. Mary did not charge the informant tax for the purchase nor did she later process the transaction through her register at the iWireless store. A later DEA test determined that the "Blue" weighed 0.2 grams and contained pyrrolidinopentiophene (á-PVP), a substance with a chemical structure substantially similar to the Schedule I controlled substance methylenedioxypyrovalerone ("MDPV") and with a pharmacological effect substantially similar to MDPV, cocaine, and methamphetamine.

Not long after these incidents, the DEA and Cedar Rapids police executed a search warrant at Mary's store. The agents and officers recovered "Blue" from a drawer under the register counter. They also located hundreds of packets containing synthetic cannabinoids around the store, including in a drawer under the counter, a back storage room, and the back office. None of the synthetic cannabinoid products were advertised in the store. Nearly all of these products contained XLR-11, and some also contained UR-144, a second synthetic cannabinoid. Labels on many of these packets noted that the product should not be consumed by humans. The agents and officers also found smoking paraphernalia, including glass pipes and rolling papers. They found no loose tobacco in the store.

The DEA and Cedar Rapids police also searched Mary's car and home. In the car, the agents and officers found an unloaded handgun and four boxes of ammunition immediately next to a box containing several containers of "Blue." They also found packets containing synthetic cannabinoids in the back pocket of the driver's seat. In Mary's home, the officers and agents found more synthetic cannabinoids and another box of "Blue." The box's label read "scouring powder" and bore the image of a silhouetted woman in front of a disco ball. Each jar of "Blue" contained between 0.2 and 0.4 grams of á-PVP.

Mary was indicted for several drug-related counts—including distribution of a controlled substance (XLR-11), see 21 U.S.C. § 841(a)(1), distribution of a controlled substance analogue (á-PVP), see 21 U.S.C. §§ 813, 841(a)(1), possession with intent to distribute a controlled substance (XLR-11), see 21 U.S.C. § 841(a)(1), possession with intent to distribute a controlled substance analogue (á-PVP), see 21 U.S.C. §§ 813, 841(a)(1)—and possession of a firearm in furtherance of a drug trafficking crime, see 18 U.S.C. § 924(c). At trial, the Government provided evidence regarding Mary's encounters with the undercover officers and the confidential informant. The Government also called expert witnesses to testify regarding the synthetic cannabinoids and á-PVP. Another Government witness testified regarding the street names of the drugs at issue.

At the conclusion of the trial, the district court instructed the jury. Regarding the controlled substance counts for XLR-11, the court explained that the Government had to prove that Mary "knew that the substance was some kind of prohibited drug." For the controlled substance analogue counts involving "Blue," the court instructed the jury:

> [T]he government must prove: (1) the defendant knew that Alpha-PVP was intended for human consumption; and (2) the defendant knew (a) the chemical structure of Alpha-PVP is substantially similar to the chemical structure of a controlled substance in Schedule I or II; and (b) Alpha-PVP either has or was represented by the defendant to have a stimulant, depressant or hallucinogenic effect on the central nervous system that is substantially similar to or greater than the stimulant, depressant or hallucinogenic effect on the central nervous system as a controlled substance in Schedule I or II.

After the jury returned its guilty verdicts on the drug-related counts, Mary renewed her motion for judgment of acquittal. She argued that the Government had failed to offer sufficient evidence regarding her knowledge. The district court denied this motion.

Earl Ramos managed the Five Star Snacks and Iowa Wireless store in Waterloo, Iowa. Beginning in 2012, Earl sold synthetic cannabinoids—including XLR-11, UR-144, AM-2201, and JWH-081—and synthetic cathinones from his store. Earl elected not to go to trial and instead pleaded guilty to one count of distributing pentedrone, a controlled substance analogue, *see* 21 U.S.C. § 841(a)(1). The court accepted his plea.

Before sentencing Mary and Earl, the district court conducted a joint evidentiary hearing on the nature of the various synthetic cannabinoids sold by the defendants. Synthetic cannabinoids are Schedule I substances; however, they are not listed in the Guidelines Manual drug-equivalency tables. The court thus sought to determine whether the synthetic cannabinoids were more closely related to pure tetrahydrocannabinol ("THC") or marijuana, a plant that naturally contains THC. This decision guided the court's conclusion about which marijuana-equivalency ratio to use when calculating the defendants' base offense levels under the sentencing guidelines. USSG § 2D1.1cmt. 6. If the synthetic cannabinoids were more closely related to THC, the Guidelines Manual dictated a 1:167 marijuana-equivalency ratio, meaning that one gram of the synthetic cannabinoid product would be treated as 167 grams of marijuana. USSG § 2D1.1 cmt. 8(D). In contrast, if marijuana were the more similar controlled substance, the applicable ratio would be 1:1. *Id.*

At the hearing, the Government called Dr. Jordan Trecki, a DEA pharmacologist, to testify regarding the pharmacological effect and potency of the synthetic cannabinoids. Dr. Trecki explained that each of the synthetic cannabinoids involved in the case has an effect on the central nervous system that is substantially similar to THC. He testified that all but two of the synthetic cannabinoids sold by the defendants are at least as potent as, if not more potent than, THC. Dr. Trecki also discussed the adverse side effects of various synthetic cannabinoids, including hallucinations, psychoses, severe agitation, and excited delirium. Finally, Dr. Trecki noted that synthetic cannabinoids are distinguishable from marijuana in several ways, including (1) the lack of a chemical moderating the effects of THC that is present in marijuana and (2) the synthetic drugs' increased likelihood of producing seizures, coma, and death. Based on this testimony, the court concluded that THC was the scheduled substance most closely related to the synthetic cannabinoids at issue. The court thus applied a 1:167 marijuana-equivalency ratio to determine the defendants' base offense levels and advisory sentencing guidelines ranges. The court ultimately sentenced Earl to 57 months' imprisonment, a sentence within his sentencing guidelines range, and Mary to 60 months' imprisonment, a downward variance from her advisory guidelines range of 97–121 months.

II.

The defendants raise several issues on appeal. Mary contends that the district court erred by denying her motion for judgment of acquittal because the evidence was insufficient to support her conviction. . . .

Knowledge is one element of drug-distribution charges under 18 U.S.C. § 841(a). *See United States v. Nichols,* 808 F.2d 660, 663 (8th Cir.1987). Mary contends on appeal that the Government failed to prove that she knew the synthetic cannabinoid products contained XLR-11 or some other controlled substance. The Government, however, was "not required to prove that the defendant actually knew the exact nature of the substance with which [s]he was dealing." *United States v. Sheppard,* 219 F.3d 766, 769 (8th Cir.2000) (quoting *United States v. Jewell,* 532 F.2d 697, 698 (9th Cir.1976) (en banc)). "[T]he 'knowingly' element of th[e] offense refers to a general criminal intent, i.e., awareness that the substance possessed was a controlled substance of some kind." *United States v. Noibi,* 780 F.2d 1419, 1421 (8th Cir.1986). "Since the factfinder can seldom know with certainty what someone actually knows, knowledge must necessarily be shown circumstantially." *Id.*

During trial, the Government presented evidence tending to show that Mary knew she was dealing with illegal drugs when she sold the XLR-11. Though Mary openly sold glass pipes and other smoking paraphernalia, the packets containing synthetic cannabinoid products were not on public display in the store nor advertised in any way. One undercover officer who took part in the controlled purchase testified that Mary produced packets of "Mr. Happy" and "Mr. Nice Guy" only after the agent requested "potpourri," a street name for synthetic cannabinoid products. The label on the packets of "Mr. Happy" and "Mr. Nice Guy" stated that the product was not for human consumption; however, the "Mr. Nice Guy" packet advertised a cotton-candy flavor. And Mary, unprompted, asked if the officers needed rolling papers with the "Mr. Nice Guy" purchase. After the agents declined, Mary charged $25 for the small, ten-gram packet of purported "potpourri." Finally, the jury heard that the search of Mary's store, car, and home yielded hundreds of packets containing synthetic cannabinoids stored out of public view. Viewed in the light most favorable to the jury's verdict, this evidence was sufficient to demonstrate Mary's awareness that she possessed and sold a controlled substance of some kind.

EXERCISE

You are a defense attorney appointed by the court to represent Cindy, who has been charged with possession with intent to distribute cocaine. She tells you that she was convicted in 2010 of felony aggravated assault and cannot possess firearms. Her friend Clarence paid her $800 to pick up a package delivered to a post office box in a neighboring state. Clarence told Cindy that the package contained guns. Cindy picked up the package, was immediately caught by federal authorities, and charged with possession to intent once the package was opened and found to contain two kilos of cocaine. What defense do you think is most likely to succeed?

Federal law also criminalizes the sale of "precursor" drugs—those that are used to make narcotics. For example, the cold remedy pseudoephedrine is commonly used to produce methamphetamine, and 21 U.S.C§ 841(c) bars its possession or distribution if the defendant knows that it will be used to manufacture a controlled substance. This creates a distinct element of knowledge that must be proven by the government.

UNITED STATES V. MUESSIG
427 F. 3d 856 (10th Cir. 2005)

TYMKOVICH, CIRCUIT JUDGE.

I.   Background

Sonny's Express Grocery and Smoke for Less are two Oklahoma City convenience stores that were operated by the Trans and Muessig at various times between June 2000 and September 2001. Both stores were subject to an undercover operation aimed at stemming illegal sales of pseudoephedrine for use in methamphetamine manufacturing.

On June 29, 2000, Detective Mark Wenthold and an informant entered Sonny's, which was then owned by Sonny and Nga Tran. Sonny Tran was working behind the counter. Wenthold and the informant spoke to Tran about buying a "large amount" of pseudoephedrine. At trial, Wenthold testified that during the course of this discussion, "it was decided that we would buy, I believe it was six bottles each, and then leave the store and immediately walk back in, and buy six bottles each again, immediately go

back out, come back in, and buy another six bottles of pseudoephedrine."
Tr. at 51–52. During one of the purchases, Wenthold told Sonny Tran that
he and his companion were "making methamphetamine with [the pills]."
Tr. at 52. Despite this, Tran continued to sell them the pills. In exchange
for the pills, Wenthold and the informant paid Sonny Tran hundreds of
dollars in cash.

On June 30, Wenthold and the informant returned to Sonny's, where Nga
Tran, Sonny Tran's wife, was working behind the counter. Following the
pattern of their first visit, Wenthold testified that he and the informant
"each bought eight bottles . . . left the store, came back in, bought the eight
bottles again, left the store, and did it a third time." Tr. at 52–53. Nga Tran
charged them $112 per eight bottles, totaling $672 in cash. During the
course of the transactions, Wenthold told Nga Tran he was willing to sell
her some of the "stuff" they planned to make, and that the "stuff" could help
her stay awake for days at a time. She told him she "wasn't into that kind
of stuff." Tr. at 53.

On April 6, 2001, Wenthold returned to Sonny's alone. During this
transaction and subsequent visits to Sonny's and Smoke for Less, Wenthold
was wired for audio and video recording. Muessig was working behind the
counter when Wenthold arrived. After she expressed reluctance to sell him
large quantities of pseudoephedrine, Wenthold urged her to telephone Nga
Tran, which Muessig did. Muessig told Nga Tran (in Vietnamese) that she
was "very afraid." Tr. at 121–122. Muessig then gave the telephone to
Wenthold, who assured Tran (in English) that he "had bought pills there
before and there hadn't been any trouble." Tr. at 56. During this
conversation, Tran invited him to visit her new store to purchase pills.
Following Wenthold's conversation with Tran, Muessig called Tran a
second time and spoke with her again.

After the two telephone conversations, Wenthold and Muessig began to
discuss the prospect of Wenthold purchasing pseudoephedrine pills.
Muessig voiced concerns that Wenthold was "with the FBI." Tr. at 56.
Wenthold told her that he had purchased pseudoephedrine pills at the store
before, and "those people didn't go to jail yet, so everything was all right."
Tr. at 56–57. This was apparently sufficiently convincing to Muessig, who
then sold Wenthold 24 boxes of pseudoephedrine tablets, for which he paid
her $250 in cash.

On April 13, at Nga Tran's invitation, Wenthold visited Tran's new
Oklahoma City store, Smoke for Less. Nga Tran was working behind the
counter. After Tran stated that she "recognized" Wenthold, she sold him 24
boxes of pseudoephedrine pills for $260. She also stated that "you scare
people," and Wenthold reassured her he was not a police officer. Tr. at 74–
76.

Wenthold returned to Sonny's on April 13, 2001. Muessig was behind the
counter, and he told her he had $500 to spend on pseudoephedrine pills.

They joked about her suspicions that he was with the FBI. Muessig joked that should refer to himself as "Mark, with the FBI" if he were to call her in the future. Tr. at 62. Before leaving the store, Wenthold purchased 36 boxes of pills for $460.

On April 19, 2001, Wenthold returned to Sonny's for the last time. Muessig was again behind the counter, and she repeated her concerns that he was with the FBI. Nonetheless, she sold him 24 boxes of pseudoephedrine pills for $300. On the same day, Wenthold also visited Smoke for Less, where Sonny Tran was working behind the counter. After a telephone call to Nga Tran, Sonny Tran told Wenthold the current price on pseudoephedrine pills. Wenthold told Sonny Tran that he "liked the bottles [of pills] because it was easy to cut open the bottles, instead of having to pop each individual pill out of the package like you have to do [with the packages]." Tr. at 77. Wenthold also discussed the process of cooking methamphetamine. Nonetheless, Sonny Tran sold him 16 bottles of pseudoephedrine tablets for $400 in cash.

On May 21, 2001, Wenthold again visited Smoke for Less. Nga Tran was working at the store, and she showed him a "blister pack" of pills, which Wenthold informed her he "didn't like," because "you had to pop each pill out." Tr. at 80. He also mentioned that he preferred bottles of pills because he "could cut the bottoms out of the bottles." Tr. at 81. Tran again told Wenthold that he "scared people," and that people "thought [he] was a police officer[.]" Tr. at 81. Despite her concerns, Tran sold Wenthold 25 bottles of pills for $700.

Wenthold made his last trip to Smoke for Less on September 27, 2001. Nga Tran was working behind the counter. Wenthold told Tran that he preferred a particular kind of bottle, because he "liked to cut the bottoms out of them." Tr. at 85. They also discussed the prospect of having the pills delivered to Wenthold, but Tran did not appear interested in accommodating such a request. Before departing, Wenthold purchased 48 bottles of pills for $1200.

After these visits, the government concluded its investigation. Indictments were filed in October 2002.

II. Discussion

A. Sufficiency of the Evidence as to Muessig and Nga Tran

Muessig and Nga Tran each argue that the government did not present enough evidence to support their convictions. We review the record de novo for sufficiency of the evidence and uphold a conviction if, viewing the evidence in the light most favorable to the government and drawing all reasonable inferences therefrom, a reasonable jury could have found the defendant guilty beyond a reasonable doubt. *United States v. Nguyen*, 413 F.3d 1170, 1175 (10th Cir.2005). In conducting this review, we accept the jury's resolution of conflicting evidence without weighing the credibility of witnesses. *United States v. Sapp,* 53 F.3d 1100, 1103 (10th Cir.1995).

Section 841(c)(2) imposes criminal penalties on "[a]ny person who knowingly or intentionally . . . possesses or distributes a listed chemical knowing, or having reasonable cause to believe, that the listed chemical will be used to manufacture a controlled substance[.]" 21 U.S.C. § 841(c)(2). Neither Muessig nor Nga Tran contest that they knowingly distributed pseudoephedrine, or that pseudoephedrine is a listed chemical. They deny only that they had "reasonable cause to believe that it would be used to manufacture a controlled substance."

We have recently held in interpreting 21 U.S.C. § 841 that it is

> not sufficient for the government to prove that the defendant knew, intended, or had reasonable cause to believe that the substance would be abused or would be used illegally. Nor is it sufficient for the government to prove that the defendant was negligent or reckless with respect to the risk that the ephedrine or pseudoephedrine he sold would be used to manufacture methamphetamine. The government must prove the defendant was aware, or had reasonable cause to believe, that the substance would be used for the specific purpose of manufacturing methamphetamine.

United States v. Truong, 425 F.3d 1282, 1288 (10th Cir.2005) (internal citations omitted). In other words, there must be a showing of "actual knowledge, or something close to it" that the precursor drugs would be used to manufacture controlled substances. *Id.*

We find that the evidence was sufficient to prove this element of the crime as to both Muessig and Nga Tran.

Muessig

Muessig argues a jury could not conclude she either knew or had reasonable cause to believe that the pseudoephedrine she sold would be used to make methamphetamine. According to Muessig, the evidence, at best, shows that she had been told that selling large quantities of the drug could "get her in trouble," but that she never had been told or knew that the drug could be converted into methamphetamine.

At trial, DEA Agent Gary Lawson testified that a person using pseudoephedrine for its intended purpose and taking the maximum dosage per day would require two years to consume the 3024 tablets Muessig sold to Wenthold over a two-week time period. Tr. at 127–128. Thus, as a preliminary matter, a reasonable jury could infer from this fact that Muessig knew that the pseudoephedrine was not being used for its ordinary medicinal purpose. Other evidence established that Muessig had reasonable cause to believe the pseudoephedrine would be used for illicit purposes. For example, when Wenthold visited her store on April 6, 2001, Muessig stated that she was "afraid" and asked whether Wenthold was affiliated with the FBI. Furthermore, Muessig refused to sell the pills before first calling Nga Tran and receiving Wenthold's assurances that he had indeed purchased large quantities of pseudoephedrine pills in the past.

On top of this foundational evidence, the government produced additional evidence from which a reasonable jury could infer culpability. First, the evidence disclosed that Muessig had knowledge about the illicit uses of pseudoephedrine. At trial, Drug Enforcement Agency Agent Gary Lawson testified that after her arrest, Muessig admitted that (1) Nga Tran's sister, Anna Nguyen, a licensed pseudoephedrine distributor, had informed Muessig of pseudoephedrine's illegal uses and that Muessig knew "drugs" were made from "pseudoephedrine"; and (2) Muessig knew large-quantity sales were a red flag, because she said "[d]on't sell too much, don't sell too much. You have to be careful. The police will get you in trouble." Tr. at 131–32. Although Muessig denied in her trial testimony that she knew pseudoephedrine was used to make controlled substances, or that Anna Nguyen had told her that pseudoephedrine could be used to manufacture illicit substances, given Lawson's testimony the jury could have concluded otherwise. On appeal, we may not resolve conflicting evidence or weigh the credibility of witnesses; the credibility determination is for the jury at trial. *See United States v. Pappert,* 112 F.3d 1073, 1077 (10th Cir.1997).

Muessig replies that no evidence was ever presented to show she received formal "notice" that the sale of pseudoephedrine for use in the manufacture of methamphetamine could expose her to criminal liability. However, formal notice, whether from pseudoephedrine distributors or the government itself, is not a required element of § 841(c)(2). Such notice is merely additional evidence that is typically employed to establish knowledge under the statute. *See, e.g., United States v. Nguyen,* 413 F.3d 1170, 1176 (10th Cir.2005) (holding that defendant's receipt of warnings from his pseudoephedrine distributors was relevant to intent); *Truong,* 425 F.3d at 1290 (finding no evidence that defendant was aware of the illegal uses of pseudoephedrine, because no relevant conversations with undercover agents, statements by the defendant, or official warnings were indicated in the record).

In other words, whether Muessig received official notice of the illegal uses of pseudoephedrine is irrelevant in light of the other evidence produced at trial. Evidence of knowledge need not come in the form of an *ex ante* official notice about the illegal uses of pseudoephedrine. A reasonable jury could infer from Muessig's conduct and admissions that she had reasonable cause to believe the pseudoephedrine would be used to make controlled substances. Accordingly, taking the evidence as a whole, we believe a reasonable jury could have found Muessig guilty of violating 21 U.S.C. § 841(c)(2).

Nga Tran

Nga Tran argues that the trial testimony was insufficient to prove she knew that the pseudoephedrine pills would be used to manufacture a controlled substance. The question, again, is the link between the large-scale sales of pseudoephedrine and the "actual knowledge or intent (or, in this Circuit, something 'akin to actual knowledge') that it would be used to manufacture methamphetamine," *Truong*, 425 F.3d 1290. On this record, we conclude that a jury could indeed find such knowledge.

To begin, Nga Tran testified at trial that she received prior notice that large-scale sales were illegal. Distributors had informed her that customers should not be allowed to purchase large quantities of pseudoephedrine tablets, and that such sales were unlawful. In fact, her sister, Anna Nguyen, was one of the distributors who supplied Sonny's and Smoke for Less. On two occasions Tran told Wenthold that he "scared people," and she expressed concern about being "set up" by the police as a result of Wenthold's conduct. Wenthold testified that he made his purchases in cash (in excess of the retail value) and acted "upset" with Tran when she tried to charge him tax on the purchases. In short, the record shows Nga Tran knew that the transactions with the undercover police were illegal.

In order to establish guilt under the statute, however, the government must also show Nga Tran knew or had reasonable cause to believe that the pseudoephedrine would be used to manufacture a controlled substance. The government's evidence supporting this element is found in both Wenthold's and Tran's testimony. Wenthold testified that on June 30, 2000, he had a conversation with Tran regarding his plans to use the pseudoephedrine for manufacturing. When asked if he ever mentioned to her that "an illegal substance" would be made with the pills, Wenthold answered, "yes, on the first occasion that I bought from her on 29th Street." Tr. at 104. Describing the conversation at issue, Wenthold stated that he offered "to trade some of the stuff that we were making with the pills. I told her it would keep her up for days and she wouldn't need any sleep and she could work very hard. She told me she wasn't into that kind of stuff." Tr. at 53, 104. In her own testimony at trial, Tran was asked whether the agent told her he would "cook methamphetamine" with the pills. She answered, "I don't remember that he tell me, or not; maybe he do, but I do not know what does that mean or I didn't know anything about that." Tr. at 187. Finally, Wenthold testified (and the videotapes clearly showed) he informed Tran he liked to cut the bottoms from the pseudoephedrine bottles, and that he did not like receiving pills in packets because they required him to punch out the individual pills.

Based on this evidence, a reasonable jury could conclude that Nga Tran knew the pseudoephedrine sales were illegal and were to be used to manufacture controlled substances. We therefore find the government established sufficient evidence to sustain her conviction under 21 U.S.C. § 841(c)(2).

EXERCISE

The defendants in the *Muessig* case operated the stores which were selling pseudoephedrine. To control the use of pseudoephedrine to make methamphetamine, sale of the cold medicine is generally now restricted to pharmacies, where it is sold behind the counter (though no prescription is required). Imagine a pharmacy clerk who sells several boxes a day to a single customer over the course of months. As a prosecutor, what facts would you need to establish before you were comfortable charging her with the illegal sale of pseudoephedrine?

D. CHEMICAL COMPOSITION OF NARCOTICS

Drug laws require an unusual degree of scientific precision, since they must distinguish between which narcotics are legal and which are not. In turn, this specificity usually requires prosecutors to be prepared to prove up the chemical composition of a controlled substance seized from a defendant through expert analysis and (if necessary) testimony. This requirement means not only that an expert needs to be available, but that the "chain of custody" relating to the drugs themselves must be carefully managed to ensure that the drugs can be proven up at trial as what was seized from the defendant and then tested for its chemical composition.

UNITED STATES V. STANLEY
24 F. 3d 1314 (11th Cir. 1994)

CLARK, SENIOR CIRCUIT JUDGE:

Defendants-appellants Charles Reynaldo Cameron and Tiffany Sherrell Stanley were convicted along with Ronald Calvin Powers of conspiracy to possess with intent to distribute and with possession with intent to distribute cocaine base, in violation of 21 U.S.C. §§ 841(a)(1) and 846. Powers' convictions and sentence were affirmed by another panel of this court. This appeal involves only Cameron and Stanley. We affirm Cameron's convictions and sentence, but we vacate Stanley's convictions, as we find that the evidence is insufficient to sustain her convictions.

FACTS

On December 12, 1991, police arrested Timothy Wayne Murray in Columbus, Georgia, on cocaine trafficking charges. Murray agreed to cooperate with police by assisting them in arresting his suppliers in Atlanta, Georgia. At the direction of the police, Murray made a telephone call from the police department in Columbus to defendant Cameron in

Atlanta. Murray telephoned Cameron's pager number and left the telephone number of the telephone line used by the police to set up undercover drug deals. At approximately 8:40 p.m. on December 12th, Cameron returned Murray's telephone call, and the police tape-recorded the ensuing conversation between Cameron and Murray. During the course of this conversation, Cameron and Murray arranged a drug deal: Cameron agreed to drive down to Columbus that evening with three and one-half ounces of cocaine base, for which Murray agreed to pay $3,600.00. Cameron agreed to telephone Murray when he arrived at the Hardee's Restaurant in Columbus.

Several hours later, Cameron telephoned Murray from the Hardee's Restaurant in Columbus. An undercover police officer drove Murray to the Hardee's Restaurant in an old pick-up truck. When they arrived at the Hardee's, Murray saw Cameron across the street at the gas station, standing beside his car pumping gas. As he approached Cameron's car, Murray saw two passengers in the car, a black female in the front passenger's seat and a black male, identified as Powers, in the back seat. Murray asked Cameron, "where the dope was," and Powers responded, "You need to talk to me." Powers then got out of the car and he and Murray walked across the street to the Hardee's Restaurant, discussing the drug deal as they walked. Powers and Murray then walked back across the street to the gas station and got into the back seat of Cameron's car. Cameron sat in the driver's seat. The woman was still in the front passenger's seat.

Cameron drove the car out of the gas station and across the street toward the back of the Hardee's Restaurant, ostensibly so Murray could obtain money for the drug deal. As Cameron drove across the street and around toward the back of the restaurant, police officers moved in the make the arrests. The undercover police officer who had driven Murray to the scene stopped Cameron's car by ramming it with the pick-up truck. Another officer observed Powers throw an automatic pistol out of the car. After apprehending the occupants of Cameron's car, the police officers searched the car and discovered cocaine base under the dashboard. The police arrested Cameron, Powers, and the woman in the front seat, identified as Stanley. The arrests were made at approximately 2:00 a.m. In a post-arrest statement, Cameron admitted ownership of the cocaine base discovered hidden under the dashboard. . . .

Cameron contends that the evidence is insufficient to sustain his convictions because the government failed to prove that the substance found in his car on the night of his arrest was cocaine base. On the night of Cameron's arrest, the police officers weighed the substance found under the dashboard of Cameron's car on scales in the police department; the substance weighed 105.6 grams. The state crime laboratory subsequently determined that the substance was cocaine base and that it weighed 88 grams. Cameron relies on this discrepancy in weight to support his argument that the government failed to establish that the cocaine base identified at trial was the same substance discovered in his car on the night of his arrest. Having carefully reviewed the record, we determine that this argument is without merit. First, the government's witnesses established a chain of custody between the substance seized on the night of Cameron's arrest and the cocaine base identified at trial. Second, the government's witnesses provided a plausible explanation for the weight discrepancy: the scales in the police department had been confiscated during a drug deal and were not properly maintained, and the police officers did not remove the plastic bags in which the cocaine base was packaged before weighing it, as the state crime lab did. Accordingly, we conclude that the evidence was sufficient to sustain Cameron's convictions.

EXERCISE

It is not unusual for defense attorneys to stipulate to the chemical composition of the drugs at issue, which frees the government from having to provide expert testimony. What reasons might a defense attorney have for making that decision, which relieves the prosecutor of the significant burden of proven a scientific fact?

Disputes over chemical composition have often related to crack cocaine, a smokeable form of cocaine that is made out by cooking powder cocaine with baking soda (sodium bicarbonate) and water to create small rocks. Distinguishing crack from powder cocaine has challenged legislatures, given that both substances have the same active ingredient and crack cocaine is made out of powder cocaine. As the Supreme Court addresses below, the federal statutes attempt to describe crack cocaine as "cocaine base," but that is an awkward definition in chemical terms. The ensuing twisted logic reveals the importance of precision in legislating, charging, and litigating narcotics laws.

DePierre v. United States
564 U.S. 70 (2011)

JUSTICE SOTOMAYOR delivered the opinion of the Court.

At the time of petitioner's conviction and sentence, federal law mandated a minimum 10-year sentence for persons convicted of certain drug offenses, 21 U.S.C. § 841(a), including those involving 50 grams or more of "a mixture or substance . . . which contains cocaine base," § 841(b)(1)(A)(iii), and a minimum 5-year sentence for offenses involving 5 grams or more of the same, § 841(b)(1)(B)(iii). This case requires us to decide whether the term "cocaine base" as used in this statute refers generally to cocaine in its chemically basic form or exclusively to what is colloquially known as "crack cocaine." We conclude that "cocaine base" means the former.

I

A

As a matter of chemistry, cocaine is an alkaloid with the molecular formula $C^{17} H^{21} NO^4$. Webster's Third New International Dictionary 434 (2002). An alkaloid is a base—that is, a compound capable of reacting with an acid to form a salt. *Id.,* at 54, 180; see also Brief for Individual Physicians and Scientists as *Amici Curiae* 2–3 (herein-after Physicians Brief). Cocaine is derived from the coca plant native to South America. The leaves of the coca plant can be processed with water, kerosene, sodium carbonate, and sulphuric acid to produce a paste-like substance. R. Weiss, S. Mirin, & R. Bartel, Cocaine 10 (2d ed.1994). When dried, the resulting "coca paste" can be vaporized (through the application of heat) and inhaled, *i.e.,* "smoked." See United States Sentencing Commission, Special Report to the Congress: Cocaine and Federal Sentencing Policy 11–12 (1995) (hereinafter Commission Report). Coca paste contains $C^{17} H^{21} NO^4$—that is, cocaine in its base form.

Dissolving coca paste in water and hydrochloric acid produces (after several intermediate steps) cocaine hydrochloride, which is a salt with the molecular formula $C^{17} H^{22} NO^{4+}Cl^-$. *Id.,* at 12; Physicians Brief 3. Cocaine hydrochloride, therefore, is not a base. It generally comes in powder form, which we will refer to as "powder cocaine." It is usually insufflated (breathed in through the nose), though it can also be ingested or diluted in water and injected. Because cocaine hydrochloride vaporizes at a much higher temperature than chemically basic cocaine (at which point the cocaine molecule tends to decompose), it is generally not smoked. See Commission Report 11, n. 15, 12–13.

Cocaine hydrochloride can be converted into cocaine in its base form by combining powder cocaine with water and a base, like sodium bicarbonate (also known as baking soda). *Id.,* at 14. The chemical reaction changes the cocaine hydrochloride molecule into a chemically basic cocaine molecule, Physicians Brief 4, and the resulting solid substance can be cooled and broken into small pieces and then smoked, Commission Report 14. This substance is commonly known as "crack" or "crack cocaine." Alternatively, powder cocaine can be dissolved in water and ammonia (also a base); with the addition of ether, a solid substance—known as "freebase"—separates from the solution, and can be smoked. *Id.,* at 13. As with crack cocaine, freebase contains cocaine in its chemically basic form. *Ibid.*

Chemically, therefore, there is no difference between the cocaine in coca paste, crack cocaine, and freebase—all are cocaine in its base form. On the other hand, cocaine in its base form and in its salt form (*i.e.,* cocaine hydrochloride) are chemically different, though they have the same active ingredient and produce the same physiological and psychotropic effects. See *id.*, at 14–22. The key difference between them is the method by which they generally enter the body; smoking cocaine in its base form—whether as coca paste, freebase, or crack cocaine—allows the body to absorb the active ingredient quickly, thereby producing a shorter, more intense high than obtained from insufflating cocaine hydrochloride. *Ibid.*; see generally *Kimbrough v. United States,* 552 U.S. 85, 94, 128 S.Ct. 558, 169 L.Ed.2d 481 (2007).

B

In 1986, increasing public concern over the dangers associated with illicit drugs—and the new phenomenon of crack cocaine in particular—prompted Congress to re-vise the penalties for criminal offenses involving cocaine-related substances. See *id.*, at 95–96, 128 S.Ct. 558. At the time, federal law generally tied the penalties for drug offenses to both the type of drug and the quantity involved, with no provision for mandatory minimum sentences. See, *e.g.*, § 841(b)(1) (1982 ed., Supp. III). After holding several hearings specifically addressing the emergence of crack cocaine, Congress enacted the Anti-Drug Abuse Act of 1986 (ADAA), 100 Stat. 3207, which provided mandatory minimum sentences for controlled-substance offenses involving specific quantities of drugs.

As relevant here, the ADAA provided a mandatory 10-year sentence for certain drug offenses involving 5 kilograms or more of "a mixture or substance containing a detectable amount of "various cocaine-related elements, including coca leaves, cocaine, and cocaine salts; it also called for the same sentence for offenses involving only 50 grams or more of "a mixture or substance . . . *which contains cocaine base.*" ADAA, § 1002, 100 Stat. 3207–2 (amending §§ 841(b)(1)(A)(ii)–(iii)) (emphasis added). The ADAA also stipulated a mandatory 5-year sentence for offenses involving 500 grams of a mixture or substance containing coca leaves, cocaine, and cocaine salts, or 5 grams of a mixture or substance containing "cocaine base." *Id.*, at 3207–3 (amending §§ 841(b)(1)(B)(ii)–(iii)).

Thus, the ADAA established a 100-to-1 ratio for the threshold quantities of cocaine-related substances that triggered the statute's mandatory minimum penalties. That is, 5 grams or more of "a mixture or substance . . . which contains cocaine base" was penalized as severely as 100 times that amount of the other cocaine-related elements enumerated in the statute. These provisions were still in effect at the time of petitioner's conviction and sentence. See §§ 841(b)(1)(A)–(B) (2000 ed. and Supp. V).

The United States Sentencing Commission subsequently promulgated Sentencing Guidelines for drug-trafficking offenses. Under the Guidelines, the offense levels for drug crimes are tied to the drug type and quantity involved. See United States Sentencing Commission, Guidelines Manual § 2D1.1(c) (Nov.2010) (USSG). The Commission originally adopted the

ADAA's 100-to-1 ratio for offenses involving "cocaine" and "cocaine base," though instead of setting only two quantity thresholds, as the ADAA did, the Guidelines "set sentences for the full range of possible drug quantities." Commission Report 1; see generally *Kimbrough,* 552 U.S., at 96–97, 128 S.Ct. 558.

The original version of § 2D1.1(c) did not define "cocaine base" as used in that provision, but in 1993 the Commission issued an amendment to explain that " '[c]ocaine base,' for the purposes of this guideline, means 'crack,' " that is, "the street name for a form of cocaine base, usually prepared by processing cocaine hydrochloride and sodium bicarbonate, and usually appearing in a lumpy, rocklike form." USSG App. C, Amdt. 487 (effective Nov. 1, 1993); see also USSG § 2D1.1(c), n. (D). The Commission noted that "forms of cocaine base other than crack (*e.g.,* coca paste . . .) will be treated as cocaine." USSG App. C, Amdt. 487.

C

In April 2005, petitioner Frantz DePierre sold two bags of drugs to a Government informant. DePierre was subsequently indicted on a charge of distributing 50 grams or more of cocaine base under §§ 841(a)(1) and (b)(1)(A)(iii). At trial, a Government chemist testified that the substance in the bags, which weighed 55.1 grams, was "cocaine base." Tr. 488, 490. She was not able to identify any sodium bicarbonate. *Id.,* at 499. A police officer testified that the substance in question was "off-white [and] chunky." *Id.,* at 455.

DePierre asked the District Court to instruct the jury that, in order to find him guilty of distribution of cocaine base, it must find that his offense involved "the form of cocaine base known as crack cocaine." App. in No. 08–2101(CA1), p. 43. His proposed jury instruction defined "crack" identically to the Guidelines definition. See *id.,* at 43–44; see also USSG § 2D1.1(c), n. (D). In addition, DePierre asked the court to instruct the jury that "[c]hemical analysis cannot establish a substance as crack because crack is chemically identical to other forms of cocaine base, although it can reveal the presence of sodium bicarbonate, which is usually used in the processing of crack." App. in No. 08–2101, at 44.

The court, however, instructed the jury that "the statute that's relevant asks about cocaine base. Crack cocaine is a form of cocaine base, so you'll tell us whether or not what was involved is cocaine base . . . ." Tr. 585 (paragraph break omitted). The jury form asked whether the offense involved "over 50 grams of cocaine base." App. to Pet. for Cert. 17a. The jury found DePierre guilty of distributing 50 grams or more of cocaine base, and the court sentenced DePierre to 120 months in prison as required by the statute.

The United States Court of Appeals for the First Circuit affirmed, rejecting DePierre's argument that § 841(b)(1)(A)(iii) should be read only to apply to offenses involving crack cocaine. 599 F.3d 25, 30–31 (2010). While noting the division on this question among the Courts of Appeals, *id.,* at 30–31, and nn. 3, 4, the First Circuit adhered to its own precedent and "read the statute according to its terms," holding that " 'cocaine base' refers to 'all forms of cocaine base, including but not limited to crack cocaine.' " *Id.,* at 30–31 (quoting *United States v. Anderson,* 452 F.3d 66, 86–87 (C.A.1 2006)). We granted certiorari to resolve the longstanding division in authority among the Courts of Appeals on this question. 562 U.S. ___, 131 S.Ct. 458, 178 L.Ed.2d 286 (2010).

II

A

We begin with the statutory text. See *United States v. Ron Pair Enterprises, Inc.,* 489 U.S. 235, 241, 109 S.Ct. 1026, 103 L.Ed.2d 290 (1989). Section 841(b)(1)(A) provides a mandatory 10-year minimum sentence for certain drug offenses involving

> "(ii) 5 kilograms or more of a mixture or substance containing a detectable amount of—
>
>> "(I) coca leaves, except coca leaves and extracts of coca leaves from which cocaine, ecgonine, and derivatives of ecgonine or their salts have been removed;
>>
>> "(II) cocaine, its salts, optical and geometric isomers, and salts of isomers;
>>
>> "(III) ecgonine, its derivatives, their salts, isomers, and salts of isomers; or
>>
>> "(IV) any compound, mixture, or preparation which contains any quantity of any of the substances referred to in subclauses (I) through (III); [or]
>
> "(iii) 50 grams or more of a mixture or substance described in clause (ii) which contains cocaine base."

We agree with the Government that the most natural reading of the term "cocaine base" is "cocaine in its base form"—*i.e.,* $C^{17} H^{21} NO^4$, the molecule found in crack cocaine, freebase, and coca paste. On its plain terms, then, "cocaine base" reaches more broadly than just crack cocaine. In arguing to the contrary, DePierre asks us to stray far from the statute's text, as the term "crack cocaine" appears nowhere in the ADAA (or the United States Code, for that matter). While the Government's reading is not without its problems, that reading follows from the words Congress chose to include in the text. See *United States v. Rodriquez,* 553 U.S. 377, 384, 128 S.Ct. 1783, 170 L.Ed.2d 719 (2008) (eschewing an interpretation that was "not faithful to the statutory text"). In short, the term "cocaine base" is more plausibly read to mean the "chemically basic form of cocaine," Brief for United States 15, than it is "crack cocaine," Brief for Petitioner 24, 28. . . .

We agree with DePierre that using the term "cocaine base" to refer to C^{17} H^{21} NO^4 is technically redundant; as noted earlier, chemically speaking cocaine *is* a base. If Congress meant in clause (iii) to penalize more severely offenses involving "a mixture or substance . . . which contains" cocaine in its base form it could have simply (and more correctly) used the word "cocaine" instead. But Congress had good reason to use "cocaine base" in the ADAA—to distinguish the substances covered by clause (iii) from other cocaine-related substances. For example, at the time Congress enacted the statute, the word "cocaine" was commonly used to refer to cocaine hydrochloride, *i.e.,* powder cocaine. See, *e.g., United States v. Montoya de Hernandez,* 473 U.S. 531, 536, 544, 105 S.Ct. 3304, 87 L.Ed.2d 381 (1985) (repeatedly referring to cocaine hydrochloride as "cocaine"); "Crack" Cocaine, Hearing before the Permanent Subcommittee on Investigations of the Senate Committee on Governmental Affairs, 99th Cong., 2d Sess., 94 (1986) (hereinafter Crack Cocaine Hearing) (prepared statement of David L. Westrate, Assistant Administrator, Drug Enforcement Admin., Dept. of Justice) (discussing production of "a white, crystalline powder, cocaine hydrochloride, otherwise known simply as cocaine").

To make things more confusing, in the scientific and medical literature the word "cocaine" is often used to refer to *all* cocaine-related substances, including powder cocaine. See, *e.g.,* J. Fay, The Alcohol/Drug Abuse Dictionary and Encyclopedia 26–27 (1988); Weiss et al., Cocaine, at 15–25; R. Lewis, Hawley's Condensed Chemical Dictionary 317 (15th ed.2007). Accordingly, Congress' choice to use the admittedly redundant term "cocaine base" to refer to chemically basic cocaine is best understood as an effort to make clear that clause (iii) does not apply to offenses involving powder cocaine or other nonbasic cocaine-related substances.

B

Notwithstanding DePierre's arguments to the contrary, reading "cocaine base" to mean chemically basic cocaine is also consistent with § 841(b)(1)'s somewhat confounding structure. DePierre is correct that the interpretation we adopt today raises the question why Congress included the word "cocaine" in subclause (II) of clause (ii). That subclause lists "*cocaine,* its salts, optical and geometric isomers, and salts of isomers" as elements subject to clause (ii)'s higher quantity threshold. §§ 841(b)(1)(A)(ii)(II), (B)(ii)(II) (emphasis added). If, as we conclude, the terms "cocaine" and "cocaine base" both mean chemically basic cocaine, offenses involving a mixture or substance which contains such cocaine will always be penalized according to the lower quantity thresholds of clause (iii), and never the higher quantity thresholds clause (ii) establishes for mixtures and substances containing "cocaine." . . .

DePierre offers four additional arguments in support of his view that the term "cocaine base" in clause (iii) is best read to mean "crack cocaine." We do not find them convincing.

A

DePierre first argues that we should read "cocaine base" to mean "crack cocaine" because, in passing the ADAA, Congress in 1986 intended to penalize crack cocaine offenses more severely than those involving other substances containing $C^{17} H^{21} NO^4$. As is evident from the pre-ceding discussion, this position is not supported by the statutory text. To be sure, the records of the contemporaneous congressional hearings suggest that Congress was most concerned with the particular dangers posed by the advent of crack cocaine. See, *e.g.*, Crack Cocaine Hearing 1 (statement of Chairman Roth) ("[We] mee[t] today to examine a frightening and dangerous new twist in the drug abuse problem—the growing availability and use of a cheap, highly addictive, and deadly form of cocaine known on the streets as 'crack'"); see generally Commission Report 116–118; *Kimbrough,* 552 U.S., at 95–96, 128 S.Ct. 558.

It does not necessarily follow, however, that in passing the ADAA Congress meant for clause (iii)'s lower quantity thresholds to apply *exclusively* to crack cocaine offenses. Numerous witnesses at the hearings testified that the primary reason crack cocaine was so dangerous was because—contrary to powder cocaine—cocaine in its base form is smoked, which was understood to produce a faster, more intense, and more addictive high than powder cocaine. See, *e.g.*, Crack Cocaine Hearing 20 (statement of Dr. Robert Byck, Yale University School of Medicine) (stating that the ability to inhale vapor "is the reason why crack, or cocaine free-base, is so dangerous"). This is not, however, a feature unique to crack cocaine, and freebase and coca paste were also acknowledged as dangerous, smokeable forms of cocaine. See, *e.g., id.,* at 70 (prepared statement of Dr. Charles R. Schuster, Director, National Institute on Drug Abuse) (reporting on the shift from snorting powder cocaine to "newer more dangerous routes of administration, such as freebase smoking"); *id.,* at 19–20 (statement of Dr. Byck) (describing the damaging effects of cocaine smoking on people in Peru).

Moreover, the testimony of witnesses before Congress did not clearly distinguish between these base forms of cocaine; witnesses repeatedly used terms like "cocaine base," "freebase," or "cocaine freebase" in a manner that grouped crack cocaine with other substances containing chemically basic forms of cocaine. See, *e.g.*, Trafficking and Abuse of "Crack" in New York City, House Select Committee on Narcotics Abuse and Control, 99th Cong., 2d Sess., 258 (1986) (statement of Robert M. Stutman, Special Agent in Charge, Drug Enforcement Admin., Dept. of Justice) ("[C]ocaine in its alkaloid form [is] commonly known on the street as crack, rock, base, or freebase"); Crack Cocaine Hearing 71 (statement of Dr. Schuster) ("In other words, 'crack' is a street name for cocaine freebase"). In fact, prior to passage of the ADAA, multiple bills were introduced in Congress that imposed enhanced penalties on those who trafficked in "cocaine base," *e.g.,*

S. 2787, 99th Cong., 2d Sess., § 1 (1986), as well as "cocaine freebase," *e.g.,* H.R. 5394, 99th Cong., 2d Sess., § 101 (1986); H.R. 5484, 99th Cong., 2d Sess., § 608 (a) (1986).

Given crack cocaine's sudden emergence and the similarities it shared with other forms of cocaine, this lack of clarity is understandable, as is Congress' desire to adopt a statutory term that would encompass all forms. Congress faced what it perceived to be a new threat of massive scope. See, *e.g.,* Crack Cocaine Hearing 4 (statement of Sen. Nunn) ("[C]ocaine use, particularly in the more pure form known as crack, is at near epidemic proportions"); *id.,* at 21 (statement of Dr. Byck) ("We are dealing with a worse drug . . . than we have ever dealt with, or that anybody has ever dealt with in history"). Accordingly, Congress chose statutory language broad enough to meet that threat. As we have noted, "statutory prohibitions often go beyond the principal evil to cover reasonably comparable evils." *Oncale v. Sundowner Offshore Services, Inc.,* 523 U.S. 75, 79, 118 S.Ct. 998, 140 L.Ed.2d 201 (1998). In the absence of any indication in the statutory text that Congress intended only to subject crack cocaine offenses to enhanced penalties, we cannot adopt DePierre's narrow construction. See *Lewis v. Chicago,* 560 U.S. ___, ___, 130 S.Ct. 2191, 2200, 176 L.Ed.2d 967 (2010) ("It is not for us to rewrite [a] statute so that it covers only what we think is necessary to achieve what we think Congress really intended").

B

DePierre also argues that we should read the term "cocaine base" to mean "crack cocaine," rather than chemically basic cocaine, because the latter definition leads to an absurd result. Cf. *EEOC v. Commercial Office Products Co.,* 486 U.S. 107, 120, 108 S.Ct. 1666, 100 L.Ed.2d 96 (1988) (plurality opinion). He contends that, because coca leaves themselves contain cocaine, under the Government's approach an offense involving 5 grams of coca leaves will be subject to the 5-year minimum sentence in § 841(b)(1)(B)(iii), even though those leaves would produce only .05 grams of smokeable cocaine. See Brief for Petitioner 41–42. While we agree that it would be questionable to treat 5 grams of coca leaves as equivalent to 500 grams of powder cocaine for minimum-sentence purposes, we are not persuaded that such a result would actually obtain in light of our decision today.

To begin with, it is a matter of dispute between the parties whether coca leaves in their natural, unprocessed form actually contain chemically basic cocaine. Compare Brief for Petitioner 15, 17, n. 10, with Brief for United States 43. Even assuming that DePierre is correct as a matter of chemistry that coca leaves contain cocaine in its base form, see Physicians Brief 2, 11, the Government has averred that it "would not be able to make that showing in court," Tr. of Oral Arg. 27, and that "coca leaves should not be treated as containing 'cocaine base' for purposes of Clause (iii)," Brief for United States 45.

It is unsurprising, therefore, that the Government in its brief disclaimed awareness of any prosecution in which it had sought, or the defendant had received, a statutory-minimum sentence enhanced under clause (iii) for an offense involving coca leaves. *Id.,* at 44. And although this question is not before us today, we note that Congress' deliberate choice to enumerate "coca leaves" in clause (ii) strongly indicates its intent that offenses involving such leaves be subject to the higher quantity thresholds of that clause. Accordingly, there is little danger that the statute will be read in the "absurd" manner DePierre fears.

C

In addition, DePierre suggests that because the Sentencing Commission has, since 1993, defined "cocaine base" to mean "crack" for the purposes of the Federal Sentencing Guidelines, we should do the same with respect to § 841(b)(1). We do not agree. We have never held that, when interpreting a term in a criminal statute, deference is warranted to the Sentencing Commission's definition of the same term in the Guidelines. Cf. *Neal v. United States,* 516 U.S. 284, 290–296, 116 S.Ct. 763, 133 L.Ed.2d 709 (1996). And we need not decide now whether such deference would be appropriate, because the Guidelines do not purport to interpret § 841(b)(1). See USSG § 2D1.1(c), n. (D) (" 'Cocaine base,' *for the purposes of this guideline,* means 'crack' " (emphasis added)).

We recognize that, because the definition of "cocaine base" in clause (iii) differs from the Guidelines definition, certain sentencing anomalies may result. For example, an offense involving 5 grams of crack cocaine and one involving 5 grams of coca paste both trigger a minimum 5-year sentence under § 841(b)(1)(B)(iii). But defendants convicted of offenses involving only 4 grams of each substance—which do not trigger the statutory minimums—would likely receive different sentences, because of the Guidelines' differential treatment of those substances with respect to offense level. Compare USSG § 2D1.1(c)(9) (providing an offense level of 22 for at least 4 grams of "cocaine base," *i.e.,* "crack") with § 2D1.1(c)(14) (providing an offense level of 12 for less than 25 grams of "cocaine," which, under the Guidelines, includes coca paste). As we have noted in previous opinions, however, such disparities are the inevitable result of the dissimilar operation of the fixed minimum sentences Congress has provided by statute and the graduated sentencing scheme established by the Guidelines. See *Kimbrough,* 552 U.S., at 107–108, 128 S.Ct. 558; *Neal,* 516 U.S., at 291–292, 116 S.Ct. 763. Accordingly, we reject DePierre's suggestion that the term "cocaine base" as used in clause (iii) must be given the same definition as it has under the Guidelines.

D

Finally, DePierre argues that, because § 841(b)(1) is at the very least ambiguous, the rule of lenity requires us to interpret the statute in his favor. See *United States v. Santos,* 553 U.S. 507, 514, 128 S.Ct. 2020, 170

L.Ed.2d 912 (2008) ("The rule of lenity requires ambiguous criminal laws to be interpreted in favor of the defendants subjected to them"). As evinced by the preceding discussion, we cannot say that the statute is crystalline. The rule, however, is reserved for cases where, "after seizing everything from which aid can be derived, the Court is left with an ambiguous statute." *Smith v. United States,* 508 U.S. 223, 239, 113 S.Ct. 2050, 124 L.Ed.2d 138 (1993)(internal quotation marks and alterations omitted). Applying the normal rules of statutory construction in this case, it is clear that Congress used the term "cocaine base" in clause (iii) to penalize more severely not only offenses involving "crack cocaine," but those involving substances containing chemically basic cocaine more generally. There is no persuasive justification for reading the statute otherwise. Because the statutory text allows us to make far more than "a guess as to what Congress intended," *Reno v. Koray,* 515 U.S. 50, 65, 115 S.Ct. 2021, 132 L.Ed.2d 46 (1995) (internal quotation marks omitted), the rule of lenity does not apply in DePierre's favor.

* * *

We hold that the term "cocaine base" as used in § 841(b)(1) means not just "crack cocaine," but cocaine in its chemically basic form. We therefore affirm the judgment of the Court of Appeals.

EXERCISE

If you were a member of Congress, how might you reform the language of 21 U.S.C. 841 so that it more clearly differentiates between powder and crack cocaine?

E. CONTINUING CRIMINAL ENTERPRISES

Among the narcotics provisions of the federal code, one of the harshest is 21 U.S.C. § 848. That statute requires a 20-year *minimum* sentence (30 with a qualifying prior conviction) if the defendant engaged in a "continuing criminal enterprise," which is defined as (1) a felony violation of the primary federal drug laws, (2) involving a "continuing series of violations" (3) where the defendant's violation was committed in concert with five or more other people, (4) that the defendant occupied "a position of organizer, a supervisory position, or any other position of management," and (5) the defendant obtained "substantial income or resources" from the enterprise. It gets harsher, too, allowing for a mandatory life sentence and even the death penalty if certain additional factors are proven.

Some of the elements of this statute (i.e., "substantial income") are relatively undefined, but others are quite precise and a failure by the government to meet the requirements of those precise standards can undermine a case.

UNITED STATES V. EILAND
738 F. 3d 338 (D.C. Cir. 2013)

Opinion for the Court by CIRCUIT JUDGE BROWN.

Appellants, Gerald Eiland and Frederick Miller, were convicted of various narcotics-related offenses. The government's evidence at trial showed that Eiland and Miller organized an extensive drug ring in the Washington, D.C. area that had ties across the country. . . .

Sometime in 2003, the Safe Streets Task Force of the FBI began investigating a drug trafficking ring in Southeast Washington, D.C. The evidence revealed a wide-ranging drug operation headed by Eiland and Miller. The operation dealt in heroin, cocaine, cocaine base, and phencyclidine (PCP) and had ties around the country and to foreign travelers. On February 13, 2004, the task force applied for and was granted court authorization to wiretap Miller's cell phone. The court approved two extensions and the wiretap lasted three months. In April, the district court permitted the task force to tap Eiland's three phones and approved an extension for one of those phones. FBI Agent Daniel Sparks provided supporting affidavits for each of the initial wiretap and extension applications. Although the conspirators often used untapped payphones to discuss their illicit activities and spoke in guarded language while on the wiretapped phones, the FBI obtained substantial evidence from the wiretaps. Following a "reverse sting" operation, the FBI arrested Eiland and Miller in August 2004. The government charged twenty-one defendants in a 100-count superseding indictment. The defendants were charged with conspiring to distribute heroin, cocaine, cocaine base, and PCP between 1999 and 2004 in Virginia, the District of Columbia, and Maryland. . . .

. . . the jury found the government had proved Miller and Eiland conspired to traffic heroin, cocaine, and cocaine base and committed the racketeering acts and CCE predicate offenses involving those same narcotics. But the jury found the government had not proved the charged offenses and acts involving the trafficking of PCP.

At appellants' sentencing hearings, the district court dismissed the narcotics conspiracy charges against Miller and Eiland as lesser-included offenses of the CCE counts. The court sentenced each to concurrent sentences of life imprisonment for RICO conspiracy and CCE, and lesser terms of imprisonment on the other counts. . . .

Miller argues, through counsel, there was insufficient evidence for the jury to convict him of engaging in a continuing criminal enterprise in violation of 21 U.S.C. § 848. To convict a defendant of CCE, the government must prove the defendant committed: "1) a felony violation of the federal narcotics law; 2) as part of a continuing series of violations; 3) in concert with five or more persons; 4) for whom the defendant is an organizer or supervisor; 5) from which he derives substantial income or resources." *Moore,* 651 F.3d at 80. Miller contends the government failed to prove he "occupie[d] a position of organizer, a supervisory position, or any other position of management" with regard to five or more people. 21 U.S.C. § 848(c)(2)(A). To satisfy this element, the government must show the defendant "specifie[d the supervisees'] activities in adequate detail." *United States v. Williams-Davis,* 90 F.3d 490, 508 (D.C.Cir.1996). The defendant must have "exercise[d] some sort of managerial responsibility." *Id.* "Delegation of management to an intermediate supervisor does not prevent lower-level subordinates from being counted in the continuing criminal enterprise statute." *United States v. Delgado,* 4 F.3d 780, 785 (9th Cir.1993). The government identifies five individuals whom it claims were Miller's supervisees: Timothy Thomas, Tyrone Thomas, Charles Brown, Darius Ames, and Jay Ingram.

There was sufficient evidence for a jury rationally to find Miller exercised a supervisory role over Tyrone Thomas and Timothy Thomas. Miller exercised a supervisory role over both of these individuals in arranging for Tyrone to transport money to Arizona and to transport cocaine back to Washington, D.C. "Drug runners can be considered managees for purposes of 21 U.S.C. § 848." *United States v. Wilson,* 605 F.3d 985, 1030 (D.C.Cir.2010). In March 2004, Miller called Tyrone and arranged for him to drive to Washington. Oct. 10, 2006 PM Trial Tr. at 71–73. Miller then told Tyrone that Timothy Thomas would introduce Tyrone to Eiland, with whom Tyrone would be exchanging the money for drugs in Arizona. *Id.* at 73–74. As Tyrone was transporting the cocaine back to Washington, Miller kept in contact with Timothy Thomas, who was checking on Tyrone's progress. Oct. 12, 2006 AM Trial Tr. at 82–83; Calls 5589, 5659, Gov't Supplemental App'x 51–53. When Tyrone told Timothy Thomas the cocaine had been lost, Miller organized the response, at one point instructing Timothy to get the baggage claim number for Tyrone's bag. Oct. 11, 2006 AM Trial Tr. at 24–26; Call 6154, Gov't Supplemental App'x 55–56. This evidence establishes Miller exercised the requisite supervisory control over both Tyrone Thomas and Timothy Thomas, organizing the transportation of money and drugs.

The government also presented sufficient evidence to establish Miller was a manager of Charles Brown. When Tyrone claimed that the cocaine he shipped by bus was lost, Miller recruited Brown to help find the cocaine. Oct. 12, 2006 PM Trial Tr. at 13–14; Call 6133, Gov't Supplemental App'x 54. At another time Miller arranged for Brown to accept a package of heroin for Miller. Oct. 18, 2006 AM Trial Tr. at 31–32.

The government's evidence with regard to Darius Ames is weaker but still sufficient to support the jury's conclusion that Ames was a supervisee of Miller. Darius Ames bagged heroin for Eiland. Oct. 4, 2006 PM Trial Tr. at 26–27. On a few occasions Miller came into the stash apartment where

Ames was bagging and took heroin. *Id.* at 43–44; Oct. 5, 2006 AM Trial Tr. at 8–14. Miller would measure out 25 grams of heroin, stretch it to 50 grams, bag it, and leave $1,000 with Ames, directing him to give the money to Eiland. Oct. 5, 2006 AM Trial Tr. at 8–14. In another instance, Eiland, who was out of town at the time, directed Ames to pick up a shoe box from Miller. *Id.* at 15–16. Miller was to call Ames when Miller was ready for Ames to pick it up. *Id.* When Miller called Ames, Ames drove to meet Miller and, following Miller's instruction, went through the alleyway to the back door and into the basement of Miller's aunt's house. *Id.* at 16; Oct. 4, 2006 PM Trial Tr. at 57. Miller proceeded to give Ames a shoebox of money that Ames took and stored for Eiland. Oct. 4, 2006 PM Trial Tr. at 57–58. Together, this evidence, although not strong, supports the inference that Ames was Miller's subordinate. Both Miller and Eiland viewed Ames as a lower-level conspirator—a gofer whom they were free to direct. Under the deferential standard we apply on reviewing a sufficiency challenge, we conclude a jury rationally could have found Ames to be a supervisee of Miller.

Nevertheless, the government failed to produce sufficient evidence to demonstrate that Jay Ingram was supervised by Miller. FBI Agent Hall testified that Ingram was a lieutenant in the organization and was Miller's cousin. Oct. 17, 2006 AM Trial Tr. at 56. But Ingram's familial relation to Miller is irrelevant, and Agent Hall's description of Ingram as a lieutenant is conclusory. The agent's opinion regarding Miller's role has no more weight than the facts upon which it is based, and those were insufficient. There was evidence that Ingram obtained PCP from Miller. Oct. 19, 2006 PM Trial Tr. at 52–53. But a buyer-seller relationship, without more, does not suggest a managerial relationship. *See United States v. Mitchell,* 49 F.3d 769, 772 (D.C.Cir.1995); *see also United States v. Witek,* 61 F.3d 819, 822–23 (11th Cir.1995) ("Buyers and sellers often need to accommodate one another when meeting and arranging for delivery. Such conduct is simply incidental to the buyer-seller relationship."). A dealer who simply sells drugs to other dealers and is paid from the proceeds of their sales, but who has no other involvement in their sales, does not exercise the managerial control required for a CCE conviction. *Id.* There was no evidence presented at trial that Miller played any ongoing role in Ingram's sales after supplying Ingram with PCP. Furthermore, the jury's verdict demonstrates that it did not deem the PCP evidence credible. The jury found Miller not guilty of all PCP-related charges.

The government points to an intercepted phone call in which Eiland, who was looking for drugs, called Miller and asked where Ingram was. Oct. 17, 2006 AM Trial Tr. at 56–57, 65; Call 1172, Gov't Supplemental App'x at 37. Miller responded that Ingram was with him. *Id.* Rashawn Briggs, a cooperating witness, also testified he once saw Eiland, Miller, and Ingram meeting outside a carry-out restaurant. Oct. 19, 2006 AM Trial Tr. at 34–36. None of this evidence suggests Miller acted in a supervisory capacity with regard to Ingram. This evidence of association is not enough to prove that Miller managed Ingram.

The government's evidence at trial was insufficient to convince a rational jury beyond a reasonable doubt that Miller acted as an organizer, supervisor, or manager for five or more individuals. Because the government failed to establish one of the elements of CCE, we vacate Miller's conviction on this count.

————————

EXERCISE

Imagine that you are the investigating agent in the case above. What additional information would you seek if the Continuing Criminal Enterprise count against Miller was going to be re-tried?

F. USE OF A COMMUNICATION FACILITY

The narcotics statutes allow prosecutors to seek a wide range of outcomes in drug cases. While the Continuing Criminal Enterprise law offers prosecutors a way to charge up from the basic narcotics statute (21 U.S.C. § 841) and ensure a long sentence through mandatory minimums, 21 U.S.C. § 843(b) gives them flexibility in the other direction. Because this statute—which criminalizes using a "communication facility" in the course of a narcotics felony—has a maximum sentence of just four years for a first offender, it allows prosecutors to charge some defendants in a way that guarantees that a judge cannot impose an especially long sentence. These charges are sometimes referred to as a "phone count."

The phone count is one device that essentially broadens the prosecutor's discretion, and lessens that of the judge—even if the judge wants a sentence over four years, she cannot impose one.

While a phone count can be used by prosecutors to limit the criminal penalty that may be exacted against a defendant, they may run into trouble if they instead try to inflate a small case into a bigger one.

ABUELHAWA V. UNITED STATES
556 U.S. 816 (2009)

JUSTICE SOUTER delivered the opinion of the Court.

The Controlled Substances Act (CSA) makes it a felony "to use any communication facility in committing or in causing or facilitating" certain felonies prohibited by the statute. 84 Stat. 1263, 21 U.S.C. § 843(b). The question here is whether someone violates § 843(b) in making a misdemeanor drug purchase because his phone call to the dealer can be said to facilitate the felony of drug distribution. The answer is no.

I

FBI agents believed Mohammed Said was selling cocaine and got a warrant to tap his cell phone. In the course of listening in, they recorded six calls between Said and petitioner Salman Khade Abuelhawa, during which Abuelhawa arranged to buy cocaine from Said in two separate transactions, each time a single gram. Abuelhawa's two purchases were misdemeanors, § 844, while Said's two sales were felonies, § 841(a)(1) and (b). The Government nonetheless charged Abuelhawa with six felonies on the theory that each of the phone calls, whether placed by Abuelhawa or by Said, had been made "in causing or facilitating" Said's felonies, in violation of § 843(b). Abuelhawa moved for acquittal as a matter of law, arguing that his efforts to commit the misdemeanors of buying cocaine could not be treated as causing or facilitating Said's felonies, but the District Court denied his motion, App. to Pet. for Cert. 20a–25a, and the jury convicted him on all six felony counts.

Abuelhawa argued the same point to the Court of Appeals for the Fourth Circuit, with as much success. The Circuit reasoned that "for purposes of § 843(b), 'facilitate' should be given its 'common meaning—to make easier or less difficult, or to assist or aid.'" 523 F.3d 415, 420 (2008) (quoting *United States v. Lozano,* 839 F.2d 1020, 1023 (C.A.4 1988)). The court said Abuelhawa's use of a phone to buy cocaine counted as ordinary facilitation because it "undoubtedly made Said's cocaine distribution easier; in fact, 'it made the sale possible.'" 523 F.3d, at 421 (quoting *United States v. Binkley,* 903 F.2d 1130, 1136 (C.A.7 1990) (emphasis deleted)). We granted certiorari, 555 U.S. 1028, 129 S.Ct. 593 (2008), to resolve a split among the Courts of Appeals on the scope of § 843(b), and we now reverse.

II

The Government's argument is a reprise of the Fourth Circuit's opinion, that Abuelhawa's use of his cell phone satisfies the plain meaning of "facilitate" because it "allow[ed] the transaction to take place more efficiently, and with less risk of detection, than if the purchaser and seller had to meet in person." Brief for United States 10. And of course on the literal plane, the phone calls could be described as "facilitating" drug distribution; they "undoubtedly made . . . distribution easier." 523 F.3d, at 421. But stopping there would ignore the rule that, because statutes are not read as a collection of isolated phrases, see *United States Nat. Bank of Ore. v. Independent Ins. Agents of America, Inc.,* 508 U.S. 439, 455, 113 S.Ct. 2173, 124 L.Ed.2d 402 (1993), "[a] word in a statute may or may not extend to the outer limits of its definitional possibilities," *Dolan v. Postal Service,* 546 U.S. 481, 486, 126 S.Ct. 1252, 163 L.Ed.2d 1079 (2006). We think the word here does not.

To begin with, the Government's literal sweep of "facilitate" sits uncomfortably with common usage. Where a transaction like a sale necessarily presupposes two parties with specific roles, it would be odd to speak of one party as facilitating the conduct of the other. A buyer does not just make a sale easier; he makes the sale possible. No buyer, no sale; the buyer's part is already implied by the term "sale," and the word "facilitate" adds nothing. We would not say that the borrower facilitates the bank loan.

The Government, however, replies that using the instrument of communication under § 843(b) is different from borrowing the money or merely handing over the sale price for cocaine. Drugs can be sold without anyone's mailing a letter or using a cell phone. Because cell phones, say, really do make it easier for dealers to break the law, Congress probably meant to ratchet up the culpability of the buyer who calls ahead. But we think that argument comes up short against several more reasons that count against the Government's position.

The common usage that limits "facilitate" to the efforts of someone other than a primary or necessary actor in the commission of a substantive crime has its parallel in the decided cases. The traditional law is that where a statute treats one side of a bilateral transaction more leniently, adding to the penalty of the party on that side for facilitating the action by the other would upend the calibration of punishment set by the legislature, a line of reasoning exemplified in the courts' consistent refusal to treat noncriminal liquor purchases as falling under the prohibition against aiding or abetting the illegal sale of alcohol. See *Lott v. United States,* 205 F. 28, 29–31 (C.A.9 1913)(collecting cases).

And this Court followed the same course in rejecting the broadest possible reading of a similar provision in *Gebardi v. United States,* 287 U.S. 112, 53 S.Ct. 35, 77 L.Ed. 206 (1932). The question there was whether a woman who voluntarily crossed a state line with a man to engage in "illicit sexual relations" could be tagged with "aid[ing] or assist[ing] in . . . transporting, in interstate or foreign commerce . . . any woman or girl for the purpose of prostitution or of debauchery, or for any other immoral purpose" in violation of the Mann Act, ch. 395, 36 Stat. 825. *Gebardi,* 287 U.S., at 116–118, 53 S.Ct. 35 (internal quotation marks omitted). Since the statutory penalties were "clearly directed against the acts of the transporter as distinguished from the consent of the subject of the transportation," we refused to "infer that the mere acquiescence of the woman transported was intended to be condemned by the general language punishing those who aid and assist the transporter, any more than it has been inferred that the purchaser of liquor was to be regarded as an abettor of the illegal sale." *Id.,* at 119, 53 S.Ct. 35 (footnote omitted).

These cases do not strictly control the outcome of this one, but we think they have a bearing here, in two ways. As we have said many times, we presume legislatures act with case law in mind, *e.g., Williams v. Taylor,* 529 U.S. 362, 380–381, and n. 12, 120 S.Ct. 1495, 146 L.Ed.2d 389 (2000), and we presume here that when Congress enacted § 843(b), it was familiar with the traditional judicial limitation on applying terms like "aid," "abet," and "assist." We thus think it likely that Congress had comparable scope in mind when it used the term "facilitate," a word with equivalent meaning, compare Black's Law Dictionary 76 (8th ed.2004) (defining "aid and abet" as to "facilitate the commission of a crime") with *id.*, at 627 (defining "facilitation" as "[t]he act or an instance of aiding or helping; . . . the act of making it easier for another person to commit a crime").

And applying the presumption is supported significantly by the fact that here, as in the earlier cases, any broader reading of "facilitate" would for practical purposes skew the congressional calibration of respective buyer-seller penalties. When the statute was enacted, the use of land lines in drug transactions was common, and in these days when everyone over the age of three seems to carry a cell phone, the Government's interpretation would skew the calibration of penalties very substantially. The respect owed to that penalty calibration cannot be minimized. Prior to 1970, Congress punished the receipt, concealment, purchase, or sale of any narcotic drug as a felony, see 21 U.S.C. § 174 (1964 ed.) (repealed), and on top of that added a minimum of two years, and up to five, for using a communication facility in committing, causing, or facilitating, any drug "offense," 18 U.S.C. § 1403 (1964 ed.). In 1970, however, the CSA, 84 Stat. 1242, 21 U.S.C. § 801 *et seq.*, downgraded simple possession of a controlled substance to a misdemeanor, 21 U.S.C. § 844(a) (2006 ed.), and simultaneously limited the communications provision to prohibiting only the facilitation of a drug "felony," § 843(b). This history drives home what is already clear in the current statutory text: Congress meant to treat purchasing drugs for personal use more leniently than the felony of distributing drugs, and to narrow the scope of the communications provision to cover only those who facilitate a drug felony. Yet, under the Government's reading of § 843(b), in a substantial number of cases Congress would for all practical purposes simultaneously have graded back up to felony status with the left hand the same offense it had dropped to a misdemeanor with the right. As the Government sees it, Abuelhawa's use of a phone in making two small drug purchases would subject him, in fact, to six felony counts and a potential sentence of 24 years in prison, even though buying the same drugs minus the phone would have supported only two misdemeanor counts and two years of prison. Given the CSA's distinction between simple possession and distribution, and the background history of these offenses, it is impossible to believe that Congress intended "facilitating" to cause that twelve-fold quantum leap in punishment for simple drug possessors.

The Government suggests that this background usage and the 1970 choice to reduce culpability for possession is beside the point because Congress sometimes incorporates aggravating factors into the Criminal Code, and the phone use here is just one of them; the Government mentions possession by a prior drug offender, a felony punishable by up to two years' imprisonment. And, for perspective, the Government points to unauthorized possession of flunitrazepim, a drug used to incapacitate rape victims, which is punishable by imprisonment up to three years. Brief for United States 20. It would not be strange, the Government says, for Congress to "decid[e] to treat the use of a communication facility in a drug transaction as a significant act warranting additional punishment" because "[t]oday's communication facilities ... make illicit drug transactions easier and more efficient .... [and] greatly reduce the risk that the participants will be detected while negotiating a transaction." *Id.,* at 23–24.

We are skeptical. There is no question that Congress intended § 843(b) to impede illicit drug transactions by penalizing the use of communication devices in coordinating illegal drug operations, and no doubt that its purpose will be served regardless of the outcome in this case. But it does not follow that Congress also meant a first-time buyer's phone calls to get two small quantities of drugs for personal use to expose him to punishment 12 times more severe than a purchase by a recidivist offender and 8 times more severe than the unauthorized possession of a drug used by rapists. To the contrary, Congress used no language spelling out a purpose so improbable, but legislated against a background usage of terms such as "aid," "abet," and "assist" that points in the opposite direction and accords with the CSA's choice to classify small purchases as misdemeanors. The Government's position is just too unlikely.

III

The judgment of the Court of Appeals for the Fourth Circuit is reversed, and the case is remanded for further proceedings consistent with this opinion.

EXERCISE

Robert Serious is a resident of Miami who imports over 100 kilos of cocaine into the United States every week. He employs a group of 28 drivers and pilots to do so, and coordinates their actions themselves. The only one besides Serious who knows the full details of his activities is his girlfriend, Sheila Lowe. She helps out some with the operation by calling the pilots to tell them where to go, directing deliveries to safe houses, and (on one occasion) firing a shotgun into a car to scare off some guys who looked like they wanted to steal cocaine from a shipment (no one was hurt). Imagine that you are the prosecutor in this federal case.

Knowing that you will need someone to testify against Serious if you hope for a conviction, what charges would you consider against Serious, Lowe, the pilots, and the drivers if they are willing to cooperate with the government?

CHAPTER SEVEN

FIREARMS

■ ■ ■

Like narcotics, firearms have been a subject of criminal law for a relatively short period of time (at least within the broader scope of history). Though some state laws restricting guns are much older, most of the frequently-used federal statutes were enacted in the 20th century.

No American jurisdiction simply bans the possession of guns (nor could they, given the Constitution's Second Amendment as it is now understood). Instead, gun laws take one of four forms, which focus respectively on the type of gun, person, action, and place. Notably, some of these laws restrict not only firearms, but the possession of ammunition and other objects related to firearms.

First, some laws expressly prohibit or restrict the possession of certain types of firearms. For example, machine guns are subject to laws we will examine in this section and few people are allowed to possess them without running afoul of the federal statute.

Other laws, rather than prohibiting specific guns, prohibit certain *people* from possessing any firearm. For example, federal law sharply restricts the gun rights of convicted felons, and makes them one of several groups for whom it is a felony to simply possess a gun.

A third type of law makes it a separate and independent crime to possess or use a firearm in the commission of an underlying offense. Under this law, what would often be one crime—for example, armed robbery— becomes two, one for the robbery and a distinct crime for the use of the firearm.

Finally, a fourth type of law focuses not on type of gun or person, but restricts the possession of guns in certain *places*, such as courthouses, schools, and airplanes.

A. ILLEGAL GUNS AND RELATED ITEMS

Some firearms are simple more dangerous than others. A machine gun is more dangerous than a small pistol, for example, because in the wrong hands it can inflict much more damage in a short amount of time. It is because of the inherent dangerousness of some types of weapons that they face greater restrictions under the law.

Federal law limits or bars the trafficking and possession of several types of guns, in a variety of ways. Part of the tax code, 26 U.S.C. § 5801 et. seq. creates criminal penalties for the failure to register and pay a tax for a wide variety of items including machineguns, short-barreled shotguns and rifles, and silencers.

A more recent statute passed in 1986 (18 U.S.C. § 922(*o*)) sets out a broad ban on the possession of machineguns apart from the older tax-based scheme:

> **(*o*)(1)**   Except as provided in paragraph (2), it shall be unlawful for any person to transfer or possess a machinegun.
>
> > **(2)**   This subsection does not apply with respect to—
> >
> > > **(A)** a transfer to or by, or possession by or under the authority of, the United States or any department or agency thereof or a State, or a department, agency, or political subdivision thereof; or
> > >
> > > **(B)** any lawful transfer or lawful possession of a machinegun that was lawfully possessed before the date this subsection takes effect.

Crucial to the use of this statute is the definition of "machinegun," which is defined at 26 U.S.C. § 5845(b) as "any weapon which shoots, . . . or can be readily restored to shoot, automatically more than one shot, without manual reloading, by a single function of the trigger." It is the burden of the government to prove that the gun in question meets this definition.

UNITED STATES V. CAMP

343 F. 3d 743 (5th Cir. 2003)

RHESA HAWKINS BARKSDALE, CIRCUIT JUDGE:

The United States appeals the FED.R.CRIM.P. 12(b) dismissal of Ernest Camp's indictment for possession of a machine gun, in violation of 18 U.S.C. §§ 922(*o*)(1) and 924(a)(2). At issue is whether the term "trigger" as used in 26 U.S.C. § 5845(b) (defining "machine gun") includes a switch that starts a motor, causing a modified semiautomatic rifle to automatically fire more than one shot. VACATED and REMANDED.

I.

Louisiana authorities executing a search warrant at Camp's home seized firearms, illegal drugs, and drug-manufacturing equipment. One firearm was a modified semiautomatic rifle; Camp had added an electrically-operated trigger mechanism (device).

When an added switch behind the original trigger was pulled, it supplied electrical power to a motor connected to the bottom of a fishing reel that had been placed inside the weapon's trigger guard; the motor caused the reel to rotate; and that rotation caused the original trigger to function in rapid succession. The weapon would fire until either the shooter released the switch or the loaded ammunition was expended.

The Bureau of Alcohol, Tobacco, and Firearms (ATF) tested the weapon and found it "capable of firing more than one shot, without manual reloading[,] by a single function of the trigger". (This finding corresponds with the definition of a machine gun found in 26 U.S.C. § 5845(b).) The ATF was able to cause the weapon to fire two three-shot bursts. As a result, the ATF concluded that the modified rifle was a "machine gun" for purposes of § 5845(b).

Camp was indicted for possession of a machine gun. *See* 18 U.S.C. §§ 922(*o*)(1) and 924(a)(2). He stipulated that he possessed the firearm, but contended it was not a "machine gun" as defined by § 5845(b). The district court treated this contention as a Rule 12(b) motion to dismiss; held an evidentiary hearing; and dismissed the indictment. It held: the "switch" was not a "trigger" for purposes of § 5845(b); the weapon required multiple functions of the primary trigger; and, therefore, the weapon, as modified, was not a § 5845(b) machine gun.

II.

The district court's application of the statute is reviewed *de novo. United States v. Jennings*, 195 F.3d 795, 797 (5th Cir.1999), *cert. denied,* 530 U.S. 1245, 120 S.Ct. 2694, 147 L.Ed.2d 965 (2000). Pursuant to § 5845(b), a "machine gun" is

> any weapon which shoots ... automatically more than one shot, without manual reloading, *by a single function of the trigger.* The term shall also include the frame or receiver of any such weapon, any part designed and intended solely and exclusively, or combination of parts designed and intended, for use in converting a weapon into a machinegun, and any combination of parts from which a machinegun can be assembled if such parts are in the possession or under the control of a person.

26 U.S.C. § 5845(b) (emphasis added).

A.

The term "trigger" is not defined by statute. *United States v. Jokel*, 969 F.2d 132, 135 (5th Cir.1992), defined a trigger, as used in 26 U.S.C. § 5845(d)(shotguns), as any "mechanism ... used to initiate the firing sequence". *See also United States v. Fleischli*, 305 F.3d 643, 655 (7th Cir.2002) (concerning machine gun, approving of *Jokel*'s definition), *cert. denied,* 538 U.S. 1001, 123 S.Ct. 1923, 155 L.Ed.2d 828 (2003); *United States v. Evans*, 978 F.2d 1112, 1113 (9th Cir.1992), *cert. denied,* 510 U.S. 821, 114 S.Ct. 78, 126 L.Ed.2d 46 (1993) (concerning machine gun, defining trigger as "anything that releases the bolt to cause . . . [the weapon] to fire" (internal quotation omitted; alteration in original)).

In *Jokel,* the defendant contended his firearm lacked a "trigger" because it required the insertion of a nail and spring in order to fire, rather than, as is traditional, pulling a small lever. Our court disagreed: "To construe 'trigger' to mean only a small lever moved by a finger would be to impute to Congress the intent to restrict the term to apply only to one kind of trigger, albeit a very common kind. *The language implies no intent to so restrict the meaning. . . ."* 969 F.2d at 135 (emphasis added). It is undisputed that the switch in Camp's device "initiated the firing sequence".

Camp attempts to distinguish his firearm by noting there is another "trigger"—the rifle's original metal lever/trigger. He contends that, for purposes of § 5845(b), this original trigger is the operative one; and, because it functioned each time the rifle was fired, the rifle, as modified, did not become a machine gun. To accept this contention would allow transforming firearms into machine guns, so long as the original trigger was not destroyed. *See Fleischli,* 305 F.3d at 655 (dismissing as "puerile" defendant's contention that firearm was not machine gun because it used electrical, rather than traditional, trigger); *Evans,* 978 F.2d at 1113 n. 2 (same).

Camp also claims the switch is merely a legal "trigger activator". At the evidentiary hearing, an ATF Agent testified that "trigger activators" involve using springs that "force the trigger back to the forward position, *meaning that you have to separately pull the trigger each time you want to fire the gun,* but it gives the illusion of functioning as a machinegun". (Emphasis added.) According to the Agent, the ATF understands such trigger activators to be legal, insofar as they do not transform legal firearms into machine guns.

We reject Camp's contention that the switch on his firearm was a legal "trigger activator". As discussed, those activators described by the ATF Agent require a user to separately pull the activator each time the weapon is fired. Camp's weapon, however, required only one action—pulling the switch he installed—to fire multiple shots. This distinction is expressly contemplated by § 5845(b), which speaks of "shoot[ing] automatically more than one shot . . . by a *single* function of the trigger". (Emphasis added.). . .

III.

For the foregoing reasons, the dismissal of the indictment is VACATED; this matter is REMANDED for further proceedings consistent with this opinion.

VACATED; REMANDED.

EXERCISE

It you were the judge in a machinegun case where the firearm in question that was manufactured as a machinegun (say, a tommy gun) but when seized had no trigger at all—it had been removed by the owner to avoid the definition of a machinegun—would you toss the case out on a motion for directed verdict? Does it matter whether or not the owner still possesses the trigger mechanism?

Proving that a gun violates the technical requirements of a statute is only one challenging element prosecutors face. The element of knowledge can also prove tricky.

Serial numbers are etched into guns to enable tracking them, and removing the serial number can make a gun relatively untraceable. Federal law (at 18 U.S.C. § 922(k) outlaws knowing possession of a firearm with an obliterated serial number, and the federal sentencing guidelines separately provide for an enhanced sentence in all gun cases where the serial number is obliterated—but does not explicitly require "knowing" possession of a gun that has had the number removed.

This raises an intriguing question: does the defendant have to know that the serial number has been removed for the sentencing guideline to apply, consistent with the statutory elements?

UNITED STATES V. ABERNATHY
83 F. 3d 17 (1st Cir. 1996)

BAILEY ALDRICH, SENIOR CIRCUIT JUDGE.

James H. Abernathy, driving a Massachusetts registered car in Providence, Rhode Island, was stopped by two policemen, one of whom, when he peered into defendant's vehicle, observed the butt of a .45 caliber Colt semi-automatic pistol sticking out from under the driver's seat. Indicted as a result, defendant initially pleaded guilty to two counts: Count I, as a convicted felon carrying a firearm that had been in interstate commerce, in violation of 18 U.S.C. § 922(g)(1); Count II, carrying an arm that had been in interstate commerce with an obliterated serial number, in violation of 18 U.S.C. § 922(k). Defendant was sentenced to 110 months imprisonment followed by three years supervised release on Count I, and to a concurrent 60 months imprisonment on Count II. Over one year later, upon defendant's motion, the entire sentence was vacated in order to reinstate his right to pursue a direct appeal, which had been dismissed for want of prosecution.

Thereafter, prior to resentencing, defendant moved to withdraw his plea. The court denied the motion and resentenced defendant to the original terms. This appeal ensued, raising the following points: (1) the lawfulness of the stop; (2) whether defendant should have been allowed to withdraw his pleas on both counts; and (3) the constitutionality of the statutes proscribing his conduct. We affirm on (1) and (3). On (2) we reverse and vacate the sentence with respect to Count II.

Withdrawal of a guilty plea prior to sentencing may be granted for "fair and just reason." *See* Fed.R.Crim.P. 32(e) (1994); *United States v. Cotal-Crespo,* 47 F.3d 1, 3 (1st Cir.), *cert. denied,* 516 U.S. 827, 116 S.Ct. 94, 133 L.Ed.2d 49 (1995). After sentencing, the defendant must show a defect attending the plea that amounts to a "miscarriage of justice," or "an omission inconsistent with the rudimentary demands of fair procedure." *United States v. Lopez-Pineda,* 55 F.3d 693, 697 (1st Cir.) (internal quotations omitted), *cert. denied,* 516 U.S. 900, 116 S.Ct. 259, 133 L.Ed.2d 183 (1995). Although the United States attaches great significance to the category to which defendant ought to be assigned, whether defendant's plea was knowing and voluntary within the meaning of Criminal Rule 11 is the most significant factor under either standard. *United States v. Allard,* 926 F.2d 1237, 1243 (1st Cir.1991).

With respect to Count I this is a routine case-the court was well warranted in finding no misunderstanding of the charge by defendant, nor was there any other flaw in the plea proceedings. Fed.R.Crim.P. 11(a)–(f).

There is a serious question, however, with respect to Count II. From the record, it appears that the court, as well as counsel for both the government and the defendant, understood that the government was not obliged to establish actual knowledge on defendant's part that the serial number had been obliterated at the time of his possession, and communicated this misunderstanding to the defendant. We find this failure to apprise defendant of the elements of the charge fundamentally inconsistent with fair procedure in an acceptance of plea proceeding. As the record contains strong support for defendant's claim that he lacked knowledge of the obliteration-at the very least it does not establish otherwise-we cannot say the error was harmless. *Compare United States v. Ferguson,* 60 F.3d 1, 4 (1st Cir.1995). *See* Fed.R.Crim.P. 11(h). It follows that defendant has a right to withdraw his plea on Count II.

Defendant's tangential suggestion that the court's imposition of a two-level enhancement to his offense level based on the obliteration also requires reversal ignores the fact that this enhancement explicitly applies "whether or not the defendant knew or had reason to believe that the firearm . . . had an altered or obliterated serial number." USSG § 2K2.1(b)(4), comment. (n. 19).

———————

EXERCISE

As the court in *Abernathy* makes clear, the government has to prove the defendant's knowledge that the serial number was obliterated to prove the charge, but not to receive a sentencing enhancement under the guidelines. What would be the policy reason for enhancing a sentence based on something the defendant did not know about his gun?

UNITED STATES V. HAILE

685 F. 3d 1211 (11th Cir. 2012)

PER CURIAM:

Randy Vana Haile and Mark Anthony Beckford were convicted of conspiracy and attempt to possess with intent to distribute marijuana and cocaine and knowing possession of several firearms in conjunction with their drug-trafficking offenses. The district court sentenced Beckford and Haile to 438 months and 468 months of imprisonment, respectively. Beckford now appeals his conviction and sentence, and Haile appeals his sentence. After a thorough review of the record and the parties' briefs, and with the benefit of oral argument, we affirm in part and reverse in part.

Haile and Beckford were charged by superseding indictment with: conspiracy to possess at least 5 kilograms of cocaine and at least 1,000 kilograms of marijuana with intent to distribute, in violation of 21 U.S.C. §§ 841(a)(1), (b)(1)(A)(vii), and 846 (Count 1); attempt to do the same, in violation of 21 U.S.C. §§ 841(a)(1), (b)(1)(A)(ii) and (vii), and 846 (Counts 2 and 3); knowing possession of 5 enumerated firearms, including a machine gun, in furtherance of a drug-trafficking crime, in violation of 18 U.S.C. § 924(c)(1)(A), (B)(i), and (B)(ii) (Count 4); possession of a firearm with an obliterated serial number, in violation of 18 U.S.C. §§ 922(k) and 924(a)(1)(B) (Count 6); and possession of an unregistered machine gun, in violation of 26 U.S.C. §§ 5841, 5845(b), and 5861(d) (Count 7). Haile was also charged with possession of a firearm by a convicted felon, in violation of 18 U.S.C. §§ 922(g)(1) and 924(a) (Count 5).

At trial, several Drug Enforcement Administration (DEA) agents testified about the reverse-sting operation that led to the defendants' arrest. The agents testified that a confidential informant (CI) provided information that Beckford, who lived in Atlanta, was seeking a marijuana supplier. At the DEA's request, the CI told Beckford about a man named Rodriguez, an undercover agent posing as a marijuana supplier.

Thereafter, the CI and Rodriguez met with Beckford in San Antonio. Rodriguez proposed a price of $300 per pound of marijuana, to which Beckford replied, "Yeah, yeah, yeah." Beckford stated that he would take 1,000 pounds, "If it's good," and that he would like the drugs to be delivered to the Jamaica Flava restaurant in Atlanta.

Before the meeting concluded, the CI asked Rodriguez, in front of Beckford, "Did you tell him about the white stuff?" Rodriguez said to Beckford, "I give you good price too." Beckford responded, "I'll call you," and the two exchanged telephone numbers. Later, on the phone, Beckford agreed to give Rodriguez a $25,000 security deposit for the marijuana and to meet with one of Rodriguez's associates, undercover agent Arrugueta, in Atlanta. At some point during the phone conversations, the two discussed guns. And the CI confirmed that Beckford had easy access to guns.

When Beckford met with Arrugueta, Haile was also present. Arrugueta asked Beckford, "Did [Rodriguez] talk to you about the tools?" Beckford replied, "Yeah, yeah, yeah. He talked to me about it." Arrugueta asked, "What kind do you have?" Beckford said, "my people . . . got the AK," which Arrugueta understood to mean any assault rifle, not just an AK-47. Arrugueta asked, "machine gun?" Beckford said, "Yep." When Arrugueta asked what Beckford's "people" wanted for the gun, Beckford said drugs, not money. Beckford said he had "like six [guns] so far" to exchange in the deal. Arrugueta, Haile, and Beckford agreed to exchange two pounds of marijuana for each gun. . .

Rodriguez and other DEA agents staged a U-Haul trailer containing hundreds of pounds of marijuana and several kilograms of cocaine at a hotel in Atlanta. Rodriguez met with Beckford and Haile in the hotel parking lot and permitted Haile to inspect the drugs. Rodriguez then asked Haile and Beckford how much money they could pay at that time. Beckford stated that he and Haile had access to $70,000 and could probably come up with more. Rodriguez said, "and the tool?" Haile asked in response, "Oh, you want the tools now?" Rodriguez said that he did, so the three continued to negotiate Haile and Beckford's payment of guns and money. Rodriguez asked, "you bring five gun?" And Beckford replied, "Yeah." Then, Beckford and Haile left to obtain the rest of the payment.

Agents stationed at Jamaica Flava then observed several men loading large, heavy bags into the back of a truck registered to Beckford. Beckford and Haile drove the truck back to the hotel, but left the parking lot when they realized Rodriguez was not present. They drove to a nearby restaurant where DEA agents arrested them.

Agents found a Glock .45 caliber pistol on Haile. In Beckford's truck, agents found: (1) $70,000 in a plastic bag in the back seat; (2) a loaded .40 caliber handgun in a holster in the center console; (3) a bag containing loose cash, Jamaica Flava business cards, and loose marijuana in the back seat; (4) two Norinco 7.62 caliber SKS rifles, one with an obliterated serial number, in the vehicle's flatbed; and (5) a 9-millimeter, an M-11 machine gun (not registered to either defendant), a bulletproof vest, and ammunition for a .40 caliber, a 7.62 caliber, and a 9-millimeter, all inside a gym bag in the flatbed. . . .

Beckford argues that the evidence was insufficient for the jury to convict him of violating 18 U.S.C. § 922(k) because, although the serial number on one of the SKS rifles in his possession was indisputably obliterated, the government failed to establish that he knew this. Section 922(k) provides:

> It shall be unlawful for any person knowingly to transport, ship, or receive, in interstate or foreign commerce, any firearm which has had the importer's or manufacturer's serial number removed, obliterated, or altered or to possess or receive any firearm which has had the importer's or manufacturer's serial number removed, obliterated, or altered and has, at any time, been shipped or transported in interstate or foreign commerce.

Id. Whether a conviction under § 922(k) requires the government to prove beyond a reasonable doubt that the defendant knew at the time he possessed the gun that the serial number was obliterated is an issue of first impression in this circuit. But other circuits have consistently held that knowledge of the obliterated serial number is an element of the offense. *See United States v. Sullivan,* 455 F.3d 248, 261 (4th Cir.2006); *United States v. Haywood,* 363 F.3d 200, 206 (3d Cir.2004); *United States v. Abernathy,* 83 F.3d 17, 19 & n. 1 (1st Cir.1996); *United States v. Fennell,* 53 F.3d 1296, 1300–01 (D.C.Cir.1995); *United States v. Haynes,* 16 F.3d 29, 34 (2d Cir.1994); *United States v. Hooker,* 997 F.2d 67, 72 (5th Cir.1993); *see also United States v. Rice,* 520 F.3d 811, 818 (7th Cir.2008) (finding, based on evidence that the defendant cleaned his guns regularly, that "the jury could have found that he knew the serial number on his [gun] was obliterated").

We join our sister circuits in holding that a defendant's knowledge of the obliterated serial number is an element of the § 922(k) offense. Importantly, § 924(a)(1)(B), which governs the penalties for violations of § 922(k), applies only to "knowing[ ]" violations. 18 U.S.C. § 924(a)(1)(B); *see Haywood,* 363 F.3d at 206 (discussing addition of "knowingly" to § 924(a)(1)(B) in 1986); *Fennell,* 53 F.3d at 1300–01 (same). Thus, for the enhanced penalties to apply under § 922(k), Beckford must have possessed a gun with an obliterated serial number and known the number was obliterated.

The government did not admit any direct evidence of Beckford's knowledge of the obliteration. But generally, "[k]nowledge of defacement of the serial number may be inferred where the defendant has possessed the gun under conditions under which an ordinary man would have inspected [it] and discovered the absence of a serial number." *Sullivan,* 455 F.3d at 261 (citing *United States v. Moore,* 54 F.3d 92, 101 (2d Cir.1995)). The government contends that Beckford had ample time to gain knowledge of whether the gun had an obliterated serial number.

We disagree. We are not persuaded that the evidence at trial was sufficient even to show that Beckford possessed the gun for a period of time during which an ordinary man would have discovered that the serial number was obliterated. Although the government established that Beckford discussed guns in general before the arrest and that agents found the gun in the flatbed of his truck (out of his reach) after the arrest, the government put forth no evidence that Beckford actually possessed the gun for any significant length of time.

The government essentially proved only that Beckford had constructive possession of the gun at the time of the arrest. But this constructive possession alone cannot be sufficient to establish Beckford's knowledge of the obliterated serial number because, if it was sufficient, the standard would eviscerate the knowledge element of § 922(k) altogether. Thus, because the government proved only constructive possession, without anything more, it failed to prove, beyond a reasonable doubt, that Beckford had knowledge of the obliterated serial number, and Beckford's conviction on Count 6 must be reversed.

EXERCISE

In *Haile*, the serial number conviction was reversed. If you were the prosecutor and could go back in time to direct the investigators to do more work, what would you ask them to do to bolster the case relating to this gun charge?

Specific characteristics such as automatic firing or an obliterated serial number make some guns illegal in most instances under federal law. The gun laws, however, also make illegal some objects that we would not usually categorize as a firearm, such as silencers and bombs, that pose a special kind of danger. Prosecution for possession of those objects often is brought under 26 U.S.C. § 5861, which is part of the tax code and requires registration of those "quasi-suspect" objects.

UNITED STATES V. DUKES
432 F. 3d 910 (8th Cir. 2006)

GRUENDER, CIRCUIT JUDGE.

Dukes resided with his girlfriend, Pamela Hoselton, in rural Red Oak, Iowa, near the home of Shane and Julie Patent. At approximately 3:00 a.m. on September 11, 2003, a drive-by shooting occurred at the Patents' home. Upon hearing the gunshots, the Patents ran to their window and observed a white Chevy Cavalier with a stripe on the side speeding away. The Patents recognized it as Hoselton's car. The Patents immediately informed the police. After police officers discovered .22-caliber bullets lodged in the side of the Patents' home, they drove past Hoselton's residence, where they observed a white Chevy Cavalier with a stripe on the side parked outside. On this basis, the police obtained a warrant to search Hoselton's car and residence for firearms and ammunition.

While searching Hoselton's residence for firearms and ammunition, police observed evidence of methamphetamine use and manufacture. They immediately obtained a second warrant to broaden the search to include evidence of methamphetamine manufacture and trafficking and to cover a mobile home on the property. The kitchen of the residence contained items such as sixteen boxes of pseudoephedrine, a box containing a by-product of methamphetamine manufacture commonly referred to as "sludge," two scanners and a .22-caliber shell casing. Elsewhere in the residence, police discovered firearms and ammunition, a small vial of methamphetamine and items associated with methamphetamine use. In a cabinet in the dining room, police discovered two objects that were suspected to be homemade firearm silencers, along with a scale. Outside the residence and in the mobile home, police found other items associated with methamphetamine manufacture, such as stripped lithium batteries, a surveillance camera and propane and carbon dioxide tanks of a type commonly used to store anhydrous ammonia for methamphetamine manufacture. Finally, police found a fanny pack near Dukes's truck that Dukes admitted belonged to him. The fanny pack contained methamphetamine and handwritten instructions for making methamphetamine.

An agent with the Bureau of Alcohol, Tobacco, Firearms and Explosives ("ATF") tested the two suspected firearm silencers. The objects were industrial mufflers for pneumatic air valves that had been modified with holes bored lengthwise through their centers, wide enough for a bullet to pass. In addition, a set of adjustable screws had been added to the end of one of the mufflers that would enable it to be firmly attached as an extension to the end of firearm barrels of various sizes. The ATF agent test-fired a firearm through each suspected silencer. The muffler with the adjustable screws demonstrated the noise reduction characteristics of a high-quality firearm silencer. The other muffler, although damaged in its initial test-firing, still yielded respectable noise reduction characteristics.

In July 2004, Hoselton called the police and asked them to return the property seized during the September 2003 search. Hoselton told the police that she and Dukes had their "asses covered" with respect to the suspected firearm silencers because they could prove similar mufflers were present at Dukes's place of employment. Hoselton also stated that she and Dukes had more of the mufflers at their house. Based on Hoselton's statement, the police obtained another warrant to search the house for firearm silencers. Upon entering the property, police observed fresh evidence of methamphetamine manufacture and again obtained a second warrant to broaden the search to include evidence of methamphetamine manufacture.

Police discovered additional fresh evidence of methamphetamine manufacture from the residence, grounds and mobile home, including a new container of methamphetamine "sludge" in a kitchen oven.

Dukes was charged with two counts of manufacturing or aiding and abetting the manufacture of methamphetamine in violation of 21 U.S.C. §§ 841(a)(1), 841(b)(1)(C), 846 and 2, one count based on the evidence from the September 2003 search and the other based on the evidence from the July 2004 search. Dukes also was charged with two counts of possessing an unregistered firearm silencer in violation of 26 U.S.C. § 5861(d). The district court denied Dukes's motion to suppress the evidence obtained from the two searches. After a three-day trial, a jury convicted Dukes on all counts. The district court sentenced Dukes to a prison term of 94 months. On appeal, Dukes argues that the original search warrant was not supported by probable cause and that there was insufficient evidence to support his convictions. . . .

The elements of possession of an unregistered firearm silencer under 26 U.S.C. § 5861(d) are that (1) the defendant knew he possessed the object, (2) the defendant knew the object was a silencer, (3) the silencer was capable of operating as designed, and (4) the silencer was not registered to the defendant in the National Firearms Registration and Transfer Record. Eighth Circuit Model Jury Instruction § 6.26.5861. Dukes challenges the sufficiency of the evidence with respect to the second element, the defendant's knowledge.

The Government's burden of proof on the knowledge element of § 5861(d) depends upon whether the firearm can be characterized as "quasi-suspect." *United States v. Walker,* 428 F.3d 1165, 1171 (8th Cir.2005) (citing *Staples v. United States,* 511 U.S. 600, 611–12, 114 S.Ct. 1793, 128 L.Ed.2d 608 (1994)). An object that appears to be a traditionally lawful firearm, such as a rifle, is not quasi-suspect. *Id.* On the other hand, an object that fits the broad statutory definition of "firearm" in 26 U.S.C. § 5845 and does not appear to be traditionally lawful, such as a hand grenade, sawed-off shotgun or Molotov cocktail, is quasi-suspect. *Id.* at 1171–72. Whether an object is quasi-suspect depends upon the likelihood that one would know from the obvious characteristics of the object that one "was engaging in illegal activity by possessing the object." *Id.* at 1172.

If the characteristics of the object render it quasi-suspect, the Government need only prove that the defendant "knowingly possessed the item." *Id.* at 1171. For a non-quasi-suspect object, the Government has the additional burden of proving that the defendant knew of the specific characteristics of the object that made it subject to § 5861. *United States v. Barr,* 32 F.3d 1320, 1323 (8th Cir.1994). In other words, for a non-quasi-suspect object, the Government must prove beyond a reasonable doubt that the defendant knew the object he possessed had the characteristics that brought it within the statutory definition of "firearm" in 26 U.S.C. § 5845. *Staples,* 511 U.S. at 602, 114 S.Ct. 1793.

On appeal, the Government takes the position that the suspected homemade firearm silencers are quasi-suspect objects. We need not decide that question, however, because in this case the jury made the necessary finding for possession of a non-quasi-suspect firearm under § 5861(d). The jury instructions required the jury to find that Dukes "knew [the object] was a firearm silencer," Jury Instruction No. 11, and correctly defined "firearm silencer" as "any device for silencing, muffling, or diminishing the report of a portable firearm," Jury Instruction No. 13. *See* 26 U.S.C. § 5845(a)(7) (cross-referencing 18 U.S.C. § 921(a) for the applicable definition of "firearm silencer"). Thus, in order to reach its guilty verdict for possession of unregistered firearms, the jury necessarily had to find that Dukes knew each muffler was a device for silencing, muffling, or diminishing the report of a portable firearm—the knowledge element required by *Staples* for non-quasi-suspect objects.

Dukes argues that there was insufficient evidence to support the jury's finding that he knew the modified mufflers to be firearm silencers. "[K]nowledge can be inferred from circumstantial evidence, including any external indications signaling the nature of the [relevant item]." *United States v. Hall,* 171 F.3d 1133, 1152 (8th Cir.1999) (quoting *Staples,* 511 U.S. at 615–16 n. 11, 114 S.Ct. 1793) (second alteration in *Hall*). In this case, Dukes admitted he was aware that the objects were designed to function as noise-muffling devices, that each had been modified with a hole bored lengthwise through its center and that one was fitted with the previously described adjustable screws. The evidence showed that the modifications rendered the devices useless for their intended function on pneumatic air valves. The evidence also showed that Dukes possessed these modified noise-muffling devices in a residence containing multiple firearms where methamphetamine was used and manufactured. Given the circumstances in which Dukes possessed the objects, a reasonable jury could conclude beyond a reasonable doubt that Dukes knew each object was modified to be a device for silencing, muffling, or diminishing the report of a portable firearm. *See Hall,* 171 F.3d at 1152 (upholding a jury's finding of specific intent to possess a firearm silencer where the object was discovered on the defendant's premises in a bag with other noise-muffling materials and a firearm, and the premises were used for methamphetamine distribution).

Therefore, the jury verdict of guilty for possession of unregistered firearm silencers was supported by sufficient evidence.

EXERCISE

Imagine a case where Jerry, an 18-year-old who is a senior in high school, goes to a garage sale at a neighbor's house. On a table he finds an item marked "mystery bag" which is selling for $75. Feeling the bag, he can tell that it contains a gun and a few small cylindrical items. He purchases the bag, takes it to school, and rips it open. Inside he finds a small handgun and two silencers. He is immediately arrested while in physical possession of the items that were in the bag.

If you are the prosecutor in this case, what additional information do you want to obtain before deciding whether or not to charge Jerry with illegal possession of a silencer? Remember that to charge the case, you need to show probable cause on each element of the crime.

———————

Like silencers, unregistered pipe bombs and similar devices are illegal under a provision of the tax law. As terrorism concerns have grown, the regulation and prosecution of bomb-makers has intensified and become more important. Explosives, however, often have a legitimate purpose for farmers, miners, and others, which makes context very important. A farmer who blows up tree stumps to expand a field and possesses explosives in a barn may be treated differently than the person in an apartment in an urban area who has a pipe bomb in his closet.

The case below examines a charge involving an improvised explosive device as part of a detention hearing to determine whether or not the defendant should be released on bond pending trial. While we often focus on trial and appeal, these decisions are important as well.

UNITED STATES V. O'NEILL
144 F. Supp. 3d 428 (W.D.N.Y. 2015)

ELIZABETH A. WOLFORD, UNITED STATES DISTRICT JUDGE

Defendant was charged by criminal complaint dated July 23, 2015, with possession of a firearm not registered to Defendant in the National Firearms Registration and Transfer Record. Attached to the complaint is an affidavit of a law enforcement officer detailing the investigation into Defendant's alleged activities, including the recovery of "improvised explosive devices," including a piece of hard cardboard tubing with sealed ends and a fuse labeled "Powder w/ Nails" (the "Nails Device"). (Dkt. 1 at ¶ 5). The Nails Device was subsequently examined and determined to contain "multiple nails, BBs and suspected flash powder." (*Id.* at ¶ 7).

On August 13, 2015, Defendant was indicted on one count of unlawful making of a destructive device (a "pipe bomb") in violation of Title 26, United States Code, Sections 5822, 5845(a)(8), 5845(f), 5845(i), 5861(f), and 5871, and one count of unlawful possession of a destructive device (a "pipe bomb") in violation of Title 26, United States Code, Sections 5841, 5845(a)(8), 5845(f), 5845(i), 5861(d), and 5871. (Dkt. 11).

The Government sought a detention hearing on the grounds that Defendant was charged with a crime enumerated in 18 U.S.C. § 3142(f)(1)(E). A detention hearing was begun on July 30, 2015, before United States Magistrate Judge Hugh B. Scott. (Dkt. 4). A continuation of the detention hearing was held on August 5, 2015, at which Judge Scott granted the Government's motion to detain Defendant. (Dkt. 8, 9).

On November 9, 2015, Defendant filed a motion before this Court to revoke Judge Scott's detention order. . . . According to the Government, the "pipe bomb" referenced in the indictment is the Nails Device, which is depicted in Government Exhibit 3 (*see* Dkt. 9–1 at 3).

As set forth below, the Court finds that the Government has standing to seek a detention hearing as to Defendant and that the Government has shown by clear and convincing evidence that Defendant poses a danger to others and the community and that no condition or combination of conditions will reasonably assure the safety of others and the community. . .

The Bail Reform Act of 1984, 18 U.S.C. §§ 3141 *et seq.,* authorizes and sets forth the procedures for the release or detention of a person pending trial, sentence, and appeal. The procedures and standards for release or detention of a person such as Defendant pending trial are set forth at 18 U.S.C. § 3142. A defendant awaiting trial must be released unless the release will present a risk of flight or dangerousness, or both, and no set of conditions can reasonably eliminate those risks. *See United States v. Berrios-Berrios,* 791 F.2d 246, 249 (2d Cir.1986) (Bail Reform Act codified "traditional presumption favoring pretrial release for the majority of Federal defendants") (quotation omitted). . . .

Having found that the Government has standing to seek Defendant's detention since he is charged with a crime under § 3142(f)(1)(E), the Court must consider whether any condition or combination of conditions will reasonably assure the appearance of such person as required and the safety of any other person and the community.

The factors that a court must consider in making this determination include the following: (1) the nature and circumstances of the charged offenses including whether the offense involves a "firearm, explosive, or destructive device"; (2) the weight of the evidence against the person; (3) the history and characteristics of the person, including such matters as the person's character, physical and mental condition, family ties, employment history, financial resources, length of residence in the community, community ties, past conduct, history relating to drug or alcohol abuse, criminal history, and record concerning appearance at court proceedings; and (4) the nature and seriousness of any risk of danger if the person is released. 18 U.S.C. § 3142(g). The Government bears the burden to demonstrate dangerousness by clear and convincing evidence, and risk of flight by a preponderance of the evidence. *Chimurenga,* 760 F.2d at 405.

Here, the nature and circumstances of the charged offenses support detention based on danger. Defendant is charged with making and possessing a pipe bomb, a destructive device for which danger is plainly contemplated by its express reference in the first of the § 3142(g) factors. The items were apparently discovered in Defendant's garage, when emergency personnel were called on July 21, 2015, after an explosion caused Defendant to suffer a significant injury to his lower leg (ultimately resulting in its amputation). In addition to the Nails Device or alleged "pipe bomb," law enforcement officers discovered what appeared to be six additional improvised explosive devices and related materials, including flash powder, potassium perchlorate, and shotgun shells. Also discovered in the garage, among other items, were numerous other cardboard tubes, thus suggesting that Defendant intended to build additional devices. The garage also displayed various wall hangings that included language such as "The KKK Wants You!," along with references to Nazis, racially derogatory language, and material supportive of the confederacy during the Civil War. Defendant allegedly admitted to law enforcement that all the items in the garage were his.

In terms of the second factor, the weight of the evidence similarly supports detention based on danger. There does not appear to be a dispute that the materials discovered in the garage, including the "pipe bomb," belonged to Defendant. Although Defendant offers the explanation that he was manufacturing explosives to remove a tree stump, and perhaps that explanation will ultimately be believed by a jury, the explosive for which Defendant has been indicted certainly does not appear on its face to be an effective method of removing a tree stump. *See U.S. v. Dodge,* 846 F.Supp. 181, 184 (D.Conn.1994) (pipe bomb is an inherently dangerous weapon "for which no peaceful purpose can be seriously suggested"). *Cf. United States v. Tagg,* 572 F.3d 1320, 1326 (11th Cir.2009) ("pipe bombs are not typically possessed by law-abiding citizens for lawful purposes"); *United States v. Jennings,* 195 F.3d 795, 798 (5th Cir.1999) ("we cannot conceive of any nonviolent or lawful uses for a pipe bomb").

Defendant's history and characteristics also weigh in favor of detention based on danger. According to the Pretrial Services Report, Defendant has been unemployed since 2009, when he lost his employment due to alcohol use. Defendant has two driving while intoxicated charges, the first (in 2009) resulting in a disposition of driving while impaired, and the second (in 2011) resulting in a misdemeanor conviction for driving while intoxicated. Defendant denied any mental health disorders to the United States Probation Office, but his mother apparently told the Probation Officer that her son is being treated for depression and anxiety and she identified a number of medications that he is prescribed. Defendant's mother also apparently acknowledged that her son drinks alcohol in the garage where the incident occurred, and Defendant himself admitted to consuming alcohol on a weekly basis. Defendant argues that notwithstanding these characteristics, he has no criminal history and his physical injuries preclude any finding of danger. Defendant also argued to Judge Scott that his mother would be an adequate custodian, if released. The Court disagrees. Defendant already resided with his mother at the time of the incident when he was allegedly constructing destructive devices and drinking alcohol on a regular basis in the garage of his mother's residence.

When Defendant's personal characteristics and history are considered in the context of the crime with which Defendant is charged, and the evidence located at the scene of the incident, detention plainly appears necessary due to Defendant's risk of danger.

Finally, the nature and seriousness of the risk supports detention. Indeed, Defendant's own injury demonstrates the dangerous nature of his activities. *See Dodge,* 846 F.Supp. at 184 (mere possession of pipe bomb presents "a 'substantial risk' of physical injury to others"); *see also Jennings,* 195 F.3d at 798 ("We hold that possession of an unregistered pipe bomb, by its very nature, creates a substantial risk of violence. . . .").

Based on the totality of the foregoing circumstances, the Court finds that the Government has established by clear and convincing evidence that Defendant would present a grave threat to others and the community if released, and no condition or combination of conditions will reasonably assure the safety of these persons and the community. Because of the Court's finding that Defendant's danger requires his pretrial detention, the Court need not address whether detention is required due to a risk of flight.

CONCLUSION

For the foregoing reasons, Defendant shall remain detained pending the trial in this matter. Defendant shall be committed to the custody of the Attorney General for confinement in a corrections facility separate, to the extent practicable, from persons awaiting or serving sentences or being held in custody pending appeal. Defendant shall be afforded a reasonable opportunity for private consultation with counsel, and on order of a court of the United States or on request of an attorney for the Government, the person in charge of the corrections facility in which Defendant is confined shall deliver him to a United States marshal for the purpose of an appearance in connection with a court proceeding.

EXERCISE

If you represented the defendant in the O'Neill case, what arguments would you have presented in trying to convince the court not to detain him pending trial? Keep in mind that the standard at issue requires the government to show "by clear and convincing evidence that Defendant poses a danger to others and the community and that no condition or combination of conditions will reasonably assure the safety of others and the community."

B. PEOPLE PROHIBITED FROM POSSESSING FIREARMS

Just as some firearms are considered more dangerous than others, some people are viewed as more dangerous that others if they possess a gun. One group that federal law identifies as deserving this extra attention consists of people who have already committed a crime.

Limitations based on individual characteristics is not limited to those who have committed crimes, though. 18 U.S.C. § 922(g) bars a strikingly large and varied group of people from possessing firearms:

(g) It shall be unlawful for any person—

(1) who has been convicted in any court of, a crime punishable by imprisonment for a term exceeding one year;

(2) who is a fugitive from justice;

(3) who is an unlawful user of or addicted to any controlled substance (as defined in section 102 of the Controlled Substances Act (21 U.S.C. 802));

(4) who has been adjudicated as a mental defective or who has been committed to a mental institution;

(5) who, being an alien—

(A) is illegally or unlawfully in the United States; or

(B) except as provided in subsection (y)(2), has been admitted to the United States under a nonimmigrant visa (as that term is defined in section 101(a)(26) of the Immigration and Nationality Act (8 U.S.C. 1101(a)(26)));

(6) who has been discharged from the Armed Forces under dishonorable conditions;

(7) who, having been a citizen of the United States, has renounced his citizenship;

(8) who is subject to a court order that—

(A) was issued after a hearing of which such person received actual notice, and at which such person had an opportunity to participate;

(B) restrains such person from harassing, stalking, or threatening an intimate partner of such person or child of such intimate partner or person, or engaging in other conduct that would place an intimate partner in reasonable fear of bodily injury to the partner or child; and

(C)(i) includes a finding that such person represents a credible threat to the physical safety of such intimate partner or child; or

> **(ii)** by its terms explicitly prohibits the use, attempted use, or threatened use of physical force against such intimate partner or child that would reasonably be expected to cause bodily injury; or

(9) who has been convicted in any court of a misdemeanor crime of domestic violence,

to ship or transport in interstate or foreign commerce, or possess in or affecting commerce, any firearm or ammunition; or to receive any firearm or ammunition which has been shipped or transported in interstate or foreign commerce.

18 U.S.C. § 922(g)(3) is unusual in that it bars gun possession based on status as an addict—something that can be difficult for the government to prove. Many people might be surprised to find that it is illegal under federal law to possess a gun if you are a marijuana user.

UNITED STATES v. CARTER
750 F. 3d 462 (4th Cir. 2014)

NIEMEYER, CIRCUIT JUDGE:

Following his conviction and sentencing for possessing two firearms while being an unlawful user of and addicted to a controlled substance (marijuana), in violation of 18 U.S.C. § 922(g)(3), Benjamin Carter appealed, contending that § 922(g)(3) infringed on his right to bear arms, in violation of the Second Amendment. We vacated the judgment and remanded the case to the district court to allow the government to substantiate the fit between § 922(g)(3) and the government's important interest in protecting the community from gun violence. *See United States v. Carter* ("Carter I"), 669 F.3d 411 (4th Cir.2012). After taking evidence from both sides, the district court held that the government had carried its burden in justifying the regulation of guns under § 922(g)(3), and Carter filed this second appeal.

Because we agree with the district court that the government adequately demonstrated a reasonable fit between its important interest in protecting the community from gun violence and § 922(g)(3), which disarms unlawful drug users and addicts, we now affirm.

I

In *Carter I,* we recited the facts:

> Responding to complaints of suspected drug activity at 735 Central Avenue, Charleston, West Virginia, a two-unit apartment building where Carter was living at the time, Charleston police investigated by knocking on doors and talking with persons who answered. After finding evidence of marijuana use in the first unit, the officers proceeded to knock on Carter's door. Carter answered and allowed the officers to enter his apartment. Upon smelling marijuana, the officers questioned Carter, who acknowledged that he had been smoking marijuana and indeed that he had been using the drug for 15 years. The officers recovered from the apartment 12 grams of loose marijuana, 15 grams of partially smoked blunts, a digital scale, $1,000 in larger bills, and $122 in smaller denominations. Carter also informed the officers about two firearms in his closet—a semi-automatic pistol and a revolver—and disclosed that he had purchased the weapons from a friend a week earlier for his defense. He later explained in more detail that he had purchased the guns because he lived in "a bad neighborhood" and needed weapons to protect himself and his nephew, who also lived with him in the apartment. Indeed, at sentencing, Carter's attorney represented to the court that one month after Carter's arrest in this case, the other unit in the apartment building was burglarized, and his neighbor was shot eight times.

Carter I, 669 F.3d at 413.

After Carter was indicted for violating 18 U.S.C. § 922(g)(3), he filed a motion to dismiss the indictment, arguing that the statute violated his Second Amendment rights. When the district court denied his motion, Carter entered a conditional guilty plea that preserved his right to appeal the court's ruling on the motion. After accepting Carter's guilty plea, the court sentenced Carter to three years' probation.

On appeal, we vacated the judgment and remanded the case to the district court for further consideration of Carter's Second Amendment challenge. We assumed that Carter's circumstances implicated the Second Amendment but held that, because he could not claim to be a law-abiding citizen, any infringement of his right to bear arms would not have implicated a "core" Second Amendment right. *Carter I,* 669 F.3d at 416; *see also District of Columbia v. Heller,* 554 U.S. 570, 635, 128 S.Ct. 2783, 171

L.Ed.2d 637 (2008). We therefore applied intermediate scrutiny to review Carter's challenge. *Carter I,* 669 F.3d at 417. Under intermediate scrutiny, the question thus became whether there was "a reasonable fit" between § 922(g)(3) and "a substantial [or important] government objective." *Id.* (quoting *United States v. Chester,* 628 F.3d 673, 683 (4th Cir.2010)) (internal quotation marks omitted).

We readily concluded that the government had advanced an important governmental interest in protecting the community from crime and, in particular, from gun violence. *Carter I,* 669 F.3d at 417. On whether disarming drug users and addicts through § 922(g)(3)reasonably served that interest—whether there was "a reasonable fit between the important goal of reducing gun violence and the prohibition in § 922(g)(3)"—we noted that the government could "resort to a wide range of sources, such as legislative text and history, empirical evidence, case law, and common sense, as circumstances and context require[d]." *Id.* at 418. We found that while the government had made plausible commonsense arguments about the risks of mixing drugs and guns, it had "presented no empirical evidence or data to substantiate them." *Id.* at 419–20. Therefore, in light of *Chester* and *United States v. Staten,* 666 F.3d 154 (4th Cir.2011), we remanded the case to the district court to "allow the government to develop a record sufficient to justify its argument that drug users and addicts possessing firearms are sufficiently dangerous to require disarming them." *Carter I,* 669 F.3d at 419.

On remand, both the government and Carter submitted a number of publications and studies to the district court about the behavioral tendencies of drug users. After considering the evidence, the court concluded that the government had carried its burden, finding that the data indicated "a correlation between violent crime . . . and drug use." While the court acknowledged that the government's studies did not prove "a strict causal nexus" between drug usage and violence, it found that "the two factors frequently coincide." In addition, it pointed to "common-sense notions" that supported the fit between drug users and violence, noting (1) that drug users are more likely to encounter law enforcement; (2) that their criminal associations increase the risk of violence; (3) that the high price of drugs is likely to lead to violent property crimes; and (4) that drug use impairs judgment. The court then concluded:

> Based upon the narrowed design of the statute, the empirical and scholarly evidence relied upon, the weight of precedent nationwide, and common sense, the United States has shouldered its burden of establishing that section 922(g)(3) is reasonably fitted to achieve the substantial governmental objective of protecting the community from crime by keeping guns out of the hands of those impaired by their use of controlled substances. The

court, accordingly, concludes that section 922(g)(3) is constitutional as applied to Mr. Carter.

From the district court's judgment on remand, Carter filed this second appeal. . . .

Focusing on the substance of the studies presented by the government to the district court, Carter contends that the data were inadequate because they related to *drug use generally* rather than *marijuana use specifically* and because they failed to prove a causal relationship between marijuana use and violence. He maintains that the studies he submitted, by contrast, demonstrated that "marijuana users are *not* prone to violent behavior." (Emphasis added).

We have little trouble concluding that the studies presented to the district court by both the government and Carter indicate a strong link between drug use and violence. A study by Carrie Oser and colleagues, offered by the government, found that probationers who had perpetrated violence in the past were significantly more likely to have used a host of drugs— marijuana, hallucinogens, sedatives, and heroin—than probationers who had never been involved in a violent episode. A 2004 survey of prisoners by the Bureau of Justice, again offered by the government, found that almost 50% of all state and federal prisoners who had committed violent felonies were drug abusers or addicts in the year before their arrest, as compared to only 2% of the general population. That survey also found that inmates who were dependent on drugs or abusing them were much more likely to have a criminal history. The government also presented a study by Lana Harrison and Joseph Gfroerer, which found that individuals who used marijuana or marijuana and cocaine, in addition to alcohol, were significantly more likely to engage in violent crime than individuals who only used alcohol. And finally, the government presented a study by Virginia McCoy and colleagues, which found that chronic cocaine and opiate users were more likely than nonusers to engage in robbery and violence.

Carter seeks to marginalize these studies, arguing first that they are too broad and discuss only "general categories of offenders, including those who abuse a range of controlled substances." He contends that, even if there is a link between "harder" controlled substances and violence, the government's evidence does not indicate that *marijuana* users are prone to violence. To the contrary, he claims that the evidence he submitted disproves such a link. Yet, even if such a particularized demonstration is necessary—an issue we need not reach—the studies presented by the government amply demonstrate a connection between marijuana use specifically and violence. The Harrison and Gfroerer study, for instance, found that, "[e]ven after controlling for other variables [,] such as age, race, income, education, and marital status, . . . using marijuana in the past year . . . [was] significantly related to criminal behavior." Also, the study by Oser and colleagues found that, among probationers, individuals who had been involved in violence were more likely to have used marijuana. Finally, the 2005 National Survey on Drug Use and Health found that individuals arrested for a serious violent or property offense in the last year were much more likely than non-arrestees to have used marijuana.

Moreover, the evidence that Carter offered to refute the link between marijuana use and violence—a study by Evelyn Wei and colleague—actually provides additional evidence that marijuana use and violence coincide. The Wei study tracked the behavioral development of "inner-city adolescent males" for ten years and found that, "at age 18, frequent marijuana users were 11 times more likely than nonfrequent users to . . . engage in violence." The study also found that marijuana use in one year frequently predicted violence in the subsequent year. Carter argues nonetheless that the Wei study militates in his favor because, when it controlled for "risk factors," the correlation between marijuana use in adolescence and violence in young adulthood was not statistically significant. In this instance, we do not think that the Wei study's failure to identify a statistically significant correlation is particularly relevant. Indeed, we note that the study, even when controlling for risk factors, *still* found that adolescents who used marijuana were almost *twice* as likely to engage in violence when they became young adults. Thus, the Wei study, far from undercutting the government's position, provides it with strong support.

Carter also objects to the government's evidence on the grounds that it demonstrated, at most, a *correlation* between marijuana use and violence and not a *causal* relationship. Quoting the Wei study, he argues that "[t]he relationship between marijuana use and violence 'is due to the selection effects whereby these behaviors tend to co-occur in certain individuals, not because one behavior *causes* the other.' " (Emphasis added) (quoting Wei et al., *Teasing Apart,* at 166).

This argument is flawed, however, because it assumes, incorrectly, that Congress may not regulate based on correlational evidence. We conclude that it may and that the government need not prove a causal link between drug use and violence in order to carry its burden of demonstrating that there is a reasonable fit between § 922(g)(3) and an important government objective. *See Staten,* 666 F.3d at 164–67(upholding § 922(g)(9)'s disarmament of those convicted of a misdemeanor of domestic violence in large part based on correlational evidence about recidivism rates). Indeed, the studies put forward by both Carter and the government in this case illustrate just how powerful correlational evidence can be. The Harrison and Gfroerer study and the Wei study both used logistic regression to show that individuals who used marijuana were much more likely to engage in violence, even controlling for multiple demographic and behavioral variables including age, race, economic status, marital status, and educational level. While eliminating these potentially confounding variables does not prove that marijuana use causes violence, it substantially bolsters the link and helps to justify regulating gun possession by marijuana users. We have emphasized that, under intermediate scrutiny, the fit between the regulation and the harm need only be reasonable, not perfect. *Carter I,* 669 F.3d at 417. The correlational evidence put forward by the parties in the present case easily clears that bar.

While the empirical data alone are sufficient to justify the constitutionality of § 922(g)(3), we find that common sense provides further support. In *Carter I,* we noted the government's argument that "due to the illegal nature of their activities, drug users and addicts would be more likely than other citizens to have hostile run-ins with law enforcement officers, which would threaten the safety of the law enforcement officers when guns are involved." 669 F.3d at 419. The government also warned that "the inflated price of illegal drugs on the black market could drive many addicts into financial desperation, with the common result that the addict would be 'forced to obtain the wherewithal with which to purchase drugs through criminal acts either against the person or property of another or through acts of vice such as prostitution or sale of narcotics.'" *Id.* Finally, the government suggested that drugs "impair [users'] mental function . . . and thus subject others (and themselves) to irrational and unpredictable behavior." *Id.* at 420 (omission in original) (internal quotation marks omitted); *see also United States v. Dugan,* 657 F.3d 998, 999 (9th Cir.2011) ("Habitual drug users . . . more likely will have difficulty exercising self-control, particularly when they are under the influence of controlled substances"). We find all three of these observations convincing, and Carter has provided no argument grounded in either logic or evidence to undercut them.

Finally, we observe that every court to have considered the issue has affirmed the constitutionality of § 922(g)(3) under the Second Amendment. *See, e.g., Dugan,* 657 F.3d at 999; *United States v. Yancey,* 621 F.3d 681, 682 (7th Cir.2010) (per curiam); *United States v. Seay,* 620 F.3d 919, 925 (8th Cir.2010); *United States v. Richard,* 350 Fed.Appx. 252, 260 (10th Cir.2009). Indeed, the majority of these courts found the statute constitutional without relying on any empirical studies. *See Dugan,* 657 F.3d at 999; *Seay,* 620 F.3d at 925; *Richard,* 350 Fed.Appx. at 260.

At bottom, we conclude that the empirical evidence and common sense support the government's contention that drug use, including marijuana use, frequently coincides with violence. Carter has failed to present any convincing evidence that would call this conclusion into question. Accordingly, we join our sister circuits in holding that § 922(g)(3) proportionally advances the government's legitimate goal of preventing gun violence and is therefore constitutional under the Second Amendment. The judgment of the district court is

AFFIRMED.

EXERCISE

Imagine that you are the United States Attorney for a large, well-populated district. Part of your job is to establish standards for the types of cases your office will accept or decline. Cases are referred to your office regularly by federal agents, local police, and task forces that include both federal agents and local police, especially in cases that involve drugs and guns. What would be your policy for taking or rejecting cases under 18 U.S.C. § 922(g)(3)?

The "interstate commerce" element of 18 U.S.C. §922(g) is construed quite broadly. The case below examines the prevailing rule that allows prosecutors to meet the interstate commerce requirement simply by showing that the gun was manufactured outside the state where the crime was committed.

UNITED STATES v. SARRAJ
665 F.3d 916 (7th Cir. 2012)

HAMILTON, CIRCUIT JUDGE.

Defendant Khalil Sarraj sought to buy guns in Illinois, allegedly for personal protection, after he was assaulted during a dispute with criminal associates. Unluckily for Sarraj, the person he asked for help acquiring guns was a confidential informant for the Bureau of Alcohol, Tobacco, Firearms, and Explosives. After determining that Sarraj was a convicted felon, federal agents sold him two handguns, both manufactured outside the state of Illinois, in a "reverse sting" operation, one in which agents posed as sellers rather than buyers of contraband. Sarraj pled guilty to one count of being a felon in possession of a firearm in violation of 18 U.S.C. § 922(g)(1). Sarraj's guilty plea was conditioned on reservation of his right to challenge the way in which the government proposed to prove the interstate commerce element of the federal crime.

On appeal, Sarraj asserts that principles of federalism and the Supreme Court's decision in *United States v. Lopez,* 514 U.S. 549, 115 S.Ct. 1624, 131 L.Ed.2d 626 (1995), require limits on the reach of section 922(g)(1). Sarraj believes that reverse sting operations violate those limits because they allow federal agents to create the required ties to interstate commerce by choosing so-called "prop" guns that were manufactured out of state. As he views the issue, this device allowed agents improperly to "federalize" what would otherwise have been a purely local gun-possession offense. Sarraj attempts to distinguish substantial precedent treating this type of law-enforcement operation as constitutional. We have previously evaluated and described the requirements for satisfying the interstate commerce element in section 922(g)(1) prosecutions, and the element was properly satisfied here.

Sarraj also fails to account for the substantial practical consequences of the rule he suggests, which could invalidate many federal prosecutions based on similar reverse stings. We decline to prohibit reverse stings when federal agents and prosecutors provide the grounds for treating the matter as a federal crime. Although defendants may prefer to be prosecuted for similar state crimes, or to escape prosecution entirely because of differing state enforcement priorities and resources, the federal Constitution is not offended by the choice of federal prosecution under concurrent federal criminal statutes, including the choice to provide a required federal nexus element of the crime. We do not review executive branch decisions concerning whether and how to investigate and prosecute state or federal crimes absent allegations of illegality or invidious bias in those decisions, and there were none in this case. We affirm Sarraj's conviction and sentence.

I. *Factual and Procedural Background*

In June 2009, defendant Sarraj was attacked in his home by two associates—alleged co-conspirators in a prescription narcotics conspiracy—during an apparent failed robbery attempt. After his attackers were sentenced in state court to just ten days in jail, Sarraj became angry and stated in open court that he would find some guns and shoot his former associates if he ever encountered them again. Sarraj knew that his prior felony conviction made it illegal for him to possess firearms. But Sarraj ignored that restriction and proceeded to enlist the help of an acquaintance in obtaining the desired guns. Sarraj said that he wanted untraceable weapons with the serial numbers filed off.

Sarraj's acquaintance was actually a confidential informant who told agents of the Bureau of Alcohol, Tobacco, Firearms, and Explosives of Sarraj's wishes. Agents prepared to pose as undercover gun sellers, selecting several weapons from the Bureau's collection of prop guns for use in reverse sting sales to prospective gun buyers. The confidential informant introduced Sarraj to the undercover agents, and the sting was carried out in an Illinois grocery store parking lot on June 24, 2009. After handling several guns and confirming that the serial numbers had been removed, Sarraj purchased a Smith and Wesson .357 revolver and a Browning/Fabrique Nationale .380 semi-automatic handgun.

To ensure that a purchase by Sarraj would violate federal law, the guns offered by the agents had been manufactured outside the state of Illinois, though their manufacturing origin was not discussed during the sale. See, *e.g.*, *United States v. Rice,* 520 F.3d 811, 815 (7th Cir.2008) (holding that "as long as a firearm moved across state lines at some point prior to the defendant's possession of it, the possession satisfies § 922(g)(1)'s 'in or affecting commerce' requirement"). Sarraj was the proud owner of the two guns for as long as it took him to walk from the agents' vehicle to his own and to stow the guns in his trunk. At that point, other agents arrested Sarraj. He was eventually charged in a one-count indictment with being a felon in possession of a firearm in violation of 18 U.S.C. § 922(g)(1).

In the district court, Sarraj filed a Motion for Modified Jury Instruction Concerning Whether ATF Prop Firearms "Affected" Interstate Commerce. The motion argued that the ATF had removed the subject guns from the stream of interstate commerce when it took the guns off the private market and added them to the Bureau's prop gun collection. Accordingly, Sarraj argued, the guns would not have been "in or affecting commerce" when they were sold to him, as needed to meet the interstate commerce requirement of section 922(g)(1). This argument, if accepted, would distinguish reverse sting operations from the scenario, common in the case law, of a felon who is merely caught with a gun that was manufactured outside the state. The district court heard argument on this issue and denied Sarraj's motion in a written memorandum. The court correctly found no support in our cases for the distinction proposed by Sarraj. . . .

As a practical matter, we have held that the required interstate nexus under section 922(g)(1) can be established "merely by evidence that the gun was manufactured outside the state in which it was possessed," from which we infer that the gun must have traveled in interstate commerce at least once. *United States v. Humphreys,* 468 F.3d 1051, 1053 (7th Cir.2006). The interstate nexus requirement is a factual predicate, not a mens rea element of the crime that would require proof of defendant's knowledge of facts supporting the nexus. See *United States v. Lindemann,* 85 F.3d 1232, 1241 (7th Cir.1996) ("Thus it has consistently been held that for statutes in which Congress included an 'interstate nexus' for the purpose of establishing a basis for its authority, the government . . . need not prove that the defendant knew the 'interstate nexus' of his actions."); *United States v. Castor,* 937 F.2d 293, 298 (7th Cir.1991) (same). A history in or affecting interstate commerce is only a necessary property of the subject gun, not something the defendant must know. That interstate history operates to establish federal authority under our Constitution of limited powers, but it does not in any way add to, or subtract from, the wrong that is addressed by felon-in-possession statutes. It follows that the defendant need not have been involved with bringing the gun into the state, nor is there a time limit or other requirement of a temporal link between the interstate movement and the defendant's possession. See *Lemons,* 302 F.3d at 771; *Rice,* 520 F.3d at 816. A firearm can be stashed away in a friend's closet for decades prior to a defendant's offending possession, and can still satisfy the required interstate nexus. See, *e.g., Lewis,* 100 F.3d at 52. By the same reasoning, the firearm can satisfy the nexus even if it has been locked up in an ATF storage locker.

Reviewing these and other prior cases, the district court correctly rejected Sarraj's arguments that the interstate nexus evaporated when government agents allegedly removed the guns from the stream of commerce by adding them to the Bureau's prop gun collection. Our cases have not endorsed, and we do not adopt here, any distinction that would allow passage of time, or acquisition by the government, to strip a firearm of its interstate nexus. We do not evaluate and weigh the scope of an effect on interstate commerce arising from a particular firearm possession. It is sufficient that the firearm once had a minimal connection to interstate commerce. This minimal nexus requirement reflects the intent of Congress in broadly criminalizing possession of firearms by convicted felons. See, *e.g., Scarborough,* 431 U.S. at 572–75, 97 S.Ct. 1963 (analyzing the legislative history of a predecessor statute and finding "no indication of any concern with either the movement of the gun or the possessor or with the time of acquisition").

On appeal, Sarraj emphasizes more his argument that federal agents should not be permitted, in the exercise of their discretion, to "federalize" local gun-possession offenses by offering suspects interstate prop guns rather than letting them buy local. We assume that federal agents will double-check their factual predicates when setting up a sting and are unlikely to waste time selling suspects guns that do not satisfy the requirements of the statute. Good federal agents will therefore opt to use interstate prop guns in every section 922(g)(1)investigation. As a practical matter, Sarraj is arguing that federal reverse sting operations are never constitutionally acceptable where federal agents supply the link to interstate commerce but could instead have called in state authorities to investigate and arrest under state law. Sarraj asserts that federal agents, by affirmatively ensuring that factual predicates for their authority are satisfied, intrude into an area of traditional state sovereignty and exercise an impermissible "general police power."

To the extent Sarraj is suggesting that federal law enforcement officials must defer to state authorities who may wish to prosecute locally under state law, we reject the suggestion. We also reject any suggestion that section 922(g)(1) prosecutions must be confined to contexts that are uniquely and necessarily federal. In enacting section 922(g)(1), Congress chose to exercise the full extent of its power over interstate commerce, treating gun possession by convicted felons as an issue of national interest in most circumstances—an interest that is concurrent with that of the several States. See *Scarborough,* 431 U.S. at 572, 97 S.Ct. 1963 ("in implementing these findings by prohibiting both possessions in commerce and those affecting commerce, Congress must have meant more than to outlaw simply those possessions that occur in commerce or in interstate facilities"). Congress intended to regulate to the full extent of its commerce power, and permit federal authorities to reach every violation where a minimal nexus was established. *Id.* Section 922(g)(1) is facially constitutional, and a single past interstate trip sufficiently affects commerce (as our cases hold), so possessing a firearm of foreign manufacture as a felon can be both a federal and a state crime. It is up to the various state and federal agencies to work out together how to share the job of investigating and prosecuting these crimes.

In general, and particularly in areas of overlapping authority, we limit our review of decisions by prosecutors to evaluating allegations of illegal conduct or invidious bias in the exercise of executive branch discretion. *E.g., United States v. Podolsky,* 798 F.2d 177, 181 (7th Cir.1986) (observing that "judges lack the information necessary to evaluate prosecutorial decisions in areas of concurrent federal and state criminal jurisdiction"). Returning then to Sarraj's core argument, we conclude that the government here did not violate Sarraj's federal constitutional rights by investigating him and prosecuting him for violation of section 922(g)(1), including by providing him the opportunity for his firearm possession to violate federal law. Sarraj does not claim that he was entrapped by the agents who sold him the guns, or that the agents violated any of his constitutional rights in the process. His only objection is to the agents' selection of the guns they would sell him to ensure the elements of a federal crime would all be met.

In analogous reverse sting cases, this court has approved of conduct by federal agents that ensured a required interstate commerce nexus. In *Podolsky,* agents offered to pay a suspect to burn down a commercial building for insurance purposes. They steered the aspiring arsonist to a building that was in fact used for interstate commerce rather than letting him burn down an unoccupied target building next door. *Id.* at 177–78. We held that although "federal agents could have turned the evidence over to the local authorities rather than induce Podolsky to commit a federal crime," the "responsibility for wise management of scarce prosecutorial and other governmental resources is not a judicial responsibility." *Id.* at 179. Similarly, in *United States v. Skoczen,* 405 F.3d 537 (7th Cir.2005), agents borrowed a truckload of cigarettes from a tobacco company in Virginia and drove them to Illinois for use in a reverse sting. We found no problem with the agents' actions, although we noted that matters "might be different" if the defendant had expressed an interest in buying local that agents had frustrated. *Id.* at 542.

We see no meaningful distinction between these cases and the reverse sting here. The agents here did not offend the Constitution with their choice to provide interstate prop guns. Accordingly, the judgment of the district court is AFFIRMED.

EXERCISE

As the *Sarraj* case recognizes, gun cases (like drug cases) are an area of near-total overlap between state and federal jurisdiction in many places. If you were a state agent making a reverse sting of the type described above, would you take your case to federal or state authorities, assuming that the state had similar penalties for felons who possess firearms? What would be your reasoning?

Another "felon in possession" case element the government must prove is that the defendant was previously convicted of a crime for which the potential sentence is more than one year. There are some potential landmines even with this seemingly straightforward requirement. One twist is created by an exception found at 18 U.S.C. § 921(a)(20), providing that the term "crime punishable by imprisonment for a term exceeding one year" does not include "any State offense classified by the laws of the State as a misdemeanor and punishable by a term of imprisonment of two years or less."

SCHRADER V. HOLDER
704 F.3d 980 (D.C. Cir. 2013)

TATEL, CIRCUIT JUDGE:

Due to a conviction some forty years ago for common-law misdemeanor assault and battery for which he served no jail time, plaintiff Jefferson Wayne Schrader, now a sixty-four-year-old veteran, is, by virtue of 18 U.S.C. § 922(g)(1), barred for life from ever possessing a firearm. Together with the Second Amendment Foundation, Schrader contends that section 922(g)(1) is inapplicable to common-law misdemeanants as a class and, alternatively, that application of the statute to this class of individuals violates the Second Amendment. Because we find plaintiffs' statutory argument unpersuasive and see no constitutional infirmity in applying section 922(g)(1) to common-law misdemeanants, we affirm the district court's dismissal of the complaint.

I.

Enacted in its current form in 1968, section 922(g)(1) of Title 18 of the United States Code prohibits firearm possession by persons convicted of "a crime punishable by imprisonment for a term exceeding one year." 18 U.S.C. § 922(g)(1). Section 921(a)(20)(B), however, exempts "any State offense classified by the laws of the State as a misdemeanor and punishable by a term of imprisonment of two years or less." 18 U.S.C. § 921(a)(20)(B). This case concerns the application of these provisions to convictions for common-law misdemeanors that carry no statutory maximum term of imprisonment.

Section 922(g)(1)'s prohibition on firearm possession applies, with some exceptions not relevant here, for life. . . .

In 1968, while walking down the street in Annapolis, Maryland, plaintiff Jefferson Wayne Schrader, then twenty years old and serving in the United States Navy, encountered a member of a street gang who, according to the complaint, had assaulted him a week or two earlier. . . . "A dispute broke out between the two, in the course of which Schrader punched his assailant." Second Am. Compl. ¶ 10. As a result, Schrader was convicted of common-law misdemeanor assault and battery in a Maryland court and fined $100. *Id.* ¶ 11. The court imposed no jail time. *Id.* Schrader went on to complete a tour in Vietnam and received an honorable discharge from the Navy. *Id.* ¶ 12. Except for a single traffic violation, he has had no other encounter with the law. *Id.*

According to the complaint, "[o]n or about November 11, 2008, Schrader's companion attempted to purchase him a shotgun as a gift," and some two months later, "Schrader ordered a handgun from his local firearms dealer, which he would keep for self-defense." *Id.* ¶ 14. Both transactions "resulted in . . . denial decision[s] by the FBI when the National Instant Criminal Background Check ('NICS') computer system indicated that Mr. Schrader is prohibited under federal law from purchasing firearms." *Id.* ¶ 15. The FBI later "advised Schrader that the shotgun transaction was rejected pursuant to 18 U.S.C. § 922(g)(1) on the basis of his 1968 Maryland misdemeanor assault conviction." *Id.*¶ 16. In a letter to Schrader, the FBI explained that he had "been matched with the following federally prohibitive criteria under Title 18, United States Code, Sections 921(a)(20) and 922(g)(1): A person who has been convicted in any court of a crime punishable by imprisonment for a term exceeding one year or any state offense classified by the state as a misdemeanor and . . . punishable by a term of imprisonment of more than two years."

At the time of Schrader's conviction, "[t]he common law crimes of assault and battery [in Maryland] had no statutory penalty." *Robinson v. State,* 353 Md. 683, 728 A.2d 698, 702 n. 6 (1999). Although Maryland later codified these offenses, *see* Md.Code Ann., Crim. Law §§ 3–201, 3–202, 3–203, when Schrader was convicted "[t]he maximum term of imprisonment [for these offenses] was ordinarily limited only by the prohibition against cruel and unusual punishment contained in the Eighth Amendment to the United States Constitution and Articles 16 and 25 of the Maryland Declaration of Rights," *Robinson,* 728 A.2d at 702 n. 6. As the FBI explained in a declaration filed in the district court, because "[a]t the time of Schrader's 1968 assault conviction, Maryland law did not set a maximum sentence for misdemeanor assault," the FBI "determined that the conviction triggered 18 U.S.C. § 921(a)(20) and 18 U.S.C. § 922(g)(1), which prohibit firearm possession by an individual convicted of a state offense classified by the state as a misdemeanor that is punishable by a term of imprisonment of more than two years." . . .

Although the category of "common-law offenses" is rather broad, varying widely from state to state, when Congress enacted section 922(g)(1) in 1968, many common-law crimes involved quite violent behavior. In Maryland, for example, attempted rape and attempted murder were common-law misdemeanors that carried no statutory maximum sentence. *See Hardy v. State,* 301 Md. 124, 482 A.2d 474, 476–77 (1984); *Glass v. State,* 24 Md.App. 76, 329 A.2d 109, 112 (1974). The offense for which Schrader was convicted—common-law assault and battery—provides another example. Before Maryland codified the crime of common-law assault in 1996, the offense included all forms of assault with the exception of certain narrow categories of statutory aggravated assaults that were defined as felonies. *See Walker v. State,* 53 Md.App. 171, 452 A.2d 1234, 1247 & n. 11 (1982). As a result, the offense "embrace[d] an almost infinite variety of fact patterns." *Simms v. State,* 288 Md. 712, 421 A.2d 957, 965 (1980). Many of these fact patterns involved serious, violent conduct, and many offenders received sentences of ten or twenty years' imprisonment. *See Thomas v. State,* 333 Md. 84, 634 A.2d 1, 8 & nn. 3, 4 (1993) (collecting cases). In one case, for example, a defendant was sentenced to fifteen years for common-law assault where he forced a man "into a car, stabbed him twice in the neck and three times in the chest, dragged him out of the car and left him bleeding in a street gutter." *Sutton v. Maryland,* 886 F.2d 708, 709 (4th Cir.1989) (en banc). As one Maryland court explained:

> [S]tatutory assaults have not preempted the field of all serious and aggravated assaults. Our Legislature has cut out of the herd for special treatment four assaults where the aggravating factor is a special *mens rea* or specific intent. This by no means exhausts the category of more grievous and blameworthy assaults. The aggravating factor in a particular case might well be the modality of an assault, and not its *mens rea*—assault with a deadly weapon, assault by poison . . ., assault by bomb. . . . Even where . . . there simply has been no specific intent, a brutal beating that leaves its victim blinded, crippled, disfigured, in a wheelchair for life, in a psychiatric ward for life, is severely aggravated. . . . Maryland has not dealt with this form of aggravation legislatively but has left it to the discretion of common law sentencing.

Walker, 452 A.2d at 1247–48; *see also Simms,* 421 A.2d at 965 ("Some 'simple assaults' may involve more brutal or heinous conduct than may be present in other cases falling within one of the statutory aggravated assaults."). . . .

Plaintiffs' argument also runs counter to the commonsense meaning of the term "punishable," which refers to any punishment capable of being imposed, not necessarily a punishment specified by statute. *See* Webster's Third New International Dictionary 1843 (1993) (defining "punishable" as "deserving of, or liable to, punishment: capable of being punished by law or right"). Because common-law offenses carry no statutory maximum term of imprisonment, they are capable of being punished by a term of imprisonment exceeding one year and thus fall within section 922(g)(1)'s purview. And because such offenses are also capable of being punished by more than two years' imprisonment, they are ineligible for section 921(a)(20)(B)'s misdemeanor exception.

EXERCISE

The *Schrader* case was not actually a criminal action; rather, Mr. Schrader was denied the ability to buy a gun by the same law that would have subjected him to a felony charge if he had purchased and possessed that gun.

Imagine that Mr. Schrader had bought the gun and was then arrested for possessing it. You are an Assistant United States Attorney and are approached by the ATF agent who has investigated the case. She wants you to prosecute Mr. Schrader under 18 U.S.C. § 922(g). What do you do?

---

18 U.S.C. § 922(g) prohibits not only the possession of firearms by a convicted felon, but also the possession of ammunition. Just as an unloaded gun with no bullets can lead to conviction, so can possession of a bullet with no gun.

UNITED STATES V. CARDOZA
129 F. 3d 6 (1st Cir. 1997)

BOWNES, SENIOR CIRCUIT JUDGE.

In July of 1995, a sixteen-year-old acquaintance of Cardoza, Myron Ragsdale, asked Cardoza to secure a handgun for him to purchase. Cardoza found a dealer willing to sell a nine-millimeter semiautomatic handgun to Ragsdale for $200.00. On the night of July 14, 1995, Cardoza and Ragsdale went to Walnut Park in Roxbury, Massachusetts, to make the gun purchase. Ragsdale paid $200.00 for the handgun and nine rounds of ammunition. Ragsdale loaded the gun with eight rounds of ammunition, and Cardoza took possession of the ninth round.

Sometime after the transaction was completed, Cardoza and Ragsdale began walking along Humboldt Avenue. As they walked, Ragsdale had the handgun in his waistband and Cardoza carried the single round of ammunition in his hand. By this time it was approximately 2:00 a.m. on the morning of July 15. They were spotted walking along Humboldt Avenue by four officers of the Boston Police's Youth Violence Strike Force who were patrolling the area in an unmarked police car. One of the officers in the car, Gregory Brown, noticed that Cardoza and Ragsdale were acting indecisively about whether to continue walking up Humboldt, or instead cross the street in front of the police car. Moving slowly, the police car approached Cardoza and Ragsdale from behind. As the patrol car approached, Cardoza and Ragsdale crossed Humboldt Avenue in order to walk up the sidewalk of Ruthven Street, a one-way thoroughfare that emptied onto Humboldt Avenue. As they crossed in front of the car, Officer Brown, who was sitting in the back seat on the driver's side, recognized Cardoza and directed the driver to make a left turn off Humboldt, and proceed the wrong way up Ruthven for a short distance. Officer Brown testified that he wanted to ask Cardoza some questions concerning a shooting incident that had occurred some days earlier. The driver took the left turn, and pulled over to the curb just off Humboldt, facing the wrong way on Ruthven Street.

Officer Brown, whose window was rolled down, called out to Cardoza, asking "What's up Freddie? What are you doing out this time of night?" Cardoza stopped, turned, and approached the patrol car. Ragsdale continued walking a short distance. Officer Brown remained in the car conversing with Cardoza through the open car window. As he talked with Officer Brown, Cardoza began to gesture with his hand, exposing the round of ammunition. Seeing the round of ammunition, Brown exited the patrol car, and began to pat-frisk Cardoza. At the same time, two other officers exited the car and approached and pat-frisked Ragsdale, discovering the handgun loaded with eight rounds of ammunition.

Cardoza was indicted on four counts. Count I charged Cardoza with being a felon-in-possession of one round of ammunition, in violation of 18 U.S.C. § 922(g)(1). . . .

Cardoza launches his appeal by arguing that the single nine millimeter bullet which he was convicted of possessing is not "ammunition" within the meaning of 18 U.S.C. § 922(g). We disagree.

Cardoza was convicted of violating the felon-in-possession statute, which makes it illegal for a convicted felon "to possess in or affecting commerce, any firearm or ammunition. . . ." 18 U.S.C § 922(g)(1) (West Supp.1997). "Ammunition" is defined as "ammunition or cartridge cases, primers, bullets, or propellent powder designed for use in any firearm." 18 U.S.C. § 921(a)(17)(A)(West Supp.1997). Cardoza suggests first that the statutory definition, by including the plural words "cases, primers, [and] bullets" bans only the possession of more than one piece of ammunition. Second, he suggests that the word "ammunition" itself always means multiple rounds. Finally, Cardoza argues that the definition of "ammunition" is sufficiently ambiguous to require application of the "rule of lenity," *United States v. Lanier,* 520 U.S. 259, ___, 117 S.Ct. 1219, 1225, 137 L.Ed.2d 432 (1997), in his favor. The court below determined that "[n]o amount of wordplay will contradict the plain meaning of the statute, an honest reading of which leads to the inexorable conclusion that a single nine millimeter bullet . . . constitutes ammunition for the purposes of [§ 922(g)(1)]." *Cardoza,* 914 F.Supp. at 686–87.

This question is one of statutory construction which we review de novo. *Strickland v. Commissioner, Maine Dep't of Human Servs.,* 96 F.3d 542, 545 (1st Cir.1996). In this instance, we need not venture far beyond the words of the statute.

We think the common sense, everyday understanding of the word "ammunition" encompasses a single bullet or cartridge. *See O'Connell v. Shalala,* 79 F.3d 170, 176 (1st Cir.1996) ("courts are bound to afford statutes a practical, commonsense reading"). Thus courts, and the public generally, refer to ammunition in terms of "rounds." *See United States v. Brimage,* 115 F.3d 73, 76 (1st Cir.1997), *cert. denied,* 522 U.S. 924, 118 S.Ct. 321, 139 L.Ed.2d 248 (1997) ("loaded with six rounds of ammunition"); *United States v. Balanga,* 109 F.3d 1299, 1300 (8th Cir.1997)("a single round of .22 caliber ammunition"). If the word "ammunition" was incapable of meaning one bullet, one would not refer to a "single round of ammunition."

To hold otherwise would result in an absurdity. *Marques v. Fitzgerald,* 99 F.3d 1, 5 (1st Cir.1996)("[A] statute may not be construed in a manner that results in absurdities or defeats its underlying purpose."). Congress enacted the Omnibus Crime Control and Safe Streets Act of 1968 (of which § 922(g)'s predecessor was a part), inter alia, to keep certain weaponry "out of the hands of those not legally entitled to possess them because of . . . criminal background. . . ." S.Rep. No. 90–1097, at 28 (1968), *reprinted in* 1968 U.S.C.C.A.N. 2112, 2113. It would therefore make little sense to interpret § 922(g) to criminalize possession of two bullets, but not one, when Congress' purpose was to deprive certain persons of any firepower.

EXERCISE

Sylvia was convicted in 1995 of health care fraud, a felony. After serving a few months in prison she was released, but had lost her job and family as a result. She was destitute thereafter. One day she picked up food at food pantry. A volunteer helping her out the door noticed one .22 bullet in the bottom of the box and said "you should get rid of that—it must have been in there when the store dropped off that box."

Sylvia proceeded to walk home. When she entered her apartment, she found that it was being searched by a drug task force who had received a tip that she was storing heroin in her apartment. They found nothing in the apartment, but while an officer was talking to her he noticed the bullet in her food box and she was arrested and charged under 18 U.S.C. § 922(g). You are her defense attorney. When you meet with her, she tells you not only that she is guilty, but that she is a heroin addict, and that she "will never ever ever pass a drug test."

The prosecutor has indicted Sylvia, and has offered a plea deal that would include a joint recommendation of a sentence of five years of probation with conditions that she maintain employment, undergo drug testing, and maintain her residence. Your research reveals that if she goes to trial and is found guilty, her sentence would likely be 12–18 months in prison. What do you recommend to your client?

In the previous chapter we examined the doctrine of constructive possession in the context of narcotics, and the same rules apply here to possession of firearms by prohibited persons such as convicted felons—in fact, the analysis of gun and drug possession is often intertwined.

UNITED STATES V. RAMOS
852 F.3d 747 (8th Cir. 2017)

KELLY, CIRCUIT JUDGE.

Gilberto Ray Ramos was convicted after trial of multiple drug offenses, as well as the offense of being a felon in possession of a firearm. He appeals those convictions, arguing that they were supported by insufficient evidence, that the district court erred in admitting an exhibit that included an Arkansas Parole Board Waiver of Revocation Hearing form he signed, and that his sentence is substantively unreasonable. We affirm in part and reverse in part.

I.   Background

Law enforcement first became interested in Ramos during a wiretap investigation of another individual, Abraham Duran. One of the wiretap monitors, Gary Gregory, testified that he had monitored and translated three calls between Duran and another individual with a telephone number ending in 0679. During one of the calls, Duran asked the individual if he needed "more." During another call, Duran told the individual to call him so Duran could "take [him] the other part." Duran was eventually arrested for and convicted of distribution of methamphetamine, and, pursuant to a plea agreement, cooperated with law enforcement officers in their investigation.

Duran testified at trial that Ramos was the individual he had been speaking to in the three intercepted calls. Duran testified that the calls related to his agreement with Ramos to distribute methamphetamine. According to Duran, he supplied Ramos with methamphetamine at Ramos' residence at the Brookhaven Apartments in Springdale, Arkansas. Duran also testified about a text message that law enforcement had retrieved from his phone. According to Duran, in the text message, Ramos was offering to sell him a .40 caliber firearm.

Detective Preston Oswalt testified that he arranged for a confidential informant, Armando Gonzales, to make controlled purchases of methamphetamine from Ramos. Based on information provided by Gonzales, Oswalt located an apartment that he believed was Ramos' at the Brookhaven Apartments. According to Oswalt, Springdale water records listed Ramos as the occupant of the apartment. Gonzales made controlled purchases of methamphetamine at the apartment on three occasions. Each time, Gonzales purchased one gram of methamphetamine for $100. After the first purchase, Oswalt showed Gonzales a known photograph of Ramos, and Gonzales confirmed that Ramos had been the one to sell him the methamphetamine. Gonzales also testified at trial. According to Gonzales, he offered to work with the police in order to reduce his punishment for drug possession charges. Gonzales also identified Ramos in court as the man who sold him the methamphetamine.

Oswalt testified that on December 5, 2014, he and other police officers executed a search warrant at the apartment. Before they executed the warrant, officers saw a man and a woman approach the apartment and knock on the door. Another woman, later identified as Jasmyn Schmid, answered the door. Oswalt testified that in his understanding, Schmid was living at the apartment at the time. Schmid and the other two individuals left the residence together in a vehicle. Officers stopped the vehicle, and questioned and searched Schmid. They found a marijuana pipe, a methamphetamine pipe, a digital scale, and user amounts of marijuana and methamphetamine, and arrested her for drug possession. Then, officers searched the apartment. In the kitchen, they found a ledger, digital scale, baggies, and cash, as well as approximately two ounces of methamphetamine in Kool-Aid containers in the freezer. In one of the two bedrooms, they found a .45 caliber pistol under the mattress, next to a pink vibrator. The bedroom closet contained men's and women's clothing. The other bedroom's closet also contained men's clothing. On February 19, 2015, law enforcement located Ramos at his mother's residence and arrested him. The officers searched the residence, and found a water bill for the Brookhaven apartment in Ramos' name. . . .

Ramos additionally argues that there was insufficient evidence to support his conviction for being a felon in possession of a firearm, because the gun was found under a mattress next to a pink vibrator, and there was women's clothing in the closet of the bedroom where it was found. Furthermore, Ramos notes, although Duran testified that Ramos tried to sell him a .40 caliber gun, the gun found in the bedroom was a .45 caliber, and neither Oswalt nor Duran ever saw Ramos with a firearm.

A conviction for being a felon in possession of a firearm under 18 U.S.C. § 922(g)(1) may be based on constructive possession. United States v. Boykin, 986 F.2d 270, 274 (8th Cir. 1993). "[C]onstructive possession requires both knowledge that the contraband is present and dominion over the premises where the contraband is located." Ways, 832 F.3d at 897. Some of our cases have concluded that dominion over the premises can be sufficient by itself to prove constructive possession, because dominion may "give[ ] rise to a strong inference of knowledge." United States v. Dooley, 580 F.3d 682, 686 (8th Cir. 2009) (explaining why some cases appear to elide the distinction between knowledge and dominion). But such an inference is not warranted under the facts of every case. See id. ("[T]his inference may be rebutted if other evidence contradicts it."). Thus, mere dominion is not always sufficient to establish constructive possession. See, e.g., Ways, 832 F.3d at 897–88; United States v. Smith, 508 F.3d 861, 867 (8th Cir. 2007); United States v. Pace, 922 F.2d 451, 453 (8th Cir. 1990).

One context where mere dominion is insufficient to show that the defendant knowingly possessed a gun is in cases involving joint occupancy. We have explained that "when there is joint occupancy of a residence, dominion over the premises by itself is insufficient to establish constructive possession." United States v. Wright, 739 F.3d 1160, 1168 (8th Cir. 2014). Rather, the government must provide additional evidence of a link between the contraband and the defendant. Id. Otherwise, a father could be imprisoned for marijuana that his son has hidden in the house, or a wife could be jailed for her husband's secret cache of illegal guns. See id. at 1174 (Riley, C.J., concurring).

Here, because Ramos jointly occupied the apartment with Schmid, the government was required to provide some evidence linking him to the gun beyond his dominion over the apartment. The government points to evidence that the officers found some men's clothes in the closet in the bedroom where the gun was found. But they also found women's clothes in that closet and men's clothes in the other bedroom's closet. Further, the gun was found under the mattress next to a pink vibrator. It is unclear whether Ramos, though he lived at the apartment, exercised any control over the bedroom where the gun was found. On this evidence, it is more than possible that Ramos was convicted because Schmid had a weapon that Ramos did not know about. A reasonable jury could not conclude beyond a reasonable doubt to the contrary.

We acknowledge the government presented evidence that Ramos tried to sell a different gun to Duran and admitted in the Waiver Form that he violated a condition of parole involving "Weapons." But neither of these facts ties Ramos to the particular gun that he was charged with possessing. Although this evidence may demonstrate that Ramos had access to a gun, as the government argues, it does not mean that he had access to *this* gun or that he even knew about it. And though the firearm likely belonged to either Ramos or Schmid or both, "a conscientious mind would have to have entertained a reasonable doubt" about whether Ramos constructively possessed it. See United States v. Hall, 999 F.2d 1298, 1299 (8th Cir. 1993). Because insufficient evidence supported Ramos' conviction for being a felon in possession of a firearm, we reverse the judgment as to that conviction.

EXERCISE

Imagine that you are a federal investigator working on federal land. While on duty, you stop a car that resembles one reported leaving the scene of an assault (and which is also speeding). When you approach the car, you observe two occupants in the two front seats. You check the license for the driver, then ask if you can search the car. The driver (who owns the car) says yes, though the passenger urges him not to. You search the car and find a gun wedged under the console between the driver's and passenger seat. The serial number on the gun has been obliterated.

The driver has a recent conviction for narcotics trafficking. The passenger has no criminal record. Both insist on talking to lawyers and will not talk to you.

Do you have probable cause to arrest the driver?

While 18 U.S.C. § 922(g) bars convicted felons and others from possessing firearms, 18 U.S.C. § 931 bars the purchase, ownership, or possession of "body armor" by those who have been convicted of a crime of violence. Body armor includes items like bullet-proof vests that are often used by the military and law enforcement.

UNITED STATES V. SERRANO
191 F. Supp. 3d 407 (S.D.N.Y. 2016)

WILLIAM H. PAULEY III, UNITED STATES DISTRICT JUDGE:

On March 1, 2016, Defendant Pedro Serrano was charged in a two-count indictment with violating 18 U.S.C. § 922(g)(1), which, inter alia, prohibits felons from possessing ammunition shipped or transported in interstate commerce; and 18 U.S.C. § 931(a), which prohibits a felon convicted of a "crime of violence" from possessing body armor that was "sold or offered for sale, in interstate or foreign commerce." Count Two charged:

> On or about November 2, 2015, in the Southern District of New York and elsewhere, PEDRO SERRANO, a/k/a, "Louis Ortiz," the defendant, after having been convicted of a felony that is a crime of violence, knowingly did possess body armor, to wit, an American Body Armor bullet-resistant vest.

(Indictment, ECF No. 10, at 2.)

Defendant moves to dismiss Count Two because: (1) the Indictment did not charge § 931(a)'s "interstate commerce" element; (2) § 931(a)is an unconstitutional exercise of Congress's Commerce Clause authority; (3) § 931(a) is unconstitutionally vague; and (4) § 931(a) violates his Second Amendment rights. Count Two is dismissed for failure to allege the essential element of interstate commerce, without prejudice to the filing of an appropriate superseding indictment. Defendant's motions are otherwise denied.

DISCUSSION

I.   Sufficiency of the Indictment

Defendant moves to dismiss Count Two of the Indictment because it fails to state an "essential element" of the charged crime: that the body armor allegedly possessed by Defendant was "sold or offered for sale" in interstate commerce.

Under the Fifth and Sixth Amendments, "[a] criminal defendant is entitled to an indictment that states the essential elements of the charge against him." United States v. Pirro, 212 F.3d 86, 91 (2d Cir.2000) (citing Jones v. United States, 526 U.S. 227, 232, 119 S.Ct. 1215, 143 L.Ed.2d 311 (1999)). When an indictment fails to contain an essential element, the Defendant suffers the risk that the "grand jury may not have understood the elements of the crime and the evidence necessary to support the indictment." Pirro, 212 F.3d at 95. "The timing of the defendant's objection is important to the level of scrutiny employed; a defendant who objects to the indictment before trial . . . is entitled to a more exacting review of the indictment." Pirro, 212 F.3d at 92 (citing United States v. Goodwin, 141 F.3d 394, 401 (2d Cir.1997)).

The statute charged in Count Two, 18 U.S.C. § 931(a), provides that it is "unlawful for a person to purchase, own, or possess body armor, if that person has been convicted of a felony" that is a "crime of violence (as defined in section 16)." While the statute refers to the statutory provision defining "crime of violence," it does not explain whether "body armor" is a defined term. Rather, the meaning of body armor, and the relevant jurisdictional element, must be found elsewhere, in 18 U.S.C. § 921(a)(35). That provision states that body armor means "personal protective body covering intended to protect against gunfire," but only when it was "sold or offered for sale, in interstate or foreign commerce." 18 U.S.C. § 921(a)(35).

Count One of the Indictment charges that Defendant "knowingly did possess in and affecting commerce ammunition . . . which had previously been shipped and transported in interstate and foreign commerce." (Indictment at 1, ECF No. 10.) But Count Two states only that Defendant "knowingly did possess body armor," with no reference to any jurisdictional element found by the grand jury. (Indictment at 2, ECF No. 10.) While the

Second Circuit has "consistently upheld indictments that 'do little more than to track the language of the statute charged and state the time and place (in approximate terms) of the alleged crime . . . [t]he Supreme Court . . . has recognized a limitation on this practice." Pirro, 212 F.3d at 93. That is, when a statutory definition "includes generic terms, it is not sufficient that the indictment shall charge the offence in the same generic terms as in the definition; but it must states the species—it must descend to particulars." Pirro, 212 F.3d at 93 (quoting Russell v. United States, 369 U.S. 749, 765, 82 S.Ct. 1038, 8 L.Ed.2d 240 (1962)). And when "one element of the offense is implicit in the statute, rather than explicit, and the indictment tracks the language of the statute and fails to allege the implicit element explicitly, the indictment fails to allege an offense." Pirro, 212 F.3d at 93 (citation omitted).

Here, because the essential jurisdictional element of § 931(a) is concealed in an unreferenced, subsidiary statutory provision, it is not sufficient for the grand jury's Indictment to "track" the "generic terms" of the overarching statute, and omit mention of the element. Accordingly, Count Two is dismissed for failure to plead the essential element of interstate commerce. This dismissal is without prejudice to an appropriate superseding indictment.

II. Commerce Clause Challenge

Defendant further argues that even if Count Two was pleaded sufficiently, § 931(a) would be an unconstitutional exercise of Congress's Commerce Clause power. Specifically, Defendant argues that prohibiting felons from possessing body armor that was "sold or offered for sale, in interstate or foreign commerce" implicates no traditional categories of commercial activity that can be regulated by Congress. Defendant adopts by reference the reasoning from Justice Thomas's dissent from a denial of certiorari in Alderman v. United States, 562 U.S. 1163, 131 S.Ct. 700, 178 L.Ed.2d 799 (2011), in which he suggested that § 931(a) may "trespass on traditional state police powers" and is in tension with United States v. Lopez, 514 U.S. 549, 115 S.Ct. 1624, 131 L.Ed.2d 626 (1995), and United States v. Morrison, 529 U.S. 598, 120 S.Ct. 1740, 146 L.Ed.2d 658 (2000).

In Lopez, the Court invalidated a provision of the Gun-Free School Zones Act of 1990 in which Congress criminalized "knowingly . . . possess[ing] a firearm at a place that the individual knows, or has reasonable cause to believe, is a school zone" because the record revealed that Congress made no legislative findings that such firearm possession "substantially affected interstate commerce." Lopez, 514 U.S. at 551, 563, 115 S.Ct. 1624. However, in enacting the Violence Against Women Act of 1994, Congress had made various legislative findings that acts of gender-motivated violence had a "substantial effect" on interstate commerce. Morrison, 529 U.S. at 614, 120 S.Ct. 1740. Nonetheless, the Morrison Court found that the mere existence of such findings was insufficient to establish that such an effect existed. Accordingly, the Court "reject[ed] the argument that Congress may regulate noneconomic, violent criminal conduct based solely on that conduct's aggregate effect on interstate commerce." Morrison, 529 U.S. at 617, 120 S.Ct. 1740.

However, in Lopez, the Court emphasized that the relevant statute contained "no jurisdictional element which would ensure, through case-by-case inquiry, that the firearm possession in question affects interstate commerce," and noted that such an element would have limited the statute to a "discrete set of firearm possessions that additionally have an explicit connection with or effect on interstate commerce." Lopez, 514 U.S. at 561, 115 S.Ct. 1624. Moreover, in Morrison, the Supreme Court observed that the relevant provision "contain[ed] no jurisdictional element," and that such an element would have supported the Government's contention that the statute was "sufficiently tied to interstate commerce." Morrison, 529 U.S. at 613, 120 S.Ct. 1740. The Court then cited with approval a criminal statute on gender-motivated violence that did include a jurisdictional element, which it observed had been "uniformly upheld ... as an appropriate exercise of Congress' Commerce Clause." Morrison, 529 U.S. at 659 n.5, 120 S.Ct. 1740.

The Second Circuit twice upheld federal firearms violations after Lopez and Morrison where the statute included a jurisdictional element requiring the Government "to provide evidence in each prosecution of a sufficient nexus between the charged offense and interstate or foreign commerce." United States v. Santiago, 238 F.3d 213, 216 (2d Cir.2001) (applying Morrison); see also United States v. Sorrentino, 72 F.3d 294, 296 (2d Cir.1995) (applying Lopez). Here, any superseding indictment charging a revised version of Count Two would also require specific proof that body armor in Defendant's possession was a "product sold or offered for sale, in interstate or foreign commerce." Accordingly, Santiago and Sorrentino compel a finding that 18 U.S.C. § 931(a) is a facially constitutional application of Congress's power under the Commerce Clause. Any as-applied challenge to the evidence of interstate nexus in this case will be addressed by the evidence that the Government offers at trial.

III. Vagueness Challenge

"Vagueness may invalidate a criminal law" when it "fail[s] to provide the kind of notice that will enable ordinary people to understand what conduct it prohibits" or if it "authorize[s] and even encourage[s] arbitrary and discriminatory enforcement." City of Chicago v. Morales, 527 U.S. 41, 55, 119 S.Ct. 1849, 144 L.Ed.2d 67 (1999). Defendant argues that three portions of § 931(a) are unconstitutionally vague: (1) the term "crime of violence," (2) the definition of "body armor"; and (3) the phrase "sold or offered for sale."

As applied to Defendant, the term "crime of violence" is not vague. In Johnson v. United States, ___ U.S. ___, 135 S.Ct. 2551, 192 L.Ed.2d 569

(2015), the Supreme Court concluded that the so-called "residual clause" of the Armed Career Criminal Act ("ACCA"), was unconstitutionally vague. The language in that clause parallels the residual clause in the statute that is used to define a "crime of violence" for purposes of § 931(a). See 18 U.S.C. § 16(b). However, Section 16 also includes a separate "force clause," under which an offense is a crime of violence if it "had as an element the use, attempted use, or threatened use of physical force against the person or property of another." 18 U.S.C. § 16(a). And Johnson notably excluded the more specific language of the ACCA's analogous "force clause" from its holding that the residual clause was vague. Johnson, 135 S.Ct. at 2563. Here, Defendant's prior conviction for Robbery in the First Degree qualifies as a "crime of violence" under Section 16(a)'s "force clause" because one inherent element of that conviction was the "immediate use of physical force" against another person. See N.Y. Penal Law § 160.00 ("Robbery is forcible stealing. A person forcibly steals property and commits robbery when, in the course of committing a larceny, he uses or threatens the immediate use of physical force upon another person . . . .").

Nor is § 931(a)'s definition of "body armor" vague as applied to Defendant. The statute defines body armor as a "personal protective body covering designed to protect against gunfire, regardless of whether the product is to be worn alone or is sold as a complement to another product or garment." 18 U.S.C. § 921(a)(35). Here, Defendant could not reasonably be confused that the identified item is body armor, given that the label reads "American Body Armor and Equipment, Incorporated," describes its contents as "ballistic pads," and identifies the vest's ability to resist numerous types of ammunition. (See Gov't Opp. ECF No. 33, Ex. A.)

Finally, the phrase "sold or offered for sale[ ] in interstate or foreign commerce" is not vague. Whether a product was "sold" or "offered for sale" is readily understandable to the average person.

IV. Second Amendment Challenge

Finally, Defendant argues that the fact that § 931(a) prohibits a felon who has committed a "crime of violence" from possessing body armor effectively violates his Second Amendment right to keep and bear arms, relying on the Supreme Court's decision in District of Columbia v. Heller, 554 U.S. 570, 128 S.Ct. 2783, 171 L.Ed.2d 637 (2008). But even assuming that "body armor" is analogous to a firearm, Heller concluded that Second Amendment protections should not "be taken to cast doubt on longstanding prohibitions on the possession of firearms by felons." Heller, 554 U.S. at 626, 128 S.Ct. 2783. Accordingly, Defendant's Second Amendment challenge is rejected.

CONCLUSION

Defendant's motion to dismiss Count Two is granted because the Indictment did not charge that the body armor allegedly possessed by

Defendant was "sold or offered for sale, in interstate or foreign commerce." Defendant's motion is denied in all other respects.

EXERCISE

Body armor only has one purpose, which is defensive: it is designed to protect someone from gunshots and other forms of attack. Why would body armor be outlawed?

C. USE OF A FIREARM IN ANOTHER OFFENSE

The firearms laws we have examined so far create criminal liability for having certain types of guns and for possessing a gun as a prohibited person. Next, let's examine criminal gun laws that bar the actual *use* of a gun. In these cases, the focus will often be on the context of the event.

18 U.S.C. § 924(c) is a principal federal gun law of this type:

(c)(1)(A) Except to the extent that a greater minimum sentence is otherwise provided by this subsection or by any other provision of law, any person who, during and in relation to any crime of violence or drug trafficking crime. . . for which the person may be prosecuted in a court of the United States, uses or carries a firearm, or who, in furtherance of any such crime, possesses a firearm, shall, in addition to the punishment provided for such crime of violence or drug trafficking crime—

> **(i)** be sentenced to a term of imprisonment of not less than 5 years;
>
> **(ii)** if the firearm is brandished, be sentenced to a term of imprisonment of not less than 7 years; and
>
> **(iii)** if the firearm is discharged, be sentenced to a term of imprisonment of not less than 10 years.

(B) If the firearm possessed by a person convicted of a violation of this subsection—

> **(i)** is a short-barreled rifle, short-barreled shotgun, or semiautomatic assault weapon, the person shall be sentenced to a term of imprisonment of not less than 10 years; or
>
> **(ii)** is a machinegun or a destructive device, or is equipped with a firearm silencer or firearm muffler, the person shall be sentenced to a term of imprisonment of not less than 30 years.

(C) In the case of a second or subsequent conviction under this subsection, the person shall—

(i) be sentenced to a term of imprisonment of not less than 25 years; and

(ii) if the firearm involved is a machinegun or a destructive device, or is equipped with a firearm silencer or firearm muffler, be sentenced to imprisonment for life.

(D) Notwithstanding any other provision of law—

(i) a court shall not place on probation any person convicted of a violation of this subsection; and

(ii) no term of imprisonment imposed on a person under this subsection shall run concurrently with any other term of imprisonment imposed on the person, including any term of imprisonment imposed for the crime of violence or drug trafficking crime during which the firearm was used, carried, or possessed.

Pulling apart § 924(c)(1)(A), there are multiple ways the crime can be committed, which are subtly different.

First, a defendant can be proven to have "used or carried" a firearm "during and in relation" to any crime of violence or drug trafficking crime. Note that the action required under that prong is to use or carry a firearm—not simply to possess. The government must also prove that the defendant performed that action during and in relation to a qualifying crime.

The second prong allows the government to prove that the defendant "possessed" a firearm "in furtherance of" a qualifying drug or violent crime. Importantly, both the action and the context elements are different under this prong. This provision was added to the original 1968 statute in 1998, to allow the law to cover situations where a defendant possessed a firearm to protect himself during a drug transaction but neither used or carried that weapon.

Also, two aspects of § 924(c)(1)(D) above are especially significant. First, defendants charged under this law are not eligible for probation. Second—and this is unusual for federal law—a sentence for this offense stacks on top of the sentence for the underlying offense, rather than running concurrently (at the same time). Thus, if a defendant possesses a gun in furtherance of selling six grams of methamphetamine, the sentence might be five years for the narcotics sale and five years for the gun possession, one after the other, for a total of ten years in prison.

The first prong of the revised statute requires that the firearm be "used" or "carried." These action elements create intriguing issues where guns are not used in the traditional ways.

WATSON V. UNITED STATES
552 U.S. 74 (2007)

JUSTICE SOUTER delivered the opinion of the Court.

The question is whether a person who trades his drugs for a gun "uses" a firearm "during and in relation to . . . [a] drug trafficking crime" within the meaning of 18 U.S.C. § 924(c)(1)(A). We hold that he does not.

I

A

Section 924(c)(1)(A) sets a mandatory minimum sentence, depending on the facts, for a defendant who, "during and in relation to any crime of violence or drug trafficking crime[,] . . . uses or carries a firearm." The statute leaves the term "uses" undefined, though we have spoken to it twice before.

Smith v. United States, 508 U.S. 223, 113 S.Ct. 2050, 124 L.Ed.2d 138 (1993), raised the converse of today's question, and held that "a criminal who trades his firearm for drugs 'uses' it during and in relation to a drug trafficking offense within the meaning of § 924(c)(1)." *Id.,* at 241, 113 S.Ct. 2050. We rested primarily on the "ordinary or natural meaning" of the verb in context, *id.,* at 228, 113 S.Ct. 2050, and understood its common range as going beyond employment as a weapon: "it is both reasonable and normal to say that petitioner 'used' his MAC-10 in his drug trafficking offense by trading it for cocaine," *id.,* at 230, 113 S.Ct. 2050.

Two years later, the issue in *Bailey v. United States,* 516 U.S. 137, 116 S.Ct. 501, 133 L.Ed.2d 472 (1995), was whether possessing a firearm kept near the scene of drug trafficking is "use" under § 924(c)(1). We looked again to "ordinary or natural" meaning, *id.,* at 145, 116 S.Ct. 501, and decided that mere possession does not amount to "use": "§ 924(c)(1) requires evidence sufficient to show an *active employment* of the firearm by the defendant, a use that makes the firearm an operative factor in relation to the predicate offense," *id.,* at 143, 116 S.Ct. 501.

B

This third case on the reach of § 924(c)(1)(A) began to take shape when petitioner, Michael A. Watson, told a Government informant that he wanted to acquire a gun. On the matter of price, the informant quoted no dollar figure but suggested that Watson could pay in narcotics. Next, Watson met with the informant and an undercover law enforcement agent posing as a firearms dealer, to whom he gave 24 doses of oxycodone hydrocholoride (commonly, OxyContin) for a .50-caliber semiautomatic pistol. When law enforcement officers arrested Watson, they found the pistol in his car, and a later search of his house turned up a cache of prescription medicines, guns, and ammunition. Watson said he got the pistol "to protect his other firearms and drugs." App. C to Pet. for Cert. 11a.

A federal grand jury indicted him for distributing a Schedule II controlled substance and for "using" the pistol during and in relation to that crime, in violation of § 924(c)(1)(A). Watson pleaded guilty across the board, reserving the right to challenge the factual basis for a § 924(c)(1)(A) conviction and the added consecutive sentence of 60 months for using the gun. The Court of Appeals affirmed, 191 Fed.Appx. 326 (C.A.5 2006) *(per curiam),* on Circuit precedent foreclosing any argument that Watson had not "used" a firearm, see *id.,* at 327 (citing *United States v. Ulloa,* 94 F.3d 949 (C.A.5 1996), and *United States v. Zuniga,* 18 F.3d 1254 (C.A.5 1994)).

We granted certiorari to resolve a conflict among the Circuits on whether a person "uses" a firearm within the meaning of 18 U.S.C. § 924(c)(1)(A) when he trades narcotics to obtain a gun. 549 U.S. 1251, 127 S.Ct. 1371, 167 L.Ed.2d 158 (2007). We now reverse.

II

A

The Government's position that Watson "used" the pistol under § 924(c)(1)(A) by receiving it for narcotics lacks authority in either precedent or regular English. To begin with, neither *Smith* nor *Bailey* implicitly decides this case. While *Smith* held that firearms may be "used" in a barter transaction, even with no violent employment, see 508 U.S., at 241, 113 S.Ct. 2050, the case addressed only the trader who swaps his gun for drugs, not the trading partner who ends up with the gun. *Bailey,* too, is unhelpful, with its rule that a gun must be made use of actively to satisfy § 924(c)(1)(A), as "an operative factor in relation to the predicate offense." 516 U.S., at 143, 116 S.Ct. 501.The question here is whether it makes sense to say that Watson employed the gun at all; *Bailey* does not answer it.

[handwritten: government's position]

With no statutory definition or definitive clue, the meaning of the verb "uses" has to turn on the language as we normally speak it, see, *e.g., Lopez v. Gonzales,* 549 U.S. 47, 53, 127 S.Ct. 625, 629–30, 166 L.Ed.2d 462 (2006); *Asgrow Seed Co. v. Winterboer,* 513 U.S. 179, 187, 115 S.Ct. 788, 130 L.Ed.2d 682 (1995); *FDIC v. Meyer,* 510 U.S. 471, 476, 114 S.Ct. 996, 127 L.Ed.2d 308 (1994); there is no other source of a reasonable inference about what Congress understood when writing or what its words will bring to the mind of a careful reader. So, in *Smith* we looked for "everyday meaning," 508 U.S., at 228, 113 S.Ct. 2050, revealed in phraseology that strikes the ear as "both reasonable and normal," *id.,* at 230, 113 S.Ct. 2050. See also *Bailey, supra,* at 145, 116 S.Ct. 501. This appeal to the ordinary leaves the Government without much of a case.

The Government may say that a person "uses" a firearm simply by receiving it in a barter transaction, but no one else would. A boy who trades an apple to get a granola bar is sensibly said to use the apple, but one would never guess which way this commerce actually flowed from hearing that the boy used the granola. Cf. *United States v. Stewart,* 246 F.3d 728, 731

(C.A.D.C.2001) ("[W]hen a person pays a cashier a dollar for a cup of coffee in the courthouse cafeteria, the customer has not used the coffee. He has only used the dollar bill"). So, when Watson handed over the drugs for the pistol, the informant or the agent "used" the pistol to get the drugs, just as *Smith* held, but regular speech would not say that Watson himself used the pistol in the trade. "A seller does not 'use' a buyer's consideration," *United States v. Westmoreland,* 122 F.3d 431, 436 (C.A.7 1997), and the Government's contrary position recalls another case; *Lopez, supra,* at 56, 127 S.Ct. at 630–31, rejected the Government's interpretation of 18 U.S.C. § 924(c)(2) because "we do not normally speak or write the Government's way." . . .

Given ordinary meaning and the conventions of English, we hold that a person does not "use" a firearm under § 924(c)(1)(A) when he receives it in trade for drugs. The judgment of the Court of Appeals is reversed, and the case is remanded for further proceedings consistent with this opinion.

It is so ordered.

JUSTICE GINSBURG, concurring in the judgment.

It is better to receive than to give, the Court holds today, at least when the subject is guns. Distinguishing, as the Court does, between trading a gun for drugs and trading drugs for a gun, for purposes of the 18 U.S.C. § 924(c)(1) enhancement, makes scant sense to me. I join the Court's judgment, however, because I am persuaded that the Court took a wrong turn in *Smith v. United States,* 508 U.S. 223, 113 S.Ct. 2050, 124 L.Ed.2d 138 (1993), when it held that trading a gun for drugs fits within § 924(c)(1)'s compass as "us[e]" of a firearm "during and in relation to any . . . drug trafficking crime." For reasons well stated by Justice SCALIA in his dissenting opinion in *Smith,* 508 U.S., at 241, 113 S.Ct. 2050, I would read the word "use" in § 924(c)(1) to mean use as a weapon, not use in a bartering transaction. Accordingly, I would overrule *Smith,* and thereby render our precedent both coherent and consistent with normal usage. Cf. *Henslee v. Union Planters Nat. Bank & Trust Co.,* 335 U.S. 595, 600, 69 S.Ct. 290, 93 L.Ed. 259 (1949) (Frankfurter, J., dissenting) ("Wisdom too often never comes, and so one ought not to reject it merely because it comes late.").

EXERCISE

You are the supervisor of the Assistant United States Attorney who initially charged and prosecuted the *Watson* case. What constructive criticism might you have for her?

Watson was charged under the first prong of § 924(c)(1)(A), which requires proof of "use" or "carrying" of a firearm. One special element that must be proven under the second prong of this gun statute—which allows a charge based on the action of possession—is that the firearm must have been possessed "in furtherance of" the underlying offense. Gray-area cases, where that relationship between the gun and the crime is hard to prove, usually involve situations where guns and drugs are located in the same space.

UNITED STATES V. HILLIARD

490 F.3d 635 (8th Cir. 2007)

RILEY, CIRCUIT JUDGE.

Following Tyrone Hilliard's (Hilliard) convictions for two drug counts and three firearm counts, the district court sentenced Hilliard to 270 months' imprisonment and 5 years' supervised release. Hilliard appeals, challenging the denial of his motion to suppress, the sufficiency of evidence to support one of his firearm convictions, and the district court's authority to calculate drug quantity for the purpose of sentencing. Finding no error, we affirm. . . .

On February 15, 2005, Pine Lawn (Missouri) Police Department Officer Craig Church (Officer Church) and another officer responded to a 911 telephone call from a residence located at 2512 Arden (Arden residence) in St. Louis County, Missouri. When the officers arrived at the Arden residence, a partially-clothed woman, identified only as Ms. Cole (Cole), answered the door and invited the officers inside. Hilliard, who was present in the front living room of the Arden residence, did not object to Cole's invitation for the officers to enter the residence.

Cole requested that Officer Church follow her into an adjacent bedroom. Again, Hilliard did not voice any objection to this request. As Cole and Officer Church proceeded to the bedroom, Cole retrieved personal items from the floor and dressed herself. Officer Church observed several pieces of women's clothing and personal items throughout the residence. Once in the bedroom, Cole retrieved a Taurus .38 caliber revolver from under the bed, gave it to Officer Church, and stated the gun belonged to Hilliard. Cole then led Officer Church into the kitchen, where she retrieved a baggie containing crack cocaine and claimed the baggie belonged to Hilliard. The officers arrested Hilliard for possession of the firearm and crack cocaine, read Hilliard his *Miranda* rights, and transported Hilliard to the Pine Lawn Police Department for booking. At the police station, Hilliard acknowledged purchasing the firearm found in the Arden residence off the street.

In August 2005, St. Louis Metropolitan Police Department officers conducted surveillance on the Arden residence because of suspected drug activity at the residence. During their surveillance, officers observed Hilliard engage in several quick transactions with visitors to the Arden residence in a manner consistent with drug deals. An officer then secured a search warrant for the Arden residence. On August 17, 2005, officers detained Hilliard outside of the Arden residence and executed the search warrant on the property. While detained, Hilliard told officers he had a handgun under his bed pillow, stating "every man should have a gun in his house." Upon searching Hilliard's bedroom in the Arden residence, officers found a .357 Magnum revolver beneath a pillow on Hilliard's bed. Officers also found approximately 237 grams of crack cocaine in the kitchen, which was just down the hall from Hilliard's bedroom. Additionally, officers found several items of expensive jewelry and $791 in money orders within the Arden residence, and later discovered over $1,100 cash on Hilliard's person.

Following Hilliard's arrest for possession of the firearm and crack cocaine, officers took Hilliard to the police station for booking, where Hilliard admitted in a written statement he possessed the crack cocaine "to pay bills." Hilliard also told officers the firearm belonged to him and he possessed the gun for protection. Hilliard admitted purchasing the firearm off the street, because, as a convicted felon, he could not legally purchase a firearm.

A grand jury indicted Hilliard on two counts of possession with intent to distribute cocaine base, in violation of 21 U.S.C. § 841; two counts of being a felon in possession of a firearm, in violation of 18 U.S.C. § 922(g)(1); and two counts of possession of a firearm in furtherance of a drug trafficking crime, in violation of 18 U.S.C. § 924(c). The district court denied Hilliard's motion to suppress. Thereafter, a jury convicted Hilliard on five of the six counts and acquitted him on one count of possession of a firearm in furtherance of a drug trafficking crime. The district court sentenced Hilliard to 270 months' imprisonment and 5 years' supervised release. This appeal followed. . . .

Hilliard contends there was insufficient evidence to support his conviction for possession of a firearm on August 17, 2005, in furtherance of a drug trafficking crime. We review de novo the denial of a motion for judgment of acquittal, *United States v. Guel-Contreras,* 468 F.3d 517, 521 (8th Cir.2006), viewing the evidence in the light most favorable to the government and accepting all reasonable inferences supporting the jury's verdict, *United States v. Johnson,* 474 F.3d 1044, 1048 (8th Cir.2007). "Jury verdicts are not lightly overturned." *United States v. Anwar,* 428 F.3d 1102, 1108 (8th Cir.2005) (quotation omitted), *cert. denied,* 547 U.S. 1072, 126 S.Ct. 1806, 164 L.Ed.2d 520 (2006). We must uphold the jury's verdict if there is an interpretation of the evidence that would allow a reasonable-minded jury to conclude guilt beyond a reasonable doubt. *Johnson,* 474 F.3d at 1048.

To secure a conviction under § 924(c)(1)(A) for possession of a firearm in furtherance of a drug trafficking crime, "the government must present evidence from which a reasonable juror could find a 'nexus' between the defendant's possession of the charged firearm and the drug crime, such that this possession had the effect of 'furthering, advancing or helping forward' the drug crime." *United States v. Sanchez-Garcia,* 461 F.3d 939, 946 (8th Cir.2006) (quoting *United States v. Hamilton,* 332 F.3d 1144, 1149 (8th Cir.2003)). A defendant's simultaneous possession of drugs and a firearm, standing alone, is insufficient to sustain a conviction. *See United States v. Spencer,* 439 F.3d 905, 914 (8th Cir.2006). Rather, there must be evidence from which the jury could infer "the defendant's possession of the firearm facilitated the drug crime, through evidence that the firearm was used for protection, was kept near the drugs, or was in close proximity to the defendant during drug transactions." *Sanchez-Garcia,* 461 F.3d at 946–47.

Relying on this court's decision in *Spencer,* Hilliard argues there was no evidence any law enforcement officer ever observed Hilliard possess a firearm during what the officers believed to be drug transactions, and the utter absence of such evidence demonstrates Hilliard's conviction stems purely from his simultaneous possession of drugs and a firearm within the Arden residence. We disagree. The jury reasonably could have concluded Hilliard's possession of the firearm facilitated the crime of possession with intent to distribute cocaine base. On August 17, 2005, officers located the .357 Magnum in Hilliard's bedroom beneath a pillow on Hilliard's bed. Hilliard's bedroom was located just down the hall from the kitchen, where officers found a substantial quantity of crack cocaine. On the same day, officers also found several pieces of expensive jewelry and $791 in money orders in the Arden residence, and over $1,100 cash on Hilliard's person. Coupled with these facts is Hilliard's unequivocal admission to officers he kept the firearm for protection.

Additionally, the government presented expert testimony through Detective Edward Clay (Detective Clay) of the St. Louis Metropolitan Police Department about the common role of firearms in protecting drug dealers and the cash they often possess, "a role that this court has long recognized." *Id.* at 947. Detective Clay also testified powerful firearms like the one found in the Arden residence are effective for this purpose because such guns can be concealed easily. The firearm's close proximity to large quantities of drugs and valuable property, Detective Clay's expert testimony regarding the use of firearms in drug trafficking for protection, and Hilliard's own admission to officers he used the firearm for protection provides sufficient evidence to support Hilliard's conviction under § 924(c)(1)(A). *See, e.g., Sanchez-Garcia,* 461 F.3d at 946–47 (finding sufficient evidence to support the defendant's conviction under § 924(c) given the firearm's proximity to saleable quantities of drugs and to drug-packing paraphernalia, as well as expert testimony regarding the common use of firearms in drug trafficking). We therefore affirm the denial of Hilliard's motion for judgment of acquittal.

EXERCISE

As a defense attorney, you represent Phyllis Newton, the sole occupant of a house that was searched by police. During that search, police found a Norinco SKS assault rifle in the corner of Newton's bedroom, and a baggie of crack cocaine with a total weight of nine grams under a pot lid in the kitchen. The bedroom is on the second floor, and the kitchen is on the first. They also found $1,300 in Newton's purse.

Ms. Newton is charged with and convicted of possession with intent to distribute cocaine base and possession of a firearm in furtherance of a drug crime under § 924(c). You have preserved appeal on the question of sufficiency of the evidence. On appeal, how might you try to distinguish your case from *Hilliard*?

D. GUNS IN PROHIBITED PLACES

State laws often prohibit or limit the possession of guns in bars, schools, churches, and other locations. One such limitation of particular federal concern is the possession of firearms and other weapons on airplanes. One question that arises in some of those cases is the defendant's state of mind—that is, whether she knew she possessed a gun and intended to take it onto a plane. The case below involves the predecessor to a substantially similar statute that was enacted in 1994 at 49 U.S.C. § 46505, limiting the ability of commercial airline passengers to carry firearms in the cabin of a plane.

UNITED STATES V. GARRETT
984 F. 2d 1402 (5th Cir. 1993)

GARWOOD, CIRCUIT JUDGE:

Like many people trying to catch a plane around the holidays, Regina Kay Garrett was in a hurry. Unlike most, she forgot that she had a gun in her purse, or so she says. The principal question we decide today is whether the federal statute that criminalizes this conduct requires any degree of *mens rea* as an element of the offense. We hold that a "should have known" standard applies.

Facts and Proceedings Below

On December 18, 1990, Regina Kay Garrett was a ticketed passenger for and attempted to board flight 457 of L'Express Airlines, a regularly scheduled commercial commuter airline, from New Orleans to Alexandria, Louisiana. Passing through the New Orleans airport security, Garrett was stopped when the security guard monitoring the X-ray scanner noticed a dark mass in the hand bag that Garrett had placed on the conveyor belt. A consensual search of the bag was conducted and a small hand gun was discovered therein. The gun, a Browning .25 caliber semi-automatic, was loaded with six rounds in the magazine and one in the chamber. Garrett told security personnel that she had forgotten that the gun was in her purse.

Garrett was charged in a one count bill of information with attempting to board an aircraft with a concealed weapon in violation of the Federal Aviation Act (the Act or the statute). *See* 49 U.S.C.App. § 1472(*l*)(1). Garrett waived her right to a jury trial and the cause was tried by consent before a United States Magistrate Judge. On January 14, 1992, the magistrate denied Garrett's motion to dismiss the bill of information. On January 23, 1992, a bench trial was held and Garrett was found guilty. Garrett was sentenced to five years' probation and a $25 special assessment. As a special condition of probation, the magistrate ordered Garrett to reside for six months in a halfway house. Garrett appealed her conviction and sentence to the district court, 18 U.S.C. § 3402, and, on May 5, 1992, the district court affirmed the magistrate's decision. Garrett made a timely appeal to this Court. 28 U.S.C. § 1291.

Discussion

. . . Garrett argues that . . . her conviction is invalid because the magistrate did not find that she had actual knowledge that the gun was in her purse. . . .

Garrett's next argument on appeal is that her conviction should be overturned because the government did not prove, nor even attempt to prove, that she had knowledge that the gun was in her purse when she attempted to board the L'Express flight. The government's position is that section 1472(*l*)(1) is a strict liability offense and contains no intent requirement whatsoever. The magistrate, eschewing both extremes, declared that "this Court is of the opinion that it would be consistent with Fifth Circuit jurisprudence and the United States Constitution to apply a 'should have known' standard to this misdemeanor offense." We agree.

A.

Whether section 1472(*l*)(1) contains a *mens rea* requirement is a question that a number of other circuit courts seemingly addressed during the 1970's. The government cites *United States v. Flum,* 518 F.2d 39 (8th Cir.) (en banc), *cert. denied,* 423 U.S. 1018, 96 S.Ct. 454, 46 L.Ed.2d 390 (1975); *United States v. Dishman,* 486 F.2d 727 (9th Cir.1973); and *United States v. Margraf,* 483 F.2d 708 (3d Cir.) (en banc), *vacated and remanded,* 414 U.S. 1106, 94 S.Ct. 833, 38 L.Ed.2d 734 (1973); for the proposition that section 1472(*l*)(1) contains no intent requirement. Garrett offers *United States v. Lee,* 539 F.2d 606 (6th Cir.1976), for the counter proposition. We believe that none of these courts were squarely presented with, or actually decided, the precise issue before us.

In *Flum,* the defendant attempted to board an aircraft with a switchblade and a butcher knife in his carry-on baggage. The issue in *Flum,* however, was not whether the defendant knew that he was carrying the knives, but rather whether he had intended to *conceal* them:

> "In this appeal Flum contends that he was convicted upon insufficient evidence since there was no evidence tending to establish that he *intended to conceal the knives* which were discovered during a preboarding search of his carry-on luggage and personal belongings." 518 F.2d at 40 (footnote omitted; emphasis added).

There is no suggestion in *Flum* that the defendant did not know that he was carrying the knives. Indeed, the court pointedly observed that, "No issue of scienter is present in this case. It is undisputed that defendant knew the nature and approximate location of each of the knives." *Id.* at 44 n. 10. On the merits, the court held that intent to conceal is not an element of a section 1472(*l*) violation.

In *Dishman,* the defendant was carrying a .22 caliber starter pistol. The question presented to the Ninth Circuit was whether the gun, which was capable only of firing blanks, was a "deadly or dangerous weapon" within the meaning of the statute. (The answer was yes.) Thus, despite such general statements as "[s]ubsection (*l*) is a non-intent statute," 486 F.2d at 732, it is clear that the defendant's knowledge was not an issue before the *Dishman* court. To the extent that *Dishman* discussed an intent requirement, what the court said was that, to be guilty of violating section 1472(*l*), one need not intend to use the weapon in a dangerous way while in flight: "Any necessary element of present or later developed intent to make use of the 'deadly and dangerous' weapon in the commission of a crime while aboard the aircraft is conspicuous by its utter absence." *Id.* at 730.

In *Margraf,* the defendant attempted to board while carrying a folding pocket knife. The question before the Third Circuit was not whether the defendant knew that he was carrying the knife or what its physical characteristics were (which he plainly did), but rather whether he knew that the knife was legally a deadly or dangerous weapon. In other words, the knowledge issue in *Margraf* was whether section 1472(*l*) contains a specific intent requirement. To be sure, there is language in *Margraf* which would suggest a broader reading. *See, e.g.,* 483 F.2d at 720 (Seitz, C.J., dissenting) ("Under the majority's standard, no intent or knowledge of any kind is required for conviction."). However, there is no doubt that the issue before *Margraf* was specific intent:

> "[Appellant] claims that it is necessary for the government to prove a specific intent to carry a 'concealed deadly or dangerous weapon' onto a plane in order for a defendant to be convicted. In other words, it is not sufficient for the government to show that a defendant was boarding a plane with a concealed deadly weapon on his person; it must go further and show that the defendant *was aware that his weapon was dangerous,* and knowing this, still intended to carry the weapon aboard." *Id.* at 709 (emphasis added).

The Third Circuit rejected this argument and instead affirmed the defendant's conviction on the ground that he "should have been aware that it could be used as a deadly weapon." *Id.* at 712.

The case cited by Garrett, *United States v. Lee,* is a procedurally peculiar case. The defendant-appellant, Billy Ray Lee, was stopped with a hand gun in his brief case. Lee claimed that he had placed the gun in the case the night before and had forgotten that it was there. Lee consented to be tried by a magistrate judge, who found him guilty as charged. On the issue of intent, the magistrate held that it was unnecessary to determine whether Lee knew that the gun was in his brief case, because the statute did not make intent an element of the offense. Lee appealed to the district court, which reversed on the ground that knowledge of the presence of the weapon is an element of the crime. The district court then remanded to the magistrate to determine whether Lee had knowingly possessed the gun. After the case was remanded, the magistrate denied Lee's motion seeking a jury trial, retried the case upon the same evidence, and once again found Lee guilty. The district court affirmed the magistrate's decision and Lee appealed to the Sixth Circuit. Lee raised as error both the magistrate's refusal to permit him to withdraw his earlier jury trial waiver and the holding that knowing possession was an element of section 1472(*l*).

The Sixth Circuit agreed with the district court that "§ 1472 required a finding that appellant knew of the presence of the concealed dangerous weapon." *Lee,* 539 F.2d at 608. In the very next sentence, however, the court explained that, "Nevertheless, Lee's conviction must be reversed because he should have been permitted to withdraw his consent to trial before a magistrate." Because Lee's conviction was reversed on that ground, the court's approval of the district court's conclusion as to section 1472(*l*)(1)'s *mens rea* requirement is dicta.

In sum, the precise issue before this Court was not present in *Flum, Dishman,* or *Margraf,* and was addressed in *Lee* only by dicta; we appear to be the first appellate court to pass on the question.

B.

In determining whether section 1472(*l*)(1) contains a *mens rea* requirement, our overarching task is to give effect to the intent of the

Congress. The Congress is fully capable of creating strict liability crimes when it is their intent to do so. *See Liparota v. United States,* 471 U.S. 419, 424, 105 S.Ct. 2084, 2087, 85 L.Ed.2d 434 (1985) ("The definition of the elements of a criminal offense is entrusted to the legislature, particularly in the case of federal crimes, which are solely creatures of statute.") (citation omitted). Of course, the Congress cannot do so in a way that transgresses constitutional boundaries. Accordingly, to give due respect both to the will of the Congress and the mandate of the Constitution, we construe the acts of Congress, whenever possible, so as to avoid raising serious constitutional questions. *See, e.g., Public Citizen v. United States Dep't of Justice,* 491 U.S. 440, 464–69, 109 S.Ct. 2558, 2572–73, 105 L.Ed.2d 377 (1989).

Our effort to discern Congress' intent must begin, of course, with the statute's language. By its explicit terms, *see supra* note 2, the statute makes no mention of *mens rea.* But before going any further, we reject a textual argument made by the government. That section 1472(*l*)(1) contains no *mens rea* requirement, the government maintains, must be inferred from the fact that the very next subsection does so explicitly. Variations of this argument have been made before. *Cf. Margraf,* 483 F.2d at 710. To be sure, the fact that section 1472(*l*)(2) speaks of willful or reckless violations of section 1472(*l*)(1) is convincing evidence that one need not act willfully or recklessly to violate section 1472(*l*)(1).

One cannot infer from section 1472(*l*)(2), however, that section 1472(*l*)(1) contains *no mens rea* requirement *whatsoever.* There is a range of culpability between recklessness or willfulness, on the one hand, and total blamelessness, on the other, the most familiar of which is ordinary negligence. Therefore, the absence of knowledge is not the necessary converse of willfulness. So too, in some contexts, it takes more than knowledge for a violation to be willful. *See, e.g., Cheek v. United States,* 498 U.S. 192, 199–204, 111 S.Ct. 604, 609–12, 112 L.Ed.2d 617 (1991) (conviction for willful failure to file a federal income tax return and willful evasion of income taxes requires the voluntary, intentional violation of a known legal duty).

Thus, we are left with a statute which is, as we see it, silent on the question of *mens rea.* Yet, "certainly far more than the simple omission of the appropriate phrase from the statutory definition is necessary to justify dispensing with an intent requirement." *United States v. United States Gypsum Co.,* 438 U.S. 422, 438, 98 S.Ct. 2864, 2874, 57 L.Ed.2d 854 (1978). The requirement of *mens rea* as predicate to criminal liability is a fundamental precept of the Anglo-American common law. As Justice Jackson eloquently stated:

> "The contention that an injury can amount to a crime only when inflicted by intention is no provincial or transient notion. It is as universal and persistent in mature systems of law as belief in

freedom of the human will and a consequent ability and duty of the normal individual to choose between good and evil." *Morissette v. United States,* 342 U.S. 246, 250, 72 S.Ct. 240, 243, 96 L.Ed. 288 (1952) (footnote omitted).

So deeply rooted is this tradition that it is presumed that the Congress intended to incorporate some requirement of *mens rea* in its definition of federal crimes, although that presumption is rebuttable. Accordingly, "the failure of Congress explicitly and unambiguously to indicate whether *mens rea* is required does not signal a departure from this background assumption of our criminal law." *Liparota,* 471 U.S. at 426, 105 S.Ct. at 2088. *See also* 1 W. LaFave & A. Scott, Substantive Criminal Law § 5.1, at 579 (1986) ("the absence of words in the statute requiring a certain mental state does not warrant the assumption that the legislature intended to impose strict liability"). In short, we will presume that Congress intended to require some degree of *mens rea* as part of a federal criminal offense absent evidence of a contrary congressional intent.

This presumption is well established, too, in the case law of this Circuit. A seminal case in this regard is *United States v. Delahoussaye,* 573 F.2d 910 (5th Cir.1978), in which defendants were convicted of duck hunting in violation of federal regulations promulgated pursuant to the Migratory Bird Treaty Act, 16 U.S.C. § 703 *et seq.* These regulations, 50 C.F.R. § 20.21(i), prohibit the shooting of migratory game birds over a baited field. Reasoning that hunters might innocently violate these regulations by hunting over a field without knowledge that it was baited, we held that "a minimum form of scienter—the 'should have known' form—is a necessary element of the offense." *Id.* at 912. "Any other interpretation," we said, "would simply render criminal conviction an unavoidable occasional consequence of duck hunting." *Id.* at 912–13.

In *United States v. Anderson,* 885 F.2d 1248 (5th Cir.1989) (en banc), defendant was convicted of violating the National Firearms Act, 26 U.S.C. § 5861 *et seq.* Concluding that this Court's "precedent permitting conviction of certain felonies without proof of *mens rea* . . . is aberrational in our jurisprudence," *id.* at 1249, we reversed his conviction on the ground that the government had failed to prove that he knew that the guns were automatic weapons (and hence prohibited by the Act). We said at the time:

> "We think it far too severe for our community to bear—and plainly not intended by Congress—to subject to ten years' imprisonment one who possesses what appears to be, and what he innocently and reasonably believes to be, a wholly ordinary and legal pistol merely because it has been, unknown to him, modified to be fully automatic." *Anderson,* 885 F.2d at 1254 (footnote omitted).

In *United States v. Wallington,* 889 F.2d 573 (5th Cir.1989), defendant was convicted of divulging information that he had obtained within the scope of his official duties as a United States Customs agent in violation of 18

U.S.C. § 1905. We rejected his arguments that the statute was overbroad and vague by construing it narrowly to apply only to information that the employee knows to be confidential. "We do not believe that Congress intended to create strict criminal liability and impose prison sentences of up to one year for innocent disclosures of information." *Id.* at 578.

In *United States v. Nguyen,* 916 F.2d 1016 (5th Cir.1990), defendant was convicted of possessing and importing a threatened species of sea turtle (*caretta caretta*) in violation of the Endangered Species Act, 16 U.S.C. § 1531 *et seq.* We affirmed and held that the Act contained no specific intent requirement: "it is sufficient that Nguyen knew that he was in possession of a turtle. The government was not required to prove that Nguyen knew that this turtle is a threatened species or that it is illegal to transport or import it." *Id.* at 1018. We distinguished *Anderson,* and refrained from reading into the Act a more demanding *mens rea* requirement, because Congress had made its intent clear: "The [House] committee explicitly stated that it did 'not intend to make knowledge of the law an element of either civil penalty or criminal violations of the Act.'" *Id.* at 1019 (quoting the legislative history).

Here, the text of section 1472(*l*)(1) provides no indication that the Congress intended to depart from the default rule of requiring some *mens rea*. Nor is there anything in the legislative history of the Federal Aviation Act that would lead us to believe that the Congress intended section 1472(*l*)(1) to be a wholly strict liability offense. At the same time, we think that a serious due process problem would be raised by application of this statute, which carries fairly substantial penalties, to someone who did not know and had no reason to know that he was carrying a weapon. *Cf. United States v. Lee,* 383 F.Supp. 1033, 1035 (E.D.Tenn.1974). Avoiding such a construction of section 1472(*l*)(1), moreover, would comport with the so-called "rule of lenity"—the principle that ambiguous criminal statutes should be construed in favor of the defendant. Therefore, in light of the principles laid down by the Supreme Court and our case law, we cannot conclude that the Congress intended section 1472(*l*)(1) to reach persons acting without any *mens rea* whatsoever.

C.

Having declined to construe section 1472(*l*)(1) as a strict liability crime, it remains to be determined what level of mental culpability will support a conviction under it. We believe that the minimum level of *scienter*—the "should have known" standard—is appropriate and consistent with our case law.

The touchstone in our analysis is the severity of the punishment authorized by the statute. *See* 1 LaFave & Scott, *supra,* § 3.8, at 343 ("Other things being equal, the greater the possible punishment, the more likely some fault is required; and, conversely, the lighter the possible punishment, the more likely the legislature meant to impose liability without fault.")

(footnote omitted). A violation of section 1472(*l*)(1) is punishable by a fine of up to $10,000 and a prison sentence of up to one year. Therefore, a violation of section 1472(*l*)(1), although a non-petty offense, is still a misdemeanor.

We believe that a "should have known" standard is consistent with our prior cases in this area. This case is most akin to *Delahoussaye,* in which we also applied a "should have known" standard. In *Delahoussaye,* as here, the crime at issue was a misdemeanor, although one punishable by a maximum of only six months in prison rather than one year. We decline today to go as far as *Anderson,* in which we required actual knowledge, because the crime at issue in that case was a felony that carried a possible sentence of ten years imprisonment. *See Nguyen,* 916 F.2d at 1016 (distinguishing *Anderson* on the ground that it involved a felony).

The outcome of *Wallington* may appear somewhat anomalous when compared to *Delahoussaye, Anderson,* and our decision today. In *Wallington,* the statute at issue, 18 U.S.C. § 1905, prohibited government agents from disclosing confidential information acquired during the performance of their duties. As here, the crime was a Class A misdemeanor with a one year maximum sentence. Nevertheless, we construed section 1905 as requiring knowledge on the part of its violators that the information was confidential. What distinguishes *Wallington,* we think, is that it was a First Amendment case. The defendant in *Wallington* had argued that the statute was impermissibly overbroad in that it would punish even innocent disclosures of information. We gave the statute a narrow construction to avoid a serious First Amendment question:

> "At least in a substantial number of cases, the requirement that government employees refrain from *knowingly* disclosing confidential information contained in government files or collected in the scope of their official duties will strike a permissible balance between the First Amendment and the practical necessities of public service." *Wallington,* 889 F.2d at 579 (emphasis added).

It seems apparent that the *Wallington* court believed a high level of *mens rea* was required for section 1905 in order to avoid serious questions of the law's validity under the First Amendment. The government may certainly penalize the deliberate disclosure of confidential information. *See, e.g., Haig v. Agee,* 453 U.S. 280, 101 S.Ct. 2766, 69 L.Ed.2d 640 (1981) (upholding revocation of passport of former CIA employee who had pledged to reveal the identities of undercover CIA agents). Nevertheless, public employees do not surrender their free speech rights completely. *See, e.g., Rankin v. McPherson,* 483 U.S. 378, 107 S.Ct. 2891, 97 L.Ed.2d 315 (1987).

Thus, *Wallington* was concerned that a serious First Amendment problem might attend any attempt to attach criminal sanctions to a public employee who in good faith, albeit negligently, believed the information disclosed was not confidential. In *Pickering v. Board of Education,* 391 U.S. 563, 88 S.Ct. 1731, 20 L.Ed.2d 811 (1968), the Supreme Court held that a public school teacher may not be dismissed for sending to a local newspaper a letter critical of the board of education "absent proof of false statements *knowingly or recklessly made by him.*" *Id.* at 574, 88 S.Ct. at 1738(emphasis added); *id.* at 582, 88 S.Ct. at 1742 (White, J., dissenting in part) ("The Court holds that truthful statements by a school teacher critical of the school board are within the ambit of the First Amendment. So also are false statements *innocently or negligently made.*") (emphasis added). *See also Florida Star v. B.J.F.,* 491 U.S. 524, 538, 109 S.Ct. 2603, 2612, 105 L.Ed.2d 443 (1989) (reversing award of damages for publishing name of rape victim under state law imposing liability without regard to *scienter* or degree of fault); *see also id.* at 546, 109 S.Ct. at 2616 (White, J., dissenting); *United States v. Hicks,* 980 F.2d 963, 973–74 & nn. 15–16 (5th Cir.1992) (crime of intimidating flight crew members, by use of vulgar and profane language, requires knowing violation). In short, *Wallington* demanded a high level of *mens rea* in the context of a statute that raised serious First Amendment concerns. That is not the case here.

We conclude that one violates section 1472(*l*)(1) if, but only if, she either knew or should have known that the concealed weapon in question was on or about her person or property while aboard or attempting to board the aircraft.

D.

There is ample evidence in the record to support the magistrate's conclusion that Garrett should have known that she was carrying the gun when she attempted to board by going through security. Garrett testified that she had traveled by air many times and that she was aware that it was illegal to try to bring a gun through airport security. And if she needed any reminder, there were two large signs in the area of the security checkpoint. The first sign, printed with large white letters upon a bright red background, stated: "CARRY NO WEAPONS OR EXPLOSIVES BEYOND THIS POINT: VIOLATORS ARE SUBJECT TO PROSECUTION UNDER FEDERAL CRIMINAL STATUTES REQUIRING PENALTIES AND/OR IMPRISONMENT." The sign also had an image of a pistol and a knife over which was superimposed a circle and a diagonal line. The other sign displayed a list of "Federal Safety and Security Inspection Rules" and informed passengers, among other things, that, "Federal regulations prohibit persons from having a FIREARM, explosive or incendiary-device on or about their person or accessible property when entering or in an airport sterile area or while aboard an aircraft."

It is also relevant that the gun was in Garrett's hand bag. Garrett testified that she owns and uses seven or eight purses and that she did not remember when she put the gun in this particular bag, which was described at trial as a large leather satchel. She stated that she did not put the gun in the bag on the day of the flight, nor did she think that day to check the bag for it. On the other hand, she testified that she knew that she previously had carried the gun in that particular bag. Garrett also testified that she had put her wallet, checkbook, and makeup in the bag on the day in question. It is inferable that she would have used the bag during the day. We think it patently reasonable to require individuals in such circumstances to be aware of the presence of a firearm in their purse or equivalent bag, or, indeed, to infer that they actually have such knowledge.

In short, there is sufficient evidence in the record to support the magistrate's finding that Garrett should have known that she was carrying a firearm.

EXERCISE

You are a defense attorney representing Leo Rightway, who was stopped at an airport checkpoint with a small handgun in his carry-on bag. Rightway asserted at the time of his arrest that he had his wife's bag and did not know that she had left her gun in the car. Rightway has a two prior misdemeanor convictions: one for carrying a gun on school grounds, and another for purchasing a gun without proper documentation.

You meet with Rightway and he is adamant that he did not know the gun was in his bag. He explains that he rarely travels by plane, but his wife, Jane Rightway, often does. She has a black canvas carry-on bag with one large compartment and a separate zippered compartment on the inside of the bag. He borrowed the bag from Jane for his trip. The gun, which is very small and light, was in the zippered compartment. He put his things in the main compartment, and never noticed the zippered compartment. Jane contacts you and says she is willing to testify that it is her gun, that she forgot it was in the bag, and that she did not tell her husband it was in the bag.

The government has offered to plead the case out to a felony conviction with a sentence of two years probation in lieu of incarceration. Assuming that the law applied to the case above applies here, do you recommend that Mr. Rightway take the deal?

We might expect federal laws to prohibit possession of guns on planes and in some sensitive federal facilities, and they do (as we saw in the previous case). However, Congress has extended federal statutes beyond these areas. For example, 18 U.S.C. § 922(q) specifically bars the possession of guns in and around schools. This version is a reformulation of the law,[1] passed after a prior version was found unconstitutional by the

---

[1]　Omnibus Consolidated Appropriations Act, 110 Stat. 309 (1996).

476 FIREARMS CH. 7

Supreme Court due to the lack of a sufficient nexus to interstate commerce.[2] The current version is more precise, and contains several big exceptions:

(q)(1) The Congress finds and declares that—

(A) crime, particularly crime involving drugs and guns, is a pervasive, nationwide problem;

(B) crime at the local level is exacerbated by the interstate movement of drugs, guns, and criminal gangs;

(C) firearms and ammunition move easily in interstate commerce and have been found in increasing numbers in and around schools, as documented in numerous hearings in both the Committee on the Judiciary the House of Representatives and the Committee on the Judiciary of the Senate;

(D) in fact, even before the sale of a firearm, the gun, its component parts, ammunition, and the raw materials from which they are made have considerably moved in interstate commerce;

(E) while criminals freely move from State to State, ordinary citizens and foreign visitors may fear to travel to or through certain parts of the country due to concern about violent crime and gun violence, and parents may decline to send their children to school for the same reason;

(F) the occurrence of violent crime in school zones has resulted in a decline in the quality of education in our country;

(G) this decline in the quality of education has an adverse impact on interstate commerce and the foreign commerce of the United States;

(H) States, localities, and school systems find it almost impossible to handle gun-related crime by themselves—even States, localities, and school systems that have made strong efforts to prevent, detect, and punish gun-related crime find their efforts unavailing due in part to the failure or inability of other States or localities to take strong measures; and

(I) the Congress has the power, under the interstate commerce clause and other provisions of the Constitution, to enact measures to ensure the integrity and safety of the Nation's schools by enactment of this subsection.

(2)(A) It shall be unlawful for any individual knowingly to possess a firearm that has moved in or that otherwise affects

---

[2] United States v. Lopez, 514 U.S. 549 (1995).

interstate or foreign commerce at a place that the individual knows, or has reasonable cause to believe, is a school zone.

(B) Subparagraph (A) does not apply to the possession of a firearm—

   (i) on private property not part of school grounds;

   (ii) if the individual possessing the firearm is licensed to do so by the State in which the school zone is located or a political subdivision of the State, and the law of the State or political subdivision requires that, before an individual obtains such a license, the law enforcement authorities of the State or political subdivision verify that the individual is qualified under law to receive the license;

   (iii) that is—

      (I) not loaded; and

      (II) in a locked container, or a locked firearms rack that is on a motor vehicle;

   (iv) by an individual for use in a program approved by a school in the school zone;

   (v) by an individual in accordance with a contract entered into between a school in the school zone and the individual or an employer of the individual;

   (vi) by a law enforcement officer acting in his or her official capacity; or

   (vii) that is unloaded and is possessed by an individual while traversing school premises for the purpose of gaining access to public or private lands open to hunting, if the entry on school premises is authorized by school authorities.

As one might guess, the definition of a school zone is crucial to the employment of the gun-free school zone law. That definition is found at 18 U.S.C. § 921(a)(25):

(25) The term "school zone" means—

   (A) in, or on the grounds of, a public, parochial or private school; or

   (B) within a distance of 1,000 feet from the grounds of a public, parochial or private school.

The gun-free school law contains an explicit knowledge requirement: the government must prove that the defendant possessed the gun someplace where the defendant "knows, or has reasonable cause to believe, is a school zone."

Because of the 1,000-foot radius, that element can become a point of contention.

UNITED STATES V. GUZMÁN-MONTANEZ
756 F.3d 1 (1st Cir. 2014)

GELPÍ, DISTRICT JUDGE.

A jury in the District of Puerto Rico convicted Marcelino Guzmán-Montañez ("Guzmán") for being a felon in possession of a firearm in violation of 18 U.S.C. § 922(g)(1) ("count one"), and for possession of a firearm in a school zone in violation of 18 U.S.C. §§ 922(q)(2)(A) & 924(a)(4) ("count two"). The District Court sentenced Guzmán to 60 months of imprisonment as to both counts.

On appeal Guzmán raises the following claims of error. First, he argues that the district court improperly admitted evidence that was both irrelevant and unfairly prejudicial. Second, he posits that the evidence presented by the government during trial was insufficient to sustain his convictions as to both counts. Finally, he contends that the sentence imposed upon him was procedurally and substantively unreasonable. We affirm the conviction as to the felon in possession count. However, we reverse the conviction and sentence as to the possession of a firearm in a school zone count. We discuss Guzmán's claims seriatim.

I.   Relevant Factual and Procedural Background

During the morning hours of March 14, 2012, Santiago Nieves-Rivera ("Nieves"), owner of a *lechonera* restaurant in Bayamón, Puerto Rico, saw a burgundy-colored car drive slowly by his establishment. Just then, the vehicle backed up and returned to his establishment. Two men exited the vehicle. They approached Nieves to order fritters. One of these men was Guzmán. Nieves found the situation very suspicious. Nervous, afraid, and while firmly holding his machete, Nieves asked both men to leave. At that moment, he noticed a silver gun tucked on the side of the waist of one of the men as they were exiting. The man carrying the gun was later identified as "the skinny one" (hereinafter "the other suspect"). As soon as they left, Nieves called the police and reported the events. He provided a physical description of the suspects and their vehicle, a burgundy Suzuki SX4 with license plate number HPH 299. Nieves did not see Guzmán carrying a gun.

The event was broadcast over the police radio as an attempted robbery. Police Officer Carmen Nieves de Jesús ("Nieves de Jesús"), while on patrol duty, subsequently saw two men exiting a vehicle parked in front of a Church's Chicken fast food restaurant at the Rexville Shopping Center in

Bayamón. The men and vehicle matched the description she heard over the radio. Quickly, she reported her identification of the individuals via radio broadcast. Officer Edilberto Mojica-Caldero ("Mojica") was patrolling the area together with officer José Arroyo-Pérez ("Arroyo-Pérez"). They heard Nieves de Jesús's radio call and headed towards the area. At the time, both police officers were wearing civilian clothing.

As Mojica and Arroyo-Pérez approached the Church's Chicken parking lot, they spotted the burgundy Suzuki vehicle. Arroyo-Pérez remained near the vehicle while Mojica observed the two men from outside the fast food restaurant. Mojica watched as Guzmán stood in line to order food. Then, he noticed a black pistol protruding from Guzmán's waistband.

From that moment on, the following events took place rapidly. Outside, marked patrol cars arrived. Immediately, the other suspect approached Guzmán and whispered something in his ear. Without delay, Guzmán left the line and walked quickly towards the bathroom. He entered the bathroom for a brief moment. As Guzmán exited the bathroom, Mojica entered the restaurant and detained both men. However, Guzmán was no longer carrying in his waistline the object Mojica had seen on him moments earlier. As the suspects were detained, officers Arroyo-Pérez and Ismael Díaz-Rivera ("Díaz") entered the bathroom searching for additional suspects. None were found.

Following the other officers' search, Mojica then searched the bathroom and found a pistol in the diaper changing station. The pistol was in plain sight, stuck between the plastic partitions of the diaper changing station. The firearm was a black Smith and Wesson pistol, model 4003 tactical, .40 caliber. The police officers who searched the bathroom before Mojica did not see the weapon. In turn, Guzmán and the other suspect were placed under arrest. Shortly thereafter, the police officers searched the burgundy Suzuki vehicle. They seized a silver Beretta pistol found inside the glove compartment. The weapon matched the description of the gun Nieves reported seeing the other suspect carry at the *lechonera*.

On March 15, 2012, a complaint was filed against Guzmán charging him with being a convicted felon in possession of a firearm. Shortly thereafter, a federal grand jury returned a two-count indictment. Both counts charged Guzmán with possessing a Smith and Wesson pistol, Model 4003 tactical, serial number VJL7561, .40 caliber. Count one charged Guzmán with being a felon in possession of a firearm in violation of 18 U.S.C. § 922(g)(1). Count two, in turn, charged him with possessing a firearm in a school zone in violation of 18 U.S.C. §§ 922(q)(2)(A) & 924(a)(4). Guzmán exercised his constitutional right to trial by jury. . . .

Regarding the second count, to prove that the events took place within a school zone, in violation of 18 U.S.C. §§ 922(q)(2)(A) & 924(a)(4), the prosecution used Mojica's testimony to establish the proximity between Church's Chicken and the Colegio Emmanuel Discípulos de Cristo ("the school"), as well as Guzmán's knowledge of being within the requisite distance. According to Mojica, the school is located 300 feet away from Church's Chicken and is visible from inside the establishment. The government also submitted as evidence a picture of the school's main gate.

After the prosecution rested, Guzmán filed a motion for acquittal under Rule 29 of the Federal Rules of Criminal Procedure, arguing that the prosecution's evidence was insufficient to sustain his convictions. The District Court denied Guzmán's motion as to count one and reserved its judgment as to count two.

The jury convicted Guzmán on both counts. After the verdict, Guzmán filed a subsequent motion under Rule 29 as to count two, since the District Court had not yet ruled on his earlier acquittal motion. The Court denied Guzmán's motion for acquittal. . . .

Under 18 U.S.C. § 922(q)(2)(A) "[i]t shall be unlawful for any individual knowingly to possess a firearm that has moved in or that otherwise affects interstate or foreign commerce at a place that the individual knows, or has reasonable cause to believe, is a school zone." A school zone is an area within a school or "within a distance of 1,000 feet from the grounds of a public, parochial or private school." 18 U.S.C. § 921(a)(25); *see United States v. Nieves-Castaño,* 480 F.3d 597 (1st Cir.2007). Guzmán contends that the prosecution's evidence was insufficient to prove the requisite element that he knew or reasonably should have known he was in a school zone while possessing a firearm. We agree.

Colegio Emmanuel de Discipulos de Cristo is a school, as defined by 18 U.S.C. § 922(q)(2)(A), that teaches pre-kindergarten to sixth grade. The school is located on Route 167, across the street from Rexville Shopping Center in Bayamon, where the Church's Chicken is located. The parties stipulated the distance between Church's Chicken and the school was less than 1,000 feet.

At trial Mojica stated that the school was visible from within the establishment, but provided no additional information. No other witness testified as to this matter. Mojica's entire testimony follows:

> MS. MONTANEZ: Q. All these events took place—this in particular of the Church and the finding of the Smith & Wesson pistol—in Church. What is nearby that restaurant?
>
> A. In the front side of the establishment there's a bilingual school for children, primary level.
>
> Q. And how far is that school from the Church's restaurant?
>
> A. I'd say less than 300 feet.
>
> Q. Okay. And how do you know that?
>
> A. I measured it.

Q. Can you see the school from the Church?

A. Correct, yes.

Q. How do you measure the distance from the Church's Chicken restaurant to the school?

A. With a scene measuring device from the traffic unit in Bayamón. From the door—

. . .

THE WITNESS: From the door towards the main gate of said school.

BY MS. MONTANEZ:

Q. And that scene measuring device you took it from where, you said?

A. That was given to me by one of the agents of the traffic division in Bayamón which—and it's used for investigation of deathly accidents.

Q. From which door you started your measurement?

A. From the main door of the establishment. That's the one I went through.

Q. Until?

A. Up to the main gate of Emmanuel school. That's the name of it.

MS. MONTANEZ: I have no more questions, Your Honor.

THE COURT: I have—let me—when you say the school main gate, do you mean the school has a fence?

THE WITNESS: Correct, yes.

THE COURT: And the gate is on that fence, and you measured to that point.

THE WITNESS: Up to the entrance gate. Yes, sir.

THE COURT: All right. Thank you. Cross-examination?

MS. MONTANEZ: Your Honor, I have, before the defense goes, the picture of the school.

THE COURT: Well, you're going to have to show it to—

MS. MONTANEZ: Yes. We can mark this as Government ID 14. (NOTE: Document being provided to the witness.)

Q. I'm showing you what has been marked as Government ID No. 14. Do you recognize that identification?

A. Yes. This is school area which is across the—from the shopping center.

Q. And why do you recognize that identification?

A. I go by it every day.

MS. MONTANEZ: Your Honor, we move into evidence Government's Identification No. 14.

THE COURT: Any objection, Mr.—

MR. GONZALEZ: No objection, Your Honor.

THE COURT: Without objection, admitted as Government's Exhibit No. 14. Do you want to publish it? (NOTE: Document retrieved from the witness.)

BY MS. MONTANEZ:

Q. I'm showing you what has been marked as Government Exhibit number 14. What does this picture show?

A. That's Emmanuel school.

Q. And is that—this is the fence you were referring to that you measured—up until the point you measured from the Church Chicken door (indicating)?

A. Correct. Yes.

Relying exclusively on the school's proximity, the prosecution took no additional measures to provide grounds to evince that Guzmán knew, or reasonably should have known, that he was in a school zone. Instead, it relied on the closeness factor as per se probative of Guzmán's awareness. Mojica specifically testified that the school, and its main gate, were visible from Church's Chicken. The record, however, shows that he failed to testify that the school's sign was visible from Church's Chicken. In fact, the school sign was first mentioned after the prosecution rested its case.

In *United States v. Haywood,* 363 F.3d 200 (3rd Cir.2004), the Court of Appeals for the Third Circuit reversed a conviction under § 922(q)(2)(A) on insufficiency grounds. As in the case before us, appellant similarly argued that providing evidence of a school's distance was insufficient to establish his knowledge of a school zone. The court agreed. "[T]he only evidence that the government produced to support this conviction is that the school is, in fact, within 500 feet of the [locale where Haywood was found armed]. However, that is not sufficiently conclusive to enable a reasonable juror to draw the inference that Haywood knew or should have known of that proximity." *Haywood,* 363 F.3d at 209. We find said ruling to be squarely on point.

It is likely that the prosecution could have shown that Guzmán had the knowledge of the nearby school, but it failed to introduce such evidence at trial. Juxtaposing the location of the fast food restaurant with the school is not enough. Additional facts were necessary, and could have easily been proven by way of testimony of police officers who were at the scene, as well as photographs or a video demonstrating that any reasonable person at the Church's Chicken would have indeed become aware of being in a school zone. The prosecution likewise could have also demonstrated that to get to the establishment Guzmán inevitably would have driven by the school. More so, because Guzmán did not live in the neighborhood, his awareness had to be readily proven. *Cf. Nieves-Castaño,* 480 F.3d at 604("Here, three minor children lived with the defendant, and it would be easy for a jury to conclude that she knew there were two schools nearby, within or just outside her housing project and less than 1000 feet away, and that she regularly passed by those schools. One school was, in fact, located next to the south entrance of the housing project."). In the case before us the government asked the jury to take a giant leap of faith, which falls considerably short of sufficiently proving its case.

The evidence presented by the government was insufficient to establish that Guzmán knew or reasonably should have known he was in a school zone. Consequently, the conviction as to count two must be vacated.

III. Conclusion

For the reasons explained above, we **AFFIRM** the conviction on count one, **REVERSE** the conviction on count two, and **REMAND** for resentencing proceedings consistent with this opinion.

EXERCISE

Armand lives in an apartment building three blocks (and 800 feet) from an elementary school. The neighborhood is somewhat dangerous. Armand runs a dry cleaning business which is on the same block and about 600 feet from the school.

One day Armand is at his apartment and his wife, Cindy, is working at the dry cleaning business. Cindy calls Armand and says that she is worried because "some suspicious characters are hanging around outside the door." Armand keeps a gun in a safe in his apartment but does not have a concealed carry permit. He removes the gun from the safe, puts it into his pocket, and runs down to the store. He enters the store through the rear, stows the gun under the counter, and talks to his wife. She points outside at the men she was talking about. Just then, the men she was talking about come into the business and announce themselves as narcotics agents from a state-federal task force. They ask if they can search the business, and Armand gives consent. The agents search the premises and find no drugs. They do find the gun, however, and Armand readily admits that it is his. He is then placed under arrest for possessing a gun in a school zone.

You are the federal prosecutor the case is referred to. The investigators have determined that Armand and his wife have no criminal history. Do you take the case or decline it?

CHAPTER EIGHT

IMMIGRATION

■ ■ ■

Most of the crimes we have examined thus far are often criminalized under both federal and state penal codes. Immigration, however, is almost entirely a federal concern. It plays a role in many state cases, however. For example, a state case may be impacted if the defendant is an undocumented alien subject to a detainer (a legal "hold" on their release from jail or prison) because of pending federal charges or a deportation order.

Many immigration cases are resolved through administrative and civil remedies, principally through deportation. Criminal law is often involved in four types of cases related to immigration: against those involved in immigrant smuggling, those who commit fraud to obtain residency or citizenship, where an alien returns to the United States after a prior deportation (particularly if they were deported after a crime was committed), and against those who employ undocumented aliens or abuse alien labor. We will look at each in turn. First, though, let's examine how federal law pre-empts state law in this area in a manner we do not see with narcotics or firearms.

A. FEDERAL CONTROL OF IMMIGRATION

ARIZONA V. UNITED STATES
567 U.S. 387 (2012)

JUSTICE KENNEDY delivered the opinion of the Court.

To address pressing issues related to the large number of aliens within its borders who do not have a lawful right to be in this country, the State of Arizona in 2010 enacted a statute called the Support Our Law Enforcement and Safe Neighborhoods Act. The law is often referred to as S.B. 1070, the version introduced in the State Senate. See also H.R. 2162, 49th Leg., 2d Reg. Sess. (2010) (amending S. 1070). Its stated purpose is to "discourage and deter the unlawful entry and presence of aliens and economic activity by persons unlawfully present in the United States." Note following Ariz.Rev.Stat. Ann. § 11–1051 (West 2012). The law's provisions establish an official state policy of "attrition through enforcement." *Ibid.* The question before the Court is whether federal law preempts and renders invalid four separate provisions of the state law.

I

The United States filed this suit against Arizona, seeking to enjoin S.B. 1070 as preempted. Four provisions of the law are at issue here. Two create new state offenses. Section 3 makes failure to comply with federal alien-registration requirements a state misdemeanor. Ariz.Rev.Stat. Ann. § 13–1509 (West Supp.2011). Section 5, in relevant part, makes it a misdemeanor for an unauthorized alien to seek or engage in work in the State; this provision is referred to as § 5(C). See § 13–2928(C). Two other provisions give specific arrest authority and investigative duties with respect to certain aliens to state and local law enforcement officers. Section 6 authorizes officers to arrest without a warrant a person "the officer has probable cause to believe . . . has committed any public offense that makes the person removable from the United States." § 13–3883(A)(5). Section 2(B) provides that officers who conduct a stop, detention, or arrest must in some circumstances make efforts to verify the person's immigration status with the Federal Government. See § 11–1051(B) (West 2012). . . .

The federal power to determine immigration policy is well settled. Immigration policy can affect trade, investment, tourism, and diplomatic relations for the entire Nation, as well as the perceptions and expectations of aliens in this country who seek the full protection of its laws. See, *e.g.,* Brief for United Mexican States as *Amici Curiae;* see also *Harisiades v. Shaughnessy,* 342 U.S. 580, 588–589, 72 S.Ct. 512, 96 L.Ed. 586 (1952). Perceived mistreatment of aliens in the United States may lead to harmful reciprocal treatment of American citizens abroad. See Brief for Madeleine K. Albright et al. as *Amici Curiae* 24–30.

It is fundamental that foreign countries concerned about the status, safety, and security of their nationals in the United States must be able to confer and communicate on this subject with one national sovereign, not the 50 separate States. See *Chy Lung v. Freeman,* 92 U.S. 275, 279–280, 23 L.Ed. 550 (1876); see also The Federalist No. 3, p. 39 (C. Rossiter ed. 2003) (J. Jay) (observing that federal power would be necessary in part because "bordering States . . . under the impulse of sudden irritation, and a quick sense of apparent interest or injury" might take action that would undermine foreign relations). This Court has reaffirmed that "[o]ne of the most important and delicate of all international relationships . . . has to do with the protection of the just rights of a country's own nationals when those nationals are in another country." *Hines v. Davidowitz,* 312 U.S. 52, 64, 61 S.Ct. 399, 85 L.Ed. 581 (1941).

Federal governance of immigration and alien status is extensive and complex. Congress has specified categories of aliens who may not be admitted to the United States. See 8 U.S.C. § 1182. Unlawful entry and unlawful reentry into the country are federal offenses. §§ 1325, 1326. Once here, aliens are required to register with the Federal Government and to carry proof of status on their person. See §§ 1301–1306. Failure to do so is a federal misdemeanor. §§ 1304(e), 1306(a). Federal law also authorizes States to deny noncitizens a range of public benefits, § 1622; and it imposes sanctions on employers who hire unauthorized workers, § 1324a. . . .

Congress has specified which aliens may be removed from the United States and the procedures for doing so. Aliens may be removed if they were inadmissible at the time of entry, have been convicted of certain crimes, or meet other criteria set by federal law. See § 1227. Removal is a civil, not criminal, matter. A principal feature of the removal system is the broad discretion exercised by immigration officials. See Brief for Former Commissioners of the United States Immigration and Naturalization Service as *Amici Curiae* 8–13 (hereinafter Brief for Former INS Commissioners). Federal officials, as an initial matter, must decide whether it makes sense to pursue removal at all. If removal proceedings commence, aliens may seek asylum and other discretionary relief allowing them to remain in the country or at least to leave without formal removal. See § 1229a(c)(4); see also, *e.g.*, §§ 1158 (asylum), 1229b (cancellation of removal), 1229c (voluntary departure).

Discretion in the enforcement of immigration law embraces immediate human concerns.

Unauthorized workers trying to support their families, for example, likely pose less danger than alien smugglers or aliens who commit a serious crime. The equities of an individual case may turn on many factors, including whether the alien has children born in the United States, long ties to the community, or a record of distinguished military service. Some discretionary decisions involve policy choices that bear on this Nation's international relations. Returning an alien to his own country may be deemed inappropriate even where he has committed a removable offense or fails to meet the criteria for admission. The foreign state may be mired in civil war, complicit in political persecution, or enduring conditions that create a real risk that the alien or his family will be harmed upon return. The dynamic nature of relations with other countries requires the Executive Branch to ensure that enforcement policies are consistent with this Nation's foreign policy with respect to these and other realities.

Agencies in the Department of Homeland Security play a major role in enforcing the country's immigration laws. United States Customs and Border Protection (CBP) is responsible for determining the admissibility of aliens and securing the country's borders. See Dept. of Homeland Security, Office of Immigration Statistics, Immigration Enforcement Actions: 2010, p. 1 (2011). In 2010, CBP's Border Patrol apprehended almost half a million people. *Id.,* at 3. Immigration and Customs Enforcement (ICE), a second agency, "conducts criminal investigations involving the enforcement of immigration-related statutes." *Id.,* at 2. ICE also operates the Law Enforcement Support Center. LESC, as the Center is known, provides immigration status information to federal, state, and local officials around the clock. See App. 91. ICE officers are responsible "for the identification, apprehension, and removal of illegal aliens from the United States." Immigration Enforcement Actions, at 2. Hundreds of thousands of aliens are removed by the Federal Government every year. See *id.,* at 4 (reporting there were 387,242 removals, and 476,405 returns without a removal order, in 2010).

B

The pervasiveness of federal regulation does not diminish the importance of immigration policy to the States. Arizona bears many of the consequences of unlawful immigration. Hundreds of thousands of deportable aliens are apprehended in Arizona each year. Dept. of Homeland Security, Office of Immigration Statistics, 2010 Yearbook of Immigration Statistics 93 (2011) (Table 35). Unauthorized aliens who remain in the State constitute, by one estimate, almost 6% of the population. See J. Passel & D. Cohn, Pew Hispanic Center, U.S. Unauthorized Immigration Flows Are Down Sharply Since Mid-Decade 3 (2010). And in the State's most populous county, these aliens are reported to be responsible for a disproportionate share of serious crime. . . .

Federalism, central to the constitutional design, adopts the principle that both the National and State Governments have elements of sovereignty the other is bound to respect. See *Gregory v. Ashcroft,* 501 U.S. 452, 457, 111 S.Ct. 2395, 115 L.Ed.2d 410 (1991); *U.S. Term Limits, Inc. v. Thornton,* 514 U.S. 779, 838, 115 S.Ct. 1842, 131 L.Ed.2d 881 (1995) (KENNEDY, J., concurring). From the existence of two sovereigns follows the possibility that laws can be in conflict or at cross-purposes. The Supremacy Clause provides a clear rule that federal law "shall be the supreme Law of the Land; and the Judges in every State shall be bound thereby, any Thing in the Constitution or Laws of any state to the Contrary notwithstanding." Art. VI, cl. 2. Under this principle, Congress has the power to preempt state law. See *Crosby v. National Foreign Trade Council,* 530 U.S. 363, 372, 120 S.Ct. 2288, 147 L.Ed.2d 352 (2000); *Gibbons v. Ogden,* 9 Wheat. 1, 210–211, 6 L.Ed. 23 (1824). There is no doubt that Congress may withdraw specified powers from the States by enacting a statute containing an express preemption provision. See, *e.g., Chamber of Commerce of United States of America v. Whiting,* 563 U.S. 582, 592, 131 S.Ct. 1968, 1974–1975, 179 L.Ed.2d 1031 (2011).

State law must also give way to federal law in at least two other circumstances. First, the States are precluded from regulating conduct in a field that Congress, acting within its proper authority, has determined must be regulated by its exclusive governance. . . .

Second, state laws are preempted when they conflict with federal law. *Crosby, supra,* at 372, 120 S.Ct. 2288. This includes cases where "compliance with both federal and state regulations is a physical impossibility," *Florida Lime & Avocado Growers, Inc. v. Paul,* 373 U.S. 132,

142–143, 83 S.Ct. 1210, 10 L.Ed.2d 248 (1963), and those instances where the challenged state law "stands as an obstacle to the accomplishment and execution of the full purposes and objectives of Congress," *Hines,* 312 U.S., at 67, 61 S.Ct. 399. . . .

V

Immigration policy shapes the destiny of the Nation. On May 24, 2012, at one of this Nation's most distinguished museums of history, a dozen immigrants stood before the tattered flag that inspired Francis Scott Key to write the National Anthem. There they took the oath to become American citizens. The Smithsonian, News Release, Smithsonian Citizenship Ceremony Welcomes a Dozen New Americans (May 24, 2012), online at http://newsdesk.si.edu/releases. These naturalization ceremonies bring together men and women of different origins who now share a common destiny. They swear a common oath to renounce fidelity to foreign princes, to defend the Constitution, and to bear arms on behalf of the country when required by law. 8 CFR § 337.1(a). The history of the United States is in part made of the stories, talents, and lasting contributions of those who crossed oceans and deserts to come here.

The National Government has significant power to regulate immigration. With power comes responsibility, and the sound exercise of national power over immigration depends on the Nation's meeting its responsibility to base its laws on a political will informed by searching, thoughtful, rational civic discourse. Arizona may have understandable frustrations with the problems caused by illegal immigration while that process continues, but the State may not pursue policies that undermine federal law.

* * *

The United States has established that §§ 3, 5(C), and 6 of S.B. 1070 are preempted. . . .

JUSTICE SCALIA, concurring in part and dissenting in part.

The United States is an indivisible "Union of sovereign States." *Hinderlider v. La Plata River & Cherry Creek Ditch Co.,* 304 U.S. 92, 104, 58 S.Ct. 803, 82 L.Ed. 1202 (1938). Today's opinion, approving virtually all of the Ninth Circuit's injunction against enforcement of the four challenged provisions of Arizona's law, deprives States of what most would consider the defining characteristic of sovereignty: the power to exclude from the sovereign's territory people who have no right to be there. Neither the Constitution itself nor even any law passed by Congress supports this result. I dissent.

I

As a sovereign, Arizona has the inherent power to exclude persons from its territory, subject only to those limitations expressed in the Constitution or constitutionally imposed by Congress. That power to exclude has long been

[handwritten margin note: Arizona has the power to exclude]

recognized as inherent in sovereignty. Emer de Vattel's seminal 1758 treatise on the Law of Nations stated:

> The sovereign may forbid the entrance of his territory either to foreigners in general, or in particular cases, or to certain persons, or for certain particular purposes, according as he may think it advantageous to the state. There is nothing in all this, that does not flow from the rights of domain and sovereignty: every one is obliged to pay respect to the prohibition; and whoever dares to violate it, incurs the penalty decreed to render it effectual." The Law of Nations, bk. II, ch. VII, § 94, p. 309 (B. Kapossy & R. Whatmore eds.2008).

See also 1 R. Phillimore, Commentaries Upon International Law, pt. III, ch. X, *233 ("It is a received maxim of International Law, that the Government of a State may prohibit the entrance of strangers into the country").

There is no doubt that "before the adoption of the constitution of the United States" each State had the authority to "prevent [itself] from being burdened by an influx of persons." *Mayor of New York v. Miln,* 11 Pet. 102, 132–133, 9 L.Ed. 648 (1837). And the Constitution did not strip the States of that authority. To the contrary, two of the Constitution's provisions were designed to enable the States to prevent "the intrusion of obnoxious aliens through other States." Letter from James Madison to Edmund Randolph (Aug. 27, 1782), in 1 Writings of James Madison 226 (G. Hunt ed. 1900); accord, The Federalist No. 42, pp. 269–271 (C. Rossiter ed. 1961) (J. Madison). The Articles of Confederation had provided that "the free inhabitants of each of these States, paupers, vagabonds and fugitives from justice excepted, shall be entitled to all privileges and immunities of free citizens in the several States." Art. IV. This meant that an unwelcome alien could obtain all the rights of a citizen of one State simply by first becoming an *inhabitant* of another. To remedy this, the Constitution's Privileges and Immunities Clause provided that "[t]he *Citizens* of each State shall be entitled to all Privileges and Immunities of Citizens in the several States." Art. IV, § 2, cl. 1 (emphasis added). But if one State had particularly lax citizenship standards, it might still serve as a gateway for the entry of "obnoxious aliens" into other States. This problem was solved "by authorizing the general government to establish a uniform rule of naturalization throughout the United States." The Federalist No. 42, *supra,* at 271; see Art. I, § 8, cl. 4. In other words, the naturalization power was given to Congress not to abrogate States' power to exclude those they did not want, but to vindicate it. . . .

In light of the predominance of federal immigration restrictions in modern times, it is easy to lose sight of the States' traditional role in regulating immigration—and to overlook their sovereign prerogative to do so. I accept as a given that state regulation is excluded by the Constitution when (1) it has been prohibited by a valid federal law, or (2) it conflicts with federal regulation—when, for example, it admits those whom federal regulation would exclude, or excludes those whom federal regulation would admit.

Possibility (1) need not be considered here: There is no federal law prohibiting the States' sovereign power to exclude (assuming federal authority to enact such a law). The mere existence of federal action in the immigration area—and the so-called field preemption arising from that action, upon which the Court's opinion so heavily relies, *ante,* at 2501–2503 —cannot be regarded as such a prohibition. We are not talking here about a federal law prohibiting the States from regulating bubble-gum advertising, or even the construction of nuclear plants. We are talking about a federal law going to the *core* of state sovereignty: the power to exclude. Like elimination of the States' other inherent sovereign power, immunity from suit, elimination of the States' sovereign power to exclude requires that "Congress . . . unequivocally expres[s] its intent to abrogate," *Seminole Tribe of Fla. v. Florida,* 517 U.S. 44, 55, 116 S.Ct. 1114, 134 L.Ed.2d 252 (1996) (internal quotation marks omitted). Implicit "field preemption" will not do.

Nor can federal power over illegal immigration be deemed exclusive because of what the Court's opinion solicitously calls "foreign countries['] concern[s] about the status, safety, and security of their nationals in the United States," *ante,* at 2498. The Constitution gives all those on our shores the protections of the Bill of Rights—but just as those rights are not expanded for foreign nationals because of their countries' views (some countries, for example, have recently discovered the death penalty to be barbaric), neither are the fundamental sovereign powers of the States abridged to accommodate foreign countries' views. Even in its international relations, the Federal Government must live with the inconvenient fact that it is a Union of independent States, who have their own sovereign powers. This is not the first time it has found that a nuisance and a bother in the conduct of foreign policy. Four years ago, for example, the Government importuned us to interfere with thoroughly constitutional state judicial procedures in the criminal trial of foreign nationals because the international community, and even an opinion of the International Court of Justice, disapproved them. See *Medellín v. Texas,* 552 U.S. 491, 128 S.Ct. 1346, 170 L.Ed.2d 190 (2008).

We rejected that request, as we should reject the Executive's invocation of foreign-affairs considerations here. Though it may upset foreign powers— and even when the Federal Government desperately wants to avoid upsetting foreign powers—the States have the right to protect their borders against foreign nationals, just as they have the right to execute foreign nationals for murder.

What this case comes down to, then, is whether the Arizona law conflicts with federal immigration law—whether it excludes those whom federal law would admit, or admits those whom federal law would exclude. It does not purport to do so. It applies only to aliens who neither possess a privilege to be present under federal law nor have been removed pursuant to the Federal Government's inherent authority.

B. IMMIGRANT SMUGGLING

Some of the most sophisticated and dangerous criminal enterprises encountered by law enforcement are in the business of smuggling undocumented immigrants into the United States. The challenges presented by these groups can extend beyond the immigration crime as an offense against the United States; often the immigrants themselves are abandoned or abused.

Because of specialization within larger organizations, some of the elements of this crime (such as knowledge and action) can be challenging to prove.

UNITED STATES V. YOSHIDA
303 F.3d 1145 (9th Cir. 2002)

TROTT, CIRCUIT JUDGE.

Yuami Yoshida ("Yoshida") timely appeals her jury conviction for her role in assisting three Chinese aliens into the United States in violation of 8 U.S.C. §§ 1324(a)(1)(A)(iv) and (a)(2)(B)(ii). Yoshida argues that there was insufficient evidence for the jury to find that: (1) she knew or recklessly disregarded the fact that the aliens were illegally entering the United States; (2) she encouraged or induced their entry into the United States; (3) she brought or attempted to bring the aliens to the United States; and (4) she did so for private financial gain or commercial advantage. We have jurisdiction pursuant to 28 U.S.C. § 1291, and we affirm.

BACKGROUND

In August 2001, in the Fujian province of the People's Republic of China ("PRC"), the families of Zhuan Dan Lin ("Zhuan"), Cheng Huang ("Cheng"), and Yue Rong Lin ("Yue") made separate arrangements with someone identified as the "Snakehead" to smuggle Zhuan, Cheng, and Yue from the PRC into the United States. Each family paid approximately $50,000 for this service to the Snakehead operation.

The aliens' journey from the PRC to the United States was comprised of three stages: (1) from the "source" country (PRC), to the "staging" country (Thailand); (2) from the "staging" country to the "transit" country (Japan); and finally, (3) from the "transit" country to the "target" country (United States).

Before embarking on the final leg of the journey, a male escort provided Zhuan, Cheng, and Yue with passports, airline tickets, and boarding passes in Japan's Narita Airport. The airline tickets for the three aliens bore the names Daisuke Masaki, Tadashi Murai, and Keiko Ishii. The male escort pointed to Yoshida, who was walking slowly at the bottom of a flight of stairs, and told the three aliens that Yoshida was their escort and that they must follow her. Once the aliens fell into line behind her, Yoshida quickened her pace and walked toward a train platform within the airport. Without communicating or making eye contact with the aliens, Yoshida entered the train and Zhuan, Cheng, and Yue followed. They continued to follow her off the train and to the Delta Airlines boarding gate. They arrived at the gate in time for the final boarding of Delta Airlines flight 78, the flight for which they had received tickets and boarding passes just moments earlier from their male escort.

Yoshida and the aliens were the last passengers to board Delta flight 78 to Los Angeles. During the flight, Yoshida sat in a row immediately behind the aliens. There is no evidence that Yoshida spoke to the aliens during the flight. Following the male escort's instructions, the aliens destroyed their passports, tickets, and boarding passes sometime during the flight to Los Angeles. The passport Zhuan partially destroyed was recovered from the airplane toilet.

Upon arrival in Los Angeles, Yoshida was patted down by an INS Supervisory Inspector. The INS inspector noticed a bulge in Yoshida's underwear. After the INS inspector demanded that Yoshida explain the bulge, Yoshida handed two baggage claim checks to the inspector. Delta Airlines records established that the two claim checks were issued at check-in in Japan in the names of Daisuke Masaki and Tadashi Murai, Zhuan's and Cheng's aliases. Yoshida did not check any luggage for herself. Zhuan and Cheng only had carry-on luggage with them and neither was provided with baggage claim checks prior to their departure from Japan. No bags with those claim numbers were ever recovered.

In addition to Yoshida's actions at Narita airport and LAX, there were other suspicious facts surrounding Yoshida's journey to the United States. Yoshida stated on her I-94 form that her destination was the Miyako Hotel, in Las Vegas, Nevada, yet no business license was issued for a hotel by this name. Moreover, Yoshida's passport indicated that she traveled frequently within Southeast Asia during October and November 2000.

Yoshida was indicted (1) for knowingly encouraging and inducing Zhuan, Yue, and Cheng to enter the United States, in violation of 8 U.S.C. § 1324(a)(1)(A)(iv), and (2) for bringing those same aliens to the United States for commercial advantage and private financial gain, knowing and in reckless disregard of the fact that they had not received prior official authorization to enter or reside in the United States, in violation of 8 U.S.C. § 1324(a)(2)(B)(ii). A six day jury trial began on February 6, 2001. Zhuan,

Cheng, and Yue testified about their trip from the PRC to the United States and the many escorts they had along the way. At the end of the trial, Yoshida moved for acquittal based on insufficient evidence, but the district court denied the motion. The jury convicted Yoshida on both counts of the indictment. Yoshida was sentenced to ten months imprisonment for violating 8 U.S.C. § 1324(a)(1)(A)(iv) ("Count One"), and thirty-six months imprisonment for violating 8 U.S.C. § 1324(a)(2)(B)(ii) ("Count Two"), to run concurrently and to three years of supervised release.

Count I, 8 U.S.C. § 1324(a)(1)(A)(iv)

Section 1324(a)(1)(A)(iv) makes it a crime to (1) encourage or induce, (2) an alien to come to the United States, (3) while knowing or in reckless disregard of the fact that such coming to, entry or residence is or will be in violation of law. 8 U.S.C. § 1324(a)(1)(A)(iv). We have held that " 'to convict a person of violating section 1324(a)(1)(A), the government must show that the defendant acted with criminal intent', i.e., the intent to violate United States immigration laws." *United States v. Barajas-Montiel*, 185 F.3d 947, 951 (9th Cir.1999) (quoting *United States v. Nguyen*, 73 F.3d 887, 893 (9th Cir.1995)).

Yoshida admits that Zhuan, Cheng, and Yue are aliens, but she claims that there is insufficient evidence that she (1) knew or recklessly disregarded the fact that the aliens were not lawfully in the United States, and (2) knowingly encouraged or induced in some way their presence in the United States. Yoshida contends that in order for the jury to convict her for encouraging or inducing an alien to illegally enter the United States, the government had to prove that she gave support or help to the aliens. Yoshida argues that her mere presence at the airport and her simultaneous boarding of the plane were insufficient to establish that she committed the crimes.

Yoshida's "mere presence" at the airport and on the flight is not the only evidence offered against her. A number of events revealed at trial creates a series of inescapable inferences leading to the rational conclusion that Yoshida knowingly "encouraged and induced" Zhuan, Cheng, and Yue to enter the United States and that she did so with knowledge or in reckless disregard of the fact that their entry was in violation of law. For example, the government offered evidence that prior to boarding the flight that would take them to the United States none of the three aliens knew for which flight their tickets were valid, from which gate the plane departed, what time the plane was to depart, or how to find the departure gate. Yoshida clearly filled in these essential blanks. Thus, it was reasonable for the jury to infer that Yoshida helped the aliens enter the United States by leading them through the airport, to the correct departure gate, to the correct airplane, at the appointed time.

Furthermore, the government presented direct evidence that Yoshida concealed baggage claim checks in her underwear bearing the fake names of two of the aliens. A reasonable explanation for Yoshida's possession of the two baggage claim checks is that she obtained them by interacting with whoever in the smuggling organization obtained the boarding passes that were given to the three aliens. The fact that she hid the claim checks in her underwear is also evidence of guilty knowledge of her illegal acts.

We reject Yoshida's argument that her possession of the baggage claim checks was insufficient for a jury to conclude that she had assisted the aliens or had any link to them. While there might be some situations involving an unlucky airline passenger who innocently walks through an airport ahead of aliens, simultaneously shows up at a gate with a group of aliens, boards an aircraft at the same time as aliens, and is seated directly behind the aliens for the duration of the flight, this situation is clearly distinguishable. The fact that Yoshida concealed the baggage claims bearing the fake names of the aliens in the bulge in her underwear is strong evidence that she was not some unlucky bystander, but rather an escort for Zhuan, Cheng, and Yue.

The government also offered circumstantial evidence that Yoshida knowingly encouraged Zhuan, Cheng, and Yue to enter the United States. Yoshida led them to the flight for which the smuggling organization had provided tickets and boarding passes only an instant before Yoshida was identified as their escort. Yoshida walked quickly after the aliens caught up with her, and she timed their arrival at the boarding gate so that they could enter the aircraft without having to wait or be questioned extensively by airline employees. Though Yoshida did not speak or make eye contact with the aliens, the aliens followed her through the airport, boarded the same plane at the same time, and sat in the row ahead of her. Further, Yoshida's I-94 form indicated that her final destination was the Miyako Hotel in Las Vegas, but no business license was found for this hotel. The jury could reasonably conclude that no such hotel existed and thus, Yoshida's stated purpose for her trip was false.

From all of this evidence, a reasonable jury could easily conclude that Yoshida knowingly led the aliens to the flight and timed their arrival at the gate to assure that she and the aliens could promptly enter the aircraft without extensive questioning. It was also reasonable to conclude that Yoshida intentionally avoided overt communication with the aliens to preserve the appearance that she was not their escort. Finally, a jury could reasonably conclude that Yoshida's real purpose for the trip was to participate in the smuggling operation, rather than to stay at a non-existent hotel. Although the government's case consisted of largely circumstantial evidence and required the jury to make reasonable inferences, circumstantial evidence can form a sufficient basis for conviction.

See *United States v. Bernard,* 48 F.3d 427, 430 (9th Cir.1995), *United States v. Loya,* 807 F.2d 1483, 1486 (9th Cir.1987). Here, the jury had ample evidence before it to conclude, beyond a reasonable doubt, that Yoshida encouraged the aliens to enter the United States, with knowledge or in reckless disregard of the fact that the aliens' entry was in violation of law.

Count II, 8 U.S.C. § 1324(a)(2)(B)(ii)

Yoshida contends that there was insufficient evidence to find (1) that she brought an alien to the United States; (2) that she did so for commercial advantage or private financial gain; and (3) that she knew or recklessly disregarded the fact that the alien did not have official authorization to enter the United States. Yoshida argues that even if there was sufficient evidence to prove Count One's "encouraging and inducing" element, Count Two's "bringing" element requires more than encouragement. She argues that bringing requires more direct activity such as physical transportation or some type of control over the method of transportation, such as driving aliens across the United States border. We do not define "bringing" so narrowly.

The statute does not define "brings to." Thus, "[i]n the absence of such a definition, we construe a statutory term in accordance with its ordinary or natural meaning." *F.D.I.C. v. Meyer,* 510 U.S. 471, 476, 114 S.Ct. 996, 127 L.Ed.2d 308 (1994).

This skirmish over the definition of the word "bring" recalls to our memory a recent dispute over the equally common word "carry." *See Muscarello v. United States,* 524 U.S. 125, 118 S.Ct. 1911, 141 L.Ed.2d 111 (1998), *United States v. Foster,* 165 F.3d 689 (9th Cir.1999) (en banc). From this authority, we conclude that "bring" must be interpreted just as the Supreme Court interpreted "carry": broadly, using its ordinary meaning. *Muscarello,* 524 U.S. at 139, 118 S.Ct. 1911.

"Bring" is defined as "to convey, lead, carry or cause to come along from one place to another, ... to escort, [or] accompany." Webster's Third New International Dictionary 278 (1976). "Bringing" an alien to the United States would include "leading," "escorting," or "causing [the alien] to come along" to the United States. Although Yoshida argues that "bring" requires some physical transport, the ordinary definition of "bring" is not so limited, and Yoshida offers no indication that Congress intended to limit "bring." The statute itself conclusively indicates that Congress intended a broad definition of bring: "brings to or attempts to bring to the United States *in any manner whatsoever.*" 8 U.S.C. § 1324(a)(2) (emphasis added).

Here, Yoshida guided Zhuan, Cheng, and Yue to an aircraft heading to the United States. In *United States v. Gonzalez-Torres,* 273 F.3d 1181, 1186–87 (9th Cir.2001), we held that an individual leading others and guiding them across the border using hand signals and gestures was guilty of bringing aliens to the United States in violation of 8 U.S.C. § 1324(a)(2). Gonzalez-Torres did not physically transport his group of aliens, he merely brought them to the United States by guiding them along the correct route.

Similarly, Yoshida walked slowly until the aliens caught up to her in the airport and then quickly led them to the appropriate flight. She then accompanied them on the flight to the United States. In addition to the aliens' testimony that Yoshida was pointed out as their escort and that she changed pace once they fell into behind her, she had the two baggage claims under the aliens' aliases hidden in her underwear. As in Count One, these facts are sufficient evidence to conclude reasonably that Yoshida was connected to the three aliens and that she brought them to the United States by leading them to the gate and assisting them in boarding the aircraft. The fact that Yoshida did not actually pilot the airplane to the United States is of little consequence. She escorted the aliens onto the airplane that eventually landed in the United States.

Yoshida additionally argues that there was no evidence showing that she would receive any private financial gain or commercial advantage. The statute, however, does not require evidence of an actual payment or an agreement to pay. *See United States v. Angwin,* 271 F.3d 786, 805 (9th Cir.2001). "It merely requires that the offense was done for the purpose of financial gain." *Id.* Here, the government presented evidence that the families of Zhuan, Cheng, and Yue paid approximately $50,000 each to the smuggling operation. Given Yoshida's frequent pattern of travel in Southeast Asia and identification as the escort for the final leg of the aliens' journey, a reasonable jury could conclude that Yoshida was a member of the smuggling operation, and, therefore expected to reap some of its financial rewards. In addition, Yoshida, as a stranger to the aliens, had no benevolent reason to lead them into the United States. It was reasonable for the jury to infer that Yoshida expected some payment for her role in leading the aliens through the Narita airport to the correct flight to the United States.

Yoshida argues also that we must presume that she did not have knowledge or a reckless disregard for the fact that the aliens lacked official authorization to come to the United States because Delta airline employees allowed the aliens to board the airplane. We reject this argument. Delta Airlines employees do not have the authority to admit aliens into the United States, and the fact that Delta allowed the aliens onto the flight does not negate the evidence that Yoshida knew or recklessly disregarded the fact that the aliens did not have authorization to enter the United States. Yoshida had baggage claim checks issued under two of the aliens' aliases. As we have previously explained, a reasonable jury could conclude that she got the baggage claims from the aliens' previous male escort and knew that the aliens were traveling under aliases and entering the United States illegally. Secreting the baggage claim checks in her underwear is also evidence of knowledge of the illegality of her acts. As in Count One, there was sufficient evidence for the jury to conclude that Yoshida knew or recklessly disregarded the fact that Zhuan, Cheng, and Yue were not authorized to enter the United States.

CONCLUSION

After reviewing the evidence in the light most favorable to the government, we conclude that there was sufficient evidence to support the jury's verdict convicting Yoshida of violating 8 U.S.C. §§ 1324(a)(1)(A)(iv) and 1324(a)(2)(B)(ii).

EXERCISE

Imagine that in the *Yoshida* case, the baggage slips had not been found on the defendant's person at LAX. You are the defense attorney, hired by Yoshida's family. Which element of the two charges do you think is most vulnerable to challenge at trial?

Some immigrant smuggling cases involve what is sometimes called "human trafficking," where syndicates transport multiple aliens for purposes of labor or prostitution. In those cases, prosecutors face the challenge of not only showing an illegal transport, but the context and reason for that transportation across national borders. The immigration crime can sometimes effectively merge with sex trafficking.

UNITED STATES V. CORTEZ-MEZA
685 Fed. Appx. 731 (11th Cir. 2017)

JULIE CARNES, CIRCUIT JUDGE:

In 2008, a federal grand jury returned a 34-count indictment charging defendant Amador Cortes-Meza and five co-defendants with various offenses related to human trafficking and forced prostitution. As the case progressed, all of his five co-defendants pled guilty to various indicted offenses, but Defendant chose to go to trial.

Over the course of a ten-day trial, nine female victims testified about Defendant's role in a years-long sex-trafficking and prostitution ring. The details of each victim's testimony varied depending on the individual's experience, but each young woman told a similar horrifying tale. While living in Mexico, each victim separately met one of the defendants and began dating or spending time with that defendant. Eventually, each woman was enticed to come to the United States—sometimes by threat, sometimes by a promise of work, and sometimes because of the victim's romantic interests in one of the defendants. The defendants arranged for the victims' illegal entry into the United States, and they were eventually brought to a number of houses around the greater Atlanta area.

Once there, however, the victims were told that they were going to have to work as prostitutes for the defendants. Each victim worked for a specific defendant—referred to as the victim's "padrote"—and was picked up by a driver who transported the victim to various locations to perform sexual acts on customers. On an average night, each victim was required to service ten to thirty customers and to give all of the money she earned to the driver or to her padrote. A victim was given a predetermined number of condoms each night, and her padrote would determine how many clients she had serviced by counting the number of condoms left at the end of the night. In this way, the padrote could determine how much money the victim owed him. The defendants also made the women clean their vaginas with alcohol after each night's work.

During the course of the prostitution operation, the defendants used violence, threats of violence against the victims and their families, insults, psychological coercion, and strict oversight to force the women to remain in their designated houses and to work as prostitutes. Two victims, RHP and LMJ, faced particularly egregious situations.

RHP met Defendant in Mexico and Defendant took her to a festival on a date. Rather than taking her back home that night, however, Defendant took RHP to a hotel an hour from her home, refused to return her home, and had sex with her against her will. Defendant then took RHP to his house, which was a five-hour drive from where RHP lived. RHP believed that Defendant was going to marry her, but was soon disabused of that notion. Defendant prohibited RHP from leaving the house or using the phone outside of his presence, and began beating her with his belt and boot for disobeying his wishes. On one occasion, Defendant brought RHP to a party and saw her talking to someone else. When they returned home, Defendant stuck RHP's head in a water tank while punching her and yelling obscenities at her, and then threw a bucket full of water at her.

RHP did not want to go the United States, but Defendant beat her whenever she expressed that sentiment. After about three months, Defendant arranged for and paid for RHP to be brought to the United States. Defendant had told RHP that she would work at a restaurant in America, but after they arrived in the Atlanta area, Defendant told RHP that she would have to work as a prostitute. When RHP refused, Defendant beat her and threatened her with further beatings if she refused to comply. On her first night in Atlanta, RHP was sent out to work. Because she kept crying, her driver returned her home after only two customers. Defendant chastised her and told her that she would have to work harder than that in the future.

Over the course of the prostitution operation, the violence only intensified and RHP was beaten any time she said that she did not want to work as a prostitute. In one instance, RHP was pushed down the stairs when she expressed her opposition to this line of work. On another occasion, one of the other women at the house escaped and called RHP to tell her to run away as well. The next day, Defendant threw RHP to the floor, kicked her, and beat her with a broom stick until the broom stick broke. Defendant then grabbed a closet rod and continued to hit RHP with it. Defendant broke RHP's finger and caused her head to bleed, but he would not take her anywhere for treatment. RHP's sister was also brought to the United States by the co-defendants, but RHP was strictly forbidden to speak with her. If the two were ever seen talking, Defendant would beat RHP and a co-defendant would beat her sister. RHP felt "destroyed" living under Defendant's control.

LMJ had a similar experience. LMJ met Defendant in a park in Mexico and Defendant invited LMJ to a party the next day. LMJ accepted. On the way to the party, Defendant asked to borrow LMJ's cell phone, but never returned it to her. Then, rather than taking her to a party, Defendant instead took her to a hotel room six hours away from her home and forced LMJ to have sexual relations with him. LMJ had no phone or money and was scared of Defendant because he would scream at her and acted aggressively towards her.

Defendant then made arrangements for a coyote to bring LMJ and Defendant into the United States, and became aggressive toward LMJ whenever she said that she did not want to go. Once they made it to the Atlanta area, Defendant told LMJ that she would have to work as a prostitute to reimburse him for the coyote's charge. LMJ had never been told that she would have to pay Defendant for the trip, and when she refused to prostitute herself, Defendant beat her and told her that it was "as if [she] was his property." Defendant also threatened LMJ, telling her that if she tried to escape, he would kill her and her family in Mexico. LMJ felt that she could not escape because she had to protect her family.

During the two and a half years that LMJ worked as a prostitute for Defendant, Defendant beat her, humiliated her, and insulted her—calling her a whore and a bitch. Defendant hit LMJ if she did not bring home enough money in a given night and also beat her if she was insubordinate or seen talking or laughing with others. One time, Defendant beat LMJ when her driver's car broke down and she was unable to service customers. Another time, at a birthday party, Defendant hit her with a TV cord until her body and face were bruised and swollen. On yet another occasion, Defendant wanted LMJ to play volleyball, but when she refused to play, Defendant took a closet rod and began hitting her with it. He then threw an iron at LMJ, hitting her in the head. Her head bled from the injury for about two weeks but no one took her to the doctor because Defendant was scared that LMJ would tell the doctor that he had hit her. The beatings humiliated LMJ, and the continuous insults and obscenities made her feel worthless. On top of all this, Defendant also required LMJ to have sex with him.

In addition to this testimony, other victims corroborated the accounts of violence against RHP and LMJ and provided their own similar testimony about Defendant's violence and coercion. Immigration and Customs Enforcement (ICE) Agents also testified at trial. The lead case agent described how two different victims were rescued during arrests of two defendants and explained that these victims provided information about the prostitution operation and the remaining defendants. Acting on this information and independent investigation, ICE agents executed search warrants on two different houses involved in the operation and arrested Defendant and the remaining co-defendants.

At trial, Defendant's primary theory of the case was that the women identified at trial had voluntarily engaged in prostitution and had not been forced to do so against their will. Defendant did not disagree that these women had been brought to the United States by him or that the women were working as prostitutes.

After considering the evidence, the jury convicted the Defendant on all 19 counts brought against him: five counts of bringing an alien into the United States through a non-designated point of entry, in violation of 8 U.S.C. § 1324(a)(1)(A)(i); eight counts of importing and harboring an alien for purposes of prostitution, in violation of 8 U.S.C. § 1328; one count of transporting a minor for purposes of prostitution, in violation of 18 U.S.C. § 2423(a); two counts of sex trafficking of a minor, in violation of 18 U.S.C. § 1591(a) & (b)(2); two counts of sex trafficking by force, fraud, or coercion (as related to RHP and LMJ), in violation of 18 U.S.C. § 1591(a) & (b)(1); and one count of conspiracy, in violation of 18 U.S.C. § 371.

At sentencing, Defendant faced a sentence of life imprisonment under the Sentencing Guidelines, but the district court varied below the guidelines range and imposed a total concurrent sentence of 480 months imprisonment. . . .

At trial, the district court allowed the United States to introduce the diary entries of four of the victim-witnesses. These diary entries included prayers, poems, and other writings made by the victims while they were living with the defendants and engaged in prostitution. We review a trial court's evidentiary rulings under the abuse-of-discretion standard. *United States v. Frazier*, 387 F.3d 1244, 1258 (11th Cir. 2004) (*en banc*). "[T]he deference that is the hallmark of abuse-of-discretion review requires that we not reverse an evidentiary decision of a district court unless the ruling is manifestly erroneous." *Id.* at 1258 (internal citations and quotation marks omitted).

After considering the district court's evidentiary rulings, we conclude that the district court did not abuse its discretion in admitting the diary evidence. The evidence, which conveyed the mental state of the women, was pertinent to confirming the coercive environment created by Defendant, which fact was relevant in proving the two counts of sex-trafficking by force, fraud, or coercion. As to Defendant's objection on hearsay grounds, many of the entries, such as the prayers, the poems, and the writer's ruminations about life, were not offered for the truth of the matter asserted. Some entries, which expressed the writer's feeling of sadness or loneliness, were admitted for the truth of the matter asserted. But these entries fell under the "state-of-mind" exception set out in Fed. R. Evid. 803(3).

Yet, even assuming, for the sake of argument, that the district court did err by admitting this evidence, Defendant has not shown that the admitted evidence had a "substantial prejudicial effect," which showing is necessary to prompt reversal of the conviction. *Yellow Pages Photos, Inc. v. Ziplocal, LP*, 795 F.3d 1255, 1275 (11th Cir. 2015). "A prejudicial effect is demonstrated when the moving party shows that the error probably had a substantial influence on the jury's verdict." *Id.* (quotation marks omitted).

Here, given the other overwhelming evidence supporting the jury's verdict at trial, Defendant has failed to show that the diary evidence had a substantial influence on the jury's verdict. The diary evidence conveyed the state of mind of the four victims while they were living with the defendants, and was pertinent only to the two counts of sex-trafficking by force, fraud, or coercion. Yet, each diarist also testified directly and in detail about what the defendants did to her and the resulting mental state during their period of captivity. Each woman was subject to cross-examination, not only about what she wrote, but also as to the matters she testified about. And, ultimately, it was the witnesses' credibility about the events they related that mattered. In addition, there was abundant other evidence supporting Defendant's conviction on these two counts. LMJ and RHP (the two victims associated with these counts) provided extensive testimony about the pattern of threats, violence, and emotional coercion that forced them to commit acts of prostitution. Several other victims corroborated specific and general aspects of this testimony. Further, besides LMJ and RHP, the seven other victims testified as to the similar force and coercion they had experienced. Six ICE agents provided testimony about their involvement in the investigation, with each further corroborating various aspects of the victims' testimony. In addition, two physicians who had treated RHP and LMJ testified and corroborated the women's testimony about specific injuries that Defendant had inflicted on them. Thus, even assuming there was error in the admission of the diary evidence, "it was harmless in light of the overwhelming evidence establishing [Defendant's] guilt." *United States v. Hersh*, 297 F.3d 1233, 1254 n.31 (11th Cir. 2002); *see also United States v. Phaknikone*, 605 F.3d 1099, 1109 (11th Cir. 2010); *United States v. Harriston*, 329 F.3d 779, 789 (11th Cir. 2003).

EXERCISE

By admitting the diaries in the *Cortez-Meza* case, the prosecutors took a risk that the case would be overturned on this appeal. Was that risk worth it to achieve a legitimate goal? And what element of which crime were the diaries probative of?

C. IMMIGRATION FRAUD

Federal law makes many types of fraud a federal criminal act if the fraud is associated with immigration and naturalization. Because the immigration process is document-intensive and decisions are sometimes based on assertions of the prospective immigrant, the possibility of fraud is often present.

Not surprisingly, immigration fraud cases often involve the same issues and questions that come up in the context of other kinds of fraud. Part of that is the element of misrepresentation. But does the misrepresentation need to be a determining factor in an immigration or naturalization action? What if a lie wouldn't have changed the outcome?

MASLENJAK V. UNITED STATES
137 S. Ct. 1918 (2017)

JUSTICE KAGAN delivered the opinion of the Court.

A federal statute, 18 U.S.C. § 1425(a), makes it a crime to "knowingly procure[ ], contrary to law, the naturalization of any person." And when someone is convicted under § 1425(a) of unlawfully procuring her *own* naturalization, her citizenship is automatically revoked. See 8 U.S.C. § 1451(e). In this case, we consider what the Government must prove to obtain such a conviction. We hold that the Government must establish that an illegal act by the defendant played some role in her acquisition of citizenship. When the illegal act is a false statement, that means demonstrating that the defendant lied about facts that would have mattered to an immigration official, because they would have justified denying naturalization or would predictably have led to other facts warranting that result.

I

Petitioner Divna Maslenjak is an ethnic Serb who resided in Bosnia during the 1990's, when a civil war between Serbs and Muslims divided the new country. In 1998, she and her family (her husband Ratko Maslenjak and their two children) met with an American immigration official to seek refugee status in the United States. Interviewed under oath, Maslenjak explained that the family feared persecution in Bosnia from both sides of the national rift. Muslims, she said, would mistreat them because of their ethnicity. And Serbs, she testified, would abuse them because her husband had evaded service in the Bosnian Serb Army by absconding to Serbia— where he remained hidden, apart from the family, for some five years. See App. to Pet. for Cert. 58a–60a. Persuaded of the Maslenjaks' plight,

American officials granted them refugee status, and they immigrated to the United States in 2000.

Six years later, Maslenjak applied for naturalization. Question 23 on the application form asked whether she had ever given "false or misleading information" to a government official while applying for an immigration benefit; question 24 similarly asked whether she had ever "lied to a [ ] government official to gain entry or admission into the United States." *Id.,* at 72a. Maslenjak answered "no" to both questions, while swearing under oath that her replies were true. *Id.,* at 72a, 74a. She also swore that all her written answers were true during a subsequent interview with an immigration official. In August 2007, Maslenjak was naturalized as a U.S. citizen.

But Maslenjak's professions of honesty were false: In fact, she had made up much of the story she told to immigration officials when seeking refuge in this country. Her fiction began to unravel at around the same time she applied for citizenship. In 2006, immigration officials confronted Maslenjak's husband Ratko with records showing that he had not fled conscription during the Bosnian civil war; rather, he had served as an officer in the Bosnian Serb Army. And not only that: He had served in a brigade that participated in the Srebrenica massacre—a slaughter of some 8,000 Bosnian Muslim civilians. Within a year, the Government convicted Ratko on charges of making false statements on immigration documents. The newly naturalized Maslenjak attempted to prevent Ratko's deportation. During proceedings on that matter, Maslenjak admitted she had known all along that Ratko spent the war years not secreted in Serbia but fighting in Bosnia.

As a result, the Government charged Maslenjak with knowingly "procur[ing], contrary to law, [her] naturalization," in violation of 18 U.S.C. § 1425(a). According to the Government's theory, Maslenjak violated § 1425(a) because, in the course of procuring her naturalization, she broke another law: 18 U.S.C. § 1015(a), which prohibits knowingly making a false statement under oath in a naturalization proceeding. The false statements the Government invoked were Maslenjak's answers to questions 23 and 24 on the citizenship application (stating that she had not lied in seeking refugee status) and her corresponding statements in the citizenship interview. Those statements, the Government argued to the District Court, need not have affected the naturalization decision to support a conviction under § 1425(a). The court agreed: Over Maslenjak's objection, it instructed the jury that a conviction was proper so long as the Government "prove[d] that one of the defendant's statements was false"—even if the statement was not "material" and "did not influence the decision to approve [her] naturalization." App. to Pet. for Cert. 86a. The jury returned a guilty verdict; and the District Court, based on that finding, stripped Maslenjak of her citizenship. See 8 U.S.C. § 1451(e).

The United States Court of Appeals for the Sixth Circuit affirmed the conviction. As relevant here, the Sixth Circuit upheld the District Court's instructions that Maslenjak's false statements need not have influenced the naturalization decision. If, the Court of Appeals held, Maslenjak made false statements violating § 1015(a) and she procured naturalization, then she also violated § 1425(a)—irrespective of whether the false statements played any role in her obtaining citizenship. See 821 F.3d 675, 685–686 (2016). That decision created a conflict in the Circuit Courts. We granted certiorari to resolve it, 580 U.S. ___, 137 S.Ct. 809, 196 L.Ed.2d 595 (2017), and we now vacate the Sixth Circuit's judgment.

II

A

Section 1425(a), the parties agree, makes it a crime to commit some other illegal act in connection with naturalization. But the parties dispute the nature of the required connection. Maslenjak argues that the relationship must be "causal" in kind: A person "procures" her naturalization "contrary to law," she contends, only if a predicate crime in some way "contribut[ed]" to her gaining citizenship. Brief for Petitioner 21. By contrast, the Government proposes a basically chronological link: Section 1425(a), it urges, "punishes the commission of other violations of law *in the course of* procuring naturalization"—even if the illegality could not have had any effect on the naturalization decision. Brief for United States 14 (emphasis added). We conclude that Maslenjak has the better of this argument.

We begin, as usual, with the statutory text. In ordinary usage, "to procure" something is "to get possession of" it. Webster's Third New International Dictionary 1809 (2002); accord, Black's Law Dictionary 1401 (10th ed. 2014) (defining "procure" as "[t]o obtain (something), esp. by special effort or means"). So to "procure . . . naturalization" means to obtain naturalization (or, to use another word, citizenship). The adverbial phrase "contrary to law," wedged in between "procure" and "naturalization," then specifies *how* a person must procure naturalization so as to run afoul of the statute: in contravention of the law—or, in a word, illegally. Putting the pieces together, someone "procure[s], contrary to law, naturalization" when she obtains citizenship illegally.

What, then, does that whole phrase mean? The most natural understanding is that the illegal act must have somehow contributed to the obtaining of citizenship. Consider if someone said to you: "John obtained that painting illegally." You might imagine that he stole it off the walls of a museum. Or that he paid for it with a forged check. Or that he impersonated the true buyer when the auction house delivered it. But in all events, you would imagine illegal acts in some kind of means-end relation—or otherwise said, in some kind of causal relation—to the painting's acquisition. If someone said to you, "John obtained that painting illegally, but his unlawful acts did not play any role in his obtaining it," you would not have a clue what the statement meant. You would think it nonsense—or perhaps the opening of a riddle. That is because if no illegal act contributed at all to getting the painting, then the painting would not have been gotten illegally. And the same goes for naturalization. If whatever illegal conduct occurring within the naturalization process was a causal dead-end—if, so to speak, the ripples from that act could not have reached the decision to award citizenship—then the act cannot support a charge that the applicant obtained naturalization illegally. The conduct, though itself illegal, would not also make the obtaining of citizenship so. To get citizenship unlawfully, we understand, is to get it through an unlawful means—and that is just to say that an illegality played some role in its acquisition.

The Government's contrary view—that § 1425(a) requires only a "violation [ ] of law in the course of procuring naturalization"—falters on the way language naturally works. Brief for United States 14. Return for a moment to our artwork example. Imagine this time that John made an illegal turn while driving to the auction house to purchase a painting. Would you say that he had "procured the painting illegally" because he happened to violate the law in the course of obtaining it? Not likely. And again, the same is true with respect to naturalization. Suppose that an applicant for citizenship fills out the necessary paperwork in a government office with a knife tucked away in her handbag (but never mentioned or used). She has violated the law—specifically, a statute criminalizing the possession of a weapon in a federal building. See 18 U.S.C. § 930. And she has surely done so "in the course of" procuring citizenship. But would you say, using English as you ordinarily would, that she has "procure[d]" her citizenship "contrary to law" (or, as you would really speak, "illegally")? Once again, no. That is because the violation of law and the acquisition of citizenship are in that example merely coincidental: The one has no causal relation to the other. . . .

Measured against all we have said, the jury instructions in this case were in error. As earlier noted, the District Court told the jury that it could convict based on any false statement in the naturalization process (*i.e.,* any violation of § 1015(a)), no matter how inconsequential to the ultimate decision. See App. to Pet. for Cert. 86a; *supra,* at 1923–1924. But as we have shown, the jury needed to find more than an unlawful false statement. Recall that Maslenjak's lie in the naturalization process concerned her prior statements to immigration officials: She swore that she had been honest when applying for admission as a refugee, but in fact she had not. See *supra,* at 1923–1924. The jury could have convicted if that earlier dishonesty (*i.e.,* the thing she misrepresented when seeking citizenship) were itself a reason to deny naturalization—say, because it counted as "false testimony for the purpose of obtaining [immigration] benefits" and thus demonstrated bad moral character. See *supra,* at 1928–1929. Or else, the jury could have convicted if (1) knowledge of that prior dishonesty would have led a reasonable official to make some further investigation (say, into the circumstances of her admission), (2) that inquiry would predictably have yielded a legal basis for rejecting her citizenship application, and (3) Maslenjak failed to show that (notwithstanding such an objective likelihood) she was in fact qualified to become a U.S. citizen. See *supra,* at 1928–1931. This jury, however, was not asked to—and so did not—make any of those determinations. Accordingly, Maslenjak was not convicted by a properly instructed jury of "procur[ing], contrary to law, [her] naturalization."

EXERCISE

You are a Member of Congress who is upset by the *Maslenjak* opinion. You think that if people misrepresent key facts at any point of the immigration and naturalization process, they should be criminally sanctioned, de-naturalized, and deported. How would you change the text of 18 U.S.C. § 1425(a) to make sure that is possible? Here is the current text of that statute:

> **(a)** Whoever knowingly procures or attempts to procure, contrary to law, the naturalization of any person, or documentary or other evidence of naturalization or of citizenship. . .

---

8 U.S.C. § 1325(c) criminalizes sham marriages for the purpose of obtaining citizenship:

> **(c) Marriage fraud**
>
> Any individual who knowingly enters into a marriage for the purpose of evading any provision of the immigration laws shall be imprisoned for not more than 5 years, or fined not more than $250,000, or both.

That would seem to be a straightforward rule. However, facts complicate matters, as is so often true in criminal law.

UNITED STATES V. ORELLANO-BLANCO
294 F.3d 1143 (9th Cir. 2002)

KLEINFELD, CIRCUIT JUDGE.

Appellant Santos Orellana-Blanco was convicted after a jury trial of marriage fraud and making a false statement on an immigration document. The theory of the prosecution's case was that he fraudulently married a woman, Beatrice Boehm, to evade restrictions in the immigration laws, and that he lied in his sworn statement and other papers by stating that he was married to her and lived with her when the marriage was actually a sham.

The government didn't charge Boehm, Orellana-Blanco's putative wife. Instead it used her as its star witness against him. She testified that the marriage was, as charged, a sham, and was intended as such by both of them from the beginning. Orellana-Blanco testified that he fully intended to live with Boehm as husband and wife when he married her, did so to the maximum extent that she would allow, and was ultimately frustrated in his attempt to live with her by her leaving him and taking a job elsewhere after cancer surgery made him impotent. At least one of these people was lying, and the jury was not too enthused about Boehm. It sent out a note during deliberations asking "Why wasn't Bobby [Beatrice Boehm] charged with fraud concerning her part in falsifying the records?"

This appeal challenges admission of an exhibit that the government used to prove Orellana-Blanco lied under oath about his marriage. The exhibit purports to be a "Record of Sworn Statement" signed by Orellana-Blanco, in connection with a "Form I-130, Petition For Alien Relative." In the document Orellana-Blanco says he lives with his wife, he is married to her, they lived together before the marriage at the same address (his wife's house), and they've lived together continuously since the marriage. Orellana-Blanco's own testimony at trial established that he had not lived continuously or at all with Boehm, in the sense of regularly sleeping in the same residence. Therefore if the exhibit came in, as it did, then his conviction was nearly assured, at least on the false statement count, and his credibility was severely undercut on the sham marriage count.

Orellana-Blanco came illegally to the United States in 1990 from El Salvador. He worked regularly, making fast food for a chain restaurant, painting airplane parts, and doing other jobs. His membership in a class protected under an injunction in an unrelated civil class action suit kept him from being deported.

In 1994, Orellana-Blanco married Beatrice Boehm at the county courthouse in Prescott, Arizona. Boehm testified that she agreed to marry him, without ever having seen him before, to help legalize him and because Orellana-Blanco's brother and sister-in-law agreed to paint her truck, which she could not otherwise afford. She testified that they met in the car on the way to the ceremony, got married (with a borrowed ring), and had dinner with the brother and sister-in-law (the witnesses). Then Orellana-Blanco dropped her off, alone, at her house. She conceded that she wasn't paid money to marry Orellana-Blanco. She testified that they had agreed they would divorce in three years, and the reason they had not was that he refused because the immigration rules turned out to require five years, and she didn't have the money to hire a divorce lawyer.

Orellana-Blanco's and Boehm's testimony conflicted on the whole course of the relationship, including whether they had ever consummated the marriage or had any sexual relationship at all. He said he'd met Boehm years before the marriage, at his brother's house, and saw her frequently thereafter. Boehm said they met on the day of the wedding. Orellana-Blanco testified that before the marriage they did such things as watch movies and go to dinner together, he helped her clean her house, they drank together, she would tell him about her problems with her son, and they had sexual relations before marriage, sometimes outdoors, sometimes at her house after watching movies if Boehm's son wasn't there. She testified that none of this had happened, except that Orellana-Blanco had helped her clean her house and lay carpet, and had mowed her lawn once. She said she never had sexual relations with him before or after marriage.

Both also testified that they never lived together. Orellana-Blanco said Boehm wouldn't let him move in, because she was hiding the marriage from her son for the first year, and after that she was still uncomfortable because of her son and asked Orellana-Blanco "to give her some time." Boehm testified that the reason they never lived together was because the marriage was intended to be a sham.

They established a joint bank account, and Boehm filed tax returns as a married person. They exchanged gifts. Orellana-Blanco also said he gave Boehm money for household expenses, which Boehm did not deny.

Three years after the marriage, Orellana-Blanco was hospitalized for surgery to remove a large cancerous tumor in his colon. The surgeon testified that he remembered talking to Boehm during this period and she was "appropriately concerned, as anybody would be if their close family member had a major operation." Boehm testified that she was at the hospital when Orellana-Blanco had his surgery and visited him once after he was released.

According to Orellana-Blanco, the marriage, such as it was, deteriorated when Boehm objected to his having withdrawn money from their joint account, although he had put money in. He testified that after his surgery, in which seventy percent of his stomach and intestine were removed, and his year of chemotherapy following it, he could no longer perform sexually, and that changed their relationship. Boehm moved to New Mexico for a new job living with a blind rancher and his senile wife and said she wanted a divorce.

The exhibit at issue, Exhibit 3, was generated in 1998, after the surgery but before Boehm moved to New Mexico. The INS interviewed Orellana-Blanco and Boehm as part of the process by which Orellana-Blanco hoped to receive his "green card," or permanent resident alien status. Boehm had already signed an I-130 Petition for Alien Relative on Orellana-Blanco's behalf, in which she swore they were married. An INS agent testified that "at a certain stage of the process, the husband and wife, in these cases, are brought in for separate interviews." Boehm and Orellana-Blanco drove together to Phoenix for their interview. Boehm testified that on their drive down to Phoenix, they agreed on what lies to tell, and, she testified, she told them under oath in her separate interview. Her signed statement under oath was not introduced into evidence.

Orellana-Blanco was interviewed by INS Adjudications Officer Brett Kendall. But Officer Kendall did not testify at the trial. There was testimony that he was on leave and was living with his parents, but the government did not produce him as a witness. Instead it offered what purported to be a sworn statement by Orellana-Blanco, described above, through the testimony of another INS agent, Adjudications Officer Radke. But Officer Radke testified that he wasn't in the room for the whole interview. The reason he was in there at all was that Kendall called him in to translate from English to Spanish and Spanish to English, because Kendall felt that his own "knowledge of the Spanish language was not adequate to find out what he needed to find out." Officer Radke gave Orellana-Blanco the oath in Spanish, translated Officer Kendall's questions, and translated Orellana-Blanco's answers when given in Spanish (Orellana-Blanco gave some answers in each language). The interview was not taped. Orellana-Blanco testified that Radke used a Spanish English dictionary during the interview, but Radke testified that he didn't. Officer Radke testified that "[p]art way through the interview Officer Kendall was satisfied that the applicant could understand English, and at that point I did not participate in the interview anymore, other than to come in to witness the signature."

The form shows answers, apparently written by Officer Kendall, usually of just a word or two, such as "11/03/47 Victoria Texas" in answer to "What is your spouse's date and place of birth?" Because Kendall did not testify, and Radke was not there for the whole interview, there is no direct evidence on whether the answers were a verbatim record of what Orellana-Blanco said, or Kendall's formulation of what he understood Orellana-Blanco to have said. Officer Radke conceded that the answers were not verbatim and would not reflect questions by Orellana-Blanco, such as his asking what a question meant. The statement is signed by Orellana-Blanco and witnessed by Officer Kendall and Officer Radke. Orellana-Blanco testified that he and the INS officers sometimes used Spanish, sometimes English, and "really we didn't quite understand each other." Officer Kendall wasn't called as a witness, so he didn't testify to the contrary, and Officer Radke wasn't at all of the interview. . . .

In addition to what purported to be Orellana-Blanco's answers, the exhibit showed what were apparently notations about the answers by Officer Kendall, who was not present at trial to be cross examined. Next to one answer, Officer Kendall had written "wrong," next to another that on his last visit to his parents Orellana-Blanco's wife did not accompany him Officer Kendall wrote and circled "alone," and Officer Kendall circled some other answers.

The district court allowed Exhibit 3 into evidence, over the objection of Orellana-Blanco's lawyer, during the testimony of another INS agent who testified as a custodian of records that the form was in Orellana-Blanco's "A-file." Orellana-Blanco was convicted and sentenced to three years of probation, which he is now serving, and he timely appealed.

Analysis

This appeal challenges one thing, admission of this damning exhibit. The challenge is on both confrontation clause and hearsay grounds. . . .

It was admitted in violation of the hearsay rule. In order to put the evidence in the exhibit before the jury, the government should have called Officer Kendall as a witness. No issue arises as to unavailability of the witness, because the government did not claim unavailability and the court did not admit the exhibit based on unavailability. The record shows that Officer Kendall was still employed by the INS, was on sick leave, and was living with his parents, and the government did not claim that he was too sick to come to court. Orellana-Blanco and the government differed sharply on what Orellana-Blanco had said to Officer Kendall, and under the confrontation clause, Orellana-Blanco was entitled to confront Officer Kendall in cross-examination to test the accuracy of what the exhibit claimed Orellana-Blanco had said.

The government's final argument is that the error if any was harmless beyond a reasonable doubt. The government concedes that if we find the exhibit inadmissible, as we have, then the false statement conviction could not stand because the exhibit "was the primary evidence supporting this charge." But, the government contends, the evidence of a sham marriage was overwhelming based on the evidence of Beatrice Boehm about her intentions from the start and the overwhelming evidence that Orellana-Blanco did not actually reside with Boehm at her mobile home.

We do not agree that the error was harmless. A marriage is a sham "if the bride and groom did not intend to establish a life together at the time they were married." As we held in *United States v. Tagalicud,* "marriage fraud may be committed by one party to the marriage, or a person who arranged the marriage, yet the other spouse may genuinely intend to marry." Thus if one spouse intended the marriage to be a sham when the ceremony took place, but the other intended it to be genuine, then the one committed marriage fraud but not the other. That Orellana-Blanco married Boehm so that he could get a green card does not make the marriage a sham, though it is evidence that might support an inference of a sham marriage. We held in *Tagalicud* that "motivations are at most evidence of intent, and do not themselves make the marriages shams." Just as marriages for money, hardly a novelty, or marriages among princes and princesses for reasons of state may be genuine and not sham marriages, so may marriages for green cards be genuine. An intent to obtain something other than or in addition to love and companionship from that life does not make a marriage a sham. Rather, the sham arises from the intent not "to establish a life together."

The jury could have concluded from the evidence that, although Boehm never intended a genuine marriage, Orellana-Blanco did. They could have concluded that, while his motivation for marriage was love for a green card rather than love for Boehm, nevertheless he planned to live with Boehm as her husband. The jury might infer that he wouldn't have been willing to mow her lawn, clean her house, and lay her carpet without getting paid for it, unless he saw these chores as a husband's or prospective husband's duties. The jury could have believed Orellana-Blanco and disbelieved Boehm regarding their sexual relations. The jury could have concluded that he wanted to move in with Boehm from the start, and didn't only because she insisted she needed time to break the news to her son, and then needed more time to accommodate her son to the marriage. And it could have concluded, if it believed Orellana-Blanco and his surgeon, that Boehm acted consistently with being Orellana-Blanco's wife until he lost his sexual abilities after his surgery, at which time she left him for the rancher. It did not have to believe any of this, but it could well have. We accordingly cannot conclude that the error in admitting the exhibit was harmless beyond a reasonable doubt.

The judgment must be REVERSED and the case REMANDED for a new trial.

EXERCISE

You are a federal agent investigating a suspected marriage fraud. It involves Laurence, who has emigrated to the United States from El Salvador, and Marie, who is a native-born US citizen. Your investigation reveals the following (and nothing else):

— Laurence and Marie exchanged several letters prior to Laurence's arrival in the United States on a tourist visa. When he arrived, he went to Marie's house and stayed with her for 58 days. On the 59th day, they were married in a small ceremony in a Catholic church.

— Two weeks after the wedding, Laurence left the state and has been absent the five months intervening. He claims that he has been working on farms in Arizona, California, Oregon, and Washington.

— Both Laurence and Marie refuse to discuss the extent of their sexual relations.

— Marie has no photographs of Laurence other than two from their wedding. Laurence has only the same two photographs.

— Your investigation has revealed that both before and after her wedding (once Laurence was away), Marie has often entertained a young man who works with her. They have been seen bowling, dining at a cafeteria, and fishing with an unidentified group of children. Surveillance video reveals that he often stayed overnight at her house.

— Financial records indicate that shortly before the wedding, Laurence's family sent Marie a check for $4,000. It is unknown what she did with that money.

Do you believe that you have probable cause to charge Marie and/or Laurence with marriage fraud?

D. RE-ENTRY AFTER DEPORTATION

Deportation is not necessarily handled as a criminal process. A first offense for illegal entry is a misdemeanor under 8 U.S.C. § 1925, which also provides for civil penalties. However, criminal prosecution is more likely when an undocumented alien returns to the United States after being convicted of a crime and then deported. 8 U.S.C. § 1326(a) makes re-entry in those circumstances a felony, with special enhancements if the alien was previously convicted of a serious crime in the United States:

(a) In general

Subject to subsection (b), any alien who—

> **(1)** has been denied admission, excluded, deported, or removed or has departed the United States while an order of exclusion, deportation, or removal is outstanding, and thereafter

> **(2)** enters, attempts to enter, or is at any time found in, the United States, unless (A) prior to his reembarkation at a place outside the United States or his application for admission from foreign contiguous territory, the Attorney General has expressly consented to such alien's reapplying for admission; or (B) with respect to an alien previously denied admission and removed, unless such alien shall establish that he was not required to obtain such advance consent under this chapter or any prior Act,

shall be fined under Title 18, or imprisoned not more than 2 years, or both.

(b) Criminal penalties for reentry of certain removed aliens

Notwithstanding subsection (a), in the case of any alien described in such subsection—

(1) whose removal was subsequent to a conviction for commission of three or more misdemeanors involving drugs, crimes against the person, or both, or a felony (other than an aggravated felony), such alien shall be fined under Title 18, imprisoned not more than 10 years, or both;

(2) whose removal was subsequent to a conviction for commission of an aggravated felony, such alien shall be fined under such title, imprisoned not more than 20 years, or both;

To bring a charge under this statute, one element that the government must prove is that the defendant actually left the country—something that requires affirmative evidence that can sometimes be difficult to procure. Immigration law depends heavily on documentation, and the retention and availability of that documentation can be decisive.

UNITED STATES V. HARVEY
746 F.3d 87 (2d Cir. 2014)

PER CURIAM:

Defendant-Appellant Godfrey Emmanuel Harvey, a citizen of Jamaica, challenges the sufficiency of the evidence supporting his conviction for illegal re-entry into the United States after he was deported because of an aggravated felony conviction. Harvey's sole argument on appeal is that the government failed to prove his physical departure from the United States on a March 7, 1992 airline flight from John F. Kennedy International Airport ("JFK") to Kingston, Jamaica.

To prove Harvey left the country, the government relied on a 1992 warrant of deportation prepared by an immigration official, which indicated that the official witnessed Harvey depart on the March 1992 flight. That official was unavailable to testify at Harvey's October 2011 trial for illegal re-entry, and the government did not present any other direct evidence that Harvey left the United States in 1992.

We hold today that such additional evidence was unnecessary: the 1992 warrant of deportation, coupled with testimony concerning the deportation procedures followed at that time, was sufficient to permit a rational juror to conclude that Harvey left the country on the date specified in the warrant. Accordingly, we AFFIRM the judgment of the district court.

BACKGROUND

Harvey first entered the United States in 1988 through Miami, Florida. He subsequently was convicted of a crime constituting an aggravated felony under the immigration laws and, in December 1991, an immigration judge ordered him deported. Some twenty years later, in May 2011, immigration authorities apprehended Harvey in the Southern District of New York and charged him with one count of illegal re-entry after deportation for an aggravated felony.

The matter proceeded to trial in October 2011. To establish that Harvey left the country, the government introduced a Form I-205 warrant of deportation dated March 7, 1992 and executed by Supervisory Detention Enforcement Officer David R. Thompson of the (former) Immigration and Naturalization Service. The warrant indicated that Officer Thompson witnessed Harvey leave the country that morning on American Airlines flight 1193, which was bound for Kingston, Jamaica. Harvey stipulated at trial that the deportation warrant bore his signature and fingerprints.

Officer Thompson died before Harvey's October 2011 trial and therefore was unavailable to testify. Instead, the government offered the testimony of Special Agent William Sansone of the Department of Homeland Security, Homeland Security Investigations, who explained the deportation procedures in effect at the time of Harvey's 1992 deportation. He testified that, when a person was deported from the United States via airplane, the immigration officer executing the deportation escorted the deportee to his seat on the aircraft, ensured that the interior of the aircraft was secure, returned to the jetway, and then remained at the aircraft door until the aircraft pulled away. The immigration official then watched the aircraft until it was out of sight, at which point the official signed the deportation warrant. Special Agent Sansone could not recall whether he had participated in Harvey's deportation, and the government did not introduce any other direct evidence of Harvey's departure from the country.

Following the close of the government's evidence, Harvey moved for a judgment of acquittal, arguing that the government's evidence failed to establish that he ever left the country. The district court denied the motion, ruling, *inter alia,* that there was "no particular reason to doubt the regularity of the procedures" by which Harvey was deported. The jury returned a guilty verdict on November 1, 2011, and, in March 2012, the district court sentenced Harvey principally to 60 months' incarceration. Harvey timely appealed the resulting March 30, 2012 judgment of conviction.

DISCUSSION

Although we review sufficiency of the evidence claims *de novo, see United States v. Sabhnani,* 599 F.3d 215, 241 (2d Cir.2010), a defendant mounting such a challenge "bears a heavy burden," *United States v. Heras,* 609 F.3d 101, 105 (2d Cir.2010) (citation and quotation marks omitted). This is because, in assessing whether the evidence was sufficient to sustain a conviction, " 'we view the evidence in the light most favorable to the government, drawing all inferences in the government's favor and deferring to the jury's assessments of the witnesses' credibility.' " *Sabhnani,* 599 F.3d at 241 (quoting *United States v. Parkes,* 497 F.3d 220, 225 (2d Cir.2007)). Following this review, we will sustain the jury's verdict if "*any* rational trier of fact could have found the essential elements of the crime beyond a reasonable doubt." *Jackson v. Virginia,* 443 U.S. 307, 319, 99 S.Ct. 2781, 61 L.Ed.2d 560 (1979).

To sustain Harvey's illegal re-entry conviction, the government was required to prove at trial that Harvey (1) is an alien (2) who was deported (3) and thereafter re-entered the United States (4) without the requisite authority to do so. *See* 8 U.S.C. § 1326(a). Only the second element— whether he was physically deported—is at issue here. On this point, Harvey argues that, aside from the deportation warrant, the government did not introduce any documentary or testimonial evidence indicating that he was on the aircraft when it left JFK or that he entered Jamaica after the flight landed. *See* Appellant Br. at 15–16. He further contends that the deportation warrant alone was insufficient to establish the fact of his departure because it contained no indication that Officer Thompson actually followed the deportation procedures outlined by Special Agent Sansone at trial. *Id.* at 16–18.

We disagree and hold, along with every other court to have considered the issue, that a properly executed warrant of deportation, coupled with testimony regarding the deportation procedures followed at that time, is sufficient proof that a defendant was, in fact, physically deported from the United States. *See United States v. Garcia,* 452 F.3d 36, 43–44 (1st Cir.2006); *United States v. Bahena-Cardenas,* 411 F.3d 1067, 1074–75 (9th Cir.2005); *see also United States v. Nelson,* 528 Fed.Appx. 314, 315 (4th Cir.2013) (summary order); *United States v. Avila-Sifuentes,* 237 Fed.Appx. 971, 972 (5th Cir.2007) (summary order). Here, the warrant of deportation specifically indicated that Officer Thompson "witnessed" Harvey's departure, and set forth the date, flight number, and time it was effected. In addition, Harvey stipulated that he signed the warrant and that it contained his fingerprints. These facts, coupled with Sansone's testimony regarding the deportation procedures in effect in 1992, were a sufficient basis from which a reasonable juror could conclude, beyond a reasonable doubt, that Harvey physically left the United States on March 7, 1992. *Cf. Garcia,* 452 F.3d at 43–44 (warrant of deportation sufficient to establish defendant's departure from the country even though the government "failed to call any witness who personally saw [him] . . . depart from the United States").

CONCLUSION

Having concluded that the evidence was sufficient to establish Harvey's guilt beyond a reasonable doubt, we AFFIRM the judgment of the district court.

EXERCISE

Imagine that you are a federal prosecutor. An immigration agent brings you a case involving alleged re-entry after deportation. The defendant was deported in 2015 to his birthplace of Aruba. Immigration officials placed the defendant on a plane to Puerto Rico, where he was to transfer to Aruba. However, the defendant claims that he left the airport in Puerto Rico and then did not leave Puerto Rico until his recent attempt to fly to your city (where he was apprehended at the airport deplaning from a flight arriving from Puerto Rico). No flight records reflect whether or not the defendant took the connecting flight to Aruba.

How do you respond to the immigration agent's request that you take the case to the Grand Jury for indictment?

E. EMPLOYMENT OF UNDOCUMENTED ALIENS AND PEONAGE

8 U.S.C. § 1324a makes it a criminal act to knowingly hire or employ undocumented aliens:

(a) Making employment of unauthorized aliens unlawful

(1) In general

It is unlawful for a person or other entity—

> **(A)** to hire, or to recruit or refer for a fee, for employment in the United States an alien knowing the alien is an unauthorized alien (as defined in subsection (h)(3)) with respect to such employment, or
>
> **(B)** (i) to hire for employment in the United States an individual without complying with the requirements of subsection (b) or (ii) if the person or entity is an agricultural association, agricultural employer, or farm labor contractor (as defined in section 1802 of Title 29), to hire, or to recruit or refer for a fee, for employment in the United States an individual without complying with the requirements of subsection (b).

(2) Continuing employment

> It is unlawful for a person or other entity, after hiring an alien for employment in accordance with paragraph (1), to continue to employ the alien in the United States knowing the alien is (or has become) an unauthorized alien with respect to such employment.

The statute requires proof that the employer knew that the alien was unauthorized. As is often true with state-of-mind proofs, context can be important because circumstantial evidence of knowledge is so often at the heart of the case for the government.

UNITED STATES V. TIPTON

518 F.3d 591 (8th Cir. 2008)

COLLOTON, CIRCUIT JUDGE.

Sadik Seferi and Nicole Tipton were convicted of hiring, harboring, and conspiring to hire and harbor unlawful aliens working at a restaurant owned by Tipton. The district court sentenced Seferi to 30 months' imprisonment and Tipton to 27 months' imprisonment. Seferi and Tipton argue on appeal that there was insufficient evidence to support their convictions. Tipton also contends that the district court erred at sentencing when it calculated the advisory guidelines range. We affirm the judgments of the district court.

I.

We recite the evidence presented at trial in a light most favorable to the verdict. According to this evidence, Tipton purchased The Galley restaurant in Vinton, Iowa, on June 2, 2005. Tipton hired, supervised, and paid the wait staff. Seferi hired, supervised, and paid the kitchen staff. Tipton and Seferi split the restaurant's profits equally.

On March 6, 2006, acting on a tip from local police, agents of the Bureau of Immigration and Customs Enforcement (ICE) executed search warrants at The Galley and at an apartment used to house Galley workers. They discovered evidence that six undocumented aliens had worked in the restaurant's kitchen since September 2005.

The ICE agents found job applications, W-4 documents, and I-9 forms for every employee of the Galley, except for the six aliens. The personnel files for some of the aliens contained counterfeit identity documents. An ICE agent described one of these documents at trial as a "fantasy document." The six undocumented aliens were paid in cash and below the minimum wage, while all other employees were paid by check. The Galley withheld income tax and paid unemployment insurance premiums for all employees except for the six aliens.

The agents discovered that Tipton provided an apartment for the undocumented aliens. The apartment was in Tipton's name, and she paid the rent and utilities. At Tipton's request, the aliens later moved out of the apartment and rented a different place. Although one of the aliens signed the second lease, Tipton selected the apartment, completed the leasing documents, and paid the $375 deposit using her personal checking account.

On March 14, 2006, a grand jury indicted both defendants under 8 U.S.C. § 1324(a)(1)(A) for harboring illegal aliens, under 8 U.S.C. § 1324a(a)(1)(A) for hiring unauthorized aliens, and under 18 U.S.C. § 371 for conspiring to hire and harbor illegal aliens. After a joint trial, a jury found both defendants guilty on all three counts, and the district court sentenced Seferi to 30 months' imprisonment and Tipton to 27 months' imprisonment. In calculating the advisory guidelines range, the court applied a specific offense characteristic under USSG § 2L1.1(b)(2)(A) for harboring six or more unlawful aliens, and increased each defendant's offense level under USSG § 3B1.4 on the ground that the defendant used a minor to commit the offense.

II.

A.

In reviewing the appellants' challenge to the sufficiency of the evidence, we consider the record in the light most favorable to the verdict. We inquire whether a jury reasonably could find proof beyond a reasonable doubt of the charged offenses. *United States v. Red Bird,* 450 F.3d 789, 791 (8th Cir.2006).

Tipton and Seferi argue that there was insufficient proof to show that they violated 8 U.S.C. § 1324a(a)(1)(A), which makes it unlawful to hire an alien for employment in the United States while knowing that the alien is an "unauthorized alien." An unauthorized alien is one who is not either lawfully admitted to the United States for permanent residence, or authorized by law to be employed in the United States. 8 U.S.C. § 1324a(h)(3).

We conclude that the evidence presented at trial was adequate to support the convictions of both defendants on this charge. There is no dispute that the six aliens were unauthorized within the meaning of the statute, and there was sufficient evidence from which a jury reasonably could infer that Tipton and Seferi knew that the aliens were unauthorized. Rather than hire these aliens based on a job application and interview, Seferi hired three of them at a truck stop without a job application, form of identification, or employment verification form. Tipton and Seferi treated the six aliens differently than they treated employees legally in the United States: they withheld no federal income tax from the aliens' wages, made no contribution to unemployment insurance on their behalf, and paid them in cash at a rate far below the minimum wage. Seferi drove the aliens to and from work from an apartment that Tipton maintained for them. These circumstances adequately support an inference that Tipton and Seferi knew the aliens were unauthorized.

We also conclude that the evidence is sufficient to support the appellants' convictions for harboring illegal aliens. The statute makes it unlawful to "harbor" an alien, knowing or in reckless disregard of the fact that the alien has come to, entered, or remained in the United States in violation of the law. 8 U.S.C. § 1324(a)(1)(A)(iii). Harboring means any conduct that "substantially facilitate[s] an alien's remaining in the United States

[handwritten margin note: Evidence was adequate to support convictions]

[handwritten margin note: Evidence also sufficient to support convictions for harboring illegal aliens]

illegally." (R. Doc. 52, Jury Instruction 14); *United States v. Rubio-Gonzalez,* 674 F.2d 1067, 1073 (5th Cir.1982). A jury reasonably could conclude that Tipton and Seferi harbored these aliens by granting them employment, by providing the aliens a place to live, daily transportation, and money to purchase necessities, and by maintaining counterfeit immigration papers for each alien. *See United States v. Sanchez,* 963 F.2d 152, 155 (8th Cir.1992); *United States v. Kim,* 193 F.3d 567, 574–75 (2d Cir.1999). The same evidence that supported a finding that Tipton and Seferi knew the aliens were unauthorized for employment also furnished an adequate basis for the jury to conclude that the appellants knew or recklessly disregarded the fact that the aliens were unlawfully in the country.

The government also presented sufficient evidence to support the conspiracy conviction. The offense of conspiracy as charged in this case requires that the defendants knowingly reached an agreement or understanding either to hire unauthorized aliens or to harbor them, and that at least one defendant took an act in furtherance of the conspiracy. *See* 18 U.S.C. § 371; *United States v. Bertling,* 510 F.3d 804, 808 (8th Cir.2007). There was sufficient circumstantial evidence of an agreement or understanding between Tipton and Seferi. The Galley restaurant was run as a joint enterprise. Tipton and Seferi resided together, and divided equally the duties and profits of the restaurant. Tipton ran the dining room and kept the restaurant's books. Seferi hired, paid, and managed the kitchen staff, including the six aliens. Tipton maintained an apartment for the aliens from which Seferi transported them to work at the restaurant. A reasonable jury thus could have concluded that the two defendants had formed an agreement with respect to hiring and harboring the undocumented aliens. Once the jury found the requisite agreement, any of the several acts discussed above satisfied the element of an overt act in furtherance of the agreement.

B.

Tipton also appeals her sentence, arguing that the district court erroneously calculated the advisory guidelines range. In particular, she challenges the district court's application of a specific offense characteristic under USSG § 2L1.1(b)(2)(A) for harboring six or more unlawful aliens, and the court's increase of her offense level under USSG § 3B1.4 for use of a minor to commit the offense. 5A specific offense characteristic applies, resulting in an increase of three offense levels, where an offense involves the "harboring of six or more unlawful aliens." USSG § 2L1.1(b)(2). The district court found that Tipton harbored six unlawful aliens, and this finding was not clearly erroneous. Four unlawful aliens were living at the apartment that Tipton rented for use by Galley workers. Seferi identified two additional aliens who were detained at the apartment as workers in the Galley kitchen. All six aliens were paid in cash below minimum wage, with no taxes withheld, and with payment recorded on a separate log apparently reserved for unlawful aliens. This evidence was sufficient to support the district court's finding that Tipton intended to harbor six unlawful aliens.

The advisory sentencing guidelines also provide that the defendant's offense level shall be increased by two levels if she "used or attempted to use a person less than eighteen years of age to commit the offense." USSG § 3B1.4. The enhancement applies even if the defendant does not know that the persons used are minors. *United States v. Voegtlin,* 437 F.3d 741, 748 (8th Cir.2006). In the district court, Tipton disputed the application of this provision on the ground that none of the six undocumented aliens was younger than eighteen years old. The district court found, however, that two of the aliens were minors, and we conclude that the finding was not clearly erroneous. One alien, J.L., testified at trial that he was only seventeen years old. At sentencing, an ICE agent testified that the statements and appearance of another alien who worked at the Galley established that this alien, R.V., was about fourteen years of age. This evidence was sufficient to support the district court's finding.

Tipton argues for the first time on appeal that § 3B1.4 does not apply, even if the aliens were minors, because Tipton did not "use" or "attempt to use" them in committing the offense. The application note to § 3B1.4 states that "use or attempted use" of a minor includes "directing, commanding, encouraging, intimidating, counseling, training, procuring, recruiting, or soliciting." USSG § 3B1.4, comment. (n.1). Consistent with that listing, we have said that "the unambiguous legislative design of section 3B1.4 is to protect minors as a class from being 'solicited, procured, recruited, counseled, encouraged, trained, directed, commanded, intimidated, or otherwise used' to commit crime." *United States v. Paine,* 407 F.3d 958, 965 (8th Cir.2005) (internal quotation omitted).

Tipton contends that there was "no particular advantage" in employing minors rather than adults, that the minors were not used as "a cover for employing illegal aliens," and that the minors were not used to escape apprehension for the offense. She relies on *United States v. Parker,* 241 F.3d 1114, 1120 (9th Cir.2001), for the proposition that a minor's "mere participation" in a crime is not sufficient to trigger application of § 3B1.4, and that the government must show the defendant "acted affirmatively to involve the minor in the crime." This argument was not advanced at sentencing, and the district court did not address it. We thus review the claim on appeal under a plain error standard. *See United States v. Olano,* 507 U.S. 725, 113 S.Ct. 1770, 123 L.Ed.2d 508 (1993).

We see no basis for relief. Tipton did act affirmatively to involve the minors in the offense. She hired them and harbored them. The plain language of the guideline encompasses use of a minor, regardless of special advantage to the defendant. The purpose of the enhancement—"to protect minors as a class"—is served by punishing the use of minors whether or not there was a comparative advantage in using minors rather than adults. It is not plain to us that these minor aliens were not "used" to commit the offense within the meaning of § 3B1.4, given that "use" includes recruitment, that the employees were necessary to commission of the offense, and that the minor aliens were hired by Tipton and Seferi for employment at the restaurant without legal authorization to work in the United States. Accordingly, we conclude that the district court made no plain error warranting relief.

* * *

For the foregoing reasons, we affirm the judgment of the district court.

EXERCISE

The *Tipton* case presents an interesting and typical combination: a statute which requires proof of knowledge (that an employee is unauthorized to work) with a sentencing enhancement triggered by hiring minors that "applies even if the defendant does not know that the persons used are minors." How can this application of different rules applying to knowledge be justified?

Not all human-smuggling cases involve prostitution. Many target employers who bring in and abuse workers for the purpose of keeping cheap labor at hand. Sometimes those workers arrived legally. While immigration law is often implicated, these cases can also involve statutes addressing peonage (compulsory service in payment of a debt, which is criminalized under 18 U.S.C. § 1581) and abuse of documents. The case below includes some factual elements—particularly regarding the way employers may control foreign workers through fear—that recur in an unfortunate number of cases and mirror some of the techniques, such as manipulation of debt, which were used to oppress sharecroppers in an earlier age.

UNITED STATES V. FARRELL
563 F.3d 364 (8th Cir. 2009)

MELLOY, CIRCUIT JUDGE.

A jury convicted Robert John Farrell and Angelita Magat Farrell of four counts of peonage in violation of 18 U.S.C. § 1581, one count of conspiracy to commit peonage in violation of 18 U.S.C. § 371, two counts of making false statements in violation of 18 U.S.C. § 1001, one count of visa fraud in violation of 18 U.S.C. § 1546, and one count of document servitude in violation of 18 U.S.C. § 1592. The Farrells appeal, arguing that the evidence was insufficient to support the jury's verdict as to the charges of peonage, conspiracy to commit peonage, and document servitude. The Farrells further argue that the district court erred in admitting certain expert testimony. Having jurisdiction under 28 U.S.C. § 1291, we affirm the convictions.

I.

The Farrells own and operate the Comfort Inn & Suites in Oacoma, South Dakota. In both 2005 and 2006, the Farrells contracted to bring nine non-immigrant workers from the Philippines to the United States under temporary visas for the stated purpose of working as housekeepers in their hotel. The Government charged the Farrells with committing crimes against four of the nine. The Farrells assert that the Government presented insufficient evidence at trial to allow a reasonable jury to convict them of peonage, conspiracy to commit peonage, and document servitude.

1"This court reviews the sufficiency of the evidence supporting a conviction de novo, viewing evidence in the light most favorable to the government, resolving conflicts in the government's favor, and accepting all reasonable inferences that support the verdict." *United States v. Phythian,* 529 F.3d 807, 811 (8th Cir.2008) (quotation omitted). This court will "reverse only if no reasonable jury could have found the defendant guilty beyond a reasonable doubt." *Id.* (quotation omitted). Thus, we recount the facts in the light most favorable to the verdict.

A. First Application for Non-Immigrant Workers—2005

While visiting family in the Philippines in 2005, the Farrells began actively recruiting Filipino workers to come and work for them in the United States. After soliciting several individuals, the Farrells submitted an I-129 Petition for a Nonimmigrant Worker ("Petition") to the Department of Homeland Security on August 17, 2005. The Petition stated that they were seeking housekeepers from October 1, 2005, until January 31, 2006, at a salary of $300 per week. The Farrells were required to pay the government a one-time processing fee of $1200 with the submission of the Petition.

In addition to the Petition, the Farrells drafted employment contracts for each of the nine workers they had solicited. As with the Petition, these contracts stated that the Farrells would employ the workers as housekeepers and that the workers would work six days per week for eight hours each day. The contracts set compensation at $6.05 per hour and also provided for holiday and overtime pay. In addition to these provisions, the contracts stated that the Farrells were responsible for housing the workers and that each worker would reimburse the Farrells $150 per month for this expense. The contracts also provided that the Farrells were responsible for the cost of transportation to and from the United States, as required by law. After the Farrells submitted the Petition and drafted the employment contracts, the workers filed their applications for non-immigrant visas with the U.S. Embassy in Manila, Philippines. The applications reflected the terms of the employment contracts as recounted above, including the promise that the Farrells would pay for the workers' transportation to and from the United States.

Prior to the consular officers' adjudication of the workers' visa applications, the workers met with the Farrells in a Manila hotel. During this meeting, the Farrells prepped the workers for the visa interviews at the Embassy. The Farrells also revealed additional details about the job, including the fact that despite the provisions in the employment contracts and the requirements of U.S. law, the Farrells would not reimburse the workers for transportation to and from the United States. The Farrells stressed, however, that the workers' visas would be denied if the workers told this information to the consular officers and that they should refrain from mentioning it. The Farrells further stated that despite the contractual provisions, the workers would not receive holiday or overtime pay. Finally, the Farrells informed the workers that the $1200 Petition-processing fee would be divided equally among them.

Thus, upon leaving for the United States, the workers were under the impression that they would be making $6.05 per hour and working eight-hour days for six days each week. They also knew that they would be responsible for reimbursing the Farrells for the cost of transportation to and from the country, as well as one-ninth of the processing fee. Despite beginning the employment relationship financially indebted to the Farrells, the workers anticipated being able to pay back the money soon after their employment began. Many looked forward to working in the United States because the Philippines is a "poor country" with a "high unemployment rate" and "great corruption," and they anticipated that even with the debt payments, they would be able to send money home to their families. The U.S. Embassy approved the visas.

When the workers arrived in South Dakota in November 2005, the employment situation was not as they had anticipated. Angelita immediately required the workers to surrender their passports, visas, and immigration documents. Many of the workers were reluctant to do so but obeyed out of the "honor and respect" Filipino culture demanded they show their employers. Upon starting their jobs, the Farrells informed the workers that instead of an hourly wage they would be paid $3 per room. Because it took around one hour to clean a room to the Farrells' standards, the workers were making approximately one-half the wage the Farrells had promised (and had included in the paperwork), which was well under minimum wage. If the rooms were not up to the Farrells' standards, Robert told the workers they would not be paid at all. The Farrells further informed the workers that each of the nine would be individually responsible for the entire amount of the $1200 processing fee, despite the fact that the Farrells only paid the fee once.

In addition to the processing fee, the Farrells began charging the workers for transportation to and from work (which had not been agreed to in the employment contract) and began charging them for personal items that the workers neither requested nor desired. Thus, once in the United States, the workers' debt increased dramatically while the income with which they anticipated being able to pay down that debt had decreased by at least one-half. Recognizing that the workers would not be able to pay their increasing debt from their hotel paychecks, the Farrells required that the workers obtain outside employment. The Farrells facilitated the workers' interviews at local fast-food restaurants and other service-industry establishments. Many of the locations where the workers interviewed eventually employed the workers, in direct violation of their visas.

Other than when at their non-hotel employment, the workers spent little time away from the hotel. This was, in part, because of the manner in which the Farrells controlled the workers' free time. The workers were not permitted to leave their shared apartment, even to visit the drug store, without asking permission from either the Farrells or the hotel manager, Alma Navarro. Frequently, the Farrells told the workers that they were not to speak with anyone outside of the hotel and that they were prohibited from socializing with Americans. The prohibition against speaking to other people went so far as to preclude the workers from speaking to the non-Filipino workers who were employed at the same hotel.

When American co-workers at one of the fast-food restaurants invited several of the workers to go bowling, Robert insisted on driving the workers to the alley and remained there to supervise them. This was despite the fact that a co-worker had volunteered to drive the workers home when they were finished. At one point, without asking permission, several of the workers accepted an invitation from the fast-food-restaurant shift manager to visit a local bar. The workers did not miss their scheduled shifts at the hotel, and there was no evidence that the activity otherwise interfered with the workers' employment there. When the workers returned from the outing, however, the Farrells summoned them into the hotel office and proceeded to reprimand them for disobeying the rules against socialization. The workers testified that they were afraid of Robert. The Farrells even told the workers that they were not to accept rides from their co-workers, meaning that many were required to walk home from work in the freezing cold and snow.

In addition to the explicit prohibitions the Farrells placed on the workers, the workers' use of their free time was also constricted by the fact that they had very little of it. Far from the eight-hour days the workers had anticipated, they regularly worked upwards of thirteen hours per day, seven days a week, frequently traveling directly from the hotel to their outside employment or vice versa. The workers' living situation was also not as anticipated. The Farrells did provide housing, but seven workers were required to share one two-bedroom apartment. The Farrells paid only $375 per month for the lease but still charged the workers $150 per person per month. The workers were not given a key to the apartment; rather, Angelita and Navarro retained possession of the key. The workers were thus forced to leave the door to the apartment unlocked at all times. Frequently, Angelita would arrive at the residence unannounced, enter the premises, and search through the workers' belongings. In another invasion of the workers' privacy, Navarro would watch while the workers opened their personal mail, all of which was sent to the hotel. The Farrells had told the workers that the apartment was not registered with the post office and that their mail would be lost if sent directly there.

Despite the volume of work, the workers' income was still insufficient to meet their mounting debt obligations. Motivated by the workers' inability to pay their debts, the Farrells instituted a debt-prioritization scheme. As part of this plan, the Farrells required each of the workers to provide a breakdown of all of the paychecks that they had received while in the country, including those from their outside employment. In this accounting, the workers were also required to indicate how much they had sent back to the Philippines and the purpose for which the money had been sent. The Farrells also required a breakdown of each of the worker's expenses in South Dakota, including food, personal items, and telephone calls. The Farrells told the workers that this accounting would allow the Farrells to determine how much money they would allow each worker to spend and send home. One worker testified that these requirements meant that she gave the Farrells over ninety percent of her weekly income. When another worker pleaded to be allowed to keep more money so she could pay for her sister's tuition in the Philippines, the Farrells refused.

To ensure that the workers adhered to their debt-prioritization scheme, the Farrells forced the workers to sign contracts guaranteeing repayment and kept detailed records of each worker's debt. The Farrells would regularly hold meetings with the workers during which they consulted their debt logs and severely berated the workers for missteps at the hotel or spending money without permission. Robert always emphasized the importance of debt repayment at these meetings, and to punctuate his point, he frequently threatened to ship the workers back to the Philippines in a "balikbayan box" if they attempted to run away or do anything behind the Farrells' backs. The Farrells also stressed that the workers were in the United States by their grace and that if the workers avoided their payment obligation the Farrells would call immigration authorities. Following each group meeting, the Farrells held individual meetings with the workers to discuss each person's debt in detail. The workers testified that they were frequently scolded for spending too much money. Ultimately, prior to the workers' first departure from the United States, the Farrells required those employed at the fast-food restaurant to endorse their last paychecks to the Farrells.

Despite paying the Farrells the majority of their earnings, as the workers' visas were set to expire, they were all in much greater debt than they had been upon arriving in the country. Each worker initially had been promised two trips to work at the hotel, but the Farrells made them write letters establishing why they deserved to return. Begrudgingly, the workers wrote letters requesting re-employment. The workers testified that they had no interest in working for the Farrells but that it would have been impossible to repay the debt by working in the Philippines. Because the Farrells had made each worker sign a debt contract and had threatened the workers with physical harm if they defaulted, the workers testified that they believed they had no other option but to return to the United States again and fulfill their contractual duties or face imprisonment or worse in the Philippines. The workers testified that they would never have come to the United States in the first place had they known the extent of debt for which they would be responsible.

B.   Second Application for Non-Immigrant Workers—2006

The Farrells submitted their second I-129 Petition in early 2006. This time, the Petition listed the workers' salaries as $242 per week. Again, prior to the workers' consular interviews, the Farrells met with the group. They explicitly told the workers not to list their prior outside employment on the visa applications because the applications would be denied. The Farrells also told the workers to tell the government that the Farrells would pay for transportation to and from the United States. The Farrells then proceeded, however, to require each worker to acknowledge an additional $1200 debt for the transportation cost. At that meeting, the Farrells also provided the workers with copies of fake checks as evidence that the Farrells had paid the workers in accordance with the previous contract. The workers testified that they had neither received nor previously seen these checks.

Upon the workers' second arrival in the United States, the Farrells again required the workers to turn over their passports and immigration documents. As before, the workers did so in deference to their employers. The workers faced the same cramped living situation, and some of them were without a bed on which to sleep. Again, the Farrells prohibited the workers from socializing and required that they even ask permission before making phone calls.

The Farrells required the workers to sign a second debt contract, and in addition to recording the workers' income and mounting debt, the Farrells instituted a rigid schedule of mandatory bi-weekly payments. To cover these payments, the Farrells required that each worker surrender his or her hotel paycheck to them and post-date additional checks in the amount of the bi-weekly payment obligation. The payment amounts depended on the individual's indebtedness, but they ranged from $361 to $431 every two weeks. With a salary of only $242 per week, of which the workers were required to pay $150 toward housing per month, plus additional amounts for non-requested expenditures and personal items, the bi-weekly payments constituted an amount greater than the workers' salaries.

As the workers' debts mounted and their ability to pay diminished, the Farrells' debt-focused meetings became increasingly hostile. The Farrells would spontaneously call the meetings late at night and require those who were not working at the hotel to come from home to attend, even if that meant rousing them from sleep. The workers were not compensated for their attendance at the meetings. As before, the Farrells would berate the workers for anything they had done wrong at the hotel and emphasize the necessity of repayment. Robert frequently warned the workers not to go "TNT" or "tago ng tago," a Tagalog saying commonly used to refer to undocumented immigrants in hiding. He told the workers that if they went TNT he would find them and ship them back to the Philippines in a balikbayan box. Severely frightened, the workers believed the Farrells would find them no matter where they were. Robert repeated this threat several times per month both outside of and during meetings. At least once, the threat appears in the minutes of a meeting.

The Farrells' tirades against the workers would often last into the early hours of the morning. On at least one occasion, after one worker refused to provide postdated checks in the amount of the bi-weekly payment, the Farrells kept her in the meeting room until six in the morning. During that time, Robert continually yelled at her despite the fact that the worker was extremely frightened and crying. Because she was scheduled to work the next morning's shift at the hotel, once the Farrells released her she began her shift without having slept. Two other workers testified that when they sent money back to their families without asking permission, they were called into the office and reprimanded, being told that the Farrells were the only ones who would decide how the workers spent their money. One of the workers testified that Robert was so angry during this meeting that he feared Robert would punch him. The worker further testified that he was unable to do anything to stop the abuse because he was paralyzed by fear and did not "know anything about [how it works] here in America." He was convinced that Robert had the power to do to the workers whatever he wanted to do.

During this entire time, only one worker was able to leave the United States. After lying about how her mother was in the hospital and dying, the Farrells allowed her to return to Manila, but they controlled her every movement up until her departure. Angelita escorted the worker to the airport and only returned her passport when it was required to pass through security and board the plane. The woman never returned to the United States to work for the Farrells, but she testified that they harassed her via e-mail and telephone to ensure that she paid her debt. Eventually, as a result of the harassing conduct, the worker contacted the U.S. Embassy in Manila and an investigation was started.

In June 2006, two other workers attempted to leave after the Farrells accused them of stealing tips from the hotel rooms and humiliated them in front of the other workers as punishment. Their desire to return to the Philippines caused immediate conflict. Following a verbal altercation at the hotel, the Farrells accompanied the workers to their apartment, rushing them to get their belongings together so that the Farrells could take them to the airport. The Farrells informed the workers that immigration authorities were waiting to deport them, and when the workers attempted to call someone and ask for help, Angelita confiscated the telephone. Eventually, Robert called the chief of police and the FBI seeking to have the workers arrested. The chief of police arrived and talked to the workers, informing them that they could stay until their scheduled return flight, which was less than one week later. The police chief acknowledged that the workers were "terrified" of the Farrells and refused to speak in front of them. When the police chief left, the Farrells stayed outside of the apartment to prevent the workers from leaving. When the workers expressed concern about being able to purchase food, the Farrells said they would have to make do with what was in the refrigerator.

Still without their passports and thus unable to leave on their own, but fearful of what would happen, the workers found an old phone from the hotel, plugged it in, and called the manager of the fast-food restaurant (where some of the workers were employed) to ask for help. The workers also called the county attorney. Sometime thereafter, the chief of police returned to the apartment because, upon reflection, he felt as though the Farrells had used him to intimidate the workers. Sensing something was wrong, both he and the county attorney arranged for the workers to be removed from the apartment and the Farrells' control. The county attorney testified that it was "very apparent" that the workers were living in fear of the Farrells.

II.

A. Peonage

Peonage is "compulsory service in payment of a debt." *Bailey v. Alabama,* 219 U.S. 219, 242, 31 S.Ct. 145, 55 L.Ed. 191 (1911). "[C]ompulsory service" is the equivalent of "involuntary servitude," *id.* at 243, 31 S.Ct. 145, which the Supreme Court has defined as "a condition of servitude in which the victim is forced to work for the defendant by the use or threat of physical restraint or physical injury, or by the use or threat of coercion through law or the legal process." *United States v. Kozminski,* 487 U.S. 931, 952, 108 S.Ct. 2751, 101 L.Ed.2d 788 (1988). Thus, in order to prove peonage, the government must show that the defendant intentionally held a person against his or her will and coerced that person to work in order to satisfy a debt by (1) physical restraint or force, (2) legal coercion, or (3) threats of legal coercion or physical force. *See id.* at 952–53, 108 S.Ct. 2751. In determining whether "physical or legal coercion or threats thereof could plausibly have compelled the victim to serve," the jury is entitled to consider "evidence of other means of coercion, or of poor working conditions, or of the victim's special vulnerabilities." *Id.*

In this case, a reasonable jury could have found that the Government proved the elements of peonage beyond a reasonable doubt. As discussed above, the workers testified extensively about their treatment while in the Farrells' employment. They testified that Robert threatened them with physical force; namely, that if they attempted to "run away" he would find them, "put them in a balikbayan box," and ship them back to the Philippines. Despite the Farrells' argument to the contrary, it is indisputable that this statement was a threat of physical force. The evidence thus supports a finding that the workers were reasonable in inferring from these statements that the Farrells were willing to harm them if they attempted to stop working and leave.

The workers also testified about the Farrells' threats to have immigration authorities arrest and deport the workers if they did not "comply" with the Farrells' directives. The Farrells also threatened to call immigration authorities (and did ultimately call the FBI and the chief of police) after two workers expressed a desire to leave. These threats of arrest and deportation came despite the fact that the workers gave no indication that they would resist returning to the Philippines. The Farrells argue that they were legally entitled to explain to the workers that their visas were contingent on continued employment at the hotel. It is another thing entirely, however, to threaten to have immigration authorities arrest the workers as a consequence of failing to abide by the Farrells' rules—rules that included a prohibition on speaking with people outside of the hotel, presumably for fear that the workers would reveal the conditions of their employment—or as a tactic to keep the workers until the end of their contracts by exploiting their fears of being imprisoned by immigration authorities if they left early. *See United States v. Veerapol,* 312 F.3d 1128, 1131, 1132 (9th Cir.2002) (finding sufficient evidence to sustain a conviction for involuntary servitude, based, in part, on the employer's statement that "the police in the United States would arrest [the victim] as an illegal alien were [the victim] to seek their help").

In addition to showing the Farrells threatened the workers with physical force, arrest, and imprisonment, the evidence further supports the jury's finding that these threats actually compelled the workers to serve in order to satisfy their debt when viewed in conjunction with the workers' working and living conditions, as well as their particular vulnerabilities. *See Kozminski,* 487 U.S. at 952, 108 S.Ct. 2751. The evidence is clear that the workers subjectively feared the Farrells. They believed Robert when he threatened to hunt them down and ship them back to the Philippines in a balikbayan box, and they feared for their lives and the lives of their children if they were not able to meet their debt obligations or left the

Farrells' employment. Their fear of Robert was not unfounded as the evidence shows he regularly lost his temper during meetings at the hotel, revealing to the workers his volatile temper and sparking fears that he would resort to physical violence. There was also sufficient evidence to show that the workers reasonably believed that their employers were "powerful people" and could indeed "hunt them down" if the workers left. For example, after the Farrells had some initial trouble obtaining visas in Manila, Robert showed the workers a letter from congress persons in South Dakota and told them that the letter would fix the problem. The visas were subsequently approved, leading the workers to believe that the Farrells were well connected politically.

The workers' employment and living conditions also provide support for the jury's conclusion that the Farrells' threats "plausibly . . . compelled the victim[s] to serve." *id.* at 952, 108 S.Ct. 2751. In short, the conditions were difficult. The workers labored lengthy back-to-back shifts at the hotel and their outside jobs—employment facilitated and required by the Farrells—to meet their mandatory bi-weekly debt payments. One worker testified that this rigorous schedule precluded sleep at least four times per week. *See Veerapol,* 312 F.3d at 1130–31(discussing circumstances such as "excessive working hours" that supported a jury finding of involuntary servitude). The Farrells also denied the workers time off when the workers so requested. *See United States v. Sabhnani,* 539 F.Supp.2d 617, 620 (E.D.N.Y.2008) (recounting numerous "abuses" that served as a basis for a conviction, including twenty-hour work days and no regular days off). In addition to the long hours, the workers were not paid in accordance with their contract and were at times paid below minimum wage.

The Farrells continually isolated the workers from others in the community by refusing to allow them to speak or socialize with non-Filipino co-workers, by channeling all mail through the hotel where it had to be opened in the presence of the hotel manager, by refusing to allow them to leave the apartment to perform even the most mundane tasks without asking for permission, and by refusing to allow the workers to travel or otherwise spend their free time outside the hotel or apartment. *See, e.g., Veerapol,* 312 F.3d at 1130–31 ("Veerapol isolated her workers . . . by prohibiting them from . . . going to stores, speaking with her houseguests and the customers at the restaurant . . . or using the telephone or mail."); *United States v. Djoumessi,* 538 F.3d 547, 549 (6th Cir.2008), *cert. denied,* ___ U.S. ___, 129 S.Ct. 948, 173 L.Ed.2d 145 (2009); *Sabhnani,* 539 F.Supp.2d at 620. In addition to this social isolation, the Farrells attempted to control every other aspect of the workers' lives. They dictated the amount of money the workers were able to send back to the Philippines and for what purpose; required the workers to post-date checks that the workers knew they would not be able to cover unless they continued working at the hotel; and kept a key to the workers' residence so that they could conduct random inspections of the premises while refusing to allow the workers a key of their own.

Furthermore, the coercive nature of the threats is amplified by the workers' "special vulnerabilities," *Kozminski,* 487 U.S. at 952, 108 S.Ct. 2751, which include the fact that the workers were in the United States under temporary-work visas sponsored by the Farrells. Many of the workers arrived in the United States with very little money and were entirely dependent upon the Farrells for their housing and transportation. The fact that the Farrells required the workers to have outside jobs also added to their vulnerability. Even if the workers believed that they could leave the Farrells' employment and seek help, the Farrells made them acutely aware that they could have them deported for holding jobs outside of the scope of their visas. This fear was not unfounded. At some point during July 2006, even after she was under investigation, Angelita sent a letter to Immigration and Customs Enforcement officials at the Minneapolis airport to inform the agency that several of the workers (who law-enforcement officials had already removed from the Farrells' control) had taken unauthorized employment at various locations while they were working for the Farrells.

The Farrells argue that the possibility of deportation alone was insufficient to provide the requisite compulsion for peonage because being deported to the Philippines was not the equivalent of "imprisonment or worse," and they cite a First Circuit case for that proposition. *See United States v. Alzanki,* 54 F.3d 994, 1004 (1st Cir.1995) ("[T]he evidence must establish that the victim reasonably believed she was left with no alternative to continued servitude that was not the equivalent of imprisonment or worse." (citation omitted)). In other words, the Farrells contend that the workers could have simply stopped working and been deported.

Even assuming, as the Farrells' argument requires, that the only thing that kept the workers laboring was a fear of being deported, we are not persuaded. Here, the threat of deportation was more than a threat of removal from the United States or a threat to legitimately use the legal process to ensure that the workers abided by the terms of their visas. The Farrells had made it clear during various meetings that they would seek to collect the money the workers owed no matter where the workers went. It would have been extremely difficult, if not impossible, for the workers to meet their debt obligations on salaries in the Philippines. Based on Robert's threats that he would hunt the workers down and harm them if they failed to pay their debts, it was not unreasonable for the workers to believe that failure to pay their debt, even when back in the Philippines, would result in physical harm. As a consequence, here the threat of deportation was, in essence, a threat of force. *See Kozminski,* 487 U.S. at 948, 108 S.Ct. 2751 ("[I]t is possible that threatening . . . an immigrant with deportation could constitute the threat of legal coercion that induces voluntary servitude . . . ."); *see also Djoumessi,* 538 F.3d at 552; *Alzanki,* 54 F.3d at 1004–05 (finding that the victim's awareness of the "severely restrictive conditions" that she would encounter in the country to which she would be deported enabled the jury to conclude that "threatened with deportation . . . [the victim] confronted an alternative to continued involuntary service which she reasonably considered at least as severe as imprisonment").

The Farrells repeatedly claim that the workers' employment was voluntary and because voluntariness is a defense to the peonage charge, it is impossible for the workers' employment to have constituted involuntary servitude. As evidence of the voluntary nature of the employment, they cite the workers' return to the United States in the spring of 2006 for a second contractual term and to the fact that they allowed one worker to return to the Philippines to care for her ailing mother. Despite their argument, however, based on the evidence recounted above, a reasonable trier of fact could have concluded that the workers were not, in fact, free to leave and that it was the Farrells' coercive acts that compelled the workers to stay in the United States and return on a second work visa in order to satisfy their debts.

The fact that the workers left the country and then returned does not automatically make their employment voluntary. As discussed above, the workers would not have been able to pay their debt by working in the Philippines, and they believed that the Farrells would physically harm them if they failed to pay. Thus, a reasonable jury could conclude that the workers believed they had no choice but to return to United States and did not do so voluntarily. *See United States v. Bibbs,* 564 F.2d 1165, 1168 (5th Cir.1977) ("[A] defendant is guilty of holding a person to involuntary servitude if the defendant has placed him in such fear of physical harm that the victim is afraid to leave, regardless of the victim's opportunities for escape."). Even assuming that there were points at which the workers could have escaped the Farrells' control, a rational jury could have concluded that the workers' employment "was involuntary for at least *some* portion of [their] stay. And that involuntary portion would suffice to sustain the conviction." *Djoumessi,* 538 F.3d at 552–53 (emphasis in original) (citing 18 U.S.C. § 1584, which requires the involuntary servitude be for "any term"). Furthermore, once in the United States, it is undisputed that the workers needed their passports and immigration documentation to leave the country. It is also undisputed that these documents remained in the possession of the Farrells during the workers' entire stay. Realistically, without these documents, the workers were required to remain in the command, if not the employment, of the Farrells.

Given the above, a reasonable jury could have found that the Government presented sufficient evidence to prove beyond a reasonable doubt that the Farrells' threats of physical force and arrest compelled the workers to serve in order satisfy their debts. The evidence establishes that the workers reasonably believed that they had no option but to continue working for the Farrells. Accordingly, the conviction for peonage is affirmed.

B.   Conspiracy to Commit Peonage

The jury concluded that the Farrells engaged in conspiracy to commit peonage in violation of 18 U.S.C. § 371. The Farrells again contest the sufficiency of the evidence stating that they did not hold the workers in a condition of peonage and had no agreement to do so. To prove conspiracy under § 371, the Government must show beyond a reasonable doubt that the Farrells knowingly "entered into an agreement or reached an understanding to commit a crime," and that at least one of the Farrells "overtly acted in furtherance of the agreement." *United States v. Bertling,* 510 F.3d 804, 808 (8th Cir.2007) (quotations omitted). "An agreement forming a conspiracy may be either explicit or implicit." *United States v. Boesen,* 541 F.3d 838, 853 (8th Cir.2008).

The jury's conviction of the Farrells of conspiracy to commit peonage was sufficiently supported by the Government's evidence. The jury could infer from the Farrells' joint and extensive involvement in the visa application procedure, in the running of the hotel, and in the administration of the housing that the Farrells knowingly entered into an agreement to hold the workers in a condition of peonage. *See United States v. Tipton,* 518 F.3d 591, 595–96 (discussing the evidence of joint involvement of the co-conspirators). Additionally, any of the acts described in detail above are sufficient to satisfy the overt-action element once the jury determined that there was an agreement. *See id.* We thus affirm the conviction for conspiracy to commit peonage.

C.   Document Servitude

The Farrells also contest the sufficiency of the evidence with regard to their conviction for document servitude. In order to prove that the Farrells committed document servitude, the Government must show that the Farrells (1) concealed, removed, confiscated, or possessed the workers' passports, visas, or other immigration documents; (2) did these acts in the course of violating the peonage statute with the intent to violate the statute; and (3) acted knowingly and intentionally. 18 U.S.C. § 1592(a).

The evidence at trial was sufficient for a reasonable jury to convict the Farrells of document servitude. The Farrells do not contest that Angelita confiscated the workers' passports, visas, and entry cards upon their arrival in the United States in both 2005 and 2006. The Farrells also do not contest that they knowingly retained possession of these documents throughout the workers' entire stay. Numerous workers testified that they did not possess their passports while working at the hotel and that the Farrells took the documents to "control" them. Angelita only returned one worker's passport when that worker was at the airport and ready to board the plane. The chief of police further indicated that even after he specifically requested that Robert turn the workers' immigration documents over to the workers, Robert still refused. It was only after the chief of police threatened to arrest him for theft that Robert complied.

In addition to having confiscated and knowingly possessed the passports, as outlined extensively above, there was sufficient evidence that the Farrells had the intent to commit peonage and retained the documents while committing peonage. Because the evidence was such that a reasonable jury could have concluded that the Farrells committed document servitude, we affirm the conviction.

EXERCISE

We tend to think of human trafficking in terms of sweatshop factories in Los Angeles or sexual slavery in New York. The *Farrell* case, however, involved a Comfort Inn located in Oacoma, South Dakota—a town of fewer than 1,000 residents which is traversed by Interstate 90. In what ways might the federal government address this problem systemically?

CHAPTER NINE

CRIMES AGAINST JUSTICE

■ ■ ■

While most of the crimes we have examined so far involve actions that hurt or threaten to hurt people, there is a small but important group of criminal acts that damage the institution of justice. This group includes the crimes of obstruction of justice, perjury, and false statements.

While these charges are sometimes brought relative to crimes involving violence, narcotics, or firearms, they also figure prominently in many high-profile cases involving investigations of public corruption and financial improprieties.

A. OBSTRUCTION OF JUSTICE

At the core of each obstruction of justice crime is a similar intent: to affect the outcome of a legal proceeding through actions that subvert that proceeding.

A number of diverse statutes can be used in these cases. Some of them deal directly with what we would typically consider obstruction. For example, 18 U.S.C. § 1510(a) addresses "Obstruction of criminal investigations:"

(a) Whoever willfully endeavors by means of bribery to obstruct, delay, or prevent the communication of information relating to a violation of any criminal statute of the United States by any person to a criminal investigator shall be fined under this title, or imprisoned not more than five years, or both.

Other statutes protect discrete actors in the criminal case, such as witnesses or jurors and cover a wide variety of communications and actions. We tend to think of jury or witness tampering in terms of goons roughing up some guy in an alley, and certainly some cases bear out that stereotype. More subtle attempts to influence jurors, though, can create challenging cases.

The primary jury tampering statute, 18 U.S.C. § 1503, broadly outlaws "whoever corruptly, or by threats or force, or by any threatening letter or communication, endeavors to influence, intimidate, or impede any grand or petit juror. . . ." This breadth sometimes tempts prosecutors to charge defendants when the underlying action falls something short of the firm application of brass knuckles.

UNITED STATES V. BONDS

730 F.3d 890 (9th Cir. 2013)

SCHROEDER, CIRCUIT JUDGE:

Barry Bonds was a celebrity child who grew up in baseball locker rooms as he watched his father Bobby Bonds and his godfather, the legendary Willie Mays, compete in the Major Leagues. Barry Bonds was a phenomenal baseball player in his own right. Early in his career he won MVP awards and played in multiple All-Star games. Toward the end of his career, playing for the San Francisco Giants, his appearance showed strong indications of the use of steroids, some of which could have been administered by his trainer, Greg Anderson. Bonds's weight and hat size increased, along with the batting power that transformed him into one of the most feared hitters ever to play the game. From the late1990s through the early-2000s, steroid use in baseball fueled an unprecedented explosion in offense, leading some commentators to refer to the period as the "Steroid Era." In 2002, the federal government, through the Criminal Investigation Division of the Internal Revenue Service, began investigating the distribution of steroids and other performance enhancing drugs ("PEDs"). The government's purported objective was to investigate whether the distributors of PEDs laundered the proceeds gained by selling those drugs.

The government's investigation focused on the distribution of steroids by the Bay Area Laboratory Co-operative ("BALCO"), which was located in the San Francisco Bay Area. The government raided BALCO and obtained evidence suggesting that Anderson distributed BALCO manufactured steroids to Bonds and other professional athletes. The government convened a grand jury in the fall of 2003 to further investigate the sale of these drugs in order to determine whether the proceeds of the sales were being laundered. Bonds and other professional athletes were called to testify. Bonds testified under a grant of immunity and denied knowingly using steroids or any other PEDs provided by BALCO or Anderson. The government later charged Bonds with obstructing the grand jury's investigation. After a jury trial, Bonds was convicted of one count of obstruction of justice in violation of 18 U.S.C. § 1503. He now appeals. We affirm the conviction.

BACKGROUND

Our earlier opinion provides the background of the government's investigation into BALCO and Bonds. *See United States v. Bonds,* 608 F.3d 495, 498–99 (9th Cir.2010). Because Bonds's grand jury testimony is central to this appeal and was not at issue in the earlier opinion, we below briefly describe his grand jury testimony and the resulting criminal trial.

On December 4, 2003, Bonds testified before the grand jury under a grant of immunity pursuant to 18 U.S.C. § 6002. The immunity order stated that "the testimony and other information compelled from BARRY BONDS pursuant to this order . . . may not be used against him in any criminal case, except a case for perjury, false declaration, or otherwise failing to comply with this order." Before Bonds testified, the government informed him that the purpose of the grand jury was to investigate any illegal activities, including the distribution of illegal substances, that Anderson and Victor Conte (the founder of BALCO) engaged in. The government also explained the scope of the immunity grant under which Bonds would testify.

Bonds testified before the grand jury that Anderson never offered him, supplied him with, or administered to him any human growth hormone, steroids, or any substance that required injection. A portion of Bonds's testimony, referred to as "Statement C," formed the basis for the later criminal charge of obstruction of justice. It is the underlined portion of the following grand jury excerpt:

Question: Did Greg ever give you anything that required a syringe to inject yourself with?

Answer: I've only had one doctor touch me. And that's my only personal doctor. Greg, like I said, we don't get into each others' personal lives. We're friends, but I don't—we don't sit around and talk baseball, because he knows I don't want—don't come to my house talking baseball. If you want to come to my house and talk about fishing, some other stuff, we'll be good friends, you come around talking about baseball, you go on. I don't talk about his business. You know what I mean?

Question: Right.

Answer: *That's what keeps our friendship. You know, I am sorry, but that—you know, that—I was a celebrity child, not just in baseball by my own instincts. I became a celebrity child with a famous father. I just don't get into other people's business because of my father's situation, you see.*

Shortly after that exchange, the government returned to the subject of drugs and asked whether Anderson provided Bonds any drugs that required self-injection. Bonds answered with a somewhat indirect denial:

Question: And, again, I guess we've covered this, but—did [Anderson] ever give you anything that he told you had to be taken with a needle or syringe?

Answer: Greg wouldn't do that. He knows I'm against that stuff. So, he would never come up to me—he would never jeopardize our friendship like that.

Question: Okay. So, just so I'm clear, the answer is no to that, he never gave you anything like that?

Answer: Right.

Bonds was later indicted on the basis of his grand jury testimony. The third superseding indictment charged him with four counts of making false statements before a grand jury in violation of 18 U.S.C. § 1623(a), and one count of obstruction of justice in violation of 18 U.S.C. § 1503. With respect to the obstruction of justice charge, the indictment read as follows:

> On or about December 4, 2003, in the Northern District of California, the defendant, Barry Lamar Bonds, did corruptly influence, obstruct, and impede, and endeavor to corruptly influence, obstruct and impede, the due administration of justice, by knowingly giving material Grand Jury testimony that was intentionally evasive, false, and misleading, including but not limited to the false statements made by the defendant as charged in Counts One through Four of this Indictment. All in violation of Title 18, United States Code, Section 1503.

Bonds's criminal trial began on March 22, 2011, but was interrupted when the government appealed an adverse evidentiary ruling. The district court had excluded on hearsay grounds evidence the government contended linked Bonds to steroid use. We affirmed the district court's decision to exclude the evidence. *Bonds*, 608 F.3d at 508. The trial then continued.

At the close of its case-in-chief, the government dismissed one of the false statement charges. On April 13, 2011, the trial jury returned its verdict. The jury convicted Bonds of the obstruction of justice charge, finding on the verdict form that Statement C was misleading or evasive. It was unable to reach a verdict on the remaining three false statement counts. The district court sentenced Bonds to 30 days home confinement and two years probation. . . .

DISCUSSION

I.

Bonds claims that he could not have been convicted of obstructing the grand jury's investigation with an answer that was misleading or evasive, no matter how far removed that answer was from the question asked, unless the answer was false. According to Bonds, because his response in Statement C that he was a "celebrity child" was factually true, his conviction should be reversed. The problem is that while Bonds was a celebrity child, that fact was unrelated to the question, which asked whether Anderson provided Bonds with any self-injectable substances. When factually true statements are misleading or evasive, they can prevent the grand jury from obtaining truthful and responsive answers. They may therefore obstruct and impede the administration of justice within the meaning of the federal criminal statute, 18 U.S.C. § 1503, a statute that sweeps broadly.

The obstruction of justice statute provides in relevant part:

> Whoever . . . corruptly or by threats or force, or by any threatening letter or communication, influences, obstructs, or impedes, or endeavors to influence, obstruct, or impede, the due administration of justice, shall be punished as provided in subsection (b).

18 U.S.C. § 1503(a).

That portion of the statute, known as the omnibus clause, is comprehensive. We have described it as being "designed to proscribe all manner of corrupt methods of obstructing justice." *United States v. Rasheed,* 663 F.2d 843, 851–52 (9th Cir.1981). The essence of the statute is that it criminalizes conduct intended to deprive the factfinder of relevant information. *See United States v. Ashqar,* 582 F.3d 819, 822–23 (7th Cir.2009); *see also United States v. Brady,* 168 F.3d 574, 577–78 (1st Cir.1999) ("It is settled . . . that 'the due administration of justice' includes the operation of the grand jury, and that depriving the grand jury of information may constitute obstruction under [18 U.S.C. § 1503]"). The language of the statute does not differentiate between obstructive statements that are false, and obstructive statements that are not false. It requires only that the defendant make his statement with the intent to obstruct justice.

We can easily think of examples of responses that are true but nevertheless obstructive. Consider a situation where a prosecutor asks a grand jury witness if the witness drove the getaway car in a robbery. The witness truthfully responds, "I do not have a driver's license." This response would be factually true, but it could also imply that he did not drive the getaway car. If the witness did in fact drive the getaway car, his answer, although not in itself false, would nevertheless be misleading, because it would imply that he did not drive the getaway car. It could also be deemed evasive since it did not answer the question.

The cases interpreting § 1503 support our conclusion that misleading or evasive testimony that is factually true can obstruct justice. Several courts have noted the material similarity between evasive or misleading testimony and false testimony. In *United States v. Griffin,* the Fifth Circuit observed that there was no material difference between an evasive answer that deliberately conceals information and a false answer, because both block the flow of truthful information. 589 F.2d 200, 204 (5th Cir.1979). The Eleventh Circuit in *United States v. Perkins* grouped evasive and false statements together when it stated that "a reasonable jury could have found that [the defendant's] answers were evasive or false in an effort to obstruct the grand jury's investigation." 748 F.2d 1519, 1527–28 (11th Cir.1984).

The Second Circuit quoted with approval the district court in *United States v. Gambino (Thomas),* No. 89-CR-431 (E.D.N.Y.), in which Judge Jack Weinstein said that "literally true but evasive and misleading testimony would support prosecution of [the defendant] for obstruction of justice." *United States v. Remini,* 967 F.2d 754, 755 (2d Cir.1992). Accordingly, we hold that § 1503 applies to factually true statements that are evasive or misleading. Bonds cannot escape criminal liability under § 1503 by contending that his response that he was a "celebrity child" was true.

Bonds next asserts that even if the obstruction of justice statute can apply to factually true statements, the evidence at trial did not establish that Statement C was evasive, misleading, or material. We must view the evidence in the light most favorable to the prosecution, *Jackson v. Virginia,* 443 U.S. 307, 319, 99 S.Ct. 2781, 61 L.Ed.2d 560 (1979), and we conclude that there was sufficient evidence to convict Bonds of obstructing justice.

The jury instructions provided that the government had to prove that Bonds, "(1) for the purpose of obstructing justice, (2) obstructed, influenced, or impeded, or endeavored to obstruct, influence, or impede the grand jury proceeding in which [he] testified, (3) by knowingly giving material testimony that was intentionally evasive, false, or misleading." Bonds does not challenge the instructions as to these elements.

Bonds made Statement C in response to a question that asked whether Greg Anderson ever gave Bonds any self-injectable substances. Bonds responded that he and Anderson did not discuss each other's "business." Bonds stated:

> That's what keeps our friendship. You know, I am sorry, but that—you know, that—I was a celebrity child, not just in baseball by my own instincts. I became a celebrity child with a famous father. I just don't get into other people's business because of my father's situation, you see.

Bonds's description of his life as a celebrity child had nothing to do with the question, which asked whether Anderson provided him with self-injectable substances. The statement served to divert the grand jury's attention away from the relevant inquiry of the investigation, which was Anderson and BALCO's distribution of steroids and PEDs. The statement was therefore evasive.

The statement was also at the very least misleading, because it implied that Bonds did not know whether Anderson distributed steroids and PEDs. Yet, the jury at trial heard testimony from the Giants former team athletic trainer who testified about a conversation he had with Bonds before Bonds's grand jury testimony. According to the trainer, Bonds stated in this conversation that he knew that Anderson distributed steroids. Bonds also told the trainer about techniques Anderson used to conceal the identities of players taking steroids. This evidence at trial showed that

Bonds's statement to the grand jury was misleading. It is irrelevant that Bonds eventually provided a direct response to the question about self-injectable substances. Section 1503 punishes any "endeavor" to obstruct. Obstruction occurred when Bonds made Statement C.

With respect to materiality, we have said that a statement is material so long as it had "a natural tendency to influence, or was capable of influencing, the decision of the decisionmaking body to which it was addressed." *United States v. McKenna,* 327 F.3d 830, 839 (9th Cir.2003) (internal quotation marks omitted). The question asking whether Anderson provided Bonds with injectable substances was well within the scope of the grand jury's investigation, since many steroids and PEDs are injectable. Bonds's evasive and misleading "celebrity child" response was capable of influencing the grand jury to minimize Anderson's role in the distribution of illegal steroids and PEDs. The statement was material. . . .

The judgment of the district court is **AFFIRMED.**

The decision in *Bonds,* above, was short-lived. The case was taken *en banc* to the entire Ninth Circuit, which quickly disposed of it in a per curium opinion:

UNITED STATES V. BONDS
784 F.3d 582 (9th Cir. 2015)

PER CURIAM:

During a grand jury proceeding, defendant gave a rambling, non-responsive answer to a simple question. Because there is insufficient evidence that Statement C was material, defendant's conviction for obstruction of justice in violation of 18 U.S.C. § 1503 is not supported by the record. Whatever section 1503's scope may be in other circumstances, defendant's conviction here must be reversed.

A reversal for insufficient evidence implicates defendant's right under the Double Jeopardy Clause. *See United States v. Preston,* 751 F.3d 1008, 1028 (9th Cir.2014) (en banc) (citing *Burks v. United States,* 437 U.S. 1, 11, 98 S.Ct. 2141, 57 L.Ed.2d 1 (1978)). His conviction and sentence must therefore be vacated, and he may not be tried again on that count.

REVERSED.

EXERCISE

If you were the prosecutor and had a chance (after the testimony quoted was received but before Bonds was charged) to re-call Bonds before the Grand

Jury, what would you have asked him? What answers would you find satisfactory?

What if the person accused of jury tampering has no personal interest in the case, but rather advocates generally for "jury nullification," which is the ability of a jury to return an acquittal despite the government meeting its burden? Does that constitute obstruction of justice?

UNITED STATES V. HEICKLEN

858 F. Supp. 2d 256 (S.D.N.Y. 2012)

KIMBA M. WOOD, DISTRICT JUDGE.

On November 18, 2010, a grand jury indicted Julian Heicklen, charging him with attempting to influence the actions or decisions of a juror of a United States Court, in violation of 18 U.S.C. § 1504, a federal jury tampering statute. The Indictment states that, from October 2009 through May 2010, in front of the entrance to the United States Court for the Southern District of New York (the "Courthouse"), Heicklen distributed pamphlets that advocated jury nullification. (Dkt. No. 1.)

Heicklen has chosen to exercise his constitutional right to represent himself, and the Court has appointed stand-by counsel to assist him. Heicklen now moves to dismiss the Indictment on the ground that it is insufficient, because it fails to allege all the required elements of the crime, and on the ground that it is duplicitous, because it alleges multiple distinct crimes in one count. Heicklen also moves to dismiss the Indictment on the ground that the statute, both on its face and as applied, is unconstitutionally overbroad in violation of the First Amendment and unconstitutionally vague in violation of the Fifth Amendment. Heicklen also moves for a jury trial and a bill of particulars, in order to clarify the nature of the charges against him.

BACKGROUND

Heicklen advocates passionately for the right of jurors to determine the law as well as the facts. The Government states that, in advocating these views, Heicklen has on several occasions stood outside the entrance to the Courthouse, holding a sign reading "Jury Info" and distributing pamphlets from the Fully Informed Jury Association ("FIJA"). (Government's Memorandum of Law in Opposition to Defendant's Motions ("Govt.'s Mem.") at 1.) The pamphlets state that a juror has not just the responsibility to determine the facts of a case before her on the basis of the evidence presented, but also the power to determine the law according to her conscience. (Govt.'s Mem., Ex. A.)

In opposition to Heicklen's motion, the Government quotes an excerpt of a transcript of a recorded conversation that it alleges Heicklen had with an undercover agent from the Federal Bureau of Investigation ("FBI"), in which the agent specifically identified herself as a juror; the agent was not actually a juror. (Govt.'s Mem. at 2.) The Government alleges that Heicklen handed that "juror" a FIJA pamphlet and a single-sided, typewritten handout. (Govt.'s Mem., Ex. A.) The handout states in relevant part that "[i]t is not the duty of the jury to uphold the law. It is the jury's duty to see that justice is done." (*Id.*) The FIJA pamphlet is entitled "A Primer for Prospective Jurors" and contains 13 questions and answers for jurors regarding what FIJA characterizes as jurors' rights and responsibilities. (*Id.*)

In considering a motion to dismiss, the Court relies on the Indictment and accepts the allegations of the Indictment as true. *United States v. Goldberg,* 756 F.2d 949, 950 (2d Cir.1985). In full, the Indictment charges that:

> From at least in or about October 2009 up to and including in or about May 2010, in the Southern District of New York, Julian Heicklen, the defendant, attempted to influence the actions and decisions of a grand and petit juror of a court of the United States, to wit, the United States District Court for the Southern District of New York, upon an issue and matter pending before such juror, and before a jury of which he was a member, and pertaining to his duties, by writing and sending to him a written communication in relation to such issue or matter, to wit, Heicklen distributed pamphlets urging jury nullification, immediately in front of an entrance to the United States District Court for the Southern District of New York, located at 500 Pearl Street, New York, New York.

DISCUSSION

I.　*The Sufficiency of the Indictment*

Heicklen argues that the Indictment does not charge all of the elements of the crime defined in 18 U.S.C. § 1504 and must be dismissed.

A.　The Legal Standard for a Motion to Dismiss an Indictment

The Sixth Amendment guarantees a defendant's right "to be informed of the nature and cause of the accusation" against him. U.S. Const., amend. VI. This guarantee is given effect, in part, by Rule 7 of the Federal Rules of Criminal Procedure, which requires the prosecution to present to a grand jury an indictment that is "a plain, concise, and definite written statement of the essential facts constituting the offense charged." Fed.R.Crim.P. 7(c). The two requirements of an indictment are that it "contains the elements of the offense charged and fairly informs a defendant of the charge against which he must defend" and that it "enables him to plead an acquittal or conviction in bar of future prosecutions for the same offense." *United States v. Resendiz-Ponce,* 549 U.S. 102, 108, 127 S.Ct. 782, 166 L.Ed.2d 591 (2007) (internal quotations omitted); *In re Terrorist Bombings of U.S. Embassies in E. Africa,* 552 F.3d 93, 150 (2d Cir.2008) (internal quotations omitted). . . .

In considering the Indictment, the Court accepts all pertinent allegations as true. *Boyce Motor Lines, Inc. v. United States,* 342 U.S. 337, 343 n. 16, 72 S.Ct. 329, 96 L.Ed. 367 (1952); *United States v. Goldberg,* 756 F.2d 949, 950 (2d Cir.1985). As the Government points out, "[t]here is little, if any, dispute about the factual background of this matter." (Govt.'s Mem. at 1.) The Indictment states that Heicklen "attempted to influence the actions and decisions" of a juror of a United States Court on "an issue or matter pending before such juror," in that, from October of 2009 through May of 2010, Heicklen "distributed pamphlets urging jury nullification, immediately in front of an entrance to the United States District Court for the Southern District of New York." (¶ 1.)

The Indictment thus identifies the relevant time period, states the specific location of the alleged crime, and provides a general description of Heicklen's activities. The Indictment is stated with sufficient specificity.

The question remaining is whether Heicklen's alleged activities, accepted as true, are prohibited by the statute. Whether or not the Indictment charges an offense squarely presents an issue of law determinable before trial. *Cf. Crowley,* 236 F.3d at 108. In order to answer this question, the Court must first determine what the statute proscribes. . . .

1.   *The Text of the Statute*

As with any exercise in statutory construction, the Court begins with the text of the statute and draws inferences about its meaning from its composition and structure. *United States v. Gray,* 642 F.3d 371, 377 (2d Cir.2011). The federal statute prohibiting influencing a juror by writing provides that

> Whoever attempts to influence the action or decision of any grand or petit juror of any court of the United States upon any issue or matter pending before such juror, or before the jury of which he is a member, or pertaining to his duties, by writing or sending to him any written communication, in relation to such issue or matter, shall be fined under this title or imprisoned not more than six months, or both. Nothing in this section shall be construed to prohibit the communication of a request to appear before the grand jury.

> 18 U.S.C. § 1504.

The Court understands the statute to contain three elements:

> (1) that the defendant knowingly attempted to influence the action or decision of a juror of a United States court;

(2) that the defendant knowingly attempted to influence that juror (a) upon an issue or matter pending before that juror, or pending before the jury of which that juror is a member; or (b) pertaining to that juror's duties; and

(3) that the defendant knowingly attempted to influence that juror by writing or sending to that juror a written communication in relation to such issue or matter.

The second element is most logically understood as containing two parallel adjectival phrases describing the type of "action or decision" of a juror that cannot be influenced—1) an action or decision of a juror upon any issue or matter pending before that juror, or before the jury of which he is a member; and 2) an action or decision of a juror pertaining to his duties. Determining the scope of the statute initially requires determining what constitutes an "issue or matter" pending before a juror and what falls within a "juror's duties."

Black's Law Dictionary defines *"issue"* as a "point in dispute between two or more parties." (9th ed.2009).

Black's Law Dictionary defines *"matter"* as either "[a] subject under consideration, esp. involving a dispute or litigation; case" or "[s]omething that is to be tried or proved; an allegation forming the basis of a claim or defense." (*Id.*).

The canon of construction known as *noscitur a sociis* (or "it is known by its associates") instructs that the meaning of a word may be determined by the words surrounding it and that courts should "avoid ascribing to one word a meaning so broad that it is inconsistent with its accompanying words, thus giving unintended breadth to the Acts of Congress." *Gustafson v. Alloyd Co., Inc.,* 513 U.S. 561, 575, 115 S.Ct. 1061, 131 L.Ed.2d 1 (1995) (internal quotation marks omitted); *Aleynikov,* 676 F.3d at 79–80. Indeed, in interpreting a statute, courts "must give effect to every word of a statute wherever possible." *Leocal v. Ashcroft,* 543 U.S. 1, 12, 125 S.Ct. 377, 160 L.Ed.2d 271 (2004). Thus "matter" should be interpreted in such a way that it neither duplicates nor encompasses "issue." A "point in dispute between two or more parties" and "[s]omething that is to be tried or proved" convey essentially the same meaning, and a broad understanding of "subject under consideration" would encompass "a point in dispute" and render "issue" superfluous. Since "issue" means a "point in dispute between two or more parties," in order for neither "issue" nor "matter" to be surplusage, it would make the most sense for "matter" to mean "case."

Similarly, the fact that the statute separately prohibits influencing the action or decision of a juror "upon an issue or matter pending before that juror" and "pertaining to his duties" means that "pertaining to his duties" must have a distinct meaning from "issue or matter pending before that juror."

Black's Law Dictionary defines "duty" as a "legal obligation that is owed or due to another and that needs to be satisfied; an obligation for which somebody else has a corresponding right." (9th ed.2009). The particular legal obligation that jurors undertake is summarized in the oath that they swear before being impaneled, stating that "you do solemnly swear that you shall well and truly try this issue now on trial and a true verdict give according to the law and the evidence." The core of a juror's duties, then, is a commitment with regard to *how* a juror renders a verdict—an obligation to give a verdict according to the law and the evidence.

The statute's separate listing of "issue or matter" and "juror's duties" thus prohibits attempts to influence the action or decision of a juror with regard to both the *substantive* questions before a juror ("issue or matter") and pertaining to the *procedural* obligations of a juror ("juror's duties"). It does not, however, treat influencing the substantive and procedural points as the same.

A defendant's actions are encompassed within the requirements of the statute's second element if he attempts to influence a juror's actions or decisions on an *issue or matter* pending before that juror *or* if he attempts to influence a juror's actions or decisions *pertaining to that juror's duties*. However, the third element of the statute requires that the influence be exerted through a written communication in relation to such *issue or matter*. No mention is made of a juror's duties, and "such issue or matter" cannot be understood to include a "juror's duties" because they are presented as two distinct objects in the previous phrase. "Where Congress includes particular language in one section of statute but omits it in another section of the same Act, it is generally presumed that Congress acts intentionally and purposely in the disparate inclusion or exclusion." *Nken v. Holder,* 556 U.S. 418, 430, 129 S.Ct. 1749, 173 L.Ed.2d 550 (2009); *Aleynikov,* 676 F.3d at 79–80. This principle has even more force, where, as here, Congress includes particular language in one element, but omits it in another element defining the very same crime.

The statute thus prohibits a defendant from trying to influence a juror upon any case or point in dispute before that juror by means of a written communication in relation to that case or that point in dispute. It also prohibits a defendant from trying to influence a juror's actions or decisions pertaining to that juror's duties, but only *if* the defendant made that communication in relation to a case or point in dispute before that juror. The statute therefore squarely criminalizes efforts to influence the outcome of a case, but exempts the broad categories of journalistic, academic, political, and other writings that discuss the roles and responsibilities of jurors in general, as well as innocent notes from friends and spouses encouraging jurors to arrive on time or to rush home, to listen closely or to deliberate carefully, but with no relation to the outcome of a particular case.

Accordingly, the Court reads the plain text of the statute to require that a defendant must have sought to influence a juror through a written communication in relation either to a specific case before that juror or to a substantive point in dispute between two or more parties before that juror. . . .

Heicklen's alleged actions do not violate 18 U.S.C. § 1504. The Indictment alleges that Heicklen "distributed pamphlets urging jury nullification, immediately in front of an entrance to the United States District Court of the Southern District of New York." (¶ 1.) Both pamphlets discuss the role of juries in society and urge jurors to follow their consciences regardless of instructions on the law.

Heicklen's pamphlets self-evidently pertain to a "juror's duties," satisfying the requirements for liability under the second element of 18 U.S.C. § 1504. To satisfy the requirements for liability under the third element of 18 U.S.C. § 1504, however, the pamphlets must have been written or distributed in relation to an "issue or matter" pending before that juror. The two pamphlets do not relate to an "issue" pending before a juror, because a juror's duties are not a point in dispute between the parties to a suit. Understanding "matter" to mean "case," the pamphlets could trigger liability under the statute's third element if they were distributed in relation to a particular case pending before a juror. But unlike in *Turney,* there is no allegation that Heicklen distributed the pamphlets in relation to a specific case. Indeed, the Government concedes that it "does not allege that the defendant targeted a particular jury or a particular issue." (Govt.'s Mem. at 28.)

The Government agrees that the pamphlets pertain to a juror's duties but argues that they also relate to "an issue or matter" because they could encourage a juror to follow her conscience instead of the law, thus affecting the outcome of a case. Every aspect of how a juror renders a verdict has the potential to influence the outcome of a case, however, and thus any communication pertaining to a juror's duties would also relate to an issue or matter. Such an expansive interpretation of "issue or matter" would render completely meaningless the distinction that the statute draws between "issue or matter" and "a juror's duties." "[A] statute should be construed so that effect is given to all its provisions, so that no part will be inoperative or superfluous, void or insignificant." *Corley v. United States,* 556 U.S. 303, 314, 129 S.Ct. 1558, 173 L.Ed.2d 443 (2009); *Aleynikov,* 676 F.3d at 80–81. Indeed, it is possible to give effect to every word of 18 U.S.C. § 1504, by finding that influencing the actions or decisions of a juror "pertaining to his duties" means something distinct from influencing the actions or decisions of a juror "upon any issue or matter before such juror" and that both types of influence must have been made by means of a written communication in relation to a specific case or point in dispute before that juror in order to be punishable.

Because the Indictment does not allege that Heicklen attempted to influence a juror through a written communication made in relation to a specific case before a juror or in relation to a point in dispute before a juror, the Court finds that the Indictment fails to state all of the elements of the offense described in 18 U.S.C. § 1504 and must be dismissed as legally insufficient.

EXERCISE

The idea of jury nullification is controversial. You are a judge overseeing a criminal case, and the defense attorney begins to make an argument on jury nullification, saying "you have the absolute right to come back with a verdict of 'not guilty,' even if the government does prove each element. . . ." At this point the prosecutor objects. How would you rule?

Jurors, witnesses, victims, and informants are specifically protected from intimidation and harm. One tricky aspect of cases where a witness has been made unavailable is measuring whether or not that witness's testimony would have mattered in the case. Is it an element of the crime of witness intimidation that the successful elimination of the potential witness was material to the outcome of a case?

UNITED STATES V. EATON

784 F.3d 298 (6th Cir. 2015)

CLAY, CIRCUIT JUDGE.

Defendant and former Barren County Sheriff Christopher Eaton ("Defendant") was convicted of two counts of witness tampering in violation of 18 U.S.C. § 1512(b)(3) by a federal jury in the Western District of Kentucky for instructing two officers in his command to give false statements in an investigation regarding the alleged excessive use of force against Billy Randall Stinnett on February 24, 2010. Defendant appeals his conviction. For the reasons stated below, we **AFFIRM**.

BACKGROUND

Procedural History

The second superseding indictment in this case, issued on November 14, 2012, charged Defendant with eight counts related to excessive force, witness tampering, and obstruction of justice based on his conduct during the arrest of Billy Randall Stinnett and the subsequent federal investigation. Deputies Aaron Bennett, Adam Minor, and Eric Guffey were also charged in the same indictment. Defendant, Bennett, and Guffey were tried in a combined trial. After nine days of trial and due deliberation, the jury returned a verdict of acquittal of all charges as to Bennett and Guffey. Defendant was acquitted on all counts except two counts of witness tampering in violation of 18 U.S.C. § 1512(b)(3). The district court subsequently denied Defendant's motion for a judgment of acquittal, and this timely appeal followed.

Factual History

On February 24, 2010, Defendant and several of his deputies were involved in the arrest of Billy Randall Stinnett following an hour-long car chase that involved three different law enforcement agencies. Stinnett crashed his van into a church in Glasgow, Kentucky and fled on foot into a blind alley next to the church. Defendant chased after Stinnett and was the first to reach him in the alley. Stinnett testified at trial that once he realized that his way out of the alley was blocked, he raised his hands behind his head and tried to get on his knees in an effort to surrender. Defendant struck Stinnett over the head with his baton, drawing blood. Stinnett fell to the ground, but Defendant continued to strike him.

Defendant was shortly followed by Deputy Eric Guffey, Deputy Aaron Bennett and Deputy Adam Minor. Stinnett was placed in handcuffs while on the ground. He testified that Defendant and the other deputies continued to strike him, punching him in the head and "all over." (R. 249, Transcript, PGID 2404.) Stinnett acknowledged kicking Defendant with his steel-toed boots in an effort to stop the blows; in return, Defendant struck him on the back of his legs with the baton. Deputy Minor testified that he and Deputy Bennett arrived on the scene as Stinnett was being handcuffed. Minor acknowledged kicking Stinnett twice, although Stinnett was handcuffed and was not resisting, and testified that Bennett punched Stinnett five to ten times hard in the head. With the last punch, Bennett broke his hand. Bennett then switched to using a baton, and Defendant approached and began striking Stinnett with his baton.

Minor eventually pulled Stinnett up and took him back towards the road. Stinnett received more abuse during this walk, including a punch to the head from a special deputy by the name of Shannon White. Minor asked Stinnett if he had any weapons on him, and Stinnett answered that he had a pocket-knife in his pocket. Minor testified that he had Stinnett sit down so that he could be searched, and that Defendant pulled a closed pocket knife from a visible clip in Stinnett's pocket. The group continued walking. In a moment allegedly captured by photo, Defendant struck Stinnett in the groin with his fist, causing Stinnett to lean over in pain. (The photo, according to some witnesses, was later deleted at Defendant's request.) Minor placed Stinnett into his vehicle and took him to the hospital to be treated for his injuries.

Three teenagers in the church witnessed the scene in the alley from a second story window. Two of the teens would later report what they witnessed to their father, who in turn reported it to the Glasgow Police

Department. The Glasgow Police Department informed the FBI of the allegations, and the FBI launched an investigation. FBI Agent Mike Brown interviewed Stinnett at the Berren County Jail on March 4, 2010 to learn his version of the arrest and document Stinnett's injuries.

On March 4, 2010, Brown also visited Defendant at the Sheriff's Office to inform him of the investigation and request evidence related to the arrest. To Brown's surprise, Defendant responded that no use-of-force reports had been prepared. Minor would later testify at trial that Defendant as a practice did not require his deputies to complete use-of-force reports because of Defendant's belief that "the more reports you write, the more you could get hemmed up." (R. 210, Transcript, PGID 34.) Brown asked Defendant to have the deputies involved in the incident draft reports to be turned over to the FBI.

Two deputies testified at trial that Defendant asked them to write false reports regarding the incident—Adam Minor, and another deputy named Steve Runyon, who had arrived on the scene when Stinnett, already in handcuffs, was being walked to Minor's car. Runyon and Defendant were long-time friends and colleagues; Defendant was grooming Runyon to replace him as Sheriff. Runyon testified that Defendant approached him at the gym on March 4, 2010. Defendant told Runyon about the FBI investigation into Stinnett's arrest. Runyon testified that Defendant told him that he needed Runyon to write a report stating that he saw a knife belonging to Stinnett at the arrest scene, although Defendant knew Runyon was not present in the alley and could not have seen any such knife. Runyon testified that when he resisted Defendant's request, protesting that he was not even familiar with the scene, Defendant drove him over to the alley where Stinnett was taken into custody to instruct Runyon on where he should say the knife was located.

Runyon testified that he felt nauseated by Defendant's efforts to persuade him to provide a false report. He was afraid to ask why Defendant needed him to write a report about the knife, and he was afraid that he would lose his job if he did not comply with the request. Runyon complied, writing falsely that he returned to the alley with Defendant and "[t]here was a gray metal type knife found lying on the ground which Stinnett claimed." (R. 211, Transcript, PGID 1756–57.) Runyon testified that Defendant told him what to write in the report, read it over when it was completed, and took it from Runyon to transmit to the FBI. Runyon also told the jury that in the following months Defendant conducted "a few closed-door meetings" with Runyon where Defendant would make comments about how Runyon had a good job, and it would be difficult for him if he lost it. (*Id.* at 1766.) Runyon said the meetings would generally end with his telling Defendant how much he appreciated his job "and a few times just begging him" to let Runyon stay until he reached retirement. (*Id.* at 1766–67.) Runyon was subpoenaed to testify before the grand jury in February 2011. At trial,

Runyon testified that he gave false testimony before the grand jury when he told them that Defendant did not tell him what to include in his report; he did disclose to the grand jury, however, that he was not present when the knife was found. Runyon testified that after the indictments came out he was isolated in the department, excluded from operations and denied opportunities to work. He told the jury that no one spoke to him for months, and that Defendant once sent another deputy home as punishment for talking to Runyon.

Deputy Minor also testified that he wrote a false report about the incident at Defendant's direction.

Minor received a call from a detective with the sheriff's office informing him of the FBI investigation and requesting that Minor complete a written report. Minor testified at trial that he wrote his report in Defendant's presence with Deputy Bennett. He described Defendant "walking around the office before we started writing the reports" and going over "this story line for us to write." (R. 209, Tr. at 1512.) Specifically, Defendant told them to state that Stinnett had "pulled a knife on [Defendant]," resisted arrest, and did not obey verbal commands. (*Id.*) Minor said as he was writing the story, Defendant continued walking around the office "going over that story again and again." (*Id.*) Minor testified that Defendant reviewed his completed report and instructed him to include additional information, including that once Stinnett was handcuffed the incident was over, and that Defendant showed Stinnett a knife and asked if it was his. Minor complied with Defendant's directions. Minor testified that the information Defendant told him to include in his report was false, and that he included it because he was afraid of losing his job if he refused the orders. Minor testified at trial that Defendant asked him to prepare a false report in order to "cover up what we had done" from "[t]he FBI." (R. 210, Transcript, PGID 1536–37.) Minor further testified at trial that he repeated the false information in a subsequent interview with FBI Agent Brown and in three different state court proceedings. Minor testified that he gave these false statements because Defendant told him to and because he was afraid he would be fired and unable to find another job in Barren County if he resisted.

DISCUSSION

Defendant challenges his conviction on five grounds. First, Defendant asserts that the evidence was insufficient to support his conviction for witness tampering. He argues that this Court should read a materiality requirement into 18 U.S.C. § 1512(b)(3) and that we should on that basis conclude that the statements he procured regarding the knife did not "relat[e] to the commission or possible commission of a Federal offense" under the statute. Second, Defendant argues that the district court erred by failing to instruct the jury on the affirmative defense under § 1512(e). Third, Defendant asserts that the district court erred in failing to give a special unanimity instruction. Because Defendant did not request either instruction at trial, we review the district court's failure to provide the instructions for plain error. Fourth, Defendant argues that the prosecutor made improper remarks in closing argument regarding Defendant's failure to testify. In the alternative, Defendant argues that his conviction should be reversed under a cumulative error standard. None of his arguments is availing.

A. Sufficiency of the Evidence

1. Standard of Review

A Rule 29 motion for judgment of acquittal "is a challenge to the sufficiency of the evidence." *United States v. Jones,* 102 F.3d 804, 807 (6th Cir.1996). This Court reviews challenges to the sufficiency of the evidence *de novo* to determine "whether, after viewing the evidence in the light most favorable to the prosecution, any rational trier of fact could have found the essential elements of the crime." *Id.* On review, this Court "may not reweigh the evidence, reevaluate the credibility of witnesses, or substitute [its] judgment for that of the jury." *United States v. Mathis,* 738 F.3d 719, 735 (6th Cir.2013).

2. Analysis

Defendant was convicted of two counts of violating 18 U.S.C. § 1512(b)(3). That statute provides, in pertinent part, that "[w]hoever knowingly uses intimidation, threatens, or corruptly persuades another person, or attempts to do so, ... with intent to ... hinder, delay, or prevent the communication to a law enforcement officer or judge of the United States of information relating to the commission or possible commission of a Federal offense," shall be fined or imprisoned, or both. § 1512(b)(3). In order to obtain a conviction under this subsection, the government must prove that the defendant (1) knowingly and willfully used intimidation, threatened, or corruptly persuaded another person, (2) with the intent to hinder, delay, or prevent the communication to a federal official, (3) of information "relating to the commission or possible commission of a Federal offense." *Id.; United States v. Carson,* 560 F.3d 566, 580 (6th Cir.2009).

The trial record in this case contained abundant evidence that supported a finding that Defendant was guilty beyond a reasonable doubt of witness tampering based on his efforts to procure false reports from Deputy Runyon and Deputy Minor. Both Runyon and Minor testified that Defendant pressured them to write false reports about the incident to be delivered to the FBI, using his position of authority to obtain compliance. Both men testified that they were not presented with a choice; rather, that Defendant instructed them on the precise false information they had to include in the report, that he read and approved their reports, and that they feared they would be fired if they did not make the statements he requested. Runyon described to the jury "closed-door" one-on-one meetings where Defendant threatened his job and Runyon begged to be allowed to stay until he reached retirement. This evidence was more than enough to support the verdict.

The principal thrust of Defendant's challenge to the sufficiency of the evidence on appeal is that both Runyon and Minor gave inconsistent testimony over time and that there was countervailing evidence in the record that could have allowed a jury to doubt the veracity of their statements. He asserts that the testimony of two "admitted perjurers" cannot support his conviction for witness tampering. This argument is without merit. The jury was entitled to believe the trial testimony of the two officers. It is not this Court's role to reweigh the evidence or to reevaluate the credibility of witnesses. *Mathis,* 738 F.3d at 735; *see also United States v. Beverly,* 369 F.3d 516, 532 (6th Cir.2004) ("[D]etermining the credibility of witnesses is a task for the jury, not this [C]ourt."). And the fact that Runyon and Minor acknowledged perjuring themselves at Defendant's request can hardly be said to weigh objectively in Defendant's favor.

Defendant also argues that whether Stinnett had a knife in his hand when Defendant approached him is not "material to the federal offense" that was being investigated. Defendant contends that the witness tampering statute incorporates a materiality requirement by specifying that the crime involves hindering the communication of "information *relating to* the commission or possible commission of a Federal offense." § 1512(b)(3) (emphasis added). Defendant's theory is that the federal offense in question was alleged excessive force used against Stinnett after he was in handcuffs, and that the statements made by Minor and Runyon related to the knife could only be relevant to Defendant's use of force against Stinnett before he was handcuffed. Finding no precedent to support his interpretation of the statute, Defendant terms this a "novel" issue.

Defendant mistakes both the facts and the law. First, as the district court found, the federal investigation was not limited to allegations of excessive force after Stinnett was taken into custody. Agent Brown sought information from Defendant about the level of force that was used in effectuating the arrest, the reasons for the use of force, and the injuries Stinnett suffered—without any restriction to events occurring after Stinnett was handcuffed. Even at trial, the government presented evidence of excessive force prior to arrest, including Stinnett's testimony that Defendant attacked Stinnett as he was attempting to surrender by placing his hands behind his head and dropping to his knees.

The government's precise theory of excessive force during the investigation or prosecution, however, is beside the point. We decline Defendant's invitation to read a materiality requirement into § 1512(b)(3). The plain language of the statute applies to efforts to hinder the communication of information "relating to" the commission or possible commission of a federal crime. Abstractly speaking, it is possible that some information may be so very attenuated from an alleged or suspected crime that efforts to prevent its communication would not support a conviction under § 1512(b)(3). For our purposes, it is plain that information "relates to" the commission or possible commission of a federal crime if it concerns the incident or occurrence in connection with which the crime may have occurred. This interpretation is consistent with the purpose of § 1512(b)(3) to protect "the integrity" of even *potential* federal investigations by ensuring that transfers of information to federal law enforcement officers and judges relating to the possible commission of federal offenses be truthful and unimpeded." *Carson,* 560 F.3d at 581 (quoting *United States v. Ronda,* 455 F.3d 1273, 1286 (11th Cir.2006)). We would undercut that purpose if we required an inquiry into the legal significance of the information at issue in relation to the theory of criminal liability eventually developed in the course of an investigation.

Here, Defendant sought to present to the FBI a false "story line" about the physical confrontation with Stinnett by requiring Minor to report untruthfully that Stinnett threatened Defendant with a knife, resisted arrest, and refused to obey verbal orders, and by requiring Runyon to corroborate that story by reporting that they found a knife on the ground at the scene of the arrest. Defendant's efforts prevented the officers from communicating to the FBI the manner in which the incident actually occurred, including the fact that the knife was found, closed, in Stinnett's pocket well after he was handcuffed. Plainly, this was information "relating to" the commission or possible commission of a federal crime in that it pertained to the incident involving the alleged excessive use of force in violation of Stinnett's civil rights.

In sum, the evidence presented at trial was sufficient to support Defendant's conviction. This Court will neither reevaluate the witnesses' credibility nor graft a heightened materiality requirement onto § 1512(b)(3).

EXERCISE

Robert, a doctor, is under investigation for Medicaid fraud, and federal investigators are coming to interview his employees at his home office in Tulsa. One key to the investigation is Robert's office manager, Laurence, who is bilingual in English and French. Robert tells Laurence to claim that he only speaks French, and to engage the investigators exclusively in that language. Robert tells Laurence that this should "get them out the whole mess." Moreover, Robert tells Laurence that if Laurance does not take this evasive measure, he will never get another paycheck.

As events play out, two of the investigators are fluent in French, and Laurence communicates with them effortlessly and is fully cooperative.

If you are the prosecutor, would you charge Robert with "Tampering with a witness, victim, or an informant" under 18 U.S.C. § 1512(b)? That provision provides:

> **(b)** Whoever knowingly uses intimidation, threatens, or corruptly persuades another person, or attempts to do so, or engages in misleading conduct toward another person, with intent to—
>
> > **(1)** influence, delay, or prevent the testimony of any person in an official proceeding;
> >
> > **(2)** cause or induce any person to—
> >
> > > **(A)** withhold testimony, or withhold a record, document, or other object, from an official proceeding;
> > >
> > > **(B)** alter, destroy, mutilate, or conceal an object with intent to impair the object's integrity or availability for use in an official proceeding;
> > >
> > > **(C)** evade legal process summoning that person to appear as a witness, or to produce a record, document, or other object, in an official proceeding; or
> > >
> > > **(D)** be absent from an official proceeding to which such person has been summoned by legal process; or
> >
> > **(3)** hinder, delay, or prevent the communication to a law enforcement officer or judge of the United States of information relating to the commission or possible commission of a Federal offense or a violation of conditions of probation supervised release, parole, or release pending judicial proceedings;
>
> shall be fined under this title or imprisoned not more than 20 years, or both.

B. PERJURY

Most of us have a basic understanding of what perjury is: lying under oath. That, in fact, is the essence of the general perjury statute at 18 U.S.C. § 1621:

> Whoever—
>
> **(1)** having taken an oath before a competent tribunal, officer, or person, in any case in which a law of the United States authorizes an oath to be administered, that he will testify, declare, depose, or certify truly, or that any written testimony, declaration, deposition, or certificate by him subscribed, is true, willfully and contrary to such oath states or subscribes any material matter which he does not believe to be true; or

(2) in any declaration, certificate, verification, or statement under penalty of perjury as permitted under section 1746 of title 28, United States Code, willfully subscribes as true any material matter which he does not believe to be true;

is guilty of perjury and shall, except as otherwise expressly provided by law, be fined under this title or imprisoned not more than five years, or both. This section is applicable whether the statement or subscription is made within or without the United States.

The general perjury statute can be subject to an unusual evidentiary requirement: the somewhat misleadingly-named "two-witness rule."

UNITED STATES V. CHAPLIN
25 F.3d 1373 (7th Cir. 1994)

RIPPLE, CIRCUIT JUDGE.

In this appeal, James M. Chaplin challenges the sufficiency of the evidence to convict him of three counts of perjury under 18 U.S.C. § 1621. Mr. Chaplin submits that the government failed to satisfy the evidentiary requirement of the two-witness rule. For the reasons that follow, the judgment of the district court is affirmed in part and reversed in part.

I

BACKGROUND

Mr. Chaplin owned a firm that contracted with the state of Wisconsin to build pit toilets at various state parks. In May 1990, the state declared the contracts in default because the work was not being completed according to schedule. The state then filed a claim against Mr. Chaplin's bonding company, Transamerica Premiere Insurance. In turn, Transamerica, which had hired another contractor to complete the project, sued Mr. Chaplin. The state sought, along with other relief, the return of certain construction materials that had been delivered to the construction site. These materials included doors, toilets, and urinals. At a state court hearing on this matter in August 1990, Mr. Chaplin testified that the materials were in a trailer in the overflow parking area of the Peninsula State Park. After the hearing, agents of Transamerica were unable to find a trailer or any construction materials at that location.

Because of the cancellation of these contracts, Mr. Chaplin filed for bankruptcy on October 15, 1990. Transamerica filed a proof of claim and initiated two adversary proceedings. In the course of the bankruptcy proceedings, Transamerica deposed Mr. Chaplin. During these depositions, Mr. Chaplin was asked under oath whether he had ever given his father-in-law, Joseph Voss, $8,000 in cash on October 23, 1990. Mr. Chaplin said that he did not recall doing so. Also, Mr. Chaplin was shown a picture, taken by Al Payment (who owned Voss' residence), depicting what appeared to be construction materials in Voss' garage. Mr. Chaplin denied ever putting the materials in the garage and stated that he did not recall ever removing them.

In November 1992, a grand jury returned a four-count indictment against Mr. Chaplin for crimes stemming from his involvement in the pit toilet project. Count One charged Mr. Chaplin with knowingly and fraudulently transferring and concealing his interest in certain property in violation of 18 U.S.C. § 152. The remaining counts charged Mr. Chaplin with committing perjury in his bankruptcy depositions in violation of 18 U.S.C. § 1621. The indictment set out the crucial deposition testimony underlying each count of perjury:

Count Two

Q. Mr. Chaplin, did you give Joseph Voss $8,000 in currency on October 23, 1990?

A. I don't recall doing that, no.

Count Three

Q. I'll represent to you that Mr. Al Payment testified in his deposition on February 6, 1992, that he took this picture [Payment exhibit 2] of his garage, on either August 23 or August 24, 1991. Did you ever deposit these materials in Mr. Payment's garage, Mr. Chaplin?

A. Assuming that what he's told you is correct, no.

Count Four

Q. Payment exhibit no. 2, Mr. Chaplin, which I'm showing you right now, Mr. Voss testified that those materials were in the garage where he resides on Laveau Lane in Oconto and that you removed them in January of 1992, did you remove any materials from Mr. Voss' garage in January of 1992?

A. Two things there, that makes a presumption that what he says is correct and then you ask the question did I remove any materials from his garage in 1992. I don't recall doing that, no. As to whether or not he may have said that I don't know about that either.

R.1.

With respect to the $8,000 payment, Voss testified at Mr. Chaplin's trial that Mr. Chaplin had asked Voss to purchase some real estate for him. To accomplish this, Mr. Chaplin gave Voss $8,000. Voss said this transfer occurred "[p]robably about Octoberof '90." Tr. 92. Banking records show that Voss deposited $8,000 on October 23, 1990. The banking records further show that, on the same day, Voss obtained a cashier's check for

$8,000 made payable to Mr. Chaplin's new corporation, Neo-Genesis, Inc., and a real estate company. An IRS examination of Mr. Chaplin's finances revealed that Mr. Chaplin had over $8,000 in unaccounted-for cash up until at least October 23, 1990.

With respect to how the materials came to be in the garage, Voss testified on direct examination as follows:

> Q. When you were living in the property on Laveau Lane did Mr. Chaplin store anything in the garage?
>
> A. Yes, he did.

Tr. 96. Voss was never asked to elaborate on how he knew that Mr. Chaplin stored the materials in the garage. Al Payment, Voss' landlord, testified that he observed some materials labelled as Mr. Chaplin's in the garage in August 1991. He indicated that the materials consisted of outhouse inserts and door frames. He took a photograph of these materials, although the labels are not visible in the picture. He admitted that he had no idea whether Mr. Chaplin put the materials there.

Voss testified that the materials had been removed from the garage by February or March 1992; he did not testify that Mr. Chaplin removed the materials. Donald Rhode, one of Voss' neighbors, testified that he saw Mr. Chaplin driving away from the Voss residence in a pickup truck. He stated that the pickup truck was carrying doors and door frames. He believed this incident occurred shortly after the first of the year in 1992.

In his testimony, Mr. Chaplin denied that he gave $8,000 to Voss for the purchase of any land. He further testified that, although he still did not recall storing any materials in the garage, after his deposition he had spoken with former employees and it was possible that the materials had been stored there.

A jury convicted Mr. Chaplin on all four counts on May 21, 1993. The district court sentenced Mr. Chaplin to serve one year of imprisonment for each of the four counts. The sentences were to be served concurrently. The court also sentenced Mr. Chaplin to make restitution in the amount of $47,410.00.

On appeal, Mr. Chaplin leaves unchallenged Count One, which charged him with concealing assets in violation of 18 U.S.C. § 152. He does, however, make a sufficiency of the evidence challenge to the remaining counts, Counts Two through Four, which charged Mr. Chaplin with committing perjury in violation of 18 U.S.C. § 1621. Specifically, Mr. Chaplin claims that, even viewing the evidence in the light most favorable to the government, no rational trier of fact could have concluded that the government proved beyond a reasonable doubt that any of the three allegedly false statements he made were, in fact, false. Mr. Chaplin submits that, in a prosecution for perjury under 18 U.S.C. § 1621, the government can secure a conviction only in conformity with the two-witness rule, and that the government failed to so conform its proof in Counts Two through Four.

A.   *Principles of Law*

A person may be convicted of perjury if (1) he was under oath before a competent tribunal, (2) in a case in which a law of the United States authorizes an oath to be administered, (3) and he gives false testimony, (4) concerning a material matter, (5) which testimony was given with the willful intent to provide false testimony. *See* 18 U.S.C. § 1621; *United States v. Dunnigan,* 507 U.S. 87, ___, 113 S.Ct. 1111, 1116, 122 L.Ed.2d 445 (1993) (stating generally accepted definition of perjury under federal law).

In the instant case, Mr. Chaplin challenges the government's proof with respect to the third element of the offense: the giving of false testimony. In attempting to establish this element, the government faces certain hurdles not present in other prosecutions. First, the Supreme Court has established a strict standard for what constitutes falsity for the purposes of § 1621. In *Bronston v. United States,* 409 U.S. 352, 93 S.Ct. 595, 34 L.Ed.2d 568 (1973), the Court held that an answer under oath that is literally true but not responsive to the question, and arguably misleading, is not a violation of 18 U.S.C. § 1621. Second, at trial, the government must meet, as a general matter, a heightened evidentiary standard for establishing falsity. Under the so-called "two-witness rule," "the uncorroborated oath of one witness is not sufficient to establish the falsity of the testimony of the accused as set forth in the indictment as perjury." *Hammer v. United States,* 271 U.S. 620, 626, 46 S.Ct. 603, 604, 70 L.Ed. 1118 (1926). The two-witness rule "does not literally require the direct testimony of two separate witnesses, but rather may be satisfied by the direct testimony of one witness and sufficient corroborative evidence." *United States v. Diggs,* 560 F.2d 266, 269 (7th Cir.), *cert. denied,* 434 U.S. 925, 98 S.Ct. 404, 54 L.Ed.2d 283 (1977); *see also Weiler v. U.S.,* 323 U.S. 606, 610, 65 S.Ct. 548, 550, 89 L.Ed. 495 (1945). The two-witness rule has two aspects: (1) the falsity of the testimony must be established by more than the uncorroborated oath of one witness, and (2) circumstantial evidence, no matter how persuasive, will not by itself support a conviction for perjury. *See* President's Commission on Law Enforcement and Administration of Justice, *The Challenge of Crime in a Free Society* 141 (1967).

The two-witness rule arose in England, during the seventeenth century. At that time, the common law courts assumed jurisdiction over perjury cases with the abolition of the Court of Star Chamber, which had followed the practice of the ecclesiastical courts of requiring two witnesses. As a result, even in the common law courts, in which the testimony of a single witness was usually sufficient, *see* 4 William Blackstone, *Commentaries* 909 (Bernard C. Gavit ed. 1941), a perjury conviction could be obtained only on the testimony of two witnesses. *See* 7 *Wigmore on Evidence* § 2040(a), at 359–60 (Chadbourne rev. 1978). The theoretical justification for this approach was that in all other criminal cases the accused could not testify, and thus one oath for the prosecution was in any case something as against nothing; but on a charge of perjury the accused's oath was always in effect in evidence and thus, if but one witness was offered, there would be merely . . . an oath against an oath.

Id. at 360. In light of modern notions of the function of the jury, this original justification of the two-witness rule provides a very weak rationale for the application of the rule in the contemporary trial setting. As the Supreme Court noted in *Weiler:*

> Our system of justice rests on the general assumption that the truth is not to be determined merely by the number of witnesses on each side of a controversy. In gauging the truth of conflicting evidence, a jury has no simple formulation of weights and measures upon which to rely. The touchstone is always credibility; the ultimate measure of testimonial worth is quality and not quantity. Triers of fact within our fact-finding tribunals are, with rare exception, free in the exercise of their honest judgment to prefer the testimony of a single witness to that of many.

Weiler, 323 U.S. at 608, 65 S.Ct. at 549. Nevertheless, despite the modern practice of allowing the jury to prefer the testimony of one to many, the Court in *Weiler* refused to abandon the two-witness rule. While the original rationale did not reflect the needs of the modern jury trial, another reason justified its maintenance:

> Since equally honest witnesses may well have differing recollections of the same event, we cannot reject as wholly unreasonable the notion that a conviction for perjury ought not to rest entirely upon an "oath against an oath." The rule may originally have stemmed from quite different reasoning, but implicit in its evolution and continued vitality has been the fear that innocent witnesses might be unduly harassed or convicted in perjury prosecutions if a less stringent rule were adopted.

> *Id.* at 609, 65 S.Ct. at 550. Thus, although criticized by some, the two-witness rule remains viable in perjury prosecutions, at least in those perjury prosecutions brought under a statute in which the rule has not been expressly abrogated. . . .

Application of the two-witness rule becomes problematic when the allegedly perjurious statement concerns the defendant's state of mind. We addressed this situation in *United States v. Nicoletti,* 310 F.2d 359 (7th Cir.1962), *cert. denied,* 372 U.S. 942, 83 S.Ct. 935, 9 L.Ed.2d 968 (1963). Defendant Nicoletti had testified during the trial of another person that he did not recall being interviewed by two FBI agents in 1959. Nicoletti was subsequently convicted for perjury for making this statement, but he argued on appeal that the evidence adduced at his trial for perjury was insufficient under the two-witness rule to sustain his conviction. The government argued that the two-witness rule was inapplicable because recollection cannot be proved by means of direct evidence, but rather only by circumstantial evidence. *Id.* at 361. We agreed with the government that it is not possible to prove a defendant's state of mind except through circumstantial evidence, and we therefore held the two-witness rule not to apply in such situations. *Id.* at 363. We noted, however, that "in the ordinary perjury prosecution . . . the false statement is not a statement of belief, but rather, a false statement of some objective fact." *Id.* at 362.

B. *Application*

1.

The circumstances of this case present an initial question of characterization that implicates the exception to the two-witness rule established in *Nicoletti*.

In Counts Two and Four, Mr. Chaplin's allegedly perjurious deposition testimony involved answers that arguably referred to his state of mind. Specifically, in Count Two, Mr. Chaplin was charged with testifying falsely when he denied giving Voss $8,000 on October 23, 1990 by saying, "I don't recall doing that, no." In Count Four, Mr. Chaplin was charged with testifying falsely when he denied removing materials from Voss' garage by again saying, "I don't recall doing that, no." Because the statements include a reference by the defendant to his state of mind, we must determine, as a threshold matter, whether the *Nicoletti* exception applies to these statements. On the one hand, to his response "I don't recall doing that," the defendant added a categorical "no." That "no" could be interpreted as converting a statement regarding merely his recollection into a flat-out denial (that he gave Voss $8,000 or that he removed the materials from the garage). On the other hand, in each answer, the "no" could be interpreted as an inconsequential tack-on at the end of his response. Upon close examination of the entire record, we do not believe that the government can escape the application of the two-witness rule by characterizing Mr. Chaplin's answers as statements of belief about his recollection of the event in question. In the indictment, the government charged that the defendant's perjurious statements were denials that he had given Voss $8,000 on the date in question and that he had removed the materials from the garage. Moreover, the record reveals that it was this theory that the government presented to the jury in its opening statement. We believe that the government must now live with the characterization of the case that it initially presented to the jury at trial.

2.

With the threshold matter of characterization resolved, we turn to a determination of whether there was compliance with the two-witness rule in this case.

a.   Count Two: The $8,000 transaction

Count Two of the indictment charged that Mr. Chaplin lied when he stated that he did not recall giving Voss $8,000 on October 23, 1990. Mr. Chaplin argues that the government failed to produce any evidence that Mr. Chaplin gave Voss $8,000 on October 23, 1990. Voss merely testified that Mr. Chaplin gave him money "[p]robably about October of '90." Tr. 92. Mr. Chaplin claims that, in the absence of any testimony from at least one witness placing the date of the transaction on October 23, 1990, the perjury conviction cannot be sustained as to count two of the indictment. The government argues that Voss' testimony and the dates on Voss' bank records show that the date of the transaction was October 23, 1990. The parties essentially disagree on two issues with respect to Count Two: (1) whether the particular date of the alleged transaction is material to the government's case; and (2) if so, whether the government may prove the date by circumstantial evidence.

The specific date of the transaction *is* material to Count Two. The indictment charged Mr. Chaplin with committing perjury when he denied giving Voss $8,000 on October 23, 1990. If, for example, Mr. Chaplin gave Voss $8,000 on October 22, 1990, then his statement would be literally true, although perhaps misleading. The literal truth of the statement would be a complete defense to perjury. *See Bronston v. United States,* 409 U.S. 352, 360, 93 S.Ct. 595, 600, 34 L.Ed.2d 568 (1973) (stating that § 1621 is not to be invoked "simply because a wily witness succeeds in derailing the questioner—so long as the witness speaks the literal truth"). The government suggests that the date of the alleged transaction is not material because, at his perjury trial, Mr. Chaplin denied ever giving Voss $8,000. We disagree. The question in this appeal is not whether Mr. Chaplin lied during his perjury trial, but rather whether he lied in his bankruptcy depositions. To establish that he did lie, the government needed proof that his answer in that bankruptcy proceeding was literally false, which necessarily includes proving that the transaction occurred on October 23, 1990.

We now consider whether the government proved that the alleged transaction occurred on October 23, 1990. As we indicated above, the two-witness rule applies to this count, and it requires the testimony of at least one witness that the testimony was false and sufficient corroborating evidence to support the assertion of that witness. *Diggs,* 560 F.2d at 269–70. The requirements of this rule were not fulfilled. The government failed to provide direct evidence of the transaction date. Voss merely testified that the transaction took place sometime in October 1990. Voss' bank records show that he deposited $8,000 in his bank account on October 23, 1990, but he could have obtained the money from Mr. Chaplin before that date. There is thus no direct evidence that Mr. Chaplin made the payment in question on October 23. This situation is comparable to the one that faced our colleagues in the Second Circuit in *United States v. Chestman,* 903 F.2d 75 (2d Cir.1990), *vacated in part on reh'g,* 947 F.2d 551 (2d Cir.1991) (en banc), *cert. denied,* 503 U.S. 1004, 112 S.Ct. 1759, 118 L.Ed.2d 422 (1992). In *Chestman,* the indictment charged that Chestman falsely testified before the SEC when he stated that he had not spoken with Loeb (a client) before the purchase of certain stock, which occurred at 9:49 a.m. The government produced evidence only that Loeb spoke with Chestman some time prior to 10:30 a.m. The Second Circuit reasoned that the government had failed to establish the falsity of Chestman's testimony because no witness could place the Loeb's phone call to Chestman before 10:30 a.m. The court concluded that the two-witness rule had not been satisfied, and, consequently, reversed Chestman's perjury conviction due to insufficient evidence. *Id.* at 81.

The government submits that Voss' testimony suggests that he received the $8,000 from Mr. Chaplin and then immediately deposited it in his bank account. Because the deposit occurred on October 23, the implication is that Voss received the money on the twenty-third as well. This suggested chronology of events does not contradict anything in Voss' testimony. Nevertheless, it does not constitute direct evidence that the money was received on October 23. On the record before us, that conclusion can be reached only by an inference; the government adduced no direct evidence that Mr. Chaplin gave Voss $8,000 on October 23, 1990. Accordingly, like the judges of the Second Circuit in *Chestman,* we hold that the government has failed to meet the requirements of the two-witness rule. Mr. Chaplin's conviction under Count Two cannot stand.

b.   Count Three: Depositing materials in the garage

Count Three of the indictment alleged that Mr. Chaplin lied when he denied depositing the materials in the garage at Voss' residence. Mr. Chaplin argues that the government failed to produce the testimony of any witness who claims to have seen Mr. Chaplin put the materials in the garage. The government points to the following testimony from Voss:

> Q.   When you were living in the property on Laveau Lane did Mr. Chaplin store anything in the garage?

> A.   Yes, he did.

Tr. 96. Viewing the evidence in the light most favorable to the government, this testimony satisfies the requirement that at least one witness testify directly to the falsity of the defendant's statement.

Mr. Chaplin raises several arguments as to why Voss' testimony does not constitute direct evidence that Mr. Chaplin deposited materials in the garage. Mr. Chaplin argues that Voss was exceedingly vague with respect to how exactly he knew Mr. Chaplin stored materials in the garage. But Mr. Chaplin failed to object at trial that Mr. Voss lacked personal knowledge of the matter. *See* Fed.R.Evid. 602. Indeed, Mr. Chaplin's attorney never asked Voss on cross-examination how he knew that Mr. Chaplin stored the materials in the garage. To the extent Mr. Chaplin is arguing that there is no direct evidence that he put the materials in the garage because Voss did not say that he saw Mr. Chaplin put the materials there, we disagree. A permissible interpretation of Voss' testimony is that he observed Mr. Chaplin store the materials in the garage or that he had first-hand knowledge that the materials were stored there at Mr. Chaplin's direction.

We also cannot accept the supposed distinction between the words "store" and "deposit." At trial, Voss indicated that Mr. Chaplin "stored" the materials in the garage; in the deposition, Mr. Chaplin denied "depositing" the materials in the garage. Mr. Chaplin now argues that there was no direct evidence that he personally "deposited" the materials in the garage, only that he "stored" them there. Relying upon this semantical distinction, he submits that, under *Bronston,* his deposition testimony was not false for purposes of § 1621. The semantical distinction is of no help to Mr. Chaplin. One of the meanings of "store" is "[t]o deposit (goods furniture etc.) in a store or warehouse for temporary preservation or self-keeping." 16 Oxford English Dictionary 790 (2d ed. 1989). Although "store" has other meanings, we must view the evidence in the light most favorable to the government. It was hardly unreasonable for the jury to conclude that Voss meant that Mr. Chaplin deposited the materials in the garage. We conclude that Voss' testimony constituted direct evidence that Mr. Chaplin deposited the materials in the garage.

In addition to direct evidence from one witness, the two-witness rule requires sufficient corroborating evidence, which we have described as "independent evidence so corroborative of the direct testimony that the two when considered together are sufficient to establish the falsity of the accused's statements under oath beyond a reasonable doubt." *United States v. Diggs,* 560 F.2d 266, 270 (7th Cir.), *cert. denied,* 434 U.S. 925, 98 S.Ct. 404, 54 L.Ed.2d 283 (1977). Here, the government presented the testimony of Al Payment. Payment testified that he observed "outhouse inserts and door frames" in the garage in August 1991. He also testified that these materials were labelled as Mr. Chaplin's. In addition, the government introduced a photograph taken by Payment showing the materials in the garage. Payment admitted that he did not know who put the materials in the garage, but such testimony from him was not necessary. Payment's testimony, which was not inherently unreliable, substantiated to a significant degree the testimony of Voss. It thus constituted corroboration sufficient to satisfy the two-witness rule. *See Weiler,* 323 U.S. at 610, 65 S.Ct. at 550 ("Two elements must enter into a determination that corroborative evidence is sufficient: (1) that the evidence, if true, substantiates the testimony of a single witness who has sworn to the falsity of the alleged perjurious statement; (2) that the corroborative evidence is trustworthy."); *see also* 7 *Wigmore on Evidence* § 2042, at 369 (Chadbourne rev. 1978) ("[C]orrboration is required for the perjured fact as a whole, and not for every detail or constituent part of it."). Together, the testimony of Voss and Payment was sufficient to establish beyond a reasonable doubt the falsity of Mr. Chaplin's deposition testimony referred to in Count Three. The two-witness rule was satisfied.

c.   Count Four: Removing materials from the garage

Count Four alleged that Mr. Chaplin lied when he stated in his deposition that he did not remove the materials from the garage at Voss' residence. Mr. Chaplin argues that the government offered no testimony from any witness that he removed the materials from the garage. The government counters that the testimony of Voss' neighbor, Donald Rhode, demonstrates that Mr. Chaplin removed the materials.

The government's evidence that Mr. Chaplin removed the materials from the garage is entirely circumstantial. Donald Rhode testified that he saw Mr. Chaplin driving away from Voss' residence in a pickup truck with a load of doors and door frames. He did not testify that Mr. Chaplin removed them from the garage; he did not even say that they were from the garage. Voss merely testified that the materials were kept in his garage until February or March of 1992. He did not say who removed them. Thus, there is no direct evidence that Mr. Chaplin removed any materials from the garage. We must make our determinations on the basis of the cold record. Whether counsel for the government failed to ask the requisite questions in his examination of the witness out of inadvertence or design is not a matter that can concern us. The required information is not in the record. Hence, the government failed to satisfy the two-witness rule with respect to Count Four.

Conclusion

For the foregoing reasons, Mr. Chaplin's convictions on Counts One and Three are affirmed. His convictions on Counts Two and Four are reversed. As is the practice in this circuit, we shall remand this case to the district court for reassessment of the sentence. *See United States v. Lowry,* 971 F.2d 55, 66 (7th Cir.1992); *United States v. Cea,* 914 F.2d 881, 889 (7th Cir.1990).

EXERCISE

The "two-witness rule" is not new, and not unique to perjury. The Biblical book of Deuteronomy set out that "One witness is not enough to convict anyone accused of any crime or offense they may have committed. A matter must be established by the testimony of two or three witnesses."[1] The United States Constitution requires two witnesses for a treason conviction.

Do you think the two-witness rule should be adopted more widely? What would be a drawback to a general application of the two-witness rule in criminal law?

Perjury is not only an independent charge, but can be a factor at sentencing even if it is not charged separately. One controversial provision of the federal sentencing guidelines, § 3C1.1, has been interpreted by courts to allow for a two-point "obstruction of justice" enhancement where a defendant testifies on his or her own behalf regarding a fact material to an element of the crime and then goes on to be convicted by a jury.

UNITED STATES V. RASH

840 F.3d 462 (7th Cir. 2016)

BAUER, CIRCUIT JUDGE.

Oscar Rash, who was convicted of possessing a firearm as a felon, *see* 18 U.S.C. § 922(g)(1), challenges the district court's decision to apply a two-level upward adjustment for obstruction of justice. At his trial Rash had conceded to possessing the gun, but the district court found at sentencing that he had also deceptively downplayed his involvement with the gun. Rash argues that, because he conceded possession, his false testimony about his connection to the gun was immaterial to his conviction. But because the district court reasonably concluded that Rash's lie could have misled the jury to acquit him, the lie was material and the adjustment for obstruction was proper. Therefore we affirm.

I.   BACKGROUND

In 2007, police caught Rash, a felon, with a gun. They caught him after they responded to a report of a man with a gun and encountered Rash. They then saw him take something, which turned out to be a gun, from his waistband and drop it. Rash was arrested, and during his interview with one of the officers he said that the gun belonged to his girlfriend, Monica. He explained that after he saw that she had left her gun in his house, he went to return it to her since he knew that he could not have a gun in his house.

Criminal proceedings followed. At trial Rash repeated what he had told the police officers—that he was merely returning the gun to Monica, the owner. But the government introduced video footage from a gun store showing that Rash had a deeper connection to the gun—he had twice accompanied

---

[1]   Deut. 19:15 (NIV).

Monica to the store to help purchase it. Rash denied any role in purchasing the gun; he testified that he "was just in the store with her," and "just walked around and was looking." At closing, Rash's attorney urged the jury to acquit Rash in part because he "did not" purchase the gun.

At sentencing, the court applied a two-level upward adjustment for obstruction of justice, *see* U.S.S.G. § 3C1.1. The court found that the store's videotape footage showed "clearly that [he was] engaged in assisting in the purchase of that gun" and that he was "not just a disinterested man in the store." The court concluded that the statements Rash made denying "helping [his] girlfriend pick up the gun and that [he was] not paying attention to her and [was] just walking around" were "clearly false," and therefore provided "a basis for points for obstructing in this case." The court noted, however, that the obstruction enhancement did "not essentially change" the Guidelines range since Rash was subject to a 15-year mandatory minimum sentence as an armed career criminal, *see* 18 U.S.C. § 924(e).

Rash's sentence later was vacated under 28 U.S.C. § 2255 after *Johnson v. United States*, ___ U.S. ___, 135 S.Ct. 2551, 192 L.Ed.2d 569 (2015), invalidated the part of the Armed Career Criminal Act that determined Rash's sentence. During his resentencing hearing in 2016, Rash's attorney argued against the proposed enhancement for obstruction of justice. When, as here, the enhancement is based on perjury, it has three elements: (1) "providing false testimony"; (2) "concerning a material matter"; (3) "with the willful intent to provide such false testimony." *United States v. Arambula*, 238 F.3d 865, 868 (7th Cir. 2001). Without disputing the first and third elements, counsel contended only that Rash's statements regarding his role in the gun store were not material because Rash had admitted at trial that he possessed a gun.

The district court disagreed and applied the enhancement. Initially it ruled that Rash's testimony was material simply because it was sworn: "What a witness has to say under oath in a determination by—in a hearing where the finder of fact needs to assess the credibility of all the proof is material." The government then argued that Rash's testimony was material because it minimized his connection to the gun and therefore could have "encourage[d] the jury to nullify and not convict him of possession. . . ." The court agreed with that logic as well. It then applied the two-level adjustment, producing a guideline range of 92 to 115 months. Without the enhancement, the guidelines would have called for a sentence between 77 and 96 months. *See* U.S.S.G. Ch. 5, Pt. A. The court imposed a mid-range sentence of 100 months.

II. DISCUSSION

We start with a brief word about mootness. Although Rash was released from prison on September 9, 2016, his appeal is not moot because he is currently serving a term of supervised release (a form of custody), and a resentencing can still provide him some relief by shortening that term. *See United States v. Laguna*, 693 F.3d 727, 729 (7th Cir. 2012); *United States v. Garcia-Garcia*, 633 F.3d 608, 612 (7th Cir. 2011); *United States v. Larson*, 417 F.3d 741, 747 (7th Cir. 2005). Consequently we proceed to the merits.

Rash argues on appeal that the district court erroneously ruled that his testimony was material and therefore improperly applied the upward adjustment for obstruction. Under § 3C1.1, testimony is material if it is information "that, if believed, would tend to influence or affect the issue under determination." U.S.S.G. § 3C1.1, cmt. n.6. The parties focus on Rash's testimony about his role in the gun store, and the government proposes two ways in which that testimony was material: First, it could have encouraged the jury to acquit through nullification. Second, it could have influenced the sentence. After considering both contentions, we agree with the first but not the second.

We begin with the nullification argument. Rash maintains that his false testimony was not material because, after he admitted to possessing the firearm, his lie about his role in its purchase was not "crucial to the question of guilt or innocence." *Arambula*, 238 F.3d at 868. *See United States v. Senn*, 129 F.3d 886, 899 (7th Cir. 1997) (defendant's admission that he accepted marijuana proved the offense; false testimony about what he did with it was immaterial, rendering the obstruction enhancement clear error), *abrogated on other grounds by United States v. Vizcarra*, 668 F.3d 516 (7th Cir. 2012); *United States v. Parker*, 25 F.3d 442, 448–449 (7th Cir. 1994) (vacating an obstruction enhancement for a defendant who admitted his guilt, but falsely stated that he stole $200 rather than $1252 from a bank); *United States v. Stenson*, 741 F.3d 827, 831 (7th Cir. 2014) (adjustment upheld in firearm possession because defendant falsely testified "that it was his cell phone, not a firearm, that the police officers saw in his possession when they arrived"); *United States v. Saunders*, 359 F.3d 874, 879 (7th Cir. 2004) (adjustment upheld because defendant lied about possessing a gun, "the central issue at his trial"); *United States v. Sheikh*, 367 F.3d 683, 687 (7th Cir. 2004) (upholding an adjustment because each defendant lied about knowingly redeeming illegally obtained food stamps, a matter that was "certainly crucial" to guilt).

But even if his false testimony was not material to whether he possessed the gun unlawfully, it was nonetheless material to his conviction for that crime. When Rash lied that he had no role in buying the gun, he sanitized his connection to it and bolstered his exculpatory claim that he possessed the gun only to return it to its owner after he found it in his house. That spin on his conduct might have swayed the jury to decide that, despite his admitted unlawful possession, it should disregard the law and acquit him. A jury has the unreviewable power to nullify the law by acquitting a defendant even when the facts and law compel conviction. *See United*

States v. Sorich, 709 F.3d 670, 678 (7th Cir. 2013); *United States v. Kerley*, 838 F.2d 932, 938 (7th Cir. 1988). Jury nullification is a material risk when, as in this case, the jury receives information that invites it to ignore the law. *See Laguna*, 693 F.3d at 731. For that reason, the government may punish advocacy of jury nullification as obstruction of justice. *See Braun v. Baldwin*, 346 F.3d 761, 763 (7th Cir. 2003). Rash's lie that he played no role in the gun's purchase might not have risked influencing the jury quite as much as the government fears. But because Rash's (false) testimony potentially invited the jury to ignore the law, his testimony created a material risk of nullification. It therefore warranted the enhancement for obstruction of justice.

We note that the district court initially made an incorrect, but ultimately harmless, overstatement when it suggested that material testimony includes anything a witness says under oath. Not all sworn testimony, even if false, is material. *See, e.g., Senn*, 129 F.3d at 899; *Parker*, 25 F.3d at 448–449. But the court later adopted the government's more limited rationale for the obstruction enhancement: Rash's lie put his illegal behavior in a favorable light, and that lie, "if believed, would tend to influence or affect," U.S.S.G. § 3C1.1, cmt. n.6, the jury to use its nullification power. So the district court's earlier misstatement was harmless. *See United States v. Hill*, 645 F.3d 900, 906 (7th Cir. 2011).

For completeness, we explain why Rash's false testimony was not material to his sentencing. False testimony is material if it could affect a defendant's sentence. *See United States v. Sapoznik*, 161 F.3d 1117, 1121 (7th Cir. 1998) (holding that a defendant obstructs justice not only when he makes it more difficult for the government convict him, but "also when he makes it more difficult for the court to give him the sentence that is his just desert"). But Rash's false testimony deflecting his role in purchasing the gun did not have a realistic possibility of affecting his sentence. Once he was convicted of unlawful possession of a firearm in 2008, he necessarily faced a mandatory minimum of 15 years under 18 U.S.C. § 924(e) as an armed career criminal. The prospect that § 924(e) was unconstitutional, rendering his testimony at trial material to sentencing, was too remote—the Supreme Court would not decide *Johnson* for another seven years.

Finally we observe that in imposing its obstruction adjustment, the district court did not find that Rash specifically intended to obstruct justice through his lie, a finding that this court has previously required. *See United States v. Gage*, 183 F.3d 711, 717 (7th Cir. 1999) (remanding a case for resentencing when the district court's obstruction enhancement did not include a specific "factual finding that [the defendant] told the lie intending to obstruct justice"). But because Rash limited his argument on appeal to the materiality of this testimony, we have addressed only that one contested issue.

III. CONCLUSION

Because Rash's false testimony was material to the risk of jury nullification for the purposes of a § 3C1.1 obstruction adjustment, we affirm.

———————

EXERCISE

Imagine that you were Rash's defense attorney. Is there a way that you could have advised him to testify that would have been exculpatory yet would not have exposed him to the enhancement for perjury?

C. FALSE STATEMENTS

One of the more controversial sections of the federal code is 18 U.S.C. § 1001, which makes some false statements to federal officials that are made while *not* under oath a felony offense:

> **(a)** Except as otherwise provided in this section, whoever, in any matter within the jurisdiction of the executive, legislative, or judicial branch of the Government of the United States, knowingly and willfully—
>
> > **(1)** falsifies, conceals, or covers up by any trick, scheme, or device a material fact;
> >
> > **(2)** makes any materially false, fictitious, or fraudulent statement or representation; or
> >
> > **(3)** makes or uses any false writing or document knowing the same to contain any materially false, fictitious, or fraudulent statement or entry;
>
> shall be fined under this title, imprisoned not more than 5 years or, if the offense involves international or domestic terrorism (as defined in section 2331), imprisoned not more than 8 years, or both. If the matter relates to an offense under chapter 109A, 109B, 110, or 117, or section 1591, then the term of imprisonment imposed under this section shall be not more than 8 years.

Most commonly, § 1001 is used when those under investigation lie to federal agents. In some circumstances, this law comes close to a direct conflict with the protections of the Fifth Amendment. One dispute, settled by the Supreme Court in the case below, was whether or not simply denying an offense—an "exculpatory no"—can serve as the basis for a charge under this statute.

UNITED STATES V. BROGAN

522 U.S. 398 (1998)

JUSTICE SCALIA delivered the opinion of the Court.

This case presents the question whether there is an exception to criminal liability under 18 U.S.C. § 1001 for a false statement that consists of the mere denial of wrongdoing, the so-called "exculpatory no."

I

While acting as a union officer during 1987 and 1988, petitioner James Brogan accepted cash payments from JRD Management Corporation, a real estate company whose employees were represented by the union. On October 4, 1993, federal agents from the Department of Labor and the Internal Revenue Service visited petitioner at his home. The agents identified themselves and explained that they were seeking petitioner's cooperation in an investigation of JRD and various individuals. They told petitioner that if he wished to cooperate, he should have an attorney contact the United States Attorney's Office, and that if he could not afford an attorney, one could be appointed for him.

The agents then asked petitioner if he would answer some questions, and he agreed. One question was whether he had received any cash or gifts from JRD when he was a union officer. Petitioner's response was "no." At that point, the agents disclosed that a search of JRD headquarters had produced company records showing the contrary. They also told petitioner that lying to federal agents in the course of an investigation was a crime. Petitioner did not modify his answers, and the interview ended shortly thereafter.

Petitioner was indicted for accepting unlawful cash payments from an employer in violation of 29 U.S.C. §§ 186(b)(1), (a)(2) and (d)(2), and making a false statement within the jurisdiction of a federal agency in violation of 18 U.S.C. § 1001. He was tried, along with several co-defendants, before a jury in the United States District Court for the Southern District of New York, and was found guilty. The United States Court of Appeals for the Second Circuit affirmed the convictions, 96 F.3d 35 (1996). We granted certiorari on the issue of the "exculpatory no." 520 U.S. 1263, 117 S.Ct. 2430, 138 L.Ed.2d 192 (1997).

II

At the time petitioner falsely replied "no" to the Government investigators' question, 18 U.S.C. § 1001 (1988 ed.) provided:

"Whoever, in any matter within the jurisdiction of any department or agency of the United States knowingly and willfully falsifies, conceals or covers up by any trick, scheme, or device a material fact, or makes any false, fictitious or fraudulent statements or representations, or makes or uses any false writing or document knowing the same to contain any false, fictitious or fraudulent statement or entry, shall be fined not more than $10,000 or imprisoned not more than five years, or both."

By its terms, 18 U.S.C. § 1001 covers "any" false statement—that is, a false statement "of whatever kind," *United States v. Gonzales,* 520 U.S. 1, 5, 117 S.Ct. 1032, 1035 (1997) (internal quotation marks and citation omitted). The word "no" in response to a question assuredly makes a "statement," see, *e.g.,* Webster's New International Dictionary 2461 (2d ed.1950) (def.: "That which is stated; an embodiment in words of facts or opinions"), and petitioner does not contest that his utterance was false or that it was made "knowingly and willfully." In fact, petitioner concedes that under a "literal reading" of the statute he loses. Brief for Petitioner 5.

Petitioner asks us, however, to depart from the literal text that Congress has enacted, and to approve the doctrine adopted by many Circuits which excludes from the scope of § 1001 the "exculpatory no." The central feature of this doctrine is that a simple denial of guilt does not come within the statute. See, *e.g., Moser v. United States,* 18 F.3d 469, 473–474 (C.A.7 1994); *United States v. Taylor,* 907 F.2d 801, 805 (C.A.8 1990); *United States v. Equihua-Juarez,* 851 F.2d 1222, 1224 (C.A.9 1988); *United States v. Cogdell,* 844 F.2d 179, 183 (C.A.4 1988); *United States v. Tabor,* 788 F.2d 714, 717–719 (C.A.11 1986); *United States v. Fitzgibbon,* 619 F.2d 874, 880–881 (C.A.10 1980); *United States v. Chevoor,* 526 F.2d 178, 183–184 (C.A.1 1975), cert. denied, 425 U.S. 935, 96 S.Ct. 1665, 48 L.Ed.2d 176 (1976). There is considerable variation among the Circuits concerning, among other things, what degree of elaborated tale-telling carries a statement beyond simple denial. See generally Annot., 102 A.L.R. Fed. 742 (1991). In the present case, however, the Second Circuit agreed with petitioner that his statement would constitute a "true 'exculpatory n[o]' as recognized in other circuits," 96 F.3d, at 37, but aligned itself with the Fifth Circuit (one of whose panels had been the very first to embrace the "exculpatory no," see *Paternostro v. United States,* 311 F.2d 298 (C.A.5 1962)) in categorically rejecting the doctrine, see *United States v. Rodriguez-Rios,* 14 F.3d 1040 (C.A.5 1994) (en banc).

Petitioner's argument in support of the "exculpatory no" doctrine proceeds from the major premise that § 1001 criminalizes only those statements to Government investigators that "pervert governmental functions"; to the minor premise that simple denials of guilt to Government investigators do not pervert governmental functions; to the conclusion that § 1001 does not criminalize simple denials of guilt to Government investigators. Both premises seem to us mistaken. As to the minor: We cannot imagine how it could be true that falsely denying guilt in a Government investigation does not pervert a governmental function. Certainly the investigation of wrongdoing is a proper governmental function; and since it is the very *purpose* of an investigation to uncover the truth, any falsehood relating to the subject of the investigation perverts that function. It could be argued, perhaps, that a *disbelieved* falsehood does not pervert an investigation. But making the existence of this crime turn upon the credulousness of the federal investigator (or the persuasiveness of the liar) would be exceedingly strange; such a defense to the analogous crime of perjury is certainly unheard of. Moreover, as we shall see, the only support for the "perversion of governmental functions" limitation is a statement of this Court referring to the *possibility* (as opposed to the certainty) of perversion of function—a possibility that exists whenever investigators are told a falsehood relevant to their task.

In any event, we find no basis for the major premise that only those falsehoods that pervert governmental functions are covered by § 1001. Petitioner derives this premise from a comment we made in *United States v. Gilliland,* 312 U.S. 86, 61 S.Ct. 518, 85 L.Ed. 598 (1941), a case involving the predecessor to § 1001. That earlier version of the statute subjected to criminal liability " 'whoever shall knowingly and willfully . . . make or cause to be made any false or fraudulent statements or representations, or make or use or cause to be made or used any false bill, receipt, voucher, roll, account, claim, certificate, affidavit, 403 or deposition, knowing the same to contain any fraudulent or fictitious statement or entry, in any matter within the jurisdiction of any department or agency of the United States . . . .' " *Id.,* at 92–93, 61 S.Ct., at 522. The defendant in *Gilliland,* relying on the interpretive canon *ejusdem generis,* argued that the statute should be read to apply only to matters in which the Government has a financial or proprietary interest. In rejecting that argument, we noted that Congress had specifically amended the statute to cover " 'any matter within the jurisdiction of any department or agency of the United States,' " thereby indicating "the congressional intent to protect the authorized functions of governmental departments and agencies from the perversion which might result from the deceptive practices described." *Id.,* at 93, 61 S.Ct., at 522. Petitioner would elevate this statement to a holding that § 1001 does not apply where a perversion of governmental functions does not exist.

But it is not, and cannot be, our practice to restrict the unqualified language of a statute to the particular evil that Congress was trying to remedy—even assuming that it is possible to identify that evil from something other than the text of the statute itself. The holding of *Gilliland* certainly does not exemplify such a practice, since it *rejected* the defendant's argument for a limitation that the text of the statute would not bear. And even the relied-upon dictum from *Gilliland* does not support restricting text to supposed purpose, but to the contrary acknowledges the reality that the reach of a statute often exceeds the precise evil to be eliminated.

There is no inconsistency whatever between the proposition that Congress intended "to protect the authorized functions of governmental departments and agencies from the perversion which might result" and the proposition that the statute forbids *all* "the deceptive practices described." *Ibid.*

The second line of defense that petitioner invokes for the "exculpatory no" doctrine is inspired by the Fifth Amendment. He argues that a literal reading of § 1001 violates the "spirit" of the Fifth Amendment because it places a "cornered suspect" in the "cruel trilemma" of admitting guilt, remaining silent, or falsely denying guilt. Brief for Petitioner 11. This "trilemma" is wholly of the guilty suspect's own making, of course. An innocent person will not find himself in a similar quandary (as one commentator has put it, the innocent person lacks even a "lemma," Allen, The Simpson Affair, Reform of the Criminal Justice Process, and Magic Bullets, 67 U. Colo. L.Rev. 989, 1016 (1996)). And even the honest and contrite guilty person will not regard the third prong of the "trilemma" (the blatant lie) as an available option. The *bon mot* "cruel trilemma" first appeared in Justice Goldberg's opinion for the Court in *Murphy v. Waterfront Comm'n of N.Y. Harbor,* 378 U.S. 52, 84 S.Ct. 1594, 12 L.Ed.2d 678 (1964), where it was used to explain the importance of a suspect's Fifth Amendment right to remain silent when subpoenaed to testify in an official inquiry. Without that right, the opinion said, he would be exposed "to the cruel trilemma of self-accusation, perjury or contempt." *Id.,* at 55, 84 S.Ct., at 1596. In order to validate the "exculpatory no," the elements of this "cruel trilemma" have now been altered—ratcheted up, as it were, so that the right to remain silent, which was the *liberation* from the original trilemma, is now *itself* a cruelty. We are not disposed to write into our law this species of compassion inflation.

Whether or not the predicament of the wrongdoer run to ground tugs at the heartstrings, neither the text nor the spirit of the Fifth Amendment confers a privilege to lie. "[P]roper invocation of the Fifth Amendment privilege against compulsory self-incrimination allows a witness to remain silent, but not to swear falsely." United States v. Apfelbaum, 445 U.S. 115, 117, 100 S.Ct. 948, 950, 63 L.Ed.2d 250 (1980). See also *United States v. Wong,* 431 U.S. 174, 180, 97 S.Ct. 1823, 1826–27, 52 L.Ed.2d 231 (1977); *Bryson v. United States,* 396 U.S. 64, 72, 90 S.Ct. 355, 360, 24 L.Ed.2d 264 (1969). Petitioner contends that silence is an "illusory" option because a suspect may fear that his silence will be used against him later, or may not even know that silence is an available option. Brief for Petitioner 12–13. As to the former: It is well established that the fact that a person's silence can be used against him—either as substantive evidence of guilt or to impeach him if he takes the stand—does not exert a form of pressure that exonerates an otherwise unlawful lie. See *United States v. Knox,* 396 U.S. 77, 81–82, 90 S.Ct. 363, 366–67, 24 L.Ed.2d 275 (1969). And as for the possibility that the person under investigation may be unaware of his right to remain silent: In the modern age of frequently dramatized "Miranda" warnings, that is implausible. Indeed, we found it implausible (or irrelevant) 30 years ago, unless the suspect was "in custody or otherwise deprived of his freedom of action in any significant way," *Miranda v. Arizona,* 384 U.S. 436, 445, 86 S.Ct. 1602, 1612, 16 L.Ed.2d 694 (1966).

Petitioner repeats the argument made by many supporters of the "exculpatory no," that the doctrine is necessary to eliminate the grave risk that § 1001 will become an instrument of prosecutorial abuse. The supposed danger is that overzealous prosecutors will use this provision as a means of "piling on" offenses—sometimes punishing the denial of wrongdoing more severely than the wrongdoing itself. The objectors' principal grievance on this score, however, lies not with the hypothetical prosecutors but with Congress itself, which has decreed the obstruction of a legitimate investigation to be a separate offense, and a serious one. It is not for us to revise that judgment. Petitioner has been unable to demonstrate, moreover, any history of prosecutorial excess, either before or after widespread judicial acceptance of the "exculpatory no." And finally, if there is a problem of supposed "overreaching" it is hard to see how the doctrine of the "exculpatory no" could solve it. It is easy enough for an interrogator to press the liar from the initial simple denial to a more detailed fabrication that would not qualify for the exemption.

III

A brief word in response to the dissent's assertion that the Court may interpret a criminal statute more narrowly than it is written: Some of the cases it cites for that proposition represent instances in which the Court did *not* purport to be departing from a reasonable reading of the text, *United States v. X-Citement Video, Inc.,* 513 U.S. 64, 77–78, 115 S.Ct. 464, 471–72, 130 L.Ed.2d 372 (1994); *Williams v. United States,* 458 U.S. 279, 286–287, 102 S.Ct. 3088, 3092–93, 73 L.Ed.2d 767 (1982). In the others, the Court applied what it thought to be a background interpretive principle of general application. *Staples v. United States,* 511 U.S. 600, 619, 114 S.Ct. 1793, 1804, 128 L.Ed.2d 608 (1994) (construing statute to contain common-law requirement of *mens rea*); *Sorrells v. United States,* 287 U.S. 435, 446, 53 S.Ct. 210, 214, 77 L.Ed. 413 (1932) (construing statute not to cover violations produced by entrapment); *United States v. Palmer,* 3 Wheat. 610, 631, 4 L.Ed. 471 (1818) (construing statute not to apply extraterritorially to noncitizens). Also into this last category falls the dissent's correct assertion that the present statute does not "mak[e] it a crime for an undercover narcotics agent to make a false statement to a drug peddler." *Post,* at 817 (opinion of STEVENS, J.).Criminal prohibitions do not generally apply to reasonable enforcement actions by officers of the law. See, *e.g.,* 2 P. Robinson, Criminal Law Defenses § 142(a), p. 121 (1984) ("Every American jurisdiction recognizes some form of law enforcement authority justification").

It is one thing to acknowledge and accept such well defined (or even newly enunciated), generally applicable, background principles of assumed legislative intent. It is quite another to espouse the broad proposition that criminal statutes do not have to be read as broadly as they are written, but are subject to case-by-case exceptions. The problem with adopting such an expansive, user-friendly judicial rule is that there is no way of knowing when, or how, the rule is to be invoked. As to the when: The only reason Justice STEVENS adduces for invoking it here is that a felony conviction for this offense seems to him harsh. Which it may well be. But the instances in which courts may ignore harsh penalties are set forth in the Constitution, see Art. I, § 9; Art. III, § 3; Amdt. 8; Amdt. 14, § 1; and to go beyond them will surely leave us at sea. And as to the how: There is no reason in principle why the dissent chooses to mitigate the harshness by saying that § 1001 does not embrace the "exculpatory no," rather than by saying that § 1001 has no application unless the defendant has been warned of the consequences of lying, or indeed unless the defendant has been put under oath. We are again at sea.

To be sure, some of this uncertainty would be eliminated, at our stage of judging, if we wrenched out of its context the principle quoted by the dissent from Sir Edward Coke, that "*communis opinio* is of good authoritie in law," and if we applied that principle consistently to a consensus in the judgments of the courts of appeals. (Of course the courts of appeals themselves, and the district courts, would still be entirely at sea, until such time as a consensus would have developed.) But the dissent does not propose, and its author has not practiced, consistent application of the principle, see, *e.g., Hubbard v. United States,* 514 U.S. 695, 713, 115 S.Ct. 1754, 1763, 131 L.Ed.2d 779 (1995) (opinion of STEVENS, J.) ("We think the text of § 1001 forecloses any argument that we should simply ratify the body of cases adopting the judicial function exception"); *Chapman v. United States,* 500 U.S. 453, 468, 111 S.Ct. 1919, 1929, 114 L.Ed.2d 524 (1991)(STEVENS, J., dissenting) (disagreeing with the unanimous conclusions of the Courts of Appeals that interpreted the criminal statute at issue); thus it becomes yet another user-friendly judicial rule to be invoked *ad libitum*.

* * *

In sum, we find nothing to support the "exculpatory no" doctrine except the many Court of Appeals decisions that have embraced it. While *communis error facit jus* may be a sadly accurate description of reality, it is not the normative basis of this Court's jurisprudence. Courts may not create their own limitations on legislation, no matter how alluring the policy arguments for doing so, and no matter how widely the blame may be spread. Because the plain language of § 1001 admits of no exception for an "exculpatory no," we affirm the judgment of the Court of Appeals.

In *Brogan*, Justice Scalia raised the "cruel trilemma": Upon being questioned by investigators, the defendant must either admit guilt, remain silent, or lie. This trilemma, in fact, is one of the strongest tools investigators have, since many people when being questioned find it very hard to remain silent; we feel an inherent need to explain ourselves.

Do you think there should be limits on police questioning to somehow mitigate this trilemma? What would those limits look like?

———————

Let's add one new dimension to the "trilemma" described in *Brogan*. What if the three options available to the target of an investigation are to (1) confess a crime, (2) lie, or (3) to remain silent and lose her job? That can be the situation where the false statement is made not only *to* but *by* law enforcement officials.

UNITED STATES v. COOK

526 F. Supp. 2d 1 (D.C.D.C. 2007)

ELLEN SEGAL HUVELLE, DISTRICT JUDGE.

Defendant Stephen Cook, a Deputy United States Marshal, was allegedly involved in an incident with Omar Hunter while Hunter was in the custody of the United States Marshal Service ("USMS") on August 30, 2005. As a result, Hunter filed a Citizen Complaint Report the same day claiming that Cook assaulted him in the sallyport in the Superior Court. Immediately after receiving the complaint, defendant's supervisor, Supervisory Deputy United States Marshal Paul Rivers, instructed defendant to complete a USM-210 Field Report and a USM-133 Use of Force Report concerning the incident. Defendant did so.

On May 11, 2006, the government filed a seven-count indictment against defendant. Count 1 charges defendant with using unreasonable force against Omar Hunter, thereby depriving him of his liberty without due process of law, in violation of 18 U.S.C. § 242. Count 2 alleges that Cook made false statements by filing a false Field Report in violation of 18 U.S.C. §§ 1001(a)(1) and (a)(2). Count 3 alleges that Cook conspired with others to submit false Field Reports and to testify falsely before the grand jury in violation of 18 U.S.C. § 371. Finally, Counts 4 and 6 allege that Cook tampered with a grand jury witness in violation of 18 U.S.C. § 1512(b)(1).

Defendant Stephen Cook has moved this Court to suppress the statements he made in his Field and Use of Force Reports, arguing that their use against him in a criminal prosecution violates his due process rights and his privilege against self-incrimination pursuant to *Garrity v. New Jersey*, 385 U.S. 493, 87 S.Ct. 616, 17 L.Ed.2d 562 (1967). (Def.'s Mot. at 1.) The Court held an evidentiary hearing on October 15, 2007, at which the defendant, Supervisory Deputy United States Marshal Paul Rivers, and Chief Inspector Stanley E. Griscavage testified. At the conclusion of the hearing, the Court ruled from the bench denying defendant's due process claim, but took defendant's *Garrity* argument under advisement and requested supplemental pleadings regarding the applicability of *United States v. Veal,* 153 F.3d 1233 (11th Cir.1998), *cert. denied,* 526 U.S. 1147, 119 S.Ct. 2024, 143 L.Ed.2d 1035 (1999). Having now reviewed the testimony, the pleadings, and the relevant law, the Court denies defendant's motion based on the following findings of fact and conclusions of law.

FINDINGS OF FACT

I. Hearing Testimony

A. Supervisory Deputy United States Marshal Paul Rivers

Supervisory Deputy United States Marshal Paul Rivers testified that he has been employed with the United States Marshal Service since October 1990. Since April 2004, Rivers has been a Supervisory Deputy in Superior Court. As a Supervisory Deputy, Rivers is responsible for handling prisoners, managing deputy rotations, and handling personnel matters for the deputies he supervises.

Rivers testified that pursuant to USMS policies and procedures, deputies are required to file a USM-210 Field Report whenever any incident occurs that is "out of the ordinary," which could include anything from finding contraband to someone falling on the stairs. If the incident involves any use of force, the deputy must also file a USM-133 Use of Force Report as well as the Field Report. Use of Force Reports are required when the physical force used is anything beyond that necessary for a "come along hold" or an "escort stand." Rivers testified that the use of both of these reports is routine. He receives Field Reports daily and between one and three Use of Force Reports per week. Upon receiving these reports, Rivers checks for spelling and grammar errors, and then forwards them to Chief Greg Petchel. He is not responsible for evaluating whether the claims have merit or for determining whether to initiate a formal administrative or criminal investigation. He simply collects the reports and forwards them to the chief.

On August 31, 2005, Rivers, who was employed as the AM cell block supervisor at the Superior Court, received from his secretary a Citizen Complaint Report that had been filed by Omar Hunter. He alleged that on August 30, 2005, an unnamed deputy had used excessive force on the complainant while he was in the custody of the USMS in the sallyport in the Superior Court. (Def.'s Ex. 1.) The physical description of the deputy did not match any of the marshals, so Rivers asked Cook, who happened to be nearby, if he knew anything about the incident. Cook identified himself as the deputy against whom the allegations had been made. Cook told him that nothing had happened-he just had to help a guy off the prisoner van. Rivers then instructed Cook to fill out the "basic" forms, the USM-210 and the USM-133, in the next couple of days, and confirmed with him which other officers had been present at the time of the alleged incident. He did not give Cook any *Garrity* warning prior to requesting the reports, nor was he aware of what *Garrity* was at the time of this incident. Rivers did not remember questioning Cook any further about the incident. He also instructed the other deputies who had been present at the scene (Deputies Sharpstene, Behringer, Greenlee, and Ramsey) to fill out USM-210 reports. Rivers testified that he did not threaten Cook or any of the other deputies with termination or any other form of discipline if they failed to file the report.

Once Rivers received the reports from Cook and the other deputies, as well as from the Deputy-in-Charge Steve Long, he turned them over to the chief. He did no further investigation and made no recommendation either written or oral to any superior. The matter did not seem urgent to Rivers, for as he explained, while he has been a supervisor there have been several major incidents, including seizures, injuries, and attacks, and this incident did not seem "like a big deal" so he spent "very little" time on it.

B. Defendant Stephen Cook

Cook testified that he has been employed at the USMS since January 2003 and is currently on leave. He did not have a smooth relationship with his supervisor Rivers, and he believed that Rivers "singled him out" for discipline. However, prior to this incident, Cook had never been subject to any form of discipline, and he had always received successful evaluations from Rivers. Cook was aware that he had previously been subjected to a "handful" of internal affairs investigations between 2003 and 2005, but he had never been interviewed in connection with any of them. He learned of these investigations only after he received letters saying that investigations had been opened and closed. Cook also testified that he had previously filled out both Field and Use of Force Reports. He had filled out between six and eight Use of Force Reports prior to this incident, sometimes on his own initiative and sometimes when told to do so by his supervisor. In all of these cases, Cook believed that he had used force.

Cook's testimony about his conversation on August 31 did not differ substantially from River's account. Cook explained that he was present when Rivers received the complaint and, after reading it, he identified himself as its subject. He was not concerned when Rivers instructed him to file a Field Report because such reports are routine. However, after he submitted the Field Report, Rivers then told him to file a Use of Force Report. Cook responded that no force had been used, but Rivers instructed him to file the report anyways. Rivers never threatened him with any possibility of discipline for failing to file, nor did Rivers question him about the incident involving Hunter. Cook described Rivers's tone as being "conversational" and admitted that Rivers never "ordered" him to file the report. He believed that it was "abnormal" for Rivers to instruct him to file a report having been told that no force had been used. He nonetheless went to the computer and "copied and pasted" the contents of his Field Report into his Use of Force Report and submitted it to Rivers. (*See* Gov't Ex. 3.)

Cook testified that at the time he believed that if he failed to file the report, he could be fired. He believed this because another deputy, Christopher Christian, had been told by the chief that he would be fired if he failed to file a report. Cook was unable to recall whether he learned about Christian's situation before or after August 31, 2005. Cook also testified that he was not familiar with the particular USM policy that explains the penalty for failing to file a report or failing to follow an order, but said that he received training prior to August 2005, at which time he was told that he was required to cooperate in an investigation by answering questions and filling out reports.

C.   Chief Inspector Stanley E. Griscavage

Stanley E. Griscavage, Chief Inspector of the Office of Internal Investigations ("OII") for the USMS, testified to the policies and procedures for reporting and investigating incidents involving the use of force. He explained that any use of force must be documented in a USM-133 Report. This report is used in the normal course of business to document incidents ranging from "physical control" to the discharge of a firearm. As an example, Griscavage indicated that no report would be necessary if an officer was required to touch a suspect in order to place handcuffs on him, but if the suspect resisted, then the force used to restrain him would be reportable. Deputies have the obligation to fill out a USM-133 Report any time they use force (*see* Gov't Reply Ex. 3 [Use of Force Report] at 3), and it is the responsibility of the supervisor to ensure that the report is completed.

After the reports of an incident are completed, they are then automatically forwarded to OII, where Griscavage reviews them. If he determines that the use of force was appropriate and proper, and absent any formal complaint, the reports are processed and filed for statistical purposes. If a formal citizen complaint is filed for which no previous USM-133 or USM-210 has been submitted, the complaint is usually sent to OII without any accompanying documentation. In such a situation, the policies and procedures are silent as to whether a supervisor should request a USM-133 or USM-210 before sending the complaint to OII. However, according to Griscavage, it is very unusual for a supervisor to request that a USM-133 or a USM-210 be completed after a citizen complaint has been filed, especially where there has been a passage of time between the alleged incident and the filing of the complaint.

If OII believes that a USM-133 report requires further investigation or if there is a formal citizen complaint that alleges excessive force, that report is automatically forwarded to both the Office of the Inspector General ("OIG") and DOJ's Civil Rights Division. The large majority of cases where no citizen complaint has been filed are reviewed and closed by OII without being forwarded. Griscavage testified that he was not familiar with the internal review process of either OIG or Civil Rights, but explained the possible outcomes of sending a case to these offices. After reviewing the complaint, Civil Rights either sends a notification that it will pursue its own investigation (usually by using the FBI) or sends a letter of declination. OIG either refers the case back to OII to handle as a management issue; retains it for its own administrative or criminal investigation; or initiates a joint investigation with OII. Griscavage explained that the forwarding of a case to OIG and Civil Rights officially opens an administrative investigation because it triggers the opening of a case in the database and the assignment of a case number. Local supervisors do not have the responsibility for determining when or if an administrative or criminal investigation should be initiated, nor do they conduct investigations. In fact, it would be "improper" for them to do so.

Once an administrative or criminal investigation has been opened, the deputy receives certain procedural protections pursuant to *Garrity,* which are explained in Article 39 of the Master Agreement between the Marshal Service and the union. (*See* Court's Ex. 3.) The deputy is notified that an administrative action is being pursued and that he has the right to seek representation. OII makes the decision when to provide the *Garrity* notice, and a line supervisor may not decide to do so before OIG and DOJ have had the opportunity to review the matter. However, *Garrity* protections do not apply prior to the initiation of the administrative or criminal investigation.

If a deputy is instructed to file a report by his supervisor, he has no choice but to respond or to face possible discipline. This decision to discipline is not made by the line supervisor. The report of insubordination is submitted to OII, which forwards it to OIG. OIG can either choose to pursue its own investigation of the matter; refer it back to OII to open an administrative action; or pursue a joint investigation with OII. Once OII has completed its investigation, it forwards its conclusions to a disciplinary panel. The panel reviews the case, issues a proposal letter based on its findings to the deciding official, and the deciding official then meets with the subject employee or reviews his or her paperwork and makes a determination as to what kind of disciplinary action is appropriate. Griscavage was unaware of any instance where a marshal with a clean disciplinary record was terminated for failing to file a necessary report.

CONCLUSIONS OF LAW

I. Governing Principles of Law

Cook argues that his Field and Use of Force Reports may not be used against him because they were obtained in violation of his Fifth Amendment right against self-incrimination. He maintains that because

Hunter's complaint alleged possible criminal conduct, Rivers's instruction to write these reports should have been accompanied by a *Garrity* warning, and in the absence of such a warning, his statements were coerced and must be suppressed. Cook's argument is based on a misunderstanding of the protections to which he is entitled under *Garrity*.

In *Garrity,* officers under investigation for corruption were warned before questioning "(1) that anything [they] said might be used against [them] in any state criminal proceeding; (2) that [they] had the privilege to refuse to answer if the disclosure would tend to incriminate [them]; but (3) that if [they] refused to answer [they] would be subject to removal from office." 385 U.S. at 494, 87 S.Ct. 616. The Supreme Court determined that the choice presented to the officers "either to forfeit their jobs or to incriminate themselves" was "likely to exert such pressure upon an individual as to disable from making a free and rational choice" and therefore could not "be sustained as voluntary. . . ." *Id.*at 497–98, 87 S.Ct. 616 (internal quotation marks omitted). The Court concluded that "the protection of the individual under the Fourteenth Amendment against coerced statements prohibits use in subsequent criminal proceedings of statements obtained under the threat of removal from office. . . ." *Id.* at 500, 87 S.Ct. 616.

"Although the Supreme Court has not recently revisited the *Garrity* line of cases, a number of the circuits have focused on the 'coercion' issue emphasized by the Court in those cases, making it a claim dependent on such a showing." *United States v. Trevino,* 215 Fed.Appx. 319, 321 (5th Cir.2007) (citing *McKinley v. City of Mansfield,* 404 F.3d 418, 436 (6th Cir.2005); *United States v. Vangates,* 287 F.3d 1315, 1321–22 (11th Cir.2002); *Chan v. Wodnicki,* 123 F.3d 1005, 1009–10 (7th Cir.1997); *Singer v. Maine,* 49 F.3d 837, 847 (1st Cir.1995); *Benjamin v. City of Montgomery,* 785 F.2d 959, 961–62 (11th Cir.1986)). To make out a *Garrity* claim, the officer must demonstrate that he had been put "between the rock and the whirlpool," *Garrity,* 385 U.S. at 498, 87 S.Ct. 616, by having to choose whether to incriminate himself or to lose his job. In this Circuit, an officer claiming the protection o f *Garrity* "must have in fact believed his . . . statements to be compelled on threat of loss of job and this belief must have been objectively reasonable." *United States v. Friedrick,* 842 F.2d 382, 395 (D.C.Cir.1988).

Cook has failed to meet his burden under *Garrity*. First, his claim that he subjectively believed he would be fired if he failed to file the Use of Force Report is, at best, dubious. Cook admitted to being unfamiliar with the USMS policy setting out the disciplinary consequences of failing to follow an order to write a report, and he further admitted that he never knew of anyone who had been terminated on these grounds. The only evidence he offered to support his belief that refusal to submit a report would be punished by termination was that another deputy claimed to have been told that he would be fired if he refused to submit a report. However, Cook was unable to remember with certainty whether he learned this information in August 2005 or thereafter, and he admitted that he knew nothing about that deputy's prior disciplinary record or any other details of the situation. When told by Rivers that he needed to write the USM-133 despite his contention that no force had been used, Cook did not object, refuse, or request representation. He simply copied the contents of his USM-210 into the USM-133 and submitted it later that day. Under these circumstances, Cook's contention that he was coerced into making the report for fear of being fired is implausible.

But even if his testimony about his subjective belief were credible, Cook has failed to demonstrate that his belief that he would be fired for refusing to submit a report was "objectively reasonable." *Friedrick,* 842 F.2d at 395. The USMS Master Agreement specifies the disciplinary actions that may be taken for specific offenses. Failure to carry out orders, work assignments, or instructions is punished on a sliding scale: a first offense may be punished by anything between a reprimand and removal; a second offense may be punished by anything between a 15-day suspension and removal; and a third offense is punished by removal. For a first time offender like Cook, removal is not mandated, nor, according to Griscavage, is it likely. Given the lack of any policy mandating removal, as well as the absence of any precedent where removal had been invoked, it would not have been objectively reasonable for Cook to believe that he would be terminated if he declined to file the reports.

Contrary to Cook's argument, *Garrity* does not stand for the proposition that a statement made in a standard report is coerced whenever an officer faces both the remote possibility of criminal prosecution if he files the report and the arguably even more speculative possibility of termination if he declines to do so. Rather, the touchstone of the *Garrity* inquiry is whether the defendant's statements were coerced and therefore involuntary. In Cook's case, both the possibility of prosecution and the possibility of termination were far too tenuous to support a finding that he was between "the rock and the whirlpool" at the time he filed his reports. In fact, the circumstances of the case, as testified to by both Cook and Rivers, support a finding that no coercion was involved when Cook decided to file the reports. *See Trevino,* 215 Fed.Appx. at 320 (finding no coercion even when off-duty officer was called into the station for questioning and escorted into the interrogation room by the Chief of Police).

Furthermore, the presumption underlying *Garrity* and its progeny is that the subject employee is under investigation at the time the challenged statement is made. *See, e.g., Garrity,* 385 U.S. at 494, 87 S.Ct. 616 (police officers interviewed as part of an internal investigation led by the Attorney General); *Lefkowitz v. Cunningham,* 431 U.S. 801, 803, 97 S.Ct. 2132, 53 L.Ed.2d 1 (1977) (public official subpoenaed to appear before a grand jury); *Friedrick,* 842 F.2d at 386 (FBI agent interviewed as part of administrative and criminal investigations). As the testimony of Griscavage clearly demonstrates, Cook was not under either administrative or criminal investigation when Rivers requested his reports. Cook cites no case, nor has the Court located any, to support the position that *Garrity* should be applied prior to the initiation of an administrative or criminal investigation. To interpret *Garrity* as defendant advocates would be both unprecedented and impracticable. It would mean that when a supervisor receives a complaint against an officer that has even the slightest potential of resulting in criminal charges, the supervisor could not follow up by requesting the standard paperwork without providing the officer with *Garrity* protections, because the request could be construed as an "order" to comply with an "investigation." This scenario would be unworkable for a number of reasons, not the least of which is that it would require line supervisors to make legal judgments about the potential criminality of the conduct alleged. Given the witnesses' testimony as to the frequency with which force is and must be used, extending *Garrity* protections to the moment a complaint is filed would create a tremendous and unnecessary administrative burden. The Court therefore declines to adopt this unwarranted extension of the *Garrity* doctrine.

Moreover, even if Cook could demonstrate that *Garrity* is applicable here, which he has not, he could not rely upon it to prevent the introduction of his reports as evidence with respect to Counts 2, 3, 4, and 6. *Garrity* provides that an officer under investigation may choose between refusing to cooperate with the investigation and losing his job or providing an incriminating statement and avoiding prosecution on that matter. "An accused may not abuse *Garrity* by committing a crime involving false statements and thereafter rely on *Garrity* to provide a safe haven by foreclosing any use of such statements in a prosecution for perjury, false statements, or obstruction of justice." *United States v. Veal,* 153 F.3d at 1243. *See also United States ex rel. Annunziato v. Deegan,* 440 F.2d 304, 306 (2d Cir.1971) (upholding perjury conviction because "appellant was not prosecuted for past criminal activity based on what he was forced to reveal about himself; he was prosecuted for the commission of a crime while testifying. . . ."); *United States v. Devitt,* 499 F.2d 135, 142 (7th Cir.1974) (holding that *Garrity* and its progeny "provide adequate protection of the witness's Fifth Amendment rights. We find no reason or justification for extending this umbrella of protection to shield a witness against prosecution for knowingly giving false testimony."); *United States v. White,* 887 F.2d 267, 274 (D.C.Cir.1989) (Ginsburg, J.) (explaining that the decision to lie is not protected by *Garrity*).

Cook attempts to escape this well-established rule by arguing that at the time he was told to write the reports, he was being investigated for both the alleged assault and a possible cover-up. (Def.'s Supp. Mem. at 3–6.) This contention is without evidentiary support. First, Cook cannot demonstrate that he was the subject of any type of investigation, least of all a criminal investigation, at the time he was instructed to write the reports. As Griscavage explained, the decision whether to initiate a criminal investigation occurs much later after the complaint and any accompanying documentation have been forwarded to OII and then to OIG and the Civil Rights Division. Both Rivers and Cook testified that Rivers had just received the complaint, which had been dropped off at the Superior Court, at the time of their first conversation. Therefore, it is simply not possible that a criminal investigation was in progress (or even contemplated) at the time Rivers told Cook to write the reports.

More importantly, there is no basis for Cook's argument that he was the subject of an investigation for a potential cover-up at the time he was asked to complete the reports. (Def.'s Supp. Mem. at 3–6.) Also, to the extent that Cook argues that Rivers was also investigating Cook's failure to file a report, this is irrelevant. Cook is not being prosecuted for failing to file a report-he is being prosecuted for filing a false Field Report and for conspiring with others to support his version of the incident by filing false reports and giving false testimony to the grand jury. Obviously, none of these offenses could have been the subject of the investigation prior to the filing of the reports, and, therefore, they could not qualify for *Garrity* immunity.

CONCLUSION

For the foregoing reasons, defendant's motion to suppress his statements [Dkt. # 7] is DENIED.

EXERCISE

In *Cook*, the Chief Inspector of the Office of Internal Investigations for the Marshal's service asserted that he "was unaware of any instance where a marshal with a clean disciplinary record was terminated for failing to file a necessary report."

Does that reflect a functioning system? And should the analysis of the "cruel trilemma" change when the defendant is a law enforcement official?

D. MISPRISION OF A FELONY

Sometimes, what is criminalized is something less than an explicit misrepresentation. 18 U.S.C. § 4 outlaws a particular kind of obstruction of justice based on knowledge of a crime, non-disclosure, and concealment:

> Whoever, having knowledge of the actual commission of a felony cognizable by a court of the United States, conceals and does not as soon as possible make known the same to some judge or other person in civil or military authority under the United States, shall

18 U.S.C
sec 4

be fined under this title or imprisoned not more than three years, or both.

Importantly, the federal version of misprision requires more than simply not turning in a felon—it also includes as an element that the defendant must "conceal" the crime.

UNITED STATES V. BRANTLEY

803 F.3d 1265 (11th Cir. 2015)

PROCTOR, DISTRICT JUDGE:

This appeal involves an infrequently charged crime: misprision of a felony in violation of 18 U.S.C. § 4. Courtnee Nicole Brantley was convicted of misprision as a result of her actions during and following a traffic stop on June 29, 2010. Brantley raises several challenges to her conviction. She argues that she was the subject of selective prosecution, the prosecution violated her Fifth Amendment privilege against self-incrimination, and there was insufficient evidence to support the verdict against her. After careful review and with the benefit of oral argument, we disagree. For the reasons stated below, we affirm Brantley's conviction.

I.   BACKGROUND

The misprision charge brought against Brantley stems from tragic events that occurred on June 29, 2010. Brantley was pulled over in a routine traffic stop. Brantley's boyfriend, convicted felon Dontae Morris, was a passenger in her car. Upon questioning by the police, he emerged from the car and shot and killed two officers. He then fled on foot as Brantley sped away. Within minutes, Brantley spoke with Morris on a cell phone, and thereafter hid the car and exchanged texts with Morris. The traffic stop itself—including the shootings—was recorded by the dashboard video camera in a police car. The video was played for the jury.

At trial, the jury ultimately found that Brantley knew about a federal felony (her convicted-felon boyfriend's possession of the firearm which he used to shoot the officers), did not report that crime to the authorities, and, in the aftermath of the murders, took affirmative steps to conceal Morris's felony from the authorities.

II.   SUMMARY OF RELEVANT FACTS

At about 2:13 a.m. on June 29, 2010, Tampa Police Officer David Curtis pulled over Brantley's car because it did not have a license tag. Brantley provided her driver's license and vehicle documentation, and Officer Curtis discussed the tag violation with her. Officer Curtis also questioned Morris, who gave Curtis his name and birthdate. Officer Curtis entered Morris's information into his patrol car's computer. An outstanding warrant came up, along with a warning that Morris had previously resisted arrest.

[handwritten margin note: pulled over for no license tag - Curtis who questioned Morris and gave his name and birthdate and the officer found Morris had a warrant.]

A backup officer, Jeffrey Kocab, arrived on the scene, and both officers approached the passenger side of Brantley's car. Officer Curtis told Morris to step out of the car. As he exited the car, Morris pulled a gun and shot Officers Curtis and Kocab in the head. Both officers died from their wounds. Morris ran in one direction, and Brantley drove off in another. The entire traffic stop—including the shootings—was captured by the dashboard video camera in Officer Curtis's vehicle.

asked morris to get out- morris shot them both

dash cam caught the crime

Within a minute of the shootings, Brantley called Morris. Two more phone calls between them soon followed. Brantley drove to an apartment complex located about three miles from the murder scene. Therefore, the calls between Brantley and Morris necessarily occurred prior to the time Brantley parked the car. Brantley parked the car a distance from the apartment in which she hid. When Brantley parked, she backed the car into a space (and up against some bushes) in order to conceal the missing license tag.

concealed missing tag

Following their phone conversations, and within minutes after the shootings, Brantley and Morris had the following exchange of text messages:

> Morris: "Your ride dont need 2 be park by the spot neither."

> Brantley: "No. Still n here, bt way round corner. I nd to move it sumwhere else tho."

> Morris: "Just lean bak til 2morrow. you phone in your name."

> Brantley: "No."

> Morris: "Bet im bout 2 turn my shiit off til 2morrow i love you."

> Brantley: "I love u with my last breath."

> Morris: "Yea just lean bak stay loyal."

> Brantley: "Of course . . . Til death do us part."

texts after shootings

Brantley's texts all included the tagline: "ON MY OWN LEVEL."

A few minutes later, Brantley sent text messages to several other people: "U havent seen me. . . . . U dont know where im at. . . . . Please dont tell anyone anything. Erase these messages!" When one of those people questioned her, Brantley explained, "Just make like I never exisisted!"

The police eventually located Brantley in an apartment some 500 yards and across a lake from where she had parked her car. During questioning, Brantley admitted that she had been pulled over, someone had been injured, and she had fled the scene. She further admitted that she had a passenger in the car, but refused to disclose Morris's last name.

Police found Brantley but refused to tell them Morris' name

Morris was arrested after three days, and was prosecuted by the State of Florida for the two murders. Brantley went to trial on the misprision of a

Federal crime - felon in possession of firearm
State crime- murder of two officers

felony charge. After the Government put on its case, Brantley rested without presenting any evidence. The case then went to the jury.

jury instructions

The jury was instructed that, in order for Brantley to be found guilty of misprision, it must find "that a federal felony as charged in Count I of the Indictment was committed[,] that the defendant had actual knowledge of the commission of the felony[,] that the defendant did not as soon as possible make known the felony to some judge or other person in civil or military authority [, and] that the defendant did an affirmative act to conceal the crime." The court further instructed that, in the event the jury found Brantley guilty, it should disclose the acts of concealment that it found she had committed. ("there's blanks for you to write in whatever act or acts you find"). Consistent with the trial court's instruction, the verdict form directed the jury (in the event it found Brantley guilty) to "describe the act or acts you find Brantley committed to conceal the crime of felon in possession of [a] firearm and ammunition."

Jury found Brantley guilty

The jury returned a verdict of guilty against Brantley on the misprision charge. In response to the special jury interrogatory, the jury explained that it found evidence of the following acts: "The defendant knowingly and willfully concealed her knowledge of the possession of a firearm and ammunition by a convicted felon from the authorities by coordinating via phone calls and text messages with Dantae [sic] Morris." After return of the verdict, the district court gave the jury the opportunity to be more specific as to the "acts of concealment" it found. The jury declined to supplement or alter its verdict. . . .

Brantley argument court rejects

Brantley next argues that the evidence was insufficient to convict her of misprision. We reject her contention. The misprision statute provides that "[w]hoever, having knowledge of the actual commission of a felony cognizable by a court of the United States, conceals and does not as soon as possible make known the same to some judge or other person in civil or military authority under the United States," is guilty of misprision. 18 U.S.C. § 4. The statute, though, has been construed to require also "some affirmative act of concealment or participation." *Itani v. Ashcroft,* 298 F.3d 1213, 1216 (11th Cir.2002).

4 elements

At Brantley's trial, the district court correctly explained that the crime of misprision is comprised of four elements. The district court's instruction regarding the elements of the crime of misprision is consistent with the definition articulated by the Third Circuit. *See Baer v. United States,* 722 F.3d 168, 176 (3rd Cir.2013). We hereby adopt the Third Circuit's definition and conclude that the elements of the crime of misprision are: "(1) the principal committed and completed the felony alleged; (2) the defendant had full knowledge of that fact; (3) the defendant failed to notify authorities; and (4) the defendant took steps to conceal the crime." *Id.* (quoting *United States v. Gebbie,* 294 F.3d 540, 544 (3d Cir.2002) (internal quotations omitted)). We also conclude that the district court properly instructed the jury that, in order to find Brantley guilty of the crime of misprision, the Government was required to prove each of those four elements beyond a reasonable doubt. . . .

The only element of the crime that Brantley has challenged on sufficiency grounds is the fourth one, requiring an affirmative act of concealment. At trial, the jury heard evidence that Brantley fled the scene after Morris shot and killed the police officers. The jurors also heard evidence indicating that in the minutes following the murder of the officers, Brantley and Morris spoke during three phone calls. The jury further heard evidence that, at around the same time, Brantley and Morris exchanged text messages about concealing the car and staying loyal. After her conversations with Morris, Brantley actually concealed the car and hid herself in a distant apartment away from the vehicle. A reasonable jury could conclude that the subject of the telephone calls was similar to the subject of the text messages—*i.e.,* they involved discussions about how and where to hide evidence (the car). The car linked Brantley to Morris and also linked Morris to the possession of the weapon involved in the murder of the two police officers, which was committed in Brantley's presence. And, Morris, who Brantley knew to be a felon, committed the murders while being in possession of a firearm.

[margin note: concealment]

In response to a question on the verdict form asking it to identify Brantley's affirmative act or acts of concealment, the jury stated that "[t]he defendant knowingly and willfully concealed her knowledge of the possession of a firearm and ammunition by a convicted felon from the authorities *by coordinating via phone calls and text messages with Dantae [sic] Morris.*" (Emphasis added). A reasonable jury could conclude based upon the evidence presented at trial that the coordination between Brantley and Morris, both phone calls and text messages, was hiding the car. . . .

[margin note: A reasonable jury could conclude from the evidence]

Finally, there was sufficient evidence of affirmative acts of concealment to support the jury's guilty verdict. "[R]eceipt or possession of evidence has regularly been considered a sufficient affirmative act to support conviction under the misprision statute." *United States v. Davila,* 698 F.2d 715, 718 (5th Cir.1983); *see also United States v. King,* 402 F.2d 694 (9th Cir.1968). So has the *removal* of evidence. *United States v. Stuard,* 566 F.2d 1 (6th Cir.1977). Again, this case does not involve a mere failure to report a crime. Rather, there is sufficient evidence of affirmative concealment of evidence—*i.e.,* the removal and hiding of evidence related to a crime (the car)—to support the jury's finding of an affirmative act of concealment. After review of this record, we cannot say that no trier of fact could have found Brantley guilty beyond a reasonable doubt. Therefore, the district court did not err in denying her a judgment of acquittal and declining to order a new trial. *See Tinoco,* 304 F.3d at 1122; *Calderon,* 127 F.3d at 1324.

[margin note: holding]

V. CONCLUSION

For the foregoing reasons, Brantley's misprision conviction is

AFFIRMED.

MARTIN, CIRCUIT JUDGE, concurring:

The shocking events out of which this appeal arises were senseless and tragic. Dontae Morris's June 29, 2010 murder of two police officers can only be characterized as a grave and unspeakable crime. But Courtnee Brantley, whose appeal we consider here, was never charged with those murders. That means our job is to evaluate her claims as they relate to the crime for which the jury convicted her—misprision of a felony in violation of 18 U.S.C. § 4. Specifically, we must determine "if a reasonable trier of fact could find that the evidence established guilt beyond a reasonable doubt." *United States v. Jiminez,* 564 F.3d 1280, 1285 (11th Cir.2009) (quotation omitted). Even viewing all of the evidence in the light most favorable to the government and drawing all reasonable factual inferences in favor of the jury's verdict, *id.* at 1284, I agree with what I gather to be the District Judge's sense that Ms. Brantley's is a close case. Ultimately, I reach the same conclusion as the majority—that there is sufficient evidence to support Ms. Brantley's conviction. I write separately, however, because I do not share the majority's view of the strength of the case against her.

As the majority notes, misprision of a felony is a rarely charged crime. In order to prove a violation of 18 U.S.C. § 4, the government must offer sufficient evidence to demonstrate: "(1) the principal committed and completed the felony alleged [here, the felony is Mr. Morris being a felon in possession of a firearm]; (2) the defendant had full knowledge of that fact; (3) the defendant failed to notify authorities; and (4) the defendant took steps to conceal the crime." *Baer v. United States,* 722 F.3d 168, 176 (3d Cir.2013) (quotation omitted). On appeal, Ms. Brantley challenges only the fourth element, arguing that the government has not offered sufficient evidence to prove that she concealed Mr. Morris's crime of being a felon in possession. This appeal concerns Ms. Brantley's second trial, because her first jury could not unanimously agree to convict her.

As I've said, in order to convict Ms. Brantley of the crime of misprision of a felony, the government was required to prove that she took an affirmative step to conceal Mr. Morris's crime of possessing a firearm as a convicted felon. *See United States v. Johnson,* 546 F.2d 1225, 1227 (5th Cir.1977). Our precedent is clear that "[t]he mere failure to report a felony is not sufficient" to establish concealment. *Id.* At the same time, I am not aware of any binding precedent from our court holding that *intent* to conceal the commission of a felony from the government (without the carrying out of the corresponding act) is sufficient to prove this element. *Cf. Neal v. U.S.,* 102 F.2d 643, 650 (8th Cir.1939) ("An intent to conceal from the government, if such intent existed, that is not carried out is not an offense under the statute."). One of our sister Circuits has recognized that even knowing where a perpetrator is hiding and having conversations with him about how to escape is not sufficient, absent some positive act of concealment. *Id.*

other circuit says it is not sufficient for concealment

In most misprision cases, a defendant's affirmative act of concealment is readily apparent. This is true of the out-of-circuit cases the majority relies upon in support of Ms. Brantley's conviction. In *United States v. Davila,* 698 F.2d 715 (5th Cir.1983), the concealment element of misprision of a felony was met because Mr. Davila agreed to hold approximately $15,000 in payoff money in the service of the underlying conspiracy to suborn perjury. *Id.* at 718. In *United States v. Stuard,* 566 F.2d 1 (6th Cir.1977) (per curiam), the defendant's actions of removing stolen whiskey from a truck, replacing it with sandbags, and driving the truck to another state were deemed sufficient affirmative acts to conceal the underlying theft. *Id.* at 1. As the majority recognizes, receipt of or hiding evidence of a felony is typically sufficient to establish an affirmative act of concealment.

this is typically sufficient

This case is not as clear. The majority holds that Ms. Brantley's affirmative act of concealment was hiding her car after she left the scene of the crime. Specifically, the majority concludes that by hiding the car she was driving, Ms. Brantley concealed evidence that Mr. Morris committed the crime of being a felon in possession of a firearm. The District Court expressed dissatisfaction with this interpretation of the evidence in its well-reasoned Order denying Ms. Brantley's motion for a judgment of acquittal. Although the question of whether Ms. Brantley concealed evidence of a crime may seem simple, a closer look is necessary.

4 reasons:)

First, it is not readily apparent to me how Ms. Brantley's automobile is evidence of Mr. Morris's crime of being a felon in possession of a firearm. Mr. Morris's gun was not in her car when she drove away. Neither did she flee with his ammunition. Nevertheless, the government asserts that the car was "evidence" of the underlying felony because police officers could have gleaned from her car a "scent sample" to aid their bloodhound in tracking Mr. Morris after his escape. I agree with the District Court that this argument strains credulity. The record before us contains no evidence that the police made any attempt to capture a scent sample even after recovering Ms. Brantley's car, despite that Mr. Morris was still missing and it would still have been possible to do so. Despite this, the majority accepts without discussion that the car was an evidentiary link between Mr. Morris and his underlying crime of being a felon in possession of a firearm.

Second, this record reveals no evidence that Ms. Brantley had the required intent to conceal Mr. Morris's felony at the time she drove away from the scene of the crime. Indeed, the government recognizes that Ms. Brantley "recoiled" after Mr. Morris shot the officers, and then "fled" the crime scene. Ms. Brantley's reaction, then, was one of shock, rather than conscious reflection. There was no evidence offered at trial to prove that Ms. Brantley drove away from the scene of the crime with the intent to keep her car from the police officers' bloodhounds.

Third, Ms. Brantley took no affirmative steps to conceal the car after communicating with Mr. Morris. It is important to carefully consider the sequence of events. First, immediately after the crime, there were three calls between Ms. Brantley and Mr. Morris, the content of which we don't know. Next, Mr. Morris texted Ms. Brantley saying, "Your ride dont need 2 be park by the spot neither," to which she responded, "No. Still n here bt way round corner. I nd to move it sumwhere else tho." She then pledged her loyalty to him.

But there is no evidence that Ms. Brantley then moved the car after sending these texts. Neither is there evidence that she tried to clean the car. Instead she stayed where she was (at her friend's apartment complex) until the police found her there. It bears repeating that our Circuit has no rule allowing intent to conceal the commission of a felony, by itself, to support a conviction for misprision. *See Neal*, 102 F.2d at 650. The texts, which were not followed up with actions, do not prove that Ms. Brantley concealed evidence of Mr. Morris's crime. And her declarations of loyalty do not alter this conclusion.

Finally, the only "affirmative act" we have to support the jury's verdict is Ms. Brantley's initial decision to park her car at a friend's apartment complex, backing into the spot in a way that her missing license tag was hidden. Certainly, Ms. Brantley's conduct in this regard could plausibly be interpreted as her intent to avoid the authorities. However, this cannot be the affirmative act that supports her conviction. Again, the "mere failure to report a felony is not sufficient to constitute a violation of 18 U.S.C.A. § 4." *Johnson*, 546 F.2d at 1227. In fact, if Ms. Brantley had remained at the scene of the crime but refused to answer questions, she would not be guilty of misprision. It follows, therefore, that rendering herself unavailable for questioning cannot be the required affirmative act of concealment.

That said, Ms. Brantley faces a very tough standard in seeking to overturn the jury's verdict. On appeal, we are required to construe all inferences in favor of the jury's verdict. Having done so, I conclude that a reasonable factfinder could find that by parking her car the way she did, Ms. Brantley intended to conceal Mr. Morris's murder of the two police officers. That murder, in turn, involved a firearm. A reasonable jury could find that Ms. Brantley surmised that the police were looking for a vehicle without tags, and with that in mind, thought that concealing her vehicle would help Mr. Morris evade detection for having possessed the firearm he used to murder the officers. Mr. Morris told her that the car "dont need 2 be park by the spot neither." And she assured him that it wasn't—it was "way round corner." Although no affirmative acts of concealment transpired after this text exchange, a reasonable factfinder could infer from her response that her earlier act of parking at her friend's apartment complex was done with the required intent to conceal. On this narrow basis, I concur in the majority's judgment that there is sufficient evidence to support Ms. Brantley's conviction.

The majority holds that the evidence adduced at trial amply supports the jury's finding. The majority so holds despite the fact that this defendant did not conceal any fruit or instrumentality of the crime. In that way, I believe this case stands in stark contrast to the typical charge of misprision of a felony. Nevertheless, the standard for a sufficiency-of-the-evidence claim places a heavy burden on a defendant: to prove that no rational factfinder could have found that the evidence established guilt beyond a reasonable doubt. Since I agree with the conclusion ultimately reached by the District Judge, that there is a reading of the evidence that supports the jury's verdict, I concur in the Judgment of the majority.

EXERCISE

You are a federal prosecutor. A Secret Service agent comes to you with a counterfeiting case. A college student, Ronald Dalt, is suspected of making counterfeit $20 bills using printing equipment at his school. Identity will be hard to show, though, since it appears that Dalt (if it was him) covered his tracks very well by using proxy accounts when he accessed the computers and used the printers. There is no conclusive video evidence. However, the paper he used was distinctive: an expensive stock with high cotton content made by Crane's, a stationary manufacturer.

The Secret Service agent went to the college bookstore and talked to the clerks. One woman, Susan Saarsgaard, worked in the stationary section the two days before the counterfeit was made. She said that she did not know Dalt, and that no one had bought that type of stationary in the past two days.

The agent then investigated credit card records and determined that Ms. Saarsgaard had sold that type of Crane's paper to Dalt the day before the counterfeit was made. Also, three pictures drawn from social media show Saarsgaard and Dalt together as part of a group of four people. Returning to the bookstore and confronting Ms. Saarsgaard with this fact, the agent found that Saarsgaard refused to speak further about the incident or anything else, and advised that she had retained a lawyer.

Would you consider charging Saarsgaard with either making a false statement or misprision of a felony (or both)? Why?

CHAPTER TEN

EXPANDING LIABILITY: ATTEMPT, CONSPIRACY, AND ACCOMPLICE LIABILITY

■ ■ ■

Criminal law casts a wide net. Those who can be convicted and sentenced include not only primary actors who commit crimes—those who pull the trigger and kill someone, for example—but those who simply attempt to commit a crime (attempt), agree to work with others to commit a crime (conspiracy), get someone else to commit a crime (solicitation), or help someone else commit a crime or evade punishment (accomplice liability). In this chapter, we will explore the shape and size of that net. Some of the most challenging and important questions in criminal law arise here.

It is the careful crafting of the elements in statutes that broadens the net. For example, attempt allows an uncompleted crime to be prosecuted by eliminating the action-outcome element (death) usually necessary in proving up a homicide. Conspiracy expands liability by criminalizing the agreement to commit a crime—which creates a new state of mind requirement (agreement itself). Accomplice liability requires the intent to help or control someone else. As we discuss each construct, elements will fade or become prominent, depending on the nature of the charge.

Attempt and conspiracy are sometimes referred to as "inchoate" crimes because they do not require completion of the crime itself—they punish planning and collusion. In contrast, solicitation, aiding and abetting, and accessory after the fact are sometimes called forms of "accomplice liability," and often do require completion of the crime to create criminal liability. All serve to expand the ability of the government to prosecute people beyond the primary actor in a completed crime.

The interaction between these charges is important and sometimes confusing. Some statutes, for example, jumble up aiding and abetting, conspiracy, and solicitation in a single statute.[1] Moreover, almost every case that could be charged under accomplice liability can also be charged as the inchoate crime of conspiracy, even though they have distinct elements.

---

[1] E.g. Minnesota Statute § 609.05.

This complexity often serves to increase the options available to prosecutors within their discretion, both in terms of charges available and individuals who are susceptible to a charge.

A. ATTEMPT

It makes sense that we would want to criminalize the mere effort to commit a crime, since this allows us to catch and prosecute criminals before they actually do harm.

Some jurisdictions have a catch-all attempt provision that applies to all crimes.[2] Others, including the federal code, include attempt as a part of some crimes but not others. For example, attempt is built into the statute that criminalizes the re-entry of deported aliens, 8 U.S.C. § 1326:

(a) In general

Subject to subsection (b), any alien who—

> **(1)** has been denied admission, excluded, deported, or removed or has departed the United States while an order of exclusion, deportation, or removal is outstanding, and thereafter

> **(2)** enters, attempts to enter, or is at any time found in, the United States, unless (A) prior to his reembarkation at a place outside the United States or his application for admission from foreign contiguous territory, the Attorney General has expressly consented to such alien's reapplying for admission; or (B) with respect to an alien previously denied admission and removed, unless such alien shall establish that he was not required to obtain such advance consent under this chapter or any prior Act,

shall be fined under Title 18, or imprisoned not more than 2 years, or both.

The key question with attempt often regards the action element—how much action is required towards the goal of accomplishing the crime? The line between planning and action can be difficult to determine. 8 U.S.C. § 1326 does little to define that, leaving it to the courts.

UNITED STATES V. RESENDIZ-PONCE
549 U.S. 102 (2007)

JUSTICE STEVENS delivered the opinion of the Court.

A jury convicted respondent Juan Resendiz-Ponce, a Mexican citizen, of illegally attempting to reenter the United States. Because the indictment

---

[2]   E.g. 720 Illinois Compiled Statute 5–8/4.

failed to allege a specific overt act that he committed in seeking reentry, the Court of Appeals set aside his conviction and remanded for dismissal of the indictment. We granted the Government's petition for certiorari to answer the question whether the omission of an element of a criminal offense from a federal indictment can constitute harmless error. . . .

Respondent was deported twice, once in 1988 and again in 2002, before his attempted reentry on June 1, 2003. On that day, respondent walked up to a port of entry and displayed a photo identification of his cousin to the border agent. Respondent told the agent that he was a legal resident and that he was traveling to Calexico, California. Because he did not resemble his cousin, respondent was questioned, taken into custody, and ultimately charged with a violation of 8 U.S.C. § 1326(a). The indictment alleged:

> On or about June 1, 2003, JUAN RESENDIZ-PONCE, an alien, knowingly and intentionally attempted to enter the United States of America at or near San Luis in the District of Arizona, after having been previously denied admission, excluded, deported, and removed from the United States at or near Nogales, Arizona, on or about October 15, 2002, and not having obtained the express consent of the Secretary of the Department of Homeland Security to reapply for admission.
>
> In violation of Title 8, United States Code, Sections 1326(a) and enhanced by (b)(2)." App. 8.

Respondent moved to dismiss the indictment, contending that it "fail[ed] to allege an essential element, an overt act, or to state the essential facts of such overt act." *Id.*, at 12. The District Court denied the motion and, after the jury found him guilty, sentenced respondent to a 63-month term of imprisonment.

The Ninth Circuit reversed, reasoning that an indictment's omission of "an essential element of the offense is a fatal flaw not subject to mere harmless error analysis." 425 F.3d 729, 732 (2005). In the court's view, respondent's indictment was fatally flawed because it nowhere alleged "any specific overt act that is a substantial step" toward the completion of the unlawful reentry. *Id.*, at 733. The panel majority explained:

> The defendant has a right to be apprised of what overt act the government will try to prove at trial, and he has a right to have a grand jury consider whether to charge that specific overt act. Physical crossing into a government inspection area is but one of a number of other acts that the government might have alleged as a substantial step toward entry into the United States. The indictment might have alleged the tendering a bogus identification card; it might have alleged successful clearance of the inspection area; or it might have alleged lying to an inspection officer with the purpose of being admitted . . . . A grand jury never

> passed on a specific overt act, and Resendiz was never given notice
> of what specific overt act would be proved at trial. *Ibid.*

Judge Reavley concurred, agreeing that Ninth Circuit precedent mandated reversal. If not bound by precedent, however, he would have found the indictment to be "constitutionally sufficient" because it clearly informed respondent "of the precise offense of which he [was] accused so that he [could] prepare his defense and so that a judgment thereon [would] safeguard him from a subsequent prosecution for the same offense."

II

At common law, the attempt to commit a crime was itself a crime if the perpetrator not only intended to commit the completed offense, but also performed " 'some open deed tending to the execution of his intent.' " 2 W. LaFave, Substantive Criminal Law § 11.2(a), p. 205 (2d ed.2003) (quoting E. Coke, Third Institute 5 (6th ed. 1680)); see Keedy, Criminal Attempts at Common Law, 102 U. Pa. L. Rev. 464, 468 (1954) (noting that common-law attempt required "that some act must be done towards carrying out the intent").

More recently, the requisite "open deed" has been described as an "overt act" that constitutes a "substantial step" toward completing the offense. 2 LaFave, Substantive Criminal Law § 11.4; see ALI, Model Penal Code § 5.01(1)(c) (1985) (defining "criminal attempt" to include "an act or omission constituting a substantial step in a course of conduct planned to culminate in his commission of the crime"); see also *Braxton v. United States,* 500 U.S. 344, 349, 111 S.Ct. 1854, 114 L.Ed.2d 385 (1991) ("For Braxton to be guilty of an attempted killing under 18 U.S.C. § 1114, he must have taken a substantial step towards that crime, and must also have had the requisite *mens rea*"). As was true at common law, the mere intent to violate a federal criminal statute is not punishable as an attempt unless it is also accompanied by significant conduct.

The Government does not disagree with respondent's submission that he cannot be guilty of attempted reentry in violation of 8 U.S.C. § 1326(a) unless he committed an overt act qualifying as a substantial step toward completion of his goal. See Supplemental Brief for United States 7–8. Nor does it dispute that "[a]n indictment must set forth each element of the crime that it charges." *Almendarez-Torres v. United States,* 523 U.S. 224, 228, 118 S.Ct. 1219, 140 L.Ed.2d 350 (1998). It instead contends that the indictment at bar implicitly alleged that respondent engaged in the necessary overt act "simply by alleging that he 'attempted to enter the United States.' " Supplemental Brief for United States 8. We agree.

Not only does the word "attempt" as used in common parlance connote action rather than mere intent, but more importantly, as used in the law for centuries, it encompasses both the overt act and intent elements. Consequently, an indictment alleging attempted illegal reentry under

§ 1326(a) need not specifically allege a particular overt act or any other "component par[t]" of the offense. See *Hamling v. United States,* 418 U.S. 87, 119, 94 S.Ct. 2887, 41 L.Ed.2d 590 (1974). Just as it was enough for the indictment in *Hamling* to allege that the defendant mailed "obscene" material in violation of 18 U.S.C. § 1461, see 418 U.S., at 117–118, 94 S.Ct. 2887, it was enough for the indictment in this case to point to the relevant criminal statute and allege that "[o]n or about June 1, 2003," respondent "attempted to enter the United States of America at or near San Luis in the District of Arizona," App. 8.

In *Hamling,* we identified two constitutional requirements for an indictment: "first, [that it] contains the elements of the offense charged and fairly informs a defendant of the charge against which he must defend, and, second, [that it] enables him to plead an acquittal or conviction in bar of future prosecutions for the same offense." 418 U.S., at 117, 94 S.Ct. 2887. In this case, the use of the word "attempt," coupled with the specification of the time and place of respondent's attempted illegal reentry, satisfied both. Indeed, the time-and-place information provided respondent with more adequate notice than would an indictment describing particular overt acts. After all, a given defendant may have approached the border or lied to a border-patrol agent in the course of countless attempts on innumerable occasions. For the same reason, the time-and-date specification in respondent's indictment provided ample protection against the risk of multiple prosecutions for the same crime.

Respondent nonetheless maintains that the indictment would have been sufficient only if it had alleged any of three overt acts performed during his attempted reentry: that he walked into an inspection area; that he presented a misleading identification card; or that he lied to the inspector. See Supplemental Brief for Respondent 7. Individually and cumulatively, those acts tend to prove the charged attempt—but none was essential to the finding of guilt in this case. All three acts were rather part of a single course of conduct culminating in the charged "attempt." As Justice Holmes explained in *Swift & Co. v. United States,* 196 U.S. 375, 396, 25 S.Ct. 276, 49 L.Ed. 518 (1905), "[t]he unity of the plan embraces all the parts."

Respondent is of course correct that while an indictment parroting the language of a federal criminal statute is often sufficient, there are crimes that must be charged with greater specificity. See *Hamling,* 418 U.S., at 117, 94 S.Ct. 2887. A clear example is the statute making it a crime for a witness summoned before a congressional committee to refuse to answer any question "pertinent to the question under inquiry." 2 U.S.C. § 192. As we explained at length in our opinion in *Russell v. United States,* 369 U.S. 749, 82 S.Ct. 1038, 8 L.Ed.2d 240 (1962), a valid indictment for such a refusal to testify must go beyond the words of § 192 and allege the subject of the congressional hearing in order to determine whether the defendant's refusal was "pertinent." Based on a number of cases arising out of congressional investigations, we recognized that the relevant hearing's subject was frequently uncertain but invariably "central to every prosecution under the statute." *Id.*, at 764, 82 S.Ct. 1038. Both to provide fair notice to defendants and to ensure that any conviction would arise out of the theory of guilt presented to the grand jury, we held that indictments under § 192 must do more than restate the language of the statute.

Our reasoning in *Russell* suggests that there was no infirmity in the present indictment. First, unlike the statute at issue in *Russell,* guilt under 8 U.S.C. § 1326(a) does not "depen[d] so crucially upon such a specific identification of fact." 369 U.S., at 764, 82 S.Ct. 1038. Second, before explaining the special need for particularity in charges brought under 2 U.S.C. § 192, Justice Stewart noted that, in 1872, Congress had enacted a statute reflecting "the drift of the law away from the rules of technical and formalized pleading which had characterized an earlier era." 369 U.S., at 762, 82 S.Ct. 1038. Other than that statute, which was repealed in 1948, there was no other legislation dealing generally with the subject of indictments until the promulgation of Federal Rule of Criminal Procedure 7(c)(1). As we have said, the Federal Rules "were designed to eliminate technicalities in criminal pleadings and are to be construed to secure simplicity in procedure." *United States v. Debrow,* 346 U.S. 374, 376, 74 S.Ct. 113, 98 L.Ed. 92 (1953). While detailed allegations might well have been required under common-law pleading rules, see, *e.g., Commonwealth v. Peaslee,* 177 Mass. 267, 59 N.E. 55 (1901), they surely are not contemplated by Rule 7(c)(1), which provides that an indictment "shall be a plain, concise, and definite written statement of the essential facts constituting the offense charged."

Because we are satisfied that respondent's indictment fully complied with that Rule and did not deprive him of any significant protection that the constitutional guarantee of a grand jury was intended to confer, we reverse the judgment of the Court of Appeals and remand the case for further proceedings consistent with this opinion.

It is so ordered.

JUSTICE SCALIA, dissenting.

It is well established that an indictment must allege all the elements of the charged crime. *Almendarez-Torres v. United States,* 523 U.S. 224, 228, 118 S.Ct. 1219, 140 L.Ed.2d 350 (1998); *United States v. Cook,* 17 Wall. 168, 174, 21 L.Ed. 538 (1872). As the Court acknowledges, it is likewise well established that "attempt" contains two substantive elements: the *intent* to commit the underlying crime, and the undertaking of *some action* toward commission of that crime. See *ante,* at 787 (citing 2 W. LaFave, Substantive Criminal Law § 11.2(a), p. 205 (2d ed.2003) (hereinafter LaFave), E. Coke, Third Institute 5 (6th ed. 1680), and Keedy, Criminal Attempts at Common Law, 102 U. Pa. L.Rev. 464, 468 (1954)). See also *Braxton v. United States,* 500 U.S. 344, 349, 111 S.Ct. 1854, 114 L.Ed.2d 385 (1991). It should follow, then, that when the Government indicts for attempt to commit a crime, it must allege both that the defendant had the intent to commit the crime, *and* that he took some action toward its commission. Any rule to the contrary would be an exception to the standard practice.

The Court gives two reasons for its special "attempt" exception. First, it says that in "common parlance" the word attempt "connote[s]," and therefore "impli[es]," both the intent and overt-act elements. *Ante,* at 787. This strikes me as certainly irrelevant, and probably incorrect to boot. It is irrelevant because, as I have just discussed, we have always required the elements of a crime to be explicitly set forth in the indictment, *whether or not* they are fairly called to mind by the mere name of the crime. Burglary, for example, connotes in common parlance the entry of a building with felonious intent, yet we require those elements to be set forth. Our precedents make clear that the indictment must "fully, directly, and *expressly,* without any uncertainty or ambiguity, set forth all the elements necessary to constitute the offence intended to be punished." *United States v. Carll,* 105 U.S. 611, 612, 26 L.Ed. 1135 (1881) (emphasis added). And the Court's argument is probably incorrect because I doubt that the common meaning of the word "attempt" conveys with precision what conviction of that crime requires. A reasonable grand juror, relying on nothing but that term, might well believe that it connotes intent plus any minor action toward the commission of the crime, rather than the " 'substantial step' " that the Court acknowledges is required, *ante,* at 787.

Besides appealing to "common parlance," the Court relies on the fact that attempt, "as used in the law for centuries . . . encompasses both the overt act and intent elements." *Ante,* at 788. Once again, this argument seems to me certainly irrelevant and probably incorrect. Many common-law crimes have retained relatively static elements throughout history, burglary among them; that has never been thought to excuse the specification of those elements in the indictment. And the argument is probably incorrect, because the definition of attempt has not been nearly as consistent as the Court suggests. Nearly a century ago, a leading criminal-law treatise pointed out that " 'attempt' is a term peculiarly indefinite" with "no prescribed legal meaning." 1 F. Wharton, Criminal Law § 229, p. 298 (11th ed.1912). Even the modern treatise the Court relies upon, see *ante,* at 787, explains—in a subsection entitled "The Confusion"—that jurisdictions vary widely in how they define the requisite *actus reus.* LaFave § 11.4(a), at 218–219. Among the variations are: " 'an act toward the commission of' some offense"; "an act 'in furtherance of' " an offense; " 'a substantial step toward the commission of the crime' "; " 'some appreciable fragment of the crime' "; and the wonderfully opaque " 'commencement of the consummation.' " *Ibid.* (footnote omitted). These are not simply different ways of saying "substantial step." The Model Penal Code definition that the Court invokes, *ante,* at 787–788, is just that: a model. It does not establish the degree of homogeneity that the Court asserts. The contention that the "federal system" has a "well-settled" definition of attempt, see Supplemental Brief for United States 22, tells us nothing; many terms in federal indictments have only one *federal* definition, not because that is the universally accepted definition, but because there is only one Federal Government.

In this case, the indictment alleged that respondent "knowingly and intentionally attempted to enter the United States of America," App. 8, so that the Court focuses only on whether the indictment needed to allege the second element of attempt, an overt act. If one accepts the Court's opinion, however, the indictment could just as well have omitted the phrase "knowingly and intentionally," since that is understood in "common parlance," and has been an element of attempt "for centuries." Would we say that, in a prosecution for first-degree murder, the element of "malice aforethought" could be omitted from the indictment simply because it is commonly understood, and the law has always required it? Surely not.

EXERCISE

Indictments usually must contain a plain statement that addresses every material element of a law. How would you amend the *Resendiz-Ponce* indictment (quoted in the opinion above) so as to include an overt act?

Another federal statute that criminalizes attempts is 18 U.S.C. 1956, which covers some forms of money laundering:

(a)(3)   Whoever, with the intent—

> **(A)** to promote the carrying on of specified unlawful activity;
>
> **(B)** to conceal or disguise the nature, location, source, ownership, or control of property believed to be the proceeds of specified unlawful activity; or
>
> **(C)** to avoid a transaction reporting requirement under State or Federal law,

conducts or attempts to conduct a financial transaction involving property represented to be the proceeds of specified unlawful activity, or property used to conduct or facilitate specified unlawful activity, shall be fined under this title or imprisoned for not more than 20 years, or both.

As with other attempt crimes, the government must prove up an overt act—a term that requires some definition.

United States v. Nelson
66 F. 3d 1036 (9th Cir. 1995)

Boochever, Circuit Judge:

Kevin Lee Nelson appeals his conviction for attempting and conspiring to structure a money laundering transaction. Undercover government agents posing as drug dealers came to the car dealership where Nelson worked, proposing to buy a car with cash. Nelson suggested ways to structure the cash purchase of a car to avoid the dealership's requirement under federal law to report cash transactions over $10,000. We reverse Nelson's attempt conviction, but affirm his conviction for conspiracy.

FACTS

In 1992, the Internal Revenue Service ("IRS") learned that two Montana drug dealers had used cash proceeds from drug transactions to purchase cars from Prestige Toyota ("Prestige"), a car dealership in Billings. The IRS also had information that the sales had been structured to avoid the IRS requirement that a retail business file a reporting form whenever it receives more than $10,000 in cash, and that Prestige salesperson William Rahlf was involved in one of the sales.

The IRS began an undercover investigation. IRS Special Agent Pam White and Raymond Malley, an agent of the Montana Criminal Investigation Bureau, set up an appointment with Rahlf and arrived at Prestige on May 29, 1992. Agent White, using the name "Pam Wright," wore a transmitter to record their conversations. Rahlf took Agents White and Malley for a test drive in a Toyota 4-Runner, during which Agent White told Rahlf that she was "in the dope business" and Malley was her supplier. She added that she wanted to buy a car with cash, but did not want a "paper trail:" "I don't want anything in my name at all." Rahlf said "It's not a problem," and volunteered that he had previously sold cars to another drug dealer. Agent White asked him if his superiors would have any problems with the deal, and Rahlf answered "We've done it before, we can do it again." Rahlf added that "[i]t won't be a big deal" to use cash and title the car in another name.

Upon their return to the dealership, Agent White showed Rahlf a bundle of cash, which was in denominations of hundreds and twenties. Rahlf began to complete a "four-square," a form the salesperson fills out with the prospective customer's offer for a car. Rahlf asked Agent White the name and address she wanted to use. Agent White told him she would offer $22,000, asked him to use the name "Joyce Brown" and a post office box, and suggested he explain her situation to his superiors. She declined to sign the four-square form.

Rahlf took the four-square in to Randy Replogle, the assistant general sales manager, and appellant Kevin Nelson. Nelson was a sales manager or "closer," who helped salespersons finalize offers. As a closer, Nelson reported to the general sales manager or "desk," who had the final authority to put the deal together. Replogle was filling in as "desk" that day for Dustin Timmons, Prestige's general sales manager. Rahlf and Replogle discussed the deal, with Nelson present.

Rahlf told Replogle that the customers got their money from the drug business, and that they wanted to buy with cash and leave no paper trail. Replogle said he thought they should not get involved in the deal, and called the owner of Prestige, Ray McLean, at his home. McLean told him not to make the deal, and to get the customers out of the store. Replogle told Nelson to tell the customers to leave.

Rahlf and Nelson returned to Agents White and Malley, and Rahlf introduced Nelson, saying that he was aware of the situation. Nelson told Agents White and Malley that retail sellers must report any cash transaction over $10,000, and that Prestige would have to fill out a form to make such a report. He also told the agents they could use the name "Joyce Brown." Nelson went back in to talk to Replogle, telling the agents that the price was the likely sticking point.

Nelson told Replogle that the customers wanted to use an assumed name, and Replogle called McLean again, who reiterated that he wanted them to ask the customers to leave. Nelson returned to Agents White and Malley, telling them that Prestige would not falsify a name on the reporting form because that would be "fraud to the bank." After discussing whether it would be all right to use a different name if it were a real person, Agent White told Nelson that Joyce Brown was her sister. Nelson then said "The hell with it, let's do it. Let me go grab—grab a paper. Keep that pencil ready on site." Nelson left.

When he returned, Nelson told Agent White that Prestige could not use "Joyce Brown" on the reporting form. He then suggested another way to get around the reporting requirement: if Agent White were to come in with a trade-in to keep the cash price under $10,000, no form would be necessary. He said "I got probably ten good friends in the same situation but when they do it, they always come in and they trade something so they keep it under $10,000 . . . so it doesn't have to be reported." He also suggested that Agent White consider buying two vehicles at Prestige for less than $10,000 each, which the dealership later could take back as trade-ins to keep the cash price of the 4-Runner below the reporting threshold. Nelson explained that he had done this "all the time" so that "we don't have the money trail." Nelson added that he was "more than willing" to do this: "All I want to do is cover my butt and cover yours at the same time." Nelson and Rahlf suggested the agents call Prestige the next day, and the agents left.

Later that evening, Rahlf contacted Jim Sinhold, a friend who worked as a salesperson at a Ford dealership, telling him that he had a female customer with "a purse full of money" who wanted to buy a car. Sinhold testified that Rahlf explained that "the deal didn't happen" at Prestige, and that Rahlf would send Agent White over. Although Rahlf testified that he thought he had told Sinhold that the customer was a dope dealer, Sinhold did not remember that, and thought Rahlf was looking for a referral fee for sending the woman over to the Ford dealership.

The next morning, when owner McLean arrived at Prestige, Nelson told him that he made the right decision when he turned down the deal the night before.

Agent White called Rahlf later that same morning. Rahlf told her that he and the agents "blew it" by telling Replogle the whole story, although Nelson was not the problem. Agent White told him the trade-in scheme sounded too complicated. Rahlf then put Prestige's general manager, Dustin Timmons, on the line, and Timmons told Agent White that she would have to get the trade-ins from other dealerships to avoid throwing up a flag. Agent White said the plan was not going to work for her. Rahlf then referred her to Sinhold at the Ford dealership to buy a Ford Explorer. Rahlf also stated "you don't need to tell [Sinhold] anything because I've already told him . . . just do whatever it is you got to do and they'll . . . make the paper work right."

Two days later, on June 1, 1992, federal agents entered Prestige with a search warrant and seized business records. Nelson and Rahlf were indicted in March 1993. On June 30, 1993, a jury found Rahlf and Nelson guilty of one count of conspiring to conduct or attempt to conduct financial transactions involving property represented to be the proceeds of unlawful controlled substance trafficking, with the intent to avoid a transaction reporting requirement, and one count of conducting or attempting to conduct such a financial transaction, both in violation of 18 U.S.C. § 1956(a)(3)(C). Nelson was sentenced to a ten-month "split sentence" in the pre-release center in Great Falls, Montana, with five months in the custody component and five months in the pre-release component of the center. . . .

18 U.S.C. § 1956(a)(3)(C) (1992), in effect at the time of Nelson's charged conduct (there have since been some technical amendments), provided that whoever, intending "to avoid a transaction reporting requirement under State or Federal law, conducts or attempts to conduct a financial transaction involving property represented by a law enforcement officer to be the proceeds of specified unlawful activity," commits an offense punishable by fines and/or imprisonment for not more than twenty years. "[T]he term 'conducts' includes initiating, concluding, or participating in initiating, or concluding a transaction. . . ." *Id.* at § 1956(c)(2). "Specified unlawful activity" includes violations of the narcotics laws. *Id.* at § 1956(c)(7)(A).

To prove a violation of this section, the Government must prove (1) that the defendant conducted or attempted to conduct a financial transaction, (2) with the intent to avoid a transaction reporting requirement, and (3) that the property involved in the transaction was represented by a law enforcement officer to be the proceeds of specified unlawful activity. *United States v. Breque,* 964 F.2d 381, 386–87 (5th Cir.1992), *cert. denied,* 507 U.S. 909, 113 S.Ct. 1253, 122 L.Ed.2d 652 (1993).

The transaction reporting requirement alleged to have been violated in this case was 26 U.S.C. § 6050(I)(a) (1990), which requires any person engaged in business "who, in the course of such ... business, receives more than $10,000 cash in 1 transaction (or 2 or more related transactions)" to report the transaction to the IRS. Subsection (f) specifically provides that it is a violation of the statute to cause or attempt to cause a business to file a required return with a material misstatement of fact, or to structure or assist in structuring (or attempt to structure or assist in structuring) a transaction, for the purpose of evading the reporting requirements. 26 U.S.C § 6050(I)(f). . . .

Nelson claims that the evidence does not show that he attempted to initiate or to participate in initiating a car sale. Nelson argues that because he was not involved at the time Rahlf completed the four-square form, he took no substantial step toward the completion of the transaction, and all his other acts were mere preparation.

An attempt conviction requires evidence that the defendant intended to violate the statute, and that he took a substantial step toward completing the violation. *See United States v. Acuna,* 9 F.3d 1442, 1447 (9th Cir.1993). To constitute a substantial step, the defendant's actions must go beyond mere preparation, and must corroborate strongly the firmness of the defendant's criminal intent. *Id.* "The conduct must be necessary to the consummation of the crime and of such nature that a reasonable observer, viewing it in context, could conclude beyond a reasonable doubt that it was undertaken in accordance with a design to violate the statute." *Id.* (quotation omitted).

Nelson advised Agent White that she could use "Joyce Brown," her "sister's" name, on the reporting form and took that idea inside to the "desk" (Replogle) for approval. Replogle told Nelson to ask the customers to leave. Telling the agents that he would do the transaction with a different name "in a heartbeat," but his superiors were unwilling, Nelson then proposed the trade-in scheme using vehicles purchased at Prestige or elsewhere for under $10,000. When the agents said they wanted to think it over and got up to leave, Nelson urged them to call him or Rahlf back.

We have already rejected Nelson's argument that § 1956 requires a higher level of intent than shown by his actions. There is no question that a jury could conclude that Nelson intended to violate the statute when he proposed structuring the car sale to avoid the reporting requirement. We now must determine whether a jury could find that Nelson's actions were a substantial step toward the violation. "It is admittedly difficult to draw the line between mere preparation to commit an offense, which does not constitute an attempt, and the taking of a substantial step toward commission of the crime, which does." *Harper,* 33 F.3d at 1147.

A substantial step is an "appreciable fragment" of a crime, an action of "such substantiality that, unless frustrated, the crime would have occurred." *United States v. Buffington,* 815 F.2d 1292, 1303 (9th Cir.1987). In *Buffington,* the defendants drove past a bank twice. One defendant entered a store nearby and observed the bank, while two others, one disguised as a woman, exited their car in the bank parking lot and focused their attention on the bank. All were armed. Nevertheless, because there was no movement toward the bank and no indication that defendants planned to enter, this court found insufficient evidence of attempted bank robbery. *Id.*

Even when the defendant's intent is clear, his actions must "cross the line between preparation and attempt" by unequivocally demonstrating that the crime will take place unless interrupted by independent circumstances. *United States v. Still,* 850 F.2d 607, 609 (9th Cir.1988), *cert. denied,* 489 U.S. 1060, 109 S.Ct. 1330, 103 L.Ed.2d 598 (1989). A witness saw the defendant in *Still* putting on a long blonde wig while sitting in his van with the motor running, about two hundred feet from a bank. The defendant put the van into reverse and drove off when the police arrived. *Id.* at 610. Although after his arrest the defendant made it clear that he intended to rob the bank, the court held that the absence of facts establishing "either actual movement toward the bank or actions that are analytically similar" required the reversal of the attempt conviction. *Id.*

To constitute a substantial step, the defendant's actions must be a "true commitment" toward completing the crime. *Harper,* 33 F.3d at 1147–48. Defendants who created a "bill trap" in an automated teller machine ("ATM"), with the intent of robbing the ATM vault when technicians eventually would arrive to clear the trap, did not take a substantial step toward bank robbery because the robbery was in the future and the defendants, who were sitting in their car in the parking lot, had not moved toward the bank. *Id.* at 1147. *Cf. United States v. Smith,* 962 F.2d 923, 926, 930–31 (9th Cir.1992) (sufficient evidence of "substantial step" toward possession of cocaine when defendant arrived with codefendant at house where cocaine was picked up, drove off later in another car, and circled parking lot of restaurant where cocaine deal was to take place before parking nearby with a shotgun in his lap); *United States v. Davis,* 960 F.2d 820, 827 (9th Cir.)(sufficient evidence of substantial step toward possession of cocaine with intent to distribute where defendant arranged meeting to discuss distribution and introduced parties when they arrived), *cert. denied,* 506 U.S. 873, 113 S.Ct. 210, 121 L.Ed.2d 150 (1992); *United States v. Candoli,* 870 F.2d 496, 503 (9th Cir.1989) (defendants seen driving by business and parking up the street, who later were stopped driving away from business with plastic bottles of gasoline in the trunk, did not commit substantial step toward arson which occurred two weeks later).

This court has not addressed the conduct that will constitute a substantial step toward a violation of § 1956. Other circuits have found sufficient evidence of an attempt to violate the statute where defendants have done more than merely discuss possible ways to avoid reporting requirements. In *McLamb,* 985 F.2d at 1287, the Fourth Circuit affirmed the conviction of an owner of a car dealership for money laundering under 18 U.S.C. § 1956(a)(3). McLamb told a salesman to break up a $14,000 cash payment into two payments under $10,000 and assisted in the transaction, for which the dealership filed no reporting form. *Id.* at 1286. He advised an undercover agent in another transaction that there were ways to avoid reporting a cash purchase of a car, advised him to break up the payment so each transaction would be under $10,000, and again discussed the deal when the agent arrived with the money, which the defendant turned over to the dealership. *Id.* at 1286–87.

These steps "went far beyond mere preparation ... to characterize McLamb, on this evidence, as a mere passive observer of these goings-on, would defy reason." *Id.* at 1292. The Sixth Circuit found a substantial step when a car sale designed to conceal drug proceeds through the use of an assumed name and the avoidance of the reporting requirement was at least half completed. The defendant prepared a purchase agreement using the name of a fictitious third party, presented the agreement to the dealership's general manager for further paperwork, assured the buyer he would not file reporting forms, and accepted over $20,000 in cash when the buyer (an undercover agent) arrived to take possession of the car. *United States v. Loehr,* 966 F.2d 201, 202–03 (6th Cir.), *cert. denied,* 506 U.S. 1020, 113 S.Ct. 655, 121 L.Ed.2d 582 (1992). In a case unrelated to the purchase of a car, the Fifth Circuit has found sufficient evidence that the defendant took a substantial step toward circumventing currency reporting requirements when

> [h]e prepared a plan, he refined it after communicating with an intended recipient of the money, he demonstrated the commercial reasonableness of the plan to the undercover agent, he received the money, and was on his way to deliver the money to the sanitizing agent in a foreign situs when he was arrested. If he had made delivery of the money the crime would have been perfected.

Fuller, 974 F.2d at 1479.

Nelson's actions in this case were far less definitive. Nelson discussed the assumed name scheme with Replogle, who had the final authority, and Replogle rejected it. He proposed the trade-in scheme to the agents, who said they would think it over. He continued to urge the trade-in idea when Agent White expressed reluctance. Nevertheless, Nelson's expressed eagerness to consummate the deal and his efforts towards doing so are evidence of intent, rather than evidence supporting a finding that Nelson took a step "of such substantiality that, unless frustrated, the crime would have occurred." *Harper,* 33 F.3d at 1147 (quotation omitted). His actions are also consistent with his job, which was to keep customers on the hook while he helped the salesperson (Rahlf) finalize the offer, which is consistent with mere preparation. Nelson did not break up a cash payment already received, *McLamb,* 985 F.2d at 1286, complete paperwork or accept a cash payment, *Loehr,* 966 F.2d at 202, or prepare a detailed plan and receive payment. *Fuller,* 974 F.2d at 1476–77.

Nelson's actions were too "tentative and unfocussed" to be an appreciable fragment of the crime of avoiding a reporting requirement. *Still,* 850 F.2d at 609. Nor were they a step toward the commission of the crime so substantial that without an intervening act the crime would have occurred. *Id.* We agree that "[w]hen criminal intent is clear, identifying the point at which the defendants' activities ripen into an attempt is not an analytically satisfying enterprise." *Harper,* 33 F.3d at 1148. We conclude, however, that even viewing the evidence in the light most favorable to the government, the evidence does not show beyond a reasonable doubt that Nelson took a substantial step toward violation of the statute. His actions were mere preparation, and were not sufficient to show an attempt to launder money.

EXERCISE

　　Imagine a case in which a defendant is charged with attempt to conceal the proceeds of a specified unlawful activity. The defendant had taken $14,000 he had made selling methamphetamine and gone to a friend who owned a coin-operated car wash. He convinced the friend to trade him the cash for $14,000 in quarters garnered from the car wash. The friend agrees, and they plan to exchange the cash for the quarters the next day. The defendant shoves the $14,000 into a gym bag and heads over towards the car wash on foot. On the way, he stops and sits down on a park bench, thinking about how he is going to get rid of all those quarters, which is a quandary. At that moment a police officer approaches the defendant, asks a few questions before asking to look in the bag, and finds the money. The defendant admits the origins of the cash and his plan. Can a case be made for attempt under 18 U.S.C. § 1956(a)(3)?

B.　CONSPIRACY

　　The distinctive essential element of conspiracy is *agreement*—that two or more people agreed to work together in some way to commit a crime. In this way, conspiracy can rope together large groups of people into one charge. Particularly in narcotics crimes, fraud, and other business-centered crimes that almost necessarily involve multiple people, conspiracy is a frequently-used charge that can exert great leverage on defendants to plead guilty and cooperate with the government in prosecuting others. This makes the definition of conspiracies—who is in and who is out—a critical question in many prosecutions.

Importantly, the rules for conspiracies involving narcotics can diverge from those for other types of conspiracies. For example (as we will see in the cases that follow), non-narcotics conspiracy cases in federal court generally require that an overt act in furtherance of the conspiracy be proven by the government, but that requirement does not apply to federal narcotics conspiracies.

One key question relating to conspiracy regards the element of intent. Usually (as we will see in the cases that follow), two kinds of intent are required: the intent to agree with another person, and the intent that the underlying crime be committed.

Another aspect of conspiracy that has proven important is the way in which it spreads responsibility. Those convicted of conspiracy are generally held liable for the foreseeable acts of co-conspirators.

1.   GENERAL CONSPIRACIES

Unlike attempt, there is one law in the federal penal code that covers conspiracy to commit crimes. This is often referred to as the "general conspiracy" statute, and is found at 18 U.S.C. § 371:

> If two or more persons conspire either to commit any offense against the United States, or to defraud the United States, or any agency thereof in any manner or for any purpose, and one or more of such persons do any act to effect the object of the conspiracy, each shall be fined under this title or imprisoned not more than five years, or both.
>
> If, however, the offense, the commission of which is the object of the conspiracy, is a misdemeanor only, the punishment for such conspiracy shall not exceed the maximum punishment provided for such misdemeanor.

Conspiracy law can be quite confusing, and can involve complicated state of mind proofs relating to agreement, intent, and knowledge.

a.   Agreement

The essence of conspiracy is agreement, a meeting of the minds. Because agreement often occurs informally, the evidence of agreement can take a wide variety of forms, and often agreement is proven only by circumstantial evidence. In the world of crime, after all, the agreement to conspire is rarely memorialized in a written contract signed by the co-conspirators.

The further away an actor is from the center of a conspiracy, the more difficult it may be to show that there was agreement.

UNITED STATES V. BURTON

126 F.3d 666 (5th Cir. 1997)

DUHÉ, CIRCUIT JUDGE:

Appellants Joshua Burton and Quinton Carr were convicted and sentenced for conspiracy to commit robbery, in violation of 18 U.S.C. § 371("conspiracy"), and for attempted robbery by force, violence and intimidation, in violation of 18 U.S.C. §§ 2113(a) and 2 ("bank robbery"). On appeal, Appellants contend the Government's evidence was insufficient to convict them of either offense and that the district court erred in adding a six-level increase to their offense levels for "otherwise using a firearm." We affirm.

BACKGROUND

On December 21, 1994, two armed men attempted to rob Bank One in Missouri City, Texas at around 2:30 p.m. The men were dressed in grey sweat suits and wore black masks. They pointed guns at the bank employees and threatened to kill the employees if they did not cooperate. After unsuccessfully attempting to enter the bank vault, the men abandoned their robbery attempt. Before leaving, the robbers threatened to blow up the bank and left two small packages they removed from a black duffel bag. The packages were actually shoe boxes containing road flares, wires and an alarm clock and could not be detonated. The only description of the robbers the bank employees could provide was that the skin around their eyes not covered by the masks revealed the men were African-American.

A witness using the ATM outside the bank saw two men in grey sweat suits run out of the bank carrying a black duffel bag, enter a parked blue car, and drive away, apparently driven by a third man. Policemen soon arrived and found the car abandoned, with the motor running, at a nearby car wash. The car was later determined to belong to Quinton Carr ("Carr"). Around midnight on December 22, the morning after the robbery attempt, Carr called the police and reported the car stolen.

The Government alleged that Joshua Burton ("Joshua") and his cousin, Wilton Burton ("Wilton"), actually entered the bank, and that Carr (Joshua's cousin and Wilton's brother) allowed his car to be used for the getaway and also picked up Joshua and Wilton after the robbery. Wilton gave a statement to police apparently implicating Joshua and Quinton in the robbery, but recanted that statement at trial, claiming he had confessed only because policemen were beating him. After a trial in which the Government relied largely on circumstantial evidence, Appellants were convicted on both counts. . . .

B. *Quinton Carr*

1. The blue Pontiac.

Police found a blue Pontiac abandoned, with its engine still running, in a car wash near the robbery scene. The key was in the ignition and the car showed no signs of having been hot wired. Police found evidence in the car linking it to Quinton Carr, including an automobile service contract in Carr's name, Carr's medical card, and cards written to Carr by his girlfriend Rita Gwen. Ed Burton testified that he saw the car in the vicinity of the bank both on the morning and the afternoon of the robbery. *See* discussion *supra* Part I.A.3.

A police operator testified that she received a call shortly after midnight on December 22 (the morning after the robbery), apparently from Carr, reporting his car stolen. Although there was some confusion about the interpretation of her report, a reasonable construction of her report was that Carr reported he had last seen the car at his cousin's apartment on December 5 but only realized it had been stolen on December 21. Christopher Spooner testified that Wilton Burton told him Carr's stolen car report was false. *See* discussion *infra* Part I.B.2. Although Carr's girlfriend Rita Gwen testified that the last time she had seen the car was on December 9 or 10 parked in front of Christopher Spooner's house, she told the grand jury that she last saw the car at Spooner's as late as December 20.

2. Testimony of Christopher Spooner.

Christopher Spooner is Asia Morgan's husband. Wilton Burton regularly spent the night at their apartment. Spooner testified that Wilton spent the night at their apartment on December 20–21 and that Wilton left with Carr on the morning of the 21st at 4:30 a.m. Spooner said Wilton and Quinton left in Quinton's car, but he did not actually see them getting into the car; he testified, however, that Quinton's car was parked in front of his apartment building on the morning of December 21.

Spooner testified that he had overheard Wilton and Quinton, talking "about bank robberies" about two weeks before the actual robbery:

Q: Did they both say things in your presence that made you understand they were talking about a bank robbery?

A: Yes.

On cross examination, Spooner stated that Wilton and Carr were "generally speaking" about bank robberies and that they did not refer specifically to the December 21 robbery.

Spooner said that Wilton had not told him that Carr was involved in the bank robbery. Wilton, however, did tell Spooner that they had used Carr's vehicle in the robbery and had then abandoned it at a car wash.

Significantly, Wilton told Spooner that Quinton Carr was going to call the police and report his car stolen and that the report would be false.

3.   Testimony of Rita Gwen.

Rita Gwen, Carr's girlfriend, testified that Carr spent the night with her on December 20–21 and left very early on the morning of December 21, the day of the robbery. She said he picked her up around noon that day and that he was driving a cream-colored Lexus. Other witnesses testified that Joshua Burton drove a cream-colored Lexus. Carr took Gwen to pay bills and dropped her off around 1:00 p.m. She saw Carr again around 3:00 p.m., when he returned to her place, still driving the Lexus, but this time accompanied by Wilton Burton. Wilton apparently remained with her and Carr for the rest of the day. Gwen also testified that Carr, at some point that evening, reported his car stolen; she could not specify whether he called around 7:00 that evening or between 10 and 11:00 p.m. *See also* discussion *supra* Part I.B.1.

4.   Conclusion

Our function in reviewing the sufficiency of the evidence is not to determine "whether the trier of fact made the correct guilt or innocence determination, but whether it made a rational decision to convict or acquit." *United States v. Ornelas-Rodriguez,* 12 F.3d 1339, 1344 (5th Cir.1994), *quoting Herrera v. Collins,* 506 U.S. 390, 402, 113 S.Ct. 853, 861, 122 L.Ed.2d 203 (1993). Here, the principle is apposite that "[w]hile each piece of evidence, viewed independently[,] may have been susceptible of innocent interpretation . . . the jury reasonably could have concluded that *when examined in the aggregate,* the evidence sufficed to establish . . . guilt." *Ornelas-Rodriguez,* 12 F.3d at 1346. (emphasis added). With that in mind, we find that the evidence was sufficient for a rational trier of fact to find Quinton Carr guilty beyond a reasonable doubt of the crimes charged.

On appeal Carr argues that the Government presented no evidence that he agreed to participate in the robbery. He contends the evidence shows he was "merely associated" with members of the conspiracy and only "aware" of the criminal plan, not that he took part in it. Carr also maintains that the jury could not infer from the use of his car in the robbery, standing alone, that he *allowed* the robbers to use it. Finally, Carr argues that his stolen car report does not allow the inference that he was aiding and abetting the robbery; even if the report was false, according to Carr, the jury could, "at best," infer that Carr was only trying to protect himself when he discovered the car had been used in a robbery.

Carr would have us unduly curtail the "responsibility of the trier of fact fairly to resolve conflicts in the testimony, to weigh the evidence, and to draw reasonable inferences from basic facts to ultimate facts." *Herrera,* 506 U.S. at 401–02, 113 S.Ct. at 861, *quoting Jackson v. Virginia,* 443 U.S. 307, 319, 99 S.Ct. 2781, 2789, 61 L.Ed.2d 560 (1979). We decline to do so. A rational trier of fact could have found that the evidence before it established far more than Carr's "mere association" with the members of the conspiracy.

The jury reasonably could have found that the use of Carr's vehicle in the robbery, coupled with his sham stolen car report, established that Carr was associated with the robbery, that he participated in it, and that he "sought by action to make the venture succeed." *See* 18 U.S.C. § 2. The jury could have found this conclusion strengthened by Carr's appearance, before and after the robbery, in Joshua Burton's Lexus. Certainly there is nothing illegal in Carr driving Joshua's car on the day of the robbery, or in his leaving early that morning with Wilton Burton, or in his showing up with Wilton soon after the robbery; but as coincidence piles upon coincidence, a rational jury is entitled to find that criminal activity may be afoot. *See Ornelas-Rodriguez,* 12 F.3d at 1346.

Finally, a rational jury could have found from Christopher Spooner's testimony that Carr and Wilton Burton were planning the bank robbery in question a mere two weeks before the robbery took place. While Spooner's testimony was vague, the jury did not have to rely solely on it to find that Carr participated in the conspiracy. The jury could also have considered Carr's familial and social relationships with the other members of the conspiracy, and, most importantly, the series of "coincidences" that strongly connected Carr and his vehicle to the robbery itself. *See Williams-Hendricks,* 805 F.2d at 503.

EXERCISE

A woman approaches a bank teller and hands her a note. The note says "This is a robbery. I have a gun. You can help by putting money in the bag I am giving you. Do not look up. Do not press the button. I just want us to help each other, ok? I need the money for my family, so please just help me." The woman passing the note is a customer of the bank who is familiar to the teller, though they do not know each other outside of the occasional transaction at the bank. No one was injured during the incident.

The teller follows these instructions and gives the woman over $4,000 of the bank's money. Is the teller a co-conspirator to the robbery, per the definition used in the *Burton* case?

Multiple conspiracies can operate at the same time and overlap. Particularly challenging can be "hub and spoke" conspiracies, where an individual or small group have separate agreements with many people to commit similar but distinct acts.

UNITED STATES V. CHANDLER

388 F.3d 796 (11th Cir. 2004)

HILL, CIRCUIT JUDGE:

On December 6, 2001, a grand jury empaneled by the United States District Court for the Middle District of Florida, Jacksonville Division, returned a 62 page indictment charging 43 defendants with conspiracy to commit mail fraud, in violation of 18 U.S.C. § 371. The defendants were alleged to have used the United States mails in furtherance of a scheme and artifice to defraud McDonald's Corporation (McDonald's). During the relevant time period, McDonald's conducted "Monopoly" style and "Hatch, Match and Win" promotional games to attract customers to McDonald's restaurants. Over twenty different games were played during this time. The games were played by visiting the restaurant, purchasing food, and collecting the game stamps that were attached to the various food products sold by McDonald's. Certain game stamps were "winners," worth substantial sums of money. McDonald's employed Simon Marketing, Inc. ("Simon") to develop, manage, and advertise the games. Jerome Jacobson was the Director of Security for Simon, with responsibility for disseminating the high-value game stamps.

The indictment alleged that Jacobson would embezzle these game stamps and conspire with friends, relatives, and others to act as "recruiters," who would in turn solicit other friends and relatives to submit the stolen winning game stamps to McDonald's and collect the prize money. Appellants George Chandler, John Henderson, Jerome Pearl and Kevin J. Whitfield were alleged to have recruited winners or redeemed stolen game stamps. Prize money, it was alleged, was shared by Jacobson and the other conspirators. The scope of the alleged conspiracy was substantial, as evidenced by both the number of defendants and the fact that game stamps were distributed nation-wide and so the "winners" were located across the country. . . .

Despite having charged a single conspiracy with two criminal objects, the government's prosecution of the case severed the connection between Jacobson's illegal act of embezzlement and the defendants' "fraudulent" redemptions. The government's position was that it did not matter *how* the defendants obtained the game stamps. The government asserted on numerous occasions that Jacobson's theft of the stamps was legally irrelevant to the culpability of the defendants for their redemptions. The government even argued that the game stamps could have been legitimately obtained by someone other than the individual that redeemed the game stamp, or even been *found on the street,* and the defendants representations would still have been fraudulent. In the government's view, it was the defendants' "misrepresentations" to McDonald's that they were "legitimate" winners that constituted the underlying illegal activity to which the defendants agreed.

The question now is what impact this view of the conspiracy had on defendants' convictions. The defendants argue that it resulted in a fatal variance between the conspiracy charged in the indictment and that proved at trial. Defendants claim that the under the government's theory of the prosecution, not only was Jacobson's embezzlement irrelevant to proof of the conspiracy, but Jacobson, himself, became irrelevant. The result was that the most the government may have proved was a series of conspiracies, not a single conspiracy. We turn now to this issue.

1.   *The Conspiratorial Agreement*

A conspiracy is an agreement between two or more persons to accomplish an unlawful plan. 18 U.S.C. § 371; *Parker,* 839 F.2d at 1477. The essence of the conspiracy is this agreement to commit an unlawful act. *Toler,* 144 F.3d at 1425. What distinguishes the offense of conspiracy from a substantive offense, is that "agreement is the essential evil at which the crime of conspiracy is directed." *Iannelli v. United States,* 420 U.S. 770, 777 n. 10, 95 S.Ct. 1284, 43 L.Ed.2d 616 (1975). The agreement itself "remains the essential element of the crime." *Id.* Thus the government must prove the existence of an *agreement* to achieve an unlawful objective and the defendant's *knowing* participation in that agreement. *United States v. Adkinson,* 158 F.3d 1147, 1155 (11th Cir.1998).

Because the essential nature of conspiracy is secrecy, a conspiracy conviction may be proved by circumstantial evidence. *Glasser v. United States,* 315 U.S. 60, 80, 62 S.Ct. 457, 86 L.Ed. 680 (1942). The government must, however, show circumstances from which a jury could infer beyond a reasonable doubt that there was a "meeting of the minds to commit an unlawful act." *Adkinson,* 158 F.3d at 1154 (quoting *Parker,* 839 F.2d at 1478).

Since no one can be said to have agreed to a conspiracy that they do not know exists, proof of *knowledge* of the overall scheme is critical to a finding of conspiratorial intent. "Nobody is liable in conspiracy except for the fair import of the concerted purpose or agreement as he understands it." *United States v. Peoni,* 100 F.2d 401, 403 (2nd Cir.1938). The government, therefore, must prove beyond a reasonable doubt that the conspiracy existed, that the defendant *knew* about it and that he voluntarily agreed to join it. *United States v. Hernandez,* 896 F.2d 513, 519 (11th Cir.1990).

We have reversed conspiracy convictions where there was no direct proof of an agreement, and the circumstantial evidence of agreement was insufficient to support such an inference. *Adkinson,* 158 F.3d at 1159 (reversing conspiracy convictions where government failed to prove defendants knowingly agreed to unlawful act); *United States v. Awan,* 966 F.2d 1415, 1434–35 (11th Cir.1992) (insufficient evidence to support finding of unlawful agreement); *Parker,* 839 F.2d at 1478 (insufficient evidence of common agreement). Proof of a true agreement is the only way to prevent individuals who are not actually members of the group from being swept into the conspiratorial net.

In this case, the indictment charged a single conspiracy in which Jacobson was the "key man" who stole the game stamps and then constructed a vast network of co-conspirators who would both redeem the game stamps and recruit others to do so. To convict the defendants of this conspiracy, the government had to prove that the defendants knew of the "essential nature of the plan" and agreed to it. *See Blumenthal v. United States,* 332 U.S. 539, 557, 68 S.Ct. 248, 92 L.Ed. 154 (1947); *Adkinson,* 158 F.3d at 1155.

2. *What the Government Proved about the Agreement*

There are *no* allegations in the indictment that any of these defendants knew of Jacobson's plan to steal the game stamps and distribute them to a vast array of recruiters and winners. There are none because Jacobson deliberately set out to keep the fact that there was any overall scheme secret from the defendants. In fact, the government conceded in its opening remarks, "[e]vidence will establish, which will be uncontroverted by the defense, that many of the winners did not know that the winning game stamps(s) that they redeemed had originally been embezzled or stolen."

At trial, Jacobson testified that he had ten different recruiters to whom he gave game stamps. These recruiters in turn found "winners" to redeem the game stamps. Jacobson testified that *not one* of his recruiters knew any of the others, or even about his theft of the stamps. Nor did any of the winners know of Jacobson, or his embezzlement of the game stamps. It was part of Jacobson's scheme deliberately to keep each recruiter and the winners developed by each recruiter separate from and ignorant of the existence of the others.

Jacobson's scheme was a classic "hub-and-spoke" conspiracy, in which a central core of conspirators recruits separate groups of co-conspirators to carry out the various functions of the illegal enterprise. *See Kotteakos v. United States,* 328 U.S. 750, 755, 66 S.Ct. 1239, 90 L.Ed. 1557 (1946); *United States v. Perez,* 489 F.2d 51, 58 (5th Cir.1973). In such a conspiracy, the core conspirators are the hub and each group of co-conspirators form a spoke leading out from the center in different directions. *Kotteakos,* 328 U.S. at 755, 66 S.Ct. 1239. The core conspirators move from spoke to spoke, directing the functions of the conspiracy. *Id.*

Jacobson's conspiracy also had a hub and spokes. He was the hub and his recruiters and winners formed the various spokes. Unlike the classic hub-and-spoke conspiracy, however, Jacobson was the *only* conspirator in the hub, and when he moved from spoke to spoke, he moved alone. There was no time at which he and another conspirator moved from spoke to spoke. . . .

The Supreme Court has characterized such a conspiracy as a "rimless wheel" because there is no rim to connect the spokes into a single scheme.

Kotteakos, 328 U.S. at 755, 66 S.Ct. 1239. In *Kotteakos,* several different defendants fraudulently obtained loans through the central key man, Brown. There was, however, no connection *between* the defendants. They were connected only to Brown. The trial court had upheld the jury's convictions of these defendants on the theory that "it was possible on the evidence for the jury to conclude that all were in a common adventure because of [each defendant's connection to Brown in one or more transactions] and the similarity of purpose presented in the various applications for loans." *Id.* at 768–69, 66 S.Ct. 1239.

The Supreme Court, however, reversed the convictions, holding that the trial court "confuse[d] the common purpose of a single enterprise with the several, though similar, purposes of numerous separate adventures of like character." *Id.* at 769, 66 S.Ct. 1239. As the Court put it:

> [T]he pattern was "that of separate spokes meeting at a common center," though we may add without the rim of the wheel to enclose the spokes. The proof therefore admittedly made out a case, not of a single conspiracy, but of several, notwithstanding only one was charged in the indictment.

Id. at 755, 66 S.Ct. 1239. Thus, where the "spokes" of a conspiracy have no knowledge of or connection with any other, dealing independently with the hub conspirator, there is not a single conspiracy, but rather as many conspiracies as there are spokes. *Id.* at 754–55, 66 S.Ct. 1239. . . .

In this case, there was no connection whatsoever between the various spokes of Jacobson's scheme. . . . Jacobson was the only person common to the ten otherwise completely separate undertakings, no other person moving with him from spoke to spoke. The government conceded early on and at trial that the spokes knew nothing about each other or, indeed, about Jacobson's theft of the game stamps and his overall scheme. Jacobson, himself, so testified. In the face of this fact, the government took the only position it could—that such knowledge was irrelevant to proof of the charged conspiracy.

This was error of constitutional proportions. In order to prove the charged conspiracy, the government had to show that the defendants knew and agreed to some scheme larger than their own spoke, involving only receipt of a game stamp from their immediate recruiter and its "illegitimate" redemption. *Iannelli,* 420 U.S. at 777, 95 S.Ct. 1284; *Toler,* 144 F.3d at 1425. Without evidence of an agreement to participate in the larger scheme charged in the indictment, the government proved only that there may have been multiple conspiracies, each with Jacobson as the unknown key man, the recruiter and, had they known of Jacobson's thefts, the redeemers. *See Barnard v. United States,* 342 F.2d 309, 312–13 (9th Cir.1965) (without some evidence that individual spokes knew about others, there was not a conspiracy for a succession of fraudulent collisions, but rather a succession of separate collision conspiracies); *United States v.*

Varelli, 407 F.2d 735 (7th Cir.1969) (reversing conviction where insufficient evidence that similar hijackings part of one overall conspiracy).

EXERCISE

What options does a prosecutor have in dealing with a hub-and-spoke conspiracy as in the case above? How might it have been successfully charged?

b. Intent

Interestingly, 18 U.S.C. § 371, in outlawing conspiracies, does not use the words "intent" or "intentionally." However, intent is the basis for not one but two essential elements of conspiracy: the government must prove that the defendant had both the intent to agree to commit a crime and the intent that the crime be completed.

Intent to agree to commit the crime is often proven up by circumstantial evidence, but that evidence must still be convincing.

UNITED STATES V. GRASSI

616 F. 2d 1295 (5th Cir. 1980)

LEWIS R. MORGAN, CIRCUIT JUDGE.

Dante Angelo Grassi and Jack Louis Gail appeal from convictions based on their participation in a series of transactions involving controlled substances and unregistered guns. The principal issues presented by this appeal concern the sufficiency of the evidence to prove a conspiracy and the fairness of the joinder of the appellants together with six other defendants in a 21-count indictment.

The indictment charged both Grassi and Gail with conspiring to distribute controlled substances and to possess, transfer and transport unregistered firearms in violation of 18 U.S.C. s 371 (count 1). Grassi was also charged with conspiring to import controlled substances in violation of 21 U.S.C. s 963 (count 2). Gail was charged with shipping firearms in interstate commerce in violation of 18 U.S.C. s 924(b) (count 17). The appellants were convicted as charged.

The evidence against the defendants consists primarily of the testimony of undercover agents and of tape recordings of the agents' conversations with the defendants during the period covered by the indictment. Having assumed the identity of smugglers of firearms and narcotics, agents Ralph Altman and Gary Peacock of the Bureau of Alcohol, Tobacco and Firearms first met with defendant Charles Watson on April 27, 1978 at Watson's place of business in Homestead, Florida. The agents explained that they had a substantial business exchanging guns for drugs with South American sources, and were exploring for new contacts who would help in the landing, off-loading and distribution of a great quantity of marijuana that would be received in the near future. The agents added that they would also be interested in obtaining weapons and pistol silencers for use in their narcotics trade. Watson asked to join in the marijuana venture, and offered to find silencers for two pistols the agents were carrying. Altman and Peacock agreed to accept Watson's help and delivered two .22 caliber pistol barrels to be fitted with silencers.

Watson later introduced the agents to his brother, defendant Carl Watson, and defendant Frank Ammirato, who, Watson explained, could supply the agents with large quantities of automatic weapons, silencers and drugs. The agents met with the Watsons and Ammirato on May 5, 1978 at the construction site of the Ramblewood Middle School in Coral Springs, Florida. Carl Watson and Ammirato gave the agents a sample of pills from a supply of amphetamines they offered to sell. Four days later the agents met with Carl Watson again and purchased 1000 amphetamines for $850. At that meeting, the agents and Carl Watson discussed the details of the pending marijuana importation, Watson's progress in finding supplies of machine guns and pistol silencers, and the possibility that Watson and his associates would offer the agents a supply of quaalude pills.

Appellant Grassi was not introduced to the agents until May 12, 1978 during another meeting at the Ramblewood School. Grassi expressed interest in the agents' marijuana importation scheme, and proposed to work with the agents if they could supply reliable personal references. Peacock gave Grassi two names of people who would vouch for their operation, and Grassi proceeded to conduct a background check.

In the weeks that followed, Ammirato and Watson met regularly with Peacock and Altman to discuss the marijuana importation venture, and to negotiate and consummate various drug and firearms sales. Other defendants were introduced and participated in these deals, but neither Grassi nor Gail were present at any meetings during this stage of the investigations.

Gail was not introduced to the agents until early July 1978. At a meeting on July 6 between the agents, Ammirato and Watson, Ammirato informed the agents that he had a contact in Chicago who could supply the agents with silencers. The next evening, Ammirato, Peacock and Altman travelled to Chicago to meet Gail Ammirato's Chicago contact. Gail sold the agents one silencer and offered to begin supplying fifty more per month. During the same meeting, Ammirato explained the various pending drug deals to Gail, and in Gail's presence told the agents that Gail would be interested in purchasing some of the quaaludes the agents were to receive from Ammirato. Gail added that he was also interested in buying cocaine.

Complications soon developed in Gail's plan to provide silencers to the agents. Gail reported that his source for silencers insisted on fitting the silencers on complete pistols so that the silencers could be tested as they were made and fitted. When the agents explained this problem to Ammirato, Ammirato said that he could procure and ship pistols to Chicago as needed.

On July 26, at a meeting at the Ramblewood School, Ammirato showed Peacock and Altman two pistols he had purchased for them. Ammirato explained that he would have one of his men carry the guns to Chicago and deliver them to Gail to be fitted with silencers. Under the observation of agents of the Bureau of Alcohol, Tobacco and Firearms, defendant Alfred Beuf flew to Chicago that day, handed a briefcase to Gail at the airport, and left on a departing flight. Informed by Ammirato that the pistols were ready, Peacock and Altman flew to Chicago two days later and purchased the two silenced pistols from Gail.

Grassi reentered the scene on July 27 when the agents met with Ammirato and Grassi at Ammirato's home. The discussion at this meeting covered the planned marijuana importation as well as the many other completed and proposed illicit transactions. Ammirato told the agents that they would not receive any more pistols or silencers until the marijuana importation was accomplished. Grassi then proposed that if the agents could provide their own planes for the marijuana importation, he would send one of his men to protect them and arrange for a purchase of fifteen to thirty kilograms of cocaine along the way. The conversation then turned to the other illicit deals, and although Grassi listened, it does not appear that he contributed to this discussion or took part in any negotiation.

Further discussions and transactions between the agents and certain defendants followed. The agents' last conversation with Gail before his arrest was at a meeting in Chicago on September 19.

Gail stated that he was still interested in obtaining quaaludes, possibly in exchange for pistols and silencers, and asked when the agents thought they would receive their quaaludes from Ammirato.

The eight defendants were arrested in late November of 1978 and joined in a 21-count indictment alleging two conspiracies and nineteen substantive offenses. Only Grassi and Gail resisted their convictions to the conclusion of the jury trial. . . .

. . . [T]here is no evidence that Grassi was a participant in the count 1 conspiracy discussions, or that he indicated, expressly or impliedly, his involvement or personal interest in the count 1 conspiracy. Rather, the record shows that Grassi attended the July 27 meeting only to protect his interests in the marijuana importation scheme.

It is a cardinal rule of conspiracy law that one does not become a coconspirator simply by virtue of knowledge of a conspiracy and association with conspirators. United States v. Falcone, 311 U.S. 205, 61 S.Ct. 204, 85 L.Ed.2d 128 (1940); United States v. Barrera, 547 F.2d 1250 (5th Cir. 1977); United States v. Chandler, 586 F.2d 593 (5th Cir. 1978). The essence of conspiracy is the agreement to engage in concerted unlawful activity. To connect the defendant to a conspiracy, the prosecution must demonstrate that the defendant agreed with others to join the conspiracy and participate in the achievement of the illegal objective. United States v. Avila-Dominguez, 610 F.2d 1266 (5th Cir. 1980).

Conspiracy law is not a dragnet for apprehending those with criminal dispositions. To prove that Grassi was aware of the illegal plan charged in count 1, and even approved of it, may impugn his character but does not place him in violation of the conspiracy laws. While evidence of knowledge and association may be combined with other circumstantial evidence to prove an agreement to join a conspiracy, United States v. Etley, 574 F.2d 850 (5th Cir. 1978); United States v. Evans, 572 F.2d 455 (5th Cir. 1978), we are unable to find any additional independent evidence against Grassi to support his count 1 conviction.

EXERCISE

Imagine that you are the leader of a group trying to produce illegal machine guns in the United States. To do so, you will have to purchase gun parts from a foreign manufacturer and then employ a machinist to grind off a part of those guns. If you were legally savvy and wanted to avoid charges of conspiracy, how would you do that?

A second intent element sometimes read into conspiracy statutes is that the defendant must have intended to achieve a specific, illegal goal. The level of specificity required can be an important question.

UNITED STATES V. SALAMEH
152 F.3d 88 (2d Cir. 1998)

Before: MESKILL, MCLAUGHLIN and CALABRESI, CIRCUIT JUDGES.

PER CURIAM:

Following a lengthy jury trial in the United States District Court for the Southern District of New York (Duffy, *J.*), defendants were convicted of various crimes related to the bombing of the World Trade Center Complex in New York City. Defendants now appeal, asserting a congeries of arguments. For the reasons that follow, we affirm the judgment of the district court but remand for re-sentencing and decline to exercise jurisdiction over certain post-trial motions pending before the district court. . . .

On April 24, 1992, Ahmad Mohammad Ajaj departed from his home in Houston, Texas, and traveled to the Middle East to attend a terrorist training camp, known as "Camp Khaldan," on the Afghanistan-Pakistan border. There he learned how to construct homemade explosive devices. During his time in Pakistan, Ajaj met Ramzi Ahmed Yousef. Together the two plotted to use their newly acquired skills to bomb targets in the United States.

In the fall of 1992, after formulating a terrorist plan, Ajaj and Yousef traveled to New York under assumed names. Ajaj carried with him a "terrorist kit" that he and Yousef had assembled in Pakistan. The kit included, among other things, handwritten notes Ajaj had taken while attending explosives courses, manuals containing formulae and instructions for manufacturing bombs, materials describing how to carry-off a successful terrorist operation, videotapes advocating terrorist action against the United States, and fraudulent identification documents.

On September 1, 1992, Ajaj and Yousef, using false names and passports, arrived at John F. Kennedy International Airport in New York. At customs, INS inspectors discovered that Ajaj's passport had been altered and, consequently, they searched his belongings. Upon discovery of the "terrorist kit," Ajaj became belligerent. The INS seized Ajaj's "terrorist kit" and placed him under arrest. Ajaj was later indicted in the United States District Court for the Eastern District of New York for passport fraud. He pled guilty and was sentenced to six months' imprisonment.

During Ajaj's encounter with the INS inspectors, he denied that he was traveling with Yousef, who proceeded unmolested to the secondary inspection area where he presented an Iraqi passport and claimed political asylum. Yousef was arrested for entering the United States without a visa. Eventually he was released on his own recognizance.

Once in New York, Yousef assembled a team of trusted criminal associates, including Mohammed Salameh, Nidal Ayyad, Mahmoud Abouhalima and Abdul Rahman Yasin. Together, the conspirators implemented the bombing plot that Ajaj and Yousef had hatched overseas. Ayyad and Salameh opened a joint bank account into which they deposited funds to finance the bombing plot. Some of that money was later used by Salameh to rent a storage shed in Jersey City, New Jersey, where the conspirators stored chemicals for making explosives. Yousef also drew on that account to pay for materials described in Ajaj's manuals as ingredients for bomb making.

The first target of the conspirators' plot was the World Trade Center. Ayyad used his position as an engineer at Allied Signal, a large New Jersey chemical company, to order the necessary chemical ingredients for bomb making, and to order hydrogen tanks from ALG Welding Company that would enhance the bomb's destructive force. Abouhalima obtained "smokeless powder," which the conspirators used to make explosives. Smokeless powder, and all the other chemicals procured by the conspirators for the bomb, were stored in the shed rented by Salameh.

Abouhalima helped Salameh and Yousef find a ground floor apartment at 40 Pamrapo Avenue in Jersey City. The apartment fit the specifications in Ajaj's manuals for an ideal base of operations. In the 40 Pamrapo apartment, Abouhalima, Salameh, Yousef and Yasin mixed the chemicals for the World Trade Center bomb, following Ajaj's formulae. Abouhalima also obtained a telephone calling card, which the conspirators used to contact each other and to call various chemical companies for bomb ingredients.

During this entire period, although Ajaj remained incarcerated, he kept in telephone contact with Yousef. By doing so, Ajaj stayed abreast of the conspirators' progress in carrying out the terrorist plot and attempted to get his "terrorist kit" into Yousef's hands. Because Ajaj was in jail and his telephone calls were monitored, Ajaj and Yousef spoke in code when discussing the bomb plot.

On February 23, 1993, Salameh rented a yellow van at DIB Leasing, a Ryder dealership in Jersey City. The conspirators loaded their homemade bomb into that van. On February 26, 1993, the conspirators drove the bomb-laden van into a below-ground parking lot on the B-2 level of the World Trade Center Complex and, using a timer, set the bomb to detonate. At 12:18 p.m., the bomb exploded, killing six people, injuring over a thousand others, and causing hundreds of millions of dollars in damage.

After the explosion, Ayyad took credit for the bombing on behalf of the conspirators by, among other things, writing an anonymous letter to the *New York Times* explaining that the attack was undertaken in retaliation for American support of Israel. The letter threatened future terrorist "missions."

Immediately after the bombing, Yousef, Abouhalima and Yasin fled the country. Abouhalima was apprehended in Egypt prior to the trial and turned over to federal agents by Egyptian authorities, but Yousef and Yasin remained fugitives. Salameh arranged to flee as well, but was arrested the day before he planned to depart when he made the ludicrous mistake of going back to the Ryder truck rental office to get his rental deposit back. On March 1, 1993, Ajaj completed his term of imprisonment on the passport fraud conviction and was released. Approximately one week later, on March 9, Ajaj was taken into government custody on an INS detainer.

In September 1993, Ayyad, Abouhalima, Ajaj, Salameh, Yousef and Yasin were indicted in the United States District Court for the Southern District of New York (Duffy, *J.*), on various charges relating to their participation in the plot to bomb the World Trade Center. Yousef and Yasin were still fugitives at the time of trial.

The trial lasted six months and involved over 1000 exhibits and the testimony of more than 200 witnesses. The defendants were convicted on all counts and each was sentenced to 240 years' imprisonment. Defendants now appeal their convictions and sentences, raising a variety of issues. . . .

Abouhalima next assails the district court's denial of his request to charge concerning the intent required to be convicted of the conspiracy. Specifically, in Abouhalima's request to charge, he averred that, based on the conspiracy as charged in the indictment, the government was required to prove specific knowledge and intent to bomb the World Trade Center. The district court disagreed and instead instructed the jury that for purposes of unlawful intent, the object of the conspiracy "is not restricted to a particular building." Abouhalima argues that the district court's instruction was error because it invited the jury to convict him without finding the mental element of the crime charged. Moreover, Abouhalima asserts that the court's "sweeping language" concerning the object of the conspiracy resulted in his conviction "for participation in a conspiracy beyond that which was charged, noticed, and alleged in the government's proof." In this regard, Abouhalima argues that through the jury charge, the court constructively amended the indictment to reflect an offense not passed on by the grand jury. Furthermore, Abouhalima asserts that the indictment's repeated references to the World Trade Center and the government's repeated references to that complex during opening statements and summation required the government to prove a specific conspiracy to bomb the World Trade Center.

We disagree. "In order to succeed when challenging jury instructions appellant has the burden of showing that the requested charge accurately represented the law in every respect and that, viewing as a whole the charge actually given, he was prejudiced." *Dove*, 916 F.2d at 45 (internal quotation marks and citations omitted). Because Abouhalima cannot show that his request to charge accurately represented the law, we do not reach the issue of prejudice.

It is well settled that the essential elements of the crime of conspiracy are: (1) that the defendant agreed with at least one other person to commit an offense; (2) the defendant knowingly participated in the conspiracy with the specific intent to commit the offenses that were the objects of the conspiracy; and (3) that during the existence of the conspiracy, at least one of the overt acts set forth in the indictment was committed by one or more of the members of the conspiracy in furtherance of the objectives of the conspiracy. *See Maldonado-Rivera*, 922 F.2d at 961; *see also United States v. Wallace*, 85 F.3d 1063, 1068 (2d Cir.1996) (for purposes of conspiracy, unlawful intent is the "specific intent to achieve th[e] object [of the conspiracy]").

The indictment does not charge the defendants with conspiring to bomb the World Trade Center. The indictment alleges that the defendants conspired "to commit offenses against the United States." Four objectives of the conspiracy, each a separate bombing violation, are alleged as follows: (i) to bomb buildings used in or affecting interstate and foreign commerce, in violation of 18 U.S.C. § 844(i); (ii) to bomb property and vehicles owned by the United States, in violation of 18 U.S.C. § 844(f); (iii) to transport explosives interstate for the purpose of bombing buildings, vehicles, and other property, in violation of 18 U.S.C. § 844(d); and (iv) to bomb automobiles used in interstate commerce, in violation of 18 U.S.C. § 33. The World Trade Center bombing is not listed as an object of the conspiracy, but merely as one of 31 overt acts alleged to have been committed in furtherance of the conspiracy. Consequently, because the World Trade Center bombing is not alleged as an objective of the conspiracy, the district court did not err in refusing to charge the jury that specific knowledge and intent was required with respect to that bombing.

There is also nothing in the record to support Abouhalima's contention that the court's instruction eliminated the specific knowledge and intent required for conviction of the charged conspiracy and thereby constructively amended the indictment. A constructive amendment occurs when the terms of the indictment are in effect altered by the presentation of evidence and jury instructions which so modify essential elements of the offense charged that there is a substantial likelihood that the defendant may have been convicted of an offense other than that charged in the indictment. *United States v. Wallace,* 59 F.3d 333, 337 (2d Cir.1995) (quoting *United States v. Mollica,* 849 F.2d 723, 729 (2d Cir.1988)); *see also United States v. Delano,* 55 F.3d 720, 729 (2d Cir.1995).

Consistent with the indictment, the government argued to the jury that the defendants engaged in a conspiracy to bomb buildings, vehicles and property in the United States and the World Trade Center bombing was one act committed in furtherance of the overall conspiracy. Furthermore, the district court's jury charge closely tracked the indictment. The jury also was given a copy of the indictment to take with it during its deliberations, which, as discussed above, clearly stated the objectives of the conspiracy. *See United States v. Jones,* 30 F.3d 276, 284 (2d Cir.1994) (perception of prejudice mitigated when jury is given a copy of the indictment). The evidence at trial established a conspiracy to bomb multiple targets and demonstrated that the conspirators successfully bombed the World Trade Center in furtherance of that conspiracy. Accordingly, there was no constructive amendment.

Finally, the government's multiple references to the World Trade Center in the indictment and during opening statements and summation did not require the court to charge conspiracy to bomb the World Trade Center. Aside from the unprecedented nature of Abouhalima's argument, those multiple references to the World Trade Center bombing were due to the fact that most of the substantive crimes charged in the indictment stemmed from that bombing. In any event, the proof at trial demonstrated that the conspiracy encompassed considerably more than just the bombing of the World Trade Center, including: (1) the existence of additional chemicals recovered from the Shed after the bombing; (2) the modified timing device found in Ayyad's home; and (3) Ayyad's continuing attempts to procure additional explosive chemicals after the bombing. The most definitive proof of the broad scope of the conspiracy and the defendants' intent to commit additional bombings after the World Trade Center was the letter sent to the *New York Times* claiming responsibility for the bombing and the similar draft letter retrieved from an erased file on Ayyad's computer disk, both of which speak to future acts of terrorism.

EXERCISE

The specific intent to commit the crime required by conspiracy is usually proven up by the plan itself—that is, the agreement on its face shows what the conspirators wanted. The need to know that plan often drives prosecutors to "flip" defendants who are within the conspiracy in order to present credible evidence about the nature and extent of the agreement.

Imagine that you are an investigator assigned to dig into a complicated fraud scheme. The three targets have worked together to sell insurance to elderly residents of nursing homes, insuring against the possibility of a foreign invasion. None of them are licensed to engage in the insurance business, and the money taken is simply converted to their own use. The principal target, John Restrio, developed the scheme and the other two market the "insurance" over the internet and through personal visits to nursing homes (they promise, and give over, a cut of the proceeds to the nursing home administrators).

What will you do to develop evidence that the three conspired to conduct this scheme?

c.   Knowledge

The element of knowledge can get hopelessly tangled up with proofs of intent in conspiracy cases, and discussions of conspiracy proofs often conflate the two. The mash-up makes some sense, as the defendant must have known enough about the scheme to form a specific intent; one is a predicate of the other, yet they are not the same thing. How much the defendant has to know about the scheme, however, sometimes does not extend to knowing the facts that underlay each element of the substantive crime.

UNITED STATES V. FEOLA
420 U.S. 671 (1975)

MR. JUSTICE BLACKMUN delivered the opinion of the Court.

This case presents the issue whether knowledge that the intended victim is a federal officer is a requisite for the crime of conspiracy, under 18 U.S.C. § 371, to commit an offense violative of 18 U.S.C. § 111, that is, an assault upon a federal officer while engaged in the performance of his official duties.

Respondent Feola and three others (Alsondo, Rosa, and Farr) were indicted for violations of §§ 371 and 111. A jury found all four defendants guilty of both charges. Feola received a sentence of four years for the conspiracy and one of three years, plus a $3,000 fine, for the assault. The three-year sentence, however, was suspended and he was given three years' probation 'to commence at the expiration of confinement' for the conspiracy. The respective appeals of Feola, Alsondo, and Rosa were considered by the United States Court of Appeals for the Second Circuit in a single opinion. After an initial ruling partially to the contrary, that court affirmed the judgment of conviction on the substantive charges, but reversed the conspiracy convictions. United States v. Alsondo, 486 F.2d 1339, 1346 (1973). Because of a conflict among the federal Circuits on the scienter issue with respect to a conspiracy charge, we granted the Government's petition for a writ of certiorari in Feola's case. 416 U.S. 935, 94 S.Ct. 1932, 40 L.Ed.2d 285 (1974).

I

The facts reveal a classic narcotics 'rip-off.' The details are not particularly important for our present purposes. We need note only that the evidence shows that Feola and his confederates arranged for a sale of heroin to buyers who turned out to be undercover agents for the Bureau of Narcotics and Dangerous Drugs. The group planned to palm off on the purchasers, for a substantial sum, a form of sugar in place of heroin and, should that ruse fail, simply to surprise their unwitting buyers and relieve them of the cash they had brought along for payment. The plan failed when one agent, his suspicions being aroused, drew his revolver in time to counter an assault upon another agent from the rear. Instead of enjoying the rich benefits of a successful swindle, Feola and his associates found themselves charged, to their undoubted surprise, with conspiring to assault, and with assaulting, federal officers.

At the trial, the District Court, without objection from the defense, charged the jurors that, in order to find any of the defendants guilty on either the conspiracy count or the substantive one, they were not required to conclude that the defendants were aware that their quarry were federal officers.

The Court of Appeals reversed the conspiracy convictions on a ground not advanced by any of the defendants. Although it approved the trial court's instructions to the jury on the substantive charge of assaulting a federal officer, it nonetheless concluded that the failure to charge that knowledge of the victim's official identity must be proved in order to convict on the conspiracy charge amounted to plain error. 486 F.2d, at 1344. The court perceived itself bound by a line of cases, commencing with Judge Learned Hand's opinion in United States v. Crimmins, 123 F.2d 271 (CA2 1941), all holding that scienter of a factual element that confers federal jurisdiction, while unnecessary for conviction of the substantive offense, is required in order to sustain a conviction for conspiracy to commit the substantive offense. Although the court noted that the Crimins rationale 'has been criticized,' 486 F.2d, at 1343, and, indeed, offered no argument in support of it, it accepted 'the controlling precedents somewhat reluctantly.' Id., at 1344.

II

The Government's plea is for symmetry. It urges that since criminal liability for the offense described in 18 U.S.C. § 111 does not depend on whether the assailant harbored the specific intent to assault a federal officer, no greater scienter requirement can be engrafted upon the conspiracy offense, which is merely an agreement to commit the act proscribed by § 371. Consideration of the Government's contention requires us preliminarily to pass upon its premise, the proposition that responsibility for assault upon a federal officer does not depend upon whether the assailant was aware of the official identity of his victim at the time he acted.

That the 'federal officer' requirement is anything other than jurisdictional is not seriously urged upon us; indeed, both Feola and the Court of Appeals, 486 F.2d at 1342, concede that scienter is not a necessary element of the substantive offense under § 111. . . .

We conclude, from all this, that in order to effectuate the congressional purpose of according maximum protection to federal officers by making prosecution for assaults upon them cognizable in the federal courts, § 111 cannot be construed as embodying an unexpressed requirement that an assailant be aware that his victim is a federal officer. All the statute requires is an intent to assault, not an intent to assault a federal officer. A contrary conclusion would give insufficient protection to the agent enforcing an unpopular law, and none to the agent acting under cover.

This interpretation poses no risk of unfairness to defendants. It is no snare for the unsuspecting. Although the perpetrator of a narcotics 'rip-off,' such as the one involved here, may be surprised to find that his intended victim is a federal officer in civilian apparel, he nonetheless knows from the very outset that his planned course of conduct is wrongful. The situation is not one where legitimate conduct becomes unlawful solely because of the identity of the individual or agency affected. In a case of this kind the offender takes his victim as he finds him. The concept of criminal intent does not extend so far as to require that the actor understand not only the nature of his act but also its consequence for the choice of a judicial forum. . . .

We hold, therefore, that in order to incur criminal liability under § 111 an actor must entertain merely the criminal intent to do the acts therein specified. We now consider whether the rule should be different where persons conspire to commit those acts.

III

Our decisions establish that in order to sustain a judgment of conviction on a charge of conspiracy to violate a federal statute, the Government must prove at least the degree of criminal intent necessary for the substantive offense itself. Ingram v. United States, 360 U.S. 672, 678, 79 S.Ct. 1314, 1319, 3 L.Ed.2d 1503 (1959). See Pettibone v. United States, 148 U.S. 197, 13 S.Ct. 542, 37 L.Ed. 419 (1893). Respondent Feola urges upon us the proposition that the Government must show a degree of criminal intent in the conspiracy count greater than is necessary to convict for the substantive offense; he urges that even though it is not necessary to show that he was aware of the official identity of his assaulted victims in order to find him guilty of assaulting federal officers, in violation of 18 U.S.C. § 111, the Government nonetheless must show that he was aware that his intended victims were undercover agents, if it is successfully to prosecute him for conspiring to assault federal agents. And the Court of Appeals held that the trial court's failure to charge the jury to this effect constituted plain error.

The general conspiracy statute, 18 U.S.C. s 371, offers no textual support for the proposition that to be guilty of conspiracy a defendant in effect must have known that his conduct violated federal law. The statute makes it unlawful simply to 'conspire . . . to commit any offense against the United States.' A natural reading of these words would be that since one can violate a criminal statute simply by engaging in the forbidden conduct, a conspiracy to commit that offense is nothing more than an agreement to engage in the prohibited conduct. Then where, as here, the substantive statute does not require that an assailant know the official status of his victim, there is nothing on the face of the conspiracy statute that would seem to require that those agreeing to the assault have a greater degree of knowledge.

We have been unable to find any decision of this Court that lends support to the respondent. On the contrary, at least two of our cases implicitly repudiate his position. The appellants in In re Coy, 127 U.S. 731, 8 S.Ct. 1263, 32 L.Ed. 274 (1888), were convicted of conspiring to induce state election officials to neglect their duty to safeguard ballots and election results. The offense occurred with respect to an election at which Indiana voters, in accordance with state law, voted for both local officials and members of Congress. Much like Feola here, those appellants asserted that they could not be punished for conspiring to violate federal law because they had intended only to affect the outcome of state races. In short, it was urged that the conspiracy statute embodied a requirement of specific intent to violate federal law. Id., at 753, 8 S.Ct. at 1269. The Court rejected this contention and held that the statute required only that the conspirators agree to participate in the prohibited conduct. See Anderson v. United States, 417 U.S. 211, 226, 94 S.Ct. 2253, 2263, 41 L.Ed.2d 20 (1974).

Similarly, in United States v. Freed, 401 U.S. 601, 91 S.Ct. 1112, 28 L.Ed.2d 356 (1971), we reversed the dismissal of an indictment charging defendants with possession of, and with conspiracy to possess, hand grenades that had not been registered, as reguired by 26 U.S.C. § 5861(d). The trial court dismissed the indictment for failure to allege that the defendants knew that the hand grenades in fact were unregistered. We held that actual knowledge that the grenades were unregistered was not an element of the substantive offense created by Congress and therefore upheld the indictment both as to the substantive offense and as to the charge of conspiracy. Again, we declined to require a greater degree of intent for conspiratorial responsibility than for responsibility for the underlying substantive offense.

With no support on the face of the general conspiracy statute or in this Court's decisions, respondent relies solely on the line of cases commencing with United States v. Crimmins, 123 F.2d 271 (CA2 1941), for the principle that the Government must prove 'antifederal' intent in order to establish liability under § 371. In Crimmins, the defendant had been found guilty of conspiring to receive stolen bonds that had been transported in interstate commerce. Upon review, the Court of Appeals pointed out that the evidence failed to establish that Crimmins actually knew the stolen bonds had moved into the State. Accepting for the sake of argument the assumption that such knowledge was not necessary to sustain a conviction on the substantive offense, Judge Learned Hand nevertheless concluded that to permit conspiratorial liability where the conspirators were ignorant of the federal implications of their acts would be to enlarge their agreement beyond its terms as they understood them. He capsulized the distinction in what has become well known as his 'traffic light' analogy:

> While one may, for instance, be guilty of running past a traffic light of whose existence one is ignorant, one cannot be guilty of conspiring to run past such a light, for one cannot agree to run past a light unless one supposes that there is a light to run past.' Id., at 273.

Judge Hand's attractive, but perhaps seductive, analogy has received a mixed reception in the Courts of Appeals. The Second Circuit, of course, has followed it; others have rejected it. It appears that most have avoided it by the simple expedient of inferring the requisite knowledge from the scope of the conspiratorial venture. We conclude that the analogy, though effective prose, is, as applied to the facts before us, bad law.

The question posed by the traffic light analogy is not before us, just as it was not before the Second Circuit in Crimmins. Criminal liability, of course, may be imposed on one who runs a traffic light regardless of whether he harbored the 'evil intent' of disobeying the light's command; whether he drove so recklessly as to be unable to perceive the light; whether, thinking he was observing all traffic rules, he simply failed to notice the light; or whether, having been reared elsewhere, he thought that the light was only an ornament. Traffic violations generally fall into that category of offenses that dispense with a mens rea requirement. See United States v. Dotterweich, 320 U.S. 277, 64 S.Ct. 134, 88 L.Ed. 48 (1943). These laws embody the social judgment that it is fair to punish one who intentionally engages in conduct that creates a risk to others, even though no risk is intended or the actor, through no fault of his own, is completely unaware of the existence of any risk. The traffic light analogy poses the question whether it is fair to punish parties to an agreement to engage intentionally in apparently innocent conduct where the unintended result of engaging in that conduct is the violation of a criminal statute.

But this case does not call upon us to answer this question, and we decline to do so, just as we have once before. United States v. Freed, 401 U.S., at 609 n. 14, 91 S.Ct. at 1118. We note in passing, however, that the analogy comes close to stating what has been known as the 'Powell doctrine,' originating in People v. Powell, 63 N.Y. 88 (1875), to the effect that a conspiracy, to be criminal, must be animated by a corrupt motive or a motive to do wrong. Under this principle, such a motive could be easily demonstrated if the underlying offense involved an act clearly wrongful in itself; but it had to be independently demonstrated if the acts agreed to were wrongful solely because of statutory proscription. . . .

It is well settled that the law of conspiracy serves ends different from, and complementary to, those served by criminal prohibitions of the substantive offense. Because of this, consecutive sentences may be imposed for the conspiracy and for the underlying crime. Callanan v. United States, 364 U.S. 587, 81 S.Ct. 321, 5 L.Ed.2d 312 (1961); Pinkerton v. United States, 328 U.S. 640, 66 S.Ct. 1180, 90 L.Ed. 1489 (1946). Our decisions have identified two independent values served by the law of conspiracy. The first is protection of society from the dangers of concerted criminal activity, Callanan v. United States, supra, 364 U.S., at 593, 81 S.Ct., at 325; Dennis v. United States, 341 U.S. 494, 573—574, 71 S.Ct. 857, 899—900, 95 L.Ed. 1137 (1951) (Jackson, J., concurring). That individuals know that their planned joint venture violates federal as well as state law seems totally irrelevant to that purpose of conspiracy law which seeks to protect society from the dangers of concerted criminal activity. Given the level of criminal intent necessary to sustain conviction for the substantive offense, the act of agreement to commit the crime is no less opprobrious and no less dangerous because of the absence of knowledge of a fact unnecessary to the formation of criminal intent. Indeed, unless imposition of an 'antifederal' knowledge requirement serves social purposes external to the law of conspiracy of which we are unaware, its imposition here would serve only to make it more difficult to obtain convictions on charges of conspiracy, a policy with no apparent purpose.

The second aspect is that conspiracy is an inchoate crime. This is to say, that, although the law generally makes criminal only antisocial conduct, at some point in the continuum between preparation and consummation, the likelihood of a commission of an act is sufficiently great and the criminal intent sufficiently well formed to justify the intervention of the criminal law. See Note, Developments in the Law—Criminal Conspiracy, 72 Harv.L.Rev., at 923—925. The law of conspiracy identifies the agreement to engage in a criminal venture as an event of sufficient threat to social order to permit the imposition of criminal sanctions for the agreement alone, plus an overt act in pursuit of it, regardless of whether the crime agreed upon actually is committed. United States v. Bayer, 331 U.S. 532, 542, 67 S.Ct. 1394, 1399, 91 L.Ed. 1654 (1947). Criminal intent has crystallized, and the likelihood of actual, fulfilled commission warrants preventive action.

Again, we do not see how imposition of a strict 'anti-federal' scienter requirement would relate to this purpose of conspiracy law. Given the level of intent needed to carry out the substantive offense, we fail to see how the agreement is any less blameworthy or constitutes less of a danger to society solely because the participants are unaware which body of law they intend to violate. Therefore, we again conclude that imposition of a requirement of knowledge of those facts that serve only to establish federal jurisdiction would render it more difficult to serve the policy behind the law of conspiracy without serving any other apparent social policy.

We hold, then, that assault of a federal officer pursuant to an agreement to assault is not, even in the words of Judge Hand, 'beyond the reasonable intendment of the common understanding,' United States v. Crimmins, 123 F.2d, at 273. The agreement is not thereby enlarged, for knowledge of the official identity of the victim is irrelevant to the essential nature of the agreement, entrance into which is made criminal by the law of conspiracy. . . .

To summarize, with the exception of the infrequent situation in which reference to the knowledge of the parties to an illegal agreement is necessary to establish the existence of federal jurisdiction, we hold that where knowledge of the facts giving rise to federal jurisdiction is not necessary for conviction of a substantive offense embodying a mens rea requirement, such knowledge is equally irrelevant to questions of responsibility for conspiracy to commit that offense.

The judgment of the Court of Appeals with respect to the respondent's conspiracy conviction is reversed.

EXERCISE

Federal insurance of the victim bank at the time of the robbery is an essential element of the crime of bank robbery in federal court.

Samuel and Sarah are planning to rob something in order to make their rent. Sarah suggests robbing a nearby gas station, but Samuel counters by saying that a gas station won't have much money and suggests robbing a nearby bank. Sarah rejects the idea, saying "that's a federal crime—I don't want to mess with the feds." Samuel tells her it is only a federal crime if the bank carries federal insurance, and that since this bank is called "First State Bank of Springfield," it is probably insured by the state and not the federal government.

It turns out Samuel is wrong. Assuming that they make a failed attempt to rob the bank, is Sarah guilty of conspiracy under 18 U.S.C. § 371?

d.   Overt Act Requirement

Like attempt, non-narcotic conspiracy charges usually require proof of an "overt act." 18 U.S.C. § 371, for example, requires the government to prove that an overt act was completed by a conspirator in furtherance of the conspiracy.

UNITED STATES V. MOHAMMED
600 F.3d 1000 (8th Cir. 2010)

LANGE, DISTRICT JUDGE.

Elias Mohamed ("Mohamed") was convicted of conspiracy to commit mail fraud in connection with a scheme to obtain fraudulently Missouri commercial driver's licenses. Mohamed appeals the denial of his motion to suppress materials found in his possession during a traffic stop and challenges a verdict director instruction that included overt acts not specifically alleged in the indictment. For the reasons set forth below, we affirm. . . .

At trial, co-conspirator White testified that he helped individuals pass the Missouri commercial driver's license examination by providing students at South Central Career Center ("SCCC"), a third-party tester under contract with the State of Missouri to administer the skills test, with answers to the written portion under the guise of translation services. White testified that in 2003 he met Osman Abdullahi ("Abdullahi"). Abdullahi operated a business named "Translation Station," where he provided translation services to students taking the written test. He informed White that he provided answers to the students together with translation services. White helped students pass the skills portion of the test by bribing one of SCCC's third-party testers, Orbin May ("May"), to assure the students passed the driving portion of the test.

White identified Mohamed as one of Abdullahi's business associates. White testified that Mohamed knew about the arrangement between White and May and that Mohamed continued to send students to White to help them pass the commercial driver's license skills test. White testified that Mohamed and Abdullahi referred between 80 and 120 students to White.

The government also provided testimony of Abdu Mohamed Osman ("Osman"). Osman testified that Mohamed sold him a Missouri commercial driver's license form D3R for $900. Osman identified the D3R found in the trunk of Mohamed's vehicle by Trooper Frisby as a document that he purchased from Mohamed to obtain a commercial driver's license. The D3R form which Osman purchased from Mohamed indicated that he had taken the skills test at SCCC and that the test was administered by May.

Ahmed Muhidin Sharif ("Sharif"), who received assistance in obtaining his Missouri commercial driver's license from Abdullahi, testified that he directed a student to Mohamed to obtain a commercial driver's license. Sharif stated that the student left with Mohamed and then returned two hours later with a completed commercial driver's license skills document showing that he had passed the skills test.

The government introduced records of Mohamed's cell phone use as evidence of the mail fraud conspiracy. The records showed that the cell phone number that Mohamed had provided to Trooper Frisby had been used in numerous telephone contacts with May, White, and Abdullahi during the time of the conspiracy. FBI Agent Clayton Bye interviewed Mohamed after his arrest and testified that Mohamed told him that he knew Abdullahi and White. Mohamed denied having translated for them or possessing any papers that would help a person fraudulently to obtain a commercial driver's license.

At trial, the district court gave a verdict director instruction, instruction 21. Paragraph 4 of jury instruction 21 stated that one element that the government must prove in order for the defendant to be found guilty is that:

> [W]hile the agreement or understanding was in effect, a person or persons who had joined in the agreement knowingly did one or more of the following acts for the purpose of carrying out or carrying forward the agreement or understanding:
>
> a.   assisted in providing translation services which actually fraudulently provided the correct answers to the Missouri CDL written test in order to allow the student to then take the CDL driving test to obtain a Missouri CDL;

b.   directed persons seeking to obtain CDL licenses to co-defendant Ernest White, knowing that White would obtain these CDL licenses in an illegal manner by fraudulent means through his relationship with codefendant Orbin May;

c.   with other persons sold outdated versions of the Missouri CDL driving exam forms without the person purchasing the form actually having taken the Missouri CDL driving test."

On January 7, 2009, a jury found Mohamed guilty of conspiracy to commit mail fraud. He was sentenced on May 28, 2009, and filed a notice of appeal on June 7, 2009. . . .

Mohamed argues that because the verdict director instruction included overt acts which were not specifically alleged in the indictment, the district court erred and Mohamed's conviction should be remanded for a new trial. Mohamed also argues that jury instruction 21, the verdict director, which was derived from Eighth Circuit Model Criminal Jury Instructions § 5.06A, violated due process of law because it did not require the jury to find that Mohamed personally committed the overt acts in furtherance of the conspiracy in order to convict him of conspiracy to commit mail fraud.

Count 1 of the indictment charged that Mohamed and fourteen other individuals conspired with one another to commit mail fraud. The indictment alleged that Mohamed committed the overt act of directing students to another co-conspirator, Ernest White, knowing that he would provide students with fraudulently obtained commercial driver's licenses. Although Mohamed argues that the jury instruction refers to overt acts not pled in the indictment, specifically that he was in possession and sold D3R documents found in his vehicle, a defendant may be found guilty of overt acts not charged in the indictment. *See United States v. Sdoulam,* 398 F.3d 981, 992 (8th Cir.2005). A variance between the indictment and proof occurs "when the essential elements of the offense set forth in the indictment are left unaltered but the evidence offered at trial proves facts materially different from those alleged in the indictment." *See United States v. Begnaud,* 783 F.2d, 144, 147 n. 4 (8th Cir.1986). In *Sdoulam,* this Court stated that "the inclusion of some overt acts in an indictment does not bar proof of other acts, and proof of other acts in furtherance of the same conspiracy does not constitute a variance." 398 F.3d at 992. The elements of the offense for which Mohamed was charged did not change when other overt acts were proven at trial, and the additional acts contained in the verdict director were not materially different from the charge in the indictment. Mohamed recognizes that *Sdoulam* is on point, but urges the court to overrule *Sdoulam* on the principle that "a person ought not to be convicted of an overt act not charged in the Indictment." This Court refuses to overrule *Sdoulam.*

Even if the overt acts were a variance, Mohamed's conviction still was proper under the circumstances. The indictment fully and fairly apprised him of the charges against him, despite the alleged variance, and therefore there was no actual prejudice to Mohamed. *See Begnaud,* 783 F.2d at 148 (defendant suffers no actual prejudice so long as an indictment fully and fairly apprises the defendant of the charges he must meet). The indictment charged Mohamed with conspiracy to commit mail fraud by assisting students to the conspiracy with obtaining licenses fraudulently. Mohamed was fully and fairly apprised of the charges that were brought against him and was able to prepare a defense to the conspiracy charge.

The district court instructed the jury that in order to prove mail or wire fraud conspiracy, the government needed to prove that "while the agreement or understanding was in effect, a person or persons who had joined the conspiracy did one or more of the following acts." Under the federal conspiracy statute, a conspiracy is committed when two or more persons conspire to commit any offense against the laws of the United States, and only requires that one or more of the co-conspirators commit an overt act to further the purposes of the conspiracy. *See* 18 U.S.C. § 371 (2009). The requisite overt act is satisfied by a single overt act committed by one coconspirator. *United States v. Falcone,* 311 U.S. 205, 210, 61 S.Ct. 204, 85 L.Ed. 128 (1940). Although Mohamed argues that such a jury instruction allows for him to be found guilty without him ever committing an overt act, the government is not required to prove that he committed an overt act. The government need show that "only one of the conspirators engaged in one overt act in furtherance of the conspiracy" and that Mohamed was part of the conspiracy. *United States v. Hermes,* 847 F.2d 493, 495 (8th Cir.1988); *see also United States v. Hobson,* 686 F.2d 628, 630 (8th Cir.1982); *United States v. Bass,* 472 F.2d 207, 213 (8th Cir.1973). Because the government proved that Mohamed knowingly joined the conspiracy, the overt act need not be shown to have been committed by him.

Accordingly, we affirm.

––––––––––––

EXERCISE

Laura and Linette are college roommates. Laura has a work-study job at the campus print shop. One day she picks up a box that is full of what looks like $20 bills. Curious, she looks at them more closely and concludes that they are counterfeit because they all have the same serial number and feel "funny." Laura swipes the box from the print shop and takes it back to her dorm room and shows it to Linette. Intrigued, Linette examines the counterfeit bills and says they are "really good!" Linette then suggests that they convert the fake bills to real money by using the bill changers in campus laundry facilities. Laura agrees enthusiastically, and they agree they will split up campus locations the next day.

The next morning, Laura wakes up early to go to class. On her way back to her room, she stops by the laundry room in the basement of the student center and slips one of the counterfeit bills in the change machine. An alarm goes off, and she is arrested. Later both are charged with conspiracy under 18 U.S.C. § 371. At trial, Linette's lawyer argues that she should not be convicted of conspiracy because she did not commit an overt act, and did not know that Laura was going to do so. As a juror, properly instructed on the law, how would you come out?

e.   Pinkerton Rule

In a 1946 decision, *Pinkerton v. United States*,[3] the United States Supreme Court held that a conspirator is liable for what others in a conspiracy do, so long as two criteria are satisfied: that the criminal act was reasonably foreseeable, and that the act was committed in furtherance of the conspiracy.

UNITED STATES V. ALLEN
425 F.3d 1231 (9th Cir. 2005)

RAWLINSON, CIRCUIT JUDGE:

A jury convicted Koran McKinley Allen of conspiracy to commit armed bank robbery, armed bank robbery, and using, carrying, or possessing a firearm during a crime of violence. On appeal, Allen maintains that there was insufficient evidence to support his firearm conviction. . . .

Allen and his co-conspirators robbed the Community Bank in Pasadena, California, of $21,619. The plan was organized by Larry Washington and his longtime friend, Derrick O'Neal. The two of them, along with co-conspirator Edward Warren, drove to Pasadena the day before the robbery and selected Community Bank as the target. O'Neal recruited three co-conspirators to assist with the robbery, and Washington told O'Neal that Washington "was going to bring a crew that he had used in another robbery." According to FBI Special Agent Taglioretti's testimony, he was informed by O'Neal of Washington's prior statement to O'Neal that Washington recruited Jerry Hughes, Allen, and another individual.

On the morning of the robbery, all involved, including Allen, met in front of Warren's home to organize and discuss the logistics of the robbery. The use of firearms was discussed, and Washington took a bag full of guns out of his Pathfinder truck, around which all the participants had gathered. Hughes also displayed his gun during the meeting. The meeting ended when Warren's mother began looking out the window of the home.

The robbers drove to Pasadena in four vehicles: a maroon van that O'Neal had stolen to use as a getaway car; Washington's white Pathfinder; a gray Escort; and a rental car. Allen, who was designated as a getaway driver, drove the maroon van. When they arrived in Pasadena, all four cars met

---

[3]   328 U.S. 640 (1946).

behind the bank in a parking area. Eventually, five members of the crew entered the bank. Allen remained behind.

During the robbery, Hughes and Joseph Alexander displayed their firearms. Hughes also used his gun to strike two bank employees. One of these employees was knocked unconscious and taken to the emergency room for a CAT scan. Upon exiting the bank, the robbers walked toward the maroon van, but Allen was not in it. As a result, the five robbers drove away in the Escort.

Warren and O'Neal remained in O'Neal's car during the robbery. They were planning to drive away from the bank, turn around, and drive back. As they were heading back toward the bank, Washington called O'Neal, explaining that he needed a ride because his truck would not start. At approximately the same time, O'Neal and Warren saw Allen walking down the street and summoned him into the vehicle. Washington phoned O'Neal a second time, and, as the two were speaking, O'Neal spotted Washington on the corner. Washington entered the backseat of the car and attempted to lie down to hide himself from view.

Officer Shannon Reece of the Pasadena Police Department was on patrol when she heard over the police radio that the Community Bank had been robbed. While Reece was at an intersection, a car stopped on the opposite side of the traffic light drew her attention. When she proceeded through the intersection, she noticed a passenger in that car attempting to hide in the backseat, so she made a U-turn and initiated a traffic stop of the vehicle. The four individuals in the car-O'Neal, Warren, Washington, and Allen-were taken into custody later that day.

All those involved in the robbery were charged with one count of conspiracy to commit bank robbery in violation of 18 U.S.C. § 371, one count of armed bank robbery in violation of 18 U.S.C. § 2113(a) and (d), and one count of using, carrying, or possessing a firearm during a crime of violence in violation of 18 U.S.C. § 924(c). Allen was convicted on all counts, and sentenced to 319 months imprisonment after the district court applied several enhancements to Allen's base offense level. This appeal followed. . . .

Under § 924(c), it is a crime to use or carry a firearm during a crime of violence or to possess a firearm in furtherance of such a crime. 18 U.S.C. § 924(c)(1)(A) (2000 & Supp.2005). Although Allen did not himself use, carry, or possess a gun in furtherance of the robbery, he could be convicted as a co-conspirator. *See Pinkerton v. United States,* 328 U.S. 640, 647, 66 S.Ct. 1180, 90 L.Ed. 1489 (1946).

The *Pinkerton* rule holds "a conspirator criminally liable for the substantive offenses committed by a co-conspirator when they are reasonably foreseeable and committed in furtherance of the conspiracy." *United States v. Long,* 301 F.3d 1095, 1103 (9th Cir.2002) (citing *Pinkerton,*

328 U.S. at 645–48, 66 S.Ct. 1180). Thus, the government "is not required to establish that [Allen] had actual knowledge of the gun[s]"; rather, "[t]he touchstone is foreseeability." *United States v. Hoskins,* 282 F.3d 772, 776 (9th Cir.2002) (citation omitted).

The district court committed no error in denying Allen's motion for a judgment of acquittal. Allen was present at the "morning of" meeting where guns were present and their use was discussed; he had a longstanding friendship with co-conspirator O'Neal who had participated in previous armed bank robberies; and, it is reasonable to infer from the nature of the plan-the overtaking of a bank by force and intimidation-that guns would be used. *See id.* at 777 (upholding a conviction under § 924(c) premised on co-conspirator liability where the defendant participated in two meetings at which the robbery was planned, was involved romantically with one of the co-conspirators who had participated in similar armed robberies, and because the nature of the plan, which required the use of force or intimidation to overtake the cash room at a K-Mart, made the use of a gun reasonably foreseeable.).

EXERCISE

Bob McBurger has a lot of stolen guns from which he has removed the serial numbers. He is also a convicted felon. He decides to sell the guns to Gordon, who is actually an undercover federal agent. Bob is arrested by Gordon when he delivers the guns and asks for payment.

When he is arrested, Bob tells Gordon that he was advised to sell the guns by his wife, Shannon. It turns out that Shannon was very upset that Bob had the stolen guns (Shannon knew that they were stolen from a neighbor and that Bob had filed off the serial numbers), and told him to "get rid of them." They agreed that Bob would find someone to sell them to. When he did, Shannon drove Bob over to meet with Gordon in a park, and then drove off when he was arrested.

Gordon intends to recommend prosecution of Bob for selling stolen guns with the serial number removed and the distinct crime of possessing guns as a felon. He is justifiably confident that a federal prosecutor will take the case and get convictions against Bob. Should he seek to have Shannon charged for conspiracy? If so, conspiracy to do what?

f.   Multiple Act Conspiracies

Sometimes a group of people agree to a conspiracy that encompasses more than one illegal goal. Is that one conspiracy, or more? If it is just one conspiracy, how does that limit the government?

UNITED STATES V. BROCE

488 U.S. 563 (1989)

JUSTICE KENNEDY delivered the opinion of the Court.

We consider here the circumstances under which a defendant who has entered a plea of guilty to a criminal charge may assert a double jeopardy claim in a collateral attack upon the sentence. Respondents, upon entering guilty pleas, were convicted of two separate counts of conspiracy, but contend now that only one conspiracy existed and that double jeopardy principles require the conviction and sentence on the second count to be set aside. The United States Court of Appeals for the Tenth Circuit held that respondents were entitled to introduce evidence outside the original record supporting their claim and directed further proceedings in the District Court. We hold that the double jeopardy challenge is foreclosed by the guilty pleas and the judgments of conviction.

I

A

Respondents, Ray C. Broce and Broce Construction Co., Inc., bid for work on highway projects in Kansas. Two of the contracts awarded to them became the subject of separate indictments charging concerted acts to rig bids and suppress competition in violation of the Sherman Act, 26 Stat. 209, as amended, 15 U.S.C. § 1. The relevant portions of the indictments are set forth in the Appendix to our opinion. The first indictment charged respondents with entering into an agreement, sometime in or about April 1978, to rig bids on a particular highway project. The second charged respondents with entering into a similar agreement, sometime in or about July 1979, to rig bids on a different project. Both indictments were discussed during plea negotiations, and respondents acknowledged in plea agreements that they were subject to separate sentences on each conspiracy charged. Plea Agreement between the United States of America and Defendant Ray C. Broce, App. to Pet. for Cert. 126a, 127a; Plea Agreement between the United States of America and Defendant Broce Construction Co., Inc., App. to Pet. for Cert. 133a, 134a.

Respondents pleaded guilty to the two indictments in a single proceeding. The District Court conducted a hearing fully in accord with Rule 11 of the Federal Rules of Criminal Procedure and found that the pleas were free and voluntary, made with an understanding of their consequences and of the nature of the charges. Respondents had counsel at all stages and there are no allegations that counsel was ineffective. Convictions were entered on the pleas. The District Court then sentenced Broce to two years' imprisonment on each count, the terms to run concurrently, and to a fine of $50,000 on each count. Broce was also sentenced for mail fraud under 18 U.S.C. § 1341, a conviction which is not relevant here. The corporation was fined $750,000 on each count, for a total of $1,500,000. Neither respondent having appealed, the judgments became final.

B

On the same day that respondents entered their pleas, an indictment was filed against Robert T. Beachner and Beachner Construction Co. charging a violation of both the Sherman Act and the mail fraud statute. The indictment alleged a bid-rigging conspiracy involving yet a third Kansas highway construction project. These defendants, however, chose a different path than that taken by the *Broce* respondents: they proceeded to trial and were acquitted. After the acquittal in the *Beachner* case *(Beachner I),* a second indictment was returned by the grand jury charging Beachner Construction Co. with three new Sherman Act violations and three new acts of mail fraud. The Sherman Act counts charged bid-rigging conspiracies on three Kansas highway projects not mentioned in *Beachner I.*

Once again, Beachner pursued a different strategy than that followed by Broce and Broce Construction Co. Prior to trial, Beachner moved to dismiss the indictment on the ground that the bid-rigging arrangements identified were merely smaller parts of one overarching conspiracy existing among Kansas highway contractors to rig highway bids within the State. In light of its acquittal in *Beachner I,* the company argued that a second prosecution would place it in double jeopardy.

The District Court granted the motion to dismiss. *United States v. Beachner Construction Co.,* 555 F.Supp. 1273 (Kan.1983) *(Beachner II).* It found that a "continuous, cooperative effort among Kansas highway contractors to rig bids, thereby eliminating price competition, has permeated the Kansas highway construction industry in excess of twenty-five years, including the period of April 25, 1978, to February 7, 1980, the time period encompassed by the Beachner I and Beachner II indictments." *Id.,* at 1277. The District Court based the finding on its determination that there had been a common objective among participants to eliminate price competition, a common method of organizing bidding for projects, and a common jargon throughout the industry, and that mutual and interdependent obligations were created among highway contractors. Concluding that the District Court's findings were not clearly erroneous, the Court of Appeals affirmed the dismissal. *United States v. Beachner Construction Co.,* 729 F.2d 1278 (CA10 1984).

One might surmise that the *Broce* defendants watched the *Beachner* proceedings with awe, if not envy. What is certain is that the *Broce* defendants sought to profit from Beachner's success. After the District Court issued its decision to dismiss in *Beachner II,* the *Broce* respondents filed a motion pursuant to Federal Rule of Criminal Procedure 35(a) to vacate their own sentences on the Sherman Act charge contained in the second indictment. Relying on *Beachner II,* they argued that the bid-rigging schemes alleged in their indictments were but a single conspiracy. The District Court denied the motion, concluding that respondents' earlier guilty pleas were an admission of the Government's allegations of two conspiracies, an admission that foreclosed and concluded new arguments to the contrary. Nos. 81-20119-01 and 82-20011-01 (Kan., Nov. 18, 1983), App. to Pet. for Cert. 112a.

A panel of the Court of Appeals for the Tenth Circuit reversed. 753 F.2d 811 (1985). That judgment was vacated and the case reheard en banc. Citing our decisions in *Blackledge v. Perry,* 417 U.S. 21, 94 S.Ct. 2098, 40 L.Ed.2d 628 (1974), and *Menna v. New York,* 423 U.S. 61, 96 S.Ct. 241, 46 L.Ed.2d 195 (1975) *(per curiam),* a divided en banc court concluded that respondents were entitled to draw upon factual evidence outside the original record, including the *Beachner II* findings, to support the claim of a single conspiracy. 781 F.2d 792 (CA10 1986). The en banc court rejected the Government's argument that respondents had waived the right to raise their double jeopardy claim by pleading guilty, holding that the Double Jeopardy Clause "does not constitute an individual right which is subject to waiver." *Id.,* at 795. It further rejected the Government's contention that respondents' guilty pleas must be construed as admissions that there had been separate conspiracies. The Court of Appeals observed that the indictments did not "specifically allege separate conspiracies," and held that "the admissions of factual guilt subsumed in the pleas of guilty go only to the acts constituting the conspiracy and not to whether one or more conspiracies existed." *Id.,* at 796.

On remand, the District Court, citing *Beachner II,* concluded that the indictments merely charged different aspects of the same conspiracy to restrain competition. It vacated the judgments and sentences entered against both respondents on the second indictment. Nos. 81-20119-01 and 82-20011-01 (Kan., June 30, 1986), App. to Pet. for Cert. 5a. In its decision on appeal from that judgment, the Court of Appeals noted that our intervening decision in *Ricketts v. Adamson,* 483 U.S. 1, 107 S.Ct. 2680, 97 L.Ed.2d 1 (1987), made clear that the protection against double jeopardy is subject to waiver. Nonetheless, it concluded that while *Ricketts* invalidated the broader rationale underlying its earlier en banc opinion that double jeopardy protections could not be waived, it left intact its narrower holding that the guilty pleas in this case did not themselves constitute such waivers. It then held that the District Court's finding of a single conspiracy was not clearly erroneous, and affirmed. Nos. 86-2166 and 86-2202 (CA10, Aug. 18, 1987), App. to Pet. for Cert. 1a. We granted certiorari, 485 U.S. 903, 108 S.Ct. 1073, 99 L.Ed.2d 232 (1988).

II

A plea of guilty and the ensuing conviction comprehend all of the factual and legal elements necessary to sustain a binding, final judgment of guilt and a lawful sentence. Accordingly, when the judgment of conviction upon a guilty plea has become final and the offender seeks to reopen the proceeding, the inquiry is ordinarily confined to whether the underlying plea was both counseled and voluntary. If the answer is in the affirmative then the conviction and the plea, as a general rule, foreclose the collateral attack. There are exceptions where on the face of the record the court had no power to enter the conviction or impose the sentence. We discuss those exceptions below and find them inapplicable. The general rule applies here to bar the double jeopardy claim.

A

The Government's petition for certiorari did not seek review of the determination that the bid-rigging described in the two *Broce* indictments was part of one overall conspiracy. Instead, the Government challenges the theory underlying the en banc judgment in the Court of Appeals that respondents were entitled, notwithstanding their earlier guilty pleas, to a factual determination on their one-conspiracy claim. That holding was predicated on the court's view that, in pleading guilty, respondents admitted only the acts described in the indictments, not their legal consequences. As the indictments did not include an express statement that the two conspiracies were separate, the Court of Appeals reasoned, no such concession may be inferred from the pleas.

In holding that the admissions inherent in a guilty plea "go only to the acts constituting the conspiracy," 781 F.2d, at 796, the Court of Appeals misapprehended the nature and effect of the plea. A guilty plea "is more than a confession which admits that the accused did various acts." *Boykin v. Alabama,* 395 U.S. 238, 242, 89 S.Ct. 1709, 1711, 23 L.Ed.2d 274 (1969). It is an "admission that he committed the crime charged against him." *North Carolina v. Alford,* 400 U.S. 25, 32, 91 S.Ct. 160, 164, 27 L.Ed.2d 162 (1970). By entering a plea of guilty, the accused is not simply stating that he did the discrete acts described in the indictment; he is admitting guilt of a substantive crime. That is why the defendant must be instructed in open court on "the nature of the charge to which the plea is offered," Fed.Rule Crim.Proc. 11(c)(1), and why the plea "cannot be truly voluntary unless the defendant possesses an understanding of the law in relation to the facts," *McCarthy v. United States,* 394 U.S. 459, 466, 89 S.Ct. 1166, 1171, 22 L.Ed.2d 418 (1969).

Just as a defendant who pleads guilty to a single count admits guilt to the specified offense, so too does a defendant who pleads guilty to two counts with facial allegations of distinct offenses concede that he has committed two separate crimes. The *Broce* indictments alleged two distinct agreements: the first, an agreement beginning in April 1978 to rig bids on one specified highway project, and the second, an agreement beginning 15 months later to rig bids on a different project. The Court of Appeals erred in concluding that because the indictments did not explicitly state that the conspiracies were separate, respondents did not concede their separate nature by pleading guilty to both. In a conspiracy charge, the term "agreement" is all but synonymous with the conspiracy itself, and as such has great operative force. We held in *Braverman v. United States,* 317 U.S. 49, 53, 63 S.Ct. 99, 101, 87 L.Ed. 23 (1942), that "[t]he gist of the crime of conspiracy as defined by the statute is the agreement . . . to commit one or more unlawful acts," from which it follows that "the precise nature and extent of the conspiracy must be determined by reference to the agreement which embraces and defines its objects."

A single agreement to commit several crimes constitutes one conspiracy. By the same reasoning, multiple agreements to commit separate crimes constitute multiple conspiracies. When respondents pleaded guilty to two charges of conspiracy on the explicit premise of two agreements which started at different times and embraced separate objectives, they conceded guilt to two separate offenses.

Respondents had the opportunity, instead of entering their guilty pleas, to challenge the theory of the indictments and to attempt to show the existence of only one conspiracy in a trial-type proceeding. They chose not to, and hence relinquished that entitlement. In light of *Beachner,* respondents may believe that they made a strategic miscalculation. Our precedents demonstrate, however, that such grounds do not justify setting aside an otherwise valid guilty plea. . . .

JUSTICE BLACKMUN, with whom JUSTICE BRENNAN and JUSTICE MARSHALL join, dissenting.

A guilty plea, for all its practical importance in the day-to-day administration of justice, does not bestow on the Government any power to prosecute that it otherwise lacks. Here, after remand, the District Court found, and the Court of Appeals affirmed, that the two indictments brought against respondents charged two parts of the same conspiracy, and therefore sought to punish respondents twice for the same behavior, in violation of the Double Jeopardy Clause of the Fifth Amendment.

The Government, see *ante,* at 762–763, does not contest the finding that in fact there was only one conspiracy. It argues, however, that the defendants' guilty pleas render this fact wholly irrelevant, and urges us to let stand convictions that otherwise are barred. Because I believe it inappropriate for a reviewing court to close its eyes to this constitutional violation, and because I find that the basis of respondents' double jeopardy challenge is obvious from a reading of the two indictments and entitles respondents to a hearing, I dissent from the majority's ruling that the guilty pleas are conclusive. . . .

EXERCISE

Broce sets out several basic rules about conspiracies. What are two of them?

The *Broce* case also presents a difficult question regarding plea agreements. Can a conviction by plea be defended when a similarly-situated defendant is acquitted? Should they be?

g. Unilateral Conspiracies

What if a scheme has only one willing participant? This is an issue where a defendant has agreed to commit a crime with an undercover agent or an informant, not knowing the status of the government actor. While some jurisdictions have legislated around the problem by allowing conspiracy to include agreements with law enforcement officials posing as schemers, that is not universal.

SEARS V. UNITED STATES
343 F. 2d 139 (5th Cir. 1965)

GRIFFIN B. BELL, CIRCUIT JUDGE:

Appellant Julian Sears, sheriff of Coffee County, Georgia, was convicted below under an indictment charging that he with Harris Johnson, Beecher Wright, and other persons unknown to the grand jury conspired to violate the Internal Revenue laws relating to the possession of an unregistered distillery. The alleged co-conspirators were jointly indicted, but a severance was granted with the result that Sears was tried separately.

I.

Appellant's first contention is that his motion for acquittal should have been granted because the evidence was insufficient to prove the conspiracy charged. This necessitates a review of the evidence. The government's case was built primarily around the testimony of Dorsey Davis, a former bootlegger who worked with government investigators as an undercover agent and informer. His testimony, corroborated in many particulars by federal agents, established the following. Davis approached government agents and offered to help secure evidence against Sheriff Sears. Davis explained that he and Sears had collaborated in the whisky business in the past, and that he wanted to see Sears caught. The federal agents agreed to employ Davis as an undercover agent, and agreed to pay him $10.00 a day for expenses plus 'a substantial sum' if he was successful in producing evidence against Sears. Davis eventually received an $800.00 fee.

Davis first contacted Sheriff Sears on July 2, 1963. He told Sears that he wanted to resume his illegal whisky operations, and asked Sears if he would furnish 'protection,' that is, permit him to carry on his bootleg activities and warn him of the movements of state and federal agents. Sears agreed to furnish this protection for $250.00 a week.

At the time of this agreement, Davis did not have a still, but he thereafter contacted Johnson and his employee Beecher Wright (the two alleged coconspirators) who had an illegal still in operation. Davis and Johnson agreed to operate the still as co-venturers and to expand the enterprise. Davis was to acquire an interest by working at the still. Davis had reapproached Sheriff Sears on September 4, 1963, told him he was ready to begin production, and tendered $250.00. After some hesitation, Sears accepted the money, and the two agreed to meet each Wednesday night in a secluded area of the woods.

The agreement between Davis and Johnson was made in the presence of federal agent Hayes who posed as the employee of Davis. Wright, the employee of Johnson, was called in to help load whisky purchased at the time from Johnson. He showed Davis and Hayes the still, helped them charge it, and then withdrew from the venture. Thereafter, according to the evidence, it was operated by Davis and Hayes, with all of the production being delivered to Johnson by them except for one purchase by government agents. Thus Johnson's connection with the still was through ownership, and Wright's through firing it up on the one occasion. Davis, the informer, and Hayes, the federal agent, were the operators. Davis met Sears in the woods on each Wednesday of the next four weeks and paid him $250.00 each time. At one of these meetings, Sears agreed to warn Davis of the presence of federal agents in Coffee County by placing a pine top in the left rut of the trail leading to the Johnson-Davis still. Sears never in fact used the pine top warning, and federal agents later moved in and destroyed the still. The indictment, trial, and conviction of Sheriff Sears followed.

On this appeal, Sears contends that the foregoing evidence shows only a conspiracy between himself and Davis, whereas he was indicted and convicted for conspiring with Johnson and Wright. Davis was not named as a co-conspirator in the indictment. Since Davis was an undercover agent secretly intending to frustrate the conspiracy, it is contended that he was incapable of being a party to the conspiracy or of serving as a connecting link between Sears on the one hand and Johnson and Wright on the other.

There was no evidence that Sears ever had any contact with Johnson and Wright or that he even knew they were assisting Davis in the operation of the still. Davis himself testified that he never mentioned their names to Sears. However, the evidence does show that Sears knew that some persons, names to him unknown, were working with Davis. A tape recording of one of the clandestine meetings between Sears and Davis shows that Sears knew Davis was not alone in his enterprise. We hold that this was sufficient to connect Sears to a conspiracy with Johnson and Wright. It is firmly established that it is not necessary for a conspirator to know the identity of his co-conspirators or the exact role which they play in the conspiracy. Rogers v. United States, 1951, 340 U.S. 367, 71 S.Ct. 438, 95 L.Ed. 344; Sigers v. United States, 5 Cir., 1963, 321 F.2d 843; United States v. Dardi, 2 Cir., 1964, 330 F.2d 316; United States v. Wenzel, 4 Cir., 1962, 311 F.2d 164; and Isaacs v. United States, 8 Cir., 1962, 301 F.2d 706. The fact that Sears' only connection with and knowledge of the unknown co-conspirators (Johnson and Wright) was through a government informer (Davis) does not vitiate the conspiracy. In Sigers v. United States, supra, we recently held that government informers may serve as the connecting link between co-conspirators.

The facts of that case were somewhat different in that the informers acted at all times in accordance with instructions furnished by the co-conspirators, but we do not deem this difference significant. By agreeing to furnish protection, Sears plainly intended to assist the unknown persons working with Davis in their illegal enterprise. He is consequently properly chargeable as a conspirator with them.

Although the evidence was sufficient to support the conspiracy charged, it was not the province of the jury to convict Sears merely upon finding that he had accepted money from Davis and furnished protection. This would establish only that Sears had combined with Davis, and as it takes two to conspire, there can be no indictable conspiracy with a government informer who secretly intends to frustrate the conspiracy. See United States v. Wray, N.D.Ga., 1925, 8 F.2d 429. In order to convict, it was incumbent upon the jury to find that Sears knew that there were others assisting Davis in his illegal whisky activities. Appellant requested a cautionary instruction to this effect which was refused by the District Court. We hold this was error. In view of the posture of the evidence and the charge actually given by the court, the jury may well have believed that it could convict Sears simply by believing that he agreed with Davis and accepted bribes from him. Consequently, the court should have given a cautionary instruction to the effect that even if the jury believed Sears had done these things, it could convict only if it further believed that he did so with knowledge that Johnson and Wright, or some anonymous persons, were also involved in the illegal enterprise.

EXERCISE

Lanny and Drew are co-workers at a grocery store. There is a small bank in the store, which Lanny knows can be accessed by a door to the employee's break room. Lanny mentions to Drew that he thinks they could get in there and steal some money. Unbeknownst to Lanny, Drew is married to an FBI agent. He tells his FBI agent husband that a co-worker is thinking of stealing from the bank. Drew's husband tells him to go through with it, and that he will then arrest Lanny.

Before going forward with the plan, Drew gets an FBI undercover identifier and is given a wire to wear. However, Lanny also brings in a buddy named Lars, who is good at opening locked doors. Lanny and Drew find a drawer of money in the federally-insured bank after Lars picks the lock. Drew and Lanny split the money while still in the bank, before other agents from the FBI come in and arrest Lanny. However, it appears that Lars did not know that there was a bank on the other side of the door he was asked to open, and refused his cut of the money. He was just helping out a buddy.

You represent Lanny. How strong is the conspiracy case against him?

h. Wharton's Rule

Some crimes, such as dueling or incest between adults, necessarily require a conspiracy. "Wharton's Rule" (a holdover from common law) directs that in that type of case, the government cannot convict for both the underlying offense and conspiracy. How far can the rule be stretched?

UNITED STATES V. BROWN
7 F.3d 1155 (5th Cir. 1993)

GARWOOD, CIRCUIT JUDGE:

Defendant-appellant Jackie Brown (Brown) participated in a money order scam operating out of Parchman State Penitentiary in Mississippi. A jury found him guilty of conspiracy to alter and pass altered postal money orders and aiding and abetting mail fraud. The district court imposed concurrent sentences of 15 months' imprisonment and 3 years' supervised release on each count, and ordered Brown to pay $1,092 in restitution. Brown appeals the district court's application of the Sentencing Guidelines and certain evidentiary rulings. We affirm.

Facts and Proceedings Below

In January 1992, Evelyn Lomoriello (Lomoriello), a sixty-five-year-old Florida retiree, began corresponding through a "lonely hearts pen-pal club" with Richard Sims (Sims), an inmate at Parchman State Penitentiary in Mississippi. In April 1992, Lomoriello began accepting collect calls from Sims. In their conversations, Sims informed her that he planned to receive several money orders from Johnny Clark, whom he represented as his case worker. Telling Lomoriello that he needed the money to pay his fines, Sims asked her to deposit the money orders in her bank account and to send $5,000 of the money to a man identified as Jackie Brown in Cleveland, Mississippi.

On April 3, 1992, Lomoriello received 8 $700 money orders, totalling $5,600. Pursuant to Sims's instructions, she deposited them in her account, sent $5,000 to Brown in Cleveland by wire transfer, paid $200 to Western Union, and kept $400 for herself to pay for the collect calls. When Lomoriello's bank discovered the money orders had been altered to reflect

$700 instead of their true $1 face values, the bank charged the $5,600 back to her account. Two weeks later, Lomoriello received a second set of altered money orders from Clark. By this time, however, police had warned her of the scam, and she turned the altered money orders over to postal authorities.

On April 6, 1992, Brown, a contract food manager at Parchman, received three Western Union drafts (one in the amount of $1,000 and two $2,000 drafts), and attempted to cash them the following day. The Western Union agent cashed only the $1,000 draft and then called the police to inform them that Brown, using Parchman prison identification, had received the money from a woman in Florida.

After learning from Lomoriello that she had been corresponding with a Parchman inmate, Detective Serio of the Cleveland Police Department attempted to contact Brown. On April 8, 1992, Brown came to the police station and turned over the two uncashed $2,000 drafts and $500 of the draft that he had cashed. The following day, Brown voluntarily returned to the police station and gave Inspector Collins a handwritten statement admitting that he had picked up the money orders at the direction of Parchman inmate Ronnie Franklin. At trial, Brown admitted he was to receive $500 for smuggling the money into Parchman.

Josephine Fortner (Fortner), a Michigan retiree, testified that she had also been corresponding with an inmate at Parchman named Richard Sims. Fortner received $3,500 in altered money orders from Johnny Blackman, who claimed to be Sims's case worker. Following Sims's instructions, she cashed the money orders, kept $500 for herself, and sent $3,000 via Express Mail to Jackie Brown at 900 White Street, Apartment 10-D, Cleveland, Mississippi. Upon discovery of the alterations, her bank charged the $3,500 to her account.

Brown was indicted and found guilty on charges of conspiracy to alter and pass altered postal money orders in violation of 18 U.S.C. § 371(count one), and aiding and abetting mail fraud in violation of 18 U.S.C. §§ 2 and 1343 (count two). . . .

Brown asserts that the district court erred in refusing to dismiss count two (aiding and abetting mail fraud) because it required proof of the same set of operative facts as count one (conspiracy). The courts have consistently ruled that the commission of a substantive crime and a conspiracy to commit that crime are separate and distinct offenses. *Pinkerton v. United States,* 328 U.S. 640, 643, 66 S.Ct. 1180, 1182, 90 L.Ed. 1489 (1946). Wharton's Rule, however, prohibits conviction for both the substantive offense and conspiracy to commit that offense if the substantive offense necessarily requires the participation and cooperation of more than one person. *United States v. Payan,* 992 F.2d 1387, 1389 (5th Cir.1993). A conviction based solely on aider and abetter liability would appear to require the involvement of at least two persons since one cannot aid and abet oneself. Nevertheless, we have recently held that Wharton's Rule does not bar separate convictions for aiding and abetting an offense and conspiring to commit that offense. *Id.* The aiding and abetting statute, 18 U.S.C. § 2, does not define an offense, but simply provides that one who aids or abets the commission of a substantive offense is punishable as a principal. *Id.* at 1390. In applying Wharton's Rule, we consider whether "it is *impossible under any circumstances* to commit the substantive offense without cooperative action." *Id.* Clearly, a single individual acting alone is capable of committing mail fraud as defined by 18 U.S.C. § 1343. Thus, the district court properly refused to dismiss count two.

EXERCISE

Pierre and Cindy are neighbors who live on a military base. They put together a weekly high-stakes poker game. Eventually, the game gets out of hand as more people join in, so they move it on-line. Soon they are caught and charged with running an illegal gambling enterprise under a federal statute targeting gambling rings that involve five or more people.

You are Cindy's attorney. Do you have a defense under Wharton's Rule?

2. NARCOTICS CONSPIRACIES

While the rules discussed above generally apply to narcotics conspiracy cases, there is one special rule and a few distinctive points of emphasis that differtiate narcotics conspiracies from those involving others types of crime.

While the general conspiracy statute at 18 U.S.C. § 371 does apply to federal narcotics cases, there is also a specialized narcotics conspiracy statute. Within federal law, both attempts to violate the narcotics laws and narcotics conspiracies are covered by 21 U.S.C. § 846:

> Any person who attempts or conspires to commit any offense defined in this subchapter shall be subject to the same penalties as those prescribed for the offense, the commission of which was the object of the attempt or conspiracy.

a. Overt Act Requirement

You will note that unlike 18 U.S.C. § 371, there is no mention of an overt act in the narcotics conspiracy statute. That becomes an important point of distinction between narcotics conspiracies and general conspiracies.

UNITED STATES V. SHABANI
513 U.S. 10 (1994)

JUSTICE O'CONNOR delivered the opinion of the Court.

This case asks us to consider whether 21 U.S.C. § 846, the drug conspiracy statute, requires the Government to prove that a conspirator committed an overt act in furtherance of the conspiracy. We conclude that it does not.

I

According to the grand jury indictment, Reshat Shabani participated in a narcotics distribution scheme in Anchorage, Alaska, with his girlfriend, her family, and other associates. Shabani was allegedly the supplier of drugs, which he arranged to be smuggled from California. In an undercover operation, federal agents purchased cocaine from distributors involved in the conspiracy.

Shabani was charged with conspiracy to distribute cocaine in violation of 21 U.S.C. § 846. He moved to dismiss the indictment because it did not allege the commission of an overt act in furtherance of the conspiracy, which act, he argued, was an essential element of the offense. The United States District Court for the District of Alaska, Hon. H. Russel Holland, denied the motion, and the case proceeded to trial. At the close of evidence, Shabani again raised the issue and asked the court to instruct the jury that proof of an overt act was required for conviction. The District Court noted that Circuit precedent did not require the allegation of an overt act in the indictment but did require proof of such an act at trial in order to state a violation of § 846. Recognizing that such a result was "totally illogical," App. 29, and contrary to the language of the statute, Judge Holland rejected Shabani's proposed jury instruction, id., at 36. The jury returned a guilty verdict, and the court sentenced Shabani to 160 months' imprisonment.

The United States Court of Appeals for the Ninth Circuit reversed. 993 F.2d 1419 (1993). The court acknowledged an inconsistency between its cases holding that an indictment under § 846 need not allege an overt act and those requiring proof of such an act at trial, and it noted that the latter cases "stand on weak ground." Id., at 1420. Nevertheless, the court felt bound by precedent and attempted to reconcile the two lines of cases. The Court of Appeals reasoned that, although the Government must prove at trial that the defendant has committed an overt act in furtherance of a narcotics conspiracy, the act need not be alleged in the indictment because " '[c]ourts do not require as detailed a statement of an offense's elements under a conspiracy count as under a substantive count.' " Id., at 1422, quoting United States v. Tavelman, 650 F.2d 1133, 1137 (CA9 1981). Chief Judge Wallace wrote separately to point out that in no other circumstance could the Government refrain from alleging in the indictment an element it had to prove at trial. He followed the Circuit precedent but invited the

Court of Appeals to consider the question en banc because the Ninth Circuit, "contrary to every other circuit, clings to a problematic gloss on 21 U.S.C. § 846, insisting, despite a complete lack of textual support in the statute, that in order to convict under this section the government must prove the commission of an overt act in furtherance of the conspiracy." 993 F.2d, at 1422 (concurring opinion). For reasons unknown, the Court of Appeals did not grant en banc review. We granted certiorari, 510 U.S. 1108, 114 S.Ct. 1047, 127 L.Ed.2d 370 (1994), to resolve the conflict between the Ninth Circuit and the 11 other Circuits that have addressed the question, all of which have held that § 846 does not require proof of an overt act.

II

Congress passed the drug conspiracy statute as § 406 of the Comprehensive Drug Abuse Prevention and Control Act of 1970, Pub.L. 91–513, 84 Stat. 1236. It provided: "Any person who attempts or conspires to commit any offense defined in this title is punishable by imprisonment or fine or both which may not exceed the maximum punishment prescribed for the offense, the commission of which was the object of the attempt or conspiracy." *Id.,* at 1265. As amended by the Anti-Drug Abuse Act of 1988, Pub.L. 100–690, § 6470(a), 102 Stat. 4377, the statute currently provides: "Any person who attempts or conspires to commit any offense defined in this subchapter shall be subject to the same penalties as those prescribed for the offense, the commission of which was the object of the attempt or conspiracy." 21 U.S.C. § 846. The language of neither version requires that an overt act be committed to further the conspiracy, and we have not inferred such a requirement from congressional silence in other conspiracy statutes. In *Nash v. United States,* 229 U.S. 373, 33 S.Ct. 780, 57 L.Ed. 1232 (1913), Justice Holmes wrote, "[W]e can see no reason for reading into the Sherman Act more than we find there," *id.,* at 378, 33 S.Ct., at 782, and the Court held that an overt act is not required for antitrust conspiracy liability. The same reasoning prompted our conclusion in *Singer v. United States,* 323 U.S. 338, 65 S.Ct. 282, 89 L.Ed. 285 (1945), that the Selective Service Act "does not require an overt act for the offense of conspiracy." *Id.,* at 340, 65 S.Ct., at 283.

Nash and *Singer* follow the settled principle of statutory construction that, absent contrary indications, Congress intends to adopt the common law definition of statutory terms. See *Molzof v. United States,* 502 U.S. 301, 307–308, 112 S.Ct. 711, 715–716, 116 L.Ed.2d 731 (1992). We have consistently held that the common law understanding of conspiracy "does not make the doing of any act other than the act of conspiring a condition of liability." *Nash, supra,* 229 U.S., at 378, 33 S.Ct., at 782; see also *Collins v. Hardyman,* 341 U.S. 651, 659, 71 S.Ct. 937, 941, 95 L.Ed. 1253 (1951); *Bannon v. United States,* 156 U.S. 464, 468, 15 S.Ct. 467, 469, 39 L.Ed. 494 (1895) ("At common law it was neither necessary to aver nor prove an overt act in furtherance of the conspiracy . . ."). Respondent contends that these decisions were rendered in a period of unfettered expansion in the law of conspiracy, a period which allegedly ended when the Court declared that "we will view with disfavor attempts to broaden the already pervasive and wide-sweeping nets of conspiracy prosecutions." *Grunewald v. United States,* 353 U.S. 391, 404, 77 S.Ct. 963, 974, 1 L.Ed.2d 931 (1957) (citations omitted). *Grunewald,* however, was a statute of limitations case, and whatever exasperation with conspiracy prosecutions the opinion may have expressed in dictum says little about the views of Congress when it enacted § 846.

As to those views, we find it instructive that the general conspiracy statute, 18 U.S.C. § 371, contains an explicit requirement that a conspirator "do any act to effect the object of the conspiracy." In light of this additional element in the general conspiracy statute, Congress' silence in § 846 speaks volumes. After all, the general conspiracy statute preceded and presumably provided the framework for the more specific drug conspiracy statute. "*Nash* and *Singer* give Congress a formulary: by choosing a text modeled on § 371, it gets an overt-act requirement; by choosing a text modeled on the Sherman Act, 15 U.S.C. § 1, it dispenses with such a requirement." *United States v. Sassi,* 966 F.2d 283, 284 (CA7 1992). Congress appears to have made the choice quite deliberately with respect to § 846; the same Congress that passed this provision also enacted the Organized Crime Control Act of 1970, Pub.L. 91–452, 84 Stat. 922, § 802(a) of which contains an explicit requirement that "one or more of [the conspirators] does any act to effect the object of such a conspiracy," *id.,* at 936, codified at 18 U.S.C. § 1511(a). . . .

What the Ninth Circuit failed to recognize we now make explicit: In order to establish a violation of 21 U.S.C. § 846, the Government need not prove the commission of any overt acts in furtherance of the conspiracy. . . .

Shabani reminds us that the law does not punish criminal thoughts and contends that conspiracy without an overt act requirement violates this principle because the offense is predominantly mental in composition. The prohibition against criminal conspiracy, however, does not punish mere thought; the criminal agreement itself is the *actus reus* and has been so viewed since *Regina v. Bass,* 11 Mod. 55, 88 Eng.Rep. 881, 882 (K.B.1705) ("[T]he very assembling together was an overt act"); see also *Iannelli v. United States,* 420 U.S. 770, 777, 95 S.Ct. 1284, 1289, 43 L.Ed.2d 616 (1975) ("Conspiracy is an inchoate offense, the essence of which is an agreement to commit an unlawful act") (citations omitted).

Finally, Shabani invokes the rule of lenity, arguing that the statute is unclear because it neither requires an overt act nor specifies that one is not necessary. The rule of lenity, however, applies only when, after consulting traditional canons of statutory construction, we are left with an ambiguous statute. See, *e.g., Beecham v. United States,* 511 U.S. 368, 374, 114 S.Ct. 1669, 1672, 128 L.Ed.2d 383 (1994); *Smith v. United States,* 508 U.S. 223,

239–241, 113 S.Ct. 2050, 2059–2060, 124 L.Ed.2d 138 (1993). That is not the case here. To require that Congress explicitly state its intention *not* to adopt petitioner's reading would make the rule applicable with the "mere possibility of articulating a narrower construction," *id.*, at 239, 113 S.Ct. at 2059, a result supported by neither lenity nor logic.

As the District Court correctly noted in this case, the plain language of the statute and settled interpretive principles reveal that proof of an overt act is not required to establish a violation of 21 U.S.C. § 846. Accordingly, the judgment of the Court of Appeals is

Reversed.

EXERCISE

You are a federal prosecutor. A DEA agent meets with you regarding a local man, Harvey Ransom. Mr. Ransom is a banker in town who was in financial trouble. Ransom met with a local drug dealer, Art Carr. Ransom tried to pitch Carr on the idea of a joint narcotic venture—Ransom would get money from the bank, Carr would buy a lot of cocaine in bulk, and then they would find people to sell it on the street.

Carr has talked with a DEA informant (though he was not aware of the man's connection to the DEA), and sought out the informant's advice on how to deal with Ransom. Carr claimed to the informant that Ransom pushed hard for the deal, but Carr was "pretty sure" that Ransom was an undercover police officer or an informant, so he put Ransom off by saying they would talk again and then ditched his phone and did not contact Ransom again.

Is there a case for conspiracy worth making?

b. Buyer-Seller Relationship

Defining who is in and out of a conspiracy can be a special challenge when dealing with narcotics operations. Because they are a business, one central question is this: Are a buyer and seller conspiring with one another? Or does that commercial transaction represent the boundary of a conspiracy?

UNITED STATES V. BROCK
789 F.3d 60 (2d Cir. 2015)

In April 2012, James Dickerson was indicted along with thirty-seven other defendants and charged in two counts—conspiracy to distribute and to possess with intent to distribute 28 grams or more of cocaine base, in violation of 21 U.S.C. §§ 841(a)(1), 841(b)(1)(B), and 846, and distribution of cocaine base, in violation of 21 U.S.C. §§ 841(a)(1) and 841(b)(1)(c). Following a four day trial, Dickerson was convicted on both counts and sentenced to 168 months, to run concurrently. On appeal, Dickerson challenges his conviction on the conspiracy, but not the substantive distribution count. As to the conspiracy conviction, we agree with Dickerson that the evidence establishes no more than his role as a mere purchaser from the conspiracy and cannot support an inference that he joined it. Consequently, we do not address his alternative argument for a new trial as to that count on the basis that a juror committed misconduct during deliberations by accessing a dictionary definition of the word "conspiracy".

The indictment targeted a drug distribution conspiracy based in the Newhallville neighborhood on the border of New Haven and Hamden, Connecticut. Joseph Jackson, the leader of the organization, employed several lieutenants, including his nephew Jayquis Brock, to distribute crack cocaine to purchasers. Brock ultimately pled guilty and testified for the prosecution pursuant to a cooperation agreement. Brock testified that he typically sold 18 "eight-balls" (each weighing approximately 3.5 grams) of crack cocaine per day at $140–150 each. Jackson allowed Brock to keep the money he earned for every ninth eight-ball he sold.

According to Brock, Dickerson was one of his regular buyers, and had been an existing customer at the time Brock joined Jackson's organization in July 2010. Dickerson typically purchased two eight-balls at a time, on several days each week, and occasionally more than once per day. Dickerson contacted Brock by calling his "dispatch" phone, which was a cell phone issued by Jackson to Brock on which purchasers could contact Brock to set up transactions. The government obtained warrants to intercept calls on the dispatch telephone and captured numerous calls between Dickerson and Brock, as well as several calls between Dickerson and Jackson. Telephone records introduced at trial showed that Dickerson contacted Brock or Jackson 129 times between June and September 2010. Of these contacts, the government introduced 31 recorded calls, all but two of which were between Dickerson and Brock. On cross-examination, Brock testified that he did not have resale agreements with his customers and, consequently, did not know or care what they did with the drugs after he sold them. Brock further testified that he did not consider Dickerson to be a member of Jackson's drug trafficking organization, although he did consider Dickerson to be a "reliable customer."

In October 2010, Dickerson was captured on video selling an eight-ball and eight $20 baggies of crack cocaine to an undercover officer, which formed the basis for the substantive distribution count in the indictment. In November 2010, Dickerson was arrested. Shortly thereafter, he met with a law enforcement agent and his attorney, and admitted that he purchased crack cocaine from Brock and others, broke down each eight-ball, and resold it in $20 baggies.

Dickerson's defense at trial to the conspiracy count was that he was a mere buyer of drugs and not a participant in the conspiracy. At the close of the prosecution's case in chief, Dickerson moved on this ground for a judgment of acquittal as to the conspiracy count. Dickerson contended that he never joined the conspiracy and was only one of its numerous customers, highlighting the fact that Brock himself testified that he viewed Dickerson as a customer and not a member of the organization.

The district court denied the motion, concluding that the government had adduced sufficient evidence that Dickerson was a member of the conspiracy. The district court held that, although the "transactions between Dickerson and Brock are by themselves insufficient to constitute the charged conspiracy. . . . other evidence presented at trial was sufficient to permit the jury to conclude beyond a reasonable doubt that Dickerson knew of the Jackson group's drug distribution scheme and agreed to join and participate in it." JA 111.

Specifically, the district court noted that the government had proved that Dickerson purchased and resold drugs in wholesale quantities on a regular basis over a period of at least a month from Brock and that Dickerson's post-arrest statements indicated that he knew Brock worked for Jackson and that the two were moving large quantities of drugs on a daily basis. These facts, according to the district court, permitted the jury to conclude that "Dickerson had not merely engaged in spot transactions with Brock" but that the two had developed an expectation of future sales such that "each side had an interest in the other's future drug-related endeavors— *i.e.*, Dickerson's interest in the continued supply of [crack] by Brock, and Brock's interest in Dickerson's continued demand for them." JA 113. This appeal followed.

DISCUSSION

"As a general matter, a defendant challenging the sufficiency of the evidence bears a heavy burden, as the standard of review is exceedingly deferential." *United States v. Coplan,* 703 F.3d 46, 62 (2d Cir.2012) (internal citations and quotation marks omitted). Specifically, we "must view the evidence in the light most favorable to the Government, crediting every inference that could have been drawn in the Government's favor, and deferring to the jury's assessment of witness credibility and its assessment of the weight of the evidence." *Id.* (citing *United States v. Chavez,* 549 F.3d 119, 124 (2d Cir.2008)).

"Although sufficiency review is *de novo,* we will uphold the judgments of conviction if 'any rational trier of fact could have found the essential elements of the crime beyond a reasonable doubt.' " *Id.*(citing *United States v. Yannotti,* 541 F.3d 112, 120 (2d Cir.2008); *Jackson v. Virginia,* 443 U.S. 307, 319, 99 S.Ct. 2781, 61 L.Ed.2d 560 (1979)).

Our precedent is clear that the mere purchase and sale of drugs does not, without more, amount to a conspiracy to distribute narcotics. *See United States v. Parker,* 554 F.3d 230, 234 (2d Cir.2009). "[T]he buyer's agreement to buy from the seller and the seller's agreement to sell to the buyer cannot 'be the conspiracy to distribute, for it has no separate criminal object.'" *Id.* at 235 (quoting *United States v. Wexler,* 522 F.3d 194, 208 (2d Cir.2008) (internal alterations omitted)). We have explained that, although the mere buyer defense "does not protect either the seller or buyer from a charge they conspired together to transfer drugs if the evidence supports a finding that they shared a conspiratorial purpose to advance other transfers, whether by the seller or by the buyer," *id.* at 234, "[e]vidence that a buyer intends to resell the product instead of personally consuming it does not necessarily establish that the buyer has joined the seller's distribution conspiracy," *United States v. Hawkins,* 547 F.3d 66, 74 (2d Cir.2008). Nor is "contact with drug traffickers," standing alone, sufficient "to prove participation in a conspiracy." *United States v. Gaviria,* 740 F.2d 174, 184 (2d Cir.1984). Although we have "avoided listing factors to guide what is a highly-specific fact inquiry into whether the circumstances surrounding a buyer-seller relationship establish an agreement to participate in a distribution conspiracy," we have identified certain factors relevant to the analysis, including "whether there was a prolonged cooperation between the parties, a level of mutual trust, standardized dealings, sales on credit [ ], and the quantity of drugs involved." *Hawkins,* 547 F.3d at 74 (internal citations and quotation marks omitted).

Here, there is insufficient evidence of a shared conspiratorial purpose among Jackson, Brock and Dickerson. While Dickerson frequently bought crack from Brock, he also purchased crack from others not involved in the Jackson organization. Brock and Jackson never sold crack to Dickerson on credit, and placed no limitations on Dickerson's ability to use or resell the product he purchased. Brock testified that he did not consider Dickerson to be a member of the organization and did not know or care what Dickerson did with the drugs after he purchased them. There was no evidence that Dickerson shared profits with Brock or any other members of the organization, that Dickerson had interactions with Jackson or Brock other than the transactions that made him a customer, or that, apart from being a customer, he assisted their operation in any capacity.

This evidence is far weaker than the evidence in previous cases where we affirmed convictions despite a mere buyer defense. *See, e.g., United States v. Rojas,* 617 F.3d 669, 672, 675–76 (2d Cir.2010) (the seller testified that he had a "longstanding" relationship with the buyer, provided the buyer with bail money because the buyer "was moving product" for him, and sold drugs to the buyer on credit because he knew that the buyer would resell a portion of the drugs); *Parker,* 554 F.3d at 239 (unrebutted evidence that a buyer recruited his roommate to help the selling organization "handle one of the drug-order phone lines" while himself making deliveries for the

[handwritten margin note: insufficient evidence of shared conspiratorial purpose— no evidence of shared profits or anything outside of him being a customer]

selling group, and that another buyer purchased crack on credit and facilitated resales of crack in smaller quantities than the selling organization usually transacted in); *Hawkins,* 547 F.3d at 75 (testimony that the buyer "repeatedly brought potential customers' needs" to the seller's attention, and that he purchased drugs on credit with the understanding that he would resell the drugs and use the profits to repay the seller). In each of these cases, significant indicia of a conspiratorial purpose existed: the defendants purchased drugs in significant quantities on credit from the selling organization and took substantial other steps to assist it such as facilitating resales, supplying bail money and recruiting other customers and sellers.

The government, however, contends that our precedent permits juries to infer a conspiratorial agreement between the seller and the buyer on the basis of the volume and frequency of drug transactions. *See* Gov't Br. 41– 46; *see also Parker,* 554 F.3d at 239 ("All three appellants purchased with such frequency and such quantity from the selling group to support a finding that each of them depended on it as a source of supply and thus had a stake in the group's success. . . ."); *Hawkins,* 547 F.3d at 77 ("In some cases, a large drug quantity may, in addition to establishing an intent to redistribute, support inferences about the relationship between the participants").

[handwritten margin note: Govt says jury is permitted to infer conspiratorial agreement on basis of volume + frequency]

It is certainly true that the volume and frequency of transactions between Dickerson and the Jackson organization is significant, and could have, under certain circumstances permitted an inference of conspiratorial intent. For example, in a footnote in *Parker,* we upheld a conspiracy conviction of a defendant without evidence that he "furnished . . . additional support to the selling group" because "his repeated purchases in wholesale quantities gave him a stake in the success" of the drug selling organization. 554 F.3d at 239 n. 6. However, that individual is differently situated than Dickerson.

The trial evidence in *Parker* established that this buyer never used crack cocaine and resold *all* of the drugs that he purchased from multiple members of the selling organization, which, in combination with the volume of sales, permitted the inference that he was closely aligned with the success of the enterprise. *See United States v. Parker, et al.,* No. 05-cr-529, Transcript of Oral Argument on Rule 29 Motion, at 17 (N.D.N.Y. Dec. 8, 2006). In contrast, Dickerson had no connection to the Jackson enterprise, other than using Brock as one of the "various" suppliers of crack cocaine for both Dickerson's personal use and resale. Further there was evidence that the Jackson organization as a whole, and Brock specifically, sold to many different buyers. Brock's trial testimony established that Dickerson was one of his forty regular customers, that Brock had no interest in what Dickerson did with the drugs, and that he saw Dickerson only as a customer.

[handwritten margin note: Brock only saw Dickerson as a customer]

volume + frequency are insufficient

Viewing the evidence as a whole, we find the volume and frequency of *these* transactions to be insufficient to move the Brock-Dickerson relationship beyond that of buyer-seller because these circumstances do not create the inference of mutual dependency we identified in *Parker.* If, for example, Dickerson operated a food truck and purchased fifty loaves of bread at five different supermarkets, each of which sold bread to fifty different food truck operators on a daily basis, those purchases and his subsequent resales of the bread would simply make him a good customer, not a member of any single supermarket enterprise. Although the volume of purchases is high, neither the food truck operator nor the supermarket is dependent on each other. By the same token, a good customer—even a very good customer—of a drug organization may still be just a customer, not a co-conspirator, if the evidence cannot support an inference of mutual dependency or a common stake.

"To sustain a conspiracy conviction, the government must present some evidence from which it can reasonably be inferred that the person charged with conspiracy knew of the existence of the scheme alleged in the indictment and knowingly joined and participated in it." *United States v. Rodriguez,* 392 F.3d 539, 544 (2d Cir.2004). We conclude that the evidence was insufficient to permit any rational juror to infer that Dickerson knowingly joined or participated in the charged conspiracy.

CONCLUSION

For these reasons, we **REVERSE** Dickerson's conviction for conspiracy to distribute and to possess with intent to distribute. Because Dickerson's 168 month sentence was driven largely by the drug weight charged in the conspiracy, we also **VACATE** Dickerson's sentence and **REMAND** for resentencing on the substantive distribution count alone.

EXERCISE

Does it make sense to draw a line around a conspiracy at buyer-seller relationships? Is Dickerson's relationship to the larger group really that different than Brock's? Remember that Brock got narcotics from Jackson, and then "typically sold 18 "eight-balls" (each weighing approximately 3.5 grams) of crack cocaine per day at $140–150 each. Jackson allowed Brock to keep the money he earned for every ninth eight-ball he sold."

c. Ongoing Conspiracy

We usually think of conspirators as those who agree to *begin* a criminal enterprise together. However, sometimes conspirators join into an ongoing criminal conspiracy. This is particularly true where the conspiracy involves an ongoing business, such as a drug trafficking network. Like any other business, they routinely add new workers and leaders, while others drop out of the operation and move on to other things.

UNITED STATES V. JOHNSON
450 F.3d 366 (8th Cir. 2006)

WOLLMAN, CIRCUIT JUDGE.

This appeal follows the convictions of Reginald Dinez Johnson, Patricia Alexander-Butler, Carl Alexander, and Terry Brown. Johnson, Alexander, and Brown were convicted of conspiracy to possess with intent to distribute cocaine and phencyclidine (PCP) in violation of 21 U.S.C. §§ 841(a)(1) and 846. . . .

We state the facts in the light most favorable to the jury verdict. *United States v. Selwyn,* 398 F.3d 1064, 1065 (8th Cir.2005). In the 1990s, Edward Quentin Anderson sold drugs in the St. Louis area. Around 1996, Anderson began buying cocaine from Lester Diggs. When a cocaine drought hit St. Louis and prices skyrocketed, Anderson and Diggs decided to buy drugs directly from suppliers in California. At first, they bought marijuana and later, cocaine and PCP.

In the beginning of this cross-country relationship, Diggs and Anderson tried different methods of transporting the drugs from California to St. Louis. Eventually, they purchased a truck with two gas tanks, one of which was outfitted with a false tank. Diggs and Anderson hired a white driver and followed him in a second vehicle. This chase vehicle served two purposes: it accompanied the vehicle that contained money on the way to California and drugs on the return trip to St. Louis, and it served as a decoy for law enforcement. Anderson testified that he did not trust the couriers with the large quantities of drugs or sums of money and that it was more likely that the police would stop the three or four black men in the chase vehicle than the white driver.

Over the course of the next seven or eight years, Anderson purchased several different vehicles with false tanks or hidden compartments and hired various white men to transport the drugs. Anderson, Brown, Diggs, Johnson, and others drove the chase vehicle, usually a van with tinted windows. Anderson testified that the group made numerous trips to California and a few trips to Texas to purchase drugs and transport them back to St. Louis.

On at least two occasions, Alexander traveled with his codefendants to purchase drugs. In 1996 or 1997, Alexander, Anderson, and Erica Bass flew to Los Angeles to purchase cocaine. Although most of the purchase money was concealed in the transport truck's false tank, Alexander carried $10,000 on the plane. After arriving in California, the group purchased cocaine. Alexander purchased half of a kilogram using his $10,000. A hired driver transported the cocaine, including Alexander's portion, to St. Louis.

On another trip, Anderson, Johnson, Alexander, Diggs, and a few others flew to Houston to buy cocaine. Although the group was unable to purchase the drugs from the intended source, Alexander found a different source and purchased half of a kilogram of cocaine. He returned to their shared hotel room, packaged the cocaine, and returned to St. Louis on a commercial flight, carrying the drugs with him.

The conspiracy experienced general success until a Kansas deputy sheriff stopped Jason Miller, a drug courier, for speeding. Miller gave consent to search the vehicle, and the deputy found six kilograms of cocaine. Miller advised the deputy that he was en route to deliver the drugs. The deputy then contacted the FBI, which arranged a controlled delivery of the cocaine to take place in a parking lot at the DePaul Health Center in St. Louis. On December 11, 2001, Anderson, Johnson, and two other men were arrested at the scene and taken to the Jennings Municipal Jail. At the time of the arrest, Johnson identified himself as Cedric Miller.

Johnson was searched either at the scene or at the Jennings Municipal Jail, and the items found on his person were placed in a plastic bag. FBI Agent Henry Vera testified that the bag contained the following items: an Illinois identification card bearing a picture of Johnson and the name of Cedric Miller, a cellular telephone, a pager, and loose slips of paper containing incriminating information. The FBI transferred the bag containing Johnson's personal property to the Jennings Police Department. After booking Johnson, the police returned the bag to the FBI. Agent Vera testified that he participated in the investigation of Johnson's personal property on December 11 or 12, 2001, and that the accompanying report was transcribed on December 16, 2001.

Following the arrests at the hospital, the group did not sell cocaine for several months. Because they experienced several financial losses, the group decided to sell PCP, which could be purchased at a price less than cocaine and sold for a similar profit. They bought the drugs in California and used the same method of transporting PCP as they had cocaine.

In February 2004, a Kansas trooper stopped one of their PCP couriers and found $28,000 in a secret compartment. The driver told the trooper that three men, including Diggs, were following him in the chase vehicle. When the chase vehicle was stopped and its occupants arrested, Diggs provided an Illinois identification card in the name of Stephen Boyd. . . .

Alexander and Brown assert that the evidence is insufficient to support their convictions of conspiracy to distribute and possess with intent to distribute cocaine and PCP. We review the sufficiency of the evidence *de novo*. *United States v. Alexander*, 408 F.3d 1003, 1008 (8th Cir.2005). We view the evidence in the light most favorable to the verdict, " 'resolving evidentiary conflicts in favor of the government, and accepting all reasonable inferences drawn from the evidence that support the jury's verdict.' " *Id.* (quoting *United States v. Espino*, 317 F.3d 788, 792 (8th

Cir.2003)). We reverse only if no reasonable jury could have found the defendants guilty. *Id.*

To establish that Alexander and Brown conspired to distribute cocaine and PCP, the government must prove: (1) that there was a conspiracy, an agreement to distribute cocaine and PCP; (2) that the defendants knew of the conspiracy; and (3) that the defendants intentionally joined the conspiracy. *Id.* (citing *Espino,* 317 F.3d at 792). A conspiracy may be inferred from circumstantial evidence; it need not be proved by direct evidence. *Id.*

[handwritten margin note: what the government must prove]

Alexander and Brown argue that they were merely present and that they neither knew of the conspiracy nor took part in it. We conclude that the evidence supports their convictions and that both Brown and Alexander contributed to the conspiracy's success.

For his part, Brown often drove or rode with his codefendants in the chase vehicle. Anderson, Diggs, Bass, and the couriers testified that Brown served in that capacity for the transport of cocaine and PCP. Miller also testified that, after his first trip from California to St. Louis, he returned the vehicle and the drugs to Anderson's house. After the drugs were taken out of the false compartment, Brown drove Miller home. From this evidence, we conclude that a jury could reasonably find that Brown knowingly and intentionally joined the conspiracy.

Similarly, the evidence is sufficient to support Alexander's conviction. According to the testimony of Anderson and Bass, Alexander accompanied them to California and Texas to purchase drugs. Alexander argues that the testimony of his codefendants was unreliable and that he was either merely present or an independent actor. The jury, however, found Alexander's codefendants' testimony credible, and "[w]e give significant weight to the jury's credibility determination." *Alexander,* 408 F.3d at 1008. From the evidence presented, a jury could reasonably deduce that Alexander knew of, and intentionally joined, the conspiracy.

EXERCISE

Imagine that Rhoda and Jim are engaged in a conspiracy to manufacture LSD. They are both chemists, and have set up a lab in the basement of their house for this purpose. For several months, they make and sell LSD in large volumes.

Pierre is their next-door neighbor. On occasion, Pierre has purchased methamphetamine from Rhoda. One day, Rhoda knocks on his door and asks if she and Jim can borrow some plastic tubing "for our basement." She offers $300, and he takes it.

If you are an investigator, what more do you want to know to prove that Pierre joined this conspiracy? How could you gather that evidence?

C. SOLICITATION, AIDING AND ABETTING, AND ACCESSORY AFTER THE FACT

In the federal code, coercing someone to commit a crime or helping another actor before or during a crime are themselves criminalized at 18 U.S.C. § 2:

> **(a)** Whoever commits an offense against the United States or aids, abets, counsels, commands, induces or procures its commission, is punishable as a principal.

> **(b)** Whoever willfully causes an act to be done which if directly performed by him or another would be an offense against the United States, is punishable as a principal.

It is also illegal to help someone escape responsibility for a crime after the crime is committed—and act that is often called "accessory after the fact." That is the title of 18 U.S.C. § 3, which provides:

> Whoever, knowing that an offense against the United States has been committed, receives, relieves, comforts or assists the offender in order to hinder or prevent his apprehension, trial or punishment, is an accessory after the fact.

> Except as otherwise expressly provided by any Act of Congress, an accessory after the fact shall be imprisoned not more than one-half the maximum term of imprisonment or (notwithstanding section 3571) fined not more than one-half the maximum fine prescribed for the punishment of the principal, or both; or if the principal is punishable by life imprisonment or death, the accessory shall be imprisoned not more than 15 years.

Unlike some states, the federal code makes solicitors and helpers before and during the crime fully responsible, while those who help out after the crime only face half of the criminally liability assessed to the primary actor.

1. SOLICITATION

Soliciting a crime—that is, coercing or causing someone else to commit a crime—is a distinct violation with a unique element (that being the action element of getting someone else to commit a crime). That said, cases that involve solicitation are often prosecuted as conspiracies, since the agreement between the solicitor and the person being solicited will usually suffice as the basis for a conspiracy charge.

You will recall that 18 U.S.C. § 2 makes a defendant liable as a principal where she "counsels, commands, induces or procures" a crime or "willfully causes an act to be done which if directly performed by him or another would be an offense against the United States." Importantly, that statute both requires that the criminal act induced be completed, and allows the solicitor to be liable as a principal. In this kind of solicitation, it is often possible to charge the solicitor directly with the underlying crime, because they intentionally caused the outcome. For example, if David pays Julie to kill Maurice and she does so, David is directly responsible for murder, since he intentionally caused the death. The fact that he utilized another person to complete the act does not insulate him from liability.

In addition to 18 U.S.C. § 2, 18 U.S.C. § 373 provides for another avenue to pursue solicitation in some cases. Unlike § 2, § 373 does not require that the criminal act solicited be completed, and does not create the same criminal liability as would be faced by an actor who completes the crime:

> **(a)** Whoever, with intent that another person engage in conduct constituting a felony that has as an element the use, attempted use, or threatened use of physical force against property or against the person of another in violation of the laws of the United States, and under circumstances strongly corroborative of that intent, solicits, commands, induces, or otherwise endeavors to persuade such other person to engage in such conduct, shall be imprisoned not more than one-half the maximum term of imprisonment or (notwithstanding section 3571) fined not more than one-half of the maximum fine prescribed for the punishment of the crime solicited, or both; or if the crime solicited is punishable by life imprisonment or death, shall be imprisoned for not more than twenty years.

One issue with a solicitation that is rooted in simply urging others to take an action is that it can conflict with real or perceived free speech rights.

UNITED STATES V. WHITE

698 F.3d 1005 (7th Cir. 2012)

Before POSNER, FLAUM, and WILLIAMS, CIRCUIT JUDGES.

PER CURIAM.

William White was charged with soliciting the commission of a violent federal crime against a juror in violation of 18 U.S.C. § 373. The alleged solicitations at issue were messages that White posted to a website that he created to advance white supremacy, which included White's 2005 statement that "[e]veryone associated with the Matt Hale trial has deserved assassination for a long time," and his 2008 publication of information related to the foreperson, "Juror A," of the jury that convicted Hale. The 2008 post disclosed Juror A's home address and mobile, home, and work phone numbers, though it did not contain an explicit request for Juror A to be harmed.

White was tried and convicted by a jury. White then filed a Rule 29 motion for entry of a judgment of acquittal, arguing that the evidence was insufficient to convict him of solicitation. The district court granted the motion, finding that the government failed to present sufficient evidence for a reasonable juror to conclude that White was guilty of criminal solicitation, and that White's speech was protected by the First Amendment. The government appeals that ruling, and White has filed a cross-appeal urging a new trial if we reverse the judgment of acquittal. After reviewing the trial record, we conclude that a rational jury could have found beyond a reasonable doubt that, based on the contents of the website, its readership, and other contextual factors, White intentionally solicited a violent crime against Juror A by posting Juror A's personal information on his website. Criminal solicitation is not protected by the First Amendment, and so we reverse White's acquittal and reinstate his conviction. Also, because White is not entitled to a new trial, we remand for sentencing.

I.   BACKGROUND

To best understand the facts of this case it is helpful to have some basic familiarity with another case involving Matthew Hale, a white supremacist convicted of solicitation under 18 U.S.C. § 373. *See United States v. Hale,* 448 F.3d 971 (7th Cir.2006) (per curiam).

The defendant in that case led a white supremacist organization known as the World Church of the Creator ("World Church"). A religious organization operating under the name "Church of the Creator" sued World Church for trademark infringement in federal court. Both parties moved for summary judgment and Judge Joan Lefkow granted the motion of Hale's organization, World Church. But we reversed and remanded for judgment to be entered in favor of Church of the Creator. After Judge Lefkow abided by our instructions, Hale informed his followers that they were "in a state of war with this federal judge." *Id.* at 978. He then sent an email to Tony Evola, a cooperating witness who had infiltrated World Church, requesting the home address of Judge Lefkow. One day later, Evola and Hale met. Evola asked Hale if they were "gonna exterminate the rat." Hale answered, "I'm gonna fight within the law" but "that information's been . . . provided" so "[i]f you wish" to "do anything yourself, you can, you know?" Evola responded, "Consider it done," to which Hale replied, "Good." *Id.* at 979. A jury convicted Hale for, among other things, criminally soliciting harm to Judge Lefkow, and he received a sentence of 40 years in prison. *Id.* at 982. The foreperson of that jury was "Juror A," the target of the alleged solicitation in this case.

William White is an avid supporter of Matthew Hale. An active white supremacist, White created and served as editor of a website, Overthrow.com, which sought to advance that cause. On February 28,

2005, only hours after Judge Lefkow's husband and mother were tragically murdered, White applauded the crimes on his website. He wrote, "Everyone associated with the Matt Hale trial has deserved assassination for a long time. . . . In my view, it was clearly just, and I look forward to seeing who else this new white nationalist group of assassins kills next." Not long afterward, in March 2005, White described an email, circulating on the internet, that contained the personal identification information of the FBI agents and prosecutors ("scumbags") who investigated and prosecuted Hale. White noted that they might be the "next targets of the unknown nationalist assassin who killed the family of Chicago Judge Joan Lefkow." He explained on his website that he would not disclose the agents' and prosecutors' personal information, however, because there was "so great a potential for action linked to such posting."

On February 13, 2007, White published on his website the address of Elie Wiesel, an internationally known Holocaust survivor, "In Case Anyone Was Looking For Him." White praised Eric Hunt, "a fan of [the] website," as a "loyal soldier" for attacking Wiesel a few days earlier, on February 1. White presented similar information about six black teenagers in Jena, Louisiana in September 2007, suggesting that they be "lynch[ed]" for their involvement in a schoolyard fight that garnered national attention due to its racial overtones. He continued this trend in 2008 by posting the personal information of individuals whom he labeled "anti-racist" or "enemies" of white supremacy. One such post, "Kill Richard Warman," advocated the murder of a noted Canadian civil rights lawyer. That particular message could be accessed from any page on the website because it could be retrieved using a hyperlink located in a static column of the site, called "Top Articles." Another post—"Kill This Nigger?"—contained images of and articles about then-presidential candidate Barack Obama. One article displayed a photograph of the presidential candidate with swastika-shaped crosshairs superimposed over his face, and stated that "White people must deny [Barack Obama] the presidency . . . by any means necessary."

Those postings, however, were mere prelude to the conduct that got White indicted for criminal solicitation. On September 11, 2008, White authored a post titled, "The Juror Who Convicted Matt Hale." In it, he disclosed personal, identifying information about Juror A. The post read:

> Gay anti-racist [Juror A] was a juror who played a key role in convicting Matt Hale. Born [date], [he/she] lives at [address] with [his/her] gay black lover and [his/her] cat [name]. [His/Her] phone number is [phone number], cell phone [phone number], and [his/her] office is [phone number].

The post further stated that the "gay Jewish [Juror A], who has a gay black lover and ties to professional antiracist groups, and who also personally knew [an individual] killed by Ben Smith, a follower of Hale, was allowed to sit on his jury without challenge and played a leading role in inciting both the conviction and harsh sentence that followed." The entry featured a color photograph of Juror A.

One day later, White uploaded an identical message to a different portion of the website. The post carried the title: "[Juror A] Updated-Since They Blocked the first photo." Apparently, Juror A's employer had blocked public access to the page on its website that contained information about Juror A and the color photograph of the juror that appeared in White's first post. White's second post stated, "Note that [Employer] blocked much of [Juror A's] information after we linked to [his/her] photograph." The photograph of Juror A that appeared was embedded in the Overthrow server so that only White could remove it.

On October 22, 2008, a grand jury indicted White for soliciting the commission of a violent federal offense against Juror A in violation of 18 U.S.C. § 373. The indictment charged that White had "solicited and otherwise endeavored to persuade another person to injure Juror A on account of a verdict assented to by Juror A, in violation of Title 18, United States Code 1503." *See also* 18 U.S.C. § 1503 (outlawing injuring or threatening to injure a federal juror). A grand jury returned a superseding indictment against White on February 10, 2009. White moved to dismiss the indictment, and the district court granted his motion after finding that White's internet postings were protected speech and that the indictment failed to sufficiently allege "corroborating circumstances" of White's criminal intent.

The government appealed. We reversed because the indictment was facially valid and White's First Amendment rights were protected by the government's burden to prove beyond a reasonable doubt that White had the requisite intent for criminal solicitation. *United States v. White,* 610 F.3d 956, 961 (7th Cir.2010) (per curiam). As we explained:

> The government informed us at oral argument that it has further evidence of the website's readership, audience, and the relationship between White and his followers which will show the posting was a specific request to White's followers, who understood that request and were capable and willing to act on it. This evidence is not laid out in the indictment and does not need to be. The existence of strongly corroborating circumstances evincing White's intent is a jury question. . . . The government has the burden to prove, beyond a reasonable doubt, that White intended, through his posting of Juror A's personal information, to request someone else to harm Juror A. After the prosecution presents its case, the court may decide that a reasonable juror could not conclude that White's intent was for harm to befall Juror A, and not merely electronic or verbal harassment.

> *Id.* at 962 (internal citations omitted).

On remand, White was tried before an anonymous jury. The government offered as evidence the postings made by White that we described above. The government also called several witnesses. FBI Special Agent Paul Messing testified that he installed highly sophisticated computer software on the computer and server that agents seized from White. The software allowed the FBI to search for specific articles and words that White personally posted on the Overthrow website. Officer John Dziedzic explained that an internet user who visited the Overthrow website before the site had been disabled could have seen all of White's postings.

The government also presented the testimony of Juror A. That testimony established that at approximately 9:30 a.m. on September 11, 2008, Juror A received a phone call from a telephone registered to White's wife. The male caller asked Juror A to confirm Juror A's name, date of birth, address, and service on the jury that convicted Hale. The caller did not, however, threaten Juror A. Less than thirty minutes after the call was disconnected, White posted Juror A's personal information on Overthrow. Juror A almost immediately began receiving harassing text messages. The messages conveyed things like "sodomize Obama," "Bomb China," "kill McCain," and "cremate[ ] Jews." Juror A testified that these messages were "all . . . really upsetting." Juror A reported receiving text messages of the same nature for the next few days. Juror A was not personally threatened, stalked, or physically harmed after White's initial post.

FBI Special Agent Maureen Mazzola also testified at trial. She described what an internet user who viewed the Overthrow website on September 11, 2008 would have seen. According to her, on that day the site's visitors would have immediately been directed to the post about Juror A. They would not have been able to see White's other posts unless they accessed them via hyperlink or viewed other portions of the website. According to Agent Mazzola, a user would have "to be either looking for it or reading every single article on the website" to access White's other posts.

The last two witnesses the government called to testify were Phil Anderson and Michael Burks. Both were former members of the American National Socialist Workers Party ("ANSWP"), a white supremacist organization that White organized and directed. After his home was searched and his computer seized, White asked Anderson to reach out to other white supremacists to find out if they were aware of any plans to harm Juror A. White expressed concern that "someone may be trying to do something" to Juror A. Anderson reported back that his associates had not seen the Juror A post and were not aware of any plans to harm Juror A.

On October 29, 2008, White was arrested. After his arrest, he sent letters to both Anderson and Burks. White requested that Anderson testify regarding "the fact that you have never done anything criminal, and do not interpret articles on Overthrow.com as criminal instructions." And White asked Burks to testify about ANSWP's "rejection of criminal activity and violent crime," and thanked him for his support. At trial, both Anderson and Burks maintained that White never instructed them to commit criminal acts and they never interpreted anything he posted on Overthrow as instructions to harm Juror A in particular.

Burks, however, acknowledged that some violent white supremacists—of whom White had knowledge and approved—might have looked to Overthrow for criminal instructions. He cited the Richard Warman post as an example. According to Burks, in addition to authoring that post, White disclosed Warman's information during a radio show and stated at that time that "this bastard has lived way too long. If somebody wants to kill him, here's his address." Burks testified that White repeated this sentiment "two or three times," and White "really didn't care if something did happen." Burks interpreted the Warman, Wiesel, and Jena Six posts as requests that people go out and do violent things. But he expressly denied ever seeing anything on Overthrow or hearing anything from White that he understood as a call to harm Juror A.

At the close of the evidence, the district court instructed the jury that the government must prove the following elements beyond a reasonable doubt:

> First, that the defendant solicited, commanded, induced, or otherwise endeavored to persuade another person to carry out a violent federal crime.
>
> Second, with strongly corroborative circumstances, that the defendant intended for another person to commit a violent federal crime.

District Court's jury instruction

The court also crafted a First Amendment instruction, which combined two of White's six proposed First Amendment instructions. The court explained:

> The First Amendment protects vehement, scathing, and offensive criticism of others; however, a solicitation, command, inducement, or endeavor to persuade another to engage in conduct constituting a violent felony as defined in these instructions is not protected by the First Amendment.
>
> If the purpose of the speaker or the tendency of his words are directed to ideas or consequences remote from the commission of the criminal act, then the speech is protected by the First Amendment.
>
> Speech is protected unless both the intent of the speaker . . . and the tendency of his words was to produce or incite an imminent lawless act.
>
> An imminent lawless act is one that is likely to occur.
>
> A statement which is mere political hyperbole or an expression of opinion does not constitute a solicitation.

> If you find that the defendant's statements were no more than an indignant or extreme method of stating political opposition to the juror in the Matthew Hale case, then you are justified in finding that no solicitation was, in fact, made and you may find the defendant not guilty.

The jury convicted White of soliciting a violent federal crime against Juror A. White filed a post-trial motion for judgment of acquittal, requesting in the alternative a new trial. The district court ruled that the government failed to present sufficient evidence to sustain White's conviction. The court found that White's posts were not objective solicitations and nothing on the website "transformed" them into solicitous instructions. Additionally, the court found that the government failed to present adequate evidence of section 373's "strongly corroborative" circumstances, which is necessary under the statute to prove intent. Finally, the court held that because the government did not prove White's criminal intent beyond a reasonable doubt, White's posts were protected speech under the First Amendment. The district court granted White's Rule 29 motion and conditionally denied his request for a new trial. Both the government and White appeal.

II. ANALYSIS

Subsection (a) of 18 U.S.C. § 373 states, in relevant part, that:

> Whoever, with intent that another person engage in conduct constituting a felony that has as an element the use, attempted use, or threatened use of physical force against property or against the person of another in violation of the laws of the United States, and under circumstances strongly corroborative of that intent, solicits, commands, induces, or otherwise endeavors to persuade such other person to engage in such conduct, shall be imprisoned. . . .

The underlying felony White allegedly solicited was harm to Juror A, which is prohibited by 18 U.S.C. § 1503 ("Whoever . . . by threats or force . . . endeavors to influence, intimidate, or impede any grand or petit juror . . . or injures any such grand or petit juror . . . on account of any verdict or indictment assented to by him, or on account of his being or having been such juror . . . shall be punished. . . ."). So to convict White of solicitation, the government had to prove beyond a reasonable doubt: (1) with "strongly corroborative" circumstances that White intended for another person to harm Juror A; and (2) that White solicited, commanded, induced, or otherwise tried to persuade the other person to carry out that crime. 18 U.S.C. § 373(a); *see also Hale*, 448 F.3d at 982 ("[T]he government had to establish (1) with 'strongly corroborative circumstances' that Hale intended for Tony Evola to arrange the murder of Judge Lefkow; and (2) that Hale solicited, commanded, induced, or otherwise tried to persuade Evola to carry out the crime.").

A. The District Court's Judgment of Acquittal Must Be Reversed Because a Reasonable Jury Could Have Convicted White of Criminal Solicitation

A judgment of acquittal must be granted when "the evidence is insufficient to sustain a conviction." Fed.R.Crim.P. 29(a). Our review is *de novo*. *United States v. Presbitero*, 569 F.3d 691, 704 (7th Cir.2009). Our job, however, is not to "reweigh the evidence nor second-guess the jury's credibility determinations." *United States v. Tavarez*, 626 F.3d 902, 906 (7th Cir.2010). Rather, we view the evidence in the light most favorable to the government and ask whether *any* rational jury could have found the essential elements of the charged crime beyond a reasonable doubt. *Presbitero*, 569 F.3d at 704. "We will set aside a jury's guilty verdict only if 'the record contains no evidence, regardless of how it is weighed,' from which a jury could have returned a conviction." *Id.* (quoting *United States v. Moses*, 513 F.3d 727, 733 (7th Cir.2008)). But the defendant "bears a heavy burden on appeal, as he must demonstrate that no rational trier of fact could decide beyond a reasonable doubt" that he committed the offense charged. *See United States v. Cervante*, 958 F.2d 175, 178 (7th Cir.1992).

We begin our analysis with our instructions to the district court on remand: "After the prosecution presents its case, the court may decide that a reasonable juror could not conclude that White's intent was for harm to befall Juror A, and not merely electronic or verbal harassment." *White*, 610 F.3d at 962. The government bore not only the burden of proving White's intentional solicitation, but it also had to prove beyond a reasonable doubt the objective of that solicitation: harm or the threat of harm to Juror A, not mere electronic or verbal harassment. *Id.; cf. United States v. Rahman*, 34 F.3d 1331, 1337 (7th Cir.1994) (requiring the government to show with "strongly corroborative" circumstances that the defendant "intended for [the solicitee] to *extort and rob* [the victim] of $60,000," and that the defendant "solicited, commanded, induced, or otherwise tried to persuade [the solicitee] to carry out the *extortion and robbery*." (emphasis added)).

A reasonable jury could have found that the government met this burden. Whether White's post was a criminal solicitation depended on context, and the government provided ample evidence of such context from which a rational jury could have concluded that the post was an invitation for others to harm Juror A, though fortunately no one accepted the invitation. The post attributed to Juror A characteristics intended to make the target loathed by readers of White's neo-Nazi website: a Jew, a homosexual with a black lover, and above all the foreman of the jury that had convicted Overthrow.com's hero, Matthew Hale—an Anti-Semitic white supremacist—of soliciting the murder of a federal judge. And whereas White previously refrained from "republish[ing] the personal information" of others involved in the Hale trial because, as White acknowledged, "there [was] so great a potential for action linked to such posting," White expressly published Juror A's personal information, including Juror A's photograph, home address, and telephone numbers.

The post has a context created by previous posts on the website that had solicited the murder of Barack Obama, Richard Warman (a Canadian civil rights lawyer and the bane of hate groups), Elie Wiesel, and six black teenagers known as the "Jena 6." Other posts had congratulated murderers or urged the murder of enemies defined in terms that would embrace Juror A. All that was missing was an explicit solicitation to murder Juror A. But the description summarized above would have made Juror A seem to loyal readers of Overthrow.com as being at least as worthy of assassination as Richard Warman, who had been described in a post, published only a few months before the Juror A post, as "Richard, the sometimes Jewish, sometimes not, attorney behind the abuses of Canada's Human Rights Tribunal," who "should be drug out into the street and shot, after appropriate trial by a revolutionary tribunal of Canada's white activists. It won't be hard to do, he can be found, easily, at his home, at [address]." And Juror A could be found at home just as easily because White posted Juror A's personal contact information along with the denunciation.

The "abuses" of the Canadian Human Rights Tribunal had been left unspecified in the denunciation of Warman, whereas Juror A was identified as instrumental in the conviction of the hero Hale: If "all [Juror A] was . . . was another anonymous voice in a dirty Jewish mob, screaming for blood and for the further impoverishment of the white worker . . . [he/she] would hardly be of note. But [Juror A] is something more. [He/She] was not only a juror at the nationally publicized trial of Matt Hale, but the jury foreman, and the architect of both Hale's conviction and his extreme and lengthy 40-year sentence." If Warman should be killed, then *a fortiori* Juror A should be killed, or at least injured. White didn't have to *say* harm Juror A. All he had to do and did do to invite violence was to sketch the characteristics that made Juror A a mortal enemy of White's neo-Nazi movement and to publish Juror A's personal contact information.

The fact that White made an effort to discourage assassination attempts against Juror A when law enforcement moved against his website shows at a minimum that he knew he was playing with fire. But a reasonable jury could have also interpreted such evidence as intent to solicit violence against Juror A followed by a change of mind when he realized that if someone harmed Juror A he could get in trouble. There was enough evidence of White's intent to solicit the murder of, or other physical violence against, Juror A, to justify a reasonable jury in convicting him.

It's true that the posts that establish the context that makes the solicitation to violence unmistakable were not links to the posts on Overthrow.com about Juror A. That is, they were not words or phrases in blue in the posts that if clicked on by the reader would appear on the reader's computer screen. Some of the explicit solicitations to murder had been published on

Overthrow.com months, even years, earlier, though others were recent. The Juror A posts had appeared between September 11 and October 3, 2008, the postings regarding Wiesel and the Jena 6 between February 3 and September 20, 2007. But the Warman and Obama death threats were recent—March 26, 2008 and September 9, 2008 respectively—the latter threat having been posted two days before the first threat against Juror A.

Regardless of when these other still-accessible posts were technically created, a reasonable jury cannot be expected to ignore the audience, who may not have been as concerned about such chronological specifics. Readers of Overthrow.com were not casual Web browsers, but extremists molded into a community by the internet—loyal and avid readers who, whether or not they remember every specific solicitation to assassination, knew that Overthrow.com identified hateful enemies who should be assassinated. A reasonable jury could infer that members of the Party were regular readers of the Overthrow website, which prominently displayed links to the Party's own website, to its streaming radio, and to its hotline. One witness testified that he learned of the Party through Overthrow.com. White identified one reader in a post on the website as a "loyal soldier" and "fan of this website," and there is similar language in other posts. Two members of the party who testified made clear their familiarity with the contents of the website over a period of years. Though these members specifically denied interpreting White's post as an invitation to harm Juror A, a reasonable jury could have thought, based on White's reaching out to them for support following the search of White's home, that they were biased in White's favor and therefore skewed their testimony in order to protect a fellow supremacist.

The government also established "strongly corroborative circumstances" of White's intent to urge the killing of, or harm to, Juror A. Typically, the government will satisfy its burden of strongly corroborating the defendant's intent by introducing evidence showing that the defendant: (1) offered or promised payment or some other benefit to the person solicited; (2) threatened to punish or harm the solicitee for failing to commit the offense; (3) repeatedly solicited the commission of the offense or expressly stated his seriousness; (4) knew or believed that the person solicited had previously committed a similar offense; or (5) acquired weapons, tools or information, or made other preparations, suited for use by the solicitee. *United States v. Gabriel,* 810 F.2d 627, 635 (7th Cir.1987) (citing S.Rep. No. 307, 97th Cong., 1st Sess. 183 (1982)). These factors are not exclusive or conclusive indicators of intent, *id.,* but they are representative examples of the types of circumstantial evidence that a rational jury could rely on to corroborate the defendant's intent. *See Hale,* 448 F.3d at 983 ("The existence of strongly corroborating circumstances is a question of fact for the jury." (citation omitted)).

[handwritten margin note: How the govt. meets its burden of proof]

Such circumstantial evidence, much of which is already recounted above, exists here. In posts on his website directed at his neo-Nazi readers, White wrote that "everyone associated with the Matt Hale trial has deserved assassination for a long time;" he expressly solicited violence against Obama, Warman, Wiesel, and the Jena 6; he praised Wiesel's assailant and appreciated that White's expressed views "may have played a role in motivating" the assailant; he went to the trouble of obtaining and publishing Juror A's contact information after expressly recognizing the "great [ ] potential for action" linked to the posting of personal contact information of other "scumbags" involved in the Hale trial; and after learning of the FBI's investigation he demonstrated awareness that his posts might induce readers to commit a violent act against Juror A.

Though the government did not present a specific "solicitee," it was unnecessary to do so given the very nature of the solicitation—an electronic broadcast which, a reasonable jury could conclude, was specifically designed to reach as many white supremacist readers as possible so that *someone* could kill or harm Juror A. 18 U.S.C. § 373 requires proof of intent "that another person" commit the felony, and White's desire for *any* reader to respond to his call satisfies this requirement. *See White,* 610 F.3d at 960 ("a specific person-to-person request is not required") (citing *United States v. Rahman,* 189 F.3d 88, 117–18 (2d Cir.1999)).

White rightfully emphasizes that the First Amendment protects even speech that is loathsome. But criminal solicitations are simply not protected by the First Amendment. *See id.; Chaplinsky v. New Hampshire,* 315 U.S. 568, 572, 62 S.Ct. 766, 86 L.Ed. 1031 (1942) ("[T]hose [words] which by their very utterance inflict injury or tend to incite an immediate breach of the peace" are not protected by the First Amendment); *see also United States v. Williams,* 553 U.S. 285, 297, 128 S.Ct. 1830, 170 L.Ed.2d 650 (2008) ("Offers to engage in illegal transactions are categorically excluded from First Amendment protection." (citations omitted)). A reasonable jury could have found that White's posts constituted "a proposal to engage in illegal activity" and not merely "the abstract advocacy of illegality." *See id.* at 298–99, 128 S.Ct. 1830. Accordingly, the First Amendment provides no shelter for White's criminal behavior.

For the above reasons, White's acquittal must be reversed. . . .

[handwritten margin note: White's acquittal reversed. 1st amend. protections don't apply]

3. White's Proposed Jury Instructions Concerning the First Amendment

White finally argues that a new trial is warranted because the district court failed to include four of his proposed jury instructions concerning the First Amendment. Briefly summarized, these include: an instruction that speech is protected when it incites imminent lawless action, an instruction that speech may not be banned simply because it is unpopular, an instruction that speech scrutinizing people involved in the prosecution of crimes (e.g., jurors) is protected, and an instruction that speech approving of past violence by others is protected.

Plain error review applies when counsel fails to "object, on the record, to the judge's refusal to tender the defendant's instructions [and] clearly state the reasons for his or her objections." *United States v. Douglas,* 818 F.2d 1317, 1320 (7th Cir.1987); *see* Fed.R.Crim.P. 30(d). The government points out that after the court expressly made its instructions ruling and asked White's counsel, "Do you have any objections, by the way, . . . or are you otherwise satisfied with the instructions?", counsel responded, "Judge, I'm pretty sure—I haven't looked at the other ones, but I'm satisfied with the elements instruction that I think is the main one." The government therefore argues that no objection was made. White counters that his proposed First Amendment instructions were vigorously debated, albeit before the district court ruled on the instructions.

We have said that, so long as defense counsel "alert[s] the court and the opposing party to the specific grounds for the objection in a timely fashion," then "[t]here is no utility in requiring defense counsel to object again after the court has made its final ruling." *United States v. James,* 464 F.3d 699, 707 n. 1 (7th Cir.2006). But in the case of the court's refusal to give a proposed instruction, some of our cases have suggested that objections must be made *after* a ruling is made, or at least after the district court indicates how it intends to rule. *See United States v. Irorere,* 228 F.3d 816, 825 (7th Cir.2000) (objection not preserved where defendant "did not object on the record at the time the district court refused to give the defendant's proposed instruction"); *United States v. Green,* 779 F.2d 1313, 1320 n. 6 (7th Cir.1985)(objection not preserved where "the defendant originally argued on behalf of his proposed instruction, but offered no further comment, much less an objection" after court adopted other instructions). And counsel can simply object by stating that he or she objects and incorporates arguments previously made. *See United States v. Hollinger,* 553 F.2d 535, 543 (7th Cir.1977) ("While the process of stating for the record that such pre-charge objections are incorporated by reference is a somewhat pro forma exercise, we are nevertheless of the opinion that the better practice would be for counsel to see that the record affirmatively shows that counsel has renewed his specific objections by the incorporation method."); *see also United States v. Requarth,* 847 F.2d 1249, 1254 (7th Cir.1988) ("Specific objections to instructions that are distinctly made at an instructions conference may be incorporated by reference."). It would have been wise for White's counsel to have at least objected and incorporated his previous arguments by reference when the district court gave him an express opportunity to do so after it had made its ruling on the instructions. *See generally Hollinger,* 553 F.2d at 543 (district court has discretion to determine when the "distinct statement of the matter to which counsel objects and the grounds of the objections are stated" pursuant to Rule 30(d)).

In any event, we need not decide whether plain error review applies, because we find that the district court did not improperly exclude his proposed instructions even on *de novo* review. *See James,* 464 F.3d at 707 (review of district court's refusal to give proposed jury instructions is *de novo*). "To be entitled to a particular theory of defense instruction, the defendant must show the following: (1) the instruction is a correct statement of the law, (2) the evidence in the case supports the theory of defense, (3) that theory is not already part of the charge, and (4) a failure to provide the instruction would deny a fair trial." *Id.*

Excluding White's proposed jury instructions was not improper. The district court essentially incorporated White's proposed instruction about speech being protected unless it incites imminent lawless action, and adopting any additional emphasis on that point as White proposed could have been misleading because it would have suggested that the solicitation of a non-immediate crime was protected, when it is not. *See White,* 610 F.3d at 960 ("solicitations[ ] remain categorically outside [the First Amendment's] protection"). And the district court essentially incorporated White's proposed instruction about unpopular speech when it told the jury that the "First Amendment protects . . . offensive criticism of others," and that speech that is nothing more than an "indignant or extreme method of stating political opposition to the juror in the Matthew Hale case" was not criminal. This latter instruction also captured White's proposed instruction about the First Amendment protecting speech that scrutinizes people involved in the prosecution of crimes, such as jurors. And White was not clearly denied a fair trial by the exclusion of his proposed instruction concerning speech approving of past violence by others. No reasonable juror would interpret the district court's instruction about what solicitation means—"an endeavor to persuade another to engage in conduct constituting a violent felony"—to mean that mere approval of past violence automatically translates into solicitation of future criminal conduct.

The district court's jury instructions concisely described the protections of the First Amendment and correctly informed the jury that criminal solicitations fall outside its protection. *See Trident Inv. Mgmt., Inc. v. Amoco Oil Co.,* 194 F.3d 772, 780 (7th Cir.1999) ("[w]e will not find reversible error in jury instructions if, taken as a whole, they fairly and accurately inform the jury about the law"). The inclusion of White's proposed instructions would have been unduly cumulative and potentially confusing, and White points to no indication that the jury failed to appreciate the protections of the First Amendment, to the extent they were relevant in this criminal solicitation case. *See DePaepe v. Gen. Motors Corp.,* 33 F.3d 737, 743 (7th Cir.1994) (" 'Inadequate jury instructions are cause for reversal only if it appears that the jury's comprehension of the issues was so misguided that one of the parties was prejudiced.' " (citation omitted)).

Therefore, the district court's exclusion of White's proposed jury instructions was not erroneous. White's argument that the cumulative impact of all the above alleged errors warrants a new trial is also without merit.

III. CONCLUSION

For the reasons stated above, the judgment of acquittal entered by the district court is REVERSED, the conviction is REINSTATED, and the case is REMANDED for sentencing. White's cross-appeal is DISMISSED.

EXERCISE

Ronald and Ramona are walking down a street when they see a man coming towards them. Ramona recognizes the man as a federal Magistrate Judge who ruled that her then-boyfriend, Rupert, be detained pending his narcotic-trafficking trial. Ramona whispers "that's him—the judge who locked up Rupert!"

Ronald says "Do what you gotta do—I'm not going to be a witness against you," and turns and walks in the opposite direction. Ramona then shoots and injures the Magistrate Judge.

If you are the prosecutor assigned to this case (and received the information above via a statement Ronald made after the incident), would you charge Ronald for solicitation under 18 U.S.C. § 373? Assume that assaulting a Magistrate Judge as retaliation for an official act is a federal crime.

2. AIDING AND ABETTING

Helping someone else commit a crime or evade responsibility for a crime is itself criminalized in American jurisdictions. In the federal code, 18 U.S.C. § 2 directs that someone who "aids, abets, counsels, commands, induces or procures" a crime is punishable as a principal. That means that accomplices face the same sentences as principals (those who directly cause the crime to be completed). Importantly, though, aiding and abetting and conspiracy are distinct crimes with unique elements. Conspiracy requires proof of agreement, while aiding and abetting does not. It is the rare case, of course, where someone helps another commit a crime without agreeing to do so.

Like conspiracy, the more troubling aiding and abetting cases often involve a much less culpable actor facing the same stiff sentence accorded the principal.

UNITED STATES V. SIMPSON

979 F.2d 1282 (8th Cir. 1992)

MAGILL, CIRCUIT JUDGE.

Sharon Kay Simpson was convicted of aiding and abetting an armed bank robbery, in violation of 18 U.S.C. § 2113(d) and 18 U.S.C. § 2(a), and of aiding and abetting the use of a firearm in the commission of a violent felony, in violation of 18 U.S.C. § 924(c)(1) and 18 U.S.C. § 2(a). In this appeal, she challenges (1) the application of 18 U.S.C. § 924(c) to an aider and abettor; (2) the imposition of the mandatory five-year minimum sentence on the firearms charge; (3) the district court's refusal to grant a continuance following a superseding indictment adding the firearms charge; and (4) the sufficiency of evidence to support the convictions in light of her defense of coercion. Simpson also requests on appeal that this court exercise its supervisory powers and dismiss the § 924(c) charge because of prosecutorial abuse. We affirm.

I.

On February 27, 1991, Mark Grotte awoke and told Sharon Kay Simpson, his live-in girlfriend, that they were going to rob the First Bank Northtown in Coon Rapids, Minnesota. Grotte had discussed robbing a bank with Simpson for some time. He initially raised the matter when he and Simpson were on vacation in Florida, and renewed these discussions upon their return to Minnesota. In January 1991, Grotte told Simpson that he planned to rob the First Bank Northtown, and that he intended to do so when there was snow on the ground.

On the morning of February 27, Grotte, who had worn a beard for most of the time Simpson had known him, told Simpson to warm up the car while he shaved. The two then left for the bank, a trip of about four miles, with Simpson driving. Grotte brought with him a .357 magnum pistol loaded with hollow-point bullets and a suitcase containing a trench coat, stocking cap, and a woman's nylon stocking.

Upon reaching the bank, Grotte told Simpson to wait, with the car running, while he feigned making a telephone call to better view the bank. Grotte then entered the bank and, brandishing the pistol, robbed it of approximately $28,000. Simpson and Grotte drove to a Budgetel motel, where Simpson rented a room. Grotte remained at the hotel for the remainder of the day and night to count the money, while Simpson went home and returned to pick him up the next day.

Acting on a confidential tip, the FBI and local police executed a search warrant for the Grotte and Simpson home on May 3, 1991. They discovered a loaded .357 magnum, 400 rounds of live ammunition and approximately $6000 cash.

Simpson was arrested later that day and confessed to driving the getaway car. She stated that she had received approximately $4000 of the proceeds from the robbery.

Simpson was charged under 18 U.S.C. § 2 and 18 U.S.C. § 2113(d) with aiding and abetting the bank robbery, but was not initially charged on the firearms count. The prosecution offered her a plea bargain with a recommendation of no prison time if she would testify against Grotte. The prosecution also warned her that she could be charged with aiding and abetting the firearms charge if she refused to cooperate. Simpson refused to testify. On August 21, 1991, the government secured a superseding indictment charging Simpson with aiding and abetting the use of a firearm in the commission of a violent felony.

The defendant sought a thirty-day continuance under the Speedy Trial Act or, in the alternative, a four-day continuance to secure the testimony of an expert concerning battered woman's syndrome. The court denied this request, but did allow the defense a one-half-day continuance. The court later granted a second one-half-day continuance at the close of the government's case.

At trial, Simpson claimed that she was coerced into driving the getaway car. She claimed that Grotte had beat her throughout their relationship, and had threatened to kill her or her daughter and parents if she did not drive the getaway car. Testimony at trial revealed that Simpson had testified at Grotte's detention hearing that Grotte never had beaten her and that she did not fear him. She also signed an affidavit to that effect.

Sharon Kay Simpson was convicted on both counts. On the bank robbery count, the court reduced her offense level by two, determining that she had been a "minor participant" in the robbery. On the firearms count, however, the court determined that it had no discretion, and sentenced her to the five-year mandatory minimum. This appeal followed.

Simpson convicted

II.

A.   Application of Section 924(c) to Aider and Abettor

This difficult issue involves the interrelationship between the federal aiding and abetting statute, 18 U.S.C. § 2, and the use of a firearm in the commission of a violent felony under 18 U.S.C. § 924(c)(1). The latter statute imposes a consecutive five-year mandatory minimum sentence. The sentencing court departed downward approximately three years on the bank robbery charge, imposing a twelve-month sentence; however, finding no discretion to depart under § 924(c), the court imposed the five-year mandatory minimum. This consecutive sentence resulted in a total sentence of approximately six years of imprisonment for Simpson, as opposed to the eight-year sentence her co-defendant, the bank robber, received.

Simpson contends that she cannot be punished as an aider and abettor under both the robbery statute and the firearms statute because Congress has not clearly stated an intention to allow such "double punishment."

The Supreme Court has held that "[w]ith respect to cumulative sentences imposed in a single trial, the Double Jeopardy Clause does no more than prevent the sentencing court from prescribing greater punishment than the legislature intended." *Missouri v. Hunter,* 459 U.S. 359, 366, 103 S.Ct. 673, 678, 74 L.Ed.2d 535 (1983). Thus, the Double Jeopardy Clause does not prohibit the government from proving violations of two criminal statutes with the same course of conduct if Congress clearly intended to subject defendants to such "double punishment." *Hunter,* 459 U.S. at 367, 103 S.Ct. at 678; *Simpson v. United States,* 435 U.S. 6, 98 S.Ct. 909, 55 L.Ed.2d 70 (1978).

Simpson contends that the government may not prosecute her for both the bank robbery and the firearms charge when all she did was drive the getaway car. She claims that although Congress clearly intended to subject those who "use or carry" a firearm to double punishment, she did not do so. Furthermore, she argues that § 924(c) does not explicitly require enhanced liability for one who "aids and abets" another who uses or carries a firearm.

We disagree. Our analysis proceeds in two steps. First, the aider and abettor statute, 18 U.S.C. § 2, clearly states that the actions of the aider and abettor become those of a principal violation. Second, 18 U.S.C. § 924(c) explicitly states that one convicted as a principal of using a firearm to commit a violent crime may be punished both for the underlying crime and for the § 924(c) charge. Because the actions of the principal here involve use of a gun falling within § 924(c)'s prohibitions, an aider and abettor, chargeable as a principal, is also clearly liable for the use of the gun.

18 U.S.C. § 2 provides that one who "aids, abets, counsels, commands, induces or procures" a crime against the United States "is punishable as a principal." This statute does not create a separate crime; instead, it makes the listed actions a primary violation of another, specific crime. *United States v. Pino-Perez,* 870 F.2d 1230, 1236–37 (7th Cir.), *cert. denied,* 493 U.S. 901, 110 S.Ct. 260, 107 L.Ed.2d 209 (1989); *Londono-Gomez v. Immigration & Naturalization Serv.,* 699 F.2d 475, 476 (9th Cir.1983). Under § 2, the *acts* of the principal become those of the aider and abettor as a matter of law. *Pereira v. United States,* 347 U.S. 1, 74 S.Ct. 358, 98 L.Ed. 435 (1954); *Nye & Nissen v. United States,* 336 U.S. 613, 620, 69 S.Ct. 766, 770, 93 L.Ed. 919 (1949) ("Aiding and abetting . . . states a rule of criminal responsibility for acts which one assists another in performing."). Finally, § 2 applies to the entire criminal code. *United States v. Jones,* 678 F.2d 102, 105 (9th Cir.1982).

Here, Mark Grotte robbed a bank using a firearm. Simpson's conduct was integral to the crime. She provided the transportation and the means of concealment. Simpson also knew that Grotte possessed a firearm and

[handwritten margin note: Her conduct was integral to the crime]

his gun became hers in the eyes of the law

planned to use it in committing the robbery. Because Simpson's actions aided the commission of the armed bank robbery, Grotte's actions, and his gun, became hers in the eyes of the law. *See United States v. Archie,* 656 F.2d 1253, 1259 (8th Cir.1981) (getaway car driver guilty of bank robbery under 18 U.S.C. § 2113(a) and 18 U.S.C. § 2); *United States v. Moore,* 936 F.2d 1508, 1526 (7th Cir.1991) (conviction of firearm under 18 U.S.C. § 2 upheld on a theory of "constructive possession" where defendant was an integral part of the armed robbery, was aware of co-defendant's possession of gun, and knew that the weapon would be used to commit the crime).

Our conclusion is supported by the Supreme Court's discussion in *Busic v. United States,* 446 U.S. 398, 100 S.Ct. 1747, 64 L.Ed.2d 381 (1980). In *Busic,* the Supreme Court considered the application of the former version of § 924(c) to one who aided and abetted the armed assault of a federal officer under 18 U.S.C. § 111. With respect to the aider and abettor, the Court stated: "Through the combination of § 111 and 18 U.S.C. § 2, he was found guilty as a principal of using a firearm to assault the undercover agents. LaRocca's gun, in other words, became Busic's as a matter of law." *Id.* at 410–11, 100 S.Ct. at 1755. The Court added, in dicta, that were LaRocca punishable under both § 111 and § 924(c), "Busic, too would have been guilty of that crime as an aider and abettor." *Id.* at 411 n. 17, 100 S.Ct. at 1755 n. 17. Simpson's situation is indistinguishable. The gun is hers as a matter of law.

Having determined that Simpson's actions in aiding and abetting the robbery make her liable for the use of the gun, it is clear that she can be held liable on the gun charge. The text of 18 U.S.C. § 924(c) demonstrates a clear congressional intent to subject primary actors to enhanced punishment for the same conduct that constitutes armed bank robbery.

> Whoever, during and in relation to any crime of violence or drug trafficking crime (*including a crime of violence or drug trafficking crime which provides for an enhanced punishment if committed by the use of a deadly or dangerous weapon or device*) for which he may be prosecuted in a court of the United States, uses or carries a firearm, shall, *in addition to the punishment provided for such crime of violence or drug trafficking crime,* be sentenced to imprisonment for five years.

18 U.S.C. § 924(c)(1) (1988) (emphasis added). Congress clearly intended that one liable for the use of a firearm in a violent felony be liable for both the underlying felony and the § 924(c) charge. Because Simpson is properly liable as an aider and abettor for the use of the gun, there is no double jeopardy problem in punishing her for the underlying crime and the enhanced gun charge.

B.   Sentencing Discretion Under Section 924(c)

Simpson also contends that the district court erred when it concluded that it had no discretion to depart from the mandatory five-year sentence for the § 924(c) charge. As noted above, the statute creating liability for aiders and abettors, 18 U.S.C. § 2, provides that the aider and abettor is punishable as a principal. Thus, by aiding and abetting the § 924(c) offense, Simpson in effect has committed it herself. She stands in the shoes of the principal, and therefore is subject to the mandatory minimum.

Simpson contends, however, that § 2 allows for discretion in sentencing. We disagree. The Seventh Circuit, sitting *en banc,* considered and rejected this contention, and we agree with their views. *United States v. Pino-Perez,* 870 F.2d 1230 (7th Cir.1989). Section 2 provides no independent basis for sentencing discretion. It does not create a separate offense, nor does it contain its own schedule of penalties. It merely provides an alternative way to commit an independent, substantive crime. Therefore, criminal liability and punishment must be imposed under the substantive offense aided and abetted, and under no other statute. *See id.* at 1236–37.

Because § 924(c) provides for a mandatory minimum, the district court had no discretion, and properly sentenced Simpson to the five-year mandatory minimum. Although the imposition of a five-year mandatory minimum sentence may seem harsh in this situation, that is an issue for Congress, not the courts. *See, e.g., United States v. Lattimore,* 974 F.2d 971, 976 (8th Cir.1992); *United States v. Halford,* 948 F.2d 1054, 1057 n. 4 (8th Cir.1991).

———————

EXERCISE

If you were the prosecutor in the Simpson case, what would you have charged to either keep or avoid the outcome above?

———————

While conspiracy and aiding and abetting often run together, they do have distinct elements and a given defendant can be guilty of one and not the other.

UNITED STATES V. LEDEZMA

26 F.3d 636 (6th Cir. 1994)

RYAN, CIRCUIT JUDGE.

Josephine Ledezma was indicted for running an illegal family business: an interstate conspiracy to transport 1,600 kilograms of cocaine. According to the indictment, Terry Zajac was one of her minions. A jury convicted Ledezma and Zajac of conspiracy to possess 1,600 kilograms of cocaine with intent to distribute, in violation of 21 U.S.C. §§ 841(a)(1) and 846 (count 1);

and aiding and abetting in the possession of 351 kilograms of cocaine with intent to distribute, in violation of 21 U.S.C. § 841(a)(1) and 18 U.S.C. § 2 (count 2). In this appeal, both defendants challenge their convictions and sentences.

We affirm Ledezma's conviction and life sentence. As to Zajac, we affirm his conspiracy conviction, reverse his conviction for aiding and abetting, vacate his sentence, and remand for resentencing.

I.

This is another in a seemingly endless stream of drug distribution cases. David Edmonds, a sheriff's deputy in Shelby County, Tennessee, was among the first witnesses to testify at trial. He explained that on November 23, 1990, he stopped a Ford van on I-40 in Memphis, Tennessee, for speeding. The deputy stated that he asked permission to search the van after his suspicions were roused by the driver's nervousness and evasiveness. The driver, Jeffrey Ferrer, consented, and the deputy found fifteen packages of cocaine under a built-in cooler. The deputy then arrested Jeffrey Ferrer and his brother Eldon Ferrer, a passenger. An inventory search revealed a total of 351 kilograms of cocaine stashed in the van. Another officer, Lanny Hughes, testified that he found a piece of paper in the van with directions from Los Angeles to Washington, D.C. via Memphis.

Corbett Hart, a Drug Task Force Coordinator for the FBI, testified that law enforcement authorities, including of the FBI and the DEA, allowed the Ferrer brothers to continue their trip to Washington, D.C. in order to make a controlled delivery and to arrest the recipients and those orchestrating the delivery. En route, the brothers continued to make check-in calls to their superiors, and Hart testified that he was present on one occasion when Jeffrey Ferrer called defendant Ledezma at her home in suburban Los Angeles. Two of those calls were taped by the FBI.

Jeffrey Ferrer testified that en route to Washington he did indeed make check-in calls to Ledezma. Ferrer described how his father introduced him to Ledezma and how Ledezma recruited him to deliver the van with a promise to pay him and his brother each $2,000. According to Ferrer, Ledezma then showed him a map of the route and ordered him to call in from specific check points. Ferrer also identified a business card found in the van with Ledezma's phone number.

Jeffrey Ferrer's father, Robert Ferrer, also testified. The elder Ferrer explained that he was recruited by Manny Castellano, Ledezma's brother, and paid $4,000 to drive a van containing cocaine to Detroit. In a curious display of paternal interest, Ferrer asked Castellano whether his two unemployed sons—Jeffrey and Eldon—could make similar deliveries. With Castellano's assistance, Ferrer secured an audience with Ledezma at her home, where he introduced his sons to Ledezma.

According to Ferrer, Ledezma proceeded to instruct the younger Ferrers on how to deliver the van. Robert Ferrer testified that Ledezma also promised to pay each of his sons $2,000 upon their return.

Robert Ferrer further explained that after his sons left Los Angeles with the van, Castellano became concerned because the younger Ferrers were not calling in from all of the agreed upon check points. When the Ferrers arrived in Washington, they called their father to inquire about returning to California. Robert Ferrer then approached Castellano who told him that the deal in Washington was off and the van had to be delivered to Amarillo, Texas. Castellano gave Robert Ferrer $1,000 and dispatched him to Washington with instructions to drive the van to Texas.

Robert Ferrer and his wife flew to Washington and met their sons. This reunion was short lived, however, because Robert Ferrer was soon confronted by the police. Ferrer agreed to work with the authorities and to make a controlled delivery of the van in Amarillo, Texas. Robert Ferrer testified that he drove the van to Texas and then flew home to Los Angeles. When he returned home to California, Ferrer called Castellano. Castellano told Ferrer that defendant Terry Zajac would pay him for the delivery. Wearing an FBI wire, Ferrer met Zajac in the parking lot of a local restaurant. Ferrer testified that Zajac took $3,500 out of the trunk of his car and gave it to him, telling him "we did a good job and that everybody was happy with the way that we were delivering the vans and not touching anything inside."

Ricardo Rios, Ledezma's cousin and Castellano's confidant, testified that he agreed to "baby-sit" a house in Fontana, California, where 1,600 kilograms of cocaine was stored. Rios described how he helped load the van destined for Washington with 351 kilograms of cocaine. Further, Rios explained how he picked up the Ferrer brothers at Ledezma's house and turned the van over to them. Several days after the Ferrers departed, Rios testified that Castellano began to suspect that the van "had a fly in it"—an unsavory metaphor suggesting that the van had been intercepted by the police. Rios testified that Castellano, fearing the conspiracy had been compromised, came with Zajac to the house where Rios was staying, and together they loaded 244 kilograms of cocaine into a GMC Blazer. They left the truck in the garage, and Rios moved from the house to an apartment with Castellano and Zajac.

Detective Richard Bitonti, a police officer in Rialto, California, testified that he executed a search warrant on December 4, 1990, for the residence in Fontana, California, and seized 244 kilograms of cocaine in the GMC Blazer parked in the garage. The following day, Detective Bitonti executed a search warrant of Ledezma's house and found an Ohaus gram scale in the garage.

Josephine Ledezma took the stand in her own defense and offered an innocent explanation for the evidence against her. She denied any knowledge of the Ohaus scale found in her garage. She explained that the Ferrer brothers had asked her for directions to Washington. Ledezma further testified that it was Robert Ferrer who insisted that his sons call her if they encountered any difficulties on their trip. Ledezma explained that she intended only to relay these messages to her brother, Manny Castellano. Finally, in response to the government's evidence that she requested that her telephone service be disconnected shortly after the Ferrer brothers failed to check in, Ledezma testified that she cut off the telephone service to her house because her father and brother were charging calls to her phone number.

Zajac also testified. He denied that he assisted Ledezma and Castellano in distributing cocaine. He also denied meeting with Robert Ferrer and paying him on behalf of Castellano.

At the close of the evidence, the defendants moved for a judgment of acquittal based on insufficient evidence. The district court denied the motions, and the case went to the jury. The jury found Ledezma and Zajac guilty of both conspiracy to possess cocaine with intent to distribute (count 1), and aiding and abetting in the possession of cocaine with intent to distribute (count 2). The district court then sentenced Ledezma to life in prison, and Zajac to 292 months imprisonment with a five-year period of supervised release. The defendants now appeal their convictions and sentences. . . .

Zajac maintains that the evidence was not sufficient to sustain his conviction for conspiracy, or his conviction for aiding and abetting.

As to the conspiracy, Zajac argues there is no direct evidence that he knowingly participated in the scheme. Of course, this court has held that the " 'connection of the defendant to the conspiracy need only be slight, if there is sufficient evidence to establish that connection beyond a reasonable doubt.' " *Barrett*, 933 F.2d at 359 (quoting *Christian*, 786 F.2d at 211). While Zajac is correct that his mere presence at Ledezma's home and his sharing an apartment with Castellano and Rios is insufficient evidence on which to convict, he ignores the fact that he actively participated in the conspiracy when he helped Castellano and Rios remove the cocaine from the house in Fontana, California. Moreover, acting as Castellano's agent, Zajac paid Robert Ferrer for driving the van from Washington, D.C., to Amarillo, Texas. Therefore, we conclude that there was sufficient evidence from which a rational jury could find that Zajac knowingly participated in the conspiracy to possess cocaine with intent to distribute.

2. Aiding and Abetting

Zajac's conviction for aiding and abetting in the possession of 351 kilograms of cocaine with intent to distribute, in violation of 21 U.S.C. § 841(a)(1) and 18 U.S.C. § 2, presents a more difficult question. The United States Code provides that "[w]hoever . . . aids, abets, counsels, commands, induces or procures [the] commission [of a crime] is punishable as a principal." 18 U.S.C. § 2(a) (1988). Judge Learned Hand read the statute to require that the defendant "in some sort associate himself with the venture, that he participate in it as in something that he wishes to bring about, that he seek by his action to make it succeed." *United States v. Peoni,* 100 F.2d 401, 402 (2d Cir.1938). Judge Learned Hand's formulation has become the accepted standard for imposing accomplice liability under 18 U.S.C. § 2(a). *See Nye & Nissen v. United States,* 336 U.S. 613, 619, 69 S.Ct. 766, 769–70, 93 L.Ed. 919 (1949); *United States v. Morrow,* 977 F.2d 222, 230 (6th Cir.1992) *(en banc),* cert. denied, 508 U.S. 975, 113 S.Ct. 2969, 125 L.Ed.2d 668 (1993).

As we observed in *United States v. Winston,* 687 F.2d 832, 834 (6th Cir.1982), "[d]rawing an exact line of sufficient participation [to support a conviction for aiding and abetting], especially in drug distribution cases, is difficult if not impossible." To prove aiding and abetting, the government must show that Zajac knew that the principals possessed cocaine with the intent to distribute it, and that Zajac assisted in their plan to deliver the cocaine. *United States v. Pena,* 983 F.2d 71, 72 (6th Cir.1993). It is not necessary, however, for the government to show that Zajac actually or even constructively possessed the cocaine. *Winston,* 687 F.2d at 834 n. 2, 835.

We think the evidence presented is insufficient to support Zajac's conviction for aiding and abetting. The first evidence of Zajac's involvement in the criminal venture is his assisting Castellano and Rios in loading a truck with 244 kilograms of cocaine, but, of course, that was unrelated to the 351 kilograms in the van driven by the Ferrer brothers. Rios's testimony establishes that Zajac entered the conspiracy several days after the Ferrer brothers left Los Angeles. Thus, Zajac did not assist his principals' possession in a typical aiding and abetting scenario under section 841 by acting as a "lookout," *United States v. Martin,* 920 F.2d 345, 348 (6th Cir.1990), cert. denied, 500 U.S. 926, 111 S.Ct. 2038, 114 L.Ed.2d 122 (1991); *United States v. Poston,* 902 F.2d 90, 94–95 (D.C.Cir.1990); a supplier, *United States v. Brantley,* 733 F.2d 1429, 1434–35 (11th Cir.1984), cert. denied, 470 U.S. 1006, 105 S.Ct. 1362, 84 L.Ed.2d 383 (1985); or a middleman procuring customers, *United States v. Frorup,* 963 F.2d 41, 43 (3d Cir.1992); *United States v. Wesson,* 889 F.2d 134, 135 (7th Cir.1989).

The government argues that the same evidence that proved Zajac's participation in the conspiracy to possess the cocaine with intent to distribute is sufficient to support Zajac's conviction for aiding and abetting in the possession of cocaine with intent to distribute. While some cases relying on *Pinkerton v. United States,* 328 U.S. 640, 66 S.Ct. 1180, 90 L.Ed. 1489 (1946), have so held, *see, e.g., United States v. Salazar,* 958 F.2d 1285, 1292 (5th Cir.), cert. denied, 506 U.S. 863, 113 S.Ct. 185, 121 L.Ed.2d 129 (1992); *United States v. Collazo,* 815 F.2d 1138, 1144–45 (7th Cir.1987), we think they are distinguishable from this case. In *Salazar* and *Collazo,* each defendant had a prolonged association with the conspiracy, an association that predated the commission of the substantive crime the defendant was convicted of aiding and abetting. Thus, the facts in *Salazar* and *Collazo* were such that it could reasonably be inferred that a defendant's continued participation in a criminal enterprise aided and abetted a coconspirator's subsequent crime. In contrast, no such inference can be drawn here where it is apparent that the specific crime of possession with intent to distribute, as it related to the 351 kilograms of cocaine in the van, had already commenced when Zajac joined the conspiracy.

The only connection between Zajac and the 351 kilograms of cocaine is the evidence that Zajac paid Robert Ferrer for delivering the van. This, however, did not occur until after the van was confiscated by the authorities. Zajac argues that the crime was over and done with by the time he paid off Ferrer, and that he cannot be convicted of aiding and abetting the substantive offense of possession of cocaine with the intent to distribute it once the principals were no longer in possession of the cocaine. The government argues that the principals' possession of the cocaine is irrelevant since all the government needs to prove is that Zajac intended to facilitate the commission of a crime by another.

We agree with the government that the essence of the crime of aiding and abetting is the defendant's offering assistance or encouragement to his principal in the commission of a substantive offense. *See* Wayne R. LaFave and Austin W. Scott, Jr., *Criminal Law* § 63 (1972); *see also* Charles E. Torcia, *Wharton's Criminal Law* § 29 (15th ed.1993). But one cannot aid and abet a completed crime. *Roberts v. United States,* 416 F.2d 1216, 1221 (5th Cir.1969); *see also United States v. Shulman,* 624 F.2d 384, 387 (2d Cir.1980); *United States v. Murry,* 588 F.2d 641, 646 (8th Cir.1978); *United States v. Keach,* 480 F.2d 1274, 1287 (10th Cir.1973). And we do not think Zajac's activity can properly be characterized as intended to help or to encourage the commission of a crime.

The United States Code makes it a crime to "possess with intent to . . . distribute . . . a controlled substance." 21 U.S.C. § 841(a)(1) (1988). Here the possession of the cocaine by the other members of the conspiracy was an accomplished fact when Zajac entered the conspiracy. Moreover, by the time Zajac paid Ferrer for making the delivery, the police had already seized the cocaine and arrested several of Zajac's coconspirators. Zajac did nothing to assist his coconspirators in the substantive offense relating to the 351 kilograms of cocaine in the van, because his coconspirators had already completed the crime. Perhaps Zajac might well have been charged and convicted under 18 U.S.C. § 3 as an accessory after the fact, or on some other theory, *see* Sharon C. Lynch, Comment, *Drug Kingpins and Their Helpers: Accomplice Liability Under 21 USC § 848,* 58 U. Chi. L.Rev. 391 (1991), on the basis that his paying Ferrer was an effort to help his coconspirators avoid detection, but such was not the indictment in this case.

We recognize that aiding and abetting a drug offense may encompass activities, intended to ensure the success of the underlying crime, that take place after delivery and after the principal no longer possesses the narcotics. In *United States v. Coady,* 809 F.2d 119, 124 (1st Cir.1987), a defendant who made assurances to the purchasers of narcotics concerning the quality of drugs previously delivered was convicted of aiding and abetting an offense under 21 U.S.C. § 841(a)(1), because his declarations were intended to secure payment for the drugs and to facilitate "the financial climax of the deal." In *United States v. Orozco-Prada,* 732 F.2d 1076, 1080 (2d Cir.), *cert. denied,* 469 U.S. 845, 105 S.Ct. 154, 83 L.Ed.2d 92 (1984), a defendant was convicted of aiding and abetting a conspiracy to distribute cocaine because he laundered proceeds from drug sales, thus furthering the distribution of the narcotics. *See also United States v. Perez,* 922 F.2d 782, 785–86 (11th Cir.), *cert. denied,* 501 U.S. 1223, 111 S.Ct. 2840, 115 L.Ed.2d 1009 (1991). In this case, however, Zajac's putative participation was not part of an on-going crime (*Coady*) nor was it a recurring contribution to a continuing crime (*Orozco-Prada*). We conclude, therefore, that there is insufficient evidence from which a rational jury could convict Zajac of aiding and abetting in the possession of cocaine with intent to distribute.

EXERCISE

Jean-Christophe decides to rob a local convenience store. He picks his target, enters the store, and draws a gun. He tells the clerk to "put all the cash in a bag" and thrusts out a blue pillowcase. He also tells the clerk to give him "all the cigarettes you have." At that point a customer in the store, LuAnn, goes behind the counter and starts taking cigarettes from a rack and putting them into the blue pillowcase as the clerk takes money out of the till and the safe. Jean-Christophe and LuAnn do not know each other and have never spoken; LuAnn just happened to be in the store and wanted to help.

When Jean-Christophe runs out, LuAnn follows him. Before they part ways on the street, Jean-Christophe gives her five packs of cigarettes and says "thanks!"

You are the prosecutor. Do you charge LuAnn? With what?

3. ACCESSORY AFTER THE FACT

18 U.S.C. § 3 allows for one-half the criminal liability of a principal for anyone who "knowing that an offense against the United States has been committed, receives, relieves, comforts, or assists the offender in order to hinder or prevent his apprehension, trial, or punishment. . . ." A key

element here is knowledge that an offense has already been committed. While this is often considered a form of accomplice liability, accessories after the fact are often seen as less culpable that those who help a criminal before and during the criminal act.

UNITED STATES V. CALDERON
785 F.3d 847 (2d Cir. 2015)

WESLEY, CIRCUIT JUDGE:

Defendants-Appellants Nelson Calderon, Wilfredo Sanchez, Eva Cardoza, and Angelo DeLeon appeal from judgments of the district court, following a jury trial, convicting them of racketeering, narcotics, and obstruction-of-justice offenses. The appellants were charged along with thirty other alleged members and associates of a violent street gang. Following a five-week trial, the jury returned a verdict finding each appellant guilty on at least one count.

On appeal, appellants raise a host of legal challenges to their convictions. All save one are disposed of by a summary order issued simultaneously with this opinion. We write here only with regard to Appellant Cardoza's conviction for accessory after the fact to murder, in violation of 18 U.S.C. § 3. This opinion addresses her argument that the evidence at trial was insufficient to establish that she was an accessory after the fact to a murder. We hold that the trial evidence was not sufficient for a reasonable jury to find Cardoza guilty of that charge.

BACKGROUND

Appellants were members and associates of a nationwide criminal organization known as the "Almighty Latin King Queen Nation" or simply the "Latin Kings." The Latin Kings operated drug markets—selling crack cocaine, powder cocaine, heroin, and marijuana—at gang-controlled locations in Newburgh, New York.

Cardoza lived with her young daughter and her boyfriend, Latin Kings member Steven Lewis (known as "Scoobz" or "Scooby"), in an apartment where she and Lewis stored drugs for the Latin Kings. Although she was not officially a member of the Latin Kings, Cardoza went on missions with gang members, collected money from drug sales, advised drug customers of Lewis's location, and sold drugs and made drug deliveries for the gang. Cardoza regularly drove Lewis to the homes of drug customers to help him make deliveries in her green Ford Explorer. Several times, narcotics customers gave cash for drugs directly to Cardoza.

This opinion deals with Cardoza's challenge to her accessory-after-the-fact conviction for helping a Latin Kings member escape after he shot and killed an aspiring member of the gang, John Maldonado (known as "Tarzan"), in retaliation for what the gang had determined was an earlier betrayal.

Maldonado and several Latin Kings members had been involved in a shooting on a block "controlled by the Bloods," a rival gang, in order to "show[ ] face." Trial Tr. 1482–83; 2684. A member of the Bloods shot at Maldonado's group from across the street; they returned fire. Police intervention halted the violence before anyone was injured.

The next day, the Latin Kings leadership planned to retaliate against the Bloods. Maldonado and a fully initiated Latin Kings member, Carlos Romero (known as "Los"), were directed to locate and kill some Bloods members. Lewis was assigned the task of helping Maldonado and Romero flee the scene. Cardoza drove Lewis and fellow Latin Kings member Luis Tambito (known as "Luch") to an intersection in Newburgh where they waited to pick up the shooters. Ultimately Lewis and Tambito were instructed by Latin Kings superiors to abandon the mission because there were no Bloods members in the area to target.

The next day, the Latin Kings again attempted to retaliate against the Bloods. This time, they sent Maldonado and another aspiring gang member, Jerome Scarlett (known as "Rudeboy"). The Latin Kings equipped both Scarlett and Maldonado with firearms. The attack on the Bloods went poorly and Scarlett was shot and killed.

Latin Kings had heard rumors that Maldonado was "infiltrating" their gang and that "he was working with the Bloods and that's why he had Rudeboy shot." Trial Tr. 1542. As a result, they suspected that Maldonado had killed Scarlett. The Latin Kings decided to retaliate by shooting Maldonado "in the middle of the street." Trial Tr. 1542. They chose gang member William Overton (known as "Tutu") for the task and provided him with a firearm for that purpose. Romero was instructed to walk Maldonado down a street under the pretense of preparing for another mission "to get back at the Bloods because [of] what happened with Rudeboy." Trial Tr. 2713. Overton was to lie in wait along the path and shoot Maldonado as he went by.

Cardoza was aware of Maldonado's suspected involvement in Scarlett's death. Romero testified that he rode with Lewis and Cardoza in the Explorer after Scarlett's death and discussed how Maldonado had "shot at Rudeboy by accident." Trial Tr. 2705. Thereafter, as part of the plan to eliminate Maldonado, Overton was told to look for "a green SUV" and that Cardoza would be driving. Trial Tr. 2907.

On the day of the murder, Overton hid behind bushes beside the street, wearing gloves, a mask, and a hoodie, and waited for Maldonado. When his victim walked by, Overton jumped out from his hiding place and shot Maldonado three times, mortally wounding him. Tambito, who was in close proximity to both Cardoza's vehicle, which was parked down the street, and the scene of the murder, testified that he heard the three shots.

After shooting Maldonado, Overton ran past Cardoza and Lewis waiting in the Explorer and on through a graveyard. Romero, who had run across the street after the shooting, testified that as Cardoza's vehicle approached Overton, he heard a female voice and saw a "hand come out from the—from the driving side start saying come on, come on" waving with her left arm toward the inside of the car. Trial Tr. 2722–23. Tambito yelled to Cardoza to "[g]o get him"—meaning Overton—and Cardoza drove her vehicle in pursuit. Trial Tr. 1581. When Overton heard sirens, he discarded his gloves, mask, and hoodie, and stashed his weapon "on somebody's porch" beneath a piece of furniture. Trial Tr. 2915–16.

Overton then met up with Cardoza and Lewis in the getaway SUV. Overton testified that once he was in the vehicle he had a conversation with Lewis and Cardoza:

> [Overton]: Yeah. I was asked if I had the gun. I told Scoobz [Lewis] that I did not have the gun. And like he just told me that—that someone would be getting in touch with me so we could—like I could show them where the gloves were, where the jacket was, where the gun was, and whoever would be doing it would be disposing of all of it.
>
> . . .
>
> [Assistant United States Attorney Benjamin Allee]: All right. And what further discussion, if any, did you have as you drove away from the block?
>
> [Overton]: They had told me that someone would come and pick me up and that someone would be in touch. That way, they would come back to wherever I was, come and get me, and we would dispose of—like I would show them where the gun, the gloves, the mask and the sweatshirt were so they can get rid of it.

Trial Tr. 2921. Cardoza drove Overton to his home in Montgomery, New York.

DISCUSSION

Cardoza argues that a rational jury could not convict her of being an accessory after the fact to a homicide committed in violation of 18 U.S.C. § 1959(a)(1), *i.e.,* the Maldonado murder, because there was insufficient evidence that she had knowledge "that the decedent was dead or dying at the time of [her] decision to provide assistance." Cardoza Br. 49 (internal quotation marks and alterations omitted). The accessory after the fact statute provides that "[w]hoever, knowing that an offense against the United States has been committed, receives, relieves, comforts or assists the offender in order to hinder or prevent his apprehension, trial or punishment, is an accessory after the fact." 18 U.S.C. § 3. Murder in aid of racketeering is one such "offense against the United States." *See United*

States v. Malpeso, 115 F.3d 155, 161 (2d Cir.1997); see also 18 U.S.C. § 1959(a)(1).

We review a challenge to the sufficiency of the evidence *de novo* and must " 'affirm if the evidence, when viewed in its totality and in the light most favorable to the government, would permit any rational jury to find the essential elements of the crime beyond a reasonable doubt.' " *United States v. Yannotti,* 541 F.3d 112, 120 (2d Cir.2008) (quoting *United States v. Geibel,* 369 F.3d 682, 689 (2d Cir.2004)). A guilty verdict may be based entirely on circumstantial evidence and guilt "may be inferred from the evidence so long as the inference is reasonable." *United States v. Morgan,* 385 F.3d 196, 204 (2d Cir.2004) (citation omitted) (internal quotation marks omitted). "The ultimate question is not whether *we believe* the evidence adduced at trial established defendant's guilt beyond a reasonable doubt, but whether *any rational trier of fact could so find." United States v. Payton,* 159 F.3d 49, 56 (2d Cir.1998).

The statute applies where, *inter alia,* a person "know[s] that an offense against the United States has been committed." 18 U.S.C. § 3. Thus, to permit a verdict of guilty, there must have been sufficient evidence that Cardoza knew that she was helping a killer after he had committed a murder. Several state courts have contemplated the nature of proof necessary to establish that one is an accessory after the fact to a murder. In some states, "a person cannot be convicted as an accessory after the fact to a murder . . . when the aid was rendered after the mortal wound was given, but before death ensued." *State v. Williams,* 229 N.C. 348, 49 S.E.2d 617, 618 (1948); *see also State v. Chism,* 436 So.2d 464, 468 (La.1983) ("A person cannot be convicted as an accessory after the fact to a murder because of aid given after the murderer's acts but before the victim's death, but under these circumstances the aider may be found to be an accessory after the fact to the felonious assault.").

The Fourth Circuit—the only circuit to have addressed this question—has expressly "decline[d] . . . to apply such a restrictive rule." *United States v. McCoy,* 721 F.2d 473, 474 (4th Cir.1983). Instead, the Fourth Circuit has held that the "defendant must have had knowledge that [the victim] was dead *or dying* at the time of his decision" to act as an accessory. *Id.* at 475 (internal quotation marks omitted and emphasis added).

We agree with the Fourth Circuit and adopt the standard that the Government must prove that the defendant knew or must have known that the victim was dead or dying at the time she decided to act as an accessory after the fact to murder.

The Government argues that the evidence was sufficient to permit a reasonable juror to infer the requisite knowledge. However, even construing the evidence in the light most favorable to the Government, no rational juror could have found that Cardoza knew that Maldonado was dead or dying during the relevant time period. *See United States v.*

Fernandez, 526 Fed.Appx. 270, 280–81 (4th Cir.), *cert. denied sub nom. Gonzalez v. United States,* ___ U.S. ___, 134 S.Ct. 342, 187 L.Ed.2d 238, *and cert. denied sub nom. Fernandez-Gradis v. United States,* ___ U.S. ___, 134 S.Ct. 456, 187 L.Ed.2d 305 (2013).

The facts the Government employs to this task are insufficient to impute knowledge of Maldonado's condition to Cardoza. Overton's testimony that he was told that Cardoza would be around the corner waiting for him provided a reasonable inference only that Cardoza knew she was driving someone away from a crime. Although there was evidence that Lewis had been told that the plan was to kill Maldonado, there was no evidence that Cardoza was present when Lewis was so informed or that he relayed that information to her. Even if Cardoza was told that Maldonado was going to be shot, there is no evidence that she knew Maldonado was dead or dying when she drove Overton away. Tambito's direction to Cardoza to "[g]o get" Overton when he ran the wrong way, while showing that Cardoza understood that she was providing getaway services, does not show that she knew what Overton's mission was or that it had been successful. Lastly, in the conversation between Overton and Lewis on the drive out of Newburgh, there is no indication that either Maldonado or the shooting were discussed.

It is probable, given her proximity to the events, that Cardoza heard the shots. Tambito testified that he was nearby and that the shots were audible to him. But as the trial evidence in this case showed, and as we have recognized in the past, "[g]uns are among the tools of the narcotics trade," *United States v. Stevens,* 985 F.2d 1175, 1188 (2d Cir.1993). Shots fired in that context are not always intended to be lethal and, even so intended, not all gunshots are fatal. The Latin Kings and the Bloods would frequently "shoot at" each other to "show face" or to protect their drug-selling territory. *See, e.g.* Tr. 1482–84; 1545; 1604–08; 1672. The jury was not entitled to infer, without more, that shots fired within earshot of Cardoza gave her knowledge that Maldonado was dead or dying.

Based on the totality of the circumstances, no rational juror could find that when she drove him out of Newburgh, Cardoza knew that Overton had shot Maldonado and that Maldonado was dead or dying. Thus, the evidence presented to convict Cardoza of being an accessory after the fact to a homicide was insufficient.

CONCLUSION

For the reasons stated above, the judgment of the district court convicting Cardoza of accessory after the fact to a federal offense in violation of 18 U.S.C. § 3 is **REVERSED.** As decided in the accompanying summary order, Cardoza's convictions on all other counts are **AFFIRMED.** The case is **REMANDED** as to Cardoza, with instructions for the district court to dismiss Count Forty-Three of the Indictment in 10 CR 392, and for resentencing on the counts of conviction.

EXERCISE

What charge would have more properly fit Eva Cardoza's actions? Is there a reason that prosecutors may have avoided pursuing that charge?

CHAPTER ELEVEN

DEFENSES

■ ■ ■

There are two types of trial defenses in a criminal case.

By far the most commonly-used defense is the attempt by a defense attorney to create reasonable doubt as to at least one of the elements of the crime. The defense need not even present evidence to press this defense; it simply needs to convince the jury that the government did not meet its burden to prove each element beyond a reasonable doubt. In the preceding chapters we have examined many cases where this type of defense is employed. We will call this type "element" defenses, since they are targeted at the government's high burden and the elements of the crime.

A second, and much less common, form of defense is the affirmative defense, where the defendant actually takes on the burden of proving a fact in order to escape liability. These affirmative defenses are often described in statutes which specify the burden born by the defendant. We have already studied one in the context of homicide: self-defense.

In this chapter, we will first examine an element defense, alibi. From there, we will move on to discuss the defenses of public authority, withdrawal and renunciation, duress, necessity, and entrapment. All of these are often defined as affirmative defenses (though the way they are treated varies between jurisdictions). The affirmative defense of insanity will be discussed in the next chapter, as part of a broader discussion of mental health.

A. ALIBI

The defense of alibi is usually an element defense, since the goal is simply to establish reasonable doubt as to the element of identification by showing that the defendant was somewhere else (or doing something else) at the time of the crime.

Relying on an alibi defense, though, presents special challenges. Federal Rule of Criminal Procedure 12.1 does not shift the burden to the defense, but does create obligations on both parties:

(a) Government's Request for Notice and Defendant's Response.

  (1) Government's Request. An attorney for the government may request in writing that the defendant notify an attorney for the government of any intended alibi defense. The request must state the time, date, and place of the alleged offense.

(2) Defendant's Response. Within 14 days after the request, or at some other time the court sets, the defendant must serve written notice on an attorney for the government of any intended alibi defense. The defendant's notice must state:

(A) each specific place where the defendant claims to have been at the time of the alleged offense; and

(B) the name, address, and telephone number of each alibi witness on whom the defendant intends to rely.

(b) Disclosing Government Witnesses.

(1) Disclosure.

(A) In General. If the defendant serves a Rule 12.1(a)(2) notice, an attorney for the government must disclose in writing to the defendant or the defendant's attorney:

(i) the name of each witness—and the address and telephone number of each witness other than a victim—that the government intends to rely on to establish that the defendant was present at the scene of the alleged offense; and

(ii) each government rebuttal witness to the defendant's alibi defense.

The fact that an alibi defense can be misconstrued by a jury as a burden-shifting mechanism means that courts must be very careful when instructing a jury on this point.

UNITED STATES V. ZUNIGA

6 F.3d 569 (9th Cir. 1993)

PREGERSON, CIRCUIT JUDGE:

Juan Carlos Zuniga was convicted of bank robbery in violation of 18 U.S.C. § 2113(a). He was sentenced to prison. He appeals because the trial court failed to give the jury a requested alibi instruction. We have jurisdiction under 28 U.S.C. § 1291. We reverse.

At 5:45 p.m., April 19, 1991, the Valley National Bank in Phoenix, Arizona was robbed. A lone robber gave a bank teller a demand note that stated: "4,000 or I'll blow your head off. At you a gun I got pointed." The teller gave the robber $1,705.00. Once the robber left the bank, an off-duty police officer, who was a customer of the bank, shouted that there were "two black men" in the robber's getaway car. Police traced the license plate number of the getaway car to Andres Gonzales Portal.

Portal told police that he had driven to the bank on April 19 with a friend, Damaso Olivera, and a casual acquaintance, Juan Zuniga. Portal, like Zuniga, is a heavy-set Black man of medium height, with a medium complexion, who speaks with a Cuban accent. Portal stated that only Zuniga had entered the bank, for about ten minutes. Portal also stated that he had no knowledge of any robbery occurring in the bank.

Police then questioned Olivera, who also stated that he had no knowledge of the robbery and that only Zuniga had gone into the bank on the day in question. Olivera also testified that he, Portal, and Zuniga drove around for 35 to 40 minutes after leaving the bank. Based on Portal's and Olivera's statements, the police arrested Zuniga and charged him with bank robbery in violation of 18 U.S.C. § 2113(a). Upon arrest, police seized a striped shirt from Zuniga's apartment that was similar to one worn by the bank robber. Later, the victim teller identified Zuniga from a photographic lineup. A police officer testified that when he questioned Zuniga alone, Zuniga identified himself in a bank surveillance photo. This admission was neither recorded nor substantiated by another officer.

At trial, defense counsel argued that Portal, who looks like Zuniga and owns a baseball cap like the one worn by the robber, was in fact the man who robbed the bank. Defense counsel also presented alibi testimony from Zuniga's wife, Tammi Woods. Woods testified that Zuniga was at home with their baby when she returned from work on April 19, 1991. Based on the time she regularly leaves work and on bus schedules, Woods testified that she arrived home at "5:15, 5:30, [or] the latest, 6:00 [p.m.]." Based on this testimony, defense counsel asked the court to give Ninth Circuit Model Jury Instruction 6.01, concerning alibi. This instruction states:

> The defendant has introduced evidence to show that he was not present at the time and place of the commission of the offense charged in the indictment. The government has the burden of establishing beyond a reasonable doubt the defendant's presence at that time and place.

proposed jury instruction

> If, after consideration of all the evidence, you have a reasonable doubt that the defendant was present at the time the crime was committed, you must find the defendant not guilty.

The issue presented by this appeal is whether the district court committed reversible error by refusing to instruct the jury on Zuniga's alibi defense. We have not yet decided whether to review a district court's denial of a proposed jury instruction de novo or for abuse of discretion. *See United States v. Frank,* 956 F.2d 872, 879 (9th Cir.1992) (citing *United States v. Slaughter,* 891 F.2d 691, 699 (9th Cir.1989)), *cert. denied,* 506 U.S. 932, 113

S.Ct. 363, 121 L.Ed.2d 276 (1992). We need not resolve this issue on this appeal because the result would be the same under either standard.

"A defendant is entitled to an instruction concerning his [or her] theory of the case if it is supported by law and has *some foundation in the evidence.*" *United States v. Mason,* 902 F.2d 1434, 1438 (9th Cir.1990) (emphasis added) (citing *United States v. Lopez,* 885 F.2d 1428, 1434 (9th Cir.1989), *cert. denied,* 493 U.S. 1032, 110 S.Ct. 748, 107 L.Ed.2d 765 (1990)). Even if the alibi evidence is "weak, insufficient, inconsistent, or of doubtful credibility," the instruction should be given. *United States v. Washington,* 819 F.2d 221, 225 (9th Cir.1987) (citing *United States v. Doubleday,* 804 F.2d 1091, 1095 (9th Cir.1986), *cert. denied,* 481 U.S. 1005, 107 S.Ct. 1628, 95 L.Ed.2d 201 (1987)).

An alibi instruction is critical because a juror, unschooled in the law's intricacies, may interpret a failure to prove the alibi defense as proof of the defendant's guilt. *United States v. Hoke,* 610 F.2d 678, 679 (9th Cir.1980). To avoid this possibility, "[w]here alibi is the defense[,] a suitable *alibi* instruction *must be given when requested.*" *Hoke,* 610 F.2d at 679 (emphasis added).

A different jury instruction cannot be an adequate substitute for an alibi instruction:

> [I]nstructions on the presumption of innocence of the accused, and of the necessity of fastening every necessary element of the crime charged upon the accused beyond a reasonable doubt, *are not enough* in cases involving the necessary presence of the accused at a particular time and place, when the accused produces testimony that he was elsewhere at the time. . . . [A]n instruction . . . *must be given* so as to acquaint the jury with the law that the government's burden of proof covers the defense of alibi, as well as all other phases of the case. Proof beyond a reasonable doubt as to the alibi never shifts to the accused who offers it, and if the jury's consideration of the alibi testimony leaves in the jury's mind a reasonable doubt as to the presence of the accused, then the government has not proved the guilt of the accused beyond a reasonable doubt.

United States v. Ragghianti, 560 F.2d 1376, 1379 (9th Cir.1977) (emphasis added) (quoting *United States v. Marcus,* 166 F.2d 497, 503 (3d Cir.1948)).

In particular, we require more than an instruction on identification of the defendant as the perpetrator of the crime. An alibi is a distinct defense. *See Woratzeck v. Ricketts,* 820 F.2d 1450, 1457 (9th Cir.1987) (defendant's "defense theory" was an "alibi defense"), *vacated, on other grounds,* 486 U.S. 1051, 108 S.Ct. 2815, 100 L.Ed.2d 916 (1988); *Thomas v. Goldsmith,* 979 F.2d 746, 748 (9th Cir.1992) ("alibi defense"); *United States v. Bryser,* 954 F.2d 79, 87 (2d Cir.) (same), *cert. denied,* 504 U.S. 972, 112 S.Ct. 2939,

119 L.Ed.2d 564 (1992); Fed.R.Crim.P. 12.1(a) (upon proper demand, defendant shall give prosecution "written notice of [her] intention to offer a defense of alibi"); *Black's Law Dictionary* 71 (6th ed. 1990) (alibi is "a defense").

An alibi defense differs from other mistaken identity defenses in an important respect: A defendant might win based on an alibi defense even if she does nothing at all to dispute the government's proof, because the alibi itself can create reasonable doubt. Without an alibi, the defendant would have to work much harder to disprove identity.

Moreover, the special treatment accorded the alibi defense under Rule 12.1 of the Federal Rules of Criminal Procedure suggests that it may deserve a special jury instruction. Rule 12.1 forces the defendant to notify the government of the "specific place or places at which the defendant claims to have been at the time of the alleged offense and the names and addresses of the witnesses upon whom the defendant intends to rely to establish such alibi." Fed.R.Crim.P. 12.1. Just as this rule focuses on the defendant's presence at the scene of the crime, the alibi instruction emphasizes the government's burden "of establishing beyond a reasonable doubt the defendant's presence at [the] time and place" of the offense. Ninth Circuit Model Jury Instruction 6.01. Insofar as Rule 12.1 ensures the prosecution receives notice of an alibi, jurors should also be alerted to the nature of the alibi so they may carefully deliberate before giving the defendant the benefit of this powerful defense.

As stated above, Zuniga's wife, Tammi Woods, testified that on April 19, 1991 she arrived home at "5:15, 5:30, [or] 6:00 [p.m.] at the latest." At that time, she found Zuniga at home, caring for their daughter. Their daughter was not dressed as if she had been outside. Woods further testified that she firmly believed that Zuniga would not leave the child at home alone.

The robbery occurred at 5:45 p.m. Olivera told police that he, Portal, and Zuniga drove around for an additional 35 to 40 minutes after leaving the bank. Woods' testimony, standing alone, was sufficient to create an issue as to Zuniga's whereabouts at the time and place of the bank robbery. Therefore, the requested alibi instruction should have been given.

The prosecution contends that even if the district court erred in refusing to instruct the jury on Zuniga's alibi defense, such error was harmless. Our precedent does not support this argument. We have held that failure to instruct the jury on the defendant's theory of the case, where there is evidence to support such instruction, is reversible per se and can never be considered harmless error. *See United States v. Escobar de Bright*, 742 F.2d 1196, 1201 (9th Cir.1984) ("[O]ur cases must be read as meaning that a failure to instruct the jury on the defendant's theory of the case is reversible per se. . . . The right to have the jury instructed as to the defendant's theory of the case is one of those rights 'so basic to a fair trial' that failure to instruct where there is evidence to support the instruction can never be considered harmless error."). The trial court, however, is not required to give a particular instruction regarding the defense's theory of the case so long as the court's instructions adequately cover the subject. If the instructions adequately cover the theory of the defense, there is no error. *See Mason,* 902 F.2d at 1438.

The record shows that none of the court's instructions either addressed or adequately covered the alibi defense. Accordingly, the court's failure to give an adequate instruction on Zuniga's alibi defense theory requires reversal of his conviction and a remand for a new trial.

REVERSED AND REMANDED.

EXERCISE

If a defendant chooses to present evidence of an alibi (usually through witnesses), the government is then allowed to call rebuttal witnesses to countermand that evidence.

Imagine that you are the prosecutor in a bank robbery case in the Southern District of New York. Trial is set for three weeks hence, and the defendant has filed an alibi notice. He claims that at the time of the robbery he was gambling in Atlantic City with his wife. Atlantic City is about 125 miles from New York City. The defendant properly filed an alibi notice listing his wife and a restaurant waiter in Atlantic City as alibi witnesses.

The FBI agent who is investigating the case is willing to gather whatever evidence you need to rebut the alibi. What should you ask her to do?

B. PUBLIC AUTHORITY

As the use of informants and undercover agents has proliferated, the defense of public authority has grown in importance. In essence, this defense asserts that a crime was committed in the service of and at the direction of law enforcement. It is asserted (successfully or not) by informants, former informants, and others who consider themselves to have been directed by legal authorities.

As with an alibi defense, federal rules require a defendant relying on this defense to provide notice in time for the government to research the claim. Federal Rule of Criminal Procedure 12.3 sets this out:

(a) **Notice of the Defense and Disclosure of Witnesses.**

    (1) **Notice in General.** If a defendant intends to assert a defense of actual or believed exercise of public authority on behalf of a law enforcement agency or federal intelligence agency at the time of the alleged offense, the defendant must so notify an attorney for the government in writing and must

file a copy of the notice with the clerk within the time provided for filing a pretrial motion, or at any later time the court sets. The notice filed with the clerk must be under seal if the notice identifies a federal intelligence agency as the source of public authority.

(2) Contents of Notice. The notice must contain the following information:

> **(A)** the law enforcement agency or federal intelligence agency involved;

> **(B)** the agency member on whose behalf the defendant claims to have acted; and

> **(C)** the time during which the defendant claims to have acted with public authority.

(3) Response to the Notice. An attorney for the government must serve a written response on the defendant or the defendant's attorney within 14 days after receiving the defendant's notice, but no later than 21 days before trial. The response must admit or deny that the defendant exercised the public authority identified in the defendant's notice.

Unlike the alibi defense, the defense of public authority is an affirmative defense, meaning that it is the defendant who bears the burden of presenting evidence and proving by a preponderance of the evidence that he was working under the direction of law enforcement. Things get confusing, though, when informants go beyond the scope of their charge.

UNITED STATES V. ALVARADO
808 F.3d 474 (11th Cir. 2015)

JULIE CARNES, CIRCUIT JUDGE:

For less than a year, Defendant Fausto Aguero Alvarado worked as an undercover confidential informant ("CI") for the United States Drug Enforcement Administration ("DEA") in Central America. Formalizing this role, he signed written agreements with federal DEA agents that set out the parameters of his duties, and thereafter assisted these agents with investigations into drug and weapons trafficking operations. After working with the agents for a few months, Defendant apparently came to the realization that he could make more money by actually dealing drugs and weapons than by merely reporting on those who do. So, deciding to make a career change, Defendant began working in earnest with some of the drug traffickers on whom he had been gathering intelligence, as well as some new acquaintances, in an effort to trade weapons for large quantities of cocaine. Not surprisingly, Defendant kept this new entrepreneurial venture to himself, conceding that he never at any time, during a criminal conspiracy that spanned sixteen months, informed his supervising federal agents what he was up to or that there was even a weapons-for-drugs transaction in the offing with his new-found working partners. In fact, these supervising agents had no idea that Defendant had been involved in the conspiracy that ultimately led to his indictment until they were later informed by other law enforcement officials who had uncovered Defendant's criminal activities.

At trial, Defendant did not deny that he and his fellow conspirators planned and took steps to trade weapons in exchange for obtaining large quantities of cocaine. His explanation, which he offered in his trial testimony before the jury, was that throughout his involvement in the charged conspiracy, he considered himself to be acting in his capacity as an informant, merely gathering intelligence as part of that role. But as to when he planned to actually share with supervising agents his sixteen months of covert "intelligence gathering," such a conversation was apparently never on Defendant's "to-do" list. . . .

In 2008, while living in Colombia, Defendant obtained some information regarding weapons and narcotics activity. Having worked as a CI in the past, he had received training in field operations and intelligence gathering. Accordingly, around April of 2008, Defendant went to the United States Embassy in Bogota, Colombia, to share his recently-gained intelligence with the DEA. After providing a previously-assigned code that identified him as a former CI, Defendant met with DEA Agents Matthews and Romain and offered them information that was potentially useful to the dismantling of a drug trafficking cartel.

Other meetings followed this first session, and Agent Romain decided that he wanted to use Defendant to infiltrate an organization in which one undercover operative was already working. Accordingly, on August 28, 2008, Defendant and Agent Romain entered into a contract formally authorizing Defendant to work as a CI. The agreement made clear that Defendant would have no immunity from prosecution for activities that were not specifically authorized by his controlling investigators. Further reinforcing that condition, the contract required Defendant to agree that he would take no independent action on behalf of the DEA or the United States government. The term of the agreement was one year, meaning that it would expire in August 2009.

Defendant then began providing Romain with information about Franklin McField-Bent, a Nicaraguan national known to authorities as the supplier of a transportation service used by drug dealers to move cocaine from the interior of Colombia, to the Nicaragua/Honduras border, to Guatemala, and then to Mexico. Romain sought Defendant's assistance as part of his effort to build a case against McField-Bent and the Titos Montes trafficking organization.

Also in August 2008, Defendant began working with DEA Agent Ball in Honduras on an investigation into a terrorist named Jamal al Yousef. Ball and Defendant worked closely together during the investigation. Some of Defendant's phone calls to targets in the Jamal al Yousef investigation were recorded under Ball's direction and Ball met with Defendant, both before and after key meetings with targets, to instruct and debrief him. Defendant was paid $8,800 for his work sometime in 2008 and worked on the investigation until March 2009.

In early September 2008, Defendant signed two other CI agreements, each with a one-year term, with DEA Agents Sanes and Peterson, who were working in Honduras and Panama, respectively. Like the first agreement with Agent Romain, these agreements reiterated that Defendant could not act independently of his controlling agents. On October 2, 2008, Defendant met with both Agents Romain and Sanes to share information about McField-Bent. Then, sometime between October and December 2008, as a result of safety and security issues, Agent Ball instructed Defendant to leave Honduras.

By January 2009, Defendant's work and contact with the above agents had largely ceased, the exception being some continued work with Agent Ball on the al Yousef terrorist investigation, which ended in March 2009. Indeed, in January 2009, Defendant emailed Agent Ball, informing him that Agent Romain had told him to "fruck off" and leave Colombia as soon as possible because "you guys didn't want to work with me" any longer. It was around this time that Agent Ball became aware of an ongoing investigation into Defendant's unauthorized criminal activities. In fact, by May, Agent Romain had left Colombia and had no further contact with Defendant. . . .

According to the evidence presented at trial, Defendant was integrally and actively involved in the charged criminal conspiracy, which spanned over sixteen months. The overarching goal of the conspiracy was to obtain large quantities of cocaine, after which the transportation services of McField-Bent would be utilized to transport the drugs from Colombia to Mexico; thereafter, the drugs would be moved across the border to the United States. Defendant focused much of his efforts on acquiring drugs by trading weapons with an individual who could supply those drugs. This individual, Jaime Velasquez, purportedly was the commander of an illicit Colombian paramilitary group known as Autodefensas, which group very much wanted weapons. In actuality, Velasquez was an undercover operative who was working for both the Colombian government and the United States Department of Homeland Security.

Defendant was introduced to Velasquez as a potential weapons supplier and, in a telephone conversation on June 12, 2009, Velasquez and Defendant discussed Velasquez's desire to order SAM-7 missiles. Defendant explained that he could be the intermediary for a potential exchange. Three days later, at an in-person meeting with Velasquez and others, Defendant stated that he worked with a "really good office," which Velasquez understood to mean a good drug trafficking organization. Velasquez suggested that they start with a deal for six grenade launchers, which Defendant would arrange to have transported from Honduras to Colombia. Defendant proposed an exchange of one kilogram of cocaine for each grenade launcher. Defendant also told Velasquez that he could exchange cocaine for weapons in Central America and that McField-Bent was in charge of the drug transportation logistics. At some point during the meeting, Defendant had a telephone conversation with McField-Bent in which he mentioned that a woman named Lina Ester Grendet had given him "the terrain, that farm already, that 1,000-meter property," which Velasquez understood to mean that Lina had given Defendant 1,000 kilograms of cocaine. Defendant explained that he was purchasing the cocaine from Lina for $7,000 per kilogram and planned to sell it for $9,500 to an individual named David.

One month later, at a meeting on July 25, 2009, Velasquez again expressed interest in purchasing missiles from Defendant. Defendant asked Velasquez if Velasquez could help him recover some money that Lina owed him. Velasquez understood Defendant to be asking him to put pressure on Lina to pay back this money to Defendant. Defendant sent Velasquez an email with Lina's contact information, including her address and a photograph of her. That same month, Defendant received two payments via wire transfer: one from Velasquez and one from Lina.

Negotiations between Velasquez and Defendant and his group concerning this guns-for-drugs initiative continued for months until, finally, in May 2010, Defendant, McField-Bent, Jeison Archibold, and a Miguel Vilella met with Velasquez, who agreed to provide 400 kilograms of cocaine to Defendant's group every twenty days in exchange for rocket-propelled grenade launchers, grenades, and other weapons. Talks continued and the deal was to be finalized with Velasquez at a meeting on October 8, 2010. But instead, Colombian officials arrested the conspirators at this meeting. Defendant, who was in Bogota and not present at that meeting, was arrested a month later.

Although the weapons-trading aspect of the conspiracy was a focus of Defendant's work, Defendant was also involved in other efforts by the group to acquire drugs independently of Velasquez. For example, in March 2010, Defendant, McField-Bent, and Archibold shipped a load of cocaine that was later seized en route to Honduras by Colombian authorities. Recorded conversations revealed discussion of an additional shipment in May 2010. In addition, as set out above, Defendant had purchased cocaine from Lina at some point prior to June 2009.

Notably, most of the above-described events occurred after the August and September 2009 expiration dates of Defendant's CI agreements with the federal agencies. All of them occurred after Agent Romain had told Defendant that the agents no longer wanted to work with him. And at no time during the sixteen-month conspiracy did Defendant ever inform any of his supervising agents that these very significant criminal acts were occurring or that he was involved in their planning. . . .

Co-defendants McField-Bent and Archibold both pled guilty, with McField-Bent later testifying as a Government witness at Defendant's trial. Defendant, however, decided to go to trial for the purpose of arguing that he had been authorized by federal agents to engage in the charged criminal activity. As required by Federal Rule of Criminal Procedure 12.3(a)(1), Defendant filed a pretrial notice of intent to present a public authority defense and included a list of federal agents for whom he had worked. The notice indicated that Defendant had worked for all the listed agents between 2008 and 2011.

In response, the Government filed a motion in limine to preclude Defendant from raising a public authority or entrapment-by-estoppel defense. The motion noted that Defendant had proffered no evidence that he was authorized to participate in any of the illicit meetings or calls occurring during the conspiracy. Indeed, having broken off contact with agents during this time period, Defendant had failed even to notify agents of those meetings and calls. Further, the written agreements that Defendant signed explicitly stated that he was not authorized to participate in any criminal activity unless specifically authorized in writing by a prosecutor or his controlling agents. In short, the motion contended that the above defenses were unavailable to Defendant absent his production of evidence demonstrating that he was specifically authorized to engage in the conduct charged in the indictment. Responding to the Government's motion, Defendant argued that the public authority defense should be available to him. He argued that he had "general" authorization to gather intelligence and therefore was not required to prove that an agent had affirmatively authorized any particular conduct. . . .

As noted, at the hearing before the magistrate judge concerning whether Defendant would be permitted to present a public authority defense, Defendant failed to present any evidence to qualify him for this defense. At trial, he had a second chance to make his case for a public authority defense when he testified in his own behalf. The district court concluded, however, that Defendant had still failed to provide an evidentiary foundation for the defense. Accordingly, the court declined to instruct the jury to consider a public authority defense, but did instruct the jury to consider whether Defendant acted with an "innocent intent." Defendant argues that the district court erred in rejecting his proposed instruction on the public authority defense. . . .

A defendant may assert a public authority affirmative defense when he has knowingly acted in violation of federal criminal law, but has done so in reasonable reliance on the authorization of a governmental official. *Id.; see also United States v. Reyes-Vasquez,* 905 F.2d 1497, 1500 n. 5 (11th Cir.1990) (a public authority defense applies when a defendant alleges that his actions were taken under color of public authority). For example, an informant who participates in a typical undercover drug sting operation at the behest of the DEA could potentially assert a public authority defense were he later to be prosecuted for his participation.

The public authority defense is narrowly defined, however, and a defendant will not be allowed to assert the defense, or to demand that the jury be instructed on it, unless he meets certain evidentiary prerequisites. First, as the name of the defense implies, a federal law enforcement officer must have actually authorized the defendant to commit the particular criminal act at issue, and the defendant must have reasonably relied on that authorization when engaging in that conduct. *United States v. Johnson,* 139 F.3d 1359, 1365–66 (11th Cir.1998)(public authority defense is only available when a defendant can show that he "relied on official government communications before acting in a manner proscribed by law," and that this reliance was reasonable).

Second, the government official on whom the defendant purportedly relied must have actually had the authority to permit a cooperating individual to commit the criminal act in question. *Id.* at 1365 ("The actual authority defense requires proof that a defendant reasonably relied upon the *actual authority* of a government official to request participation in an illegal activity." (emphasis added)). If, contrary to the defendant's genuine belief, the official possessed no such authority, then the public authority defense cannot be asserted. *See Baptista-Rodriguez,* 17 F.3d at 1368 n. 18 ("[R]eliance on the *apparent* authority of a government official is not a defense in this circuit. . . ."); *United States v. Anderson,* 872 F.2d 1508, 1516 (11th Cir.1989) (disallowing defendants' reliance on apparent authority of CIA agent because the latter lacked actual power to authorize violation of laws); *United States v. Rosenthal,* 793 F.2d 1214, 1236 (11th Cir.1986), *modified on other grounds,* 801 F.2d 378, *cert. denied,* 480 U.S. 919, 107 S.Ct. 1377, 94 L.Ed.2d 692 (1987) (same). . . .

As explained above, a defendant who seeks an instruction on a public authority defense must produce evidence that (1) a government official authorized him to take what would otherwise be an illegal action; (2) that this official had the actual authority to permit the action; and (3) that the defendant reasonably relied on the official's authorization. There is no dispute here that the controlling agents with whom Defendant worked had the authority to approve his participation in the undercover drug conspiracy that was charged in the present indictment. There are few disputes, and none of them material, between the agents and Defendant as to their communications. Yet, taking the evidence in the light most favorable to Defendant, which means taking as true his testimony, we agree with the district court that Defendant failed to provide evidence that the agents had ever authorized him to participate in the sixteen-month conspiracy that led to his indictment. Indeed, the vagueness and generality of Defendant's testimony, by itself, reinforces a conclusion that he simply lacks any evidence to support an argument that supervising agents had authorized his activities, or that he could have reasonably understood them to have done so.

Recapping our earlier summary of the evidence, for about a six-month period of time, between August 2008 and March 2009, Defendant acted as an informant under the supervision of DEA agents in Central and South America who were trying to uncover illegal drug importation activity. Formalizing his relationship with the agents, Defendant signed written agreements which provided that he was immune from prosecution only for ~ *immune only for activities specifically authorized* activities specifically authorized by his controlling agents and that he agreed to take no independent action on behalf of American law enforcement interests without such authorization.

As to this drug investigation, neither Defendant nor the two testifying agents, Ball and Romain, offered much detail as to exactly what assistance he provided, nor did they give much information about the number or nature of interactions between them. What we do know from the evidence presented is that in January 2009, Agent Romain had essentially told Defendant that their working relationship was over. Defendant himself admitted that Agent Romain had told him to "fruck off" and leave Colombia as soon as possible because "you guys didn't want to work with me" anymore.

Defendant did not leave Colombia. And, notwithstanding this seemingly unambiguous message from Agent Romain that Defendant's services as an informant were no longer wanted or needed, Defendant nonetheless claims that he believed he was working on behalf of the DEA agents over the next sixteen months, albeit without their knowledge, and that he believed his activities to be authorized by the agency. Yet, at no time during this sixteen-month period did Defendant make any effort to let these agents know what he was accomplishing as their informant. Which is too bad, because Defendant had a lot to tell. Indeed, taking Defendant at his word that, at least in his own mind, he was continuing to function as an informant while in the thick of drug activity that would have obviously intrigued the agents, his silence is inexplicable. By at least the spring of 2009, Defendant was having conversations with his soon-to-be co-conspirators about involving himself in their drug dealing. And in June 2009, Defendant met with the purported commander of an illegal paramilitary group and discussed the latter's willingness to provide Defendant large quantities of drugs in return for Defendant's sale of grenade launchers, surface-to-air missiles, and other weapons.

Surely, Defendant realized that the agents would be keenly interested in this development so that they could deploy standard investigative techniques, such as the interception of telephone calls and visual monitoring, to build their case. Yet again, Defendant said nothing. Further, over the entirety of the charged conspiracy, Defendant was involved in other drug-related endeavors with McField-Bent and Archibold—two individuals in whose activities he knew the agents to be interested—with one of their drug shipments having been seized by Colombian authorities. But again, radio silence from Defendant. Finally, in May 2010, Defendant was kidnapped by a drug cartel and held for three days before escaping: a dramatic event about which his handlers would surely want to be informed. Yet once again, Defendant kept this news to himself. In short, Defendant participated in numerous acts in furtherance of the criminal conspiracy, including telephone calls, meetings, money transfers, and drug deals. Yet, he told his former supervising agents nothing about any of these events.

In fact, Defendant agrees that none of the criminal acts he committed during the sixteen-month term of the conspiracy was explicitly authorized by the agents. How could they have been, given Defendant's failure to ever inform the agents of what he was doing? He also acknowledges, as he must, that his written agreements with the agencies prohibited him from taking any actions not authorized by his handlers. His only explanation for his violation of the agreements' requirement that he only undertake illegal activity that was approved by the agents was to recount Agent Romain's alleged statement, in an undescribed context, that the written documents were "merely formalities." In addition, Defendant testified that he did not think he needed to inform the agents what he was doing because they had earlier told him that they had the technological capabilities to listen in to all his telephone calls and to discern, through GPS, where he was at all times. So, according to Defendant, he inferred that the agents knew everything he was doing and, by their silence, he assumed they necessarily had approved his actions. Finally, Defendant claims that because he had never been formally deactivated by the agents, he could still consider himself an informant. He makes this claim notwithstanding having been told that the agents no longer wanted to work with him, notwithstanding the absence of any request by agents for his assistance during the period of the conspiracy, and notwithstanding his awareness that the written agreements between him and the agency had expired during the beginning of the sixteen-month period described in the indictment.

Defendant's argument can be boiled down to the following: up until the time an informant is formally deactivated, any criminal conduct he engages in is deemed to be authorized by the law enforcement agency, even if agents have no knowledge of the informant's actions, so long as the informant (1) believes that his status as an informant relieves him of the obligation to obtain approval for his chosen actions or (2) assumes that the agency has

[margin handwritten note: Defendant's argument —]

probably learned elsewhere about his criminal conduct, and infers authorization from the agency's subsequent silence.

Of course, what is lacking in Defendant's interpretation of the term "authorization" is anything remotely approaching the definition that is actually applied to that word. Black's Law Dictionary defines the word "authorize" as meaning, "To formally approve; to sanction <the city authorized the construction project>." BLACK'S LAW DICTIONARY (10th ed.2015). The phrase "authorization of an action" connotes first, an awareness of the intended action by the person authorizing it and second, a communication to the person undertaking the action. An assumption that one is not required to obtain approval or that the approving official may well know of the intended action is not the same thing as having gotten authorization to take the action. And it is the actual affirmative communication by a law enforcement agent that transforms an informant's assumption of authorization into the approval that is required for the public authority defense to apply.

We are aware of no caselaw that supports an interpretation that so turns on its head the word "authorize." The sparse authority in analogous cases that we have found surely does not support Defendant's peculiar interpretation. *See United States v. Mergen,* 764 F.3d 199, 205 (2d Cir.2014) (For the public authority defense to apply, the defendant must "in fact" have been authorized by the Government to engage in what would otherwise be illegal activity. Thus, the fact that defendant was acting as an informant on other matters for the FBI and had even brought to its attention a planned arson did not confer on him the authorization of the Bureau to participate in that arson); *Giffen,* 473 F.3d at 41 (where official encouraged defendant to continue with his informant activities, the former had not authorized the defendant to commit illegal conduct not mentioned in the previous disclosures); *Abcasis,* 45 F.3d at 43–44 (public authority defense will not "support a claim of an open-ended license to commit crimes in the expectation of receiving subsequent authorization"); *cf. United States v. Goodwin,* 496 F.3d 636, 644 (7th Cir.2007) (reiterating district court's conclusion that defendant was not entitled to assert a public authority defense because he "was attempting to play both sides of the street" when "engaged in freelance drug dealing distinct from the controlled deals that he made at the government's instruction as a then-confidential informant").

In short, Defendant's proffered evidence is little more than a recitation of his purported, and rather convenient, assumptions, not proof of authorization by the supervising agents. In reaching this conclusion, however, we caution that adherence to formalistic requirements is not a prerequisite to a finding of approval by the appropriate official. For example, had the DEA agents here verbally approved of Defendant's participation in the criminal conspiracy, the fact that the confidential informant's agreement had already expired or that a new written document had not been issued would not necessarily preclude a finding that authorization had been given. Likewise, we are not holding that, in every case, authorization must be so specific that an informant will be required to seek out and receive instruction for each discrete act that he takes. Further, a course of conduct between the agents and the informant and the latter's reasonable reliance on past communications may, in appropriate circumstances, give rise to an inference of authorization.

In sum, for us to infer authorization of a particular action, the communications and course of dealing between an informant and his supervising agents must be such that the informant would reasonably understand he is authorized to engage in the particular conduct at issue. And his conduct "must remain within the general scope of the solicitation or assurance of authorization." *Abcasis,* 45 F.3d at 43–44. This means that "[w]hether a defendant was given governmental authorization to do otherwise illegal acts through some dialogue with government officials necessarily depends, at least in part, on precisely what was said in the exchange." *Giffen,* 473 F.3d at 39; *cf. United States v. Burt,* 410 F.3d 1100, 1104 (9th Cir.2005) (finding that defendant was entitled to a public authority instruction where she testified that federal agents gave her no instructions as to how to conduct herself and told her that as long as she was gathering information for them, her actions would not be illegal).

Here, though, a conclusion that Defendant lacked authorization to engage in this sixteen-month criminal conspiracy is not a close call. And absent such authorization, Defendant had no entitlement to violate the law with impunity nor any right to a public authority instruction that would vindicate that claimed expectation. Accordingly, we conclude that the district court did not err in refusing to instruct the jury to consider whether Defendant had acted under public authority in committing his offense.

EXERCISE

Lorne is a government informant who is paid about $50,000 a year to buy heroin and provide information to federal agents. He became an informant after being convicted of a felony fraud charge. He sometimes works on "reverse stings," where he poses as a seller rather than a buyer of heroin, or introduces an undercover officer as a seller to those seeking heroin.

On one reverse sting, things go terribly wrong. He has introduced a DEA agent to Marcel, a local heroin dealer who needs a new supplier. They meet in a restaurant parking lot to consummate the transaction. However, Marcel becomes convinced that Lorne is going to rob him. Marcel pulls a gun and begins firing. He hits and kills the DEA agent. As Marcel shoots at him, Lorne takes the fallen officer's gun and returns fire towards Marcel in self-defense. Lorne accidentally shoots a by-stander, a 14-year-old boy, who was in the restaurant directly behind Marcel. There is a public outcry over the incident, with one headline announcing "Ex-con Shoots Kid with Cop's Gun."

Could Lorne assert the defense of public authority if he is charged with felon in possession of a firearm?

C. WITHDRAWAL, ABANDONMENT, AND RENUNCIATION

Sometimes, defendants in a criminal case rely on the defense that they pulled out of a criminal activity before it was completed. Most often, this is in relation to charges—attempt and conspiracy—that themselves do not require completion of the crime. The terms "withdrawal," "abandonment," and "renunciation" do not have consistent and clearly distinct meanings, and what will matter is the definition of the defense found in a statute or precedential opinion within the controlling jurisdiction.

This defense is sometimes phrased not as an affirmative defense but as a way of showing reasonable doubt as to the action element or intent.

One question which has been answered differently in different jurisdictions is whether or not this defense is allowed in cases where attempt is charged and an overt act was completed.

UNITED STATES V. YOUNG
613 F.3d 735 (8th Cir. 2010)

SHEPHERD, CIRCUIT JUDGE.

Following trial, a jury convicted James William Young of one count of attempting to entice a minor to engage in sexual activity, in violation of 18 U.S.C. § 2422(b). The district court sentenced Young to 160 months imprisonment, a $100 special assessment, and 10 years supervised release. Young appeals, challenging his conviction, the refusal of his proffered jury instructions on abandonment and entrapment, and his sentencing enhancements for misrepresentation of identity and obstruction of justice. *See* United States Sentencing Commission, *Guidelines Manual*, §§ 2G1.3(b)(2)(A), 3C1.1. For the following reasons, we affirm.

I.

On November 4, 2008, at 3:50 p.m., Young, a 33-year-old married father of three, entered an adult online chat room entitled "romance, adult," on Yahoo! Instant Messenger. Young utilized the screen name "Funminqc" and sent an instant message to an individual with the screen name "Erj94e." The person at "Erj94e" responded and disclosed that her name was "Emily" and that she was a 14-year-old female. Unbeknownst to Young, in reality "Emily" was undercover Dewitt, Iowa Police Officer Shai Cruciani of the Internet Crimes Against Children Task Force.

Emily and Young chatted for approximately one hour. After Emily disclosed that she disliked band, Young told Emily that he worked as an engineer for Alliant Energy, although, in reality, he was a band director at a high school in Clinton, Iowa. Young asked Emily if she had a boyfriend and she responded that she did not. Young also told Emily that he was not married, discussed the possibility of a future meeting and provided Emily with his cell phone number. Young sent Emily a picture of himself, and Emily sent Young a photograph that had been digitally modified to appear to be of a 14-year-old female.

Young and Emily chatted online and exchanged emails on several occasions between November 4 and November 13, 2008. During their discussions, Young continued "grooming" Emily by never indicating that he was a band director and discussing topics he knew would be of interest to her. As the chats progressed, they became more sexually explicit in nature, including references to sexual acts the two might perform with each other. Specifically, Young inquired if Emily had "ever done oral . . . ever had a guy lick you?" (Trial Tr. vol. II, 147.) When she responded "no," Young stated, "K, well may have to give you that experience." (*Id.*)

Emily eventually agreed to meet Young in person. Emily told Young that she had seen a Super 8 Motel close to Westbrook Park in DeWitt, Iowa. Young offered to obtain a room at the Super 8. Young warned Emily to keep their relationship and planned meeting private. Young specifically told Emily not to tell anyone because "[he] would be locked up" for "being with a minor." (*Id.* at 149.)

During one of the final online conversations between Emily and Young, the discussion progressed to include graphic details of an anticipated sexual encounter, with Young indicating that he wanted to "kiss, touch, and lick" Emily and suggesting that the two have sexual intercourse at the motel. (*Id.* at 155.) Young and Emily exchanged emails to arrange the details of their meeting, which was to take place on November 13, 2008. Emily suggested that Young pick her up at Westbrook Park, but the two eventually decided that she would walk to the Super 8 Motel. Emily indicated that she would be dressed in jeans and a pink coat. Young planned to arrive at approximately 3:00 p.m., check into a room, and leave a note containing Emily's name and his room number on the windshield of his car.

On November 13, 2008, Young used his personal credit card to reserve a room at the Super 8 Motel in Dewitt, Iowa. Young then drove to the Super 8 followed by several undercover police officers. Upon his arrival at the motel at approximately 3:10 p.m., he attempted to reserve a room at the front desk, however his credit card was declined. Young told the motel clerk that he was going to withdraw cash and then return. Young next drove to a U.S. Bank Automated Teller Machine ("ATM"), where Young appeared to attempt a cash withdrawal. Young's account, however, had insufficient funds and Young called the Super 8 clerk and cancelled his reservation due to his inability to secure any payment.

Young next drove to a middle school and high school near the Super 8. Young traveled back and forth between the schools and motel several times and circled the parking lots. Young eventually drove to Westbrook Park. Officer Tamii Gordy, another undercover officer with the Dewitt Police Department, was standing in the park dressed in jeans and a pink coat. When Young saw the undercover officer, he began honking and yelling. Officers then arrested Young.

The officers gave Young his *Miranda* warnings and Young agreed to an interview. This interview occurred prior to Young's discovery that "Emily" was not, in fact, a 14-year-old female. During the interview, Young indicated that he had "feelings that [he was] not proud of for the last 15 years" and that he had been online chatting with a 14-year-old girl named Emily. (*Id.* at 169.) Young indicated that the chat topics included, "sex once, playing cards, eating pizza, that they were supposed to meet in the hotel room for four hours, possibly take a bath because she liked to take baths, [and] they had talked about touching and kissing and oral." (*Id.* at 137–38.) When asked whether a sexual encounter would have occurred between himself and Emily in the hotel room, Young responded that "he didn't know if it would [have been] 100 percent innocent while in the room." (*Id.* at 138.)

During the search incident to Young's arrest, officers discovered a condom on Young's person. After obtaining a search warrant for Young's car, officers recovered a note with the name "Emily" written on it and a bottle of bubble bath. . . .

Young pled not guilty and stated that he had been "tempted" by Emily, that his online conversations were merely fantasies, and that he had not intended to go through with the planned sexual encounter, but had traveled to the Super 8 out of concern for Emily's safety. Young testified that he had used a "maxed out credit card" because he had never expected to obtain a room. (Trial Tr. vol. III, 317–18.) He also stated that he had driven to the ATM to watch for Emily and not to withdraw money. Finally, he testified that, after cancelling the reserved room, he had driven around in search of Emily only to ensure that she was safe.

Young requested that the jury be instructed on his abandonment and entrapment defenses. Young's proffered abandonment instruction read:

> One of the issues in this case is whether the defendant abandoned his attempt. If the defendant abandoned his attempt he must be found not guilty. The government has the burden of proving beyond a reasonable doubt that the defendant did not abandon his attempt. When the actor's conduct would otherwise constitute an attempt it is an affirmative defense that he abandoned his effort to commit the crime or otherwise prevented its commission under

[handwritten margin note: Young's proposed jury instruction]

the circumstances manifesting a complete and voluntary renunciation of his criminal purpose. Renunciation of criminal purpose is not voluntary if it is motivated, in whole or in part, by circumstances, not present or apparent at the inception of the actor's course of conduct, that increase the probability of detection or apprehension or that make more difficult the accomplishment of the criminal purpose. Renunciation is not complete if it is motivated by a decision to postpone the criminal conduct until a more advantageous time or to transfer the criminal effort to another by similar objective or victim.

. . .

In his proposed abandonment instruction, Young cited the Model Penal Code, in which the provisions concerning criminal attempt include references to the affirmative defense of voluntary renunciation. *See* Model Penal Code § 5.01(4). The code section provides that the defense applies only when the defendant:

> abandon[s] his effort to commit the crime or otherwise prevent[s] its commission, under circumstances manifesting a complete and voluntary renunciation of his criminal purpose. . . . [R]enunciation of criminal purpose is not voluntary if it is motivated, in whole or in part, by circumstances, not present or apparent at the inception of the actor's course of conduct, that increase the probability of detection or apprehension or that make more difficult the accomplishment of the criminal purpose. Renunciation is not complete if it is motivated by a decision to postpone the criminal conduct until a more advantageous time or to transfer the criminal effort to another but similar objective or victim.

Id. The Model Penal Code lists two considerations for recognizing such a defense in attempt crimes: (1) "renunciation of criminal purpose tends to negative dangerousness," and (2) "to provide actors with a motive for desisting from their criminal designs, thereby diminishing the risk that the substantive crime will be committed." Model Penal Code § 5.01(4) cmt. 8 (Official Draft and Revised Comments 1985).

Issue

This issue of whether a defendant is entitled to an abandonment defense once an attempt has been completed, i.e., the defendant has the requisite intent and has completed a substantial step towards the crime, is an issue of first impression in our circuit. While we have stated, "[i]n an attempt case, abandonment precludes liability," *United States v. Robinson,* 217 F.3d 560, 564 n. 3 (8th Cir.2000), we relied upon *United States v. Joyce,* 693 F.2d 838 (8th Cir.1982) in making that comment. *Joyce,* however, involved abandonment of an attempt prior to the completion of the attempt. *Id.* at 841. We hold today that a defendant cannot abandon an attempt once it has been completed.

We emphasize that all of our sister circuits that have faced this issue have either held that a defendant cannot abandon a completed attempt or have alluded to such a determination. *See United States v. Crowley,* 318 F.3d 401, 410–11 (2d Cir.2003) (not formally addressing the issue but noting, "[t]he only other circuits that have formally addressed the question have rejected the defense as a matter of federal law"); *United States v. Shelton,* 30 F.3d 702, 706 (6th Cir.1994) ("[W]ithdrawal, abandonment and renunciation, however characterized, do not provide a defense to an attempt crime."); *United States v. Bussey,* 507 F.2d 1096, 1098 (9th Cir.1974) ("A voluntary abandonment of an attempt which has proceeded well beyond preparation as here, will not bar a conviction for the attempt."); *United States v. Wales,* 127 Fed.Appx. 424, 432 (10th Cir.2005) (unpublished) ("[N]either this circuit nor any other circuit to have addressed the issue has held that abandonment or renunciation may constitute a defense to the completed crime of attempt.").

Specifically, in *Shelton,* the Sixth Circuit rejected the Model Penal Code's approach and held that "withdrawal, abandonment and renunciation, however characterized, do not provide a defense to an attempt crime." 30 F.3d at 706. The court explained:

> As noted, the attempt crime is complete with proof of intent together with acts constituting a substantial step toward commission of the substantive offense. When a defendant withdraws prior to forming the necessary intent or taking a substantial step toward the commission of the offense, the essential elements of the crime cannot be proved. At this point, the question whether a defendant has withdrawn is synonymous with whether he has committed the offense. After a defendant has evidenced the necessary intent and has committed an act constituting a substantial step toward the commission of the offense, he has committed the crime of attempt, and can withdraw only from the commission of the substantive offense. We are not persuaded that the availability of a withdrawal defense would provide an incentive or motive to desist from the commission of an offense, especially since the success of the defense presupposes a criminal trial at which the issue would be submitted to the jury for decision. A remote chance of acquittal would appear to have an even more remote chance of deterring conduct. We recognize, of course, that attempt crimes pose unique issues. However, the interest of defendants in not being convicted for mere thoughts, desires or motives is adequately addressed by the government's burden of proving that the defendant took a substantial step toward the commission of the substantive offense.

Id. (quotation omitted).

We have previously held that completed crimes, other than attempt, cannot be abandoned. *See United States v. Ball,* 22 F.3d 197 (8th Cir.1994). Specifically, in *Ball,* defendants who had been convicted of entering a bank with intent to commit robbery, in violation of 18 U.S.C. § 2113(a), argued that the district court erred by refusing "an instruction on a defense theory: that, even had the defendants entered the bank with intent to commit a robbery, they subsequently abandoned or withdrew from their intention when they left the bank without pointing a gun or announcing a stick-up." *Id.* at 199. We held that the abandonment defense did not apply because the crime had been completed once the defendants entered the bank. *Id.*

Because our circuit has already determined that the abandonment defense: (1) can apply to uncompleted attempt crimes, *see Joyce,* 693 F.2d at 841–42, and (2) has been rejected as a defense to completed crimes other than attempt, *see Ball,* 22 F.3d at 199, logically flowing from this analysis is the conclusion that, when a defendant has completed the crime of attempt; i.e., has the requisite intent and has taken a substantial step towards completion of the crime, he cannot successfully abandon the attempt because the crime itself has already been completed. We therefore adopt the Sixth Circuit's approach in *Shelton,* specifically reject the Model Penal Code approach, and hold that the defense of abandonment is not warranted once a defendant completes the crime of attempt. We acknowledge, that "[a]fter a defendant has evidenced the necessary intent and has committed an act constituting a substantial step toward the commission of the offense, he has committed the crime of attempt, and can withdraw only from the commission of the substantive offense," not the attempt of such offense. *Shelton,* 30 F.3d at 706.

As discussed above, Young completed his attempt because he had the requisite intent and took a substantial step towards completion of the enticement crime, all supported by the evidence discovered in his car, his travel to the hotel and attempt to check in, and his search for Emily once he could not obtain the hotel room. Because Young completed "the essential elements" of his attempt, *Shelton,* 30 F.3d at 706, he cannot now claim that he abandoned that plan. We therefore conclude that the district court committed no error in its decision to refuse Young's proffered abandonment instruction.

EXERCISE

Imagine that the key overt act by the defendant alleged by the government in *Young* was his paying for a motel room with his credit card. You represent the defendant.

Now imagine the following alternative scenario. It turns out that the defendant reserved the motel room using a credit card. He was not billed at that time. On the day he was to meet the victim, the defendant changed his mind at the last minute. In the motel parking lot, he turns around and goes home. However, since he did not cancel his guaranteed reservation, his credit card is charged for the unused room. Do you think he should be able to get an instruction on withdrawal in the Eighth Circuit? Does he need one?

As with other criminal law topics, conspiracy complicates the question of withdrawal. To withdraw from a conspiracy, it often requires an affirmative act rather than simply backing away. That makes withdrawal a difficult defense in conspiracy cases.

UNITED STATES V. MALONEY
71 F.3d 645 (7th Cir. 1995)

ESCHBACH, CIRCUIT JUDGE.

This is yet another in an unfortunately long line of public corruption cases which have left a blot on the escutcheon of Chicago justice. Thomas J. Maloney, a former judge in the Circuit Court of Cook County, appeals from his conviction on charges of racketeering conspiracy, racketeering, extortion under color of official right, and obstruction of justice, in violation of 18 U.S.C. §§ 1962(d), 1962(c), 1951, and 1503, respectively, in connection with his taking bribes in cases before him. Among his many grounds for appeal, Maloney contends that he should have been granted a new trial due to the government's failure to disclose improper benefits bestowed upon two "El Rukn" witnesses. The district court denied Maloney's motion, finding that further impeachment of these witnesses would not have changed the outcome. We affirm.

I.

Thomas Maloney assumed his position on the bench in 1977 and remained there until his retirement in 1990. According to the jury's findings, during that time he took bribes and agreed to "fix" four cases, including three murder cases, and obstructed justice in relation to the investigation of these bribes. Generally, these bribes were accomplished through the use of a "bagman," or intermediary between the lawyer desiring the fix and the judge. Maloney used a bailiff, Lucius Robinson, as his bagman until Robinson's reputation became a liability during the "Greylord" investigation of Chicago judges. Maloney then switched to Robert McGee, who practiced law with Maloney from 1973 until 1977. . . .

The final bribe charged in the indictment took place a few years later. In June 1985, Earl Hawkins and Nathan Fields, members of the El Rukns, were charged with murdering two men. Judge Maloney was assigned the case and Swano represented Hawkins. Swano assured Hawkins that he could win a decision in his favor in a bench trial if Hawkins could raise enough money for the Judge. Hawkins referred him to Alan Knox, a "senior" El Rukn general, who approved the fix. Swano testified that he met with McGee in January or February of 1986 to discuss the fix and they arrived at a figure of $10,000. According to Swano, McGee talked with Maloney and confirmed the figure, but McGee told Swano that the fix was conditional upon Swano putting on a "a good case" so Judge Maloney would not look bad. Swano then informed the El Rukns that the bribe was on, although he padded the figure to $20,000 to ensure some money for himself. He had some difficulty, however, collecting the bribe money from the El Rukns. Finally, the morning of trial, surveillance records indicate Swano left court and went to the El Rukn headquarters to get the money, and that Knox later arrived at the courthouse with a bulge in his pocket which appeared to be a roll of bills. Swano called McGee to confirm the fix and gave him a file folder with the money at the Mayor's Row restaurant. The case proceeded to a bench trial. On June 17th and 18th, the State put on its case where three eyewitnesses identified Hawkins as the murderer.

By this time, the FBI had become suspicious of Judge Maloney and Hawkins/Fields case, and its agents were watching the trial closely. This attention, coupled with the strength of the State's case, prompted Judge Maloney to have second thoughts. Thus, McGee called Swano at 11:23 a.m. on June 19th in the anteroom outside Judge Maloney's chambers to inform him that he needed to "give the books back that he had given him the other day." Swano, hoping to salvage the fix, told McGee to "hold onto the books" at least until the defense could put on its case. According to Hawkins' testimony, Swano came back from the Judge's chambers and told him that Judge Maloney had returned the bribe money. Swano testified, however, that he had in fact persuaded McGee to talk to Judge Maloney about continuing the fix and was, at least temporarily, successful. Swano also testified that he confirmed the existence of the fix with Judge Maloney himself on two occasions. By the end of trial on June 26th, though, Judge Maloney apparently believed that Swano had not lived up to his end of the bargain by putting on a good defense case. McGee called Swano on the evening of the 26th to inform him the fix was off. The next morning Maloney told Swano that a lawyer had left a file for him in his chambers and directed a deputy sheriff to retrieve it. When Swano went to the Judge's chambers, Maloney handed Swano the file of money he had passed to McGee at the start of the trial. Hawkins and Fields were found guilty by the Judge and subsequently sentenced to death. . . .

Maloney asserts that the district court erroneously refused to read his withdrawal instruction despite the evidence that the Hawkins bribe was returned. . . .

In making this determination, we must remember that withdrawal requires an affirmative act on the part of the conspirator. He must either confess to authorities, or "communicate to each of his conspirators that he has abandoned the conspiracy and its goals." *United States v. Sax,* 39 F.3d 1380, 1386 (7th Cir.1994). Mere inactivity is not sufficient; the conspirator must "affirmatively renounce[ ] the goals of the criminal enterprise," *United States v. DePriest,* 6 F.3d 1201, 1206 (7th Cir.1993), by taking steps to "defeat or disavow the conspiracy's purpose." *Sax,* 39 F.3d at 1386.

Maloney asserts that the return of the Hawkins bribe was an affirmative act inconsistent with the conspiracy's purpose. This, however, ignores the conditional nature of the bribe and the circumstances surrounding it. Many indictments and convictions of judges had already occurred at this time as a result of the Greylord investigation. According to Swano, McGee told him that Judge Maloney agreed to accept the $10,000 bribe conditional upon Swano putting on "a good [defense] case." (Tr. 2571). Swano elaborated on what the members of the conspiracy understood this to mean in the instant case:

> The judge was worried about looking bad on a serious double-murder case like this. And I had to have the witnesses together and I had to do the case the way I described it to him; that the state had a weak identification case; that we had nullified Sumner and that we had, in fact, the eyewitnesses that would contradict the testimony of the state's witnesses. (Tr. 2571).

Swano emphasized "it wasn't a hundred percent guarantee. We had to put on a good defense." (Tr. 2586). This is what he told the El Rukns when he explained the fix to them. Thus, when McGee called to end the fix, he explained that "the State witnesses were too good, and the case was going too good for the State." (Tr. 2669). Several witnesses testified that the presence of FBI agents in the building and the courtroom during Hawkins' trial was obvious and a clear indication that the case was being closely monitored for a possible fix. Thus, the threshold standard for the appearance of propriety was raised. When Swano failed to effectively rebut the state's case, the fix was called off for good. According to Hawkins, Swano explained that "the case was too hot and he didn't want to go through with it no more . . . that somebody had leaked it—somebody in the organization had leaked it to the FBI." (Tr. 1559–60). There was no evidence introduced that Maloney would be unreceptive to future bribes; the only evidence at all on the matter revealed merely that this bribe under these circumstances did not comport with the conspiracy's objectives and criteria for the fixing of cases. Maloney's return of the bribe was therefore more akin to a deal gone sour than an affirmative attempt to defeat the purposes of the conspiracy. In *United States v. Pofahl,* 990 F.2d 1456, 1484 (5th Cir.), *cert. denied,* 510 U.S. 898, 114 S.Ct. 266, 126 L.Ed.2d 218 *and cert. denied,* 510 U.S. 996, 114 S.Ct. 560, 126 L.Ed.2d 460 (1993), a conspirator was scheduled to go to Guatemala to help arrange a shipment of drugs. After learning that a co-conspirator had been arrested, the conspirator canceled his scheduled trip. He argued that this was an affirmative act to withdraw from the conspiracy. The court disagreed, holding that "Nunn's decision to cancel his trip to Guatemala in the face of possible arrest is hardly an affirmative action to defeat the conspiracy." *Id.* It was an attempt to evade detection by canceling an act which was supposed to be in furtherance of the conspiracy, but this cannot equate to a withdrawal. By the same token Maloney may have canceled a bribe intended to be in furtherance of the RICO and extortion conspiracies, but this did not withdraw him from those conspiracies.

Maloney counters that the absence of any evidence of bribes after the return of the Hawkins bribe confirms that this was intended to signal a withdrawal. He admits that the inactivity itself cannot signal a withdrawal, *see, Sax,* 39 F.3d at 1386, but argues that it evidences his intent to withdraw when the bribe was returned. This ignores the intermittent character of the conspiracy. After the Greylord investigation became public knowledge in 1983, the conspirators waited almost three years before attempting another bribe. As long as Judge Maloney remained on the bench, "the central criminal purpose" of the conspiracy, to fix cases whenever feasible, had not yet ended or been accomplished. *United States v. McKinney,* 954 F.2d 471, 475 (7th Cir.), *cert. denied,* 506 U.S. 1023, 113 S.Ct. 662, 121 L.Ed.2d 587 (1992).... Thus, it was not error to deny Maloney's proposed withdrawal instruction.

EXERCISE

The *Maloney* opinion reflects the common view that in a conspiracy case the defense of withdrawal requires much more than passive inactivity—that, in fact, the defense must be predicated on either a confession to the authorities or a statement of renunciation to all of the others involved. One might think it unlikely that a prosecutor would ever seek to charge someone who had done one or both of those things.

Imagine a case where a co-conspirator, Roberto, foiled a counterfeiting scheme by informing the police that his colleagues were printing up counterfeit bills. Because of Roberto's tip, authorities were able to arrest all of the co-conspirators before any counterfeit bills hit the street.

Why might a prosecutor want to charge Roberto?

D. DURESS

The defense of duress rests on the assertion that one was forced to commit a criminal act by another through threat of death or injury. As described in the dissent in the case below, duress will generally excuse criminal conduct only if (1) a threat of imminent death or serious bodily injury led the defendant to commit the crime, (2) the defendant had no reasonable, legal alternative to breaking the law, and (3) the defendant was not responsible for creating the threat.[1]

But who bears the burden? Is this an affirmative defense that requires the defendant to present evidence?

DIXON V. UNITED STATES
548 U.S. 1 (2006)

JUSTICE STEVENS delivered the opinion of the Court.

In January 2003, petitioner Keshia Dixon purchased multiple firearms at two gun shows, during the course of which she provided an incorrect address and falsely stated that she was not under indictment for a felony. As a result of these illegal acts, petitioner was indicted and convicted on one count of receiving a firearm while under indictment in violation of 18 U.S.C. § 922(n) and eight counts of making false statements in connection with the acquisition of a firearm in violation of § 922(a)(6). At trial, petitioner admitted that she knew she was under indictment when she made the purchases and that she knew doing so was a crime; her defense was that she acted under duress because her boyfriend threatened to kill her or hurt her daughters if she did not buy the guns for him.

Petitioner contends that the trial judge's instructions to the jury erroneously required her to prove duress by a preponderance of the evidence instead of requiring the Government to prove beyond a reasonable doubt that she did not act under duress. The Court of Appeals rejected petitioner's contention, 413 F.3d 520 (C.A.5 2005); given contrary treatment of the issue by other federal courts, we granted certiorari, 546 U.S. 1135, 126 S.Ct. 1139, 163 L.Ed.2d 943 (2006).

I

At trial, in her request for jury instructions on her defense of duress, petitioner contended that she "should have the burden of production, and then that the Government should be required to disprove beyond a reasonable doubt the duress." App. 300. Petitioner admitted that this request was contrary to Fifth Circuit precedent, and the trial court, correctly finding itself bound by Circuit precedent, denied petitioner's request. *Ibid.* Instead, the judge's instructions to the jury defined the elements of the duress defense and stated that petitioner has "the burden of proof to establish the defense of duress by a preponderance of the evidence." *Id.,* at 312.

Petitioner argues here, as she did in the District Court and the Court of Appeals, that federal law requires the Government to bear the burden of disproving her defense beyond a reasonable doubt and that the trial court's erroneous instruction on this point entitles her to a new trial. There are

---

[1]   United States v. Bailey, 444 U.S. 394, 409–410 (1980).

two aspects to petitioner's argument in support of her proposed instruction that merit separate discussion. First, petitioner contends that her defense "controverted the *mens rea* required for conviction" and therefore that the Due Process Clause requires the Government to retain the burden of persuasion on that element. Brief for Petitioner 41. Second, petitioner argues that the Fifth Circuit's rule is "contrary to modern common law." *Id.*, at 14.

II

The crimes for which petitioner was convicted require that she have acted "knowingly," § 922(a)(6), or "willfully," § 924(a)(1)(D). As we have explained, "unless the text of the statute dictates a different result, the term 'knowingly' merely requires proof of knowledge of the facts that constitute the offense." *Bryan v. United States,* 524 U.S. 184, 193, 118 S.Ct. 1939, 141 L.Ed.2d 197 (1998)(footnote omitted). And the term "willfully" in § 924(a)(1)(D) requires a defendant to have "acted with knowledge that his conduct was unlawful." *Ibid.* In this case, then, the Government bore the burden of proving beyond a reasonable doubt that petitioner knew she was making false statements in connection with the acquisition of firearms and that she knew she was breaking the law when she acquired a firearm while under indictment. See *In re Winship,* 397 U.S. 358, 364, 90 S.Ct. 1068, 25 L.Ed.2d 368 (1970). Although the Government may have proved these elements in other ways, it clearly met its burden when petitioner testified that she knowingly committed certain acts—she put a false address on the forms she completed to purchase the firearms, falsely claimed that she was the actual buyer of the firearms, and falsely stated that she was not under indictment at the time of the purchase—and when she testified that she knew she was breaking the law when, as an individual under indictment at the time, she purchased a firearm. App. 221–222.

Petitioner contends, however, that she cannot have formed the necessary *mens rea* for these crimes because she did not freely choose to commit the acts in question. But even if we assume that petitioner's will was overborne by the threats made against her and her daughters, she still *knew* that she was making false statements and *knew* that she was breaking the law by buying a firearm. The duress defense, like the defense of necessity that we considered in *United States v. Bailey,* 444 U.S. 394, 409–410, 100 S.Ct. 624, 62 L.Ed.2d 575 (1980), may excuse conduct that would otherwise be punishable, but the existence of duress normally does not controvert any of the elements of the offense itself. As we explained in *Bailey,* "[c]riminal liability is normally based upon the concurrence of two factors, 'an evil-meaning mind [and] and evil-doing hand . . . .' " *Id.*, at 402, 100 S.Ct. 624 (quoting *Morissette v. United States,* 342 U.S. 246, 251, 72 S.Ct. 240, 96 L.Ed. 288 (1952)). Like the defense of necessity, the defense of duress does not negate a defendant's criminal state of mind when the applicable offense requires a defendant to have acted knowingly or willfully; instead, it allows the defendant to "avoid liability . . . because coercive conditions or necessity negates a conclusion of guilt even though the necessary *mens rea* was present." *Bailey,* 444 U.S., at 402, 100 S.Ct. 624.

The fact that petitioner's crimes are statutory offenses that have no counterpart in the common law also supports our conclusion that her duress defense in no way disproves an element of those crimes. We have observed that "[t]he definition of the elements of a criminal offense is entrusted to the legislature, particularly in the case of federal crimes, which are solely creatures of statute." *Liparota v. United States,* 471 U.S. 419, 424, 105 S.Ct. 2084, 85 L.Ed.2d 434 (1985). Here, consistent with the movement away from the traditional dichotomy of general versus specific intent and toward a more specifically defined hierarchy of culpable mental states, see *Bailey,* 444 U.S., at 403–404, 100 S.Ct. 624, Congress defined the crimes at issue to punish defendants who act "knowingly," § 922(a)(6), or "willfully," § 924(a)(1)(D). It is these specific mental states, rather than some vague "evil mind," Brief for Petitioner 42, or " 'criminal' intent," *Martin v. Ohio,* 480 U.S. 228, 235, 107 S.Ct. 1098, 94 L.Ed.2d 267 (1987), that the Government is required to prove beyond a reasonable doubt, see *Patterson v. New York,* 432 U.S. 197, 211, n. 12, 97 S.Ct. 2319, 53 L.Ed.2d 281 (1977) ("The applicability of the reasonable-doubt standard, however, has always been dependent on how a State defines the offense that is charged in any given case"). The jury instructions in this case were consistent with this requirement and, as such, did not run afoul of the Due Process Clause when they placed the burden on petitioner to establish the existence of duress by a preponderance of the evidence.

III

Having found no constitutional basis for placing upon the Government the burden of disproving petitioner's duress defense beyond a reasonable doubt, we next address petitioner's argument that the modern common law requires the Government to bear that burden. In making this argument, petitioner recognizes that, until the end of the 19th century, common-law courts generally adhered to the rule that "the proponent of an issue bears the burden of persuasion on the factual premises for applying the rule." Fletcher, Two Kinds of Legal Rules: A Comparative Study of Burden-of-Persuasion Practices in Criminal Cases, 77 Yale L.J. 880, 898 (1967–1968). In petitioner's view, however, two important developments have established a contrary common-law rule that now prevails in federal courts: this Court's decision in *Davis v. United States,* 160 U.S. 469, 16 S.Ct. 353, 40 L.Ed. 499 (1895), which placed the burden on the Government to prove a defendant's sanity, and the publication of the Model Penal Code in 1962.

Although undisputed in this case, it bears repeating that, at common law, the burden of proving "affirmative defenses—indeed, 'all . . . circumstances of justification, excuse or alleviation'—rested on the defendant." *Patterson,*

432 U.S., at 202, 97 S.Ct. 2319 (quoting 4 W. Blackstone, Commentaries *201); see also *Martin v. Ohio,* 480 U.S., at 235, 107 S.Ct. 1098; *Mullaney v. Wilbur,* 421 U.S. 684, 693, 95 S.Ct. 1881, 44 L.Ed.2d 508 (1975). This common-law rule accords with the general evidentiary rule that "the burdens of producing evidence and of persuasion with regard to any given issue are both generally allocated to the same party." 2 J. Strong, McCormick on Evidence § 337, p. 415 (5th ed. 1999). And, in the context of the defense of duress, it accords with the doctrine that "where the facts with regard to an issue lie peculiarly in the knowledge of a party, that party has the burden of proving the issue." *Id.,* at 413. Although she claims that the common-law rule placing the burden on a defendant to prove the existence of duress "was the product of flawed reasoning," petitioner accepts that this was the general rule, at least until this Court's decision in *Davis.* Brief for Petitioner 18. According to petitioner, however, *Davis* initiated a revolution that overthrew the old common-law rule and established her proposed rule in its place.

Davis itself, however, does not support petitioner's position. . . .

. . . petitioner's reliance on *Davis* ignores the fact that federal crimes "are solely creatures of statute," *Liparota,* 471 U.S., at 424, 105 S.Ct. 2084, and therefore that we are required to effectuate the duress defense as Congress "may have contemplated" it in the context of these specific offenses. . . . Assuming that a defense of duress is available to the statutory crimes at issue, then, we must determine what that defense would look like as Congress "may have contemplated" it.

As discussed above, the common law long required the defendant to bear the burden of proving the existence of duress. Similarly, even where Congress has enacted an affirmative defense in the proviso of a statute, the "settled rule in this jurisdiction [is] that an indictment or other pleading . . . need not negative the matter of an exception made by a proviso or other distinct clause . . . and that it is incumbent on one who relies on such an exception to set it up and establish it." *McKelvey v. United States,* 260 U.S. 353, 357, 43 S.Ct. 132, 67 L.Ed. 301 (1922); see also *United States v. Dickson,* 15 Pet. 141, 165, 10 L.Ed. 689 (1841) (calling this "the general rule of law which has always prevailed, and become consecrated almost as a maxim in the interpretation of statutes"). Even though the Safe Streets Act does not mention the defense of duress, we can safely assume that the 1968 Congress was familiar with both the long-established common-law rule and the rule applied in *McKelvey* and that it would have expected federal courts to apply a similar approach to any affirmative defense that might be asserted as a justification or excuse for violating the new law.

This conclusion is surely more reasonable than petitioner's hypothesis that *Davis* dramatically upset a well-settled rule of law. Petitioner cites only one federal case decided before 1968 for the proposition that it has been well established in federal law that the Government bears the burden of disproving duress beyond a reasonable doubt. But that case involved a defendant's claim that he "lacked the specific intent to defraud required by the statute for the reason that he committed the offense under duress and coercion." *Johnson v. United States,* 291 F.2d 150, 152 (C.A.8 1961). Thus, when the Court of Appeals explained that "there is no burden upon the defendant to prove his defense of coercion," *id.,* at 155, that statement is best understood in context as a corollary to the by-then-unremarkable proposition that "the burden of proof rests upon the Government to prove the defendant's guilt beyond a reasonable doubt," *ibid.* Properly understood, *Johnson* provides petitioner little help in her uphill struggle to prove that a dramatic shift in the federal common-law rule occurred between *Davis* and the enactment of the Safe Streets Act in 1968.

Indeed, for us to be able to accept petitioner's proposition, we would need to find an overwhelming consensus among federal courts that it is the Government's burden to disprove the existence of duress beyond a reasonable doubt. The existence today of disagreement among the Federal Courts of Appeals on this issue, however—the very disagreement that caused us to grant certiorari in this case, see n. 1, *supra*—demonstrates that no such consensus has ever existed. See also *post,* at 2452–2453 (BREYER, J., dissenting) (discussing differences in treatment of the duress defense by the various Courts of Appeals). Also undermining petitioner's argument is the fact that, in 1970, the National Commission on Reform of Federal Criminal Laws proposed that a defendant prove the existence of duress by a preponderance of the evidence. See 1 Working Papers 278. Moreover, while there seem to be few, if any, post-*Davis,* pre-1968 cases placing the burden on a defendant to prove the existence of duress, or even discussing the issue in any way, this lack of evidence does not help petitioner. The long-established common-law rule is that the burden of proving duress rests on the defendant. Petitioner hypothesizes that *Davis* fomented a revolution upsetting this rule. If this were true, one would expect to find cases discussing the matter. But no such cases exist.

It is for a similar reason that we give no weight to the publication of the Model Penal Code in 1962. As petitioner notes, the Code would place the burden on the government to disprove the existence of duress beyond a reasonable doubt. See ALI, Model Penal Code § 1.12, p. 88 (2001) (hereinafter Model Penal Code or Code) (stating that each element of an offense must be proved beyond a reasonable doubt); § 1.13(9)(c), at 91 (defining as an element anything that negatives an excuse for the conduct at issue); § 2.09, at 131–132 (establishing affirmative defense of duress). Petitioner argues that the Code reflects "well established" federal law as it existed at the time. Brief for Petitioner 25. But, as discussed above, no such consensus existed when Congress passed the Safe Streets Act in 1968. And even if we assume Congress' familiarity with the Code and the rule it would establish, there is no evidence that Congress endorsed the Code's views or incorporated them into the Safe Streets Act.

In fact, the Act itself provides evidence to the contrary. Despite the Code's careful delineation of mental states, see Model Penal Code § 2.02, at 94–95, the Safe Streets Act attached no explicit *mens rea* requirement to the crime of receiving a firearm while under indictment, § 924(a), 82 Stat. 233 ("Whoever violates any provision of this chapter . . . shall be fined not more than $5,000 or imprisoned not more than five years, or both"). And when Congress amended the Act to impose a *mens rea* requirement, it punished people who "willfully" violate the statute, see § 104(a), 100 Stat. 456, a mental state that has not been embraced by the Code, see Model Penal Code § 2.02(2), at 94–95 (defining "purposely," "knowingly," "recklessly," and "negligently"); *id.,* Explanatory Note, at 97 ("Though the term 'wilfully' is not used in the definitions of crimes contained in the Code, its currency and its existence in offenses outside the criminal code suggest the desirability of clarification"). Had Congress intended to adopt the Code's structure when it enacted or amended the Safe Streets Act, one would expect the Act's form and language to adhere much more closely to that used by the Code. It does not, and, for that reason, we cannot rely on the Model Penal Code to provide evidence as to how Congress would have wanted us to effectuate the duress defense in this context.

IV

Congress can, if it chooses, enact a duress defense that places the burden on the Government to disprove duress beyond a reasonable doubt. In light of Congress' silence on the issue, however, it is up to the federal courts to effectuate the affirmative defense of duress as Congress "may have contemplated" it in an offense-specific context. *Oakland Cannabis Buyers' Cooperative,* 532 U.S., at 491, n. 3, 121 S.Ct. 1711 (internal quotation marks omitted). In the context of the firearms offenses at issue—as will usually be the case, given the long-established common-law rule—we presume that Congress intended the petitioner to bear the burden of proving the defense of duress by a preponderance of the evidence. Accordingly, the judgment of the Court of Appeals is affirmed. . . .

JUSTICE BREYER, with whom JUSTICE SOUTER joins, dissenting.

Courts have long recognized that "duress" constitutes a defense to a criminal charge. Historically, that defense "excuse[d] criminal conduct" if (1) a "threat of imminent death or serious bodily injury" led the defendant to commit the crime, (2) the defendant had no reasonable, legal alternative to breaking the law, and (3) the defendant was not responsible for creating the threat. *United States v. Bailey,* 444 U.S. 394, 409–410, 100 S.Ct. 624, 62 L.Ed.2d 575 (1980); see also 2 W. LaFave, Substantive Criminal Law § 9.7(b), pp. 74–82 (2003) (hereinafter LaFave); *ante,* at 2440, n. 1 (opinion of the Court). The Court decides today in respect to *federal* crimes that the defense must bear the burden of both producing evidence of duress and persuading the jury. I agree with the majority that the burden of production lies on the defendant, that here the burden of persuasion issue is not constitutional, and that Congress may allocate that burden as it sees fit. But I also believe that, in the absence of any indication of a different congressional intent, the burden of persuading the jury beyond a reasonable doubt should lie where such burdens normally lie in criminal cases, upon the prosecution.

EXERCISE

Imagine you are a defense attorney in federal court. The case above is binding precedent. Your client is Robert Munger, who is accused of illegally entering a military facility. Specifically, he rammed his car through a locked gate in a security fence at a Department of Energy facility where nuclear materials were kept. Shortly after he burst through the fence he ran into a security pole that disabled his car. At the time there was another man in his car, identified as Louis Therot. Therot was not charged and has since left the country and cannot be located or reached.

Your client claims that he drove into the facility under duress. He says had picked up Therot as a hitchhiker as he drove by the facility. As they drove, Therot found a gun that Munger kept under the car seat. Munger knew that the gun was loaded (it was his gun, after all). Therot insisted that Munger get out of the car and give him the keys. Munger tried to grab the gun away from Therot and as they struggled he drove through the gate by accident. At the time of the incident, police did find a loaded gun under the car seat.

Your client wants you to pursue a defense of duress. Is it worthwhile to do so?

E. NECESSITY

If duress goes to whether an action was voluntary or not, the defense of necessity is aimed at whether the action is wrong in the first place. In short, the defense of necessity usually is available where a defendant can make a strong case that she avoided a greater evil by committing the crime she is charged with. Some would consider the assertion of self-defense (which we studied in the section on homicide) a variation on the defense of necessity.

As with duress, necessity is often formulated as an affirmative defense that must be proven by a preponderance by the defendant. Also like duress, this will often require that the defense bring in significant evidence.

UNITED STATES V. RIDNER
512 F.3d 846 (6th Cir. 2008)

MERRITT, CIRCUIT JUDGE.

The defendant, Scotty Ridner, appeals the district court's *in limine* ruling that denied him the opportunity to present a necessity defense at trial to charges of being a felon-in-possession of ammunition. As a result of the adverse ruling, Ridner entered into a conditional guilty plea, reserving his right to appeal the court's order precluding the necessity defense. We are constrained to hold that the district court's pre-trial order preventing a criminal defendant from asserting a defense at trial is proper according to this Circuit's precedent although we note that the issue has never been addressed by the Supreme Court. The district court held that the defendant failed to establish a *prima facie* case of necessity pursuant to the five-factor test set forth in *United States v. Singleton,* 902 F.2d 471, 472 (6th Cir.1990). Because we agree that the defendant has failed to present evidence to satisfy two of the *Singleton* factors, we affirm the district court's opinion.

On July 29, 2003, the McCreary County Sheriff's Office and the Kentucky State Police approached the home of Ella Mae Goodin in search of Scotty Ridner. Ella Mae Goodin is the ex-wife of Scotty's brother, Freddy Ridner. Prior to the officers' arrival, Freddy and Scotty were sitting on the front porch. Upon seeing the approaching officers, Scotty ran through the residence and exited the back door. Because the officers had an active arrest warrant for Scotty, they chased him and eventually apprehended him a short distance from the home. The officers proceeded to search Scotty and found him in possession of three rounds of shotgun ammunition. One of the officers escorted Scotty to a patrol car while the others returned to Ella Mae Goodin's residence to conduct a search of the premises. Within the home, they found a 12-gauge shotgun under the sofa.

Prior to this event, Scotty's criminal record included three violent felonies as defined in 18 U.S.C. § 924(e)(2)(B). On April 21, 2004, a grand injury indicted Scotty Ridner for being a convicted felon in possession of a 12-gauge shotgun and three rounds of 12-gauge ammunition in violation of 18 U.S.C. §§ 922(g)(1) and 924(e)(1). In anticipation of trial, the United States filed a motion *in limine* to prevent the defendant from producing any testimony or evidence that related to a necessity defense. Specifically, Ridner proposed to argue that he was only carrying ammunition to keep it away from his brother who was allegedly acting suicidal the morning of the arrest. The district court conducted a hearing on this motion on March 1, 2006, at which only Scotty Ridner testified. His version of events is as follows: He spent the night prior to the arrest at his niece's trailer, which is proximately located to Ella Mae Goodin's home. Shortly after he awoke in the morning, Freddy Ridner and Ella Mae Goodin walked down to the niece's home and asked Scotty to walk to their home with them. During this walk, Ms. Goodin allegedly told Scotty that Freddy "was acting funny again, talking crazy" which traditionally meant, according to Scotty, that Freddy is "talking suicide" or "fixing to take a seizure." Joint Appendix (JA) at 112. Upon reaching the home, Scotty and Freddy decided to sit on the front porch. Freddy went into the house and returned with a cup of coffee and three shotgun shells. While sitting on the porch, the two brothers allegedly discussed Freddy's desire to retrieve his gun from a pawnshop. Further, Scotty testified that Freddy "was talking that morning that he was going to kill hisself [sic]. He said he would be better off dead than having to live like he was." J.A. at 113. When Ms. Goodin brought Freddy another cup of coffee, he dropped the shells while switching hands. Scotty maintains that he picked up the shells and put them in his pocket "just a few minutes" before the officers arrived. J.A. at 113. To justify picking up the shells, Scotty testified that his brother Graylan shot and killed himself in 1992 in front of Scotty and that Freddy had attempted suicide, also with a gun, "a few years before." J.A. at 111, 114. He further testified that Freddy was in better spirits by the time the police arrived because Scotty had given him cigarettes. After the police arrived, Scotty ran through the front door and out the back with the shells in his pocket. Scotty admitted that he did not know of any gun located in the house on that particular day and that his primary concern was that his brother would attempt to retrieve the gun from the pawnshop, which he thought might be a 12-gauge shotgun.

Whether or not a defendant has established a *prima facie* case of necessity is a question of law which this Court reviews *de novo*. *United States v. Johnson*, 416 F.3d 464, 468 (6th Cir.2005).

A defendant charged with being a felon-in-possession of a firearm may assert the necessity defense. *United States v. Singleton*, 902 F.2d 471, 472 (6th Cir.1990) (explaining that even though the statute under which the defendant is charged does not provide an affirmative defense of justification, the defense still exists under common law). In essence, a "necessity defense, like other justification defenses, allows a defendant to escape responsibility despite proof that his actions encompassed all the elements of a criminal offense." *United States v. Maxwell*, 254 F.3d 21, 27 (1st Cir.2001). This defense is limited to rare situations and should be "construed very narrowly." *Singleton*, 902 F.2d at 472. The Seventh Circuit, when analyzing this defense under similar facts, concluded "[t]he defense of necessity will rarely lie in a felon-in-possession case unless the ex-felon, not being engaged in criminal activity, does nothing more than grab a gun with which he or another is being threatened (the other might be the possessor of the gun, threatening suicide)." *United States v. Perez*, 86 F.3d 735, 737 (7th Cir.1996). When the issue arises in a pre-trial motion, as opposed to a court's refusal to give an accurate jury instruction, the rule is the same: the defendant must proffer evidence that is legally sufficient to support the defense. *Johnson*, 416 F.3d. at 468. The defendant's preliminary burden is "not a heavy one" and is met even where there is "weak supporting evidence." *United States v. Riffe,* 28 F.3d 565, 569 (6th Cir.1994). Further, the trial judge's duty is to require a *prima facie* showing by the defendant on each of the elements of the defense. *Johnson,* 416 F.3d at 467–68 ("Where 'an affirmative defense consists of several elements and testimony supporting one element is insufficient to sustain it even if believed, the trial court and jury need not be burdened with testimony supporting other elements of the defense.'") (quoting *United States v. Bailey,* 444 U.S. 394, 416, 100 S.Ct. 624, 62 L.Ed.2d 575 (1980)).

In *Singleton,* the Sixth Circuit adopted a five-factor test to determine when a defendant is entitled to a jury instruction presenting the necessity defense. 902 F.2d at 472–73. The court emphasized that "the keystone of the analysis is that the defendant must have no alternative—either before or during the event—to avoid violating the law." *Id.* at 473 (citing *United States v. Bailey,* 444 U.S. 394, 410, 100 S.Ct. 624, 62 L.Ed.2d 575 (1980)). Instructions on the defense are proper if the defendant produces evidence upon which a reasonable jury could conclude by a preponderance of the evidence that each of the following five requirements is met:

> (1) that defendant was under an unlawful and present, imminent, and impending threat of such a nature as to induce a well-grounded apprehension of death or serious bodily injury;

> (2) that defendant had not recklessly or negligently placed himself in a situation in which it was probable that he would be forced to choose the criminal conduct;

> (3) that defendant had no reasonable, legal alternative to violating the law, a chance both to refuse to do the criminal act and also to avoid the threatened harm;

> (4) that a direct causal relationship may be reasonably anticipated between the criminal action taken and the avoidance of the threatened harm; . . . and

> (5) [that the defendant] did not maintain the illegal conduct any longer than absolutely necessary.

United States v. Newcomb, 6 F.3d 1129, 1134–35 (6th Cir.1993) (quotations omitted) (citing *Singleton,* 902 F.2d at 472–73).

The district court found that the defendant failed to produce sufficient evidence to satisfy the first and fifth *Singleton* requirements. Although the first criterion is phrased in terms of harm to the defendant himself, this Circuit also applies the necessity defense when "a defendant is acting out of a desire to prevent harm to a third party." *Newcomb,* 6 F.3d at 1136. Under the first element, the defendant must be under an "unlawful and present, *imminent,* and impending threat of such a nature as to induce a well-grounded apprehension of death or serious bodily injury." *Id.* at 1134.

(emphasis added). The district court held that the defendant failed to meet this requirement because it found that no reasonable jury could conclude that Scotty or his brother had a well-grounded fear of death or serious injury. The court reached this conclusion after focusing on the parts of Scotty's testimony wherein he indicated that he was unaware if any guns were present in Freddy's house and that he did not believe there was a gun located on the premises. Therefore, the closest gun that Scotty knew about at the time of the incident was at the nearby pawn shop. The court determined that the time it would take Freddy to retrieve a gun to use the ammunition vitiated the immediacy of the threat. Further, the court cited the Sixth Circuit case, *United States v. Hargrove,* 416 F.3d 486 (6th Cir.2005), for the proposition that Scotty had to demonstrate that his brother was in immediate danger, not just that his brother might contemplate committing suicide in the future. In *Hargrove,* the defendant testified that he carried a firearm solely for his own protection after he was robbed. 416 F.3d at 489. He further testified that on the morning of his arrest a man threatened him but did not follow him when he drove away in his vehicle. *Id.* The court found that the circumstances fell short of constituting a "present, imminent, and impending [threat]" because the defendant could only support his defense with "speculation and conjecture" that did not reveal any immediate threat to his life. *Id.* The logical connection between these two cases is clear: the legitimacy and nature of the threat cannot compensate for the lack of immediacy. Even assuming that Scotty Ridner genuinely believed that Freddy was contemplating suicide, Scotty was unaware of any gun located nearby that Freddy could use to carry out his threat. Consequently, we agree with the district court that the defendant has failed to meet his burden with respect to the first *Singleton* factor.

Scotty also fails to satisfy the fifth factor. It requires the defendant to show that "he did not maintain the illegal conduct any longer than absolutely necessary." *United States v. Newcomb,* 6 F.3d 1129, 1135 (6th Cir.1993). The district court held that Scotty failed to present evidence to satisfy this requirement because he attempted to escape with the ammunition when the police arrived. Although he testified that he only possessed the ammunition for a few minutes before the police arrived, the police chased him for a quarter of a mile before arresting him. Further, Scotty testified that when the police arrived and the shells were in his pocket, Freddy's spirits had picked up and he was laughing. At this point, the court concluded the threat had subsided and Scotty could have handed the ammunition to the police and explained why he had taken possession of it. The Third Circuit analyzed a defendant's escape in the context of a felon-in-possession case in *United States v. Paolello,* 951 F.2d 537 (3d Cir.1991). In *Paolello,* a convicted felon became involved in a confrontation in which he felt threatened. *Id.* at 542. Afraid of being attacked, Paolello knocked the gun out of the other man's hands, picked it up and fled down an alley.

Id. One of the arresting officers testified that he chased the defendant down the alley, ordered him to stop running, and identified himself as a policeman, but the defendant did not stop. *Id.* The court considered the defendant's testimony wherein he explained that he ran because he was afraid that the armed man might send his friends after him and that he responded to the policeman's command as soon as he heard it. *Id.* The court noted that if it believed Paolello's account, then he did not maintain possession any longer than necessary. *Id.* However, the court countered that if Paolello was aware he was being chased by a policeman, "it would severely undercut Paolello's justification defense because it would appear that Paolello had an opportunity to dispose of the gun and stop running earlier than he did, so that he possessed the firearm longer than absolutely necessary." *Id.* The court found that the defendant put forth sufficient evidence to meet the first factor because the issue involved a credibility determination that would be judged by the jury. Under our facts, Scotty Ridner does not contest that he ran from the police officers when they arrived. Further, he does not maintain, as Paolello did, that he was running to escape harm; rather, it is clear that he was running to escape arrest. Scotty had the opportunity to dispose of the ammunition when the police arrived because they could have protected his brother from that moment forward. Consequently, no reasonable jury could find that Scotty did not possess the ammunition longer than absolutely necessary.

For the foregoing reasons, we AFFIRM the judgment of the district court.

EXERCISE

Samuel is deeply concerned with the environment, and convinced that the government is withholding studies that show the specific impact on global warming of certain human activities. He reads one morning in USA Today that a former employee of the federal government has stated that such reports exist and are being hidden by the government.

Because he is a trained hacker, Samuel is able to access a federal agency's databank and retrieve the report. He sends the report to the New York Times, which publishes it to great acclaim. Forced to admit the truth of the information contained in the now-public report, the federal government takes steps to address that factor relating to global warming.

Samuel is charged with unauthorized access to government data (technically, he is charged with using an "access device," a password, without authorization). You represent him, and he wants to press the defense of necessity. How do you advise him?

F. ENTRAPMENT

Entrapment is an affirmative defense that (in the federal system) requires the defendant to show by a preponderance of the evidence that but for police involvement and enticement he would not have committed the crime. An entrapment defense will generally fail if the defendant was predisposed to commit the crime.

UNITED STATES V. MAYFIELD

771 F.3d 417 (7th Cir. 2014)

SYKES, CIRCUIT JUDGE.

Leslie Mayfield was indicted for conspiring with a coworker and a drug courier to rob a stash house controlled by the courier's suppliers. The conspiracy was a setup; the drug courier was an undercover government agent and the coworker was an informant. At his trial Mayfield wanted to present a defense of entrapment, but the government opposed it and moved in limine to preclude the defense, arguing that there wasn't enough evidence to show that the government induced the crime or that Mayfield lacked the predisposition to commit it. Mayfield responded with a narrative of the informant's persistent campaign to secure his participation in the stash-house robbery and his repeated resistance to the scheme. The district court granted the government's motion and barred the defense. The jury, uninstructed on the entrapment issue, convicted Mayfield of several federal crimes stemming from the conspiracy. . . .

Entrapment is a defense to criminal liability when the defendant was not predisposed to commit the charged crime before the intervention of the government's agents and the government's conduct induced him to commit it. The two elements of the defense—lack of predisposition and government inducement—are conceptually related but formally and temporally distinct. We define the two elements here and resolve some conflicting strains in our caselaw about the relationship between them.

Procedurally, the entrapment defense is an issue of fact for the jury. The defendant is entitled to an entrapment jury instruction if he can show that some evidence supports both elements of the defense. When the issue is raised before trial on the government's motion to preclude the defense, the court must accept the defendant's factual proffer as true and not weigh the evidence against the government's counterstatement of the facts.

Here, Mayfield proffered enough evidence to justify giving the issue to the jury. He provided some facts showing that he was not predisposed to commit the charged crimes prior to being approached by the informant, and he narrated a story of substantial government inducement going beyond the mere offer of a chance to rob a stash house. His story may be false or unpersuasive, but that's for the jury to decide. The district court erred by crediting the government's evidence over Mayfield's and precluding the entrapment defense before trial. We vacate the judgment and remand for a new trial.

I. Background

We take the facts from Mayfield's pretrial proffer (most of which was excluded pretrial) and the evidence introduced at trial. Mayfield was convicted of residential burglary in 1987 at age 18 and served time in jail for this crime. In 1994 he was convicted of several violent crimes stemming from an armed carjacking; he received a lengthy prison sentence. While in prison he earned a GED, an associate degree in general studies, and vocational certificates in commercial custodial services and cosmetology. He was released in 2005 and returned home to Waukegan, Illinois, where he participated in the Second Chance Program operated by the Urban League of Lake County, the Waukegan Township Coalition to Reduce Recidivism, and Cease Fire Waukegan.

But not all was well. At some point after his release from prison (we don't know exactly when), Mayfield was charged with unlawful possession of a firearm. That prosecution was still pending when the events in this case took place. In 2008 he moved with his fiancée from Waukegan to Naperville, ostensibly to escape gang violence.

Although jobs for convicted felons were hard to come by, Mayfield managed to find sporadic work. After moving to Naperville, he found a temporary job in nearby Bolingbrook that allowed him to work a 40-hour workweek. He started this new job in late April or early May of 2009 and soon thereafter met Jeffrey Potts, a coworker with whom he had much in common. Potts was also a felon with convictions for drug trafficking, robbery, and gun possession. The two men commiserated about their financial straits, their difficulty finding permanent jobs, and their struggle to support their families. What Mayfield did not know was that his new friend was supplementing his income as a confidential informant for the Bureau of Alcohol, Tobacco, Firearms, and Explosives ("ATF").

As an informant Potts was supposed to identify targets for sting operations and, as in this case, participate in the stings. He selected Mayfield as a target because he knew that Mayfield had a criminal record. What followed, according to Mayfield, was a concerted effort to entrap him into committing a stash-house robbery.

In his first overture to Mayfield, Potts explained that he had returned to selling cocaine and invited Mayfield to join him in the drug trade. Mayfield rebuffed this offer. A few days later Potts learned that Mayfield had a pending gun-possession charge, so he tried another tack. He told Mayfield of a one-time opportunity "that was worth a lot of money." His drug supplier was planning to "stickup" his wholesaler, a robbery that would net tens of thousands of dollars in cocaine. Potts invited Mayfield to participate in the robbery in return for a share of the profits. Mayfield rejected the invitation.

Potts persisted. Each day at work he tried to persuade Mayfield to join the conspiracy by appealing to his concerns about money. He urged Mayfield to think about the financial needs of his family, saying "I know you [are] tired of working for this chump change" and "I know you need this money," among other similar lines of persuasion. Potts also flaunted his expensive Dodge Ram pickup truck, telling Mayfield that he bought it with $40,000 he had "earned" in another drug robbery. Mayfield continued to decline the offers.

On June 25, 2009, Mayfield's car was damaged in an accident. He borrowed money from a family member to have the car towed but did not have enough to pay for the needed repairs. He missed three days of work before he found another way to get to his job in Bolingbrook. When Potts asked him why he had missed work, Mayfield told him about the accident and explained his financial predicament. Potts unexpectedly gave him $180 in cash to pay for the car repairs.

Two days later Potts returned to the subject of the stashhouse robbery, again pressuring Mayfield to join the conspiracy. Mayfield equivocated but did not agree to anything. The following week Potts tried again. When Mayfield continued to resist, Potts gestured to a Gangster Disciples tattoo on Mayfield's arm. The tattoo dated from Mayfield's membership in the street gang before his carjacking conviction; he knew that failure to repay a debt risked harsh punishment from the gang. When Potts said he was still associated with the Gangster Disciples, Mayfield took it as a warning that he would be in danger if he did not quickly pay up. By the end of the day, Mayfield agreed to participate in the stash-house robbery conspiracy.

According to the standard ATF script for the sting, a fictional drug courier was disgruntled with his organization and wanted to rob one of its stash houses. Mayfield was to meet with the courier to discuss logistics, then recruit a crew, gather weapons, and help the courier carry out the robbery. Mayfield contends that because he was still reluctant to participate, Potts went off script and instead urged him to play along with the plan to rob the stash house but at the last minute rob *the courier* instead, which would be a less risky way to repay the debt—or at least not as dangerous as running into a guarded stash house.

Potts and Mayfield met with the "drug courier"—actually undercover Special Agent Dave Gomez—on July 23, 2009. Depending on whose version is believed, this meeting involved not one but *two* setups: Gomez and Potts were setting up Mayfield for prosecution; Mayfield and Potts were setting up Gomez for a robbery. Gomez told the pair that he normally received instructions to transport cocaine about once a month and that the shipments typically involved six to eight kilograms. He also said his organization typically kept 20 to 30 kilograms at its guarded stash houses, the locations of which were kept secret until just before the transport.

Recordings of this meeting indicate that Mayfield helped plan the robbery. He told Gomez that he had experience in knocking off stash houses but had not done a robbery quite like this one before. He said he felt like he was going in blind and suggested that the "element of surprise" would be essential. He assured Gomez that the people he was going to recruit were "for real" and agreed to gather the guns, bulletproof vests, and other equipment for the robbery. Mayfield claims it was all a bluff.

On July 27, 2009, Gomez and Mayfield spoke again by phone, and Mayfield reported that his recruits were ready to meet. Gomez and Mayfield kept in touch by phone for about two weeks, and the next meeting took place on August 9, 2009. Mayfield brought along Montreece Kindle, who in turn brought Nathan Ward and a person known only as "New York." The group went over the strategy and logistics of the operation. Mayfield again emphasized the need for surprise. Kindle, "New York," and Gomez discussed the possibility that the guards at the stash house might have to be killed. "New York" bragged about his ability to distribute the cocaine obtained in the robbery. Gomez asked the group if the robbery was too much for them to handle. "New York" and Kindle said it was not. Finally, Gomez made clear that if they thought they couldn't handle the job, they could call it off.

Mayfield claims that after the meeting with Gomez, he informed his crew that the actual plan was to rob Gomez, not the stash house, and that they were to play along to dupe him into believing that they were serious about the stash-house robbery. Later that evening Gomez called Mayfield to let him know the robbery would happen the following night. Mayfield then called Potts, ostensibly to say he was prepared to rob Gomez to settle the debt and be done with the whole affair. Potts did not answer the call.

Mayfield tried again to reach Potts the next day, and again Potts did not answer the call. Mayfield then called a friend, Dwayne White, who agreed to come meet him. White had no transportation, so Mayfield arranged for Kindle and Ward to pick him up. White, Kindle, and Ward met at Mayfield's apartment, and the group drove in Ward's van to meet Gomez in a parking lot in Aurora, Illinois, the prearranged meeting spot.

Gomez was waiting in the parking lot in a Cadillac Escalade. Mayfield got out of the van to speak with Gomez, who explained that he planned to get out of town right after the robbery but wanted his share of the cocaine placed in a storage locker. Gomez told Mayfield to get into the Escalade so he could show him the location of the storage facility. The two men left the parking lot in the Escalade, with White, Kindle, and Ward following behind in Ward's van.

When they arrived at the storage facility, all five men got out of their vehicles. Gomez then noticed White, whom he had not met before. Mayfield said that White was his little brother and assured Gomez that he was "100." Gomez asked White whether he understood the plan to rob a stash house, and White said he did. Gomez then asked if everyone was ready. When he got a positive response, he gave the arrest signal. ATF agents swarmed the scene and arrested the four men. Inside Ward's van agents discovered a sawed-off shotgun, a .40-caliber Glock semiautomatic pistol, a .44-caliber revolver, two bulletproof vests, and a duffel bag large enough to hold 25 to 30 kilograms of cocaine. They also recovered a .357 Magnum revolver from Gomez's Escalade, apparently tossed there by Mayfield after he saw Gomez give the arrest signal.

Mayfield and the others were charged with conspiracy and attempt to distribute cocaine, see 21 U.S.C. § 846, possession of a firearm in connection with a drug crime, see 18 U.S.C. § 924(c)(1)(A), and possession of a firearm by a felon, see id. § 922(g)(1). The case against Mayfield, White, and Ward proceeded to trial before the same jury; the charges against Kindle were tried separately because he had given a post arrest statement that inculpated the others. The government moved in limine to prevent Mayfield from presenting an entrapment defense, arguing that the following evidence established his predisposition as a matter of law: (1) his criminal record; (2) his recorded statements to Gomez that he had committed similar stash-house robberies; (3) his extensive preparation and arsenal at the time of arrest; and (4) his failure to abort the plan when Gomez gave him the opportunity.

Mayfield opposed the government's motion with a formal response and a six-page handwritten "statement of fact." Together, these two documents amounted to a proffer on Mayfield's entrapment defense and narrated the events we have recounted above. The proffer's description of the interactions between Potts and Mayfield is reasonably detailed, emphasizing that Mayfield repeatedly rebuffed Potts's advances and that Potts played on Mayfield's indebtedness and Potts's affiliation with the Gangster Disciples. The description of the planning and execution of the robbery scheme is more cursory, but the proffer indicates that Potts coached Mayfield on what to say at the various meetings with Gomez and provided the weapons for use in the robbery. (The government denies this, of course.) Mayfield's initial proffer addressed only the issue of inducement; he took the position that once a defendant has presented sufficient evidence of government inducement, the burden shifts to the government to convince the jury beyond a reasonable doubt either that its agents did not induce the crime or that the defendant was predisposed to commit it.

The district court granted the government's motion and precluded the entrapment defense. . . .

Mayfield was convicted on all counts, and the judge sentenced him to a whopping 322 months in prison. A divided panel of this court affirmed. The panel majority concluded that the judge properly excluded the entrapment defense because Mayfield ultimately accepted the government's offer to participate in the robbery, which though perhaps routine as stash-house robberies go was nonetheless highly dangerous. *See Kindle,* 698 F.3d at 408–09. The majority reasoned that only a person already predisposed to such a risky crime would choose to participate, so Mayfield must have been predisposed. *Id.* Judge Posner dissented, concluding that Mayfield offered enough evidence to get his entrapment defense before the jury. *Id.* at 412–16 (Posner, J., dissenting). We granted rehearing en banc.

II. Discussion

Some of our recent entrapment cases have given conflicting signals about the substance of the defense, the procedure for raising and presenting it, and the quantum of evidence necessary to get the issue before the jury. The government commonly seeks to block the defense before trial, proffering evidence that its agents did not induce the crime, the defendant was predisposed to commit it, or both. These are the two formal elements of entrapment, but our circuit's caselaw could be clearer about the relationship between them and what the defendant must do to overcome the government's motion in limine to preclude the defense at trial. To that end, we begin with some history.

A. History

Entrapment is a relative newcomer to the catalog of criminal defenses. It's not just that the defense is new; it's that entrapment-like *activity* is new, having arisen as law enforcement professionalized and developed techniques of artifice and deception in the pursuit of criminals. Still, courts were slow to recognize entrapment as a defense to criminal liability. This statement from a nineteenth century state appellate decision colorfully captures the judiciary's resistance:

> Even if inducements to commit crime could be assumed to exist in this case, the allegation of the defendant would be but the repetition of the plea as ancient as the world, and first interposed in Paradise: "The serpent beguiled me and I did eat." That defence was overruled by the great Lawgiver, and whatever estimate we may form, or whatever judgment pass upon the character or conduct of the tempter, this plea has never since availed to shield crime or give indemnity to the culprit, and it is safe to say that under any code of civilized, not to say christian ethics, it never will.

Bd. of Commis. of Excise of Onondaga Cnty. v. Backus, 29 How. Pr. 33, 42, 1864 WL 3628, at *6 (N.Y.1864). By the turn of the twentieth century, however, state courts and lower federal courts had begun to recognize some form of an entrapment defense. The Supreme Court eventually followed suit.

1. *Adoption*

The Supreme Court's first significant encounter with the entrapment defense came in *Casey v. United States,* 276 U.S. 413, 48 S.Ct. 373, 72 L.Ed. 632 (1928). When jail officials suspected a lawyer of smuggling narcotics into the jail for his clients, they laid a trap. They recruited a prisoner and instructed him to summon the lawyer and offer him $20 in exchange for a delivery of morphine. The lawyer made the deal and smuggled the drug in. A jury convicted him of drug trafficking, and his case made its way to the Supreme Court. In the view of a majority of the justices, entrapment wasn't properly before the Court. Writing for the majority, Justice Holmes intimated that a defense of entrapment might be available in an appropriate case, but held that the Court should not rule on the issue on its own initiative. *Id.* at 418–19, 48 S.Ct. 373.

Justice Brandeis dissented, arguing in favor of recognizing an entrapment defense. His premise was that courts have both the authority and responsibility not to partake in the disreputable conduct of other agents of government and thus should not preside over the prosecutions of entrapped defendants:

> The obstacle to the prosecution lies in the fact that the alleged crime was instigated by officers of the government; that the act for which the government seeks to punish the defendant is the fruit of their criminal conspiracy to induce its commission. The government may set decoys to entrap criminals. But it may not provoke or create a crime and then punish the criminal, its creature. If [the defendant] is guilty . . ., it is because he yielded to the temptation presented by the officers. *Their conduct is not a defense to him.* For no officer of the government has power to authorize the violation of an act of Congress, and no conduct of an officer can excuse the violation. *But it does not follow that the court must suffer a detective-made criminal to be punished. To permit that would be tantamount to a ratification by the government of the officers' unauthorized and unjustifiable conduct.*

Id. at 423–24, 48 S.Ct. 373 (Brandeis, J., dissenting) (emphases added) (footnote omitted). For Justice Brandeis, then, the rationale for an entrapment defense was grounded in the court's duty to ensure the integrity of its own proceedings: "This prosecution should be stopped, not because some right of [the defendant's] has been denied, but in order to protect the government. To protect it from illegal conduct of its officers. To preserve the purity of its courts." *Id.* at 425, 48 S.Ct. 373. . . .

But when the Court eventually adopted the entrapment defense in *Sorrells v. United States,* Justice Brandeis's rationale did not carry the day. *Sorrells* involved a Prohibition-era prosecution for possession and sale of whiskey. An undercover government agent pressured the defendant into providing him with liquor. The agent was introduced to the defendant by a common friend and exploited their shared status as veterans of World War I in an effort to persuade the defendant to get some alcohol. The defendant initially resisted the agent's repeated appeals to camaraderie. When the defendant finally relented—after the fifth request, by one witness's account—he left the scene and returned a few minutes later with a half-gallon of whiskey. Testimony of other witnesses suggested that the defendant had no existing ties to the bootlegging business.

The Supreme Court reversed the trial court's refusal to submit the issue of entrapment to the jury, but expressly rejected the "judicial integrity" justification for the defense:

> We are unable to approve the view that the court, although treating the statute as applicable despite the entrapment, and the defendant as guilty, has authority to grant immunity, or to adopt a procedure to that end. It is the function of the court to construe the statute, not to defeat it as construed. Clemency is the function of the Executive. . . . Where defendant has been duly indicted for an offense found to be within the statute, and the proper authorities seek to proceed with the prosecution, the court cannot refuse to try the case in the constitutional method because it desires to let the defendant go free.

287 U.S. at 449–50, 53 S.Ct. 210. Instead, the Court based its decision on a loose (some might say implausible) theory of statutory interpretation:

> We are unable to conclude that it was the intention of the Congress in enacting this statute that its processes of detection and enforcement should be abused by the instigation by government officials of an act on the part of persons otherwise innocent in order to lure them to its commission and to punish them. We are not forced by the letter to do violence to the spirit and purpose of the statute.

Id. at 448, 53 S.Ct. 210. This rationale endured despite repeated attacks from the Brandeis camp. *See Hampton,* 425 U.S. at 490, 96 S.Ct. 1646; *Russell,* 411 U.S. at 432–33, 93 S.Ct. 1637; *Sherman,* 356 U.S. at 372, 78 S.Ct. 819.

The debate over the justification for the entrapment defense is not merely academic; it determined the elements of the doctrine and even now has important practical implications for how the defense is litigated. Most importantly, the Court's choice of rationale eventually determined the content of the defense and the priority and weight given its constituent parts. . . .

Recall that the ground of principle underlying the Brandeis view was that courts have the authority and responsibility to protect the integrity of the judicial process from the corrupting influence of disreputable police conduct that *creates* rather than detects and captures criminals. Disreputable police conduct is disreputable regardless of the characteristics of the defendant, and the doctrinal test favored by the Brandeis camp reflected this conception. As articulated by Justice Frankfurter: "[The] test [for entrapment] shifts attention from the record and predisposition of the particular defendant to the conduct of the police and the likelihood, objectively considered, that it would entrap only those ready and willing to commit crime." *Sherman,* 356 U.S. at 384, 78 S.Ct. 819. This "objective" test held sway with almost everyone who agreed with Brandeis that the entrapment defense is rooted in the need for courts to protect their own integrity.

But because the Court ultimately grounded the defense in statutory interpretation—the premise that Congress could not possibly have intended to criminalize conduct instigated by government agents—a different test emerged, one that placed decisive weight on the defendant's predisposition. Hence the doctrine that the defense of entrapment consists of *two* elements—government inducement and the defendant's lack of predisposition—with predisposition standing as the "principal element." *Russell,* 411 U.S. at 433, 93 S.Ct. 1637. The relationship between this "subjective" test and the statutory-interpretation rationale is not entirely clear, but the basic idea seems to be that Congress could not have intended to criminalize the conduct of "otherwise innocent" persons (i.e., those not "predisposed") who were ensnared by government ploys.

The adoption of the statutory-interpretation rationale also dictated whether the entrapment defense is a question for the judge or the jury. Judge Friendly neatly explained the point:

> The Supreme Court has long been divided as to who should decide [the entrapment] issue, the majority holding for the jury and a strong minority for the judge. The view of the *Sorrells* majority [that entrapment is a jury question] followed logically from its concept that a case of entrapment was implicitly excepted from the statutory definition of the crime; the minority's view flowed with equal logic from its concept that the defense was for the protection of the court's "own functions and the preservation of the purity of its own temple."

United States v. Riley, 363 F.2d 955, 957 (2d Cir.1966) (quoting *Sorrells,* 287 U.S. at 457, 53 S.Ct. 210 (Roberts, J., concurring) (citations omitted)). The majority view won out; it's now well established that entrapment is a jury question.

2. *Elaboration*

Sorrells established that the defendant may raise an entrapment defense and the test for entrapment had something to do with the defendant's characteristics and the circumstances surrounding the government's undercover operation. But the doctrine was skeletal and details had to be hammered out. Much of this was accomplished in a single case, albeit one that involved two trials and several appeals.

Joseph Sherman was a recovering heroin addict. *Sherman,* 356 U.S. at 371, 373, 78 S.Ct. 819. His record included a 1942 conviction for narcotics distribution and a 1946 conviction for possession of narcotics. *Id.* at 375, 78 S.Ct. 819. In the summer and fall of 1951, he was working to kick the habit with the aid of a Dr. Grossman, when by chance he met another of Grossman's patients, one Kalchinian. *Id.* at 371, 78 S.Ct. 819. Federal agents caught Kalchinian dealing drugs and recruited him as an informant; his task was "to go out and try to induce a person to sell narcotics." *United States v. Sherman,* 200 F.2d 880, 881 (2d Cir.1952). So when Kalchinian crossed paths with Sherman at a pharmacy where both were waiting to have prescriptions filled, Kalchinian started a campaign to persuade Sherman to help him obtain heroin. 356 U.S. at 371, 78 S.Ct. 819. Claiming to be suffering from withdrawal, he repeatedly asked Sherman for help finding the drug; Sherman repeatedly refused. *Id.* After a number of these requests, Sherman acquiesced and several times obtained quantities of the narcotic, which he shared with Kalchinian in exchange for half the purchase price, plus cab fare and other expenses. *Id.;* 200 F.2d at 881. Sherman was arrested and charged with selling narcotics. 356 U.S. at 370, 78 S.Ct. 819.

The first time the case went to trial, the jury rejected Sherman's entrapment defense. On appeal he challenged the entrapment jury instruction and also argued that the district court should have found entrapment as a matter of law. Writing for the court, Judge Learned Hand agreed that instructional error had occurred and warranted a new trial. What is most significant about the Second Circuit's opinion is that Judge Hand gave the entrapment defense its two formal elements: "[I]n [cases of entrapment,] two questions of fact arise: (1) did the agent induce the accused to commit the offence charged in the indictment; [and] (2) if so, was the accused ready and willing without persuasion and was he awaiting any propitious opportunity to commit the offence." 200 F.2d at 882.

A second jury convicted Sherman. He again complained that the court should have directed a verdict in his favor, and this time his appeal went all the way to the Supreme Court. The Court agreed that the evidence established entrapment as a matter of law. *Sherman,* 356 U.S. at 373, 78 S.Ct. 819. Three aspects of the Court's opinion deserve note.

First, the Court firmly rejected the proposal of the concurring justices to abandon the subjective test of *Sorrells* and adopt the objective test under which a defendant's predisposition is irrelevant. *Id.* at 376, 78 S.Ct. 819; *see also id.* at 378–85, 78 S.Ct. 819 (Frankfurter, J., concurring). Second, the Court implicitly endorsed Judge Hand's two-element formula:

> To determine whether entrapment has been established, a line must be drawn between the trap for the unwary innocent and the trap for the unwary criminal. The principles by which the courts are to make this determination were outlined in *Sorrells*. On the one hand, at trial the accused may examine the conduct of the government agent; and on the other hand, the accused will be subjected to an appropriate and searching inquiry into his own conduct and predisposition as bearing on his claim of innocence.

Id. at 372–73, 78 S.Ct. 819 (internal quotation marks omitted).

The last point concerns the Court's treatment of Sherman's narcotics convictions. During the second trial, the government introduced the convictions to show that Sherman was predisposed to commit the crime. At the time of the charged conduct, the convictions were five and nine years old, respectively. *Id.* at 375, 78 S.Ct. 819. The Court found the passage of time significant, holding as a matter of law that the two convictions were insufficient to prove that Sherman "had *a readiness to sell narcotics at the time Kalchinian approached him,* particularly when we must assume from the record he was trying to overcome the narcotics habit at the time." *Id.* at 375–76, 78 S.Ct. 819 (emphasis added).

This aspect of the case is important in several respects. The premise is that predisposition is not an immutable characteristic or one-way ratchet. Past convictions for similar conduct may show predisposition, but only if reasonably close in time to the charged conduct, and even then only in combination with other evidence tending to show predisposition. More abstractly, the Court's decision implies that predisposition requires more than a mere desire, urge, or inclination to engage in particular conduct, for surely Sherman was "predisposed" to obtain and share heroin with a fellow addict in that sense. The Court used the word "readiness" and amplified the point later on in the opinion; the Court explained that the predisposition inquiry focuses on whether the defendant "otherwise would . . . have attempted" the crime without government intervention. *Id.* at 376, 78 S.Ct. 819.

In other words, predisposition is chiefly probabilistic, not psychological. *See United States v. Hollingsworth,* 27 F.3d 1196, 1203 (7th Cir.1994) (en banc) (explaining that a predisposed person is one who "is likely to commit a particular type of crime without being induced to do so by government agents" so that "by arranging for him to commit it now, in circumstances that enable the government to apprehend and convict him, the government punishes or prevents real criminal activity"). . . .

B. Synthesizing the Doctrine: Inducement, Predisposition, and the Relationship Between the Two

It should be clear from this trip through the Supreme Court's key entrapment cases that although the defense has two distinct elements—government inducement and lack of predisposition—the elements are conceptually related. *See Mathews*, 485 U.S. at 63, 108 S.Ct. 883(explaining that the defense has "two *related* elements: government inducement of the crime, and a lack of predisposition on the part of the defendant" (emphasis added)). We addressed the relationship twenty years ago in our en banc decision in *Hollingsworth*. There we noted that the two elements of the entrapment defense are formally distinct but related in the sense that inducement is "evidence bearing on predisposition: the greater the inducement, the weaker the inference that in yielding to it the defendant demonstrated that he was predisposed to commit the crime in question." *Hollingsworth*, 27 F.3d at 1200. . . .

. . . Where the government's agents merely initiate contact with the defendant, solicit the crime, or furnish an opportunity to commit it on customary terms, the government has not "induced" the crime within the meaning of the entrapment doctrine and the defense should be unavailable without the need for a more complex inquiry into evidence of predisposition. . . .

Clarity and consistency would be served if we made a fresh start with a definition of inducement. We hold that inducement means more than mere government solicitation of the crime; the fact that government agents initiated contact with the defendant, suggested the crime, or furnished the ordinary opportunity to commit it is insufficient to show inducement. Instead, inducement means government solicitation of the crime *plus* some other government conduct that creates a risk that a person who would not commit the crime if left to his own devices will do so in response to the government's efforts. The "other conduct" may be repeated attempts at persuasion, fraudulent representations, threats, coercive tactics, harassment, promises of reward beyond that inherent in the customary execution of the crime, pleas based on need, sympathy, or friendship, or any other conduct by government agents that creates a risk that a person who otherwise would not commit the crime if left alone will do so in response to the government's efforts.

* * *

Moving on to predisposition, our circuit has long used a nonexclusive list of five factors to determine whether the defendant was predisposed to commit the charged crime. Formally adopted in 1983, *see Kaminski*, 703 F.2d at 1008, our test includes the following factors:

> (1) the defendant's character or reputation; (2) whether the government initially suggested the criminal activity; (3) whether

> the defendant engaged in the criminal activity for profit; (4) whether the defendant evidenced a reluctance to commit the offense that was overcome by government persuasion; and (5) the nature of the inducement or persuasion by the government.

Pillado, 656 F.3d at 766; *see also United States v. Hall,* 608 F.3d 340, 343 (7th Cir.2010); *Santiago-Godinez,* 12 F.3d at 728. No one factor controls, and the "most significant is whether the defendant was reluctant to commit the offense." *Pillado,* 656 F.3d at 766.

Multifactor tests are common in our law but they can be cryptic when unattached to a substantive legal standard, as this one is. Knowing what factors to look *at* is useless unless one knows what to look *for.* Without a legal definition of predisposition, jurors are left to weigh the listed factors in the abstract, or perhaps to weigh them against an intuitive understanding of the term. Some concepts in our law are appropriately left to the common sense and collective wisdom of the jury. *See United States v. Hatfield,* 591 F.3d 945, 949–50 (7th Cir.2010) (explaining that the term "reasonable doubt" is best left undefined); *United States v. Glass,* 846 F.2d 386, 387 (7th Cir.1988) ("Jurors know what is 'reasonable' and are quite familiar with the meaning of 'doubt.'"). The concept of predisposition is not so well understood that it belongs in this category. Our multifactor test for predisposition would be more useful if we defined the term.

Again we take our cues from the Supreme Court's key entrapment cases. We know from *Sherman* and *Jacobson* that predisposition requires more than a mere desire, urge, or inclination to engage in the charged criminal misconduct. Sherman surely had an inclination or urge to obtain narcotics; he was struggling to overcome an addiction, after all. *Sherman,* 356 U.S. at 371, 78 S.Ct. 819. If the mere urge was enough to make him predisposed to sharing drugs, the outcome of the case would have been different. Similarly, Jacobson may have been predisposed in the sense of having an inclination to view child pornography, but the Supreme Court rejected that understanding of predisposition:

> Petitioner's responses to the many communications prior to the ultimate criminal act were *at most indicative of certain personal inclinations,* including a predisposition to view photographs of preteen sex and a willingness to promote a given agenda by supporting lobbying organizations. Even so, petitioner's responses hardly support an inference that he would commit the crime of receiving child pornography through the mails. Furthermore, *a person's inclinations and fantasies . . . are his own and beyond the reach of government. . . .*

Jacobson, 503 U.S. at 551–52, 112 S.Ct. 1535 (emphases added) (footnote and internal quotation marks omitted). In short, a person who resists his baser urges is not "predisposed" simply because he experiences them.

This conclusion follows from the animating principles of the entrapment doctrine. A legitimate sting takes an actual criminal off the streets and thus reduces the actual crime rate. *See United States v. Manzella,* 791 F.2d 1263, 1269 (7th Cir.1986). The entrapment defense guards against government overreach in this context, "reflect[ing] the view that the proper use of the criminal law in a society such as ours is to prevent harmful conduct for the protection of the law abiding, rather than to purify thoughts and perfect character." *Hollingsworth,* 27 F.3d at 1203. When government agents "tempt [ ] [a] person to commit a crime that he would not otherwise have committed, punishing him will not reduce the crime rate; it will merely deflect law enforcement into the sterile channel of causing criminal activity and then prosecuting the same activity." *Manzella,* 791 F.2d at 1269.

Predisposition thus refers to the likelihood that the defendant would have committed the crime without the government's intervention, or actively wanted to but hadn't yet found the means. In *Sherman* the Court asked whether the defendant "otherwise would . . . have attempted" the crime absent the government's effort to beguile him, 356 U.S. at 376, 78 S.Ct. 819, and concluded that he would not have. The Court used the word "readiness": It was the government's burden "to prove petitioner had a *readiness* to sell narcotics at the time [the informant] approached him." *Id.* at 375, 78 S.Ct. 819 (emphasis added). In *Jacobson* the Court described entrapment as "the apprehension of an otherwise law-abiding citizen who, if left to his own devices, likely would have never run afoul of the law." 503 U.S. at 553–54, 112 S.Ct. 1535. . . .

Relatedly, we have long emphasized that evidence of the defendant's reluctance to commit the crime looms large in the analysis of predisposition. *See, e.g., Pillado,* 656 F.3d at 766 (explaining that the most significant factor in predisposition analysis is "whether the defendant was reluctant to commit the offense"); *Hall,* 608 F.3d at 343 (same); *United States v. Blassingame,* 197 F.3d 271, 281 (7th Cir.1999) (same); *Theodosopoulos,* 48 F.3d at 1444 ("The most important factor is whether the defendant exhibited a reluctance to commit the offense that government agents overcame."); *Kaminski,* 703 F.2d at 1008 (same). Other evidence of the defendant's conduct after the initial contact by the government's agents—for example, his actions or statements during the planning stages of the criminal scheme—also may be relevant to the determination of predisposition. All this evidence must be considered with care, of course; by definition, the defendant's later actions may have been shaped by the government's conduct.

Better evidence of the defendant's predisposition may come from his past conduct. Entrapment is one of the few areas in the criminal law in which past is legitimately considered to be prologue. . . .

C. Procedure

Generally speaking, entrapment is a question for the jury, not the court. *Jacobson,* 503 U.S. at 549, 112 S.Ct. 1535; *Mathews,* 485 U.S. at 63, 108 S.Ct. 883; *McGill,* 754 F.3d at 457; *Pillado,* 656 F.3d at 763. As we've explained, the subjective basis of the defense makes entrapment a fact question for the jury to decide "as part of its function of determining the guilt or innocence of the accused." *Sherman,* 356 U.S. at 377, 78 S.Ct. 819; *see also Mathews,* 485 U.S. at 62–63, 108 S.Ct. 883.

Two important procedural questions remain: (1) What is the burden of proof for entrapment and who bears it? (2) Under what circumstances may the court preclude a defendant from asserting the defense at all?

1. *Burden of Proof*

"Where . . . the defense of entrapment is at issue, . . . the prosecution must prove beyond reasonable doubt that the defendant was disposed to commit the criminal act prior to first being approached by [g]overnment agents." *Jacobson,* 503 U.S. at 548–49, 112 S.Ct. 1535. This statement admits of no ambiguity: The government bears the burden, and the level of proof is beyond reasonable doubt. *See also Pillado,* 656 F.3d at 763; *Santiago-Godinez,* 12 F.3d at 728. . . .

2. *Raising the Entrapment Defense*

Because entrapment is a fact question on which the government bears the burden of proof, the defendant is entitled to a jury instruction on the defense "whenever there is sufficient evidence from which a reasonable jury could find entrapment." *Mathews,* 485 U.S. at 62, 108 S.Ct. 883; *see also Plowman,* 700 F.3d at 1057; *Theodosopoulos,* 48 F.3d at 1444; *Santiago-Godinez,* 12 F.3d at 727. We have held that to obtain a jury instruction and shift the burden of disproving entrapment to the government, the defendant must proffer evidence on both elements of the defense. *See Plowman,* 700 F.3d at 1057; *Pillado,* 656 F.3d at 763; *Santiago-Godinez,* 12 F.3d at 728. But this initial burden of production is not great. An entrapment instruction is warranted if the defendant proffers "some evidence" that the government induced him to commit the crime and he was not predisposed to commit it. *Pillado,* 656 F.3d at 764 ("[A] defendant must proffer some evidence on both elements of the entrapment defense to warrant the instruction. . . ."); *see also Theodosopoulos,* 48 F.3d at 1445; *Gunter,* 741 F.2d at 153. Put another way, "[a]lthough more than a scintilla of evidence of entrapment is needed before instruction on the defense becomes necessary, the defendant need only point to evidence in the record that would allow a rational jury to conclude that he was entrapped." *McGill,* 754 F.3d at 457; *see also Santiago-Godinez,* 12 F.3d at 727. . . .

D. Application

We now return to Mayfield's case. Did he proffer enough evidence to create an entrapment issue for trial? Accepting the facts in his pretrial proffer as true and drawing reasonable inferences in his favor, we conclude that he did.

Mayfield's proffer contains sufficient evidence from which a reasonable jury could find that the government induced him to commit the crime. Potts targeted Mayfield at a moment of acute financial need and against a backdrop of prolonged difficulty finding permanent, family-supporting work. Potts also appealed to Mayfield's friendship and camaraderie and to their common struggle as convicted felons trying to make a living. Appeals of this sort are among the oldest tactics recognized as forms of government inducement. *See, e.g., Sorrells,* 287 U.S. at 441, 53 S.Ct. 210. Moreover, Potts gave Mayfield money in order to create a debt that he knew Mayfield would be unable to repay and then exploited that debt by alluding to his status as a member of the Gangster Disciples. Drawing inferences in Mayfield's favor, this action was arguably calculated to convey an implied threat of violence if the debt was not repaid. Threats obviously qualify as inducements. Finally, Potts pestered Mayfield over a substantial period of time; a reasonable jury could find that this persistent pressure amounted to harassment.

We do not need to decide whether any of these tactics standing alone would suffice to establish inducement; some of them almost certainly would not. But together, they are enough to permit a reasonable jury to conclude that the government induced Mayfield to commit the crime. That is, a rational jury could find that the government's actions created a risk that a person who otherwise would not have committed the crime would do so in response to the government's efforts.

It's true that when push came to shove, Potts offered Mayfield an opportunity to participate in what was apparently a typical stash-house robbery, at least as far as the record shows. If the government had done nothing more than make this opportunity available, then its actions would not qualify as an illegitimate inducement. But the government did more; it paired the reward of a stash-house robbery with an extended campaign of persuasion that played on Mayfield's financial need and culminated in a veiled threat of reprisal from a vicious street gang. A rational jury could find that the government induced him to commit the crime.

Mayfield also proffered enough evidence to permit a rational jury to find reasonable doubt about his predisposition to commit the stash-house robbery at the time Potts first approached him with the offer. Mayfield repeatedly rejected Potts's entreaties over the course of several weeks, relenting only when faced with an implied threat that the Gangster Disciples street gang might retaliate against him if he did not repay his debt. Accepted as true, Mayfield's initial reluctance and continued resistance is substantive evidence that he was not predisposed to commit the crime when Potts first proposed it.

True, the government offered its own evidence that Mayfield had a serious criminal record, and that once he accepted Potts's overture, he recruited a crew and actively participated in planning the scheme, and also bragged about having experience robbing stash houses. However substantial or substantiated the government's evidence may seem to the court, its weight is a question for the jury. If Mayfield had been allowed to present his entrapment evidence at trial, he might have persuaded the jury that it was all a bluff.

As a logical and legal matter, Mayfield's active engagement in the scheme *after* the government's extended efforts to procure his participation has limited bearing on his predisposition when the government first proposed it. If a jury were to conclude that the government's conduct might have ensnared a person who otherwise would not have committed the crime, the fact that Mayfield, once ensnared, actively participated in it doesn't tell us much about his predisposition. *See Evans,* 924 F.2d at 716 (explaining that if the defendant "was indeed entrapped, it is irrelevant that the entrapment was so effective as to make him not only a willing but an eager participant"). Moreover, as we've explained, the trial judge cannot weigh the competing evidentiary proffers and accept the government's as more persuasive than the defendant's. That's exactly what the judge did here, and quite expressly. Of course, Mayfield can't escape his criminal record, which contains a conviction for armed carjacking. But he proffered evidence that after his release from prison, he joined antirecidivism programs and found honest work in an effort to go straight and not return to a life of crime. Even without this evidence of rehabilitation, the fact that Mayfield committed a different kind of robbery in the past is not conclusive evidence that he was predisposed to commit *this crime*—a stash-house robbery—when Potts first proposed it. *See Sherman,* 356 U.S. at 375–76, 78 S.Ct. 819.

In the end, the inferences to be drawn from the evidence as a whole are varied and ultimately for the jury. Mayfield proffered enough evidence to defeat the government's motion in limine. The district court should not have precluded him from presenting his entrapment evidence at trial.

III. Conclusion

To recap, entrapment is a defense to criminal liability when the defendant was not predisposed to commit the charged crime before the intervention of the government's agents and the government's conduct induced him to commit it. The two elements of the defense—lack of predisposition and government inducement—are conceptually related but formally and temporally distinct.

The predisposition element focuses on the defendant's circumstances *before* and *at the time* the government first approached him with a proposal to commit the crime. A defendant is predisposed to commit the charged crime if he was ready and willing to do so and likely would have committed it without the government's intervention, or actively wanted to but hadn't yet found the means.

As for the inducement element, the fact that the government initiated contact with the defendant, suggested the crime, or created the ordinary opportunity to commit it is not sufficient; something more is required, either in terms of the character and degree of the government's persistence or persuasion, the nature of the enticement or reward, or some combination of these. Conduct by the government's agents amounts to inducement if, considering its character and the factual context, it creates a risk that a person who otherwise would not commit the crime if left alone will do so in response to the government's persuasion.

Procedurally, entrapment is an issue of fact for the jury. The defendant is entitled to present the defense at trial if he shows that some evidence supports it. This initial burden is not great; the defendant must produce some evidence from which a reasonable jury could find government inducement and lack of predisposition. If he can make this showing, the court must instruct the jury on entrapment and the government must prove beyond a reasonable doubt that the defendant was predisposed to commit the charged crime, or alternatively (but less commonly), that there was no government inducement. When the issue is raised before trial on the government's motion to preclude the defense, the court must accept the defendant's factual proffer as true and not weigh it against the government's evidence.

Applying these substantive and procedural principles here, we conclude that Mayfield's proffer was sufficient to overcome the government's motion in limine. The district court erred by crediting the government's evidence over Mayfield's and precluding him from presenting his entrapment evidence at trial. He is entitled to a new trial.

VACATED and REMANDED.

EXERCISE

Ramona is deeply addicted to opiates and has been for four years. After a particularly difficult week, in which she crashed her car and hit one of her children hard enough to require a visit to the emergency room to have the child's arm examined for a break, Ramona's husband persuades her to enter an in-patient treatment program. Despite having lost several jobs because of her addiction, Ramona has never been arrested or convicted of a crime.

After two weeks in rehab, Ramona can't take it anymore. She walks out of the rehab center at night and goes to a local motel. There, she searches the street for anyone who could help her find opiates. Eventually, she falls into conversation with Larry, who is a vegetable stocker at a 24-hour grocery. Ramona explains her situation and asks if he can help her get any opiates. She says she will do "anything" to get them. Larry is actually a part-time police informant. After hearing Ramona out and commiserating with her situation, Larry tells her to come back the next night.

The next day, Larry tells his "handler" at the DEA about Ramona. The handler thinks he recognizes the name "Ramona" as someone who previously had sold a large amount of methamphetamine in the city. (It turns out this is a different person, not Ramona). Larry is given $500 in cash and given instructions. He is to tell Ramona that she should take the $500 to an apartment nearby and purchase opiates. She will get to keep half and Larry (he claims falsely) will sell the other half. Ramona does so, and is charged with possession with intent to distribute Fentanyl.

You are the prosecutor to whom the case is referred. Your supervisor says you should take it unless there is "a good case" for entrapment. What do you tell your supervisor?

CHAPTER TWELVE

MENTAL HEALTH AND ABILITY— COMPETENCE AND INSANITY

∎ ∎ ∎

American criminal law is deeply entangled with issues of mental health and ability. Practitioners find that they deal regularly with people suffering from a variety of mental health issues that drive criminality and create enduring problems in a system often unsuited to handle questions rooted in psychiatry.

Judges and juries, respectively, are charged with making two crucial mental-health and mental ability determinations: competence and insanity. Competence is the ability of a defendant to understand the legal process and work with an attorney, and is determined by a judge. If a defendant is not legally competent, the legal proceeding—whether it is an initial appearance, an arraignment, a trial, or sentencing—cannot proceed. Competence has to do with the defendant's mental health or ability at the time of the court appearance.

Insanity is a separate doctrine that has to do with the defendant's mental health or ability at the time of the crime, not at the time of a legal proceeding, and is usually an affirmative defense that serves to negate the defendant's guilty state of mind. Jurisdictions handle this doctrine differently: some allow for a verdict of "not guilty by reason of insanity," while others have a possible verdict of "guilty but insane." Standards for insanity vary as well. In a jury trial, insanity is an issue for the jury to determine.

While insanity is relatively rarely raised, competence is evaluated, if only informally at the initial appearance, in every case. During an initial appearance a magistrate or judge will often pay attention to the mental abilities and stability of a defendant, especially if there is some cause for concern based on demeanor or articulation.

A. COMPETENCE

Some people, because of diminished mental ability or mental health issues, simply are not able to be processed by the criminal law system because they cannot understand their rights or the proceedings, or are unable to communicate effectively with their lawyer. Typically, when competence is an issue in a federal case, a judge will have the defendant professionally evaluated before determining whether or not the defendant is competent.

In federal courts, 18 U.S.C. § 4241 sets out the procedure to be followed:

(a) Motion to determine competency of defendant.—At any time after the commencement of a prosecution for an offense and prior to the sentencing of the defendant, or at any time after the commencement of probation or supervised release and prior to the completion of the sentence, the defendant or the attorney for the Government may file a motion for a hearing to determine the mental competency of the defendant. The court shall grant the motion, or shall order such a hearing on its own motion, if there is reasonable cause to believe that the defendant may presently be suffering from a mental disease or defect rendering him mentally incompetent to the extent that he is unable to understand the nature and consequences of the proceedings against him or to assist properly in his defense.

(b) Psychiatric or psychological examination and report.—Prior to the date of the hearing, the court may order that a psychiatric or psychological examination of the defendant be conducted, and that a psychiatric or psychological report be filed with the court, pursuant to the provisions of section 4247 (b) and (c).

(c) Hearing.—The hearing shall be conducted pursuant to the provisions of section 4247(d).

(d) Determination and disposition.—If, after the hearing, the court finds by a preponderance of the evidence that the defendant is presently suffering from a mental disease or defect rendering him mentally incompetent to the extent that he is unable to understand the nature and consequences of the proceedings against him or to assist properly in his defense, the court shall commit the defendant to the custody of the Attorney General. The Attorney General shall hospitalize the defendant for treatment in a suitable facility—

  (1) for such a reasonable period of time, not to exceed four months, as is necessary to determine whether there is a substantial probability that in the foreseeable future he will attain the capacity to permit the proceedings to go forward; and

  (2) for an additional reasonable period of time until—

    (A) his mental condition is so improved that trial may proceed, if the court finds that there is a substantial probability that within such additional period of time he will attain the capacity to permit the proceedings to go forward; or

(B) the pending charges against him are disposed of according to law;

whichever is earlier.

There are some fundamental underlying problems with competency evaluations. One is that each of the actors who might initiate an evaluation are limited in their ability do so. The prosecutor and the judge have very limited contact with the defendant, and communication is often through the defendant's attorney. While the defendant's attorney has greater access, she can be limited by the ethical restrictions on revealing attorney-client communications.

Another issue can be the time taken to evaluate the defendant, particularly where the crime is relatively minor, given that the defendant may be in custody for this evaluation without having completed even an initial appearance on the charge. This can effectively result in a jail sentence for an individual based solely on mental illness or ability.

UNITED STATES V. KIMBLE

2012 WL 2049885 (WD La. May 22, 2012)

REPORT AND RECOMMENDATION

MARK L. HORNSBY, UNITED STATES MAGISTRATE JUDGE.

Defendant Bobby Lee Kimble is a 40 year old male charged with conspiracy, wire fraud, and health care fraud in connection with automobile accidents. He suffers from mild to moderate mental retardation with an IQ between 55 and 58. The issue before the court is whether Defendant is competent to stand trial. An evidentiary hearing was held before the undersigned on May 15, 2012. For the reasons that follow, the undersigned recommends that Defendant be found not competent to stand trial.

Applicable Law

A criminal defendant may not be tried unless he is competent. *Pate v. Robinson,* 383 U.S. 375, 378 (1966); *Washington v. Johnson,* 90 F.3d 945, 949–950 (5th Cir.1996). An erroneous determination of competence threatens a fundamental component of our criminal justice system—the basic fairness of the trial itself. *Cooper v. Oklahoma,* 517 U.S. 348, 364 (1996).

In *Dusky v. United States,* 362 U.S. 402, 402 (1960), the Supreme Court established the following test for competency: "Whether [the defendant] has sufficient present ability to consult with his lawyer with a reasonable degree of rational understanding—and whether he has a rational as well as factual understanding of the proceedings against him." *See also Carter v. Johnson*, 131 F.3d 452, 459 (5th Cir.1997); *Moody v. Johnson*, 139 F.3d 477, 480–481 (5th Cir.1998). In *Drope v. Misssouri*, 420 U.S. 162, 171 (1975), the court added an additional element to the test of compentency— the defendant must be able to "assist in preparing his defense." Thus, to be competent, a defendant must:

1.   Be able to consult with his lawyer with a reasonable degree of rational understanding;

2.   Be able to otherwise assist in his defense;

3.   Have a rational understanding of the criminal proceedings; and

4.   Have a factual understanding of the proceedings.

[handwritten margin note: Test for competence:]

A hearing on the issue of competency must be held if there is reasonable cause to believe the defendant may presently be suffering from a mental disease or defect rendering him mentally incompetent to the extent that he is unable to understand the nature and consequences of the proceedings against him or to assist properly in his defense. 18 U.S.C. § 4241. Mental retardation may render an individual incompetent to stand trial. *United States v. Forrest*, 2010 WL 4626089 (W.D.La.2010), citing ABA Criminal Justice Mental Health Standards, Section 7.4(b).

[handwritten margin note: Must have reasonable cause to believe defendant is mentally incompetent for hearing]

The defendant is entitled to court appointed counsel at the hearing, the opportunity to testify and present evidence, to subpoena witnesses on his own behalf, and to confront and cross-examine the witnesses who appear at the hearing. § 4247(d). If, after the hearing, the court finds by a *preponderance of the evidence* that the defendant is presently suffering from a mental disease or defect rendering him incompetent, the court is required to commit him to the custody of the Attorney General for treatment in a suitable facility. § 4241(d).

Analysis

A.   Relevant Facts

There is no question that Defendant suffers from mild to moderate mental retardation. His intelligence is significantly below average. The records show that he has an IQ of between 55 and 58. (The average IQ of the population is 100.) Defendant's answers to questions on the IQ test were consistent with those given by preschool and early grade-school children.

Defendant was in special education beginning in the first grade. He quit school when he was about 20 years old. He does not possess a 6th grade reading ability. He has cognitive limitations and physical problems from a serious car accident in 2001. His concentration and long-term memory are impaired. He cannot identify his daily pain medicines, and he denies having a primary physician.

Defendant received a score of 55 on the Global Assessment of Functioning ("GAF") test, which measures the extent of his impairment in various areas of functioning. A GAF of 51–60 reflects "moderate symptoms" or moderate difficulty in social, occupational or school functioning (i.e., few friends, conflicts with peers or co-workers). Defendant has never lived alone, and currently resides with his parents. His father manages his money (SSI benefits).

B. Competing Expert Opinions

The determination of Defendant's competency, or lack thereof, to stand trial is a particularly difficult one for the court, because of conflicting conclusions from two highly regarded experts: Dr. George Seiden and Dr. Glenn Ahava. Dr. Seiden is a physician specializing in psychiatry and forensic psychiatry. It is Dr. Seiden's opinion that Defendant is not competent to stand trial. Dr. Ahava is a clinical and forensic psychologist. Dr. Ahava opines that Defendant is competent to stand trial. Dr. Seiden found that Defendant did not understand his constitutional rights. Defendant stated that the right to remain silent meant "You're under arrest." He did not believe he had a right to a lawyer during questioning, and he could not understand why he would want to have an attorney present during questioning. Defendant believed that, if he did not answer questions, he would go to jail.

Dr. Seiden also found that Defendant did not understand the role of the courtroom participants. Defendant stated that the role of the U.S. Attorney was to "sentence you." He could not explain the role of a jury. He also could not explain the concept of a plea bargain.

Dr. Seiden notes that at least some of Defendant's impairment is remediable with proper education; however, Defendant's concentration and cognitive impairments are not remediable. The undersigned interprets this to mean that (and by way of example), while Defendant may be taught that he has the right not to testify, he cannot intelligently exercise or waive that right.

Dr. Ahava administered several additional psychological tests to Defendant. His report and testimony at the hearing share many similarities with the findings by Dr. Seiden. Dr. Ahava agrees that Defendant likely meets the criteria for Mild Mental Retardation and that Defendant has been enduring cognitive limitations from the 2001 car accident. However, Dr. Ahava believes that, if certain basic accommodations can be made, "the defendant appears to possess the knowledge and ability to proceed to trial." Dr. Ahava's proposed accommodations are:

Dr. Ahava's proposed accommodations

1. Requiring court hearings to be shorter in duration;

2. Require Defendant to obtain all of his pain medication from one (and only one) primary care physician [this would allow coordination and control over the medications];

3. Require Defendant to take his pain medication at prescribed intervals during the proceedings;

3. Require that all communications between the court and Defendant be pursued in the simplest language possible; and

4. Require that Defendant repeat back, in his own words, those provisions of the communications that are central to the topic at hand.

Conclusion

unrealistic —

Dr. Ahava's proposed accommodations, particularly the last two, are not realistic in this case. This is a multi-defendant conspiracy case. It is unreasonable to attempt to require that witnesses, counsel, and the court use overly simplistic language during the trial. It is also unreasonable and impractical to stop the trial frequently so that Defendant can repeat trial testimony back to his counsel in his own words to ensure that Defendant has a clear understanding of the proceeding.

reasoning—

The issue is close, but the evidence satisfies the undersigned that Defendant is not competent to stand trial at this time. Defendant does not have sufficient present ability to consult with his lawyer with a reasonable degree of rational understanding; he does not understand his constitutional rights; he cannot make a knowing and voluntary waiver of his rights; he does not have a rational or factual understanding of the proceedings against him; he does not understand the nature and consequences of the proceeding; and he cannot assist in his defense.

Accordingly;

IT IS RECOMMENDED that Defendant Bobby Lee Kimble be found not presently competent to stand trial;

IT IS FURTHER RECOMMENDED that Defendant Bobby Lee Kimble be committed to the custody of the Attorney General for restoration of competency at a medical referral center, for a reasonable period, not to exceed four (4) months, as is necessary to determine whether there is a substantial probability that Defendant will in the foreseeable future attain the capacity to stand trial. 18 U.S.C. § 4241(d)(1). Because Defendant is on bond, and he is not considered a danger to himself or others, he should be allowed to self-report to the U.S. Marshal.

EXERCISE

You are federal Magistrate Judge. A defendant appears before you on a minor mail-theft felony with a likely sentence of 0–6 months under the advisory sentencing guidelines. At the initial appearance, he refuses to speak in response to your questions, staring straight ahead.

The pretrial services officer, who attempted to interview the defendant prior to the appearance, tells you that the defendant refused to say anything to her after she advised him that he "had the right to remain silent." Trying to break the impasse, you call over to the federal defenders' office and ask that he be appointed temporary counsel for the purpose of completing the initial appearance. A defender appears and talks to the defendant in the hallway, but reports that the defendant won't talk to her, either, or even look at her.

Should you send the defendant to be evaluated for competence, under the standard set out in 18 U.S.C. § 4241? To complete the competency evaluation, the defendant will be sent to a Federal Medical Center several states away.

[handwritten margin note: possibly - but could just know his rights to remain silent]

When a defendant is found not competent, one option is to impose treatment in the hopes that the defendant will be made competent. This, of course, raises troubling issues about forced medication of individuals who have not been convicted of a crime.

UNITED STATES V. SELL
539 U.S. 166 (2003)

JUSTICE BREYER delivered the opinion of the Court.

The question presented is whether the Constitution permits the Government to administer antipsychotic drugs involuntarily to a mentally ill criminal defendant—in order to render that defendant competent to stand trial for serious, but nonviolent, crimes. We conclude that the Constitution allows the Government to administer those drugs, even against the defendant's will, in limited circumstances, *i.e.,* upon satisfaction of conditions that we shall describe. Because the Court of Appeals did not find that the requisite circumstances existed in this case, we vacate its judgment.

I

A

Petitioner Charles Sell, once a practicing dentist, has a long and unfortunate history of mental illness. In September 1982, after telling doctors that the gold he used for fillings had been contaminated by communists, Sell was hospitalized, treated with antipsychotic medication, and subsequently discharged. App. 146. In June 1984, Sell called the police to say that a leopard was outside his office boarding a bus, and he then asked the police to shoot him. *Id.,* at 148; Record Forensic Report, p. 1 (June 20, 1997 (Sealed)). Sell was again hospitalized and subsequently released. On various occasions, he complained that public officials, for example, a State Governor and a police chief, were trying to kill him. *Id.,* at 4. In April 1997, he told law enforcement personnel that he "spoke to God last night," and that "God told me every [Federal Bureau of Investigation] person I kill, a soul will be saved." *Id.,* at 1.

In May 1997, the Government charged Sell with submitting fictitious insurance claims for payment. See 18 U.S.C. § 1035(a)(2). A Federal Magistrate Judge (Magistrate), after ordering a psychiatric examination, found Sell "currently competent," but noted that Sell might experience "a psychotic episode" in the future. App. 321. The Magistrate released Sell on bail. A grand jury later produced a superseding indictment charging Sell and his wife with 56 counts of mail fraud, 6 counts of Medicaid fraud, and 1 count of money laundering. *Id.,* at 12–22.

In early 1998, the Government claimed that Sell had sought to intimidate a witness. The Magistrate held a bail revocation hearing. Sell's behavior at his initial appearance was, in the judge's words, " 'totally out of control,' " involving "screaming and shouting," the use of "personal insults" and "racial epithets," and spitting "in the judge's face." *Id.,* at 322. A psychiatrist reported that Sell could not sleep because he expected the Federal Bureau of Investigation (FBI) to " 'come busting through the door,' " and concluded that Sell's condition had worsened. *Ibid.* After considering that report and other testimony, the Magistrate revoked Sell's bail.

In April 1998, the grand jury issued a new indictment charging Sell with attempting to murder the FBI agent who had arrested him and a former employee who planned to testify against him in the fraud case. *Id.,* at 23–29. The attempted murder and fraud cases were joined for trial.

In early 1999, Sell asked the Magistrate to reconsider his competence to stand trial. The Magistrate sent Sell to the United States Medical Center for Federal Prisoners (Medical Center) at Springfield, Missouri, for examination. Subsequently the Magistrate found that Sell was "mentally incompetent to stand trial." *Id.,* at 323. He ordered Sell to "be hospitalized for treatment" at the Medical Center for up to four months, "to determine whether there was a substantial probability that [Sell] would attain the capacity to allow his trial to proceed." *Ibid.*

Two months later, Medical Center staff recommended that Sell take antipsychotic medication. Sell refused to do so. The staff sought permission to administer the medication against Sell's will. That effort is the subject of the present proceedings.

B

We here review the last of five hierarchically ordered lower court and Medical Center determinations. First, in June 1999, Medical Center staff sought permission from institutional authorities to administer antipsychotic drugs to Sell involuntarily. A reviewing psychiatrist held a hearing and considered Sell's prior history; Sell's current persecutional beliefs (for example, that Government officials were trying to suppress his knowledge about events in Waco, Texas, and had sent him to Alaska to silence him); staff medical opinions (for example, that "Sell's symptoms point to a diagnosis of Delusional Disorder but . . . there well may be an underlying Schizophrenic Process"); staff medical concerns (for example, about "the persistence of Dr. Sell's belief that the Courts, FBI, and federal government in general are against him"); an outside medical expert's opinion (that Sell suffered only from delusional disorder, which, in that expert's view, "medication rarely helps"); and Sell's own views, as well as those of other laypersons who know him (to the effect that he did not suffer from a serious mental illness). *Id.,* at 147–150.

The reviewing psychiatrist then authorized involuntary administration of the drugs, both (1) because Sell was "mentally ill and dangerous, and medication is necessary to treat the mental illness," and (2) so that Sell would "become competent for trial." *Id.,* at 145. The reviewing psychiatrist added that he considered Sell "dangerous based on threats and delusions if outside, but not necessarily in[side] prison" and that Sell was "[a]ble to function" in prison in the "open population." *Id.,* at 144.

Second, the Medical Center administratively reviewed the determination of its reviewing psychiatrist. A Bureau of Prisons official considered the evidence that had been presented at the initial hearing, referred to Sell's delusions, noted differences of professional opinion as to proper classification and treatment, and concluded that antipsychotic medication represents the medical intervention "most likely" to "ameliorate" Sell's symptoms; that other "less restrictive interventions" are "unlikely" to work; and that Sell's "pervasive belief" that he was "being targeted for nefarious actions by various governmental . . . parties," along with the "current charges of conspiracy to commit murder," made Sell "a potential risk to the safety of one or more others in the community." *Id.,* at 154–155. The reviewing official "upheld" the "hearing officer's decision that [Sell] would benefit from the utilization of anti-psychotic medication." *Id.,* at 157.

Third, in July 1999, Sell filed a court motion contesting the Medical Center's right involuntarily to administer antipsychotic drugs. In September 1999, the Magistrate who had ordered Sell sent to the Medical Center held a hearing. The evidence introduced at the hearing for the most part replicated the evidence introduced at the administrative hearing, with two exceptions. First, the witnesses explored the question of the medication's effectiveness more thoroughly. Second, Medical Center doctors testified about an incident that took place at the Medical Center *after* the administrative proceedings were completed. In July 1999, Sell had approached one of the Medical Center's nurses, suggested that he was in love with her, criticized her for having nothing to do with him, and, when told that his behavior was inappropriate, added " 'I can't help it.' " *Id., at* 168–170, 325. He subsequently made remarks or acted in ways indicating that this kind of conduct would continue. The Medical Center doctors testified that, given Sell's prior behavior, diagnosis, and current beliefs, boundary-breaching incidents of this sort were not harmless and, when coupled with Sell's inability or unwillingness to desist, indicated that he was a safety risk even within the institution. They added that he had been moved to a locked cell.

In August 2000, the Magistrate found that "the government has made a substantial and very strong showing that Dr. Sell is a danger to himself and others at the institution in which he is currently incarcerated"; that "the government has shown that anti-psychotic medication is the only way to render him less dangerous"; that newer drugs and/or changing drugs will "ameliorat [e]" any "serious side effects"; that "the benefits to Dr. Sell . . . far outweigh any risks"; and that "there is a substantial probability that" the drugs will "retur[n]" Sell "to competency." *Id.,* at 333–334. The Magistrate concluded that "the government has shown in as strong a manner as possible, that anti-psychotic medications are the only way to render the defendant not dangerous and competent to stand trial." *Id.,* at 335. The Magistrate issued an order authorizing the involuntary administration of antipsychotic drugs to Sell, *id.,* at 331, but stayed that order to allow Sell to appeal the matter to the Federal District Court, *id.,* at 337.

Fourth, the District Court reviewed the record and, in April 2001, issued an opinion. The court addressed the Magistrate's finding "that defendant presents a danger to himself or others sufficient" to warrant involuntary administration of antipsychotic drugs. *Id.,* at 349. After noting that Sell subsequently had "been returned to an open ward," the District Court held the Magistrate's "dangerousness" finding "clearly erroneous." *Id.,* at 349, and n. 5. The court limited its determination to Sell's "dangerousness *at this time* to himself and to those around him *in his institutional context.*" *Id.,* at 349 (emphasis in original). Nonetheless, the District Court *affirmed* the Magistrate's order permitting Sell's involuntary medication. The court wrote that "anti-psychotic drugs are medically appropriate," that "they represent the only viable hope of rendering defendant competent to stand trial," and that "administration of such drugs appears necessary to serve the government's compelling interest in obtaining an adjudication of defendant's guilt or innocence of numerous and serious charges" (including fraud and attempted murder). *Id.,* at 354. The court added that it was "premature" to consider whether "the effects of medication might prejudice

[Sell's] defense at trial." *Id.,* at 351, 352. The Government and Sell both appealed.

Fifth, in March 2002, a divided panel of the Court of Appeals affirmed the District Court's judgment. 282 F.3d 560 (CA8 2002). The majority affirmed the District Court's determination that Sell was not dangerous. The majority noted that, according to the District Court, Sell's behavior at the Medical Center "amounted at most to an 'inappropriate familiarity and even infatuation' with a nurse." *Id.,* at 565. The Court of Appeals agreed, "[u]pon review," that "the evidence does not support a finding that Sell posed a danger to himself or others at the Medical Center." *Ibid.*

The Court of Appeals also affirmed the District Court's order requiring medication in order to render Sell competent to stand trial. Focusing solely on the serious fraud charges, the panel majority concluded that the "government has an essential interest in bringing a defendant to trial." *Id.,* at 568. It added that the District Court "correctly concluded that there were no less intrusive means." *Ibid.* After reviewing the conflicting views of the experts, *id.,* at 568–571, the panel majority found antipsychotic drug treatment "medically appropriate" for Sell, *id.,* at 571. It added that the "medical evidence presented indicated a reasonable probability that Sell will fairly be able to participate in his trial." *Id.,* at 572. One member of the panel dissented primarily on the ground that the fraud and money laundering charges were "not serious enough to warrant the forced medication of the defendant." *Id.,* at 574 (opinion of Bye, J.).

We granted certiorari to determine whether the Eighth Circuit "erred in rejecting" Sell's argument that "allowing the government to administer antipsychotic medication against his will solely to render him competent to stand trial for non-violent offenses," Brief for Petitioner i, violated the Constitution—in effect by improperly depriving Sell of an important "liberty" that the Constitution guarantees, Amdt. 5. . . .

We turn now to the basic question presented: Does forced administration of antipsychotic drugs to render Sell competent to stand trial unconstitutionally deprive him of his "liberty" to reject medical treatment? U.S. Const., Amdt. 5 (Federal Government may not "depriv[e]" any person of "liberty . . . without due process of law"). Two prior precedents, *Harper, supra,* and *Riggins v. Nevada,* 504 U.S. 127, 112 S.Ct. 1810, 118 L.Ed.2d 479 (1992), set forth the framework for determining the legal answer.

In *Harper,* this Court recognized that an individual has a "significant" constitutionally protected "liberty interest" in "avoiding the unwanted administration of antipsychotic drugs." 494 U.S., at 221, 110 S.Ct. 1028. The Court considered a state law authorizing forced administration of those drugs "to inmates who are . . . gravely disabled or represent a significant danger to themselves or others." *Id.,* at 226, 110 S.Ct. 1028. The State had established "by a medical finding" that Harper, a mentally ill prison inmate, had "a mental disorder . . . which is likely to cause harm if not treated." *Id.*, at 222, 110 S.Ct. 1028. The treatment decision had been made "by a psychiatrist," it had been approved by "a reviewing psychiatrist," and it "ordered" medication only because that was "in the prisoner's medical interests, given the legitimate needs of his institutional confinement." *Ibid.*

The Court found that the State's interest in administering medication was "legitima[te]" and "importan[t]," *id.*, at 225, 110 S.Ct. 1028; and it held that "the Due Process Clause permits the State to treat a prison inmate who has a serious mental illness with antipsychotic drugs against his will, if the inmate is dangerous to himself or others and the treatment is in the inmate's medical interest," *id.*, at 227, 110 S.Ct. 1028. The Court concluded that, in the circumstances, the state law authorizing involuntary treatment amounted to a constitutionally permissible "accommodation between an inmate's liberty interest in avoiding the forced administration of antipsychotic drugs and the State's interests in providing appropriate medical treatment to reduce the danger that an inmate suffering from a serious mental disorder represents to himself or others." *Id.*, at 236, 110 S.Ct. 1028.

In *Riggins,* the Court repeated that an individual has a constitutionally protected liberty "interest in avoiding involuntary administration of antipsychotic drugs"—an interest that only an "essential" or "overriding" state interest might overcome. 504 U.S., at 134, 135, 112 S.Ct. 1810. The Court suggested that, in principle, forced medication in order to render a defendant competent to stand trial for murder was constitutionally permissible. The Court, citing *Harper,* noted that the State "would have satisfied due process if the prosecution had demonstrated . . . that treatment with antipsychotic medication was medically appropriate and, considering less intrusive alternatives, essential for the sake of Riggins' *own safety or the safety of others.*" 504 U.S., at 135, 112 S.Ct. 1810 (emphasis added). And it said that the State "*[s]imilarly* . . . might have been able to justify medically appropriate, involuntary treatment with the drug by establishing that it could not obtain an adjudication of Riggins' guilt or innocence" of the murder charge "by using less intrusive means." *Ibid.* (emphasis added). Because the trial court had permitted forced medication of Riggins without taking account of his "liberty interest," with a consequent possibility of trial prejudice, the Court reversed Riggins' conviction and remanded for further proceedings. *Id.*, at 137–138, 112 S.Ct. 1810. JUSTICE KENNEDY, concurring in the judgment, emphasized that antipsychotic drugs might have side effects that would interfere with the defendant's ability to receive a fair trial. *Id.*, at 145, 112 S.Ct. 1810 (finding forced medication likely justified only where State shows drugs would not significantly affect defendant's "behavior and demeanor").

These two cases, *Harper* and *Riggins,* indicate that the Constitution permits the Government involuntarily to administer antipsychotic drugs to a mentally ill defendant facing serious criminal charges in order to render that defendant competent to stand trial, but only if the treatment is medically appropriate, is substantially unlikely to have side effects that may undermine the fairness of the trial, and, taking account of less intrusive alternatives, is necessary significantly to further important governmental trial-related interests.

This standard will permit involuntary administration of drugs solely for trial competence purposes in certain instances. But those instances may be rare. That is because the standard says or fairly implies the following:

First, a court must find that *important* governmental interests are at stake. The Government's interest in bringing to trial an individual accused of a serious crime is important. That is so whether the offense is a serious crime against the person or a serious crime against property. In both instances the Government seeks to protect through application of the criminal law the basic human need for security. See *Riggins, supra,* at 135–136, 112 S.Ct. 1810 (" '[P]ower to bring an accused to trial is fundamental to a scheme of "ordered liberty" and prerequisite to social justice and peace' " (quoting *Illinois v. Allen,* 397 U.S. 337, 347, 90 S.Ct. 1057, 25 L.Ed.2d 353 (1970) (Brennan, J., concurring))).

Courts, however, must consider the facts of the individual case in evaluating the Government's interest in prosecution. Special circumstances may lessen the importance of that interest. The defendant's failure to take drugs voluntarily, for example, may mean lengthy confinement in an institution for the mentally ill—and that would diminish the risks that ordinarily attach to freeing without punishment one who has committed a serious crime. We do not mean to suggest that civil commitment is a substitute for a criminal trial. The Government has a substantial interest in timely prosecution. And it may be difficult or impossible to try a defendant who regains competence after years of commitment during which memories may fade and evidence may be lost. The potential for future confinement affects, but does not totally undermine, the strength of the need for prosecution. The same is true of the possibility that the defendant has already been confined for a significant amount of time (for which he would receive credit toward any sentence ultimately imposed, see 18 U.S.C. § 3585(b)). Moreover, the Government has a concomitant, constitutionally essential interest in assuring that the defendant's trial is a fair one.

Second, the court must conclude that involuntary medication will *significantly further* those concomitant state interests. It must find that administration of the drugs is substantially likely to render the defendant competent to stand trial. At the same time, it must find that administration of the drugs is substantially unlikely to have side effects that will interfere significantly with the defendant's ability to assist counsel in conducting a trial defense, thereby rendering the trial unfair. See *Riggins,* 504 U.S., at 142–145, 112 S.Ct. 1810 (KENNEDY, J., concurring in judgment).

Third, the court must conclude that involuntary medication is *necessary* to further those interests. The court must find that any alternative, less intrusive treatments are unlikely to achieve substantially the same results. Cf. Brief for American Psychological Association as *Amicus Curiae* 10–14 (nondrug therapies may be effective in restoring psychotic defendants to competence); but cf. Brief for American Psychiatric Association et al. as *Amici Curiae* 13–22 (alternative treatments for psychosis commonly not as effective as medication). And the court must consider less intrusive means for administering the drugs, *e.g.,* a court order to the defendant backed by the contempt power, before considering more intrusive methods.

Fourth, as we have said, the court must conclude that administration of the drugs is *medically appropriate, i.e.,* in the patient's best medical interest in light of his medical condition. The specific kinds of drugs at issue may matter here as elsewhere. Different kinds of antipsychotic drugs may produce different side effects and enjoy different levels of success.

We emphasize that the court applying these standards is seeking to determine whether involuntary administration of drugs is necessary significantly to further a particular governmental interest, namely, the interest in rendering the defendant *competent to stand trial.* A court need not consider whether to allow forced medication for that kind of purpose, if forced medication is warranted for a *different* purpose, such as the purposes set out in *Harper* related to the individual's dangerousness, or purposes related to the individual's own interests where refusal to take drugs puts his health gravely at risk. 494 U.S., at 225–226, 110 S.Ct. 1028. There are often strong reasons for a court to determine whether forced administration of drugs can be justified on these alternative grounds *before* turning to the trial competence question. . . .

The Medical Center and the Magistrate in this case, applying standards roughly comparable to those set forth here and in *Harper,* approved forced medication substantially, if not primarily, upon grounds of Sell's dangerousness to others. But the District Court and the Eighth Circuit took a different approach. The District Court found "clearly erroneous" the Magistrate's conclusion regarding dangerousness, and the Court of Appeals agreed. Both courts approved forced medication solely in order to render Sell competent to stand trial.

We shall assume that the Court of Appeals' conclusion about Sell's dangerousness was correct. But we make that assumption *only* because the Government did not contest, and the parties have not argued, that particular matter. . . .

Regardless, as we have said, we must assume that Sell was not dangerous. And on that hypothetical assumption, we find that the Court of Appeals was wrong to approve forced medication solely to render Sell competent to stand trial. For one thing, the Magistrate's opinion makes clear that he did *not* find forced medication legally justified on trial competence grounds alone. Rather, the Magistrate concluded that Sell *was* dangerous, and he wrote that forced medication was "the only way to render the defendant *not dangerous and* competent to stand trial." App. 335 (emphasis added).

Moreover, the record of the hearing before the Magistrate shows that the experts themselves focused mainly upon the dangerousness issue. Consequently the experts did not pose important questions—questions, for example, about trial-related side effects and risks—the answers to which could have helped determine whether forced medication was warranted on trial competence grounds alone. Rather, the Medical Center's experts conceded that their proposed medications had "significant" side effects and that "there has to be a cost benefit analysis." *Id.,* at 185 (testimony of Dr. DeMier); *id.,* at 236 (testimony of Dr. Wolfson). And in making their "cost-benefit" judgments, they primarily took into account Sell's dangerousness, not the need to bring him to trial.

The failure to focus upon trial competence could well have mattered. Whether a particular drug will tend to sedate a defendant, interfere with communication with counsel, prevent rapid reaction to trial developments, or diminish the ability to express emotions are matters important in determining the permissibility of medication to restore competence, *Riggins,* 504 U.S., at 142–145, 112 S.Ct. 1810 (KENNEDY, J., concurring in judgment), but not necessarily relevant when dangerousness is primarily at issue. We cannot tell whether the side effects of antipsychotic medication were likely to undermine the fairness of a trial in Sell's case.

Finally, the lower courts did not consider that Sell has already been confined at the Medical Center for a long period of time, and that his refusal to take antipsychotic drugs might result in further lengthy confinement. Those factors, the first because a defendant ordinarily receives credit toward a sentence for time served, 18 U.S.C. § 3585(b), and the second because it reduces the likelihood of the defendant's committing future crimes, moderate—though they do not eliminate—the importance of the governmental interest in prosecution. See *supra,* at 2184.

V

For these reasons, we believe that the present orders authorizing forced administration of antipsychotic drugs cannot stand. The Government may pursue its request for forced medication on the grounds discussed in this opinion, including grounds related to the danger Sell poses to himself or others. Since Sell's medical condition may have changed over time, the Government should do so on the basis of current circumstances.

The judgment of the Eighth Circuit is vacated, and the case is remanded for further proceedings consistent with this opinion.

It is so ordered.

EXERCISE

One problem with forced medication is that it can be difficult to administer consistently as a prisoner is transported and held in a jail. Imagine again that you are Magistrate Judge. You recommended that Dwight Diggins, a man charged with mail fraud, be evaluated for competence. The District Judge accepted your recommendation, and authorized the Federal Medical Center to use medication, even if the defendant resisted, to make Mr. Diggins competent.

At the FMC, Diggins was given medication and after two months the staff declared that he was now competent. Two weeks later, he has again appeared in your courtroom, and is exhibiting highly erratic behavior. Upon inquiry, you find that he has been held at a local jail and not given the required medication. What do you recommend to the District Judge?

If a competency evaluation reveals that the defendant is not competent and cannot be made competent, the Court has limited options. It cannot proceed with the criminal case. In some cases, the court may have the former defendant civilly committed under 18 U.S.C. § 4246 if it finds by clear and convincing evidence that releasing the subject would "create a substantial risk of bodily injury to another person or serious damage to property of another." Similarly, § 4248 allows for the civil commitment of "sexually dangerous persons."

This leaves to the court the tricky question of committing to confinement a mentally ill person who has not been convicted, based on the interpretation of terms like "dangerousness."

UNITED STATES V. STEIL
916 F.2d 485 (8th Cir. 1990)

BOWMAN, CIRCUIT JUDGE.

Jeffrey Allen Steil appeals an order of the District Court granting the government's 18 U.S.C. § 4246 (1988) petition. We affirm.

Born in 1962, Steil has a long history of psychiatric problems. He began having auditory hallucinations at age six and attempted suicide in 1981 and 1985. Also in 1985, shortly after identifying his father as the Green River Killer, Steil had intercourse with his puppy. He then shot, killed, and buried it because he believed it to be a threat to his future children. Steil later exhumed the puppy's body and took it to a veterinarian when he heard voices telling him it was alive. An anxiety attack followed this incident, and Steil was first hospitalized, then committed. He was discharged on December 23, 1985, after being diagnosed as suffering from paranoid schizophrenia and mixed substance abuse.

In late 1987, Steil began a cross-country journey from his home in Seattle. He planned to travel to New York City to obtain financing for his flying saucer. From there, he hoped to present the plans for his saucer to the government for defense purposes. The trip had another purpose; to track the Green River Killer. Steil believed the Killer had put blood on his bed sheets in Seattle.

On route to the East Coast, Steil was stopped by the state police in northern Ohio. The police found an unregistered, loaded, sawed-off, ten gauge shotgun on the front seat of Steil's car, as well as some marijuana. The arresting officer noted that Steil appeared to have psychological problems, but was cooperative during the arrest. Steil admitted shortening the barrel of the gun.

Steil was interviewed by Special Agents from the Bureau of Alcohol, Tobacco, and Firearms. The agents noted that Steil was agitated, that he had difficulty maintaining a consistent train of thought, and that he did not realize that he was in Ohio. Steil explained to the agents that he previously had been to Washington, D.C. to see the President and wished to give the Chief Executive the plans for his saucer.

Steil was charged with illegal possession of a sawed-off shotgun, a violation of 26 U.S.C. § 5861(d) (1988). On November 5, 1987, the United States District Court for the Northern District of Ohio ordered a psychiatric examination to determine Steil's responsibility for his conduct and mental competence to stand trial. In an order filed February 8, 1988, that court found Steil to be suffering from a mental disease or defect rendering him mentally incompetent to understand the nature and consequences of the proceedings against him or to assist properly in his defense. The court committed him to the custody of the Attorney General for a period not to exceed four months for a determination of the probability of attaining capacity to permit the trial to proceed. On February 23, 1988, Steil was sent to the Federal Medical Center in Rochester, Minnesota [hereinafter FMC].

At an October 13, 1988, hearing, the court found no substantial probability of Steil's attaining capacity to permit trial to proceed in the foreseeable future. The FMC was ordered to examine Steil to determine whether his release would create a substantial risk of bodily injury to another person or serious damage to the property of another. The court considered the matter again on February 28, 1989. It concluded that Steil was suffering from a mental disease or defect as a result of which his release would create a substantial risk of bodily injury to other persons. Pursuant to 18 U.S.C. § 4246, Steil was remanded to the custody of the Attorney General for the purpose of finding a suitable state placement.

No suitable state placement was available, and, on May 8, 1989, the government filed in the United States District Court for the District of Minnesota a petition to determine the present mental condition of an imprisoned person due for release pursuant to Section 4246. Filed with this petition were two significant documents: (1) a certificate of mental disease or defect and dangerousness executed by the director of the FMC, Dr. Joseph B. Bogan; and (2) a Pre-Release (Dangerousness) Evaluation. The petition requested a finding of dangerousness and an order committing Steil to the custody of the Attorney General for hospitalization and treatment pursuant to Section 4246.

Pursuant to the petition, a hearing was held before a United States Magistrate. Two government witnesses testified. The Chief of Psychology at the FMC, Dr. Michael R. Furlong, Ph.D. in Clinical Psychology,, testified that Steil suffers from paranoid schizophrenia and is dangerous due to his mental illness. This testimony was based upon his own evaluation as well as the opinions of at least four other mental health professionals who found Steil to be mentally ill and dangerous. Dr. Furlong commented that, in his professional opinion, Steil was dangerous because he confused his hallucinations and delusions with the events around him and responds to them as if they are real. As examples, the doctor cited the events surrounding Steil's arrest and the scores of threatening letters Steil has written to public figures. Steil's case manager, Stephen O'Conner, testified that he was unable to locate a suitable state institution willing to accept Steil. Steil, represented by counsel, called no witnesses, nor did he testify.

In his Report and Recommendation, the Magistrate concluded that the government "[had] not shown by clear and convincing evidence that [Steil] should be indefinitely committed to the custody of the Attorney General" and recommended that the government's Section 4246 petition be denied. Report & Recommendation at 19. The Magistrate based this recommendation upon two premises: (1) that there is a tendency to over-predict the potential dangerousness of mentally ill persons; and (2) that Steil had no history of violent behavior toward other people, nor was he convicted of a crime prior to the shotgun incident.

The District Court, after a de novo review of the files, records, and proceedings, disagreed with the Magistrate's recommendation and granted the government's petition. The court observed in its order that at least five mental health professionals had evaluated Steil and found him to be mentally ill and dangerous, and it found that the government had shown by clear and convincing evidence that Steil remains dangerous to others.

In this appeal, Steil contends that the District Court erred in finding that the government had met its burden of showing by clear and convincing evidence that his release would present a substantial risk of bodily injury to another person or serious damage to the property of another as a result of his mental illness. We disagree.

"Section 4246 provides for the indefinite hospitalization of a person who is otherwise due to be released from commitment but who is suffering from mental disease or defect as a result of which his release would create a substantial risk of harm to the person or property of another." *United States v. Gold,* 790 F.2d 235, 237 (2d Cir.1986). Subsection (d) of Section 4246 states in part:

> (d) **Determination and disposition.**—If, after the hearing, the court finds by clear and convincing evidence that the person is presently suffering from a mental disease or defect as a result of which his release would create a substantial risk of bodily injury to another person or serious damage to property of another, the court shall commit the person to the custody of the Attorney General.

. . .

"Dangerousness is certainly not an alien term to trial judges." *United States v. Cox,* 719 F.2d 285, 287 (8th Cir.1983), *cert. denied,* 466 U.S. 929, 104 S.Ct. 1714, 80 L.Ed.2d 186 (1984). " 'In bail and sentencing proceedings, trial judges routinely consider . . . the potential danger a defendant poses to society.' " *Cox,* 719 F.2d at 287 (quoting *United States v. Schell,* 692 F.2d 672, 675 (10th Cir.1982)). A finding under 18 U.S.C. § 3142(g)(4) (1988) (Bail Reform Act of 1984 with regard to a defendant's potential danger to the community is reviewable under the clearly erroneous standard). *United States v. Maull,* 773 F.2d 1479, 1486–88 (8th Cir.1985); *see also United States v. Hurtado,* 779 F.2d 1467, 1470–73 (11th Cir.1985); *cf. Marino v. Vasquez,* 812 F.2d 499, 509 (9th Cir.1987) (under Fed.R.App.P. 23, which relates to the release on bail of state prisoners seeking habeas corpus relief in federal court, a district court's findings of fact as to a petitioner's potential danger to the community are entitled to a deferential standard of review). Consistent with this authority, we hold that the clearly erroneous standard governs our review of a district court's Section 4246 finding of dangerousness.

In the present case, the District Court found that the government has established by clear and convincing evidence that Steil is mentally ill and, if released, would pose a substantial risk of bodily injury to, or serious damage to the property of, another. The record amply supports this finding, and any contention that it is clearly erroneous is without merit. At least five mental health professionals have found Steil mentally ill and dangerous, and there is no medical opinion to the contrary in the record before us.

"It has to be recalled that the government's role here is not that of punitive custodian of a fully competent inmate, but benign custodian of one legally committed to it for medical care and treatment—specifically for psychiatric treatment." *United States v. Charters,* 863 F.2d 302, 312 (4th Cir.1988), *cert. denied,* 494 U.S. 1016, 110 S.Ct. 1317, 108 L.Ed.2d 493 (1990). In its custodial role, the government of course must fulfill its statutory duties. Most importantly, the Attorney General must continue to make all reasonable efforts to place Steil in a suitable state facility, *see* 18 U.S.C. § 4246(d), and to prepare annual reports concerning Steil's mental condition and the need for his continued hospitalization. *See* 18 U.S.C. § 4247(e)(1)(B) (1988). We hope that Steil's placement in an appropriate state institution will be arranged soon, but we recognize that such a placement depends upon finding a state institution that is willing to accept Steil. We are confident that the government will continue its efforts in this regard.

The order of the District Court is affirmed.

EXERCISE

Where a defendant has been found not competent and cannot be made competent, the court often has a difficult choice: it may either release the prisoner or impose civil commitment. If the person is released, there is no probation or other tool to keep track of the former defendant. Would it ever be appropriate to release a sex offender who was found not competent? In what circumstances?

B. THE DEFENSE OF INSANITY

Defendants with the most serious and continuing mental health issues are likely to be found not competent to stand trial, and thus never are in a position to assert a defense of insanity. One of the oddities of the process is that to assert insanity, one must be competent at the time of trial. This is possible, however, since the two processes analyze different questions at different points in time.

18 U.S.C. § 4242 establishes the procedure for asserting a defense of insanity in federal court:

(a) Motion for pretrial psychiatric or psychological examination.—Upon the filing of a notice, as provided in Rule 12.2 of the Federal Rules of Criminal Procedure, that the defendant intends to rely on the defense of insanity, the court, upon motion of the attorney for the Government, shall order that a psychiatric or psychological examination of the defendant be conducted, and that a psychiatric or psychological report be filed with the court, pursuant to the provisions of section 4247(b) and (c).

(b) Special verdict.—If the issue of insanity is raised by notice as provided in Rule 12.2 of the Federal Rules of Criminal

Procedure on motion of the defendant or of the attorney for the Government, or on the court's own motion, the jury shall be instructed to find, or, in the event of a nonjury trial, the court shall find the defendant—

(1) guilty;

(2) not guilty; or

(3) not guilty only by reason of insanity.

The federal definition of insanity, in turn, is laid out in 18 U.S.C. § 17, and is a variation of the "M'Naghten standard" developed in the 1800's:

(a) Affirmative defense. It is an affirmative defense to a prosecution under any Federal statute that, at the time of the commission of the acts constituting the offense, the defendant, as a result of a severe mental disease or defect, was unable to appreciate the nature and quality or the wrongfulness of his acts. Mental disease or defect does not otherwise constitute a defense.

(b) Burden of proof. The defendant has the burden of proving the defense of insanity by clear and convincing evidence.

This formulation is the result of a 1984 statute that changed the definition of insanity in a way that can impact some cases, including those where Post Traumatic Stress Disorder is at issue.

UNITED STATES V. BROWN
326 F.3d 1143 (10th Cir. 2003)

MURPHY, CIRCUIT JUDGE.

. . .

I. INTRODUCTION

Defendant Edward J. Brown ("Brown") was indicted on one count of conspiracy to possess with intent to distribute and distribution of methamphetamine in violation of 21 U.S.C. §§ 841(a)(1), 841(b)(1)(A), and 846; one count of using a firearm during and in relation to a drug trafficking offense in violation of 18 U.S.C. § 924(c)(1); and one count of being a felon in possession of a firearm in violation of 18 U.S.C. §§ 922(g), 924(a)(2). Pursuant to a conditional plea agreement, Brown pleaded guilty to conspiracy to possess with intent to distribute and distribution of methamphetamine and use of a firearm during and in relation to a drug trafficking offense. The district court sentenced Brown to consecutive terms of 121 months on the former count and 60 months on the latter count. The district court also ordered a $1000 fine and five years of supervised release.

Brown argues on appeal that he was deprived of his Fifth and Sixth Amendment guarantees of due process under the United States Constitution when the district court granted the government's motion in limine to exclude evidence of Brown's mental condition from consideration by the jury. Exercising jurisdiction pursuant to 28 U.S.C. § 1291, this court **affirms**, concluding that although psychological or psychiatric evidence negating specific intent may be admissible, Brown relied upon an impermissible legal theory for admitting the evidence and failed to identify a relationship between the proposed testimony and his *mens rea*.

II. BACKGROUND

On March 22, 2001, Brown was indicted on three counts for his participation in a multi-state methamphetamine operation. At arraignment, Brown pleaded not guilty to the three charges.

Subsequent to entering his pleas, Brown filed a motion to obtain a psychological examination by Dr. Fred Lindberg for the purpose of preparing a defense. The district court granted the motion. On July 30, 2001, Brown submitted notice in accordance with Fed.R.Crim.P. 12.2(a) that he intended to rely upon insanity as a defense to all charges. In addition, Brown submitted notice in accordance with Fed.R.Crim.P. 12.2(b) that he intended to "present expert testimony relating to a mental disease or defect or other mental condition of [Brown] bearing upon issue of [his] guilt."

Thereafter, the government sought an order to compel Brown to submit to a psychiatric and medical examination conducted by the Bureau of Prisons. The district court granted the government's motion and ordered Brown to be examined for purposes of determining competency and legal sanity. Brown was then re-arraigned and he entered pleas of not guilty by reason of mental illness or disease to the charges.

On December 12, 2001, the district court held a competency hearing. At the hearing, Dr. Lindberg testified that Brown suffered from post-traumatic stress disorder and chemical dependency. Dr. Lindberg also testified that, as a result of his condition, Brown did not have the capacity to conform his conduct to the requirements of the law. He also stated that at the time of his arrest, Brown did not have the capacity to "make the correct choices." Dr. Lindberg, however, concluded that Brown was not legally insane and was competent to stand trial. The Bureau of Prisons psychologist, Dr. Ronald Riggs, similarly testified that Brown was competent to stand trial and was not insane at the time he committed the offenses. Dr. Riggs also noted that, if treated, Brown may have the capacity to conform his conduct to the requirements of the law. The district court determined that Brown was competent to stand trial.

On December 21, 2001, the government filed a motion in limine seeking to exclude any testimony offered by Brown concerning his alleged mental disease or defect. Brown responded that he intended to rely on the psychological testimony of Dr. Lindberg to prove that his post-traumatic stress disorder and severe addiction to methamphetamine prevented him from formulating the necessary *mens rea* of specific intent.

At the motion hearing, the district court determined that the proposed testimony was inadmissible based on the evidence before it, namely the transcript of Dr. Lindberg's testimony at the competency hearing. The court concluded that Dr. Lindberg's testimony reflected an improper justification defense or impermissible evidence of volition and did not "establish a link or relationship between the specific psychiatric evidence offered and the mens rea at issue in this case." The court, however, was willing to reconsider the matter upon presentation of further evidence establishing such a link or relationship. Relying on *United States v. Cameron,* 907 F.2d 1051 (11th Cir.1990), the district court then granted the government's motion to exclude the testimony because the offer of proof was "limited" and "would not tend to disprove the necessary element of specific intent with regard to the conspiracy and possession with the intent to distribute charges."

On January 19, 2002, Brown entered into a conditional plea agreement. Pursuant to the agreement, Brown pleaded guilty to the conspiracy charge and the unlawful use of a firearm charge on the condition that he be allowed to pursue an appeal of the district court's order granting the government's motion in limine to exclude psychological testimony at trial. Brown was subsequently sentenced to consecutive terms of 121 months' imprisonment for the conspiracy and distribution charge and 60 months' imprisonment for the unlawful use of a firearm charge and five years of supervised release.

III. DISCUSSION

Brown argues that he is entitled to have a jury consider Dr. Lindberg's testimony concerning his mental condition for determination of whether he had the capacity to form the necessary *mens rea*. This court reviews a district court's exclusion of expert testimony for an abuse of discretion. *United States v. Diaz,* 189 F.3d 1239, 1246 (10th Cir.1999).

The standard for the defense of insanity is reflected in the Insanity Defense Reform Act ("IDRA"), 18 U.S.C. § 17. IDRA states:

> It is an affirmative defense to a prosecution under any Federal Statute that, at the time of the commission of the acts constituting the offense, the defendant, as a result of a severe mental disease or defect, was unable to appreciate the nature and quality of the wrongfulness of his acts. Mental disease or defect does not otherwise constitute a defense.

18 U.S.C. § 17(a). Prior to the enactment of IDRA in 1984, this court followed the insanity test established by the American Law Institute Model

Penal Code ("ALI"). *United States v. Denny-Shaffer,* 2 F.3d 999, 1003 n. 1 (10th Cir.1993). The ALI test provided that a defendant would not be criminally responsible for conduct if "as a result of mental disease or defect, he lacked substantial capacity either to appreciate the wrongfulness of his conduct or to conform his conduct to the requirements of the law." *Id.* (quotation omitted). In enacting IDRA, Congress eliminated the volitional branch, which is the latter portion of the ALI test. *Id.* In addition, IDRA "eliminated all other *affirmative defenses or excuses* based upon mental disease or defect." *Cameron,* 907 F.2d at 1061. Thus, IDRA bars the introduction of evidence of a defendant's mental disease or defect to demonstrate that he lacked substantial capacity to control his actions or reflect upon the consequences or nature of his actions. *United States v. Worrell,* 313 F.3d 867, 872 (4th Cir.2002).

Brown essentially contends that evidence of his mental condition is admissible to negate specific intent. This court has not addressed whether psychological or psychiatric expert testimony is admissible to negate specific intent. Several circuits, however, have concluded that evidence of a defendant's mental condition is admissible for the purpose of disproving specific intent. *Id.* at 873; *see also United States v. Kimes,* 246 F.3d 800, 806 (6th Cir.2001), *cert. denied,* 534 U.S. 1085, 122 S.Ct. 823, 151 L.Ed.2d 705 (2002); *United States v. Schneider,* 111 F.3d 197, 201 (1st Cir.1997); *United States v. Childress,* 58 F.3d 693, 729–30 (D.C.Cir.1995); *United States v. Twine,* 853 F.2d 676, 679 (9th Cir.1988); *United States v. Newman,* 849 F.2d 156, 165 (5th Cir.1988); *United States v. Pohlot,* 827 F.2d 889, 897 (3d Cir.1987). The circuits reaching such a result generally rely on the distinction between psychiatric evidence that provides a justification or excuse for criminal conduct and psychiatric evidence that assists the trier of fact in determining whether the prosecution has satisfied its burden of proving each element of the crime. *Worrell,* 313 F.3d at 873; *see also Cameron,* 907 F.2d at 1060 (noting that Congress intended to preclude psychiatric evidence as a legal excuse but not to negate specific intent); *Pohlot,* 827 F.2d at 897 (commenting that admitting psychiatric evidence to negate *mens rea* is not a defense but only a challenge to an element of the offense). The circuits, however, recognize that evidence of a defendant's impaired volitional control or inability to reflect on the consequences of his conduct remains inadmissible. *Cameron,* 907 F.2d at 1066; *see also Worrell,* 313 F.3d at 872; *Pohlot,* 827 F.2d at 890.

This court similarly agrees that psychological or psychiatric evidence that negates the essential element of specific intent can be admissible. The admission of such evidence will depend upon whether the defendant clearly demonstrates how such evidence would negate intent rather than "merely present a dangerously confusing theory of defense more akin to justification and excuse." *Cameron,* 907 F.2d at 1067. Because there is a risk that such evidence will mislead or confuse the jury, district courts must carefully scrutinize proposed psychiatric evidence to determine whether the evidence rests upon a legally acceptable theory for negating intent. *Id.* While "IDRA does not prohibit psychiatric evidence of a mental condition short of insanity when such evidence is offered purely to rebut the government's evidence of specific intent, . . . such cases will be rare." *Worrell,* 313 F.3d at 874.

In *Worrell,* the defendant sought to introduce the expert testimony of a forensic psychiatrist who opined that the defendant was "quite impaired psychiatrically" around the time of the offense. *Id.* at 870. The district court excluded the testimony. *Id.* at 871. The United States Court of Appeals for the Fourth Circuit concluded that the district court did not err in excluding the evidence because the proposed testimony was not relevant to the issue of specific intent. *Id.* at 874. The court noted that the expert's opinion did not even address the defendant's intent, or lack thereof, for the particular offense charged. *Id.* Similarly, in *Cameron,* the defendant argued that the proffered psychiatric evidence would have shown that her mental condition "rendered her incapable of forming the specific intent necessary to commit the crimes charged." 907 F.2d at 1067. The United States Court of Appeals for the Eleventh Circuit concluded, however, that Cameron failed to specifically explain how the psychiatric evidence demonstrated that she did not intend to distribute cocaine. *Id.* The *Cameron* court noted that "[t]he proper focus should be on the proffered link or relationship between the specific psychiatric evidence offered and the *mens rea* at issue in the case." *Id.* at 1067 n. 31.

In this case, Brown sought to introduce evidence that his mental capacity precluded him from forming the requisite specific intent. For proof, Brown relied on Dr. Lindberg's conclusion that Brown did not have the capacity to conform his conduct to the requirements of the law. Specifically, Brown sought to rely upon testimony that he was unable to make "correct choices" because of his mental condition. Similar to the evidence in *Worrell* and *Cameron,* Dr. Lindberg's testimony did not address Brown's intent, or lack thereof, for conspiracy to possess with the intent to distribute and distribution of methamphetamine. Dr. Lindberg did not opine on how Brown's post-traumatic stress disorder, coupled with chemical dependency, was either related to or tended to negate the requisite specific intent element. Thus, Brown fails to connect his mental condition with any legally acceptable theory that he lacked specific intent. Furthermore, although the district court was willing to consider evidence that would link Dr. Lindberg's testimony to the government's proof of specific intent, Brown failed to offer such support.

Additionally, Brown's reasons for offering Dr. Lindberg's testimony, which were to show that Brown failed to conform his conduct to the requirements of the law and failed to make correct choices because of his mental condition, equates to proof that Brown lacked the capacity to control or reflect upon his conduct. Such evidence is inadmissible psychological or psychiatric evidence. *See Cameron,* 907 F.2d at 1066 (stating that evidence of the defendant's inability to reflect upon or control behavior is inadmissible because it does not negate specific intent). Accordingly, the district court did not abuse its discretion in excluding evidence of Brown's mental disease or defect.

IV. CONCLUSION

Based upon the foregoing reasons, the district court's exclusion of psychological evidence is AFFIRMED.

EXERCISE

Imagine that you are the defense attorney for the defendant in the *Brown* case, and that the case was remanded for a new trial on other grounds. This allows for a complete do-over of the defense case. What would you do differently?

Because the insanity defense is relatively rarely employed, shifts the burden to the defense, contains an unusual standard of proof within criminal law ("by clear and convincing evidence"), and involves the delicate interpretation of expert testimony, trial courts are usually quite careful in crafting instructions to the jury regarding this defense.

UNITED STATES V. BROWN
635 Fed. Appx. 574 (11th Cir. 2015)

PER CURIAM:

After a five-day trial at which he presented a defense of not guilty by reason of insanity, Korrigan Brown was convicted of conspiracy to commit Hobbs Act robbery, Hobbs Act robbery, and using a firearm during a crime of violence. He challenges his convictions and his sentence.

I.

On December 14, 2012, Brown called his childhood friend Lamel Lattimore and asked him to come over to his house. At Brown's house Lattimore agreed to drive the car while they committed a robbery. They drove to another friend's house, and Brown borrowed a firearm from him and put it in a backpack. Brown and Lattimore met up with Nathan Holmes, who had committed armed robberies with Brown "more than three times" before. Holmes agreed to participate in a robbery that day, went into his house and retrieved his firearm, and left in the car with Lattimore and Brown.

They drove to a Chevron station in Miami Beach, but their armed robbery attempt ended unsuccessfully when an employee summoned the police, causing them to flee without any money. The Chevron robbery was recorded on surveillance video.

Because that robbery attempt was unsuccessful, the three men tried again at a Wendy's restaurant in Hialeah. Lattimore parked the car at Wendy's, and Brown and Holmes got out with their firearms and the backpack. After they entered Wendy's, Brown pointed his firearm at the cashier and told him to open the cash registers. The cashier handed Brown the money from the registers, which he put in his backpack. Brown and Holmes ran out of the restaurant. That robbery was also recorded on surveillance video.

As the three men pulled away in Lattimore's car, a witness called 911 and reported that the Wendy's had just been robbed and the robbers were fleeing in a gray car. Responding to the 911 call, Officer Orlando Salvat began following Lattimore's car and eventually stopped it. The dispatcher confirmed, based on information from the 911 caller who was watching the events unfold, that it was the car with the Wendy's robbers in it. Based on that information, Salvat drew his gun and ordered everyone in the car to get out and put their hands on the roof of the car. Lattimore and Holmes complied. Brown exited the car and fled, carrying the backpack. Salvat and another officer who had arrived at the scene fired shots at Brown but missed. Brown kept running. He was eventually apprehended by officers using a K-9 and tasers.

In the truck where Brown had been hiding, there was a backpack, a pair of gloves, and a cell phone. The cell phone's call records later showed that it had been used to make a call to Lattimore on the morning of the robberies and to make calls while it was being transported toward the Chevron just before that first robbery. A t-shirt with a bloodstain was later found in Lattimore's car; the DNA in the blood matched Brown's.

A superseding indictment charged Brown, Lattimore, and Holmes with conspiracy to commit Hobbs Act robbery (Count 1) as well as the Hobbs Act robberies of the Chevron (Count 2) and the Wendy's (Count 4), all in violation of 18 U.S.C.1951(a), and use of a firearm during a crime of violence (Counts 3 & 5), in violation of 18 U.S.C. § 924(c)(1)(A). Brown pleaded not guilty and provided notice under Fed.R.Crim.P. 12.2, stating that he intended to rely on an insanity defense at trial. Lattimore and Holmes pleaded guilty and later testified at Brown's trial.

Brown's trial lasted five days. Defense counsel admitted during voir dire and in his opening statement that Brown had participated in the robberies, but he asserted that Brown was insane. Despite counsel's admission, the parties did not stipulate to all of the elements of Hobbs Act robbery. They did stipulate that the Chevron and Wendy's were businesses operating in foreign commerce and that the robbery of them had "obstructed, delayed and affected interstate and foreign commerce." *See* 18 U.S.C. § 1951(b)(3) (defining "commerce" as used in the statute as interstate or foreign commerce).

The government called ten witnesses: employees from the Chevron station and the Wendy's, officer Salvat and the K-9 officer, a police ID technician, a criminologist, an FBI agent, a cell phone records custodian, and Brown's co-conspirators Lattimore and Holmes. Defense counsel cross-examined the government's witnesses. Most of his questions were related to mental illness and the insanity defense, but not all of them. Some of them were about factual matters such as: why Officer Salvat decided to stop the defendants' car even though it did not match the description given by dispatch (a Honda, not a Nissan; gray, not "dark"); whether any firearm, clothing, or "masking equipment" was found in the police-marked perimeter where Brown had fled after the car was stopped; and whether the cell phone data revealed who possessed the cell phone that was alleged to be Brown's at the time of the robberies. Defense counsel also attempted to establish through cross-examination that the firearm Brown was carrying was not loaded.

Brown moved for a judgment of acquittal at the close of the government's case, asserting that it had failed to prove its case. After that motion was denied, Brown called six witnesses in an attempt to establish his insanity defense: his stepfather, his mother, his friend, the mother of that friend, and two mental health experts. Both of the experts testified that they had diagnosed Brown with bipolar disorder. The government presented a mental health expert who testified that Brown was malingering and had shown no signs of bipolar disorder.

In his closing argument, defense counsel once again admitted that Brown had participated in the robberies, said that the only issue was whether he was insane at the time the crimes were committed, and argued that clear and convincing evidence established Brown's insanity. For each of the five counts, the verdict form contained three options: guilty, not guilty, and not guilty by reason of insanity. The jury found Brown guilty on all counts. It also specifically found that Brown used or carried a firearm in relation to the robberies, that he possessed it in furtherance of the crimes, and that he had brandished it.

Brown was subject to mandatory minimum consecutive sentences on the firearms convictions. The district court imposed a total sentence of 435 months imprisonment. This is Brown's appeal.

II.

Brown contends that the district court erred in rejecting his proposed jury instructions about the burden of proof on the insanity defense and about the mandatory minimum punishment he faced if convicted. "We review a district court's refusal to give a requested jury instruction for abuse of discretion." *United States v. Martinelli,* 454 F.3d 1300, 1309 (11th Cir.2006) (quotation marks omitted). "A district court's refusal to give a requested instruction is reversible error if (1) the requested instruction was a correct statement of the law, (2) its subject matter was not substantially covered by other instructions, and (3) its subject matter dealt with an issue in the trial court that was so important that failure to give it seriously impaired the defendant's ability to defend himself." *Id.*

A.

Brown acknowledges that the Insanity Defense Reform Act of 1984 establishes that insanity is an affirmative defense and that a defendant has the burden of proving it by clear and convincing evidence. *See* 18 U.S.C. § 17. That statute, titled "Insanity Defense," provides:

> (a) Affirmative defense.—It is an affirmative defense to a prosecution under any Federal statute that, at the time of the commission of the acts constituting the offense, the defendant, as a result of a severe mental disease or defect, was unable to appreciate the nature and quality or the wrongfulness of his acts. Mental disease or defect does not otherwise constitute a defense.

> (b) Burden of proof.—The defendant has the burden of proving the defense of insanity by clear and convincing evidence.

Id.

The district court gave the Eleventh Circuit Pattern Jury Instruction on the insanity defense, which basically tracks the statute. *See* 11th Cir. PJI—Criminal 15 (2010). The district court instructed the jury as follows:

> Now, there is an issue about the Defendant's sanity when the charged offense occurred. If you find beyond a reasonable doubt that the Defendant committed the offense, you must consider whether the Defendant was "not guilty only by reason of insanity."

> A defendant is "insane" only if the defendant is unable because of severe mental disease or defect to appreciate the nature and quality or wrongfulness of an act. But mental disease or defect does not otherwise constitute a defense.

> On the issue of insanity, it is the Defendant who must prove his insanity by clear and convincing evidence. Clear and convincing evidence is evidence sufficient to persuade you that the Defendant's claim is highly probable. It is a higher standard of proof than a preponderance of the evidence, but less exacting than proof beyond a reasonable doubt.

> A "preponderance of the evidence" is enough evidence to persuade you that the Defendant's claim is more likely true than not true.

> If the defendant proves insanity by clear and convincing evidence, then you must find the Defendant not guilty only by reason of insanity.

> So there are three possible verdicts: Guilty, not guilty, and not guilty only by reason of insanity.

The proposed instruction that Brown submitted to the district court, which the court rejected, was: "On the issue of insanity, the Defendant must be proven sane at the time of the charged offense beyond a reasonable doubt, as previously defined in these instructions." Brown argues that after he produced "some evidence" to support his insanity defense, the government should have had the burden of proving beyond a reasonable doubt that he was not insane when he committed the crimes. He argues that shifting the burden to him after he had produced some evidence of his insanity was a due process violation because the government was relieved of having to prove every element of the charged offenses.

Brown's proposed jury instruction would have put the insanity burden of proof on the government, which is contrary to the plain language of 18 U.S.C. § 17. In effect, the instruction would have made sanity an element of the charged offenses. Put another way, the instruction he wanted was: The government must prove beyond a reasonable doubt that Brown was sane at the time he committed the charged offenses because Brown has presented some evidence that he suffered from mental illness.

This Court has already held that putting the burden of proof on the defendant to prove insanity by clear and convincing evidence, as 18 U.S.C. § 17 does, is constitutionally permissible. *United States v. Freeman*, 804 F.2d 1574, 1576 (11th Cir.1986). The plain language of § 17 and the *Freeman* decision foreclose Brown's arguments about the jury instructions he requested. The jury instructions that the court gave did not relieve the government of its burden of proving every element of the charged crimes (except to the extent of Brown's stipulation about interstate or foreign commerce). The district court did not err by refusing to give Brown's requested instruction on the burden of proof.

EXERCISE

So, why *not* require the government to prove that the defendant was sane at the time of the crime? Wouldn't that be consistent with the burden of proof in other areas, where we expect the government to prove the defendant's state of mind as to intent and knowledge?

Because the insanity defense focuses on the defendant's mental condition at the time of the offense, it must be determined with clarity when the offense actually occurred.

UNITED STATES V. ALVAREZ-ULLOA

784 F.3d 558 (9th Cir. 2015)

TASHIMA, CIRCUIT JUDGE:

Jesus Alvarez-Ulloa ("Ulloa") appeals his conviction for illegal reentry under 8 U.S.C. § 1326(a) and the district court's order revoking his supervised release based on the jury's guilty verdict in the illegal reentry case. During jury selection, Ulloa unsuccessfully challenged three of the government's peremptory strikes under *Batson v. Kentucky,* 476 U.S. 79, 106 S.Ct. 1712, 90 L.Ed.2d 69 (1986). At trial, Ulloa asserted the insanity defense, arguing that as a former boxer he suffered from brain damage that prevented him from understanding the nature of his presence in the United States. After the jury deadlocked, the district court clarified that the insanity defense would not apply if while Ulloa was illegally present in the United States he was sane for a long enough period to have left the country. The jury subsequently returned a guilty verdict.

On appeal, Ulloa contends, first, that the district court erred in rejecting his *Batson* challenges, and, second, that the supplemental instruction impermissibly coerced the jury and constructively expanded the indictment. We have jurisdiction under 28 U.S.C. § 1291. We affirm.

I.

Over a period of about twelve years, between approximately 1984 and 1996, Ulloa was first an amateur and later a professional boxer. Although Ulloa was raised and appears to have lived primarily in Arizona, he is a citizen of Mexico, a designation responsible for many of his recent legal problems.

In 2010, Ulloa was removed to Mexico following a conviction for attempted illegal reentry after deportation, in violation of 8 U.S.C. §§ 1326(a), (b)(2). Ulloa subsequently reentered the United States. Local police found and detained Ulloa in October 2011 at a resort in Phoenix after he reportedly attempted to steal a copy of the roster of the Arizona Cardinals. . . .

At trial Ulloa stipulated that he had been found on or about October 23, 2011, in Phoenix, noting that it would be "surprising" if the government failed to prove the elements of illegal reentry. Ulloa intended to build his case on the insanity defense, alleging that, due to injuries he sustained during his career as a professional boxer, he was unable to understand the wrongfulness of his actions. The government presented evidence that Ulloa had been previously deported and was found in the United States in October 2011, and evidence suggesting that Ulloa did not have a mental disease or defect. Ulloa presented evidence suggesting that he in fact suffered from chronic traumatic encephalopathy, a disease which— according to his expert witness—could have rendered him legally insane.

Under the jury instructions, for Ulloa to be found guilty under § 1326(a), the government was required to prove that: (1) Ulloa "was deported from the United States on or about December 17, 2010," (2) Ulloa "voluntarily entered the United States," (3) "after entering the United States, [Ulloa] knew that he was in the United States and knowingly remained," (4) "on or about October 23, 2011, [Ulloa] was found in the United States," and (5) "[Ulloa] was an alien at the time of [his] entry into the United States." The court further instructed that "[a] defendant is insane only if at the time of the crime charged, one, the defendant had a severe mental disease or defect; and two, as a result, the defendant was unable to appreciate the nature and quality or the wrongfulness of his acts."

Several hours after the jury began deliberations, the court received a note from the foreperson, which stated:

> The jury needs clarification on the defendant's mental state needed to consistently meet the, quote, 'insane,' close quote, criteria for the entire time he was here illegally, (from 2010–2011). Specifically, if the defendant had any moments of mental clarity during that time or he was able to appreciate the nature and quality or wrongfulness of his acts, does that negate the defense of insanity?

After consulting with the parties, the court answered the question by referring the jury to the original jury instructions. Thereafter, the jury sent out another note stating:

> We currently seem to be unable to reach a unanimous decision on a verdict and would like some direction from the court on what to do at this point.

The court responded:

> If the Court gives a more specific answer to your previous question, would you wish to continue to deliberate to try to reach a unanimous verdict?

After the jury replied affirmatively, the court provided the jury with the following supplemental instruction in response to its question:

> The insanity defense would be negated if, after entering the United States, the Defendant ceased to be insane for a long enough time that he reasonably could have left the United States, and he then knowingly remained in the United States for that time.

Thirty-seven minutes later, the jury returned a guilty verdict. The district court subsequently sentenced Ulloa to 48 months' imprisonment. . . .

Ulloa next contends that the district court's supplemental instruction impermissibly coerced the jury's verdict in violation of the Sixth Amendment. Although we review the decision to give a supplemental jury instruction for abuse of discretion, *see United States v. Solomon,* 825 F.2d 1292, 1295 (9th Cir.1987), we review *de novo* whether a trial court's actions impermissibly coerced a jury's verdict, *United States v. Williams,* 547 F.3d 1187, 1202 n. 14 (9th Cir.2008).

In resolving Ulloa's challenge, we first examine whether the supplemental instruction was substantively correct. Ulloa was charged with the crime of being "found in" the United States after having been removed, one of "three distinct substantive offenses" under § 1326(a). *United States v. Covian-Sandoval,* 462 F.3d 1090, 1094 (9th Cir.2006). It is an affirmative defense to any federal crime, including those under § 1326, that "at the time of the commission of the acts constituting the offense, the defendant, as a result of a severe mental disease or defect, was unable to appreciate the nature and quality or the wrongfulness of his acts." 18 U.S.C. § 17(a).

Although we have not had occasion to apply the insanity defense to the "found in" offense under § 1326(a), our precedents offer guidance on how the defense operates. Illegal reentry is a continuing offense, meaning that the offense "commences with the illegal entry, but is not completed until discovery." *United States v. Hernandez-Guerrero,* 633 F.3d 933, 936 (9th Cir.2011). When a defendant asserts an affirmative defense to a continuing offense, he generally must show that the requirements for the defense were satisfied for the entire period in question. *See United States v. Bailey,* 444 U.S. 394, 412, 100 S.Ct. 624, 62 L.Ed.2d 575 (1980) (noting that an individual using a duress defense to defend a charge of escape, another continuing offense, "must ... offer evidence justifying his continued absence from custody as well as his initial departure"); *see also United States v. Williams,* 791 F.2d 1383, 1388 (9th Cir.1986). Continuing offenses, by their nature, contemplate extended periods of proscribed criminal conduct. It would be anomalous for a defense that negates culpability for only one portion of a continuing offense's criminal period to completely bar conviction.

The Tenth Circuit dealt with a case which involved a situation similar to the case at bench, in which the defendant asserted duress as a defense to an illegal reentry charge under § 1326(a). *See United States v. Portillo-Vega,* 478 F.3d 1194 (10th Cir.2007). There, the defendant claimed that he illegally reentered the United States because he feared persecution at the hands of Mexican police. *Id.* at 1198–99. The court reasoned that for the defendant to be entitled to a duress instruction, he needed to adduce evidence to show not only that he reasonably feared death or serious bodily injury when he reentered, but also throughout the duration of his illegal stay. *Id.* at 1201. The logic of *Portillo-Vega* applies with equal force to the insanity defense, which is historically and conceptually analogous to duress. *See Powell v. Texas,* 392 U.S. 514, 535–36, 88 S.Ct. 2145, 20 L.Ed.2d 1254 (1968) (plurality opinion). To succeed in his defense, Ulloa thus needed to prove that he was legally insane for virtually the entire duration of his illegal stay, such that he could not reasonably have left the United

States. We therefore conclude that the district court's supplemental instruction was substantively correct. . . .

EXERCISE

You are the judge in a case against a single defendant charged with conspiracy to manufacture marijuana. The defendant, Lisa Stucco, agreed with David Thompson that they would start a small marijuana farm on some land Lisa owns. David would get young plants and provide them to Lisa, who would plant and grow them. When the plants became mature, David would sell the marijuana, and they would split the profits. However, David bought the plants from an undercover police officer and, once caught, agreed to cooperate against Lisa. He gave her the plants as directed by the police officer, she planted them, and three weeks later (before the plants were mature) she was arrested and charged with narcotics conspiracy.

In the middle of those three weeks, Lisa was arrested on an unrelated charge of car theft and sent for outpatient mental health evaluation by a state court that was unaware of the federal narcotics investigation. The doctor conducting the evaluation concluded that Lisa was suffering from severe delusions resulting from the use of narcotics and schizophrenia. He ordered a follow-up in two days to conduct more tests. She did not show up for the follow-up evaluation, and was then arrested on the federal charges.

Assuming that the evidence shows that an insanity defense instruction is warranted in Lisa's case, how would you define the time period during which she must meet the definition of insanity if her insanity defense is to prevail?

Can you assert the defense of insanity if your incapacitation is the result of voluntary intoxication? While jurisdictions vary in their answer to this question, the analysis below is common.

UNITED STATES V. GARCIA
94 F.3d 57 (2d Cir. 1996)

WALKER, CIRCUIT JUDGE:

Defendant Felix Garcia appeals from his conviction before the United States District Court for the District of Connecticut (T.F. Gilroy Daly, *District Judge*). On appeal, Garcia claims that: (1) the district court erred in instructing the jury that in order to find that Garcia satisfied his burden of proving insanity, his severe mental disease, rather than his alcohol and drug use at the time of the commission of the crime, must have been the cause of his inability to appreciate the wrongfulness of his actions. . . .

BACKGROUND

During mid-afternoon on March 28, 1994, in response to a radio report that a man was threatening others with a gun, Bridgeport, Connecticut Police Officer James Kirkland was dispatched to 1111 Barnum Avenue in Bridgeport. On arrival, he saw a group of people on the sidewalk and, upon inquiring, was advised that the man with the gun was going up the street. Officer Kirkland saw the man, later identified as Defendant Felix Garcia, about forty yards away walking with a bicycle. Officer Kirkland then drove alongside Garcia in a marked police car, rolled down the driver's window, and asked Garcia: "What's up?" Garcia dropped the bicycle and responded: "Nothing's up." Garcia then reached for his waist and pulled out a gun. Officer Kirkland drew his weapon and fired a shot out of the driver's window into Garcia's stomach. Garcia thereafter was arrested.

On October 20, 1994, a grand jury indicted Garcia for possession of a firearm by a convicted felon, in violation of 18 U.S.C. § 922(g)(1). After entering a plea of not guilty, Garcia moved for a competency evaluation. Judge Daly granted the motion on December 8, 1994 and, following the evaluation, Garcia was found competent to stand trial. On January 13, 1995, Garcia filed a notice of intent to rely on an insanity defense, pursuant to Rule 12.2 of the Federal Rules of Criminal Procedure. Trial commenced on May 3, 1995. Garcia presented his insanity defense, but on May 4, 1995, the jury rejected it and rendered a guilty verdict. On September 29, 1995, the district court sentenced Garcia under the armed career criminal provision of 18 U.S.C. § 924(e)(1) to a term of imprisonment of 192 months, to run concurrently with any sentence to be imposed by the State of Connecticut, to be followed by a five year term of supervised release. Judgment was entered on October 2, 1995. Garcia subsequently pled guilty in state court to attempted assault on a police officer and was sentenced to a term of imprisonment of ten years, to run concurrently with his federal sentence. On appeal, Garcia raises no objection to his sentence; his challenge is solely to his district court conviction.

DISCUSSION

I. The Insanity Defense Issue

Garcia argues that the district court erred in its insanity defense instruction to the jury to the effect that a finding of mental disease or defect could not be based upon Garcia's alcohol or drug consumption. Before we turn to the instruction at issue, we recount the evidence relating to the insanity defense raised at trial.

José Solano, Garcia's nephew, testified that he saw Garcia at approximately 12:00 p.m. on the day of the shooting when Garcia was working on a bicycle in the rear yard of Solano's apartment at 1111 Barnum Avenue. According to Solano, Garcia was acting "normal," "nice," and "calm" and was "happy" at that time. Solano also testified that Garcia showed Solano a gun, which Garcia claimed a friend had given to him.

According to his testimony, Solano left home for a few hours and returned at approximately 2:30 or 3:00 p.m. with his sister and his friend, Edwin Maldonado. When they arrived, they heard Solano's dogs barking in Solano's third floor apartment. As they approached the apartment, Maldonado, who had been living with Solano for several months, shouted to the dogs to shut up. Garcia, who was in the apartment making a sandwich and heard Maldonado yell at the dogs, came out of the apartment, grabbed Maldonado, threw him against the door, and told him never to tell the dogs to shut up. Shortly after Solano told Garcia to stop fighting with Maldonado, Garcia let go of Maldonado but continued to yell, and threatened Maldonado with the gun he had earlier shown to Solano. At Solano's request, Garcia eventually left the apartment, all the while yelling, swearing, and threatening both Solano and Maldonado. At that point, Solano telephoned his mother, Minerva Solano (Garcia's sister), and also called the police. Solano testified that, at this time, Garcia was acting "angry," "sounded like evil," and "sounded like he . . . had a demon or something."

When Minerva Solano arrived, Garcia was still in the yard. When his sister asked him to leave, he did so, taking his bicycle with him. As he was leaving, he yelled: "They're going to get you, they're going to get me." He also threatened to blow up the block and said that Hitler was coming, that this was a communist world, and that "demons are going to get you."

At trial, both sides put on psychiatric testimony. The psychiatrists for both sides testified to Garcia's long history of drug and alcohol use, beginning in his pre-teen years. Dr. Paul T. Amble, the defense psychiatrist, stated that Garcia had reported to him that on the day of the shooting and prior to the incident, he had smoked approximately nine or ten vials of crack cocaine and had drunk half a pint of brandy. Both Dr. Amble and Dr. Jeffrey Gottlieb, the government's psychiatrist, testified as to their awareness that Garcia had undergone numerous psychiatric evaluations in the past and that he had, on previous occasions, been diagnosed with bipolar disorder (also known as manic depression). They were also aware that, in the past, Garcia had received different diagnoses such as organic brain syndrome, secondary substance abuse, anti-social personality disorder, and substance abuse disorder.

Not surprisingly, the views of the psychiatrists differed as to the nature of Garcia's mental state at the time of the incident. Dr. Gottlieb testified for the government that Garcia's primary diagnosis was substance dependence—primarily on cocaine and alcohol—coupled with antisocial personality disorder. Dr. Gottlieb stated that Garcia's "behavior [was] entire [l]y consistent with someone who was, in common parlance, . . . really high and probably drunk too." In contrast, Dr. Amble testified for the defense that Garcia suffered, and had long been suffering, from the severe mental disease of bipolar disorder, and that he was in a manic phase and suffered from delusional thinking on March 28, 1994. Dr. Amble also testified, however, that he could not "rule . . . out completely" the possibility that Garcia's behavior was "simply the product of substance abuse."

On appeal, Garcia claims that the district court erred when it instructed the jury that to find that Garcia had met his burden of proving insanity, his inability to appreciate the wrongfulness of his actions must have been caused by severe mental disease rather than by alcohol and drug use. This issue is one of first impression in this circuit.

The district court charged the jury as follows:

> Now, the effects of the voluntary use of drugs or alcohol do not constitute, nor may they legally give rise to a severe mental disease or defect. The voluntary use, if any you find, of drugs or alcohol also must be disregarded in determining whether the Defendant could appreciate the nature and quality of his acts or the wrongfulness of his acts. However, if you find that at the time in issue the Defendant had a severe mental disease or defect, and that the disease or defect gave rise to an inability to appreciate the nature or quality or wrongfulness of his acts, then the Defendant's consumption of drugs or alcohol, whether voluntary or involuntary, cannot preclude his defense of insanity.

The district court rejected the following instruction offered by Garcia:

> There has been evidence at this trial regarding the defendant's substance abuse. Substance abuse, standing alone, does not constitute a severe mental illness. On the other hand, if you find that the substance abuse either caused or was caused by a separate mental illness, then you can consider both the mental illness and the substance abuse in assessing whether or not the defendant was able to know and appreciate the quality or wrongfulness of his actions.

As we previously have stated, "[a]lthough a defendant is entitled to a jury charge reflecting his theory of defense, that theory must have a valid basis in law and fact." *United States v. Ruggiero,* 934 F.2d 440, 450 (2d Cir.1991). We believe that the district court correctly rejected Garcia's proposed charge because Garcia's theory had no basis in fact. Although the jury was apprised of Garcia's long history of substance abuse, it heard no evidence that Garcia's substance abuse either caused or was caused by his bipolar disorder.

The district court told the jury, in effect, that voluntary substance abuse must not be taken into account in determining whether a severe mental disease or defect exists in the first instance, but where such a disease or defect is found to exist, voluntary substance abuse will not defeat an insanity defense. Our review of the charge is de novo. *See United States v. Kwong,* 69 F.3d 663, 667 (2d Cir.1995), *cert. denied,* 517 U.S. 1115, 116 S.Ct. 1343, 134 L.Ed.2d 491 (1996). Because the charge is not covered expressly by the text of the Insanity Defense Reform Act of 1984 ("IDRA"), 18 U.S.C. § 17, in examining the charge for error, we are required to look to the congressional intent behind the IDRA and to existing caselaw.

Congress enacted the IDRA, the first federal legislation on the insanity defense, largely in response to public concern over the acquittal of John W. Hinkley, Jr. for the attempted assassination of President Reagan. In enacting the IDRA, Congress made two substantial changes to the federal insanity defense. First, it narrowed the definition of insanity that had evolved from the caselaw. Second, it shifted to the defendant the burden of proving the insanity defense by clear and convincing evidence. S.Rep. No. 225, 98th Cong., 1st Sess. 222, 225–26 (1983), *reprinted in* 1984 U.S.C.C.A.N. 3182, 3407. Of significance to this case, Congress, speaking through the Senate Judiciary Committee, stated: "The committee also intends that, as has been held under present case law interpretation, the voluntary use of alcohol or drugs, even if they render the defendant unable to appreciate the nature and quality of his acts, does not constitute insanity or any other species of legally valid affirmative defense." *Id.* at 229. Statements of congressional intent are rarely so clear.

Garcia claims, however, that the statement by the Senate Judiciary Committee regarding voluntary intoxication means only that "a drug addict or alcoholic cannot assert an insanity defense based solely upon [his] addicted status." He suggests that Congress did not mean to imply that where one suffers from a mental disease or defect as well as voluntary alcoholism or substance abuse, each of which alone is insufficient to satisfy the IDRA's requirement of a "severe mental disease or defect [rendering one] unable to appreciate the nature and quality or the wrongfulness of his acts," he may not prove that together the conditions satisfy the statute's requirement. The government responds that "[c]ombining a mental disease or defect that is itself insufficient under the IDRA, with the impermissible consideration of voluntary substance abuse, to result in a valid defense of insanity under the IDRA, is wholly illogical. This would constitute nothing short of rewarding the voluntary abuse of drugs and alcohol in direct contradiction of the intent of Congress in passing the IDRA." The caselaw on this issue, although limited, recognizes as much, and we agree.

To date, only the Ninth Circuit has considered this issue. *United States v. Knott,* 894 F.2d 1119 (9th Cir.), *cert. denied,* 498 U.S. 873, 111 S.Ct. 197, 112 L.Ed.2d 158 (1990). On facts similar to this case, the *Knott* Court held that the jury could not consider a defendant's voluntary drug use or intoxication at the time of his crime in combination with his schizophrenia in determining whether the defendant was unable to appreciate the nature and quality or wrongfulness of his acts. Rather, in order to satisfy the requirements of the IDRA with respect to proving insanity, the defendant would have had to demonstrate that his schizophrenia alone prevented him from appreciating the nature and quality of his acts. *Id.* at 1121.

Garcia argues against our adopting the view set forth in *Knott*. Instead, relying on our decision in *United States v. Torniero*, 735 F.2d 725 (2d Cir.1984), *cert. denied,* 469 U.S. 1110, 105 S.Ct. 788, 83 L.Ed.2d 782 (1985), he urges us to find error in the district court's charge. Garcia's reliance on *Torniero,* however, is misplaced. In *Torniero,* we stated that "[s]ubstance abuse may only be used as the basis of an insanity defense if the affliction brings about actual insanity." *Id.* at 733. The *Torniero* case, however, involved involuntary intoxication and the above-quoted statement is thus dicta. Furthermore, there was no evidence presented that Garcia's bipolar disorder, the mental disease or defect at issue, was caused by his substance abuse. In addition, our decision in *Torniero* preceded passage of the IDRA, which, as we have already noted, significantly changed federal insanity defense law.

EXERCISE

Imagine that you are the prosecutor in the *Garcia* case above. The defendant has been convicted but not yet sentenced. At sentencing, the defense attorney argues that while voluntary intoxication did not suffice as a basis for a defense of insanity, it should be a mitigating circumstance and result in a lower sentence for the defendant. How do you respond?

Some might argue that at times intoxication by an addict is involuntary—that they cannot resist the addiction. Should that kind of "involuntary" intoxication be an allowable basis for an insanity defense, provided that the addiction can be proven?

UNITED STATES V. TAYLOR
224 F.Supp.3d 1262 (N.D.AL. 2016)

KARON OWEN BOWDRE, CHIEF UNITED STATES DISTRICT JUDGE.

Defendant John Robert Taylor has a history of schizophrenia, severe alcohol abuse, and numerous felony convictions. He lives in a van outside of Pickensville, Alabama without power or running water and is known to hear voices and speak to those voices. After an altercation in which Mr. Taylor attempted to fire a loaded gun at a police officer, the Government charged him as a felon in possession of a gun under 18 U.S.C. § 922(g)(1).

Mr. Taylor notified the court in writing on June 20, 2016 of his desire to waive his request for a jury trial. (Doc. 24). The court conducted the trial of this case on July 11 and 12, 2016. The court found the Government proved beyond a reasonable doubt that Mr. Taylor is a felon, that he possessed the gun, and that the gun had traveled in interstate commerce. The only issues remaining before the court are whether Mr. Taylor is entitled to an insanity defense and whether he *knowingly* possessed a gun on the date in question.

For the reasons discussed below, the court finds Mr. Taylor is not entitled to an insanity defense and that he knowingly possessed a gun, and thus is guilty as charged.

I. Factual and Procedural Background

The Grand Jury returned a one-count Indictment on October 29, 2015, charging Mr. Taylor with the offense of felon in possession in violation of 18 U.S.C. § 922(g)(1). Upon his filing of a notice of intent to plead not guilty by reason of mental disease or defect (doc. 13), the Government moved for an order directing that Mr. Taylor undergo a mental examination, pursuant to 18 U.S.C. § 4242(a). (Doc. 14). On February 4, 2016, the court granted the motion, and Mr. Taylor was sent to FCI Fort Worth for evaluation.

On April 27, 2016, psychologist Lisa Bellah, Ph.D., issued a written report stating, in substance, that "[t]here [was] insufficient evidence to suggest that Mr. Taylor suffered from a severe mental disease or defect at the time of his arrest that interfered with his ability to appreciate the nature, quality or wrongfulness of his alleged offense conduct." (Doc. 19 at 13). Dr. Bellah further noted that, while Mr. Taylor has been diagnosed as having schizophrenia, he has not received mental health treatment on either an inpatient or outpatient basis since 1999; he has not consistently taken psychotropic medication for approximately 20 years; and the course of his illness has been atypical for schizophrenia and more consistent with long-term alcohol abuse. *Id.* at 3, 5, 7–8. Instead, Dr. Bellah opined that "Mr. Taylor's primary diagnosis is severe and long-term abuse of alcohol. . . . Prognosis is considered poor. Mr. Taylor has a long term addiction to alcohol." *Id.* at 8. Dr. Bellah testified that alcoholism is an Axis I mental disease or disorder.

Dr. Bellah's report and her trial testimony play a critical role in the issues currently before the court: to what extent, if any, Mr. Taylor's chronic alcohol addiction affects his guilt and his ability to act "knowingly."

Trial began on July 11, 2016 and lasted barely one-and-a-half days. At the end of all the evidence, and after hearing arguments of counsel, the court found that the Government proved beyond a reasonable doubt that Mr. Taylor had prior felony convictions, that he possessed a gun on April 3, 2015, and that the gun had traveled in interstate commerce. The court reserved ruling on the remaining element of whether Mr. Taylor "knowingly" possessed the gun.

In doing so, the court found the testimony of the arresting officer, Deputy Tony Thrasher, credible. He testified that he stopped by the B-Mart convenience store in Aliceville, Alabama to buy a drink. As he approached the door, he saw Mr. Taylor arguing with the store clerk. Deputy Thrasher smelled alcohol on Mr. Taylor's breath and attempted to arrest him for public intoxication. Mr. Taylor refused to comply and began walking away. Deputy Thrasher ordered Mr. Taylor to stop, drew his Taser, and advised Mr. Taylor he would Tase him if he did not stop. Mr. Taylor spun around, pointed a loaded gun at Deputy Thrasher, and repeatedly tried pulling the trigger. Fortunately for all, the gun's safety was on.

Next, Deputy Thrasher immediately discharged the Taser, striking Mr. Taylor in the chest and stunning him. Mr. Taylor dropped his arm, but still held the gun. Although Deputy Thrasher continued to Tase him, Mr. Taylor stumbled toward a parked car, tossed the gun into the open window of the car, and eventually fell over. Deputy Thrasher immediately took Mr. Taylor into custody, secured him in the police car, and then retrieved the gun from the car. Willie Brown, a correctional officer at the Pickens County Jail, testified that Mr. Taylor complied with instructions when he was brought in to the jail.

The Government also offered proof that, at that time, Mr. Taylor was a convicted felon, and the .38 caliber Derringer pistol was manufactured in Chino, California, so it had traveled in interstate commerce.

As mentioned previously, the report and testimony of Dr. Bellah play a critical role in determining whether Mr. Taylor "knowingly" possessed the gun. Both Dr. Bellah's report and the voluminous medical records of Mr. Taylor's treatment at VA facilities reflect that he was diagnosed and treated for paranoid schizophrenia in the late 1970s, that he has been in and out of the hospital for treatment, and that he has a long history of alcohol abuse. *See* (Doc. 19 at 3–5, 7–8). Further, Mr. Taylor has not taken medications for paranoid schizophrenia for approximately twenty years. *Id.* at 5, 12. Thus, in her opinion, Mr. Taylor's paranoid schizophrenia is in remission and his primary current diagnosis is severe and long-term alcohol abuse. *See id.* at 8. She testified that schizophrenia or alcohol-related causes are not mutually exclusive, and that alcohol can exacerbate symptoms of mental illness.

The Defense presented testimony from Mr. Taylor's long-time friend, Jacqueline Taggart. Ms. Taggart testified about Mr. Taylor's eccentric lifestyle and unusual behavior, stating that he had an aversion to being around more than two or three people, wore copious amount of clothing in summer when walking ten miles, and placed large rocks around his residence.

Ms. Taggart also testified that she took Mr. Taylor to get groceries on April 1, 2015. Ms. Taggart testified she observed Mr. Taylor talking as if a another person was in the back of the car during the trip, but that she only saw Mr. Taylor. Ms. Taggart also stated Mr. Taylor talked to himself throughout the day.

II. Discussion

A. Mr. Taylor failed to prove he is not guilty because of mental disease or defect.

Mr. Taylor attempts to avoid criminal responsibility by arguing that involuntary intoxication rendered him legally insane at the time of the incident. *See* (Doc. 39). To meet his burden of proof, Mr. Taylor must prove that (1) he suffers from a severe mental disease or defect, and (2) as a result of the severe mental disease or defect, he could not appreciate the nature and quality of his conduct, or the wrongfulness of his actions. 18 U.S.C. § 17. Mr. Taylor asserts that "[i]ntoxication because of physiological and psychological conditions is at issue . . . because [he] suffers from paranoid schizophrenia and severe alcohol use disorder and these conditions caused *involuntary* intoxication of alcohol resulting in an inability to appreciate the wrongfulness of his actions. . . ." *Id.* at 3.

The Government argues that Dr. Bellah's testimony that Mr. Taylor's schizophrenia was in remission and he had not received mental health treatment or medication in twenty years establishes that Mr. Taylor cannot prove he was suffering from a severe mental disease or defect during the relevant time; i.e., he cannot satisfy the first of the three prongs required to prove an insanity defense. (Doc. 40 at 5).

The Government relies on *Poolaw v. United States*, 588 F.2d 103 (5th Cir. 1979), to argue that the Eleventh Circuit "does not recognize alcoholism as a severe mental disease or defect that supports a finding of not guilty by reason of insanity." (Doc. 40 at 6). *Poolaw*, however, predates the vast scientific and medical revelations of the last thirty years about the brain, which recognize drug and alcohol addiction as a disease. *See, e.g.*, Joanna S. Fowler, et al., *Imaging the Addicted Human Brain*, SCIENCE & PRACTICE PERSPECTIVES, April 2007, at 4–16, *available at* http://www.ncbi.nlm.nih.gov/pmc/articles/PMC2851068.

The Government's reference to "a social disorder like alcoholism" (doc. 40 at 7) ignores this evolution in the understanding of alcoholism and also ignores Dr. Bellah's testimony that alcoholism is an Axis I mental disease or disorder. Dr. Bellah's testimony provides evidence that alcoholism is a mental disease or defect. In *Poolaw*, however, the court did not have the benefit of more recent science. Thus, the court is not persuaded by the Government's reliance on *Poolaw* in this matter.

Indeed, the Office of the Surgeon General has recently stated, "Research on alcohol and drug use, and addiction, has led to an increase of knowledge and to one clear conclusion: Addiction to alcohol or drugs is a chronic but treatable brain disease that requires medical intervention, not moral judgment." U.S. Dep't of Health and Human Servs., Off. of the Surgeon

Gen., *Facing Addiction in America: The Surgeon General's Report on Alcohol, Drugs, and Health, Executive Summary* at ES-3 (Nov. 2016) [hereinafter "Facing Addiction"], *available at* http://addiction.surgeon general.gov.

The understanding of alcohol use disorders has evolved as science has gained a greater appreciation of how the brain operates. The Defense—and the court—question whether case law has kept pace with that evolution.

Mr. Taylor points to the progression of the Diagnostic and Statistical Manual of Mental Disorders (DSM) to explain the evolution in understanding alcohol use disorders:

The First and Second Editions of the DSM, published in 1952 and 1968 respectively, categorized "alcoholism" as a subset of personality disorders and neuroses. *See* http://pubs.niaaa.nih.gov/publications/aa30.htm (last visited July 25, 2016). In 1980, the Third Edition of the DSM (DSM-III) eliminated the term "alcoholism" in favor of two distinct categories of "alcohol abuse" and "alcohol dependence." *Id.* The DSM-III also moved these two categories under "substance use disorders" rather than personality disorders. *Id.* . . .

The DSM was revised again in 1994 (DSM-IV) and kept the two subcategories. But in 2013, the drafters of DSM-V found the terms "Alcohol Abuse" and "Alcohol Dependence" misleading. DSM-V replaced the terms "Alcohol Abuse" and "Alcohol Dependence" with the umbrella term "Alcohol Use Disorder" to better describe "a distinct syndrome that includes compulsive drug-seeking behavior, loss of control, craving[,] and marked decrements in social and occupational functioning." Lloyd I. Sederer, The DSM-5: The Changes Ahead (Part 2), The Huffington Post (Nov. 19, 2011) *available at* http://www.huffingtonpost.com/lloyd-i-sederer-md-DSM-5_b_ 961966.html; *see also See* [sic] American Psychiatric Ass'n, Substance-Related and Addictive Disorders, DSM-5 Collection (2013) *available at* . . . The DSM-V uses sub-classifications of mild, moderate, and severe to categorize the disorder. . . .

The addicting nature of alcohol is also well known. The American Psychiatric Association (APA), which publishes the DSM, defines "addiction" as:

> a complex condition, a chronic brain disease that is manifested by compulsive substance use despite harmful consequence. People with addiction (severe substance use disorder) have an intense focus on using a certain substance, such as alcohol or drugs, to the point that it takes over their life. They keep using alcohol or a drug when they know it will causes [sic] problems. Yet a number of effective treatments are available and people can recover from addiction and lead normal, productive lives.

> People with a substance use disorder have disturbed thinking, behavior and body functions. Changes in the brain's wiring are what cause people to have intense cravings for the drug and make it hard to stop using the drug. Brain imaging studies show changes in the areas of the brain that relate to judgment, decision making, learning, memory and behavior control.

See https://www.psychiatry.org/patients-families/addiction/what-is-addiction (last visited July 21, 2016). The APA's website on Addiction explains "[p]eople with addictive disorders may be aware of their problem, but be unable to stop it even if they want to." *Id.*

(Doc. 39 at 4–6).

The U.S. Surgeon General recognizes drug and alcohol addiction as a pressing public health crisis, and a report released by the Office of the Surgeon General on November 17, 2016 estimates that 20.8 million Americans over the age of 12 have a substance use disorder. "Facing Addiction," *supra*. This number approximates the number of people who have diabetes in the United States and is one-and-a-half times the number of people who have any type of cancer. "Surgeon General Murthy Wants America to Face Up to Addiction" (Nov. 17, 2016), *available at* http://www.npr.org/sections/health-shots/2016/11/17/502402409. The Surgeon General's Report summarizes the evolving understanding of substance use disorders as follows: "severe substance use disorders, commonly called addictions, were once viewed largely as a moral failing or character flaw, but are now understood to be chronic illnesses characterized by clinically significant impairments in health, social function, and voluntary control over substance use." "Facing Addiction," *supra* at 2–1.

The Government also argues that Mr. Taylor is not entitled to the benefit of the insanity defense because he has not proved by clear and convincing evidence that he could not appreciate the nature and quality of his conduct or the wrongfulness of his actions at the time of the incident. *See* (Doc. 40 at 11–12; Doc. 43 at 5–6). Indeed, neither side offered direct or even circumstantial evidence regarding Mr. Taylor's level of intoxication on April 3, 2015, and the court would have to speculate to conclude he was intoxicated to such an extent as to be legally insane. Moreover, the evidence shows that while Deputy Thrasher was Tasing him, Mr. Taylor attempted to dispose of his gun by tossing it into a parked vehicle, suggesting Mr. Taylor understood the nature and quality or wrongfulness of his conduct at the time of the incident.

In addition, Mr. Taylor offered nothing to dispute the evidence that he had received neither mental health treatment since 1999 nor taken medication for schizophrenia for approximately twenty years. Finally, while Jacqueline Taggart, Mr. Taylor's friend, testified that she observed him behaving strangely on April 1, 2015, her testimony does nothing to prove Mr. Taylor's state of mind at the time of the incident two days later.

Accordingly, the court finds Mr. Taylor has failed to meet his burden of proving, by clear and convincing evidence, that he could not appreciate the nature and quality of his conduct or the wrongfulness of his actions on the date in question.

Even if severe alcohol use disorder may be a severe mental disease or defect that could support an insanity defense, the court concludes Mr. Taylor has not shown he is entitled to the benefit of such a defense here. By denying the insanity defense to Mr. Taylor in this case, the court does not foreclose its use in other cases when a defendant with severe alcohol use disorder may prove he is unable to appreciate the nature and quality of his conduct or the wrongfulness of his actions because of involuntary intoxication.

EXERCISE

Few would dispute that America suffers from widespread addictions to drugs and alcohol. Does it do more to address those problems if we allow them to excuse or mitigate crime, insist that they have no impact one way or the other, or should we punish people more harshly if their crime is the result of an addiction?

CHAPTER THIRTEEN

SENTENCING

■ ■ ■

The focus of this book has been on the elements of crimes in charging, plea negotiation, and at trial. Sentencing is a very different thing. The elements of a crime are no longer the central focus—they have been proven through plea or a trial verdict—and a wealth of other considerations (such as prior criminal history) come into play. In modern practice, sentencing is an important point for fact-finding and needs to be understood to fully grasp the broad scope of the project of criminal law. After all, only a small fraction of charged cases go to trial, but nearly all of them include a sentencing.

Sentencing systems vary widely from one American jurisdiction to another. Some feature sentencing guidelines that either limit or advise judges. Others have chosen to forego guidelines. While every jurisdiction imposes some kind of restriction on judges through statute, those restrictions diverge between systems as well.

In the federal system, a judge must take into account two primary inputs when sentencing: statutes and the federal sentencing guidelines. The sentence actually served is almost entirely determined by the judge, since there is no parole in the federal system.

Statutes serve two functions. Some limit the judge's discretion and require that a judge sentence above a mandatory floor (we call these mandatory minimums) or below a ceiling (statutory maximums). Others, such as 18 U.S.C. § 3553, guide the judge's discretion and require consideration of specific goals.

The federal sentencing guidelines are advisory to the trial court (and have been since the Supreme Court ruled in *United States v. Booker*, 543 U.S. 220 (2005)). While the judge must properly calculate a guideline range, it can vary from that range provided the resulting sentence is "reasonable."

Putting all of this together, we see that a judge's options at sentencing are defined and limited by statute. Within those options, the judge must consider the guidelines and the goals set out in 18 U.S.C. § 3553.

A. STATUTORY MINIMUMS AND MAXIMUMS

Nearly every federal statute contains a statutory maximum sentence, a cap above which a judge cannot go (one of the rare exceptions is treason;

18 U.S.C. § 2381 contains a mandatory minimum of five years but no upper limit). Relatively few federal statutes contain a mandatory minimum sentence. However, some of the statutes that do contain a mandatory minimum sentence provision are among those most often used by federal prosecutors, including 21 U.S.C. § 841 (which covers narcotics trafficking) and 18 U.S.C. § 924(c) (use or possession of firearms in association with certain crimes).

1. STATUTORY MAXIMUM SENTENCE

Judges often find facts at sentencing; in fact, doing so is an essential part of determining the sentencing range under the federal guidelines. But does the Constitution allow a judge to find facts that move a sentence above the maximum sentence for the underlying crime? The case below addressed that question in the context of state law, but laid the groundwork for later decisions that profoundly changed sentencing law in federal courts.

APPRENDI V. NEW JERSEY
530 U.S. 466 (2000)

JUSTICE STEVENS delivered the opinion of the Court.

A New Jersey statute classifies the possession of a firearm for an unlawful purpose as a "second-degree" offense. N.J. Stat. Ann. § 2C:39–4(a) (West 1995). Such an offense is punishable by imprisonment for "between five years and 10 years." § 2C:43–6(a)(2). A separate statute, described by that State's Supreme Court as a "hate crime" law, provides for an "extended term" of imprisonment if the trial judge finds, by a preponderance of the evidence, that "[t]he defendant in committing the crime acted with a purpose to intimidate an individual or group of individuals because of race, color, gender, handicap, religion, sexual orientation or ethnicity." N.J. Stat. Ann. § 2C:44–3(e) (West Supp. 1999–2000). The extended term authorized by the hate crime law for second-degree offenses is imprisonment for "between 10 and 20 years." § 2C:43–7(a)(3).

The question presented is whether the Due Process Clause of the Fourteenth Amendment requires that a factual determination authorizing an increase in the maximum prison sentence for an offense from 10 to 20 years be made by a jury on the basis of proof beyond a reasonable doubt.

I

At 2:04 a.m. on December 22, 1994, petitioner Charles C. Apprendi, Jr., fired several .22-caliber bullets into the home of an African-American family that had recently moved into a previously all-white neighborhood in Vineland, New Jersey. Apprendi was promptly arrested and, at 3:05 a.m., admitted that he was the shooter. After further questioning, at 6:04 a.m., he made a statement-which he later retracted-that even though he did not know the occupants of the house personally, "because they are black in color he does not want them in the neighborhood." 159 N.J. 7, 10, 731 A.2d 485, 486 (1999).

A New Jersey grand jury returned a 23-count indictment charging Apprendi with four first-degree, eight second-degree, six third-degree, and five fourth-degree offenses. The charges alleged shootings on four different dates, as well as the unlawful possession of various weapons. None of the counts referred to the hate crime statute, and none alleged that Apprendi acted with a racially biased purpose.

The parties entered into a plea agreement, pursuant to which Apprendi pleaded guilty to two counts (3 and 18) of second-degree possession of a firearm for an unlawful purpose, N.J. Stat. Ann. § 2C:39–4a (West 1995), and one count (22) of the third-degree offense of unlawful possession of an antipersonnel bomb, § 2C:39–3a; the prosecutor dismissed the other 20 counts. Under state law, a second-degree offense carries a penalty range of 5 to 10 years, § 2C:43–6(a)(2); a third-degree offense carries a penalty range of between 3 and 5 years, § 2C:43–6(a)(3). As part of the plea agreement, however, the State reserved the right to request the court to impose a higher "enhanced" sentence on count 18 (which was based on the December 22 shooting) on the ground that that offense was committed with a biased purpose, as described in § 2C:44–3(e). Apprendi, correspondingly, reserved the right to challenge the hate crime sentence enhancement on the ground that it violates the United States Constitution.

At the plea hearing, the trial judge heard sufficient evidence to establish Apprendi's guilt on counts 3, 18, and 22; the judge then confirmed that Apprendi understood the maximum sentences that could be imposed on those counts. Because the plea agreement provided that the sentence on the sole third-degree offense (count 22) would run concurrently with the other sentences, the potential sentences on the two second-degree counts were critical. If the judge found no basis for the biased purpose enhancement, the maximum consecutive sentences on those counts would amount to 20 years in aggregate; if, however, the judge enhanced the sentence on count 18, the maximum on that count alone would be 20 years and the maximum for the two counts in aggregate would be 30 years, with a 15-year period of parole ineligibility.

After the trial judge accepted the three guilty pleas, the prosecutor filed a formal motion for an extended term. The trial judge thereafter held an evidentiary hearing on the issue of Apprendi's "purpose" for the shooting on December 22. Apprendi adduced evidence from a psychologist and from seven character witnesses who testified that he did not have a reputation for racial bias. He also took the stand himself, explaining that the incident was an unintended consequence of overindulgence in alcohol, denying that he was in any way biased against African-Americans, and denying that his statement to the police had been accurately described. The judge, however, found the police officer's testimony credible, and concluded that the evidence supported a finding "that the crime was motivated by racial bias." App. to Pet. for Cert. 143a. Having found "by a preponderance of the evidence" that Apprendi's actions were taken "with a purpose to intimidate" as provided by the statute, *id.,* at 138a, 139a, 144a, the trial judge held that the hate crime enhancement applied. Rejecting Apprendi's constitutional challenge to the statute, the judge sentenced him to a 12-year term of imprisonment on count 18, and to shorter concurrent sentences on the other two counts. . . .

. . . In his 1881 lecture on the criminal law, Oliver Wendell Holmes, Jr., observed: "The law threatens certain pains if you do certain things, intending thereby to give you a new motive for not doing them. If you persist in doing them, it has to inflict the pains in order that its threats may continue to be believed." New Jersey threatened Apprendi with certain pains if he unlawfully possessed a weapon and with additional pains if he selected his victims with a purpose to intimidate them because of their race. As a matter of simple justice, it seems obvious that the procedural safeguards designed to protect Apprendi from unwarranted pains should apply equally to the two acts that New Jersey has singled out for punishment. Merely using the label "sentence enhancement" to describe the latter surely does not provide a principled basis for treating them differently.

At stake in this case are constitutional protections of surpassing importance: the proscription of any deprivation of liberty without "due process of law," Amdt. 14, and the guarantee that "[i]n all criminal prosecutions, the accused shall enjoy the right to a speedy and public trial, by an impartial jury," Amdt. 6. Taken together, these rights indisputably entitle a criminal defendant to "a jury determination that [he] is guilty of every element of the crime with which he is charged, beyond a reasonable doubt.". . .

We do not suggest that trial practices cannot change in the course of centuries and still remain true to the principles that emerged from the Framers' fears "that the jury right could be lost not only by gross denial, but by erosion." *Jones,* 526 U.S., at 247–248, 119 S.Ct. 1215. But practice must at least adhere to the basic principles undergirding the requirements of trying to a jury all facts necessary to constitute a statutory offense, and proving those facts beyond reasonable doubt. As we made clear in *Winship,* the "reasonable doubt" requirement "has [a] vital role in our criminal procedure for cogent reasons." 397 U.S., at 363, 90 S.Ct. 1068. Prosecution subjects the criminal defendant both to "the possibility that he may lose his liberty upon conviction and . . . the certainty that he would be stigmatized by the conviction." *Ibid.* We thus require this, among other, procedural protections in order to "provid[e] concrete substance for the presumption of innocence," and to reduce the risk of imposing such deprivations erroneously. *Ibid.* If a defendant faces punishment beyond that provided by statute when an offense is committed under certain circumstances but not others, it is obvious that both the loss of liberty and the stigma attaching to the offense are heightened; it necessarily follows that the defendant should not-at the moment the State is put to proof of those circumstances-be deprived of protections that have, until that point, unquestionably attached. . . .

In sum, our reexamination of our cases in this area, and of the history upon which they rely, confirms the opinion that we expressed in *Jones*. Other than the fact of a prior conviction, any fact that increases the penalty for a crime beyond the prescribed statutory maximum must be submitted to a jury, and proved beyond a reasonable doubt. With that exception, we endorse the statement of the rule set forth in the concurring opinions in that case: "[I]t is unconstitutional for a legislature to remove from the jury the assessment of facts that increase the prescribed range of penalties to which a criminal defendant is exposed. It is equally clear that such facts must be established by proof beyond a reasonable doubt." 526 U.S., at 252–253, 119 S.Ct. 1215 (opinion of STEVENS, J.); see also *id.,* at 253, 119 S.Ct. 1215 (opinion of SCALIA, J.). . . .

The New Jersey procedure challenged in this case is an unacceptable departure from the jury tradition that is an indispensable part of our criminal justice system. Accordingly, the judgment of the Supreme Court of New Jersey is reversed, and the case is remanded for further proceedings not inconsistent with this opinion.

It is so ordered.

EXERCISE

Note that in *Apprendi* the government agreed to a plea deal that dismissed the first-degree counts which could have allowed for a sentence over ten years without any judicial determinations of fact. Instead of pressing forward with that count, the government signed off on a plea agreement that seemed to allow the sentence to exceed ten years only if the judge determined that a hate crime had been committed.

What value might the government have gotten out of the approach they chose, other than length of sentence? The outcome in the Supreme Court aside, do you agree with that decision?

2. STATUTORY MINIMUMS

One of the more controversial aspects of federal sentencing has been the use of mandatory minimum sentences for certain drug crimes. One of those mandatory minimum provisions is found at 21 U.S.C. § 841(b)(1)(B), and covers narcotics trafficking crimes including distribution and possession of narcotics with the intent to distribute. That statute provides, in part:

(B) In the case of a violation of subsection (a) of this section involving—

    (i) 100 grams or more of a mixture or substance containing a detectable amount of heroin;

    (ii) 500 grams or more of a mixture or substance containing a detectable amount of—

        (I) coca leaves, except coca leaves and extracts of coca leaves from which cocaine, ecgonine, and derivatives of ecgonine or their salts have been removed;

        (II) cocaine, its salts, optical and geometric isomers, and salts of isomers;

        (III) ecgonine, its derivatives, their salts, isomers, and salts of isomers; or

        (IV) any compound, mixture, or preparation which contains any quantity of any of the substances referred to in subclauses (I) through (III);

    (iii) 28 grams or more of a mixture or substance described in clause (ii) which contains cocaine base;

    (iv) 10 grams or more of phencyclidine (PCP) or 100 grams or more of a mixture or substance containing a detectable amount of phencyclidine (PCP);

    (v) 1 gram or more of a mixture or substance containing a detectable amount of lysergic acid diethylamide (LSD);

    (vi) 40 grams or more of a mixture or substance containing a detectable amount of N-phenyl-N-[1-(2-phenylethyl)-4-piperidinyl] propanamide or 10 grams or more of a mixture or substance containing a detectable amount of any analogue of N-phenyl-N-[1-(2-phenylethyl)-4-piperidinyl] propanamide;

    (vii) 100 kilograms or more of a mixture or substance containing a detectable amount of marihuana, or 100 or more marihuana plants regardless of weight; or

    (viii) 5 grams or more of methamphetamine, its salts, isomers, and salts of its isomers or 50 grams or more of a mixture or substance containing a detectable amount of methamphetamine, its salts, isomers, or salts of its isomers;

such person shall be sentenced to a term of imprisonment which may not be less than 5 years and not more than 40 years. . . . If any person commits such a violation after a prior conviction for a felony drug offense has become final, such person shall be sentenced to a term of imprisonment which may not be less than 10 years and not more than life imprisonment. . . .

The current law reflects an amendment made in 2010; prior to that, crack cocaine was sentenced consistent with methamphetamine and was subject to these enhancements if the defendant was connected to 5 grams or more of that substance.

These enhancements have been subjected to, and survived, challenges under the Eighth Amendment.

UNITED STATES V. FORD

839 F.3d 94 (1st Cir. 2016)

MASTROIANNI, DISTRICT JUDGE.

James F. Ford, with assistance from his wife Darlene and his sons Paul and Jim, directed a marijuana-growing operation out of a home in Monroe, Maine. Acting on a tip from Jim's girlfriend, police executed a search warrant and interviewed James, who openly described the sophisticated operation and discussed his previous marijuana-growing case in Massachusetts. After a trial, a jury convicted him on the four counts charged in the superseding indictment: conspiracy, manufacturing over 100 marijuana plants, maintaining a residence for marijuana manufacturing, and possessing a firearm as a felon. The district court applied a statutory mandatory minimum and sentenced James to 120 months in prison followed by eight years of supervised release. On appeal, James challenges his convictions and his sentence. Finding no reversible error, we affirm.

I. Background

On the evening of November 15, 2011, Maine drug enforcement officers, via loudspeaker, ordered the occupants of James's and Darlene's home to exit and executed a search warrant. The officers discovered a large marijuana-growing operation and two disassembled firearms under a makeshift bed outside of one of the cultivation rooms.

Later that evening, James discussed the operation in detail during a recorded interview. He described the intricate set-up, which he was "pretty proud of," but lamented the chores and expenses required by the operation. For example, James explained he had to empty air-conditioner buckets every morning or else they would "run over." He also had to collect water from a spring in Dixmont, Maine, using a 150-gallon tank, because the well water at the home was "horrible" and would "kill" the plants. In addition, James's crop "had bug problems," but he used hypoaspis miles, a type of mite, to control fungus gnats attracted to the marijuana plants. James told the officers he normally yielded either eight or twelve pounds of marijuana every nine weeks, had produced thirty-seven total harvests, and had sold each pound for approximately $2,000. He deciphered some of the acronyms on a calendar officers found in the home, explaining "H1" referred to harvest one and "H2" meant harvest two.

Notably, James volunteered during the interview "you already know that I got popped in Mass" when explaining his previous growing operation in Wakefield, Massachusetts, which had been uncovered through a confidential informant. James revealed he paid his attorney in Massachusetts over $20,000 yet still "ended up with a frigging . . . felony conviction because they forced me to plea bargain." He further disclosed that he lost a house in connection with the bust, which he thought was unfair because the property was not purchased with "drug money" and his "name wasn't even on the search warrant.". . .

At sentencing, James objected to application of 21 U.S.C. § 841(b)(1)(B)(vii), which prescribes a ten-year mandatory minimum for manufacturing 100 or more marijuana plants if the individual was previously convicted of a felony drug offense. . . . The district court. . . did note, however, that in light of the state legalizations "we are in sort of an odd time for purposes of marijuana." After calculating a Sentencing Guideline range of 97 to 121 months of imprisonment, which produced a range of 120 to 121 months when combined with the statutory minimum, the court sentenced James to 120 months in prison to be followed by eight years of supervised release. . . .

Lastly, James contends his ten-year mandatory-minimum sentence for manufacturing marijuana is grossly disproportionate to the offense and, therefore, violates the Eighth Amendment. He points to the public's evolving views on marijuana, including state-law decriminalization and legalization (medicinal and recreational) measures. He also cites the federal government's general policy of not prosecuting cultivation and distribution activities that are in compliance with "strong and effective [state marijuana] regulatory and enforcement systems." Memorandum from James M. Cole, Deputy Att'y Gen., U.S. Dep't of Justice, for All U.S. Att'ys 2 (Aug. 29, 2013), available at https://www.justice.gov/iso/opa/resources/3052013829132756857467.pdf. We review this Eighth Amendment challenge de novo. United States v. Raymond, 697 F.3d 32, 40 (1st Cir. 2012).

"The Eighth Amendment, which forbids cruel and unusual punishments, contains a 'narrow proportionality principle' that 'applies to noncapital sentences.'" Ewing v. California, 538 U.S. 11, 20, 123 S.Ct. 1179, 155 L.Ed.2d 108 (2003) (plurality opinion) (quoting Harmelin v. Michigan, 501 U.S. 957, 996–97, 111 S.Ct. 2680, 115 L.Ed.2d 836 (1991) (Kennedy, J., concurring in part and concurring in judgment)). This principle, however, " 'does not require strict proportionality between crime and sentence' but rather 'forbids only extreme sentences that are grossly disproportionate to the crime.'" Graham v. Florida, 560 U.S. 48, 60, 130 S.Ct. 2011, 176 L.Ed.2d 825 (2010)(quoting Harmelin, 501 U.S. at 997, 1000–01, 111 S.Ct. 2680 (Kennedy, J., concurring in part and concurring in judgment)). In determining whether a sentence is grossly disproportionate, we first undertake a threshold comparison between "the gravity of the offense and the severity of the sentence." Id. at 60, 130 S.Ct. 2011. If, after making this threshold comparison, "we conclude there is no 'gross disproportionality . . . the inquiry ends there.'" United States v. Lyons, 740 F.3d 702, 731 (1st Cir. 2014) (quoting Raymond, 697 F.3d at 40).

We also must be mindful of our "substantial deference to the broad authority that legislatures necessarily possess in determining the types and limits of punishments for crimes." Solem v. Helm, 463 U.S. 277, 290, 103 S.Ct. 3001, 77 L.Ed.2d 637 (1983). After all, "the Constitution 'does not mandate adoption of any one penological theory.'" Ewing, 538 U.S. at 25, 123 S.Ct. 1179 (quoting Harmelin, 501 U.S. at 999, 111 S.Ct. 2680 (Kennedy, J., concurring in part and concurring in judgment)). In light of this deference and the rigorous standard for demonstrating gross disproportionality, "a reviewing court rarely will be required to engage in extended analysis to determine that a sentence is not constitutionally disproportionate." Solem, 463 U.S. at 290 n.16, 103 S.Ct. 3001. Indeed, "'[o]utside the context of capital punishment, successful challenges to the proportionality of particular sentences have been exceedingly rare.'" Ewing, 538 U.S. at 21, 123 S.Ct. 1179 (plurality opinion) (quoting Rummel v. Estelle, 445 U.S. 263, 272, 100 S.Ct. 1133, 63 L.Ed.2d 382 (1980)); see id.at 19–20, 123 S.Ct. 1179 (upholding California's "three strikes" law and the imposition of a 25 years to life sentence for stealing golf clubs); Harmelin, 501 U.S. at 996, 111 S.Ct. 2680 (upholding a sentence of life in prison without parole for possession of more than 650 grams of cocaine); Hutto v. Davis, 454 U.S. 370, 374–75, 102 S.Ct. 703, 70 L.Ed.2d 556 (1982) (upholding a sentence of forty years for possession and distribution of nine ounces of marijuana).

James's challenge fails at the threshold inquiry. We recognize that, for Eighth Amendment purposes, "courts must look beyond historical conceptions to 'the evolving standards of decency that mark the progress of a maturing society.'" Graham, 560 U.S. at 58, 130 S.Ct. 2011 (quoting Estelle v. Gamble, 429 U.S. 97, 102, 97 S.Ct. 285, 50 L.Ed.2d 251 (1976)). Those evolving standards certainly now point towards a markedly different level of acceptance of marijuana than in the past. "But within extremely broad limits, Congress—which unlike the judiciary is popularly elected—sets both sentencing policy and the prescribed range of sentences for federal drug crimes. . . ." United States v. Jones, 674 F.3d 88, 96 (1st Cir. 2012). And, despite the evolving consensus on marijuana policy, manufacturing marijuana remains a serious crime under federal law, subject to the penalties set forth in 21 U.S.C. § 841(b). See United States v. Ford, 625 Fed.Appx. 4, 7 (1st Cir. 2015) (unpublished opinion).

In the end, James's arguments as to federal marijuana sentencing policy are more appropriately directed at the Executive and Legislative branches. "Relief in cases such as this—if there is any—must come, in the first instance, in the exercise of restraint and wisdom in the charging decision of the prosecutor, or in the exercise of the clemency power; both are executive not judicial functions and leave us powerless to intercede to grant relief." Paladin, 748 F.3d at 454.

III. Conclusion

For the reasons given, we **affirm**.

EXERCISE

Imagine that you are the head of a federal law enforcement task force charged with addressing narcotics. Informants tell you that there is a "medium-sized" grow operation for marijuana only a mile away from your office. On further investigation, you get reliable information that the house in question has (at any given time) 25 to 30 marijuana plants under cultivation.

If you go into the house and arrest the growers, they will be subject to the mandatory minimum sentences in 21 U.S.C. § 841(b)(1)(B), because the federal prosecutor in your district always tries to impose them (and can argue that over the past two years, over 100 plants have been grown).

What do you do?

The sentencing enhancements applying to narcotics cases under 21 U.S.C. § 841(b) include several that boost both mandatory minimum and maximum sentences based on prior convictions. These enhancements only come into play if the prosecutor seeks them. This discretion is given to prosecutors under 21 U.S.C. § 851:

(a) Information filed by United States Attorney

(1) No person who stands convicted of an offense under this part shall be sentenced to increased punishment by reason of one or more prior convictions, unless before trial, or before entry of a plea of guilty, the United States attorney files an information with the court (and serves a copy of such information on the person or counsel for the person) stating in writing the previous convictions to be relied upon.

Federal administrations vary in the direction they provide to prosecutors in using this significant direction, which in some instances can lead to a mandatory sentence of life in prison. Ultimately, though, individual prosecutors are the primary deciders in how these enhancements are used.

UNITED STATES V. YOUNG

960 F. Supp. 2d 881 (N.D. Iowa 2013)

MARK W. BENNETT, DISTRICT JUDGE. . . .

This case presents a deeply disturbing, yet often replayed, shocking, dirty little secret of federal sentencing: the stunningly arbitrary application by the Department of Justice (DOJ) of § 851 drug sentencing enhancements. These enhancements, at a minimum, double a drug defendant's mandatory minimum sentence and may also raise the maximum possible sentence, for example, from forty years to life. They are possible any time a drug defendant, facing a mandatory minimum sentence in federal court, has a prior qualifying drug conviction in state or federal court (even some state court misdemeanor convictions count), no matter how old that conviction is.

Recent statistics obtained from the U.S. Sentencing Commission (Commission)—the only known data that exists on the eligibility and applications of the DOJ's § 851 decision making—reveal jaw-dropping, shocking disparity. For example, a defendant in the Northern District of Iowa (N.D. of Iowa) who is eligible for a § 851 enhancement is 2,532% more likely to receive it than a similarly eligible defendant in the bordering District of Nebraska. Equally problematic is that, at least prior to August 12, 2013, decisions to apply or waive § 851enhancements were made in the absence of any national policy, and they are still solely within the unreviewed discretion of the DOJ without any requirement that the basis for the decisions be disclosed or stated on the record. This is true even for non-violent, low-level drug addicts. These decisions are shrouded in such complete secrecy that they make the proceedings of the former English Court of Star Chamber appear to be a model of criminal justice transparency. *See In re Oliver,* 333 U.S. 257, 266–271, 68 S.Ct. 499, 92 L.Ed. 682 (1948) ("The traditional Anglo-American distrust for secret trials has been variously ascribed to the notorious use of this practice by . . . the English Court of Star Chamber."). Attorney General Holder's August 12, 2013, Memorandum to the United States Attorneys and Assistant Attorney General for the Criminal Division: Department Policy on Charging Mandatory Minimum Sentences and Recidivist Enhancements in Certain Drug Cases (Holder 2013 Memo), while establishing a national policy for § 841 enhancements, does nothing to pull aside the cloak of secrecy shrouding the nationwide disparities in the application of § 851 enhancements.

I. INTRODUCTION—DEFENDANT DOUGLAS YOUNG

Defendant Douglas Young, whose situation brings the issue of the § 851 enhancement before me now, pleaded guilty to conspiracy to distribute 28 grams or more of cocaine base following a prior conviction for a felony drug offense (count 1) and possession with intent to distribute 28 grams or more of cocaine base (count 2) in violation of 21 U.S.C. §§ 846, 841(b)(1)(B), and 851. His preliminary Presentence Investigation Report revealed, *inter alia,* that he is a 37-year-old African-American male with a Total Offense Level of 29, and 3 criminal history points, putting him in Criminal History Category II. Mr. Young's advisory U.S. Guideline range was 93 to 121 months. His entire criminal history scoring consisted of one offense—a conviction in Cook County, Illinois, in 1996, at age 20, for the manufacture/delivery of a controlled substance—cocaine base. He received probation, which he successfully completed without notation of any probation violations. His mandatory minimum sentence of 60 months is doubled to 120 months as a result of a § 851 enhancement for this 17-year-old conviction, and his maximum sentence of 40 years is increased to life, as well. However, after objections were filed by defense counsel, Mr. Young argued that his one prior conviction should receive no criminal history points, and the AUSA, the U.S. probation officer, and I agreed. Thus, Mr. Young is in Criminal History Category I and is now safety-valve eligible. . . .

II. THE OVERVIEW

A. How The § 851 Enhancement Works

I turn now to the § 851 enhancement issue in this and other cases. Pursuant to the penalty provisions set forth in 21 U.S.C. § 841(b)(1), enhanced penalties, including increased mandatory minimum and maximum terms of imprisonment, apply if the defendant has a prior conviction for a "felony drug offense." "Felony drug offense" is defined as "an offense that is punishable by imprisonment for more than one year under any law of the United States or of a State or foreign country that prohibits or restricts conduct relating to narcotic drugs, marihuana, anabolic steroids, or depressant or stimulant substances." 21 U.S.C. § 802(44). This sweeping definition includes many state drug convictions that the various states define under state law as misdemeanors. Unlike criminal history scoring under the Federal Sentencing Guidelines, no conviction is too old to be used as an enhancement. These enhancements are usually referred to as "§ 851enhancements" because 21 U.S.C. § 851 establishes and prescribes certain notice and other procedural requirements that trigger them.

In my experience, many § 851 enhancements involve only relatively minor state drug offenses classified as some variation of a misdemeanor under state law. Many predicate prior offenses are also decades old, where the defendant never served so much as one day in jail, and often paid only a small fine.

The highest penalties in federal drug cases are for convictions under 21 U.S.C. § 841(b)(1)(A). This subsection applies when the offense of conviction involves specifically identified drugs coupled with specific quantities of those drugs. A first-time drug offender convicted under § 841(b)(1)(A) faces a statutory mandatory minimum sentencing range of ten years and a maximum sentence of life. With a prior "felony drug conviction," the mandatory minimum doubles to twenty years. With two prior "felony drug convictions," a mandatory life sentence must be given. 21 U.S.C. § 841(b)(1)(A). On the other hand, § 841(b)(1)(B) applies to offenses involving lower quantities of drugs. A five-year mandatory minimum applies with no "prior felony drug" convictions, while a prior "felony drug" conviction, doubles the mandatory minimum to ten years.

B.   A Brief History Of Recidivist Enhancements And § 851

The modern history of experimentation with enhancements for prior drug convictions can be traced back to the 1964 amendments to the Narcotic Drug Import and Export Act of 1958. This statutory scheme automatically required the mandatory minimum sentence to be doubled when the offender had a qualifying prior drug conviction. Title II of the Comprehensive Drug Abuse Prevention and Control Act of 1970, better known as the Controlled Substances Act (CSA), repealed and replaced the Narcotic Drug Import and Export Act. Pub. L. No. 91–513, 84 Stat. 1236 (Oct. 27, 1970), codified at 21 U.S.C. §§ 801–904. The CSA afforded judges and prosecutors some leeway for the application of the prior drug conviction enhancement. The CSA also replaced mandatory minimum sentences with maximum sentences for what has become 21 U.S.C. § 841.

The House Committee, in reporting on the House bill, explained the reasons for revising the penalty structure:

> The foregoing sentencing procedures give maximum flexibility to judges, permitting them to tailor the period of imprisonment, as well as the fine, to the circumstances involved in the individual case.

> The severity of existing penalties, involving in many instances minimum mandatory sentences, have led in many instances to reluctance on the part of prosecutors to prosecute some violations, where the penalties seem to be out of line with the seriousness of the offense. In addition, severe penalties, which do not take into account individual circumstances, and treat casual violators as severely as they treat hardened criminals, tend to make convictions somewhat more difficult to obtain. The committee feels, therefore, that making the penalty structure in the law more flexible can actually serve to have a more deterrent effect than

existing penalties, through eliminating some of the difficulties prosecutors and courts have had in the past arising out of minimum mandatory sentences.

H. Rep. No. 91–1444, 91st Cong., 2d Sess., 1970 U.S.Code Cong. & Admin. News, pp. 4566, 4576.

In *United States v. Noland,* 495 F.2d 529 (5th Cir.1974), the first appellate case to be decided under the enhancement section of the 1970 CSA, the court understood this flexibility to be used in situations where neither the prosecutor, nor the court thought the enhancement desirable or necessary. *Id.* at 532. The court in *Noland* determined that it was up to the U.S. Attorney to seek enhancement if the sentence was to be doubled. Judge Sidney Thomas noted, in discussing *Noland,* that "the statutory scheme was completely everted: rather than requiring courts to impose mandatory minimums regardless of prosecutorial desire, courts were prohibited from enhancing sentences unless the government had timely filed an information stating that it intended to seek an enhanced sentence based on specific prior convictions." *United States v. Severino,* 268 F.3d 850, 863 (9th Cir.2001). So, the Congressional motivation for the injection of prosecutorial discretion for the sentencing enhancement was to overcome the temptation for prosecutors *not* to charge offenders in situations where the court was likely to impose an unduly harsh sentence because of a qualifying prior drug offense. This is the opposite of the application of § 851 enhancements as currently applied in the N.D. of Iowa, where it is applied in four out of five eligible cases.

C.   Lack Of A National DOJ § 851 Policy

Until earlier this week, the DOJ did not appear to have a national policy for the 94 districts as to when or why to seek a § 851enhancement and, in the N.D. of Iowa, there was no discernible local policy or even a whiff of an identifiable pattern. I have never been able to discern a pattern or policy of when or why a defendant receives a § 851 enhancement in my nearly 20 years as a U.S. district court judge who has sentenced over 3,500 defendants, mostly on drug charges. I asked one of our district's most respected supervisors of probation officers to inquire among all of this district's probation officers who write pre-sentence reports if any could discern a pattern. I received the following response: "I had a chance to talk with each of the writers and the consensus is that there really is no rhyme or reason to when the § 851 [enhancement] is filed and when it is not." I have also repeatedly asked defense counsel, on the record, if they are able to discern a pattern as to when their clients, who are eligible for a § 851 enhancement, receive it and when it is waived. Not a single defense lawyer has ever been able to articulate a pattern—other than the criminal defense lawyers from Omaha, Nebraska, who routinely indicate that, had the case been in the District of Nebraska, the § 851 notice would have been waived. These on-the-record statements by the Omaha criminal defense lawyers are validated by the data from the Commission. These data establish that, for the three-year sampling period, an eligible defendant in the N.D. of Iowa had a whopping 2,532% greater likelihood of receiving a § 851 enhancement than the same defendant in the District of Nebraska.

In eight of the Nation's ninety-four federal districts, § 851 enhancements have been waived in every case, regardless of whether the defendant pleads, goes to trial, or cooperates, with or without receiving a substantial assistance motion. In many other districts, the § 851enhancements were used as a plea hammer to induce a defendant to plead—then withdrawn when the defendant did plead. In the N.D. of Iowa, already this year, I have sentenced numerous defendants with § 851 enhancements, regardless of whether they pled, or pled and cooperated, and did or did not receive a substantial assistance motion. Indeed, in one case, the § 851 notice was not waived where a defendant pled, cooperated, was given a U.S.S.G. § 5K1.1 motion, but not an 18 U.S.C. § 3553(e) motion, so that the defendant received the full brunt of the doubling of her mandatory minimum sentence, even though she was the least culpable defendant in a small methamphetamine conspiracy. She received the second longest sentence of any of her co-defendants. *United States v. Newhouse,* 919 F.Supp.2d 955, 987–88, 992 (N.D.Iowa 2013).

At long last, on August 12, 2013, Attorney General Holder issued his 2013 Memo establishing a national policy on charging mandatory minimum sentences and recidivist enhancements in drug cases. In pertinent part, the Holder 2013 Memo addressed § 851 enhancements, as follows:

> **Recidivist Enhancements:** Prosecutors should decline to file an information pursuant to 21 U.S.C. § 851 unless the defendant is involved in conduct that makes the case appropriate for severe sanctions. When determining whether an enhancement is appropriate, prosecutors should consider the following factors:
>
> - Whether the defendant was an organizer, leader, manager or supervisor of others within a criminal organization;
>
> - Whether the defendant was involved in the use or threat of violence in connection with the offense;
>
> - The nature of the defendant's criminal history, including any prior history of violent conduct or recent prior convictions for serious offenses;
>
> - Whether the defendant has significant ties to large-scale drug trafficking organizations, gangs, or cartels;
>
> - Whether the filing would create a gross sentencing disparity with equally or more culpable co-defendants; and

- Other case-specific aggravating or mitigating factors.

In keeping with current policy, prosecutors are reminded that all charging decisions must be reviewed by a supervisory attorney to ensure adherence to the Principles of Federal Prosecution, the guidance provided by my May 19, 2010 memorandum, and the policy outlined in this memorandum.

Holder 2013 Memo at 3.

D.   The Wheel of Misfortune

The lack of any national or local policy, at least until August 12, 2013, rendered application of § 851 enhancements both whimsical and arbitrary—something akin to the spin of a "Wheel of Misfortune"—where similarly-situated defendants in the same district, before the same sentencing judge, sometimes received a doubling of their mandatory minimum sentences and sometimes did not. The same was true for similarly-situated defendants in the same district, before different judges, and similarly-situated defendants spanning the ninety-four districts. Also, the opposite problem of unwarranted uniformity existed, where, owing to the absence of a national policy, the most objectively deserving defendants were never subject to an enhancement in the eight districts that never apply § 851 enhancements. Given the arbitrary nature of § 851 enhancements, there were no assurances that the most objectively deserving defendants, nationwide, were actually the defendants receiving enhancements. Likewise, there were no assurances that the least deserving defendants, nationwide, were the ones that actually received a waiver. The purpose of the Sentencing Reform Act of 1984 (SRA) was to

> [P]rovide certainty and fairness in meeting the purposes of sentencing, avoiding unwarranted sentencing disparities among defendants with similar records . . . while maintaining sufficient flexibility to permit individualized sentences, where appropriate; and to "reflect, to the extent practicable, advancement in knowledge of human behavior as it relates to the criminal justice process." 28 U.S.C. § 991(b)(1), Congress further specified four "purposes" of sentencing that the Commission must pursue in carrying out its mandate: "to reflect the seriousness of the offense, to promote respect for the law, and to provide just punishment for the offense"; "to afford adequate deterrence to criminal conduct"; "to protect the public from further crimes of the defendant"; and "to provide the defendant with needed . . . correctional treatment." 18 U.S.C. § 3553(a)(2).

Mistretta v. United States, 488 U.S. 361, 374, 109 S.Ct. 647, 102 L.Ed.2d 714 (1989). The lack of a national, regional, intra-state, or local policy on § 851 enhancements rendered that stated purpose as illusory as David Copperfield's Vanishing Statue of Liberty.

If humans continue to be involved in federal sentencing, there will always be some disparity. . . . Indeed, there is some disparity because no two federal district court judges, over numerous cases, are likely to apply the Guidelines and the § 3553(a) factors in precisely the same way. Nevertheless, there is no unwarranted disparity because judges are applying congressionally-mandated factors and their decisions are subject to appellate review. Where there is now a national policy by the DOJ, with defined factors for the 94 U.S. Attorneys and the thousands of Assistant U.S. Attorneys to apply, I can accept that different federal prosecutors, like different federal judges, could, in the utmost good faith, apply the same factors differently and reach different results—that's what happens when individuals exercise judgment. What should be totally unacceptable and shocking to federal judges of all stripes, the DOJ, Congress, and the American public were the effects of a total lack of a national policy prior to August 12, 2013. What we had until then was a standardless Wheel of Misfortune regime. The Commission's data and my experience illustrated the dangers of such a regime: Individual prosecutor's wholly-insulated § 851 charging decisions resulted in both unwarranted sentencing disparity and unwarranted sentencing uniformity—the worst case scenario imaginable.

E.   Other Problems With The Arbitrary Workings Of § 851 Enhancements

Wholly apart from these critical considerations of arbitrary application and lack of transparency by the DOJ, the serious and pervasive structural deficiencies in § 851 enhancements that existed prior to August 12, 2013, often led to bizarre and incomprehensibly unfair results. For example, take two low-level drug addict co-defendants who, prior to August 12, 2013, pled guilty to and were sentenced for the same conspiracy to manufacture a small amount (as little as five grams) of homemade methamphetamine, made from cough medication purchased at a local drug store. One was non-violent; the other had a long history of violence. They were both fifty years old and lived next to each other, and both worked the night shift at a local manufacturing plant. Bob had a thirty-year-old prior aggravated misdemeanor conviction in Iowa for possession of a small amount of marijuana. In 1993, he paid a $100 fine, was given probation, never served a day in jail, and successfully completed his short term of probation. He had no other prior convictions. His co-defendant, John, had one prior armed robbery conviction in 2000, served an eight-year prison sentence, and violated his parole on several occasions before he was discharged in 2011. John also had four assault convictions before his armed robbery conviction. John would likely have received a mandatory minimum five-year sentence, but because Bob's prior misdemeanor drug conviction is a predicate to a § 851 enhancement, and John's prior robbery and assault convictions are not, Bob would likely have received, at a minimum, the mandatory minimum sentence of ten years in a district where § 851 enhancements were routine. This was justice? Indeed, a major drug trafficker in federal court would not receive a recidivist enhancement with a prior state court murder conviction, but a low-level drug addict would receive such an enhancement with a prior qualifying state court misdemeanor drug conviction. This was justice?

I am optimistic that fair application of the Holder 2013 Memo will rectify this problem going forward.

III. ANALYSIS OF THE COMMISSION'S § 851 DATA

A.   Overview Of The Underlying Data On § 851 Enhancements

The grim state of affairs for § 851 enhancements prior to the national policy established by the Holder 2013 Memo is starkly revealed by an examination of the Commission's § 851 data on the one occasion that it collected such information. Every year, pursuant to its statutory mandate, the Commission publishes national data collected from federal sentencings spanning all ninety-four districts. In 2011, the Commission conducted the first and only, additional targeted coding and analysis project on nationwide application of 21 U.S.C. § 851 recidivist enhancements as part of the REPORT TO THE CONGRESS: MANDATORY MINIMUM PENALTIES IN THE FEDERAL CRIMINAL JUSTICE SYSTEM (Commission's 2011 REPORT). Ninety-three of the ninety-four districts reported data, and the Commission described in detail its methodology for its targeted § 851 study. The Commission's 2011 REPORT itself notes, "[This] study of drug offenses and mandatory minimum penalties demonstrates a lack of uniformity in application of the enhanced mandatory minimum penalties." Commission's 2011 REPORT at 253. . . .

C.   The Eighth Circuit—§ 851 Application Disparity

The average application rate of § 851 enhancements for districts in the Eighth Circuit is 28%. App. D. The application rates in the Eighth Circuit range from 84% in the S.D. of Iowa, to 0% in the W.D. of Arkansas. *Id.* Of the ten districts in the Eighth Circuit, Iowa's two districts are responsible for enhancing the sentences of 63% of the eligible offenders. . . .

Prosecutors in the N.D. of Iowa applied this enhancement at a higher rate than all other districts in the Eighth Circuit except the S.D. of Iowa. Iowa's two federal district applied the § 851 enhancement to more defendants than the rest of the districts in the Eighth Circuit combined. App. D. The N.D. of Iowa alone, applied the § 851 enhancement at a rate more than twice the amount of six other districts in the Eighth Circuit combined.25 Eligible defendants in the N.D. of Iowa were 1,183% more likely to receive at least a § 851 enhancement than the average of other districts in the Eighth Circuit excluding the S.D. of Iowa.

Although the N.D. and S.D. of Iowa differ in application by only five percentage points, the difference that geography can make in sentencing becomes apparent when the N.D. of Iowa is compared to the three federal districts, other than the S.D. of Iowa, that border the N.D. of Iowa. Apps. C, D. Nebraska is only one mile south of the federal courthouse in Sioux City, Iowa, where I preside, yet defendants are 2,532% more likely to face a § 851 enhancement in the N.D. of Iowa than in the D. of Nebraska. Ironically, a very significant percentage of my drug cases, including those where a § 851 enhancement is applied, could have been venued and prosecuted in Nebraska. The South Dakota border is four miles to the west, but federal prosecutors in the D. of South Dakota apply the enhancement at one-twentieth the rate federal prosecutors apply it in the N.D. of Iowa. Defendants in Minnesota, an hour-and-a-half drive to the north, were less than one-tenth as likely to be subjected to a § 851 enhancement as defendants in the N.D. of Iowa.

EXERCISE

The Holder memo referred to in the *Young* case was replaced by the Trump administration, as is typical in new administrations. The new memo arguably gave more discretion to local prosecutors in employing § 851 enhancements.

Imagine that you are the appointed United States Attorney for the district where you live. You have the ability to create a policy directing the use of § 851 enhancements by the prosecutors in your office. Would you create such a policy? What would it require or direct?

Prosecutors can wield great discretion not only in seeking sentence enhancements, but by purposely directing a sentence in how they charge a case. Particularly in cases involving narcotics and guns, a wide variety of charges could apply, meaning that a prosecutor can limit a judge's options in one direction by choosing charges with high minimum sentences or the other by choosing one with a low maximum sentence. The power of a prosecutor to create a severe sentence is heightened when charges are sentenced "consecutively"—that is, such that the sentence for one charge doesn't start until another is finished, so that the sentences are "stacked" on top of one another.

UNITED STATES V. ANGELOS

345 F. Supp. 2d 1227 (D. Utah 2004)

CASSELL, DISTRICT JUDGE. . . .

Defendant Weldon Angelos stands now before the court for sentencing. He is a twenty-four-year-old first offender who is a successful music executive with two young children. Because he was convicted of dealing marijuana and related offenses, both the government and the defense agree that Mr. Angelos should serve about six to eight years in prison. But there are three additional firearms offenses for which the court must also impose sentence. Two of those offenses occurred when Mr. Angelos carried a handgun to two $350 marijuana deals; the third when police found several additional handguns at his home when they executed a search warrant. For these three acts of possessing (not using or even displaying) these guns, the government insists that Mr. Angelos should essentially spend the rest of his life in prison. Specifically, the government urges the court to sentence Mr. Angelos to a prison term of no less than 61 ½ years—six years and a half (or more) for drug dealing followed by 55 years for three counts of possessing a firearm in connection with a drug offense. In support of its position, the government relies on a statute—18 U.S.C. § 924(c)—which requires the court to impose a sentence of five years in prison the first time a drug dealer carries a gun and twenty-five years for each subsequent time. Under § 924(c), the three counts produce 55 years of additional punishment for carrying a firearm.

The court believes that to sentence Mr. Angelos to prison for the rest of his life is unjust, cruel, and even irrational. Adding 55 years on top of a sentence for drug dealing is far beyond the roughly two-year sentence that the congressionally-created expert agency (the United States Sentencing Commission) believes is appropriate for possessing firearms under the same circumstances. The 55-year sentence substantially exceeds what the jury recommended to the court. It is also far in excess of the sentence imposed for such serious crimes as aircraft hijacking, second degree murder, espionage, kidnapping, aggravated assault, and rape. It exceeds what recidivist criminals will likely serve under the federal "three strikes" provision. At the same time, however, this 55-year additional sentence is decreed by § 924(c).

The court's role in evaluating § 924(c) is quite limited. The court can set aside the statute only if it is irrational punishment without any conceivable justification or is so excessive as to constitute cruel and unusual punishment in violation of the Eighth Amendment. After careful deliberation, the court reluctantly concludes that it has no choice but to impose the 55 year sentence. While the sentence appears to be cruel, unjust, and irrational, in our system of separated powers Congress makes the final decisions as to appropriate criminal penalties. Under the controlling case law, the court must find either that a statute has no conceivable justification or is so grossly disproportionate to the crime that no reasonable argument can be made its behalf. If the court is to fairly apply these precedents in this case, it must reject Mr. Angelos' constitutional challenges. Accordingly, the court sentences Mr. Angelos to a prison term of 55 years and one day, the minimum that the law allows. . . .

Weldon Angelos is twenty-four years old. He was born on July 16, 1979, in Salt Lake City, Utah. He was raised in the Salt Lake City area by his father, Mr. James B. Angelos, with only minimal contact with his mother. Mr. Angelos has two young children by Ms. Zandrah Uyan: six-year-old Anthony and five-year-old Jessie. Before his arrest Mr. Angelos had achieved some success in the music industry. He started Extravagant Records, a label that produces rap and hip hop music. He had worked with prominent hip hop musicians, including Snoop Dogg, on the "beats" to various songs and was preparing to record his own album.

The critical events in this case are three "controlled buys" of marijuana by a government informant from Mr. Angelos. On May 10, 2002, Mr. Angelos met with the informant, Ronnie Lazalde, and arranged a sale of marijuana. On May 21, 2002, Mr. Angelos completed a sale of a eight ounces of marijuana to Lazalde for $350. Lazalde observed Mr. Angelos' Glock pistol by the center console of his car. This drug deal formed the basis for the first § 924(c) count.

During a second controlled buy with Lazalde, on June 4, 2002, Mr. Angelos lifted his pant leg to show him the Glock in an ankle holster. Lazalde again purchased approximately eight ounces of marijuana for $350. This deal formed the basis for the second § 924(c) count.

A third controlled buy occurred on June 18, 2002, with Mr. Angelos again selling Lazalde eight ounces of marijuana for $350. There was no direct evidence of a gun at this transaction, so no § 924(c) count was charged.

On November 15, 2003, police officers arrested Mr. Angelos at his apartment pursuant to a warrant. Mr. Angelos consented to a search. The search revealed a briefcase which contained $18,040, a handgun, and two opiate suckers. Officers also discovered two bags which contained approximately three pounds of marijuana. Officers also recovered two other guns in a locked safe, one of which was confirmed as stolen. Searches at other locations, including the apartment of Mr. Angelos' girlfriend, turned up several duffle bags with marijuana residue, two more guns, and additional cash. . . .

The jury found Mr. Angelos guilty on sixteen counts, including three § 924(c) counts: two counts for the Glock seen at the two controlled buys and a third count for the three handguns at Mr. Angelos' home. The jury found him not guilty on three counts—including the two additional § 924(c) counts for the two guns at his girlfriends' home. (The court dismissed one other minor count.)

Mr. Angelos' sentence is presumptively governed by the Federal Sentencing Guidelines. Under governing Guideline provisions, the bottom line is that all counts but the three § 924(c) counts combine to create a total offense level of 28. Because Mr. Angelos has no significant prior criminal history, he is treated as first-time offender (a criminal history category I) under the Guidelines. The prescribed Guidelines' sentence for Mr. Angelos for everything but the § 924(c) counts is 78 to 97 months.

After the Guideline sentence is imposed, however, the court must then add the § 924(c) counts. Section 924(c) prescribes a five-year mandatory minimum for a first conviction, and 25 years for each subsequent conviction. This means that Mr. Angelos is facing 55 years (660 months) of mandatory time for the § 924(c) convictions. In addition, § 924(c) mandates that these 55 years run consecutively to any other time imposed. As a consequence, the minimum sentence that the court can impose on Mr. Angelos is 61 ½ years—6 ½ years (78 months) for the 13 counts under the Guidelines and 55 consecutive years for the three § 924 convictions. The federal system does not provide the possibility of parole, but instead provides only a modest "good behavior" credit of approximately 15 percent of the sentence. Assuming good behavior, Mr. Angelos' sentence will be reduced to "only" 55 years, meaning he could be released when he is 78 years old.

Before turning to Mr. Angelos' specific challenges to § 924(c), it is helpful to understand the history of the statute. Title 18 U.S.C. § 924(c)was proposed and enacted in a single day as an amendment to the Gun Control Act of 1968 enacted following the assassinations of Martin Luther King, Jr. and Robert F. Kennedy. Congress intended the Act to address the "increasing rate of crime and lawlessness and the growing use of firearms in violent crime." Because § 924(c) was offered as a floor amendment, there are no congressional hearings or committee reports regarding its original purpose, and the court is left only with a few statements made during floor debate. For example, Representative Poff, the sponsor of the amendment, stated that the law's purpose was to "persuade the man tempted to commit a Federal felony to leave his gun at home."

As originally enacted, § 924(c) gave judges considerable discretion in sentencing and was not nearly as harsh as it has become. When passed in 1968, § 924(c) imposed an enhancement of "not less than one year nor more than ten years" for the person who "uses a firearm to commit any felony for which he may be prosecuted in a court of the United States" or "carries a firearm unlawfully during the commission of any felony for which he may be prosecuted in a court of the United States." If the person was convicted of a "second or subsequent" violation of § 924(c), the additional penalty was "not less than 2 nor more than 25 years," which could not run "concurrently with any term of imprisonment imposed for the commission of such felony." In the 36 years since its passage, the penalties attached to § 924(c) have been made continually harsher either by judicial interpretation or congressional action. . . .

Mr. Angelos first contends that 18 U.S.C. § 924(c) makes arbitrary classifications and irrationally treats him far more harshly than criminals guilty of other much more serious crimes. He raises this claim as an equal protection challenge. The court will first set forth the law on such arguments and then turn to the merits of Mr. Angelos' claim. . . .

Mr. Angelos does not argue that his claim is subject to a heightened standard of review. The law is well-settled on the subject. As explained by the Supreme Court:

Every person has a fundamental right to liberty in the sense that the Government may not punish him unless and until it proves his guilt beyond a reasonable doubt at a criminal trial conducted in accordance with the relevant constitutional guarantees. . . . But a person who *has* been so convicted is eligible for, and the court may impose, whatever punishment is authorized by statute for his offense, so long as that penalty is not cruel and unusual . . . and so long as the penalty is not based on an arbitrary distinction that would violate the Due Process Clause of the Fifth Amendment. In this context . . . an argument based on equal protection essentially duplicates an argument based on due process.

This holding places on Mr. Angelos a heavy burden of proof. First, "statutory classifications will not be set aside on equal protection grounds if any ground can be conceived to justify them as rationally related to a legitimate government interest." Second, "those attacking the rationality of the legislative classification have the burden 'to negate every conceivable basis' which might support it." The government "has no obligation to produce evidence to sustain the rationality of a statutory classification," nor does Congress have to " 'articulate its reasons for enacting a statute' " "[U]nder a rational basis analysis, [Congress] need not articulate the precise reasons why it chose to impose different sentences for different crimes; nothing in the Constitution prevents [Congress] from making classifications along non-suspect lines if there is a rational basis for doing so." A statute can be both over-inclusive and under-inclusive and still pass rational basis review. In sum, rational basis review is "a paradigm of judicial restraint" which "presumes that . . . even improvident decisions will eventually be rectified by the democratic process and that judicial intervention is generally unwarranted no matter how unwisely we may think a political branch has acted." It is on this basis that the court will proceed. . . .

As applied in this case, the classifications created by § 924(c) are simply irrational. Section 924(c) imposes on Mr. Angelos a sentence 55 years or 660 months. Added to the minimum 78-month Guidelines sentence for a total sentence of 738 months, Mr. Angelos is facing a prison term which more than doubles the sentence of, for example, an aircraft hijacker (293 months), a terrorist who detonates a bomb in a public place (235 months), a racist who attacks a minority with the intent to kill and inflicts permanent or life-threatening injuries (210 months), a second-degree murderer, or a rapist.

When multiple § 924(c) counts are stacked on top of each other, they produce lengthy sentences that fail to distinguish between first offenders (like Mr. Angelos) and recidivist offenders. As John R. Steer, Vice Chair of the United States Sentencing Commission, has explained:

> [C]onsider the effects if prosecutors pursued every possible count of 18 U.S.C. § 924(c). . . . The statute provides for minimum consecutive sentence enhancements of 25 years to life for the second and subsequent conviction under the statute, even if all the counts are charged, convicted, and sentenced at the same time. Pursuing multiple § 924(c) charges at the same time has been called "count stacking" and has resulted in sentences of life imprisonment (or aggregate sentences for a term of years far exceeding life expectancy) for some offenders with little or no criminal history.

Consider the way in which the § 924(c) counts stack up on Mr. Angelos. He is currently 24 years old. He is to receive at least 78 months for the underlying offenses. Stacked on top of this is another 5 years for the first § 924(c) conviction. Stacked on top of this is another 25 years for the second § 924(c) conviction. And finally, another 25 years is stacked on top for the third § 924(c) conviction. Even assuming credit for good time served, Mr. Angelos will be more than 55-years-old before he even begins to serve the final 25 years his sentence. This happens not because Mr. Angelos "failed to learn his lessons from the initial punishment" and committed a repeat offense. Section 924(c) jumps from a five-year mandatory sentence for a first violation to a 25-year mandatory sentence for a second violation, which may occur just days (or even hours) later. It is not a recidivist provision. . . .

For the reasons outlined in the previous section, § 924(c) imposes unjust punishment and creates irrational classifications between different offenses and different offenders. To some, this may seem like a law professor's argument—one that may have some validity in the classroom but little salience in the real world. After all, the only issue in this case is the extent of punishment for a man justly convicted of serious drug trafficking offenses. So what, some may say, if he spends more years in prison than might be theoretically justified? It is common wisdom that "if you can't do the time, don't do the crime."

The problem with this simplistic position is that it overlooks other interests that are inevitably involved in the imposition of a criminal sentence. For example, crime victims expect that the penalties the court imposes will fairly reflect the harms that they have suffered. When the sentence for actual violence inflicted on a victim is dwarfed by a sentence for carrying guns to several drug deals, the implicit message to victims is that their pain and suffering counts for less than some abstract "war on drugs."

This is no mere academic point, as a case from this court's docket will illustrate. Earlier today, shortly before Mr. Angelos' hearing, the court imposed sentence in *United States v. Visinaiz,* 344 F.Supp.2d 1310 (D.Utah 2004), a second-degree murder case. There, a jury convicted Cruz Joaquin Visinaiz of second-degree murder in the death of 68-year-old Clara Jenkins. On one evening, while drinking together, the two got into an argument. Ms. Jenkins threw an empty bottle at Mr. Visinaiz, who then proceeded to beat her to death by striking her in the head at least three times with a log. Mr. Visinaiz then hid the body in a crawl space of his home, later dumping the body in a river weighted down with cement blocks.

Following his conviction for second-degree murder, Mr. Visinaiz came before the court as a first-time offender for sentencing. The Sentencing Guidelines require a sentence for this brutal second-degree murder of between 210 to 262 months. The government called this an "aggravated second-degree murder" and recommended a sentence of 262 months. The court followed that recommendation. Yet on the same day, the court is to impose a sentence of 738 months for a first-time drug dealer who carried a gun to several drug deals!? The victim's family in the Visinaiz case—not to mention victims of a vast array of other violent crimes—can be forgiven if they think that the federal criminal justice system minimizes their losses. No doubt § 924(c) is motivated by the best of intentions—to prevent criminal victimization. But the statute pursues that goal in a way that effectively sends a message to victims of actual criminal violence that their suffering is not fully considered by the system.

Another reason for concern is that the unjust penalties imposed by § 924(c) can be expected to attract public notice. As shown earlier, applying § 924(c) to cases such as this one leads to sentences far in excess of what the public believes is appropriate. Perhaps in the short term, no ill effects will come from the difference between public expectations and actual sentences. But in the longer term, the federal criminal justice system will suffer. Most seriously, jurors may stop voting to convict drug dealers in federal criminal prosecutions if they are aware that unjust punishment may follow. It only takes a single juror who is worried about unjust sentencing to "hang" a jury and prevent a conviction. This is not an abstract concern. In the case of *United States v. Molina* the jury failed to reach a verdict on a § 924(c) count which would have added 30 years to the defendant's sentence. Judge Weinstein, commenting on "the dubious state of our criminal sentencing law" noted that "[j]ury nullification of sentences deemed too harsh is increasingly reflected in refusals to convict." In the last several drug trials before this court, jurors have privately expressed considerable concern after their verdicts about what sentences might be imposed. If federal juries are to continue to convict the guilty, those juries must have confidence that just punishment will follow from their verdicts. . . .

Mr. Angelos is probably receiving a sentence far in excess of what many other identically-situated offenders will receive for identical crimes in other federal districts. The court has been advised by judges from other parts of the country that, in their districts, an offender like Mr. Angelos would not have been charged with multiple § 924(c) counts. This is no trivial matter. The decision to pursue, for example, a third § 924(c) count in this case makes the difference between a 36-year-sentence and 61-year sentence. In short, § 924(c) as applied in this case seems to create the serious risk of massive sentencing disparity between identically-situated offenders within the federal system. And the problem of disparity only worsens if we acknowledge the fact that Mr. Angelos would not have been charged with federal crimes in many other states. For all these reasons, the government could not plausibly defend § 924(c) on an eliminating-disparity rationale. . . .

Instead, the rationale advanced by government is deterrence and incapacitation: the draconian provisions of § 924(c) are necessary to deter drug dealers from committing crimes with those firearms and to prevent Mr. Angelos from doing so in the future.

The deterrence argument rests on a strong intuitive logic. Sending a message to drug dealers that they will serve additional time in prison if they are caught with firearms may lead some to avoid firearms entirely and others to leave their firearms at home. The Supreme Court has specifically noted "the deterrence rationale of § 924(c)," explaining that a fundamental purpose behind § 924(c) was to combat the dangerous combination of drugs and firearms. Congress is certainly entitled to legislate based on the belief that § 924(c) will "persuade the man tempted to commit a Federal felony to leave his gun at home."

Congress' belief is, moreover, supported by empirical evidence. Generally criminologists believe that an increase in prison populations will reduce crime through both a deterrent and incapacitative effect. The consensus view appears to be that each 10% increase in the prison population produces about a 1% to 3% decrease in serious crimes. For example, one recent study concluded that California's three strikes law prevented 8 murders, 4000 aggravated assaults, 10,000 robberies, and 400,000 burglaries in its first two years of operation. One study found that Congress' financial incentives to states to which (like the federal system) force violent offenders to serve 85% of their sentences decreased murders by 16%, aggravated assaults by 12%, robberies by 24%, rapes by 12%, and larcenies by 3%. While offenders "substituted" into less harmful property crimes, the overall reduction in crime was significant. While no specific study has examined § 924(c), it is reasonable to assume—and Congress is entitled to assume—that it has prevented some serious drug and firearms offenses.

The problem with the deterrence argument, however, is that it proves too much. A statute that provides mandatory life sentences for jaywalking or petty theft would, no doubt, deter those offenses. But it would be hard to view such hypothetical statutes as resting on rational premises. Moreover, a mandatory life sentence for petty theft, for example, would raise the question of why such penalties were not in place for aircraft hijacking, second-degree murder, rape, and other serious crimes. Finally, deterrence comes at a price. Given that holding a person in federal prison costs about $23,000 per year, the 61-year-sentence the court is being asked to impose in this case will cost the taxpayers (even assuming Mr. Angelos receives good time credit and serves "only" 55-years) about $1,265,000. Spending more than a million dollars to incarcerate Mr. Angelos will prevent future crimes by him and may well deter some others from being involved with drugs and guns. But that money could also be spent on other law enforcement or social programs that in all likelihood would produce greater reductions in crime and victimization.

If the court were to evaluate these competing tradeoffs, it would conclude that stacking § 924(c) counts on top of each other for first-time drug offenders who have merely possessed firearms is not a cost-effective way of obtaining deterrence.

It is not enough to simply be "tough" on crime. Given limited resources in our society, we also have to be "smart" in the way we allocate our resources. But these tradeoffs are the subject of reasonable debate. It is not the proper business of the court to second-guess the congressional judgment that § 924(c) is a wise investment of resources. Instead, in conducting rational basis review of the statute, the court is only to determine whether "any ground can be conceived to justify [the statutory scheme] as rationally related to a legitimate government interest." "Where there are 'plausible reasons' for Congress' action, [the court's] inquiry is at an end." In *Busic* referring to *Simpson,* the Supreme Court recognized that § 924(c) could lead to "seemingly unreasonable comparative sentences" but that "[i]f corrective action is needed it is the Congress that must provide it. It is not for us to speculate, much less act, on whether Congress would have altered its stance had the specific events of this case been anticipated." The Court further noted that "in our constitutional system the commitment to separation of powers is too fundamental for us to pre-empt congressional action by judicially decreeing what accords with 'commonsense and the public weal.'"

Accordingly, the court reluctantly concludes that § 924(c) survives rational basis scrutiny. While it imposes unjust punishment and creates irrational classifications, there is a "plausible reason" for Congress' action. As a result, this court's obligation is to follow the law and to reject Mr. Angelos' equal protection challenge to the statute. . . .

In addition to raising an equal protection argument, Mr. Angelos also argues that his 55-year sentence under § 924(c) violates the Eighth Amendment's prohibition of cruel and unusual punishment. In this argument, he is joined in an *amicus* brief filed by a distinguished group of 29 former United States District Judges, United States Circuit Court Judges, and United States Attorneys, who draw on their expertise in federal criminal law and federal sentencing issues to urge that the sentence is unconstitutional as disproportionate to the offenses at hand.

Mr. Angelos and his supporting *amici* are correct in urging that controlling Eighth Amendment case law places an outer limit on punishments that can be imposed for criminal offenses, forbidding penalties that are grossly disproportionate to any offense. . . .

. . . The court is keenly aware of its obligation to follow precedent from superior courts—specifically the Tenth Circuit and, of course, the Supreme Court. The Supreme Court has considered one case that might be regarded as quite similar to this one. In *Hutto v. Davis,* the Supreme Court held that two consecutive twenty-year sentences—totaling forty years—for possession of nine ounces of marijuana said to be worth $200 did not violate the Eighth Amendment. If *Davis* remains good law, it is hard see how the sentence in this case violates the Eighth Amendment. Here, Mr. Angelos was involved in at least two marijuana deals involving $700 and approximately sixteen ounces (one pound) of marijuana. Perhaps currency inflation could equate $700 today with $200 in the 1980's. But as a simple matter of arithmetic, if 40 years in prison for possessing nine ounces marijuana does not violate the Eighth Amendment, it is hard to see how 61 years for distributing sixteen ounces (or more) would do so. . . .

Indeed, in *Davis* the Supreme Court pointedly reminded district court judges that "unless we wish anarchy to prevail within the federal judicial system, a precedent of this Court must be followed by the lower federal courts. . . ." Under *Davis,* Mr. Angelos' sentence is not cruel and unusual punishment. Therefore, his Eighth Amendment challenge must be rejected. . . .

With Mr. Angelos' constitutional challenges to the 55-year sentence on § 924(c) counts resolved, the remaining issue before the court is the sentence to be imposed on the other counts. Mr. Angelos raises a constitutional challenge to the 78–97 month sentence called for by the Sentencing Guidelines for his thirteen other offenses. He notes that the Guidelines calculation rests on enhancements that were never submitted to the jury, in particular enhancements based on the quantity of drugs involved and the amount of money laundered. . . .

Without the Guidelines, the court is free to make its own determination of what is an appropriate sentence for these thirteen offenses. In making that determination, the court consults the Guidelines as instructive but not binding. If the sentence on these thirteen counts was the only sentence that Mr. Angelos would serve, a sentence of about 78–97 months might well be appropriate. But the court cannot ignore the reality that Mr. Angelos will also be sentenced to 55 years on the § 924(c) counts, far in excess of what is just punishment for all of his crimes. In light of this 55-year sentence, and having considered all of the relevant factors listed in the Sentencing Reform Act, the court will impose a sentence of one day in prison for all offenses other than the § 924(c) counts. Lest anyone think that this is a "soft" sentence, in combination with the § 924(c) counts, the result is that Mr. Angelos will not walk outside of prison until after he reaches the age of 70.

Having disposed of the legal arguments in this case, it seems appropriate to make some concluding, personal observations. I have been on the bench for nearly two-and-half years now. During that time, I have sentenced several hundred offenders under the Sentencing Guidelines and federal mandatory minimum statutes. By and large, the sentences I have been required to impose have been tough but fair. In a few cases, to be sure, I have felt that either the Guidelines or the mandatory minimums produced excessive punishment. But even in those cases, the sentences seemed to be within the realm of reason.

This case is different. It involves a first offender who will receive a life sentence for crimes far less serious than those committed by many other offenders—including violent offenders and even a murderer—who have been before me. For the reasons explained in my opinion, I am legally obligated to impose this sentence. But I feel ethically obligated to bring this injustice to the attention of those who are in a position to do something about it.

A.   Recommendation for Executive Commutation

For all the reasons previously given, an additional 55-year sentence for Mr. Angelos under § 924(c) is unjust, disproportionate to his offense, demeaning to victims of actual criminal violence—but nonetheless constitutional. While I must impose the unjust sentence, our system of separated powers provides a means of redress. The Framers were well aware that "[t]he administration of justice . . . is not necessarily always wise or certainly considerate of circumstances which may properly mitigate guilt." In my mind, this is one of those rare cases where the system has malfunctioned. "To afford a remedy, it has always been thought essential in popular governments, as well as in monarchies, to vest in some other authority than the courts power to ameliorate or avoid particular criminal judgments." Under our Constitution, the President has "the Power to grant Reprieves and Pardons for Offenses against the United States. . . ." One of the purposes of executive clemency is "to afford relief from undue harshness." This power is absolute. "The executive can reprieve or pardon all offenses after their commission, either before trial, during trial or after trial, by individuals, or by classes, conditionally or absolutely, and this without modification or regulation by Congress."

Given that the President has the exclusive power to commute sentences, the question arises as to whether I have any role to play in commutation decisions, *i.e.*, is it appropriate for me to make a commutation recommendation to the President. Having carefully reviewed the issue, I believe that such a recommendation is entirely proper. The President presumably wants the fullest array of information regarding cases in which a commutation might be appropriate. Moreover, the Executive Branch has indicated that it actively solicits the views of sentencing judges on pardon and commutation requests. The Office of the Pardon Attorney in the Department of Justice is responsible for handling requests for pardons and commutations. According to the U.S. Attorney's Manual Standards for Consideration of Clemency Petitions, the Pardon Attorney "routinely requests . . . the views and recommendations of the sentencing judge" on any request for commutation.

I therefore believe that it is appropriate for me to communicate to the President, through the Office of the Pardon Attorney, my views regarding Mr. Angelos' sentence. I recommend that the President commute Mr. Angelos' sentence to a prison term of no more than 18 years, the average sentence recommended by the jury that heard this case. The court agrees with the jury that this is an appropriate sentence in this matter in light of all of the other facts discussed in this opinion. The Clerk's Office is directed to forward a copy of this opinion with its commutation recommendation to the Office of Pardon Attorney. . . .

The 55-year sentence mandated by § 924(c) in this case appears to be unjust, cruel, and irrational. But our constitutional system of government requires the court to follow the law, not its own personal views about what the law ought to be. Perhaps the court has overlooked some legal point, and that the appellate courts will find Mr. Angelos' sentence invalid. But applying the law as the court understands it, the court sentences Mr. Angelos to serve a term of imprisonment of 55 years and one day. The court recommends that the President commute this unjust sentence and that the Congress modify the laws that produced it. The Clerk's Office is directed to forward a copy of this opinion with its commutation recommendation to the Office of Pardon Attorney and to the Chair and Ranking Member of the House and Senate Judiciary Committees.

EXERCISE

Imagine that you are a federal prosecutor assigned the cast of George Glass, a 19-year-old. Based on a reliable tip that he was growing marijuana, a local task force receives a warrant and searches his house. They find seven immature marijuana plants under a grow light, and seize the plants, some notes, and Mr. Glass's computers, phones, and tablets (which were covered by the search warrant). Upon inspecting the contents of the seven electronic devices seized, investigators find at least one image of child pornography on each device (six of the devices have one image, and one contains three images). Each image had been received by Mr. Glass via email. The images are familiar to the investigators, as they are widely distributed on the internet, and depict 12 and 13 year old female victims engaging in sexual acts with adults. Each image depicts different victims (they are not multiple copies or versions of the same image). This appears to be a clear violation of 18 U.S.C. § 2252A(a)(2)(A). Mr. Glass has no prior criminal history.

The statute sets out a mandatory sentence of five to twenty years per count. Under 18 U.S.C. § 3584(a), the sentencing judge can sentence multiple counts either concurrently (so they run at the same time) or consecutively (so that they stack up and run one after the other). You know that in child porn cases, the judge assigned to the Glass case always stacks the sentences for multiple counts where (as here) there are unique devices and images, and sentences at the mandatory minimum for each.

You talk to your supervisor, and she says it is up to you to make the charging decision, but you must charge all images on one device in a separate count. This means that your charging decisions will largely determine the sentence: If you charge one count, the defendant will get a five year sentence, and if you charge six counts the defendant will receive a sentence of 30 years. What will you do?

B. SENTENCING GUIDELINES

The federal system, like many state systems, employs a set of sentencing guidelines that judges must consult before formulating a sentence. Those guidelines establish a range of months of incarceration, based on a grid that takes two factors into consideration: the seriousness of the offense and the defendant's criminal history. The "offense level" scores range from one to 43, while there are six criminal history categories on the other axis. That creates a grid of potential outcomes:

SENTENCING TABLE
(in months of imprisonment)

Offense Level	Criminal History Category (Criminal History Points)					
	I (0 or 1)	II (2 or 3)	III (4, 5, 6)	IV (7, 8, 9)	V (10, 11, 12)	VI (13 or more)
1	0–6	0–6	0–6	0–6	0–6	0–6
2	0–6	0–6	0–6	0–6	0–6	1–7
3	0–6	0–6	0–6	0–6	2–8	3–9
4	0–6	0–6	0–6	2–8	4–10	6–12
5	0–6	0–6	1–7	4–10	6–12	9–15
6	0–6	1–7	2–8	6–12	9–15	12–18
7	0–6	2–8	4–10	8–14	12–18	15–21
8	0–6	4–10	6–12	10–16	15–21	18–24
9	4–10	6–12	8–14	12–18	18–24	21–27
10	6–12	8–14	10–16	15–21	21–27	24–30
11	8–14	10–16	12–18	18–24	24–30	27–33
12	10–16	12–18	15–21	21–27	27–33	30–37
13	12–18	15–21	18–24	24–30	30–37	33–41
14	15–21	18–24	21–27	27–33	33–41	37–46
15	18–24	21–27	24–30	30–37	37–46	41–51
16	21–27	24–30	27–33	33–41	41–51	46–57
17	24–30	27–33	30–37	37–46	46–57	51–63
18	27–33	30–37	33–41	41–51	51–63	57–71
19	30–37	33–41	37–46	46–57	57–71	63–78
20	33–41	37–46	41–51	51–63	63–78	70–87
21	37–46	41–51	46–57	57–71	70–87	77–96
22	41–51	46–57	51–63	63–78	77–96	84–105
23	46–57	51–63	57–71	70–87	84–105	92–115
24	51–63	57–71	63–78	77–96	92–115	100–125
25	57–71	63–78	70–87	84–105	100–125	110–137
26	63–78	70–87	78–97	92–115	110–137	120–150
27	70–87	78–97	87–108	100–125	120–150	130–162
28	78–97	87–108	97–121	110–137	130–162	140–175
29	87–108	97–121	108–135	121–151	140–175	151–188
30	97–121	108–135	121–151	135–168	151–188	168–210
31	108–135	121–151	135–168	151–188	168–210	188–235
32	121–151	135–168	151–188	168–210	188–235	210–262
33	135–168	151–188	168–210	188–235	210–262	235–293
34	151–188	168–210	188–235	210–262	235–293	262–327
35	168–210	188–235	210–262	235–293	262–327	292–365
36	188–235	210–262	235–293	262–327	292–365	324–405
37	210–262	235–293	262–327	292–365	324–405	360–life
38	235–293	262–327	292–365	324–405	360–life	360–life
39	262–327	292–365	324–405	360–life	360–life	360–life
40	292–365	324–405	360–life	360–life	360–life	360–life
41	324–405	360–life	360–life	360–life	360–life	360–life
42	360–life	360–life	360–life	360–life	360–life	360–life
43	life	life	life	life	life	life

Zones: Zone A (levels 1–8 area), Zone B, Zone C, Zone D.

November 1, 2016

Relative to some state systems, the federal guidelines are particularly complex. For example, to determine the offense level for a theft under guideline § 2B1.1, adjustments are directed based on a remarkable range of factors: the amount of loss, the number of victims, whether substantial hardship was caused, whether the theft was from a national cemetery, whether the theft involved government health care, whether the theft involved a trade secret or auto parts, and whether or not a dangerous weapon was possessed, among others. The purpose of this discussion is not to provide a thorough training in federal guideline calculations; unfortunately, the system is far too complex to do that here. Rather, the goal is to get a sense of how the system works.

Until 2005, the federal guidelines were mandatory and restricted judges to sentencing within the range provided unless relying on a "departure" allowed for in the guidelines themselves. For example, guideline § 5k1.1 allows for a downward departure from the guidelines when the defendant provides "substantial assistance" in a case against someone else.

This mandatory scheme changed with the Supreme Court's in *United States v. Booker*, 543 U.S. 220 (2005). There, the Court first held that the mandatory guidelines, since they allowed upper ranges to go up according to a judge's decision, violated the jury right described in *Apprendi v. New Jersey*, 530 U.S. 466 (2000). The Court then found (in a second opinion with a different majority) that the proper remedy to the problem was to make the guidelines advisory rather than mandatory, while emphasizing that a sentence would be reviewed for "reasonableness" under the standards set out in 18 U.S.C. § 3553.

After *Booker*, the problem of calculating a correct guideline range still challenges the primary actors at criminal sentencing.

MOLINO-MARTINEZ V. UNITED STATES
136 S. Ct. 1338 (2016)

JUSTICE KENNEDY delivered the opinion of the Court.

This case involves the Federal Sentencing Guidelines. In sentencing petitioner, the District Court applied a Guidelines range higher than the applicable one. The error went unnoticed by the court and the parties, so no timely objection was entered. The error was first noted when, during briefing to the Court of Appeals for the Fifth Circuit, petitioner himself raised the mistake. The Court of Appeals refused to correct the error because, in its view, petitioner could not establish a reasonable probability that but for the error he would have received a different sentence. Under that court's decisions, if a defendant's ultimate sentence falls within what would have been the correct Guidelines range, the defendant, on appeal, must identify "additional evidence" to show that use of the incorrect Guidelines range did in fact affect his sentence. Absent that evidence, in the Court of Appeals' view, a defendant who is sentenced under an incorrect range but whose sentence is also within what would have been the correct range cannot demonstrate he has been prejudiced by the error.

Most Courts of Appeals have not adopted so rigid a standard. Instead, in recognition of the Guidelines' central role in sentencing, other Courts of Appeals have concluded that a district court's application of an incorrect Guidelines range can itself serve as evidence of an effect on substantial rights. See, *e.g., United States v. Sabillon-Umana*, 772 F.3d 1328, 1333 (C.A.10 2014) (application of an erroneous Guidelines range " 'runs the risk of affecting the ultimate sentence *regardless of* whether the court ultimately imposes a sentence within or outside'" that range); *United States v. Vargem,* 747 F.3d 724, 728–729 (C.A.9 2014); *United States v. Story,* 503 F.3d 436, 440 (C.A.6 2007). These courts recognize that, in most cases, when a district court adopts an incorrect Guidelines range, there is a reasonable probability that the defendant's sentence would be different absent the error. This Court granted certiorari to reconcile the difference in approaches.

I

A

The Sentencing Guidelines provide the framework for the tens of thousands of federal sentencing proceedings that occur each year. Congress directed the United States Sentencing Commission (USSC or Commission) to establish the Guidelines. 28 U.S.C. § 994(a)(1). The goal was to achieve "'*uniformity* in sentencing ... imposed by different federal courts for similar criminal conduct,' as well as '*proportionality* in sentencing through a system that imposes appropriately different sentences for criminal conduct of different severity.'" *Rita v. United States,* 551 U.S. 338, 349, 127 S.Ct. 2456, 168 L.Ed.2d 203 (2007). To those ends, the Commission engaged in "a deliberative and dynamic process" to create Guidelines that account for a variety of offenses and circumstances. USSC, Guidelines Manual § 2, ch. 1, pt. A, intro. comment., p. 14 (Nov. 2015) (USSG). As part of that process, the Commission considered the objectives of federal sentencing identified in the Sentencing Reform Act of 1984—the same objectives that federal judges must consider when sentencing defendants. Compare 28 U.S.C. § 991(b) with 18 U.S.C. § 3553(a). The result is a set of elaborate, detailed Guidelines that aim to embody federal sentencing objectives "both in principle and in practice." *Rita, supra,* at 350, 127 S.Ct. 2456.

Uniformity and proportionality in sentencing are achieved, in part, by the Guidelines' significant role in sentencing. See *Peugh v. United States,* 569 U.S. ___, ___, 133 S.Ct. 2072, 2082–2083, 186 L.Ed.2d 84 (2013). The Guidelines enter the sentencing process long before the district court imposes the sentence. The United States Probation Office first prepares a presentence report which includes a calculation of the advisory Guidelines range it considers to be applicable. Fed. Rules Crim. Proc. 32(d)(1)(A)–(C); see generally 18 U.S.C. § 3552(a). The applicable Guidelines range is based on the seriousness of a defendant's offense (indicated by his "offense level") and his criminal history (indicated by his "criminal history category"). Rules 32(d)(1)(B)–(C). The presentence report explains the basis for the Probation Office's calculations and sets out the sentencing options under the applicable statutes and Guidelines. Rule 32(d)(1). It also contains detailed information about the defendant's criminal history and personal characteristics, such as education and employment history. Rule 32(d)(2).

At the outset of the sentencing proceedings, the district court must determine the applicable Guidelines range. *Peugh, supra,* at ___, 133 S.Ct., at 2082–2083. To do so, the court considers the presentence report as well as any objections the parties might have. The court then entertains the parties' arguments regarding an appropriate sentence, including whether the sentence should be within the Guidelines range or not. Although the district court has discretion to depart from the Guidelines, the court "must consult those Guidelines and take them into account when sentencing." *United States v. Booker,* 543 U.S. 220, 264, 125 S.Ct. 738, 160 L.Ed.2d 621 (2005).

B

The Guidelines are complex, and so there will be instances when a district court's sentencing of a defendant within the framework of an incorrect Guidelines range goes unnoticed. In that circumstance, because the defendant failed to object to the miscalculation, appellate review of the error is governed by Federal Rule of Criminal Procedure 52(b).

Rule 52, in both its parts, is brief. It states:

> "(a) HARMLESS ERROR. Any error, defect, irregularity, or variance that does not affect substantial rights must be disregarded.

> "(b) PLAIN ERROR. A plain error that affects substantial rights may be considered even though it was not brought to the court's attention."

The starting point for interpreting and applying paragraph (b) of the Rule, upon which this case turns, is the Court's decision in *United States v. Olano,* 507 U.S. 725, 113 S.Ct. 1770, 123 L.Ed.2d 508 (1993). *Olano* instructs that a court of appeals has discretion to remedy a forfeited error provided certain conditions are met. First, there must be an error that has not been intentionally relinquished or abandoned. *Id.,* at 732–733, 113 S.Ct. 1770. Second, the error must be plain—that is to say, clear or obvious. *Id.,* at 734, 113 S.Ct. 1770. Third, the error must have affected the defendant's substantial rights, *ibid.,* which in the ordinary case means he or she must "show a reasonable probability that, but for the error," the outcome of the proceeding would have been different, *United States v. Dominguez Benitez,* 542 U.S. 74, 76, 82, 124 S.Ct. 2333, 159 L.Ed.2d 157 (2004). Once these three conditions have been met, the court of appeals should exercise its discretion to correct the forfeited error if the error " 'seriously affects the fairness, integrity or public reputation of judicial proceedings.' " *Olano, supra,* at 736, 113 S.Ct. 1770 (brackets omitted).

II

The petitioner here, Saul Molina-Martinez, pleaded guilty to being unlawfully present in the United States after having been deported following an aggravated felony conviction, in violation of 8 U.S.C. §§ 1326(a) and (b). As required, the Probation Office prepared a presentence report that related Molina-Martinez's offense of conviction, his criminal history, his personal characteristics, and the available sentencing options. The report also included the Probation Office's calculation of what it believed to be Molina-Martinez's Guidelines range. The Probation Office calculated Molina-Martinez's total offense level as 21. It concluded that Molina-Martinez's criminal history warranted 18 points, which included 11 points for five aggravated burglary convictions from 2011. Those 18 criminal history points resulted in a criminal history category of VI. That category, combined with an offense level of 21, resulted in a Guidelines range of 77 to 96 months.

At the sentencing hearing Molina-Martinez's counsel and the Government addressed the court. The Government acknowledged that the Probation Office had "recommended the low end on this case, 77 months." App. 30. But, the prosecution told the court, it "disagree[d] with that recommendation," and was "asking for a high end sentence of 96 months"— the top of the Guidelines range. *Ibid.* Like the Probation Office, counsel for Molina-Martinez urged the court to enter a sentence at the bottom of the Guidelines range. Counsel asserted that "77 months is a severe sentence" and that "after the 77 months, he'll be deported with probably a special release term." *Id.,* at 32. A sentence of 77 months, counsel continued, "is more than adequate to ensure he doesn't come back again." *Ibid.*

After hearing from the parties, the court stated it was adopting the presentence report's factual findings and Guidelines calculations. It then ordered Molina-Martinez's sentence:

> It's the judgment of the Court that the defendant, Saul Molina-Martinez, is hereby committed to the custody of the Bureau of Prisons to be imprisoned for a term of 77 months. Upon release from imprisonment, Defendant shall be placed on supervised release for a term of three years without supervision. *Id.,* at 33.

The court provided no further explanation for the sentence.

On appeal, Molina-Martinez's attorney submitted a brief pursuant to *Anders v. California,* 386 U.S. 738, 87 S.Ct. 1396, 18 L.Ed.2d 493 (1967). The attorney explained that, in his opinion, there were no nonfrivolous grounds for appeal. Molina-Martinez, however, submitted a *pro se* response to his attorney's *Anders* brief. In it he identified for the first time what he believed to be an error in the calculation of his criminal history points under the Guidelines. The Court of Appeals concluded that Molina-Martinez's argument did not appear frivolous. It directed his lawyer to file either a supplemental *Anders* brief or a brief on the merits of the Guidelines issue.

Molina-Martinez, through his attorney, filed a merits brief arguing that the Probation Office and the District Court erred in calculating his criminal history points, resulting in the application of a higher Guidelines range.

The error, Molina-Martinez explained, occurred because the Probation Office failed to apply § 4A1.2(a)(2) of the Guidelines. See USSG § 4A1.2(a)(2) (Nov. 2012). That provision addresses how multiple sentences imposed on the same day are to be counted for purposes of determining a defendant's criminal history. It instructs that, when prior sentences were imposed on the same day, they should be counted as a single sentence unless the offenses "were separated by an intervening arrest (*i.e.,* the defendant is arrested for the first offense prior to committing the second offense)." *Ibid.*

Molina-Martinez's presentence report included five aggravated burglary convictions for which he had been sentenced on the same day. The Probation Office counted each sentence separately, which resulted in the imposition of 11 criminal history points. Molina-Martinez contended this was error because none of the offenses were separated by an intervening arrest and because he had been sentenced for all five burglaries on the same day. Under a correct calculation, in his view, the burglaries should have resulted in 5 criminal history points instead of 11. That would have lowered his criminal history category from VI to V. The correct criminal history category, in turn, would have resulted in a Guidelines range of 70 to 87 months rather than 77 to 96 months. Had the correct range been used, Molina-Martinez's 77-month sentence would have been in the middle of the range, not at the bottom.

Molina-Martinez acknowledged that, because he did not object in the District Court, he was entitled to relief only if he could satisfy Rule 52(b)'s requirements. He nevertheless maintained relief was warranted because the error was plain, affected his substantial rights, and impugned the fairness, integrity, and public reputation of judicial proceedings.

The Court of Appeals disagreed. It held that Molina-Martinez had not established that the District Court's application of an incorrect Guidelines range affected his substantial rights. It reasoned that, when a correct sentencing range overlaps with an incorrect range, the reviewing court " 'do[es] not assume, in the absence of additional evidence, that the sentence [imposed] affects a defendant's substantial rights.'. . .

The Court of Appeals for the Fifth Circuit stands generally apart from other Courts of Appeals with respect to its consideration of unpreserved Guidelines errors. This Court now holds that its approach is incorrect.

Nothing in the text of Rule 52(b), its rationale, or the Court's precedents supports a requirement that a defendant seeking appellate review of an unpreserved Guidelines error make some further showing of prejudice beyond the fact that the erroneous, and higher, Guidelines range set the wrong framework for the sentencing proceedings. This is so even if the ultimate sentence falls within both the correct and incorrect range. When a defendant is sentenced under an incorrect Guidelines range—whether or not the defendant's ultimate sentence falls within the correct range—the error itself can, and most often will, be sufficient to show a reasonable probability of a different outcome absent the error.

A

Today's holding follows from the essential framework the Guidelines establish for sentencing proceedings. The Court has made clear that the Guidelines are to be the sentencing court's "starting point and . . . initial benchmark." *Gall v. United States,* 552 U.S. 38, 49, 128 S.Ct. 586, 169 L.Ed.2d 445 (2007). Federal courts understand that they " '*must* begin their analysis with the Guidelines and remain cognizant of them throughout the sentencing process.' " *Peugh,* 569 U.S., at ___, 133 S.Ct., at 2083. The Guidelines are "the framework for sentencing" and "anchor . . . the district court's discretion." *Id.,* at ___, ___, 133 S.Ct., at 2083, 2087 "Even if the sentencing judge sees a reason to vary from the Guidelines, 'if the judge uses the sentencing range as the beginning point to explain the decision to deviate from it, *then the Guidelines are in a real sense the basis for the sentence.*' " *Id.,* at ___, 133 S.Ct., at 2083.

The Guidelines' central role in sentencing means that an error related to the Guidelines can be particularly serious. A district court that "improperly calculat[es]" a defendant's Guidelines range, for example, has committed a "significant procedural error." *Gall, supra,* at 51, 128 S.Ct. 586. . . .

These sources confirm that the Guidelines are not only the starting point for most federal sentencing proceedings but also the lodestar. The Guidelines inform and instruct the district court's determination of an appropriate sentence. In the usual case, then, the systemic function of the selected Guidelines range will affect the sentence. This fact is essential to the application of Rule 52(b) to a Guidelines error. From the centrality of the Guidelines in the sentencing process it must follow that, when a defendant shows that the district court used an incorrect range, he should not be barred from relief on appeal simply because there is no other evidence that the sentencing outcome would have been different had the correct range been used. . . .

In the ordinary case the Guidelines accomplish their purpose. They serve as the starting point for the district court's decision and anchor the court's discretion in selecting an appropriate sentence. It follows, then, that in most cases the Guidelines range will affect the sentence. When that is so, a defendant sentenced under an incorrect Guidelines range should be able to rely on that fact to show a reasonable probability that the district court would have imposed a different sentence under the correct range. That probability is all that is needed to establish an effect on substantial rights for purposes of obtaining relief under Rule 52(b).

The contrary judgment of the Court of Appeals for the Fifth Circuit is reversed, and the case is remanded for further proceedings consistent with this opinion.

It is so ordered.

EXERCISE

It is worth reviewing just how many people miscalculated the sentencing guidelines in the *Molino-Martinez* case. The prosecutor didn't get it right. Neither did the defense attorney. The probation officer failed in calculating the sentencing range in the presentence investigation report. Then the judge got it wrong. Eventually it was the *defendant* who caught the error. What is to be learned from this about the use of complex sentencing guidelines? What structural changes would help avoid this problem?

Another question left open under *Booker* was whether or not sentencing judges could go outside the guidelines (or "vary" from them) based solely on the belief that the applicable guidelines were too harsh. Before the guidelines (and the underlying statute) were revised in 2010, this question frequently came up in the context of the sentencing scheme for crack cocaine, where one gram of crack was sentenced in the same manner as 100 grams of powder cocaine. Some judges, objecting to the resulting high sentences, categorically rejected that ratio and substituted their own.

SPEARS V. UNITED STATES
555 U.S. 261 (2009)

PER CURIAM.

Steven Spears was found guilty of conspiracy to distribute at least 50 grams of cocaine base and at least 500 grams of powder cocaine, in violation of 21 U.S.C. §§ 841(a)(1), (b)(1)(A), (b)(1)(B), 846. At sentencing, the District Court determined that the drug quantities attributable to Spears yielded an offense level of 38, that his criminal history justified placing him in the Guidelines' criminal history category IV, and that the resulting advisory Guidelines sentencing range was 324 to 405 months' imprisonment. The District Court was of the view that the Guidelines' 100:1 ratio between powder cocaine and crack cocaine quantities, see United States Sentencing Commission, Guidelines Manual § 2D1.1(c) (Nov.2006) (USSG),* yielded an excessive sentence in light of the sentencing factors outlined in 18 U.S.C. § 3553(a). Relying in part on decisions from other District Courts, see *United States v. Perry,* 389 F.Supp.2d 278, 307–308 (RI 2005); *United States v. Smith,* 359 F.Supp.2d 771, 781–782 (E.D.Wis.2005), which in turn relied on a report from the Sentencing Commission criticizing the 100:1 ratio, see United States Sentencing Commission, Report to Congress: Cocaine and Federal Sentencing Policy 106–107, App. A, pp. 3–6 (May

2002) (hereinafter Report to Congress), the District Court recalculated Spears' offense level based on a 20:1 crack-to-powder ratio. That yielded an offense level of 34 and a sentencing range of 210 to 262 months' imprisonment. The District Court sentenced Spears to 240 months in prison, the statutory mandatory minimum. See *United States v. Spears,* 469 F.3d 1166, 1173–1174 (C.A.8 2006) (en banc) *(Spears I).*

On cross-appeal, the Government argued that "the district court erred by categorically rejecting the 100:1 quantity ratio and substituting its own ratio in calculating Spears's sentence." *Id.,* at 1174. The Eighth Circuit reversed Spears' sentence and remanded for resentencing, holding that "neither *Booker* nor § 3553(a) authorizes district courts to reject the 100:1 quantity ratio and use a different ratio in sentencing defendants for crack cocaine offenses." *Id.,* at 1176. This Court vacated the judgment of the Eighth Circuit, and remanded for further consideration in light of *Kimbrough v. United States,* 552 U.S. 85, 128 S.Ct. 558, 169 L.Ed.2d 481 (2007). *Spears v. United States,* 552 U.S. 1090, 128 S.Ct. 858, 169 L.Ed.2d 709 (2008).

On remand, the Eighth Circuit again reversed Spears' sentence and remanded for resentencing. 533 F.3d 715, 716 (2008) (en banc) *(Spears II).* It concluded, again, that the District Court "may not categorically reject the ratio set forth by the Guidelines," *id.,* at 717, and " 'impermissibly varied by *replacing* the 100:1 quantity ratio inherent in the advisory Guidelines range with a 20:1 quantity ratio,' " *ibid.*(quoting *Spears I, supra,* at 1178). Spears again petitioned for a writ of certiorari. Because the Eighth Circuit's decision on remand conflicts with our decision in *Kimbrough,* we grant the petition for certiorari and reverse. 1In *Kimbrough,* we held that "under *Booker,* the cocaine Guidelines, like all other Guidelines, are advisory only," 552 U.S., at 91, 128 S.Ct., at 560, and that "it would not be an abuse of discretion for a district court to conclude when sentencing a particular defendant that the crack/powder disparity yields a sentence 'greater than necessary' to achieve § 3553(a)'s purpose, *even in a mine-run case,*" *id.,* at 110, 128 S.Ct., at 563 (emphasis added). The correct interpretation of that holding is the one offered by the dissent in *Spears II:*

> "The Court thus established that even when a particular defendant in a crack cocaine case presents no special mitigating circumstances—no outstanding service to country or community, no unusually disadvantaged childhood, no overstated criminal history score, no post-offense rehabilitation—a sentencing court may nonetheless vary downward from the advisory guideline range. The court may do so based solely on its view that the 100-to-1 ratio embodied in the sentencing guidelines for the treatment of crack cocaine versus powder cocaine creates 'an unwarranted disparity within the meaning of § 3553(a),' and is 'at odds with

§ 3553(a).' The only fact necessary to justify such a variance is the sentencing court's disagreement with the guidelines—its policy view that the 100-to-1 ratio creates an unwarranted disparity." 533 F.3d, at 719 (opinion of Colloton, J.) (citations omitted).

Kimbrough considered and rejected the position taken by the Eighth Circuit below. It noted that "a district court's decision to vary from the advisory Guidelines may attract greatest respect when the sentencing judge finds a particular case 'outside the "heartland" to which the Commission intends individual Guidelines to apply.'" 552 U.S., at 109, 128 S.Ct., at 563 (quoting *Rita v. United States,* 551 U.S. 338, 351, 127 S.Ct. 2456, 168 L.Ed.2d 203 (2007)). The implication was that an "inside the heartland" departure (which is necessarily based on a policy disagreement with the Guidelines and necessarily disagrees on a "categorical basis") may be entitled to less respect. Our opinion said, however, that the "crack cocaine Guidelines . . . present no occasion for elaborative discussion of this matter because those Guidelines do not exemplify the Commission's exercise of its characteristic institutional role." 552 U.S., at 109, 128 S.Ct., at 563. *Kimbrough* thus holds that with respect to the crack cocaine Guidelines, a categorical disagreement with and variance from the Guidelines is not suspect.

That was indeed the point of *Kimbrough:* a recognition of district courts' authority to vary from the crack cocaine Guidelines based on *policy* disagreement with them, and not simply based on an individualized determination that they yield an excessive sentence in a particular case. The latter proposition was already established pre-*Kimbrough,* see *United States v. Booker,* 543 U.S. 220, 245–246, 125 S.Ct. 738, 160 L.Ed.2d 621 (2005), and the Government conceded as much in *Kimbrough.* 552 U.S., at 102, 128 S.Ct. at 571 n. 13. That the Government did not prevail in *Kimbrough* proves that its concession—"that a district court may vary from the 100-to-1 ratio if it does so 'based on the individualized circumstance[s]' of a particular case," *ibid.*—understated the extent of district courts' sentencing discretion.

In drawing a distinction between "individualized, case-specific" consideration of the Guidelines' ratio and categorical rejection and replacement of that ratio, the Eighth Circuit relied in part, *Spears II, supra,* at 717, on the following passage from *Kimbrough:*

> "The [district] court did not purport to establish a ratio of its own. Rather, it appropriately framed its final determination in line with § 3553(a)'s overarching instruction to 'impose a sentence sufficient, but not greater than necessary' to accomplish the sentencing goals advanced in § 3553(a)(2)." 552 U.S., at 111, 128 S.Ct., at 575.

This says that it was "appropriate" for the District Court in *Kimbrough* not to specify what ratio it was using, but merely to proceed with § 3553(a) analysis. The Eighth Circuit read that to mean that district courts, in the course of their individualized determinations, *may not categorically disagree with the Guidelines ratio, and (consequently) may not substitute their own ratio for that of the Guidelines.* If it meant that, our vacating of the Eighth Circuit's judgment in *Spears I* would have been inexplicable, because that supposedly impermissible disagreement and substitution was precisely the reason for *Spears I*'s reversal of the District Court. See *Spears I,* 469 F.3d, at 1175–1176. As a logical matter, of course, rejection of the 100:1 ratio, explicitly approved by *Kimbrough,* necessarily implies adoption of some other ratio to govern the mine-run case. A sentencing judge who is given the power to reject the disparity created by the crack-to-powder ratio must also possess the power to apply a different ratio which, in his judgment, corrects the disparity. Put simply, the ability to reduce a mine-run defendant's sentence necessarily permits adoption of a replacement ratio.

To the extent the above quoted language has obscured *Kimbrough*'s holding, we now clarify that district courts are entitled to reject and vary categorically from the crack cocaine Guidelines based on a policy disagreement with those Guidelines. Here, the District Court's choice of replacement ratio was based upon two well-reasoned decisions by other courts, which themselves reflected the Sentencing Commission's expert judgment that a 20:1 ratio would be appropriate in a mine-run case. See *Perry,* 389 F.Supp.2d, at 307–308; *Smith,* 359 F.Supp.2d, at 781–782; Report to Congress 106–107, App. A, pp. 3–6.

The alternative approach—adopted by the Eighth Circuit—would likely yield one of two results. Either district courts would treat the Guidelines' policy embodied in the crack-to-powder ratio as mandatory, believing that they are not entitled to vary based on "categorical" policy disagreements with the Guidelines, or they would continue to vary, masking their categorical policy disagreements as "individualized determinations." The latter is institutionalized subterfuge. The former contradicts our holding in *Kimbrough.* Neither is an acceptable sentencing practice.

EXERCISE

In *Spears,* the Court premised its finding on the fact that in creating the 100-to-1 ratio between powder and crack cocaine, the Sentencing Commission did "not exemplify the Commission's exercise of its characteristic institutional role." This was because the Commission followed Congress's lead rather than its own empirical study. Importantly, the *Kimbrough* and *Spears* decisions allowed sentencing judges to categorically reject the guidelines, but did not require them to do so. Within a structure that had handed much of the discretion in sentencing to prosecutors, this apportioned some back to judges.

Imagine that you are a federal District Court Judge. Congress has passed a statute that creates a new law making physicians criminally responsible if patients get addicted to drugs they prescribe. Though it does not establish mandatory minimum sentences, Congress directs the United States Sentencing Commission to create guidelines that will punish these physicians consistent with the sentences faced by street dealers who sell an analogous amount of the same or a similar drug. Specifically, the law says that one gram of prescribed OxyContin that leads to addiction will result in the same sentence as that called for when a defendant sells one gram of heroin.

Before you is a typical case under the new law: Dr. Anders Luke prescribed OxyContin to a patient suffering from debilitating back pain. The patient received over 400 grams of the drug. The resulting sentence, if you follow the guidelines, would be over five years. Would you categorically reject the ratio created by the guidelines at the direction of Congress?

C. JUDICIAL DISCRETION AND THE GOALS OF SENTENCING

Federal Judges are constrained by statutes and advised by guidelines when they sentence defendants. Given those inputs, the Supreme Court was clear about what should guide district judges within their discretion when they sentence and appellate courts in their review in *United States v. Booker*, 543 U.S. 220, 261 (2005): "Section 3553(a) remains in effect, and sets forth numerous factors that guide sentencing. Those factors in turn will guide appellate courts, as they have in the past, in determining whether a sentence is unreasonable." Booker made the entirety of § 3553(a) central to sentencing in the federal system.

18 U.S.C. § 3553(a) is comprehensive in its scope:

(a) **Factors to be considered in imposing a sentence.**—The court shall impose a sentence sufficient, but not greater than necessary, to comply with the purposes set forth in paragraph (2) of this subsection. The court, in determining the particular sentence to be imposed, shall consider—

> (1) the nature and circumstances of the offense and the history and characteristics of the defendant;
>
> (2) the need for the sentence imposed—
>
> > (A) to reflect the seriousness of the offense, to promote respect for the law, and to provide just punishment for the offense;
> >
> > (B) to afford adequate deterrence to criminal conduct;
> >
> > (C) to protect the public from further crimes of the defendant; and

(D) to provide the defendant with needed educational or vocational training, medical care, or other correctional treatment in the most effective manner;

(3) the kinds of sentences available;

(4) the kinds of sentence and the sentencing range established for—

(A) the applicable category of offense committed by the applicable category of defendant as set forth in the guidelines—

(i) issued by the Sentencing Commission pursuant to section 994(a)(1) of title 28, United States Code, subject to any amendments made to such guidelines by act of Congress (regardless of whether such amendments have yet to be incorporated by the Sentencing Commission into amendments issued under section 994(p) of title 28); and

(ii) that, except as provided in section 3742(g), are in effect on the date the defendant is sentenced; or

(B) in the case of a violation of probation or supervised release, the applicable guidelines or policy statements issued by the Sentencing Commission pursuant to section 994(a)(3) of title 28, United States Code, taking into account any amendments made to such guidelines or policy statements by act of Congress (regardless of whether such amendments have yet to be incorporated by the Sentencing Commission into amendments issued under section 994(p) of title 28);

(5) any pertinent policy statement—

(A) issued by the Sentencing Commission pursuant to section 994(a)(2) of title 28, United States Code, subject to any amendments made to such policy statement by act of Congress (regardless of whether such amendments have yet to be incorporated by the Sentencing Commission into amendments issued under section 994(p) of title 28); and

(B) that, except as provided in section 3742(g), is in effect on the date the defendant is sentenced.

(6) the need to avoid unwarranted sentence disparities among defendants with similar records who have been found guilty of similar conduct; and

(7) the need to provide restitution to any victims of the offense.

It is section (a)(2) above that explicitly sets out the traditional goals of sentencing—retribution, deterrence, incapacitation, and rehabilitation—as the goals of federal sentencing, along with the other listed goals (such as (a)(6)'s instruction to "avoid unwarranted sentencing disparities. . ."). This is significant because the federal sentencing guidelines do not mention the traditional goals at all, and when the guidelines were mandatory judges were actively restricted from seeking to pursue some of those goals at times by the guidelines themselves. For example, a judge who felt rehabilitation was possible in a particularly case through non-custodial drug treatment was barred from doing so if the guidelines required a long custodial sentence.

The courts have often struggled with the balance between considering the sentencing guidelines as an advisory baseline and the other factors of § 3553(a) that often can pull a judge away from the guidelines' directives. Also difficult was the application of the "reasonableness" criteria by appellate courts.

GALL v. UNITED STATES
552 U.S. 38 (2007)

JUSTICE STEVENS delivered the opinion of the Court.

In two cases argued on the same day last Term we considered the standard that courts of appeals should apply when reviewing the reasonableness of sentences imposed by district judges. The first, *Rita v. United States,* 551 U.S. 338, 127 S.Ct. 2456, 168 L.Ed.2d 203 (2007), involved a sentence *within* the range recommended by the Federal Sentencing Guidelines; we held that when a district judge's discretionary decision in a particular case accords with the sentence the United States Sentencing Commission deems appropriate "in the mine run of cases," the court of appeals may presume that the sentence is reasonable. *Id.,* at 351, 127 S.Ct., at 2465.. . . We now hold that, while the extent of the difference between a particular sentence and the recommended Guidelines range is surely relevant, courts of appeals must review all sentences—whether inside, just outside, or significantly outside the Guidelines range—under a deferential abuse-of-discretion standard. We also hold that the sentence imposed by the experienced District Judge in this case was reasonable.

I

In February or March 2000, petitioner Brian Gall, a second-year college student at the University of Iowa, was invited by Luke Rinderknecht to join an ongoing enterprise distributing a controlled substance popularly known as "ecstasy." Gall—who was then a user of ecstasy, cocaine, and marijuana—accepted the invitation. During the ensuing seven months,

Gall delivered ecstasy pills, which he received from Rinderknecht, to other conspirators, who then sold them to consumers. He netted over $30,000.

A month or two after joining the conspiracy, Gall stopped using ecstasy. A few months after that, in September 2000, he advised Rinderknecht and other co-conspirators that he was withdrawing from the conspiracy. He has not sold illegal drugs of any kind since. He has, in the words of the District Court, "self-rehabilitated." App. 75. He graduated from the University of Iowa in 2002, and moved first to Arizona, where he obtained a job in the construction industry, and later to Colorado, where he earned $18 per hour as a master carpenter. He has not used any illegal drugs since graduating from college.

After Gall moved to Arizona, he was approached by federal law enforcement agents who questioned him about his involvement in the ecstasy distribution conspiracy. Gall admitted his limited participation in the distribution of ecstasy, and the agents took no further action at that time. On April 28, 2004—approximately 1½ years after this initial interview, and 3½ years after Gall withdrew from the conspiracy—an indictment was returned in the Southern District of Iowa charging him and seven other defendants with participating in a conspiracy to distribute ecstasy, cocaine, and marijuana, that began in or about May 1996 and continued through October 30, 2002. The Government has never questioned the truthfulness of any of Gall's earlier statements or contended that he played any role in, or had any knowledge of, other aspects of the conspiracy described in the indictment. When he received notice of the indictment, Gall moved back to Iowa and surrendered to the authorities. While free on his own recognizance, Gall started his own business in the construction industry, primarily engaged in subcontracting for the installation of windows and doors. In his first year, his profits were over $2,000 per month.

Gall entered into a plea agreement with the Government, stipulating that he was "responsible for, but did not necessarily distribute himself, at least 2,500 grams of [ecstasy], or the equivalent of at least 87.5 kilograms of marijuana." *Id.*, at 25. In the agreement, the Government acknowledged that "on or about September of 2000," Gall had communicated his intent to stop distributing ecstasy to Rinderknecht and other members of the conspiracy. *Ibid.* The agreement further provided that recent changes in the Guidelines that enhanced the recommended punishment for distributing ecstasy were not applicable to Gall because he had withdrawn from the conspiracy prior to the effective date of those changes. In her presentence report, the probation officer concluded that Gall had no significant criminal history; that he was not an organizer, leader, or manager; and that his offense did not involve the use of any weapons. The report stated that Gall had truthfully provided the Government with all of the evidence he had concerning the alleged offenses, but that his evidence was not useful because he provided no new information to the agents. The report also described Gall's substantial use of drugs prior to his offense and the absence of any such use in recent years.

The report recommended a sentencing range of 30 to 37 months of imprisonment. The record of the sentencing hearing held on May 27, 2005, includes a "small flood" of letters from Gall's parents and other relatives, his fiancée, neighbors, and representatives of firms doing business with him, uniformly praising his character and work ethic. The transcript includes the testimony of several witnesses and the District Judge's colloquy with the assistant United States attorney (AUSA) and with Gall. The AUSA did not contest any of the evidence concerning Gall's law-abiding life during the preceding five years, but urged that "the guidelines are appropriate and should be followed," and requested that the court impose a prison sentence within the Guidelines range. *Id.,* at 93. He mentioned that two of Gall's co-conspirators had been sentenced to 30 and 35 months, respectively, but upon further questioning by the District Court, he acknowledged that neither of them had voluntarily withdrawn from the conspiracy.

The District Judge sentenced Gall to probation for a term of 36 months. In addition to making a lengthy statement on the record, the judge filed a detailed sentencing memorandum explaining his decision, and provided the following statement of reasons in his written judgment:

> The Court determined that, considering all the factors under 18 U.S.C. 3553(a), the Defendant's explicit withdrawal from the conspiracy almost four years before the filing of the Indictment, the Defendant's post-offense conduct, especially obtaining a college degree and the start of his own successful business, the support of family and friends, lack of criminal history, and his age at the time of the offense conduct, all warrant the sentence imposed, which was sufficient, but not greater than necessary to serve the purposes of sentencing. *Id.,* at 117.

At the end of both the sentencing hearing and the sentencing memorandum, the District Judge reminded Gall that probation, rather than "an act of leniency," is a "substantial restriction of freedom." *Id.,* at 99, 125. In the memorandum, he emphasized:

> [Gall] will have to comply with strict reporting conditions along with a three-year regime of alcohol and drug testing. He will not be able to change or make decisions about significant circumstances in his life, such as where to live or work, which are prized liberty interests, without first seeking authorization from his Probation Officer or, perhaps, even the Court. Of course, the Defendant always faces the harsh consequences that await if he violates the conditions of his probationary term. *Id.,* at 125.

Finally, the District Judge explained why he had concluded that the sentence of probation reflected the seriousness of Gall's offense and that no term of imprisonment was necessary:

> Any term of imprisonment in this case would be counter effective by depriving society of the contributions of the Defendant who, the Court has found, understands the consequences of his criminal conduct and is doing everything in his power to forge a new life. The Defendant's post-offense conduct indicates neither that he will return to criminal behavior nor that the Defendant is a danger to society. In fact, the Defendant's post-offense conduct was not motivated by a desire to please the Court or any other governmental agency, but was the pre-Indictment product of the Defendant's own desire to lead a better life. *Id.*, at 125–126.

II

The Court of Appeals reversed and remanded for resentencing. Relying on its earlier opinion in *United States v. Claiborne,* 439 F.3d 479 (C.A.8 2006), it held that a sentence outside of the Guidelines range must be supported by a justification that " ' "is proportional to the extent of the difference between the advisory range and the sentence imposed." ' " 446 F.3d 884, 889 (C.A.8 2006) (quoting *Claiborne,* 439 F.3d, at 481, in turn quoting *United States v. Johnson,* 427 F.3d 423, 426–427 (C.A.7 2005)). Characterizing the difference between a sentence of probation and the bottom of Gall's advisory Guidelines range of 30 months as "extraordinary" because it amounted to "a 100% downward variance," 446 F.3d, at 889, the Court of Appeals held that such a variance must be—and here was not— supported by extraordinary circumstances.

In reviewing the reasonableness of a sentence outside the Guidelines range, appellate courts may therefore take the degree of variance into account and consider the extent of a deviation from the Guidelines. We reject, however, an appellate rule that requires "extraordinary" circumstances to justify a sentence outside the Guidelines range. We also reject the use of a rigid mathematical formula that uses the percentage of a departure as the standard for determining the strength of the justifications required for a specific sentence. . . .

As we explained in *Rita,* a district court should begin all sentencing proceedings by correctly calculating the applicable Guidelines range. See 551 U.S., at 347–348, 127 S.Ct. 2456. As a matter of administration and to secure nationwide consistency, the Guidelines should be the starting point and the initial benchmark. The Guidelines are not the only consideration, however. Accordingly, after giving both parties an opportunity to argue for whatever sentence they deem appropriate, the district judge should then consider all of the § 3553(a) factors to determine whether they support the sentence requested by a party. In so doing, he may not presume that the Guidelines range is reasonable. See *id.,* at 351, 127 S.Ct. 2456. He must make an individualized assessment based on the facts presented. If he decides that an outside-Guidelines sentence is warranted, he must consider the extent of the deviation and ensure that the justification is sufficiently compelling to support the degree of the variance. We find it uncontroversial that a major departure should be supported by a more significant justification than a minor one.

After settling on the appropriate sentence, he must adequately explain the chosen sentence to allow for meaningful appellate review and to promote the perception of fair sentencing. . . .

As an initial matter, we note that the District Judge committed no significant procedural error. He correctly calculated the applicable Guidelines range, allowed both parties to present arguments as to what they believed the appropriate sentence should be, considered all of the § 3553(a) factors, and thoroughly documented his reasoning. The Court of Appeals found that the District Judge erred in failing to give proper weight to the seriousness of the offense, as required by § 3553(a)(2)(A), and failing to consider whether a sentence of probation would create unwarranted disparities, as required by § 3553(a)(6). We disagree. Section 3553(a)(2)(A) requires judges to consider "the need for the sentence imposed . . . to reflect the seriousness of the offense, to promote respect for the law, and to provide just punishment for the offense." The Court of Appeals concluded that "the district court did not properly weigh the seriousness of Gall's offense" because it "ignored the serious health risks ecstasy poses." 446 F.3d, at 890. Contrary to the Court of Appeals' conclusion, the District Judge plainly did consider the seriousness of the offense. See, *e.g.,* App. 99 ("The Court, however, is bound to impose a sentence that reflects the seriousness of joining a conspiracy to distribute MDMA or Ecstasy"); *id.,* at 122. It is true that the District Judge did not make specific reference to the (unquestionably significant) health risks posed by ecstasy, but the prosecutor did not raise ecstasy's effects at the sentencing hearing. Had the prosecutor raised the issue, specific discussion of the point might have been in order, but it was not incumbent on the District Judge to raise every conceivably relevant issue on his own initiative.

The Government's legitimate concern that a lenient sentence for a serious offense threatens to promote disrespect for the law is at least to some extent offset by the fact that seven of the eight defendants in this case have been sentenced to significant prison terms. Moreover, the unique facts of Gall's situation provide support for the District Judge's conclusion that, in Gall's case, "a sentence of imprisonment may work to promote not respect, but derision, of the law if the law is viewed as merely a means to dispense harsh punishment without taking into account the real conduct and circumstances involved in sentencing." *Id.,* at 126. Section 3553(a)(6) requires judges to consider "the need to avoid unwarranted sentence disparities among defendants with similar records who have been found guilty of similar conduct." The Court of Appeals stated that "the record does not show that the district court considered whether a sentence of probation would result in unwarranted disparities." 446 F.3d, at 890. As with the seriousness of the offense conduct, avoidance of unwarranted disparities was clearly considered by the Sentencing Commission when setting the Guidelines ranges. Since the District Judge correctly calculated and carefully reviewed the Guidelines range, he necessarily gave significant weight and consideration to the need to avoid unwarranted disparities.

Moreover, as we understand the colloquy between the District Judge and the AUSA, it seems that the judge gave specific attention to the issue of disparity when he inquired about the sentences already imposed by a different judge on two of Gall's codefendants. The AUSA advised the District Judge that defendant Harbison had received a 30-month sentence and that Gooding had received 35 months. The following colloquy then occurred:

> THE COURT: ... You probably know more about this than anybody. How long did those two stay in the conspiracy, and did they voluntarily withdraw?
>
> "MR. GRIESS: They did not.
>
> "THE COURT: They did not?
>
> "MR. GRIESS: They did not voluntarily withdraw. And they were in the conspiracy, I think, for a shorter period of time, but at the very end.
>
> "THE COURT: Okay. Thank you.
>
> "MR. GRIESS: A significant difference there, Your Honor, is that they were in the conspiracy after the guidelines changed and, therefore, were sentenced at a much higher level because of that. App. 88.

A little later Mr. Griess stated: "The last thing I want to talk about goes to sentencing disparity .... Obviously, the Court is cognizant of that and wants to avoid any unwarranted sentencing disparities." *Id.,* at 89. He then discussed at some length the sentence of 36 months imposed on another codefendant, Jarod Yoder, whose participation in the conspiracy was roughly comparable to Gall's. Griess voluntarily acknowledged three differences between Yoder and Gall: Yoder was in the conspiracy at its end and therefore was sentenced under the more severe Guidelines, he had a more serious criminal history, and he did not withdraw from the conspiracy.

From these facts, it is perfectly clear that the District Judge considered the need to avoid unwarranted disparities, but also considered the need to avoid unwarranted *similarities* among other co-conspirators who were not similarly situated. The District Judge regarded Gall's voluntary withdrawal as a reasonable basis for giving him a less severe sentence than the three codefendants discussed with the AUSA, who neither withdrew from the conspiracy nor rehabilitated themselves as Gall had done. We also note that neither the Court of Appeals nor the Government has called our attention to a comparable defendant who received a more severe sentence.

Since the District Court committed no procedural error, the only question for the Court of Appeals was whether the sentence was reasonable—*i.e.,* whether the District Judge abused his discretion in determining that the § 3553(a) factors supported a sentence of probation and justified a substantial deviation from the Guidelines range. As we shall now explain, the sentence was reasonable. The Court of Appeals' decision to the contrary was incorrect and failed to demonstrate the requisite deference to the District Judge's decision. . . .

The District Court quite reasonably attached great weight to Gall's self-motivated rehabilitation, which was undertaken not at the direction of, or under supervision by, any court, but on his own initiative. This also lends strong support to the conclusion that imprisonment was not necessary to deter Gall from engaging in future criminal conduct or to protect the public from his future criminal acts. See 18 U.S.C. §§ 3553(a)(2)(B), (C).

The Court of Appeals clearly disagreed with the District Judge's conclusion that consideration of the § 3553(a) factors justified a sentence of probation; it believed that the circumstances presented here were insufficient to sustain such a marked deviation from the Guidelines range. But it is not for the Court of Appeals to decide *de novo* whether the justification for a variance is sufficient or the sentence reasonable. On abuse-of-discretion review, the Court of Appeals should have given due deference to the District Court's reasoned and reasonable decision that the § 3553(a) factors, on the whole, justified the sentence. Accordingly, the judgment of the Court of Appeals is reversed.

It is so ordered.

―――――――――

EXERCISE

By backing down the efforts of the Court of Appeals to restrict the discretion of sentencing judges, the Supreme Court's decision in *Gall* reinforced the idea that those sentencing judges would have broad discretion so long as they grounded their decisions in the sentencing factors set out in 18 U.S.C. § 3553(a). If you were the sentencing judge in the *Gall* case, what sentence would you have chosen, and how would you justify that choice?

―――――――――

Judges discuss the statutorily-mandated goal of deterrence in two ways. One is "general deterrence," which seeks to use the sentence to deter others from committing similar crimes. The second is "specific deterrence," which is an effort to deter the specific defendant being sentenced from committing further crimes.

UNITED STATES V. SANCHEZ-LOPEZ

858 F.3d 1064 (7th Cir. 2017)

PER CURIAM.

Jesus Sanchez-Lopez pleaded guilty to unauthorized presence in the United States after removal, *see* 8 U.S.C. § 1326(a), and was sentenced to twenty-four months' imprisonment—a term ninety days above the properly calculated guidelines range. Mr. Sanchez-Lopez contends that the district court erred when, in an effort to deter future illegal reentry by Mr. Sanchez-Lopez, it deviated from the Guidelines and sentenced him to a lengthier term than the sentence he had served the last time he was convicted of the same offense. Because the district court thoroughly explained its reasons and acted well within its discretion, we affirm the sentence.

I

BACKGROUND

Mr. Sanchez-Lopez came to the attention of immigration authorities after local police arrested him for retail theft at a Home Depot in June 2016. Mr. Sanchez-Lopez was indicted for illegally reentering the United States after removal, *see* 8 U.S.C. § 1326(a), and pleaded guilty shortly thereafter.

A probation officer compiled a report detailing Mr. Sanchez-Lopez's long history of criminal activity in and removal from the United States. He first entered the country without authorization and settled in Wisconsin in 1994. The majority of his convictions over the years were driving-related: four DUIs, one hit-and-run accident, and three charges of driving with a suspended license. His criminal history, however, also includes convictions for battery, sexually assaulting an eleven-year-old child, and criminal escape. Mr. Sanchez-Lopez first was removed in January 2010, but Border Patrol agents arrested him in Arizona only seven months later. Mr. Sanchez-Lopez was convicted of attempted reentry after removal, sentenced to eighteen months' imprisonment, and removed for the second time in November 2011.

Mr. Sanchez-Lopez told the probation officer that he had reentered the United States, despite the risk of criminal prosecution and removal, because his common-law wife suffered serious work-related injuries and needed care. Mr. Sanchez-Lopez said that he returned to Wisconsin sometime in 2013 but could not remember the date. His wife told the district court that he had returned in January 2014. If Mr. Sanchez-Lopez returned to the United States *after* October 2013, his convictions for battery and sexual assault of a child fall out-side the ten-year period factored into his criminal-history score. Taking a cautious approach, the probation officer excluded those convictions when calculating his criminal history category, but noted that the court might wish to consider those convictions nonetheless.

With respect to Mr. Sanchez-Lopez's offense, the probation officer employed a base offense level of eight, *see* U.S.S.G. § 2L1.2(a), and Mr. Sanchez-Lopez received a four-level up-ward adjustment because he had been removed after a conviction for a felony, *see id.* § 2L1.2(b)(1)(D). After a two-level decrease for acceptance of responsibility, *id.* § 3E1.1(a), Mr. Sanchez-Lopez's total offense level was ten. When combined with Mr. Sanchez-Lopez's criminal history category of IV, this yielded a guidelines range of fifteen to twenty-one months' imprisonment. If the judge had believed that Mr. Sanchez-Lopez entered the country during or before October 2013—and his convictions for battery and sexual assault thus factored in to his criminal-history score—his guidelines range would have been twenty-one to twenty-seven months.

The district judge began the sentencing hearing by ex-pressing misgivings about the appropriateness of a sentence within the guidelines range:

> The difficulty that I'm having with that range is that the defendant has reentered after receiving a sentence of 18 months from the District Court in Arizona. I understand, to the defendant's credit, that he reentered and has not offended, as far as we know, again. Hopefully that includes not drinking and not driving while drunk as well as no further battery offenses.

> But I'm offsetting that against the fact that the defendant benefits by a favorable calculation . . . in terms of his criminal history as well as, as I say, the fact that it would seem some graduated penalty is appropriate for reentry, notwithstanding the defendant's representation that he did so solely to assist his girlfriend . . . .

The Government then requested that the court sentence Mr. Sanchez-Lopez to twenty-one months' imprisonment, the top of the guidelines range, arguing that a graduated penalty is appropriate given his prior conviction for the same offense.

Mr. Sanchez-Lopez's counsel made no specific sentencing recommendation to the court. Counsel pointed out, however, that Mr. Sanchez-Lopez had not been *convicted* of any new crimes since returning to the country (the retail theft charges having been dropped after he was picked up by immigration authorities) and urged the court to consider that his wife's illness prompted his return.

After a short allocution by Mr. Sanchez-Lopez, the court explained the rationale behind its decision to impose a twenty-four-month sentence. The court said it wanted to give Mr. Sanchez-Lopez some credit for having cared for his wife after returning to the United States and for not having "engaged in at least serious criminal conduct." But, the court explained, Mr. Sanchez-Lopez's inability to control himself while drinking made him a danger to society, and, according to the court, his "noble reason for returning" was offset by the seriousness of having reentered the country after twice being removed. The court also considered Mr. Sanchez-Lopez's "very lengthy criminal record," including his convictions for battery and sexual assault of a child that, because of their age, were excluded from the guidelines calculation. It then elaborated on its reason for deviating ninety days above the guidelines imprisonment range:

> As previously noted, the present offense is the defendant's second criminal conviction for illegal reentry after deportation. And having been sentenced to 18 months the first time, the Court is concerned about sending a message if not to those who reenter this country for lots of economic and other hardship reasons, at least sending a message to this defendant that he simply has to make a life in Mexico, notwithstanding whatever pulls there may be for him to attempt to return again to this country.

> Taking into consideration the nature of the offense as well as the defendant's personal history and characteristics, I am persuaded that a custodial sentence slightly above the guideline range is reasonable and no greater than necessary to hold the defendant accountable, protect the community, provide the defendant the opportunity for rehabilitative programs and achieve parity with the sentences of similarly-situated offenders.

II

DISCUSSION

Mr. Sanchez-Lopez challenges the district court's ninety-day variance above his guidelines imprisonment range. Rather than attacking the sentence as substantively unreasonable, he argues that the court erred by taking into account his previous § 1326(a) sentence because "there is no recognized sentencing factor that a person must serve a higher sentence for a later offense ... for no other reason than that it took place afterwards." Mr. Sanchez-Lopez contends that the court failed to make an individualized assessment of the circumstances of his crime, but instead "treated the notion of incremental punishment as a general policy matter with scant regard for whether it was appropriate in this case."

We cannot accept this contention. Right from the start the district judge told Mr. Sanchez-Lopez what troubled him about the guidelines range, then handled the hearing succinctly, crisply, and carefully. The court thoughtfully considered Mr. Sanchez-Lopez's personal characteristics, including the nature of his previous convictions, the fact that he had not committed "serious offenses" since reentering, his reason for returning to Wisconsin, and the danger posed to society by his many arrests for drunk driving. But the court honed in on one particular concern in fashioning an appropriate sentence—the need to deter Mr. Sanchez-Lopez from continuing to enter the country illegally—and that decision was entirely proper given that 18 U.S.C. § 3553(a)(2)(B) specifically instructs sentencing courts to consider the need "to afford adequate deterrence to criminal conduct." *See United States v. Perez-Molina*, 627 F.3d 1049, 1050–51 (7th Cir. 2010) (affirming sentence more than double the guidelines range that was imposed based on "the particular need to deter [the defendant] from further reentry"); *United States v. Huffstatler*, 571 F.3d 620, 622, 624 (7th Cir. 2009) (rejecting reasonableness challenge to sentence substantially above guidelines range where district judge cited fact that previous sentences had not deterred defendant and need to protect society from future serious crimes). The district court acted well within its discretion in concluding that Mr. Sanchez-Lopez could best be deterred by serving a longer sentence than he received the last time he committed the same offense. . . .

CONCLUSION

The judgment of the district court is affirmed.

———————

EXERCISE

Imagine that you are the defense attorney at the sentencing of Oliver Tyler, who was convicted by guilty plea of selling twelve grams of methamphetamine, a fairly typical offense in the large jurisdiction where you work.

At sentencing, the prosecutor says "Judge, I'm tired of these meth cases. They just keep coming. We need you to go over the top of the guideline range, really make this sentence count, so that we can send a message to everyone else who sells meth. If we are going to deter anyone, the same old sentences aren't going to work."

How do your respond to the government's argument for an above-guideline sentence based on the principle of general deterrence?

———————

Mental health can be a tricky issue at sentencing. We previously discussed the role of competence and the defense of insanity, which usually come into play before sentencing (though a defendant must be competent at sentencing, as well). Mental health can, of course, be a factor that directly affects sentencing, as well. While it is often presented as a mitigating factor, this is sometimes met with skepticism.

UNITED STATES V. DAVIS
764 F.3d 690 (7th Cir. 2014)

ROVNER, CIRCUIT JUDGE.

By all accounts, Margaret Davis relished her role as the "Mother Teresa" of the west side of Chicago. As a long time nurse and assistant professor of nursing at Chicago State University, she ran several different public health programs aimed at improving the health care of the African-American community. In addition to her roles at African American AIDS Network, Health Works of Cook County, Healthy Start, Southeast Chicago, and the Healthcare Consortium of Illinois, she was also a program director for the Chicago Chapter of the National Black Nurses Association (CCBNA). In her position as program director for CCBNA, Davis solicited and oversaw public and private grants, contracts, and funds awarded to CCBNA. Between December 2005 and March 2009, Davis solicited and obtained contracts and grants totaling approximately $1,062,000 from various Illinois state agencies.

Unfortunately for the intended beneficiaries of those funds, Davis and her co-conspirator diverted a large portion of the money for their own and other unintended uses. This appeal is limited to one specific aspect of sentencing so we need not elaborate on the details of the scheme other than to say that the court estimated that, over the course of three and a half years, Davis diverted approximately $377,000. She did so by, among other things, writing checks to herself, friends, and family members; concealing conflicts of interest; hiring unqualified family members and other acquaintances for positions in projects; forging co-signatures; and falsifying information.

Davis pleaded guilty to one count of mail fraud and one count of money laundering and waived her right to appeal the reasonableness of the sentence, but reserved the right to appeal any procedural error committed by the district court or the amount of restitution, the latter of which she does not appeal.

Under the terms of the plea agreement, the parties concurred that based on the factors contained in 18 U.S.C. § 3553, Davis could be sentenced to, and the government would recommend, no higher than a below-guidelines sentence of 41 months' imprisonment—a significant break from the advisory guidelines range calculation of 57–71 months. The agreement preserved Davis' ability to challenge the guideline calculation and argue for whatever sentence she deemed appropriate. Davis waived the right to appeal the reasonableness of the sentence but reserved the right to challenge on appeal any procedural error at sentencing. She now claims that the district court erred procedurally by failing to adequately take into account her mental health when considering mitigating factors.

The mental health history that Davis claims was ignored was summarized in a presentence investigation report submitted to the court prior to sentencing. The report revealed that in 2007, doctors diagnosed Davis with bipolar disorder following an incident of steroid-induced psychosis that resulted from treatment for multiple sclerosis. Davis informed the probation officer who prepared the presentence report that while that particular episode brought forth the diagnosis, she had been experiencing symptoms associated with bipolar disorder since the 1970s. In February 2009, approximately three years after the charged scheme to defraud began, and a few months before it ended, Davis was hospitalized for having thoughts of and planning suicide. And then in October 2009, she was hospitalized again after an episode of mania, during which time she was abnormally agitated and complained of decreased cognitive function. She underwent a neuropsychological evaluation on March 24, 2010, which revealed psychological distress including significant symptoms of depression, somatic complaints, and bizarre sensory experiences. Just a little more than six months later, from October 10 through October 27, 2010, she was again hospitalized at Rush University Medical Center following a manic episode. She returned to the hospital from February 10–25, 2011, due to worsening depression and problems with caring for herself. Davis reported to the probation officer that, at the time of the interview, her mental health was stabilized through medication, counseling, anger management, and sleep management.

After revealing these facts, the presentence report specifically noted that Davis' mental and emotional conditions might be relevant in determining whether a departure was warranted pursuant to United States Sentencing Guidelines (U.S.S.G.) § 5H1.3, and that under U.S.S.G. § 5K2.13 an adjustment might be warranted if Davis committed the offense while suffering from a significantly reduced mental capacity which substantially contributed to the commission of the offense. Finally, the presentence report noted that the court could consider a sentence outside of the advisory Guidelines based on Davis' mental and physical conditions pursuant to 18 U.S.C. § 3553(a)(1), which requires a sentencing court to consider a defendant's history and characteristics.

Prior to sentencing, Davis filed a 105-page sentencing memorandum with 56 exhibits—400 pages in all. Davis' argument that her mental health was a mitigating factor was the seventh of eight arguments in the memorandum.

To support her claim, she provided her mental health records and the 2012 and 2013 statements of five treating mental health professionals from several different health care facilities. One treating psychiatrist wrote to the court that "it is highly likely that [Davis] had at least some of these clinical manifestations [of mania and major depression as part of bipolar I disorder] during the period she committed the crime(s)." R. 115. She also presented reports written by two retained forensic health care professionals. The first, Dr. Bernard Rubin, M.D., from the University of

Chicago, reviewed Davis' records, but did not see her in person nor treat her. He found that Davis had psychological and physical difficulties which began to limit her capacities for insight and judgment, including impulse control, as early as mid-2006 to early 2007. The second retained expert, Sheryl Dolezal, Psy.D., described Davis' hypomanic behavior and physical and mental health conditions that lead to mood swings, aggression, emotional outbursts, paranoia, impulsivity and compromised judgment and decision making, which Dr. Dolezal opined began prior to 2007. She wrote that, "Although Ms. Davis' choices/crimes . . . cannot be blamed entirely on her mental health or [multiple sclerosis], it is likely that they had some impact on her judgment and emotional state at the time." (R. 103, Exh. 52, p. 8). She also noted, "How much of these behaviors were driving her poor judgment and decision making is difficult to determine, but are likely a factor." *Id.* The sentencing memorandum also pointed out that certain members of the CCBNA had noticed symptoms of mental health problems dating back to 2006 and worsening from 2007 to 2010 (R. 103, p. 67).

The sentencing memorandum urged the court to address her mental condition and the effect it had on her ability to "exercise the power of reason and control her behavior." (R.103, p. 78–79). At the sentencing hearing, the government countered that despite the fact that Davis suffered from mental health ailments, there was no evidence that her mental condition had a substantial connection to the offense or that it warranted deviation from the Guidelines. (R. 139, p. 229).

The district court judge began the sentencing hearing by noting that she had reviewed the presentence report, the plea agreements, Davis' sentencing memorandum, and all of the supporting exhibits and the many letters and spreadsheets detailing the investigation. At the end of the hearing she imposed a below-guidelines sentence of forty one months.

Davis appeals arguing that the district court committed procedural error by failing to acknowledge and respond to Davis' argument about the mitigating role that her mental illness should have had on the sentence. . . .

The district court's discussion of Davis' mental health at the sentencing hearing was indeed brief. In fact, her entire discussion of the sentencing factors took only nine pages of transcript space. Given Davis' considerable mental health history, a more thorough discussion would have been helpful. Brevity, however, is not a sign of inadequacy. *See, e.g., Stinefast,* 724 F.3d at 931–32. And in this case, the district court addressed Davis' mental health issues (and her physical health issues which contributed to her mental health problems) approximately six times in those nine pages of transcript. In that way, the discussion of her mental health permeated the discourse.

The district court judge first emphasized that she had considered the factors set forth in 18 U.S.C. § 3553(a), particularly Davis' history and characteristics. (R. 139, Tr. 10/8/13 at p. 270). She then went on to say, "Your case is especially hard for me because of your personal history, your medical conditions, even the difficulty the case agents had with calculating the loss amounts." *Id.* We also know that the district judge considered Davis' mental health when considering motivation, stating, "we have issues of motivation here. I don't understand them. The psychiatrists don't understand them." *Id.* at p. 271.

After noting that she had considered all of the issues presented, the district court judge concluded, "You're responsible for your conduct. I do believe, truthfully, that [Assistant U.S. Attorney] Mr. Bass considered all the sentencing factors in coming to his recommendation for your sentence. And, certainly, those factors include your mental health and your physical condition with your MS, which I'm very glad to say is controlled at this time." *Id.* at p. 272. Further noting Davis' mental health condition, the district court judge encouraged Davis to continue with treatment through psychotherapy and medication, both in prison and after her release. *Id.* at 272, 275, 277. She also ordered that as a condition of probation Davis participate in psychiatric services or a program of mental health counseling and treatment, and that she take all prescribed medications as directed by the treatment providers. *Id.* at 275. These multiple discussions demonstrate that Davis' mental and physical health were not only considered, but forefront in the judge's mind during sentencing.

We conclude, therefore, that the district court adequately considered, discussed, and then rejected Davis's argument that her sentence should be lowered due to her mental health condition. The judgment of the district court is AFFIRMED.

EXERCISE

In the Davis case, the sentencing judge evaluated mental health as part of the "history and characteristics of the defendant" prong of 18 U.S.C. § 3553(a)(1), but did not expressly evaluate the defendant's mental health in terms of how it would impact each of the traditional goals of sentencing (retribution, deterrence, incapacitation, and rehabilitation) set out in (a)(2). Accepting Davis's claim of mental health issues at face value, do you think those issues weigh in favor of a higher or lower sentence in light of each of these traditional goals?

CHAPTER FOURTEEN

THE THEORY OF CRIMINAL LAW

■ ■ ■

Theory has been saved for last not because it is insignificant, but because it is important. And because it is important, it is crucial to first know how criminal law is structured and how it works before we apply theory to that structure.

One of the things made clear in all of the cases that came before is that many legal outcomes are determined not just by the law on the books, but within the discretion of a single person: a prosecutor, a judge, occasionally a defense attorney. One great question of legal theory is what guides them, or should guide them, when they employ that discretion—what guiding principles do they use, and should they use? After all, deep tragedies can be both caused and prevented by the employment of theory, or the lack of it, when a decision-maker chooses a defendant's fate. Without a theoretical framework, principled action is impossible; criminal law becomes amoral without theory in the form of principled purpose. We spend billions of dollars, incarcerate millions of people, and even make life-and-death decisions (in capital cases) on less than complete certainty as part of the criminal justice process every year. Criminal law as a function of government imposes huge costs, and that requires moral justification in the choices we make.

Much of what is presented as "criminal law theory" is, in fact, primarily about sentencing and that ultimate outcome of a case rather than guilt or innocence. Because plea-based modern sentencing is rooted in the choices prosecutors make (and, sometimes, the responses of defense attorneys and judges), these theories go to the choices made even at the start of a case.

Why prosecute people at all? In short, it is because society wants to have some effect on the individual defendant or others, such as potential criminals we want to deter and victims we want to recompense for their losses. Here, we will explore five purposes for the project of criminal law. Four of them were mentioned in the preceding chapter on sentencing, as part of 18 U.S.C. § 3553(a).

The first is punishment or retribution—the use of criminal law to hurt and humiliate a defendant in response to the defendant's hurtful actions. Punishment is a part of almost any sentence, and underlies the broadest purpose of criminal law: to mark certain acts as wrong.

The second is deterrence—the use of criminal law to convince the defendant or others to avoid committing wrongful acts in the future.

The third is incapacitation—the use of criminal law to affirmatively restrict the freedom of a defendant to prevent him or her from doing further harm in the future.

The fourth is rehabilitation—the use of criminal law to require a defendant to change bad behaviors and underlying causes.

The fifth is restoration—the use of criminal law to "restore" the relationship between the offender and the community (and the victim if there is one).

A. RETRIBUTION AND PUNISHMENT

We begin with the theory of retributive justice: the idea that causing deprivation, pain or humiliation to a wrongdoer is a proper goal of government. While many examinations of this question are rooted in abstract principles, it is possible to look deeply at this question in the context of a real-life set of facts.

In 1972, the Supreme Court struck down the use of capital punishment in Georgia and Texas in the remarkable case of *Furman v. Georgia*, 408 U.S. 238 (1972), which consolidated three cases from those two states. The men facing execution were William Furman, Lucious Jackson, and Elmer Branch. Each Justice wrote an opinion—five concurring and four dissents—and several of them directly addressed the question of retribution and its role in the use of death as a punishment, particularly in an environment of racial disparities. These opinions reveal a raw and genuine set of views in the context of a life-and-death decision the Court had to make.

As you read these excerpts (which are no substitute for a reading of the complete set of opinions), think about your own view on the idea of retribution as a legitimate goal of criminal law.

FURMAN v. GEORGIA
408 U.S. 238 (1972)

MR. JUSTICE DOUGLAS, concurring. . .

Jackson, a black, convicted of the rape of a white woman, was 21 years old. A court-appointed psychiatrist said that Jackson was of average education and average intelligence, that he was not an imbecile, or schizophrenic, or psychotic, that his traits were the product of environmental influences, and that he was competent to stand trial. Jackson had entered the house after the husband left for work. He held scissors against the neck of the wife, demanding money. She could find none and a struggle ensued for the scissors, a battle which she lost; and she was then raped, Jackson keeping the scissors pressed against her neck. While there did not appear to be any long-term traumatic impact on the victim, she was bruised and abrased in the struggle but was not hospitalized. Jackson was a convict who had escaped from a work gang in the area, a result of a three-year sentence for auto theft. He was at large for three days and during that time had committed several other offenses-burglary, auto theft, and assault and battery.

Furman, a black, killed a householder while seeking to enter the home at night. Furman shot the deceased through a closed door. He was 26 years old and had finished the sixth grade in school. Pending trial, he was committed to the Georgia Central State Hospital for a psychiatric examination on his plea of insanity tendered by court-appointed counsel. The superintendent reported that a unanimous staff diagnostic conference had concluded 'that this patient should retain his present diagnosis of Mental Deficiency, Mild to Moderate, with Psychotic Episodes associated with Convulsive Disorder.' The physicians agreed that 'at present the patient is not psychotic, but he is not capable of cooperating with his counsel in the preparation of his defense'; and the staff believed 'that he is in need of further psychiatric hospitalization and treatment.'

Later, the superintendent reported that the staff diagnosis was Mental Deficiency, Mild to Moderate, with Psychotic Episodes associated with Convulsive Disorder. He concluded, however, that Furman was 'not psychotic at present, knows right from wrong and is able to cooperate with his counsel in preparing his defense.'

Branch, a black, entered the rural home of a 65-year-old widow, a white, while she slept and raped her, holding his arm against her throat. Thereupon he demanded money and for 30 minutes or more the widow searched for money, finding little. As he left, Jackson said if the widow told anyone what happened, he would return and kill her. The record is barren of any medical or psychiatric evidence showing injury to her as a result of Branch's attack.

He had previously been convicted of felony theft and found to be a borderline mental deficient and well below the average IQ of Texas prison inmates. He had the equivalent of five and a half years of grade school education. He had a 'dull intelligence' and was in the lowest fourth percentile of his class. . . .

MR. JUSTICE BRENNAN, concurring. . .

At bottom, then, the Cruel and Unusual Punishments Clause prohibits the infliction of uncivilized and inhuman punishments. The State, even as it punishes, must treat its members with respect for their intrinsic worth as human beings. A punishment is 'cruel and unusual,' therefore, if it does not comport with human dignity. . . .

Although pragmatic arguments for and against the punishment have been frequently advanced, this longstanding and heated controversy cannot be explained solely as the result of differences over the practical wisdom of a particular government policy. At bottom, the battle has been waged on moral grounds. The country has debated whether a society for which the dignity of the individual is the supreme value can, without a fundamental inconsistency, follow the practice of deliberately putting some of its members to death. In the United States, as in other nations of the western world, 'the struggle about this punishment has been one between ancient and deeply rooted beliefs in retribution, atonement or vengeance on the one hand, and, on the other, beliefs in the personal value and dignity of the common man that were born of the democratic movement of the eighteenth century, as well as beliefs in the scientific approach to an understanding of the motive forces of human conduct, which are the result of the growth of the sciences of behavior during the nineteenth and twentieth centuries.' It is this essentially moral conflict that forms the backdrop for the past changes in and the present operation of our system of imposing death as a punishment for crime. . . .

There is, then, no substantial reason to believe that the punishment of death, as currently administered, is necessary for the protection of society. The only other purpose suggested, one that is independent of protection for society, is retribution. Shortly stated, retribution in this context means that criminals are put to death because they deserve it.

Although it is difficult to believe that any State today wishes to proclaim adherence to 'naked vengeance,' Trop v. Dulles, 356 U.S., at 112, 78 S.Ct., at 604 (Brennan, J., concurring), the States claim, in reliance upon its statutory authorization, that death is the only fit punishment for capital crimes and that this retributive purpose justifies its infliction. In the past, judged by its statutory authorization, death was considered the only fit punishment for the crime of forgery, for the first federal criminal statute provided a mandatory death penalty for that crime. Act of April 30, 1790, s 14, 1 Stat. 115. Obviously, concepts of justice change; no immutable moral order requires death for murderers and rapists. The claim that death is a just punishment necessarily refers to the existence of certain public beliefs. The claim must be that for capital crimes death alone comports with society's notion of proper punishment. As administered today, however, the punishment of death cannot be justified as a necessary means of exacting retribution from criminals. When the overwhelming number of criminals who commit capital crimes go to prison, it cannot be concluded that death serves the purpose of retribution more effectively than imprisonment. The asserted public belief that murderers and rapists deserve to die is flatly inconsistent with the execution of a random few. As the history of the punishment of death in this country shows, our society wishes to prevent crime; we have no desire to kill criminals simply to get even with them. . . .

MR. JUSTICE STEWART, concurring. . .

On that score I would say only that I cannot agree that retribution is a constitutionally impermissible ingredient in the imposition of punishment. The instinct for retribution is part of the nature of man, and channeling that instinct in the administration of criminal justice serves an important purpose in promoting the stability of a society governed by law. When people begin to believe that organized society is unwilling or unable to impose upon criminal offenders the punishment they 'deserve,' then there are sown the seeds of anarchy-of self-help, vigilante justice, and lynch law. . . .

MR. JUSTICE MARSHALL, concurring. . .

In order to assess whether or not death is an excessive or unnecessary penalty, it is necessary to consider the reasons why a legislature might select it as punishment for one or more offenses, and examine whether less severe penalties would satisfy the legitimate legislative wants as well as capital punishment. If they would, then the death penalty is unnecessary cruelty, and, therefore, unconstitutional.

There are six purposes conceivably served by capital punishment: retribution, deterrence, prevention of repetitive criminal acts, encouragement of guilty pleas and confessions, eugenics, and economy. These are considered seriatim below.

A.   The concept of retribution is one of the most misunderstood in all of our criminal jurisprudence. The principal source of confusion derives from the fact that, in dealing with the concept, most people confuse the question 'why do men in fact punish?' with the question 'what justifies men in punishing?' Men may punish for any number of reasons, but the one reason that punishment is morally good or morally justifiable is that someone has broken the law. Thus, it can correctly be said that breaking the law is the sine qua non of punishment, or, in other words, that we only tolerate punishment as it is imposed on one who deviates from the norm established by the criminal law.

The fact that the State may seek retribution against those who have broken its laws does not mean that retribution may then become the State's sole end in punishing. Our jurisprudence has always accepted deterrence in general, deterrence of individual recidivism, isolation of dangerous persons, and rehabilitation as proper goals of punishment. See Trop v. Dulles, 356 U.S., at 111, 78 S.Ct., at 603–604. (Brennan, J., concurring). Retaliation, vengeance, and retribution have been roundly condemned as intolerable aspirations for a government in a free society.

Punishment as retribution has been condemned by scholars for centuries, and the Eighth Amendment itself was adopted to prevent punishment from becoming synonymous with vengeance.

In Weems v. United States, 217 U.S., at 381, 30 S.Ct., at 554, the Court in the course of holding that Weems' punishment violated the Eighth Amendment, contrasted it with penalties provided for other offenses and concluded:

> [T]his contrast shows more than different exercises of legislative judgment. It is greater than that. It condemns the sentence in this case as cruel and unusual. It exhibits a difference between unrestrained power and that which is exercised under the spirit of constitutional limitations formed to establish justice. The State thereby suffers nothing and loses no power. The purpose of punishment is fulfilled, crime is repressed by penalties of just, not tormenting, severity, its repetition is prevented, and hope is given for the reformation of the criminal. (Emphasis added.)

It is plain that the view of the Weems Court was that punishment for the sake of retribution was not permissible under the Eighth Amendment. This is the only view that the Court could have taken if the 'cruel and unusual' language were to be given any meaning. Retribution surely underlies the imposition of some punishment on one who commits a criminal act. But, the fact that some punishment may be imposed does not mean that any punishment is permissible. If retribution alone could serve as a justification for any particular penalty, then all penalties selected by the legislature would be definition be acceptable means for designating society's moral approbation of a particular act. The 'cruel and unusual' language would thus be read out of the Constitution and the fears of Patrick Henry and the other Founding Fathers would become realities.

To preserve the integrity of the Eighth Amendment, the Court has consistently denigrated retribution as a permissible goal of punishment. It is undoubtedly correct that there is a demand for vengeance on the part of many persons in a community against one who is convicted of a particularly offensive act. At times a cry is heard that morality requires vengeance to evidence society's abhorrence of the act. But the Eighth Amendment is our insulation from our baser selves. The 'cruel and unusual' language limits the avenues through which vengeance can be channeled. Were this not so, the language would be empty and a return to the rack and other tortures would be possible in a given case.

Mr. Justice Story wrote that the Eighth Amendment's limitation on punishment 'would seem to be wholly unnecessary in a free government, since it is scarcely possible that any department of such a government should authorize or justify such atrocious conduct.'

I would reach an opposite conclusion-that only in a free society would men recognize their inherent weaknesses and seek to compensate for them by means of a Constitution.

The history of the Eighth Amendment supports only the conclusion that retribution for its own sake is improper. . . .

[fn 163] There is too much crime, too much killing, too much hatred in this country. If the legislatures could eradicate these elements from our lives by utilizing capital punishment, then there would be a valid purpose for the sanction and the public would surely accept it. It would be constitutional. As THE CHIEF JUSTICE and Mr. Justice POWELL point out, however, capital punishment has been with us a long time. What purpose has it served? The evidence is that it has served none. I cannot agree that the American people have been so hardened, so embittered that they want to take the life of one who performs even the basest criminal act knowing that the execution is nothing more than bloodlust. This has not been my experience with my fellow citizens. Rather, I have found that they earnestly desire their system of punishments to make sense in order that it can be a morally justifiable system. . . .

MR. CHIEF JUSTICE BURGER, dissenting. . .

Two of the several aims of punishment are generally associated with capital punishment-retribution and deterrence. It is argued that retribution can be discounted because that, after all, is what the Eighth Amendment seeks to eliminate. There is no authority suggesting that the Eighth Amendment was intended to purge the law of its retributive elements, and the Court has consistently assumed that retribution is a legitimate dimension of the punishment of crimes. See Williams v. New York, 337 U.S. 241, 248, 69 S.Ct. 1079, 1083, 93 L.Ed. 1337 (1949); United States v. Lovett, 328 U.S. 303, 324, 66 S.Ct. 1073, 1083, 90 L.Ed. 1252 (1946) (Frankfurter, J., concurring). Furthermore, responsible legal thinkers of widely varying persuasions have debated the sociological and philosophical aspects of the retribution question for generations, neither side being able to convince the other. It would be reading a great deal into the Eighth Amendment to hold that the punishments authorized by legislatures cannot constitutionally reflect a retributive purpose. . . .

MR. JUSTICE BLACKMUN, dissenting. . .

Cases such as these provide for me an excruciating agony of the spirit. I yield to no one in the depth of my distaste, antipathy, and, indeed, abhorrence, for the death penalty, with all its aspects of physical distress and fear and of moral judgment exercised by finite minds. That distaste is buttressed by a belief that capital punishment serves no useful purpose that can be demonstrated. For me, it violates childhood's training and life's experiences, and is not compatible with the philosophical convictions I have been able to develop. . . .

It is not without interest, also, to note that, although the several concurring opinions acknowledge the heinous and atrocious character of the offenses committed by the petitioners, none of those opinions makes reference to the misery the petitioners' crimes occasioned to the victims, to the families of the victims, and to the communities where the offenses took place. The arguments for the respective petitioners, particularly the oral arguments, were similarly and curiously devoid of reference to the victims. There is risk, of course, in a comment such as this, for it opens one to the charge of emphasizing the retributive. But see Williams v. New York, 337 U.S. 241, 248, 69 S.Ct. 1079, 1083, 93 L.Ed. 1337 (1949). Nevertheless, these cases are here because offenses to innocent victims were perpetrated. This fact, and the terror that occasioned it, and the fear that stalks the streets of many of our cities today perhaps deserve not to be entirely overlooked. Let us hope that, with the Court's decision, the terror imposed will be forgotten by those upon whom it was visited, and that our society will reap the hoped-for benefits of magnanimity.

Although personally I may rejoice at the Court's result, I find it difficult to accept or to justify as a matter of history, of law, or of constitutional pronouncement. I fear the Court has overstepped. It has sought and has achieved an end. . . .

MR. JUSTICE POWELL, dissenting. . . .

The concept of retribution-though popular for centuries-is now criticized as unworthy of a civilized people. Yet this Court has acknowledged the existence of a retributive element in criminal sanctions and has never heretofore found it impermissible. In Williams v. New York, 337 U.S. 241, 69 S.Ct. 1079, 93 L.Ed. 1337 (1949), Mr. Justice Black stated that,

'Retribution is no longer the dominant objective of the criminal law. Reformation and rehabilitation of offenders have become important goals of criminal jurisprudence.' Id., at 248, 69 S.Ct., at 1084.

It is clear, however, that the Court did not reject retribution altogether. The record in that case indicated that one of the reasons why the trial judge imposed the death penalty was his sense of revulsion at the 'shocking details of the crime.' Id., at 244, 69 S.Ct., at 1081. Although his motivation was clearly retributive, the Court upheld the trial judge's sentence. Similarly, Mr. Justice Marshall noted in his plurality opinion in Powell v. Texas, 392 U.S. 514, 530, 88 S.Ct. 2145, 2153, 20 L.Ed.2d 1254 (1968), that this Court 'has never held that anything in the Constitution requires that penal sanctions be designed solely to achieve therapeutic or rehabilitative effects.'

While retribution alone may seem an unworthy justification in a moral sense, its utility in a system of criminal justice requiring public support has long been recognized. Lord Justice Denning, now Master of the Rolls of the Court of Appeal in England, testified on this subject before the British Royal Commission on Capital Punishment:

Many are inclined to test the efficacy of punishment solely by its value as a deterrent: but this is too narrow a view. Punishment is the way in which society expresses its denunciation of wrong doing; and, in order to maintain respect for law, it is essential that the punishment inflicted for grave crimes should adequately reflect the revulsion felt by the great majority of citizens for them. It is a mistake to consider the objects of punishment as being deterrent or reformative or preventive and nothing else. If this were so, we should not send to prison a man who was guilty of motor manslaughter, but only disqualify him from driving; but would public opinion be content with this? The truth is that some crimes are so outrageous that society insists on adequate punishment, because the wrong-doer deserves it, irrespective of whether it is a deterrent or not.

The view expressed by Lord Denning was cited approvingly in the Royal Commission's Report, recognizing 'a strong and widespread demand for retribution.' Mr. Justice STEWART makes much the same point in his opinion today when he concludes that expression of man's retributive instincts in the sentencing process 'serves an important purpose in promoting the stability of a society governed by law.' Ante, at 2761. The view, moreover, is not without respectable support in the jurisprudential literature in this country, despite a substantial body of opinion to the contrary. And it is conceded on all sides that, not infrequently, cases arise that are so shocking or offensive that the public demands the ultimate penalty for the transgressor.

EXERCISE

Retribution is an important consideration in non-capital cases, as well. Do you think that it should be a factor considered by judges in cases where there are no victims, such as a narcotics transaction? If so, which of the justifications given in *Furman* would support your view?

Retribution theory put into practice by legislators, lawyers and judges is necessarily going to be connected to how a given decider rank-orders various wrongs, and that ordering inevitably differs from one person to another. Is an immigration crime "worse" than a theft? Individuals may disagree on that question, but the broader society makes a choice through statutory minimums and maximums and (sometimes) sentencing guidelines that provide for different punishments for different offenders. Because we issue discrete punishments to convicted defendants, there is a functioning rank-order system in place, whether intentionally created or not.

While some think retribution should be a major consideration in financial crimes, others would disagree.

UNITED STATES V. COLE

622 F. Supp. 2d 632 (N.D.Ohio 2008)

JAMES S. GWIN, DISTRICT JUDGE:

With this sentencing opinion, the Court seeks to provide a thorough explanation of its imposition of a non-guideline sentence in the case of Defendant Robert G. Cole ("Cole"). . . .

On August 11, 2008, the United States filed an Information charging Cole with securities fraud in violation of *15 U.S.C. §§ 78j(b)* and 78ff. On September 5, 2008, the Defendant was arraigned. On the same date, the United States and the Defendant executed a Federal Rules of Criminal Procedure Rule 11(c)(1)(A) plea agreement in which Defendant Cole pled guilty to securities fraud.

As part of the plea agreement, Cole testified that he had worked for Diebold, Inc., an Ohio corporation headquartered in North Canton, Ohio. Diebold manufactures and sells ATMs, bank security systems, and electronic voting terminals. Diebold common stock trades on the New York Stock Exchange. Defendant Cole worked for Diebold as a sales representative in the Oklahoma area. As a sales representative, Cole regularly received confidential information from Diebold concerning Diebold's North American regional bank business. Diebold prohibited corporate employees from trading in Diebold securities when those employees possessed material nonpublic information. Cole knew of this policy.

Diebold regularly forecasted future earnings expectations to the public. The charges brought against Defendant Cole relate to his trading of Diebold shares in the interim between two of these forecasts. On July 27, 2005, Diebold announced its second quarter earnings and provided earnings guidance for the third quarter ending on September 30, 2005. It also provided guidance for 2005 as a whole. In a public conference call, Diebold predicted that Diebold's earnings would be $0.62 to $0.67 per share in the third quarter of 2005 and $2.60 to $2.70 per share for the entire 2005 year. Diebold projected third quarter revenue increases of 9 to 11 percent.

After it issued these projections, Diebold's earnings prospects diminished. On September 13, 2005, Diebold sales managers gave Cole and other sales representatives financial reports detailing third quarter orders and sales information. From these reports, Cole learned non-public information—specifically that Diebold was not meeting its sales targets for either the third quarter of 2005 or for 2005 as a whole. Moreover, Cole learned that Diebold's year-to-date revenues from United States regional banks only amounted to 78.8 percent of its target revenues. Other information that

Cole received gave further indication that Diebold would fail to meet its revenue targets.

On September 15, 2005, and within days of receiving the non-public information mentioned above, Defendant Cole began purchasing Diebold "put option" contracts at a total cost of $70,110.

Based on the same general information that Diebold had earlier given Cole, on September 21, 2005 Diebold publicly released earnings guidance that suggested lower-than-forecasted quarterly and annual earnings. With this guidance, Diebold reduced its predicted sales to American financial institutions by $50 million. As a result of this September 21, 2005 earnings warning, Diebold's stock price fell more than 16 percent from the previous day's closing price.

In the days following Diebold's September 21, 2005 earnings forecast, Cole sold all his put option contracts for approximately $579,190, realizing profits of $509,080. After Cole's put options were investigated, he disgorged all the profits that he had made. On August 4, 2008, Defendant Cole paid $509,080 to the government. Shortly thereafter, on August 11, 2008, the United States named Defendant Cole in a one count Information filed in the Northern District of Ohio. On September 5, 2008, Cole pled guilty to the Information charging him with one count of securities fraud in violation of *15 U.S.C. §§ 78j(b)* and 78ff. Defendant Cole appeared for sentencing on November 20, 2008. At that hearing, the Court sentenced Cole to imprisonment for one year and one day followed by two years of supervised release. The Court also imposed a $180,000 fine together with a special assessment of $100. With this opinion, the Court explains the reasons for the chosen sentence. . . .

Retribution, involves the calculation of moral culpability, with society gauging the seriousness of the offense and the response that society believes an appropriate response to the offense. In general, retribution imposes punishment to reflect respect for the dignity of the victim. Stated otherwise, society stands with victims and exacts punishment in rough approximation to the detriment caused by the defendant. Retributive or "just deserts" theory considerations study the defendant's past actions and the effect of these actions on the victim or victims of the crime, not the defendant's probable future conduct or the effect that his or her punishment might have on others in society. In recent years, retribution has played a more important, if not dominating, role in sentencing determinations. *See, e.g.* Model Penal Code: Sentencing, Tentative Draft No. 1, April 9, 2007) ("The general purposes of the provisions on sentencing [ ] in decisions affecting the sentencing of individual offenders: to render sentences in all cases within a range of severity proportionate to the gravity of offenses, the harms done to crime victims, and the blameworthiness of offenders. . . .")

To address the retributive goals of sentencing, the Court considers the effect of Defendant Cole's acts. In enacting the Securities Act of 1933, *15 U.S.C. § 77a et seq.*, and the Securities Exchange Act of 1934, *15 U.S.C. § 78a et seq.*, Congress established a regulatory system that requires disclosure of all material aspects of transactions involving securities. Federal securities laws dictate that investors can be protected only if all relevant aspects of market transactions are fully and fairly disclosed and if investment decisions are made based upon information available to all investors.

Defendant Cole's misappropriation of non-public information undermines a cornerstone of our investment regulation policy. Moreover, when Cole used his knowledge of Diebold's reduced orders to purchase put options in September 2005, he disadvantaged other, legitimate investors in his September 2005 purchase of put options. Society deserves retribution resulting from the damage Cole imposed upon persons involved with the September transactions and to the securities markets generally. With regard to fulfilling the need for the sentence to impose retribution, this Court finds that Cole should be punished significantly. . . .

Defendant Cole has a commendable past: a productive work history, a lack of any past criminal history, admirable military service, community involvement, and a history of having sacrificed to raise two children. His sole explanation for his crime was greed, however, even though his earnings placed him in the top 3% of wage earners. Moreover, with his actions, Cole betrayed his employer's trust and cheated market participants.

The imposed term of imprisonment, while lower than the guideline range, still represents a significant period of incarceration considering Cole's age and physical condition. The fine, while higher than the guideline range, serves to adequately protect society from similar conduct. This Court is mindful of the motivation for this crime and also of Cole's diminished standard of living resulting from the fine. At roughly 20% of the wealth that Cole has worked for over 40 years to accumulate, this fine appropriately deters the rest of society from engaging in similar conduct.

The Court therefore finds that a sentence of one year and one day, joined with the restitution that has already occurred and a fine of $180,000, reflects the seriousness of the offense, promotes respect for the law, provides just punishment for the offense, affords adequate deterrence to criminal conduct, and protects the public from further crimes of the Defendant. *See 18 U.S.C. § 3553(a)(2).*

EXERCISE

In the case above, the judge chose to sentence below the guideline range for incarceration, and above the guideline range for a fine. How does the sentence comport with the court's reasoning on the need for retribution?

While retribution has always been a basis for criminal punishment, alternative bases were proposed during the enlightenment by John Stuart Mill, Jeremy Bentham, and others. Bentham's thinking was particularly influential. He opined generally that the choices of governmental actors should be guided by a "principle of utility" which requires a preference for those paths which lead to happiness for the greatest number of citizens and away from paths that lead to pain, evil, and unhappiness.[1]

Utilitarian principles are often discussed by philosophers but rarely are explicitly recognized by criminal law practitioners in the course of doing their work. The influence of these ideas can be seen, though, in the "problem-solving" approach taken by some and the parsimony principle embedded in 18 U.S.C. § 3553(a), which provides that a sentence shall "sufficient, but not greater than necessary, to comply with the purposes set forth in paragraph (2) of this subjection"—paragraph two being the listing of the four traditional goals of sentencing.

UNITED STATES V. WEEKLY

128 F.3d 1198 (8th Cir. 1997)

ORDER MODIFYING OPINION

Prior Report: 118 F.3d 576.

With permission of the panel, Judge Bright's dissent is modified to read as follows:

BRIGHT, CIRCUIT JUDGE, dissenting.

I dissent.

This case provides a disturbing glimpse into the underbelly of prosecuting non-violent, first time drug offenders under mandatory minimum sentences. The district court sentenced Donna Romero, a first time offender and the mother of three young children, to a five-year mandatory minimum term of incarceration. Her request for a reduced sentence under the safety valve provision of 18 U.S.C. § 3553(f) and U.S.S.G. § 5C1.2 was denied. In my view, this case should be remanded for resentencing because the sentencing judge relied on irrelevant evidence of a lie detector test to deny Romero application of the safety valve.

---

[1]   Jeremy Bentham, An Introduction to the Principles of Morals and Legislation, 2 (Oxford, New York 1907).

Romero and Grajeda transported drugs from Phoenix to St. Louis. Romero told the authorities that she did not organize or plan this trip, but merely accompanied Grajeda at his request. Romero acknowledged that she knew they were doing something illegal.

Romero sought relief from a five-year mandatory minimum sentence for this first offense by requesting application of the safety valve provision. Initially, Romero appeared to meet the requirements of the safety valve provision and the presentence report recommended its application in her case. The safety valve provides that a defendant must not have more than one criminal history point, must not use violence during the commission of the offense, the offense must not result in serious physical injury, the defendant must not be an organizer of the offense, and the defendant must truthfully provide all relevant information to the government regarding the offense. 18 U.S.C. § 3553(f). Application of the safety valve provision permits a district judge to sentence a defendant below the statutory mandatory minimum, but within the Sentencing Guideline Range. In this case, Romero could be sentenced between forty-six and fifty-seven months in prison.

Grajeda, the apparent husband of Ms. Romero and the father of two of her young children, had a different view of the circumstances. He asserted that Romero was responsible for transporting the drugs and that he merely joined her for the ride. In an apparent attempt to resolve the conflicting stories of Romero and Grajeda, the prosecutor arranged for Grajeda to take a lie detector test. Romero, on advice from counsel, declined to submit to a test. After Grajeda "passed" the lie detector test, the prosecutor opposed application of the safety valve provision for Romero and objected to the presentence report. Eventually the probation office prepared an "Addendum to the Presentence Report" recommending, based on the government's objection, that the court not apply the safety valve provision to Romero.

The district court relied exclusively upon Grajeda's polygraph in denying Romero the safety valve. The reliability of polygraph evidence has long been considered suspect, *Brown v. Darcy,* 783 F.2d 1389, 1394–97 (9th Cir.1986), and its admission into evidence is rarely granted. *See, e.g., United States v. Williams,* 95 F.3d 723, 728–730 (8th Cir.1996) (affirming denial of admission of polygraph into evidence). In the rare instance where it is utilized, courts require careful foundation such as a qualified polygraph expert and appropriate questioning. *See, e.g., United States v. Kwong,* 69 F.3d 663, 668 (2d Cir.1995) (polygraph results inadmissible because "the questions posed to Kwong were inherently ambiguous no matter how they were answered"), *cert. denied,* 517 U.S. 1115, 116 S.Ct. 1343, 134 L.Ed.2d 491 (1996). The prosecution presented no such foundation here.

Let us review the relevance of Grajeda's lie detector test which was the focus of a hearing prior to sentencing. The polygraph examiner never testified. The government offered no evidence regarding the qualifications, if any, of the examiner. No report was presented to the district court. It is unknown if the examiner even made a report. Sent. Tr. at 27. We do not know the questions the examiner asked Grajeda, sent. tr. at 27–28, or Grajeda's answers. Indeed, the only testimony relating to the polygraph examination came from an individual, Agent Don Mendrala, who allegedly spoke with the examiner by telephone. The entire testimony on direct examination relating to the polygraph test is as follows:

Q. Who administered the polygraph examination?

A. Special Agent Ben Scott, Benjamin Scott.

Q. And his duties, he is employed by whom?

A. Employed by DEA as a polygraph examiner. At the time he was assigned to our New Orleans office.

[At this point, defense counsel objected to the line of questioning, but was apparently overruled. The questioning continued]

A. Currently assigned to our Washington D.C. office.

Q. And he traveled to St. Louis and administered a polygraph examination of Mr. Grajeda regarding his role in the offense, is that correct?

A. That's correct.

Q. And based upon your conversations with Ben Scoff, the examiner, did he render an opinion as to whether or not Mr. Grajeda passed or was telling the truth during that examination?

A. He indicated to me that he was truthful.

Q. And that no deception was indicated?

A. None at all.

Q. That's all, Judge.

Sent. Tr. at 25.

At sentencing, of course, the usual federal rules of evidence do not apply. But the evidence presented in this case lacked any trustworthiness or reliability whatsoever. In a word, the "evidence" of Grajeda's lie detector test was worthless. As such, it was entitled to no consideration by the district judge.

Moreover, Grajeda's obvious intent to sacrifice his wife and children resulted in part from the actions of the prosecutor. The United States Attorneys in drug cases often turn family member against family member with the result invariably being the destruction of the family and harm to the children. A recent article in *The Atlantic Monthly* provided an example of such a situation:

> Federal prosecutors in Montana threatened her [Israel] with a long prison sentence. Although Israel possessed only eight ounces of marijuana at the time of her arrest, under the broad federal conspiracy laws she could be held liable for many of her husband's crimes. Israel was thirty-one years old, the mother of four young children. She had never been charged with any crime. Judge Jack Shanstrom warned her in court that without a promise of cooperation "you are not going to see your children for ten plus years."

> Nevertheless, Israel refused to testify against her husband. She was sentenced to eleven years in federal prison without parole. Her husband was sentenced to twenty-nine years without parole. Her children were scattered among various relatives.

Eric Schlosser, "More Reefer Madness", *The Atlantic Monthly,* Apr. 1997, at 96.

When Romero refused to take a lie detector test, the prosecutor did not simply retract his recommendation for the safety valve provision. Instead, he pursued a harsher sentence for obstruction of justice, as if a five-year sentence for this first-time offender was somehow insufficient punishment. Of course, it is the children who suffer for turning "family values" on its head in this fashion. The district court properly denied the government's request for an obstruction of justice adjustment. Sent. Tr. at 33.

The sad outcome of this case results from a sentencing structure which improperly confers immense discretionary power upon the prosecutor. He or she exercises substantive control over the sentencing process by determining what charges to pursue and whether to disagree with the recommendation contained in the presentence report. As this case demonstrates, the prosecutor, not bound by the rules of evidence, is free to introduce worthless evidence to "prove" a point regardless of its relevance. Unfortunately, "prosecutors sometimes forget that the prosecutor's special duty is not to convict, but to secure justice." *United States v. Guerra,* 113 F.3d 809, 818 (8th Cir.1997) (citations omitted).

The trial judge, on the other hand, is confined by the sentencing guidelines, the criminal code, the presentence report and the charges filed by the prosecutor. In short, the sentencing judge has little flexibility to do what he or she thinks is right. Furthermore, if the judge departs downward, prosecutors will often take an appeal. In my experience, the federal courts of appeal all too often side with prosecutors and not the district judges in these situations.

In my view, sentencing in many federal drug cases is unworthy of American justice, and it pains me that our citizens are often sentenced to lengthy prison terms under circumstances similar to those presented here. What is most disturbing, perhaps, is that this case is not unusual in any significant respect from the seemingly endless drug cases we review. It is precisely the ordinariness of the manner in which we lock away Donna Romero for five years that appalls me. In the end, it is simply another example of excessive mandatory sentences, the use of improper evidence and the destruction of families that results from this country's treatment of its non-violent drug offenders.

A recent study by the Drug Policy Center of the Rand Corporation, representing the first detailed examination of the cost effectiveness of mandatory minimum sentences, concluded that "Mandatory minimum sentences are not justifiable on the basis of cost-effectiveness at reducing cocaine consumption or drug-related crimes[.]" *Study Questions Costs of Shift to Harsher Cocaine Sentences,* N.Y. Times, May 13, 1997, at A13; *see also United States v. Hiveley,* 61 F.3d 1358, 1363–66 (8th Cir.1995) (Bright, J., concurring). This case causes me to reflect on the words of the great English legal philosopher Jeremy Bentham: "Every particle of real punishment that is produced, more than what is necessary, is just so much misery run to waste." Jeremy Bentham, *Principles of Penal* Law, 1 The Works of Jeremy Bentham 398 (John Bowring ed., 1962).

Therefore, I would reverse and remand for resentencing.

EXERCISE

In *Weekly*, Judge Bright highlights an intriguing detail about the case. It appears that the prosecutor sought a higher punishment in retribution for the defendant's refusal to take a lie detector test, "as if a five-year sentence for this first-time offender was somehow insufficient punishment."

While that may surprise some students, it is one permutation of a dynamic that is quite familiar to practitioners, and in some instances there is a good argument to support such choices by the prosecution. For example, there is nearly always a "trial price" exacted when a federal defendant does not plead guilty, and the federal sentencing guidelines (at § 3E1.1) explicitly direct that outcome based on the defendant's assertion of a constitutional right.

One primary justification for punishing the assertion of rights by the defendant is to increase the efficiency of criminal justice. Does that justify the decision in *Weekly* to seek a higher sentence because the defendant refused to take a lie detector test?

B.　DETERRENCE

Deterrence is the goal of altering future behavior through the use of criminal law in the present. Specific deterrence is directed at the defendant, while general deterrence seeks to affect those other who might commit similar crimes in the future. Courts only sometimes distinguish between the two with clarity.

UNITED STATES V. WALKER

252 F.Supp.3d 1269 (D.Utah 2017)

CLARK WADDOUPS, UNITED STATES DISTRICT JUDGE.

Defendant John Eugene Walker appears before this court for resentencing following the Tenth Circuit Court of Appeal's reversal and remand of his prior sentence. *See United States v. Walker*, 844 F.3d 1253 (10th Cir. 2017).

BACKGROUND

On December 11, 2013, Mr. Walker pled guilty to two counts of bank robbery, in violation of 18 U.S.C. § 2113(a). On May 13, 2014, the court deferred sentencing for thirteen months to allow Mr. Walker to enroll in a residential treatment program. Mr. Walker returned to the court for sentencing on September 22, 2015. Based on the Presentence Report ("PSR"), the court calculated Mr. Walker's total offense level at 29 with a criminal history category of VI, resulting in a Guideline range of 151 to 188 months with a period of one to three years of supervised release or one to five years of probation. The statutory maximum for this offense is 240 months. *See* 18 U.S.C. § 2113(a). There is no mandatory minimum. The court originally imposed a sentence of time served followed by 36 months of supervised release, a $200 special assessment, and $3,695.50 in restitution. The court imposed the standard conditions of supervised release, as well as special conditions relating to restitution, drug and alcohol testing, and mental health treatment.

The government appealed the sentence, and the Tenth Circuit reversed and remanded, finding the sentence substantively unreasonable in light of the statutory sentencing factors and precedent. *Walker*, 844 F.3d at 1255. In particular, the Tenth Circuit found this court focused "almost exclusively" on one sentencing factor, while "fail[ing] to give any weight to" other relevant sentencing factors. . . .

On May 29, 2013, a grand jury indicted Mr. Walker on two counts of bank robbery, in violation of 18 U.S.C. § 2113(a). . . . Mr. Walker pled guilty to both counts of the indictment. Mr. Walker pled to the following facts:

> On May 3, 2013, [Mr. Walker] robbed the U.S. Bank located at 888 East 4500 South, in Salt Lake City, Utah while dressed as a construction worker and carrying a dark colored messenger style bag. Upon entering the bank, [Mr. Walker] approached the teller counter and demanded money from the teller. The teller complied and gave [him] approximately $2152.50 in U.S. currency, which [he] put in the bag and left the bank.

> On May 22, 2013, [Mr. Walker] robbed the Zions Bank located at 8955 South 700 East in Sandy, Utah while dressed in women's clothing and carrying a light blue purse. After entering the bank, [Mr. Walker] approached the teller counter, placed the purse on the teller counter and demanded money. The teller complied and gave [him] approximately $1543 in U.S. currency, which [he] put in the purse and left the bank. . . .

The PSR submitted in advance of sentencing reports that Mr. Walker has a long criminal history, which is only surpassed by his long addiction to alcohol and drugs. Mr. Walker began using alcohol at an early age and has been an alcoholic "all his life." He began using methamphetamine daily in his twenties. In 1987, Mr. Walker committed armed bank robberies in Nevada, for which he was incarcerated approximately 14 years (paroled in 2001). While in prison, he used meth intravenously at least once per month until he got clean in 1997. In 2004, he committed another bank robbery, this time in Utah, for which he served five years in prison (until 2009) and three years on supervised release (until 2012). During the years when Mr. Walker was not incarcerated, he was convicted of several felony drug possession charges and misdemeanor DUI/intoxication charges. From April 2009 through 2012, Mr. Walker successfully completed a term of supervised release and was apparently clean for three years, but he relapsed on meth in 2013. After completing Teen Challenge in June 2015, Mr. Walker had been clean from all substances for nearly two years.

At sentencing, Mr. Walker first objected to the career offender enhancement in the PSR, but, after hearing argument from the parties, the court found that the enhancement applied. The court accepted the PSR and calculated Mr. Walker's total offense level at 29 and criminal history category at VI (with or without the career offender enhancement), resulting in a Guideline range of 151 to 188 months. . . .

On resentencing, the court has received additional evidence spanning from Mr. Walker's commission of the two bank robberies in May 2013 through his pretrial/post-release conduct as of April 2017.

First, the Probation Office submitted a Supplemental Memorandum to the PSR. Probation Officer Renee Lewis stated that since the September 2015 sentencing, Mr. Walker has been supervised in the Northern District of Ohio. His supervising probation officer in Ohio, Adam Jones, reported that Mr. Walker has complied with all conditions of supervision, including maintaining employment, paying restitution monthly, and completing random drug testing with no positive results. Mr. Walker works for R.B.P. One, Inc. as a painter and has earned several raises. He and his wife live a modest life, and he continues to work on restoring his relationships with his siblings and children. Mr. Walker also continues to see a mental health counselor once a month and has remained sober with no relapses. He attends church, self-improvement classes offered by his church, and

Alcoholics Anonymous (AA) meetings. He has led several AA groups, which have given him the opportunity to speak about his experiences and sobriety.

The court also received a written statement from Angie Skinner, Mr. Walker's court-ordered mental health counselor and a Licensed Clinical Christian Counselor. Ms. Skinner reports that Mr. Walker has made "significant improvement in every area of his life and has taken his recovery very seriously." She reports that he has been clean since April 29, 2014, and that he no longer has cravings for drugs or alcohol. Mr. Walker got married on December 31, 2015. Ms. Skinner considers him "a contributing member of society" who "provides for his family and is a faithful husband and father." Along with the church and AA meetings, Mr. Walker has completed volunteer work at his church, including painting and repairs. . . .

Chanelle Torgerson was the first victim to testify. Ms. Torgerson worked for U.S. Bank as a head teller on May 3, 2013, during the robbery. When Mr. Walker entered the bank screaming, Ms. Torgerson thought he was a grumpy customer and approached him to try to diffuse the situation. Mr. Walker, who was dressed as a construction worker and had what looked like a soft cooler bag with him, was yelling "top and bottom, top and bottom" at another teller named Austin. When Ms. Torgerson realized that this was a robbery, she began handing him the money in her top and bottom drawers, including a tracker. She described Mr. Walker as ignorant and confused, and reported to officers afterwards that he was high and "not himself." She did not like how he was screaming and being disrespectful toward them. Mr. Walker kept screaming for more money, and Ms. Torgerson kept saying her drawers were empty, at which point Mr. Walker left. Ms. Torgerson had never been part of a robbery before, and she testified that it has affected her life "a little bit." She continued: "When I go into the bank, I have to be more paranoid now that this trial has been back up and everyone is bringing it back up, like, I have anxiety when I see construction workers. I know it's weird, but it happens." A counselor spoke to the employees the Monday after the robbery, but Ms. Torgerson has not sought counseling since. Ms. Torgerson felt that the contact brought about by the resentencing had re-opened some of the experiences associated with the robbery. . . .

Under section 3553(a)(2)(B), the court is to consider the need to deter the defendant and others. *Walker,* 844 F.3d at 1257. The Tenth Circuit found this court's prior conclusion that imprisonment was unnecessary to deter Mr. Walker reasonable. *Id.* The court again finds Mr. Walker is not currently a threat to the public and that the evidence shows no further need to deter him.

"[E]xemplary postsentencing conduct may be taken as the most accurate indicator of '[a defendant's] present purposes and tendencies and significantly to suggest the period of restraint and the kind of discipline that ought to be imposed upon him.' " *Pepper*, 562 U.S. at 492–93, 131 S.Ct. 1229 (quoting *Pennsylvania ex rel. Sullivan v. Ashe*, 302 U.S. 51, 55, 58 S.Ct. 59, 82 L.Ed. 43 (1937)). Mr. Jones, Mr. Walker's probation officer, reports that Mr. Walker has been compliant with all terms of supervised release for the past three years, both before and after the prior sentencing. Mr. Walker stresses that he has changed, and that the "old," drug-addicted John Walker is finally gone. Evidence from every person around Mr. Walker, from his family to his community to his mental health counselor and probation officer, uniformly and amply supports this conclusion. The court can very clearly tie Mr. Walker's self-rehabilitation to an identifiable source (Teen Challenge) that is extremely successful at producing individuals who remain clean and sober. Twenty years of prison sentences failed to accomplish the deterrence achieved by a self-motivated defendant and a tough, yet effective treatment program.

Even if the court were not to accept Mr. Walker's representations—though the court can find no evidence to undercut them—and the government is correct that only a looming prison sentence motivates Mr. Walker's recovery and good behavior, such logic suggests that a probation sentence with looming prison time upon any violation would more effectively and efficiently effect the purposes of deterrence. Incarceration, on the other hand, would appear to undermine that self-motivated recovery and may even increase the likelihood of Mr. Walker's reoffending in the future. . . .

The Sentencing Commission also found that half of offenders (including career offenders) were rearrested in less than two years following their initial release from prison or placement on probation, and that fewer individuals were rearrested in each subsequent year following release. Mr. Walker is now going on four years without rearrest. Approximately 4.7% of offenders are rearrested in their fourth year following release. But Mr. Walker is categorized as a career offender, and the Commission noted that career offenders and armed career criminals have a higher rearrest rate than other offenders (69.5% compared to 48.7%) and that offenders committing robbery are some of the most likely to be rearrested (67.3%).

These data, while conflicting, confirm that Mr. Walker has a greater risk of reoffending than most, a reality also substantiated by his history of addiction and criminal history. There is also evidence in the record, however, that contradicts these statistics. Mr. Jones testified that Mr. Walker's PCRA measures him at a low to moderate risk of recidivism and that Mr. Walker's criminal history, because it is a static factor, may be keeping him at that level. In addition, Mr. Walker's enormous recovery and demonstrated changes in mindset and behavior strongly suggest Mr. Walker has finally broken the iterative loop of addiction-crime-incarceration and that sending Mr. Walker back to prison for another ten years will not achieve any deterrent effect at this point. The Commission found that offenders sentenced to probation had a lower rearrest rate than those sentenced to imprisonment (35.1% compared with 52.5%), while the highest recidivism rates were associated with offenders receiving longer sentences. While a term of incarceration will certainly incapacitate and punish Mr. Walker, the court finds that it will do little to deter Mr. Walker from committing future robberies and may actually precipitate a relapse into addiction and crime. *See* NIJ, *Five Things* ("Prison is an important option for incapacitating and punishing those who commit crimes, but the data show long prison sentences do little to deter people from committing future crimes.").

Additionally, the court finds Mr. Walker's improved familial relationships and relationships with his community also support the lack of any need to further deter Mr. Walker at this point. Studies show that supportive family connections predict reduced recidivism, while breaking up families leads to increased recidivism. Kimberly Bahna, *"It's a Family Affair"—The Incarceration of the American Family: Confronting Legal and Social Issues,* 28 U.S.F. L. Rev. 271, 275 (1994). . . . Courts have considered family ties important to sentencing decisions. In the Commission's 2010 survey of United States district judges, 62% said that family ties and responsibilities are "ordinarily relevant" to the consideration of a departure or variance. U.S.S.C., *Results of Survey of United States District Judges January 2010 through March 2010,* Table 13 (June 2010). . . . In 2003, a majority of district court judges surveyed indicated that more emphasis was needed on (1) age; (2) mental condition; and (3) family ties and responsibilities. *See* Linda Drazga Maxfield, Office of Policy Analysis, U.S.S.C., *Final Report: Survey of Article III Judges on the Federal Sentencing Guidelines,* Chapter II B. 2. (Mar. 2003). . .

In sum, the court finds incarcerating Mr. Walker and removing him from the strong system of support and accountability that he has built around himself would not measurably deter him and would more likely cause a backslide into relapse, and thus further criminal conduct, than a probationary sentence. *See United States v. Rodriguez,* 724 F.Supp. 1118, 1119 (S.D.N.Y. 1989) ("The imposition of a year's jail sentence would serve no end, but ritualistic punishment with a high potential for destruction. Indeed, putting the defendant in jail for a year would be the cause most likely to undo his rehabilitation.").

But individual deterrence is only one side of the deterrence analysis. Sentencing courts need also consider the deterrent effect a sentence of incarceration for this crime will have on others. As the Tenth Circuit noted, "[g]eneral deterrence . . . is one of the key purposes of sentencing . . ." *Walker,* 844 F.3d at 1257 (quoting *United States v. Medearis,* 451 F.3d 918, 920 (8th Cir. 2006)); *see also United States v. Milo,* 506 F.3d 71, 76 (1st Cir. 2007) ("The need to deter others is under federal law a major element in criminal sentencing."). Beyond these general statements, however, the court finds the recent research shows general deterrence is more effectively accomplished in circumstances already addressed in, or less applicable to, this case.

Because theories of deterrence involve the attempt to induce crime-eschewing behavior in response to the threat of punishment, researchers (and courts) have attempted to better understand the circumstances in which deterrence is and is not effective. The NIJ, culling from Professor Nagin's 2013 article summarizing the current state of theory and empirical knowledge about deterrence, states that sending a convicted individual to prison is not a very effective way to deter crime and that increasing the severity of punishment does little to deter crime. *See* NIJ, *Five Things.*

Nagin states the conclusion more precisely: is it the "*certainty of apprehension* and not the severity of the legal consequence ensuing from apprehension" that is a more effective deterrent. Daniel S. Nagin, *Deterrence in the Twenty-First Century*, Crime and Justice in America: 1975–2025, at 202 (2013) [hereinafter *Deterrence*]. Nagin also concludes that "there is little evidence that increases in the length of already long prison sentences yield general deterrent effects that are sufficiently large to justify their social and economic costs." *Id.* at 201. Inherent in this statement, as the NIJ and the government also point out, is that short to moderate prison sentences may still be a deterrent. But "it is clear that lengthy prison sentences cannot be justified on a deterrence-based, crime prevention basis." *Id.* at 202.

These conclusions acknowledge at least some delusion in the concept that severe punishment effects general deterrence. The court does not doubt that incarceration has some general deterrent effect; however, this effect does not work on the level of precision that a sentencing court must in crafting sentences that truly effectuate sentencing purposes. For example, would the public, including would-be defendants, be more deterred by a sentence of 12 months incarceration, or 60 months, or 120 months? Most of the public is unaware of how harsh federal sentences can be, which suggests that the incremental severity of sentence does not act as an effective general deterrent. *See* Nagin, *Deterrence* at 204 ("Not surprisingly, the surveys find that knowledge of sanction regimes is poor. . . . [F]or individuals for whom sanction threats might affect their behavior, it is preposterous to assume that their perceptions conform to the realities of the legally available sanction options and their administration."). According to Nagin, the more effective general deterrence comes from better visibility of policing, which increases certainty of punishment, rather than increasing the severity of punishment on the back end. *See id.*at 201, 252–53.

Moreover, current theories of deterrence are inconclusive on the differential deterrent effects of different sanctions, e.g., imprisonment versus probation. *See id.*at 253 ("Theories of deterrence, however, specify sanction threats in the singular, not in the plural. Theories of deterrence that conceive of sanctions in the singular do not provide the conceptual basis for considering the differential deterrent effect of different types of sanction options."). Nagin concludes that lengthy prison sentences can only be justified on retributive grounds:

> [These conclusions] suggest that lengthy prison sentences cannot be justified on deterrent grounds, but rather must be justified either on crime prevention through incapacitation or on retributive grounds. The crime prevention efficiency of incapacitating aged criminals is dubious, and thus the case for lengthy prison sentences must rest on retributive considerations.

Id. If the general deterrent effect of different sanctions is indeterminate, and lengthy imprisonment simply calls back the purposes of retribution, the court cannot reasonably conclude that a lengthy term of imprisonment in this case will effectuate the specific purpose of general deterrence.

Finally, courts recognize that general deterrence is more effective in certain contexts. In *United States v. Musgrave*, 761 F.3d 602 (6th Cir.2014), the Sixth Circuit identified white-collar crime as "especially susceptible to general deterrence." *Id.* at 609. "Because economic and fraud-based crimes are more rational, cool, and calculated than sudden crimes of passion or opportunity, these crimes are prime candidates for general deterrence." *Id.* (quoting *United States v. Peppel*, 707 F.3d 627, 637 (6th Cir. 2013)). As discussed previously, addiction induces irrational behavior, and robbery is a particularly irrational crime. "[S]everity of punishment clearly continues to have some deterrent effect—albeit less than it would were the universe of potential criminals an overall rational bunch." *United States v. Courtney*, 76 F.Supp.3d 1267, 1304 n.13 (D.N.M. 2014). . . . Drug-addicted bank robbers are a less-than rational bunch, and the court finds the effect on general deterrence of sending Mr. Walker away for a lengthy period of incarceration is marginal in this context. Neither Mr. Walker's crime nor his sentence is likely to be highly publicized. The chance that a would-be bank robber would learn of Mr. Walker's sentence of probation and, by that information, be less deterred from robbing a bank, thinking he would only receive a sentence of probation, is so remote as to defy any meaningful conclusion that this case requires a longer, custody sentence.

Consideration of general deterrence "becomes particularly important when the district court varies substantially from the sentencing guidelines." *Walker*, 844 F.3d at 1258. The court has considered general deterrence and finds the evidence is, at best, inconclusive as to whether a lengthy term of imprisonment of Mr. Walker would provide any deterrent effect. Matched with the finding that there is no need for specific deterrence in Mr. Walker's case, the court finds that the purposes of deterrence are well-served by a probationary sentence. . . .

CONCLUSION

Overall, the court finds the balance of sentencing factors weighs toward a substantial variance from the Guideline range and toward a non-custody sentence in this case. The nature of the offense and Mr. Walker's criminal history weigh strongly toward incarceration. "Just punishment" also weighs toward incarceration, but less so than in other cases because Mr. Walker's lifelong addiction mitigates the underlying purpose of retribution. The court does not find that a custody sentence would promote respect for the law in light of Mr. Walker's significant recovery efforts. Further, the goals of incapacitation and general deterrence appear to be indeterminate in this case and, when combined with the lack of any concern for specific deterrence here, they point no more strongly toward incarceration than a noncustodial sentence. The need for restitution weighs slightly away from incarceration. And the extraordinary circumstances of Mr. Walker's current characteristics and rehabilitation weigh strongly against incarceration. Finally, the need to avoid sentencing disparities weighs toward incarceration, but the court finds any disparities warranted in these circumstances.,,,

For these reasons, the court sentences Mr. Walker to ten years of probation, with a mandatory review in five years, two years of home confinement, 500 hours of community service, and restitution, with the requirements and other details to be set forth in the Amended Judgment.

EXERCISE

The opinion above cites to the theory that certainty of conviction—that is, of getting caught—is more important than length of sentence in creating deterrence. If this is true, how should we change our allocation of resources devoted to criminal law, and what negative consequences might that shift create?

In considering general deterrence, one factor may be the prevalence of that crime in the community. If there is more crime, there is both more of a need (and more of an opportunity) to deter people from choosing to commit crimes.

UNITED STATES V. FUENTES-ECHEVARRIA

856 F.3d 22 (1st Cir. 2017)

HOWARD, CHIEF JUDGE.

Raymond Fuentes-Echevarria challenges the procedural reasonableness of a forty-eight-month sentence imposed following his guilty plea for illegal possession of a machine gun. He also brings an ineffective assistance of counsel claim. After careful consideration, we affirm his sentence and dismiss his ineffective assistance claim without prejudice.

I.

On September 15, 2014, police officers stopped Fuentes, who was driving his Honda Accord in reverse in the middle of a street, near a known drug trafficking point in San Juan, Puerto Rico. While one officer issued a ticket to Fuentes, a canine trained to detect narcotics, accompanied by another officer, marked two separate locations on Fuentes's vehicle. Fuentes fled the scene and was not arrested.

Officers subsequently sealed Fuentes's vehicle, transported it to police headquarters, and obtained a search warrant. A subsequent search of the vehicle revealed a secret compartment near the center of the dashboard. From the compartment, officers seized a .40 Glock pistol modified to fire automatically, several gun magazines, and 108 rounds of ammunition. On September 18, 2014, a grand jury returned a sealed indictment charging Fuentes with illegal possession of a machine gun, in violation of 18 U.S.C. § 922(o) and § 924(a)(2).

Fuentes was arrested about a year later, in July 2015. He initially pled not guilty, and a trial was scheduled. But he ultimately moved to change his plea mere days before the trial was set to begin, and entered a straight plea—that is, without a plea agreement—to the sole charge in the indictment.

Fuentes's Presentence Report ("PSR"), to which he did not object, indicated that his criminal history category was I, and that his Base Offense Level ("BOL") was eighteen, pursuant to U.S.S.G. § 2K2.1(a)(5). However, because Fuentes accepted responsibility, his total offense level ("TOL") was reduced to sixteen, see U.S.S.G. § 3.E1.1(a), thus setting the applicable Guidelines Sentencing Range ("GSR") at twenty-one to twenty-seven months. At the sentencing hearing, Fuentes recommended a bottom-of-the-GSR sentence of twenty-one months, while the government asked for sixty.

After reviewing the facts of this case and expressing a heightened need for community deterrence, the judge sentenced Fuentes to forty-eight months' imprisonment, followed by thirty-six months of supervised release.

On appeal, Fuentes challenges the reasonableness of his sentence on two grounds. He contends that the district court erred by failing to apply an additional one-level reduction to his TOL for acceptance of responsibility under § 3E1.1(b). He also argues that the district court's reliance on certain community factors did not justify the upward variance. Finally, Fuentes brings an ineffective assistance of counsel claim. We address each in turn. . . .

... we proceed to Fuentes's next challenge, which he preserved below. Fuentes maintains that the court's decision to impose a forty-eight-month variant sentence "lacked factual support," because it was heavily premised on the court's concern with "general violence" in the community. For instance, he points to the sentencing court's statement that it was "sick and tired of violent crimes and guns." He posits that the court went "too far" in "speculat[ing] about the lives of violent criminals," at the expense of failing to consider facts specific to his case.

When a court imposes a variant sentence, "its reasons for doing so 'should typically be rooted either in the nature and circumstances of the offense or the characteristics of the offender.'" United States v. Flores-Machicote, 706 F.3d 16, 21 (1st Cir. 2013) (quoting Martin, 520 F.3d at 91). While Fuentes is correct that the court had an eye towards community deterrence in fashioning his sentence, we have "repeatedly" explained that "[d]eterrence is widely recognized as an important factor in the sentencing calculus." United States v. Díaz-Arroyo, 797 F.3d 125, 129 (1st Cir. 2015) (quoting Flores-Machicote, 706 F.3d at 23) (alteration in original); see also 18 U.S.C. § 3553(a)(2)(B). Indeed, community context can "inform[ ] and contextualize[ ] the relevant need for deterrence." Flores-Machicote, 706 F.3d at 23. The district court did not abuse its discretion by allowing its assessment that there was an "arsenal [of weapons] out there in the streets" to bear on its conclusion that a strong deterrent was warranted in this case.

Although "[i]t is possible for a sentencing judge to focus too much on the community and too little on the individual," id. at 24, that did not happen here. The sentencing court identified several case-specific factors, beyond the need for general deterrence, to support its view that Fuentes's offense was "out of line with a heartland case" for which the calculated GSR would have been appropriate. Among these were the fact that Fuentes's modified firearm was housed in a secret compartment, and that it was found with extended magazines and 108 rounds of ammunition, some of which was suitable for an AK-47 rifle. Moreover, the court found it significant that Fuentes's traffic stop occurred near a known drug trafficking area, and that he fled the scene. The sentencing judge's discussion of these case-specific facts blunts Fuentes's claim that community factors improperly shaded his variant sentence.

EXERCISE

You are a federal prosecutor. Your community has suddenly seen an influx of a particularly potent and dangerous kind of heroin. Overdose deaths doubled (from 12 to 24 a month) in the course of two months after this new type of heroin appeared. Because it is being distributed in a particularly furtive way, only one seller of the new type of heroin has been identified. His name is Harley Reince, and you are assigned to his case.

The investigation reveals that Mr. Reince is 25 and has been addicted to heroin for about three years. According to an informant, Reince was in debt to his supplier and agreed to sell the new heroin product on the street in exchange for a forgiveness of his debt. You and the investigators have pressed Mr. Reince to provide information on his supplier, but he has steadfastly refused and you have no other leads.

Mr. Reince is convicted at trial of distributing heroin. At sentencing, will you ask for an above-guideline sentence based on the need for deterrence?

C. INCAPACITATION

The theory of incapacitation directs that a sentence be crafted so as to "protect the public from further crimes of the defendant," according to 18 U.S.C. § 3553(a)(2)(C). The most common way to achieve incapacitation is through incarceration, though execution achieves the goal with greater certainty. As theory, it is fairly simple: an incarcerated person cannot harm those outside of the prison walls.

In their 1995 book *Incapacitation: Penal Confinement and the Restraint of Crime*, Franklin E. Zimring and Gordon Hawkins begin by laying out the current state of this idea:

Incapacitation now serves as the principal justification for imprisonment in American criminal justice: offenders are imprisoned in the United States to restrain them physically from offending again while they are confined. The singular importance of incapacitation as a purpose of imprisonment is of relatively recent vintage. In the 1970's, the rhetoric of rehabilitation was a dominant feature of the literature and discussion of imprisonment, and the deterrence justification was more prominent than incapacitation in debates about punishment. It is only in the last 15 years that something approaching a consensus about its priority of restraint has begun to emerge.

Not only is the dominance of incapacitation a recent phenomenon, it is based on almost unexamined principles. Neither the arguments in support of using incapacitation simply to restrain the offender nor the evidence to support the proposition that such incapacitation lowers community crime rates has been subjected to careful scrutiny or detailed analysis.

Two sentence types in particular are often supported through appeals to society's interest in the incapacitation of particularly dangerous people: execution, and life without the possibility of parole. With the imposition of these sentences, there is total or near-total incapacitation, reflecting a complete absence of hope that the defendant can change his or her behavior. That conclusion can be troubling when the defendant is very young.

GRAHAM V. FLORIDA
560 U.S. 48 (2010)

JUSTICE KENNEDY delivered the opinion of the Court.

The issue before the Court is whether the Constitution permits a juvenile offender to be sentenced to life in prison without parole for a nonhomicide crime. The sentence was imposed by the State of Florida. Petitioner challenges the sentence under the Eighth Amendment's Cruel and Unusual Punishments Clause, made applicable to the States by the Due Process Clause of the Fourteenth Amendment. *Robinson v. California,* 370 U.S. 660, 82 S.Ct. 1417, 8 L.Ed.2d 758 (1962).

I

Petitioner is Terrance Jamar Graham. He was born on January 6, 1987. Graham's parents were addicted to crack cocaine, and their drug use persisted in his early years. Graham was diagnosed with attention deficit hyperactivity disorder in elementary school. He began drinking alcohol and using tobacco at age 9 and smoked marijuana at age 13.

In July 2003, when Graham was age 16, he and three other school-age youths attempted to rob a barbeque restaurant in Jacksonville, Florida. One youth, who worked at the restaurant, left the back door unlocked just before closing time. Graham and another youth, wearing masks, entered through the unlocked door. Graham's masked accomplice twice struck the restaurant manager in the back of the head with a metal bar. When the manager started yelling at the assailant and Graham, the two youths ran out and escaped in a car driven by the third accomplice. The restaurant manager required stitches for his head injury. No money was taken.

Graham was arrested for the robbery attempt. Under Florida law, it is within a prosecutor's discretion whether to charge 16- and 17-year-olds as adults or juveniles for most felony crimes. Fla. Stat. § 985.227(1)(b) (2003) (subsequently renumbered at § 985.557(1)(b) (2007)). Graham's prosecutor elected to charge Graham as an adult. The charges against Graham were armed burglary with assault or battery, a first-degree felony carrying a maximum penalty of life imprisonment without the possibility of parole, §§ 810.02(1)(b), (2)(a) (2003); and attempted armed robbery, a second-degree felony carrying a maximum penalty of 15 years' imprisonment, §§ 812.13(2)(b), 777.04(1), (4)(a), 775.082(3)(c).

On December 18, 2003, Graham pleaded guilty to both charges under a plea agreement. Graham wrote a letter to the trial court. After reciting "this is my first and last time getting in trouble," he continued "I've decided to turn my life around." App. 379–380. Graham said "I made a promise to

God and myself that if I get a second chance, I'm going to do whatever it takes to get to the [National Football League]." *Id.,* at 380.

The trial court accepted the plea agreement. The court withheld adjudication of guilt as to both charges and sentenced Graham to concurrent 3-year terms of probation. Graham was required to spend the first 12 months of his probation in the county jail, but he received credit for the time he had served awaiting trial, and was released on June 25, 2004.

Less than 6 months later, on the night of December 2, 2004, Graham again was arrested. The State's case was as follows: Earlier that evening, Graham participated in a home invasion robbery. His two accomplices were Meigo Bailey and Kirkland Lawrence, both 20-year-old men. According to the State, at 7 p.m. that night, Graham, Bailey, and Lawrence knocked on the door of the home where Carlos Rodriguez lived. Graham, followed by Bailey and Lawrence, forcibly entered the home and held a pistol to Rodriguez's chest. For the next 30 minutes, the three held Rodriguez and another man, a friend of Rodriguez, at gunpoint while they ransacked the home searching for money. Before leaving, Graham and his accomplices barricaded Rodriguez and his friend inside a closet.

The State further alleged that Graham, Bailey, and Lawrence, later the same evening, attempted a second robbery, during which Bailey was shot.

Graham, who had borrowed his father's car, drove Bailey and Lawrence to the hospital and left them there. As Graham drove away, a police sergeant signaled him to stop. Graham continued at a high speed but crashed into a telephone pole. He tried to flee on foot but was apprehended. Three handguns were found in his car.

When detectives interviewed Graham, he denied involvement in the crimes. He said he encountered Bailey and Lawrence only after Bailey had been shot. One of the detectives told Graham that the victims of the home invasion had identified him. He asked Graham, "Aside from the two robberies tonight how many more were you involved in?" Graham responded, "Two to three before tonight." *Id.,* at 160. The night that Graham allegedly committed the robbery, he was 34 days short of his 18th birthday.

On December 13, 2004, Graham's probation officer filed with the trial court an affidavit asserting that Graham had violated the conditions of his probation by possessing a firearm, committing crimes, and associating with persons engaged in criminal activity. The trial court held hearings on Graham's violations about a year later, in December 2005 and January 2006. The judge who presided was not the same judge who had accepted Graham's guilty plea to the earlier offenses.

Graham maintained that he had no involvement in the home invasion robbery; but, even after the court underscored that the admission could expose him to a life sentence on the earlier charges, he admitted violating probation conditions by fleeing. The State presented evidence related to the home invasion, including testimony from the victims. The trial court noted that Graham, in admitting his attempt to avoid arrest, had acknowledged violating his probation. The court further found that Graham had violated his probation by committing a home invasion robbery, by possessing a firearm, and by associating with persons engaged in criminal activity.

The trial court held a sentencing hearing. Under Florida law the minimum sentence Graham could receive absent a downward departure by the judge was 5 years' imprisonment. The maximum was life imprisonment. Graham's attorney requested the minimum nondeparture sentence of 5 years. A presentence report prepared by the Florida Department of Corrections recommended that Graham receive an even lower sentence—at most 4 years' imprisonment. The State recommended that Graham receive 30 years on the armed burglary count and 15 years on the attempted armed robbery count.

After hearing Graham's testimony, the trial court explained the sentence it was about to pronounce:

> Mr. Graham, as I look back on your case, yours is really candidly a sad situation. You had, as far as I can tell, you have quite a family structure. You had a lot of people who wanted to try and help you get your life turned around including the court system, and you had a judge who took the step to try and give you direction through his probation order to give you a chance to get back onto track. And at the time you seemed through your letters that that is exactly what you wanted to do. And I don't know why it is that you threw your life away. I don't know why. . . .

> "So then it becomes a focus, if I can't do anything to help you, if I can't do anything to get you back on the right path, then I have to start focusing on the community and trying to protect the community from your actions. And, unfortunately, that is where we are today is I don't see where I can do anything to help you any further. You've evidently decided this is the direction you're going to take in life, and it's unfortunate that you made that choice.

> "I have reviewed the statute. I don't see where any further juvenile sanctions would be appropriate. I don't see where any youthful offender sanctions would be appropriate. Given your escalating pattern of criminal conduct, it is apparent to the Court that you have decided that this is the way you are going to live your life and that the only thing I can do now is to try and protect the community from your actions.

The trial court found Graham guilty of the earlier armed burglary and attempted armed robbery charges. It sentenced him to the maximum sentence authorized by law on each charge: life imprisonment for the armed burglary and 15 years for the attempted armed robbery. Because Florida has abolished its parole system, see Fla. Stat. § 921.002(1)(e) (2003), a life sentence gives a defendant no possibility of release unless he is granted executive clemency. . . .

In cases turning on the characteristics of the offender, the Court has adopted categorical rules prohibiting the death penalty for defendants who committed their crimes before the age of 18, *Roper v. Simmons,* 543 U.S. 551, 125 S.Ct. 1183, 161 L.Ed.2d 1 (2005), or whose intellectual functioning is in a low range, *Atkins v. Virginia,* 536 U.S. 304, 122 S.Ct. 2242, 153 L.Ed.2d 335 (2002). . . .

Roper established that because juveniles have lessened culpability they are less deserving of the most severe punishments. 543 U.S., at 569, 125 S.Ct. 1183. As compared to adults, juveniles have a " 'lack of maturity and an underdeveloped sense of responsibility' "; they "are more vulnerable or susceptible to negative influences and outside pressures, including peer pressure"; and their characters are "not as well formed." *Id.,* at 569–570, 125 S.Ct. 1183. These salient characteristics mean that "[i]t is difficult even for expert psychologists to differentiate between the juvenile offender whose crime reflects unfortunate yet transient immaturity, and the rare juvenile offender whose crime reflects irreparable corruption." *Id.,* at 573, 125 S.Ct. 1183. Accordingly, "juvenile offenders cannot with reliability be classified among the worst offenders." *Id.,* at 569, 125 S.Ct. 1183. A juvenile is not absolved of responsibility for his actions, but his transgression "is not as morally reprehensible as that of an adult." *Thompson, supra,* at 835, 108 S.Ct. 2687 (plurality opinion).

No recent data provide reason to reconsider the Court's observations in *Roper* about the nature of juveniles. As petitioner's *amici* point out, developments in psychology and brain science continue to show fundamental differences between juvenile and adult minds. For example, parts of the brain involved in behavior control continue to mature through late adolescence. See Brief for American Medical Association et al. as *Amici Curiae* 16–24; Brief for American Psychological Association et al. as *Amici Curiae* 22–27. Juveniles are more capable of change than are adults, and their actions are less likely to be evidence of "irretrievably depraved character" than are the actions of adults. *Roper,* 543 U.S., at 570, 125 S.Ct. 1183. It remains true that "[f]rom a moral standpoint it would be misguided to equate the failings of a minor with those of an adult, for a greater possibility exists that a minor's character deficiencies will be reformed." *Ibid.* These matters relate to the status of the offenders in question; and it is relevant to consider next the nature of the offenses to which this harsh penalty might apply. . . .

With respect to life without parole for juvenile nonhomicide offenders, none of the goals of penal sanctions that have been recognized as legitimate— retribution, deterrence, incapacitation, and rehabilitation, see *Ewing,* 538

U.S., at 25, 123 S.Ct. 1179 (plurality opinion)—provides an adequate justification. . . .

Incapacitation, a third legitimate reason for imprisonment, does not justify the life without parole sentence in question here. Recidivism is a serious risk to public safety, and so incapacitation is an important goal. See *Ewing, supra,* at 26, 123 S.Ct. 1179 (plurality opinion) (statistics show 67 percent of former inmates released from state prisons are charged with at least one serious new crime within three years). But while incapacitation may be a legitimate penological goal sufficient to justify life without parole in other contexts, it is inadequate to justify that punishment for juveniles who did not commit homicide. To justify life without parole on the assumption that the juvenile offender forever will be a danger to society requires the sentencer to make a judgment that the juvenile is incorrigible. The characteristics of juveniles make that judgment questionable. "It is difficult even for expert psychologists to differentiate between the juvenile offender whose crime reflects unfortunate yet transient immaturity, and the rare juvenile offender whose crime reflects irreparable corruption." *Roper, supra,* at 572, 125 S.Ct. 1183. As one court concluded in a challenge to a life without parole sentence for a 14-year-old, "incorrigibility is inconsistent with youth." *Workman v. Commonwealth,* 429 S.W.2d 374, 378 (Ky.1968).

Here one cannot dispute that this defendant posed an immediate risk, for he had committed, we can assume, serious crimes early in his term of supervised release and despite his own assurances of reform. Graham deserved to be separated from society for some time in order to prevent what the trial court described as an "escalating pattern of criminal conduct," App. 394, but it does not follow that he would be a risk to society for the rest of his life. Even if the State's judgment that Graham was incorrigible were later corroborated by prison misbehavior or failure to mature, the sentence was still disproportionate because that judgment was made at the outset. A life without parole sentence improperly denies the juvenile offender a chance to demonstrate growth and maturity. Incapacitation cannot override all other considerations, lest the Eighth Amendment's rule against disproportionate sentences be a nullity.

The Constitution prohibits the imposition of a life without parole sentence on a juvenile offender who did not commit homicide. A State need not guarantee the offender eventual release, but if it imposes a sentence of life it must provide him or her with some realistic opportunity to obtain release before the end of that term. The judgment of the First District Court of Appeal of Florida is reversed, and the case is remanded for further proceedings not inconsistent with this opinion.

It is so ordered.

EXERCISE

Larry Faust is a 30-year-old man with long history of bipolar disorder and criminal behavior. He has three prior crimes of violence (two aggravated assaults and a simple assault) and two serious cocaine trafficking convictions. You are a sentencing judge, and Faust is before you having been convicted at trial of selling cocaine in the parking lot of a high school.

The government is seeking a life sentence, and there is no parole in the federal system. They rely on testimony from an expert witness they called at sentencing, a psychiatrist who asserted that Faust is a "sociopath" who will always commit serious crimes and resists treatment for his mental illness. On cross examination, the expert is asked if Faust is likely to kill if he receives a sentence that allows for freedom in his lifetime and the expert responded "probably not."

As the trial judge, you can issue any sentence up to life in prison. Is a life sentence for Faust justified by the goal of incapacitation?

D. REHABILITATION

18 U.S.C. § 3553(a)(2)(D) requires judges to consider certain types of rehabilitative possibilities when sentencing a defendant, mandating that a judge "consider. . . the need for the sentence imposed. . . to provide the defendant with needed educational or vocational training, medical care, or other correctional treatment in the most effective manner. . . ."

While rehabilitation has lost its position as a primary focus at sentencing, it still weighs into the considerations of decision-makers within criminal law.

UNITED STATES V. BANNISTER
786 F.Supp.2d 617 (E.D.NY 2011)

JACK B. WEINSTEIN, DISTRICT JUDGE. . .

Almost filling the jury box were the defendants—Damien Bannister, Darrell Bannister, Christopher Hall, Cyril McCray, Eric Morris, Roger Patrick, James Ross, Derrick Tatum, Indio Tatum, Jawara Tatum, and Pedro Torres—eleven males, ranging in age from twenty-one to forty-nine, ten African American and one Hispanic. Fully occupying the well of the court were counsel for the defendants, assistant United States attorneys, agents of the Federal Bureau of Investigation, and a phalanx of United States Marshals. Jammed into the gallery were defendants' anxious mothers, girlfriends, other family members, and friends.

The indictment embraced twenty-three counts connected by a conspiracy to sell, and the selling of, crack cocaine and heroin in the hallways of, and the streets surrounding, a public housing project in Brooklyn between September 2007 and January 2010. Guns were carried. The lives of the residents were made miserable by the attendant depravity and violence. These were serious crimes.

The unspoken questions permeating the courtroom were: How did these eleven come to this pass, and what should be done with them if they were convicted, as all of them eventually were, by guilty pleas? Some of the unsatisfactory answers in such all-too-frequent urban tragedies are discussed in the memorandum that follows.

The issue of what should be done about these defendants, and others like them, is central to the law's rationale for the heavy mandatory minimum incarceratory sentences being imposed in this case. For a number of the defendants, they are much heavier than are appropriate. One of our most thoughtful jurists reminds us, "[o]ur resources are misspent, our punishments too severe, our sentences too long." Justice Anthony M. Kennedy, Address at the American Bar Association Annual Meeting, San Francisco, Ca. (Aug. 9, 2003).

As a group, defendants grew up in dysfunctional homes characterized by a combination of poverty, unemployment, undereducation, crime, addiction to drugs and alcohol, physical and emotional abuse, and the absence of an adult male role model. They attended low-functioning public schools with limited resources to help students with their in- and out-of-school difficulties. Most dropped out of school, habitually abused drugs and alcohol from an early age, and found little lawful employment. They became involved in a gang of illegal narcotics distributors, which turned to guns and violence, contributing to the degradation of their community.

While the defendants are before this court because of choices they themselves have made, the limited options available to them are partly the fixed artifacts of history. Their story begins hundreds of years ago with the enslavement of African Americans. It runs through Reconstruction, Jim Crow, northward migration, *de jure* and *de facto* segregation, decades of neglect, and intermittent improvement efforts by government and others.

Protection of the public requires serious terms of incarceration. But enforcement of the harsh mandatory minimum sentences required by Congress imposes longer terms of imprisonment than are necessary. Such long years of incarceration and separation from relatives generally increase the likelihood of further crime by these defendants and their children.

Nevertheless, strong efforts will be made by the Bureau of Prisons to help educate the defendants and provide occupational training. Drug and alcohol treatment will be made available. Upon their release from prison, the court's probation service will provide strict, day-to-day supervision and assist in attempts to obtain essential jobs. . . .

The effectiveness of prisons as places for maximum rehabilitation is called into question by high rates of recidivism. "More than 40 percent of murders and robberies are committed by people on probation, parole, or pretrial release." Kleiman, *supra,* at A5. A 2002 study of 272,111 former state prisoners in fifteen states indicated high rates of recidivism within three years of release from prison: 68 percent were rearrested for new offenses, almost exclusively felonies and serious misdemeanors; 52 percent were returned to prison for new offenses or technical violations; 47 percent were convicted of new offenses; and 25 percent were resentenced to prison for new offenses. Patrick A. Langan & David J. Levin, Bureau of Justice Stat., Dep't of Justice, *Recidivism of Prisoners Released in 1994* 1 (2002). Thirty percent of ex-convicts were arrested for a serious offense in the first six months after release. *Id.* at 3.

Demographic data correlate with higher risks of recidivism. In the 2002 study, men were more likely to be rearrested than women (68 percent versus 58 percent) and African Americans more than Whites (73 percent versus 63 percent). *Id.* at 7. The risk of recidivism is inversely correlated with age; prisoners released as teenagers were those most likely to be rearrested or reconvicted within three years, and those released at the age of forty-five or older were the least. *Id.* at 7. The highest rearrest rates were seen for those initially convicted of property offenses: 74 percent. *Id.* at 8. Prisoners convicted of violent crimes and drug crimes had lower rearrest rates: 62 percent and 67 percent, respectively. *Id.*

The ability to relate such factors to recidivism risks has led some to suggest strong reliance on them in determining the length of prison sentences. *See* Am. L. Inst., Model Penal Code: Sentencing § 6B.09 cmt. A at 56 (Preliminary Draft No. 5, 2007) (not yet adopted). It has been argued that these instruments can reduce prison populations by allowing the release of inmates who pose little risk to the public. Bernard E. Harcourt, *Risk as a Proxy for Race* 1 (U. Chi. L. Sch., John M. Olin Law and Economics Working Paper No. 535, Public Law and Legal Theory Working Paper No. 323). The reliability of risk assessment tools may be undermined by faulty assumptions. From the 1920s to the 1970s, race and nationality were explicitly relied upon in making such determinations. Racial disparity continues today through the use of prior criminal history as a tool for determining sentence length. Criminal history may be a reflection less of a defendant's risk of recidivism than of disparities in investigation, arrest, prosecution, and sentencing.

Except for the incapacitation effect of incarceration, there is little apparent correlation between recidivism and the length of imprisonment. Those who serve five years or less in prison have rearrest rates of 63 to 68 percent, with no discernible pattern relating to sentence length. A 2002 study did note a lower rearrest rate—54 percent—among those who served more than five years. No conclusions regarding these longer sentences can be drawn because the report did not differentiate among them by length. It appears that among low-risk offenders, recidivism may to a limited extent be fostered, not prevented, by lengthy imprisonment.

Among low-risk offenders, those who spent less time in prison were 4% less likely to recidivate than low-risk offenders who served longer sentences. Thus, when prison sentences are relatively short, offenders are more likely to maintain their ties to family, employers, and their community, all of which promote successful reentry into society. Conversely, when prisoners serve longer sentences they are more likely to become institutionalized, lose pro-social contacts in the community, and become removed from legitimate opportunities, all of which promote recidivism. Wright, *supra,* at 7; *but see* Langan & Levin, *supra,* at 11 ("No evidence was found that spending more time in prison raises the recidivism rate.").

Because prisons are often located in rural areas, and because convicts' families and friends have limited ability to travel, convicts' relationships with people on the outside—the people most likely to motivate convicts to lead straight lives—may be eroded seriously during long terms of imprisonment. *See* Jeremy Travis, et al., Urban Inst. Justice Pol'y Ctr., *Families Left Behind: The Hidden Costs of Incarceration and Reentry* 1 (rev. ed. 2005) (reporting that incarcerated fathers and mothers are housed an average of 100 and 160 miles, respectively, from their children); *id.* (stating that over half of incarcerated parents report never receiving a personal visit from their children).

Programs such as those for drug and alcohol treatment, adult basic education, vocational training, and prison industries reduce recidivism by 8 to 15 percent. Petersilia, *supra,* at 17. *See also id.* at 34 (reporting a study of inmates in three states that found that those who underwent prison education programs were 23 percent less likely than other inmates to be re-incarcerated). Treatment for mental disabilities may have an even greater positive impact. Nearly a third of state prisoners and a quarter of federal prisoners suffer from a mental condition or physical impairment. Ten percent of state prisoners and 5 percent of federal prisoners have a learning disability. Among state prisoners, 19 percent are completely illiterate and 40 percent functionally illiterate, compared to 4 percent and 21 percent, respectively, of the non-incarcerated population. In 1999, 51 percent of released prisoners lacked a high school education, and 11 percent had an eighth-grade education or less.

Coinciding with the nationwide push for stiffer prison sentences since the 1970s has been a de-emphasis on the rehabilitation of criminals and a preference for lengthy incapacitation. When rehabilitative measures were retained, it was often with the purpose of keeping inmates manageable, not in reducing recidivism. The continued existence of programs effective at combating recidivism both for current and released prisoners may be threatened by budgetary pressures. *See* Kevin Johnson, *Budget Cuts Slice Programs for Ex-Inmates,* USA Today, Feb. 9, 2011, at 7A (reporting concerns that state government spending for parole and probation departments may be reduced, depleting resources for drug treatment, supervision of offenders, and housing and job assistance).

Recidivism may be promoted by the behavior traits prisoners develop while incarcerated. To survive, they "tend to develop characteristics institutionally selected for survival: circumspection, canniness, coldness, and cruelty." Perkinson, *supra,* at 368. After release, the negative traits cultivated in prison may be received as virtues on the street. "[P]rison usually enhances one's prestige on the street, particularly in terms of . . . values like toughness, nerve, and willingness to retaliate for transgressions." Anderson, *supra,* at 292. . . .

A number of the sentences. . . are excessive because of the requirement of statutory mandatory minimum terms of incarceration under present case law. They cannot as yet be said to violate the Constitution. . . .

Judges approach the grave responsibility of sentencing criminals with all the thoughtfulness and limited insight that their knowledge and wisdom can muster. "Sentencing . . . is in its essence subjective. . . . It is not possible to determine a condign sentence without looking closely at all relevant facts and circumstances, and making a nuanced decision." Hon. John L. Kane, *Sentencing: Beyond the Calculus,* Litig., Fall 2010, at 5. *See also* Hon. David L. Bazelon, *Questioning Authority: Justice and Criminal Law* 27 ("We have to conduct this searching inquiry into the criminal's life history, not to excuse, but to appreciate the conditions that inevitably attend and may lead to criminal behavior. Focusing on the individual offender is not part of the problem of crime; it is part of the solution.").

Mandatory minimum sentencing provisions, leaving no alternative but lengthy incarceration, prevent the exercise of this fundamental judicial duty. Such laws are "overly blunt instruments, bringing undue focus upon factors (such as drug quantities) to the exclusion of other important considerations, including role in the offense, use of guns and violence, criminal history, risk of recidivism, and many personal characteristics of an individual defendant." Sessions, *supra,* at 42. It is difficult to conceive of a system of mandatory minimum sentences that could effectively anticipate and provide for such factors.

For nonviolent, low-level drug crimes, the goals of sentencing—general and specific deterrence, incapacitation, retribution, and rehabilitation—could in most cases be achieved with limited incarceration, through a system of intense supervised release utilizing home visits; meetings with parole officers; a combination of counseling, drug and alcohol treatment, education, job training, and job placement; and electronic monitoring to prevent flight, promote positive choices, and deter and detect incipient crime. Such a regime would likely be more effective in reducing crime and much less costly than imprisonment. Given discouraging economic, social, and psychological conditions, it seems doubtful that the long sentences of incarceration imposed will appreciably reduce crime.

Pragmatism and a sense of fairness suggest reconsideration of our overreliance on incarceration. Though defendants are hemmed in by circumstances, the law must believe that free will offers an escape. Otherwise, its vaunted belief in redemption and deterrence—both specific and general—is a euphemism for cruelty. These defendants are not merely criminals, but human beings and fellow American citizens, deserving of an opportunity for rehabilitation. Even now, they are capable of useful lives, lived lawfully.

EXERCISE

You are a defense attorney representing Lori Banker, who has been convicted at trial of conspiracy to distribute a large amount of heroin. She was a lower-level player in a large conspiracy; her role was limited to packaging the heroin, and her involvement was driven by her addiction to heroin. She got involved in the conspiracy after she fell into debt to the group, and now she was paid primarily in heroin.

She has never received treatment for her addiction, and this is her first conviction. She is 46 years old.

Banker tells you that she very much wants to get clean. Her sentencing guideline range is 87–108 months, which is advisory. What sentence will you request of the court, and how will you argue for that sentence using the goal of rehabilitation?

It would seem that sometimes rehabilitation might require incarceration. For example, if a defendant had flunked out of addiction treatment programs as an outpatient, the circumstances of confinement might lead to better success if narcotics are unavailable in prison. However, 18 U.S.C. § 3582(a) pushes the other way, directing that sentencing judges "shall consider the factors set forth in section 3553(a) to the extent they are applicable, recognizing that imprisonment is not an appropriate means of promoting correction and rehabilitation."

TAPIA V. UNITED STATES
564 U.S. 319 (2011)

JUSTICE KAGAN delivered the opinion of the Court.

We consider here whether the Sentencing Reform Act precludes federal courts from imposing or lengthening a prison term in order to promote a criminal defendant's rehabilitation. We hold that it does.

I

Petitioner Alejandra Tapia was convicted of, *inter alia*, smuggling unauthorized aliens into the United States, in violation of 8 U.S.C. §§ 1324(a)(2)(B)(ii) and (iii). At sentencing, the District Court determined that the United States Sentencing Guidelines recommended a prison term of between 41 and 51 months for Tapia's offenses. The court decided to impose a 51-month term, followed by three years of supervised release. In explaining its reasons, the court referred several times to Tapia's need for drug treatment, citing in particular the Bureau of Prison's Residential Drug Abuse Program (known as RDAP or the 500 Hour Drug Program). The court indicated that Tapia should serve a prison term long enough to qualify for and complete that program:

> The sentence has to be sufficient to provide needed correctional treatment, and here I think the needed correctional treatment is the 500 Hour Drug Program.
>
> . . . .
>
> "Here I have to say that one of the factors that—I am going to impose a 51-month sentence, . . . and one of the factors that affects this is the need to provide treatment. In other words, so she is in long enough to get the 500 Hour Drug Program, number one." App. 27.

("Number two" was "to deter her from committing other criminal offenses." *Ibid.*) The court "strongly recommend[ed]" to the Bureau of Prisons (BOP) that Tapia "participate in [RDAP] and that she serve her sentence at" the Federal Correctional Institution in Dublin, California (FCI Dublin), where "they have the appropriate tools . . . to help her, to start to make a recovery." *Id.*, at 29. Tapia did not object to the sentence at that time. *Id.*, at 31.

On appeal, however, Tapia argued that the District Court had erred in lengthening her prison term to make her eligible for RDAP. App. to Pet. for Cert. 2. In Tapia's view, this action violated 18 U.S.C. § 3582(a), which instructs sentencing courts to "recogniz[e] that imprisonment is not an appropriate means of promoting correction and rehabilitation." The United States Court of Appeals for the Ninth Circuit disagreed, 376 Fed.Appx. 707 (2010), relying on its prior decision in *United States v. Duran*, 37 F.3d 557 (1994). The Ninth Circuit had held there that § 3582(a) distinguishes between deciding to impose a term of imprisonment and determining its length. See *id.*, at 561. According to *Duran*, a sentencing court cannot impose a prison term to assist a defendant's rehabilitation. But "[o]nce imprisonment is chosen as a punishment," the court may consider the defendant's need for rehabilitation in setting the length of the sentence. *Ibid.*

We granted certiorari to consider whether § 3582(a) permits a sentencing court to impose or lengthen a prison term in order to foster a defendant's rehabilitation. 562 U.S. ___, 131 S.Ct. 817, 178 L.Ed.2d 551 (2010). That question has divided the Courts of Appeals. Because the United States agrees with Tapia's interpretation of the statute, we appointed an *amicus curiae* to defend the judgment below. We now reverse. . . .

Our consideration of Tapia's claim starts with the text of 18 U.S.C. § 3582(a)—and given the clarity of that provision's language, could end there as well. As just noted, that section instructs courts to "recogniz[e] that imprisonment is not an appropriate means of promoting correction and rehabilitation." A common—and in context the most natural—definition of the word "recognize" is "to acknowledge or treat as valid." Random House Dictionary of the English Language 1611 (2d ed.1987). And a thing that is not "appropriate" is not "suitable or fitting for a particular purpose." *Id.,* at 103. Putting these two definitions together, § 3582(a) tells courts that they should acknowledge that imprisonment is not suitable for the purpose of promoting rehabilitation. And when should courts acknowledge this? Section § 3582(a)answers: when "determining whether to impose a term of imprisonment, and, if a term of imprisonment is to be imposed, [when] determining the length of the term." So a court making these decisions should consider the specified rationales of punishment *except for* rehabilitation, which it should acknowledge as an unsuitable justification for a prison term.

As against this understanding, *amicus* argues that § 3582(a)'s "recognizing" clause is not a flat prohibition but only a "reminder" or a "guide [for] sentencing judges' cognitive processes." Brief for Court-Appointed *Amicus Curiae* in Support of Judgment Below 23–24 (hereinafter *Amicus* Brief) (emphasis deleted). *Amicus* supports this view by offering a string of other definitions of the word "recognize": " 'recall to mind,' 'realize,' or 'perceive clearly.' " *Id.,* at 24 (quoting dictionary definitions). Once these are plugged in, *amicus* suggests, § 3582(a)reveals itself as a kind of loosey-goosey caution not to put *too* much faith in the capacity of prisons to rehabilitate.

But we do not see how these alternative meanings of "recognize" help *amicus* 's cause. A judge who "perceives clearly" that imprisonment is not an appropriate means of promoting rehabilitation would hardly incarcerate someone for that purpose. Ditto for a judge who "realizes" or "recalls" that imprisonment is not a way to rehabilitate an offender. To be sure, the drafters of the "recognizing" clause could have used still more commanding language: Congress could have inserted a "thou shalt not" or equivalent phrase to convey that a sentencing judge may never, ever, under any circumstances consider rehabilitation in imposing a prison term. But when we interpret a statute, we cannot allow the perfect to be the enemy of the merely excellent. Congress expressed itself clearly in § 3582(a), even if armchair legislators might come up with something even better. And what Congress said was that when sentencing an offender to prison, the court shall consider all the purposes of punishment except rehabilitation—because imprisonment is not an appropriate means of pursuing that goal.

Finally, for those who consider legislative history useful, the key Senate Report concerning the SRA provides one last piece of corroborating evidence. According to that Report, decades of experience with indeterminate sentencing, resulting in the release of many inmates after they completed correctional programs, had left Congress skeptical that "rehabilitation can be induced reliably in a prison setting." S. Rep., at 38. Although some critics argued that "rehabilitation should be eliminated completely as a purpose of sentencing," Congress declined to adopt that categorical position. *Id.,* at 76. Instead, the Report explains, Congress barred courts from considering rehabilitation in imposing prison terms, *ibid.,* and n. 165, but not in ordering other kinds of sentences, *ibid.,* and n. 164. "[T]he purpose of rehabilitation," the Report stated, "is still important in determining whether a sanction *other than a term of imprisonment* is appropriate in a particular case." See *id.,* at 76–77 (emphasis added).

And so this is a case in which text, context, and history point to the same bottom line: Section 3582(a) precludes sentencing courts from imposing or lengthening a prison term to promote an offender's rehabilitation. . . .

EXERCISE

Unremarked upon in *Tapia* is the odd fact that the federal government both provides an extensive drug rehabilitation program in federal prisons—a fact that seems to reflect a belief that they can be successful—while providing a bar that prevents judges from considering in-prison rehabilitation programs. Is there a way in which this could make sense?

Imagine that you represent a defendant who very much wants to participate in the in-prison drug rehabilitation program. How would you approach sentencing so as to best ensure that outcome, given the holding in *Tapia?*

E. RESTORATIVE JUSTICE

Restorative justice is a model for criminal law that focuses on restoring relationships, including the relationships between offender and victim and offender and society. It has been influential in the development of juvenile law and special-interest courts such as drug courts, veterans' courts, and mental health court.

Unlike the four ideas described above, restorative justice does not have an explicit statutory mandate in federal law. However, this theory of justice has grown in influence, and is considered by some decision-makers as they make decisions.

Vermont has even included the basic principles of restorative justice in their code, at 28 V.S.A. § 2a:

(a) State policy. It is the policy of this State that principles of restorative justice be included in shaping how the criminal justice system responds to persons charged with or convicted of criminal offenses, and how the State responds to persons who are in contempt of child support orders. The policy goal is a community response to a person's wrongdoing at its earliest onset, and a type and intensity of sanction tailored to each instance of wrongdoing. Policy objectives are to:

(1) Resolve conflicts and disputes by means of a nonadversarial community process.

(2) Repair damage caused by criminal acts to communities in which they occur, and to address wrongs inflicted on individual victims.

(3) Reduce the risk of an offender committing a more serious crime in the future, that would require a more intensive and more costly sanction, such as incarceration.

(b) Implementation. It is the intent of the General Assembly that law enforcement officials develop and employ restorative justice approaches whenever feasible and responsive to specific criminal acts, pursuant to 3 V.S.A. §§ 163 and 164, concerning court diversion, 13 V.S.A. chapter 221, concerning sentencing, and the provisions of this title, concerning persons in the custody of the Commissioner of Corrections. It is the further intent of the General Assembly that such restorative justice programs be designed to encourage participation by local community members, including victims, when they so choose, as well as public officials, in holding offenders accountable for damage caused to communities and victims, and in restoring offenders to the law-abiding community, through activities:

(1) Which require offenders to:

(A) acknowledge wrongdoing and apologize to victims;

(B) make restitution for damage to the victims, consistent with provisions of 13 V.S.A. chapter 221 and of this title;

(C) make reparation for damage to the community by fulfilling a community service; and

(D) when relevant, successfully complete treatment addressing the offense or other underlying problematic behavior, or undertake academic or vocational training or other self-improving activity.

(2) Which aid in the recovery of victims, recognizing that victims, particularly of violent crime, often suffer lifelong effects and, accordingly, must feel safe and involved in any program offered to assist them.

(3) Which help in identifying the causes of crime and ways community members and municipal and State government can reduce or prevent crime in the future.

In the absence of such explicit guidance in the federal system, judges sometimes simply apply their own notions of what restorative justice might be.

UNITED STATES v. CUNNINGHAM
2014 WL 3002207 (N.D. Cal. 2014)

LARRY ALAN BURNS, DISTRICT JUDGE.

Former United States Congressman Randy Cunningham has filed a motion asking the court to terminate the remaining two years of his supervised release. Cunningham has completed the 100-month custodial sentence that the court imposed, as well as a term of confinement in a half-way house and in home confinement. He has also served over a year of the three-year term of supervised release that the court originally imposed.

Mr. Cunningham was also ordered to pay restitution and back taxes in the amount of approximately $1,800,000, and the Internal Revenue Service has been collecting that debt since shortly after he was remanded to custody. The IRS continues to garnish approximately $60,000 a year from Mr. Cunningham's various retirement payments.

Since his release from custody, Mr. Cunningham has performed extensive volunteer work. The court has received letters from religious and civic leaders and from civic and veterans' organizations supporting Mr. Cunningham, and urging the termination of his supervised release.

The Government opposes Cunningham's motion. As a matter of policy, the Government says it does not support early termination of supervised release unless a person has completed two-thirds of his supervised release term and paid his monetary penalties in full. The court also sought input from Mr. Cunningham's probation officer, Mr. Joel Humphrey. Mr. Humphrey reports that Mr. Cunningham has been very compliant while on supervised release and has been easy to supervise. He verifies Mr.

Cunningham's extensive civic and charitable work, and does not oppose his request for early termination of supervised release.

Under 18 U.S.C. § 3583(e)(1), a court is authorized to terminate a term of supervised release and discharge a defendant from the obligation any time after the expiration of one year of supervised release. The factors that must be considered in making the decision include: the nature and circumstances of the offense; the history and characteristics of the offender; the need for deterrence and for protecting the public; the need to provide the offender with educational or vocational training or medical care; the United States Sentencing Guidelines, including pertinent policy statements; the interest in avoiding sentencing disparity between similarly situated offenders; and the need to secure restitution.

This court has thought through and weighed all of these factors. There is no question that Mr. Cunningham's offenses were aggravated, involving serial corrupt acts and deception. And the deception didn't end with his sentencing. Mr. Cunningham subsequently attempted to obstruct justice by submitting a false affidavit in Brent Wilkes' case claiming that Wilkes had not bribed him. Although this court and the court of appeals gave short shrift to the affidavit, Mr. Cunningham perpetuated his dishonest behavior by submitting it.

The court has reconsidered Mr. Cunningham's history, especially his heroic military service. Despite his later misdeeds, Mr. Cunningham well served our nation in the armed forces, and his meritorious legacy can never be taken from him and should not be diminished. The court has also considered, as it should, the extensive civic and charitable volunteer work Mr. Cunningham has performed since his release from custody.

Mr. Cunningham has no history of violence or of illegal behavior, generally, so the court perceives no need to further deter him from wrongdoing or to protect the public from him.

The court is informed that Mr. Cunningham continues to battle prostate cancer. However, as an honorably discharged combat veteran, he is entitled to seek medical care from the Veteran's Administration and doesn't need to rely on the criminal justice system. Nor, because he is a retired person on a pension, is there any need to provide him with educational or vocational training.

In opposing Mr. Cunningham's motion, the Government has not pointed to any Guideline provision or policy statement that precludes early termination, and the court is unaware of any. The Government simply has a policy and is sticking to it. It must be acknowledged, however, that the overarching objective of the Guidelines is fair and uniform sentencing. This court routinely grants early termination of supervised release to offenders who paid their debts to society and have righted themselves. Granting this form of dispensation is consistent with the parsimony clause in 18 U.S.C.

§ 3553(a), which directs courts, as a general matter, to impose sentences that are "sufficient, but not greater than necessary" to achieve the objectives of sentencing. The court assumes that this directive applies not just to the length of a sentence, but also to the term of supervised release.

As for the need to secure restitution, the Government's policy of opposing termination if restitution is still owed is undoubtedly based on the legitimate assumption that collecting restitution is easier if the offender remains on supervised release. But that's not necessarily so here because, in addition to his criminal restitution obligation, Mr. Cunningham is on the hook civilly to the IRS. Indeed, the IRS has been collecting on the civil judgment it obtained against Mr. Cunningham—not on this court's criminal restitution order—confiscating about a third of his net income every month. The garnishments won't end even if Mr. Cunningham's supervised release is terminated.

As a final consideration, and as an adjunct to the § 3553 formula factors, the court believes that the concept of simple forgiveness should be part of the equation here. Forgiveness is a moral quality and a social good, and is important to a system of restorative justice. "The quality of mercy is not strained," and there comes a time to forgive. Mr. Cunningham served a long jail sentence in this case. He spent time in a halfway house, and under house arrest. And since June 2013, he has been supervised by a United States Probation officer. Besides these direct consequences that he suffered for his illegal actions, he lost his home, his marriage, and his reputation. At some point, once justice has been served, the system must take care to avoid erecting roadblocks that might prevent an offender from reintegrating into society and becoming a productive and useful citizen again.

Mr. Cunningham's motion to terminate his supervised release is GRANTED as of July 1, 2014.

IT IS SO ORDERED.

EXERCISE

Did the judge's actions in Cunningham fulfill the restorative justice goals described in the Vermont statute cited above?

Perhaps the strongest influence restorative justice has had on contemporary criminal law is through creating a focus on restitution and the effort to make victims financially whole. That goal has ancient roots.

UNITED STATES V. FERRANTI

928 F.Supp. 206 (E.D.NY 1996)

WEINSTEIN, SENIOR DISTRICT JUDGE:

For the reasons indicated below, defendant, who was found guilty of arson resulting in death and other crimes, must be sentenced to a term of just less than life imprisonment. Maximum monetary penalties, and restitution are also required.

II. FACTS

Defendant owned and operated a retail women's clothing store on the ground floor of a three-story building in Maspeth, Queens. On the upper floors were four residential apartments.

The business was not profitable. Defendant had fallen behind on rent. Fire insurance premiums were not current. Notice of imminent cancellation of the policy had been given.

In the Fall of 1991, defendant began planning to set fire to the store in order to collect insurance proceeds and to avoid payment of future rent on what had become a burdensome lease. He paid the overdue premiums to ensure that his policy for fire damage would be in force. Months before the event he boasted of his plan to set the fire. He recruited a friend, Thomas Tocco, through his brother, Mario Ferranti, to help set the fire.

On February 24, 1992, at 5:00 p.m., an employee shut off the lights and locked the doors of the store, planning to return next morning. Later that same night someone possessing one of the two available keys entered. The bulk of the merchandise was removed. An old electric space heater was placed in the rear to make it appear that this was an accidental electrical fire. Flammable liquid was spread near the heater. At approximately 11:00 p.m. the fire was lighted by defendant or someone working under his direction.

The Fire Department arrived quickly. Fire and smoke were intense. Some of the building's eight residents had already fled in panic.

To ensure that no one was left in the building, two firefighters, Lieutenant Thomas A. Williams and Michael J. Milner, searched the front portion of the second floor. Visibility was nil. Heat was intense. Lieutenant Williams directed Milner to break open a floor-to-ceiling window to help ventilate the area. As Milner did so, he observed a passing shadow. It was Lieutenant Williams who fell to the pavement. Death was almost instantaneous.

Two dozen firefighters suffered minor injuries. Several tenants required treatment for smoke inhalation. Their possessions were destroyed. They were left homeless. Destruction of the building was close to complete. The fire also damaged adjoining premises.

The next day, fire marshals collected strong evidence of arson. Nine days after the fire, investigators located defendant. He claimed to know nothing about the fire, falsely stating that he had been visiting a girlfriend in New Jersey since the day prior to the fire. He lied about the financial difficulties his store was having. He lied when he asserted that the store was fully stocked with merchandise at the time of the fire. . . .

There are adverse allegations of defendant's conduct that have not led to conviction. They include being a "slumlord" who used violence against tenants and others. Defendant denies their truth. His close family ties with his parents, siblings, wife, ex-wife and son are urged on his behalf. None of these derogatory or supportive contentions need to be considered on this sentence. The crime itself provides overwhelming evidence of depravity. . . .

When applicable, pecuniary penalties serve more than punishment purposes; they provide tort-like remedies to institutions, communities, and victims who suffer the consequences of criminal conduct. Such quasi-remedial measures fall well within constitutional due process requirements. The analogous but more developed procedure used by the respected French criminal-civil system demonstrates that restitution as an added feature of criminal law is not inconsistent with due process. The private restitutory portion of the penalty reflects an important change in the direction of our criminal law to amalgamate tort-like functions with criminal prosecutions.

The archaic necessity of self-help to punish and compensate tended to create feuds and tensions inconsistent with a peaceful centrally controlled society. An important step in limiting private vengeance was the eye-for-an-eye and tooth-for-a-tooth edict of the bible and like limits in other early codes.

Later, tort law based on negligence rather than accident without fault, constituted another step forward in controlling private retributory conduct. Strict liability in limited contexts to provide both deterrence and compensation constitutes a still developing further advance. . . .

Unlike the still fairly clear line between civil and criminal remedies in Anglo-American law, the French system has long utilized criminal prosecutions to provide for victim compensation. In France, as in most Romanistic legal systems, the victim plays an important part in the criminal proceeding. The principle of discretionary criminal prosecution applies in France with respect to the public prosecutor's office. The French Code of Criminal Procedure Art. 40 ¶ 1 (Gerald L. Kock & Richard S. Frase trans. rev. ed. 1988) [hereinafter French Code of Criminal Procedure]. The victim can, by means of the *action civile* raise an official complaint even if that is contrary to the wishes of the public prosecutor. French Code of Criminal Procedure Art. 1 ¶ 2. The *action civile* does two things: it initiates a claim for compensation, and it begins a public criminal action. Martine Merigeau, *Evaluation of the Practice of Compensation within Recent*

Victim-related Crime Policy in France in Victims and Criminal Justice 240–241 (Gunther Kaiser, Helmut Kury, Hans-Jorg Albrecht ed. 1991).

The French victim's right to initiate public criminal action provides an important check on prosecutorial discretion. Moreover, the right to demand civil damages in the criminal court allows a broader scope for the French court to assess the extent of compensation for damages than does the American counterpart of restitution. The victim can insist that the examining magistrate investigate and help document the civil claim. The court must rule on the civil claim; damages awards are enforceable both as a condition of probation and as a civil judgement. *See* Richard S. Frase, *Comparative Criminal Justice as a Guide to American Law Reform: How Do the French Do It, How Can We Find Out, and Why Should We Care?,* 78 Cal.L.Rev. 542, 670–71 (1990); *see also, e.g.,* Ruth Bader Ginsburg & Anders Bruzelius, *Civil Procedure in Sweden,* 145–150 (1965) (court in which criminal prosecution is instituted has ancillary competence to adjudicate related civil claims).

Under Article 3 of the French Code of Criminal Procedure the civil action may be pursued at the same time and before the same court as the prosecution. This civil claim may include "all heads of damages, material as well as bodily or moral, which flow from the acts that are the object of the prosecution." French Code of Criminal Procedure Art. 3 ¶ 2; *see also* Stephen Schafer, Compensation and Restitution to Victims of Crime, 21 (2d ed. 1970).

A French victim has the choice of bringing the civil action in civil or criminal court. If brought in the criminal court, the *action civile* is subject to the statute of limitations applied to the specific crime. In all other respects this civil action conforms to the French Rules of Civil Procedure. For example, although the conviction part of a felony trial is heard by a jury, the court dismisses the jury before hearing the parties with respect to the civil damages claims made by the victim against the accused or by an acquitted accused against the victim. French Code of Criminal Procedure Art. 371 ¶ 1. The victim retains the right to enforce the claim for restitution against the prisoner's earnings while he is incarcerated. Schafer, *supra,* at 23.

The United States is in a state of transition on restitution. How far it will move toward an integrated criminal-civil-administrative system in areas such as mass torts or environmental delicts, what effect recovery for restitution will have on the tort law system's collateral benefits rule, how much cooperation there will be between the public prosecutor, administrative agencies and private persons, and many other issues are just beginning to be addressed. *See generally* ABA Standards for Criminal Justice, Sentencing, 107–112 (1994) (new section on restitution). The discussion that follows in Parts IX-XIII, *infra,* has made as few assumptions about new developments as possible, utilizing traditional criminal law conceptions in-so-far as the new statutes permit. . . .

Restitution is an "[a]ct of restoring; restoration of anything to its rightful owner; the act of making good or giving equivalent for any loss, damage or injury; and indemnification." Black's Law Dictionary, 1477 (4th ed. 1968). Statutory-based restitution is a payment to victims of crime by an offender to cover losses incurred as a result of the crime. The payment can take the form of either money or services to the victim or the state. *See generally* Elmar Weitekamp, *Recent Developments on Restitution and Victim-Offender Reconciliation in the U.S.A. and Canada: An Assessment,* in Victims and Criminal Justice 425 (Gunther Kaiser, Helmut Kury, Hans-Jorg Albrecht ed. 1991).

Payment for wrongs committed in the form of restitution to victims has a long history. It has always been closely intertwined with conceptions of punishment and justice. The law of Moses required fourfold restitution for stolen sheep and fivefold for the more useful ox; the Middle-Eastern law Code of Hammurabi (c. 1700 B.C.), which focused on implementing deterrent measures through severe and cruel punishments and imposition of restitution for property offenses, could demand up to thirty times the value of damage caused. . . .

The Roman Law of the Twelve Tables (449 B.C.) required thieves to make restitution payments to their victims starting at double the value of the stolen goods. The value of the payment due would increase depending on the circumstance in which such stolen goods were found or confiscated. *See* Van Ness at 7. In England, prior to the Middle Ages, elaborate and detailed systems of victim compensation were developed by the Anglo-Saxons, placing the victim's right to compensation at the forefront of punishment considerations. *Id.*

Views on criminality and punishment shifted in England beginning with the reign of William the Conqueror and the growth of central government administration. The King or State began to take center stage and was treated as the paramount "victim" of offenses, to whom offenders had to make payment. Offenses were thought of as crimes against society, rather than against the individual. *See generally* Roger Meiners, *Victim Compensation* (1978). Until recently this was the approach in the United States.

In this country victim restitution has recently emerged in the criminal justice system, initially through legislation passed by individual states, as either an alternative to incarceration or as an added component of the sentence. *Id.,* 25–39. At the federal level, the Victim and Witness Protection Act of 1982 emphasized victims' interest in the sentencing stage. Pub.L. 97–291, 1982 U.S.C.C.A.N. 2515–2516. These interests include the right to be heard at sentencing, *Id.* at 2517–2520, and the right to restitution. *Id.* at 2519–2520; 18 U.S.C. § 3663.

The enactment of these modern statutes has increased the obligation of courts to consider the victims' need for emotional healing and financial compensation within the context of criminal law. Their special interests are evaluated separately from those of the government. The legislative history of the Victim and Witness Protection Act emphasized the need for "legislative action to assist victims . . . [to correct] the insensitivity and lack of concern for the witness" that has marked the structure of our criminal justice system. Pub.L. 97–291, 1982 U.S.C.C.A.N. 2515–2516. The objective is to try to make the victims as whole as possible—both financially and psychologically.

Under the Victim and Witness Protection Act restitution may be ordered. 18 U.S.C. §§ 3663–3664. Section 3663(a)(1), reads as follows:

The court . . . may order, in addition to or in lieu of any other penalty authorized by law, that the defendant make restitution to any victim of such offense.

Section 3663 allows exercise of a broad discretion in providing restitution. The following types of payment are authorized:

> (b)(1)   in the case of an offense resulting in damage to or loss or destruction of property of a victim of the offense—
>
>> (B) if return of the property . . . is impossible, impractical, or inadequate, pay an amount equal to or greater of—
>>
>>> (i) the value of the property on the date of the damage, loss, or destruction, or
>>>
>>> (ii) the value of the property on the date of sentencing, less the value of any part of the property that is returned;
>
> (2) in the case of an offense resulting in bodily injury to a victim—
>
>> (A) pay an amount equal to the cost of necessary medical and related professional services . . .
>>
>> (C) reimburse the victim for income lost by such victim as a result of such offense;
>
> (3) in the case of an offense resulting in bodily injury also results in the death of a victim, pay an amount equal to the cost of necessary funeral and related services; . . .

Restitution is called for because of the nature of the crime committed by defendant, the damage his acts caused, and the extent of the assets he possesses. The arson caused injury and death as well as extensive physical and economic damage to the building, tenants and firefighters. It put a large number of lives at risk. Defendant has shown contempt for our justice system, as demonstrated by his attempts at manipulating and intimidating key witnesses and his lies to investigators.

Defendant has failed to provide information about his assets through pre-sentencing discovery proceedings. He has not contested his ability to pay restitution or fines claimed by the government. He has the ability to pay all the restitution due under the statute as well as the fine imposed and cost of incarceration. Since much of defendant's assets are in the form of real estate holdings and some appear to be jointly owned, liquidation will be necessary to comply with the restitution and fine order. . . .

A total restitution amount of $1,455,799.79 shall be paid to the victims as follows: $56,569.40 to Michelle and Shelly Anthony; $18,506.00 to Estelle and William Cortes; $5,670.86 to Zbigniew and Jaowica Kwiatkowski; $7,168.50 to Charles Wagner; $16,385.15 to Ronald Bass; $136,131.20 to Thomas A. Ripley; $275,453.89 to Cigna Fire Underwriters; and $939,914.79 to the New York City Fire Department.

EXERCISE

Judge Weinstein notes that some legal systems blur the line between civil and criminal law. In the United States, the prosecutor does not represent the victim. In fact, there often is tension between the prosecutor and the victim, as the prosecutor may not choose the course of action (for example, in cutting a plea deal) that the victim would prefer.

Would it be a good idea to have an attorney appointed to represent an indigent *victim* and participate in the criminal case as a co-equal to the defense attorney and prosecutor?

Criminal law is a central function of government, and plays a key role in the success or failure of societies. Maintaining a balance between safety and freedom is a project that is and will be both contentious and brutally important.

That importance comes from what is at stake: lives and liberty. The tall buildings, fancy offices, and lengthy discourses of civil law will always be about money; criminal law is about blood and greed and sex and death. The practice of criminal law is the management of tragedy. It is a world where people—capital jurors—are paid $40 a day to decide whether or not a man standing a few yards away should live or die. It is a realm where a wrong decision by a prosecutor can result in a woman being raped and killed. It is a place of deep meaning.

Elegy Ending with a Cell Door Closing
by Reginald Dwayne Betts

& the Judge told him to count
the trees in the parking lot
where there were only cars. Zero.
The same number of stars
You could see on a night in the city.
& the judge told him the parking lot will
be filled with trees, oaks & spruces
& pines & willow trees & grass & maybe
horses before he smells the city
on a Sunday afternoon; & another word
for this story is azalea, the purple bouquet
his mother buried her face against,
her skin another purplish bruise—
he pled not guilty, & in the courtroom
he washed his hands against the air,
as if to say fuck everything;
imagine, he had no hair on his face
that afternoon & he'd never held a razor,
not even inside his mouth, the best weapon
a man could ask for unless you lost
the first fight he'd see in prison,
a baseball bat turning the razor under
the bad man's tongue into a kind of prayer—
made the man wash the air with his hands,
too, & anyone who'd seen this & recalled
that day in court, would know the washing
as a kind of suicide, because before
the roots of trees splinter that asphalt, we will
all call some grave home &
that the chubby kid who a whole
neighborhood called Fats will lose
every memory he's had in the wildfire
a man smashed by a rusted bat.[2]

---

[2] From Reginald Dwayne Betts, Bastards of the Reagan Era, pp. 43–44 (2015) (as amended by Betts for this use).

INDEX

References are to Pages
